HISTORY
OF
HUMANITY
Scientific and Cultural Development

The *History of Humanity: The Nineteenth Century* sees the publication of the sixth and penultimate volume in the invaluable History of Humanity series published in association with UNESCO. Volume VI covers the nineteenth century, globally speaking, a period of huge change. With essays from an international team of specialist contributors, the *History of Humanity* explores humankind's cultural and scientific development, covering such diverse aspects as the Industrial Revolution, religion, architecture and medicine, as well as looking in depth at the changes that took place within each region of the world.

The *History of Humanity: The Nineteenth Century* is an invaluable source of information for students and scholars of history and anthropology, and includes special features such as maps and illustrations that complement the text, making this volume highly readable. Collected as a whole, the series provides the user with a comprehensive guide to the history of different cultures across different periods of time.

History of Humanity
Scientific and Cultural Development

In memory of Paulo E. de Berrêdo Carneiro,
President of the first International Commission
for a Scientific and Cultural History of Mankind
(1952–1969) and of the present Commission from
1979 to 1982.

HISTORY OF HUMANITY

Scientific and Cultural Development

Volume VI
The Nineteenth Century

EDITED BY

P. Mathias (United Kingdom)
N. Todorov (Bulgaria)

CO-EDITED BY

S. Al Mujahid (Pakistan)   F. Iglesias (Brazil)
O. Chubarian (Russian   Shu-li Ji (China)
Federation)   I. D. Thiam (Senegal)

Routledge
Taylor & Francis Group

LONDON AND NEW YORK

UNESCO

First published 2005
by the United Nations Educational, Scientific and Cultural Organization
7 Place de Fontenoy, 75352, Paris 07 SP
and
by Routledge
2 Park Square, Milton Park, Abingdon, Oxon, OX14 4RN
Simultaneously published in the USA and Canada
by Routledge

Routledge is an imprint of the Taylor & Francis Group

© 2005 UNESCO

Typeset by Newgen Imaging Systems (P) Ltd, India
Printed and bound in Great Britain by TJ International Ltd, Padstow, Cornwall

British Library Cataloguing in Publication Data
A catalogue record for this book is available from the British Library

Library of Congress Cataloging in Publication Data
A catalog record for this title has been requested

ISBN 92-3-102815-4 (UNESCO)
ISBN 0-415-09310-4 (Routledge)

PREFACE

Koïchiro Matsuura
Director-General, UNESCO

'Our civilization is the first to have for its past the past of the world, our history is the first to be world history'.[1] As the year 2000 recedes, the phenomenon described seventy years ago by Jan Huizinga becomes an ever more sensible reality. In a bounded and increasingly interconnected world, we necessarily find ourselves a part of that emerging global civilization that constitutes the matrix of our collective destinies.

The years immediately following the Dutch historian's assertion were indeed to illustrate, and in the most horrific manner, the interdependence of the world community. The planet on which millions of humans wished for nothing more than to live in peace and well-being presented the unnatural spectacle of a world at war. Land, sea and air routes were patrolled day and night by armadas venting fury on all that was most precious and vital to the inhabitants. The dreadful hurt that the populations sustained, physically and morally, dispelled *in perpetuum* a number of illusions and faced humanity with a stark choice – that of being, in the words of Albert Einstein, 'one or none'.

Thenceforth the grave danger attendant on inter-racial, and consequently inter-cultural, ignorance was conspicuous to thinking minds. A flawed consciousness of our common humanity must be incompatible with the survival of a world armed with knowledge of such awesome potential. Clearly the only course of action, the only way forward, lay in building bridges between peoples, in forging a resilient awareness of the unity inherent in human diversity.

Such was the background to UNESCO's decision in 1947 to produce a truly universal work of international cooperation that would provide 'a wider understanding of the scientific and cultural aspects of the history of mankind and of the mutual interdependence of peoples and cultures and of their contributions to the common heritage'.[2] That initiative, which was one of UNESCO's earliest projects, sprang from the Organization's fundamental principles and was widely acclaimed, although not a few saw in it a Sisyphean undertaking at which past attempts had signally failed.

Three years later, in 1950, the first International Commission for a History of the Scientific and Cultural Development of Mankind began the task of fashioning a history that – in the words of René Maheu – would 'present to man the sum total of his memories as a coherent whole'. As the distinguished international team of collaborators took shape and as the first results of its work began to appear in the Commission's review the *Journal of World History*, it became clear that new ground was being broken in pursuit of this ambitious goal. When some fifteen years later the first edition began to appear in six languages, the reception accorded to the work confirmed – some inevitable reservations apart – the success of this 'first attempt to compose a universal history of the human mind from the varying stand points of memory and thought that characterize the different contemporary cultures'.

The compilers of the first edition of the *History of Mankind* were conscious that all historiography is 'work in progress', that in the continuous flux of history nothing is fixed, neither facts nor interpretations. In 1969, Paulo de Berrêdo Cameiro declared: 'The day will come when what we have written . . . will, in its turn, have to be replaced. I like to think that our successors will attend to this, and that a revised edition of the work we have begun may be published at the dawn of a new millennium'.

That day came. The General Conference of UNESCO decided in 1978 that the work should be revised, and two years later the Second International Commission met to formulate its aims.

Much has changed since the publication of the first edition. In recent years, the historical sciences have been enriched by contributions from many disciplines, giving rise to new methods of investigation and bringing to light new facts, particularly in the realm of 'prehistory'. At the same time, a heightened awareness of cultural identity has intensified the demand for a corresponding decentralization of historical viewpoints and interpretations. UNESCO has both heeded and nurtured this trend by undertaking a series of regional histories, one of which – *General History of Africa*[3] – has been completed while others are in active

---

1 See Huizinga, J., 'A Definition of the Concept of History'. In: Klibansky, R. and Paton, H. J. (eds) *Philosophy and History*, Oxford, 1936, p. 8.

2 See UNESCO, 1947 General Conference; Second Session. Paris. Resolution 5.7.

3 The complete version of the *History of Mankind* has been published in Arabic, English and French, and the abridged version in English and French.

preparation. Finally, history itself has moved on, altering in the process the perspectives from which the past is viewed.

For all these reasons, and to take account of some valid criticisms of the original version, it was decided that the new edition of the *History of the Scientific and Cultural Development of Humanity*, to be called simply the *History of Humanity*, should not be merely a revision, but rather a radical recasting of its predecessor. Its goal – to provide an account of the history of humanity in terms of its varied cultural and scientific achievements – remains unchanged, but the view it offers of its subject is – it is hoped – more detailed, more diverse and broader in scope.

More than fifteen years after the launching of the project, it is my privilege to present this new *History*, which has built upon and extended the pioneering work of those dedicated scholars responsible for the first edition. I should like to express my admiration and deep gratitude to the members of the Second International Commission and to the some 450 distinguished specialists from all geocultural backgrounds who have contributed to this historic undertaking. Readers will, I feel sure, make known their own views in the years to come. In committing this work to their scrutiny, the International Commission – and, through it, UNESCO – is taking the final step in the task entrusted to it by the community of Member States represented at the General Conference. Each of us, I am sure, stands to benefit from this concerted testimony to our common past and act of faith in our shared future.

CONTENTS

FOREWORD

Charles Morazé
former President of the International Commission

Among the great tasks assigned to UNESCO by the Constitution is the duty to promote and encourage mutual knowledge and understanding throughout the world. While many of the divergences which divide people date from a distant past, an analysis of their historical antecedents discloses links which draw them nearer to one another, brings to light their contributions to a common patrimony of humanity, reveals the ebb and flow of cultural exchanges and emphasizes their increasing tendency to become integrated into an international community.

This is how Paulo E. de Berrêdo Carneiro, President of the International Commission (1952–69), expressed himself in the opening paragraph of the Preface to the *History of the Scientific and Cultural Development of Mankind* in 1963. Today, it would be difficult to say anything about humanity's 'increasing tendency to become integrated into an international community', unless an attempt is made to assess the outcome of this 'tendency' as reflected in the state of the world since. Today, few events remain local. Information on any minor or major occurrence is communicated to almost everyone immediately and an action undertaken in one part of the world inevitably has its repercussions in the others. Those who experience fully this 'planetariza- tion', sense the 'integration' of all human beings into an international community less as a 'tendency' than as a *fait accompli*. But what about the subordinates who are more or less associated, or the vast excluded majority of people? These others put the question in completely different terms. What they seem to ask is: can a 'common patrimony of humanity' be achieved solely through an integration based on scientific and technical developments? What then can we do to ensure an equal access to such means for all when the more fundamental task of reducing existing differences in the very standards of living lags far behind?

The idea of writing a history of the development of humankind was first put forward by Julian Huxley, the Executive Secretary of the Preparatory Commission of UNESCO. In 1946 Huxley wrote that 'the chief task before the Humanities today would seem to be to help in con- structing a history of the development of the human mind, notably in its highest cultural achievements'. He under- scored the major role that historians would play in the rea- lization of what he called a 'gigantic enterprise'. Huxley later

outlined a project which was to be submitted to the future UNESCO. In 1950, in accordance with a resolution passed by the General Conference of UNESCO, an International Commission was set up and the publication of a *History of the Scientific and Cultural Development of Mankind* in six volumes was approved. The first volume appeared in 1963.

What was this 'gigantic enterprise', conceived by Huxley worth? In most cases, the volumes were not well received by critics. They did not question the data included. What they objected to mainly were the criteria for the selection of data and the interpretations offered. Yet a closer look at these criticisms revealed that, skilled as they were at pointing out certain flaws and misconceptions, these commentators hardly ever came up with concrete suggestions that would lead to any improvement of the work in the future. On the whole, however, we were left with the impression that notwithstanding its shortcomings, a very large number of readers found the work commendable, particularly as a first step towards the achievement of an 'essential task'.

No elucidation, rational or otherwise, of the origins or the evolution of human beings can be offered once and for all, as if by divine revelation. Writing a history of the development of humankind necessarily constitutes a work that one has to return to over and over again. Nearly thirty years passed by before UNESCO decided to take up once more a work that could by no means be regarded as fin- ished. Requested by the new Member States, a recasting of the first edition deserved the wholehearted support of all those who helped establish the Organization. The changes which have taken place over these last thirty years rendered necessary and amply justified a revision and revaluation of history, and the members of the International Commission were the first to acknowledge such a need. There were, of course, other and more imperative reasons. Two of these should be pointed out here.

The first concerns developments in the area of research methodology since the 1960s. Over the last three decades historical knowledge has increased considerably and has turned from factual history to a greater interest in anthro- pological research. Although they still remain far from being fully capable of answering all the questions that we ask today – or for that matter the more serious of those posed thirty years ago – the added insight that present studies offer us deserves to be transmitted to a larger public. The second, and perhaps less obvious reason, springs from the very role that the writing of history can, and should play in increasing our level of awareness. A writing, or as in the present case, a rewriting of the history of human scientific and cultural evolution signifies not only taking stock of the new data available but also helping one and all in evaluating and assessing the various implications, positive and also negative, of all the changes. Justifying science in the name of all its benefits and advantages amounts to refusing to accept the damaging effects it can have. We have gradually accustomed ourselves to the presence of many latent nuclear volcanoes without compensating for the technological risks. Not enough has been done to counterbalance the excessive monetary investments needed to build up such arsenals with sufficient funds to help confront the problems and miseries afflicting one section of humanity and which is on the way to becoming a danger for the other. Technological development has also begun to seriously endanger animal and plant life on this planet. Factors such as these plead for greater vigilance.

Universal histories and histories of the world abound. So many have already been published and continue to be published that one could question the need to bring out yet another one. No doubt many readers will be surprised at this venture. Each in his own way will of course judge this work better or worse than another of its kind. There is, however, one major difference. Other works of history enjoy a certain freedom that has in a sense been denied to the present one. They are free to choose themes, periods and regions that suit best the demands of a particular readership and a specific conception of history. Such works can thereby claim a certain cohesion of the elements introduced; a cohesion which also helps establish a certain uniformity of expression and style. The present work is founded on an entirely different principle; a maximum of diversity. This diversity proves to be, on the one hand, so great that it is difficult to stop it from becoming disparate and, on the other, not great enough to allow for a convenient regrouping of elements into types. The fault lies not in the venture itself nor in those who took up the task. It lies mainly in the present state of historical knowledge. The analytic nature of historical research today blocks the way to synthesis, to the kind of approach required in the writing of a history that can be considered truly universal.

This work can serve only as a history of the world and not as a universal history. This, of course, is already a great deal. We should not count on the diffusion of a universalism, which is the subject of reflection by a very small, privileged minority, as long as all cultures are not equally represented and historians from all parts of the world are not endowed with the same means and cannot claim the same status, social and otherwise.

Not claiming to attain the unattainable does not, however, mean renunciation. The roads to universalism are full of bends and curves. But, they all lead to the same destination; one history for one united world. Since this history could not reach the highest common factor, it had to tend towards the lowest common multiple. And in this respect, the present work has not failed in its mission.

In 1950 we opted in three days for a plan that would take thirteen years to complete. With a view to ensuring a unity of style and presentation, we decided that each of the six volumes would be written by a single author. Such ideas had to be abandoned. Some thirty years later, the New Commission decided to take more time over the distribution of the work to be done among seven and not six volumes, each well coordinated with the other and allowing free play to as many authors as would be necessary to cover a maximum of domains. The selection of the criteria on which the new history would be based first led to a detailed examination of the comments made by the readers of the first edition. After many debates and discussions, all agreed that it would not do simply to juxtapose a series of regional histories one after the other. Then one of the two possible solutions had to be chosen; dividing history either into themes or into periods and analysing each according to themes and regions. The first option – an idea that had already been put forward before 1948 – would perhaps have helped bring out in a more significant manner the factors which render manifest the common destiny of mankind. But the present state of historical research, which in most cases and owing to an ever-increasing acquisition of skills, proceeds in the form of temporal as well as regional specializations, constituted a real obstacle to the realization of such a scheme. It was therefore decided that each of the seven volumes would be devoted to a single period and would contain a thematic and regional section.

Yielding to the constraints imposed by the state of knowledge and research today does not, however, solve all probable problems. Let us take a look at the issue point by point.

The idea of splitting the past into defined periods pleased no one, as most historians view it as an organic whole. But, taking everything into consideration, had the objective been to separate one cultural component from another or, for example, the physical from the cultural or the religious from the profane, this surgery would have turned literally into a vivisection. Opting for the lesser evil, the Commission thus decided to work on chronological sections. This, at least, allowed for the preservation of a certain unity within each group.

Already in the 1950s it had become evident that the form of periodization upheld by the European tradition loses its signification when applied to the other parts of the world. Terms such as 'Antiquity', 'the Middle Ages' or 'modern times' do not correspond to much insofar as Asia is concerned, and perhaps even less for what concerns Africa. Admittedly, we continue using such words for the sake of convenience. We cannot totally discard them, but we should try at least not to trust them fully.

The importance of each period is measured more in terms of what humankind has contributed to each than in terms of a duration defined by astronomy. The 'Grand Discoveries' of the sixteenth and the seventeenth centuries led to some spectacular changes in the history of the world. A sudden growth of ideas and of commercial capitalism accompanied by or resulting from military conquest gave rise to migrations that brought about the creation of a new map of the world and new conceptions of humanity's destiny. This moment marks a turning point that we have ever since sensed as an acceleration of history. It was, therefore, decided that three volumes of the present work would be devoted to the period succeeding these significant changes and transformations as against only four which would cover the entire preceding period, starting from the origins of humankind and leading up to the sixteenth century. The Commission also decided to devote more and more pages to the more recent years. The fifth volume thus covers three centuries; the sixth, one and a half; and the seventh only about seventy-five years.

A word of caution is, however, necessary. We often make use of a concept of progress that is based on the quantitative and not the qualitative value of what has been achieved. Manufactured goods, consumer items and exchanges, whether they concern concrete objects or ideas, can be more or less quantified. But, as we do not possess any means of measuring happiness or well-being, we cannot infer therefrom that the quantitative and the qualitative values of this progress are the same, particularly insofar as the world in general is concerned. This notion of progress should not, moreover, hinder a proper appraisal of all that was contributed to history by our ancestors, to whom we owe our existence and our way of living.

Great care was taken to avoid putting an undue emphasis on what could be considered as being only the European landmarks of history. The years 1789 and 1914, although highly significant in the history of Europe, served only nominally as points of reference. It was understood that, depending on the case, the ethnocentrism implied by these dates would be reduced as much as necessary through a proper and adequate treatment of the issues preceding or following them. Similarly, to avoid falling into the traps of Western traditionalism, it was considered necessary to cease using the Christianization of the Roman Empire as a mark of the end of the Ancient World and the beginning of the Middle Ages and, therefore, to include the first years of the Hegira in the third volume, which covers the period from 700 BC to AD 700, the middle of which comes before the beginning of the era acknowledged – belatedly – also by the Muslims.

The Commission's choice does not conflict greatly with the Chinese system of dating, because around the same epoch the same phenomenon appeared in both the east and west of Eurasia: The awakening of tribes in these Central Steppes who until then had been restricted to a disorderly, Brownian form of movement of particular groups, and who henceforth united together and set off to conquer the largest empire that the world has ever known. Events such as this draw our attention to the advantages of following a calendar determined not according to the permanent aspects of the planets but according to the variations of climate. Indeed, the Mongols would not have reached such a high degree of power had the climate not favoured the humidification of the pasture lands which nourished their horses. However, it will be a good while before we have available a calendar based on climatic variations. We still lack information on some vital factors; the evaluation of harvests, the extension or the regression of lacustrine and forest areas, phyto-graphical analyses, and so on. Only when we have obtained such necessary data can we think of establishing a new type of periodization that can be verified through metereological calculations extrapolating and applying to the past our present conjectures about the influence of solar explosions on the atmosphere.

The period to be treated in the fourth volume was therefore set by the end of Volume III (the seventh century) and the beginning (the sixteenth century) of Volume V. Volumes I and II have been devoted to the many thousands of years constituting the origins of humanity. The richness of the new data at our disposal made it necessary to treat separately the period spreading from the third millennium to the beginning of the seventh century before our era.

This division into seven volumes, dictated by a combination of factors ranging from the abstract to the practical – amongst the latter, being that of ensuring the more or less equal size of the volumes – is more or less in keeping with historical facts. Beyond all specific differences, five principal stages can be recorded in human evolution: the use of material tools accompanied by the emergence of cultures destined to be full of meaning for a long time to come; the moulding of a geo-politics or a geo-culture signalled by the appearance of major works of all kinds, all of which were to be of lasting value; partitive convulsions that forced in advance the distinction of cultural identities through the play of mutual influences; conceptions resulting from a closed human universe whose planetary course lies within a limitless space; the intensification of centres of development under the pressure of a capitalism that has become industrial and an industry that is becoming scientific – phenomena which push to the outskirts the excess of constraints from which the thus privileged zones escape. The seventh volume will thus deal with the issue of these new currents and the tidal waves that they provoke; facets that lead to the birth of a new type of polarization and as a result of which traditional cultures fall into abeyance.

Such bird's-eye views as those offered here are not misleading because they are crude; they seem questionable because they escape our sight when we keep ourselves too close to the ordinary facts. And it is in this that we mainly confront the limitations of our methods of research. No one is unaware of the difficulties that continue to affect all attempts to provide a synthetic view of humankind's common destiny. There is no answer to these difficulties from which the present subdivision of each volume into themes and regions suffers; into themes to bring out what all human beings share in common; into regions to mark the diversities.

In each volume, the thematic parts should have been the easiest to work out. Several problems were, however, encountered. In order to ensure that the cultures that benefit from the spectacular development that we witness today be no longer favoured beyond measure, it was considered necessary to reduce the importance granted to theoretical innovations and their applications and therefore to refrain from using scientific discoveries as chronological pointers. Had this not been the case, the distribution of themes would have been a simple matter. It would have sufficed to begin with a survey of the scientific and technical knowledge acquired over a given period of time, and then retrace the causes in their sequential order.

Now, from the moment when it becomes necessary for history to tone down the privileges conferred on some by the process of evolution – and, more particularly, to question a system of values rooted in an overly univocal notion of progress – it also becomes necessary to standardize the distribution of themes by including more 'ordinary' references: For example, by starting with a description of the physical and natural conditions in order to arrive at the scientific through the demographic and the cultural. This not only increased the uniformity of the volumes but also offered the major advantage of emphasizing the ways of living. Whatever they are, these must first satisfy the basic physiological needs – a vital minimum dictated by the instincts of survival and rendered partially relative by the differences of climate. Each culture responds to this in its own manner, and according as much to its natural environment as to the habits that it inherits. Certain acquired needs are then added to this vital minimum – superfluous needs turned into necessary ones and established in varying degrees according to the social hierarchies and geohistorical differences. Moreover, as human beings are not only biological but also thinking and feeling entities, each material culture is accompanied by a culture that can be called 'spiritual' in the widest sense of the term, and that also varies according to the situation already mentioned. Finally, even though the conditions are not identical, material culture and spiritual culture are interrelated.

This enunciation of the common grounds on which all human lives are established stands to reason and would seem evident to any lay person. It could also, however, lead us to think that it is easy to find historians ready to develop each theme. The present state of historical knowledge proves that it is not so and, as always, for the same reason. Insignificant as this problem may be, the solution lies in turning one's back on analytical methods and adopting an approach that would be one of synthesis.

Undoubtedly, current research and investigations help us in our evaluation of material and spiritual cultures, but separately. We are completely ignorant about the interconnections between the two. Where does this notorious deficiency come from? Two main reasons can be put forward.

The first concerns the elaboration of a global history. Indeed, when it comes to local or regional histories, each confined to a particular epoch, the data that we possess helps us either to deal with some of the problems or to contribute by offering some information. But when one problem or another needs to be looked at from a global point of view, then we confront a major difficulty; which elements of the data available should be included in an inventory of an absolutely common heritage? In other words, what advances made at one place or another, or at one point of time or another, effectively contributed to what can be called 'general progress'? The workshops of historians can boast of few if any historians at all who specialize in the evaluation of 'generalities'! When the need for one arises, then it has to be admitted that the courageous few who have undertaken such a task suffered from the absence of sufficient information and were compelled to work in conditions that rendered their merits highly eminent but curbed considerably their influence.

This first reason leads to the second, the absence of criteria that would make it possible to distinguish effectively the subjective from the objective, as much in the work accomplished as in the reputations won. Here we touch upon an issue that is too important to dismiss without fuller attention.

The studies on primitive or savage societies, particularly those conducted over the last fifty years, carried anthropology to a high degree of what must be called the 'intelligence' of cultures. Indeed, in these societies, myth plays a fundamental role. It legitimizes matrimonial and social behaviour as well as customs and ways of living – the way one eats, dresses and organizes one's life inside and outside one's own dwelling. In an even more significant manner, it legitimizes humankind's spiritual behaviour as much in times of war as in peace. This global aspect of myth itself leads us to the heights from which, at one glance, we can view not only the various behaviours as a whole, but also, and as a result, the very logic that sustains them.

Historical evolution disperses myth, without however abolishing the mythological function. It provokes the growth of branches and favours ramifications. What had been thanks to myth, at one and the same time, religion and literature, moral and political, art and technique, breaks up later into more and more subdivided areas of knowledge; differentiations that led namely to the belief that the logic of myth or of the sacred is gainsaid by that of science. 'Science'; this word, which obstructs more than all others what we term historical intelligence. In the original sense of the word, science means knowledge, with no distinction implied between knowledge and know-how. Today this same word has taken on such a specific meaning that for a vast majority of the most highly informed minds, science denotes truth, as against the falsity of myth. Yet, many eminent scholars acknowledge that this 'truth' contains a part of myth and that it is indeed thanks to this that methods and knowledge advance. It is by working within the mythological that we reduce the part of myths, something of which always survives in the very heart of science.

The barriers that have been most resolutely built against the 'intelligence' of history have their sources in the gradual formation of separate enclaves of investigation. Social, economic, political, literary history and so on; each domain follows its worn path and rarely meets the other, or never enough to allow for the establishment of criteria common to all that could constitute the basis for a truly universal history of scientific and cultural developments. The worst form of such separation can be found in the cosmic distance that has been introduced between the history of religion and that of science, and this, in spite of some highly remarkable, though rare, attempts to make them move towards each other via the social and the philosophical. No significant results should be expected until the gaps between ordinary language and scientific language are bridged, particularly when the latter makes use of mathematical terms so fully exploited by the initiated few and so little accessible to the secular mass.

This brings us back to the question of the limitations of this edition referred to earlier; limitations concerning the basic logical presuppositions on which a truly universal history of humankind should be founded. It is only on the basis of certain common features that one culture can comprehend something that is part of another culture and that the people of today can understand a little of what lies in the past. But then, given the present state of our knowledge and the manner in which the basic logical presuppositions are handled, our history will remain beyond the reach of the general public, however enlightened, for which it is intended.

None the less, a certain merit – perhaps less significant than hoped for – makes this second edition worthy of our attention. By eliminating the notion that the cultures rendered marginal by 'progress' represent groups of people 'without history', the study of cultures wherein myth is dispersed among all kinds of domains could only gain from the experience of those whose lives are, even today, steeped in a mythology that they all consider fundamental. We have not as yet reached our goal, but the step taken marks a sure improvement in terms of our understanding of history. And, as readers will themselves find out, it is this aspect of the thematic part of each volume that makes this work truly exceptional.

We now come to the question of the treatment of regions in each volume. To begin with, let us look at a major ambiguity, which threatened the very conception of these sections. An example will suffice. To which region does Newton belong? To Cambridge? England? Europe? The West? The world? There is no doubt that the universality of his law of gravitation makes him a part of the common heritage of humanity. Yet, undoubtedly this law discovered by a particular man, at a particular place and point of time, would seem to have miraculously descended from the skies, if we did not take into account the facts of the discovery, the circumstances leading to it and the manner in which the law was adopted by all. Should we have then talked about Newton in one way in the thematic chapter and in another in the regional? Although the difficulties involved in solving such a problem are great, they turn out to be less so when confronted with yet another problem that would have resulted from any attempt to merge the two parts into one; for, in that case, the question would have been, which one? A fusion of all into the regional would, to a great extent, have simplified the task, given that we are dealing with specializations in different fields. But it would have led to the very unpleasant need to emphasize the merits of one culture at the cost of the others. A fusion of all into the thematic? In that case, Newton's law would have been stripped of its socio-cultural characteristics and this would have led to some kind of sanctification of the 'genius'. Needless to say, what has been noted as regards Newton applies to all thinkers, discoverers and to all that humankind has created.

Some readers will perhaps regret the fact that this history, whose dominant note is certainly transcultural, does not succeed better in overcoming certain problems resulting from habits and preconceived notions. We all talk about Asia, Africa and Europe. Originally, these were names given to Greek nymphs and were used to distinguish the three principal, cardinal points of the world perceived by the Mediterranean navigators: the east, the south and the north, respectively. To these seafarers the west was nothing but a vast indecipherable stretch, presumably a part of the legendary Atlantis. As for the continent of America, its name was curiously given to it by a cartographer who, while outlining a map of this continent, used the information supplied to him by Amerigo Vespucci – thus depriving Christopher Columbus of the recognition he deserved. In the case of the nymphs as well as in that of the cartographer, we can no longer distinguish the subjective from the objective. What was in fact a very subjective decision in the first place now appears to be very objective because it is commonly accepted by everyone. We cannot change something that has been so firmly established over the years, but the often very serious problems and disadvantages that result from the ethnocentrism implied by such customs need to be pointed out.

Depending on the epochs, Egypt is at times best understood when considered as African and at others when its civilization is regarded as having acquired much of its significance from a dual Nile-Euphrates identity. Similarly, instead of remaining Mediterranean, southern Europe became continental when the centre of gravity of exchanges and developments shifted to the Atlantic. China constitutes another example. This Middle Kingdom felt the effects of the existence of other continental regions when its Great Wall no longer protected it from the conquerors it tried later to assimilate, or when it yielded, perhaps for too long a period, to the attacks of the seamen and naval forces coming from the other end of the world, that is, from Europe.

Geographical perspectives change from one era to the other. But it is difficult to incorporate such changes and align them with the periodization adopted for a work on history. Those responsible for planning the seven volumes

had to devise the ways and means of solving such problems. At times they had to have recourse to certain subterfuges so as to prevent the periodization from turning into some kind of a jigsaw puzzle and requiring a frequent arrangement and rearrangement. This entailed, however, the risks of introducing certain anachronisms.

Such risks are in no way negligible. To a modern mind, for example, the commerce or the conquests in ancient times across the deserts of Sinai appear as manifestations of the hostilities existing between Africa and Asia. This distinction between the two continents becomes nonsensical when applied to the period when Egypt did not see itself as African nor Assyria as Asian. Each region thought of itself first as constituting in itself the whole universe or as representing in itself the whole universe as defined by its own gods. We must be aware of the dangers of accepting such ideas, which still survive in the unconscious, affect our conscious minds, and foster notions of rights and privileges detrimental to the development of universalism.

The need to determine the number of pages to be devoted to each 'contingent' arose from certain customs that, although anachronic, generate at times very strong emotions and influence our decisions. It also arose from the fact that the distrust of ethnocentrism expressed itself in terms that were very ethnocentric. Including Cro-Magnon man in an inventory of 'European' sites amounts to attributing to him a label that contradicts all that was felt in times when existence could not be conceived of except in terms very different from those related to our planetary territoriality. Similarly, the concept of Africa was itself foreign to the African empires or kingdoms, each constituting for each a world in itself and, at the same time, a world which belongs to all. Readers will themselves correct such imperfections, which have resulted from a need to adopt a pragmatic approach.

Applying modern notions of geography to any period of the past relieves us of the dizziness felt when we look down into the immense depths of time, yet it is in these depths that cultural but also natural interactions, direct or indirect, multiplied; a swarming mass much too indecipherable to allow for the delineation of linear ancestry. It is, therefore, better to avoid distinguishing overmuch our distant common ancestors. Physical evolution leads perhaps to the formation of races. But as the human species can be known through its customs, faculties and cerebral activities, this privilege common to all reduces practically to nothing the particularisms that some not always disinterested viewpoints defined formerly as racial.

The human species cannot really be differentiated except as ethnic groups and through customs that defy any simplistic typology. A strong capacity for adaption, peculiar to humans, enables them to invent a practically limitless number of solutions to the problems posed by all kinds of environments, and even more so by circumstances that the smallest events modify and great events transform altogether. In this lies the most amazing aspect of history: the infinite variety of answers that each individual or collectivity finds to the questions put to it by destiny. The more history accelerates its pace and becomes more specific, the more our destiny becomes enigmatic. This is because every human being is a human being and no single one resembles another.

The end of the colonialisms that believed or claimed themselves to be the civilizers of this world led to the birth of many new nations and many new member states of international organizations. 'New' in what sense? The establishment of a 'New World Order' is bound to remain a Utopian idea as long as history has not explained how a local body of historical cultures finally engendered what it has over the centuries referred to as 'civilization'; a word full of contradictions. Intended as universal and respectful to other cultures, this civilization turned out to be materialist and destroyed many cultures as a result of the superiority that it attributed to its own system of laws and rights. Two heavy tasks thus face historians; acknowledging the universalism that lies hidden beneath all particularisms and agreeing among themselves on what should be made generally known in this respect.

An elucidation of the past requires personal as well as collective efforts. This twofold process should therefore have found spontaneous expression in a work meant to aid the advancement of knowledge. The Commission recommended therefore that, in addition to the thematic and regional parts, a third part be added that would have comprised specific supplements on details that needed developing, problems that needed solving, and finally an exposition of different and opposing opinions on interpretations in dispute. This project met with overwhelming difficulties, and some explanation is called for.

This international history, which had been conceived as a result of dialogues and discussions, would evidently have gained considerably from an exposition of the differences in interpretation in their proper dimensions. It would have been more lively and instructive and have given readers more food for thought. Unfortunately, the dispersion of authors to be included and chosen from the whole world demanded means and time that we did not have. The editors, who already had a heavy task, could not have undertaken this extra work without assistance, in particular from committees specifically chosen and brought together in the light of the subjects to be discussed. Taking into account the costs of travel and accommodation, the already high cost of the operation would have almost doubled. No doubt a day will come when, debates on themes and regions

being easier than they are now, it will be possible to expound history as it is revealed by a confrontation of knowledge and viewpoints on particular questions concerning all humanity.

Until the state of knowledge and of historical research in the world has reached this convergent point, we are obliged to give up the idea of showing the divergences that future workshops of historians will have to face. We have, however, provided notes at the end of articles, which have been written so as to ensure maximum diversity and the broadest possible participation. A certain arbitrariness persists, of course. But this will remain unavoidable as long as the excesses that analyses lead to are not minimized through the elaboration of syntheses based on criteria derived from irrefutable logical presuppositions – presuppositions that help establish universal certitudes. Let us not forget, however, that innovations originate only within the gaps of certitude.

One of the merits of this work lies in that it has succeeded in enlisting the collaboration of a very large number of people, representing a large number of regions and cultures. The Commission also encouraged the formation of local working groups responsible for obtaining and organizing the data to be included in the various chapters. This present work marks perhaps only the beginning of such collective efforts. Nevertheless, it permits us to anticipate satisfactory results. Knowing oneself well in order to make oneself better known constitutes a major contribution to mutual understanding. In this respect, historical research resembles an awareness of unconscious phenomena. It brings into the daylight what in the nocturnal depths of individual or collective existences gives them life, so to speak, in spite of themselves or against their will.

This publication will no doubt give rise to many criticisms. If these turn out to be harsh, they will justify the project, whose main objective is to arouse us from our dogmatic slumber. Historical events take care of this much more efficiently, but at a much higher price.

GENERAL INTRODUCTION

Georges-Henri Dumont
President of the International Commission (1994)

Societies are making greater demands than ever on history, but urgent as they might be, these demands by various groups are not altogether straightforward. Some societies look to historians to define their identity, to buttress the development of their specific characteristics or even to present and analyse the past as confirming a founding myth. Conversely, other societies influenced both by the *Annales* school of historiography and by the geographical, chronological and thematic enlargement of history, aspire to the building of bridges, the ending of self-isolation and the smoothing out of the lack of continuity that is characteristic of the short term.

In 1946 those attending the meeting of the first Preparatory Commission of UNESCO agreed that it was part of the fundamental mission of the United Nations Educational, Scientific and Cultural Organization to lay the foundations for a collective memory of humanity and of all its parts, spread all over the world and expressing themselves in every civilization. The International Scientific Commission came into being four years later with the apparently gigantic task of drafting a *History of the Scientific and Cultural Development of Mankind*. Publication of the six volumes began in 1963, marking the successful conclusion of an international endeavour without parallel, but not without risks. Success with the general public was immediate and lasting, notwithstanding the reservations expressed by the critics, who often found certain choices disconcerting but were not consistent in the choices and interpretations they proposed as alternatives.

For its time – not that of its publication but that of its long preparation – the first edition of the *History* must be seen as a daring achievement, having a number of faults inherent in the very nature of historical knowledge, but opening up new avenues and encouraging further progress along them.

In 1978, the General Conference of UNESCO decided to embark on a new and completely revised edition of the *History* because it realized that the considerable development of historiography, the improvement in what are called its auxiliary sciences and its growing links with the social sciences, had combined with an extraordinary acceleration of day-to-day history. What it did not know, however, was that the pace of this acceleration would continue to increase until it brought profound changes to the face of the world.

It scarcely needs saying that the task laid upon the International Scientific Commission, under the chairmanship of the late Paulo de Berrêdo Carreiro and then of my eminent predecessor, Professor Charles Morazó, was both enormous and difficult.

First of all, international teams had to be formed, as balanced as possible, and cooperation and dialogue organized between the different views of the major collective stages in the lives of people, but without disregarding the cultural identity of human groups.

Next, attention had to be given to changes in chronological scale by attempting a scientific reconstruction of the successive stages of the peopling of our planet, including the spread of animal populations. This was the goal pursued and largely attained by the authors of the present volume.

Lastly, steps had to be taken to ensure that traditional methods of historical research, based on written sources, were used side-by-side with new critical methods adapted to the use of oral sources and contributions from archaeology, in Africa for the most part.

To quote what Professor Jean Devisse said at a symposium in Nice in 1986 on 'Being a historian today': 'If we accept that the history of other people has something to teach us, there can be no infallible model, no immutable methodological certainty: listening to each other can lead to a genuine universal history'.

Although historians must be guided by a desire for intellectual honesty, they depend on their own views of things, with the result that history is the science most vulnerable to ideologies. The fall of the Berlin Wall a few weeks after I assumed office symbolized the end of a particularly burdensome ideological division. It certainly makes the work of the International Scientific Commission easier whenever it has to come to grips with the past/present dialectic from which history cannot escape.

In a way, the impact of ideologies will also be lessened by the fact that the Chief Editors of each volume have sought the invaluable cooperation not only of experienced historians but also of renowned specialists in disciplines such as law, art, philosophy, literature, oral traditions, the natural sciences, medicine, anthropology, mathematics and economics. In any event, this interdisciplinary, which helps dissipate error, is undoubtedly one of the major improvements of this second edition of the *History of Humanity* over the previous edition.

Another problem faced was that of periodization. It was out of the question systematically to adopt the periodization long in use in European history, that is Antiquity, the Middle Ages, and modern times, because it is now being extensively called into question and also, above all, because it would have led to a Eurocentric view of world history, a view whose absurdity is now quite obvious. The seven volumes are thus arranged in the following chronological order:

Volume I   Prehistory and the beginnings of civilization
Volume II   From the third millennium to the seventh century BC
Volume III   From the seventh century BC to the seventh century AD
Volume IV   From the seventh to the sixteenth century
Volume V   From the sixteenth to the eighteenth century
Volume VI   The nineteenth century
Volume VII The twentieth century

It must be stated at once that this somewhat surgical distribution is in no way absolute or binding. It will in no way prevent the overlapping that there must be at the turn of each century if breaks in continuity and the resulting errors of perspective are to be avoided.

In his preface, Professor Charles Morazé has clearly described and explained the structure of each of the volumes, with a thematic chapter, a regional chapter and annexes. This structure, too, may be modified so as not to upset the complementarity of the pieces of a mosaic that must retain its significance.

When the International Scientific Commission, the Chief Editors of the volumes and the very large number of contributors have completed their work – and this will be in the near future – they will be able to adopt as their motto the frequently quoted saying of the philosopher Etienne Gilson:

> We do not study history to get rid of it but to save from nothingness all the past which, without history, would vanish into the void. We study history so that what, without it, would not even be the past any more, may be reborn to life in this unique present outside which nothing exists.

This present will be all the more unique because history will have shown itself to be not an instrument for legitimizing exacerbated forms of nationalism, but an instrument, ever more effective because ever more perfectible, for ensuring mutual respect, solidarity and the scientific and cultural interdependence of humanity.

THE INTERNATIONAL COMMISSION

for the New Edition of the History of the Scientific and Cultural Development of Mankind

---

President: G.-H. Dumont (Belgium)

Members of the International Commission:
I. A. Abu-Lughod (The Palestinian Authority)
A. R. Al-Ansary (Saudi Arabia)
J. Bony (Ivory Coast)
E. K. Brathwaite (Barbados)
G. Carrera Damas (Venezuela)
A. H. Dani (Pakistan)
D. Denoon (Australia)
M. Garanin (Yugoslavia, Fed. Rep. of)
T. Haga (Japan)
F. Iglesias (Brazil)
H. Inalcik (Turkey)
S. Kartodirdjo (Indonesia)
J. Ki-Zerbo (Burkina Faso)
C. Martinez Shaw (Spain)
E. Mendelsohn (United States of America)

Bureau of the International Commission:
A. R. Al-Ansary (Saudi Arabia)
E. K. Brathwaite (Barbados)
G. Carrera Damas (Venezuela)
A. H. Dani (Pakistan)
E. Mendelsohn (United States of America)

Honorary Members:
S. A. Al-Ali (Iraq)
P. J. Riis (Denmark)
T. Yamamoto (Japan)

Former Presidents:
P. E. B. Carneiro (Brazil) (deceased)
C. Morazé (France)

Secretariat (UNESCO):
J. P. Bouyain, Programme Specialist
B. Appleyard (Ms)
M. Vallés (Ms)
E. M'Bokolo (Democratic Republic of the Congo)
K. N'Ketia (Ghana)
T. Obenga (Congo)
B. A. Ogot (Kenya)
Pang Pu (China)
W. Sauerlander (Germany)
B. Schroeder-Gudehus (Ms) (Canada)
R. Thapar (Ms) (India)
I. D. Thiam (Senegal)
K. V. Thomas (United Kingdom)
S. L. Tikhvinsky (Russian Federation)
N. Todorov (Bulgaria)
G. Weinberg (Argentina)
M. Yardeni (Ms) (Israel)
E. Zürcher (the Netherlands)

R. Thapar (Ms) (India)
I. D. Thiam (Senegal)
K. V. Thomas (United Kingdom)
S. L. Tikhvinsky (Russian Federation)
N. Todorov (Bulgaria)

Former Members:
E. Condurachi (Romania) (deceased)
G. Daws (Australia)
C. A. Diop (Senegal) (deceased)
A. A. Kamel (Egypt) (deceased)
M. Kably (Morocco)
H. Nakamura (Japan)
J. Prawer (Israel) (deceased)
S. Zavala (Mexico)

HISTORY OF HUMANITY
SCIENTIFIC AND CULTURAL
DEVELOPMENT
IN SEVEN VOLUMES

VOLUME I
Prehistory and the Beginning of Civilization

Editor: S. J. De Laet (Belgium)
Co-Editors: A. H. Dani (Pakistan)
            J. L. Lorenzo (Mexico) (deceased)
            R. B. Nunoo (Ghana)

VOLUME II
From the Third Millennium to the Seventh Century BC

Editors: A. H. Dani (Pakistan)
            J-R. Mohen (France)
Co-Editors: C. A. Diop (Senegal) (deceased)
            J. L. Lorenzo (Mexico) (deceased)
            V. M. Masson (Russian Federation)
            T. Obenga (Congo)
            M. B. Sakelladou (Greece)
            B. K. Thapar (India) (deceased)
            Xia Nai (China) (deceased)
            Zhang Changshou (China)

VOLUME III
From the Seventh Century BC to the Seventh Century AD

Editors: E. Condurachi (Romania) (deceased)
            J. Hermiann (Germany)
            E. Zürcher (the Netherlands)
Co-Editors: J. Harmatta (Hungary)
            J. K. Litvak (Mexico)
            R. Lonis (France)
            T. Obenga (Congo)
            R. Thapar (Ms) (India)
            Zhou Yiliang (China)

VOLUME IV
From the Seventh to the Sixteenth Century

Editors: M. A. Al-Bakhit (Jordan)
            L. Bazin (France)
            S. M. Cissoko (Mali)
            A. A. Kamel (Egypt) (deceased)

Co-Editors: M. S. Asimov (Tajikistan) (deceased)
            P. Gendrop (Mexico) (deceased)
            A. Gieysztor (Poland)
            I. Habib (India)
            J. Karayannopoulos (Greece)
            J. K. Litvak/P. Schmidt (Mexico)

VOLUME V
From the Sixteenth to the Eighteenth Century

Editors: P. Burke (United Kingdom)
            H. Inalcik (Turkey)
Co-Editors: I. Habib (India)
            J. Ki-Zerbo (Burkina Faso)
            T. Kusamitsu (Japan)
            C. Martinez Shaw (Spain)
            E. Tchernjak (Russian Federation)
            E. Trabulse (Mexico)

VOLUME VI
The Nineteenth Century

Editors: P. Mathias (United Kingdom)
            N. Todorov (Bulgaria)
Co-Editors: S. Al Mujahid (Pakistan)
            O. Chubarian (Russian Federation)
            F. Iglesias (Brazil)
            Shu-li Ji (China)
            I. D. Thiam (Senegal)

VOLUME VII
The Twentieth Century

Editors: E. K. Brathwaite (Barbados)
            S. Gopal (India)
            E. Mendelsohn (United States of America)
            S. L. Tikhvinsky (Russian Federation)
Co-Editors: I. A. Abu-Lughod (the Palestinian Authority)
            I. D. Thiam (Senegal)
            G. Weinberg (Argentina)
            Tao Wenzhao (China)

LIST OF TABLES

LIST OF MAPS

LIST OF PLATES

THE CONTRIBUTORS

Agboteka, Francis (Ghana); spec. modern West African history; formerly Professor, University of Cape Coast; Fellow, Historical Society of Ghana, Chairman, Organization for Research on Eweland (ORE).

Akamatsu, Paul A. (France); spec. modern and contemporary Japanese history and research; Director, Centre National de la Recherche Scientifique (CNRS), Paris.

Al Mujahid, Sharif (Pakistan); spec. Muslim Freedom Movement (1857–1947), contemporary history of Pakistan; retired Professor of Journalism and Communication; Director, Freedom Movement Archives, University of Karachi.

Ann-Baron, Ok-Sung (France); spec. cultural history of ancient Korea; former Assistant Lecturer, Institut National des Langues et Civilisations Orientales (INALCO) and Musée National des Arts Asiatiques Guimet (France); former Researcher, Centre d'Etude de la Société et de la Culture Coréennes (CECSC), University of Rouen, France.

Bah, Thierno (Guinea, Conakry); spec. military and history of ancient and modern Central Africa; founder member of the Association of African Historians; Professor, University of Yaoundé I (Cameroon).

Barker, Theo, C. (United Kingdom); spec. economic history, Emeritus Professor, University of London.

Bensaude-Vincent, Bernadette (France); Professor of History and Philosophy of the Sciences, University of Paris X-Nanterre.

Berend, Ivan (United States of America); spec. history.

Béranger, Jean (France); spec. modern history, and early modern history; Professor, University of Sorbonne and Director of research, Ecole Pratique des Hautes Etudes (EPHE), Paris.

Berthon, Jean-Pierre (France); spec. modern and contemporary Japanese religions; Researcher, Centre National de la Recherche Scientifique (CNRS), East Asia Institute, Collège de France, Paris.

Bhebe, Ngwabi (Zimbabwe); spec. political and cultural history of Zimbabwe and southern Africa; Professor of History, University of Zimbabwe; President of the Historical Society of Zimbabwe.

Blomme, Jan (Belgium); spec. history of economic development; Director of Research Department of the Antwerp Port Authority.

Blondel, Christine (France); spec. history of physics (eighteenth and nineteenth centuries); Researcher, Centre National de la Recherche Scientifique (CNRS), Paris.

Carrera Damas, Germán (Venezuela); spec. history, methodology and technical documental investigation; founder of the Cathedral of Theory and Method of History; Professor, Central University of Venezuela.

Charleux, Isabelle (France); spec. history of Mongolian art; Doctor, University of Paris IV.

Chater, Khalifa (Tunisia); Professor of Modern and Contemporary Histories, Faculty of Letters and Human Sciences, University of Tunis, Director-General of National Library of Tunis.

Cheah Boon-Kheng (Malaysia); spec. social and political history of Malaysia and southeast Asia; retired Professor of History, School of Humanities, Universiti Sains Malaysia in Penang, Malaysia. Vice-President of the Malaysian Branch of the Royal Asiatic Society.

Chinchilla, Perla (Mexico); spec. Mexican historiography and cultural history, Professor, Universidad Iberoamericana, responsible for the nineteenth century volume of History of the Sciences in Mexico.

Chubarian, Alexander, O. (Russia); spec. history of Europe and the European idea in the nineteenth/twentieth centuries; corresponding member of the Russian Academy of Sciences; Director of the Institute of Universal History.

Clément, Olivier (France); spec. Orthodox world, Professor, Orthodox Institut Saint-Serge, Paris.

Collard, Patrick (Belgium); spec. modern Spanish and Latin American literature and culture; Professor, University of Ghent; member, Belgian Royal Academy of Overseas Sciences.

Coulibaly, Elisée (Burkina Faso); spec. history of archaeology; Chargé de Mission, National Museum of Arts of Africa and Oceania (Paris), senior researcher, mining history and metallurgy, University of Paris I, CNRS, France.

Crouzet, François (France); spec. economic history of the eighteenth and nineteenth centuries, particularly Britain and France; Emeritus Professor of Modern History, University of Paris-Sorbonne; Member of the Academia European; Corresponding Fellow of the Royal Academy of Belgium and of the British Academy.

Dani, Ahmad, H. (Pakistan); spec. archaeology; Professor, University of Islamabad; Director, Centre for the Study of Central Asian Civilisations; Director of Taxila Institute of Asian Civilizations.

Delissen, Alain (France); Lecturer at Ecole des Hautes Etudes en Sciences Sociales (EHESS), (Centre Corée); Holder of *Aggregation*, Doctorate in History, degree in Korean.

Denoon, Donald (Australia); Professor of History, University of Papua New Guinea.

Diallo, Thierno, M. (Guinea – Senegal); spec. Islam, Faculté des Lettres et Sciences Humaines, University of Paris XII – Val-de-Marne Créteil.

Dilagowa, Hanna (Poland); spec. history of the nineteenth and twentieth centuries of Central Eastern Europe; Emeritus Professor, Catholic University, Lublin.

Fievé, Nicolas (France); spec. history of medieval, pre-modern and modern architecture and urbanism in Japan; Researcher, Centre National de la Recherche Scientifique (CNRS), Paris.

Fremdling, Rainer (Germany); spec. economic history of modern times, in particular the process of industrialization; Professor of Economic and Social History, University of Gröningen, the Netherlands.

Gadille, Jacques (France); President and Founder, International Centre of Research and Exchange on the Diffusion of Christianity out of Europe.

Ghomsi, Emmanuel (Cameroon); Professor of African History, University of Yaoundé I; member, Bureau of the Association of African Historians.

Golubkova, Tatiana, V. (Russia); spec. history of philosophy; Docent at the Moscow State Pedagogical University.

Goossaert, Vincent (France); spec. social history of Chinese religion; Chargé de Recherches, Centre National de la Recherche Scientifique (CNRS), Paris.

Grau, Conrad (Germany); spec. East European history; Professor, Academy of Sciences of the former GDR; Researcher, history of German-Russian scientific relations.

Guellouz, Azzedine (Tunisia); spec. history, Arabic and French letters.

Guerra Martiniere, Margarita (Peru); spec. history of Peru and Latin America in the nineteenth and twentieth centuries; Professor, Department of Humanities. Pontificia Universidad Católica del Perú (PUCP) and Department of Sciences of Education. Universidad Femenina del Sagrado Carazón (UNIFE); member of Instituto RIVA-Agüero (PUCP).

Iglesias, Francisco (Brazil); deceased; spec. general history of Latin America; economic, social and politic history; Professor, Universidade Federal de Minas Gerais.

Ionov, Igor, N. (Russia); Senior Researcher at the Institute of Russian History and of the Institute of Universal History of the Russian Academy of Sciences.

Itandala, Buluda, A. (Tanzania); spec. east African history at the University of Dar es Salaam and the Open University of Tanzania; Vice-President of the Historical Association of Tanzania.

Ji, Shu-li (China); spec. philosophy of science, comparative study of Western and Chinese cultures; Professor of the Philosophical Institute of Shanghai Academy of Social Sciences.

Kambou-Ferrand, Jeanne, M. (Burkina Faso); spec. History of Contemporary Africa; Associate Researcher (CRA), Université de Paris.

Kecskeméti, Charles (France); spec. history of Hungarian political institutions and ideas (eighteenth/nineteenth century); Doctor, University of Paris I.

Kiéthéga, Jean-Baptiste (Burkina Faso); spec. African archaeology; Lecturer; Director, Archaeology Laboratory, University of Ouagadougou; Chevalier des Arts et Lettres de la République Française; Prix Prince CLAUS 1998.

Koelbing, Huldrich, M. (Switzerland); Emeritus Professor of the History of Medicine, University of Zurich.

Le Callenec, Sophie (France); spec. history of religions in Sub-Saharan Africa; Université des Réseaux d'Expression Françaises (UREF), Paris.

López-Ocón, Leoncio (Spain); spec. history of science in Spain and Latin America; Researcher at the Centre of History Studies, CSIC, Universidad Complutense de Madrid.

Madeira Santos, Maria, E. (Portugal); spec. history of Portuguese-speaking Africa; Director, Centre of History Studies and Cartography of Antigua at the Institute of Scientific and Tropical Investigation.

Mahalingam Carr, Indira (India); Professor of University of Kent, Canterbury. Reader, international commercial law and Senior Visiting Fellow at the Institute of Advanced Legal Studies, London.

Mathias, Peter (United Kingdom); Professor of the University; Researcher at Jesus College, Cambridge; member of International Association of History and Economy; President Emeritus, Royal Academy of Danish Sciences and Letters.

Mayeur, Françoise (France); Emeritus Professor of contemporary history, University of Paris-Sorbonne.

van Meerten, Michelangelo (Belgium); spec. economic development of nineteenth and twentieth centuries; Fellow, Institute de Recherches Economiques et Sociales, Université Catholique de Louvain; Visiting Professor, Department of Economics and Enterprise, Universitat Pompeú Fabra, Barcelona.

Mitani, Hiroshi (Japan); spec. history of nineteenth-century Japan; Professor, Department of Area Studies, Graduate School of Arts and Sciences, University of Tokyo.

Morazé, Charles (France); Professor, Institute d'Etudes Politiques de Paris I; member-founder of the National Foundation of Political Sciences and Fondation National de la Maison des Sciences de l'Homme; Commandeur des Palmes Académiques; member of the 1st International Commission of the Scientific and Cultural Development for the History of Humanity and former President of the Commission.

Mworoha, Emile (Burundi): spec. modern history; Professor of History, University of Burundi; Director-General of Culture and Communication and Director-General of Politics and Planning at the ACCT. (Agence de Coopération Culturelle et Technique), Paris.

Niane, Djibril, T. (Guinea); spec. African oral traditions (Mandigo world); Professor and former Director of the L. S. Senghor Foundation, Dakar, Senegal; Editor of Vol. 4 of UNESCO's *General History of Africa*; former Dean of the Faculty of Literature and Director of the Organization for Memory and Heritage, Conakry, Guinea. Palmes académiques; Dr honoris causa of Tufts University, Massachusetts.

Niculescu, Remus (Romania); spec. history of modern art; former Director (1992–98), Institute of Art History, Romania Academy.

Ortega-Gálvez, Maria, L. (Spain); spec. history and sociology of science; Associate Professor, Autonomous University of Madrid.

Park, Seong-Rae (Korea); spec. history of science in Korea and East Asia; Professor, Department of History, Hankuk University of Foreign Studies, Seoul.

Pollard, Sidney (United Kingdom) deceased; spec. labour history and economic development of Europe; formerly Professor of Economic History at Sheffield (UK), and latterly at the University of Bielefeld (Germany); Fellow of the British Academy.

Poulat, Emile (France); historian; Professor; Director of Research (since 1968) Centre National de la Recherche Scientifique (CNRS); Director of Studies, Ecole des Hautes Etudes en Sciences Sociales (EHESS); founder member and former Director of Sociology of Religion Group (CNRS); Chairman of honour of the Centro de Estudios de las Religiones en Mexico (CEREM) (Mexico); Médaille du réfractaire, Doctor honoris causa of Laval University, Quebec (Canada).

Rafeq, Abdul-Karim (Syria); spec. modern Arab history; former Chairman and Professor of Modern Arab History, Department of History, University of Damascus; Bickers

Professor of Arab Middle East Studies, College of William and Mary, Virginia, USA.

Rajaonah V. Faranirina (Madagascar); spec. urban, social and cultural history of Madagascar in the nineteenth and twentieth centuries; Teaching-Researcher, University of Antananarivo.

Rasmussen, Anne (France); spec. cultural history of France and international, scientific and intellectual exchange in the nineteenth and twentieth centuries; Senior Researcher, Center of Historical, Scientific and Technological Research, Cité des Sciences et de l'Industrie, Paris.

Reiniche, Marie Louise (France); spec. social and religious anthropology of India; Director of studies at Ecole Pratique des Hautes Etudes (EPHE), Religious Studies Section, Sorbonne, Paris; Head of an EPHE research team: 'The Indian World-Anthropology of a Civilization'.

Romero, Luis, A. (Argentina); spec. social and cultural history of contemporary Argentina; Professor, University of Buenos Aires.

de Roux, Rodolfo (Colombia); spec. history of Latin American catholicism; Professor, University of Toulouse II (France).

Sarkar, Sumit (India); spec. modern Indian social and political history; Professor of History, Delhi University.

Schroeder-Gudehus, Brigitte (Canada); spec. international relations and political history of science and technology (nineteenth and twentieth centuries); Professor, University of Montreal, Department of Political Science, and at the Institute of History and Socio-Politics of Science; Director, Centre of Research in the History of Sciences and Technology, CNRS/Cité des Sciences et de l'Industrie, Paris.

Somé, Roger (Burkina Faso, Italy); philosopher; researcher; member of the board of directors of *Journal des Africanistes* of the Musée de l'Homme (Paris).

Statham, Pamela (Australia); spec. nineteenth-century Australian and British economic history, and nineteenth and twentieth-century business history; Senior Lecturer, University of Western Australia.

Stearns, Peter, N. (United States of America); spec. history of emotions in the United States and in European social history; Dean of the College of Humanities and Social Sciences, Carnegie-Mellon University.

Stepaniants, Marietta T. (Russia); spec. history of philosophy; Professor, Head of Department, Institute of Philosophy, Russian Academy of Sciences.

Tchernjak, Efim B. (Russian Federation); spec. British history and the history of international relations in the sixteenth to eighteenth centuries; Professor (retired).

Thiam, Iba Der (Sénégal); spec. modern and contemporary history, Faculty of Letters and Human Sciences, University Cheikh Anta Diop, Dakar, Senegal.

Todorov, Nikolaï (Bulgaria); spec. Balkan history; Academician; Professor, University of Sofia; Director, Institute of Balkan Studies of the Bulgarian Academy of Sciences.

Tsamutali, Alexei, N. (Russia); spec. history of Russian culture; Professor, St-Petersburg Affiliate Institute of Russian History.

Vernoit, Stephen (United Kingdom); spec. Islamic art and architecture; Research Fellow, St Anthony's College, Oxford (1991–93); lecturer, Al-Akhawayn University, Ifrane, Morocco.

Vervliet, Raymond (Belgium); spec. literary historiography (esp. *fin-de-siècle* literature in Europe); Professor of Comparative Literature and Literary Sociology; President of the Flemish Association of General and Comparative Literature; Member of the ICLA.

Wang, Gung Wu (Singapore); spec. history of Chinese and Asian Studies; Professor of Far Eastern History, Australian National University; President, Australian Academy of the Humanities.

Van der Wee, Herman (Belgium); Emeritus Professor of Social and Economic History, University of Louvain (Belgium); Visiting Fellow at the research institutes of Princeton (USA), Oxford (UK), Washington DC (USA), Canberra (Australia), Bloomington (USA), and Wassenaar (Netherlands).

Wondji, Christophe (Ivory Coast); spec. African history; Professor, University of Abidjan and France.

PREFACE TO VOLUME VI

Peter Mathias

There is no ideal, universally acceptable, way of structuring a volume such as this. It must be comprehensive if it is to fulfil its aims of being a 'history of mankind', in the sense of providing the reader with a survey of all the main aspects of historical development in all the main countries and societies. Yet, at the same time, it cannot escape being selective. Human history is infinite in its diversity. Even if this study of change and continuity in the nineteenth century did not have to be confined to a single volume, a multi-volume history could still not cover all aspects in detail – one would simply draw the line of selectivity at a different point. Specialist studies on ever-more differentiated manifestations of historical reality will continue to be written. More general works of synthesis will continue to modify interpretations of history – as new knowledge accumulates, as perspective change with the evolution of time – and also because of the intrinsic subjectivity of the historian's work – however rigorous and 'scientific' the procedures for producing new sources or analysis data. History, it has often been remarked, remains a depressingly inexact science – indeed not a science at all according to the criteria to be found in some of the sections of the volume concerned with the evolution of scientific methodologies of the nineteenth century. Even the attempt to structure the volume as a comprehensive encyclopaedia or historical dictionary would preclude the sustained treatment of single items but, more importantly, prevent essays in synthesis and interpretations of the broad sweep of change. Descriptions of myriad individual trees preclude a vision of the forest as a whole. Some shape of the patterns of change and stability, of trends and interactions, needs to be established if the story of the evolution of human society in its broadest parameters over this critical century is to be meaningful.

As wide a range of professional historians as possible needed to be invited to make contributions within their own areas of expertise, mostly, but not invariably, based in the regions of the world on which their contributions were focused. In addition to the authors of texts, additional advisors made their contributions, and acted as editors themselves for arranging some specialist contributions. The editors had the responsibility, with the committee, for the final choice of advisors and authors, as well as for the planning and coordination of the volume as a whole. The authors retained personal authority (and responsibility) for theirs contributions, as agreed by the editors.

The network of contributions is designed to reflect the multi-national, multi-cultural kaleidoscope of the historical experience covered. However, the choice of the authors was not the only main issue facing the directing committee and the general editors. How was the volume to be structured? Should it be organized in a thematic way, following the evolution of different aspects of development – economy, polity, technology, the sciences, arts, music, religion *et al.* – or should the structure be that of following all these trends as they were manifest within the boundaries of different countries and regions: a set of spatial and national case histories rather than a series of themes? Each mode has advantages and disadvantages: the gains carry with them corresponding liabilities. In particular, many historical processes are not to be identified within national frontiers, nor do they respond to the coherence of national identities. But national frameworks and the dynamics they embody do exert powerful influences upon thematic change. And readers of the volume who identify with their own countries, as well as having both wider and more local horizons, will want to read about the experiences of their nations in the nineteenth century in an integrated way.

Seeking to capture the advantages of both modes of organization (and to minimize the drawbacks of each) the volume has been drawn up in two sections. The first – thematic – follows up the main aspects of change in chapters which concentrate upon different subjects. The second – regional – takes each main region (rather than each individual country) as the focus within which to look at the main aspects of change in an integrated way.

Needless to say invidious choices were still inescapable. In particular, different sections had to be scheduled for more or less extensive coverage. The tyranny of the overall length of the text was always present. There will always be contention about the relative length which the organizers of the volume decided to devote to different subjects and to different regions. No value judgement is implied about the intrinsic importance or the themes and cultures in question. In the perspective of historical change in the nineteenth century the editors had to make judgements about the relative significance of developments, in their view, and make allocations of space accordingly. Needless to say these judgements are challengeable because they cannot be based on agreed detailed criteria or totally objective viewpoints.

They will also differ according to the periods covered by different volumes in the present series. What is not in dispute, however, is that the evolution of human society in the nineteenth century, in all its manifestations, embraced historical change and development so deep-seated and profound as to largely shape the course of humanity for the twentieth and succeeding centuries. It is that wider perspective which this volume in the new UNESCO history of humanity seeks to document and to make understandable.

A

INTRODUCTION

INTRODUCTION

Peter Mathias

Each volume of the new UNESCO *History of Humanity* covers a period which can claim to have witnessed momentous change in the evolution of human society. The evolving panorama of humankind on the planet is manifest throughout, and who can say, *sub specie aeternitatis*, which phases of change will have proved the most portentous for the long-term future of humanity? It is the primary role of a history such as this to document the story of change within its period, to understand the pattern of evolution in its manifold manifestations and to assess its wider meaning, rather than to cast moral judgements or to make facile comparisons.

But change has evolved at a different pace in different millennia and over different centuries. Change has been more pervasive in some societies than in others – affecting a wider or narrower range of human activities and the human consciousness, impacting upon different levels of society; diffused over greater or more limited regions of the world; influencing different ranges of cultures and social groups within cultures. Stability, or slow evolution, rather than dramatic change characterized many societies in this period but it is right, in an introduction, to concentrate on the forces of change rather than those of inertia if we are to understand how the world differed in 1914 from what it had been in 1789 or 1800.

The 'chronological' nineteenth century – or, even more, the 'long' nineteenth century between the French Revolution of 1789, followed by world-wide wars, and the First World War of 1914, which engulfed the globe on an even more pervasive and lethal scale – must surely rank as one of the great pivotal epochs in the evolution of economies, societies and cultures. No region of the world proved to be beyond the influence of major forces of change; no culture was immune, directly or indirectly. Where some indigenous cultures did not themselves originate any major impetus for change beyond their own regions, virtually all economies and cultures reacted and responded to the thrust of change derived from beyond their boundaries, in turn influencing the process of cultural interaction which was never uni-directional (as was also the case with economic and political interactions). In many places, in regions of Asia and Africa in particular, such influences came with conquest and colonization in the nineteenth century; in others such influences were already the heritage of and evolution from previous centuries (as in Latin America). But formal subjugation was perhaps the lesser means whereby what was loosely termed 'Westernization' spread across much the world from Europe, North America and their outposts of settlement in Australasia, South Africa and North Africa.

Economic 'globalization' took on a new force, although 'globalization' as a process can be identified from the sixteenth century with European imperial expansion, colonization and trade, accompanied by strategic imperatives, already being played out in the New World, India, South East Asia and across the Pacific. Major civilizations resisted being drawn in fully to the 'magnetic field' of European expansion – China in particular – while the interiors of other vast land masses in Asia and Africa were scarcely penetrated save by intrepid adventurers, except where great rivers offered access.

Trade, with the development of commodities which were the constituents of trade, and the commercial (and sometimes naval) infrastructure that trade demanded, was the greatest engine for the transformation of the world economy in the nineteenth century and was the carrier of so much cultural penetration. This was so in contexts free of imperial administration or control, whether British, French, Belgian, Dutch, German or Danish. 'Informal empire' or the 'imperialism of free trade' are phrases designed to capture some meaning of this process, but it was operational also within Europe and within North America, because these areas also had 'peripheries' subjected to similar influences.

Trade flows brought economic interdependency, but with the initiative largely held by the merchants, bankers, and railway and shipping companies of the industrializing Western European countries. The expansion of their economies, the demands of their growing urban populations, their rising wealth, created an ever-increasing need for raw materials and foodstuffs originating beyond their own territories, while their technological capabilities provided the means whereby such demands were translated into effect. Their capital largely underpinned this process of global economic expansion by funding investment in the infrastructures required by new economic activities and the trade, which was their realization.

So pervasive and profound were the effects of European expansion that the global process has been called the 'Europeanization' of the world economy or more generally the 'Westernization' of the world process. This is a claim not just of economic, technological or financial processes but also for cultural – for example the growing dominance of 'Western' science and the intellectual *weltanschauung* which was integral with the methodology of 'science' and the experimental method, one principal aspect of what identified as archetypal 'Western' culture. The leading edge of advance was certainly Western in so many manifestations, and much of non-Western science, mathematics, astronomy and medicine did not progress with comparable momentum. This is not to say that Western science and medicine, for example, was uninfluenced by the then manifestations of other cultures, and some, but not so

3

much, rapport was gained from such interaction on the side of non-Western science and medicine. In the main, however, in this period the meeting of Western and non-Western was more confrontational than assimilative; a collision of non-communicating alternatives rather than a movement towards synthesis or symbiosis. This was true also in the main of philosophies and religions. Only at the margin and on the fringes were essays in cultural integration being explored.

Although in the broadest of historical perspectives of change, it may be recognized that 'Westernization' if not Europeanization was a more dominant and more invasive trend in the world as a whole than ever before, this was not uni-directional and certainly not without counter-currents in the tide. Many regions were not directly transformed by technology or integration into urban, national or international markets. Much traditional agriculture, whether producing crops or herding livestock, continued impervious, it seemed, to influences for change. The peasant lives of many millions in the most populous countries such as India and China were not transformed. Oxen ploughed with implements known for centuries, if not millennia, even by the side of railway tracks, as now they can be seen in the shadow of factories and power stations. Over the great plains of Central Asia, as in many upland mountain regions elsewhere, sheep and goats were being guarded on their seasonal migrations of transhumance as they had been for generations. This great survivability owed much to the strong coherence of local village society integrated by family and wider kinship links. It was also usually dependent upon a high degree of self-sufficiency in the growing and consuming of local food and drink. But local continuities were often a surface stability resting upon profound underlying transformations. Even traditional agriculture produced cash-crops, and an unchanging context of the local relations of production could at the same time be integrated with a wider, and modernized, economic system. This was true for plantation economies as it was for peasant farming. Other modes of dependence on the new world of capitalistic relationships enabled the old world of traditional family economies to survive – temporary employment for some family members elsewhere, work in mines or with fishing fleets, or as servants; seasonal work following the harvest in the commercialized agriculture of other countries, service in foreign armies, migration either permanent or temporary. A shifting symbiosis, by such various means, enabled some continuity with traditional rural societies, although the tide was running strongly towards the new economic bases for social existence to which family relationship had to adapt – often at great social cost.

Even though the integration of the world economy was far from complete, at the end of the century the dynamic of development between the primary producers and the industrializing economies had become a dominant feature of the global economy. At this period it was understandable that the process was dubbed 'Europeanization' or 'Westernization' but, in longer perspective into the twentieth century, modernization and industrialization proved truly global in their scope – as Japan was already revealing by 1914. Modernization – in many manifestations – also characterized many basically agrarian economies, such as Argentina, Canada and Australasia in the nineteenth century. The prominence of Europe in this process during the nineteenth century was transitory, as the next century and beyond was to demonstrate.

The process of 'modern economic growth' or 'sustained economic development' or 'the process of industrialization' as it has been variously designated, was initiated in North Western Europe, with roots stretching back over a long period, but becoming manifest as a new phenomenon in the evolution of economy and society in the later eighteenth century (in Britain most prominently) and then as a widening phenomenon in nineteenth-century Western Europe and the United States. Although in some respects a questionable term, the early phases of this continuing, cumulative process are universally known as the 'Industrial Revolution' – and many sections of this volume explore its implications. More accurately, and in the longer perspective, it is better identified as the onset of industrialization as a world process.

This can be plotted quantitatively as the attainment of higher rates of growth of economies (in terms of income per capita) sustained over the long term – a trend rather than just a fluctuation. Being cumulative in this way, what, in comparison with some twentieth-century case histories, were modest rates of growth of 2–3 per cent per annum (in Britain during the classic period of the Industrial Revolution growth rates did exceed 1.9 per cent) nevertheless became a transforming experience. Industrialization and modernization (the two processes being interdependent) were not simply a transformation of economic relationships and the structure of the economies involved. Economic change was integral with political, social and cultural transformations beyond the short term, if constraints on economic change itself were to be relaxed and the forces of inertia kept less dominant than the forces for change.

This introduction is not the place to explore these dynamics in depth. But, in relation to the detailed exploration of historical change during the nineteenth century in all its parameters, which forms the chapters of this volume, some general comments are in order about the process of transformation as a whole. It was, in essence, a wealth-creating process (as it still is). The world experienced a massive accumulation of capital in the aggregate as well as in its global redistribution on an unprecedented scale. At its heart lay an unprecedented growth of productivity, integrated with great increases in the inputs of labour, capital and resources as the process of progressive integration continued. Rising productivity – the growing efficiency in the utilization of resources or greater output in relation to inputs – came from diverse sources. Improved technology and progressive technical change, specialization of function and division of labour, lower transport costs and improved communication (culminating in the instantaneous transfer of information), more effective institutions and legal systems (closely linked to the political process), an efficient state, assured private property rights, better education and the growth of new skills (or, as economists put it, 'investment in human capital'), more efficient business organization, economies of scale and scope (within the firm and beyond the firm). This list is not complete but it contains many of the main constituents which, in various degrees, produced during the nineteenth century the greatest and most sustained rise in productivity which the world had ever seen. As 'transaction costs' collectively were lowered, the incentives for economic growth increased accordingly, relative to the constraints against change.

The countries whose merchants, industrialists, shippers and financiers had the initiative and control of these processes gained most – in many contexts almost all – of the rising economic surplus. In addition, economic change was disruptive and immiserating for those whose livelihoods and traditional bases of social living were undercut by change. Almost all change produces hardships for some and invites hostility, at least in the short term, however beneficial to those within the expanding orbit of new activities and in the aggregate. The adverse economic, social and cultural consequences of economic transformations are much in evidence in this volume. But this is not to say that positive immiseration – as distinct from a failure to enjoy the fruits of economic growth – was an inevitable aspect of the dynamic. In purely material terms those countries participating in international markets proved to benefit more than those which remained isolated (as the contrasting wealth of different African countries at the later point of decolonization revealed). In the industrializing and progressive agricultural modernizing economies, real wages – the command over consumption given by money wages – did rise, despite what may well have been a trend towards a greater inequality of income and wealth. When the economic surplus increased from rising productivity, producing a rising 'ceiling', the scope for greater inequality grew. In any case it would be difficult to argue in favour of a more equitable distribution of wealth and consumption above subsistence level in pre-industrial, pre-modern societies for the great bulk of the populace in settled agrarian societies. Benefits in real income from economic growth were slow in coming. Real wages in England, the country leading the advance of industrialization and urbanization, did not increase significantly, it seems, before the 1850s, doubtless affected by high rates of growth of population. After 1850, however, increases in the standard of living became sustained, and this was the case for most such countries (led by the United States). Where economic change was associated with high rates of population growth there could be attrition of living standards if numbers grew faster than resources. Where population increased without changes in productivity the prospects were bleak, and famine would be a recurrent threat. At subsistence level, and without 'significant' reserves, societies were at risk from natural disasters in the absence of economic growth. This remained the fate of much of humanity.

For the exploited people of European colonial territories, the consequences of empire in the nineteenth century were not wholly adverse. Law and order (if harshly enforced), administrative stability and some infrastructure investment (railways, dams, some irrigation and flood control, some anti-famine measures and some elements of a medical service, particularly in India) have to be entered on the positive side of the balance sheet of colonialism. These modest gains were bought at a high political social and also fiscal cost. It should be added that, in the different context of post-colonial times (beyond the scope of this volume), economic growth, the encouragement of modern industry and commercial agriculture became the professed objective of public economic policy in all newly independent countries.

Many attempts have been made to quantify the gains and losses of imperialism – for both the imperial powers and their colonies. This is part of the wider debate about the consequences of relationships between 'core' and 'periphery', between the industrializing powers and the primary-product exporters. No one disputes that 'gains from trade' were shared unequally in many parts of the world – that the terms of trade for commodities and income from services (which could be as large as the values of commodity trade) were skewed in favour of the international traders, shippers and financiers. In the context of formal empire the conclusion seems to be that, in the case of the British Empire at least (much the largest), the colonies did not produce a direct profit on public account for the British government. The costs of administration and defence, servicing government loans and the like, remained higher than income from local taxation. However, this calculation does not capture the gains in the private sector accruing from the imperial connection – the profits of business operating in the colonies and capital accumulated there (much of which was repatriated), all the business activity and profits created by trade between the colonies and the imperial powers. Even if colonial governments 'lost' by having to service loans, those who gained were the bondholders, who overwhelmingly were resident in the 'imperial' countries. The balance sheet of imperialism for the private sector was surely positive. This does not touch the effects of empire on global power relationships. And who can say what the 'counterfactual' would have been if the resources – financial, economic, human – that sustained empires had been redeployed within the metropolitan economies and societies? Certainly, influences of empire (as with the wider international trading and financial system) on the metropolitan countries were far-reaching. In the absence of imperial commitments, the history of the imperial powers would have been very different – economically, politically, in naval, military and strategic issues, in the cultures of their elites, in the symbolism of national identity.

The progressive invasion of countries and cultures by the forces of 'Westernization' or 'Europeanization' was not simply a uni-directional process, although that was certainly the main thrust of change and development. Vigorous intra-regional trading patterns flourished in South East Asia, of which the commerce in rice remained important, without the benefit of European initiative or control. Mid-century Japan quickly became an indigenous source for energizing its region (utilizing Western precedent but firmly under Japanese initiative). Japan certainly 'Westernized' – in industry, technology, transport, in the institutions of a modern state (civil and military), developing commitments in 'modern' medicine, Western science, music and art (symbolized by the *yoga* school of painting). At the Exposition Universelle in Paris of 1900, 177 Japanese artists exhibited 269 works – 'traditional' and 'Western' – in the fourth largest national contribution, after France (1,066 exhibitors), the United States (251), Great Britain (223) and Germany (200) amongst submissions from thirty countries. The rapid emergence of 'Western'-style universities and colleges after 1860, becoming indigenous within Japan, became a principal force for Westernization, but this process was responsive to national initiatives and perceived national need. In no sense did the assimilation of 'Western' influences, – from all leading Western countries – Britain, the United States, Germany and France in particular – entail the rejection of Japanese cultural traditions (although lively debates ensued over such manifestations as dress, particularly for men, where 'Western' dress became an embodiment of 'modernization' which related more to the roles of men than women). A dichotomy more than general cultural assimilation ensued, two traditions living side-by-side rather than integrating. But the 'Japaneseness' of Japanese culture was strengthened by the nationalism encouraged by Japan's expansion and demonstrable success on the international scene, particularly following victory in the war against Russia. Comparable sequences of the experience of Japan in relation to the impact of Western culture are revealed in Latin America or the Middle East, but the Japanese story is perhaps the most dramatic: both because of the extent of its isolation from Western influences in the two centuries beforehand and then for the speed and extent of its embrace of Westernization after the mid-nineteenth century.

Although European 'high culture' – opera, music, fine art – became dominant internationally, with France asserting her leadership in the visual arts (expressed in the distribution of exhibits in a series of international exhibitions in Paris), counter-currents were not absent. Collecting Japanese prints became fashionable amongst leading artists in Europe for example. 'Chinoiserie' maintained its popularity. The substantial import trade to Europe in Chinese and Japanese ceramics acknowledged their primacy in quality (as long before the nineteenth century). African art (whether sculpted in wood or the bronzes of Benin) inspired Picasso. 'Primitive art', although derogatory in its original implications as a typical piece of Euro-centric labelling, became acknowledged as the expression of sophisticated cultures. Africa joined Asia in the secular temples of European cultures: 'natural history' and ethnology museums throughout Europe embody this new awareness.

Although Europe was the originating point for so much economic, financial, political and cultural expansionism in the nineteenth century, by its end the impact of the United States upon Europe had become prominent. American industry and agriculture had become the largest in scale, the most technologically progressive and the most cost-effective, overshadowing the most powerful national economies in Europe – but the United States was not dominant internationally in trade, shipping and finance. American superiority in strategic branches of manufacturing explained an invasion of Europe by American firms by 1914: Ford, Singer, Kodak, Standard Oil and others became household names symbolizing American material success in providing what the whole modernizing world wanted. American business culture and lifestyles, in such manifestations as advertising, retailing, the steel-framed buildings and skyscrapers, elevators and hotels, based upon the highest national level of disposable income, spread in the wake of American business. This was not just a growing presence on the economic scene. European aristocratic families were re-invigorated (particularly financially) by marrying into American wealth. Fashionable American artists like Sargent and Whistler were lionized on the European scene, just as an important part of the artistic heritage of Europe found its way to the United States. The great museums and galleries there (most created from new private fortunes) grew into public totems of Western civilization. In effect the *haute bourgeoisie* and aristocratic cultures became international currencies across Europe and the east coast of the United States.

The changes in world history, beginning in the late eighteenth century but revealing their full potential in the nineteenth (and continuing since then) have been argued to be more profound than any since the establishment of settled agriculture and the domestication of animals several millennia earlier. Some see the onset and subsequent spread of industrialization – a continuing and cumulative process – as the 'great divide' or the 'great discontinuity' in human history, when judged in this very long term.

It is certainly the most challenging trend to be documented and explained in this volume of the UNESCO *History of Humanity*. This is the underlying dynamic of change, the consequences of which led to the increasing prominence of 'Europeanization' or the 'rise of the West'. It used to be a common assumption (amongst Western historians) that these developments, absolute and relative, can be traced back to the sixteenth century and that the centuries from 1500 to 1800 revealed the progressive differentiation between the experience of Europe, Asia, Africa and the New World. At the end of the (European) Middle Ages the world was more 'Sino-centric' than 'Euro-centric'. Europe, from a non-European perspective, was seen as peripheral amongst world civilizations as a whole – less advanced that the leading countries of Asia, where China's presence was dominating – and on the defensive against Arab and Ottoman expansion.

Much revision has come to this perspective in the past generation. It is now not thought that Western Europe had 'pulsed ahead' of the most advanced regions of Asia significantly, if at all, by 1800, and that there was no great 'economic distance' between them on the eve of industrialization. Large parts of Asia were far from poor or backward compared with Europe. Indeed, it can be argued that, before the great breakthrough in rates of growth and productivity associated with economic modernization and industrialization – centred initially on Western Europe – there could not have been substantial differences in wealth between all 'advanced organic societies', simply because prevailing techniques and organization in agriculture, commerce and handicraft industry did not produce a great economic surplus for the mass of the population beyond subsistence, and the possibilities of redistribution (beyond a small elite) were therefore limited, in comparison with later contexts.

The possibility remains that the institutional structures, legal and political regimes, technical advances and 'scientific culture' emerging in Europe in three centuries before 1800 fostered (or did not block) the potential momentum for evolution and change as much as was the case in Asia, even if this had not expressed itself in dramatic contrasts in the relative wealth of Western Europe and Asia by 1800. In North Western Europe, also, population pressures against resources were mitigated by various social mechanisms, such as late age of marriage and a significant percentage remaining non-married. At all events, in 1800, the world economy was not European-centred or characterized by a European form of capitalism.

The 'great divide', historically in comparison with earlier periods and regionally in the relationship between the 'West' and the 'East', had begun to emerge by 1800, but was fully revealed by 1914. Differences in wealth, resulting from long-sustained differences in rates of growth, were then manifold – possibly a hundredfold between the most advanced and the less advanced. Africa fared worse than Asia in this respect. Asian economies expanded in a context of population growth, but did not develop progressively in terms of income per head, in comparison with Western Europe and North America. This came as much from the stability of Asia as from the 'rise of the West'. Some have argued that advanced regions of Asia were caught in a 'high-level equilibrium trap' where labour was increasingly abundant and cheap in relation to resources and capital, providing little incentive for technical change through mechanization, which would have offered the main escape route from productivity levels limited by hand-technology in both agriculture and industry. For others this was compounded by the heavy hand of state bureaucracy or the 'feudal' powers of landlords. The main reasons, whatever they may be, are likely to lie within the countries concerned – particularly for a vast country such as China, where external trade throughout the nineteenth century was a small percentage of national income (5–10 per cent at most; and trading relations with Europe much smaller).

The international trading sector was more strategic for growth or stagnation than this quantitative measure reveals, while for a small economy the external influences would be greater than for a larger, which might generate more internal forces for momentum or inertia. At all events, the contrasting experiences of China and Japan in this dynamic of change in the nineteenth century raise profound issues for interpretation with Western countries.

B

THEMATIC SECTION

I

THE CHANGING SOCIO-ECONOMIC CONTEXT

Peter Mathias and Sidney Pollard (the late)

with a contribution from *Ivan Berend*

PREFACE

Peter Mathias

A single volume which sets out to encompass all the main manifestations of human history – in their infinite variety across the world – during the nineteenth century faces an impossible task of compression and generalization. In this opening chapter, as with the other chapters in the thematic section of the book, the text is inescapably a synthesis. It is impossible to provide a taxonomy of socio-economic life and change: the range of individual contexts, each unique in some respects and to a certain degree, is vast and encompasses the economic development of humankind over centuries if not millennia. This is because settlement patterns, land, pasturage and animal husbandry, the working environment of forest and jungle, the exploitation of seas, lakes and rivers, and handicraft production methods, had changed only slowly, if at all, in many regions. Man was still responsive to habitat in these socio-economic contexts as much as imposing change upon that habitat. In varying degrees, the equilibrium between resources, technology, output and sustaining local populations remained unstable, and when this equilibrium was upset by natural disaster or pressure of population on resources it was human society that suffered the consequences rather than the dis-equilibrium inducing a change in technology or other initiatives to sustain (or expand) output. The economic fate of man in the face of potentially hostile environments over much of the world proved an unending struggle. If this was the economic foundation of an often elemental material existence, it co-existed with impressive cultural manifestations.

In other regions of the world, made clear in the following pages, the balance of initiative between man and nature was swinging decisively – more dramatically in the nineteenth century, perhaps, under the impetus of industrialization and 'modern' economic growth, directly and indirectly, and certainly on a greater scale and at a faster pace than had been known in any previous epoch of human history. Changes between the end of the eighteenth century and the outbreak of the First World War, saw, on trend, a decisive change in the pace of development, both within certain regions, and in the relations between countries, with the growth of a more integrated world economy on new dynamics. The twentieth century, in its turn, was to see these trends grow further and faster.

This chapter sets out the basis of the main trends which determined economic and social change in the nineteenth century, inevitably concentrating on the dynamics of development rather than the inertia of stability: the historical process is always a dynamic between the forces of change and the inertia of older structures consolidated in technological, economic, political, social and cultural terms.

THE DEMOGRAPHIC CHALLENGE

Population and the dynamics of change

Population represents one of the basic parameters of the collective human condition. World distribution of population in the nineteenth century, and its trends, puts the relative scale of societies into perspective. When demographic data are translated into terms of output and income then the relationships between population, resources, technology and all the other inputs which reflect changes in productivity as well as total output are brought into play and the dynamics of change revealed. It is not so much aggregate scale of output (determined at the minimum by the basic needs to sustain population) or total aggregate numbers which determined change in the world – and saw the transformation, directly and indirectly, of human society in the nineteenth century – as the dynamic of development in processes of production, transport, trade and finance. This dynamic of change had long historical roots in Europe, as elsewhere, before the nineteenth century, but the pace, scale and nature of such changes were unprecedented from the late eighteenth century, and have become even more momentous for continuing change in the century after 1900.

Europe and North America, the latter from a very low starting point of 16 million (5.3M for the USA) and Europe from 187M in 1800, experienced the most dynamic population growth over the century (see Table 1). Europe's population more than doubled by 1900 while North

Table 1 World population growth, 1800–1950 (millions).

	1800	*1850*	*1900*	*1950*
Europe	187.0	266.0	401.0	559.0
United Kingdom	16.1	27.5	41.8	50.6
Great Britain[a]	10.7	20.9	37.1	–
Ireland	5.2	6.5	4.5	–
Germany	24.6	35.9	56.4	69.0[b]
France	27.3	35.8	39.0	41.9
Russia	37.0	60.2	111.0	193.0[c]
Spain	10.5	n/a	16.6	28.3
Italy	18.1	24.3	32.5	46.3
Sweden	2.3	3.5	5.1	7.0
Belgium	n/a	4.3	6.7	8.6
Netherlands	n/a	3.1	5.1	10.0
North America	16.0	39.0	106.0	217.0
United States	5.3	23.7	76.0	151.7
South America	9.0	20.0	38.0	111.0
Asia	602.0	749.0	937.0	1302.0
Africa	90.0	95.0	120.0	198.0
Oceania	2.0	2.0	6.0	13.0
World total	906	1,171	1,608	2,400

Notes

a Census dates, 1801, 1851 and 1901.

b West Germany.

c 1946.

Sources: W. S. Woytinsky and E. S. Woytinsky, *World Population and Production*: Trends and Outlook (New York, 1953) pp. 34–44. Great Britain and Ireland from B. R. Mitchell and P. Deane. *Abstract of British Historical Statistics*, Cambridge, 1962, pp. 8–10. Rondo Cameron, *A Concise Economic History of the World*, 3rd edn, Oxford University Press, New York, 1997.

America's grew fifteenfold from 16M to 106M (76M in the case of the USA). This was at a much greater rate than the rest of the world, except for the 'white' dominions in Australasia and Canada. Moreover, demographic change in Europe and North America was integrated with profound economic and social developments. The dynamic of change in the 'trans-atlantic region' was also linked demographically through massive interregional migration flows, as noted below.

Population growth in North America (as in Canada, Australia, New Zealand, Argentina and some other Latin American countries) constituted a distinct pattern. These offered vast, in some regions virtually empty lands, of reasonable fertility in a resource-rich, labour-scarce context. In addition, abundant other natural resources of minerals and forests lay open to exploitation, where capital and enterprise, settlement and improved transport made this possible. The growth of population in such a context could lead to rapid economic growth, provided always that the institutional structure was appropriate and that progressive technology and investment enhanced levels of productivity, and therefore the extent of surpluses and incomes being produced.

It was not only the leaders in industrialization who could prosper from rising numbers. The United States became the world's leading producer of primary produce in the nineteenth century (cotton, cereals, meat, fats, timber, minerals, etc.) and a leading exporter of such produce, as well as becoming the greatest industrial power and wealthiest economy by the First World War. Other economies, expanding mainly through the growth of their primary

product sectors (agriculture, forestry, mining), where orientated through exports to the growth of the international economy, were able to maintain or enhance income levels comparably in relation to their populations: Canada, Australia, New Zealand, Argentina, Denmark, Sweden and Finland are amongst this group. Reliance on the primary sector thus did not condemn a country to falling behind the industrializing countries. Qualifications are necessary. Where primary produce exporters enhanced their levels of income this was associated with a modernized infrastructure (including commercial, financial infrastructure and the political/administrative structures, not only ports and railways). And their prosperity derived from exports to the main expanding regions of the world, where populations were rising, sectors other than agriculture growing fastest and urbanization producing a rising percentage of non-food producers. Equally, in such contexts the exponential growth of industry made even greater demands on raw-material imports – to the great advantage of those countries which had low-cost minerals to sell on the world market. The precious metals were always integrated into the world market, so newly discovered low-cost mining areas in the world provided a basis for settlement, population growth and economic expansion – whether Australia, Central and South Africa or California.

The European context of population growth showed great contrasts to these resource-rich labour-scarce regions, with a great diversity of contexts within Europe itself. Given the low rate of growth in the pre-industrial period, with long, established structures, the potential for sustained increases in numbers could respond to economic opportunities as they developed. This was mainly on a regional basis, between countries, and between regions within countries. Britain, North Western Europe (Belgium and Northern France on the same coalfield), other 'nodes' in France, western Germany, Switzerland, and localities in the Austro-Hungarian Empire became the main industrializing centres. Population growth was linked with internal migration, urbanization (the rising percentage of population living in towns), and the growth of industrial and mining districts. The coalfields exercised a powerful 'centripetal' pull in this process of demographic growth and redevelopment. Changes in the structure of European economies integral with the process of expansion lay at the centre of this dynamic. In the third quarter of the nineteenth century less than half the inhabitants of Britain's major industrial towns and ports had been born there.

Europe had produced its own demographic impetus in these ways, as well as contributing to expanding the basis of the world economy by migration. But the internal regional contrasts were great. Southern Italy, much of Spain, regions of the Balkans, Eastern and Central Europe, and Russia did not see population growth associated with progressive agriculture or changes of structure associated with sustained economic growth. In such regions, as noted, demographic growth meant migration, immiseration (or holding already minimal levels of consumption), the survival of much local self-subsistence, and the slow growth of internal markets, commercial and physical infrastructures in rural society.

Migration: demography and development

Asia dominated the world's population at the beginning of the nineteenth century (over 600M) as in 1900 (*c*.937M), out of a world total of *c*.900M in 1800 and *c*.600M a century later. Europe's population increased almost threefold to Asia's twofold over the same period, despite losing c.60M by migration mainly to the United States (35M) but also, for British emigrants (18M) to the 'white' dominions, and with growing Spanish, Portuguese and Italian communities in Brazil and Argentina. Before 1913, 1M people were leaving Europe annually. In Ireland the population halved from 8M in the aftermath of the great famine of 1846 and with continuing emigration. In addition, Norway, Scotland and England lost most as a share of their total population.

The movement was mainly to 'new world' areas of settlement rather than to tropical colonies and the acquisitions of empire. In 1830 it is reckoned that only 100,000 Europeans lived in tropical colonies and in 1914 1.6M – 0.2 per cent of their total population. Only 175,000 Europeans (principally English and Scottish, apart from Irish soldiers) were in India – a mere 0.1 per cent of total numbers there. By contrast over 97 per cent of the population of Canada, Australia and New Zealand were white settlers; and 21 per cent of South Africa's population. In early nineteenth-century America 45 per cent of total numbers were white (possibly 11M Africans had been taken as slaves to the new world over the preceding centuries); with 2–3M Asians also taken overseas as 'indentured labourers' to work in plantations, railways and mines. One of the largest movements of permanent settlement from Europe to a North African 'colony' enclave came with the French administration of Algeria after 1830, where 400,000 Europeans settled over the next half-century. In Japanese mainland Asian settlements in Formosa and Manchuria, growing at the end of the century, almost half a million Japanese in 1913 constituted 2.5 per cent of the total in the regions, corresponding closely to the general world pattern of colonization.

Other regions of the world were much more thinly populated. Oceania – scattered over the vast Pacific region – totalled 2M in 1800 and 6M in 1900; Africa 90M in 1800 and 120M a century later. Apart from Europe and the areas of European settlement (including the United States) population growth was modest in the nineteenth century – about 20 per cent. Doubtless where economic growth was not resilient population was constrained by a variety of causes: numbers checked by maintaining an equilibrium between land and output by traditional methods of agriculture, working through the age of marriage, numbers remaining unmarried, migration and the harsher 'Malthusian' checks of famine, disease, war and natural disasters where numbers grew greater than sustainable resources. Japan's population, it seems, followed a largely European pattern. Demographic constraints (with a high age of first marriage) held the potential higher rise of numbers in check while the intensive use of land with progressive (although unmechanized) agriculture produced an 'industrious' revolution, keeping demographic growth and the growth of resources broadly in balance (even though this pattern did not produce a progressive increase in income per head in parallel with the leading industrializing countries). Unlike Japan, the mainly agricultural economy of Ireland experienced a Malthusian tragedy (intensified by the prevailing institutional context); and migration helped to purge potential Malthusian pressures in poor agricultural regions of Scandinavia, Italy, Central and Eastern Europe. India also was to experience disastrous regional famines by the end of the century (and into the twentieth) – a phenomenon compounded of poverty and lack of commercialized regional markets and poor transport

as well as food shortages. This was the demographic fate for peoples whose numbers grew out of balance with employment opportunities and resources.

Of course the area across which economic opportunity correlated with demographic pressure varied greatly. As noted above, this involved transatlantic and intercontinental movement on a vast scale. But it also operated between different regions of the same country: with internal migration to growing industrializing centres (where employment was expanding rapidly), to coalfields, to towns and to main ports. This was a complex process integral with change in economic structure and rising wealth where rates of growth were sustained. Industrial and mining employment grew faster than agricultural in such regions. Industrialization became integral with urbanization. Employment in services (predominantly urban) grew with a progressively differentiated economy, rising numbers in public administration, clerical functions, medicine and teaching, the extension of personal services and domestic services with rising incomes. Most of this employment was in small-scale units, and with traditional technology for the most part until the latter decades of the century (when the typewriter, the sewing machine and new household equipment began to make inroads).

Thus, through migration, population increase became geared into economic transformation. This was not the only demographic mechanism. Where agricultural production could be expanded – by more intensive methods, plantation development (usually labour-intensive, whether in cotton, tea, coffee, rubber and other crops), 'peasant crop' expansion then employment could expand with the increase of agricultural output, not only by changes in economic structure. In the second half of the century the mechanization of harvesting in North America, the progressive cereal farming regions of Britain and North Western Europe resulted in great productivity gains – a progressive increase in output with much less increase pro rata in labour inputs, and, in certain places, a fall in numbers employed. Agricultural productivity could advance by several routes, and this could enhance income per head, depending on how the aggregate gains in output per head were distributed between landlords (receiving rent), farmers and peasants (gaining profits) and labourers (earning wages). Where workable land lay empty, numbers could expand in agriculture with traditional methods and technology, but yielding only stagnant levels of productivity and facing the probability of diminishing returns if numbers rose faster than the cultivated area.

Economic growth could prove symbiotic with population growth in a 'happy circle' with contrasting dynamics to the 'vicious circle' of Malthusian constraints. Increasing numbers, where the context was responsive, might induce economic activity, and the migration of jobs to local population rather than the reverse. This was the case with 'proto-industrial' growth in some regions, as in expanding textile and small-metal industries in the English Midlands (both in rural and urban contexts). Greater employment opportunities could encourage demographic growth by lowering the age of first marriage, encouraging a higher marriage rate and the formation of new households. Better (and/or more regular) employment could improve nutrition, lead to less demographic 'wastage' in miscarriages and infant deaths, and lead to a healthier, more vigorous workforce (for which levels of nutrition were influential). Migration could enhance these advantages where the 'pull' lay to regions of rising activity and the offer of more employment. Migrants were mainly in the young adult age groups, with a propensity for the more active, ambitious and forward-looking to respond to opportunity. Moreover, migrants created a mobile labour force, attracted to the 'pressure points' in the labour markets at reception areas which gave added gains in the mobilization of 'human capital', bleak though the conditions of mass-migration were. Much subsequent mobility for relatives or friends, and reverse repatriation, compounded the dynamics of migration once 'social' and 'community' bridgeheads had been established, but for most the act of migration was a commitment to a new way of life in a new environment.

One further relationship between demographic growth, economic change and migration needs to be stressed: the impact upon the regions from which the migrants were leaving. The employment situation (or the land/labour ratio) would be more favourable to those remaining than would have been the case without outward migration. Wage rates might be higher than they would otherwise have been. The marginal product of labour could be greater. The marginal economic effects of migration could be greater than that suggested by the ratio between the migrants and the established population. In general terms, however, the marginal product of those who could have stayed on in their established communities and traditional economic roles – particularly in overcrowded agricultural communities or the floating population of towns – would be far lower than the marginal product of these additions to the labour force in the countries and regions to which they moved. This was the greatest economic gain from migration, even if bought at a high social cost of disrupted families.

Completing the circle of links between demographic change and migration is the flow of remittances sent by emigrants back to their families, coupled with the transfer of accumulated savings by emigrants who returned to the land of their birth in later years. Italians in New York and Buenos Aires helped to sustain their families in Puglia and the south; so accordingly did the Irish in New York, Boston and Baltimore, Germans in Milwaukee, Swedes in Minnesota, Scottish Presbyterians in Canada, English settlers in New Zealand. In this century British links with kin and culture in the United States and the 'white' dominions were forged more extensively and intimately than with Europe. The economy of Ireland, in particular, was greatly sustained from this nexus. Girls from rural Quebec worked for a few years in the textile mills of Amoskeg and Lowell, sending some of their wages home before they returned themselves to marry. Seasonal migrations for work created the same symbiosis between the worlds of traditional ways of life and the new in diverse contexts across the world. Irish working the harvests in England; shepherds in the 'trans-humance' between mountains and the valley villages; domestic servants and nurses coming from the country to the towns, fishing communities, naval and maritime employment, gangs building railways in remote countries – the list is endless. Thus, even the traditional was sustained by the new, in terms of family continuity and links between surpluses earned from employment in the new contexts of economic growth and the older contexts of life and work under attrition. Some symbiosis was sustained in these ways, as well as the confrontations between old and new, where falling agricultural prices and international competition from modernized industry increasingly threatened communities based on traditional agriculture and handicraft industries.

Levels of wealth and rates of growth

The dynamics of the links between population and the political, institutional, social and economic transformations, which are subsumed under the name 'economic growth' or 'modernization', are complex as the first section of this chapter has discussed. The key variables in these linkages are discussed in the remaining sections of this chapter, and in the subsequent chapters of the thematic section of the volume. They are then construed within different regional contexts in the second part of the book to provide the empirical basis for the arid statistics elaborated here. However, it is only by producing comparable data, on a common basis, that a general analysis of changes in historical perspective can be made. The common currency for such comparative analysis in the long run lies in the use of reconstituted national income data, which gives a monetized calculation for the total size of an economy, its sectoral composition and various distributions (for example the size of the public sector versus the private sector; production, consumption and investment, foreign trade, the balance of payments, etc.). Such monetized calculations contain inescapable limitations, which cannot be discussed here. They can be supplemented by physical measurements (output figures in weight or volume, consumption measures, calorie counts, etc.) but these also come with problems of comparability, particularly when utilized over long time periods and across cultures. No such quantification yields a calculus of satisfactions or happiness, or cultural uniqueness or environmental quality. But these formulae are the best yet devised to measure changing levels of wealth and income – which bring the potential, at least, for greater satisfactions by widening choice and options – and they are the professed objectives for maximization in the policies of most countries in the world today.

The nineteenth century saw faster rates of growth and more massive accumulations of wealth and capital than had been known in any earlier epoch. With this went a progressive increase in inequalities of income and wealth between different regions and countries, making the nineteenth century unique also in respect of these divergences (which have not been reversed between the wealthiest industrialized countries and the poorest of the 'Third World' in the twentieth century).

The growing gap between rich and poor countries, between the traditional economies and the progressive economies, did not develop so much because the poor countries got poorer (most people in these societies were close to what subsistence meant in different contexts) – most indices show some gains – but because the rich were able to get so much richer through the accumulation of capital, thanks to the advances in productivity which became progressively realizable during the century. A long-running debate continues as to whether these growing inequalities of income derived from the operation of the international economy whereby income levels of the Third-World primary producers, exporting to richer countries, were actually pushed down by this dynamic or whether they simply did not win rewards from trade as did the trading partners who held most of the financial, commercial, managerial and technical assets employed and thus reaped most of the gains. Other chapters in the volume discuss the issue. Income disparities within countries, rich or poor, remained great and probably increased with the potential of higher ceilings of wealth and income. Notably, however, some primary-product exporters did prosper, and even for the tropical exporters, income levels were probably greater than in regions not drawn into the international economy. Nigeria and Ghana, for example, were richer than most countries in tropical Africa, and Argentina was by far the wealthiest country in South America in 1914.

Perhaps, when the nineteenth century opened, the gap in average incomes between India, the Ottoman Empire and Europe (including the poorest regions of Mediterranean countries, Central and Eastern European regions and Russia) was not large. Before 1800, some estimates suggest, however, that North Western European countries were 20–40 per cent richer than present developing countries – the result of a large number of interacting variables developing over the previous centuries. Amongst these were capital accumulation, commercial wealth from both external trade and the commercialization of internal markets, a progressive agriculture, a long record of productive investment, albeit mainly utilizing 'artisan technology' in industry, relative intellectual freedom with an intellectual culture favourable to the exploration of nature, and experimental methods encouraging gradual advances in empirical techniques. Critically important institutional advances developed individual property rights and legal regimes favourable to commercial progress – such as the assured legal status of private assets and the transferability of such assets (including financial assets) which establishes the preconditions for functioning markets. Roman law and the English common law created a particularly favourable context. The exercise of arbitrary power in economic dealings was progressively curtailed. That, and the reduction of risk and uncertainty by better communication and transport, the slow but cumulative subjection of natural hazards to human will, reduced transaction costs and encouraged enterprise.

The two parts of Table 2, with wide margins of uncertainty, reveal the contrasting dynamics through the latter part of the nineteenth century. Initially, England and the Netherlands were roughly on a par for GDP per capita, with Belgium about 75 per cent of this level, France at about 65 per cent, Spain at 50 per cent and Poland (representative of Eastern Europe) at 25 per cent. Britain increased its lead over the other European countries, being in advance of them in the process of industrialization (characterized by more rapid technical changes, a higher degree of urbanization, more rapid sectoral change with industry and services expanding much faster than agriculture, and a more extensive specialization in the international economy on both the export and the import side). After 1870, however, rates of growth slackened in Britain (they were always modest at 2–2.5 per cent p.a. in the earlier period) and most other European countries began to catch up, although the Mediterranean countries, Central and Eastern Europe very gradually, and from a low base. GDP per capita in Southern and Eastern Europe rose by 50 per cent between 1870 and 1914, while in Western Europe the rise was about 75 per cent. Asian, African and most Latin American countries, although increasing wealth and income in absolute terms, fell behind the leaders relatively.

The United States proved exceptional in terms of income levels, rates of growth, the scale of its economy and

its progressiveness in technical advances in all sectors (including services). Real wages had been higher in America than in England – characteristic of a resource-rich labour-scarce country attracting immigrants – but to this was now added the momentum of economic development on an unrivalled scale. America was potentially a 'super-economy' spanning half a continent with an extraordinary range of natural resources for agricultural, forest, industrial and mining products of all kinds. The balance of government regulation, public initiatives and individual freedom to pursue private advantage encouraged enterprise. The inertia of a lingering feudal heritage or absolutist regime did not exist in North America as it did in varying degrees in some European countries (although not so much in North West Europe). Although an importer of much new technology and capital from Britain during the first half of the century, the United States was already flexing its muscles as a rapidly industrializing economy, as well as a major exporter of primary products (raw or lightly processed as with cotton, cereals and timber, or with greater value-added in leather, meat and fats) and manufactured goods. Between 1850 and 1914 the United States became the largest and richest industrial country, although the UK remained the largest exporter and importer in 1913, as continued growth in a relatively small country produced progressive international specialization in the exports of manufactured goods (textiles, metal products – and coal) and imports of foodstuffs and raw materials. In 1900, UK exports totalled US$34.4 per capita, and American exports $18.6 per capita.

The fast pace of growth of population in the United States (from 5.3M to 76M) – boosted by immigration and much

Table 2 World economy: income and growth.

	Growth of GDP per capita (1870–1913)		
A GDP per capita ($US in 1980 prices)			
	1870	*1990*	*% p.a.*
USA	1591	2911	2.0
UK	1875	2798	1.0
Japan	425	677	1.6
India	345	378	0.6
China	331	401	0.5
Brazil	283	436	1.2
Ghana	292	405	0.9

B Per capita income and growth rates in nineteenth-century Europe relative to UK level (UK = 100)			
	1870	*1910*	*1870–1910* *(rate of growth)*
France	58	61	1.09
Germany	48	61	1.09
Belgium	77	81	1.03
Denmark	61	78	1.55
Sweden	48	60	1.49
Italy	46	50	1.00
Spain	43	51	1.37
Habsburg Empire	32	42	1.63
Poland	21	27	1.53
Russia	34	32	0.7

Sources: Maddison (1983; 1989; 1991); D. F. Good, *Journal of Economic History*, LIV (December 1994).

faster than any other main country – gave added impetus to the expansion of the economy. The process of expansion was integral with economic development (industrialization, urbanization, structural change, a progressive primary sector), which produced faster rates of growth than elsewhere and an unparalleled rise in the rate of growth of productivity. This, in turn, led to the United States having the largest economy in the world by 1914, and the highest income per capita (as Tables 2 and 3 reveal). The rate of growth of the American economy, in the aggregate and per capita, (at 4 per cent p.a. and 2 per cent p.a. in constant prices) was twice that of the UK and well ahead of the fastest growing European economies, which were now growing rather faster than the UK, although from a lower base. After 1870, as the first industrial nation, Britain was experiencing the initial consequences of the spread of industrialization as a global phenomenon. In 1870 GDP per capita was still higher in the UK than in USA (US\$1,875 in 1980 prices compared with \$1,591) but this had been reversed by 1900 (when the figure for the USA was \$2,911 and that for the UK \$2,798). Within Europe, however, the long lead established by Britain in economic and industrial development still put her ahead of all other countries by a factor of 30–40 per cent for Western European countries, 50 per cent for Mediterranean countries and 60–70 per cent for Central and Eastern European regions). 'Catching up' had started, with all European countries except Russia growing faster than Britain, in the case of Denmark and Sweden half as fast again.

The basic patterns of world development under the dynamic of industrialization and modernization emerged clearly in the nineteenth century, projected into the next century. A 'core' of progressive economies able to take advantage of the opportunities of growth (internal as well as through their commitments in the international economy) prospered to an extent unique to that date in human history. The impetus was not always industrial, as has been stressed, but the agriculturally-based economies in the favoured

group were characterized by the progressive processing of their products – producing higher value-added through rising productivity. This dynamic was integral with other facts of modernization – urbanization, a modernized physical infrastructure and transport system, an indigenous financial communications and commercial infrastructure, and an appropriately modernized political, legal and administrative system.

For this group of 'core' countries and regions, growth and rising incomes produced convergence (with the United States, however, leading in income and, by ever greater strides, in scale of output and population). The gap in rates of growth and income levels between this advantaged group and the majority of humanity, living in countries lagging in terms of economic growth and modernization, grew wider. The possibilities for faster growth were much enhanced by the processes of historical changes during the nineteenth century; for those countries unable to take advantage of them, by contrast, their relative poverty became more prominent. This covered many regions in Asia, all of Africa, the Near East, continental Russia, much of South East and Eastern Europe, and most of Latin America. Japan, by contrast, from the Meiji Restoration in 1868, showed a quite different dynamic of modernization and economic development, under state initiatives, which set her on the path to modern economic growth, even if chronologically well behind the leading economies until the twentieth century.

Economic expansion, as distinct from economic development, was experienced by many of these less-favoured contexts. Population growth could co-exist with rising agricultural output (from the extension of the cultivated area or more intensive cultivation), which increased the total size of such economies but, with traditional technology and methods of production, did not raise levels of productivity significantly (indeed, expansion of this sort in such a context was all too likely to lead eventually to diminishing returns). Nor could it lead to long-term improvements in real income. For this the nature of the economy had to be transformed.

Traditionally the analysis of historical change, economic and social as well as political, has been made in terms of nation states. Governments produce statistics on a national basis and comparative performance is customarily measured in terms of such national data. This can be seriously misleading when seeking to understand the dynamics of economic change (particularly for countries where the economy was responding mainly to market forces rather than to state decrees). Industrial growth (with associated commercial, urban, transport development) was more a regional than a uniformly national phenomenon – sometimes based on coalfields, which ran across national frontiers (as in Southern Belgium and Northern France) or regional within the borders of a national state. Just as great contrasts existed in the record of growth and wealth between states (where per capita data is just the arithmetic quotient of dividing GDP by population totals) so great contrasts developed in different regions within the same country, following a similar logic. This was particularly the case where countries were large and patterns of regional activity diverse. Real wages and regional GDP in the south of the USA showed a growing lag with the industrial regions, a gap which did not converge before 1914 even though there were no formal barriers to internal migration. The advanced agricultural regions of the Po valley in Northern Italy contrasted with the impoverished,

Table 3 Growth of output (aggregates and per capita) in selected countries, 1820–1913 (annual average compound growth rates in constant prices).

	1820–1870		1870–1913	
	Aggregate	*Per capita*	*Aggregate*	*Per capita*
Australia	–	–	3.4	0.6
Austria	(1.4)	0.7	2.4	1.5
Belgium	2.7	1.9	2.0	1.0
Canada	–	–	3.8	2.0
Denmark	1.9	0.9	2.7	1.6
Finland	–	–	3.0	1.7
France	1.4	1.0	1.7	1.5
Germany	2.0	1.1	2.8	1.6
Italy	–	–	1.5	0.8
Japan	(0.4)	0.0	2.5	1.5
Netherlands	2.4	1.5	2.1	0.9
Norway	(2.2)	1.0	2.1	1.3
Sweden	(1.6)	0.6	2.8	2.1
Switzerland	(2.5)	1.7	2.1	1.2
UK	2.4	1.5	1.9	1.0
USA	4.4	1.4	4.1	2.0
Average	2.1	1.1	2.5	1.4

Source: A. Maddison, *Phases of Capitalist Development* (Oxford, 1982).

over-populated rural South. Within the UK, rural Scotland, Wales and much of Ireland showed the same relative poverty compared with other regions. The same was true of France, Scandinavia, Spain, Russia and other large land masses. National averages become misleading in such contexts, and mask the regional reality of where the impetus for growth and change was principally based.

The varying record of change and stability (or stagnation), growth and income levels discussed above were consequential on the changing technology of production, investment and finance, together with changes in the organizational basis of the economy. Output in the aggregate, and rising productivity (output relative to the inputs required) were the net result of the transformation of many variables (not only the technological) and their interrelationships, as has been stressed. The succeeding sections discuss three of the most important aspects of the economic changes taking place in the nineteenth century.

CHANGES IN THE BASIS OF OUTPUT AND PRODUCTIVITY: THE IMPETUS OF INDUSTRIALIZATION AND MODERNIZATION

The changing technology of production

The discussion about technology and technical change has to be highly synoptic, with so much omitted, given the infinite variety and the increasing diversity of output during the century. Handicraft industries were universal, whether mining, fishing, forestry, manufacturing in textiles and metals, or food and drink processing. Some production, under the patronage of royal, noble, or just wealthy clients, were luxuries of the highest quality, commanding premium prices in the connoisseur markets today. The forging of Japanese steel for swords, for example, was of supreme technical quality and not dependent on European metalworking traditions. Many handicrafts entered more than local trade, for example Indian cotton textiles, Chinese porcelain, English and French clocks. Interregional, and international trade in a bewildering variety of textiles in all fibres had been complex for many generations.

The basic characteristic of handicraft production was smallness of scale by unit of production, hand tools, and the skill of the artisan (men and women). The use of nonhuman power in production was extremely limited, and provided by draught animals and wind and water power in traditional 'mill' industries (for grain milling, pumping out mines, draining fen land and polders, sawing timber, working bellows in larger ironworks, and similar functions). Technical advances were slow within this basic technology and productivity gains came principally from the increasing division of labour and specialization of labour, which – as Adam Smith pronounced – was principally determined by the size of the market. In certain instances, supremely in the clock and watch industries of Geneva, Paris and London, the division of labour, and the distribution of processes of production in urban and rural centres, had become extremely intricate. Textiles, and small metal products had become large industries in many contexts, but unit costs remained high without significant economies of scale (except in trading relations).

In the long-term perspective we can see that technical progress through the mechanization of production was the key to increasing scale from individual units of production, lower costs (particularly labour costs) and rising productivity. Other complementary developments in the context of production were necessary for these gains to be realized, but innovation and technical change was at the heart of the matter.

Judged as a process, innovation (inventions which led to successful use and diffusion in a market context) was not just random, driven by chance, the product of intellectual curiosity, scientific knowledge, or individual genius – although all of these played their part at different points. Propensities or inducements to innovation came by way of opportunities for comparative advantage, often by differential costs with existing products, but also by way of the introduction of new products without immediate competition. Inducements could be positive or negative – a pull and/or a push effort. Relative costs of labour (in relation to output per worker – which, in turn, depended on the technology) and the availability of skills were also relevant.

Mechanization in terms of modern industrialization was directly a function of machinery and power (if with many other contextual variables). This, in turn, depended on the emergence of a 'mineral fuel' technology, associated developments in the iron and later steel industry, metalworking and engineering skills. Engineering, as an industry, was a creation of the Industrial Revolution. Power engineering was central to the process of advance. A favourable resource position in coal, iron-ore and other minerals was more important for the 'heavy' industries than for textiles because of the greater importance of fuel costs and transport costs in final product prices. Fuel-intensive industries needed to be located close to coalfields or ports. Britain was uniquely favoured for the growth of coal-based industries – having abundant coalfields within close proximity, and adjacent to all metal ores except tin and copper. At the same time the British economy was favoured by progressive shortcomings and rising costs in traditional resources: timber for fuel and sites for large-scale water power, in the Midlands and South of England. Here was the double inducement of being pushed out of traditional technology based on the resource pattern of centuries and being pulled by cost advantage to the new matrix of resources and technology. This was also true of comparative costs between Britain and other countries (with the possible exception of Belgium at this time). The heritage was much older than the nineteenth century: metal industries, most urban industries and most domestic house fuel in Britain were already based on coal and coke long before 1800, as was, for example, food processing such as malting, brewing and distilling.

The statistics of total coal production and per head of the population send their own message in this respect. Aggregate data are listed in Table 4. Britain produced more coal than the rest of Europe put together until the last decade of the century (when Germany, in particular, and on a more continental scale the United States, came into the full flood tide of industrialization. In 1913 Britain's coal production, at 300M tons (of which about a third was exported to neighbouring European countries and coaling stations for ships across the world) remained the highest in Europe. The figures of coal output relative to population show the same perspective (see Table 5).

Innovations in the coal industry reveal a paradox. Expansion, especially for deep mines, depended for drainage and hoisting on steam power, and new techniques of

Table 4 Coal production, selected countries (M metric tons, annual averages) (bituminous, lignite, anthracite).

	1800	1850–4	1870–4	1911–13
Austria-Hungary	–	1.4	9.2	50.7
Belgium	–	6.8	14.7	24.8
France	–	5.3	15.4	39.9
Germany	–	9.2	41.4	247.5
Italy	–	–	0.1	0.6
Russia	–	–	1.0	30.2
Sweden	–	–	0.05	0.36
UK	11.2	50.2	123.2	275.4
USA (short tons)	0.1	10.6	64.2	525.6

Sources: B. R. Mitchell, *Fontana Economic History of Europe* (The Emergence of Industrial Societies: 2) (London, 1973), statistical appendix. *Historical Statistics of the United States* (US Department of Commerce, Washington, 1960).

Table 5 Coal output per capita (main economies only) (figures in metric tons).

	1830–4	1911–13
Belgium	0.59	3.35
France	0.07	1.01
Germany	0.07	3.81
UK	0.95	6.09
USA (short tons)	0.30	5.55

Sources: B. R. Mitchell, *Fontana Economic History of Europe* (The Emergence of Industrial Societies: 2) (London, 1973), statistical appendix. *Historical Statistics of the United States* (US Department of Commerce, Washington, 1960).

ventilation, which integrated the industry with the new technology for which it was providing a key raw material. By 1913 in the most advanced coal industry – the American – more than half the bituminous coal was being cut mechanically (but less than 1 per cent of the harder anthracite) – a development of the previous twenty years – and a small fraction mechanically washed. These percentages were much lower in Europe, notably in the UK. The paradox thus lay in a most strategic industry for the new industrial economy expanding rapidly (with 1M miners at work in the UK in 1913) depending on medieval methods of physical labour by pick-and-shovel below ground, helped by pit ponies. This technological symbiosis of medieval and modern was almost as much a characteristic of industrial development in the nineteenth century as the confrontation of manual labour by machine. In serving urban termini, the railways produced the greatest new demand for horses in the nineteenth century, and for two generations the mechanization of spinning in the British textile industry produced an army of hand-loom weavers. This collaboration of old and new technology then became a feature of an international division of labour between Lancashire-spun yarn, and hand-loom weaving industries on the continent, in India and then in Japan.

The greatest technological heritage from the eighteenth to the nineteenth century was steam-power, and its attendant metal-working skills in rolled-wrought iron, large castings, and precision components such as plane-surfaces for steam-proof valves and pipes. The rising skills of the mechanical engineers were themselves dependant on improving methods in metal smelting with falling costs as the size of blast furnaces, forges, rolling and stripping mills increased. Water power supplied massive power for the primary metal industries (as for the first generation of large spinning mills in the textile industries in England, the continent and New England). Water power, as well as water transport, remained an important constituent of total capacity, if being overtaken by steam, which offered greater choice of location sites with lower costs of production (in relation to labour, markets and the coalfields), and removed a constraint on scale. Metal-working technology played a collateral role: early machine tools, such as the screw-cutting lathe, originating in arsenals in Holland and London in the late eighteenth century, where skills were at their highest, were followed by a proliferation of lathes, cutting and bending, grinding, shaping and stamping machines which had spread effects over a widening range of industries. With this went ever more accurate techniques of measurement. Self-governing mechanisms evolved from the windmill technology and the steam-pressure governor, which regulated the speed of eighteenth-century fixed engines.

Engine technology was itself proliferating by the opening decades of the new century; engines of many variants in all sizes for many different purposes (most of which James Watt had been reluctant to contemplate). Rotary motion from the fixed engine was already a tried technology (the first cotton spinning mill had been powered by steam in 1785); with efficient pumping engines in deep mines of all sorts (coal being by far the most important in the aggregate), and water-supplies for large cities (Paris and London being the leaders), breweries and distilleries. Trevithick and Hornblower were already mastering the technology of high-pressure engines, without reciprocating overhead beams, which was a precondition of engines for railways and ships (if not successfully for road carriage, despite much experimentation).

As power-weight-and-size ratios steadily improved, a wider range of engines could be put to use in a growing variety of contexts. Small engines on work benches were in use by 1820. Steam power became 'divisible', working large series of individual machines in textile mills through the provision of overhead iron shafting and leather belting. In this way steam power became available for renting with small workshops in the Birmingham and Sheffield metal trades; this was quickly adopted in the equivalent centres of the secondary metal-processing industries on the continent and in the United States. There is no space here to pursue the major innovations in power technologies alternative to steam during the century: gas-engines, and then internal combustion and diesel, with electric motors of increasing range. The electrical engineering industries ranged from the largest equipment for power-generation to fractional-horse power electric-motors, which helped to transform productivity in smaller factory and workshop trades, generating advances which had previously belonged to the large-scale production units in the primary side of the metal industries and textiles. With the electric telegraph of Samuel Morse (and others) of 1832 and subsequently the telephone, electric lighting, phonograph, and other electrical apparatus (symbolized by the protean inventions of Thomas Edison), quite new dimensions were given to the advance of technology. These innovations, as also advances in the fine-chemical industry, explosives, dyestuffs, special steels, optical glass and some others, had a particularly close relationship with advances in scientific knowledge and its application to industry. This was also true of certain advances in agriculture, with the work of Justus von Liebig at Giessen, and the Rothamsted Experimental Field Station set up by Sir John Lawes, a pupil of Liebig, in 1843, in England. As such these aspects of technical change may more appropriately be discussed in Chapter 3 – 'Industrialization and scientific and technological progress'.

Mechanization spread like a virus – following the dictates of relative costs and productivity – over ever wider areas of production in manufacturing industry as the century advanced. When innovations valorized steel as a cheap mass-produced metal after the 1860s, greater precision was made possible for machinery, as strength-weight ratios improved. More elaborate machine tools, automatic stamping machines and the like gave new standards of accuracy and exact replication. The Ruhr became a major European centre for this new metal technology. This trend had been clear in small-arms manufacture, predating but given new impetus from the Colt factory in Hartford, Connecticut of 1855. The system of construction from component and replaceable parts, for which precision manufacture was a precondition, became known as the 'American system' in tribute to its origin. Typewriters, sewing machines (both for domestic and industrial use), other office machinery, small arms and other 'assembly' type operations from components spread into the mass-produced metal-product industries, although the moving assembly line did not appear until Henry Ford invented it early in the next century (1913) for manufacturing motor cars. Even before then, the motor industry, growing in scale in France, Britain, Germany and other leading European centres of the mechanical engineering industry, exemplified the new 'assembly' techniques of replaceable parts. The family names of Peugeot, Renault and Citroën in France, Daimler and Benz in Germany, Morris and Austin in England, became as well known in Europe for their cars as that of Henry Ford in the United States. But by 1914 the new world was teaching the old in the techniques of mass production and assembly.

This type of mechanization gave smaller units of production the opportunity of reaping great gains in productivity. Small power units – steam, diesel, electric – made ranges of smaller machines viable. In the boot and shoe industry, for example, soles were stamped out by machine, and uppers stitched and 'closed' by commercial sewing machines. Sewing machines (hand operated or with foot-treadles, subsequently hitched to power) transformed productivity in the garment trades after 1870, hitherto lagging in productivity compared with the mechanized primary sides of textiles in spinning (with preparatory processes), weaving and finishing. Singer became a household name as the principal suppliers of domestic sewing machines across the world (with production facilities soon established in Europe) as did Remington (1874), for typewriters and Kodak for cameras. Typewriters and other office equipment began to make inroads of rising productivity in the service industries, long laggards compared with manufacturing industry, as did the telephone.

The iron industry, with non-ferrous metal smelting and refining (using the reverberatory furnace), was firmly set within the 'mineral-fuel technology' of coke-smelted, 'puddled' and rolled iron in Britain by the conclusion of the Napoleonic Wars, but with charcoal smelting still the rule in Sweden, Russia and most other European centres of iron-making except Belgium and Northern France. The hot-blast invented in Glasgow by J. B. Nielson in 1828 (he was manager of the local gasworks) valorized new varieties of iron-ore for the blast furnace. Great expansion ensued with the blast for the furnaces, tilt-hammers, the steam-hammer after 1838, and rollers all operated by steam. As Table 6 indicates, the course of iron production broadly followed that of coal – the two were closely linked with many interrelationships. Cast-iron became a leading constructional material, rolled wrought iron was the basic material for railway track. Urbanization, mechanization, iron ships, and the proliferating uses of iron made this a basic industry for modernizing economies. Units of production in the primary metal industries became vast, and highly capitalized, in contrast to steel production (in this early period) and the secondary metal industries using refined iron and steel as their raw materials. In the 1840s Sir John Guest's ironworks in South Wales employed over 6,000 workers and produced over 20,000 tons of pig iron annually.

The initial innovation which transformed the world's steel industry in the second half of the nineteenth century was also British – Henry Bessemer's 'converter' of 1856. This was followed by the Franco-German technology of the Siemens-Martin open-hearth furnace, the Martins, father and son, being professional metallurgists, unlike Bessemer.

Table 6 Pig iron and steel production, selected countries (thousands of metric tons, average p.a.).

	1800–14	1850–4	1880–4		1910–13	
	Pig iron	Pig iron	Pig iron	Steel	Pig iron	Steel
Austria-Hungary	–	221	591	–	2,204	2,450
Belgium	–	201	699	170	2,171	2,280
France	200	561	1,918	460	4,664	4,090
Germany	–	245	2,893	990	14,836	16240
Italy	–	–	23	150	366	980
Russia	200	231	477	250	3,870	4,200
Sweden	–	155	418	300	667	620
UK	248	2,716	8,295	2,860	9,792	6,930
USA*	–	642	4,770	1,559	30,941	28,081

Note

* pig iron in short tons; steel in long tons.

Sources: B. R. Mitchell, *Fontana Economic History of Europe* (The Emergence of Industrial Societies: 2) (London, 1973), statistical appendix. *Historical Statistics of the United States* (US Department of Commerce, Washington, 1960).

In 1878, an amateur chemist, S. G. Thomas (who worked in a police court), invented the 'basic' process valorizing the use of cheap phosphoric ores, which were widely available in Britain, Germany, Lorraine and Luxembourg. Before this steel was a semi-precious metal, affordable only for specialized uses in small objects, such as cutlery, blades and 'edged' tools. After the innovations it became cheap as a mass-produced product, and the steel industry followed the same logic of development, and broadly the same distribution as with iron. The Ruhr (with Krupps at Essen), Lorraine, and Franche-Compté became major continental steel regions, with great expansion also following in the Russian steel industry, particularly in the Donetz basin, experiencing a major 'spurt' of industrialization from the 1880s.

Rolled steel became a basic structural material, largely replacing wrought and cast-iron (being stiffer than wrought iron, stronger weight-for-weight, less brittle than cast-iron). The 'RSJ' (rolled steel joist) removed constraints on the height of buildings, and the mild-steel plate and rivetting did the same for the size of ships.

Further technological innovation followed through the advance of chemical knowledge applied to metallurgy in creating alloy or 'special steels' with chromium and manganese. France (innovating the electrical pyrometer), Germany (with the most sophisticated chemical industry in Europe) and Sheffield, lagging in other developments, led this field. Armoured plating, armaments, steel for high-speed machine tools, cutlery, surgical instruments and other specialized uses provided the main markets. Latterly, American innovations in galvanizing, pickling, annealing, improved plant design and the like led the way in more general increases in productivity. In 1890, at advanced plants, three tons of fuel were used in creating one ton of steel; by 1914, it was less than a ton. The American industry, with large plants, giant firms, using cheap ores from the Lake Superior region, dominated world steel production, as with coal.

Technology in the textile industry (the world's largest industry after agriculture) had made the vital initial bridgeheads away from handicraft methods before 1800, above all the cotton industry, which led the way in innovations, to be followed by other fibres, wool, linen, hemp, jute and silk (for weaving). Mechanization of silk reeling in 'filatori' worked by water power had spread in Italy and France in the eighteenth century – the one main branch of textiles where Britain did not lead innovation. The complex figured weaving of silk had also been successfully 'automated' by the French Jacquard loom after 1804.

Spinning and its preparatory processes for cotton were the first to be mechanized: Kay's flying shuttle, Crompton's 'mule', Arkwright's water frame and roller spinning had set the new technology in the late eighteenth century, with 'ring-spinning' from the United States following in the 1850s. Eli Whitney's 'cotton gin' of 1793, made the cleaning of raw cotton a cheap mass-produced operation.

Iron machinery linked to massive water power brought the first massive gains in productivity in spinning, in Britain, followed by continental countries and the New England mills. Jedediah Strutt's new mill of 1804 in Derbyshire was worked by a single water-wheel – 18ft in diameter, 23ft wide; power was delivered by vertical and horizontal iron shafts, elaborately geared, with leather belting over five floors to over 4,000 cotton spindles, as well as to carding,

reeling, doubling and twisting machines. Almost a thousand employees worked in the mill.

The effects on productivity were dramatic: more than 50,000 hours were needed to spin 100 lbs of cotton by Indian hand-spinners in the eighteenth century; with Richard Roberts' automatic mule of 1825 this had fallen to 135. A commentator spoke of a sequence of eleven different machines deployed to produce yarn, 'the operations chasing each other', adding 'the cotton mill presents the most striking example of the domination obtained by human science over the powers of nature of which modern times can boast'.

Power weaving was successfully innovated only after 1821, for cotton, and spread much more slowly than power-spinning. The sequence followed the same path: progressive adoption of steam power with the new textile technology, increases in scale, development of large plants, great speeding up of output, a fall in unit costs with rising productivity, and pressure being put on handicraft workers as piece-rates fell. International diffusion was slower in weaving than spinning, with complementarity developing between machine-spun yarn from Britain supplying hand-loom weaving handicraft industries in other countries, until the 'catching up' and diffusion spread to the next stage.

The scale of the growth of the cotton industry was the greatest of all the textile industries as Table 7 indicates. Britain's initial dominance of modernization techniques produced an early start, which kept her in the lead in output and exports throughout the century. Scale was such that international trade in raw cotton became massive – the first truly international specialization of a major industry – while the requirements of bleaching and dyeing produced the largest growth in the chemical industry, where techniques were principally led by France and Germany (see Chapter 3). Mechanized printing by rollers, which revolutionised productivity in this finishing process, had begun with Oberkampf in Paris in 1802. Switzerland and France led this technology for the fine cotton industry; automatic weaving of silk began in Switzerland in the 1870s.

By the 1820s textile machinery makers had specialized out in Britain within the mechanical engineering industry – profit-making firms seeking markets for their capital goods whether at home or abroad, as later in Germany, Belgium, France and the United States. The process of industrialization had produced an indigenous mechanism for diffusing technology, as with the capital goods industries more generally – from iron, to steam engines and locomotives. Platt's of Oldham became a principal supplier of textile machines (including ring-spinning machines, which

Table 7 Capacity of the European cotton industry (no. of spindles in thousands; percentage of UK capacity).

	1834	1877	1913
Austria–Hungary	800 (8)	1,558 (4)	4,909 (9)
Belgium	200 (2)	800 (2)	1,492 (3)
France	2,500 (25)	5,000 (13)	7,400 (13)
Germany	626 (6)	4,700 (12)	11,186 (20)
Italy	–	880 (2)	4,600 (8)
Russia	700 (7)	2,500 (6)	9,212 (16)
Switzerland	580 (6)	1,850 (5)	1,398 (3)
UK	10,000 (100)	39,500 (100)	55,700 (100)

Source: B. R. Mitchell, *Fontana Economic History of Europe* (The Emergence of Industrial Societies: 2) (London, 1973), statistical appendix.

20

Lancashire was slow to adopt) to various European countries, New England, India and Japan.

This account of advancing textile technology perforce concentrates on the 'leading edge' of change. Scant justice is therefore done to the large textile industries in other parts of the world: India, China and Japan (in cottons and silks) still mainly operating with handicraft technology before the twentieth century, although some mechanized spinning mills had been established. The regional chapters of the volume help to repair this omission.

Although railways dominate the story of inland transport innovation in the nineteenth century, the importance of developments in canal and river navigation needs to be stressed. Although long predating this period, great investment took place – enlarging canals to take large-barge industrial traffic, linking major river systems across Europe and within the United States. For low-cost bulk transfers where speed was not critical, water transport sustained mining and industrial regions as well as the growing cities. Over 2,500 km of canals came into use in France between 1815 and 1850, creating then, and over the next quarter-century, new long-distance connections within France, and with wider regions. Paris became linked with the northern coalfields and with St Etienne coal to the south. Canals linked the Rhone and the Marne to the Rhine. Barges, which were to reach 1,000 tons in capacity, traversed the Rhine, making the river a key artery for regional development – from Switzerland, the Ruhr, Belgium, the Netherlands and France down to the North Sea littoral. The Manchester Ship Canal served a similar role on a much smaller scale in England.

The technology for the first generation of successful locomotive-driven railways (there had been tramways using horses before) after 1825 was almost exclusively British: the high-pressure steam engine, the steam blast (whereby the steam from the boiler was thrown up the chimney), flanged wheels, cast-iron (then rolled-iron) rails, iron frameworks and wheels for locomotives and carriages. British engineering firms such as George and Robert Stephenson, supplied overseas orders, in Europe and North America, as well as customers in the UK, but the technology was quickly indigenized in all the advanced countries. Within a decade locomotives were being made in Belgium, France and the United States. The diffusion (for successful operating devices, as opposed to experimental engines) was much more rapid than for steam-power before 1815.

Early railways in England had been projected in anticipation that freight traffic (particularly coal) would be the principal market. In the event, passenger traffic provided the main initial impetus. Soon the main cities were linked by rail, and urbanization proved to be a great generator of traffic and passengers: railways removed the main constraint on the growth of large inland cities by being able to provide for a much greater intensity of use than road, canal or river (particularly for passenger traffic). The larger ports, responding to the great flows of international trade in foodstuffs, raw materials, coal, minerals and manufactured goods being generated by the expansion of the international economy, became the site of processing industries as well as transit centres. They needed to be serviced by railways, as did industrial regions and coalfields, where the intensity of demand for inland transport capacity was at its highest. The railways, for inland transport, added an extra dimension of efficiency in speed, certainty and lower costs for both passenger and freight. With the other applications of steam

power they became the most important single agency for transforming economies and societies in the nineteenth century. As with other metal-based mechanical engineering technologies, technical change in the railways (in such matters as power-weight ratios for locomotives, braking systems, signalling, the electric telegraph, comfort for passengers and carrying capacity for freight) brought progressive advances in technical efficiency, costs and productivity, as the inherent potential in the basic technology became progressively realized throughout the century and beyond.

Table 8 shows the main features of the diffusion of railways (mileage opened being a reliable proxy for investment and scale of commitment). Developments were led by the advanced European countries (with the UK in the lead, initially, closely followed by Belgium) and by the United States. This is particularly apparent if track-mileage is considered in relation to the geographical extent of countries and their population (see Table 1). During the second half of the century the scale of railway investment in the United States became unrivalled, as did the scale of American mining, heavy industry, urbanization and primary production in agriculture – which the railways helped to make possible. Unlocking the economic potential of great land masses, inconceivable except through the railways, brought benefits to regions hitherto remote from integration in the world economy. Some of the main linkages were as follows: Paris-Rome (1846) – the line built by Thomas Brassey, using English 'navvies', who subsequently built railways in many countries; Paris-Brussels (1846); Moscow-St Petersburg (1850s); the Gotthard Tunnel through the Alps (1882), the Orient Express (London-Paris-Vienna-Constantinople, 1888); the Trans-Siberian Railway (1891). In the United States the East Coast was linked with California in 1869; and in Canada the Canadian Pacific Railroad opened coast-to-coast in 1885. These transcontinental routes, although important in strategic terms, did not integrate national economies to a full extent: railways from

Table 8 Railways (kilometres of track open: selected countries).

	1840	1870	1910
Austria-Hungary	144	9,589	43,280
Belgium	344	2,897	4,679
Denmark	–	770	3,445
Finland	–	483	3,651
France	497	15,544	40,484
Germany	469	18,876	61,209
Italy	20	6,429	18,090
Netherlands	17	1,419	3,215
Norway	–	359	2,976
Portugal	–	694	2,888
Romania	–	316	3,437
Russia	27	10,731	66,581
Spain	–	5,442	14,675
Sweden	–	1,727	13,829
Switzerland	–	1,426	4,716
UK	2,411	24,759	37,658
USA	4,509	84,675	607,212

Sources: B. R. Mitchell, *Fontana Economic History of Europe* (The Emergence of Industrial Societies: 2) (London, 1973), statistical appendix. *Historical Statistics of the United States* (US Department of Commerce, Washington, 1960).

Table 8a Railways (kilometres of track open: selected countries).

Africa	1840	1870	1910
Algeria	–	265	3,277
Angola	–	–	851
Benin	–	–	307
Cameroon	–	–	107
Egypt	–	1,184	4,321
Ethiopia	–	–	310
Ghana	–	–	270
Guinea	–	–	324
Ivory Coast	–	–	182
Kenya	–	–	940
Madagascar	–	–	272
Malawi	–	–	182
Mauritius	–	106	209
Mozambique	–	–	516
Namibia	–	–	1,593
Nigeria	–	–	673
Réunion	–	–	126
Senegal	–	–	947
Sierra Leone	–	–	410
South Africa	–	–	12,208
Sudan	–	–	1,992
Tanzania	–	–	718
Togo	–	–	195
Tunisia	–	–	1,517
Zaïre	–	–	1,235
Zambia and Zimbabwe	–	–	3,582

Source: Mitchell, B. R., *International Historical Statistics, Africa, Asia and Oceania 1750–1993*, 3rd edn, Macmillan, Basingstoke, 1998, pp. 673–8.

Table 8b Railways (kilometres of track open: selected countries).

	1840	1870	1910
North America			
Barbados	–	–	45
Belize	–	–	40
Canada	25	4,211	39,799
Costa Rica	–	–	619
Cuba	82	1,382[1]	3,229
Dominican Republic	–	–	241
El Salvador	–	–	156
Guatemala	–	–	724
Haïti	–	–	103
Honduras	–	–	170
Jamaïca	–	37	298
Mexico	–	349	19,748
Nicaragua	–	–	275
Panama	–	76	76
Puerto Rico	–	–	354
Trinidad	–	–	130
South America			
Argentina	–	732	27,713
Bolivia	–	–	1,207
Brazil	–	745	21,326
Chile	–	732	5,944
Colombia	–	–	988
Ecuador	–	–	587
Guyana	–	32	153
Paraguay	–	91	373[2]
Peru	–	669	2,995
Surinam	–	–	133[3]
Uruguay	–	20	2,488
Venezuela	–	13	858

Notes
1 1880.
2 1911.
3 1909.

Source: Mitchell, B. R., *International Historical Statistics, the Americas 1750–1993*, 4th edn, Macmillan, Basingstoke, 1998, pp. 539–47.

the west coast to Chicago and from Chicago to the East Coast, for example, saw the vast growth of interregional traffic in the United States more than coast-to-coast traffic.

Strategic considerations were prominent in railway projection in continental Europe, where governments took the major initiatives in national planning and financing. By the Franco-Prussian war of 1870, military logistics had become determined by the railways. This was also the case in the government sponsorship of railways in India, spurred by the mutiny of 1857; even if the considerations of military deployments largely coincided with commercial priorities. Between 1845 and 1870, over 5,000 miles of railway were constructed in India – the largest mileage outside of Europe and North America at that date – with £95M of foreign capital invested, and dividends guaranteed out of tax revenues where necessary. The first railway in Africa opened in Egypt between Alexandria, Cairo and Suez in 1856–7, predating the Suez Canal of 1869, but not attracting mass freight transfers. Later, railways in the mining regions of Africa did unlock inland resources on a major scale. In general, however, taking the worldview, railway investment was coterminous with economic development – and integral with it. By 1870, only about 9,000 miles of railway were in operation outside Europe and North America (over half of this being in India) – only 7 per cent of the world's total.

Space does not allow a wider discussion of the effects of railway development, but these were protean. They include a great increase in the scale of mobility of people (for which railways were considered subversive of traditional social subservience); a great boost to mechanical and civil engineering; great developments in banking and the capital markets (because of the unprecedented scale on which capital had to be mobilized); the creation of a new rentier, shareholding class; advances in accountancy and company law; the evolution of new management structures for large-scale organizations; new concepts in the measurement and coordination of time; and the evolution of new regulatory systems by the state. This is in addition to technological innovations largely induced by the railways with spread-effects beyond them (such as the electric telegraph). Some of these issues find a place in other sections of this volume.

Steam-technology was quickly applied to navigation, once high pressures and the 'direct action' engine had avoided the great weight and slow movement of a rocking beam on a low-pressure engine, saving space and allowing a much lower centre of gravity. This made power-weight ratios acceptable for propelling ships. An international ferment of experimentation led by engineers in France, Britain (Scotland as well as England) and the United States was in progress as the century opened, with earlier river routes pioneered on the Delaware, the Seine, the Saone, the Hudson and the Clyde.

Table 8c Railways (kilometres of track open: selected countries).

	1840	1870	1910
Asia			
China	–	–	8,601
Cyprus	–	–	98
India	–	7,678	51,658
Indochina	–	99	1,717
Indonesia	–	–	5,145
Iran	–	–	9
Japan	–	–	8,661
Korea	–	–	1,031
Malaya	–	–	867
Philippines	–	–	206
Sabah and Sarawak	–	–	209
Sri Lanka	–	119[1]	930
Taiwan	–	–	436
Thailand	–	–	896
Turkey	–	180[2]	6,558[3]
Oceania			
Australia	–	1,529	28,049
New Zealand	–	–	4,490

Notes
1 1871.
2 1869.
3 1909.

Source: Mitchell, B. R., *International Historical Statistics, Africa, Asia and Oceania 1750–1993*, 3rd edn, Macmillan, Basingstoke, 1993, pp. 679–88.

These were mainly for paddle steamers, carrying passengers, but the role of the steam tug was quickly established for hauling barges on inland waters and sailing ships (whether commercial or naval) temporarily stranded while waiting for a suitable wind or tide. By 1820, thirty-four paddle steamers were plying British waters; France had 229 steamers by 1842. Where speed and reliability were at a premium (as for passengers, mail or specialized freight of small bulk) steam vessels quickly came to dominance on short hauls as paddle-steamers without complex gearing.

The further extension of steam shipping hinged on the amount of coal which could be carried – a function of the size of vessel, its carrying capacity, the efficiency of the engines, the method of propulsion and – critically – the length of the voyage. The immediate constraint was always the limitations on bunkering capacity, despite steam-ships using sails when in the open seas on long voyages. The first vessel to cross the Atlantic from London to New York was the small paddle-ship *Sirius*, sailing the 3,000 miles in 19 days in 1838. The *Great Western*, built in Bristol by I. K. Brunel, the great railway and bridge engineer, specifically for the transatlantic trade, took 15 days to New York shortly afterwards – arriving with 200 tons of coal still in her bunkers. She also carried sails.

Paddle-steamers remained common on short-distance and long-distance river routes where fuel could be picked up *en route*, into the twentieth century, but most advances in steam vessels after 1835 came with screw-propulsion, pioneered mainly in Britain and the United States. The operative patents were taken out independently by John Ericsson (a Swedish engineer working in Britain and the USA) and Sir Francis Pettit Smith in 1836. The first transatlantic crossing by a steam-ship using propellers came in 1843 (Brunel's *Great Britain* – displacing almost 3,000 tons and iron-hulled).

Innovations continued. Vessels became progressively larger and more powerful. Wood gave place to wrought-iron hulls and then to steel plates after mass-produced steel was pioneered in the 1860s. Screw propulsion was intrinsically more efficient than paddles (which lost energy in thrashing the water) but this demanded more rapidly operating engines and gearing, which encouraged progressively higher pressures and new designs. The most important advance came with the compound-expansion engine, re-using steam under diminishing pressures, the key patents being those of John Elder in 1862. The triple- and quadruple-expansion marine engine then became the standard technology for steam propulsion in the last quarter of the nineteenth century, when the era of the steam-turbines, pioneered by Sir Charles Parsons of Newcastle-on-Tyne (patents 1884), and oil-fired furnaces (for the most modern naval vessels by 1914) began.

The grandest manifestations of steam technology at sea came with ocean-going liners – successively grander, more powerful, more luxurious than anything else afloat – prestige palaces for national shipping lines in fierce competition for the luxury market. A similar transformation (using much of the same technology and ship-building capacity) took place in naval vessels, in conjunction with advances in armaments and armour-plating. Scale in size, steam power and guns dominated naval strategies in battlefleets across the world at the outbreak of the Great War in 1914.

If steam-technology and iron and steel vessels had the leading edge in shipping technology in the nineteenth century, steam was slow to conquer the trans-oceanic, long-distance cargo-routes for non-perishables, where sail remained dominant until the twentieth century – the long haul of grain or tea to Europe from the Far East and wool and wheat from Australasia (although meat demanded refrigeration and steam ships) and comparable trades from South America and the West Coast of the United States. Wooden hulls had given way to wrought iron and steel on such trade routes before sail had given place to steam.

Unlike other areas of technical innovation and industrial growth, where Britain came under challenge from other leading industrial countries after 1870, her dominance in shipping technology, ship-building and ship-owning remained without a rival until after 1914. This was based on the fact of an established position from the beginning of the new matrix of mineral-fuel technology, steam power and associated skills, with an unparalleled natural resource advantage. Being the greatest sea-trading country in the world throughout the nineteenth century, British shipping enjoyed the largest home market. But the efficiency of the ship-building and ship-utilizing industries was such, enjoying sustained comparative advantage in costs, that most of the world's long-distance trade, whether British or not, was being carried by British ships up to 1914, and British shipyards built more ships than the rest of the world put together. Most of the determinant marine patents in this same epoch remained British. It was a dominance not set to survive long in the next century.

A major new extractive industry, based on geological exploration, a new technology and largely new markets, began in 1859, when the first modern oil well was drilled in Pennsylvania. Baku followed in 1871–2 (a Swede, Robert Nobel, being the leading entrepreneur), with Hungary, Romania, Borneo, Burma and Sumatra quickly following, and Iran in 1903. The oil industry was born international and multi-national. On the basis of new chemical analysis and refining technology, growth was rapid – the main initial demand being for kerosene for domestic lighting cooking and heating, before the internal combustion engine (using 'diesel' and various other grades of refined petroleum) and naval ships' boilers became the major markets. World output of crude oil reached 20M tons by 1900 and about 55M tons by 1914 – small in relation to coal, which provided over 80 per cent of modern energy sources, but already of great significance to the growth of modernized economies 'at the margin'. American oil, now being produced in several states, dominated world output, with 65 per cent of the total. Before its break-up by anti-trust legislation in 1911, Standard Oil, owned by John D. Rockefeller, controlled over 80 per cent of American production, sales and exports. Caucasian oil supplied over 16 per cent of the total; Hungary and Romania about 7 per cent; Asia about 3 per cent (where Shell, the Anglo-Dutch firm of Henry Deterding and Marcus Samuel, was establishing a major presence). Thus a major new industrial legacy was given to the twentieth century from the nineteenth.

Space precludes even the barest description of much technical change and innovation, which contributed to the transformations of the nineteenth century. A list of some omissions emphasizes the range of developments: the glass industry, transformed like non-ferrous metal production to a scale of output comparable to iron and steel; ceramics, cement, tin-plate, rubber, the gas industry; paper making (moving from rags to wood-pulp); printing (more particularly for mass-produced newspapers), large-scale brewing and distilling, refrigeration, canning (as the food-processing industries expanded), bread-making, biscuits and confectionery (transformed by Perkins' 'travelling' gas oven), milling (led by Hungarian multiple-reduction systems), cigarette-making (revolutionized by the American Bonsack machine after 1881); soap and margarine (the latter a quite new industry); artificial fibres (with the rayon industry growing rapidly after 1900), musical instruments (in particular the piano, with large-scale output after the adoption of the iron frame). Equivalent transformation came in distribution and retailing (department stores led by Bon Marché in Paris after 1860 – closely followed in all the largest cities in Europe and the United States – mail order firms selling by catalogues, led by Montgomery Ward and Sears Roebuck in the United States, serving the rural market in particular; multiple stores, especially in the food trades). Thomas Lipton had more than 500 shops open in Britain by 1899, with extensive manufacturing and packing stations in various countries, selling almost over 50 tons of tea per day in his shops and to 5,000 wholesale tea agents. In 1914 the Maypole Dairy Company had almost 1,000 branches and sold a third of all the margarine in Britain – 1,000 tons per week, made in their own factories. It is important to recognize that large-scale developments were not confined to industry.

In much of the world, traditional handicraft methods and small-scale shop-keeping continued to dominate activity. But innovations brought a new industrial impetus in the decades before 1914, based largely on oil, steel, motor cars, aircraft, electrical engineering, artificial fibres, consumer durables, and food and drink processing.

The financial dimensions of development

Economic growth in the nineteenth century was integral with the growth in the number and diversity of financial institutions, which supported (and sometimes led) developments. Unprecedented increases in the capital-intensity of economic activity brought unprecedented innovations in finance, which were closely linked to the demands of scale. Railways and urban infrastructures (financing urban development itself, urban water, public utilities, local transport) made the greatest demands, but mining and large-scale industrial development (in particular in heavy industry) demanded new levels of capitalization. The extensions of rural settlement demanded funding through land-banks. Irrigation and water could be capital-intensive in dams, reservoirs and infrastructures. For major Western European countries, led by the United Kingdom, France and Germany, although their own economies were becoming more capital-intensive, major flows of internal savings went abroad, financing infrastructures in other countries. In 1913 almost half of Britain's domestic savings were flowing overseas (net national savings were 13.2 per cent of net national product, while net domestic capital formation was 7.5 per cent of NNP). Industrialization and economic growth produced financial surpluses, in addition to making greater demands on savings for capital investment. Net domestic capital formation in Germany rose from 8.5 per cent of NNP to 15 per cent between 1857 and 1913; that of Italy from 4.6 per cent to 9.9 per cent.

Small private banks – mainly family firms – had been features of European economies, since the thirteenth/fourteenth centuries in Italy. Central banks began with the Bank of England in 1694, and were founded in the nineteenth century as modern nation states emerged. Napoleon established the Bank of France in 1800. A central bank, closely linked with the national currency, state borrowing and government influence over the monetary system, was a characteristic institution of modernized independent states. Banks of all kinds proliferated as economics grew, diversified, urbanized; as international trade expanded, international financial transfers increased, and populations living and working in a monetized environment sought secure institutions for their savings, domestic borrowings and insurance. There were mortgage banks, land-credit banks, rural credit institutions funding peasant, small-scale agriculture, savings banks, and local cooperative banks. Trade unions and friendly societies assumed savings-bank (as well as insurance) functions. In Britain, and America, more than continental countries, insurance companies became a major independent presence in the long-term financial markets, while banks fulfilled this role rather more in other countries. By 1914, building societies in Britain were institutionalizing the financing of domestic houses independently of banks and insurance companies. By 1873, 1,534 such societies existed in Britain (some designed to be terminal) with assets of £65M in 1913.

At the local level, universally, in village as well as town society, money lenders, and pawnbrokers (some, as in Italy, with a municipal *imprimatur*) served an important, if sometimes exploitative, role. Across the world there was a strong Jewish presence in local money-lending, while at the other end of the financial spectrum, Jewish families were also prominent in the wealthiest of private banking circles, in France, Germany, Eastern Europe, and in Britain (more than in the United States). The Rothschilds were pre-eminent, with a presence in all the main European financial centres. Private bankers in Europe developed in particular as 'investment' bankers (or merchant bankers in the present idiom), putting together syndicates for major investments in government loans, taking initiatives (and organizing finance and shareholding) for railway projects, urban improvement, mines and heavy industry across Europe. France and Germany were the main investors in Central and Eastern Europe, and in Russia in the 1890s massive loans were raised to fund railway constructions, mining, heavy industry and Caucasian oil, under the initiative of S. Y. Witte, Minister of Finance, in a 'forced draught' of late industrialization.

In Britain the Barings matched the London Rothschilds in organizing and underwriting foreign loans raised in London, and funding the immense credits centring in London from overseas trade. They were particularly prominent in financial dealings between Britain and the United States, Britain and Argentina, although, with the Rothschilds, they provided the financial backing for re-establishing the European legitimist monarchies after Napoleon. The private bankers prospered whenever governments (who guaranteed the payment of interest in terms of gold or sterling) raised loans for railways, wars or luxury spending (with sometimes dire results, as with Egypt in the 1870s and 1880s).

By 1914, £4,000M in 'portfolio' investment – apart from direct investment – had been invested abroad from Britain – over 40 per cent of the world's total foreign lending – with 21 per cent going to the United States, principally for railways but also for developing ranches and mines. Similar investment followed British migrants and business to the Dominions (Canada, Australia, New Zealand, South Africa), taking 37 per cent; to Latin America (principally Argentina), 18 per cent; and to India (9 per cent). Continental Europe – Spain, Italy, Central and Eastern Europe, and Russia – was the main domain for France and Germany, where their enterprise followed their banks and their capital. French foreign investments totalled about £2,000M (fully a quarter being in Russia); German foreign investments £1,250M; Belgian, Dutch and Swiss on a smaller scale. Only around 6 per cent of British foreign investment (£250M) went to Europe as spheres of financial and industrial influence were staked out.

The main banking innovations of the nineteenth century concerned deposit-banking, multi-branched banking, and new types of corporate banking institutions evolved to fund highly capitalized enterprise. Deposit banking with the use of cheques was long established in Britain (from the seventeenth century) but did not evolve significantly elsewhere until after 1800 (partly for legal reasons). Joint-stock banks (common in Scotland before 1800) were allowed in England after 1826 and became the general form for larger banks on the continent after 1850, increases in the size of firm offering improved stability. This allowed growth in scale (by expansion and absorption of private banks) into multi-branched operations for 'retail' deposit banks with branches in the high streets of most towns. In 1825, 715 banks existed in the UK. By 1913 numbers were down to 88 (only 29 private bankers were left) but bank branches totalled 8,610.

A similar consolidation, although less intense, was proceeding in France, where deposit banks such as the Crédit Lyonnais spread their networks after 1860. Such national branch systems did not characterize American banks, however, because federal legislation blocked interstate banks, leaving, a 'unit' banking structure. This also became the pattern in Japan for retail banking. Capacity in the American banking system grew at a formidable rate, collaterally with the scale of economic development: there were 506 registered banks in 1834, 1,937 in 1870 and no less than 25,000 by 1913.

As 'monetization' spread, banks became the custodians of a rising share of nations' savings; cheque and other transfers by way of banks assumed a greater share of total transactions, while financial assets increased in diversity and range. The assets of financial institutions in European centres were growing at 5–6 per cent p.a. in 1861–1913. The aggregates of cash and currency increased throughout, with predominance in the early stages of evolution of financial structures in advanced economies, but over time their role lessened in comparison with that of bank assets. In 1850 cash and currency formed 24 per cent of all money stocks in England, with Bank of England assets at 11 per cent and commercial bank notes and deposits 65 per cent. This was a more advanced ratio than anywhere else. By 1913, coin and Bank of England notes were 12 per cent of the total; bank deposits 85 per cent.

Financial structures were deepening as well as widening in response to the increasing range of demands for financial accommodation both short and long. Most world foreign trade (and until the mid-century most internal trade in England) had been financed by way of bills of exchange. This vast, expanding market induced into existence a new financial intermediary: the bill-broker or discount house, which became a major presence in the London money market. For the advanced countries as a whole, in 1913, the distribution of assets between financial institutions has been calculated as: central banks 12 per cent; deposit banks 59 per cent, thrift institutions (savings banks, thrift and loan, building societies, etc.) 14 per cent, insurance 10 per cent, miscellaneous 15 per cent. Independent thrift institutions did not evolve so much beyond Britain and the United States. Specialized mortgage banks fulfilled this role rather more in continental countries by 1913, holding between 12 and 23 per cent of the assets of all financial institutions there. The share was 12 per cent in Japan and no less than 70 per cent in Egypt.

Demands for long-term credit for heavily capitalized undertakings where evolution came late demanded specialized financial institutions. Capitalization had increased with the growing scale of heavy industry, public utilities, transport and urban developments, but mobilized wealth had not increased *pro rata* in later developers, nor had a long-term public capital market evolved to the same extent as in Britain through stock exchanges – the major alternative to raising long-term capital in the private sector apart from the banking systems.

Industrial firms, when beginning in a small way, could raise the modest initial capital to get started from private sources or trade credits, thence increasing their capital assets from retained profits – 'auto-financement' – using banks for short-term commercial credit. This was the standard pattern across the world for family and partnership enterprise. Even with the rapid emergence of large-scale multi-national corporations in the United States after 1860 (in mining, oil, chemicals, motor cars, steel, etc.), retained earnings was still a principal source of capital growth, and family control often remained dominant within the corporate form.

At the same time the Amsterdam and London stock exchanges had become institutionalized over a century before 1815, their main business being the market in government securities, resulting from state borrowings to pay for the escalating costs of war. The permanent, long-term, national debt in Britain had reached £840M in 1820 (almost three times larger than GNP), and a shareholding class had been educated in buying stocks and shares. The full market-panoply of financial intermediaries, brokers and agents had evolved round the stock exchange, closely linked with bankers handling investments for their customers. The evolution of this long-term capital market produced a structural difference between Britain and continental countries, with the United States following British precedent. In Britain all new capital for railway investment (with a share value of £1,300M in 1914) had been raised privately on commercial terms through shares issued on the stock exchange. In virtually all other instances the state was involved in raising capital, offering concessions or guaranteeing dividends. The funding of public utilities, heavy industry and mining (where retained profits did not suffice) took a similar course. British banks, including the 'national' high-street banks did not normally lend long for equity investment, while British merchant banks looked to foreign trade and overseas investment for their business rather than to large-scale enterprise within Britain.

In the absence of this degree of development of a public capital market, and a large share-holding class willing to trust their savings in this market, specialized long-term funding institutions grew up in France, Germany and elsewhere on the continent to fill this gap. In retrospect it may have been one of the 'advantages of backwardness' that such a profoundly important new funding method for 'lumpy' capital investment was created. Continental economies gained much from the innovation of investment banks (*banques d'affaires*) – and not just in terms of the capital raised. Joint-stock banking offered the advantages of scale, as did the general spread of joint-stock companies in other fields after 1860, which quickly provided the institutional basis for all large-scale enterprise.

The early growth of heavy industry and railways in Belgium, brought precocious structural advances to the banking system there, with the Société Générale (1822), and the Banque de Belgique (1835), taking on the role of long-term funding. The principal investment banking movement in Europe, however, began with the foundation of the Crédit Mobilier in France in 1852 (under government stimulus for railway development). Although this collapsed in 1967 (its founders the Pereire brothers waged an interminable feud with the Rothschilds), the Crédit Mobilier inspired a progeny. In France in the 1860s the Crédit Industriel, Crédit Lyonnais (1863), Paribas, and the Société Générale became major deposit banks and 'mixed banks' combining retail banking, with longer-term loans for equity investment. Investment banks occupied a major role, which became more important relatively in Germany, and thence Russia, Spain, Italy and elsewhere, than in France. The four great German 'mixed' banks – the Deutsch Bank, Dresdener Bank, Darmstadter, and Disconti Bank – were all in business by 1872 and continued to dominate the scene. The Credit Anstalt in Vienna (founded with French and German capital in 1856) promoted similar investment in railways, public utilities, mining and heavy industry in Austria-Hungary, as did comparable banks in other countries.

By holding long-term equity shares (which controlled voting rights in companies) investment banks were drawn into matters of corporate strategy as well as the supply of capital. They were instrumental, it seems, in organizing cartels in the German mining and steel industries. They could also potentially monitor performance and check on management efficiency, in a way which was wholly alien to banks and institutional shareholders (or private investors) in Britain. These entrepreneurial roles of continental investment banks may have been exaggerated, but they were not absent. The Credit Anstalt became linked with forty-three industrial firms, while in 1912 the Deutsch Bank had its representatives on the boards of directors of 159 firms.

Changing organizational base

The basis of enterprise

Much emphasis is now placed on the institutional framework of countries as an important influence upon propensities for growth or consolidating the forces of inertia. This range of explanation goes beyond questions of natural resources or economic and technical variables, penetrating to the heart of a country's political, legal and cultural processes. Awareness of these issues is closely linked with the appreciation of the significance of the growth of market economies (the locus for so much of economic change), which, in turn, focuses attention on the necessary conditions for the successful operation of markets and their evolution. Much of this evolution long-antedated the nineteenth century, and could spread by established precedent: commercial success contained its own impetus where conditions were propitious and external forces did not block change. Despite constraints, market forces and institutions developed both within individual countries, and exemplified commercial and financial relationships between countries, in the portentous growth of the international economy during the nineteenth century.

Private property rights are one pillar of a market economy, as mentioned above. A 'free' market cannot operate unless the ownership of assets and their tradability is assured, their market value ascertainable by bidders having open access to the market. This was true already for land, property (with variations), commodities and chattels, but a precondition for capitalist development required the transferability of financial assets in particular: paper- instruments covering money transfers, bank deposits, cheques (as bills of exchange had long been), stocks and shares, and other media of value and exchange. Contracts required enforceability: market regulations needed an ultimate legal sanction, because all markets involved an equilibrium between individual freedom and regulatory frameworks.

A market economy depends on the freedom to negotiate prices. Theoretically a perfect market depends on perfect information – an unrealized abstraction – but the fewer constraints (from whatever source) the more accurately will prices embody commercial reality. The lower information/transaction costs become, the more efficient will be the allocations determined through the market. Improved information flows and falling costs of information characterized the nineteenth century. Price 'currents', newspapers, carried price information and expanded their circulation greatly; technical literature developed to disseminate information on internal and international exchanges. International commodity markets became the most sophisticated (and efficient) manifestations of market mechanisms, with the Chicago wheat exchange of 1848, and London becoming the main centre of international exchanges in tea, coffee, metals, jute and sugar. Liverpool and Manchester set world prices for raw cotton.

Railways and the electric telegraph transformed the flows of market information. For the first time news could travel faster than a galloping horse or a ship under sail or steam. The electric telegraph girdled the globe within a decade after 1866, transforming the commercial operation of the international economy. Europe was linked to North America in 1866, to South Africa in 1868, to India and Japan in 1871, to South America in 1873–5, and to Australia by 1876. Chapter 2 has more discussion on the implications of these linkages.

Personal freedom, with access to all careers, became generalized in the early nineteenth century. Discrimination against religious minorities faded but limitations on the civic status of Jews were lifted only gradually. England was in advance of continental countries in this relaxation, although Jewish bankers in London could only obtain the Freedom of the City in 1851, and Lionel Rothschild became the first Jewish Member of Parliament in 1858. Problems of 'derogation' of nobility being formally debarred from careers in business were resolved – for the very rich – by ennobling Jewish bankers in Austria-Hungary. Napoleon's regimes in Europe cleared away much of the debris of surviving feudal apparatuses, establishing modern Roman-law legal codes in the French style. Personal freedom and flexible commercial law systems (whether Roman Law as in the Netherlands or the Common Law – judge-made law – in England) had long characterized North Western European countries. This set a basic parameter for development, even though some anomalies, such as the 'serf-entrepreneur' in Russia or the samurai-turned-entrepreneur in Japan, saw an old world coalescing with a new.

Before generalization of incorporated enterprise with limited liability in the mid-decades of the nineteenth century (mentioned elsewhere in this chapter), accommodation had been made for the organization of some larger-scale operations. Most Western European countries had privileged (often monopoly) companies trading to the East Indies and elsewhere, where risks were high and large capital essential. Other ventures could be incorporated by special legislation. The ownership of mines or ships (one of the 'lumpiest' forms of capital at the beginning of the century) could be made divisible by various means. The partnership form of enterprise proved adaptable for such purposes in many contexts. The *société en commandite* in France, for example, allowed sleeping partners with liability limited to their own capital. However, in all countries the dominant form of enterprise was the individually owned business, the family business and the small partnership. This was true of most professional as well as commercial and industrial enterprise in the private sector in most contexts in the world throughout the century.

This form of small-scale organization, with management closely tied to ownership (unlike the large joint-stock company with operations controlled by professional salaried managers) was in large measure a response to doing business in a context of high risk. Levels of risk and uncertainty were being diminished in the context of advanced countries in the nineteenth century (with better communications, better institutional arrangements, insurance, etc.) but were still high and had not diminished very much in many countries. Fraud was commonplace, particularly associated with stock-exchange flotations and the fleecing of ignorant or unwary investors. This concentrated on the upswing of economic cycles, when critical standards were low, to be revealed in the following depression. Shareholders were cheated by the payment of dividends out of capital rather than genuine profits and by many other sharp practices. Overseas mining

adventures were particularly subject to such practices: accountancy rules and company law advanced, but usually in the wake of scandals. High risk made it difficult to run multi-branched firms, to control agents at a distance, to prevent fraud. Management control needed to be exercised directly by the owner or partners of an enterprise. Such a context placed a high premium on dealings between known individuals where a bond of trust and confidence had become established. The greater the risk the higher this premium, which made kinship a profoundly important organizing principle for enterprise. Access to credit, for example, a pre-condition for conducting business, was central to such inter-personal relationships, spreading outwards by personal 'networking'. Personal trust and creditworthiness in turn depended on personal reputation built from the perceptions of others over time. The strength of minority groups in business, where religion as the focus for identity in a minority created an effective matrix for kinship and inter-personal links, can be explained in large part by this logic. Huguenots, Quakers, Mennonites and others in Europe had their equivalents in Armenians, Parsees, and Chinese minority groups throughout South East Asia and elsewhere, while Jewish trading and financial elites worldwide embodied similar characteristics. This phenomenon was, it seems, almost irrespective of the formal theologies which such religiously identified minorities espoused.

Personal, family and small-partnership enterprise continue to dominate total business and professional activity into the twentieth century. However, when seen in longer-term historical perspective, the nineteenth century saw a potent strategic innovation – the large-scale business organization, already by 1914 operating on a multi-national scale. Other sections of this chapter have mentioned the financial and legal dimensions of this development under the form of joint-stock companies with limited liability issuing publicly-tradable stocks and shares. This removed constraints on the growth of scale in individual firms, which raised the organizational issues considered here.

Before the nineteenth-century, large-scale organizations, demanding bureaucratic management controls, were all outside the private sector – in the administration of armies, navies and state bureaucracies. The first major exceptions to this pattern came with the railway companies. Vast capital assets, a powerful shareholding interest, state regulatory systems, and great investment in mechanical and civil engineering works, demanded large organizations, under corporate firms. The intricacies of running the system raised managerial problems of an intricacy unknown in industrial or commercial enterprise in that period. New cadres of middle-management, supervisory and clerical staff were required, a process replicated when equivalent increases in scale came to industrial, mining and retailing firms after the 1860s. New techniques of management control aided by management accountancy, monitoring all aspects of performance by way of regular statistical reporting to head office, evolved to maintain efficiency and create internal coherence within large organizations. The 'administrative revolution' of the nineteenth century was not confined to governments.

The expansion of the large-scale organization came by merger as much as internal growth, with the latter decades of the century showing a spate of take-overs, mergers and cartels as large-scale business in the 'modernized' sectors consolidated. This was characteristic of 'heavy' industry (coal-mining, iron and steel, cement, chemicals, etc.) but covered transport (railways and shipping lines), oil, banking, railways, and consumer goods industries such as soap, tobacco, margarine, sewing cotton, brewing. Scale became unprecedented. In 1902 United States Steel had 168,127 employees. The capitalization of the Pennsylvania Railroad (controlling 11,400 miles of track in 1906) was $1,218M. Almost 80 per cent of the American rail system was owned and run by thirty-two companies. Britain's rail system of 20,000 miles was dominated by four national companies in 1914, capitalized by way of 'pyramiding' amalgamations at £1,300M. Bankers across the world organized the financing of such mergers.

Trade associations and cartels became strategic organizational devices to coordinate policies between large firms. In Britain large-scale 'horizontal' trade associations formed amongst competing firms in textiles. J. and P. Coats brought fourteen firms together in 1897 to produce a virtual monopoly in sewing cotton. The Salt Union of 1888 amalgamated sixty-four firms; the United Alkali Company of 1891, forty-eight firms in bleaching and heavy chemicals. William Lever controlled 60 per cent of United Kingdom soap production in 1914. Some of these amalgamations (as in tobacco) were countering American 'invasions'. In Britain they were mainly defensive – to shore up prices – and had few gains from rationalizing production or increasing productive investment. Many were costly failures, but amalgamations did not diminish.

The cartel movement was most advanced in German heavy industry by the last decade of the century. Almost all the output of Ruhr coal was 'cartelized' in the Rheinland-Westphalia Coal Syndicate (1893). The German Steelworks Association followed for most Ruhr steel in 1904, with a major chemical cartel of Hoechst, Casella, BASF and Bayer shortly after. In contrast to Britain, German cartels played a more positive role. Because the investment banks controlled a significant percentage of the equity capital of such constituent firms, they were instrumental in organizing cartels and could impose rationalization measures upon them. The first attempts were made at international cartels and price agreements in chemicals and oil, but these did not make significant advances until the inter-war period.

In Japan an equivalent path of evolution of the large-scale company merger, amalgamation and 'oligopoly' was taking place in the modernized sectors of the economy after 1868, if under a rather different organizational form. A few giant firms grew largely by taking over previously government-sponsored enterprises. The *zaibatsu* were more like 'conglomerates', family-controlled holding companies with enterprises in diverse industries. Mitsui and Mitsubishi were the most prominent; Sumitomo and Yasuda had integrated businesses in mining, iron and steel, shipbuilding and engineering, but also investments in textiles, shipping lines and foreign trade. Unlike Europe or the United States, the main *zaibatsu* in Japan developed banks as an integrated part of their firms, operating as the financial arm of their holding companies, as well as offering financial services elsewhere. This was the most dramatic example of the modern manifestation of integrated business operations.

In Europe and Japan the growth of scale and the rise to dominance of a few firms in many industries, controlling a significant percentage of total national output in their hands, did not invoke government response until the inter-war years. In the United States, where the giant firms in oil, steel, chemicals, coal and railroads had become more prominent than elsewhere, responding to the unprecedented opportunities for growth which the American economy afforded, it was otherwise. The first 'anti trust' legislation against the threat of monopoly came with the Sherman Act of 1890, extended by the Clayton Act of 1914. That this legislation had an impact was not in doubt: the national 'empire' in oil created by John D. Rockefeller was broken up in 1911, the greatest state intervention in modern industry known to that date.

One consequence of these developments was the rise of 'white-collar' employment. State-created, state-regulated activities were increasingly administered by salaried bureaucrats forming a distinct professional cadre of civil servants, operating at central government and local government levels (for city administration); at state as much as federal level in the United States. Large-scale organizations such as the army and navy, customs and excise authorities had more long-standing full-time salaried administrators, but what had been called a 'revolution in government' added public bureaucracies on a large scale during the century. 'White-collar' employment in the service sector, with national schooling, and the medical and legal professions, added to the spread of 'professionalization' and the 'salariat' trends, which were also progressive within railways, public utilities and larger-scale businesses.

By 1911, 8 per cent of UK employees in manufacturing industry were in 'white-collar' functions. Leading firms had several thousand employees in their head offices (Siemens in Germany had over 3,000). This was a portent for changes in the structure of employment in the twentieth century.

The role of the state

In considering processes of change in the nineteenth century, the role of the state, whether positive or negative, can never be ignored. At the most elemental level, physical security for persons, property and assets under an assured legal system – with the anticipation of continuity – is a precondition for success. This becomes more vital as economic activity and institutions become more complex and operate on a widening scale. The state guarantees the enforceability of legal systems: all markets must have legal (ultimately political) legitimation. The state was the largest single influence in economies and societies in the nineteenth century, not just for the modernizers. State structures and bureaucracy were strong in China and quickly became so in Japan after the Meiji Restoration of 1868. The state mobilized resources on a scale greater than any private organization through its control of taxation and the ability to raise loans on the security of tax revenues. Where governments directly controlled the money supply (which was not general in Europe or the New World, where the gold standard prevailed) then 'paper' inflation could provide extra resources, if only temporarily. The largest single commitments lay in the military and naval expenditures of states, an inheritance from the eighteenth century, which continued.

Some states still owned or controlled great assets, inherited from royal demesnes, with lands including minerals. This had ceased to be significant in Britain, France and Holland, but in Scandinavia and Prussia, for example, public assets had remained important, and this was also the case in the United States. The federal government controlled public land of 1,810M acres in 1789, during the nineteenth century distributing 120M acres free in land grants, 127M acres for transport (particularly land for railways), selling a further 324M acres, and maintaining 842M acres in the public domain by the twentieth century – by far the largest landholder. Large public domains still existed in Russia and many other countries. All states had major roles in economic policy making. Protection of agriculture was a near universal attribute, giving political protection for landowners and peasants, including in the United Kingdom before 1846, when protectionism was abandoned. Industrial tariffs, initially mainly anti-British, characterized all the other main European industrial economies and the United States. The decision of Britain to abandon protection, was, of course, no less a political act than imposing tariffs, bitterly fought out in Parliament. It was also state action, which abolished certain monopolies (such as foreign trading companies) and swept away most of the old restrictive regulations of mercantilism.

Whatever kinds of economic policies pursued, states became regulatory bodies over widening ranges of activity. Urbanization and industrialization were processes breeding regulations: safety when travelling and at work; control of working conditions, particularly for women and children in factory and mine inspectorates, health and sanitation regulations invoking public health authorities at central and local government level, urban planning, transport, and other fields.

Regulatory regimes proliferated for such diverse institutions as public utilities, police and prisons, transport, immigration, lighthouses and rescue at sea, harbour controls, posts and telegraph, patents. Regulatory controls over business and banking made the presence of the state of direct importance in the operation of the banking system. Central banks (whether formally state institutions or informally so, as in Britain) accepted responsibilities for ensuring stability over the monetary systems as a whole (with central banks opening branches in the provinces to limit over-issues of private bank notes, etc.).

The structure of banking systems was also much subject to regulation. Prohibition against joint-stock banking held back developments in scale of operation and thereby increased one source of the instability which prohibitions against incorporated, limited-liability enterprise were designed to prevent. General statutory access was given to incorporation and limitation of liability in the mid-century in most countries. This gave momentum to the expansion of enterprise (particularly removing a constraint against larger-scale operations), but gave scope for greater fraud and speculation in stock-exchange manias. Every individual transport undertaking needed a private Act of Parliament in Britain (as did all incorporated enterprise until the general statutes), emphasizing the importance of the state.

Apart from establishing the regulatory systems demanded by all modern urban societies, probably the most positive effects of state initiative (with state funding) came with the promotion of national education systems – a characteristic of all such countries (as Chapter 7 elaborates). There is a close connection between levels of wealth and investment in human capital through education. This was not only true in regard to literacy and numeracy at primary level; but in continental countries in Europe for the promotion of 'tertiary' education in universities, *technische Hochschulen* spreading from the mid-century; having originated in the Ecole Polytechnique of Paris, a prototype for the *grandes écoles* established by Napoleon. *Ecoles* for road engineers and mining dated from the *ancien régime*. French initiatives became the inspiration for Europe as a whole, and

this followed the eighteenth-century values of the Enlightenment. 'Land-grant' colleges in the United States were another example of state initiatives in funding an educational system. This precedent was directly transferred to Japan when the first agricultural college was founded in Hokkaido under American initiative in the 1870s. Private provision of education was extensive at all levels, but public funding was critical for mass basic education at one end of the spectrum and for universities and research institutes at the other. The United Kingdom lagged relatively: amongst the advanced countries national, compulsory, free, state-funded education came only after 1870, while major university and research investment did not happen until the end of the century, despite much campaigning.

Britain, with a highly centralized and modernized state apparatus developed during the nineteenth century, was unique as a 'minimum' state in that the public sector was extremely small in relation to the national income. In 1850 public sector spending was 11 per cent of GNP, with the annual servicing costs of debt absorbing more than half, and military expenditure in peacetime was about 3 per cent of GNP, leaving all other central state expenditure at only 2.4 per cent of GNP. No great state investment programmes were pursued for the productive sides of the economy, no state funding of railways, no state promotion of innovation (except by way of military spending), no public underwriting of private investment by central government (although some greater initiatives could be found in city administrations). The UK provides a norm in this respect, against which the greater roles of the state may be judged in all other countries, including the United States.

A long tradition of states promoting enterprise existed, especially under the absolutist monarchies of the *ancien régime*. Royal manufactories, industrial capacity for military *materiel* and mining, encouraging new skills and the immigration of artisans who would bring with them advanced technology, were the most characteristic of such state efforts. The long-term results for the nineteenth century were not encouraging. Few major innovations came from military technology before the mid-nineteenth century: most enterprise prospered in the private sector (subject to the disciplines of a market economy). State manufactures were in luxury industries, for status products where cost was not an issue, and for armaments. Subsidized production engendered inefficiency and waste, with the functional efficiency of enterprise perpetually put at risk by the more pressing priorities of political patronage. An important technical contribution, however, was made in early civil engineering by military cadres such as the *Corps des Ponts et Chaussées* in France and the Corps of Army Engineers in the United States.

As mentioned in other sections of this chapter, the role of the state in promoting enterprise, indirectly more than by direct management, was widened during the nineteenth century. This was more particularly so in those countries coming to industrialization late – Eastern Europe, Spain, Italy, Russia, and, above all, Japan. Market mechanisms and institutions had not evolved in these countries to be able to sustain developments spontaneously in the same way as in Western Europe or the United States. Coming late in time, the scale of technology in mining and heavy industry had become larger, and more capital-intensive, making greater demands on investment funds for 'lumpy' investment, which demanded the prior accumulation of savings and special institutions for mobilizing capital. As we have seen, railways and public utilities providing the infrastructure of urban development were an integral part of the process. Where the flow of internal savings proved inadequate, such projects also became dependant on imported capital, which provided critical initiatives for investment. Thus, in late nineteenth-century contexts where the need for such strategic investment was greatest, effective response from the private sector responding just to market incentives was least possible.

In such circumstances all roads led back to state initiatives. In any case these states had a tradition of centralized political power. Land in the public domain could be granted. To attract financial syndicates led by powerful *banques d'affaires*, all kinds of concessions could be provided; strong corporate banks could be established which linked powerful individuals within the country to foreign capital. Little happened without official approval and encouragement; the favoured concessionaires enjoyed many privileges. This was promoting development at a high cost, but where market disciplines were absent this form of institutionalizing capital-intensive investment became inevitable. This thesis explaining the enhanced role of the state in 'late developers' was put forward by Alexander Gerschenkron for European economies in the nineteenth century, but nowhere does it apply more dramatically than to Japan. A modernized apparatus of state and economy was almost wholly absent there at the change of regime in 1868. The astonishingly rapid transformation of Japan from then onwards owed its momentum to initial state initiatives making bridgeheads into all sectors for development: railways, shipyards, engineering, iron and steel, textiles, mining, chemicals, education, the banking system. By 1914 major industrial and financial conglomerates – the *zaibatsu* – had emerged, as has been cited earlier in the text.

FOLLOWER ECONOMIES AND THE EUROPEAN PERIPHERY

Peter Mathias

This chapter has concentrated on the 'leading edge' of industrial advance and the modernization of economies and societies in the nineteenth century. Subsequent thematic chapters explore different aspects of these processes in more detail, while the regional chapters in the second section of the volume relate such changes to their national and regional contexts in all their diversity. Here only the briefest discussion can cover the outlines of what was, in relation to the core economies' leading patterns of urban and industrial growth, a highly diverse periphery. Economic integration was proceeding both internationally and within countries as transport, commercial and financial systems and state administrations developed. Effective national states were a prime basis for this. International trade, supported by financial and investment flows, brought virtually every country and region more fully into an international economy of growing complexity. Primary products – whether for food, industrial or energy requirements – in bewildering variety provided still the main basis for international exchange, increasingly supplemented by trade in industrial goods, both consumer and capital goods, the latter supporting the growth of the former. Progressive countries prospering on agricultural exports tended to enhance the

degree of processing and thus gain greater added value. Sweden is an example in wood products and pulp for paper; Hungary (in contrast to Romania and Russia) in milled and processed grain and sugar.

Many great interior land masses, where climate or geography were extreme and transport investment too costly to produce an economic gain, remained largely insulated from becoming integrated in the world economy. Within countries, particularly those which were large, with mountains or desert regions and difficult communications, great diversities in economic development prevailed. Nodes of modernized and urban sectors co-existed with extensive regions of a more primitive economic base, some highly populated and others scantily settled. China, India, Russia, Canada and Australia are examples of such regional diversity and contrasting economic development, but in lesser degree regional contrasts were prominent in Spain, Italy and Scandinavia, while the same phenomenon, if on a lesser scale, was to be found in the core industrial economies of Britain, France, Germany and the United States.

A characteristic of these regions isolated from a commercial nexus and remote from the dynamics of development – both within economies and between countries – was poverty. Such regions tended to experience slower growth in income per head (if not always growth in the size of their economies). Economic expansion (as distinct from economic development) allowed a rising population to be sustained where extra land and resources existed but, without a rise in productivity which only economic development – changes in the economic system – could bring, income levels per capita could not increase over the long run. Malthusian problems, where they did not produce crises, were relieved by mass emigration – for Europe overseas as much as internal migration. Thus came a widening discernible gap in living standards and modernization during the century in these regions peripheral to the industrializing economies of Western Europe. All showed regionally, and usually in the main cities, some trends of progressive transformation, quickening after 1860, and between 1896 and 1914. This was characteristic of rates of growth, urbanization (especially in the growth of large cities, capital cities in particular), state structures and state initiatives, some development of a modernized financial and banking system, some development of railways and mining (where natural resources allowed) and other attributes of modernized countries. In almost all these regions, however, the primary sector (agriculture, forestry, fishing) remained the largest single sector of the productive economy, even if progressively modernising and geared into economic advance through exports and/or the supply of urban markets. There also tended to be a correlation between the level of national wealth and the extent of literacy.

In these regions of Europe the impetus for economic growth was largely derivative rather than indigenous – derived from the dynamic being generated from the industrializing and urbanizing 'core' regions. This came about from diverse but usually integrated mechanisms: the more advanced regions taking exports of primary products, foodstuffs and raw materials, supplying manufactured and capital goods, making transfers of modern technology, direct investments, business and financial linkages, supplying exported capital through 'portfolio' investment for railways and infrastructures.

From such bridgeheads 'spread effects' could develop: agricultural processing industries, engineering industries to 'indigenize' functions previously supplied by imports – in short, the progressive development of an internal dynamic to serve the requirements of a modernizing economy, in commercial and financial spheres as well as the industrial and technological. Export opportunities would also diversify as such modernization proceeded and the momentum of development became self-sustaining internationally and within economies. Even before this, most countries in Europe had a pre-existing handicraft industrial base to some extent. Artisan-based textile and small metal industries were widely scattered, with a 'proto-industrial' tradition going back centuries in particular localities. The largest cities, particularly where courts and noble residences were sited, had concentrations of skilled craftsmen in the luxury trades doing precision work of great intricacy.

Amongst the most successful of the European 'peripheral' economies was Sweden, favoured by its resources endowment in relation to international demand. Growth rates rose from about 3 per cent p.a. after 1850–9 to 6 per cent p.a. by 1880–1914. Initially textiles and the forest industries (particularly wood pulp for paper in the latter decades) provided the main industrial thrust, supported by a long tradition of mining and metals. Engineering and food-processing developed from this and largely grew out of this matrix. The share of exports in total industrial output grew from 10–15 per cent to over 25 per cent in 1860–80, but the strategic role of experts may well not be fully revealed by this percentage of the aggregate. Sweden's path of development was emulated in a similar sequence subsequently for other Scandinavian countries, if originating on a different natural resource base (apart from Finland). Denmark diversified from arable agriculture to farm and dairy produce (much aided by a successful cooperative movement), responding to British and German urban markets. By the end of the century Denmark claimed to supply the Englishman's typical breakfast of butter, bacon and eggs in a mass export trade across the North Sea.

For the Norwegian economy forest products, together with fishing and then an internationally important merchant marine, provide the main specializations, although all Scandinavian countries diversified with a growing industrial sector as they advanced. Textiles, food and drink processing (particularly brewing) metals and engineering were characteristic of the paths of growth. Good design (linked to educational and training institutions) aided this industrial evolution in furniture, glass, ceramics, textiles and other sectors. Food processing and brewing capitalized on local agricultural production. As elsewhere, the engineering industries proliferated, with early close connections to supplying equipment for the primary sectors (agricultural and dairy equipment, machinery and tools for forest industries, food and drink processing and the like).

Great disparities in development characterized different regions of the Austrian (Austro-Hungarian) Empire. The western regions (the 'Czech Lands') were the most advanced and, after 1860, showed a slightly faster growth rate than the UK but from a much lower base, leaving per capita wealth and living standards much lower than in Western Europe. Agriculture remained dominant (and the main source for exports) but the Empire has been called an 'industrialized agricultural state'. Structural transformation was in progress, noticeably after 1860. As elsewhere, the textile industries – wool, linen and then cotton – led industrial development, on the earlier basis of rural handicraft industry, with some heavy industrial zones based upon

ore deposits and coal. By the 1880s, it could be claimed that a 'factory industrial revolution' was taking place in the Czech Lands.

The Empire gave some institutional coherence in industrial, commercial, financial and policy terms within this great diversity. Liberal economic policies were the main trend of the 1860s (as in Western Europe), to be followed after 1873 by more restrictive policies and protectionism, partly in response to the inflows of cheap transatlantic grain, partly to encourage nascent industries. Centralized initiatives from Vienna aided the evolution of a modern banking system (on French and German lines), while the state-sponsored railway development and the import of capital was directed to transport and public utilities. This gave impetus to a 'revolution from above' with growing links to German and French financial and industrial interests. The Empire also offered favoured markets for industries in the Czech Lands and for Hungarian agricultural produce.

Similar sequences marked developments in Hungary, by 1914 a case of 'semi-successful peripheral industrialization' in I. Berend's phrase. Capital imports from France, Germany and Austria by way of state and municipal bonds and debentures were instrumental in creating a modern transport infrastructure in railways (22,000 km by 1913) and river navigation. Agrarian production and exports, increasingly in processed forms such as milled wheat, maize and sugar, gave an important boost to the economy, particularly after serfdom was abolished in 1848. In Hungary's case the key technical innovations behind agricultural success were indigenous: roller-milling with multiple-reduction systems (in contrast to traditional grinding methods) led Europe and ensured the technical superiority of the Hungarian milling industry. This invention had come from the Ganz engineering firm of Budapest, which became one of the most successful electrical engineering enterprises of Central and Eastern Europe, supplying whole ranges of equipment from generating plant and electrical urban tramways to dynamos. Ganz, with the Hungarian State Railway Machine Works of 1872, were important points of technological growth, if limited in their 'spread-effects' in this period.

Budapest, as the political and administrative joint capital with Vienna after 1867, followed Vienna in attracting massive urban investment as two great social and cultural magnets – significant in economic terms for the Empire – in what was to prove the final flourishing of the united Empire.

The 'Mediterranean' economies of Italy, Spain, Portugal and Greece showed lags in modern developments in the nineteenth century comparable, or greater than, most of the other 'peripheral' European regions beyond the industrialized core of the Western countries. Per capita income, in all the Mediterranean economies, as in East and Central Europe, declined relative to the West, even if increasing slowly in absolute terms. Here the main break in trend, with rapid industrialization, was to come only after the Second World War. This was a 'Latin' pattern of development, grounded in climate, geography, culture and institutional traditions, which delayed modernization and resulted in relative backwardness. In the second half of the century Italy and Spain had levels of per capita income roughly half those of Britain and France, on average, with Portugal half as low again. Italy experienced a much greater impetus to modernization after 1860 than the other Mediterranean economies. Urbanization was weak, in contrast to levels in

Italy. Agricultural surpluses were meagre in most of their regions (wine areas were a partial exception), a consequence of low productivity agriculture disconnected in large measure from export and urban markets, unresponsive to commercial incentives. Changes in tenurial relations (by way of much expropriation of entailed land) in Spain did open the way for agricultural development in the following century. Two thirds of the occupied population of Spain were still employed on the land in 1900–13.

Southern areas of Italy also followed this pattern, but agriculture in the north, across the plains of the Po and the Ticino rivers, and in the Veneto, was highly productive and commercially responsive, with long-standing investment in irrigation and canal and river networks. Equally, Italy had a long-standing industrial tradition in urban industries and proto-industrialization dating back to the thirteenth century, with extensive foreign markets, sophisticated urban cultures and accumulated wealth. Textiles led Italian industrial development, as in Spain and in many other regions of Europe, but the premier textile in Italy was silk, rather than wool, flax or cotton (as elsewhere), and in silk production Italy led Europe. Large mechanized mills for silk reeling ('filatori') were established in Lombardy in the seventeenth century, long predating the mechanization of cotton-spinning in Britain. Thomas Lombe pirated this invention to introduce it to Derby in England at the beginning of the eighteenth century. In the nineteenth century there was faster growth in the production of silk yarn than finished silk fabrics in Italy, feeding the manufacture of silk products in France and elsewhere, together with other branches of a modernized textile industry in cotton and wool.

A strong tradition of successful metal industries also developed in the mountain districts of North Italy, which in many respects paralleled the pattern of industrial growth in Switzerland, where a proto-industrial tradition in textiles and in small-scale metal manufacture, as in clock- and watch-making, had been well established. The exploitation of ore deposits in Elba during the century enabled a heavy industry dimension to be added to Italian industrialization – latterly encouraged by hydro-electric power, which created a resource advantage rather than a liability for a remote mountainous region, as in Switzerland. Spain, too, was bountifully endowed with a wide range of metal ores (iron, copper pyrites, lead, zinc and mercury). Except for mercury, located far inland in Almaden, most were accessible to the coast and hence formed the basis for growing exports, mainly organized by foreign enterprise. Unlike Italy, however, Spain did not develop important modern metal industries. Making small steel artefacts, as in Toledo, belonged to a much older handicraft tradition. Textiles (wool and cotton) were the leading industrial sector in Spain in the nineteenth century.

Italy's industrial resources, like its modernized agriculture, were highly concentrated in a few northern provinces. The economic development of this most advanced region, although following a different path of growth, was closer to that achieved by Western Europe, but in the national context was dragged down in the aggregates by the mainly underdeveloped and unindustrialized southern provinces. In the north of Italy 'spread effects' – reflected in the indigenization of railway technology, engineering enterprise associated with textile production, food processing, urban industries and the like – consolidated the regional impetus of modernization to a much greater extent

than in Spain and Portugal. Even so, much modernized technology was originally import-dependent.

Similar parallels in the process of modernization in Italy and Spain, with similar contrasts in pace and degree, were apparent in other aspects of development. Government initiatives were prominent in the import of capital and the promotion of railways in both countries. Protection, it seems, encouraged industrial growth at the end of the century. The basis of a modern banking system evolved rapidly in Italy after unification in 1870 – overtaking the proud medieval tradition of banks, which Italy had pioneered. This was not matched in Spain during the nineteenth century. Both railways development and banking – hallmarks of a modernizing economy in this period – were much more retarded in Spain than in Italy, in response to a much less developed and articulated economy. Both geographical obstacles and institutional inertia held back progress in Portugal and Spain compared with Italy.

RURAL AND URBAN RELATIONSHIPS

Sidney Pollard

Since the dawn of recorded history there have been towns, communities, which differed in important respects from the countryside surrounding them. The nineteenth century saw great changes in this area of social life, as in so many others. Above all, there was a sharp increase in the relative weight of the urban population within an overall population increase, and a widening of the range of functions undertaken by towns.

There is no clear or generally accepted definition of what constitutes a 'town'. In some countries, the statistics employ an arbitrary number, such as 2,000 or 5,000 people as the recognized minimum, though with the growth of towns and their share in the total, the minimum has tended to increase. In other countries, the definition is a legal one: towns are places with charters giving them certain rights and privileges, usually including the right to collect taxes. Elsewhere still, it is the function and the economic activity, which may be taken as the criterion of a town. Rural life is characterized by an exclusive or predominant concentration on agriculture and supporting activities; places in which industry, services or governmental activities prevail, we classify as urban. Commonly all these go together: towns are largish concentrations of population living in a relatively confined area, with some form of self-government and engaged mainly in activities other than agriculture. However, in the nineteenth century there were increasing numbers of cases which fell between these categories, as hamlets and villages thickened up into conglomerations without a recognized centre or local government, while older privileged towns shrank into obscurity.

Urban and rural areas were not only different from each other: they were also linked by a relationship of mutual dependence by performing certain functions for each other. Basically, and following the practice of centuries of tradition, the surrounding areas provided food and certain industrial raw materials, such as flax, wool or leather, for the towns, while the latter provided the countryman with industrial products and some services. These relationships had become more complex in the seventeenth and eighteenth centuries; in the nineteenth, there were to be greater changes still.

The declining share of the agricultural population

As in the case of the dividing line between town and countryside, the definition of the agricultural population is by no means clear-cut. All we can say is that at the beginning of the nineteenth century, the population of Europe, as well as North America and other parts of the world, was overwhelmingly agrarian; putting it differently, it may be said that the work of several families on the land was necessary to provide the surplus which would keep one non-agricultural family in food and other necessary agrarian products. For our purposes, we may include in the agricultural population those working in arable cultivation and in animal husbandry, as well as in fishing and in forestry. We may also include the landowners who might not have worked themselves, but lived on their estates and depended on them for their income.

In France at the time of the Revolution, then one of the most advanced regions of Europe, the proportion of the population dependent on agriculture in that sense amounted to at least 90 per cent. The same ratio applied to the United States. In Eastern Europe it was higher still. By the mid-nineteenth century it had fallen sharply and declined further to around 50 per cent in France in 1913. Those employed directly in agriculture numbered 70 per cent of the European population in 1800 and 57 per cent (outside Russia) in 1860. By 1895, the agricultural population of Germany had fallen to 35.5 per cent; in Austria-Hungary it was just over 50 per cent at the turn of the century, in the Scandinavian countries just below that figure. In Russia and the Balkans it was still close to 90 per cent. Only in Belgium, where the non-agrarian population had exceeded 50 per cent by 1850, and in Britain, where the proportion of the labour force in agriculture had declined to 25 per cent as early as 1840, was the transformation far in advance of this.

Given the rapid increase of total population and the fall in the agricultural *share* in it, which often meant very slow growth, or stagnation in *absolute* numbers in that sector, and given that the natural population increase on the land was at least as fast as in the towns, there must have been a considerable emigration from the villages. Some people migrated into the towns; others, as noted elsewhere in this volume, emigrated, mainly to overseas destinations. There was also some transformation of former agrarian villages into industrial towns by the introduction of industrial employment there.

Migration on any scale implies either a pull or a push factor: people were attracted to a new location, or they felt that life had become impossible where they were. Both were at work in this period. One significant factor virtually everywhere was that pay was low on the land relatively to other employment, working conditions were harsh, and urban life appeared more attractive in other respects, too, though migrants did not always take the higher costs and the atrocious hygienic conditions in towns fully into account. Rising numbers in villages, where the supply of land was limited and no employment opportunities existed for the landless, meant that people moved, not to find better jobs, but to find any jobs at all.

Productivity and specialization in agriculture

If the proportion employed on the land declined, yet consumption levels as well as the output of agrarian raw materials were on the increase, at least one of two things must have happened. Either productivity increased, or there was a rise in imports from outside regions. Both occurred to a large extent in our period. The expansion of overseas trade bringing food and raw materials to the industrialized parts of Europe is treated elsewhere in this volume; here we are concerned with the rising productivity on the land.

In Europe itself there was little spare land available. In Britain, the last stages of enclosure coupled with crop rotations, which eliminated the fallow, had begun in the mid-eighteenth century and were virtually completed in less than a hundred years. Thereafter there was little additional land to be had; on the contrary, the cheap grain which came flooding into Europe from overseas in the last third of the century induced farmers to turn arable into grassland for animal husbandry which, though profitable, reduced the number of people that could be fed from each hectare. There was enclosure and land consolidation into larger plots also in France and Germany. Much spare land was still available to be taken under cultivation in Scandinavia and Russia. There was extension of cultivation also in the Balkans, and much fertile land was gained by taming the mouth of the Danube. Drainage and irrigation, respectively, extended the available agricultural land in Italy and the Iberian Peninsula. Some gains could be made from eliminating the fallow year. In East-Elbian Prussia, for example, the land in fallow was reduced from 2.8 million hectare in 1800 to 1.1Mha in 1907, while the land under food crops increased from 4.6Mha to 10.1Mha, partly at the expense of grassland.

Nevertheless, the numbers of additional hectares was strictly limited, and population soon outgrew any increase from that source. The really extensive additional land resources were found in North America, in South America, in Australia and New Zealand and other overseas territories, and it was these which, through international trade, helped to prevent a Malthusian famine resulting from the unparalleled population increase in Europe.

At the same time, there were also technical changes to permit larger output per hectare as well as per person, thus, freeing labour for non-agrarian pursuits. While not as spectacular as the new technology in industry, technical change, in the broadest sense, was more rapid than ever before.

One source of rising farm output was the introduction or extension of new crops. The potato became a leading cheap food, capable of feeding very large numbers per cultivated acre. Other root crops, such as turnips, also spread, and the sugar beet began its victorious march across the northern plains of Germany from the late 1830s, and in the Low Countries and France from the mid-century, after having failed as a crop to beat the blockade under Napoleon. Tobacco came to be grown in quantities in several Mediterranean countries, and maize cultivation was extended in the Hungarian plain and in the Balkans. The quantities of maize harvested in Hungary, for example, rose from 9.8 million quintals in 1842 to an average of 48.1 million quintals in 1910–13. The strains of cereals, the main food source in Europe, were systematically improved, and new varieties, such as millet and buckwheat, extended in cultivation. Improved crop rotations, including leguminous plants, also helped to increase yields.

Possibly the most significant innovation to raise productivity was the use of artificial fertilizers. First introduced in the 1840s, by such researchers as Liebig in Germany,

Boussingault in France and Lawes in Britain, they by-passed the threatened shortage of animal manure. Some were imported from abroad, such as guano from Peru. Others were the product of an increasingly scientific chemical industry in Europe, such as the fixing of nitrogen from the air, discovered early in the twentieth century. One estimate of the quantities of mineral fertilizer applied, expressed in kilograms of pure plant nutrients per hectare in the period 1910–13, put the Netherlands at the top with 164, followed by Belgium at 69, Germany at 50 and the United Kingdom at 28. Even Poland registered 17 kg and Italy 14 kg.

Manpower also came to be saved by machinery. Belgium had 23,000 power-driven threshers in 1910, France had 234,000 in 1892 and Germany 1,436,000 in 1907. Some of the models then in use could be bought for as little £10–20 in Britain. Of mechanical reapers it was estimated that Britain had 40,000 in use in the 1870s and Germany had 301,000 in 1907. In the United States, which was far ahead in this field, 73,000 reapers, had been sold by McCormick as early as 1858, and the annual output of grain harvesters had risen to 250,000 by 1885. The total value of all American farm equipment increased fivefold, from $246M in 1860 to $1,200M in 1910. All these machines were constantly being improved and cheapened.

The European farming community also managed to sustain an astonishing increase in the livestock carried. Thus the number of cattle (in millions) rose from 5.0 in 1840 to 9.2 in 1910 in Austria, from 5.6 to 7.2 in Hungary, from 11.8 to 14.5 in France, from 0.8 to 2.3 in Denmark, from 7.1 (1850) to 11.7 in the United Kingdom and from 15.0 (1860) to 20.2 in Germany. The numbers of pigs in the five countries of Denmark, Germany, France, Sweden and Ireland together rose from 12M in 1840 to 32M in 1910.

There were still enormous differences between different parts of Europe. Thus the yield in grain cultivation, that is, the ratio of the grain harvested to the seedcorn, was up to four times as high in the West as in Russia; animals weighed more than twice as much; the milk yield could be threefold. Quality control, particularly well developed in Denmark, could make the produce far more valuable. Potentially there was thus still room left for further increase, provided capital, knowledge and skills could be made available in the backward regions. Overseas, on the vast farms and ranches in the Americas and in Oceania, extensive agriculture produced less per acre, but far more per man.

One other source of increasing output deserves mention: specialization, made possible by the improved means of transport and communication, allowed peasants and farmers in each region to produce what their soil and climate were best suited for, which both increased quantity and improved quality overall. Thus, in France, wine production moved south, into more suitable areas, as soon as transport to the consuming areas in the north of the country was cheapened; the Mediterranean countries developed the cultivation of citrus fruit and olives for export; and farmers within reach of large industrial cities in Britain, the Netherlands or Denmark, specialized in market gardening, dairying and the like, where closeness to the market mattered, importing feedstuffs from overseas where they could be produced more cheaply.

In the course of the century, the large majority of the rural community had turned from subsistence farming to supplying markets. This meant dependence on market fluctuations, for inputs as well as outputs, and the danger of effective competition from other regions in their own country or from abroad. It also meant the growing danger of infection of cattle or of plant diseases, the most devastating of which turned out to be the phylloxera which devastated French vineyards in the 1870s and 1880s, as well as those of Spain and Italy.

Traditionally, technological change is assumed to spread much more slowly in the countryside than in urban industry. This is partly because the farming units tend to be smaller and less well provided with capital, but also because peasants and farmers were believed to be more conservative in outlook – possibly with good reason – and also less educated and informed. There was some justification for assuming villages and hamlets to be cultural backwaters.

Schools came later to them, even when one country after another made elementary schooling universal and compulsory. Their teachers were poorly paid and often had to teach several year-groups together in one classroom. Children tended to disappear at certain times in the crop year, or were kept away in the winter when snow blocked roads. Secondary schools would be found in towns only. Similarly, country people had access to fewer newspapers, few professionals lived in the villages, and those who did, like squires and parsons, had few cultural contacts with the typical villager.

Culturally as well as politically, the town was thus in a position of hegemony over its surrounding countryside. Country folk, apart from the landowning upper classes, were looked down on as ignorant, barely literate even where they had had some schooling, slow in thought and dependent for their ideas on what they could learn from the urban population. Yet, at the same time, city people frequently also had a sneaking admiration for the bucolic culture, and there was a widespread tendency to romanticize rural morals as against alleged urban decadence. The peasantry was often assumed to be a dependable, loyal, stable element in society. Traditional values, a sense of reality, deep religiosity, and attachment to family were other qualities for which country folk were admired. Yet such romanticizing neglected the abject poverty and oppressive dependence on the landlord class, the looser sexual morals, often induced by gross overcrowding, the poor medical provision, and the slyness and greed with which peasant smallholders were also often associated. The peasantry might possibly be held to have been a more contented class than their urban equivalents, but it was certainly also, by comparison, culturally deprived.

Social and property relationships in agriculture

Agricultural specialization depended to large extent on natural conditions, such as climate and soil, and also on distance from the markets. But additionally, the structure of landholding and property relations, themselves not unconnected with the lie of the land, influenced the kind of agriculture pursued.

A relatively well-to-do, capitalist farmer class, owning or renting their land, was typical for England and Scotland. Employing wage labour, and usually able and willing to make use of modern techniques, including farm machinery, they worked for the market and had access to the necessary market information. Some were sufficiently independent to associate socially with their squires. In North America, farmers would employ less labour but far more machinery.

They were even more dependent on distant markets, and more likely to be in debt to merchants and bankers.

In hilly areas, conditions imposed a stockbreeding economy. Farmers often owned their land; but if it was rented, they tended to have secure and heritable tenancies, one aspect of the earlier liberation from feudal conditions generally found in the mountains. They depended on the market not only for the sale of their animals or dairy products, but also often for food for their own table. Such relationships were found in upland Britain, in Alpine countries and in Scandinavia.

A free peasantry was also the norm in many lowland areas in Western Europe, including France, the Low Countries and western Germany. Typically theirs were family farms, though the larger would employ wage labour, while the holders of the smallest would have to make up their income by working part-time in other pursuits or by temporary migration. Mixed farming, both in the sense of arable jointly with animal husbandry, but also of production partly for the market, partly for subsistence, was often found there. Many owned the land they worked; others, particularly in the Netherlands and adjoining regions, enjoyed secure tenancies. Personal freedom had come to these villagers at different times in the past, but in the nineteenth century it was no longer questioned.

There were also regions with a free peasantry but without security of holding. These would not merely have a less favourable tenure, they were also normally poorer. Examples were to be found in Ireland (until towards the end of the century) and in the *métayage* (share-cropping) tenancies in southern France and Italy, especially in wine and fruit regions.

At the beginning of the century, there were still large numbers of unfree peasants. Their conditions of unfreedom differed, as did the manner in which their labour was exploited. The most fettered were those on private estates in Russia, where personal unfreedom included the right of landlords to sell them with their land. Freedom came with the Emancipation Edict of 1861, which left the peasants to pay for their freedom in instalments over forty-nine years, keeping a share, varying in size in different parts of the country, of the land they previously worked. They were the poorest, most backward, most oppressed by rents and taxes of all European peasants, even after liberation.

In East Elbian Prussia, emancipation was set in train by laws of 1807 and 1811, but was not fully completed until the revolution of 1848. In the Austrian Empire, emancipation laws were passed in the same year after earlier easements of the conditions of serfdom, culminating in the edict of 1789. In the Balkan lands gradually liberated from the Ottoman Empire, moves to peasant emancipation spread over much of the nineteenth century.

Typically in former servile areas such as Russia and East-Elbian Germany, much land was left in the hands of landowners in the form of large estates. These estates had to be worked by 'free' labour, hired in different ways, which often derived from the traditional agrarian structure. On the estates of East Germany, for example, which developed almost into a region of monoculture of rye or other grain for export to the West, four main categories, each with their own sub-categories, could be distinguished: living-in servants, labourers working under contract, dependent small-holders required to perform labour services on the estates or the large farms, and wage labourers and migrant workers not under contract.

Large estates, in the form of latifundia, were found also in Southern Italy and Southern Spain. Worked by hired, dependent, poverty-stricken labour, they were frequently technically backward and inefficient.

The working of timber resources in Scandinavia, Russia, the Alpine lands and the Carpathians, developed yet other forms of labour and ownership. Fishing was often a cooperative venture of owners and crews, but more near-capitalistic relationships were also found.

Agricultural policies

Because of the economic as well as social weight of agriculture, policies relating to the agrarian sector frequently played a major part in the political life of Europe. The background in many countries was that the political and social power of the landed classes, inherited from a past when they were economically dominant, was coming under threat as the rising economic significance of industry, transport and the services tended to shift political influence towards those non-agrarian interests. The loss of aristocratic power in rural areas had not proceeded very far: even in 1913, it still maintained control over nearly all of Europe, including Great Britain, but it had had to fight to retain it.

One key issue was agricultural protection, by tariffs, import restrictions or subsidies, to benefit the whole of the agricultural interest, including farmers and peasants, but above all the landlords. After a brief liberal phase in 1860–80, most of Europe, but excluding Britain and the Low Countries, had gone protectionist again, with a subtle distinction between industrial and agricultural protection. Industry as a rule used the 'infant industry' argument: it had to be protected in its early, weak stage of growth until it was strong enough to meet foreign competition; in other words, protection was to be an aid to expansion. Agricultural protection, by contrast, was usually defensive: it was to hold positions against overseas imports, in other words, to prevent decline. In the United States and Canada, on the other hand, which at that time were agricultural exporters, it was the industrial lobby which pressed for the highest possible protection.

Among other issues high on the political agenda was the liberation of the serfs and the compensation to be paid to landlords for the loss of their unfree cheap labour supply. Although, as we have seen, emancipation tended to occur when the ruling classes were in a state of weakness, either in the revolution year of 1848 or after a lost war – 1807 in Prussia, 1861 in Russia – the terms were usually quite generous to them.

In some countries, including Ireland, security of agrarian tenure was an issue; in others it was allotments, in others still, rural housing. The burden of tithes paid to the church and the distribution of taxes, as well as the level of rents, were other important issues.

Urbanization

Since much of manufacturing and services, including administration, is usually located in towns, the expansion of the share of the industrial and service sectors in the economy was bound to be accompanied by their growth. However, there was a noticeable trend towards urbanization in the nineteenth century, even in regions and countries which showed little or no industrial development.

It has been estimated that in 1800, the urban population of Europe, taking 5,000 people as the lower limit, accounted for between 9 and 11 per cent of the total; taking 2,000 as the limit, it lay between 13–16 per cent. It grew sixfold to 1910, by which time (given that the total was also expanding) it reached a share of around one half. In France, a country of slow overall growth, the urban population increased from 4.2M in 1811 to 13.8M in 1911; in Sweden, from 200,000 in 1800 to 1,300,000 in 1920; while the three leading Dutch cities, Amsterdam, Rotterdam and The Hague, grew from 302,000 in 1795 to 1,035,000 in 1899. Northern Italy had one city of over 200,000 in 1840, but four in 1901; towns between 20,000 and 200,000 grew from 23 to 66 in those years. German urbanization had its biggest spurt, like industry itself, after unification. There were eight cities there of over 100,000 in 1871, but forty-eight in 1910: Gelsenkirchen, in the Ruhr district, grew tenfold in forty years.

Overseas, the trend towards urbanization was possibly even more pronounced: while in 1800 no city in the USA or the countries of European settlement had as many as 100,000 people, and at most 10 per cent of the population was urban, by 1913 there were several cities exceeding one million and urbanization had proceeded as far as in Europe.

It is safe to assume that general trend was connected with the growth of population, which was found in all parts of Europe, though proceeding at different rates. Where, as in many regions of Central Europe, village land was held in tight ownership by peasants and was in any case in short supply, this growth meant that in every age cohort some people could find no land and had to leave their village. Those who moved into the nearby towns found in some cases, as in Bavaria or Switzerland, that settlement there was not easy either, and might mean living without full civic and other rights. In Russia even after emancipation, legal and fiscal restrictions limited the numbers who could migrate from the villages into the towns. In Britain under the Settlement Acts, some localities were reluctant to allow those without property to live long enough in one place to gain a 'settlement' with rights to be relieved by the local Poor Law authorities in case of need. By contrast, where industrial or commercial employment opportunities were expanding, employers, who usually controlled the town governments, were only too eager to welcome new settlers looking for jobs. In this manner, the equation between rising population and a growing share of the kind of jobs found mostly in towns was brought into balance by migration.

There were various types of town, which expanded in numbers and economic and cultural significance in this period. The fastest and most spectacular growth commonly occurred among the industrial towns. Many of these had grown out of villages or small unincorporated towns, for which their status, unprotected by guild or other restrictions, might itself have been one of the reasons why manufacturers settled there. It has to be remembered that much of the manufacturing employment in the era preceding industrialization and in its early phases was of the domestic or proto-industrial type in village homes. This was sometimes linked to a central workshop, which might be mechanized, to undertake the finishing stages, such as dyeing or calico printing, situated in a town. Incorporating the surrounding semi-industrial areas helped the new industrial towns to be among the fastest growers.

Older towns not only frequently maintained restrictions on settlement and on uncontrolled manufacturing; there, rents and wages would also be higher, and the use of water power could be expensive or limited because grain and other mills occupied all the best sites. By contrast, in villages and on greenfield sites labour and rents were cheap, and the actual location could be picked for its available water power or coal supply. Once a number of firms of one common trade, such as textiles or metal fabrication, had settled on a site, others would be attracted because of the labour skills, the market information or the raw materials available there. In due course, an infrastructure would be built up, including roads and canals, a water supply, schools or a police force, encouraging further concentration. Nevertheless, it was precisely in such towns that the worst overcrowding resulted as building could not keep up with needs, and that hygienic conditions were the most atrocious, and the supply of civic services lagged most seriously as local government either did not exist at all or was unable to cope. It is reports from such places in Lancashire and Yorkshire, the Upper Loire valley, Alsace or the Walloon country, the Ruhr or northern Bohemia-Moravia, or, a little later, the Ukrainian coal and iron belt, which furnish the worst horror stories of the industrialization period.

Closely related were the mining towns, which had sprung up around coal or metal workings. Many of these were in isolated areas, without a civic background, too, and depended on immigrant labour, attracted often by the high wages to be earned. In their case, infrastructure provision tended to be even more inadequate, since there was normally no democratic method available for applying pressure on the single employer, or a group of closely related ones, who generally had total control over local civic and social life as well as over the employment of the miners and their families.

Capital cities, of countries and provinces, also expanded. In part this was the result of the growth of the scope of government and of the numbers of the governed. In part it reflected economic growth, which permitted the luxury expenditure of the rich to increase and gave rise to new products and imported exotic goods on which to spend it. Typically, the ruling classes congregated in the capital cities at least for the 'season', as improved transport made commuting from their country estates easier. They naturally attracted skilled craftsmen and personal servants to pander to their needs. The luxury market might also be expanded by the location of the courts of law, the university, the stock exchange and the theatres, together with the officer class of the garrisons to be found in the capital. Some capital cities, such as Athens or Naples, could grow to considerable size without industrialization.

This would explain the pull factor. There was also the push, particularly in the less advanced countries in Europe and overseas, which drove people off the land, and if they were unable to find industrial employment, they drifted into the capital cities or emigrated. Poverty in shantytowns in the outer suburbs was a characteristic of many of them, both before and after industrialization.

Ports and trading towns, including river ports, were the only ones to have grown substantially in the preceding phase, which is sometimes referred to as commercial capitalism. Where they imported raw material for the processing industries or, in the second half of the century, foodstuffs for the industrial population of their hinterland, or where they were the export outlets of its mineral or manufactured products, economic development provided an additional impetus for growth, over and above that applying to all cities. Mass emigration led to the expansion of the port cities handling that traffic, including Liverpool, Hamburg, Trieste and Genoa.

There were also urban centres which are best described as railway towns, either because they were major junctions of important railway lines and their traffic connections, like Crewe or, on a different scale, Chicago, or because of major railway building works there. Lastly, resort towns developed, which attracted visitors to drink the healing waters, breathe the fresh mountain air, or bathe in the sea. Railway, and steam-ship connections made travelling to them available to ever increasing numbers. Some became centres of elegant living, and retired people found them to be desirable places of residence, not least because they would find likeminded company there. The jobs available in hotels, boarding houses and in personal service brought in immigrants of a different class looking for work.

Characteristics of urban life

One main characteristic of urban life was the weakened links to the land, though in many Italian, Spanish, North African and Mexican cities there were still large numbers of agricultural workers employed in latifundia or peasant plots outside. But there were many other significant differences from existence in rural communities. Commonly two types of urban functions are stressed: the contribution of towns to industrialization and growth, and their occasional parasitic character.

Towns were providing the setting for the intellectual and cultural contributions of a nation: scholars, thinkers, inventors and leading entrepreneurs would settle there, attracted by the presence of others like them and by the facilities such as libraries and printing presses. Towns in that sense were generative, attracting the creative minds fleeing the conformism of rural life, and seeking the stimulus of the intellectual market place. Scientific discoveries and technical inventions are often said to have arisen in towns for that reason, though significantly, the Industrial Revolution itself had its origins in small, provincial towns and villages rather than in the rich and advanced cities of Britain. Great Britain as a whole, the pioneer industrial country, was among the least urbanized parts of Europe in the later eighteenth century. By contrast, the most urbanized regions of Europe at the time, including Italy, the Netherlands, Spain and Portugal, were a long way from being industrial pioneers.

Towns might not only contain localized concentrations of immigrants from particular provinces, but also from abroad. These would, together with artists, poets or men of particular skills, such as the Spitalfields silk weavers in London, create sub-cultures, which would enrich the country as a whole. The common assumption that towns were also the favoured haunts of criminals does not stand up to investigation, yet clearly some types of crime and criminal and anti-social behaviour were found in the larger cities only. Crowds large enough to mount demonstrations and make revolutions were another feature of towns and cities.

The most concentrated markets for industrial goods, both of the mass-produced kinds and of the luxury kind, were found in towns, which encouraged new methods to supply them. Even where much of the culture and of the purchasing power of a country were located in its manor houses and rural palaces, the shopping, the propagation of new fashions and styles, the discussions on their value, the demonstrations and lectures, were in the towns and cities. For some of the technical breakthroughs of the age, the dense populous concentrations to justify them economically were found in towns, at least in their critical early stages: these included gasworks and electric power stations, telephones and electric trams.

But cities, as we have seen, and particularly national and provincial capitals, would sometimes attract immigration beyond their actual needs. They might also expand to a size unrelated to the best economic interests of the productive part of the country, or become the place for idlers and wastrels, spending the produce of their estates instead of investing it in productive improvements. They fostered and strengthened the idea that there was higher social standing to be achieved by discriminating spending than by careful husbanding. In that sense they were parasitic. Similarly, where countries were oppressed by exploitative, unrepresentative ruling classes, their governance and administration were a burden, rather than a necessary part of national income, and thus the cities from which they were governed were another expression of that parasitism.

Pollution and noise, dirt and disease were other aspects of town life. The inconveniences felt were a commonplace among contemporaries, but historians are more impressed by the very high death rates, particularly of infants, in towns. Most nineteenth-century towns and cities, which registered such an astonishing growth, would actually have suffered a decline in population if it had been left to the natural balance between births and deaths: their population increase depended on immigration mainly from the healthier country areas. In that sense, also, they were parasitic on the rest of society. It says something for the pull they exerted, or the push effect of life in the village, that in spite of their lethal conditions, towns continued to attract millions of immigrants in our period.

THE CONTEXT OF WORK

Labour in agriculture

The kind of work available and its conditions changed profoundly for most people with the onset of industrialization and modernization. There was, as we have seen, a substantial and continuous transfer of work from agriculture to industry and from the countryside into the towns. There were also profound changes within each of these two sectors.

On the land, there had survived a great variety of forms of remuneration for the people who actually did the work. At the beginning of the nineteenth century, only a small minority, hardly going beyond the labourers on the larger British and northern French farms, and some labourers on East German estates, were simply paid a money wage. By the end of the century, this had become the norm in many, perhaps most areas.

The incentive for the labourer to work without imposing too great a managerial burden on the part of the employer or proprietor was provided by a number of distinct methods. One was the sheer compulsion of serfdom, maintained in the worst cases, like that prevalent in Russia and Prussia, by the right of the owner to administer severe punishments, such as flogging. Serfdom, as noted above, was abolished in the course of the century, but over much of Russia it was replaced by a system which made the village community as a whole responsible for meeting its tax and redemption payments target, so that each peasant was obliged to deliver up his part of the duty by the pressure of all the others.

On the latifundia, which might occupy up to three quarters of the land in Southern Spain, Southern Italy and Portugal, labour was nominally free but worked under oppressive conditions approximating to compulsion. Further north in Italy, as well as in Southern France, systems of crop sharing (*métayage*) were common. The owner provided the land and much of the capital, while the peasant provided the labour, and they shared the proceeds, not necessarily on a 50–50 basis. On the face of it, it was an intelligent way of inducing the working family to do its best without much direct supervision, which might have been difficult in mountainous and remote areas. However, it tended to perpetuate a low level of innovative investment and led to much cheating, and it exposed the peasantry to hardship and poverty in years of poor harvests.

More widespread was a system which remunerated the worker on estates or farms by a plot of land, and possibly also part of the harvest, in return for an appropriate number of days of labour, or tasks performed on the master's farm or estate. Ireland showed a variety of payments in land or in kind, as well as in money, the labourer conversely either paying for his plot in labour or in money rent. A similar variety of remuneration systems, in which the labourer was paid in housing or a plot of land as well as in produce, might be found in East Germany, another region of large estates. However, the tendency was towards simple wage labour, possibly with some tied housing, usually paid by the day, but in harvest or peak times supplemented by task work for the labourer and members of his family. All regions were marked by an apparently unstoppable advance of pure money wage payment.

Domestic industry

By the end of the eighteenth century, much of the manufacturing in Europe was carried on within the system known as domestic industry or, in some cases, as *proto-industry*. There were innumerable regional variations. These depended on local traditions, on the forms of land ownership and the agricultural year, on the type of industry involved, and on the organization of merchanting and marketing of the goods produced. No generalization can cover all of these in detail, but some common or widespread features may be noted.

As the name implies, the actual work was carried on in the worker's own home rather than on the master's premises. This meant that the worker had some discretion as to the hours of work he or she put in, and on their timing. It was therefore possible to work only part-time, which might mean either part of each day while bringing up a family or looking after house or farm generally, or certain times of the year when there was little to do on the fields. Domestic industry was, in fact, quite widespread where upland stock rearing left much free time in the winter when roads were impassable and the cattle were safely housed in their byres, but it was found in all types of agrarian organization.

In some cases, particularly in the later nineteenth century when trades became overstocked, uncontrolled and possibly competing with machine industry, workers had to be at their loom or anvil every hour that God sent to make ends meet. In these conditions there was little value in the freedom of choice over working hours.

Almost by definition, domestic or cottage industry meant that little machinery or other costly capital equipment was involved: at most a loom or primitive jenny, a small furnace or anvil might be needed. The system also kept to the traditional family framework. Thus while the father might be at the weaving loom, wife and daughters would provide his yarn by spinning and younger children would be employed in preparatory work. Discipline and training would be maintained within the family. It has been held that since young people could quickly earn a full wage under this system, they tended to marry early, and since children could help in the work from a very young age, couples were encouraged to have many children. In consequence the domestic system has been said to have encouraged a rapid increase in population, which in turn drove down wages. There is, however, no conclusive evidence to show that regions of proto-industry had faster population increase or lower incomes than other regions.

This kind of organization could be adapted to many types of industry. It was most widespread in textile manufacture, since textiles were by far the most important manufactured goods within the consumption pattern of the day. There were few regions of Europe without their domestic textile industry, whether linens, woollens or, more rarely, cottons and silks, together with smallwares, hosiery and lace. Some regions were known for their high-quality work, others for their cheap and coarse products. Metal goods, such as nails, tools or chains, formed another group of commodities made in domestic work, as did wooden articles, straw hats and gloves. Some districts specialized in composite products, such as watches from Geneva and the Jura Mountains, Black Forest clocks or Erzgebirge toys and musical instruments. It is worth noting that in most cases, though not necessarily where composite products were concerned, the goods which left the workers' household were complete and of a certain standard, such as a bale of cloth or a bag of nails. Though not a craftsman in the traditional sense, the worker still had some relationship to his work, and not infrequently some pride in its quality.

Several developments were to change that in the course of the century. Behind these changes was frequently an increasing division of labour and a removal of certain stages of production from hand work to centralized or machine manufacture, turning the worker in the remaining domestically produced stage increasingly into a mere cog in a machine over which he had little control.

It is necessary to consider the merchanting aspects of this system. Behind its growth was the expansion of markets on an international scale and the productive efficiency, which the specialization had helped to make possible. In one form of marketing, the worker was responsible for buying in his raw material and selling the finished article: thus on market day the woollen or worsted weaver of the West Riding of Yorkshire would take his woven piece made during the week to one of the market halls specially built in the larger towns, such as Halifax, Leeds or Wakefield, with the intention of selling it to one of the merchants in attendance there. He was not merely a maker, he was also an independent entrepreneur. The East-Westphalian linen weaver who had Bielefeld as his marketing town, acted in a similar manner. Weavers of this type were people of some status in their community. This method is sometimes known as the *Kaufsystem*.

The merchant who bought the cloth would see to the finishing of it, and to selling it, sometimes to foreign or overseas regions of the globe. Having knowledge of the distant market, he might make use of it to place orders with weavers for goods to be made to his specifications. He might also provide the raw materials, and it would then be but a small step to retain possession of them during the production process, paying the weaver or other worker involved a piece wage. Once that happens, the producer is no longer a buyer and seller, but has become a wage worker who does not own the material on which he is engaged any more. The merchant, meanwhile, is on the way to become an industrial capitalist. This is known as the *Verlagsystem*.

Yet a further stage might arise when the equipment used by the worker has become too expensive for him to buy, or he is simply too poor to afford any expenditure of that kind at all. In that case, the capitalist could provide it, charging a rent for its use to be deducted from the weekly wage. By that stage, there is hardly any pretence of independent entrepreneurship on the part of the operative. It is worth noting that these are not necessarily stages in sequence of a process, though they might be in the history of an individual family, but could be found simultaneously, existing side-by-side. Nevertheless, a growing loss of independent status, and a broad drift into something akin to wage labour, was clearly in evidence.

Bearing in mind the technical limitations of production, transport and communication of the day, this was a highly efficient system. It brought together the producer, who might be skilled or at least efficient in his or her routinized job, working within a region which specialized in it, and a widely spaced circle of customers who would have otherwise no means of contacting efficient or experienced producers: the merchants formed a class of intermediaries who were rich in capital, able to finance the goods in transit and assemble large consignments for transport on an efficient scale. At the same time, there was also an upstream movement of information from the consumer to the producer, as knowledgeable merchants picked up what the market wanted or what the latest fashion was going to be and relayed it to the producer in his remote cottage. Most significantly, proto-industry, being highly competitive at every level, strongly encouraged technical and marketing innovation and progress.

Yet the system was not without its drawbacks and dangers, which became increasingly clear as the century progressed. Ultimately, employment for the family in domestic industry depended on distant markets and on the skill with which their demand was being met. Therefore, unlike the traditional guild craftsman or village baker, the domestic worker faced a fluctuating demand for his products, its sources and uncertain prosperity quite outside his control; phases of unemployment or erratic income were a feature of the worker's life. In its origins, domestic work had often been a by-employment, or a source of income for only some members of a family. The family still had its own plot, which provided for its subsistence and possibly even the feed for a horse to take its goods to market, as well as sustenance in slack industrial times. Alternatively, its members found work on neighbouring farms. With growing specialization, a result of an increasing division of labour and a necessity in the quest for greater efficiency, the agrarian links had often withered away and the worker had nothing to fall back on in trade depressions. In any case, by the later nineteenth century his village environment might have turned into a densely settled proto-industrial region with little land to spare for growing local produce.

To this was added the growing threat of mechanization. In their early days, the new technical inventions of the industrial revolution tended to help, rather than undermine, the domestic worker. The spinning machines, among the first mechanical aids to be introduced, did indeed made the hand spinners redundant, but they also so cheapened the yarn that sales of textiles boomed, and weavers enjoyed a golden age of prosperity. Similarly, mass-produced iron cheapened and widened the markets for nails and other iron goods, and altogether, rising incomes offered growing opportunities for many domestic manufacturers.

Sooner or later, however, the machine ceased to be an ally and became an enemy, as it began to replace the manual work itself that was previously done in the home. At first, the new machines, as for example the power looms of the 1800s and 1810s, were crude and not very efficient, but in time they were sufficiently improved to drive the manual workers out of the cheaper standard lines into the more complex, high quality goods, and ultimately even out of those. In textiles spinning became mechanized first, then weaving and lastly even dressmaking and tailoring. In a long phase of attrition, the hand workers in these trades would struggle on, preferring low wages on what they knew, to factory work or perhaps emigration, by lowering their prices, exploiting themselves and their children, until even that could not sustain them and they were forced to give up altogether.

In a final stage, domestic labour of this kind moved into the towns, out of the countryside where proto-industry had had its main base. The sweated clothing workers of the East End of London were matched by the *midinettes* of Paris who brought the city world fame as a centre of fashion and fashion goods. Towards the end of the nineteenth century, next to dressmaking, the making of paper goods, cardboard box-making and similar extremely badly paid jobs, often undertaken by women or immigrants, represented a final stage of exploitation of a system which had once covered the most advanced techniques, carried on by most respectable working families of the age.

'Outwork' of this kind had, however, become comparatively rare in some countries. According to their respective censuses of 1907, it employed a mere 2.9 per cent of all manufacturing labour in the United Kingdom and 4.7 per cent in Germany. In Belgium, on the other hand, it was calculated to cover 27 per cent of labour in manufacturing in 1896, and 25 per cent in France in the same year.

Handicraft labour

Such industry as there had been in the Middle Ages had generally been dependent on the craftsman or artisan. One characteristic of the craftsman was that he possessed recognized skill, which might include a good deal of appropriate knowledge, derived from a more or less formal apprenticeship served for a number of years, usually five or seven, under a qualified master. This type of worker continued to have central importance, though circumstances were changing and some artisans were now fulfilling a different role.

Traditionally, the handicraftsman could count on establishing a workshop of his own in which he handled materials bought in by himself, working, commonly bespoke, for a circle of local or regional customers who provided a steady market secured by the exclusive power of his guild. Some of these survived into the nineteenth century, a few even until today. The premises of saddlers and cobblers, butchers and bakers, plumbers and, nowadays, small garages, electrical and television repair shops, still contain men and women of this type.

However, the economic changes of the age transformed the framework within which most of them worked. On the positive side, the rise of large-scale manufacture moved certain types of skilled men from workshops of their own into the larger workshops and factories where their personal freedom might be less, but the pay often better and more regular. Thus the larger engineering factories would employ iron moulders or brass founders, former carpenters, clockmakers and others, to build or repair machines, and frequently these craftsmen would keep their status and retain a good deal of freedom, at least in the earlier decades of the century, as to how their work was carried out. In the same way skilled dyers and calico printers, typesetters and bookbinders, printers, instrument makers and cabinet makers, would work for wages in large capitalistic premises without losing their skill or the rate of pay that went with it. Building workers, stonemasons, bricklayers, plasterers or glaziers, too, might work for large contractors on the same basis.

New industries created the need for new types of crafts. Thus in engineering there were now fitters, patternmakers and boilermakers to be trained up, there were new specialists in pottery, in paper making or among glass makers. There were also jobs that clearly required skills, know-how and a sense of responsibility without the need for the traditional formal apprenticeship years, but instead a learning period of variable duration on the job before the worker was fit to take on the key posts. Among the most significant of these occupations were hewing in the coal mines, puddling and furnace work in iron and steel making and in metal smelting generally, locomotive driving and marine engine maintenance.

Meanwhile, there were changes also in the practice of training. It was no longer in the masters' interest to control or limit the numbers of entrants to their trade: on the contrary, they wanted to open up entry so as to allow them to have the pick of labour and drive wages down to the level of the less exclusive trades. For that very reason, it was the men themselves and their trade unions, as soon as these were established, who insisted on formal apprenticeships and refused to work alongside 'illegal' men. The corollary of this was that it was craftsmen in the works, and no longer the masters, who were responsible for and did the teaching and training. By the end of our period, some theoretical or formal knowledge, such as of mechanical drawing, elementary mechanics, chemistry or electricity, was becoming increasingly necessary, and came to be provided by the public authorities in many countries in technical schools of various kinds. At the same time, the very largest employers, particularly those dominating the labour market of a town or a particular area, rediscovered the value of skills among their work force, and provided some of the formal training

themselves, as long as they could be sure that their trained people would not leave them for other employers, taking their acquired skills with them.

There was also a negative side to progress, as far as the crafts are concerned. Many of the traditional crafts were, either replaced by machines or they were made redundant altogether as their product or service was no longer wanted. The weavers, once a most respected trade, have already been noted. Others, like furniture makers, tailors and shoemakers, were put under increasing pressure by machine competition and, apart from a small minority working on high-quality goods, either competed with machine-trade products on ever worsening terms, or were reduced to semi-skilled routines on the new factory processes. Other crafts, like wigmakers or candlemakers, faded out altogether.

Factories and other large-scale enterprises

Large-scale enterprises, employing up to hundreds of workers each, were not unknown before the nineteenth century. Royal dockyards, numerous coalmines, some royal porcelain, small arms or even textile manufactories, might fit that description. Yet they were the exception. In the nineteenth century, they became far more common and, in some trades, they became the norm. Moreover, while formerly the workers operated side-by-side, merely being housed together under common supervision to make up large units, in the new technology they were more often collaborating in serving a single set of equipment, such as a steel furnace or rolling mill, or they became dependent on a set of machines driven by a single motive power which set the pace. In those conditions they were made adjuncts to the mechanical apparatus rather than being in control of their working tools.

Typical for that type of work place was the textile factory. The machine spinning of cotton from the 1760s onward is commonly considered to have been the first mechanized trade, though silk was 'thrown' or spun in large premises before that. The 'factory' is often taken to be symbolic of the new industrial age, though there were numerous other large-scale enterprises. In addition to the mines and steelworks noted already, there were shipyards, gasworks, railways, and the construction of large public buildings and other enterprises employing large numbers of workers together with substantial capital sums.

Yet many smaller units survived. There were also great differences between industries: for all establishments together, the average number of employees was 67 in the United States in the early twentieth century, 64 in Britain, 26 in France and 14 in Germany, though these averages were affected by the inclusion of numerous tiny units. If we eliminate these and take only establishments employing twenty people or more each, the average size was 766 workers in the French iron and steel industry, but only 114 in textiles; for the USA the figures were 548 and 126, and for Germany, 378 and 46.

From the start, factories and other large-scale enterprises posed new problems both for labour and for management, especially where craft skill and pride lost their former significance. New and tough forms of discipline were introduced, with fines and other punishments for slackness, absence or disturbing behaviour, such as talking or singing at work, which men and women had done naturally when working in their own homes. Conversely, among the early factory labour, attendance was often irregular, jobs were frequently changed and at harvest time workers would disappear in droves to bring in the harvest in their former villages, often for what were still family farms.

Mill workers, moreover, were largely women and children, fairly defenceless and easily exploited. From the 1830s, onwards, one government after another found it expedient to protect the more vulnerable among them by legislation laying down maximum hours of work, prohibiting night work or work with dangerous substances, and enforcing safety rules on fencing machinery, as well as hygienic regulations such as providing washing facilities or whitewashing walls. Gradually, inspection and minimum safety rules were also enforced for underground mines or tall building sites, while safety regulations referring to railways and ships were designed to protect travellers as well as employees.

In the early days of textile mills, children might still be employed by or with their parents or older brothers and sisters, but more and more, people now found themselves working in an environment entirely outside their families. The employer himself was increasingly distant, and relations in the larger works between him and the individual worker were becoming wholly impersonal. But even fellow workers were strangers, and new forms of solidarity and common loyalties had to be evolved. Home and work became two quite separate spheres. Moralists deplored the loss of family discipline, and the temptations which the working together of young men and women – let alone the congregating in inns and beer houses after work – without the direct control of their elders would subject them to; and although their fears turned out to be exaggerated, there was no doubt that changes in public and private moral behaviour were induced by the new working environment.

There were important differences between large units springing up in major towns, and enterprises in villages or greenfield sites where they found the main or sole source of industrial employment. Factory or mining villages, that is to say, settlements either created deliberately by an enterprise in order to assemble a labour force around it, or developed from a smaller pre-existing community, were common in most industrial countries, and tended to produce their own form of paternalism, their own peculiar form of exploitation, or a mixture of both. Often the houses were provided by the employer, together with social institutions such as a church, a school, an insurance scheme or medical attention. Self-interest and a sense of social responsibility combined to make employers in the most favourable cases provide other benefits, such as pensions for widows of workers, or grain bought in bulk and sold cheaply in times of high prices. At the other extreme, some employers would exploit their enormous power over their settlement by paying in truck or forcing their workers to patronize the factory shop charging exorbitant prices; others used the tied cottage as means of control by threatening to evict those who showed any sign of resistance to wage levels or conditions of work.

In larger towns, employers had fewer means of direct social control over their work force, though it was often exerted indirectly by domination over the town or city government. At the same time, there was also less sense of social obligation, and no help for dependent workers in periods of slack employment. Mill hands were sacked with little compunction for disciplinary offences, as well as a method of cost reduction when orders fell off.

Uncertain employment, or longish periods of unemployment in the recurrent depressions which had become part of the industrial age, or as a result of bankruptcy on the part of the employers, were among the most serious negative aspects of modern forms of work organization. For the early part of the century it is difficult to find reliable percentages of unemployment because of poor data sources on the one hand, and a great deal of part-time work by those who would have preferred full-time employment, on the other. Comparisons across countries would be even more difficult. For the years c.1890–1913, when some more reliable statistics exist, it may be estimated that unemployment in Britain fluctuated round an average of 4–5 per cent, in France around 7–8 per cent, in Belgium around 3 per cent and in Germany about 2.5 per cent.

Things were particularly difficult when slackness of trade in one particular industry would affect many factories of a town simultaneously, so that there was no alternative source of income available. New poor law and charity provisions had to be devised to deal with breakdowns of that kind in the urban industrial communities.

Service industries and white-collar occupations

Industrial innovation and expansion, especially where these depended on distant markets inland or even abroad, required more complex and more sophisticated service institutions than economies consisting largely of subsistence farming and local urban craftsmen to supply the manufactured goods. The expanding commercial relationships needed not only new means of transport which had to be built and staffed, but behind them there also had to be a great deal of clerical work, organizing, monitoring, sensing new directions of demand, providing information and security. But the specialization did not end there. Banking and other forms of finance, as well as insurance, became features of the new system, as did growing needs for legal advice in drawing up contracts and settling disputes. Extended requirements for information were met in part by newspapers, printed share lists or shipping gazettes, all needing writers, editors and clerks.

But there was need also within the industrial works for clerks, accountants, foremen and managers, possibly also for technical draughtsmen, designers and translators. What has come to be called 'white collar' employment became a feature not merely of the service trades, but of productive industry itself.

These demands for different types of skilled clerical labour occurred at a time when literacy among the poorer classes could by no means taken for granted. As elementary education spread in this period, in part as a consequence of the growing need for literate people in various walks of life, the relative privileges of clerks, writers and cashiers, such as better pay on a monthly rather than a weekly basis, a more secure position and possibly a pension in old age, were correspondingly reduced but by no means altogether extinguished.

Within the larger enterprises themselves, a new class thus began to insert itself into the growing gap and the increasing social distance between the capitalist employer no longer working at the bench himself and his wage worker. Sometimes referred to as part of the 'new middle classes', these had something in common with both those above and those below them, but had essentially also separate interests of their own. They were often more valuable to the employer because of their special knowledge of the firm, its internal structure and outside relationships, and thus more difficult to replace. In consequence, they commonly felt themselves to be part of the management team, with a shared sense of responsibility. Unlike manual workers, most of them therefore looked askance at organization to face their employer as a group and had little loyalty to their 'class': they tended to wish to be treated as individuals.

As technical requirements increased in various sectors of the economy, diverse groups of these white-collar workers were acquiring skills and know-how approaching those of the recognized older professions, the law, the church and medicine. The creation of new professions proper, recognized as such on that basis, was a long-drawn out process in most countries, proceeding at different speeds, determined in part by different economic needs but also in part by different legal systems and social traditions.

From one point of view, what mattered was technical competence and reliability: customers expected engineers to be able to build bridges that would stand up, or accountants to be able to balance the books on the basis of a real appraisal of the situation. But the proof of competence might depend on certificates from recognized teachers, on self-regulating professional societies or on government-controlled admission procedures, none of which was entirely reliable in the early build-up of a profession. Nor were recognized training schemes easily established. But the public also expected a degree of professional ethics, a sense of obligation to the profession and to the interests of the client in place of the crude profit maximization that drove the industrialist.

Some beginnings could be found in the eighteenth century, but the main period for the professionalization of a number of key occupations was the nineteenth century. It was reached by different paths in different countries, but a similar final structure lends credence to the view that there was an inherent need in modern industrial society for specialists of this kind. They formed another element of the 'new middle classes' of the age.

THE SOCIAL AND INSTITUTIONAL DYNAMIC

New urban and industrial elites

The economic and social changes of the age increased the weight of industry and of urban populations in society. They thereby opened the way for new elites, based on those sectors, to rise to the top.

In earlier centuries, right up to the end of the *ancien régime*, it could be said that, broadly speaking, rural government was in the hands of the landed nobility and gentry. The towns were either governed in the same way simply as part of the regional administration, or in the case of the privileged and chartered ones among them, they were controlled by a traditional urban elite. In some parts of Europe, including Northern Italy and Switzerland, it was the cities which controlled the surrounding countryside.

There was a great variety among the traditional urban elites, so that it is difficult to generalize about them. Most

consisted of merchants rather than craftsmen, and they had long since shed whatever democratic elements there had been in their original constitution, normally representing congeries of self-appointed or recruited cliques. Two main changes occurred in the course of the nineteenth century: town government came increasingly to be dominated by the thrusting, upwardly mobile, industrial and new commercial entrepreneurial classes; and it also became increasingly democratic. However, even where elections took place with an electorate which reached down into the lower orders, it was as a rule the economic leaders of local industry and commerce, together with the top professionals, who were chosen to govern the towns and to fill their top judicial posts.

Reaching outward from the towns, these elites also began to capture positions of national power in parliaments, ministries, provincial governorships and the like. Essentially, the traditional landed nobility still kept control over the main bastions of power, including not merely governments and courts, but also top diplomatic, military and civil service positions. There was thus a great deal of continuity. Yet inroads were continually being made into these positions of power by the new classes, whose economic base was beginning to exceed the agrarian sector in significance. There were great differences between countries. Apart from the United States and other countries of overseas settlement, which had never been blessed by an aristocracy, it was the French bourgeoisie, which had gained more than most, together with that of the Netherlands and of Switzerland, among the smaller nations. The United Kingdom came next, together with Germany and the Scandinavian countries, followed by the Hapsburg Empire and the Italian and Iberian peninsulas, with the Russian Empire bringing up the rear. It is evident that the progress of the replacement of the landed hereditary ruling classes by the industrial and commercial ones was closely connected with the rate of progress of industrialization and modernization in each country.

Social prestige, however, still attached to the land and to ancient title rather than to recent wealth, and there was a tendency observable in practically every country, for merchants and industrialists, having made their fortune, to seek to consolidate their social position by acquiring both title and estate. Among the clearest evidence for this eagerness to join the existing elite rather than establishing their own was the practice of members of the new elites to send their sons into the traditional top schools designed for preparing boys for governance and gracious living, including *Gymnasien*, *lycées* and in Britain 'public' schools, which retained their emphasis on classical learning, rather than building new schools to provide practical subjects needed in business life. Only gradually would the classical school be transformed to serve the real needs of the new elites.

Social conflicts

It does not surprise that the lower orders were not always satisfied with the way they were being governed by the elites. Social protest was known among the peasantry and the urban and rural proletariat before the onset of industrialization. The most commonly experienced form was the food riot, a feature not only of towns and countryside dependent on imported foodstuffs which in times of famine or poor harvest would be priced out of their reach, but also familiar in food export regions when high prices induced farmers to export their produce while local labourers starved. Other riots concerned conscription, increases in taxation or rents, changes in Poor Law provisions, rural evictions and the introduction of machinery.

The most sustained and spectacular rural protest occurred in the course of the French Revolution. Though it had numerous roots, in national politics and taxation issues, in the writings of Enlightenment authors and in grievances among the middle classes, among others, that revolution also had among its roots a movement of social protest on the part of the peasantry and the urban poor. Details differ enormously, in line with the great variety of conditions in rural and urban France, yet the protests had much in common over the whole of the country.

The revolution years had been preceded by a slow attrition of ancient peasant and communal rights, as landlords and large owners tried to use the new market opportunities to enrich themselves, by enclosures, by ploughing up waste land and by exploiting their various privileges and local monopolies. To these were added immediate issues, which filled the *cahiers de doléances* that emerged from the provinces in 1789. The bad harvests and shortages of 1787–9 led to a doubling of wheat prices in the main producing areas of Northern France. The peasantry suffered as producers and as consumers, as wine growers, dairy farmers and wheat growers. The urban poor suffered greater hardships still.

According to the history books, it was mainly the Parisian crowd which dictated events in the revolution years. Yet in the villages there had been almost continuous unrest in many areas since December 1788. In 1789 and after, there were assaults on millers, granaries and food convoys, and attacks on game laws, tithes and taxes. *Châteaux* were burnt down together with their manorial rolls. At the end of decades of upheavals which followed, it is generally agreed that the peasant had gained the most from the revolution.

Apart from that exceptional sequence of events, pre-industrial riots and public protests tended to be localized, sporadic and without organization or permanent leadership. Even where it spread over extensive areas, like the English labourers' revolt of 1830, it lacked organization or permanence and left few traces after it was over, apart from the usual brutal retribution exacted by the frightened ruling classes. Though some of these protests had a clear class basis, such as riots over threshing machines or over evictions, others, and particularly food riots, had a mixed social basis. They were crowd actions, often led by women, yet, though the actors in them might appear to the local elites to consist of mindless mobs, there was often a clear concept of what has been termed a 'moral economy' – for example, the demand for 'fair' prices – which the people believed to have been violated.

In the relatively advanced British economy, this kind of unstructured rural protest petered out after the mid-nineteenth century, to be ultimately replaced by labourers' trade unions. Elsewhere, modernization came later. Thus in Italy traditional food riots occurred in the north and centre in 1846–7, in which the populace attacked grain merchants and carters, inducing the Austrian government to forbid the export of wheat or corn and at the same time send in Croatian troops to restore order. In Southern Italy, the revolutionary year of 1848 saw communal lands occupied, private woods burned, animals stolen or killed, and tax and land records destroyed. There were riots in many large Italian cities once more in 1868.

In Germany, another country with great regional differences, collective protests tended to coincide with upheavals in France in 1830, and especially in 1848; but most of the disturbances recorded for 1830–3 and 1846–7, were food riots and, not surprisingly, these were largely urban: between 1816 and 1847, 55 per cent of disorders occurred in cities, which at the time contained only 15 per cent of the population. The Irish 'land war' which began in 1879 was the last of these largely unorganized manifestations in Western Europe. There has recently been a major revision of this episode, which used to be described as a reaction against brutal oppression and evictions by largely absentee landlords. If not caused by abject poverty, as was once thought, yet the Irish peasantry had grievances enough. Appropriately, the last significant food riot in Europe as a whole occurred in St Petersburg and preceded the revolution of 1917.

Industrialization changed the nature of protest. Increasingly, it was found to be more effective if backed by organization, which then tended to become permanent. This did not all happen at once; on the contrary, there was a transitional phase when protest of a traditional kind mingled with more modern forms of organization. Thus at Rouen in a strike in 1830, the crowds moved from factory to factory as food rioters had done in the past in their protest action. In a similar way in the 'plug plot' of 1842, the Lancashire cotton workers marched from mill to mill to close each one by putting the boilers out of action, in pursuit both of a protest over unemployment and hunger on the one hand, while pushing the demand for the political Charter, on the other.

These and similar protests were frequently against hardships imposed by industrialization itself. Some consequences, such as poor housing, appalling hygienic urban conditions or the loss of access to land, formed parts of a background rather than being the immediate triggers for action. Against that background, there was little give in the system when things went wrong. Moreover, the early stages of industrialization had seen falling real wages in many towns in Britain, Belgium, France and Germany, as well as in the Austrian Empire and in Russia later. This decline was caused by a mixture of rising prices, possible falling quality of food and other commodities, and actual cuts in wages. In those deteriorating conditions, even a small cut in the rate of pay, a reduction in employment, or a rise in the price of a major item of food, might be enough to set off a major protest. Many of those making up the revolutionary crowds fighting in Paris, Vienna, Berlin and elsewhere in 1848, were workers in trades in which conditions had deteriorated either because of machines, or because of over-stocking with uncontrolled entrants.

Another example of a transitional kind of protest was furnished by the Luddite riots in English textile districts in 1811 and 1817, ostensibly against the new machinery, which gave a generic name to machine breaking as such. Examples of machine breaking were found in all parts of the continent, particularly in the difficult years of 1819 and 1830. Possibly the most famous of them was the Silesian cotton weavers' violent revolt of 1844. Significantly, it started only after a petition to the authorities had been rejected, and there was a simultaneous tax strike and revolt by Silesian peasants beginning in 1843. Selective violence occurred once again in the Silesian food riots of 1847. Other important machinery riots occurred among Krefeld silk workers in 1826 and Leipzig printers in 1830.

Some protests took the form of strikes and go-slows. These, however, merge into the origins and rise of trade unions.

Trade unions and friendly societies

Trade unions, permanent associations of people in the same occupation, formed to improve their wages and conditions, were the most natural defensive organizations of workers having to negotiate with their employers from an inherent position of weakness. From the beginning, many of them also used their funds to provide unemployment, sickness and even retirement benefits, as well as a reserve in case of disputes; many, indeed, started as insurance clubs which were forced by circumstances into representing their members in industrial disputes. If negotiations failed, strikes or related forms of labour withdrawal, such as go-slows or sit-ins, were the main instruments of pressure open to the men, as sackings and lockouts were those of the employers.

Unions were known in Britain in the eighteenth century. They were generally formed by skilled workers on a local basis, but some select trades, which had something like a national labour market, such as hat makers, organized within a wider catchment area. Maintaining houses of call as centres of information about jobs and to support journeymen on the move was an early form of self-help, additional to accumulating benefit funds. The associations of French journeymen known as *compagnonnages* engaged in activities which were not wholly dissimilar. In the less advanced German conditions, the journeymen were tied more closely to their master craftsmen, and young artisans commonly went on the tramp in order to complete their technical training rather than because they were forced to look for jobs outside their home town. Elsewhere in Europe, trade unions made their appearance a good deal later still.

While the 'friendly society'-type of insurance functions which the trade unions developed were sometimes appreciated by the authorities, in industrial disputes these invariably took the side of the employers. In their early decades, unions everywhere faced prohibition and persecution, which, in turn, tended to drive members to look beyond their narrow crafts, to see themselves as being moulded together into a class with common class interests against the classes which held the reins of government.

In Britain, a modest and circumscribed form of legality for trade unions appeared first, based on the legislation of 1824 and 1825. Real freedom, however, was not secured until 1875. The unions which arose under that legislation were mainly of skilled, male workers, who formed organizations within local or at most regional geographical limits. Logic dictated that men should seek to cover the extent of their own labour market, and no more. When railways began in the 1840s to widen the range in which workers might seek jobs and employers recruit their labour, national organizations began to emerge. After some earlier, abortive attempts, the Amalgamated Society of Engineers (ASE), formed in 1851 out of smaller localized and specialized associations, is generally held to have been the first modern 'model' trade union. Others of the same kind soon followed. Apart from these, it was the miners, who were among the best organized, grouped, like the industry itself, into clearly demarcated regions. Despite their valuable benefit funds, which helped to retain the loyalty of their members, union fortunes and membership tended to fluctuate in line with trade conditions. The great worldwide boom of the early 1870s saw a substantial jump in trade union membership, and was marked by a successful reduction of the normal working day from 10–10.5 to 9–9.5 hours in many organized trades. There followed a decline during the depression of the 1880s, and a much more powerful surge forward from 1889 onward. In that phase, workers from outside the range of craftsmen were organized on a broad base for the first time, although, like dockers or gas workers, they were by no means without skill.

In France, trade unions had been outlawed by the revolutionary legislation of 1791. Later, it was to be skilled workers, like masons and carpenters, engineers and printers, tailors and shoemakers, who formed the first modern-type unions within the July Monarchy. Savage repression led to a number of violent clashes before 1848. That year saw a brief period of freedom, but despite some easing of legislation in the Second Empire, especially by the Act of 1868, trade unions were not allowed to develop properly until the Act of 1884 gave them a reasonable degree of freedom. There were, however, *conseils de prud'hommes*, first set up in Lyons in 1806, to deal with local grievances. These were later copied in Belgium and Italy. Strikes became legal in Belgium in 1867 and in Austria in 1870. Trade unions themselves were legalised in Austria in 1867, in the Netherlands in 1872 and in Spain in 1876. Russia, as always, was somewhat behind this broad European movement; her repressive trade union legislation was not eased until after 1905.

Among the larger European economies, it was the German trade societies which showed the closest affinities to the British development. Repression there, however, lasted much longer. In the Kingdom of Saxony, trade unions were legalized only in 1861, in the Grand Duchy of Baden it was 1867 and in the North German Federation not until 1869. Anything approaching full rights of organization had to wait until the 1890s. In the brief liberal revolutionary period of 1848–9 a short-lived Workers' Brotherhood had been formed in Berlin, and there were other local associations of skilled workers for various purposes; but under German law, conditions were too repressive to allow much in the way of clandestine unionism. The view, which was once widespread, that German trade unions were more ideologically motivated, and more under the control of politicians of the (Marxist) Social Democratic Party, is now discredited, though there were links between them. By and large, German unions, like those elsewhere, existed to defend the immediate interests of their members. In 1877 there were only 50,000 of them. Then followed the Anti-Socialist Law, and some years after its repeal, in 1895, membership had climbed to 332,000.

In the boom of the 1890s, trade unions registered an enormous expansion of membership in all parts of Europe, both in terms of numbers and in the range of occupations, which now became organized. There followed a cyclical decline in the early years of the new century, but by 1913 trade union membership had climbed to altogether new heights. Thus in Germany it reached three million, made up of three distinct groupings, those associated in the 'free' or socialist association with over 2.5M million members, the liberal (or Hirsch-Duncker) unions of craftsmen, with 107,000 members, and the Catholic grouping, with 343,000 members in 1914. In addition, there were unfree or 'yellow' unions established by some large employers. Even these together, however, represented only a small fraction of the potential membership.

In Britain, membership had climbed to over 4.1M, in France it was over one million, in Italy, perhaps 250,000 and in German Austria, well over 400,000. Increasingly, factory workers, including many women, and less skilled employees were to be found in the ranks of the trade unions, though there tended to be some differences between the craft and the more 'general' societies. The former were not only able to count on a greater degree of loyalty on the part of their members, since their skill was a valuable possession which men cherished, but also because, being better paid and more regularly employed, they could afford to accumulate benefit funds in their societies which they were loath to abandon. Unskilled workers, and especially those not attached to a particular firm or even industry, were unable to pay for benefit funds and therefore had less to lose: they tended to flock to a union in times of dispute, but to leave again when the excitement was over.

There were also national characteristics in trade union behaviour. British and German unions, being relatively well endowed and somewhat bureaucratized, tended to prefer peaceful solutions to disputes; Britain, in fact, had far more collective agreements than other European states. The French, on the other hand, and even more so the Italian and Spanish unions, tended to go for quick solutions by lightning strikes, since they frequently lacked the resources to sustain long disputes. In France, the number of strikes per year rose from about 150–200 in the 1870s to an average of 700–1,000 in the early years of the new century, the number of strikers involved rising from around 30,000 to 300,000 in the same period. Significantly, it was in France – as well as in Italy and Spain – that 'syndicalism' took root most firmly, including the notion that it would be successful industrial action, organized by the trade union movement, rather than political activity in the accepted sense, which would end the capitalist system and usher in socialism. In Italy, syndicalism was particularly strong among railwaymen, in the Po valley agricultural regions, and in the old anarchist centres of Ancona, Massa-Carrara and Rome.

Elsewhere, too, the years 1910–14 were a period of widespread industrial conflict. Thus, in Germany there were 681,000 strikers in 1910 and over a million in 1912, and in Britain there were 831,000 in 1911 and over 1.2M in 1912, the peak years. Measured as a proportion of the non-agricultural wage earners, the numbers of strikers reached exceptionally high levels in virtually every Western country in the years of unrest 1910–13, except in Sweden, where 1909 saw the high point. Strikers per 100,000 workers numbered 10,900 in Finland's peak year, 10,600 in the United Kingdom, 10,000 in Norway and 7,700 in Italy. All the rest, apart from peaceful Switzerland, registered 2,900 or over.

Unlike trade unions, the friendly societies established for mutual aid and social companionship enjoyed a modicum of freedom at the hands of governments, though in times of conflict they, too, became suspect as organizations strengthening the bargaining power of labour. Their membership was not exclusively working class, but largely so. In Britain it exceeded in numbers that of trade unions over the whole of the nineteenth century, and in France there were over 2,000 societies in the 1840s, many of them being trade unions driven into that disguise by government persecution. In Germany, working-class educational and cultural associations were particularly highly developed.

There were cooperative societies, both of mainly working-class consumers and producers, founded in all major advanced countries. The consumer movement was especially strong in Britain, agricultural cooperation in Denmark and Germany, and mutual credit societies in most countries, especially Germany and the USA.

The Poor Laws and protective legislation

Paupers, including the old and the sick, were traditionally looked after by local institutions, many of them maintained by charitable foundations. The population increase, together with the bunching of people in larger towns, the growing incidence of industrial unemployment, and the break-up of the tradition of looking after elderly family members within the farm household, made a new approach necessary. In the early days of industrialization, when relations between those requiring relief and the representatives of authority were becoming less personal and pauperism threatened to overwhelm the relief funds, the Poor Law provisions might become harsher, as was the case in Britain in 1834 and in Sweden in 1871. But whether they did or not, there was an increasing tendency for dealing with them on a national basis while keeping to a traditional structure.

By the end of the century this had clearly become inadequate, and an altogether new approach, based on state-backed insurance, was tried out and spread to most countries with astonishing rapidity in the years before 1914. The pioneer country was Germany, where sickness insurance was enacted in 1883, occupational injuries (workmen's compensation) legislation dated from 1884, and old-age pensions from 1889. Bismarck's motivation for introducing this German insurance scheme was mixed. In part, it arose out of the party-political need for parliamentary support, but, more significantly, Bismarck wished to take the wind out of the socialist sails by offering concessions to the working classes which would counteract the propaganda drive that maintained that Germany was class-ridden society in which wage earners were oppressed and discriminated. By being given pensions, in particular, workers were to acquire a stake in society. There was possibly also a lingering tradition of the old-fashioned Prussian *Junker* (squire) who, while insisting that he was absolute master, also recognized his responsibility for the welfare of those entrusted to his care. It is not without significance that workers in the Prussian nationalized undertakings managed by the *See-handlung* had enjoyed health care and sickness benefits from the eighteenth century as part of the same tradition. Miners, likewise, had been granted special welfare protection for centuries in the German states.

Similar motivations – staving off revolution on the one hand, and expressing mutual dependence of aristocratic ruler and the ruled on the other – may have induced other authoritarian states to follow the German example. In the more democratic societies, including Britain, France and the Netherlands, the drive to look after those who were, for one reason or another, no longer capable of looking after themselves, came at least in part from the bottom rather than the top of society. Having acquired some political power by their vote, the lower orders were enabled to demand measures to reduce the worst of the fear which blighted their lives, namely poverty and helplessness induced by old age, sickness or injury sustained at work.

In detail, the provisions enacted by various countries differed a great deal; in some cases, they extended to the working population only, or they depended on private provision subsidized by the state, or they were circumscribed in other ways. Yet something was done almost everywhere. Workmen's compensation, in which the onus was placed on the employer, was possibly the most widespread. Apart from the western countries, it was also introduced in Greece, Romania and even Russia, as well as Spain and Portugal before 1914. Health insurance, also, spread to Eastern and Southern, as well as Western and Northern Europe. Old age pensions were not quite as widespread, Finland, Norway and Switzerland, as well as most of Eastern Europe, having made no provision before 1914. Unemployment insurance, curiously, was not introduced into Germany until 1927. It was, however, to be found, though limited in various ways, in Denmark, France, Norway and Britain before 1914. It is worth noting that in the brief months of the Paris revolution of 1848 when the city's artisans shared in a modicum of power, they used it to open 'national workshops' to provide an income from work for those out of a job in the crisis year. However, in most cases unemployment before 1914 appeared as a short-term, cyclical crisis problem rather than as the inherent feature of the system which it was to become after 1919.

A second early root of the welfare state may be found in the efforts to protect the weakest of all, children and women at work in factories, which, as noted above, was to turn, a good while later, into general factory protection legislation. Again, motives were mixed. In the more democratic states, it was pressure from below, from the workers themselves, assisted by individual philanthropists, doctors and social scientists, which brought about change, generally against bitter opposition from the employing classes. In the more authoritarian countries, such as Prussia or Russia, it was the state bureaucracy which saw the protection of some of its citizens as part of its governmental obligation. However, in both cases, factory legislation seemed to follow an almost inevitable course, beginning as well-meaning legal measures, which remained dead letters because they lacked means of enforcement, to be transformed in due course by the introduction of an inspectorate, which made the legislation effective.

Britain, as the pioneer factory economy, grappled with the problem first. The earliest legislation, dealing technically with apprentices, dated from 1802. After several more interesting, but ineffective attempts, the first factory act with teeth was passed in 1833. Its power derived from the newly established inspectorate; even then, however, there were numerous loopholes exploited by unscrupulous masters and by parents desperate for the additional earnings of their children, while the inspectors themselves, of whom there were far too few, had to be cautious in their role of enforcement. However, once the dam was broken and restriction became accepted in principle, further extensions, including those relating to safety in mines, to dangerous substances, and ultimately to even those protecting adult male workers, were somewhat easier to introduce.

The earliest continental country to follow along the same path was Switzerland. It was the Canton Zurich which passed its first child labour law in 1815, made effective in 1837. Others followed, and the federal labour law of 1877 was at the time the most advanced on the continent. For reasons noted above, Imperial Russia was another country early in the field with legislation in 1835, but made effective only in the 1880s.

There was a set of early child labour provisions in Prussia in 1824–5, induced at least in part by the fear of the military that undernourished crippled children would make poor soldiers – a thought which was also to inspire similar legislation elsewhere. Like a later law of 1839, it remained ineffective. Only in 1853 was an inspectorate added and the act began to bite. A similar tale could be told of Hannover, Oldenburg, Saxony and Thuringia, and early, ineffective child labour laws were also passed in France (1841), Austria (1842) and Venice and Lombardy (1843). In these countries, as elsewhere in Europe, effective provisions spread rapidly in the 1880s. As in the case of social insurance, there was an evident tendency for legislation, once it had proved itself in the leading countries, to be copied elsewhere, obeying a kind of 'spirit of the age', even though the economic base might not have reached the same advanced stage everywhere.

Other social problems were tackled on a local scale by the urban authorities. These took over, or obtained, powers and obligations to build, pave and maintain streets and bridges, and look after sewerage, lighting and cleansing. They might also become responsible for the provision of clean water, gas, and even electricity, though in the early stages these were usually supplied by private companies for the more affluent families' houses only. Urban transport at cheap rates made workers more mobile, allowing them to move to the more open suburbs, while widening the labour market for individual employers in towns. Civic enterprise would often then yield a surplus, which was used to relieve the local rates or permit other civic ventures, including parks and recreation grounds. Here was a major cause of the reduction of the high death rates – particularly of infants – associated with towns in the early stages of industrialization and urbanization.

Socialist ideologies

It is most unlikely that conditions actually worsened for large numbers of people over longer periods in the nineteenth century; it was rather that shortcomings were felt more strongly because it was evident that opportunities for improvement existed and were not used. Moreover, given the larger concentrations of people and of wealth, particular grievances tended to be expressed more consistently than before. In addition, in the new environment, voices were raised for the first time in criticism of and attacking the economic and social system as a whole. The most widely propagated alternative to industrial 'capitalism' was the ideology of socialism.

The concept of 'socialism' encompasses a variety of solutions to the problems of the age. They all have in common that they set out to abolish the rule of capital over labour, and thus, in practical political terms, they sought and usually obtained the support of the working classes. In most countries, socialist, and labour or workers' parties, became interchangeable terms. We can distinguish at least four main strands of the ideology, though the list is by no means an exhaustive one.

One form, with particular appeal to skilled men in traditional crafts, proposed a form of cooperative organization which would eliminate the capitalist and preserve the whole produce of labour – a concept common also to other varieties of socialism – for the actual producer. It flourished especially in France and Britain about the mid-nineteenth century, but failed to deal with industries requiring massed capital which workers' cooperatives were unable to raise. In that respect, alone among socialists, the adherents of this form of cooperation were looking backward rather than forward to the opportunities provided by the new technologies.

A second variety concentrated on the waste and inefficiency of capitalist markets, which it proposed to overcome by planning and, usually associated with it, by the public ownership of the means of production. The French aristocrat Henri de Saint-Simon was an early representative of this line, which was expressed most strongly by the British Fabian Society. It does, however, form an element in all forms of socialism.

A third strand stresses the immorality rather than the inefficiency of capitalist markets. The defence of the poor against the rich and the powerful is part of a long Judaeo-Christian tradition. The further element of oppression inherent in modern industrial society was a major concern of Robert Owen in Britain and the Lassalleans who formed the first German socialist party in 1863. This aspect of taking the side of the weak against the strong, too, is an important ingredient in all forms of socialism.

Lastly, there is 'scientific Socialism', developed by Karl Marx and Friedrich Engels. This includes elements of all the others, but possesses the additional power of claiming to have discovered laws of history which predict an inevitable clash between the ruling capitalists and the exploited workers, which the latter were destined to win. Their victory would usher in the reign of socialism and the end of all oppression of class by class. This particular variety clearly associates the modern proletariat most closely with the idea of socialism, and gives it the most explicit hope for the future. It proved much the most successful, and apart from Britain, where Marxism never captured more than a tiny sect, it became the official ideology of virtually every socialist or workers' party on the continent, with particular strength in Germany, France, Austria and Russia.

Marxist parties were, in theory, revolutionary parties, since their doctrine predicted a violent clash for which it was their duty to prepare. In practice, however, they were more concerned, as were non-Marxist socialists, with alleviating the hardships of working-class life, and in particular with strengthening trade unions and social and welfare legislation. Denounced by consistent Marxists as 'reformism', this work played a not insignificant part in the social progress recorded in this chapter. Only among the Russian Marxists, who were working in exile or clandestinely in a country in which any kind of social progress seemed hopeless, was there a significant grouping, in the form of the Bolsheviks under Lenin, who worked consistently for a revolutionary solution as their overriding aim.

BIBLIOGRAPHY

ALDCROFT, D. H.; SUTCLIFFE, A. (eds) 1999. *Europe in the International Economy, 1500–2000*. E. Elgar, Cheltenham.

BEREND, I. T.; RANKI, G. 1974. *Economic Development in East-Central Europe in the XIXth and XXth Centuries*. Columbia University Press, New York.

BOSERUP, E. 1989. *The Conditions of Agricultural Growth*. Allen and Unwin, London.

CHURCH, R. A. 1994. *The Coal and Iron Industries (The Industrial Revolution)*. Blackwell, Oxford.

CIPOLLA, C. M. (ed.) 1973. *The Fontana Economic History of Europe: The Industrial Revolution*. Collins, London.

FIELDHOUSE, D. K. 1973. *Economy and Empire, 1830–1914*. Weidenfeld, London.

FLOUD, R.; MCCLOSKEY, D. (eds) 1994. *The Economic History of Britain since 1700*. Cambridge University Press, Cambridge.

HABAKKUK, H. J.; POSTAN, M. M. (eds) 1965. *The Cambridge Economic History of Europe*. Vol. 6. Cambridge University Press, Cambridge.

HOBSBAWM, E. J. 1962. *The Age of Revolution 1789–1848*. World Publishing Co., New York.

HUGHES, T. P. 1989. *American Genesis*. Viking Press, New York.

KENWOOD, A. G.; LOUGHEED, A. L. 1983. *The Growth of the International Economy 1820–1980*. Allen and Unwin, London.

KIRBY, M. W. 1983. *The Decline of British Economic Power since 1870*. Allen and Unwin, London.

KUZNETS, S. 1966. *Modern Economic Growth*. Yale University Press, New Haven.

LANDES, D. S. 1969. *The Unbound Prometheus*. Cambridge University Press, Cambridge.

MADDISON, A. 1982. *Phases of Capitalist Development*. Oxford University Press, Oxford.

——. 1991. *Dynamic Forces in Capitalist Development, 1995. The World Economy, 1820–1992*. OECD, Paris.

MATHIAS, P. 1983. *The First Industrial Nation*. Methuen, London.

MILWARD, A. S.; SAUL, S. B. 1973. *The Economic Development of Europe, 1780–1870; 1870–1914*. Allen and Unwin, London.

MITCHELL, B. R.; DEANE, P. 1962. *Abstract of British Historical Statistics*. Cambridge University Press, Cambridge.

——. 1975. *European Historical Statistical Appendix: Fontana Economic Historical of Europe*. Collins, London.

——. 1993. *International Historical Statistics Africa, Asia, Oceania 1750–1989*. Macmillan, Basingstoke.

——. 1998. *International Historical Statistics: the Americas 1750–1993*. Macmillan, Basingstoke.

MOKYR, J. 1990. *The Lever of Riches: Technological Creativity and Economic Progress*. Oxford University Press, Oxford.

NORTH, D. C.; THOMAS, R. P. 1973. *The Rise of the Western World*. Cambridge University Press, Cambridge.

POLLARD, S. 1981. *Peaceful Conquest: the Industrialisation of Europe, 1760–1970*. Oxford University Press, Oxford.

ROSTOW, W. W. 1978. *The World Economy: History and Prospects*. University of Texas Press, Austin.

SCHUMPETER, J. 1934. *The Theory of Economic Development*. Harvard University Press, Cambridge MA.

SINGER, C.; HOLMYARD E.; HALL, A. R.; WILLIAMS, T. (eds) 1967. *A History of Technology*. Vol II, Clarendon Press, Oxford.

SYLLA, R.; TONIOLO, G. (eds) 1991. *Patterns of European Industrialisation: the Nineteenth Century*. Routledge, London.

TEICH, M.; PORTER, R. (eds) 1996. *The Industrial Revolution in National Context: Europe and the United States of America*. Cambridge University Press, Cambridge.

TEMIN, P. 1964. *Iron and Steel in Nineteenth-Century America*. MIT Press, Cambridge MA.

TRACEY, M. 1989. *Government and Agriculture in Western Europe*. Part 1, New York University Press, New York.

UNITED STATES DEPARTMENT OF COMMERCE. 1960. *Historical Statistics of the United States*. Washington DC.

VIAL, J. 1967. *L'Industrialisation de la Sidérurgie française 1814–1864*. Mouton, Paris.

WARNER, C. K. (ed.) 1966. *Agrarian Conditions in Modern European History*. Macmillan, London.

2

THE INTERNATIONAL CONTEXT

INTRODUCTION

Herman Van der Wee, coordinator

Even during the Dark Ages interregional and intercontinental migrations and commercial contacts had never been absent. During the entire first millennium of the Christian era, great waves from the heart of Asia into the Middle East and into Europe happened in continuous succession. During the same period the intracontinental migration in America moved from north to south. The Arabs, at the same time, conquered large parts of Asia, Africa and Europe.

Migration calmed down at the beginning of the second millennium. Expansion of commercial networks now became predominant. Muslim merchants enlarged and fortified their networks in subcontinental Asia. Chinese merchants did the same in South East Asia, the European merchants at that time moving into the Middle East.

The creation of commercial networks intensified when the Europeans, at the end of the Middle Ages, began exploring the oceans. Their endeavours would lead to the great discoveries in the West- and East Indies, and beyond, and to the conquest of huge colonial territories. During the following centuries the European governments were turning these conquests overseas and the commercial networks linked with them, into colonial empires, bringing both under control of the emerging nation states. Conquests and networks during the Early Modern period were, no doubt, a significant first step to the integration of the world economy. But the rise of the nation states in Europe and the mercantilistic policies this generated undermined the process of that integration, limiting it to a mere tendency within the boundaries of each colonial empire.

The nineteenth century inaugurated a new era of economic development and of economic integration. It was the century of the Industrial Revolution bringing in its footsteps the transport revolution. It was also the century of accelerated population growth, of mass migration, liberalism and nationalism. These phenomena were all European by origin, but did not remain exclusively European. Soon they would have a powerful impact on the rest of the world, as much on America as on Asia, Africa and Australia. The European demographic revolution, for example, generated a huge migration movement within Europe, in particular from the countryside to the towns, but it generated at the

same time an even more spectacular migration movement from Europe to the Americas, to Northern and Southern Africa, to Australia and to New Zealand. This migration movement out of Europe would be a determining factor of economic development in the countries receiving European migrants. It would be a particularly decisive factor in the move to industrialization in the Americas. Population growth also generated a migration movement within Asia and from Asia to other continents, but it never was on the same scale as the European migration movement. In Sub-Saharan Africa, migration within the continent was not on a large scale either. Insofar as it did occur, it was linked to the creation of the western and southern empires of the late eighteenth and nineteenth centuries.

Europe's economic predominance in the nineteenth century would generate also a new expansion of colonialism, combined with rising nationalism in Europe itself. European economic primacy strengthened by technological progress in the armament industries and in the medical sector, stimulated a gradual geographic extension of colonialism, particularly in Africa. Second, except in the cases of Portugal and Spain, both facing independence movements in their Latin American colonies, it enabled the European sovereign countries to tighten their political and economic ties with the colonies. In other words the combination of primacy and nationalism turned colonialism into imperialism.

Europe's economic primacy had another important effect. It enabled the colonial powers to introduce a policy of economic liberalism, opening the borders of their empires to a free worldwide circulation of raw materials, manufactured goods, capital, and labour. In this way Europe made a new major contribution to the development of a fully integrated world economy. This move towards full economic integration on a world scale started around the middle of the nineteenth century, at the initiative of British interests, and would last until the First World War.

This chapter will analyse in more detail and in more depth the phenomena of migration, colonialism and integration during the nineteenth century. It will also put these phenomena in their proper international context. Both are remarkable and fascinating stories.

2.1

EUROPE, AMERICA AND AFRICA

Jan Blomme

THE GROWTH OF AN INTEGRATED WORLD ECONOMY

The nineteenth century was a period in which there was a substantial increase in the mobility of the factors of production, labour and capital. Concurrently, a brisk expansion in international trade took place, the causes for which were both material and institutional: in the first place, industrialization in Europe and the United States brought about a number of important innovations in transport, which considerably reduced the cost of transporting bulk goods by land and sea; in the second, the policy of trade liberalization pursued by the European powers served gradually to establish a new world order.

The internationalization of the production factors, labour and capital

There was indeed already a certain degree of mobility of factors of production existing prior to the nineteenth century: the slave trade between Africa and America, for example, which, although ignominious, was 'an economically profitable solution' to the scarcity of labour in the plantation economies of the new world. Prior to 1800, too, there was already a fairly substantial degree of emigration from the Iberian Peninsula to Latin America, and one could already speak of a certain specialization of labour between the various continents as regards specific luxury goods. However, it was only during the nineteenth century that a real, large-scale world economy came into being in which not only luxury, but also mass-produced goods were systematically traded between continents. At the same time, an international redistribution of labour and capital took place of an extent never seen before.

The demographic revolution

Around 1740 a very considerable expansion of the Western world's population began, and for the first time in Europe there were average annual growth rates of above 0.5 per cent. Indeed, the average growth rates for the periods 1750–1800, 1800–1850 and 1850–1900 were 0.58 per cent, 0.71 per cent and 0.87 per cent respectively. The acceleration in growth was strongest at the time the Industrial Revolution was taking a definitive hold on the European continent. In North America, the average annual rates of growth for 1800–1850 and 1850–1900 were markedly higher (2.98 per cent and 2.3 per cent respectively),

although here substantial immigration added to strong natural expansion, itself brought about chiefly by the fall in the mortality rate during a period in which the birth rate was still very high.

Between 1800 and 1900, world population increased from 900M to approximately 1,600M, more rapidly in Europe and North America than elsewhere. The population of Europe in 1800 can be put at 200M, about 22 per cent of the then world total. A hundred years later, around 1900, it had risen to slightly more than 400M or approximately 25 per cent of the world total (or more than 30 per cent, if the overseas population of European descent is included).

The revolution in transport and communications

The transport and communications revolution in the nineteenth century did not come about purely by chance. With the industrial revolution inducing an increase in industrial production and with the attendant growth in demand, the requirement grew for improved trunk routes with a view to the rapid distribution of products and the cheap exchange of goods. The new means of transport and communication would in turn boost industrial production and commerce, and enhance international labour mobility, so that a cumulative process of positive, interacting factors came into play.

Better transport opportunities permitted a greater volume of goods to be handled, as markets were broadened and there was an improved supply of raw materials; they allowed production to be concentrated, thereby encouraging specialization and permitting economic advantages of scale to be realized. Consequently, they made for substantial gains in productivity, which was to bring about major growth in real incomes.

The improvements to the transport infrastructure fall into two groups: improvements to the existing network itself and innovation as regards the means of transport, of which the steamship and the steam locomotive were the most important during the nineteenth century.

The first successful experiments with steamships took place as early as 1807, with Robert Fulton (1765–1815) as the first to illustrate the opportunities of powering ships by steam. However, the introduction of the steamship into international transport was a rather slow process, unlike the situation with steam railways, The first steamships were driven by paddle-wheels and for this reason were not suitable for the open seas; it was to take until 1833 before a steamship could cross the Atlantic Ocean without sails, with the first regular transatlantic service beginning only in 1838.

The marine screw propeller was developed around that time (the 1840s) and iron began to replace wood in ship-building from the 1860s, though not itself being replaced by steel until the end of the nineteenth century. Nevertheless, the iron steamship was not an immediate success for ocean shipping, as the great supplies of coal that it had to carry meant that the space left over for freight was too limited. Consequently, steamships carried primarily mail, passengers and valuable, small volume freight. Moreover, new competitive types of sailing-ship were being brought into service, such as the long, small clippers with an enormous area of sail that could carry up to five thousand tonnes and achieve a greater rate of knots than steamships. Until 1870, the sailing-ship had the upper hand, but thereafter found it ever more difficult to compete against the increasing tonnage of the iron, later the steel, steamship. Likewise sealing the fate of the sailing-ship was the opening of the Suez Canal in 1869, which was unnavigable for clippers. The total amount of freight carried by steamships rose from 27M tonnes in 1873 to 63M tonnes in 1898; over the same period, steamships increased their share in the total amount of freight shipped from barely 12 per cent to approximately 65 per cent. With the ending of the First World War, the days of sail were over.

Because of the sharp reduction in transport costs, consequent on the introduction of the steamship, it became possible for the first time to include heavier bulk goods on a large scale in international trade, a development that represented an enormous boost to the growth of intercontinental trade after 1870.

It was shown that steam traction offered possibilities for land transport, too, and, in 1825, George Stephenson (1781–1848) laid the first railway line able to employ locomotives, the Stockton and Darlington Railway. A feature of Great Britain was that the establishment of railway lines was left virtually entirely to private initiative, and the first of them were indeed set up by small, independent companies, though many of these were merged around the mid-nineteenth century into just a few large companies, such as the Great Western, the London and North-Western, the Midland and the Great Northern.

On the European continent, the state was usually more involved in the development and promotion of railways, the first example of state intervention in their laying being represented by Belgium, where as early as 1833 a start was made with the construction of a railway network funded by the state; within the space of about ten years, all the main lines had been laid, enabling Belgium to capture a major proportion of the transit trade of North Western Europe. Also in France, the establishment of the railways came about through a close cooperation between state and private initiative. Although railway lines were laid between Leipzig and Dresden and between Leipzig and Magdeberg in 1835 and 1839 respectively, it was only after 1850 that there was any great development of the railway network in Germany and, from the outset, the railways were state property in most German states. It was only during the second half of the nineteenth century, too, that such other European countries as the Netherlands, Austria, Hungary, Switzerland, Spain, etc. experienced their railway boom.

In Europe, as well as in the United States and Russia, the second half of the nineteenth century was also the period of the transcontinental lines. The connection between Northern and Southern Europe was laid between 1855 and 1884, with the 1870s already seeing the first railway tunnels being bored through the Alps. The Orient Express, linking London to Constantinople via Paris, began to run in 1883, and from 1888, with the construction of the Vienna-Constantinople-Baghdad railway link, Central Europe had a direct connection with the Middle East. In the United States, a transcontinental line was opened in 1869 with the Pacific Railways, and, in imperial Russia, the Trans-Caspian and the Trans-Siberian railways were laid during the 1880s and 1890s respectively.

Between 1840 and 1870, the number of kilometres of railway in the world increased from 5,500 to 130,500. The rate of growth accelerated after 1870 and in 1910 the total was already as much as 640,000km. The construction of new railway networks was further facilitated by the developing capital markets, channelling substantial savings from the new emerging middle classes into this new investment opportunity. In Europe, the breakthrough of railways contributed chiefly to the creation of large internal markets. Elsewhere in the world, railways were more an instrument to facilitate the export of mineral and agricultural products.

The railway revolution exercised an enormous influence on the economic development of Europe and the world during the nineteenth century and thus can indeed be considered as bringing about a real revolution in transport and communication. Railways were the symbol of the general progress realized by humanity during that century, and psychologically brought the conviction that man could change the world through technological progress. A second psychological impact that they had on society was to break the isolated, rather regional vision of earlier generations, whereby place was made for a national and even international recasting of the world picture. In the political field, the railways reinforced the unification of national states, serving in the United States to bring unity between North and South and between East and West, and in Russia between the Asiatic and European territories. In the industrial field, they gave a major boost to the coal, iron and (later) steel industries; they made labour mobility more flexible, thereby once again favourably influencing industrial expansion. In the commercial field, they facilitated distribution and trade, pushed costs down, and at the same time brought more uniformity to markets (whereby, for example, prices became national rather than regional). Railways, lastly, were also extremely important for the development of industrial and financial capitalism.

The final decade of the century saw the advent of the motor car, brought about by the introduction of the internal combustion engine onto the market; however, it was only after 1920 that the commercial road vehicle began to offer stiff competition to the goods train and the inland navigation vessel.

Parallel with the advances made in the transport and traffic sectors was the increase in the scope of communications. The invention of the cable telegraph in 1832 by Samuel Morse (1791–1872) and of the telephone in 1876 by Alexander Graham Bell (1847–1922) made instantaneous and secure communication over long distances possible, thereby making the world economy much more transparent. In 1866, the first transatlantic cable was laid, permitting immediate communication between Europe and North America. Another enormous success was the invention of wireless telegraphy (radio) by Gugliemo Marconi (1874–1937) in 1895.

International migratory movements

The substantial increase in the population of Europe was already generating serious Malthusian tensions between people and land at the end of the eighteenth century. Initially, the increase was matched by a rise in European agricultural production: not only was the area devoted to agriculture expanded by land reclamation, but labour and land productivity were further increased by the application of new scientific methods.

It appeared around 1850, however, that the European agricultural Revolution was not going to be sufficient to cope with the further growth in population, but the renewed threat of Malthusian tension was this time averted by massive emigration overseas. The essential economic function of international migration during the nineteenth century was to redistribute a proportion of Europe's agrarian population among the new overseas regions, though the massive exodus to other continents also represented the start of large-scale overseas development.

Overseas emigration got under way around 1820, and from 1840 assumed massive proportions. Depending on the statistics employed, the number of migrants between 1821 and 1914 was between 46M (emigration statistics) and 51M (immigration statistics, which are probably more reliable). Other statistics give a total of about 60M between 1815 and 1914. It may therefore seem plausible to put the total number of migrants in the course of the nineteenth century at something between 50 and 60 million. The great majority of emigrants (95 per cent) were Europeans, the rest being primarily from Asia. Besides the 'voluntary' emigrants were also an appreciable number of black Africans (more than 2M) who, via the slave trade, were the victims of forced migration to principally the American continent.

With nearly 32M immigrants, or approximately 60 per cent of the total, the United States was the most important destination. Canada attracted just over 4M (8 per cent of the total), about 12M settled in Latin America (23 per cent), by preference in Brazil and Argentina, and a further 5M or so (10 per cent) departed for the British dominions of Australia, New Zealand and South Africa. The initial wave of emigration lasted until about 1880, and was chiefly from Western Europe to North America, Argentina and Brazil. In total, there were about 16M emigrants from the British Isles (i.e. including Ireland) alone. Apart from the British and Irish, there were also large groups of Germans (5M) and Scandinavians (3M million).

The motives for emigrating were numerous. Generally, it was a mixture of 'push' and 'pull' factors that led to the decision to emigrate, the push factors having to do with circumstances in the country of origin (poverty, war, etc.), and pull factors being an indication of the attraction of the country of destination (discovery of precious metals, agricultural frontier, higher standard of living, etc.). Socio-economic circumstances formed the major motive for emigration. Especially in countries or regions where the countryside was overpopulated and industrialization was to limited to accommodate the increasing rural population, many tried to escape extreme poverty by emigration (cf. The Irish after the Great Potato Famine, 1845–7).

Stories about important discoveries of gold in the Far West and Australia, and about the agricultural successes of the pioneers in the American Midwest, convinced would-be migrants that emigration offered them the chance to break loose from the proletarianization brought about by the Industrial Revolution in Europe. The discovery of goldfields in remote regions indeed had a profound psychological effect. Gold was found in the United States (California and Oregon) between 1848 and 1852, in Australia between 1851 and 1877, in New Zealand in 1857 and in South Africa in 1884; once the gold rush was over, many gold-seekers chose to settle in the territory where they had prospected and to develop it agriculturally.

Other less compelling motives were the political disillusion among many European liberals after the Restoration in 1815, the religious differences between Irish and British, the propaganda conducted by local authorities in Europe for overseas emigration to rid themselves of the increasing burden of public poor-relief, and the pessimistic writings of Thomas Robert Malthus (1766–1834) and William Godwin (1756–1836) in connection with threatening overpopulation in Europe.

The second phase of emigration (from roughly 1880 to 1920), the motivation for which was virtually wholly economic, was restricted chiefly to the inhabitants of the Mediterranean and Slavic worlds, with 8M Italians, 4.6M Spaniards and Portuguese, and about 6.5M Russians, Poles, Bulgarians, Hungarians Czechs and Rumanians moving in the first instance to North America, but also to Argentina and Brazil. The North American continent attracted non-Europeans, too, such as Chinese and, to a less extent, Japanese. Lastly, the abolition of the slave trade during the second half of the nineteenth century also prompted an international migration from the Indian sub-continent.

Mass immigration from abroad went hand-in-hand with large-scale agricultural development of the overseas territories, various factors playing a part in this. The industrial expansion of Europe and probably of the East Coast of America, too, stimulated the demand for industrial crops and for grain production. Indeed, the spread of agricultural machines in the Midwest and the advances in transport infrastructure brought about by the American railway revolution and the advent of steam navigation made it possible for agricultural surpluses to be easily transported from the United States and other remote areas to Western Europe. Around 1870 began the so-called agricultural invasion, whereby enormous quantities of grain arrived in Western Europe from the United States (and later Canada, Argentina, Australia, New Zealand, Russia and Romania). This large-scale overseas trade in grain was soon followed by large-scale overseas trade in meat and fruit, which reached Western Europe in refrigerated ships, and by a large-scale overseas trade in wool and hides; the overseas trade in cotton dated from an earlier period. The agricultural invasion thus spectacularly galvanized the development of territories abroad. In some of these, government aid contributed considerably to the opening up of new areas to cultivation. Already from the mid-nineteenth century, the governments of states in the American Midwest were taking concrete measures to facilitate the appropriation of uncultivated land, a policy that reached its climax in the Homestead Act of 1863, whereby citizens or immigrants were able to acquire title to 160 acres (or about 65 hectares) of uncultivated land free, provided they declared themselves prepared to develop the land and to continue to work it for at least five years.

The significance of the mass migration and of the large-scale overseas development cannot easily be overestimated. The immigration was of vital importance for the economic and political development of the overseas territories: there was first of all the fact of its numerical extent, and it must not be forgotten that only the most dynamic and enterprising elements among the European population dared to make the leap into the far unknown and that pioneering was of itself a particularly arduous and often also thankless undertaking. Furthermore, immigration and the opening-up of the western territories of the United States enabled a giant continental economy to be built up in North America; it was in fact at this time that the basis was laid for the development of American world hegemony in the twentieth century. Specialization arose within this continental economy, whereby the East Coast concentrated on industry, the Midwest on grain production and the South West on ranching.

For Europe, the wave of overseas emigration and development represented a possible solution to increasing Malthusian tension. Population pressure in Europe declined and at the same time the expansion of intercontinental trade boosted the import of cheap agricultural products. In the countries of destination themselves, with their scarcity of labour, immigration promoted the exploitation of their enormous natural resources, which served to benefit the integration of the world economy.

An extremely tragic chapter in the history of the great migrations was the Atlantic slave trade between Africa and America. It began in the sixteenth century and its aim, then too, was to provide cheap labour for the plantation economies. The demand for African slaves was, to a large extent, due to the partial destruction of the local American Indian population. From 1650 onwards, it achieved increasing proportions; the exact number of Africans that were transported to America as slaves still remains a source of great controversy, with estimates varying between 10 and 40 million, although a number of about 10–12M seems to be most plausible (only those who survived the journey). About 2,000 per year during the sixteenth century, the number of slaves transported rose steadily to reach a peak of 80,000 in 1780, and it was only at the beginning of the nineteenth century that the European and North American powers took the first measures to restrain this shameful trade. Notwithstanding legislation abolishing the practice, still a great number of Africans were transported to the New World as slaves during the first half of the nineteenth century, the trade reaching a new peak in the 1840s: according to some estimates, indeed, approximately a further 2M Africans were shipped to America between 1810 and 1870. It was only during the third quarter of the nineteenth century that this forced migration was finally halted, when anti-slavery legislation was also adopted in the Latin American countries (from 1850 in Brazil and from 1860 in Cuba). A particular effect of this time-lag in Latin American abolitionist legislation was the geographical shift in the slave trade, its centre of gravity moving during the nineteenth century from the Atlantic west coast first to southern Africa (the Congo and Mozambique) and subsequently to the eastern part of Africa.

A further effect of the population increase was that an ambitious movement got under way in Europe from the second half of the eighteenth century to develop home regions, i.e. moorland, polders, fallow land, marshes, fens and other uncultivated ground. This urge to develop, combined with a search for work in the recently industrialized regions, led to a number of important migratory flows within Europe herself.

Both France and England attracted many immigrants from surrounding countries. Numerous East Europeans migrated to the West, where they established themselves mainly in France and Germany. Among them also a lot of Jews fleeing a new wave of pogroms in Eastern Europe. Also important was the large-scale migration eastwards connected with agrarian development, approximately 4.2M West Europeans departing for Russia between 1828 and 1915, about two thirds of whom came from Germany and Austria. Mainly after 1890, major internal migration eastwards and southwards took place in Russia itself towards the Asiatic part of the country, about 7M Russians moving to Siberia, East Asia and Turkmenistan, about four fifths of them farmers and the rest prisoners and exiles.

The urge towards intracontinental migration and colonization was not restricted to Europe alone: indeed, the western frontier migration in the United States represented one of the most important movements to open up land in the history of humankind. Other major migrations to open up land for agriculture, albeit on a significantly smaller scale than in the United States, took place in Latin America, South Africa and Australia.

International capital movements

Integration of the world economy was further advanced by the export of capital, i.e. investment abroad. Accounting for 88 per cent of all investment, Europe was by far the most important provider of capital in the world during the nineteenth century; within Europe, Great Britain was the unquestionable leader.

Foreign investment served to bring about a substantial expansion of world trade, because it promoted international specialization and the division of labour. Furthermore, it formed in time the major conduit for the transfer of technological expertise and, in a number of countries where it was applied directly to industrialization projects, it also made a decisive contribution to the growth of their gross national product.

During the first half of the nineteenth century, foreign investment was still fairly modest: from the time the Napoleonic Wars ended to the 1850s, a total of approximately US$2 billion was invested abroad, a figure that had already trebled by 1870. The great period of international lending began primarily after this date, with a renewed burst after 1900, by when the outstanding amounts totalled $23 billion; by 1914, this figure was to rise to $43 billion, nearly eight times greater than in 1870.

There are various reasons for this remarkable increase, many of them having to do with the growth of specialized financial institutions and with the introduction of more sophisticated financial instruments serving to reduce the risk attendant on foreign investment. No less important was the growth of the middle class, whose dynamic role in the Industrial Revolution had enabled it build up substantial financial resources. On the eve of the First World War, British foreign investment amounted to 43 per cent of the world total. Between 1870 and 1914, the British invested an average of 4 per cent of their national income abroad, a figure that was as high as 7 per cent between 1905 and 1913! Given that Great Britain had a negative trade balance, the requisite means for foreign investment came from invisible earnings, income generated by the British merchant fleet and surpluses on the balance of payments. Until 1850, the

British invested chiefly in Europe and the United States; thereafter, the focus of investment shifted from Europe to Latin America and principally to the British colonies and dominions.

Behind Great Britain, France was the next most important investor abroad, accounting for 20 per cent of the world total. During the first half of the nineteenth century, the French invested mainly in neighbouring countries, but subsequently turned their attention to Southern and Eastern Europe and to the Middle East. After 1891, Russia became one of the most favoured countries for French investment, so much so that in 1914 she probably accounted for more than a quarter of it. Smaller industrial countries, such as Belgium, the Netherlands and Switzerland, also played a relatively important role on the international capital market, boasting a 12 per cent share in total foreign investment in the late nineteenth century.

Germany was initially an importer of capital and, from the mid-nineteenth century built up a strong industrial base with French, British and Belgian capital that, in time, permitted her even to generate an export surplus and thereby to redeem the foreign investment. Towards the end of the century, Germans themselves began to invest abroad, primarily in the neighbouring countries of Central Europe. The United States, too, was at first an importer of capital, having large-scale resource to foreign capital – chiefly British – in order to open up her immense agricultural and industrial frontier. Until the outbreak of the First World War, indeed, she was the world's greatest beneficiary of foreign investment and it was only after 1918 that, in consequence of the enormous loans she had made to the allies during the war, she moved from being a net debtor country to being the most important creditor nation in the world.

Russia brought up the rear of the major beneficiaries of foreign investment during the nineteenth century: the Russian railway network, the large modern metal works of the Donets basin and elsewhere, and the chemical and textile industries were all in great measure constructed with foreign capital. The effect of these investments on the Russian economy was indeed very substantial, whereby the basis was laid for the initial breakthrough of the Russian industrial revolution at the end of the nineteenth century. As a result, the very high growth figures for the Russian economy between 1870 and 1914 have largely to be ascribed to foreign investment at the time. During the 1880s, the return on investment was extremely high, but fell back appreciably after 1895. The major investors were the French and the Belgians, who were in fact to lose their investment completely with the revolution of 1917.

In 1914, approximately half of all investment abroad was in Europe (27 per cent) and North America (24 per cent). Latin America accounted for nearly one fifth (19 per cent), Asia for just 16 per cent, Africa and Oceania for modest shares of 9 per cent and 5 per cent respectively. Of the foreign investment in Africa, more than 60 per cent went to South Africa alone.

As is the case with all investment, foreign investment, too, has to offer a sufficient return in order to permit not only an annual dividend to be paid, but also the original investment to be repaid. In this respect, the return on investment abroad during the nineteenth century varied considerably: in certain regions, the investment was exceptionally successful and generated both dividends and considerable capital gains, too; in others, productive application and repayment of the funds made available proved to be a much more difficult affair.

Foreign investment in the Scandinavian countries and in the British dominions of Australia, New Zealand and Canada proved to be particularly successful, and at the same time contributed decisively to the development of a modern economy in those countries. The explanation for this success can be put down to both the extent of the amount invested (which, although fairly modest in absolute terms, was greater per head of the population than anywhere else) and to the fact that the investment was in productive sectors. This sort of investment strategy, combined with a traditionally high level of general education, goes far to explain the rapid economic growth and high standard of living achieved by these countries by the beginning of the twentieth century.

Investment in Latin America, Asia and Africa as a whole was very considerable, but rather on the low side per head of population. Additionally, the level of general education was lower and the institutional structure less developed; consequently, it was only with difficulty that economic growth in the modern sense got under way. The most important result of foreign investment in these countries was to permit development of their natural resources, though without this fundamentally altering their economic structure, except in the case of Japan. Although these countries were now able to take an active part in the international economy, they remained largely dependent on the West for the consumption of industrial manufactured goods and were, furthermore, extremely vulnerable to fluctuations in trade, as their exports were usually limited to a few strategic mining or agricultural products. In some cases, foreign investment was thus not able at all to generate local development and, on the contrary, kept some regions from developing a solid economic structure. Only very seldom did they resort to processing their own raw materials so as to be able to export manufactured goods with a higher value added.

Even more sombre was the return on foreign investment in North Africa and Southern and Southeastern Europe. A considerable proportion of this investment in both the private and public sectors was not applied productively, so that repayment of interests invested often had to be suspended.

Institutional aspects: the breakthrough of free trade

From mercantilism to liberalism in world trade (1790–1880)

Besides the primitive means of transport and communication, a further obstacle to the expansion of trade during the *ancien régime* was the policy of trade protection that was pursued, with most governments placing artificial barriers on both domestic and foreign trade, aiming thereby to protect the national interest. From the sixteenth century, the growth of large national states with a centralized administration, such as France, England and Spain, had led to an intensification of national feelings. In economic terms, this development translated into a body of protectionist measures called mercantilism. Governments pursuing a mercantilistic policy attached exceptionally great importance to a positive balance of trade, as it was believed in the economic paradigm of the time that the import of precious metals increased national prosperity.

A systematic examination of the objections of physiocrats and of other philosophers to the mercantilistic policy of government was carried out by Adam Smith (1723–90), who worked these objections into a coherent theory in his book, *An Enquiry into the Nature and the Causes of the Wealth of Nations* (1776) that was to become famous. Two main propositions in his argument had far-reaching significance. First, by his efforts, an individual can promote his own well being better than the state, which means that the interests of the individual and those of society are immutable. Second, a free trade policy in respect of foreign commercial relationships ought to supplement internal liberalism: with free trade, each country could, unhindered, concentrate indeed on the production of its best specialities; in this way, an international distribution of labour would come about, which would be superior to national self-sufficiency and enhance overall world prosperity. Whereas Adam Smith emphasized differences in *absolute production costs* to commend the advantages of free trade, David Ricardo (1772–1823), in a later publication, *Principles of Political Economy* (1819) pointed also to the importance of *relative differences in cost*, a concept that was later to form the basis of the modern theory of international trade. The propositions of Adam Smith and David Ricardo were in harmony with the nineteenth-century optimism about the creativity of the individual, an optimism originating in the Enlightenment.

Great Britain set the pace in the gradual dismantling of mercantilism, Adam Smith's views being accepted already at the end of the eighteenth century by several British statesmen. However, the outbreak of war with France in 1793 served to postpone the definitive breakthrough of British liberalism in trade, and the ending of the war even saw a temporary reinforcement of British protectionism.

In 1815, in anticipation of a decline in the price of corn, seen as inevitable on the restoration of peace after Napoleon's defeat in 1814, the great landowners in Great Britain secured the promulgation in Parliament of the notorious Corn Laws, which banned the import of foreign grain if the price fell below a fixed minimum and which imposed import duties on a decreasing scale if prices rose above that minimum. It was precisely on the issue of these Corn Laws, indeed, that the battle between protectionism and free trade was fought. Shortly after the end of the Napoleonic Wars, there was already a shift in public opinion and, in 1820, a group of London businessmen petitioned Parliament for a policy of international free trade to be pursued. In fact, the sharp growth in the population and increasing urbanization made it impossible for a policy of self-sufficiency in food to be conducted and, with the influence of businessmen and industrialists on the rise, the campaign for free trade won more and more ground. The industrialists, in particular, argued that the free import of grain would serve to depress the price of corn, thereby bringing about a fall in the cost of living and likewise in wages in industry (i.e. industrial production costs), and that British industrial exports would rise in consequence.

An Anti-Corn Law League was set up in 1839 in the modern textile centre of Manchester, with Richard Cobden (1804–65) as one of its leaders. This anti-protectionist movement rapidly gained substantial influence, so much so that from 1841 it spurred the revision of a number of import duties on various food products. In 1845, the potato harvest failed throughout Europe, leading to rising food prices and to acute famine everywhere, the situation being particularly dramatic in Ireland, where the potato was the staple food of the rural population. To combat the food crisis, the prime minister of the time, Robert Peel, defied the will of the majority of his own party, the Whigs, and in January 1846 repealed the Corn Laws definitively.

The repeal of the Corn Laws marked the end of a long period of British protectionism. Under the influence of William E. Gladstone (1809–98), Chancellor of the Exchequer during the 1850s and 1860s, and later to become Prime Minister, the policy of free trade was developed further. Import tariffs were thoroughly reviewed in 1853 and 1860, so that eventually only forty-eight products remained of the 1,150 previously subject to import duty, the import duties retained being solely those on non-British goods, such as wine, tobacco, coffee, tea and spices; moreover, they were reduced to symbolic levels. In 1849, the infamous Navigation Laws of the seventeenth century were repealed. Around the middle of the nineteenth century, thus, Great Britain set herself up as the champion of free trade, thereafter pursuing a policy of absolutely free trade, naturally because this served her interests best. Indeed, given the country's political supremacy and lead in industry and commerce, free trade was the most appropriate means of guaranteeing a ready market for British manufactured goods throughout the entire world, and of squeezing traditional and possibly competitive industries elsewhere.

On the European continent, British commercial liberalism was viewed with mixed feelings. In fact, with Great Britain's 'Continental Blockade' of Napoleon from 1806 to 1814, the countries of the continent had only just experienced a resurgence of mercantilism. Moreover, Napoleon had erected high tariff barriers around France and her subject territories, and had thereby halted the movement for free trade that had begun in France with the French Revolution.

After Napoleon's defeat and the conclusion of peace in 1815 (the period of the Restoration), France retreated into a still more outspoken conservative protectionism, with the intention of screening her traditional textile industry from British competition: besides a total ban on wool and cotton articles, high import duties were also levied on raw materials and semi-manufactured goods.

The foreign policy of Napoleon III (President of France from 1848 to 1852 and Emperor from 1852 to 1870) was aimed at achieving friendship with Great Britain, not only to gain political recognition for his regime, but also for reason of prestige, more particularly to have France again playing a leading role in Europe, not least in economic terms. Although there was a majority in the French Assembly for the retention of a protectionist policy, Napoleon III was able to invoke his prerogatives that gave him the exclusive right to conclude treaties with foreign powers. The idea of free trade also found a number of protagonists in the academic world, as there had long been a school that included, among others, the French economists, Frédéric Bastiat (1801–50) and Jean-Baptiste Say (1767–1832), who provided an intellectual buttress to the principle of free trade. Substantial influence was also exerted by Michel Chevalier (1806–79), Professor of Economics at the Collège de France and member of the French Senate; it was via his friend, Richard Cobden (1804–65), pioneer of the Anti-Corn Law legislation, that an approach was made to the British Chancellor of the Exchequer, Gladstone, in order to prepare the way for a treaty liberalizing trade between the two countries.

Underpinned by the ideas of the French economists and by the early successes of the French industrial revolution, the famous 'Cobden Treaty' was concluded in January 1860 with Great Britain, which was to usher in the era of liberalism in France. The intention was to use a liberalizing trade policy to force French industrialists into modernization investment. With the exception of those on a number of luxury articles, it abolished all British import duties on French products, lifted the ban on British textile products and lowered the tariffs on other British goods to an average of about 15 per cent *ad valorem*. The French thus substituted their policy of protectionism by one providing a moderate degree of protection for the French economy. The treaty not only liberalized commercial relations between the two countries, but also represented the signal for a whole series of bilateral trade agreements between various nations: the Cobden Treaty indeed included the 'most favoured nation' clause, whereby any reduction in customs duties granted by either of the two parties to a third nation automatically applied to the other. France concluded similar treaties with virtually all other European countries during the early 1860s, and this served steadily to reduce import duties and tariffs throughout Europe in the years after 1860.

In Germany, the particularist traditions of the past had been set aside by as early as 1825 and the first customs unions or *Zollverein* created. In that year, the South German Union was set up, but fell apart when, in 1829, Bavaria sought a rapprochement with the North German Union established in 1828. For a time, there was also a Middle German Union, a heterogeneous collection of states including Saxony, Thuringia and Hanover. On 1 January 1834, the fully constituted German *Zollverein* came into force, a merger of the three, which united seventeen German states and a population of 23 million Germans in a single, common free-trade area, with uniform legislation for import, export and transit duties, and a uniform currency, weights and measures system. The most important participant and the undisputed leader was Prussia.

In 1871, finally, the customs union was integrated into the German empire and included all German states, with the exception of the free cities of Hamburg and Bremen, which acceded only in 1888. Exerting a very great influence on German trade policy was the economist Friedrich List (1789–1846).

Prompted by the Cobden Treaty, Belgium in 1861–3 concluded free trade treaties with France, Great Britain and the German *Zollverein*. In 1863, a substantial boost to the future growth of the Antwerp port and of Belgian transit trade was given by minister Hubert J. W. Frère-Orban (1812–96), with the compounding of the Scheldt toll, imposed in 1830 on Belgium by the Netherlands. Frère-Orban was a great promoter in Belgium of the notion of free trade, which won more ground in public opinion now that it had meanwhile appeared that Belgium, as a European country of transit and as a country exporting industrial manufactured goods, had every advantage in unobstructed foreign trade.

In the United States, the fear of renewed British competition after the Napoleonic Wars led to the enactment of the protectionist Tariff Act of 1816. Between 1830 and 1857, however, import duties were gradually scaled down, whereby the United States began to follow the same trend towards free trade as the European countries, only for this movement to be brusquely interrupted by the American Civil War (1860–5), when, for fiscal reasons, import duties

were again increased sharply. Even thereafter, these war tariffs remained the basis for the protection of the fledgling American industry.

The institutional framework of Europe's free trade structure rapidly acquired monetary and financial adjuncts. From the beginning of the nineteenth century already, Great Britain had consolidated the system of the gold standard, although most other European countries retained the silver standard or bimetallism until the final quarter of the nineteenth century. However, due partly to the dominance of Great Britain in international trade, most continental countries adopted the gold standard during the century's final two decades. The gradual generalization of the gold standard proved enormously beneficial for international trade. For many decades to come, a single criterion of value was to be used in both the internal trade of each country and general international trade. This led to a dramatic simplification of commercial traffic and to a growing general confidence in world trade. At the same time, advances in financial techniques facilitated the organization of foreign transfers and investment.

Together with the revolution in transport and communications, the rise in industrial output and the broadening of demand, the policy of free trade brought about the spectacular rise in world trade after 1840. Indeed, it was during the decades following the Cobden Treaty that the ideal of free trade was to reach an initial climax and international trade to achieve exceptionally spectacular expansion, with annual growth rates of up to 10 per cent during the third quarter of the nineteenth century.

Reversion to protectionism? (1880–1914)

As a result of the gradual integration of the world economy during the nineteenth century, there was a convergence of price movements to each other across national borders. During the nineteenth century, too, cyclical price and economic fluctuations moved more rapidly than ever from one country to another, the fluctuations being caused by the interaction of real and monetary factors. In general, falls in prices held for a long time, whereas a downturn in production was rather of short duration. After the Napoleonic Wars, for both real (a rise in productivity, due to technological innovation) and monetary reasons, the level of prices fell, only to rise again around the middle of the century following a number of major discoveries of gold (in California in 1849 and in Australia in 1851). From 1873, however, for a period of twenty years, the price level of most products began again to decline, a trend that was accompanied by a slowdown in economic growth and a weakening of the international free trade movement.

Due to the general use of agricultural machines in the Midwest of America, to the laying of transcontinental railways and to the breakthrough of transatlantic steam navigation, grain could be imported cheaply into the European market, and this resulted in a steep fall in prices that plunged European agriculture into deep distress.

The initial reaction to the crisis was a tendency to increase protection for national agriculture, with free trade being temporarily abjured and protective government measures announced. For Europe, agrarian protectionism softened the hard edges of overseas competition, but at the same time reinforced agricultural conservatism. A second, more positive reaction was a movement towards structural renewal of European agriculture, whereby more emphasis was placed on dairy products, an area in which European farmers could better bring their comparative advantages into play; structural reform, however, was slow to get under way. Added to this was the fact that, during the 1870s and 1880s, there was an insistent call from industrial circles for protectionist measures to be taken, a call reinforced by the revival of nationalist sentiment after the Franco-Prussian War (1870).

In unified Germany, an alliance between the Prussian landed nobility in the east and the industrial entrepreneurs in the west of the country gave the signal for a general increase in customs tariffs (1879), and analogous measures rapidly followed in Italy (1878, 1887), Austria (1882), Switzerland (1884, 1891, 1906) and elsewhere. Russia, that had always remained fairly isolated, instituted an ultra-prohibitive tariff in 1891. Initially, France hesitated, first proceeding to a revision of import duties in a moderately protectionist move in 1881, but then, in 1892, taking a somewhat harder line with the introduction of a minimum tariff that allowed of no exceptions (called the 'Méline tariff' after the Minister of Agriculture, Jules Méline [1838–1925]).

Protectionist views sprang up in Great Britain, too, including the notion of 'fair trade' and the idea of 'imperial preference' launched by minister Joseph Chamberlain (1836–1914). Chamberlain had a dual purpose in seeking protection: on the one hand, to safeguard British manufactured goods from foreign competition, which was now having a serious impact, and, on the other, to link the economies of the colonies and the mother country more closely by forming a customs union that would unite the entire British Empire within a system of colonial preference. However, the British government did not for the time being pursue these suggestions further, so that policy remained predominantly liberal until after the First World War. This was important, as Britain's ascendancy in the world during this period was so great that her fidelity to free trade continued to exert a tangible influence on overall world trade. Furthermore, monetary and financial liberalism, resting on the international mobility of capital and on the gold standard, was preserved and full mobility of labour retained.

There was also a refusal on the part of a number of smaller countries to abandon free trade; these including Belgium and the Netherlands that had built up substantial transit trade during the preceding decades.

All these factors thus explain why, despite all the tendencies towards protectionism, trade still remained largely liberal until 1914. The return to protectionism after 1873 therefore has to be considerably qualified. Although international trade thereafter grew less expansively, the annual rates of growth achieved continued to be fairly high (about 4.5 per cent) in the decade before the First World War. During the nineteenth century, thus, a real world economy was developed, the degree of whose integration was not to be surpassed until around 1960.

The extent and structure of international trade

What immediately stands out in the study of international trade during this period is the exceptional growth that was chalked up, per capita volume of international trade rising between 1800 and 1913 by a factor of twenty-five. The sharpest growth was recorded during the period of liberalization and industrialization between 1840 and 1870; thereafter the rate of expansion slowed down.

A second general fact is that world trade grew much more rapidly than world production during the same period. Consequently, the liberalization of international trade served as an important motor for general economic development. Conservative estimates put the increase in per capita world production between 1800 and 1913 at 0.73 per cent per year, as against a rate of 3.3 per cent for per capita world trade. Due to world trade expanding four times more rapidly, thus, the ratio of world trade to world production rose during this period by a factor of eleven, meaning that the share of total world trade (imports and exports together) in world output increased from barely 3 per cent in 1800 to an extraordinary 33 per cent in 1913. The growth itself was more pronounced in Europe than in the United States and Australia. These latter were already fairly substantially integrated into the world economy at the beginning of the period, thereby reducing their growth potential. Moreover, their abundance of raw materials served to boost the development of the domestic market rather than of world trade.

During the nineteenth century, Europe dominated world trade, in 1876–80 controlling 67 per cent of the total import and export of goods in the world, a share that was still as high as 62 per cent in 1913; the same period saw the share of the North American countries rising from 9.5 per cent to 13.2 per cent. This absolute predominance of the European countries in world trade has, however, to be qualified, because approximately two thirds of the European share indeed consisted of intra-European trade.

Throughout the nineteenth century, Great Britain was the absolute leader as regards trade, although a gradual decline in this supremacy can be noted, her share in total world trade in raw materials between 1876–80 and 1913 narrowing from 32.8 per cent to 25.2 per cent, and in manufactured goods from 46.9 per cent to 33.5 per cent. Exports were a major element in the economies of European countries during the nineteenth century, accounting for 15–20 per cent of national income in Great Britain, Germany and France. In smaller countries with a more favourable geographic position, such as Belgium, the Netherlands and Switzerland, the percentage was still higher.

Until about 1875, the share of food and raw materials from the temperate zones in international trade had been rising at the expense of products from tropical zones; thereafter, however, the situation was reversed, due in part to the advent of European colonialism. Another conspicuous feature was the marked stability of the share of raw materials and finished products in world trade, although the latter group exhibited a shift from textile to metal goods during the final quarter of the nineteenth century.

Finally, the expansion of international trade also brought a new, multilateral payments network into being. Most industrializing countries had substantial balance-of-payment deficits *vis-à-vis* the countries producing raw materials, and Great Britain, although also a major importer of raw materials, was the most important exporter of finished goods to non-European, raw material producers; the income from this export surplus, together with Britain's invisible income from services, generated sufficient foreign currency to cover her deficit on the trade balance with other industrialized countries, and in this way the latter received the necessary foreign exchange to be able in turn to finance their current account deficits with the countries producing raw materials.

The rise of a multilateral payments system gave the world economy an additional stimulus, as the system permitted large-scale credit operations to be mounted and large-scale clearing of debit and credit balances to be conducted, as well as minimizing flows of gold. On the other hand, it has to be said that the stability of the world system rested to a very substantial extent on the surplus that the British could achieve on their current account, based on British exports of finished goods to non-European, raw material producers, and willingness to lend, both short- and long-term.

COLONIALISM AND IMPERIALISM IN AFRICA

The geographic and demographic context

The closing years of the nineteenth century and the beginning of the twentieth saw an aggressively colonial policy being conducted by the European powers, though they were not alone in this. Indeed, Japan, once Western technology had taken root there, pursued a policy in Asia that differed very little from that of the European powers in Africa and, from the period of the McKinley administration (1898–1900) onwards, the United States, too, began to follow a markedly imperialist policy whereby – within the space of a few years – such countries as the Philippines and Puerto Rico were to come under her dominion.

It is normally the case for a difference to be made between *imperialism* and *colonialism*. In conducting an imperial policy, a country seeks economic and political expansion at the cost of other countries, thereby attempting to place them in a relationship of economic and political dependence; such expansion may be by means of indirect control or outright annexation. Colonialism can be defined as a specific form of imperialism, whereby the colonizing country exerts an extreme form of political control over the colonized territories, as well as assuming their government, although it is a fact that colonies did indeed retain a specific status *vis-à-vis* their mother country.

In no other continent was there such a spectacular expression of European colonialism and imperialism during the nineteenth century as in Africa: around 1800, the European presence was still rather peripheral and marginal, but, by 1910, a few West European powers had virtually completely divided up the continent among themselves and placed it under colonial government.

Africa is an immense continent with a pronounced regional and geographical diversity, and an appreciation of this diversity is important if historical developments are to be correctly interpreted. Six more or less clearly delineated regions can be determined, each with its own individual and historical characteristics. The first is North Africa, which is situated between the Mediterranean Sea and the Sahara desert, and has a relatively mild climate. Below the Sahara, in the west and centre, is an extensive stretch of savannah, also known as the Western Sudan, which, together with the Atlantic coastal areas (Upper and Lower Guinea), forms West Africa. To the east, the savannah merges into the fertile Ethiopian Highlands and still further towards the Red Sea into the arid Somali Plain. To the south of this extensive savannah, the African continent becomes the enormously extended plateau of Central Africa. The western part is occupied by the Zairian rain forest that, more to the south, merges into savannah. East Africa, stretching from Somalia to Mozambique, is generally drier and less fertile, although the Kenyan Highlands and the inter-lacustrine area (around present-day Uganda) form an exception to this. Southern Africa, lastly, is an extension of the great African plateau and consists of a fairly small and, in the eastern portion, fertile coastal strip with open and dry savannah more to the centre.

As regards population, North Africa is inhabited by a predominantly arabized population with the physical features of the Southern European and Arabic peoples. The inhabitants of the Ethiopian Highlands, too, probably stem from this population group.

Two groups of the Negroid type dominated Africa south of the Sahara. The first is that of the Bantu-speaking people, predominantly sedentary farmers who, over many centuries, had migrated from West Africa southwards and had colonized a substantial portion of Central and Southern Africa. The second group, the Nilotes – by and large nomadic cattle-herders – originally inhabited the area around the Upper Nile valley and had migrated towards the eastern part of Africa. This breakdown is, of course, too schematic, as there were major exceptions in both areas of Sub-Saharan Africa: the Fulani, for example, who were an important ethnic grouping in West Africa, with a long tradition in extensive cattle-herding. Among the numerous other, but smaller, ethnic groups can also be mentioned the Berbers in the Maghrib in North Africa, as well as the San and the Khoi that still inhabit parts of Southern Africa. Yet other small groups, lastly, are constituted by the descendants of the European and Indian colonists whose settlement of South Africa dates only from the seventeenth century.

Partly as a result of geographical circumstances, such as the absence of bays and inland seas and the presence of an extensive desert between the Mediterranean North and the tropical South, Sub-Saharan Africa remained a relatively isolated part of the continent up to the end of the nineteenth century.

However, this does not mean that there were no cultural or trade contacts before 1800. During the seventh century, most of North Africa was converted to the Muslim religion, albeit that in Egypt a sizable Christian minority (the Copts) has survived to the present day. Furthermore, Islam very quickly came to exercise substantial sway in the Sudanic Belt via the Nile and the caravan routes through the Sahara, although the natural religions predominated until the end of the eighteenth century. Islam also penetrated into East Africa via the Arab traders in the coastal towns and gradually into the interior too.

The European presence was still very modest in 1800. With the exception of South Africa, it was confined south of the Sahara to a number of forts along the coast. Although inter-cultural contacts were limited before the nineteenth century, certain exchanges were to have major long-term consequences. The Portuguese, for example, introduced a number of new food crops, including manioc, maize and groundnuts, which later were to become the most important staple food in large areas of Africa. The influence of such new, cultivated crops came only slowly to be felt, and even by the end of the nineteenth century their spread into the interior was not wholly completed. The greatest indirect influence had by the Europeans on the continent was via the Atlantic slave trade. Slave trading with the Arab nations had indeed always existed, but – except during the nineteenth century – was quantitatively much less extensive than the trade on the continent's west coast.

The very limited degree to which the Europeans penetrated the African continent prior to the end of the nineteenth century can be ascribed to their enhanced vulnerability to African tropical diseases, more than to the specific geographical circumstances. This resulted in the influence of the maritime revolution on Africa being very limited, contrary to the situation in such other continents as America and, to a less extent, Asia. Fatal diseases were primarily yellow fever and *falciparum malaria*. Malaria, for example, was hyperendemic in the greater part of tropical Africa: the disease was transmitted by mosquitoes, which were found not only in the rain forests and swamps, but also in the open savannah. In the new environment of disease, newly arrived Europeans died at a frightening rate. Until the mid-nineteenth century, the annual mortality rate was between 250 and 750 per thousand, meaning that on average half died within a year of their arrival. Studies of mortality in the British armed forces between 1818 and 1836, for example, indicate that the mortality rate was 13 per thousand for England and Gibraltar, 10 at the Cape of Good Hope, between 75 and 85 for India or the West Indies, but no less than 480 per thousand for Sierra Leone!

The Europeans' exceptional vulnerability to sickness applied specifically to tropical Africa and not to Northern or Southern Africa. The environment of disease in Northern Africa was the same as that on the other side of the Mediterranean Sea and the mortality rate for Southern Africa, too, was comparable to that for Europe. These levels show clearly why the European colonization of Sub-Saharan Africa was so tardy: the risk of dying was much greater in the tropics and, within the tropical world, Africa was by far the most dangerous environment for Europeans to live in. It is thus evident why European colonialism and imperialism were concentrated principally upon Northern and Southern Africa until deep into the nineteenth century: mortality, and consequently the cost of military and commercial expeditions in terms of human lives, was much lower there than in the rest of the continent.

The international context and the internal political development of Africa during the nineteenth century

A number of changes that the African continent underwent between 1800 and 1880 were brought about by exogenous circumstances, the major external factor being the increasing opposition in Europe to the slave trade, expressed in abolitionism. In numerous African regions, a period of transition began whereby the centuries-old slave trade was abolished to give way to new trade flows. An immediate consequence of the abolition was the creation of two new African states: Sierra Leone and Liberia. More generally, this transition served to reinforce the European presence and, furthermore, to put the social structure in various African kingdoms under serious pressure. European technological innovations were introduced into the continent unevenly as regards time and location, resulting in the local balance of power in certain regions being upset and providing the opportunity for the rise of the so-called 'secondary empires'.

The point has to be made that in Africa – the international context and external factors aside – there was also a strong internal political dynamism during the nineteenth century. The major internal forces were the revival of Islam in West Africa, resulting in a number of religious wars (the *jihads*),

and the rise of the Zulu nation, which in Southern Africa set in motion a number of extensive migrationary movements (the *Mfecane*).

The abolition of the slave trade and the foundation of Sierra Leone and Liberia

The spread of the ideas of the Enlightenment and of new economic theories that advanced the notion that free trade and free labour were more efficient than protectionism gradually brought into being an anti-slavery movement during the second half of the eighteenth century.

Britain took the lead in this movement and through diplomacy and military action, attempted to place a curb on the Atlantic slave trade. Although other nations also declared the slave trade illegal and France and the USA, too, sent out a few small squadrons, only Britain was effectively prepared to fund a fleet of any size in Africa on a permanent basis, dispatching a permanent detachment of the Royal Navy (the West African or Preventive Squadron) to the west coast, with its base in Sierra Leone. However, the West Africa Squadron comprised only a few ships and this policing, intervention force posted only partial successes in halting slave-trading. Nevertheless, certain researchers estimate that up to a quarter of slave ships were intercepted. Other studies state that about 160,000 slaves were freed on the high seas, approximately 8 per cent of the total shipped from Africa between 1810 and 1870. The coast of more than 3,000 kilometres north of the equator was much too long for these few ships to monitor, and the slave traders also reacted by building newer and faster ships. Moreover, captured traders could be brought to justice only in one place in Africa, Sierra Leone. The relatively modest results achieved by the introduction of military means prompted the British authorities to negotiate slave treaties with a number of West African chiefs of the interior, pursuant to which the local chiefs would abolish the slave trade and encourage trade in local products; however, success was again limited and there would be an end to the Atlantic slave trade only after the American Civil War and after such Latin American countries as Brazil and Cuba had promulgated their own anti-slavery laws after 1850.

As mentioned above, the fight against slavery was to lead to the foundation of two new countries, Sierra Leone and Liberia. The creation of the first nation was an indirect result of a decision of the English judge, Mansfield, who in 1772 pronounced that slavery was not permitted on British territory. At that time, there were about 14,000 black slaves in Britain (often domestic servants of planters who had retired from the West Indies) and many on being freed had difficulty in sorting out a reasonable existence for themselves. Their interests were defended by a number of abolitionists who in 1786 set up a Committee for Relieving the Black Poor. The committee came up with the idea of allowing these blacks to return to Africa, the first of whom, with the help of the British government, settled in Sierra Leone in 1787. Other groups followed later, among them 1,200 ex-slaves (the so-called Nova Scotians) who had fought on the side of the British during the American War of Independence and had afterwards lived in Canada for a number of years. For the economic government of the settlement, a company was set up, the Sierra Leone Company. However, as the community appeared to be barely economically viable and had come into conflict with the local inhabitants, it was taken over by the British government in 1808 as the first British crown colony. Due to the establishment in Freetown of the Court of Mixed Commission to try captured slave traders, the population of the crown colony expanded rapidly with freed slaves from the seized vessels.

The foundation of Liberia was also rooted in the 'problem' of freed slaves in the United States. In 1800, the number of free blacks in the USA totalled about 200,000 and was growing rapidly. A repressive policy on the part of the southern states towards this population group led to a growing fear in the northern states of a massive influx of free and runaway blacks, and laws were passed to prevent this. In order to do something about this increasing polarization, a number of American abolitionists formed the American Colonization Society, and in 1820 a first group of eighty-eight immigrants settled in Liberia ('Land of the Free'). Here, too, governing the new settlement proved not to be without its problems, but, contrary to the British govern-ment in respect of Sierra Leone, the American government held aloof, an attitude that served to accelerate Liberia's political development; in 1847, indeed, the local authorities (the colony had been governed by blacks since 1841) proclaimed Liberia a sovereign republic, adopting the constitution of the USA as basis for their own.

The commercial origins of the increasing European presence in Sub-Saharan Africa

The substitution of slave trading by trade in new export products from West Africa during the nineteenth century was an initial reason for the increasing European presence in Sub-Saharan Africa. The switch to new products took place much more smoothly here, as from time immemorial this region had, besides slaves, numerous other products, such as gold, hides, timber, gum, palm oil and beeswax, and exported a few industrial products, such as beads and cotton materials.

There was a marked increase in trade in Central Africa, too. Where previously traders from the coast penetrated only into the immediate interior, the entire continent was traversed during the course of the nineteenth century. Commerce was at first in the hands of Africans, but Arab traders gradually entered the field, followed later by Europeans. Three large commercial networks existed, the Atlantic Network on the west coast, the Mediterranean Network via the upper reaches of the Nile, and the Indian Ocean network on the east coast, which was part of a larger, worldwide commercial network. The Atlantic network was in fact a double one: the first, the great river network, coincided more or less with the Congo-Zaire basin; the second, the Luso-African network, stretched eastwards from the coast of Angola. Around 1870, the westward-expanding Atlantic and the eastward-expanding Indian Ocean networks met in what is presently Zaire, and an intracontinental network effectively came into being. When, after 1850, the export of slaves declined steeply in consequence of the anti-slavery campaigns, exports of principally ivory, as well as of tobacco, palm oil and peanuts, rose substantially. In the Angolan coastal region, the slave trade was all-dominant and the transfer to a more diversified range of export products proved to be exceptionally difficult.

In East Africa, the switch from slave-trading to trading in material goods proved to be a much slower process. Indeed, the slave trade even increased around the mid-nineteenth century, boosted by two major developments: the rise of a plantation economy in the Indian Ocean region and, paradoxically enough, the intensification of the abolitionist campaign of the British in the Atlantic area. Already in the eighteenth century, the French had introduced sugar plantations on the Mascarene Islands, including Mauritius and Reunion, while Omani Arabs from the Persian Gulf had begun the cultivation of cloves on the island of Zanzibar. Both sugar and cloves were capital-intensive crops and created a substantial demand for cheap (slave) labour. Because of the increasing repression of the slave trade in West Africa, the centre of gravity of the trade shifted to new regions where British control was less manifest: first to Portuguese-controlled areas and thereafter to East Africa. Here, too, the British were soon to take action. They concluded treaties with the Sultan of Zanzibar, which resulted in the slave market on that island being officially closed in 1873.

The transfer to trade in material goods was further encouraged by the brisk expansion in the trade of ivory, closely linked to the greater demand from Europe that sent prices soaring. Whereas previously only hard ivory from West Africa was used to manufacture knife handles, the softer ivory from East Africa could now be used for new, upcoming products, such as combs, piano keys and billiard balls.

The gradual abolition of the slave trade and the transition to legal trading practices set in train a number of funda-mental economic and political changes. The European slave traders and their African intermediaries had in time to implement a radical switchover: the new export products had much lower profit margins and new trading systems had to be developed.

For many African communities, such as those on the Senegambia or on the Oil Rivers in West Africa, among the Kamba in Kenya or the Duala in Gabon and others else-where, this switchover resulted in a loss of political stability: new social groupings formed and threatened the monopoly of power held by the earlier kings or middlemen. More-over, the reorganization of trade caused great changes in the social fabric throughout Africa. Old aristocracies made way for new elites, whereby no longer did solely inherited status play an important part, but also, and increasingly, did wealth.

It quickly became clear to several observers that the slave trade could only be efficiently combated if an (economic) alternative could be put in place. Certain Europeans, such as James McQueen (1778–1870) in his book *A Geographical and Commercial View of Northern and Central Africa* (1821) and Thomas Fowell Buxton (1786–1845) with his publica-tion *The African Trade and Its Remedy* (1839), therefore proposed that the presence of European traders and agri-cultural scientists be encouraged; these people could sti-mulate and guide the switch to legal forms of trade that abolitionism had now made pressing.

Until the beginning of the nineteenth century, the European presence in Africa was limited to a number of thinly populated and scattered settlements along the coast, most of which were, besides, populated more with Afro-Europeans than with actual whites. From the outset of the nineteenth century, a more active development policy was conducted from the French and English posts. Already in the 1820s, the French attempted to start up plantations in Senegal and to employ steamboats to drum up trade with more inland areas. This first project failed, however, as a result of the high mortality among the white administrators, lack of capital and the scarcity of African workers, who were not prepared to work at the wages offered. In the 1840s, the British, too, undertook similar efforts to man more inland trading posts and to employ steamboats on the rivers, but they were also forced to suspend their operations by the high mortality among whites. During the period prior to 1880, France and England organized a number of explorations to more inland areas, the purpose of which was rather to bring a limited coastal area under direct control or to gain informal control of kingdoms situated further in the interior. In addition, the attempt was made to persuade local rulers to lay out plantations to produce products for the European market, and to give European traders a degree of protection. In this way, the French came to focus their attention chiefly on Senegal where, during the administration of the energetic governor, Louis Faidherbe (1818–89), the basis was laid between 1854 and 1865 for subsequent French penetration into West Africa; The British expended a great deal of energy in the exploration of the Niger delta (the Oil Rivers), where, in implementation of the plans proposed by McQueen and Buxton, a permanent steamboat service was established on the Niger in 1857. During the years thereafter, a number of trading posts were set up along this line.

Another side effect of the burgeoning of new trade products and the attendant interest in exploration of the interior was that the intermediate position of the traditional African traders was frequently put under threat, so that conflict situations quickly arose with the European trading companies; for certain European nations, this provided a further excuse to intervene actively on the ground and to extend their sphere of influence further into the interior.

The rise of new local empires

The rise of a number of new local empires (sometimes also called secondary empires) concerns the expansion of a number of African states that was based on the use of new, generally European (military) technology, but without direct European political control. It is clear that those African states whose contacts with Europeans gave them access to a new generation of military equipment before anyone else, possessed an important comparative advantage over neighbouring states. In regions that had frequent contact with Europeans, the supply of the latest military technology was fairly regular and the technology rapidly acquired, so that the initial lead enjoyed by a particular nation was quickly cancelled out and the balance of power restored. In the more remote areas of the African continent, however, the advantage for anyone who possessed modern military technology was more marked and the initial edge could also be maintained much longer. For example, the Viceroy of Egypt, Mohammed Ali (1769–1849), was able in 1820 to conquer the Nilotic Sudan (the present-day Sudan) with a relatively small force – barely 4,000 men – but one that was equipped with modern arms, and to hold the country under Egyptian-Turkish government until 1884. A further example is provided by the European colonists in South Africa. A few thousand well armed Boers moved into the South African interior (the Great Trek), where they were able to exploit to the full the difference in military technology with the much more numerous local Africans. Other instances of the building of secondary empires were

the Kingdom of Samori Touré in West Africa (the late 1860s to 1898) and the expansion of a centralized empire in the Ethiopian Highlands during the second half of the nineteenth century. Politically, these nations were often very unstable; the origin of their successful expansion lay rather in the exploitation of a temporary ascendancy as regards military technology, an ascendancy that disappeared as soon as the annexed peoples were able to acquire similar means to restore the balance of power.

The increasing European presence, 1800–80

As regards European colonialism and imperialism, the history of Africa during the nineteenth century can be divided into two periods. Between 1800 and about 1880, European influence gradually expanded, although it was only in the north and south – outside the actual tropics – that there was a question of actual colonization. Elsewhere, the European presence remained still marginal, albeit that the number of Europeans grew and the European settlements at the periphery of the continent became more numerous and extensive. Furthermore, this was the period of the great journeys of exploration, whereby the African interior was mapped. Between 1880 and 1910, a much more aggressive policy was pursued; during these three decades, the entire continent, with a single exception, was overrun and carved up among the colonial powers.

European imperialism in North Africa prior to 1880

At the dawning of the nineteenth century, North Africa was divided according to two political-administrative systems: on the one hand, the independent, but politically unstable Morocco under the Alawite dynasty; on the other, the semi-independent states of Algeria, Tunisia, Libya and Egypt, which gave only nominal recognition to the suzerainty of the Ottoman Empire. Although at the beginning of the nineteenth century these states were still de jure provinces (sultanates) of this empire, their government was de facto in the hands of a military caste of one-time slaves who had previously been recruited abroad (the Mamluks in Egypt, for instance).

Because of its geographical location and relatively mild climate, North Africa's contacts with Europe have always been much more intensive than with the rest of Africa; indeed, up to and including the early decades of the nineteenth century, the North African states still regarded themselves as the equals of the European nations, as shown by, among other things, the maintenance of mutual diplomatic missions. They also reserved the right to levy taxes on Mediterranean shipping in their sphere of influence. However, such levies were regarded as piracy by the Western powers and as a curb on nascent world trade, an argument that would soon be invoked to justify intervention.

The gradual decline of the Ottoman Empire and its satellite states as military powers in the course of the nineteenth century and the incapacity of local rulers to recreate the European model of nation-forming and of administrative and technological development, are undoubtedly the major general factors in explanation of the success of European colonization focused on North Africa. In their efforts to maintain their sovereignty, certain of the North African rulers attempted to accelerate modernization of their country. Ironically enough, these efforts were to increase the European presence and in time European influence, too. As soon as the internal political and administrative stability of any of the North African countries started to weaken or financial dependence in respect of the external world to grow, the political influence of that external world began to expand. It is manifestly clear that the above-sketched pattern of colonization and imperialism varied from country to country, depending on specific historical and local circumstances; how varied the process of colonization really was is evident from the following concise survey of the different North African countries.

At the end of the eighteenth century, Egypt was temporarily occupied by French troops under Napoleon (Battle of the Pyramids, 1798). However, occupation by the French proved to be no more than a brief interlude, and in the decades after their departure in 1801 the country once again came under the sway of the caste of Ottoman military rulers. One of them, Mohammed Ali (1769–1849), in 1806 set Egypt on the road to modernization. He built up what was for the first time a standing army and a modern navy, and took energetic steps to improve agriculture by introducing the cultivation of cotton and by applying irrigation on a large scale. Furthermore, he sent many young Egyptians abroad, chiefly to France, with the intention of giving them a thorough grounding in Western science and technology. However, Ali did not achieve success across the board: for example, the emphasis on cotton-growing was to make Egyptian agriculture too dependent on a single cash crop (monoculture); moreover, agriculture was dependent upon price fluctuations abroad over which it had no control. Nor did Ali's efforts to build up a sound industrial structure (factories for arms, sugar and textile production) really get off the ground. All in all, however, the reforms set in train by Ali were not insubstantial: for example, de facto independence was achieved from the Ottoman Empire, and Egypt became an important producer of cotton and could boast a well trained army and a reasonably well instructed civil service. Additionally, the reforms were carried through without any real financial commitments being contracted in respect of the European great powers.

On his death in 1849, Mohammed Ali was succeeded by Abbas I (1813–54), who in turn was succeeded in 1853 by Muhammad Said (1822–63), under whose rule a start was made on the construction of the Suez Canal to link the Mediterranean with the Red Sea, a project headed by the French engineer Ferdinand de Lesseps (1805–94), and one in which Egypt participated under rather unfavourable conditions. During the rule of Said, Egypt gradually began to borrow money from foreign bankers and after his death in 1863 his successor, Ismail Pasha (1830–95), was to expand the system of foreign loans considerably in a renewed attempt to modernize the country. Under Ismail, the country's independence from the Ottoman Empire was reinforced. Furthermore, nearly 1,500 kilometres of railway and 8,000 kilometres of telegraph line were laid, and 450 bridges, 4,500 primary schools and a modern port in Alexandria were built, the number of Europeans employed in these projects increasing substantially from about 10,000 during the 1830s to approximately 100,000 in 1875. However, a great deal of money was spent on purely prestige projects, such as the extravagantly expensive opening ceremony for the Suez Canal in 1869 (£1M sterling) or the financing of two totally abortive military

expeditions to Ethiopia (1875 and 1876) in the idle hope of creating a great Egyptian empire in Africa.

By the end of the 1870s, Egypt's foreign debt had grown to £100M, as against 'only' £13M at the time of Said's death in 1863. Egypt was now not even in a position to guarantee the payment of interest on her loans. Britain, although not having participated in the Suez Canal project, profited from the situation by buying Egypt's shares in the canal for an exceptionally low price (only £4M). This purchase, made under the English prime minister of the time, Benjamin Disraeli (1804–81), was prompted by a conscious policy of controlling the transport routes to India. The persistent worsening of the situation in Egypt led in 1878 to Britain and France stepping in and forcing the Egyptian authorities to accept joint Anglo-French control of their finances. In reality, this meant that the Egyptian nation once again had to relinquish a substantial portion of its sovereignty to a foreign power, a development that led to full subjugation by Britain in 1882, with Egypt remaining virtually part of the British Empire until 1922.

The above process of how Egypt had to yield the autonomy she had only recently acquired to the European powers can also be discerned in other North African countries. Initially, the rulers of these countries struggled gradually to loosen the ties with Ottoman authority. Thereafter followed attempts to modernize the country using Western capital and Western advisers. Many of these attempts came to nothing, but resulted in an inexorable increase in European control, first in financial matters and subsequently – when problems of repayment arose – in the political and administrative affairs of the country.

In Tunisia, the financial situation under the rule of Mohammed es Sadek (1812–82), the Bey, was becoming ever more parlous around the middle of the nineteenth century, and in 1869 an international commission was set up to put the situation to rights. In return for the extinction of debt, Mohammed es Sadek was forced to grant major economic concessions to European companies. During the years thereafter, the Bey attempted to curb French influence by opening up relations with Italy, hoping thereby that the rivalry between the two countries would stave off imminent colonization; in vain, because France reacted to his approach to Italy by placing Tunisia under military occupation in 1882 (the Treaty of Bardo) and by officially annexing the country in 1883 (the Treaty of Marza) as a protectorate.

In Libya, Ottoman dominion remained intact until 1911, the year of the Italian invasion, although European influence in the form of loans and concessions had already increased sharply before then.

The conquering of Algeria by the French was a special case. During the preceding centuries, intense commercial relations had existed between the two countries, whereby Algeria exported considerable quantities of grain and olive oil to France. However, the early nineteenth century saw tensions beginning to arise in connection with, among other things, the repayment of loans (Algeria was a creditor of France); prompted by a bizarre incident (the 'fly-whisk incident' in which the French consul, Deval, claimed that he had been struck with a fly-whisk by the Bey in a heated discussion), the French blockaded Algiers in 1827, capturing it in 1830. As motivation for the invasion, the French stated that their intention was to suppress piracy, but it was generally accepted that the underlying reason was an attempt by Charles X (1757–1836), the French king, to enhance the prestige of his regime by military action and, linked to this, to establish a colony in the traditional sense of the word.

The capture of Algiers was the signal for the full conquest of Algeria, though it was to be another forty years before this was completed. The military campaign was a difficult, lengthy and expensive undertaking. During the first years of the war, the major opponent of the French was Abdel Kader (1808–83), a Berber Muslim, who succeeded in unifying the various Berber fractions in a *jihad* against the 'unbelievers'. Abdel Kader was a man of remarkable organizational qualities and military capabilities; he led a successful guerrilla war against the French troops and, partly by employing the scorched earth tactic, built up a strong resistance movement against them during the early years. In consequence of this, the French commanders – General Desmichels (1779–1845) in 1834 (the Desmichels Treaty) and General Bugeaud (1784–1849) in 1836 (the Treaty of Tafna) concluded treaties in which an effective *status quo* was accepted and whereby it was agreed that the French presence in Algeria would remain limited and the *de facto* independence of the region under the control of Abdel Kader be recognized. In reality, the French had no intention of accepting a definitive agreement; the war was resumed in 1839 and gradually the French regained the military initiative. In 1847, Abdel Kader was forced to surrender, though it was to be the early 1860s before the French finally occupied the entire region. A decade later in 1871 and for the last time in the nineteenth century, rebellion broke out among the Berbers in the Kabylie, a mountainous region in the east of the country, a revolt that was only put down with great difficulty.

In this sense, the conquest of Algeria was a special phenomenon, as nowhere else in Africa had an important area been occupied so early and with the use of such military might. A unique feature was also the enormous scale of the attendant influx of Europeans: in 1839, there were still only 25,000 *colons*; barely thirty years later, in 1871, they numbered 245,000, 130,000 of whom were French. This influx had far-reaching consequences for the Berbers, who were systematically driven from the best land and to such an extent that approximately four fifths of the fertile land in the regions of the Tell and the High Plateaus fell into the hands of colonists.

As a result of the intrusion of the French into Algeria, Morocco, too, was confronted with European colonialism and imperialism. Just as Egypt and Tunisia, she formed a special case, being an arena where the interests of various European nations came into conflict with each other. For Britain, it was control over the entrance to the Mediterranean Sea and protection of the route to India. For France, Moroccan sovereignty was a thorn in the side, because of the support given by Morocco to the Algerian resistance. Spain, for her part, had commercial interests in Morocco going back centuries. The rivalry among the various European powers reinforced the position of the Sultans, who were able to sustain the independence of their country until the beginning of the twentieth century by playing off one against the other. Indeed, it was only when the European powers came to give each other a free hand in specific territories through the means of treaties and agreements that effective conquest by a European power became possible, though this is not to deny that there was already substantial European interference in Morocco throughout the nineteenth century. In 1828, the British blockaded Tangiers, and other Moroccan ports and towns were bombarded by the Austrians and the French in 1829 and 1851 respectively, partly in retaliation for the seizure of merchant shipping by Morocco; war broke out between France and Morocco in 1844. War with Spain followed in 1851, with Tetuan being captured and a further march into the interior only being prevented by British intervention. In 1860, an agreement especially advantageous to Spain was concluded, whereby an extensive stretch of land around Melilla was ceded by Morocco and numerous trading privileges granted. This situation was very quickly to provoke comparable demands on the part of the French and British. In order to curb the interference of the European powers, the Sultans attempted to modernize their country, but, as in the case of most other North African nations, this served only to draw them gradually into debt and thereby increase their vulnerability.

European imperialism and colonialism in South Africa: the Great Trek of the Boers

Outside North Africa, it was only in the southern part of the continent that there was to be a considerable increase in the European presence during the period prior to 1880. At the beginning of the nineteenth century, the migration of the Bantu-speaking peoples had not yet ended and some groups such as the Xhosa were beginning to settle in the south east of the present state of South Africa between the Fish and Sunday rivers.

The Dutch East India Company had a settlement on the Cape of Good Hope in the south west since 1652, a supply station for ships of the company en route to the Dutch possessions and trading locations in the Far East. Towards the end of the seventeenth century, there was a rapid increase in the white population, partly as a result of the immigration of French Protestants, who at that time constituted about one third of the local European population. As their numbers grew, the European colonists began to swarm out. They practised chiefly an extensive form of cattle-farming, which led to a rapid increase in the area colonized, as the average cattle-farmer at that time required a good ten square kilometres for his farm to be viable. The relative isolation of the white colonists, who were far fewer in number than the other African peoples, intensified their sense of community and was gradually to lead to a feeling of racial superiority towards the black population, an attitude reinforced by the fact that manual work was performed principally by black slaves or Khoi servants. Another factor that played a role in this was the Calvinist religion with its strong emphasis on predestination, whereby the white farmers regarded the difference between races, as well as their own privileged position, as the will of God. From the intermingling of the white population with the Khoi and the San there arose a separate group of people, the Cape Coloured, and from the contacts between the Dutch-speaking Boers and their personnel developed Afrikaans (a local idiom, based on Dutch with influences of African languages and some English), which became the spoken language of the majority of the white population.

In the course of the eighteenth century, the white colonists pushed further into the south east where they came into contact with the Xhosa. Claims over land and cattle rapidly led to bitter rivalry between the two population groups, culminating in 1779 and 1793 in war between them (the First and Second Xhosa Wars of Resistance, otherwise known as the Kaffir Wars). During the war of 1793, the Boers established in the frontier region temporarily rejected the authority of the Dutch East India Company, until in 1795 the entire Cape region was conquered by the British. At the same time, the number of Boers in the eastern frontier region continued to grow, and the resulting tension between land area and population further intensified the competition over land and cattle with the Xhosa until war broke out again in 1799. War between the Xhosa and the colonists on the eastern frontier remained endemic and flared up anew in 1812, 1818–19, 1834–5, 1846, 1850–3 and lastly in 1877–8, when the Xhosa were finally defeated.

The Cape region remained under British control for the rest of the nineteenth century. Influenced by missionaries and the ideas of the Enlightenment, the British took a much more positive attitude towards the rights of the black population than the Dutch during the preceding period. In this respect, a number of laws were adopted, including the 50th Ordinance (1828), which previewed full equality between free Africans and whites, but this progressive stance on the part of the British was treated with great suspicion by the ultra-conservative Boers. In 1833, slavery was abolished throughout the British Empire and, after a short transitional period that ended in 1838, the freed slaves came under the regulation of the 50th Ordinance. These measures served to build up the frustration of the Boers to such an extent that the decision was taken to emigrate to new regions where British authority did not run or could no longer be enforced.

In 1836, thus, began a great movement of emigration, better known as the Great Trek, which was larger in extent than anything that had taken place during the previous waves of colonization; furthermore, the intention was to establish an independent state where the British policy of equality between the races would not obtain. The Great Trek was northwards, because Xhosa resistance was too strong in the east.

Between 1835 and 1841, about 6,000 Boers crossed the Orange River into the plains of what was to become the Orange Free State, and thereafter across the Vaal River into what was later Transvaal. Subsequently, a number of them headed towards the coast and, after having defeated the Zulus at the Battle of Blood River (1838), penetrated further eastwards into Natal. The march of the Boers with their ox-wagons and their camps or *laagers* (defensive circles of wagons) in time became romanticized, gaining mythical proportions. This migration was indeed a remarkable feat, given the means available at the time and the fact that it was undertaken in a little known and hostile environment, but the drive of the white Boers into new territories was coupled with the occupation of the land of the black people already established there. Until deep into the nineteenth century, this situation was the cause of a persistent struggle between Boer and African, which substantially destabilized the region (cf. the Battle of Vegkop, 1836, whereby the Boers were forced to withdraw temporarily). Generally, the struggle was decided in favour of the better armed and more mobile Boers, albeit that the last independent African peoples continued to resist until the end of the nineteenth century: it was not until 1879 and 1898 respectively that the Pedi in the east and the Venda in the north of Transvaal were defeated. In this new frontier region during the ensuing decades, the Boers organized a number of

small Boer republics that had only a limited affinity with each other.

The Great Trek posed a difficult dilemma for the British authorities in the Cape Colony. Where previously contacts between white colonists and the black population had been restricted to the eastern frontier, the new wave of migration provided the cause for conflict about the possession of land throughout the entire territory of South Africa. For the British, the Cape Colony was important chiefly because of its strategic position. Was it also their duty to establish their authority over the areas captured by the Boers and thus to protect and guarantee the rights of the local population? Or was it sufficient to maintain British jurisdiction over the Cape Colony and to abandon to the migrating Boers sovereignty over an interior that was often not particularly fertile and offered little economic return? In other words, was it worth the trouble to wage often costly and uncertain war to bring regions under British jurisdiction without immediate advantages for the mother country?

The occupation of Natal and the Boers' conflicts with the local population led to British reaction as early as 1841 and, after the dispatch of a small military force, the region was formally annexed to the Cape. Thereupon, the majority of Boers decided to quit Natal, again making the trek over the Drakensberg to the modern Orange Free State and Transvaal, where a number of the original participants in the Great Trek were already settled. In Natal, the place of the departing Boers was taken by British colonists, who developed a pronouncedly commercial form of agriculture there. Fairly quickly, the British planters were confronted by a problem of finding cheap labour. Shortly after the middle of the nineteenth century, a solution was sought in attracting cheap Indian labour to work the sugar plantations, and in this was the beginning of the African Indian community in South Africa. In 1847, following the War of the Axe (1846), the region between the Fish and Kei rivers, the earlier eastern frontier region, was incorporated into the Cape Colony under the name of British Kaffraria. The same happened to the Boer country between the Orange and the Vaal Rivers that, under the name of the Orange River Sovereignty, was temporarily annexed to the Cape Colony. However, war broke out in 1851 between the Boers and the Basuto led by their energetic king, Moshesh. When it appeared that the Boers and their British administrators were gaining little success by the war, renewed opposition arose among the British to a too active (and expensive) policy of intervention in Boer-controlled areas. In 1852 and 1854 respectively were signed the Sand River Convention and the Bloemfontein Convention, whereby the British undertook not to intervene north of the Vaal and the Orange Rivers, thereby implicitly accepting the independence of the Boer republics of Transvaal and Orange Free State.

In 1856, a constitution was drawn up in the Transvaal and the various groups of white colonists there were brought together under the name of the South African Republic, but efforts to achieve political unity with the Orange Free State failed. In this latter, the latent conflict between Basuto and Boer over the possession of land and cattle led to two new wars (the First and Second Orange Free State–Lesotho Wars, 1858 and 1865). The second went against the Basuto and, in order to maintain a degree of independence as regards the Boers, the now very aged king Moshesh pressed for British protection. In 1865, Basutoland (the present Lesotho) was annexed on the insistence of the

British governor, Woodhouse, and placed under British colonial rule, a rule that was temporarily assumed by the Cape Colony in 1871.

The annexation of Basutoland represented a further reversal of the British policy of detachment that had been set out ten years earlier with the Sand River and Bloemfontein Conventions.

From the 1860s onwards, economic motives, as well as political motives, came increasingly to play a major part in the renewed interventionist policy of the British in respect of the independent Boer republics. Indeed, the discovery of diamond fields around Kimberley in 1858 opened up new prospects for the exploitation of the interior. Previously, the South African interior had offered a few opportunities for barely profitable, extensive farming, but it became clearer during the 1860s that an enormous potential for mining existed. Although both Boer republics laid claim to the diamond fields, the region was brought under Cape Colony administration in 1871. The rising economic importance of South Africa (railway building, development of export-oriented agriculture) found its political embodiment in the efforts of the British Colonial Secretary, Lord Carnarvon (1831–90), to bring the various territories in South Africa together in a confederation. When in 1870 the Transvaal Republic was struggling with serious financial problems, he took advantage of its weak position to establish temporary British authority in 1877.

Overall, however, the renewed British policy of uniting the white states and of subjugating the remaining independent African states met with little success. Sir Bartle Frere (1815–84), sent by Carnarvon as High Commissioner to South Africa to set up the confederation, attempted in 1879 to annex the Zulu kingdom under Cetewayo, but met with heavy resistance. Although the British eventually gained the upper hand (after the Battle of Ulundi) and Cetewayo was taken prisoner, they were not to proceed to annex the Zulu kingdom, but to limit themselves to administrative reform. Elsewhere, too, the efforts to form a confederation made very difficult headway. When, in 1880, the Basuto rose up against the Cape Colony government because of a law forbidding Africans to carry guns (War of the Guns, 1880) and the Cape troops became stalemated, an agreement was concluded whereby Basutoland was made a British crown colony (1884). In the Transvaal itself, the Boers continued to harbour a pronounced resentment against the British administration, a resentment that was intensified by the levying of new taxes and the refusal to permit them to set up a representative council for self-government. In 1880–1, the Boers rose up in revolt (the First Anglo-Boer War) and defeated the British troops (at, among others, the Battle of Majuba, 1881). Gladstone, who had just become British prime minister, sought and found a compromise solution, whereby (in the Pretoria Convention, 1881) Transvaal was granted self-government, but the foreign affairs of the republic would remain under British tutelage. For the moment, the British policy of forming a confederation was derailed, and it was to be more than two decades before the British position in South Africa could be consolidated.

The great journeys of exploration and European penetration in the rest of Africa

Another important development of the years to 1880 was the mapping of the African interior. In part, this geographical unlocking of the African continent had to do with the rise of Romanticism; in part, it was purely scientific (to do primarily with geography, ethnography, anthropology, botany and zoology). Other motives also played a role: missionary fervour, ambition, adventure, the search for precious metals or simply prospecting for interesting trading opportunities.

The European explorers were confronted with great risks. In the first place was the vulnerability, mentioned above, of white travellers to tropical diseases, which led to numerous expeditions ending with the death of the white participants. A further problem was the sometimes hostile attitude of the local population and more particularly of local traders who feared that their intermediary role in the trade with the coast would be threatened; this hostility resulted in a number of explorers meeting a violent end. Moreover, the circumstances of travel were not seldom such as to make extreme demands on the physical powers of resistance of travellers. Because sleeping sickness (*trypano-somiasis*) was prevalent among animals in many regions along the equator, it was often impossible to use beasts of burden, so that very long distances had regularly to be covered by foot. Added to this was the fact that recourse was usually had to a large number of bearers, which sent the cost of such expeditions rocketing. It is therefore no coincidence that most explorers routed their expeditions along river systems where possible; indeed, the various river networks were the only available infrastructure whereby the interior could be opened up for (European) trade, without too great an investment. The great enigma was the course and the source of the mighty African rivers, and the challenge their discovery. In numerous instances, the European explorers received no little help in their journeys from the local knowledge of the African and Arab traders already active in the areas concerned before the advent of the Europeans.

The West African interior was the first Sub-Saharan region to be explored by Europeans from the late eighteenth century onwards. It was already known from various sources that a mighty river, the Niger, existed in Western Sudan, but one of the key questions concerned its course. Among other things to solve this enigma, the African Association (Association for Promoting the Discovery of the Interior Parts of Africa) was founded in 1788 on the initiative of Sir Joseph Banks (1743–1820) and certain other individuals, and between then and 1805 organized six expeditions. Thereafter, the Association was to be sponsored by the British government, whereby England became the leading nation as regards exploration of the African continent, certainly until the mid-nineteenth century. Two routes offered themselves for expeditions seeking to discover the course of the Niger: the first was to the north via the Mediterranean Sea, more particularly via Tripoli, where the Sahara belt was the narrowest; the second, more southerly approach was from the south western coastal areas (Upper and Lower Guinea), that ran partly through the tropical rain forest.

The first European who showed that the Niger actually existed was the Scot, Mungo Park (1771–1805), who, commissioned by the Association, reached the town of Segou (in present-day Mali) in 1795 via the westerly route. To his amazement, he noted that the river on whose banks the town stood indeed flowed to the eastward. A second journey to the interior that he organized for the British government in 1805 ended in tragedy: of the thirty-eight members of the expedition, only five, among them Park, reached Segou alive. In the descent of the Niger by boat, they were all to perish in the rapids at the town of Bussa.

When the story of this journey gained wider circulation, it gave rise to the wildest speculations about the line of this watercourse: some confused the Niger with the Senegal or the Congo river; according to others, it flowed into an inland sea in the desert or even into the Mediterranean; still others claimed that it was a tributary of the Nile!

The other expeditions sent out by the Association failed, too: some explorers died during the expedition; others, such as Major Daniel Houghton (1791–c.1840), disappeared without trace. The expeditions organized directly by the British government also exacted a high toll in human lives: not one of the leaders of the three expeditions dispatched via the southerly route between 1805 and 1816 survived the journey. Various other attempts followed, but it was only in 1830 that, under instructions from the British government, the brothers, John (1807–39) and Richard Lander (1804–34), succeeded in establishing the entire course of the Niger from Bussa to the estuary of the river in the Atlantic Ocean.

An important motive for many Europeans to explore the West African interior, besides the mapping of the course of the Niger, was to discover the mysterious town of Timbuktu, known only through tales. In 1827, the young Frenchman, René Caillé (1799–1838), gained his objective in penetrating to the interior via the coast of present-day Guinea to reach the town. It proved a disappointment to him: it had flourished in the sixteenth century, but little of its earlier prosperity now remained. He finally succeeded in travelling through the Sahara with a caravan and then via Morocco back to France, where he received a hero's welcome, an indication of the great interest that existed at that time for such explorations.

A remarkable figure in the opening-up of this region to the Europeans was the German, Heinrich Barth (1821–65), who, sent out by the British government, spent five years in central and western Sudan, returning to England in 1855 via Tripoli. He was an extremely erudite man and at the same time a geographer, historian, linguist and anthropologist, whose account of his travels in *Travels and Discoveries in North and Central Africa* (1857) is among the most important and best documented descriptions of West Africa and currently still one of the most important sources about West African society at that time.

Nevertheless, it was finally to be the south western (Atlantic) and not the northerly (trans-Saharan) route that became the major line of advance in opening up West Africa. A substantial part in this development was played by a government expedition led by Dr William Balfour Baikie (1825–64) that in 1854 worked its way up the Niger, demonstrating that a part of the river and its delta was suitable for shipping, which offered interesting prospects for trade between the interior and the European coastal settlements; from this point of view the trans-Saharan route was far less interesting, as the enormous problems of transport would always heavily mortgage the profitability of any commercial undertaking. Moreover, by using quinine as a prophylactic against malaria, he showed that the disastrous rate of mortality among Europeans could be halted: not one man died of disease on the whole trip.

The exploration of Eastern and Central Africa took another fifty years to get under way, possible reasons for this time-lag being the greater distance of these regions from Europe, the activities of the Arab traders in them, who did their utmost to protect their territory from outsiders, and the more modest European presence along the coast. Central to the exploration was the search for the sources of the Nile and the mapping of the Congo basin (in what is now Zaire). Although their precise location had little relevance in itself, finding the sources was a goal surrounded in mystery that fired a series of journeys of exploration that here, too, were gradually to open up the interior. The area of the great lakes had already been visited by various missionaries, among them Johannes Rebmann (1820–76) and Johann Ludwig Krapf (1818–81). Rebmann was the first European to cast eyes on Mount Kilimanjaro (1848) and, together with Kraft, he laid the basis for a first dictionary and grammar of Swahili, the *lingua franca* of East Africa. In 1856, two English explorers, Richard Francis Burton (1821–90) and John Hanning Speke (1827–64), were sent out to Africa by the English Royal Geographical Society, the effective successor to the Association, to explore the area around the great lakes that the Arabs along the coast spoke of; two years later, in 1858, they discovered Lake Tanganyika. When Burton fell ill, Speke continued on to another great inland sea that he named Lake Victoria. On a second journey to this lake in 1860, he followed its shore to the west and arrived as the first white man in the Kingdom of Buganda. Here, he came upon a river that flowed northwards out of the lake, that he intuitively felt to be the Nile. During a subsequent journey in 1863, he was to encounter this river again downstream at Gondokoro, which convinced him that he had found the upper course of the Nile. His conclusion was sharply disputed by his earlier companion, Burton, and was to lead to a polemic that only years later would be decided in favour of Speke.

A major part in the exploration of the African continent south of the great lakes was played by David Livingstone (1813–73), an English doctor and missionary. In 1849, he set out from South Africa into the interior, discovering first Lake Ngami and subsequently travelling westwards to the Atlantic Ocean, where he reached Luanda in 1854. Shortly thereafter, he journeyed straight across the continent to the Indian Ocean, which he reached in 1856. En route, he followed in part the course of the Zambezi, discovering the river's cataracts that he named the Victoria Falls. He returned to the interior in 1858, journeying via Lake Nyasa to Lake Tanganyika.

Besides opening up a major portion of the African continent in geographical terms, Livingstone was also an important advocate in the struggle against slavery, which precisely during this period was substantially on the increase in East Africa; a child of his time, he proposed that the practice of slavery could be combated by colonizing Africa, and preferable from, if not by, England.

Another noted explorer in this region was Henry Morton Stanley (1841–1904), whose attitude towards the African population during his travels was far more aggressive than Livingstone's. Contrary to the latter's usual practice of journeying with a small retinue of trusted men, Stanley's expeditions were up to seven hundred strong, of which often only a handful remained at an expedition's conclusion, and he did not hesitate to shoot his way where necessary through the region to be explored. Much of Central Africa was explored by him between 1874 and 1877, when, as a journalist working for the *New York Herald*, he set out to find Livingstone. In 1875, he sailed round Lake Victoria, where he established that the river indicated by Speke was the only river that flowed out of the lake, and that Lake Victoria could thus indeed be considered the source of the Nile. During his journey, he descended the Congo River further westwards, and after a trek of 999 days reached the Atlantic Ocean. After making a number of other journeys, he was a few years later to enter the service of the Association internationale du Congo. This had been set up in 1876 by King Leopold II of Belgium with the purpose of exploring the continent, suppressing slavery and bringing 'civilization'; in practice, the Association was a means to reinforce the king's influence on the continent. Within this context, Stanley was charged with the task of setting up trading posts and negotiating and concluding agreements with the local African chiefs.

Generally speaking, knowledge of the African continent was considerably increased by these journeys: whereas in 1850 enormous stretches of the maps of the interior of the continent were blank, by around 1880 they had been substantially filled in; although many details were still missing, the broad outline of the great river systems, the geography and the inhabited areas of the various peoples were now known. Furthermore, many of the traveller's accounts painted a rosy picture of the opportunities for eventual economic exploitation. The carving-up of Africa had begun.

Conclusions: European colonialism and imperialism in Africa before 1880

The first eighty years of the nineteenth century brought many changes to Africa. After a long and difficult struggle, slavery had been virtually stamped out, except in East Africa. In its place in West Africa a more diversified package of export products was developed, though elsewhere in Sub-Saharan Africa such diversification remained limited and there was often wasteful exploitation of the local ecosystem. Although European intervention in Africa was fairly modest until 1880, the influence of such countries as France and England had increased considerably in comparison with the situation around 1800. The pressure of European colonialism was already palpable in particularly those regions – North and South Africa – where there was not too great a mortality risk for whites.

Apart from a thousand or so slaves, prisoners captured during raids by Algerian pirates on European ships, there were practically no Europeans whatever in Algeria at the start of the nineteenth century; by 1875, after the French conquest, there were already 275,000 colonists, not counting an army of occupation about 60,000 strong. In Egypt, which counted virtually no Europeans around 1790, the number rose from 5,000 in 1834 to nearly 100,000 in 1880; in Morocco from less than 200 in 1820 to almost 3,000 in 1877; and in Tunis from 800 in 1834 to 15,000 in 1870. The European presence also increased substantially on the colonized islands around Africa: by 1875, there were more that 50,000 whites on the French island of Reunion and approximately 10,000 on British Mauritius.

The number of Europeans remained very limited in Sub-Saharan Africa, with the exception of South Africa, where it had grown considerable from 22,000 in 1790 to about 300,000: of these, 237,000 or nearly 80 per cent lived in the Cape Colony, 18,000 in Natal, 30,000 in the Transvaal and 15,000 in the Orange Free State.

Elsewhere, it was only in the Portuguese possessions that any colonization could be risked. Even then, there were fewer than 2,000 whites in Angola in 1845, and probably still fewer in Mozambique. White numbers in the trading posts along the coast were extremely low, too: St Louis, the capital of Dakar and the most important European settlement in West Africa, counted no more than 177 Europeans in 1850, and Sierra Leone, the major British colony in tropical Africa at the time, only 125 whites in 1870!

Taken overall, the population of European origin that had settled in Africa and the islands around rose from about 32,000 in 1790 to circa 750,000 in 1875, the majority concentrated in the north, the south and the islands. A substantial increase indeed, though, in the light of the then African population of approximately 90,000,000, the European 'presence' can hardly be described as imposing.

1880–1914: the breakthrough of European colonialism in Africa

Towards the end of the 1870s, the process of colonialism and imperialism in Africa accelerated. Around 1875, European powers controlled still only 10 per cent of African territory, but, during the three following decades, the entire African continent, with the exception of Ethiopia and Liberia, came to be divided up among them. Contrary to the situation during the rest of the nineteenth century, when European penetration was limited to those regions whose climate Europeans could tolerate and to a restricted number of coastal strips, the interior, too, was now brought under direct foreign control. The question therefore arises of why it was precisely during these thirty years that this acceleration took place.

The explanations for what came to be known as the 'scramble for Africa' can be classified according to three major groupings – the general, the European and the African – depending on their contextual emphasis.

The general context: technology and ideology

The search for an explanation for the rapid colonization of the African continent during the latter part of the nineteenth century usually takes too little account of general factors. It is not to be forgotten, for example, that there was widespread and large-scale application of new medical, industrial and military technology in Western Europe in the years after 1850. This, among other things, enabled a number of European nations at relatively limited cost to dominate the African kingdoms not only economically, but also politically and militarily.

As previously described, the mortality rate among Europeans in tropical Africa was extremely high during the first half of the nineteenth century. The deadly consequences of malaria in particular led to such losses among the first colonists and traders that the Guinea coast in the 1820s became known as the 'white man's grave'. Until and including certainly the second third of the century, the Sub-Saharan environment of sickness therefore formed an insurmountable, natural obstacle to any successful attempt at large-scale colonization of the interior.

A major change in this situation was to be wrought around mid-century by breakthroughs in medical science. Already during the 1840s it had been discovered by European explorers in South America that quinine, extracted from the bark of the cinchona tree, proved in regular doses an efficient prophylactic against malaria, and from as early as the beginning of the 1850s it was effectively used by European members of expeditions to the African interior. The most important consequence of its introduction was that the disastrous mortality rate among newly arrived Europeans fell sharply from about 500 per thousand annually to between 50 and 100 per thousand. By way of comparison, the mortality rate in Europe during the same period for the same age group was approximately 10 per thousand. A further step in the fight against malaria was the discovery around the turn of the century that mosquitoes formed an unmistakable link in the transfer of the disease. With the introduction of various measures to combat them and the application of new medical techniques, it proved possible to push down the mortality rate among Europeans shortly before the First World War to a level barely higher than in Europe itself.

It was during this period, too, that the European powers succeeded in extending their lead in military technology further, so much so that most African peoples, even those equipped with firearms, had virtually no chance of success in a military confrontation with the encroaching foreign powers. Until the 1870s, however, the European powers were unable to turn their military superiority to full account. For example, the heavier weapons, such as cannons, could not always be efficiently deployed, due to the lack of a suitable transport infrastructure; troops were confronted with even greater problems, as the larger beasts of burden, such as the horse, could not survive in regions where *trypanosomiasis* (sleeping sickness) was prevalent. In numerous situations, therefore, it was only possible to employ light infantry, which initially put the local armed forces on more or less an equal footing with the invading troops. The Ashanti of Ghana, for instance, defeated a British army in 1826 and had no difficulty in holding the British at bay during the subsequent decades; indeed, it was only in 1874 that their capital, Kumasi, was captured by a British force. As late as 1874, it was still possible for a black army in South Africa to defeat a British force in the field (e.g. at the Battle of Isandhlwana).

Numerous new and more efficient light weapons were taken into service by the European armies around the middle of the nineteenth century, the use of breach-loading guns with rifled barrels from the 1850s onwards and the arrival of repeating guns in the 1870s bringing about a substantial increase in the rapidity of fire, the range and the accuracy of the classic shoulder arm.

For their part, most African troops were still using muskets that on the battlefield were no match for this new generation of light weapons, though the advantage of the muskets was that they could be repaired and gunpowder and projectiles for them easily produced locally. More modern weapons came only gradually and to a limited extent into the hands of the Africans, but could only be obtained through foreign (European) suppliers, a dependence that made the situation of the Africans even more vulnerable. A definitive end to the balance of power came with the introduction into the field of the enormous firepower of the machine gun by the invading European armies. It was around 1870 that the first machine guns, the French *mitrailleuse* and the American Gatling gun, came onto the market; equipped with a revolving barrel, they had a very rapid rate of fire, but initially exhibited many technical shortcomings, which were only solved with the invention of the Maxim gun in 1889. Never was the difference in military technology so great as during the period from 1880 to 1914.

Another advantage not to be ignored that the European powers enjoyed was conferred on them by their having been involved much longer in the process of developing the apparatus of a modern state than most African kingdoms. From the late eighteenth century, the majority of European countries had undergone a radical process of administrative reform that gave them a pronounced edge in organizational matters; in this respect, for example, their often well developed government services allowed them to deploy and control their civil servants efficiently in the expansion of their colonial empires. Linked to this, too, was the greater professionalism of the European officer corps that came about during the nineteenth century, further enhancing the effectiveness of military campaigns. The same period saw the major European powers – England as early as 1806 and France from 1887 – establishing numerous special institutions to train colonial administrators to govern the overseas territories. Moreover, the administrative coordination of these far-flung areas was further promoted by the new breakthroughs in the field of transport and communications technology (steamships, railways, the telegraph, etc.), whereby auxiliary troops and material help could be conveyed fairly rapidly and relatively easy contact with the mother country maintained.

The late nineteenth century also brought with it a reinforcement of the European sense of superiority over other non-European peoples, a reinforcement that was closely linked with the triumph of Western capitalism. Never before had the difference between the West and the rest of the world as regards technology and production been so great as during the second half of the nineteenth century, when industrialization became definitively established in most countries of the North Atlantic region and resulted in ever increasing industrial output, major railway networks and imposing fleets, as well as a constant flow of innovation in the most varied fields.

Up to and including the second third of the nineteenth century, a sort of cultural chauvinism predominated that has also been described as 'conversionism', whereby it was assumed that other nations desired to integrate Western culture and technology into their own societies as rapidly as possible and that this would be a fairly easy process. The European sense of superiority was now also being increasingly expressed in a racial bias, as a consequence of new discoveries in biology and, more particularly, of the breakthrough of Darwin's theory of evolution. This theory provided a sort of justification for the socio-racist theories that surfaced around this time and that reached a pitch at the end of the nineteenth century in the theory of Social Darwinism propounded and popularized by Herbert Spencer who, paradoxically enough, was himself an outspoken anti-imperialist. In this theory, Darwin's ideas were applied to the human race as a whole and the theory of evolution used to define the relationships between social groups and races as the 'survival of the fittest'.

The success of the theory of Social Darwinism helps to explain how the doctrine of trusteeship arose, in which non-European peoples were presented as more or less permanently inferior and in which it was argued that, in their interest, it was better to accept a sort of European enlightened despotism. Within this idea of trusteeship, in other words, colonizing the African continent was seen as Europe's 'moral' duty (cf. the expression 'the white man's burden' in colonial India).

Due to a combination of factors that converged during the final decades of the nineteenth century, and to medical and military breakthroughs in Europe, together with an increasingly racist, ideological current, a general climate was created that permitted acceleration of the process of European colonialism and imperialism. However, it goes without saying that, in discussing the actual annexing of territories overseas, account had to be taken of the factors at play in Europe, as well as on the African continent itself.

The European context

Until recently in historical writings, great attention was still being paid to the consequences of nineteenth-century industrialization to explain the late nineteenth century wave of European colonization. In this sense, the 'climax of European colonial imperialism' (1880–1914) was ascribed to the industrialized economies' search for new markets and to their efforts to secure the supply of raw materials. Furthermore, the new overseas territories were able to absorb a part of the rapid population increase attendant on industrialization.

This theory of economic necessity was developed primarily within the Marxist paradigm. In 1916, for example, V. I. Lenin (1870–1924) published a pamphlet entitled 'Imperialism, the Highest Stage of Capitalism', which was to gain substantial appeal throughout the rest of the twentieth century. Lenin's study was a reaction to the success of the reformist socialist parties, and was an effort to adapt the theories of Marx to the changed political constellation of the early twentieth century. More particularly, Lenin argued that the enlargement of scale and the concentration in the capitalist economies would in time result in downward pressure on profits. Due to the accumulation of capital, production would increase substantially, but in its own region would come up against insufficient purchasing power. In order to be able to sell their surplus stocks and to employ their surplus capital, businessmen, in Lenin's view, would prompt their governments to conduct a consciously imperialist policy. However, the economic motives that were thus invoked to explain imperialism are certainly not the exclusive product of Lenin's thinking; indeed, he borrowed many ideas from the British liberal, John A. Hobson (1858–1940).

In the decades after decolonization, too, much attention was still given to economic arguments to explain (neo) colonialism. Nevertheless, a closer analysis suggests that it is hardly likely that the economic interpretation provides the fundamental explanation for the wave of colonization that marked the late nineteenth century.

The strong population growth in Europe during the nineteenth century was not resolved in emigration to the new colonies; indeed, European migrants opted to settle in areas of the United States, the British Dominions or parts of Latin America, where cultural differences were less pronounced and the climate comparable to that in Europe.

Furthermore, it was not necessary for the European powers to establish political dominance in overseas territories in order to have access to raw materials or to sell their surplus production. The greater part of the trade of European countries was with each other and with the United States; trade with the colonial territories represented only a relatively modest part of the total: before 1914, for example, France was sending only 10 per cent of her exports to her colonies. It has also to be noted that the possession of colonies did not necessarily mean that the colonial power in question also had a monopoly of trade: both France and Germany, for instance, sold great quantities of goods to British India. Investment of surplus capital, too, was all in all fairly limited. It is true that Great Britain invested substantial sums abroad, but more than half of the total went to independent countries; less than 10 per cent of the total amount invested abroad by France was in her own colonies, the rest went to other European countries, principally Russia; Germany's investment in her overseas territories was negligible. European capital investment in Africa indeed remained very modest, except in Egypt and South Africa.

Although from a macroeconomic point of view there was certainly no direct necessity to colonize, it can with difficulty be denied that trade competition between the various countries induced a number of psychological effects that served to accelerate the process of colonization; such a situation could arise, for instance, when more than one European power was conducting trade in a particular region. In 'frontier areas' with many European colonists, such as Algeria and South Africa, strong pressure could also arise for new territories to be annexed, sometimes against the will of the mother country.

In general, it may be stated that there was an area of tension between the aggressive attitude of Europeans domiciled in Africa (the 'men on the spot'), who often had a direct personal interest in the annexation of new territories, and the more conservative-minded governments in Europe. These governments were usually much more cautious about getting involved in colonizing adventures, because of the financial consequences of military campaigns, the danger of continuing escalation and the consequences for their relationships with other Western powers.

Currently, more attention is being paid to political motivation than to economic interpretation to explain the wave of colonization of the late nineteenth century. Following the Napoleonic Wars, national conflicts in Europe were rather short-lived affairs until shortly after the middle of the century; indeed, a great deal of political energy was expended in unifying Germany and Italy. After the Franco-Prussian War of 1870, however, nationalist emotions flared up more strongly. For the French, colonial imperialism formed an outlet for a French army thirsting for revenge. Among other nations, colonialism was resorted to as a means of distracting attention from domestic problems. National prestige and the fear of losing out in the dividing-up of the African continent therefore probably played a more important part than purely economic motives in explaining the more intense colonization pressure in those years.

The African context

The conquest of the African continent at the end of the nineteenth century was aided by the far-reaching changes that took place in African society during the nineteenth century. The rise of a number of local states as a result of the religious *jihads* in West Africa and the present Sudan, the migratory movements (*Mfecane*) in Southern Africa and the commercial changes in Central Africa created marked political instability, and these intra-African conflicts were often exploited by Europeans who, by continually changing alliances with local rulers, succeeded in pursuing a 'divide and rule' policy.

Additionally, the resistance of the African population to the invading troops was further weakened by a number of ecological disasters that afflicted the continent prior to and during the conquest.

Cattle plague, probably introduced via the provisioning of European troops along the Red Sea, took just a few years from 1890 to spread from Somalia to the rest of Africa. It resulted in massive depletion of cattle stocks and wild life: some estimates state that three quarters of African cattle stocks died during these years as a result of the great Rinderpest epizootic. In consequence of this enormous death toll among cattle, serious famine struck, affecting chiefly the cattle-herding peoples. Estimates of death during this period are particularly dramatic: for example, the 1890s probably saw half of the Masai in German East Africa dying from hunger; other statistics suggest that 10 to 50 per cent of the population of Central Kenya perished as a result of a combination of famine and epidemic sickness; and famine is often deemed to be responsible for the deaths of a third of the Ethiopian population in these years; solely the people of West Africa appear to have largely escaped the huge mortality then predominating in the greater part of Africa.

During the same period, there was a rapid spread of several new diseases or, probably in consequence of the generally weaker physical condition of the population, existing diseases became much more virulent in character. In this respect, the sudden contraction of the cattle population led to the expansion of the bush vegetation, the natural environment of the tsetse fly, the carrier of sleeping sickness or *trypanosomiasis* (also called the Black Death of Africa because of the enormous ravages that it caused during the early colonial period). Certain estimates put the number of deaths from sleeping sickness in the region between the Congo river and the eastern shore of Lake Victoria at half of the population, and observers reckon that a third of Uganda's population died during the sleeping sickness epidemic of 1902. A particularly high toll was also claimed by other diseases, too, such as smallpox, typhoid, cholera and measles; furthermore, serious skin injuries that could lead to gangrene were being caused by sand flies or 'jiggers' that in less than twenty years had spread throughout Africa from the Congolese coast, where they had been imported from Brazil in the 1870s.

The effect of these new diseases was further enhanced by the substantial degree of labour mobility during this period, which brought peoples into an environment of disease without their having the immunity that the local population had to certain sicknesses. Moreover, epidemics often broke out in places with a large concentration of people, such as regions where mining or plantations had been introduced, or where railways were being laid. Besides the actual physical and psychological impact of these ecological and epidemiological crises on the resistance of the African to the encroaching foreign powers, regional depopulation (as was the case among the Kikuyu in Central Africa) was also to favour the appropriation of extensive areas by white colonists.

The great military campaigns to conquer the interior began around 1885, and the end of that decade saw the start of the confrontation with the more strongly organized local empires. The rapid annexation of African territories quickly led to a number of clashes between the European powers, and to reduce the risk of an armed conflict Bismarck (1815–98) and the French premier, Jules Ferry (1832–93), organized the Berlin West African Conference in 1884–5, in which fourteen Western countries participated. This conference is often wrongly portrayed as being solely a meeting at which the division of Africa among the colonial powers was decided; among the things the conference actually did was to lay down a number of basic principles for the European conquest, whereby the claims of the colonizing powers to regions could be recognized by the other nations only if they had been formally notified of them and if the colonizing power set up a real administration in the area in question. However, the most important negotiations that were conducted concerned the right of free navigation of the Congo and Niger basins. At the same time, a number of agreements were concluded to guarantee free trade in the colonized areas and to abolish slavery, and the independent state of Congo under the personal rule of King Leopold II of Belgium was recognized.

The European nations were quick to realize that it would take relatively little time to gain military victory if supplies of European weapons to the stronger African empires could be cut off, and, at a conference in Brussels in 1889–90 on slavery, agreement was reached between the European countries to implement an arms blockade for modern weapons against African kingdoms offering resistance.

Overall, the 1880s can be described as the decade of the 'scramble for Africa', the 1890s as the period of conquest and the years between 1900 and the First World War as the years of consolidation. The general pattern during the conquest was of a short military confrontation with the local ruler, followed by annexation of the territory, though it was often the case that there was a massive uprising a few years later, after the initial shock of the conquest had been absorbed and the population was confronted with the new reality. It was chiefly this phase in the colonization of Africa that was especially bloody. Suppression of these insurrections proved to be more difficult than the actual conquest, and a high price had to be paid for it in both economic terms and human lives.

In North Africa, the Moroccan rulers succeeded in playing the European powers off against each other until the early years of the twentieth century, by which time the country had been able to build up a modern army; it was thus only between 1908 and 1912, after a substantial French army had been deployed, that Morocco was forced to capitulate. In 1912, following a short war, the Ottoman Empire ceded Tripoli to the Italians, who gave the name Libya to their new colony.

In West Africa, it took the French the best part of fifteen years to build up a colonial empire. Segou, the capital of the Tukuloor Empire (in present-day Mali) fell in 1890, and the Mossi Empire in what is now Burkina Faso was overrun in 1896. Notable in this region was the tough resistance put up by Samori Touré (*c.*1830–1900), who, from the 1860s, had succeeded in building up an efficiently organized state in what are now parts of Guinea, Mali and Burkina Faso; however, he, too, was finally defeated in 1898, though only after his supply-line for modern weapons via Sierra Leone had been threatened from 1896 onwards by agreements between France and Great Britain.

Between 1892 and 1896, British forces occupied consecutively the Ibo kingdom, the territories of the Ashanti and Dahomey, and parts of Nigeria; in 1893 and 1894, the Germans created their own colony in Cameroon; and between 1901 and 1903 the northerly emirates in Nigeria came under British control.

To protect their interests in Egypt, the British attempted to bring the upper Nile valley, present-day Sudan, under their control before another foreign power could seize the chance. In 1885, after an uprising led by Muhammad Ahmad (1844–5), the Mahdi (an Islamic religious leader), this region became independent of the Turko-Egyptian administration that had been set in place in 1820. Under the successors of the Mahdi, the country was built up into an independent theocratic nation between 1885 and 1898, in which latter date a sizable Anglo-Egyptian army under General H. H. Kitchener (1850–1916) penetrated further into the Sudan from Egypt. After military resistance was broken (at the Battle of Omdurman, 1898), the country was annexed by the British. Shortly thereafter, the British came into contact with French troops more to the south in Fashoda, and it was only after emergency negotiations in London and Paris that war was averted between the two nations.

Smaller states in Central and East Africa were usually too weakly organized to have any chance of offering successful resistance, the Arab empires in the Eastern Congo basin being defeated by troops of the Congo Free State between 1892 and 1895, and the Germans in East Africa in what is now Tanzania inflicting a military defeat on the Nyamwezi and the Chagga. A few years after the conquests, there followed much larger-scale popular uprisings against the new rulers, chiefly in Central and Eastern Africa. The second phase of resistance was usually substantially more massive and often more widespread, as shown by, among other things, the uprising of the Ndebele and the Shona in what was then Rhodesia (1896–7), the insurrection of the coastal peoples in Tanzania (the Abushiri Rising, 1889) and the rebellion of the Maji-Maji in German East Africa (1905–7).

The discovery of diamonds in the 1850s and of rich gold reserves in the mid-1880s transformed the rather poor agricultural economy of Southern Africa and served to give the region a more industrialized character. A major role in the further opening up of this part of the continent in the late nineteenth century was played by the Englishman, Cecil Rhodes (1853–1902), a successful businessman in diamond and gold mining who became premier of the Cape Colony in 1890. Via the British South Africa Company that he had set up, Rhodes obtained a concession from the British government in 1889 to administer and mine a region north of the Transvaal that was later to be called Rhodesia (present-day Zimbabwe and Zambia).

The strategic importance of the Boer republic of the Transvaal was increased dramatically and quickly by the discovery there of important gold reserves. Paul Kruger (1825–1904), the president of the Transvaal, came into conflict with Rhodes by refusing to join a South African Union and by his reluctance to establish a link from the Transvaal with the Cape Colony's railway network. With the complicity of Rhodes, a plot was hatched to bring this country under British control (the Jameson Raid, 1895), but failed. Relations between the republic and Great Britain remained tense and in 1899 the Second Anglo-Boer War broke out. Initially, the Boers scored a number of successes against the British, but eventually in 1902 were forced to capitulate after an exhausting guerrilla war. In exchange for their surrender, the British made a number of important concessions: not only did the Boers gain a sort of self-government, but the black African population was deprived of all political rights. The Treaty of Vereeniging

(1902), which embodied these conditions, was to affect race relations in South Africa right up to the end of the twentieth century.

The most successful resistance to European colonial imperialism came from regions where strong local empires had arisen and which throughout the nineteenth century had been relatively isolated from coastal ports or regions with a substantial European presence, or both. A prime example of this is offered by the Ethiopian nation, which was the only African state that managed to maintain its political independence. During the nineteenth century, Ethiopia had developed a relatively considerable degree of stability that rested partially on the loyalty that had already existed earlier to the emperor, as well as on the careful creation of an arsenal of modern weapons. These weapons were financed by tolls levied on the slave trade, the routes for which passed through the Ethiopian Highlands, though without the country itself being involved in the trade. Purchasing from the Italians, who were active in the frontier regions, the Ethiopian emperor, Menelik II (1844–1913), was able to build up this arsenal in time to inflict a heavy defeat on an Italian army that had invaded Ethiopia (the Battle of Aswoda, 1896).

By 1900 or thereabouts, the conquest and carving-up of Africa was largely accomplished, although pockets of resistance continued to exist here and there until the 1920s.

Contrary to their objectives in their wars on the European continent, the Europeans' aim in Africa was to establish a permanent political dominance and consequently a permanent European presence in the newly conquered territories. However, as opposition at home meant that most European countries were concerned to keep down the cost of continual military operations, local rulers were often able to negotiate with the conquerors from a position of relative strength. In several cases, the European powers were therefore prepared to make concessions to the African leaders of the defeated countries; indeed, a substantial number of African rulers, including the Fulbe emirs in Northern Nigeria, retained a considerable degree of power just by choosing the right time and the appropriate manner to negotiate with the British.

Another marked feature of the initial phase of the process of colonization was the role played by large industrial and commercial groups. Such companies as the Royal Niger Company, the Imperial British East Africa Company, the British South Africa Company (BSA Co.), the German East Africa Company and, to a certain extent, the Congo Free State often took the initiative in the actual conquest and exploitation of the annexed territories, and they were supported in this by their respective mother countries, which could thereby conduct an imperialist policy without having to give direct account for it before their national parliaments. However, the role of these groups in the actual administration of the African colonies was largely played out already before the First World War, with the exception of the BSA Co. in Rhodesia, which retained administrative authority until 1923.

By the beginning of the twentieth century, most African territories had been annexed by the European powers. For the majority of African peoples, this meant the loss of their political self-determination, but just as bad was the fact that the carving-up of the continent paid barely any or no regard to ethnic borders, a situation whose consequences would continue still to be felt in the post-colonial period. One positive aspect of colonialism was the imposition of *pax colonial* that put an end to the internal tribal wars that plagued the continent during the nineteenth century.

It nevertheless has to be emphasized that, within the context of African history, the colonial period was relatively short. Indeed, during those years preceding the First World War, when the European countries were engaged in administrative and economic consolidation of their overseas territories, several African leaders were born who, half a century later, were to lead their countries to independence.

2.2

ASIA

Michelangelo van Meerten

MOBILITY OF LABOUR

The migration from Asia

Migration from Asia to other continents was already taking place in the eighteenth century. But the migration in greater numbers really got under way in the nineteenth century. It was the abolition of slavery in the British Empire in 1834 that would boost migration. An increasing shortage of labour in the tropical and semi-tropical parts of the British Empire was met in particular by an inflow of labourers from India. The successful spread of the abolition of slavery beyond the British Empire resulted in similar labour shortages elsewhere as well. These were met by an inflow of Chinese and, towards the end of the nineteenth century, Japanese labourers. Though migration from these three countries would be quite impressive in numbers, it remained small in terms of the total populations of the countries.

The migration from India was strictly organized in a system of indenture (or the 'coolie system'). This system consisted of a contract for generally five years, during which the labourer committed himself to work for a fixed wage and to pay for the cost of his passage. After the initial period the contract could be renewed, but the possibility existed as well to settle permanently in the receiving country, with the freedom to follow the vocation of his choice. After 1857, a third option consisted of returning home at the expense of the receiving country. Indentured workers were often used to undercut wages of free workers. The indentured labour was frequently abused, and the labourers were often hardly better off than slaves. Moreover, mortality during the voyage was high. Because of these abuses, the Indian colonial government several times suspended the recruiting of labour, and towards the end of the nineteenth century controls to check abuses became more effective. The first steps to abolish the system of indentured labour from India would be taken in 1916–17.

The indenture system provided Indian labourers principally to British colonies in tropical areas. Up to 1870, Indian migration to other continents was mainly to the Caribbean islands, Guyana, Mauritius, South Africa, East Africa and the Fiji islands. But Indian labourers also went to French colonies in the Caribbean, the island of Reunion and to Surinam. Most of the migrants embarked from Calcutta and came from the United Provinces and Bihar. The south of India, with the ports of Madras and the French possessions, provided a far smaller number of migrants.

As most of the Indian migrants came from rural areas, migration did ease the pressure of population on existing resources. Famines and epidemics provoked peaks in migration and provided supplementary reasons to migrate. From the 1860s onwards, growing demand for labour in India itself and in other Asian countries led to a gradual decline in intercontinental emigration. At the turn of the century only Guyana, Trinidad, South Africa and the Fiji islands still received a sizeable number of Indians.

As the indentured labour system was not designed to lead to permanent settlement of the Indian migrants, most of them returned home afterwards. Cultural differences, sometimes hostility from the populations in the receiving countries, and the fact that migrants were predominantly male, provided little incentives for Indian labourers to stay. Overall data, including on emigration to Asia, show that between 1834 and 1900 about three quarters of all Indian emigrants eventually returned home. The percentages of Indian emigrants that chose to remain in Africa, America and Oceania, ranged, however, between 66 (Africa) and 100 per cent (Oceania) of all Indian emigrants to these continents. Estimates of total Indian emigration to other continents give a number of over one million between 1834 and 1900. Almost 750,000 of them remained in their receiving countries. A census for 1921 shows 266,000 Indians in Mauritius, 161,000 in South Africa, 65,000 in East Africa, 272,000 in the British Caribbean and Guyana, and 61,000 in Fiji.

Increasing labour shortages in the overseas colonies of Western European countries led in the 1830s to the first recruiting of Chinese labourers, despite official prohibition. The forced opening-up of China in the 1840s, resulting in treaties allowing recruiting in the 1850s and 1860s, led to an important increase in the number of Chinese that were contracted as indentured labourers.

Most of the Chinese migrants came from the coastal regions of the Chinese mainland. As far as the British and French colonies were concerned, they were mainly employed in the same areas where Indian labourers had been contracted. Thus between 1852 and 1884 some 18,000 Chinese worked in the Caribbean, and over 14,000 in Guyana. But Chinese indentured labourers were also recruited to work on the guano beds in Peru, where some 80–100,000 Chinese arrived between 1849 and 1874. Cuba attracted Chinese labourers to work on the sugar plantations. In 1862, their number amounted to 60,000.

An additional demand for Chinese labour sprang up with the discoveries of gold in Australia, the United States of America and Canada. Chinese labourers had already been attracted to Australia in 1848, but their numbers would rise considerably with the discovery of gold in New South Wales in the 1850s. In 1861, their number had risen to over 38,000. In the same period Chinese labourers were brought to California. Subsequently, a considerable number of Chinese labourers were put to work in the construction of railways. Estimates put the total number of Chinese immigrants arriving in the United States until the end of the nineteenth century at over 300,000. The discovery of gold in Canada at the end of the 1850s would lead to a large inflow of Chinese labour, which played an important part in the construction of the transcontinental railways. But apart from an inflow of indentured labour, the opportunities offered in Australia, the United States and Canada also attracted free Chinese immigrants.

The competition from Chinese labourers, which was reinforced by the low fixed wages of the indenture system, would lead to increasing protest from the indigenous population or from other mainly European immigrants. In Australia Chinese immigration was restricted as early as 1855. The United States prohibited US citizens and ships from participating in the transport of Chinese indentured labourers in 1862. In 1877, Spain concluded a treaty with China prohibiting the recruitment of indentured Chinese labourers for all its possessions. This prohibition was thereafter extended to nearly all countries. The United States extended the prohibition to free immigration from China in 1894. A similar check to Chinese immigration was passed in Australia at the turn of the century, while Canada imposed an increasing head tax on Chinese.

In the last quarter of the nineteenth century Chinese intercontinental emigration thus became more and more restricted. As generally the majority of Chinese labourers eventually returned home after the expiration of their contracts, the number of Chinese in other continents gradually decreased. Between 1904 and 1910, for instance, over 170,000 Chinese were contracted in Transvaal in South Africa. Most of them were repatriated, and in 1922 there were only about 5,000 Chinese left. In that same year 35,000 Chinese resided in Australia, almost 62,000 in the United States, and 12,000 in Canada. Only in Peru and Cuba did a large number of Chinese remain, estimated at 45,000 and 90,000 respectively.

In Japan, emigration was prohibited until 1866. Emigration of Japanese labourers would only start in 1885, when a first agreement was signed for Japanese labourers to work on sugar plantations in Hawaii. Thereafter, emigration took off. Japan even encouraged this overseas migration, as it was considered to contribute to the nation's economic expansion through the remittances sent home by emigrants. Up to 1907 almost 179,000 Japanese would migrate to Hawaii. The United States (mainly its West Coast) was a second important destination, receiving over 72,000 Japanese emigrants up to 1907. As in the case of Chinese labourers, Japanese immigration increasingly met with protests. This resulted in a 'gentlemen's agreement' by which the Japanese government was to limit emigration to the United States to selected categories of migrants. While the USA was restricting the immigration of Japanese labourers, new destinations appeared in South America. Sugar and rubber plantations in Peru, and coffee plantations in Brazil would attract increasing numbers of Japanese labourers after the turn of the century.

The Asian world

Intracontinental migration in Asia goes back many centuries. But the increasing integration of Asia in the world economy in the nineteenth century, population growth, and improved transportation would alter and speed up these migratory movements. India and China provided the majority of migrants to other less densely populated Asian countries. Towards the end of the century India and China would be joined by Japan as a source of migrants.

Indian labourers were already found in all ports of South East Asia at the end of the eighteenth century. After the abolition of slavery in the British Empire the number of Indian migrant labourers rose spectacularly. Their main destinations in Asia were Ceylon (Sri Lanka), the Straits Settlements (Malaysia and Singapore), and Burma (then a part of British India). In the period from 1834 to 1900, the number of intracontinental Indian migrants is estimated at more than 12M. As over 9.5M of these migrants eventually returned home, net Indian migration will have amounted to some 2.7M. The period from 1900 to 1915 would see a further 5.5M intracontinental Indian migrants. Net migration in this latter period is estimated at over 850,000.

The migration of Indian labourers to Ceylon got under way in the 1830s and 1840s, when coffee began to be introduced on the island on a large scale. At the end of the 1850s, coffee had become the staple crop and main export product. The scarcity of labour and the fact that indigenous independent peasants were reluctant to leave their rice fields for low wages and harsh conditions on the coffee plantations, led planters to recruit Indian labourers. Population pressure and even lower wages in India, in turn, would stimulate the migration of Indians to Ceylon. The work on the coffee plantations was mainly concentrated around the time of harvest, that is between August and November. Most Indian labourers therefore returned home after each harvest season. The instability of the supply of Indian labourers in the 1840s led the planters to adopt the system of indentured labour, under which labourers were bound by longer-term contracts. Recruitment of Indian labourers frequently would be carried out by a selected group of Indian labourers, the so-called *kangani*, who acted as middlemen recruiting themselves up to twenty other labourers. The recruiting system of labourers for Ceylon, which was also practiced for Malaysia and Singapore, therefore often is referred to as the *kangani*-system. Between 1834 and 1870, almost 1.5M Indians migrated to Ceylon. Though migrations was to a large extent seasonal, net migration in this period represented some 600,000. A second phase of Indian migration to Ceylon started in the 1880s, when the new cash crops of tea and rubber were introduced to the island. Tea required a far more permanent work force than coffee and thus favoured a more permanent settlement. According to British colonial statistics, Ceylon received over 2.8M Indian migrants between 1880 and 1913. Net migration would amount to about 1M. In 1921 the total number of residents in Ceylon, from Indian origin was over 1.4M, representing 31 per cent of the total population of the island. The majority of the Indians residing in Ceylon came from the southern provinces of India, that is the Madras Presidency.

Indian migration to Malaya and the Straits Settlements (Malaysia and Singapore) started in the early nineteenth century. Plantations and mining were the main sectors recruiting Indian labourers under the *kangani*-system.

Generally, these labourers received the lowest wages, lower than those of Chinese labourers. As for most of the nineteenth century emigration to Malaysia and Singapore was unrestricted, the area also attracted an important number of free Indian immigrants. The total number of Indians in Malaysia and Singapore in 1921, amounted to over 470,000.

The establishment of British rule over Burma, in the second half of the nineteenth century, ending with the incorporation of the entire country into the British Empire in 1885, would lead to an important migration of Indians to this relatively less densely populated area. Indian labourers were engaged in mining and agriculture. Burma was to become a major supplier of rice to the Indian subcontinent.

Immigration from other Asian countries to India in turn was rather small. The Nepalese were by far the largest group of immigrants. Living standards in Nepal were below those in India, and many Nepalese were engaged in the colonial public service. In 1921, their number was estimated at 274,000.

Though Chinese intracontinental migration was an old phenomenon as well, emigration had been prohibited in 1718. Emigration would pick up again after the conclusion of treaties in the 1840s, imposing the opening-up of China in that period. The main areas of destination were the Straits Settlements (Malaysia and Singapore), Java, Indonesia, the Philippines, Thailand, Burma, Indochina (Vietnam, Cambodia and Laos) and Taiwan. At the beginning of the twentieth century Manchuria became another destination for Chinese migrants.

The first Chinese settlers in Malaysia were attracted by the British East India Company in 1787. Soon after the British had established themselves at Singapore, the first Chinese immigrants arrived there. From 5,000 in 1826, their number rose to 50,000 in 1850, and almost 220,000 in 1911. In the latter year the inhabitants of Singapore from Chinese origin represented over 72 per cent of the city's total population. Though the Straits Settlements did attract indentured labourers, the majority of Chinese immigrants paid for their own voyage and established themselves freely. Chinese port statistics report over 2M Chinese who gave the Straits Settlements as their destination between 1876 and 1901. Net migration for that period amounted to 1.4M. Some of the Chinese travelling to the Straits Settlements went to other destinations from there. Thus the number of Chinese established in the Straits Settlements at the turn of the century was slightly less than a million.

The islands of Java and Sumatra (Indonesia, then the Dutch East Indies) were other important destinations for Chinese emigrants. Though port statistics only report a migration of some 87,000 Chinese to Indonesia between 1876 and 1901, the number of Chinese residents was estimated at 600,000 at the turn of the century and at over 1.8M in 1922.

The Philippines were another destination for Chinese emigrants. After the Spanish-American war in 1898, however, the USA's Chinese Exclusion Act applied to the Philippines, making further immigration practically impossible. At the turn of the century some 80,000 Chinese resided in the Philippines.

A much larger Chinese community was reported for Thailand, where their number at the turn of the century was estimated at 2.5M. Vietnam (then Indochina) and Burma had Chinese communities around 1900 of, respectively, 150,000 and 40,000.

Taiwan (or Formosa as it was then called) and Manchuria, are to some extent special cases as both were part of China at the beginning of the nineteenth century. After 1683, when Taiwan became a prefecture of the mainland coastal province of Fukien, Chinese settlers gradually had introduced mainland agricultural production methods on the island. Chinese migration changed over time from seasonal workers to permanent settlers, and in 1811 the Chinese population of the island was estimated at slightly over 2M. Under the threat of foreign colonization of the island, Taiwan became a province in 1887 and the provincial government started to subsidize immigration from the mainland. The Chinese population of the island at that time was some 3.2M. In 1895, however, the island would pass to Japanese rule, as result of the Sino-Japanese war, and Chinese immigration would almost come to a standstill. Chinese migration to Manchuria, on the other hand, was forbidden by the ruling Manchu dynasty until the beginning of the twentieth century. Despite this prohibition, illegal immigration to Manchuria took place during the nineteenth century. In 1893 its Chinese population was estimated at 5.3M. The opening-up of Manchuria would lead to significant immigration, and by 1913 its Chinese population exceeded 20M.

Most Chinese emigrants came from the coastal provinces of Fukien and Kwantung. Emigration slowed down population growth and thereby eased the pressure on natural resources and food supplies. The emigrants in turn contributed to the development of new areas, and increased export production in the countries that received them.

Japanese emigration was officially allowed only after 1866, when the prohibition on emigration was lifted. But the passports needed to leave the country were not supplied to any significant extent until 1885. Though Japan launched in this period an impressive programme to modernize its economy, changes were not quick enough as to prevent an emigratory outflow. The main intracontinental destinations of Japanese migrants were Japan's neighbouring countries, China, Korea, Taiwan and Asiatic Russia. Contrary to the Indians and Chinese, relatively few Japanese went to other Asian countries. Competition with Indian and Chinese low-wage labourers made these destinations unattractive to Japanese. Japanese migration to the Straits Settlements and to the Philippines up to 1913 hardly exceeded 10,000, and most of the migrants returned home.

Japanese migration to China, Korea and Taiwan closely followed the expansion of Japanese interests in these countries. Up to 1895, only 8,400 Japanese went to China, and few established themselves there. The concessions and privileges Japan acquired in 1895 after the Sino-Japanese war, and in 1905 after the Russo-Japanese war, led to an important increase in the number of Japanese migrants, and in the number of Japanese residents, particularly in Manchuria. In 1910, 36,000 Japanese resided in China, half of them in Manchuria. The establishment of Japanese colonial rule over Taiwan in 1895 after the Sino-Japanese war equally led to a considerable inflow of Japanese, which was encouraged by the colonial government. The number of Japanese residents on the Island increased from almost 38,000 in 1900 to 135,000 in 1915. Most of them were engaged in manufacturing industries. Up to 1905, when Korea became a Japanese protectorate, over 78,000 Japanese had migrated to the peninsula, but few had established themselves there permanently. After 1905, and particularly after the annexation of Korea in 1910, the number of

Japanese residents rose considerably. In 1910, their number amounted to over 170,000, and in 1920 to almost 350,000.

Asiatic Russia received the largest number of Japanese migrants. Between 1868 and 1913 almost 120,000 Japanese migrants went to Asiatic Russia. Most of these migrants were travelling traders and fishermen. Up to the First World War the number of permanently residing Japanese in Asiatic Russia did not exceed 10,000.

THE INTEGRATION OF THE WORLD MARKET: THE LIBERALIZATION OF TRADE IN JAPAN DURING THE NINETEENTH CENTURY

During the first half of the nineteenth century Japan stuck to the policy of national isolation it had pursued for centuries. Foreign trade was occasional and very limited in scale. The only Western European country that was allowed to trade with Japan was the Netherlands. This situation came to and end when American gunboat diplomacy forced Japan to open itself to trade in 1854. Through the treaties of 1858 and 1866 Japan had to extent the right of trade to other European powers. These treaties restricted Japan's autonomy in trading and fishing, and Japan had to limit tariffs on imports and exports to 5 per cent. After the reforms of the Meiji Restoration in 1868, Japanese imports and exports would grow spectacularly. In the period up to 1913, a profound change took place in the structure of Japan's foreign trade. From importing manufactured products and machinery, and exporting raw materials and semi-manufactured products as raw silk, the country shifted to importing raw materials and exporting manufactured products.

Up to 1867, Japan was ruled by the Tokugawa dynasty. Economic policy and administration were shared by the Tokugawa government (known as *bakufu*) and domain administrations (*han*). The principal policy aims of the *bakufu* were the maintenance of stability and assuring the rice harvest which was their main source of income. Since the seventeenth century, Japan had isolated itself from the rest of the world, prohibiting the presence of foreigners, and travelling abroad by Japanese subjects. Nevertheless, some trade relations with the outer world existed. Official foreign trade was concentrated in Japan's only international port, Nagasaki, and controlled by the *bakufu*. The scale of foreign trade was very limited and consisted mainly of traffic with China. The only non-Asian presence was that of the Dutch, who were allowed a permanent delegation at the island of Deshima in the port of Nagasaki. As the Dutch, for most of the period, were allowed to send one ship each year to Japan, traffic was very limited. The principal product the Dutch procured in Japan was copper. Apart from this official trade in Nagasaki, there existed a tolerated trade with China via the Ryukyu islands (Okinawa).

In the first half of the nineteenth century, Japan's isolation became increasingly threatened because of the successful European penetration of China. As a result of the Opium Wars, China was forced to open up to foreign trade and to grant privileges to Britain and other European powers. The gains from trade with Japan were, however, considered too small by the British as to justify an expedition to force the country to open up to foreign trade. It was the increasing trade with China, and not so much trade prospects with Japan, that would lead to the opening-up of

the country by the Americans. The extension of its territory to the Pacific brought the United States into direct trade relations with the Chinese. The fact that Japan was directly on the shipping route from San Francisco to Shanghai and disposed of supplies of coal, induced the Americans to send an expedition to the Island in 1853, to ask for the right of call at Japanese ports. The commander of the expedition, Commodore Perry, made it clear that he was willing to use force if the Japanese would not give in to the American requests. Realizing their weak position, the Japanese finally gave in and in March 1854 an agreement was signed that gave the Americans basically the right to call upon a limited number of Japanese ports to purchase coal and other supplies. The same year similar agreements were signed with Britain and Russia. With the latter a first convention was signed to settle the boundaries of both countries with regard to the Kurils.

Further pressures on Japan resulted in treaties in 1857 and 1858, with Britain, France, the Netherlands, Russia and the United States, which were to open several Japanese ports to trade and give foreigners extra-territorial status. These treaties met with widespread resistance in Japan itself, and the presence of foreigners brought about frictions. Incidents involving the death of a British merchant led to clashes with British warships, and an international expedition against the country, and finally, in 1866, to an agreement that would open up a large number of Japanese ports to free trade and lower Japanese tariffs to a uniform rate of 5 per cent.

The forceful opening up of the country had profound effects. In the first place it added to already existing tensions within Japanese society due to shifts in economic power benefiting an expanding class of merchants, and weakening the financial power of the ruling Tokugawa. The opening-up to foreign trade affected Japanese industries through important changes in relative prices. The existing cotton and sugar industries had a hard time competing with imports, while the increasing foreign demand for tea and silk led to a considerable rise of the price of these export products. Furthermore, the existence in Japan of a much lower silver to gold parity than the international one, led to a considerable outflow of gold from the country and a devaluation which resulted in a considerable rise of the overall price level. The effect of this inflation was a significant redistribution of wealth and income within Japanese society. Last, but not least, the treaties and their economic effects severely damaged the prestige of the existing ruling Tokugawa, and led to an increasing awareness of the country's backwardness. As a result, the idea won ground that the only way to resist foreign penetration would be to modernize the Japanese economy by imitating the West. The combined changes eventually led to a breakdown of the existing order and a revolution in 1868, known as the Meiji Restoration, which overthrew the Tokugawa Shogun and restored power to the Emperor.

The Meiji reform carried out by a coalition of samurai and merchants radically changed Japanese economic policy. Steps were taken to liberalize the Japanese economy, to reform institutions, education and public finances, to create a new banking system and to import Western technology. Through government initiative, modern industries were set up or subsidized by means of cheap long-term credit. The modernization of the country's transport and communication networks was partly financed through foreign loans, which later on would finance the wars with China and Russia.

The ensuing modernization of Japan was reflected in the composition of foreign trade. Initially, the opening-up of Japan to foreign trade almost wiped out its cotton industry, while it greatly stimulated the production of silk and tea. Tea and raw silk became the country's principal export products. The principal imports consisted of cotton and wool textiles and machinery. Exports were mainly oriented towards Europe and the United States, while Britain became Japan's principal supplier. The trade surplus prior to the Meiji Restoration soon turned, thereafter, into a persistent deficit. This persuaded the government to stimulate the creation of import-substituting industries that were heavily subsidized. After the monetary reforms at the beginning of the 1880s, many of these firms were sold to the private sector. Closely linked to financial institutions, many of them would form the heart of the so-called *zaibatsu* or large holding companies. Trade and maritime transport were at first dominated by foreigners. The *zaibatsu* imitated Western trading companies by creating similar ones with representations abroad. These would turn out to be an important tool in conquering foreign markets towards the end of the century. With government support, a maritime company was created that would successfully take over the role of foreign transportation companies.

Low wages and a depreciating value of the silver standard yen, favoured Japanese exports of manufactured products. At the beginning of the twentieth century cotton textiles made up over twenty-three per cent of Japanese exports, with China, India and the new Japanese colonies being the main export markets. Between 1880 and 1913, Japan's exports grew at an annual rate of 8.4 per cent, representing 13 per cent of national income in 1913. At the same time a shift took place in Japan's imports, which increasingly consisted of raw materials mainly imported from other Asian countries.

The indemnities received from China after the Sino-Japanese war of 1894–5 would allow Japan to adopt the Gold Standard in 1897. Japan's industrialization and military successes further allowed the country to abolish the extra-territorial rights of foreign residents in Japan in 1899, and to regain the right to determine its own tariffs in 1911.

IMPERIALISM AND COLONIALISM

Historical and geographical aspects of colonization: historical survey of the role of Japan in Asia

During the period of national isolation Japan showed no interest in expanding its rule beyond the four islands that made up Japan proper. This situation came to an end with the forced opening-up of the country to foreign trade in 1853, and the subsequent Meiji Restoration in 1868. In its drive to modernize the country following the models offered by Western Europe and the United States, the new Japanese government also became acquainted with the dominant view in the West, that colonies were vital for economic expansion and prestige of the nation.

Three further elements contributed to Japanese overseas expansion in the last quarter of the nineteenth century. The first was the increasing inroads in East Asia made by European nations: the British established their rule over Burma, the French over Indochina, the Russians over the territories north of China, and all nations were gaining footholds in China. The increasing European colonial presence was perceived as a possible threat to Japan. Second, the increasing weakness of China, in particular to foreign claims and concessions, made a coalition with the Chinese to check foreign expansion quite illusionary; at the same time it reinforced the idea that Japan also would be able to acquire territory at the expense of the Chinese; Third, and last, the successful industrialization of Japan increasingly required access to overseas markets, and to raw materials which were scarce in Japan itself. Thus the control of the supply of raw materials increased Japan's interests in Korea and, eventually, Manchuria.

After having settled the question of its national boundaries, the successful development of the Japanese economy enabled the country to increase its military power. Financed by foreign loans, Japan engaged in a conflict with China in 1894–5, which would yield Taiwan and Japanese influence in Korea. The conflict with Russia in 1904–5 would yield the southern half of Sakhalin and Port Arthur, and Japanese influence in Manchuria. Japan's colonies and overseas expansion would involve important capital movements from Japan in order to develop infrastructure and industries. Moreover, the copying of the Japanese institutions and education system in Taiwan and Korea often is considered to have laid a foundation for the subsequent successful economic growth of these two countries.

One of the issues the new Japanese government of the Meiji Restoration had to deal with was to determine Japan's boundaries. Apart from the four islands making up the Japanese mainland there were Japanese settlers on the Kurils and the island of Sakhalin. A further claim bore upon the Ryukyu kingdom with Okinawa, south of Japan, and the Bonin and Kazan islands south east of Japan. The first issue was settled in 1874–5, by leaving Sakhalin to Russia and obtaining recognition of Japanese rule over all the Kurils. The settlement of the status of the Ryukyu Islands turned out to be more complicated. Though the islands had been tributary to China, incorporating them in 1871 was not a problem. But the killing of inhabitants of the islands by Taiwanese would lead to a punitive expedition against Taiwan, which had formerly been part of China. This greatly undermined a treaty concluded with China in 1871, which contained a clause for mutual assistance in case of foreign aggression. Japan thus appeared more and more as a rival to China rather than an ally. The Ryukyu, Bonin, and Kazan islands officially became part of Japan in 1876.

Japanese and Chinese interests would clash in Korea, which had a tributary relationship to China. Japanese interests in Korea at first were related to its nearby and strategic geographical location. Concern would grow with attempts by Western powers to open up Korea, which diverted Japaneses attention from domestic problems of restructuring and modernizing and focused it on Korea. The first Japanese step to increase its influence in Korea was a gunboat expedition in 1876 to open up the country, thus imitating the way Japan had itself been opened two decades earlier. Consequently, a treaty was signed giving Japan access to the country on even more advantageous terms than Japan had had to accept from the Western powers. The advantageous position of the Japanese, however, would be short-lived, as similar treaties were concluded with Western powers in the early 1880s. Moreover, subsequent internal conflicts within Korea brought the country back under Chinese domination with the stationing of Chinese troops.

Conflict over Korea ultimately led to the Sino-Japanese war of 1894–5. Defeating the Chinese, Japan obtained Taiwan, the Chinese withdrawal from Korea, a privileged status in China and a large indemnity in gold. Further Japanese claims to a foothold in Manchuria were thwarted by the tripartite intervention of Russia, France and Germany. The annexation of Taiwan only became effective after the crushing of a widespread revolt on the island. The outcome of the war did, however, give Japan the status of a major power. As such it was allowed to take part in putting down the Boxer Rebellion in 1900, and in the ensuing peace negotiations with China. Moreover, her new status also allowed Japan to renegotiate the 'unequal' treaties it had been forced to accept when opening up, and to conclude an alliance with Britain in 1902.

In the meantime Russia had considerably expanded its influence in Manchuria and increasingly threatened Japan's influence in Korea. As Korea and even Manchuria increasingly were considered as vital Japanese markets and suppliers of raw materials, this ultimately resulted in the Russo-Japanese war of 1904–5. Financed by foreign loans, this war brought Japan a military victory, the southern half of Sakhalin, the Kwantung Leased Territory and the South Manchurian Railway Zone in Manchuria (mainly consisting of the ports of Dalny [Dairen] and Port Arthur). The Japanese supplanted the Russian presence in Manchuria, though exclusive privileges there were prevented by the mediation of the United States. Even before peace talks with Russia had started, Japan turned Korea into its protectorate. Subsequent revolts in the peninsula against Japanese domination were quashed, and the Japanese grip was further tightened by the formal annexation of Korea as a colony in 1910.

The expansion of Japanese influence involved not only an increasing overseas military presence, but also overseas Japanese migration and investment. Despite peace settlements after Japanese victories over China and Russia, and the pacification of the new Japanese overseas territories, the resulting empire could only be maintained by a strong military presence. Japan's military forces overseas were relatively large compared to those of the European colonial powers. This implied a financial burden, but also the increasing power of the military in Japan's foreign policy.

The Japanese view of their role in Asia evolved with their successful expansion. From helping other Asian nations to modernize their institutions and economies, their outlook became more analogous to current Western colonial views, as the Japanese were to consider themselves superior, and thus entitled to dominate and guide other Asian nations. It implied amongst other things an attempt to assimilate Japan's colonial subjects and to erase the latter's culture and proper identity. Japanese emigration to the newly acquired territories thus not only formed an outlet for Japan's growing population, but was also encouraged for its role in reinforcing Japan's overseas presence.

The incorporation of Japanese overseas territories into the Japanese economy and the opening up of Manchuria required important investment not only in railroads, ports, and roads, but also in warehouses and banking. The colonial government further engaged in mining, and promoted the establishment of Japanese business. Up to the First World War the main role for Taiwan and Korea, was to supply Japan with foodstuffs, that is rice, and in the case of Taiwan, sugar. To this end the Japanese rationalized and modernized the agricultural sectors in both colonies. Korea and

Taiwan increasingly also provided an outlet for Japanese manufacturing exports, in particular cotton textiles, although exports to India and China remained far more important.

In order to develop their colonial economies, the Japanese realized the importance of schooling and health, and that extending the availability of modern medical services in combination with improved diets would produce an important fall in death rates. The provision of elementary education reached increasing numbers of Koreans and Taiwanese. However, as almost all higher offices and functions in the colonies remained reserved for Japanese, the immediate benefit of such schooling was rather limited. The Japanese education system and agricultural modernization are often considered to have laid the foundations for the economic growth of both countries after the Second World War.

The colonial systems: Japan

Between 1895 and 1913, Japan had acquired a colonial empire comprising Taiwan, Korea, Kwantung (Manchuria), and the southern half of Sakhalin. Since the latter's population would soon principally consist of Japanese settlers, and Kwantung was a leased territory, Japanese colonial rule would be most characteristic in Taiwan and Korea. When Japan obtained them in 1895, it had no experiences of colonial rule or a clear-cut vision about colonial management. Gradually a policy would be developed that in many aspects resembled European colonial rule. In other aspects, however, Japanese colonial policy would be specifically Japanese.

As in European colonial policy, Japan's colonies primarily had to serve Japanese interests. Apart from serving as a demonstration of Japan's status as a modern power, the colonies were to provide Japan with foodstuffs in order to feed its growing population and to avoid expensive food imports from other countries. An important part of colonial policy in Taiwan and Korea thus consisted of modernizing the agricultural sector in order to increase the production of rice. Taiwan would also become an important supplier of sugar.

Establishing effective Japanese rule over Taiwan and Korea met with guerrilla resistance in both territories, which was suppressed by the Japanese army. In both colonies a considerable military presence would be maintained and the military had a dominant role in the administration of the colonies. The military governors of Taiwan and Korea had almost unlimited powers, and were directly accountable to the Emperor. This meant that control of the Diet (the Japanese parliament) and Japanese ministries was weak, and therefore that the colonial administration could enjoy significant autonomy.

Internal control over the colonies was carried out by an efficient Japanese police force, which was assisted by selected local representatives. In Taiwan the Japanese restored the Chinese *pao chia* system of collective responsibility in maintaining law and order. Next to their task of control, the well-trained Japanese police had an important function in local administration, collecting taxes and providing administrative and technical assistance to local communities. They thus played an important part in modernizing the colonial economies. Colonial administration further relied on civil servants trained at the best

Japanese universities. Though highly competent and efficient, these officials were transferred from colony to colony, and thus rarely had much contact with the indigenous population.

A clearly distinct feature of the Japanese colonial system related to the racial and cultural affinities between the Japanese and their colonial subjects, which generally did not exist in the European colonial empires. This opened the way to complete integration of the empire through the assimilation of the indigenous colonial populations. Japanese colonial rule thus promoted the adoption of the Japanese language and way of life. Both Japanese migration to the colonies and colonial education contributed an important role in achieving assimilation. This in turn, and particularly in Korea, would lead to increasing suppression of indigenous culture and identity. Despite the formal aim of integration, the Japanese enjoyed social and economic privileges in their colonies. The indigenous population had practically no access to employment in the colonial administration and clearly had the status of second-class citizens.

As with the European colonial powers, Japan saw its mission as one to improve the welfare of its colonies and enlighten its colonial subjects. The period of time in which these aims were to be carried out was, however, unspecified and unlimited: no provision was made for any kind of home rule for the colonies.

As Japan's financial resources were needed to continue the modernization of its home economy, there was not much room for transfers to its colonies. Though foreign loans provided some funds for Taiwan, the colonies mainly had to finance their modernization themselves. Cadastral surveys there allowed the introduction of a land tax, which together with indirect taxes on consumption and several monopoly profits would make up the main source of income for the colonial governments. These resources were used to construct railways and communications, the net income of which subsequently would also become an important source of income. Apart from providing an infrastructure, colonial governments invested in raising agricultural output through irrigation and other development programmes. Mining and specific industries also saw direct government involvement. Increasingly, colonial governments would provide incentives to attract investment from the Japanese private sector. The economic development of the colonies would further be stimulated through education and health programmes which were to improve the health and quality of the local workforce and subsequently their productivity. To a large extent the colonial administrations based their strategies on the experiences of Meiji Japan that had brought about the successful modernization of the Japanese economy.

The available evidence on the development of Taiwan and Korea seems to indicate that Japanese colonial policy was successful in bringing about economic growth. Up to the First World War agricultural output of the colonies increased considerably. Though most of the increase in agricultural output was exported to Japan, it also enabled the colonies to feed a growing domestic population. As food supplies for local consumption were relatively low, particularly in Korea, and increasing only very slowly, Japan's colonial agricultural policy has often been labelled as exploitation.

The economic gains and losses of the Japanese colonial system to Japan and to the colonial populations have been, and still are, the subject of debate. Allegedly Japan largely benefited from its colonies, that were successfully transformed into suppliers of food and raw materials to Japan and markets for Japanese manufacturing industries. Moreover, colonial enterprises and investments yielded high profits to Japanese firms. The importance of the colonies in this respect, however, should not be exaggerated. The share of colonial trade in total Japanese foreign trade remained quite small. The same can be said about the share of colonial profits in total profits of Japanese firms. The benefits for Japan from its colonies can, however, also be measured in terms of yielding Japan the status of a colonial power and in accrued access to the Chinese market.

Similarly, Korea and Taiwan are often considered at least to have benefited from the colonial institutions by way of agricultural reforms and Japanese educational efforts. Here again, it seems, the direct benefits during Japanese colonial rule were rather small. Both Koreans and Taiwanese did enjoy improving health conditions and some improvement in their standard of living. But better education gave them no access to better jobs in colonial administration or in Japanese-owned firms. Moreover, they had to face the suppression of their own culture and identity. On the other hand, the institutions, agrarian reforms and education system put in place by Japan probably did provide a base for their economic growth after independence.

BIBLIOGRAPHY

BEASLY, W. G. (ed.) 1989. The Foreign Threat and the Opening of the Ports. In: Jansen, M. B. *The Cambridge History of Japan, Vol. 5: The Nineteenth Century.* Cambridge University Press, Cambridge, pp. 259–307.

CASTLES, S.; MILLER, M. J. 1993. *The Age of Migration. International Population Movements in the Modern World.* Macmillan Press, Hong Kong.

CRAWCOUR, E. S. (ed.) 1989. Economic Change in the Nineteenth Century. In: Jansen, M. B. *The Cambridge History of Japan, Vol. 5: The Nineteenth Century.* Cambridge University Press, Cambridge, pp. 569–617.

——. (ed.) 1988. Industrialization and Technological Change, 1885–1920. In: Duus, P. *The Cambridge History of Japan, 6: The Twentieth Century.* Cambridge University Press, Cambridge, pp. 385–450.

DUUS, P. 1995. *The Abacus and the Sword. The Japanese Penetration of Korea. 1895–1910.* University of California Press, Berkeley.

FINDLAY SHIRRAS, G. (ed.) 1969. Indian Migration. In: Willcox, W. F. *International Migrations. Vol. 2. Interpretations. (Demographic Monographs Vol. 81).* Gordon and Breach, New York, pp. 591–616.

HAGGARD, S.; KANG, D.; MOON, C. 1997. Japanese Colonialism and Korean Development: A Critique. *World Development,* Vol. 25, No. 6, pp. 867–81.

HANLEY, S. B.; YAMAMURA, K. 1977. *Economic and Demographic Change in Pre-industrial Japan 1600–1868.* Princeton University Press, Princeton.

HATA, I. (ed.) 1988. Continental Expansion, 1905–1941. In: Duus, P. *The Cambridge History of Japan, 6: The Twentieth Century.* Cambridge University Press, Cambridge, pp. 271–314.

HO, S. P. S. 1978. *Economic Development of Taiwan. 1860–1970.* Yale University Press, New Haven.

ICHIHASHI, Y. (ed.) 1969. International Migration of the Japanese. In: Willcox, W. F. *International Migrations. Vol. II. Interpretations. (Demographic Monographs Vol. 8).* Gordon and Breach, New York, pp. 617–36.

IRIYE, A. (ed.) 1989. Japan's Drive to Great-power Status. In: Jansen, M. B. *The Cambridge History of Japan, 5: The Nineteenth Century*. Cambridge University Press, Cambridge, pp. 721–82.

KIMURA, M. 1995. The Economics of Japanese Imperialism in Korea, 1910–1939. *Economic History Review*, Vol. 48, No. 3, Oxford, pp. 555–74.

LUDOWYK, E. F. C. 1966. *The Modern History of Ceylon*. Praeger, New York.

MACPHERSON, W. J. 1995. *The Economic Development of Japan, 1868–1941*. Cambridge University Press, Cambridge.

MADDISON, A. 1991. *Dynamic Forces in Capitalist Development. A Long-run Comparative View*. Oxford University Press, Oxford.

——. 1969. *Economic Growth in Japan and the USSR*. Allen & Unwin, London.

MEYERS, R. H.; PEATTIE, M. R. (ed.) 1984. *The Japanese Colonial Empire, 1895–1945*. Princeton University Press, Princeton.

MIZOGUCHI, T. 1979. Economic Growth of Korea under the Japanese Occupation. Background of Industrialization of Korea 1911–1940. *Hitotsubashi Journal of Economics*, Vol. 20, No. 1, Tokyo, pp. 1–19.

OHKAWA, K.; SHINOHARA, M. 1979. *Patterns of Japanese Development. A Quantitative Appraisal*. Yale University Press, New Haven.

PANDITARATNE, B. L.; SELVA NAYAGRAM, S. (ed.) 1973. The Demography of Ceylon, An Introductory Survey. In: De Silva, K. M. *History of Ceylon. From the Beginning of the Nineteenth Century to 1948*. Vol. 3, University of Ceylon, Colombo, pp. 285–302.

PEATTIE, M. (ed.) 1988. The Japanese Colonial Empire, 1895–1945. In: Duus, P. *The Cambridge History of Japan, 6: The Twentieth Century*. Cambridge University Press, Cambridge, pp. 217–70.

PERKINS, D. H. 1969. *Agricultural Development in China 1368–1968*. Edinburgh University Press, Edinburgh.

POTTS, I. 1990. *The World Labour Market: A History of Migration*. Zed Books, London.

SMITH, T. C. 1988. *Native Sources of Japanese Industrialization 1750–1920*. University of California Press, Berkeley.

VISARIA, L.; VISARIA, P. (ed.) 1983. Population. In: Kumar, D. *The Cambridge Economic History of India*. Vol. 2, Cambridge University Press, Cambridge, pp. 463–532.

WILLCOX, W. F. (ed.) 1969. *International Migrations. Vol. 1. Statistics. (Demographic Monographs Vol. 7)*. Gordon and Breach, New York.

3

INDUSTRIALIZATION AND SCIENTIFIC AND TECHNOLOGICAL PROGRESS

Rainer Fremdling

CONCEPT AND SPREAD OF THE INDUSTRIAL REVOLUTION

The Industrial Revolution is traditionally considered the most important event in the history of humanity since the Neolithic period:

> between 1780 and 1850, in less than three generations, a far-reaching revolution, without precedent in the history of Mankind, changed the face of England. From then on, the world was no longer the same. Historians have often used the word revolution to mean a radical change, but no revolution has been as dramatic as the Industrial Revolution – except perhaps the Neolithic Revolution.
>
> (Cipolla, 1975: 7)

The Industrial Revolution marks the beginning of a self-sustained process towards modern economic growth with increasing income per capita (Kuznets, 1966). For a long time Britain, the first industrial nation (Mathias, 1969), was regarded as the model for all the Industrial Revolutions achieved in the follower countries (Landes, 1969: 124). During the eighteenth century a cluster of innovations had led to the rise of industry and the emergence of the factory system in Britain. According to Landes, these innovations could be subsumed under three principles:

> the substitution of machines – rapid, regular, precise, tireless – for human skill and effort; the substitution of inanimate for animate sources of power, in particular, the introduction of engines for converting heat into work, thereby opening to man a new and almost unlimited supply of energy; the use of new and far more abundant materials, in particular, the substitution of mineral for vegetable or animal substance.
>
> (Landes, 1969: 41)

The classic, traditional view of the Industrial Revolution in general focuses on two related aspects: an unprecedented change of techniques, accompanied by a rising income per capita.

This traditional view of industrialization has been questioned in at least three respects: When Cameron labels the term 'Industrial Revolution' a misnomer he first of all doubts its *revolutionary* character (Cameron, 1989: 163–5). Calculations of aggregate growth rates of income, indeed, do not show a rapid increase within a short period of, say, thirty years for Britain (Crafts, 1994), and hence indicate no take-off in a Rostowian[1] sense. Furthermore a continuous flow of small improvements attained by tinkering on the job (von Tunzelmann, 1981) proved at least equally important as the spectacular Schumpeterian[2] 'basic' innovations.[3] Second, there were different paths leading to modern economic growth (O'Brien and Keyder, 1978). There is, moreover, convincing evidence that the British growth path was the exception rather than the norm (Crafts, 1984). Third, the uniqueness of the growth process ushered in with the Industrial Revolution has raised scepticism. In the course of the economic history of Western Europe one can identify at least two long waves of growth (eleventh–thirteenth centuries, fifteenth–sixteenth centuries) before the Industrial Revolution. Those phases of expansion, however, ended up in the Malthusian[4] trap, with population growth reaching the ceiling built in by the limits to growth. There are apprehensions that the same might happen with modern economic growth: The Neo-Malthusian Report of the Club of Rome (1972) generalized Malthus' view for the entire earth and predicted a global environmental catastrophe, if population growth and the actual use of resources for production and consumption did not change radically (Meadows *et al.*, 1972).

Notwithstanding these objections to the traditional view of industrialization, it seems rather clear that on a worldwide scale there was a revolutionary break with the past. As this break did not force up the rate of economic growth all at once 'it is appropriate to think about the Industrial Revolution primarily in terms of accelerating and unprecedented technological change' (Mokyr, 1990: 82). Economic growth has to be seen as the outcome of a broader process, which includes also productivity gains, and the growth of output in agriculture and the service sector. A successful industrialization, however, was sufficient to economic growth. And since the so-called Industrial Revolution, modern economic growth has after all been a worldwide phenomenon. According to the calculations of world's economic growth by the British and Dutch scholar Angus Maddison, this break with the past becomes palpable: between 1500 and 1820 world population grew annually by 0.29 per cent, gross domestic product (GDP) per capita by 0.04 per cent, and the world's GDP by 0.33 per cent. Between 1820 and 1992, however, the same categories witnessed a growth rate of 0.95 per cent, 1.21 per cent and 2.17 per cent respectively (Maddison, 1991: 20). Growth performance since 1820 has been dramatically superior to that in earlier history.

> Before our present 'capitalistic' epoch, economies were predominantly agrarian, and economic advance was largely extensive. In response to demographic pressure, economic activity was successful over the long term in sustaining living standards, but technology was virtually stagnant and evidence of advances in economic well-being is very meagre.
>
> (Maddison, 1995: 19)

Taking separate nations with their performance individually (see Table 9) belittles this fundamental achievement of modern economic growth in the history of humanity. The desirable global approach should not blur the different paths the specific nations or world regions have taken since the Industrial Revolution.

In Table 9 for selected countries in certain world regions the level of gross domestic product (GDP) per capita and the size of the population is given for the benchmark years 1820, 1913 and 1992. The empirical basis and the underlying methodology of the GDP figures in 1990 US dollars may be questioned for those early years of 1820 and 1913,

and also for the above-mentioned growth rates between 1500 and 1820. Given our present knowledge about the nineteenth century and economic growth in earlier centuries, they provide a rough but correct picture of relative performance levels among nations and world regions. Since GDP per capita is still the best single indicator of welfare levels and the standard of living, the relative performance among nations also reveals information about the average well-being of people in different regions of the world. Leading performers have been Western European countries and offshoots of European settlements in North America and the Pacific. The major exceptions have been Japan from the late nineteenth century onwards and recently some newly industrializing countries in South East Asia. The other big Asian nations with their huge population have still acquired no more than moderate income levels. Latin American countries did not perform badly during the nineteenth century and the early decades of the twentieth century. From then on, however, they have fallen far behind the leading group in terms of economic growth. Southern European countries have caught up recently, whereas Eastern European countries still have to suffer under

Table 9 Gross domestic product (GDP) per capita and population of selected countries, 1820, 1913, 1992 (in 1990 international dollars and thousands).

Country	1820		1913		1992	
	GDP	Population	GDP	Population	GDP	Population
Africa						
Egypt	–	–	508	12,144	1,927	54,679
Ghana	–	–	648	2,043	1,007	15,800
South Africa	–	–	1,451	6,153	3,451	37,600
Asia						
China	523	381,000	688	437,140	3,098	1,167,000
India	531	175,349	663	251,906	1,348	881,200
Indonesia	614	17,927	917	49,934	2,749	185,900
Japan	704	31,000	1,334	51,672	19,425	124,336
Latin America						
Argentina	–	534	3,797	7,653	7,616	33,003
Brazil	670	4,507	839	23,660	4,637	156,012
Mexico	760	6,587	1,467	14,970	5,112	89,520
Eastern Europe						
Czechoslovakia	849	7,190	2,096	13,245	6,845	15,615
Hungary	–	4,571	2,098	7,840	5,638	10,313
USSR	751	50,398	1,488	156,192	4,671	292,375
Southern Europe						
Greece	–	–	1,621	5,425	10,314	10,300
Spain	1,063	12,203	2,255	20,263	12,498	39,085
Western Europe						
France	1,218	31,250	3,452	41,463	17,959	57,372
Germany[1]	1,112	14,747	3,833	37,843	19,351	64,846
Italy	1,092	20,176	2,507	37,248	16,229	57,900
Netherlands	1,561	2,355	3,950	6,164	16,898	15,178
UK	1,756	19,832	5,032	42,622	15,738	57,848
North America/Australia						
USA	1,287	9,656	5,107	97,606	21,558	255,610
Canada	893	741	4,213	7,852	18,159	28,436
Australia	1,528	33	5,505	4,821	16,237	17,529

Note

1 Population of the territory of the Federal Republic (1989 boundaries). More adequate are the following figures: 1820, German states without Austria, 24,905; 1913, Imperial Germany, 66,978; 1990, Federal Republic with the former GDR, 79,638. See also Maddison 1991.

Source: Maddison 1995, pp. 23f, 104–16.

the heritage of mismanaged planned economies of the defaulted communist regimes. Taken as a whole, Africa has remained the poorest continent, though with substantial variations among different countries. It seems pretty clear that those world regions or countries which underwent an industrial revolution already in the nineteenth century, have had the best performance in modern economic growth until today.

Being the first industrial nation, Britain had taken the technical lead in the second half of the eighteenth century. Early industrializing countries were the United States, Belgium, France and some German states (e.g. Saxony, Prussia). During the second half of the nineteenth century industrialization gained momentum in the Netherlands as well as in Scandinavia, in parts of the Austro-Hungarian Empire, in Switzerland, Italy and Japan. In Southern and Eastern Europe, in imperial Russia and in some other parts of the world industrialization then had not become a country-wide process yet, but was restricted to certain enclaves within a country. In spite of being scattered in many a place, the process became a worldwide phenomenon, insofar as a country or region either itself underwent industrialization or was involved in the international network of finance and trade which was dominated by the industrialized powers. This network did not only potentially maximize worldwide production, if one follows a Ricardian view, but with its informal and formal empires (colonialism) it could be a means of economically exploiting large parts of the world to the benefit of the first industrial nations. A famous example is the Dutch *Cultuurstelsel* (cultivation system, 1830–70) in colonial Indonesia. It meant a forced cultivation of colonial crops (e.g. sugar, coffee, tea and tobacco) destined for European markets. At the peak of this exploitation, between 1856 and 1866, the Dutch government's revenues were increased by 30 million guilders yearly for a state budget of less than 110 million guilders. The modernization of Dutch infrastructure (canals, railways, roads) could have been financed easily with this money. (Maddison and Prince, 1989; Van der Eng, 1993). To improve on the production of tropical agricultural products (such as bananas, rubber, cocoa, coffee, cotton and peanuts) which the European powers obtained from their African colonies, France, Germany, Great Britain and the Netherlands built a network of botanic gardens in their respective African colonies from before 1880 and onwards. These gardens served as experimental parks on the basis of new scientific knowledge from Europe (Bonneuil, 1997a).

Although the self-sustained character of modern economic growth is still active, a mere extension of the present industrial system of the Western countries (the OECD countries in the 1990s) to other countries might lead to a limit of growth. The industrial system has right from the beginning concentrated on new sources of energy, and the corollary of a widespread industrialization would be the widespread use of (fossil) energy (Clark, 1990).

INDUSTRIAL TECHNOLOGY AND INNOVATION

The following concentrates on certain innovations and industries, namely the steam engine, the iron and steel industry and the use of electricity. A somewhat broader view of the consequences of these and other innovations of the Industrial Revolution is presented in Chapter 1. An account of scientific progress as such is not undertaken because well into the nineteenth century technological (or technical) progress seems to have moved ahead of scientific progress.

During the Industrial Revolution the most important driving forces for innovations were focused on exploring new sources of fuel and on economizing on fuel consumption. Fuel was needed both for heating purposes and for generating mechanical energy. Thus the most important innovations of the Industrial Revolution in Britain were based on hard coal-consuming techniques. Britain was relatively well endowed with this raw material, whereas wood had become rather expensive long before the eighteenth century. For simple heating purposes (bituminous) hard coal was a perfect substitute for the hitherto generally used wood both in industry and household. It was as early as the seventeenth century that Britain experienced and tackled the problems which German economist Werner Sombart (1863–1941) labelled the 'wood constraint' (*Holzbremse*). As a forerunner of the 'limits to growth' admonishments, 'wood constraint' threatened also the further growth of continental economies at the end of the eighteenth century. As has been put forward by Wrigley (1988), the inherent limits of the pre-industrial 'organic economy' could not be overcome just by resorting to a new source of abundant heat energy, but new methods of deriving mechanical energy were required as well.

The corresponding device for the mechanization of production was the coal-consuming steam engine. As the prime mover applied in large factories (e.g. for textiles) and as the driving force of the railway and the steamboat, the steam engine became the embodiment of the industrial age. Nevertheless, traditional sources of mechanical power, in particular the windmill, the water wheel and draught animals, remained important far into the nineteenth century (von Tunzelmann, 1978, esp. ch. 6). Even in Great Britain, which was rich in coal, the major innovations in textiles at the end of the eighteenth century had been developed for water- or horse-driven mills.

> With regard to individual innovations, one can note that virtually all the celebrated eighteenth-century inventions in textiles were created for either animal or simply manpower. [Famous innovators of the British textile industry such as] Hargreaves and Crompton were avowedly improving the lot of female spinners in cottage industry. Paul and Wyatt, Arkwright, and Cartwright all began with animals. Even for the spinning-mule, waterpower was applied in incorporating the invention into factory industry before the steam engine.
>
> (von Tunzelmann, 1978: 160)

With these caveats in mind, the history of the steam engine reveals essential characteristics of the interrelationship between the Industrial Revolution on the one hand and scientific and technological progress on the other hand. The steam engine is conventionally associated with the Briton James Watt (1736–1819) who took out his first patent on this innovation in 1769. As with many inventions and their application to economic purposes, Watt's achievement has to be seen as part of a long tradition of a process of trial and error (Mokyr, 1990: 84–90). Basically the first generation of steam engines rested on the simple knowledge that the atmosphere could be used as a source of power if a vacuum was created. Torricelli in Italy (1643–4), von Guericke in Germany (around 1660) and probably the Chinese and even people in ancient Alexandria (Hero, around 100 BC) knew about this principle and used it for fancy experiments. But not before the eighteenth century was this scientific knowledge translated into innovations, above all in England. After the French natural scientist Papin (1690) and the English amateur inventor Savery (1698) had developed prototypes of the 'atmospheric' steam engine, it was the English blacksmith Newcomen who for the first time constructed an economically successful engine, installed in a coal mine near Wolverhampton in 1712. In this machine, condensation repeatedly created vacua through cooling the heated air in a cylinder. By this an alternate motive power drove a beam, which was used to pump water out of mines. Newcomen's atmospheric steam engines were used in English tin and coal mines in order to drain the water. This innovation spread to continental Europe during the first half of the eighteenth century. But the diffusion of this technology was limited, as the machine's enormous appetite for fuel made it a costly device. That is why this steam engine was almost exclusively applied for the drainage of coalmines, a location where the necessary fuel (coal) was available cheaply.

It was precisely the savings in fuel consumption which made Watt's steam engine such a success. The Watt engine raised fuel efficiency by nearly five times compared with Newcomen's design. This was due to several technical improvements: The piston cylinder was separated from the condenser, so that the cylinder could be kept hot constantly. Furthermore, John Wilkinson's boring machines produced cylinders of great accuracy, which helped to obtain a far better seal compared to the Newcomen machine. These and other improvements saved fuel, and therefore use of the steam engine was now less confined to locations close to coalfields. Watt also designed a transmission mechanism, which converted the up-and-down motion into a rotary motion. This way the steam engine became the prime mover for machines in the textile industry and various other applications, such as the steam locomotive and sea-going vessels called steamers.

Watt was seemingly not that typical of the inventors and innovators who shaped the technical change of the first industrial nation. As suggested by Mathias, 'Most innovations were the products of inspired amateurs, or brilliant artisans trained as clock-makers, millwrights, [or] blacksmiths'. That obviously does not apply to James Watt, who was part of the academic community. Watt was thus familiar with scientific experiments. But it seems to be a myth that his invention of the separate condenser arose out of listening to lectures on latent heat at Glasgow University (von Tunzelmann, 1978: 11). So not even Watt may perhaps any longer be referred to as a man of science, who formed an exception to the rule that 'By and large innovations were not the result of the formal application of applied science, nor a product of the formal educational system of the country'. In particular, 'the dozen and more inventors and improvers of techniques in steam power, and the entire pioneering of high-pressure engines, was in the amateur, and the blacksmith tradition' (Mathias, 1983: 121–30).

After Watt's patent had expired in 1800 a new generation of inventors and innovators improved the steam engine in its efficiency, which always meant saving fuel, and found various applications for its use. Technically most important was the creation of high-pressure machines. In 1802, the Englishman Richard Trevithick built a steam engine with a pressure ten times as high as the atmosphere. In Europe and

in North America in the course of the nineteenth century, numerous people constructed ever better steam engines. And 'better' is measured in terms of fuel input in relation to power generation. Besides high pressure, it was the principle of compounding which saved fuel. Compound steam engines comprised several cylinders where the same steam could be used subsequently.

The diffusion of the steam engines depended not only on their fixed costs, i.e. the price of the machine, but also on their variable costs, i.e. the costs of coal consumption. These costs changed a lot over time, among different types of machines and among geographical locations, i.e. depending on access to a coalfield. And of course the cost relative to alternative (traditional) sources of power, i.e. wind, water, animal and human power potentials, remained crucial. In essence all these factors are considered by von Tunzelmann's study (1978). He briefly compares Britain with the United States and Belgium. The Newcomen steam engine spread fast in Britain and within decades even in continental European countries. It was used for pumping water out of coalmines. According to an estimate, around 1800 roughly 2,500 steam engines had been built, of which about one third had been designed by Watt. It was not before the 1790s that steam engines were used on a large scale in textile factories. The heyday of the steam engine was yet to come during the nineteenth century. Eventually not only were stationary engines used in factories, mines, etc. as prime movers, but also steam engines served to improve transport over land (railways) and on water (steamships) considerably. Chapter 1 provides more details on the introduction of the steam-ship.

The other major coal-consuming technology involved the iron and steel industry (Church, 1994).

> How do we assess the importance of the iron industry in the Industrial Revolution? The economist's test of the importance of any invention is its substitutability: if it had not been invented, would another technology have done? By that criterion, the steam engine and cotton look less of a strategic invention than the advances in iron. It is conceivable to imagine an Industrial Revolution based on waterpower and linen or wool – in fact in many places that is precisely what happened. There was no substitute for iron, however, in thousands of uses, from nails to engines. As its price fell, iron invaded terrains traditionally dominated by timber, such as bridges, ships and eventually buildings.
>
> (Mokyr, 1994: 26f.)

Only a few parts of the world lack iron ore. With charcoal (made from wood) serving as a fuel, this iron ore could be smelted into iron nearly everywhere. So the traditional iron and steel industry was widely spread all over the world. As soon as hard coal was used for producing iron and steel, regions endowed with plentiful coal deposits became the primary sites of heavy industry. But even in pioneering Britain it took nearly a century before hard coal had supplanted charcoal as a fuel for smelting and refining iron (Hyde, 1977). Major technical problems made it difficult to find an economically viable alternative to the traditional charcoal technology.

The simplified scheme (see Table 10) allows a survey of the transition from charcoal to hard coal in the primary iron industry at a glance (Fremdling, 1986). In liquid state pig iron (stage 1) could be cast into forms for obtaining cast iron products. In order to shape iron with a hammer, pig iron had to be refined (stage 2). Refining meant a reduction of the carbon content, thereby turning the brittle, hard pig

Table 10 Primary iron industry.

Stage of production	Process		Product
	Traditional	Modern	
First stage	Smelting in the blast furnace		
	with charcoal	with coke	pig iron
Second stage	Refining		
	in a hearth	in a puddling furnace	wrought
	with charcoal	with hard-coal	iron
Third stage	Shaping		
	by the hammer	by a rolling mill	bar iron (rails)

iron into a tough but soft wrought iron. Shaped into bars, it was sold, for example, to smiths, who produced agricultural implements, horse shoes, etc.

Around 1700, the British primary iron industry lagged far behind that of Sweden, the world market leader of that time. The small British sector had high costs and could survive only behind protective walls. But in spite of import duties, the growing indigenous demand for wrought iron was mainly met by imports from Sweden and later from Russia as well. Still in 1788, those imports exceeded domestic production. Not before the eighteenth century did the British primary iron industry change fundamentally. In 1709, after a lengthy process of trial and error, the Englishman Abraham Darby of Coalbrookdale succeeded in substituting hard coal (or its derivative, coke) for charcoal in the blast furnace. He had found an economically viable way of using coke-smelted pig iron as an input for cast iron products. For wrought iron, the input of charcoal pig iron remained cheaper until well into the second half of the eighteenth century. The diffusion of coke-fired blast furnaces in Great Britain did not accelerate before the 1750s. Initially it was the demand for cast iron products which propelled this diffusion. Especially for construction purposes, cast iron served as a substitute for timber, bricks and stone. The famous iron bridge crossing the river Severn close to Coalbrookdale was built in 1779. It is a still-existing monument of this cast iron age.

Throughout the eighteenth century, prices for charcoal increased, whereas hard coal became relatively cheaper. It was thus ever more rewarding to find a process which allowed the use of hard coal for the production of wrought iron. But direct contact between the hard coal and the heated object could produce undesired chemical reactions, as impurities in the coal, such as sulphur and phosphorus, could be transferred to the melting metal. This contamination could make the metal brittle and technically inferior to the metal refined with traditional charcoal. So the main technical problem was to keep hard coal and the molten pig iron apart while refining the iron. Nobody knows how many attempts failed before this problem was finally solved. It took several generations to overcome these difficulties through trial and error methods. Most likely the Wood Brothers already in the 1760s had found an economically viable way. They used clay pots, which separated the reheated pig iron from the hard coal, thus avoiding undesirable chemical reactions during the refining process.

Probably half of all British wrought iron was produced by applying the potting process of the Woods when Henry Cort took out his famous patent on the puddling and rolling process in 1784. The inside of a bricked-up puddling furnace consists of three parts: low walls separate the bowl or working area from the fire grate on the one side and from the chimney on the other, thereby keeping the hard coal apart from the iron. Built only half-high, these walls leave the upper area of the entire furnace open so that the hot firing gases pass over the pig iron in the smelting chamber (bowl area), heating and smelting it, and then escape through the chimney. Puddling remained a handicraft, with very strong men stirring the molten mass by hand and turning and lifting the refined iron.

In addition to this new refining process, Cort also introduced rolling as a superior method of shaping the wrought iron into bars. The technologies based on hard coal spread very fast in Great Britain. Riden (1977) estimated that in 1750–4 just 7 per cent of pig iron was smelted by using coke (made from hard coal) in the blast furnace; by 1785–9 it made up nearly 90 per cent. At the beginning of the nineteenth century, after the Napoleonic Wars, Britain boasted the largest and most productive, thus the cheapest, primary iron industry in the world. Britain's former disadvantage, namely expensive wood, had become notorious by the beginning of the eighteenth century, but a century later it had turned into an advantage because it encouraged hard-coal based technologies. This development was possible only because Britain produced an innovative response to her resource endowments.

What were the consequences of the process innovations of the coke-fired blast furnace, the puddling furnace and the rolling mill on the iron industries of other countries? If these innovations were highly superior to the traditional procedures, not only technically but economically as well, the new techniques should have spread rapidly. This implies that the old-fashioned iron industry based on charcoal should have perished. But this did not occur for quite a long time. Traditional or partly modernized procedures could endure very well within their districts and their traditional markets. Moreover, when spreading over continental Europe or North America the new techniques did not strictly follow the British model, but varied in different ways. The following examples of adaptations to the British hard-coal techniques in Prussia, France and Belgium exemplify fundamentally different ways of reacting to the British challenge. The inclusion of additional countries would not have yielded more significant information on the transfer of this important technology of the first Industrial Revolution. For more information on other European countries, North America and Japan, and on the adoption of liquid steel processes in the second half of the nineteenth century, see the articles in Church, 1994; Temin, 1964; Allen, 1977; Inwood, 1992; and Abe and Suzuki, 1991.

At a very early date, the state-owned ironworks of Malapane, Gleiwitz and Königshütte (Krolewska Huta) in Prussian Upper Silesia were the first on the continent to continuously use coke for smelting pig iron. Upper Silesia was well endowed with hard coal, but was also rich in wood. Starting already in the 1790s, the early transfer of hard coal technology is widely, if rather uncritically, esteemed as a striking success. But for quite a long time coke smelting remained a heterogeneous element in an economically viable but technically rather backward method. In its technical backwardness the Upper Silesian wrought iron industry neither applied the then available modern techniques of employing hard coal (namely potting and puddling) nor resorted to more efficient methods of charcoal technology. The technical problems of coke smelting were solved, but still these ironworks did not make profits by the innovation. Prussian technocrats are to blame for introducing coke smelting that early. They had been mistaken, when imagining a programme for industrial development, to believe themselves capable of putting the British model quickly into practice in Upper Silesia. Uncritically, the Prussian technocrats had jumped to the conclusion that technical feasibility meant economic success. It did not, and thus coke smelting in Upper Silesia produced no serious consequences for the rest of the iron industry there relative to other regions until the 1830s.

Before the prohibitive duties of 1822 were levied, only a few French ironworks made an effort to follow the British model (Gille, 1968; Vial, 1967; Woronoff, 1984). The coalfields of Creuzot, for instance, already had blast furnaces in 1783–4. But before the brothers Schneider in 1836 set out to make Le Creusot one of France's most successful engineering and iron works, the enterprise had been a relative failure. The conditions after 1822 seemed to favour establishing British-type ironworks in France. By then imports from Britain had shown that there was a demand for hardcoal iron. With import tariffs guaranteeing a high price level, big profits seemed to be in prospect. In expectation thereof, ironworks proliferated in the coal districts of the Loire valley and the Massif Central. Following the British model they were built straight away as big ironworks, comprising several stages of production. But these new establishments did not enjoy economic success until well into the 1830s. Technical problems at the outset were solved gradually, but the new locations presented serious shortcomings: unlike in Britain, the iron ore had to be transported from afar, which raised the costs of production enormously. Moreover, the sites of the new iron industry were located away from the centres of consumption, which increased costs. To make matters worse, in these centres, the new products had to compete with those of higher quality produced by the traditional or partly modernized iron industry. The newcomers could not undercut the prices of the old-established firms enough for them to enter the markets. Thus for a long time the changing economic structure did not entail the decline of the traditional iron producing regions.

Dutch-Belgian Wallonia was rich in hard coal. It was the only continental European region to follow the British model successfully even before the construction of railways (Reuss et al., 1960). Since the middle of the 1820s numerous works comprising coke blast furnaces as well as puddling and rolling mills were built in the coal mining areas around Liège and Charleroi. Excelling the others, the factory of the British-Dutch-Belgian entrepreneur John Cockerill at Seraing, as early as 1825 integrated all stages of production from engineering to the supply of raw materials. The natural resources of Wallonia were similar to those in British iron producing regions, with ore and coal situated close together. Transportation costs and moderate protective duties screened Wallonia from British competition, while the Dutch government pursued an ambitious programme of industrial development based on the British model.

Thus, except for Wallonia, the first efforts to transfer British high technology to the continent by building coke blast furnaces solely or as part of integrated ironworks failed economically until well into the 1830s. But apart from imitation, the British model encouraged the traditional iron industry to apply various strategies of adaptation. Hence this sector did not remain passive, but underwent a development common in the field of technology, for instance in sailing ships, where an obsolescent technique finally reached its highest technical and productive level shortly before it disappeared. Accordingly, calculations made for Sweden, the German Siegerland district and Württemberg show that smelting iron traditionally with charcoal increased its productivity considerably in the decades from the 1820s to the 1850s, which is exactly the crucial period for the modern iron industry's diffusion on the continent (Fremdling, 1986: 155–61). The improvements were achieved through extraordinary retrenchments on charcoal, which had the highest share of the costs of smelting iron. In some traditional iron producing areas output grew enormously. Only in the 1850s did this growth reveal itself as a short-lived success. And even then, several contemporary experts did not at all foresee that the traditional iron producing areas that disposed of nothing but wood and iron ore would more or less sink into insignificance through the expertise of large-scale technology coming from Britain.

The traditional iron industry struggled for survival both by increasing the productivity of smelting iron with charcoal and by elaborately integrating parts of the new technique. The small forges could, for instance, substitute the new puddling furnace for the old refining furnace without changing the rest of the operations. Detached from the other modern techniques from Britain, the craft of puddling began spreading over many regions of the traditional iron industry already in the 1820s. As puddling furnaces were fuelled with hard coal, the charcoal was left for the blast furnaces and the rise in charcoal prices was slowed down. These partial modernizations were widespread over the most important regions with a traditional iron industry in Germany and France, namely the Siegerland and the Champagne district respectively. The bar iron produced by mixing old and new techniques was of as good a quality as traditional iron but much cheaper. In the beginning the iron made entirely from hard coal had been of inferior quality and thus had to compete against both the traditional iron and the new product of the combined technique. In the middle of the 1830s, i.e. before railway construction took off, this combination of 'old' and 'new' explains why already roughly half of the bar iron in France and one third in Prussia was processed in the modern puddling furnace (using hard coal), whereas less than 20 per cent (France) and 10 per cent (Prussia) of the pig iron was smelted in a modern, coke-fired blast furnace.

In the middle of the 1830s, continental Europe began constructing railways. This created a crucial demand for the modern iron sector in Germany and France, whereas in Belgium further expansion of the modern iron industry was powerfully supported by the railways. The prohibitive duty levied until the 1850s hindered French railway companies from buying British or Belgian rails. Railway demands made modern ironworks in the French coal mining areas economically viable for the first time. For rails did not require wrought iron of the highest quality, which the traditional or partly modernized ironworks offered – low-quality iron sufficed. Except for the deep economic slump after the Revolution of 1848, increasing demand made both the traditional and the modern iron industry expand well into the 1850s. Individual French ironworks made different use of this opportunity. Some modern works, such as Decazeville, made themselves closely dependent on railway construction, thereby failing to gain a footing in other segments of the market. Some others, such as Le Creusot, went beyond rail production and learned how to make hard coal iron in ever-greater qualities and to offer it at prices low enough for them to capture markets which had hitherto been the domain of the traditional iron industry. In the long term this process would have ruined iron production based on charcoal in any case. But in France the customs policy induced a sudden decline of that industry around 1860. Already in the 1850s Napoleon III had taken measures to reduce tariffs or to undermine the protective customs structure. In 1860 the Cobden-Chevalier Treaty between Britain and France finally established a system of rather moderate tariffs. The production costs of the traditional ironworks were too high for them to hold their ground against the sudden import competition. Within a few years they shrank and sank into insignificance. Neither were all modern ironworks up to the tough competition from abroad. Decazeville, once the greatest rail producer in France, became a mere coalmine. Having been forced to make drastic adaptations in the late 1850s, the surviving modern French iron industry consolidated and expanded rapidly during the 1860s. Now that the railways had connected producers and consumers, the remote location of the modern iron industry within the coalfields was no longer an unbridgeable gulf.

From the beginning of railway construction onwards the German iron industry partly took a similar course, but there were significant differences as well. Unlike France, the German Customs Union admitted imports to a large extent. Thus Germany at first imported railway iron from Belgium and Britain. Under the protection of an import duty on bar iron, even though moderate, the coal districts soon attracted rail producers. In Upper Silesia and Saarland large ironworks were established comprising all stages of production, whereas the Rhineland and Westphalia (the Ruhr basin) built only puddling and rolling mills at the beginning. They worked up imported coke pig iron from Britain and Belgium. Little by little these modern works gained the markets of the traditional iron industry. In parallel with France, by the 1860s the traditional sector hardly counted any more. But having had to cope with competition from imports already since the early 1840s at the latest, the old-established German iron industry was spared a precipitate decline, which had been the fate of the French industry, but it shrank rather steadily instead. The Siegerland district adapted to hard-coal technology and thus survived, even if degraded to a secondary centre. Interlacing with the Ruhr district as the predominant new centre, the Siegerland provided ore and pig iron and received coal from the Ruhr in exchange. The Ruhr district was the region to generate by far the most dynamic forces of evolution. Among all iron producing regions mentioned so far the Ruhr district was the very last to adapt to *all* new hard-coal techniques. Puddling and rolling mills had long been established, before coke smelting advanced towards the Ruhr in the 1850s. But then the area achieved the highest rate of increase. Table 11 shows how the hard-coal technologies spread in the three continental countries under consideration.

New major technological changes arrived in the second half of the nineteenth century with the introduction of liquid-steel production. These techniques finally replaced the puddling furnaces. It then became common to refer to

Table 11 Iron production in Belgium (B), France (F) and Prussia (P), 1836–1870 (thousands of metric tons and percentages).

Year		Pig iron production		Bar iron production	
		By coke or mixed fuel		By hard coal	
		1,000 tons	%	1,000 tons	%
1836	B	101.4–115.8	67.5–71.5	–	–
	F	308.4	15.0	210.6	47.3
	P	88.7	50.5	32.1	–
1837	B	118.1	72.1	–	–
	F	331.7	15.9	224.6	51.0
	P	99.5	9.6	58.7	31.8
1842	B	81.3	90.8	–	–
	F	399.5	25.6	284.8	61.1
	P	101.0	18.0	79.3	39.5
1847	B	248.4	89.5	80.9	–
	F	591.6	42.6	376.7	74.3
	P	137.9	–	158.5	70.2
1848–50	B	151.5	89.8	65.9	–
	F	430.8	40.9	255.3	71.4
	P	126.7	22.7	117.8	59.3
1851–60	B	274.3	95.7	143.1	–
	F	780.0	58.6	480.0	79.9
	P	305.5	38.3	239.8	85.4
1861–70	B	442.2	99.2	358.8	–
	F	1191.5	84.1	767.0	90.6
	P	819.9	91.5	–	–

Source: Fremdling, 1986, p. 359.

all types of wrought iron as 'steel'. In 1856 the Englishman Henry Bessemer (1813–98) took out a patent to produce steel directly from molten pig iron by blowing air through it. For this method of refining no additional fuel was necessary when the metal was kept liquid after leaving the blast furnace. Bessemer and others (e.g. the American William Kelly and the Scot Robert Mushet) had to solve quite a lot of problems to produce commercially viable steel. At first Bessemer's steel did not turn out to be the cheap substitute for the expensive crucible steel as had been expected. Furthermore, it took years of trial and error to improve the quality of the steel before it could be used for the production of rails for the railway. At length, the Bessemer steel rails became more tenacious and elastic, thus more durable than rails rolled from puddled wrought iron. Second, another problem was not solved for more than two decades after Bessemer's invention. Pig iron smelted from phosphoric ores could not be refined in the Bessemer converter. Not before 1878 did the Englishmen Sidney Thomas and Percy Gilchrist find a solution to this problem. By adding limestone to the firebricks in the converter, the harmful phosphorus could be neutralized. This caused a chemical reaction, which resulted in basic slag. In Germany, where the Thomas process spread rapidly, this basic 'Thomas-Mehl' slag became a foremost artificial fertilizer for agriculture, and was even exported in large quantities, for example to the Netherlands. With this basically slight technical modification of the converter, the rich phosphorus minette deposits in French-German Lorraine could be used for the rapidly expanding production of Thomas steel.

In the middle of the 1860s another refining method was introduced. For the open hearth or Siemens-Martin process, the experiences and experiments of several experts in three countries (France, Germany and Great Britain) were combined. In a furnace the molten metal is exposed to extremely high temperatures. Without being stirred by a puddler the metal is refined. Refining iron in the open hearth takes a very long time, but the length of time leaves more time to control the process, so that the yield is of superior quality. Another important advantage is that scrap iron serves as a major input in the open hearth. But, similar to the Bessemer converter in the beginning, the open-hearth process could not be used for refining pig iron produced from phosphorus-bearing ores. And likewise, the 'basic' process in which the furnace was lined with basic materials, was applied to the open hearth about ten years later (1888).

In contrast to the diffusion of the earlier innovations (namely coke smelting, puddling and rolling) the new liquid-steel process spread in France, Germany, Belgium and the United States without a considerable time lag behind Britain. Puddling was not replaced immediately, though. The decision to substitute liquid-steel processes for puddling depended on economic considerations (cost and price differences), as well as on the physical properties of the new steel products. As only the basic variant of the open-hearth process produced a steel as good as the soft puddled iron in Germany, puddled iron dominated until 1889, thereafter declining rapidly. A famous building made of puddled iron is the still-existing Eiffel Tower in Paris, which was completed in 1889.

The first important customers for the new steel were the railway companies. By the beginning of the 1860s, it had already been proven that the stronger Bessemer rails would last longer than the softer, but still cheaper, puddled rails. During the 1870s the efficiency of the converter was improved considerably, so that the prices for Bessemer rails dropped. Not only could Thomas steel utilize a different input, but it also had properties different from Bessemer steel. The soft Thomas steel allowed a diversification of end products. Now that they could produce general iron, wire, tubes, pipes, and sheet metal out of Thomas steel, the steel mills gave up their puddling furnaces for good. It was mainly on the European continent, particularly in Germany, that steel mills specialized in Thomas steel. Steel consumers here were content with this cheap mass product, although it was of medium quality. After 1900, however, most of the new steel mills were open-hearth plants. Major customers of the high-quality steel were shipyards. This partly explains why British steel mills had switched to the open-hearth process earlier and on a larger scale. In the course of time Germany and Britain specialized in different market sectors: medium-quality steel production in Germany, high-quality in Britain (Wengenroth, 1986).

At the turn of the century, the iron and steel industry was regarded not only as a major sector in modern industrialized countries, but also quite often as the embodiment of a nation's cultural achievements and its power; as the saying goes: 'Iron is the State'. And this did not only hold good for peacetime but surely also for wartime. The German technical historian Ludwig Beck stated that 'the progress of the iron industry is so closely connected with any progress in modern culture and civilization, that the very consumption of iron per capita presents the proper yardstick of industry, welfare, and the power of nations' (Beck, 1899). In this overweening assertion, the fact that America and Germany came to surpass Britain's iron and steel production has often been seen as symbolic of British decline. By 1890, the United States had taken the lead in producing pig iron and steel, while Germany would surpass Britain in steel production in 1893, and in pig iron production in 1903. Until far into the twentieth century, coal and steel remained critically important strategic sectors. Not by accident did the process of West European unification begin with the founding of the European Coal and Steel Community in 1951.

The strategic significance of the steel industry substantiates the paramount importance of hard coal as a new source of energy. Although hard coal had been available for thousands of years, it had been of minor importance before the Industrial Revolution. Thereafter even regions or countries less endowed with this raw material could adopt coal-using technologies (Fremdling, 1996) because cheap transport became available in the second half of the nineteenth century. This was the consequence of improved coal-fired steam engines applied to locomotives and ships. Here we have a good example of industrialization being driven by circular chains of causes. Cheaper transport widened the markets for coal sales and allowed the widening application of coal-using techniques remote from the coal mining districts. This in turn increased the output of coal in the mining areas, and via economies of scale and new connections, transport became ever cheaper. Thus the combination of forward and backward linkage effects caused self-sustaining growth in the world economy.

In the form of coal tar, the 'new' raw material of hard coal furthermore served as a major input for a modern organic chemical industry. In 1856, the Englishman William Henry Perkin (1838–1907) accidentally discovered the synthetic version of the dyestuff aniline purple when trying to produce artificial quinine, a medicine for malaria. Aniline purple, called mauveine, replaced in the long run the natural dye mauve. This discovery marked the beginning of numerous efforts to find dyes based on coal tar. Until then dyes had only been obtained from plants or animals. Coal tar was a by-product (or, better, a waste-product) of the production of lighting-gas from hard coal. In the following decades, mainly German chemists synthethized more and more artificial dyes (e.g. alizarin, indigo), which became increasingly viable substitutes for natural dyes. They were mainly used in the textile industry. The still existing German giant enterprises Bayer, BASF, and Hoechst developed their strength on artificial dyestuffs. In chemistry German firms and scholars at universities took the technological lead. Around 1880 about half of the worldwide production of synthetic dyes came from Germany. On the eve of World War I (1913) the share comprised between 80 and 90 per cent.

A new source of energy has been exploited from the end of the nineteenth century onwards, namely crude oil. In the middle of the twentieth century it had replaced hard coal to a large extent, but before 1913, the direct substitution had been rather limited. In 1913, crude oil provided no more than 5 per cent of worldwide energy consumption, whereas hard coal still contributed roughly three quarters of the energy supply (Clark, 1990: 31). Of course, the advent of the automobile resulted in rapid increase in the use of gasoline (petrol) from crude oil (see also Chapter 1).

As this contribution focuses on the Industrial Revolution, no independent account of scientific progress as such is due. The relevant question remains as to what extent sciences were related to technical progress at that time. Kuznets claimed that modern economic growth was based on the epochal innovation of 'the extended application of science to problems of economic production' (Kuznets, 1966: ch. 1). As against that, most economic or technical historians maintain that this hardly applies to the Industrial Revolution proper: until far into the nineteenth century, no decisive influence on technological progress is ascribed to advances in scientific knowledge (Cameron, 1989: 195). And until about the 1860s, scientists rather strived to explain the practice of industrial achievements *ex post facto* than to put scientific knowledge itself into practice, exceptions notwithstanding. These scholars even went so far as to claim that scientists then learned more from practice than the other way round. A more balanced view, not contradicting this basic statement, was put forward by Joel Mokyr (1990: 113). It is widely believed that before the middle of the nineteenth century, technological progress moved more or less independently of scientific progress, and that since then the interaction between science and technology has gradually become closer. As we have seen, this view is only partially correct. Science, and especially the work of some individual scientists, was not totally irrelevant to technological change before 1850. Between 1600 and 1850, technology learned some things from science, and more from scientists. In few cases, however, can we conclude that a particular invention depended crucially on a breakthrough in the scientific understanding of the chemical or physical, let alone biological, processes involved. After 1850, science became more important as a handmaiden of technology. A growing number of technologies, from waterpower to chemicals, depended on or were inspired by scientific advances. Yet the number of technological discoveries that were purely empirical has not declined, even if their relative importance has fallen.

When discussing the connections between science and technology during the British Industrial Revolution, Ian Inkster (1991: 69ff.) identifies a 'seeming confusion' among different scholars. In his proposed solution he maintains first that, already during the British Industrial Revolution, certain fields of endeavour owed a considerable debt to science, such as the chemical industry. Second, he argues that 'the availability of specific scientific and technical information was important in creating the host of incremental and adaptive innovations which in many instances followed upon important inventions'. If, furthermore, this kind of information was gradually becoming available among different social groups and localities in Britain, this would explain why in British society the Industrial Revolution and its related technical progress can be viewed as both driven by experience and by the application of science. If an important law of nature, say that of leverage, is fully embodied in a machine, this law becomes widely known and can be applied by people who do not know the underlying scientific formula. If this kind of information is not acquired predominantly by any formal education, one cannot maintain a clear-cut distinction between science and empiricism.

In the middle of the eighteenth century, England had more 'technicians' than continental countries. All those engineers, mechanics and craftsmen had been trained on-the-job or as apprentices without much of a formal education. Technical knowledge, however, was widely spread through informal lectures, scientific societies, and technical literature (Mokyr, 1990: 240f.) and above all through handling technical products and processes. This British comparative advantage may also explain why the British were so successful in putting inventions to use, even if they had originated on the continent. For one thing, the basic scientific knowledge of that time seems to have been widely established in Britain (Inkster) and for another thing, British science 'was predominantly experimental and mechanical, whereas French science was largely mathematical and deductive' (Mokyr, 1990: 242, referring to Kuhn). This British interrelation between science and practice proved a highly favourable environment for the application of science, innovation and improvement.

Even at the time of the first industrial revolutions, branches of the electrical and chemical industries required a high degree of scientific knowledge and training. Until the end of the eighteenth century, electrical phenomena had widely been regarded as curiosities before they became a field of serious science. During the first half of the nineteenth century, several electrical phenomena, which finally proved useful for practical purposes, were discovered by research. In 1807, the Englishman Humphrey Davy discovered electrolysis, which was used in the electroplating industry from the 1830s. In the following decade his assistant Michael Faraday made a host of discoveries and inventions not only in the field of electricity. Based on the principle of electromagnetism he invented the electric motor in 1821 and the dynamo in 1831. As an economically efficient generator was still lacking, electric motors were not cheap enough to compete with steam engines.

As a consequence, electricity did not come into widespread use through power transmission but through the electric telegraph. Several inventors were associated with this message transmission; one was the American Samuel Morse, who since 1837 developed his 'needle system' and the code named after him. As described by Mokyr (1990: 125f.), 'The telegraph, like the railroad, was a typical nineteenth-century invention in that it was a combination of separate technological inventions that had to be moulded together'. It took decades of subsequent inventions and improvements before the long-distance telegraph over land and below the sea became reliable. Hardly one third of the transatlantic cables laid before 1861 survived that year. The long-distance means of communication by telephone and telegraph were introduced into India and the African colonies very soon, as they helped the European powers with the conquest and administration of these territories. Besides its military, political and personal use in transmitting messages, the telegraph for the first time allowed a fast coordination of international financial and commodity markets. Like the railway, it was a network crossing state borders and as such required international cooperation. The ensuing International Telegraph Union of 1865 was one of the several international agreements concerning railway and postal services and foreign trade.

Major problems had still to be solved in the generation of electrical energy. The breakthrough came in the 1860s when several inventors independently discovered the principle of the 'self-excited' generator. One of them was the German Werner von Siemens, who did not detect the principle by theoretical reasoning, but rather by intuition when constructing magnoelectric detonators for the Prussian army in 1866. Siemens had made a fortune out of telegraphy, and was hence familiar with applying electricity. Combining all the virtues of a successful entrepreneur, technician and scientist, Siemens realized the commercial possibilities. From 1868 onwards, his firms successfully sold small dynamos. The Belgian Z. T. Gramme was the first to construct and sell larger dynamos in the 1870s. With the arrival and improvement of dynamos from the 1870s onwards, more and more factories, stores, theatres and public buildings installed the well-known arc lamps for lighting. Between 1878 and 1880, the Englishman Joseph Swan and the American Thomas Edison perfected the incandescent electric lamp almost simultaneously. The new bulb was substituted for arc lighting and created a boom in the electrical industry both in Europe and the United States. One should keep in mind, however, that for further decades gas (made from hard coal) remained a viable alternative for electric light. Other applications of electricity were the electric street car and small electric motors for factories. This soon paved the way for household appliances as well.

Before the advent of centralized power stations, every building with electric lighting possessed its own power source, where the generators were driven by a steam engine, a gas motor or even a water wheel. In the long run, centralized power stations with networks spanning several quarters of a city or a whole municipal community became the rule. The first was opened by Edison in New York City in 1882; Berlin followed in 1885. For these 'public' networks spanning municipal property, the approval of the community was necessary. When the enterprises turned out to be highly profitable, more municipalities ran the networks and power stations themselves. Alternating current emerged victorious from the battle between different current systems because it was better suited for long-distance transmission. At the end of the nineteenth century, even the most powerful steam engines turned out to suffer a serious bottleneck in generating electricity. The limited rotational velocity of the reciprocating steam engine did not reach the high speed required by a dynamo. It was, however, still steam which solved the problems of generating enough electrical power. Hard coal heated the water in devices such as the steam turbine, which had been developed in the 1880s by the Englishman Charles Parsons and the Swede Gustav de Laval. Furthermore, there was the hydraulic turbine, which already in the 1820s and 1830s had been developed by French engineers to convert the force of falling water into energy. In the 1870s, in South Eastern France, this device was already attached to a dynamo. As put forward by Cameron (1989: 198f.) 'This apparently simple innovation had important long-range consequences, for it enabled regions poor in coal but rich in water power to supply their own energy requirements'. The hydraulic turbine finally freed the generation of electric power from coal after the steam engine had tied it for decades to the most important source of energy of the Industrial Revolution, namely hard coal.

The application of electricity in the course of the nineteenth century anticipates a few features characteristic of the so-called 'second Industrial Revolution'. First of all, inventions and innovations seem to have been much more firmly based on scientific progress than during the first round of the Industrial Revolution. (The empirical element of trial and error in solving practical problems remained very important.) Second, scientific and technological progress became an international phenomenon with different people searching for the solution of the same problems in places all over Europe and the United States. As a consequence, in a *convergent* development, new inventions were implemented in the leading industrial powers without any significant delay. And third, the use of electricity itself evolved into a large technical system comprising the generation, transmission and transforming of power into its final uses such as kinetic power, light or heat. The interrelatedness with other branches of industry (e.g. the coal-fired steam engine) required a highly developed industrial system with a complex network of complementary and substitutional devices. Convergence notwithstanding, at the same time there were divergences as well. In a divergent development, the structure of networks like these revealed different styles among countries.

In the second half of the nineteenth century, the American System of Manufactures emerged, and for some it was distinctly different from the British or European skill-intensive systems (Habakkuk, 1967; Broadberry, 1997). Due to higher labour costs (thus different factor costs as compared to Europe in general), capital-intensive mass production characterized American industry. It has often been maintained that, in the search for labour-saving inventions, the American system generated more and faster innovations from the late nineteenth century onwards than its European counterparts. Among others the professional inventor Thomas A. Edison (1847–1931) – electricity; the automobile tycoon Henry Ford (1863–1947) – the assembly line; and Frederick W. Taylor (1856–1915) – scientific management – stand as synonyms for a superior American manufacturing system (Hughes, 1989). For many people this 'competitive managerial capitalism' (Chandler, 1990) has become the model of industrial achievement after Britain's relative decline as the industrial super power after the first round of industrial revolutions. Recent studies corroborate that labour productivity in American industry was significantly higher than in England as early as the first half of the nineteenth century (Broadberry, 1994). To what extent could the American System of Manufactures have been copied and to what extent did it form the technological frontier? First of all the American practice was responsive to a specific resource endowment (scarce labour, abundant land and natural resources) with corresponding relative factor costs. Thus a simple copy or transfer of American technology into other countries was limited in any case. Furthermore, different technical systems or styles of technique among different societies do not solely depend on different factor costs but probably also represent cultural and, of course, institutional differences among peoples (Radkau, 1989: 37).

The impact of educational institutions on the economic performance of a nation is not in doubt. The following comments concern formal professionalized higher education in the field of science and engineering and its impact on technological progress. Twisting this argument, many historians jump to the conclusion that Britain's alleged relative decline as compared to Germany and, of course, to the United States, must have been caused by a somehow inferior scientific and technological formal education. Prior to 1914,

A nation such as Britain, with its wide 'audience' for science, might actually seem to be falling behind in science. . . . But in terms of the creation of new, abstract knowledge, in terms of the diffusion of information through the social system and in terms of the sustenance of routine 'ordinary inventiveness' . . . throughout the industrial system, Britain may well have been significantly ahead of most nations at this time.

(Inkster, 1991: 130)

In this line of argument, governmental intervention in some fast growing nations for building modern universities and other formal institutions might be regarded as an indication that these countries (e.g. Germany, Japan or Russia) simply needed more help to both concentrate and professionalize their small base of modern science. To sum up this seeming contradiction, public investment in formal education is necessary for societies with a poor economic performance in order to acquire knowledge for technological progress. But those investments are no measure for the level and diffusion of technological knowledge appropriate in a given society, as traditions other than formal education might have built up and spread that knowledge, as occurred in Britain.

The relationship between scientific knowledge and industrial production became ever more professionalized and institutionalized. One outcome of the French Revolution and the government of Napoleon was the creation of specialized schools for science and engineering or applied research. The Ecole Polytechnique (1794) and the Ecole des Arts et Métiers (1804) served as models for other countries. Similar technical (high) schools or technical universities (later they acquired the same status as the classic universities) were founded in the Habsburg monarchy in Prague (1806), Graz (1811) and Vienna (1815); in Swiss Lausanne (1853) and Zurich (1855); and in Delft (1863) in the Netherlands. Particularly in Germany, these institutions were established or existing technical schools adopted partly to incorporate the curriculum of the French model. As Germany was not a unified centralized state, all the independent medium-sized states not only had their classic universities from the past but now, mostly in their capital cities, they possessed their technical universities, among them Dresden (1828) in Saxony; Karlsruhe (1825) in Baden; Stuttgart (1829) in Württemberg; Darmstadt (1836) in Hesse, Munich (1868) in Bavaria; and Hanover (1831). In Prussia the Technische Hochschule Charlottenburg of Berlin (1879) was the successor of two older technical schools for architecture and manufacturing. At these Technischen Hochschulen, students got a formalized training in applied sciences in close cooperation with industry; for example the Technische Hochschule Berlin-Charlottenburg worked closely together with the electro-technical firm of Siemens. The professorship for this field of science and engineering was sponsored by the same firm and the exchange of staff members guaranteed a mutual reinforcement of science and its application. In this educational system the engineer was thus scarcely a practical man any more but rather became a professional with a formal academic education. With the celebration of the centenary of Humboldt's Berlin University in 1910, another innovative research institution was established in Berlin: the Kaiser-Wilhelm-Gesellschaft, today named the Max-Planck-Gesellschaft. Here government and wealthy industrialists, bankers, etc. jointly sponsored top-level independent research institutes in the sciences. With this institutional innovation Albert Einstein, for example, could be attracted to Berlin, where in 1913 he became director of the Kaiser Wilhelm Institute for Physics. The Technische Hochschule and the German university in general became the model for university reforms in other advanced countries. The most prominent example was the United States, where in the 1870s educators turned to Germany rather than England or France when reforming higher education. Subsequently other countries fell in line as well, including Britain and France.

Britain was the first country to introduce a patent law, as early as 1624. In France a similar law was not enacted before 1791, and the other continental countries followed even later. In Germany, an effective national patent law came into being in 1877. The economic impact of such a law might entail positive as well as negative effects on economic development. The advantage is simple and straightforward: patent laws encourage technological progress, for the pioneer entrepreneur in a competitive system has to be allowed to reap the profits of his or her innovation, otherwise there is no incentive to innovate. But the disadvantage is just as simple and straightforward: being protected by a patent, the innovation cannot be copied by competitors. Hence diffusion is delayed and, furthermore, the patent-holder has less incentive to improve their original invention-innovation. Because of this ambiguity, governments in market-oriented economies compromised by restricting patent protection to a limited period of around fifteen years.

Great inventors (e.g. Watt or Bessemer, who reaped their profits under patent protection) are often quoted in order to praise the benefits of patent laws. However, the drawbacks of such an institutional arrangement probably preponderate. Holding a patent and not effectively using it might very well block any technical progress in this field. The famous example is Watt himself, who hampered the development of high-pressure steam engines (Mathias, 1983: 123). Another problem arises when several people are involved in an invention. Moreover, various improvements have often to be achieved before an invention becomes an innovation (Mokyr, 1990: 248ff.). It makes a difference, however, whether the patent protects a product or a process. In dyestuffs, the American patent law protected the product whereas in Germany it was the process. This protection is advanced as an incentive for other chemical firms in Germany to try and discover alternative processes of producing the same product. Even if they failed, they gained experience through which they often found a new product. The conclusion must be that it is not clear whether patent laws promoted technological progress or hampered it.

AGRICULTURAL PRODUCTION

Agriculture was a strategic sector to achieve modern economic growth. Table 12 presents sectoral employment shares for a selected number of countries for benchmark years between 1870 and 1992. The trend is revealed that, with generally increasing incomes, the share of people employed in agriculture went down. Fewer and fewer people were needed to produce food for the rest of the ever-growing population (on population figures, see Table 9). In addition, see Chapter 1 on agriculture. An adjustment made for imports and exports of food does not change this basic statement. Employment shares rose in the other two sectors, industry and services. It should be noticed, however, that the European pattern to some extent differs from other parts of the world. Whereas in Europe industrial employment became the foremost sector before services took the lead, in most other countries services absorbed the bulk of employees and industry remained the 'second employer' after agriculture had shrunk.

The shrinking of agricultural employment in the course of modern economic growth indicated no stagnation in the sector; on the contrary, it meant first of all increasing

Table 12 Sectoral employment shares in agriculture, industry and services (% of total employment) 1870, 1913, 1950, 1992.

	USA	France	Germany	UK	Japan	China	Russia
Agriculture, forestry, fisheries							
1870	50	49	50	23	70	–	–
1913	28	41	35	12	60	–	70
1950	13	28	22	5	48	77	46
1992	3	5	3	2	6	59	17
Mining, manufacturing, construction and utilities							
1870	24	28	29	42	–	–	–
1913	30	32	41	44	18	–	–
1950	34	35	43	45	23	7	29
1992	23	28	38	26	35	22	36
Services							
1870	26	23	22	35	–	–	–
1913	43	27	24	44	22	–	–
1950	54	37	35	50	29	16	25
1992	74	67	59	72	59	20	47

Source: See Maddison, 1995, p. 39.

productivity of the agricultural labour force. Second, according to Engel's Law,[5] with increasing income proportionally less is spent on food. Based on his empirical research, Engel had laid down the law, which – more technically formulated – means that the income elasticity of demand for food is below 1. Third, tariff protection of indigenous agriculture hampered the shift of the work force towards industry or services. As these three factors did not occur in every country at the same time, shifting sectoral shares of employment differed over time and among countries. To reveal this pattern, Table 11 presents figures for different countries.

Agrarian reforms are often regarded as a precondition of improvements in agriculture. Even so, it is very difficult to assess to what extent institutional reforms paved the way for higher agricultural productivity. According to the approach of the new institutional economics, a new arrangement of property rights, which brings the private rate of return closer to the social rate of return, strengthens the incentive to improve productivity (North and Thomas, 1973). In this line of reasoning, the feudal heritage from medieval times would have proved an obstacle to technical progress in agriculture. Roughly sketched, a feudal system means that people are placed within a hierarchy by birth. They are tied to their position through unequal rights and duties. Land is the most important pre-industrial factor of production and land is decisive, as certain property rights concerning the use of land define personal status. Abolishing the feudal heritage meant a change in land tenure.

In Britain, the enclosure movement put an end to the common use of large areas of land, and also the of open-field system. Large, compact farms emerged with clearly defined property rights applied to the landed proprietors and their tenant farmers. In France, the Revolution simply expropriated the landed aristocracy and the church. The peasants became the proprietors of their rather small farms; whereas in Prussia, the reforms after 1807 strengthened the large estates of the landlords, the 'Junkers'. In order to get rid of their obligations flowing from serfdom the peasants had to cede land (or to make huge payments) to their former feudal masters (for more details and examples, see Cameron, 1989: 302). As for the United States, one should

not forget that until the American Civil War (1861–5) agriculture in the South was largely organized as a slave plantation system. The slave population had originally been brought from black Africa. With the victory of nascent industrial capitalism in the North and Midwest, these slaves were freed. The economic viability of the slave economy was a focus of the 'New Economic History' approach[6] in the United States. In the beginning the findings raised some controversy, but now it is accepted that the slave plantation system was a profitable enterprise, and not obsolete in economic terms (Fogel and Engerman, 1974).

At the beginning of the nineteenth century, Britain boasted the most productive agriculture in Europe, as she had introduced the system of convertible husbandry rather early. This was an alternative to the traditional rotation pattern of arable followed by fallow, in that pasture was integrated. The grazing of animals such as cattle or horses reduced fallow and restored the fertility of the soil at the same time. Even after the 1840s, when the Corn Laws were repealed, both British agriculture and industry reached their peaks in performance as compared to other nations. Technical improvements such as light iron ploughs, steam threshers, mechanical harvesters and commercial fertilizers increased productivity. In contrast to Germany and France, Britain did not reintroduce protective tariffs when cheap American grain reached her markets. Like Denmark and the Netherlands, she stuck to free trade, and during the second half of the nineteenth century her agriculture switched more and more to higher-value products such as high-quality meat and dairy products. Frequently, imported grain was used as animal feed. Not only Britain but also most of the industrializing economies constantly raised their agricultural productivity. The highest levels of labour productivity, however, were reached in 'free born' nations such as North America, Argentina, Australia and New Zealand. Abundant in land and not hampered by any feudal heritage, they developed a highly commercialized agriculture, which applied technical improvements very efficiently. Their exports, however, brought about radical changes in West European agriculture. With the drastic reduction of overseas transport costs, cereals from overseas penetrated European markets, which in the 1860s were no longer protected. Around 1880, the two most important continental powers, Germany and France, resumed protection for their agriculture. This resort to protectionism partly explains why in 1913 the share of agricultural employment in Germany and France was that much higher than in free-trade Britain. As France and Germany became the core countries of the European Community from 1958 onwards, EC agricultural policy clearly bears the impress of those countries' historical heritage from the nineteenth century.

ECONOMIC TIES AMONG COUNTRIES AND REGIONS OF THE WORLD

During the nineteenth century, international trade increased much faster than production. Between 1800 and 1913, worldwide production per capita grew a little more than 7 per cent per decade, whereas foreign trade increased in volume by about 33 per cent per decade. These rough estimates reflect the hitherto unprecedented speed by which the economic ties among nations and regions of the world integrated (Bairoch, 1973). The enormous increase of world trade cannot be ascribed to the commerce between Europe and overseas countries, but it rather resulted from an intensified trade among the most advanced nations within Europe. And even in the regions beyond Europe, commerce between Europe and the European overseas settlements dominated. In 1913, two thirds of world trade (by volume) was still concentrated on Europe, with Britain maintaining a quarter of the whole until the end of the century and beyond (16 per cent in 1914). Germany and France were the other large trading nations, with 12 and 7 per cent respectively of the total in 1913. European dominance did not diminish until 1913, although the share of North America had increased by then (14 per cent in 1913). Subsequently, Britain in particular lost ground.

The growth of international trade was made possible mainly by drastically reduced transaction costs. First of all the transportation costs for passengers and goods decreased vastly, especially so in the second half of the nineteenth century. Harley (1989) compiled freight rates of coal shipments for a period including that of the decisive transition from the wooden sailing vessel to the iron steamer. Prior to the 1860s, he registers no falling trend in the overall level of freight rates. But thereafter the rates declined dramatically until the early 1890s, and in subsequent years they fell, if more moderately. Before 1914, on shipments between British and continental ports the rates dropped to 40 per cent of the level of the 1850s, and on long distances (to South America) they went down to one third. Brentano (1911) analysed the influence of declining freight rates from America on the price of wheat in London (all prices refer to one quarter of wheat). In 1868, freight from Chicago to New York cost about 7 shillings for shipments on water and railway combined and about 10s by rail only. The freight on steamboats to Liverpool cost 4.6s. In 1902, the corresponding rates were about 2.3s and 1s. The price of wheat in Britain declined from 64s to 28s between 1868 and 1902. On the European continent, freight rates for railway and inland navigation likewise dropped drastically during the second half of the nineteenth century. The peak of European railway construction coincided with the peak of European colonialism. From the late 1880s onwards, the colonial powers built railway lines connecting the seaport towns with the capitals and the economic centres of the

different African territories. See Chapter 1 on the general consequences of railways.

The decline of transportation costs undermined the free trade movement in Europe. This movement was part of a general adoption of liberal ideas and thus motivated by corresponding political attitudes. During the 1850s and 1860s, many European countries abolished restrictions on founding enterprises, making even joint-stock companies possible without an individual charter. The construction of railways was deregulated and left to the workings of the free market. Concerning customs policy, Britain had moved to free trade during the 1840s. In their strong commitment to liberalism, leading politicians and elite groups tried to translate their ideas into practice by creating a free trading zone in Western and Central Europe. In 1860, France and Britain concluded the Cobden-Chevalier Treaty, which planned to abolish most import duties. As it incorporated a most-favoured-nation clause, the free trade zone bilaterally agreed upon could easily be extended multilaterally. Belgium joined the treaty in 1861, Prussia followed in 1862, Italy in 1863, Switzerland in 1864, Sweden, Norway, Spain and the Netherlands in 1865. But the unexpectedly large-scale export of overseas cereals to Europe, in combination with the long-term economic slump (the first Great Depression) from the 1870s onward, shook the liberal system. Germany and France, in particular, resorted to the reintroduction of protective tariffs, even though they could not reverse the reduction in transportation costs. So the long established ties between many economies were not broken. Communications were further facilitated by innovations such as the telephone and telegraph, while the emergence of the gold standard under British leadership bestowed a stable currency system on the core countries of the industrializing world. In short, the late nineteenth century witnessed a unique freedom for people, commodities and capital to move from one country to another.

A CONCLUDING REMARK ON INDUSTRIALIZATION

In the long run industrialization greatly raised the living standards of those countries which industrialized in the first round. This meant higher income levels, improved education and longer life expectancy. Hence it is understandable that with this experience of the nineteenth century in mind, many decision-makers of today are quite sure of the beneficial effects of further and broader industrialization as a solution to existing worldwide (economic) problems of humanity.

NOTES

1 In Rostow's (US American) stage theory, every country will pass through five different stages of economic growth: 'the traditional society. The preconditions for take-off. The take-off. The drive to maturity. The age of high mass-consumption' (Rostow, 1960). Crucial is the 'take-off'. This Industrial Revolution marks the beginning of sustained growth of per capita income. The transition of a revolutionary nature is characterized by its short duration (around thirty years), by a substantial increase in the investment ratio (from below 5 to above 10 per cent of national income) and by the first appearance of leading sectors, which drive economic growth through successive

major technical innovations. This theory of unbalanced growth was a model for development policies proposed and pursued by the United States of America in the 1960s, and it was of great influence in newly industrializing countries like South Korea. Furthermore, Rostow's view provoked scholarly controversies in economic history: e.g. the contribution of the leading sector *railways* to economic growth during the nineteenth century (Fogel, 1964; O'Brien, 1983).

2 The term 'innovation' was introduced by the Austrian-German-US American economist Joseph Schumpeter in his doctoral dissertation in 1911. *Die Theorie der wirtschaftlichen Entwicklung* (translated into English in 1934 as *The Theory of Economic Development*) tries to explain the driving force behind capitalist economic growth. The *Pionierunternehmer* (pioneer entrepreneur) introduces inventions, or new combinations of the factors of production, into the economic system, thus accomplishing innovations. Schumpeter distinguished five different types of innovation: (a) new products, (b) new production processes, (c) new sales markets, (d) new sources for raw materials and intermediate products, (e) new organizations or new institutions. The term 'basic' innovation ('basic innovations'), however, was coined by neo-Schumpeterians, e.g. Mensch (1979).

3 'The Industrial Revolution was not the Age of Cotton or of Railways or even of Steam entirely; it was an age of improvement' (McCloskey, 1981: 118).

4 The Englishman Thomas Robert Malthus (1766–1834) asserted that there was tension between population growth and the potential growth of food supply. Populations, nations and peoples are caught in a Malthusian trap (with famines, widespread disease and hence high death rates) when population growth has outstripped the available means of subsistence. See Malthus: *An Essay on the Principle of Population*, 1798.

5 The German statistician Ernst Engel (1821–96) was head of the statistical offices of Saxony and Prussia.

6 In this approach developed in the 1960s, standard economic theory and econometrics are applied in historical research. Hence some named it 'Cliometrics'.

BIBLIOGRAPHY

ABE, E.; SUZUKI, Y. (eds) 1991. *Changing Patterns of International Rivalry: Some Lessons from the Steel Industry*. Tokyo University Press, Tokyo.

ALLEN, R. C. 1977. The Peculiar Productivity History of American Blast Furnaces, 1840–1913. *Journal of Economic History*, No. 37, pp. 605–33.

BAIROCH, P. 1973. European Foreign Trade in the Nineteenth Century: The Development of the Value and Volume of Exports. *Journal of European Economic History*, No. 2, pp. 5–36.

BECK, L. 1899. *Die Geschichte des Eisens in technischer und kultur-geschichtlicher Beziehung*. Part 4. Friedrich Vieweg und Sohn, Braunschweig.

BONNEUIL, C. 1997a. Le jardin d'essais de Conakry, Le lieu où s'invitent les tropiques. *La recherche* 300, Juillet-Août 1997, pp. 76–80.

——. 1997b. Mettre en ordre et discipliner les tropiques. Les Sciences du Végétal dans l'Empire français, 1870–1940. Doctoral thesis, University of Paris VII.

BRENTANO, L. 1911. *Die deutschen Getreidezö 11e*. Stuttgart.

BROADBERRY, S. N. 1994. Comparative Productivity in British and American Manufacturing During the Nineteenth Century. *Explorations in Economic History*, No. 31, pp. 521–48.

——. 1997. *The Productivity Race. British Manufacturing in International Perspective, 1850–1990*. Cambridge University Press, Cambridge.

CAMERON, R. 1989. *A Concise Economic History of the World*. Oxford University Press, New York.

CHANDLER, A. D. 1990. *Scale and Scope. The Dynamics of Industrial Capitalism*. Harvard University Press, Cambridge MA.

CHURCH, R. A. (ed.) 1994. *The Coal and Iron Industries* (The Industrial Revolution, vol. 10). Economic History Society/Blackwell, Oxford.

CIPOLLA, C. M. (ed.) 1975. Introduction. In: Cipolla, C. M. *The Industrial Revolution* (The Fontana Economic History of Europe), Fontana/Collins, Glasgow, pp. 7–21.

CLARK, J. G. 1990. *The Political Economy of World Energy*. Harvester Wheatsheaf, New York.

CRAFTS, N. 1984. Patterns of Development in Nineteenth Century Europe. *Oxford Economic Papers*, No. 36, pp. 438–58.

——. 1994. The Industrial Revolution. In: Floud, R. and McCloskey, D. (eds) *The Economic History of Britain since 1700*. Cambridge University Press, Cambridge, pp. 44–59.

FOGEL, R. W. 1964. *Railroads and American Growth: Essays in Econometric History*. Johns Hopkins University Press, Baltimore.

FOGEL, R. W.; ENGERMAN, S. 1974. *Time on the Cross: The Economics of American Negro Slavery*. Little, Brown, Boston MA.

FREMDLING, R. R. 1986. *Technologischer Wandel und internationaler Handel im 18. und 19. Jahrhundert, Die Eisenindustrien in Grossbritannien, Belgien. Frankreich und Deutschland*. Duncker & Humblot, Berlin.

——. 1994. Foreign Trade Patterns, Technological Change, Cost and Productivity in the West European Iron Industries, 1820–70. In: Church, R. A. (ed.) *The Coal and Iron Industries*. Economic History Society/Blackwell, Oxford, pp. 322–43.

——. 1994. Foreign Competition and Technological Change: British Exports and the Modernization of the German Iron Industry from the 1820s to the 1860s. In: Church, R. A. (ed.) The *Coal and Iron Industries*. Economic History Society/Blackwell, Oxford, pp. 345–74.

——. 1996. Anglo-German Rivalry on Coal Markets in France, the Netherlands and Germany, 1850–1913. *The Journal of European Economic History*, No. 25, pp. 599–646.

GILLE, B. 1968. *La Sidérurgie française au X1Xe Siècle*. Libraire Droz, Geneva.

HABAKKUK, H. J. 1967. *American and British Technology in the Nineteenth Century, The Search for Labour-Saving Inventions*. Cambridge University Press, Cambridge.

HARLEY, K. C. 1989. Coal Exports and British Shipping, 1850–1913. *Explorations in Economic History*, No. 26, pp. 311–38.

HUGHES, T. P. 1989. *American Genesis: A Century of Invention and Technological Enthusiasm, 1870–1970*. Viking Penguin, New York.

HYDE, C. K. 1977. *Technological Change and the British Iron Industry 1700–1870*. Princeton University Press, Princeton.

INKSTER, I. 1991. *Science and Technology in History: An Approach to Industrial Development*. Macmillan, Houndsmill.

INWOOD, K. E. 1992. The Influence of Resource Quality on Technological Persistence: Charcoal Iron in Quebec. *Material History Review*, pp. 49–56.

KUZNETS, S. 1966. *Modern Economic Growth*. Yale University Press, New Haven.

LANDES, D. S. 1969. *The Unbound Prometheus*. Cambridge University Press, Cambridge.

MCCLOSKEY, D. 1981. The Industrial Revolution 1780–1860: A Survey. In: Floud, R. and McCloskey, D. (eds) *The Economic History of Britain since 1700*. Cambridge University Press, Cambridge, pp. 103–27.

MADDISON, A. 1991. *Dynamic Forces in Capitalist Development*. Oxford University Press, Oxford.

——. 1995. *Monitoring the World Economy 1820–1992*. OECD, Paris.

MADDISON, A.; PRINCE, G. (eds) 1989. *Economic Growth in Indonesia, 1820–1940*. Foris Publications, Dordrecht.

MATHIAS, P. 1969. *The First Industrial Nation*. 2nd edn 1983, Methuen, London.

MEADOWS, D. H.; MEADOWS, D. L.; RANDERS, J.; BEHRENS III, W. W. 1972. *The Limits to Growth*. Universe Books, New York.

MENSCH, G. 1979. *Stalemate in Technology*. Ballinger, Cambridge MA.

MOKYR, J. 1990. *The Lever of Riches, Technological Creativity and Economic Progress*. Oxford University Press, New York.

——. 1994. Technological Change, 1700–1830. In: Floud, R. and McCloskey, D. (eds) *The Economic History of Britain since 1700*, Cambridge University Press, Cambridge, pp. 12–43.

NORTH, D. C.; THOMAS, R. P. 1973. *The Rise of the Western World. A New Economic History*. Cambridge University Press, Cambridge.

O'BRIEN, P. (ed.) 1983. *Railways and the Economic Development of Western Europe, 1830–1914*. Macmillan Press, London.

O'BRIEN, P.; KEYDER, C. 1978. *Economic Growth in Britain and France 1780–1914. Two Paths to the Twentieth Century*. George Allen & Unwin, London.

RADKAU, J. 1989. *Technik in Deutschland, Vom 18. Jahrhundert bis zur Gegenwart*. Suhrkamp, Frankfurt a.M.

REUSS, C.; KOUTNY, E.; TYCHON, L. 1960. *Le Progrès Economique en Sidérurgie Belgique. Luxembourg, Pays-Bas 1830–1955*. Editions Nauwelaerts, Louvain.

RIDEN, P. H. 1977. The Output of the British Iron Industry before 1870. *Economic History Review*, No. 30, pp. 442–59.

ROSTOW, W. W. 1960. *The Stages of Economic Growth*. Cambridge University Press, Cambridge.

——. 1978. *The World Economy: History and Prospects*. University of Texas Press, Austin.

SCHUMPETER, J. 1911. *Theorie der wirtschaftlichen Entwicklung*. Berlin, Duncker & Humblot. (English trans. 1934. *The Theory of Economic Development*. Harvard University Press, Cambridge MA).

TEMIN, P. 1964. *Iron and Steel in Nineteenth-Century America*. MIT Press, Cambridge MA.

VAN DER ENG, P. 1993. 'Agricultural Growth in Indonesia since 1880'. Doctoral thesis, University of Gröningen.

VIAL, J. 1967. *L'industrialization de la sidérurgie française 1814–1864*. Mouton, Paris.

VON TUNZELMANN, G. N. 1978. *Steam Power and British Industrialization to 1860*. Clarendon Press, Oxford.

——. 1981. Technical Progress During the Industrial Revolution. In: Floud, R. and McCloskey, D. (eds) *The Economic History of Britain since 1700*. Cambridge University Press, Cambridge, pp. 143–63.

——. 1995. *Technology and Industrial Progress. The Foundations of Economic Growth*. Edward Elgar, Aldershot.

WENGENROTH, U. 1986. *Unternehmensstrategien und technischer Fortschritt, Die deutsche und britische Stahlindustrie 1865–1895*. Vandenhoeck & Ruprecht, Göttingen. (English trans. 1994. *Enterprise and Technology: the German and British Steel Industries, 1865–1895*. Cambridge University Press, Cambridge).

WORONOFF, D. 1984. *L'industrie sidérurgique en France pendant la révolution et l'Empire*. Editions de l'Ecole Pratiques des Hautes Etudes en Sciences Sociales, Paris.

WRIGLEY, E. A. 1988. *Continuity, Chance and Change. The Character of the Industrial Revolution in England*. Cambridge University Press, Cambridge.

4

MATHEMATICS, EXACT SCIENCES AND NATURAL SCIENCES

Charles Morazé

INTRODUCTION: SCIENTIFIC DEVELOPMENTS AND SOCIO-CULTURAL CHANGE

It is well known that the so-called 'industrial revolutions' radically changed people's ways of life and their cultures, as well as the relationships between people within a given nation. We also know that these changes depended to differing extents on scientific advances: the influence of science, slight in the first industrial revolution (around 1780–1820), became more marked in the second one (around 1880–1914), and considerable thereafter, when such 'revolutions' became too numerous to count. However, our task in this chapter is to clarify how ordinary expansion became exponential. In using the term 'how', some distinctions can be made. For example, there is the 'how laboratories serve industry' and the 'how industry in return provides the laboratories with the equipment they need to innovate': this 'loan expecting some return' has been sufficiently well analysed for us to conclude that there are cumulative effects, and the results do explain, at least superficially, the exponential growth of science and industry. Of course, any history not content with evaluating superficial events must investigate further. Laboratories need not only equipment, but first and foremost, theories. Without theories they would not know what to look for – and how to do it – and would be unable to interpret their results.

At the very heart of the history of scientific discoveries and inventions lies the history of theories. And since these theories are expressed in mathematical terms, their history appears to correlate closely with that of mathematics as a whole. In examining this correlation, the question arises as to which of these two types of science conditions, the one based on experiment, the other on precise and purely formal reasoning, conditions the other. The century was riven by contradictory views, usually based upon the same conviction, expressed by Newton, and before him by Galileo, that nature expresses itself in mathematical terms. A retrospective study of the events swings one's preference in favour of formal and so-called operational reasoning, because it inherently obeys the conditions of exactitude. In fact it is observed that in most cases the mathematical formulations precede, by years at least, the physical theories that make use of them to explain the observed and tested phenomena. In the opposite situation – where mathematics

rapidly responds to an experimental need, it had not predicted – the historian faces virtually the same problem: what happened, on either side, to cause the operational abstraction to precede the experiment, or to follow it so closely?

Let us apply the term 'spearhead theory' (a term adopted by a meeting of experts held at UNESCO in 1978) to the progressive and growing number of abstract formulations, that led to the view of the natural world, foreseen by Galileo and defined by Newton, extending up to another view of the world proposed by Einstein, and ultimately adopted by the scientific community. This theory avoids the question of which science – exact or experimental – conditions the other, by internalizing it. In fact a theory of this kind combines, within the same coherent entity, that portion of mathematics that is indispensable to astronomical and physical theories with the portion that these theories borrow from mathematics, or encourage it to provide. These exchanges define a theoretical locus, which is destined to become a specific branch of scientific knowledge: rational mechanics. This form of mechanics, feeding off the other two types of science that it brings together, advances in parallel with them. And since it governs their similarities, it also governs their applications, and thereby occupies a central position in the curriculum for training engineers. Of course, not all industries are essentially mechanical, but all are in part, to varying degrees.

At its most elementary level, mechanics demands most from ingenious observation of a skilled person's gestures in order to reproduce them in machines. Looms and spinning machines – the jewels of the first industrial revolution – developed independently of the rational mechanics that was already essential for studying the movement of heavenly bodies. The same applied to the clock- and watchmakers, even though the latter owed the spring, whose oscillations have the same effect as those of the pendulum, to Huygens. No less striking is the example of chemistry, one of the first crafts to industrialize products, some of which – on a much smaller scale and with different names – had been known and used for many centuries.

Chemistry not only reminds us that the spearhead theory cannot be reduced to rational mechanics, but should be regarded as an entity, but also draws attention to a major aspect of the history of science and of history in general.

During the nineteenth century, and thereafter, it was said many times that modern science owed its success to the fact that it had replaced the qualitative by the quantitative. This is not untrue, but it is much too simplistic. The 'qualities' handed down from Aristotle (hot, cold, dry, wet) were quantified long before the Renaissance, although in terms that made exact reasoning abstruse. In popular terms, quantities are expressed as natural numbers: modern algebra will invent many more that are completely abstract, and this abstraction will suit quasi-qualitative algorithms, sharing with natural numbers only the property that they can be used in operations.

Those sciences that were developing before the nineteenth century, and which during that period grew exponentially, owe their universality to all that Europe borrowed from most of the cultures still vivid at that time. But is this an adequate explanation? One may ask, whether the sciences whose development flowered in the nineteenth century were ungrateful enough to help, through their industrial applications, enslave the cultures to whom they owed their universalism. If not the sciences, what other cultural factors underlie their flourishing?

Here historians of science are divided into two schools. According to one of them – the 'internalists' – scientific development apparently follows only its own internal logic. According to the other – the 'externalists' – scientific development depends on concepts provided by or inspired by social and cultural circles. In this confrontation, each side marshals arguments, which vary according to the periods or fields studied: variations that permit a reconciliation. Beyond a certain level, science develops of its own accord, until the conceptual resources that enables it to overstep that level are exhausted. On the other hand, any particular step forward takes place as a result of instances of conceptual renewal, that correspond with the changes or mutations modifying social and cultural progress.

The fact of accepting this duality facilitates inquiry, reducing it to listing those milestones, the passing of which coincides with a discontinuity in the history of how existence is perceived. History offers us a choice between three main epochs: the Renaissance – the currents of influence change direction; the eighteenth century – criminal and civil law no longer express the will of God but conform with human rights; the second industrial 'revolution' – urban activities begin to win the day over rural activities.

The nineteenth century was the great century of science, but also that of Europe. Its ships criss-crossed the seas with no fear of competition from non-European nations, so that it dominated by the power of its trade, its finance and its weapons. Competition grew only between European countries and, within them, between companies seeking to gain the same rights: to be free and statutorily equal; to no longer have to fear the monopolies built on privilege. Europe was a hive of activity: anything contributing to the undefined progress of the human race could be expected of it, and for this progress Europe opened up unlimited prospects, primarily for its own profit. This was particularly true as the initiatives taken were so varied. The French Revolution had intended to overturn the monarchies, then the empires, to subject them all to a single one: ambition had collapsed in a bloody failure; Europe was the pure essence of diversity, as were all its nations both existing and emerging.

Such great events excite and fire the imagination: everything appears possible. The passing century, shaken from time to time by other disturbances or revolutions, was to ruin many dreams, but not those that science would progressively accomplish, confident as it was in nature and its laws. As Friedrich Gauss declared, on one of the very few occasions that this pious man showed signs of exultation, 'nature is my goddess; I am the liege man of her laws'.

But what becomes of nature when science transforms its manifestations; and what becomes of these laws, when science throws doubt on the simple approach that raised Newton to the rank of master of them all? Towards the end of the century, Ernest Renan was to say that imagination existed 'to give relief from life in dreams, not to take over life itself'. But what imagination? In any event not that of scientists who, trusting the imaginary, were to move from discovery to discovery regarding all as correct, particularly as the most fundamental of them were to transform the human way of life as well as the way in which human beings saw life itself.

Romanticism is not just a premonition of the future; equally it represents nostalgia for the past. The same applies to science, primarily the exact sciences – let us say 'mathematics' and that which forms part of it within the spearhead theory: none of these innovations will be accepted unless, while contradicting or modifying existing certainties, it makes intelligible that portion of truth earlier regarded as authentic.

One may ask how the 'spirit of the century' nourished scientific intuition and inspiration. To go by the scientific biographies, historical research has found none declaring a direct influence; also very few admitted not knowing the source of ideas and concepts unconnected with learning and rejected before being refocused in old contexts wherein lay their explanation. Taking a broad view of this astonishing story, one can only note that a century marked by a diversity of experience is marked also by an unprecedented increase in the number of theoreticians becoming personally involved in theoretical progress. To each his genius, and to all, although to varying extents – participation in the mathematical developments of the century. We can illustrate this by a number of examples.

Karl Friedrich Gauss, the 'Prince of Mathematicians', was born in 1777 into a poor family. He is said to have been outstandingly precocious by the age of three. He played with numbers and number series so brilliantly that his teacher, having taught him all he knew, secured the protection of the Duke of Brunswick for his pupil. From college – where the master, in turn, was soon out of his depth – the young prodigy entered the university where his impact was no less. Having demonstrated his ability (how to divide a circle into seventeen equal parts, demonstrating the fundamental theorem of algebra), he published continuously (in Latin), turned down the Academy of St Petersburg, and agreed to direct the Göttingen Observatory and to teach mathematics there. A discreet, shy man, he accumulated vast quantities of notes in books which would be understood only after his death. Acknowledged as the 'world's leading geometer' by Laplace, Gauss was a polymath. Consulted during the surveying of Hanover, he invented a form of geodesy that took account of the curvature of the earth. As an astronomer, he prepared, amongst other studies, a paper on the perturbations affecting the planetary system. As a physicist, he calculated an absolute measurement of the earth's magnetism, and excelled equally in optics, elucidating refraction in glass lenses. He was to pass the final years of his life (which ended in 1855), in learning and excelling in the Hebrew language. Revolutions, wars, political and social events passed him by unnoticed.

Quite unlike him was Augustin Cauchy, also an eminent mathematician, but with monarchist convictions that ensured him a tumultuous life from 1830 on. Born in 1789, Cauchy's work – particularly on wave propagation on the surface of a heavy liquid – merited the honours and official posts given to him in 1816 and which he gave up when the bourgeois King Louis Philippe picked up in the street the crown fallen from the head of the legitimate Bourbon. He went into exile in Switzerland, and then on to Turin to a professorial chair that the king of Sardinia created specially for him. He did not hold it for long, and at the Prague Hardshin rejoined Charles X, who had found refuge there and entrusted the education of his eldest son to his guest. When this task was over, the 1848 Paris Revolution brought home a Cauchy determined not to continue his work, unless he could avoid swearing fealty to anyone. His enormous output reflects the character of a man both rigid and generous (he gave away to charitable causes the salary he received from a government supported essentially by businessmen). In his rigidity, Cauchy remained faithful to his original vocations: algebraic analysis, differential calculus and the theory of curves. Interested in everything, as he read he invented, and from time to time improvised notations that ran the risk of remaining incomprehensible, without a patient effort to translate these personal notations into formalisms brought into common use by the need – never fully met, but always an obsession – to provide mathematics with a language accessible to all who contributed to, or used it.

We must emphasize this difference between Gauss and Cauchy. The former's influence was slow to develop because he outstripped his peers; that of Cauchy was not felt immediately because he would not yield to accepted convention. But, despite too precocious an intelligence or too improvised a style, mathematics still progressed according to internal rather than external conditions, until intuitive understanding prevailed: not merely the inspirer of 'vague objects', as Romantic poets suggested in order to 'escape from life through dreams'; much rather the revealer of 'values of correlation', as Lazare Carnot suspected around 1800 before Henri Poincaré, a hundred years later, attributed this intuition to the action of the unconscious on the rational mind. We shall assume, as a fixed point, that the 'vague objects' of Romanticism also stem from the unconscious, without overstepping the subconscious, where 'fuzzy images' are elaborated before, in fact, being converted into literature or the visual arts. We shall also assume that the unconscious stems from correlations between the id, the ego and the superego, the task of the ego being to ensure that the influence of the superego – fashioned by the social and cultural environment – is overcome by the imperatives emerging from an id made up only, when it is merely a question of mathematics, of cerebral interconnections activated by specific learning and 'directed thinking'.

It is sometimes said that if Evariste Galois had not been assassinated – in 1832, at the age of twenty – in a duel which this extreme liberal had himself provoked – or if Henrik Abel had not succumbed – in 1829, at the age of twenty-six – to tuberculosis caused by hardship, the history of mathematics would have been very different. The course of history was altered, obviously, because they would have been involved for longer. However, mathematical development as such would have been affected only slightly. The decisive importance of their contributions was recognized too late for them, but recognized none the less when

circumstances made it possible for this to happen for the greater posthumous glory of their authors. And it is impossible to guess whether these victims of the times had any control over circumstances which laid them low in their lifetime. Gauss lived better; this made little difference to his intuitive premonitions.

Let us merely consider two possible reasons why recognition comes too late, and let us trust Felix Klein, whose Erlangen Programme (1872) attributed the major innovations bringing in successful developments to the beginning of the nineteenth century. From this we shall see that we can rely on the Romantic period to bring out most clearly the origins of theoretical advances that looked to the world of the imagination to resolve problems insoluble by mathematics based on 'reality'.

REVELATORY ENIGMAS

It had been suspected for more than a century, that the number of possible solutions to an equation was equivalent to its degree. This 'fundamental theorem of algebra' had been the subject of a demonstration by d'Alembert, which was subsequently regarded as inadequate. In fact such a demonstration was difficult because, for the theorem to be precise, the solutions would have to admit that a negative or 'imaginary' number was as 'real' as a positive number.

Around 1800, Lazare Carnot did, in fact, accept that negative or imaginary quantities were useful or even essential in calculations, but would not agree that they should appear in the solutions. This was no more than a question of ways of expressing oneself, objects of pure language or, as we would say today, significant objects deprived of all significance. The same author proposed to deal with them as 'correlation values', no doubt meaning that in themselves they represented nothing, but were merely indicators of relationships between entities that did, in fact, represent reality. However, accepting only positive roots when solving equations is tantamount to returning algebra to prehistoric times. For the previous 150 years or so, algebra had being dealing with problems that the rule and compass could not resolve. Let us borrow the idea of symmetry from geometry: this is to move into one and the same 'metaphysics' (both word and topic were highly fashionable at the time and remained so for some decades) and thus avoid regarding negative quantities as being less than nothing.

This summary ignores a number of episodes that took place during the first three decades of the nineteenth century: they were significant in a 'real' way to the extent that we shall speak of them again.

In Gauss's time, people were already speaking of 'imaginary' planes or spaces; by the end of the century they preferred to say 'abstract spaces'. A different time, a different tone: with the imaginary having won the battle of precision, the imagination, in the ordinary sense of the term, thereby became suspect, even though abstractions and abstractions of abstractions never ceased to employ it according to rules that became equally abstract in seeking to be precise.

This turning-point in conceptual development took place around the middle of the century; in any event it was already in the past when Felix Klein in 1872 published his opening dissertation ('Considerations of New Research into Geometry', better known under the name of the Erlangen Programme). The author (who qualified 'imaginary' geometry as hyperbolic, and Riemannian geometry as elliptical) became well known especially through his extension of the 'theory of groups'.

With regard to this review we can conclude that, even if it was less vague, it would not lead to a rational 'metaphysics' of algebras or abstract spaces. A precise description – hence long and detailed – would merely render even more surprising the contribution made to the clarification of physical phenomena (taking place in normal space) by abstractions which even the toughest and most experienced imagination is unable to visualize. These two concepts – the 'group' and abstract spaces – can be dealt with here in no more than an allusive way; and notably to illustrate the expression of Robert Oppenheimer, the atomic physicist, who was concerned by the gulf that made it impossible to translate into any natural language the formal procedures making mathematical theories effective, even when they are applied directly to calculating physical phenomena.

Let us begin by considering the abstraction which, as from the middle of the century, resulted in the adjective 'imaginary' going out of fashion in scientific speech – it had survived thus far – to the benefit of the adjective 'abstract', which more precisely qualifies algorithms or formal procedures devoid of fantasy. This substitution took place virtually coincidentally with the time when – in poetry, attitudes and customs – Realism marked the end of Romanticism. Talking of 'abstract spaces' is to give them the status of 'reality', even though it is a very different reality from the concrete.

Albert Einstein was to summarize this phenomenology in two words: 'the narrowness of the mind'. Similarly, human vision must scan the different parts of a landscape before the cerebral functions can assemble these multiple perceptions into a single image: the landscape that the memory retains as an entity – even though allowing the memory to bring out one of the aspects that stood out at the outset – or quite differently thereafter. As the emotive imagination, so the rational mind. The rational mind analyses item-by-item that which the cerebral unconscious unites into a single entity and which subsequent analysis will restructure, sometimes identically, sometimes differently.

If historians did not refer to this process which the narrowness of the mind forces them to divide into alternate phases of analysis and synthesis, they would run the risk of being misled when drawing up a list of innovations. True innovations are rare. One could not apply the term to those propositions, which, although certainly new, do no more than clearly express formal patterns already present in the unconscious. True innovation means enriching or re-orientating the unconscious. The expression 'scientific revolution' must be handled with care. It clearly applied to the period when reference to the doctrine of the Trinity saw the emergence of and was replaced by other systems of reference, notably the one known as Cartesian, though not due to Descartes alone nor stated or suggested only by him. In fact such a substitution process opened the way to a large number of subsequent innovations, because it radically reforms the functions of the unconscious and that which they inspire in the conscious mind.

From this point of view, the Erlangen Programme was a true innovation, but was not revolutionary because Felix Klein, in his turn and in his own way, submitted the 'comparative considerations relative to new research and geometry' to the algebraicists. After Gauss, Balyai, Lobatchewski and their 'imaginary geometries', Bernhard Riemann had – posthumously – provided him with an example of abstract geometry. Obviously Riemann questioned neither the negative nor the complex numbers. His 'hypotheses serving as a basis for geometry' hold as true those infinitely small entities through which the infinitesimal calculus, the integral calculus (the 'reverse' of the former, but less easily generalized) and the calculus of variations saw startling progress – even though it severely tested the intelligence with the difficulties or impossibility of 'integrating'. Having access to so much earlier knowledge (Newton and his fluxions, Leibniz and his infinitesimals, Lagrange and his calculus of variations), all considerably improved since, all that remained for Riemann to do was to give an explicit definition of a 'space' implicitly assumed by these types of numbers and calculations. Abstraction was shown and demonstrated to be so real that this *Privat-dozent* (university lecturer) aged only twenty-eight in 1854, was able to convince people of the existence of surfaces without thickness made up of sheets without thickness. Curvature can be analysed by a reference frame moving from point to point: points that may be so infinitely close that the surface to which they belong can be regarded as flat (in Euclidian terms).

Conceived intuitively, abstraction is an ancient concept. Euclid's infinitely thin lines, his surfaces without thickness, his points without dimension were already Figuratively 'abstracted' from concrete objects with mass and dimensions. However, when the problem is posed the other way round, and when it is a matter of using – as if they were exact – algorithms from which the mind is unable to extract anything sensible, this means that there also exists a nonsense that can only reside in the unconscious. Such a supposition makes it understandable that the sacred universe is of the same extraction as the 'imaginary' or abstract spaces. All of them reflect realities looking for instances of the boundaries being overstepped. It was less than a hundred years before the formal operational procedures began to seek the criteria of precision in the opposite direction to that in which one might have expected them to be found. Prior to Gauss or Cauchy, conviction was verified in geometrical representations that conformed to the data of the Euclidian 'synthesis' based objectively on concrete experience. As a result, the algorithms that facilitated the operations were regarded as artifices of language to exclude results. After Riemann and Klein, these same algorithms were regarded as real, since the abstract spaces were derived from them and demonstrated their internal cohesion.

Towards the end of the nineteenth century and early in the twentieth, mathematics made the most of this U-turn, and was to justify it by formulating axioms specific to each of the concepts generated abstractly in this way. In order to conceive of new ones – concerning spaces or numbers – it is sufficient to change axioms, the number of which is *a priori* limited. No sensible intuition would allow so much freedom; however, another intuitive function overcame that which was inspired by concrete experience. Rather than abstract experience – in human terms a nonsense – let us rather say internal and imperceptible experience, because it was accomplished of its own accord in the shadows of the unconscious.

Lessons from the cosmos throw mechanics into question

For thousands of years, mankind had expected the stars to throw light on human destiny. Astrology, based on ancient experience, looked to the heavens for answers. The constellations – named as they still are today – immortalized mythological heroes. The planets shared the properties of substances used in alchemy; their motion, conjunction and opposition showed how a particular date of birth meant good or bad luck: such beliefs still persist in Europe, despite all its scientific progress. However, during the sixteenth century the observers of the night sky had begun to perceive there a form of logic by sacrificing this anthropomorphism to more rational interpretations, dictated by the fact that the earth was no longer the centre of the universe. From the circular orbits of Copernicus to the ellipses of Kepler, and the calculation of the sizes of these elliptical areas using the method of fluxions, Newton entirely overturned these old ways of conceiving the world. Reason triumphs when the motions of celestial bodies can be explained by a single formula, that authenticates the new mechanics on which it was based. 'Natural' motion – the motion of a body on which no force acts – ceases to be circular and becomes linear (just as passing time ceases to be felt as repetitive and becomes progressive and unidirectional). If the planets in their orbits follow an elliptical path about a focus, it is that they are subjected to an attraction for which Newton borrowed the word from alchemy and refused to speak about the 'reality' designated in this way.

These reminders would have been worthless, if Laplace and his many admirers and supporters had not believed that a celestial mechanics and a rational mechanics, mutually legitimizing one another, represented eternal truth. In fact, this dual reign lasted only a short time. Reason held sway until the middle of the nineteenth century, whereupon abstract reasoning as well as concrete observations and experiments began to suggest that things were not so simple.

The discovery of the planet Ceres, and the calculation of its orbit by the youthful Gauss – still a student – had little effect on opinion occupied by much more spectacular events. Some forty years later – in 1845 – science was again on the agenda, particularly that of the astronomers vying with one another to understand the perturbations affecting the orbit of the planet Uranus, discovered by William Herschel in 1781. Although the celestial body that might be causing these aberrations was not discovered, the simplicity of Newton's famous law was to be put in doubt. A matter of this importance deserved the attention of the observatories. Greenwich received information from John Adams that was sufficient to resolve the enigma, but did not take the trouble to check the accuracy of the data collected by so young a colleague – who was only twenty-six. In Paris, Urbain Le Verrier, unaware of what was happening in Cambridge, did the calculations himself, obtained the same results, and sent them to Joseph Gall, the Berlin astronomer, who discovered an immense but very distant planet: Neptune. This success was all the more spectacular in that it was achieved virtually simultaneously in three centres of European science: no-one doubts that operational reasoning, based upon a simple law, can in fact be predictive. The supporters of what came to be called 'scientism' missed no opportunity to quote and re-quote this example as if it were a universal paradigm, even though other problems threw doubt on its generality.

Celestial mechanics has to accommodate factors other than those used by Newton.

The causes of this success and its exaggeration are the same: the value placed on astronomy as the prime repository of scientific truth, and the improvements made to the instruments capable of observing the sky. Kings, governments, princes and wealthy individuals established observatories in Europe, but their performance proved to be very uneven. In the universities, the post of astronomer was particularly sought after, since the routine work, especially that at night, was carried out by one or more assistants, leaving him the time to think about the data and work out new kinds of calculation and theory. It was possible by simple observation to prepare charts of hundreds and thousands of stars to be swapped by colleagues, or rivals until some international conference collects these charts into one – which was to happen in due course. One day the 'nebulas' came to be recognized as masses of stars rather than indistinct clouds of matter, and it was finally explained that galaxies could take a spiral form.

Much time had passed since Newton made his own instrument and Herschel, not content with making one for himself, ensured his financial independence by selling systems to others. The nineteenth century saw the emergence of a variety of craft skills for casting and polishing clear glass, and building telescope tubes and mechanisms enabling them to move slowly and follow the star under observation. The principle of the telescope – a mirror extending its focal length – was known to Galileo; many improvements were made to it later: for example, a mirror made of glass instead of a reflecting metal surface. Herschel had seen Uranus through a telescope, 2 metres long with an aperture of 15 centimetres. Around 1850, the length had increased to 17 metres and the aperture to over 180 centimetres. And lens systems overcame the aberrations produced around the edges of eyepieces and objectives.

Microscopes obviously benefited from similar technological advances. As to aberration, another invention gained from this defect.

Everyone knows that a prism breaks down white light into coloured rays that form a spectrum. Through successive improvements – some simple, others very complicated – before the end of the century the spectrograph was producing several thousand rays for each centimetre of spectrum. These spectral rays vary according to what chemical substances the light source is burning. And if one of these substances forms a barrier between the light source and the objectives, the corresponding rays turn black. Finally, if the light source moves, the rays do the same, which makes it possible to determine whether objects are approaching or receding, as well as their speed. No less than telescopes or field glasses, spectrography – later backed up by photography – can be used to analyse the stars, and determine their components and their movements. The problems raised by vast distances, far exceeding what Newton or Herschel could have imagined, also exceed what rational mechanics – now become conventional – calculated on the basis of simple Figures and postulates, such as the 'principle of least time or least action' – the principle adopted by Hamilton – implying that nature acts with the maximum of economy. Indeed, it was not necessary to look so far to find the same uncertainty: the planet Mercury deviates in its orbit when it approaches too close to the sun, which, instead of attracting it, repels it.

These new data – and not only they – would have given immediate support to a feeling of Riemann: space is not completely empty, and the objects it contains modify its geometry. Towards the end of the century, it was more appropriate to speak of diverse kinds of mechanics worked out on a case-by-case basis than of one only, assumed to be based on objective principles independent of the constraints imposed by the implications. What the physicists and astrophysicists expect from the newly multiform mechanics are procedures that more conveniently employ the formal rules of operational reasoning.

This reference to 'convenience' which we owe to Henri Poincaré, gives the lie to the claims of rational mechanics, which believed, at the beginning of the century, that it was founded in 'truth'. A hundred years later, it reflects a malaise affecting this discipline, which can no longer defend the absolutism of 'principles', weakened by too many uncertainties, primarily concerning the concept of velocity. This unexpected concept draws its legitimacy not only from experiment and observation but also from reasoning, that was too careless about the circularity of definitions: for example, those wherein mass is the quotient of a weight divided by an acceleration which produces a weight when multiplying a mass. Equally – just as Poincaré noted and affirmed – whatever system one conceives, it will only be possible to demonstrate relative velocities. Relativistic mechanics came into its own once 'there is no logical reason for considering existing mechanical systems as the only ones possible' (Pieer Duhem).

In 1851, Léon Foucault hung a weight, weighing nearly 30 kg on a 70 m wire from the top of a dome (the Panthéon in Paris): the plane of oscillation of this pendulum described one complete revolution in 24 hours. The experiment drew crowds who supposed it was to convince of the rotation of the earth. However, the phenomenon would have been the same if it were space that was revolving around the earth. No argument is valid unless based on a fact of a quite different kind: if it was space that revolved, the calculations would be much more complicated. But is nature simple? And if simplicity facilitates reasoning to such an extent and – in the case of Einstein – for such spectacular and disturbing results, is it not a fact that by distrusting natural complexities, formidable and opposite effects are ultimately to be expected? The nineteenth century, with its European style of science and the benefits drawn from it, obviate any fear of such a backlash – or other forms of violence already in the pipeline. The century – even in its most abstract sciences – continued on its way towards a universe of forces.

The two origins of a new theory on the calculation of forces

The century was still only in its second quarter, when two theoreticians of about the same age, and unaware of each other's existence, constructed the bases, each in his own way, for a new method: the fundamental method for vector calculus and vector space. They lived at the two ends of Europe, one in Dublin, the other in Stettin, and their intellectual development could not have been more different. Hermann Grassmann, living quietly on the shores on the Baltic, continued the work of his father by formulating a Theory of Extension – *Ausdehnungslehre* – the beginnings of which was worked out only just prior to 1800. W. R. Hamilton, older by four years, was already a celebrity

in England and on the continent, before he astonished his peers by introducing the first of the 'hypercomplex' numbers, the end product of a current of research that began in the sixteenth century.

We shall begin by considering the case of Grassmann, the least well known although not the least important. His theory formalizes the constitution of abstract spaces and the forms they may contain by attributing everything to a series of generations: a point engenders a line; a line engenders a surface, and so on, however large the number of dimensions: each step increases by one the degree – *Stufe* – of the previous one of which it 'extends' the orientation. Grassmann does not talk of 'vectors' but of 'distance between an arrival and a departure' – *Strecke* – when considering a line, but the concept applies equally well to the element of any number of dimensions.

Such an abstract theory that broke away so utterly from previous practice would not be understood until later, when at the end of the century the axioms qualifying vector spaces were recognized. It is possible to recognize, translated into algorithms, the qualifications of activity spaces generated by what today we call socio-economic development: a form of development designed as it were with no limitations other than those due to aesthetics. W. R. Hamilton was living at the very heart of these socio-economic developments, when he found himself led unawares to discover the first of the hypercomplex numbers, which he thought of calling 'grammarithms' before opting for the term 'quaternions'. This new type of number in fact comprises four entities that are factors of the same number of units: one real, the other three 'imaginary', which the author identifies as 'vectors', multiples of three 'vector' units. With a story as strange as that of this discovery, it is worth summarizing how it was achieved, the precedents and what came after.

No other story makes so clear the influence of social and cultural factors on a conceptual revolution. That which the seventeenth century still called 'impossible gulfs' of 'false numbers' gave rise in the nineteenth century to algorithms, that were the most Figurative and most useful in concrete terms to physics and mechanics.

Also, quite apart from the operational properties these quaternions possessed initially and still possess today – to which Hamilton devoted two enormous volumes written during his last twenty years – the concept of a vector and the ideas generated spawned many descendants. All are of considerable interest.

We should note that the American Academy of Sciences was first to honour Hamilton for his quaternions; we should also note that Grassmann had no time for imaginary quantities, and we should finally note that this period saw the first axiomatic formulations. New ideas of capital were coming into management at the time when mathematical certainty was changing ground. The rise of the United States made their mathematicians influential in a field hitherto mainly occupied by the Europeans, particularly in the West. The research carried out by young German logicians – for example, Gottlob Frege in arithmetic – continued along the lines established by the Grassmann father and son team. These and other innovations diverted attention from earlier concerns such as those that tried to give an operational meaning to the 'impossible roots' of 'false' numbers.

In this new cultural context, Great Britain, still a centre of routes, increasingly open to the West and the East, made its contribution to these pragmatic and conceptual reforms.

In Belfast and then in Edinburgh, the mathematician Peter Gunthie Tait was to break with his former mentor W. R. Hamilton – after vainly trying to convince him – to provide the vector algorithms needed by James Maxwell, who was in the process of formalizing the results of his experiments with electromagnetic fields, induction and force.

FROM A NATURE CONSISTING OF OBJECTS TO A NATURE MADE UP OF FORCES

The great century of science brings us face to face with a paradox: the more mathematics aspires to abstraction, the more European life declines into a materialism which it then passes on to the rest of the world. We should not be surprised at the gulf of incomprehension appearing between operational formalism and 'natural' languages. On the one hand, in calculation and reasoning, imaginary quantities are regarded as real, infinitesimal quantities as accessible and space as having any number of dimensions that are also more precise than ordinary space. On the other hand, all that matters is machines producing more, crossing oceans and continents more quickly, and transmitting orders and information virtually immediately – quite apart from those engines of war that are even more deadly by virtue of the refinements they owe to science that claims to be universal.

So where does the breakdown occur? Is it between abstract theories and practical applications? Of course, the one cannot exist without the other, when all the experimental sciences are based on practice or stem from – or even reform – theories when they do not lead on to new ones. Scientific progress advances from breakdown to breakdown, each made good in turn by purely conceptual innovations and rising to levels that are higher the deeper their roots penetrate into the unconscious. Can so many innovations be called 'scientific revolutions'? One might as well speak of a 'continuous revolution' that owes everything to its origins; owing everything to that moment where the unconscious shed its old holy certainties underlying religion and embraced new convictions, wagering – without knowing where this would lead philosophy – that the human mind could penetrate and appropriate the secrets hidden from it by the gods.

In other words, around 1780, evolving science had already passed the most decisive stage of its 'continuous revolution'. This form of selective evolution had brought about the initial breakdown, the root cause of those that followed, and had also supplied the intellectuals with all they needed to move from one innovation to another in rapid stages. Let us outline the state of experimental science at the end of the eighteenth century.

In order to link up with mathematics and its numerical calculations, the experimental sciences needed 'units' or systems of units making them coherent with one another until such time as the units themselves could be made coherent. As far as the measurement of time was concerned, the sexagesimal system had been passed down from the ancient Chaldeans: it had been convenient (although approximate) to divide the solar year into 12 lunar months, the noon-to-noon day into twice 12 hours, the hour into 60 minutes and the minute into 60 seconds. This circular approach also prevailed for the degrees of a circle: the only

unit entitled to claim a natural origin. As regards lengths, areas, volumes, weights and degrees of temperature, a few arbitrary systems emerged, reflecting cultural differences, which were not immediately overtaken by the metric system even after the CGS (centimetre, gramme, second) system rallied support from those involved in the analysis of small or infinitesimally small phenomena. However these difficulties appeared minor compared with another problem that went to the heart of basic concepts.

Devising a formal treatment for motion – as Newton had managed to do – meant that weight and mass must no longer be confused. Weight is the product of mass and 'acceleration' (here, that due to gravity). Mass designates a quantity of material regardless of what happens to it in any kind of attractive 'field': the question is what 'units' should be chosen to calculate a quantity deprived of any factual independence, disguised as it always is by various sets of various forces that act on it, or indeed come from it, or cause it to change state (from solid to liquid, from liquid to gas). Nobody could fail to be amazed by the erudition, quantity and variety of research generated by these differences between weight, mass and acceleration. As far as mass is concerned one might as well say that it is a pure concept: its 'reality' as a 'thing' is manifest only through the effects it produces.

Of course, to have atoms and forces is not necessarily to know their respective positions or functions. But these two concepts led to so much discussion that sooner or later minds were alerted and came to suggest experiments that founded an atomic theory involving a form of mechanics based on forces. Towards the end of the eighteenth century, all kinds of discoveries were made at virtually the same time: they opened up a new era for chemistry and the physics of electricity and magnetism. With minds too narrow to encompass and formulate overall views, progress along these new paths was slow; there were disputes, agreements and understandings. But since, in a manner of speaking, the future was predestined by the fact that mass and weight must no longer be regarded as the same thing, the remainder of the century was virtually sufficient, for it to be discovered how the world becomes more intelligible, once it is seen as a set of forces rather than as a set of objects. Two principal series of difficulties had to be overcome: first, defining units for each type of mass; second, deciding between the competing hypotheses regarding the propagation of forces.

These statements deserve some explanation. They are based on historical data, but data that are of little or no interest to schools of history in the traditional sense. These schools lack neither resources nor methods to throw light on events, but are unable to do so other than by comparing them either to their antecedents, or to personal initiatives stemming from equally individual reasoning, or to collective circumstances conditioned by the past and in turn conditioning initiatives and their scope. In this situation, none of the many approaches that succeeded one another made the intellectual approach universally predictive. On the contrary, in the fields covered in Newton's *Principia* that which is intelligible, and even that which can be predicted, are identified with that which can be calculated.

As the nineteenth century progressed, the observatories calculated increasingly precise values for the masses of the planets compared with that of the earth or the sun, which alone has no weight because, being central to the system, it is the cause of gravity without being exposed to it (at least at its centre, because according to another postulate – self-evident according to what happens on earth and above the earth – every outer region is attracted by that which lies within: hence the notion of 'centre of gravity').

If gravitational forces were the only ones to exist, every mass would thereby be defined. However, there are others, for example electromagnetic force. Interestingly, this other force propagates at a certain velocity – which was to be calculated as equal to that of light – whereas the force of gravity acts instantaneously.

Of course, the nineteenth century sought to produce theories – ultimately vain – to explain this difference. And the question became more complicated when other differences, concerned in particular with modes of propagation, had to be faced. As early as the seventeenth century, rudimentary measurements suggested that light – like sound – was propagated as waves, the frequency of which varied in the way that colours vary. Newton produced another explanation for this variation: the projection in straight lines of infinitesimally small particles each coloured blue, yellow or red and such that, when mixed to differing extents, they produce all the others. This merely made the confusion worse, especially as regards matter. Were these infinitesimal particles material? And although sound waves agitate the air, light waves could only pass through what was supposed to be 'empty' if this space was apparently taken up by an elastic medium – the 'ether' – devoid of meaning. It was not until the twentieth century that mathematics brought particles and vibrations into one and the same formulation; even this was an abstract formulation with no concrete meaning.

While awaiting this theoretical answer, the nineteenth century marked time. Starting from a definite distinction between mass and force, the question was still what made matter massive in space or in an ether infinitely more tenuous than the subtlest of gases. In this search, what help could the nineteenth century expect from research seeking to discover and elucidate forces?

If matter was always solid and always had the same density, a single type of force would suffice to hold it together. But the same mass of a given type of matter may be solid like ice, liquid like water or gaseous like steam. So the force must vary with temperature, at least in intensity. The problem becomes more complicated if light is propagated in the form of particles: the question is whether they are particles of matter and, if so, as from what degree of heat do particles free themselves from the mass to pass through space, or perhaps the ether?

Whatever example – or theory – one considers, the issues raised by matter, force and heat appear inseparable. If Newton's inheritance had provided the nineteenth century with an unequivocal definition of energy, these various questions could be given an answer which, if not universal, would at least be limited to the expression of a relationship between matter and energy. But the most current definition of energy is still what it was around 1850: 'that which a system contains if it is capable of producing work'. Such a definition refers to different entities; it refers, with 'system', to the universe of abstraction and, with 'work', to the world of concrete experience: a world made up of masses that are either stationary or moving with the implication of velocity, inertia or acceleration.

Thus, science does not achieve synthesis without first proceeding to partial analysis. Each of these partial analyses is linked to calculation only when definitions concerning their scope have been agreed – i.e. based upon locally specific situations. How is it that formulae drawn up in such diverse ways occasionally coincide with integrating theories? We know that the unconscious plays its part, but it is a role dictated by experience in a particular environment. In the case of experimental sciences, this environment goes beyond that of the laboratories, encompassing areas where there is a two-way trade in the benefits of inventions and the benefits of production.

Questions of matter

Of the four elements of Empedocles, the first to be cast out by the new chemistry was fire, the most noble form of matter for the ancient philosophers who had seen it in the sun and the stars, and had noted that every earthbound flame tended to reach up to these sacred heights, their 'natural home'. During the previous century, many medical chemists supported the concept of one of their colleagues who had taught the 'phlogiston' theory at the university of Halle. Phlogiston was believed to be an immaterial substance present in certain 'earths' and which escaped from them to produce light and heat; however, the experiments of Lavoisier, carried out with a candle and scales, refuted this claim: the flame results from 'combustion' and the fact, that it shines is due to the fact that it causes particles of the lowest material kind to incandesce. In this case, the residual matter resulting from the combustion weighs the same as those present at the beginning: 'nothing is lost, nothing is created, every thing is changed', and the operation conserves mass. Since phlogiston had no weight or mass it did not exist.

Even so, Lavoisier did not entirely win the day; quite apart from the fact that students in Berlin burned him in effigy, something had to be done about heat. For many decades it was identified as 'caloric', a fluid so difficult to define that the topical encyclopaedia of Panckouke devoted over a hundred pages to listing its properties. The ideas of heat and dryness – 'qualities' otherwise relative to fire – had already found refuge in thermometry and hydrometry. As for light, its speed of propagation had already been calculated fairly well, even though little could be said about its independence. Lavoisier – put to death under the Convention on the grounds that he owed his wealth to his participation in levying of taxes – left a substantial inheritance to the new chemistry, going far beyond what he had taught about combustion.

Fire requires a fuel – for example coal or any other flammable material – along with a source of oxygen: air must be such a source because it activates flames. However, the ambient air does not only contain one gas, since another remains under the bell jar where the experiment is carried out. The first is called 'oxygen' – which produces oxides or acids – and the second 'nitrogen': a 'lifeless' gas, which is of no use either to the flame or to breathing. To these new words will be added other neologisms resulting in the formulation of a lexicon, a chemical 'Nomenclature' upon which all those involved in this new chemistry would collaborate. This Nomenclature draws a distinction between simple and compound substances, all the latter named according to a convention whereby it is possible to see of what the compound consists, and how it is formed: an enormous and endless task resulting in volume succeeding volume. Also a painstaking task: air was merely a 'mixture' of two gases, but when in the early 1780s, a gas – finally isolated – burned in air to form water, this water was no longer regarded as simple: it was a 'combination' of the oxygen with what has to be called 'hydrogen' – a simple substance which generates water. Another example: when 'dephlogisticated muriatic acid' became chlorine, itself a simple substance also capable of producing acids, oxygen would keep its name even though it had lost its position as the unique 'oxidizing agent'.

From complication to complication and correction to correction, the Nomenclature would have lost its value if its beginnings – and even more its later enhancements – had not suggested new concepts concerning matter. John Dalton, a self-taught Englishman owing his title of Professor in Manchester to no one but himself (he was only twenty-six when the wealthy Lavoisier passed away), abandoned mathematics to devote himself to chemistry. His enthusiasm for rational laws led him to look for them in matter, and he found them in its behaviour and composition. Preferring to live in poverty rather than to give up his work, he used simple proportions – proved by experiment – to show in elementary images (small circles inscribed in rectangles) how 'atoms' combine to form molecules. It was thus that the 'atomic theory' emerged in chemistry, although initially receiving little consensus. It required several years and considerable support from physics, magnetism and electricity.

Later experiments were to prove him wrong, but it was first necessary to overcome the confusion by turning to proportional calculations in which the weight approach is as important as the volumetric one: a virtually inexhaustible topic of discussion at least until the middle of the nineteenth century. In the meantime in Stockholm, Jacob Berzelius – a physician turned chemist – had proposed a new system of notation, which is still in use today. The simple substances were designated in the Nomenclature by the first letter of their name written in upper case, possibly followed by a lower case letter, so as to distinguish Cl (chlorine) from C (carbon) and followed by a subscript number indicating proportions when it formed combinations. Thus it is possible to write: $HH + O = H_2O$. This notation is extremely limited in the information it provides: amongst other things it ignores is the fact that the combination process may give off heat or in fact absorb it. But it does say everything that can be said about the proportions: an aspect then regarded as essential.

In 1871 a Russian chemist, Dimitri Mendeleev (1834–1907), described a 'system of elements' (system of 'atoms') based upon what was known of simple substances and their chemical weights, in the form of suggestions, which were to prove accurate and highly significant. The chemical weights were expressed in whole numbers, from 1 for hydrogen to 207 for lead (the numbering has been modified since). His table had gaps, some natural and others due to lack of information, that the future would provide. These numbers would prove to be those of the electrons. Chemistry is not an exact science but it is predictive, and this is of particular importance. Indeed, it was to prove such through the progress made in the field of electromagnetic physics.

As early as 1812, Berzelius had assumed that chemical combinations resulted from an electro-positive component merging with an electro-negative element: this assumption was too precipitate and too simple, and was too great a generalization of data obtained at the beginning of the century. Two electrodes immersed in water separate the hydrogen from the oxygen: each of these two simple substances has its own polarization. Electricity had only just been found to have 'dynamic' properties and the suggestion was already growing (or rather insinuating itself into unconscious minds), that its dynamism acted on matter itself capable of dynamism. The fact became practical reality eight or nine decades later; equivalent to two generations of scientists.

However, chemists and physicists, even when they work together, do not have the same priorities. For the former, the nomenclature came first; the latter were not to name their unit until 1880. This reversal of priority only deserves mention – in the framework of the nineteenth century – as an illustration of the trend away from a universe of objects to a universe of forces. Chemistry (with which de Jaucourt, the encyclopaedist, identified cooking) was already occupying 'homo sapiens'; magnetism was as old as the Chinese compass, and static electricity – using amber – had already interested the predecessors of the Greeks. To begin with, the only important thing here is the change from static to dynamic electricity.

Its history is extremely simple, and covers the two decades during which the French Revolution developed, broke out and ended. Luigi Galvani – dissecting frogs to observe animal electricity – saw that a muscle trembled in contact with a copper wire once this wire was rubbed on iron. Alessandro Volta, more interested in this physical phenomenon than in animal electricity, wrote in 1796 that 'the contact between two different conductors particularly those made of metal . . . with wet conductors . . . stimulates the electrical fluid and imposes a pulse on it'. The 'cell' was born, and with it a continuous fluid, which, in its continuity, differed from the sparks produced separately by electrostatic machines. The Paris Ecole Polytechnique had a battery of cells, at the time the biggest in Europe, and hence a continuous fluid, which, soon capable of being produced anywhere, lent itself to further experiments. These included the one already mentioned, the 'electrolysis' of water, which is separated into hydrogen and oxygen.

This series of innovations left little room for chance; indeed it left no room at all if we pay attention to the convictions of Henri Poincaré and his colleagues. The unconscious prepares the discoveries of the conscious mind. It may well invite it to 'think laterally', as Galvani did when he looked for animal electricity and found gold.

Moreover, this 'fluid' possessed too many original properties for it long to bear a name relating it to the flow of heat, the behaviour of which already looked suspect to the new chemistry. Watermills – of, which there were still large numbers despite the initial success of steam-driven machines – were to provide images that were more suitable for dynamic electricity. People were to talk of it as a 'current' and its intensity, and again of a potential 'drop' or difference. And as to its links to magnetism, these were to give rise to all kinds of experiments from 1820 onwards.

It was already one hundred years since observers had noted the effects of lightning on iron, giving it the property of 'lodestone' (magnetite). The importance of the compass to ships at sea drew attention to the magnetic field of the earth, which draws the needle to the north. Gauss did calculations and devised a formal treatment to specify the data of a problem raised by this type of magnetism and its generalization. In the meantime, once the 'currents' made the electrostatic spark unfashionable, a Swedish observer (Hans Christian Oersted) found – after vain research with sparks – that an electric current deviated a magnetized needle placed above a conducting wire connected to a cell. From then on, the two phenomena of electricity and magnetism were bound up together, never to be separated.

From the many arguments before, during and after the establishment of this fact, let us select the theories and postulates of Adrien-Marie Ampère. The Figures representing the electrical and magnetic phenomena enclose an angle the sine of which can be calculated. 'Molecular' currents – those of magnetization – circulate around particles. Here Ampère is predicting the future and even prefigures the substance of vector calculus. With his 'solenoid' (a word he invented for the sort of tube formed by the wire windings), Ampère devised an instrument which experimenters could subsequently no longer do without. However, too rationally, aware of his objective of developing a mathematical treatment for magnetism induced by 'continuous' current, he missed an opportunity that was nevertheless within his grasp: to establish the principles of calculations concerned with alternating currents, leading on to producing alternators and transformers. Others would do it instead, based, it would appear, on practical work. In any event, the first, extremely limited electronic circuits would distribute only direct current. The system was to become widespread only with alternating current. Laboratories in the twentieth century had to invent 'rectifiers' to advance their investigations of direct currents.

These investigations were already well advanced by the middle of the nineteenth century. Agreement had been reached on certain concepts (for example, that of 'quantity of electricity') while others were still being clarified: 'resistance' to the current, the dissipation of some of this amount of electricity as heat when the wire is too thin; the nature of 'insulators' and what took place in a 'dielectric' interrupting a conductor; observation of what occurred in air at low pressure or in a vacuum. One interpretation of electrolytic phenomena – like that of water – suggested that 'ions' (electrical charges) transported simple molecules either to one electrode or to another: the 'anode' and the 'cathode' (words derived from the Greek: motion upwards or downwards).

These developments answered certain questions, but raised new ones. The situation was practically ripe for the establishment of a coherent system of units to which the 1880s would give the names of scientists: the volt, the ampère, the watt, the coulomb, etc., words which were to enter all the usual dictionaries. As to the nature of electricity and the way in which it is propagated, since the word 'fluid' no longer had any meaning in this connection, the argument began – as it had done at another time with regard to light – between high-speed particles and waves carried by an ether sometimes described as a super-gas: a fourth state of matter.

The increase in the number of laboratories, the spread of professionalism in the universities, and the improved facilities for transport and communications give a febrile aspect to the activities of this most fertile period. They were made even more creative by the gradual breaking down of the boundary between physics and chemistry. We shall consider here only the essential experiments of a veritable avalanche – all of them significant once they are related to operational reasoning. Thus it was impossible to identify these essential experiments until the continuously changing kaleidoscope of opinions – particularly troublesome, as each was solidly based – had settled down.

For example, the followers of Faraday opted for a recidivist interpretation of the atomic type, which their hero had challenged after Maxwell had converted the same experimental results into vector calculus. As Ampère had predicted, the electric current is not in the plane supporting the magnetic fields traversed by lines of force. The question was what vectors transported: it could only be infinitesimal particles. The laboratories in Germany, for their part, preferred the wave approach, which may have inspired – even unconsciously – Hertz (the inventor of 'Hertzian' or radio waves). If there are two open and separate circuits, a spark generated deliberately in one of them causes a similar spark in the other.

The argument between the two concepts was not to be settled by the end of the century. However, the 'particle' concept does explain other phenomena: for example the deviation by a magnet of radiation emerging from the cathode in a tube containing air at low pressure. Also, Mendeleev's classification and related later work suggested that atomic weights increased in whole numbers.

Rather than ions, let us consider electrons inside atoms, whose negative charge causes them to orbit around a positively charged nucleus, and which are sometimes capable of escaping from this new type of gravitation: the puzzles are thereby resolved.

Introducing the electron into matter does not make it any more important. On the contrary, it gives infinitely greater importance to empty space, as in the solar system where the planets orbit around a central mass. The theory of Niels Bohr, the preparatory work for which was done in Cambridge by Ernest Rutherford – the calculator of the deviation of types of radiation other than those already known – was to exploit this analogy in 1913.

To achieve this result, Rutherford had to quantify 'energy': a concept so difficult to define.

The problem of energy

The Greeks would have been astonished to learn that the most natural of opposites were not *dynamism*, potential force, and *energy*, force in action, but instead between matter and anti-matter (1958), the latest fashionable explanation of the primeval explosion that provided the universe with its energy supply. Science in the nineteenth century was still far from promulgating such a heretical hypothesis at a time when the postulates underlying physical theories were still dominated by an all-prevailing materialism.

However, the less important mass becomes in the analysis of objects, the more force gains on the path leading to a matter-energy equivalence. The dictionary of physical 'units' illustrated this situation as the laboratories discovered more and more of the microscopic world. The CGS (centimetre, gramme, second) system was formulated shortly after the electrical and magnetic phenomena had resulted in agreement on the volt, the ampère, and other related units: the dyne was then added as the unit of force and the erg as the unit of work. As to the joule, it underwent a particularly significant change of meaning.

In the early 1840s, James Prescott Joule – a brewer by profession but a physicist by choice – had proposed a unit of equivalence between heat and work. In a very simple rig, paddles rotated in a tank of water, the temperature of which rose and, since the paddles were rotated by a weight whose descent determined the work applied, the experimenter could easily calculate the desired equivalence. A German theoretician – Hermann von Helmholtz – seized upon this result to bring a latent concept – that of 'energy' – into the open, and generalized its meaning.

Any body capable of accomplishing work possesses mechanical energy that disappears only when transformed into another form, notably heat, but also – and even thereby – electrical or chemical energy. And since an inadequately conducting electric wire heats up – as every electrician knows – the 'joule' unit was to become, during the 1880s, a 'unit of work', the equivalent to the energy dissipated in one second by a current of 1 ampère flowing through a resistance of 1 ohm. It became normal to attribute to the 'joule effect' not only the heat gains expected from the electrical 'radiators' but also the unfortunate losses of energy due to a defective installation.

One may ask whether it was reasonable to elevate the notion that energy is preserved as well as converted, to the level of a principle. And was as much said of 'work', the concept on which the idea of energy is based? Does not this notion borrow from the unconscious that which it adds – without being aware of it – to the concept of work? It was found possible to replace this concept by that of 'kinetic energy' which, according to Laplace, is conserved 'so long as the kinetic energy of a body is taken to mean the product of its mass and twice the integral of its velocity, multiplied by the differential of the velocity function, which expresses force': thus this is really an algorithm which tells us nothing about the 'reality' of energy, as it is manifest outside Newton's universal gravitation. Caution teaches us to adopt a symbolic entity to be defined on a case-by-case basis – as a 'convenience' as Henri Poincaré might have said – even though the relevant theories have advanced by postulating universality.

If the joule was to be precisely defined, a no less precise definition of the calorie was needed. Such a convention was more difficult to formulate than the one concerning mass, which gravitation makes relative to weight. The calorie must also refer to a rise in temperature, the degrees of which are not equivalent. At present the calorie is defined as the amount of heat needed to raise the temperature of one gramme of water from $14.5°C$ to $15.5°C$ at 'normal' atmospheric pressure: a necessary detail since so many different factors had to be taken into account. One in particular: contradicting the 'conservation' of energy: heat energy degrades.

This degradation was the subject of a substantial set of theories, thermodynamics, the first rudiments of which were formulated by Sadi Carnot, the son of Hyppolyte, author of a paper on the motive power of fire. Steam ('steam engines') Figured only as an intermediate stage between the fire where the fuel burns and the piston whose reciprocating motion turns a wheel. When the steam enters the cylinder (where it tends to decompress by virtue of the approximate so-called Mariotte's law which, in the seventeenth century, stated that the volume increases when the pressure decreases), the piston moves back. This withdrawal continues when the steam tends to liquefy. Following these two active 'strokes', there is a third stroke during which the wheel returns the piston to its original position in such a way that a new entry of steam causes the 'Carnot cycle' to start again. This brief treatment gives an idea of the theories – complex as well as fruitful – to which these observations led the way. Somewhat whimsical comments were made, when entropy and absolute zero were extended, to encompass the development of a global universe, whose energy resources were unknown.

The first third of the nineteenth century had passed before the idea of 'negentropy' – compensating for entropy – became known; this concept is essential to research into information and communications as well as in biology (dealt with at the end of this chapter). We should note that the second half of the nineteenth century intuitively suggested some aspects of negentropy and explicitly prepared the way for these basic discoveries.

Of course negentropy existed before it was named. Crystallography fascinated thousands of people unaware of being 'crystallographers' when, for example, craftsmen, supervised by their patron pharaohs, manufactured in their crucibles jewels that were deceptively like the gems found in the mines, in terms of colour, transparency and brilliance. The attraction of precious stones generated passions, which stimulated – more than anything else – the physicists, chemists and others familiar with the different forms of crystals, how they are formed and how they grow. Questions such as how solutions crystallize out; how molecules already present in a structure dictate the locations of other molecules that join them; how the nucleus of one atom loses an electron that is attracted by another; whether 'free' electrons exist; where they come from; what becomes of them; how these electrons propagate electricity along a 'conducting' (originally synonymous with 'vector' or 'carrier') wire; what becomes of them in an 'insulator' or as they pass through a dielectric. Besides the insoluble puzzle of gravitation – how a planet 'knows' where the other celestial bodies attracting it are located – there were many others, all less insoluble and which the century attempted to resolve one-by-one as it discovered, suspected and assumed forces other than gravitation – initially the electromagnetic force – that act like gravitation in atoms or between atoms, even though not instantaneously, but at a calculable speed which is found to be equal to the 'velocity' of light.

Other, concomitant questions arose, generating theories whose contradictions – if any – were resolved or awaited the resolution of more universal theories, invariably with the support of abstract formulae worked out or yet to be worked out by mathematics. These questions included one in particular: precisely what was the ether, which was apparently expected to do for light what the surrounding air does for sound; and how could this ether, initially conceived as a medium for transmitting vibrations, be simultaneously so penetrating and so penetrable as to affect neither the path nor the nature of the particles?

Moreover, the years 1881–95 were a time for looking again at problems and formulae. If the ether does not affect the velocity of light, then the earth's rotation causing its surface to move at very high speed must add to or subtract from this velocity, depending on whether the measuring instruments are facing west or east (a north-south orientation has no effect, unless the poles are reversed). Edward Morley repeated experiments already carried out by Albert Michelson; the intervening six years changed nothing, and the velocity remained the same; it was unaffected by the composition of forces. Perhaps an 'ether wind' rotates with the earth? But how, to what extent and with what consequences for other phenomena? In 1895, Hendrick Lorentz gave back the ether its immobility, modifying – as a result of this velocity being regarded as another 'physical constant' – the mathematical equations and formulae applied to mechanics.

The ether – whether 'super gas', a 'fourth state of matter' or the 'subtle matter' of Descartes, but without his 'vortices' – still offered a convenient means of supporting the wave theory of light and the forces involved. However, colours, as analysed by the spectroscope, raised a quite different problem. It will be recalled that a sodium flame is seen yellow, but if a strong white light passes through the vapour, the yellow turns to black. Whence new experiments deduced that very short and very long wavelengths are not governed by the same laws. This compromised the idea of an 'equipartition of energy', and another theory suddenly entered the mind of Max Planck: energy is not propagated continuously but in quanta (1900).

Could it be that energy, now invading virtually the entire sphere of matter, existed in the same way? What can be said of mathematical formulae and of their propensity to explain certain forms of existence? Or could it be, indeed, that the mathematical terms in which nature is expressed – since Hamilton, Riemann and their contemporaries – are 'infinitely small' and as close as possible to a point, although never zero? The second answer, conceptual in nature, agrees with the first, which draws an analogy. Both designate an endless process stemming from history and from its contradictions and paradoxes, such as those involving entropy and negentropy. Biology was to find its own scientific status, by conceiving of the selective evolution of species as the result of mutations, each proving analogous to a generally progressive modification of messages.

FROM LIFE CONSIDERED TO BE A SPECIFIC CREATION TO LIFE AS THE PRODUCT OF NATURAL EVOLUTION

'Life is the opposite of death'. When he wrote these words at the beginning of the article on Life in Diderot's Encyclopaedia, the gentle knight of Jaucourt did not err through an excess of metaphysics. And yet this philosopher – always ready when the publishers were seeking authors – summarizes in his own way the essence of what we have just described: life compensates, by enhancing order, that which physical entropy degrades in enhancing disorder. This kind of symmetry had haunted minds since existence had led them to express – in mythological or rational terms – the coexistence of so many opposites.

There are few fields where, as in biology, science appeared to be based most directly on the collective and personal historical past. In this connection, the great century of modern science illustrates a paradox. Clearly, Darwin and his *Origin of Species* (1859) formed part of this diachronic perspective so rich in events, with contemporary agriculture giving him an initial idea; however, this idea was biased by inadequate knowledge of what was going on in contemporary exact and experimental science. Had he known more about it, he would have hesitated to generalize what he learned from those raising livestock in his neighbourhood: that characteristics acquired during life were passed on by heredity to benefit their descendants.

How is it that so powerful a mind was in such a hurry to produce so revolutionary a work without taking more precautions? One explanation suggested by Julian Huxley – grandson of a supporter of the great discoverer – shows us a Darwin both anxious and in a hurry: in a hurry to beat a rival who was about to propose the same theory; anxious

that he would have to oppose the still very widespread religious beliefs (particularly in the English universities recently given over to theology). Moreover, Darwin had to marshal so much knowledge amassed through observation, lectures, and discussions that no historian would have expected even such a great scientist also to push forward experiments still in their infancy – and with physical and chemical theories still in dispute – with no knowledge of what the end result would be. Let us remember the twenty-five years of struggle that faced Louis Pasteur (from his 'animalcules' of 1861 to his vaccination of 1885) in order to prove that a chemist can cure a child suffering from a mortal disease after being bitten by a mad dog.

It was nevertheless microbiology which, in the twentieth century, was to provide the answer to questions that Darwin did not ask about heredity and the transmission of traits not acquired but innate. The medical profession, so proud of the rapid progress made at the beginning of the century, hindered rather than supported research into micro-organisms. In 1865, Ignaz Semmelweis ended his days in a lunatic asylum, driven mad by the scorn he received from leading physicians he had suggested should wash their hands as they moved from the dissecting room to the delivery room.

In this context of the pseudo-transmission of acquired traits, social experience deceives science, though serving it so well in so many other fields, notably those of operational abstractions. That historical evolution should transmit cultural gains from age to age is self-evident, even if mental mutations take place in certain circumstances. However, when the mutation takes on the scale of a conceptual revolution, science can no longer return to its age-old habits of thought. This is the case when financiers wager on the future, rather than remaining bound by largely repetitive practices: thus a linear and exponential view of time replaced the circular concepts of a period lived and relived in an identical manner. Biology was to acquire its status as an operational science only by adopting experimental principles requiring their results to be expressed using 'imaginary' or abstract formulae.

Here we shall show how an Augustine monk established the notion of a 'gene' on the basis of combinational calculus, with necessary reference to the calculation of probabilities. And this discovery – regarded these days as fundamental – did not produce the slightest reaction until the very end of the century. One may ask how 'genetics' managed to overcome such an astonishing delay.

In fact, not only was it known that a living form could be born only from a living form, but it was discovered during the decade and that which followed, that these forms consisted of cells and that a cell could come only from another cell. This suggests that the unconscious already contained the idea that reproduction was an information process: the eighteenth century spoke of moulding and moulds; the nineteenth century was moving, initially without knowing it, towards a quasi-linguistic concept of generation. And the transfer of meaning that affected the word 'information' first prevented and then encouraged this change from an analogy with the mould to an analogy with language.

Of all the obstacles this development had to overcome, the most challenging appears to have been due to the fact that two superficial observations suggested 'spontaneous generation'. Vermin and worms grovel amongst putrefaction, which, if made up of waste or the products of death, could not support life, unless this was to emerge sponta-neously. But when the putrid gave rise to fermentation and the inherent yeasts belonging to the realm of living matter, sooner or later it had to be admitted that these superficial observations had generated an illusion. To cor-rect this mistake, it was necessary to experiment on the virtually invisible and to theorize about what was as yet unsayable.

Chemistry had long been preparing the way, and alchemy for even longer. It is too difficult precisely to date the moment when bread became more palatable because the baker introduced 'raising' – a process omitted on Jewish feast days. What are these 'yeasts' that make fermented beer into a better drink than barley beer? People had been intrigued by 'fermentation' for thousands of years, because the yeasts reproduced themselves, so to speak, of their own accord, and could be used again and again indefinitely. Also, the 1840s saw notions which had been named in the British Isles – catalysis and catalysts – spread over the continent. The words come from the Greek meaning 'dissolution', which had long intrigued the Franciscan laboratories. These catalysts, essential to certain chemical reactions, remain unchanged in the process. So long as the 'spiritualists' regarded matter as living, this process of catalysis or dis-solution was explained entirely by the presence of an active agent that lost nothing in the process. Drawing a distinction between organic and inorganic invited the nineteenth century to construct new words to designate minuscule but indispensable agents acting as catalysts for living processes. Thus 'diastase' – from the Greek for 'separator' – entered the dictionaries in the early 1830s; 'enzyme' – from the Greek for 'yeast' – at the end of the 1870s, hence at the same time as 'microbes'.

We should note that this 'catalysis' is as multi-faceted as it is useful in assisting reactions in inorganic chemistry, and is essential to those in organic chemistry. A pertinent question is whether it contributes to dividing chemical entities or in fact to producing new ones. Another is whether the agents in these operations are involved while neither losing nor gaining anything, or whether they in fact lose at the beginning what they gain back at the end. And whatever the truth, is this difference equivalent to that which sepa-rates the inorganic from the organic? So many difficulties in the way of investigating these microscopic activities help explain why the nineteenth century had no idea that biol-ogy might hold a counterpart to physical entropy. One can imagine what struggles and bitter disputes must have been involved for the positivist era to wonder again about con-cepts that its materialism had utterly rejected.

Marcellin Berthelot (1827–1907) is an example. As a citizen, Berthelot undertook to defend secular life in a Republic that was secular in the French style; as a chemist – he was one of the precursors of biochemistry – Berthelot did much more than Newton or Goethe in teaching people and getting them to understand alchemy, to which he devoted a book, the only one of its kind in Europe. It was to the Holy Spirit that the old conventional labora-tories attributed the fact that matter behaves, is converted and improves, as if it were living. A non-believer would claim that pure matter did not explain everything: matter owes its 'organization' (an abstract term) to its ability to lend itself to organic synthesis such as takes place in living tissue.

It had been known at least since the invention of the bain-marie (named after an Egyptian woman scholar of the pre-Christian era, not some latter-day expert cook, like Mrs Beeton in the United Kingdom, as both common and cultivated persons were inclined to think) that an excess of heat could kill just as much as an excess of cold. The Franciscan 'laboratories' had since discovered that a sub-stance to be distilled should be heated but not to the point of causing it to explode. These phenomena were explained by imagining that matter was inhabited by a form of life or a kind of 'spirit'. The invention of thermometry and calori-metry made clear the conditions in which the temperature ceases to fall as water crystallizes into ice and ceases to rise as water is turning into steam. But much more would have been needed for any sufficiently syncretic theory to embrace all kinds of physics and chemistry to make these phenomena understandable and calculable.

Through the adoption of a particular unit, the kilocalorie per gramme-molecule, the first few decades of the twen-tieth century were to achieve success in a calculation made complicated by the need to allow for ions and ionization as well as heat of dissociation and sublimation. When applied to the formation of sodium chloride from solid sodium and chlorine gas, the chemical reaction shows the experimenter the different stages of synthesis, demonstrating that each stage either requires or dissipates heat as a function of ionization processes: that of gaseous sodium absorbs heat, that of chlorine gives it off. In total these endothermic and exothermic reactions supply nearly 100 kilocalories per gramme-molecule. When the formation of a compound proves to be exothermic, as it does in this case, it contributes to entropy.

This example – particularly as it is recent – gives an initial idea of the problems the nineteenth century encountered in determining what living matter owed to inanimate matter, from which it was so different. If sea salt – previously considered to be a 'pure' substance as an utterly simple combination of chlorine and sodium ($NaCl$) – proved at the end of the century to have been formed only as a result of heat transfer, the measurement of which caused so much disturbance, how was it possible to determine what took place in the formation of 'giant molecules', the 'first' of which in terms of size (they were called 'proteins' around 1838, from the Greek protos, meaning first) were to reach molecular weights of up to 500,000? Enzymes are similar, but of a much higher molecular weight, to the extent that they can act on them as catalysts.

In the nineteenth century, biology was just beginning to outline methods and theories concerned with substances with such complex properties and actions. Here we shall do no more than offer simplistic views about research, that is less easy to describe the more painstaking it becomes. We should note to begin with that proteins and enzymes are not regarded as living matter, even though they are indis-pensable to life.

As soon as it was possible to distinguish oxygen from nitrogen it was clear that life – through breathing – took from the atmosphere (or from an aquatic environment into which a little of this atmosphere penetrates) the supply of oxygen necessary for combustion that keeps the organism at a given temperature. So where does the fuel come from? Plants offer a first kind of food, giving rise to the question as to where the constituents come from. They were said to come from the earth – or from humus – but this was before Justus von Liebig returned from China, where he had learned the importance of nitrogenous fertilizers: this period suggested that life was nothing more than a process of physical chemistry. However, cells are not composed of plant or animal substances in their original state. These substances have to be broken down and remade in a different way to enable them to be taken up and oxygenated by the supplies brought by arterial blood from the lungs, while venous blood carries away the waste. Of course, while the blood seems here as nothing more than a carrier, the enzymes have much more to do. As agents in digestion, the enzymes leave the cells – sometimes in the form of glandular secretions – and behave as if each was charged with a particular 'mission'. Many kinds of enzyme exist, each one having the task of identifying a particular substance, merging with it, breaking it down, and selecting the element which it will then take wherever it is needed. In order to do its 'job', the enzyme possesses 'resources' similar to those of inorganic catalysts, but developed to a much higher degree of complication. The extremely large number of enzyme functions appear to depend on a kind of pre-existing overall 'plan', developed at the expense of a great deal of time and testing so varied that 'checks' are carried out in order to correct occasional mistakes.

After Darwin – born in 1809 – had published his monumental work, two other decisive works were preparing the way for ultimate reform: those of Mendel and Pasteur, both born in 1822. The former believed in the existence of 'genes', whose dual nature lent itself to combinations. The latter answered a question, which Darwin had not asked, about the origins of life: two crystals, otherwise identical, are distinguished by a feature previously unnoticed concerning the polarization of light. The second section of this chapter will be an example of dissymmetry.

From natural history to morphology

History as a 'natural' phenomenon had long been of interest to the critical mind, particularly since, in the fourth century BC, the Greek Evhemer attempted to relate to the events of real life, that which was believed to pertain to the gods, heroes of divine origin, the subjects of sacred myths and popular legend: all these were poetic transfigurations held sacred by religions and preserved by the arts – since called 'literature', 'sculpture' or 'architecture'. The following fifteen centuries gave words the time to live and reproduce with similar or different meanings. The thirty-six volumes of Buffon's *Natural History* describe plants and animals with an elegance of style specific to him, and which gained him his reputation; there was also an outline of the ancient history of the earth, including a few more or less satisfactory hypotheses – less satisfactory when they contest the 'classifiers' such as Linné, whose *Philosophia Botanica* had introduced the divisions and subdivisions continued by his son; more satisfactory when he guesses something about methods of reproduction. It was fashionable at the time to be a 'collector', and vast rooms were filled with cupboards containing all kinds of discoveries reflecting nature's ingenuity in giving a thousand forms to its minerals as well as – to employ Goethe's words – to everything that moved and lived. In this era of 'pre-romanticism', nature consoled and encouraged, while Newton's heavens now responded only to abstract questions, while early mechanics announced developments with serious consequences for human existence, and immediately before the occurrence of fast-evolving events.

At the beginning of the nineteenth century, under a rationalist sky, through troubled and oft-changing times, and while physics advanced, a word of obscure origin entered the scientific dictionaries. 'Biology' was not yet in a position to dethrone natural history, but it was only a matter of time. It was merely a question of waiting for matter to transmogrify into a system of forces, a system which biology was to insist it had produced. In fact, the hiatus seems shorter to us today than it did to contemporary minds, unable to grasp the single entity that resulted from such different types of research. In the era of Legendre, astronomy, mechanics and algebra had already gone beyond the stage where Newton conjoined them, and where his successors merely had to get them to work together. However, as the new chemistry was still using little more than simple arithmetic, the emerging biology was only just at the stage of wondering what its role would be in the classification of the 1,001 kinds of specimens already more or less well catalogued, to which were being added the practically numberless contributions of explorers like Alexander von Humboldt, travelling the world, listing tropical species – particularly flora – not without attempting (in his 'Cosmos, an Essay') to describe what they had learned of the physical aspects of the earth. Even towards the end of the century, Thomas Huxley, who, as a defender of Darwin, supported the resemblances between homo sapiens and the anthropoid apes, assigned to biology too vague a task (the study of phenomena related to living matter) for this to lead to a discipline, let alone a method.

However, to the historical eye taking a distant view of what became of the scientific spirit at the time biology was emerging, there appears not only an adequate number of mental developments, but also a route leading from the first chemical innovations to a concatenation of biological reasoning. The two cases are extremely different and each deserves separate consideration.

Let us move on to the 'route' which new chemistry opened for emerging biology. This is better known, but not entirely clear. What a contrast, at the end of the seventeenth century, between so many cabinets filled with nature's curiosities and the very little which Lavoisier needed to distinguish, in the air we breathe, the 'oxygen' which sustains the flame and the nitrogen in which it goes out. The French word for nitrogen, 'azote', comes from the Greek meaning 'lifeless', which to the authors of the Nomenclature appeared too peremptory when a second term, 'nitrogène', came to be associated with the same meaning. Nitre – a word of Latin origin – proved to be a compound of nitrogen, oxygen and potassium. Some of its properties were known much earlier when, under the name of 'saltpetre' it was used for making gunpowder: it also makes soil more fertile. The nitrogen fixed in plant tissue moves into animal tissue, where it is rejected for the benefit of the plants. This came to be called the 'nitrogen cycle': an elementary cycle involving the most humble but essential manifestations of life. One may ask whether this nitrogen does not deserve a place alongside the oxygen we breathe, having been supplied by the diurnal respiration of plants, and only by that source. Thus the initial lessons of the new chemistry were already paralleling biology and two of the decisive functions that it would have to investigate: breathing and nutrition.

This 'functionalism' was apparently of little interest to an era that it did not impress. It provided little additional explanation about what was already known of the moderate level of heat specific to living matter: too high, it turns to fever; too low, it heralds the cold of the tomb. To keep it just right and to ensure that it consumes without being consumed, the *bain-marie* was to be the process used for nearly two thousand years after a certain Marie, an Egyptian alchemist, had demonstrated the advantages of slow 'maceration' and 'distillation' allowing two substances the time to unite in order that what would ultimately be called the male and female 'principles' should give birth to a 'child principle' that was 'purer' by being better preserved while preserving the fragile 'essences' it contained.

Perhaps the period owed it to its antecedents to place less emphasis on the new chemical reactions, than on living organs and organisms, when these were produced in specific conditions. Goethe, an alchemy enthusiast, invented the word 'morphology' to designate the study of the outer form of living creatures, and applied it in particular to botany as if to stress the contrast between plants and inert minerals, the surfaces, facets and sections of which he had admired and shown to others, even though he was not the first to do so: in the mines, miners and mineralogists had long scrutinized ores and minerals, not without some commercial interest, but also as a matter of taste, curiosity and the need to understand the nature of objects giving the earth its visible or hidden features.

What must have happened in the bowels of the earth to produce so many different forms, brought to the light of day by excavations, usually for utilitarian purposes? Sometimes they are crystals of priceless purity, contained in gangues that concealed their brightness or translucency: their regular structure recalling geometry even though it differed between various ways of conceiving their formation. Sometimes they are living beings, or the remains of living beings, whose morphology is so similar to those still extant that the ground enclosing them had obviously been earlier the site of a lake or sea, or even entirely exposed to the air and sunlight still today necessary to life. It was thus obvious that the surface of the earth had often changed its form, so that climbers could discover on mountain summits or slopes traces, calcified imprints, and remains of skeletons and shells: 'fossils' such as were dug out of old pits or collected in the flat strata of former seas or lakes, evidently piled up in the 'strata' as they occurred, in old sea and lake beds since dried out. We might add that these 'sedimentary' rocks – whatever altitude they may have been raised to in the meantime – rested upon underlying rocks of different kinds, such as gneiss or granite, attributable either to older – or primitive – formations or to volcanic eruptions.

The more geological research was done and the more it embodied verifiable assumptions – such as 'overthrust strata' which, by rearing up too high, fall in folds over and above the neighbouring zones – the more it became clear that the earth's crust experienced all kinds of vicissitudes, for example the raising of blocks as a result of contractions, or the carving out of peaks and valleys (U-shaped under glaciers or V-shaped under rivers) by glacial or river erosion: present-day orography reflects the extreme length of this process, made up of episodes each extremely slow and of no less extreme complexity. The nineteenth century would have worked out the basics before a more general explanation revealed continental drift, a phenomenon of sliding 'plates' which, in the depth of the earth's crust, moves the continents closer together or wider apart and, in particular, detaches the 'new' world from the old.

Let us return to what distinguishes biology from natural history. The former, like geology – even though largely independent of it, at least until the time when the evolutionary approach would be forced to give way to changes in soil, climate, relief and even continental continuity and discontinuity – is obliged, as a result of its conceptual beginnings, to reason in terms of historicity, if not of history, just when the word already means much more than faithful description, as in 'natural history'. Since biology by its very vocation seeks to explain living phenomena as rationally as possible, it will succeed in doing so only in so far as diachrony – time, duration and change – is rational. History as such is an extension of it, the more lacking in reasons as it is an extension of biology and geology: precisely because human will is involved, whereas it obviously could not be so in the purely 'natural' forerunners and, therefore, closer to determinisms sometimes equivalent to finalities.

Let us also turn back to morphology: in many of its aspects it involves the implementation and use of functions. Some of them are similar in any living creature, but not all: this is well-known, such as fish, birds or quadrupeds. There are as many types of relationship between functions – whether common or specific – as there are environments suitable for sustaining life. It is up to morphology – initially the study of external forms – to link these forms to relationships, or systems of functions. The problem did not give rise to too much controversy, which ran into the sand once it was a question of assuming or approving the origins of 'forms' and that which they imply as regards functions.

Morphology – a little less than a science and a little more than a method – appeared, under the pen of Goethe in 1822, almost as a philosophy still bearing the teleological stamp: a bird provided with wings to fly, carnivores with jaws to crush living flesh, and herbivores with teeth for grazing. However, this simplistic approach does not do justice to a linguistic innovation which slowly spread, carrying an originally more elaborate meaning in describing the 'harmony' of forms, until the nineteenth century was to prefer the word 'homologue' with its devotion to geometry and crystallography. In biology, this semantic development came to an end around the time when the British universities ceased to group a variety of subjects under the name of natural philosophy, of which Newton had proved the 'mathematical principles'. Although the philosophy involved in the harmony of forms, and then their homology, was also called natural in its time, it was in fact no more than 'naturalist': abstract notions – such as that of 'structure' – were to be added, and came closer to the demonstrable. By the end of the century, finalism no longer explained anything very much. Biology, seeking for causality, found only the historical type thereof, except that this research continues to deal with structures, each one regarded as a-chronic, in other words, not related to the passage of time, to the extent that it persists in a creature formed and renewing itself in a practically identical manner by 'reproduction'.

While the eighteenth century had directed to 'monsters' what remained of a fascinated curiosity inherited from past centuries, the subsequent generations were less interested in these accidents of reproduction than in reproduction proper, what it preserved of structures, and the structures themselves. Cuvier astonished his peers – including Goethe, who regarded him as his mentor – with the intelligence he applied in reconstituting an entire animal from a fragment of skeleton. Skilful in the art of comparison, Cuvier applied his art with great confidence. Determining the whole of a given structure means understanding the relationships that support its elements by virtue of observing these relationships many times; the form of an element – even if it is unique – tells all one needs to know to obtain a general view. Cuvier's unequalled erudition enabled him to extend this comparative method to the study of extinct animals. Together with the advances in geology (so named around the middle of the seventeenth century), this method was to make it possible to date what had just been named the three kingdoms: animal, vegetable and mineral. The nineteenth century was to do so, with increasing success. Relevant questions are whether it is enough to date in order to understand, and whether what is best for vertebrates is best for other species.

Geoffroy-Saint-Hilaire, a brilliant rival of Cuvier, sought to generalize his results. To begin with, convinced that the bones of the skull extended those of the spinal column, he pushed the argument much farther. Why speak of invertebrates when, in fact, their structure is merely the reverse of the other, causing to live inside the vertebrae that which the other causes to live around its column? All very well as regards the bones of the skull, but few specialists would sacrifice the branched classification for this too rational, if not fanciful, simplification. The English universities in particular were to reserve their best reception for Cuvier, whose 'The Revolutions of the Globe' were more in line with theology – the teaching of which still took priority. It was sufficient to interpose additional disasters between the Creation and the Flood: between each one the principle of 'correlation of forms' applies; after each, and therefore in new conditions, life starts again and creates morphologies different from those that disappeared.

Two parallel discoveries: evolution and genetics

November 1859 is a date usually acknowledged as of unequalled significance in the history of biology: Charles Robert Darwin published his *On the Origin of Species by Means of Natural Selection*. In eight days the first edition – 1,250 copies – passed from the publisher to its readers; it was reprinted and successive editions had similar success. Translated into many languages, the book invaded the continent. Polemics began. It had the advantage of popularity: no scientific book had so immediately raised so much curiosity. It is easy to understand what attracted readers who were in too much of a hurry and too poorly prepared to understand the details of so much erudition: humankind descended from monkeys! Blasphemy for some, rational evidence for others who were awaiting this revelation but lacking the courage to take the lead. Darwin was admirable also for his courage: so much anxiety before taking the decision! Once the deed was done, Darwin reinforced his arguments and set them out in 1871, in *The Descent of Man and Selection in Relation to Sex*. The doctrine of evolution had finally found its guru. His supporters remained constant from one generation to the next, constant in an admiration which did not weaken even after that early scholarship should in fact have been clarified, extended and even redirected.

It was a long time since scientific rationalism had eliminated God from its theories. But at this juncture religion awoke, rose up, and counter-attacked, probably not without hope of gaining the support of a humanism that had grounds for disquiet about a theory that took its conclusions to such extremes. How, 'if man is merely an improved monkey' would he have produced such art and literature, operated so many railways as well as connecting the continents by telegraph? And as for Thomas Huxley, an ardent defender of Darwin, was it in the name of his outstanding research on shrimps that he drew such outlandish conclusions? Would he venerate as an ancestor the monkey that his trainer made 'sapiens' as he held it at the end of a string to amuse the people in the street? Even so the Darwinists did not give way. Thus a German immigrant in Brazil wrote a *Für Darwin* in which he admired his mentor particularly as his own research into crustaceans suggested that the embryogenesis of an animal quickly passed through the stages that take thousands of years for 'phylogenesis': a word invented around 1870 – by Haeckel in Jena – to denote the slowly progressive evolution of the 'races' that constitutes species (thirty years later, people would say 'ontogenesis' for individual formations developing from the egg to the adult).

Moreover, after the 1830s, the added interest in 'prehistory' ('prehistory' is thirty years younger) identified three 'ages' – stone, bronze, and iron – forcing people to think that humankind gains in aptitude without changing morphology. Such progress could only be attributed to a change in collective environment: an environment other than natural (although subjected to the vicissitudes of nature) and which the twentieth century would qualify as 'cultural'. This suggests the conclusion that human performance and skills changed as history progressed, and that it is impossible to judge 'prehistoric' humanity on the basis of what it later became.

Seen from this standpoint, Darwin's success corresponds to a certain state of knowledge and to the inequalities of its distribution arising from differences in aspirations and ambitions, and resulting in locally prejudicial and generally favourable misinterpretations in that, from dispute to dispute, arguments would emerge based upon that which other sciences and new experiments had to contribute to biology, and to a Darwinism that was much corrected after owing its initial success, and its revolutionary scope, to very simple principles.

The grandson of one Erasmus Darwin, a naturalist whose Romanticism had celebrated the marvels of the botanic garden in verse, Charles Darwin, advised by his Cambridge professor, embarked on the *Beagle* for a five-year exploration of South America and certain Pacific islands. Partly convinced by the theories of Jean-Baptiste Lamarck, he returned uncertain that this 'evolutionism' was sufficient in calling upon changes in the 'environment' to explain the acquisition of new 'practices' that created lasting and transmissible organs. His exploration of the islands, notably the Galapagos, suggested to him that a number of species did better in isolated groups than on the neighbouring continent where they were diversified as a result of propinquity, rivalry and competition. Malthus in his *Essay on the Principle of Population* in 1798, concluded that populations tend to grow geometrically, and not arithmetically as do resources: to the extent that unless the proliferation of poor families was prevented, humankind would collapse into the direst poverty. This concern was felt so strongly at the beginning of the century that the government of William Pitt and his successors had set up poorhouses – in which couples were separated with only their survival being guaranteed – and workhouses – where men and women worked to serve and benefit the community, since it would not be appropriate to burden the taxpayers with the costs that the 'parishes' could no longer bear since community property had been shared out among private owners.

Charles Darwin read Malthus to learn the principles of that which he had seen vividly in his youth: to the producers, all the resources of production so long as they do it well enough to adapt to the competition; to the unfortunate, well-organized (in other words the cheapest possible) charity, so long as they do not reproduce, and unless any rural exodus brings them into the industrial cities, where they will be at the mercy of entrepreneurs seeking precisely what they represent, namely, effective labour to be paid at the lowest possible price. For these migrants, there was only one way out: to become entrepreneurs themselves. That was precisely 'natural selection'. The parliament in London framed in laws and institutions that which, on the continent, took place of its own accord: whoever is not involved in production and its profit falls within what the 'philanthropists' call 'the dangerous classes', as if they have no recourse but theft or other crime. Charles Dickens described this condition's misery and its evil, and how to escape from it through virtue, not without first having learned from improvised experts how to beg by inspiring pity, and how to steal without being caught.

At such a price, all can prosper. In their spacious estates, the horticulturists select their plants, improve their cropping, and try out beneficial hybrids, while the livestock breeders do even better for their animals. In the growing cities, it is merely a question of who will sell the best cheapest, thanks to judicious acquisitions of machines and raw materials. It is enough to extend to the animal and vegetable kingdoms of the palaeontological eras the lessons learned from experience and from 'may the best man win'. Lessons taken up in France by François Guizot and his 'enrichissez-vous' (get rich). Lessons learned from those who had been concerned with the sepoys' revolt ('revolution' in Marxist terms): massacre for massacre, the army of the East India Company was overwhelmed and came under the direct command of the Queen's government, the only power able to send reinforcements. A few years later, Darwin was to be buried in Westminster Abbey, amongst the greatest of men.

Clearly, Darwin did not have to look so far in order to verify his natural selection. Aloof from political and worldly honours, he aspired only to overtake one of his peers: Alfred Russell Wallace, author of *On the Tendency of Varieties To Depart Indefinitely From The Original Type*. Darwin was familiar with this memorandum based upon the principle of natural selection. The idea was, as they say, in the air.

In poor health, Darwin left London in 1842, for Kent, where friends — a botanist, a zoologist and a geologist — urged him to be the first to publish: another kind of selection, but selection all the same and a form of selection which sought, as in the English countryside, not only to obtain better strains of plant or livestock by careful crossbreeding, but also to be first to put them on the market. Enclosed in his genius, Darwin made haste in the same way, as did all of those looking to share in British prosperity and to make their mark.

This was a very natural encounter, therefore, and so desired by the social and cultural environment that success comes to whoever expresses himself most clearly, argues most pertinently by means of verifiable detail, and also

suddenly strikes the imagination at the most sensitive spot: the animal ancestors of humankind.

It was also an outstanding success, therefore, in that it passed unchanged through the turmoil of opposition, but a relative success. Persuading people that species evolve and advance by natural selection is not the whole story: it is necessary to understand how every particular species perpetuates itself so long as its environment permits. Cuvier did this brilliantly on the basis of a descriptive morphology. He was to be accused of 'creationism', but wrongly, because he drew a distinction between different development 'schemes' and adopted for his own the old idea of a ranking of living creatures. What he and his period were unable to do was to discern how living creatures reproduced themselves identically. Darwin was no more explicit — even though he did speak of reproductive cells alongside cells capable of acquisitions: the 'how' was nevertheless absent.

Nobody in the circle of Darwin and his admirers could have suspected that precisely at the same time, in a far-off Moravian monastery, a monk was beginning to find an answer.

At the very end of the nineteenth century and in the first few years of the twentieth, scientific terminology was enriched by new words appearing in Germany, such as 'chromosome', and 'gene' in England; a new branch of biology could no longer do without them, 'genetics', a neologism as a noun but in use for more than fifty years as an adjective. The same applied to 'somatic', qualifying that which is specific to the (human) body since the early 1870s and opposed, like 'soma', to the germinative, to germinal and to genes, when genetics used this word to name research and knowledge concerning heredity, taken from the Latin and known well before Rome. It was a concept long familiar in matters of private or dynastic succession, a concept very slowly adapted to circumstances more shaken by history than shaking family affairs, but a concept suddenly giving rise to an enormous conceptual system.

One wonders whether Johann Mendel had any idea of the extent of the conceptual revolution he was starting with no means of controlling it. His own authorities, showing less equanimity, perhaps became worried about it by appointing him bishop, as if to separate him from research whose consequences might disturb the faithful. Mendel remained unknown, dying too soon to suspect the immense reputation that would posthumously fall to him. In discovering the laws of heredity, Mendel virtually pointed out which concrete though infinitesimally small objects transmitted it. One might, briefly, have believed that life stemmed from nothing more than a mathematical set of various objects, each one individual and all transmissible, although invisible. This view fell into line with that of Mendeleev: 'elements' (atoms) having the same chemical weight are identical; they become different elements if their weight decreases or increases by one or more units, each representing what would be called in the early twentieth century an 'electron', but still unknown when Mendeleev's table was convincing the chemists, just as Mendel's calculations were passing unnoticed even though their results showed some similarity, or even an obvious analogy, with those of the Russian scientist. The time was favourable to the resurgence of the idea of spontaneous generation. One could ask whether this coincidence was due as much to chance as to the ignorance affecting biologists and chemists. We can counter this hypothesis, made highly unlikely by such an obvious historical coincidence, by another: the logic of an era continually searching for residual units does find some here and there to meet conceptual needs – inspired in particular by the exact sciences – without waiting for practical science to discover all the concrete meanings designated by these agreed and abstract symbols. As appears fair, the wait was to be longer for living matter. The whole issue of living matter must embrace a greater number of questions, more differentiated and more subtle than the issue of matter. One may regard it as significant – at least historically – that the development of biology, particularly genetics, was to do better – along with Mendelism – than the physics of energy which, in 1900, gained the theory of 'quanta': the same type of residual unit but more identifiable with life than is simple matter.

This development calls for two comments: first, it did not begin with Mendel (or Darwin), and second, biology would have to be saved from the embarrassment in which it had been placed by the idea that life could emerge spontaneously from matter. For reasons of clarity, we shall give chronology priority over logic and deal with the second aspect before the first.

In the 1870s, biology was indebted to Louis Pasteur for having formally rejected – with the proof in his hand – the idea of spontaneous generation. This idea, in turn popularly accepted, scientifically disputed and then experiencing a return to fashion, was based upon the new data produced by higher-powered microscopes. Where the eye could no longer see anything, high magnifications showed apparently living motion. Indeed, leaven, fermentation processes, yeasts and moulds showed it, although these merely stemmed from chemical substances. This was of little importance in ancient times when even minerals were supposed to be living; once this belief was swept away, how could it be that alcohol, for example, takes part in fermentation even though its molecule is made up only of chemical atoms? For Pasteur, this was the effect of minute creatures present by chance, and called 'microbes' by the end of the 1870s. The proof: nothing of the kind is produced in a very clean tube kept away from all outside contact. As a result, the words 'contaminare', 'contaminatio', contaminate and contamination were once again to undergo a transfer of meaning: the 'sacer', the wholly untouchable by the profane; the spirit soiled by sin; the body, affected by foulness, infected by some disease; and, finally – still in the pejorative sense and again invisible – health threatened by a 'microbe'.

Around 1840, 'bacilli' and 'bacteria' designated a minuscule rod hardly visible under the microscope, and assumed to be vegetable in nature: it multiplied when an extension was cut in two. Towards the end of the nineteenth century, bacteriology and microbiology were the names of new types of research equipped with much more powerful microscopes, but still discovering nothing that resembled spontaneous generation. Pasteur had never doubted it. Neither physician nor biologist but a chemist, he had become interested at the age of twenty-three in crystallography and the problem raised by the asymmetry of certain crystals (tartrates): half the edges and corners of these crystals exert different effects from those in the other half: they deviate ('polarize') light either to the right or to the left, and this property is specific to ingredients of living creatures. Where matter obeys laws of symmetry, life makes use of asymmetry: impossible to mix them up.

Four years, five years (or more) of research on 'tartrates': Pasteur needed all this time to gain the skill and reputation which attracted the attention of industrialists involved in 'fermentation'. The question is not simple and was to undergo all kinds of extensions in the twentieth century, after – towards the end of the 1850s – it had enabled the young chemist to leap the gulf between chemistry and biology. This was in fact a rediscovery because, although the tartrates owe their name to Paracelsus – apparently inspired by Tartrus, the underworld, to designate that which prevents the coupling of the male and female principles – 'tartar', as a material thing, was a source of embarrassment for centuries to alchemists and distillers who could not understand why this 'salt' (a 'son' principle) which was deposited on the walls of the vessel, facilitated distillation by encouraging fermentation. Pasteur resolved the doubt. First, no type of matter is 'living' as Paracelsus (and others after him) had believed. Second, the polarization phenomenon is double-acting: the tartrates polarize light either to the right (and are 'dextrorotatory') or to the left ('laevorotatory'), and therefore participate in life; but when they are mixed in equal parts, all polarization ceases as in the crystal of pure material. The tartrates are used for all kinds of beneficial purposes in medicine. In boilers (including those in stills when they are too gas-tight) tartar slows down boiling but it also corrodes and causes explosions.

Without dwelling on matters related to the history of medicine, we should point out that, thanks to Pasteur, vaccines and vaccinations were to meet so many therapeutic needs because they were based on what Jenner had worked out and tested on diseases that could be passed on from cows (vacca) to human beings: the living organism secretes its own defence mechanisms and acquires more, when small amounts of an innocuous disease are injected, which preserve it from much more dangerous threats. This confirms the 'vital' importance of imbalance and of reactions to imbalance. In this game, life wins the day so long as it is not unduly diverted from a situation of equilibrium, not a fixed point, but a simple passing through.

Life is made up of movement, agitation and heat; it does not stand still, and this made it difficult for biology to discover any primary ingredient such as the physical atom from which molecules are formed. It was thought to have been found in the 'cell' until there was discovered – inside a cellular 'membrane' – 'protoplasm' ('first constructed thing' – thus named from the Greek in Germany before emerging some twenty years later), 'cytoplasm', part, or 'medium', which surrounds the 'nucleus' itself surrounded by its own membrane. Constantly affected by neologism or transfers of meaning, so research became complicated by discoveries until the end of the century and even later. In 1911, English came up with 'gene' (from the Greek for birth) soon after Mendel, his book and his smallest units of hereditary transmission. Incidentally, it took a further twenty years for the vocabulary to distinguish 'genotype' and 'phenotype' (the first: heredity, the second: that acquired), and that was still not the end of the matter.

This etymological diversion recalls a journey in stages made up of surprises, assumptions, discussions, contradictions and agreements, the essence of which can be summed up in an obligation: to reconcile Darwin – which suggests the transmission of acquired traits – with Mendel whose calculations imply that only the innate preserves the continuity of the species, which suggests to the evolutionists that it is therefore on the innate that attention should be focused in order to understand how one species can be derived from another.

Such research was not straightforward because it had to overcome contradictions. 'Races' can be crossed and can reproduce together; the species is not thereby modified. The nineteenth century spoke of human races, thus connoting distinctive features. All belong to the human species: two human beings of different race can marry and produce children according to Mendel's 'laws'. As to 'pure' races or 'cross-bred' races (a more frequent instance than had been believed), however diverse, none can be said to be superior to the others. The evaluation – deprived of any biological basis – can only be subjective; hence a matter of opinion that may possibly refer to cultures, but only in an arbitrary manner since cultural history has no objective criterion to judge what was, what is, or will be best for the human being, or, preferably, for humanity. The problem of 'progress' remains entire so long as it is a question of the human species in general: no culture has advanced, is advancing or will advance independently of the others. And if it did – despite any historical likelihood – no individual would be entitled to claim superiority on the basis of his or her culture rather than himself or herself.

And yet nobody doubts that the evolution of living creatures progressed from the single-cell amoeba to the so-called higher vertebrate with a brain whose size increased in quantum leaps from one species to another and even within a given human species. If there exists something which, in the plant and animal kingdoms, resembles by its function the 'cultures' in the human kingdom, it can only be 'associations' of species: the herbivore feeds on plants, the carnivore on herbivores or other carnivores.

If we eliminate the plants, nothing can live, owing to lack of food and even of oxygen. The notion of 'association of species' goes beyond that of 'natural environment' on which it nevertheless depends. Evolution has to be considered as an entity in which the nature of climate and soil does not act alone. Adaptation is associative, or rather 'distributive', using the term in its algebraic sense: a single factor, no matter which, operates on all the others.

Besides this overall view, another is needed to explain gradual evolution: this other view is microscopic and regards the Mendelian gene as the smallest component in heredity. If we accept the hypothesis – often verified but still hypothetical – that acquired traits have no effect on the innate (or that the somatic has no effect on the genetic, another way of speaking and thinking), then how does one highly elementary creature generate another, which proves better adapted? Higher up on the creative ladder, what takes place in genes that combine half the maternal and half the paternal genes to produce a creature of a new species? One wonders whether this novelty was produced during embryonic development (which can be seen to traverse very rapidly stages fairly similar to those gradually traversed over geological eras). Or, indeed, was this novelty produced at the moment when two 'gametes' (from *gamos*, marriage) conjoin after being separated in 'meiosis' (separation into two parts, in 1890, after having signified recovery from a disease in 1842)? Or again at some time before genes are produced and transmitted?

The problem appears to have been overcome by a Dutch botanist, Hugo de Vries, when he proposed the principle of 'mutations' (a German word around 1901): a sudden variation affecting a descendant to the extent of generating an individual whose species is different from that which produces it.

The century came to an end with this sort of reincarnation, better regarded conceptually as a 'transformism',

which regained force only just before it lost the battle. From Lamarck's assumptions about the mind up to genetic mutations, an accelerating flow of discoveries had made the indications provided by microscopes of increasing magnification substantially more precise. They were more particularly concerned with the 'cell'. At first it had been expected to be a kind of atom of living matter; it became a whole world made up of parts ranging from very small to the infinitesimally small – the gene in fact – and possessing functions the importance of which was greater the less discernible they are.

At the beginning of the nineteenth century, medicine sought to distinguish diseases according to the organs they affected. These organs are made up of 'tissues', some of them specific to particular organs, others common to all: for example that which was to be called 'conjunctive tissue' (in the 1860s), which binds organs or parts of organs together and which, owing to this general property, had originally been called 'cellular tissue'. In fact all tissues are cellular, made up of adjacent cells that may or may not be specialized, and reproducing in such a way that it became clear that a cell can be born only from a similar cell. These cells feed notably on pure water, through 'osmosis' (1872: a kind of 'thrust' exerted on the membrane that allows only the solvent to pass through). Towards the end of the 1860s, the term 'nucleus' was applied to a more or less spherical corpuscle whose specific membrane contains an essence in which, some thirty years later, were to be found 'chromosomes', coloured bodies so-called because chemical dyes render them distinct on a microscope slide, on which are placed the thinnest possible slices cut with the microtome (a kind of razor mounted on a fairly massive mechanical structure to enable the very fine wire to cut slices so thin that they are transparent).

If Carl-Wilhelme Naegeli, a reputed specialist in the study of cells, particularly plant cells, had had such advanced instruments with all that they reveal, he would not have shown so much indifference when he received Mendel's memoranda. However, it is precisely against this lack of interest that can be measured the distance between two biological concepts, or rather two types of research, which did not come together until the twentieth century.

Carl-Wilhelme Naegeli taught botany in Zurich – in the canton where he was born – until in 1857, his skills earned him a similar post in Munich, not far from Brno, where monk Gregor was cultivating his monastery garden. It was no surprise that the latter should call upon the former. Moreover, the two fields of research look very close, at least when viewed retrospectively: the Swiss scientist hoped to find the secret of the transmutation of species by observing what are known as phanerograms (plants whose fruit-bearing organs are visible) forming a branch in which the types are poorly defined; the other, an expert in combinational reasoning, discovered an application, as if by surprise, in what happens to peas he was attempting to hybridize. What can one expect from calculations on paper when microscopes are available that already magnify 400 times? To each his own way of seeing. But as one was looking in the opposite direction from the other, he lost all opportunity of perceiving that his correspondent was working on the same subject.

A typical case? One could mention many others; this calls for a general remark. Advances in calculation follow their own path; advances in observation follow theirs. Normally, these two types of progress intersect, re-intersect and respond to demand. Of course, the social environment must lend itself to these encounters. In our case, a laboratory equipped to look at the infinitesimally small: what has it to do with columns of Figures traced out by a monk responsible for a piece of land intended for growing vegetables?

And yet an outstanding scientist had within his grasp the answers to a problem which Darwin did not raise, even though he had collected the data by travelling to the ends of the earth.

One may ask how it is possible to understand the history of science without reference to the history of humanity.

5

THE DEVELOPMENT OF MEDICINE

Huldrich M. Koelbing

FOREWORD

In the nineteenth century medicine became, more than ever before, a science based, as far as possible, on experimental investigation and rigorous scientific reasoning. The achievements of twentieth-century medicine in the treatment and prevention of disease would not have been possible without the enthusiasm and painstaking endeavour of physicians, surgeons, and scientists of the preceding century.

This new, self-confident medical science claimed, of course, universal recognition. But its introduction in countries with a non-European cultural tradition was often experienced as a cultural shock – in spite of the benefits it brought, for example in fighting infectious diseases. This is particularly true of a country with a great, old culture of its own like China.

HOSPITALS, MEDICAL RESEARCH AND EDUCATION IN THE EARLY NINETEENTH CENTURY

Already in the eighteenth century, the spirit of Enlightenment made public authorities realize their responsibility for the maintenance and restoration of the health of their subjects. Philanthropy as well as considerations of utility were the motives for this: a healthy population was now appreciated as the greatest wealth of the state. Thus, the Austrian emperor Joseph II founded at Vienna a big 'general infirmary' (the Allgemeines Krankenhaus, 1784). The dreadful conditions prevailing in many older hospitals were sharply criticized by keen observers such as John Howard (1726–90), the well-known English prison reformer, or the Paris surgeon Jacques-René Tenon (1724–1816). In an official report, published on the eve of the French Revolution, Tenon characterized the venerable Hôtel-Dieu of Paris as 'the most unhealthy and most uncomfortable of all hospitals', where, on an average, two of nine patients died (Ackerknecht, 1967). On the other hand, the Frenchman was enthusiastic about the English hospitals he had visited (Jetter, 1973).

In the years following the Revolution, the Paris hospitals were reorganized. First of all, they were separated from such institutions as alms-houses and prisons, so as to give them a purely medical character. Their administration was centralized. In 1794 the National Convention instituted a new type of medical education, based on the hospitals. These

also became now centres of medical research. A new kind of scientific medicine arose, the 'hospital medicine' of the nineteenth century, called so by Erwin H. Ackerknecht. Its foremost strongholds were, in the first instance, Paris, London, Dublin, and – in the middle of the century – Vienna. Early medical centres in the USA were Philadelphia, Harvard, and New York, but many American students were eager to complete their professional education in Europe.

In German-speaking and other countries, for example in Italy, medical education and research developed in close connection with universities. This proved to be an advantage later in the century, when the basic sciences became more and more important for medicine.

Careful clinical observation, on the other hand, became also the basis of psychiatry as a recognized branch of medicine. This started also in France, with Philippe Pinel (1745–1826) and Jean-Etienne-Dominique Esquirol (1772–1840).

On the whole, throughout Europe, education on an academic level now became the rule for all practitioners. The old, unfortunate separation of the craft of surgery from the science of medicine drew to an end. It was clearly the aim of the French reform to overcome this separation: the study of medicine became much more practical. Students should not primarily learn by reading but by seeing patients and working on them: 'Peu lire, beaucoup voir, beaucoup faire' (Ackerknecht, 1967: 32).

A NEW CONCEPTION: CLINICAL MEDICINE BASED ON PATHOLOGICAL ANATOMY

In 1761, Giovanni Battista Morgagni (1682–1771), of Padua had published the great work of his life: 'On the Seats and Causes of Diseases as Shown by Anatomy' (De Sedibus et Causis Morborum per Anatomen Indagatis Libri Quinque). In doing so, he had introduced, as Virchow put it, 'the anatomical idea' ('den anatomischen Gedanken') (Virchow, 1894) into clinical medicine. In the same year, Leopold Auenbrugger (1722–1809), of Vienna had proposed percussion of the chest as a rewarding help to diagnosis. But not before the nineteenth century were Morgagni's and Auenbrugger's teachings put into practice on a large scale. In the hospitals of Paris, a post-mortem dissection was now always done when a patient had died: the anatomical lesion explained in retrospect the sick person's sufferings. For doctors, however, it was more important to find out the nature and seat of a disease while the patient was still alive and might be helped. In 1808, Jean-Nicolas Corvisart (1755–1821), physician in ordinary to the Emperor Napoleon, translated and commented Auenbruger's 'inventum novum', which so far had remained nearly unnoticed. About ten years later (in 1819) Professor René-Théophile-Hyacinthe Laennec (1781–1826), described the first stethoscope and taught physicians, as well as students, the useful art of auscultation of the lungs and the heart. In this way, medical diagnosis could be built on firm ground: pathological anatomy revealed the visible and palpable changes which disease produced in different parts of the body, and physical examination – percussion and auscultation – enabled physicians to recognize them in their patients.

In order to establish the new approach, great numbers of patients, and of post-mortems were needed; the new hospital medicine was primarily an affair of *big* hospitals. The great amount of collected observations favoured also the application of statistics to medical problems, including therapeutics. Statistics had already largely been used in British medicine in the eighteenth century; but from 1825, Pierre-Charles-Alexandre Louis (1787–1872) of Paris systematized it. By his 'numerical method' ('la méthode numérique') Louis proved, for example, that copious bloodletting, which still was confidently used by many practitioners, in reality, did no good at all to the poor patients (1835).

While a post-mortem dissection yields just a static picture of a morbid condition at a particular moment, the combination of a great number of such observations may reveal the whole natural history of a given disease, for example tuberculosis. Because he noted frequently, in his post-mortems, the marks of healed tuberculous lesions in the lungs, the Vienna pathologist Karl Rokitansky (1804–78) came even to the important conclusion that, without any doubt, tuberculosis must be a curable disease (1847). This seemed at first unbelievable, but it stimulated a few doctors to develop the climatic cure of consumption and the sanatorium movement.

On the other hand, many physicians, mainly interested in making faultless diagnoses, became most sceptical about therapeutics. This trend culminated, in the 1840s, in the so-called therapeutic nihilism of some Vienna physicians who proclaimed their perfect disbelief in any remedies.

Clearly, the new conception of disease was a localistic one: disturbance of bodily functions was exclusively seen as a sequel of altered anatomical structure. This, of course, was easier to demonstrate than pathogenic nervous influences or humoral disorders, and biochemistry was still in its infancy.

But while a new science of medicine emerged from the distressing atmosphere of the Paris hospitals, the smart people of the French capital showed their enthusiasm for old Doctor Samuel Hahnemann (1755–1843) and his young wife Madame Mélanie with their homoeopathic pills, so well adaptable to the manifold ailments of any particular patient.

MICROSCOPIC VIEWS

The study of pathological changes in tissues and organs became even more rewarding by the systematic use of the microscope as propagated, first and foremost, by Rudolf Virchow (1821–1902). At first, the promising career of the young 'protector' at the Charité hospital of Berlin had been interrupted in 1849, because of his revolutionary activities, but in the same year he became professor of pathological anatomy at Würzburg in Bavaria. Here he worked out his concept of cellular pathology. In 1856 he was recalled to Berlin, and here he published, two years later, his famous book (Virchow 1858). What Virchow presented was in reality not just a new system of pathology, but a comprehensive cellular biology: the cell is, according to Virchow, not only the elementary unit in the composition of the living body, but also the source of every vital activity, normal or pathological. In addition, cells never originate, as many scientists believed, in amorphous matter such as exudates, but stem exclusively from other, already existing cells: 'omnis cellula e cellula'. In short, the cell was for Virchow the personification of life. He exhorted students and doctors 'to think microscopically'; the microscope, he affirmed, brings us the natural processes at least 300 times nearer. Virchow's cellular pathology proved particularly helpful for a better understanding of tumours and their genesis. By the way, in spite of having become a highly respected professor, Virchow did not give up politics. As a liberal deputy in the Prussian parliament, he opposed, vigorously but unfortunately in vain, Bismarck's authoritarian course. On the other hand, he was an outstanding anthropologist, too (Ackerknecht, 1952).

Also for the study of blood and its diseases, microscopy became essential, especially in combination with appropriate staining methods based on the affinities of different stains for specific chemical components of the blood cells. And above all, the microscope made bacteria visible. But in order to detect and define the pathogenic action of these extremely small organisms, biological experiments were needed.

By such experiments, arranged in strictly logical sequences, Louis Pasteur (1822–95), revealed the wide range of microbial activity in causing diseases of plants, animals, and man. And, as Virchow had demonstrated for cells, Pasteur proved also for microorganisms that there is no spontaneous generation from amorphous matter, but only filiation through generations of living beings of the same kind (1864). When, in 1882, Robert Koch (1843–1910) discovered the tubercle bacillus and proved that it was responsible for all forms of tuberculosis, bacteriology began to supersede pathology as the dominating branch of scientific medicine.

BASIC EXPERIMENTAL RESEARCH AND SOME PRACTICAL APPLICATIONS

Morphology, rich in precious information as it is, cannot reveal much about the vital processes in health and disease. But as, biologically speaking, *homo sapiens* is a vertebrate, research done on the living bodies of other vertebrates, from frog to ape, can tell us much about the working of our own organism. As early as the second century AD, Galen of Pergamon used this procedure, i.e. vivisection, to demonstrate the production of urine by the kidneys, and in the seventeenth century William Harvey ascertained the circulation of blood by a series of experiments on various animals.

In the nineteenth century, however, experimentation became the paramount method of medical research. Experimental evidence was accepted as the most truthful one – although it might be invalidated by other experiments. Such experiments might concern the chemical substances present in the body, blood and other body fluids, isolated parts or entire animals, microbes, drugs, and poisons. For the French physiologist François Magendie (1782–1855), only experimental medicine could claim to be a science. Consequently, he insisted upon experimental evaluation of purified drugs in order to obtain safe guidelines for their therapeutic use; thus, he started experimental pharmacology.

Claude Bernard (1813–78), a pupil of Magendie's and his successor as a professor of physiology at the Collège de France, worked out the philosophy of medical experimentation in his lucid *Introduction to the Study of Experimental Medicine* (*Introduction à l'étude de la médecine expérimentale*, 1865). The book is still worth reading. It teaches how to experiment intelligently: disciplined reasoning is no less important than skilful operating, if not more so.

In his book, Bernard touches also the moral aspect of animal experimentation: according to him, any experiment on a living animal is permitted, provided it may prove useful for man. For Bernard, the gain of knowledge was obviously a value of the highest order and therefore, without any doubt, useful for man, too. Discussions about the immorality of vivisection, which were running high at that time, were, according to Bernard, absurd and absolutely useless.

Not all physiologists were so peremptory about the unlimited right to experiment on living animals. Bernard's German counterpart, for example, Carl Ludwig (1816–95) at Leipzig, urged that every measure be taken to diminish the pain and discomfort of an animal subjected to an experiment, and he even joined a league for the protection of animals.

While Virchow focused his attention on the activities of the allegedly autonomous cell, Bernard followed the idea that the organism is a system of harmoniously cooperating parts. It must, therefore, possess harmonizing mechanisms, for example in the form of nervous impulses regulating blood circulation or sugar metabolism. Bernard created also the notion of internal secretion; but it was still a long way from this to our conception of endocrinology, which comprehends a most subtle, wonderfully balanced system of regulatory activities, mediated by those chemical messengers which Ernest H. Starling (1866–1927) termed 'hormones' in 1905.

About the turn of the century, too, Ivan Petrovitch Pavlov (1849–1936) of St Petersburg elucidated the important role of nervous regulatory mechanisms and particularly of conditioned reflexes in the control of appetite and digestion. Whereas for Bernard the capability of our organism to move and act freely in the outer world depended on its perfect inner organization as a physicochemical machine, Pavlov introduced into this machine a kind of psychology. But the psychical manifestations were, in his conception, subject to the same rigid determinism, which rules the material world.

Of course, all these developments went hand in hand with the constant growth of biochemistry, i.e. the investigation of the material constituents of the body. Hence, laboratory tests became increasingly important for medical diagnosis and the control of treatment.

Towards the end of the nineteenth century, the results of basic physiological research became more and more fertile for clinical medicine. Let us just give two examples.

In 1890, Oscar Minkowski and Joseph von Mering were able to produce diabetes mellitus in a dog by removing its pancreas. In this way, the seat of the disturbance could be located in the pancreatic islands described earlier by Paul Langerhans, and finally, the remedy for the disease was found in the hormone insulin, which is produced by these small islands (Frederick Grant Banting and Charles Herbert Best, 1921–2).

The other example is the vaccine against rabies, devised by Louis Pasteur on the basis of his microbiological studies in 1885. As rabies has an incubation period of several weeks, anti-rabic vaccination may still be efficient when given after infection by the bite of a rabid animal. This success in the management of a disease, which before was invariably fatal, caused a worldwide sensation. Along this line of inventive investigation, the complex science of immunology has developed in the twentieth century.

HOW TO CURE PATIENTS: CHANGING PRINCIPLES IN THERAPEUTICS

'I firmly believe that if the whole *materia medica*, as now used, could be sunk to the bottom of the sea, it would be all the better for mankind – and all the worse for the fishes'. This was the opinion of young Oliver Wendell Holmes (1809–94), physician, poet, and later professor of anatomy and physiology at Harvard, after having studied at Paris with Pasteur. It has already been mentioned that the new clinical medicine, which so carefully established the diagnosis and natural history of diseases, threw discredit upon the drugs and other remedies used so far, particularly bleeding and other measures aimed at removing the 'bad humours' from the body.

On the other hand, Magendie's experimental medicine included also drug therapy with experimentally tested preparations. In the first decades of the nineteenth century, the active components of several medicinal plants were isolated: quinine, caffeine, morphine, codeine, strychnine, and others. This made it possible for physicians to use pure substances with known therapeutic and toxic properties – let us not forget that the Greek word pharmakon meant a medicine as well as a poison and that, according to old Paracelsus, 'the dose alone ensures that something is not a poison'. Later in the century came synthetic drugs such as the still popular aspirin (acetylo-salicylic acid, 1899).

The application of soluble drugs was made easier by the hypodermic syringe introduced by the French physician Charles-Gabriel Pravaz in 1853. Pure drugs and hypodermic injection: a great advance indeed. But at the same time, this progress favoured abuse. Morphinism became a medical and social problem, and in the 1880s, physicians tried cocaine to cure morphinists. Thus, cocaine addiction began, more than a century ago, as an oestrogenic condition.

The chemical synthesis of medicaments as well as the extraction of pure substances from medicinal herbs became, in the end, an industrial activity. Inventors and producers began to take out patents for their drugs. The first to do so was the German chemist Ludwig Knorr who, in 1884, put the febrifuge 'Antipyrin' on the market. Physicians viewed this new trademark pharmacy with distrust. Many of them thought it immoral to derive profit from a medicament as if it were just an ordinary merchandise. This, however, had been done for ages. For instance, in the sixteenth and seventeenth centuries, the import from South America to Europe of guaiac (praised as an antisyphilitic) and of Peruvian bark (against malaria) was a most profitable affair. Another apprehension of physicians was that the pharmaceutical industry might enforce an unwholesome uniformity of prescription upon them, but a century later, we are rather worried by the perplexing variety of their products.

Towards the end of the century, immunisation and serotherapy became powerful means to conquer a number of infectious diseases. Pasteur's anti-rabic vaccine has already been mentioned. His pupils Emile Roux (1853–1933) and Alexandre Yersin (1863–1943) found that the deleterious effects of diphtheria and tetanus infections depend on the toxins produced by the respective bacilli. At Koch's institute in Berlin, Emil Behring (1854–1917) and his Japanese collaborator Shibasaburo Kitasato (1852–1931) could demonstrate that the serum of animals immunized with diphtheria toxin was able to cure the disease in man (1890). In this way, many patients, particularly children, were saved, and Behring was awarded the first Nobel Prize in medicine for this discovery in 1901. His colleague Paul Ehrlich (1854–1915), showed that the interaction between toxin and antitoxin is a quantitative one: it is not sufficient just to inject some serum; it is absolutely necessary to give an adequate amount of it to neutralize the entire toxin present in the body. Ehrlich, another Nobel Prize laureate, was a man who most rigorously applied scientific thinking to medical problems. This enabled him also to develop, with the assistance of Sahachiro Hata (1873–1938) from Japan, the first chemotherapeutic agent, the antisyphilitic 'Salvarsan' (1910).

In our century, chemotherapy as well as immunization – preventive even more than curative – have contributed enormously to fighting infectious disease all over the world, justifying to some extent the prediction of the Irish immunologist Sir Almroth Edward Wright (1861–1947) that the physician of the future would be an immunizator.

THE RISE OF SURGERY

In the course of the nineteenth century, surgery acquired a prestige it never had before; the surgeon performing major operations became the brilliant star among doctors. Several factors contributed to this evolution. In the first instance, surgery was now recognized as a legitimate branch of scientific medicine. Then, the localistic view prevailing in pathology favoured surgical treatment: when a tumour, for example, was no longer interpreted as a mere symptom of corruption of the body fluids but as a disease of its own, namely as a circumscribed heap of enormously growing cells, you might confidently hope to cure it completely by cutting it out.

But surgical interventions used to be atrociously painful. It was, therefore, necessary to carry them out as speedily as possible. Thus, in 1846, the London surgeon Robert Liston amputated a whole leg within 28 seconds. But in the same year, on 16 October 1846, the Boston surgeon John Collins Warren (1778–1856) successfully performed the first operation under general anaesthesia; he did so on the proposal of Thomas Green Morton (1819–68), who narcotized the patient with ethylic ether. This deed, by the way, was

the first great contribution of America to world medicine. Henceforward, it was possible calmly to execute big operations.

But the result of a surgical intervention was, all too often, ruined by a fatal post-operative sepsis. The cause of this – bacterial infection – was revealed by Joseph Lister (1827–1912), professor of surgery at Glasgow, later at Edinburgh and London. Inspired by Pasteur, Lister proclaimed in 1867 his 'antiseptic principle', advocating strong disinfecting measures to be applied during the whole course of an operation. The final answer to the problem, however, was asepsis, an elaborate system of precautions to avoid any infection while operating. In this way, surgeons gained access to the most hidden places in the body. Of course, interventions on so delicate organs as the lungs, the heart, or the brain have to deal with many additional difficulties. For more superficial operations, methods of local anaesthesia were invented, starting with cocaine instillation in the eye as proposed by young Carl Koller of Vienna in 1884.

RADIOLOGY AND RADIOTHERAPY

In the last days of the year 1895, Wilhelm Conrad Röntgen (1845–1923), professor of physics at Würzburg university, announced the discovery of a new class of rays, which he called X-rays (Röntgen 1895: 132–41; 1896: 11–16, 17–19). His discovery was immediately and enthusiastically taken up by surgeons and physicians, because Röntgen's electromagnetic rays provided them with a means to actually look at the inner parts of the body and to visualize a considerable number of their pathological lesions: fractures of bones, tuberculous lesions in the lungs, or, with some additional device, ulcers of the stomach, etc. X-ray diagnosis proved to be an ideal complement to the older diagnostic techniques such as auscultation and percussion; in a wonderful way, it served the great purpose of recognizing the effects of disease (or injury) on the organs of the human body. It was an uncomfortable surprise to see, somewhat later, that X-rays, if not used with the utmost care, could also do much harm; especially nurses and technicians operating X-ray apparatus had to suffer from severe and often mutilating burns.

The following years brought the discovery of radioactivity. Henri Becquerel observed the radiation of uranium in 1896; two years later, Marie and Pierre Curie isolated the element radium; these three physicists worked at Paris, but Marie Curie, née Sklodowska, was a fervent Polish patriot.

Röntgen's rays, as well as the emissions of radioactive elements, showed a power to destroy tumours. This really is a cellular therapy, as the radiation hinders the multiplication of cells. Gösta Forsell (1876–1950) of Sweden was the pioneer who worked out the method of radium therapy for cancer of the uterus. To his radiotherapeutic clinic at Stockholm he gave the name of 'radium home' ('Radiumhemmet'), thus stressing his conviction that tumour patients need not only a technically optimal treatment but also a friendly atmosphere, which gives them, hope and confidence.

EUROPEAN MEDICINE OVERSEAS

The new medicine which had originated in Europe claimed universal validity inasmuch as its basis was science, i.e. a reliable and ever-growing knowledge of nature, which holds true everywhere. For scientifically minded physicians, it was a matter of course to apply their methods of investigation and action also to the medical problems of overseas countries. When, for example, in 1850 the German Wilhelm Griesinger was appointed physician in ordinary to Pasha Abbas of Egypt, he and his young assistant Theodor Bilharz carefully performed a great deal of post-mortems and thereby discovered some parasites responsible for widespread diseases: the hookworm *ankylostoma duodenale* (Griesinger, 1854), which causes severe anaemia, and *schistosoma haematobium* (Bilharz, 1851), the causative agent of the disease now known as bilharziasis and characterized by bloody urine – a scourge which harassed the inhabitants of the Nile Valley from times immemorial. (In 1910, Sir Armand Ruffer found calcified eggs of the parasite in the kidneys of two mummies of the period of the twentieth dynasty, 1186–1070 BC.)

Towards the end of the century, microbiological research elucidated the causes of such disastrous infections as yellow fever, cholera, malaria, and plague; more about this will be said below. About the same time, institutions for the study of overseas diseases were founded: in 1899, Sir Patrick Manson (1844–1922), who had spent many years of his professional life in China, founded the London School of Tropical Medicine. In French colonies, the regional *Instituts Pasteur* contributed unremittingly to the investigation and prevention of tropical diseases.

A particular kind of medical activity in Asia and Africa was that of the missionary doctors, or medical missionaries. For Protestant missionaries in West Africa, preaching the Gospel was a kind of making amends for the dreadful wrong done to Africans by the white slave-traders, but they deemed it their duty, too, to help the native people in everyday matters, to provide for their education, and to give them some medical assistance. The latter task was entrusted to doctors who took service with the missionary companies. Thus, for example, in Ghana the first small hospital was opened in 1900, at Aburi, by the Swiss doctor Rudolf Fisch of the Basel Mission (Fischer, 1991).

In Ghana as well as in other countries, confrontation, or at least competition between European and African medicine was inevitable. Earlier in the century, when the white man who came to Ghana fell sick with malaria (the Gold Coast [Ghana] was dubbed 'the white man's grave') those who accepted the mild treatment of African healers fared much better than their fellow patients who underwent the bleeding procedures still popular with European doctors. Down to the end of the century, many missionaries preferred native herbal medicine to drugs imported from Europe. Africans, on the other hand, recognized the superiority of the missionary doctor in the cure, for example of yaws and in surgery including cataract operations. It was harder, however, to convince them of the benefits of smallpox vaccination.

EAST ASIA: MODERN MEDICINE COMES TO CHINA AND JAPAN

In China and Japan the great event in the medical history of the century was also the rise of modern scientific medicine, the introduction of the so-called Western medicine. This took, however, a remarkably different course in the two countries. For China, 'Western medicine was', as Ralph C. Croizier puts it (1968: 37), 'an integral part of Western cultural aggression and ultimately of Chinese cultural revolution'.

The cultural revolution Croizier speaks of is the May 4th Movement of 1919, when the Chinese rose against Japan's attempt to take over the rights and positions that defeated Germany had formerly acquired in China. The May 4th Movement called for a vast modernization of the Chinese way of life, in order to restore national dignity and independence. Up to this point, modern 'Western' medicine had not met with such considerable reluctance. This contrasts sharply with the attitude of the Japanese who, already in the Meiji period (1868–1912), eagerly and actively adopted it.

China

The points of departure for Western medical activity in China were situated on the south coast: the small Portuguese colony of Macao on the west side of the Canton River, and Canton itself. Before 1840, Canton was the only place open to foreign trade, and also the only Chinese city where Europeans and Americans were allowed to live, although in strict segregation.

The first element of European medicine to be introduced into China was Jennerian vaccination against smallpox. It was practised by Portuguese doctors at Macao and put to use on a larger scale, in 1805–6, by Alexander Pearson, surgeon to the British East India Company (Wong and Wu, 1932: 142ff.).

Most important for the permanent introduction of Western medicine were, however, the medical missionaries. In 1834, the Reverend Doctor Peter Parker, who had studied at Yale both medicine and theology, instituted at Canton a hospital and dispensary for poor Chinese patients. This charitable establishment soon became famous for the treatment of eye diseases; ophthalmology, and surgery in general, were of great immediate use to the native population. Parker and his colleagues also trained young Chinese in medicine; Parker's assistant Kwan Ato (d. 1874) was the first Chinese to be come a specialist in surgery. In 1866, a medical school was formally installed at Canton Missionary Hospital; its curriculum included also a course in 'Practical and Chinese medicine' given by Dr Kwan Ato (Wong and Wu, 1932: 246). As early as 1879, Canton Medical School accepted female (Chinese) students, too. Its most illustrious student, however, was Sun Yat-Sen (1866–1925), who was to become, in 1911, the first president of the Chinese Republic. After one year at Canton (1886–7), he moved to the new College of Medicine at Hong Kong, where he graduated in 1892; but soon after he became completely absorbed in his political activity.

It was the merit of missionary doctors also to introduce modern medical literature in Chinese. First of all, in the 1850s, the Englishman Benjamin Hobson, translating from English standard works, compiled a series of basic textbooks. But in 1850, a genuine Chinese book on anatomy and therapeutics was also published. Its author was Wang Ch'ing-jen, a learned physician eager to correct the anatomical errors of ancient writers, setting against the traditional views his own observations which he had made on the bodies of victims of epidemics, of executed wrong-doers, and of animals (Wong and Wu, 1932: 222). In his endeavour, Wang Ch'ing-jen may rightly be called a Chinese Vesalius.

By repeated military action and by the Unequal Treaties enforced upon the Chinese, the Western powers successively opened the Middle Kingdom to their trade, their missions, and their medicine. Interestingly enough, the Chinese Maritime Customs provided a new opportunity for foreign doctors to work in China. From 1863, this civil service branch was directed most efficiently by an Englishman, Sir Robert Hart, who instituted the Customs Medical Service. For appointment as Customs Medical Officers, Hart preferred graduates of Scottish medical schools. One of these was Patrick Manson. Both as a physician and an investigator of parasitic diseases including malaria, Manson worked in China from 1866 to 1889. In the inaugural speech he made in 1887 as the first dean of the Hong Kong College of Medicine, Manson praised the Chinese people for their moral and intellectual qualities and predicted them a glorious future. Back in Britain, he rescued his former student Sun Yat-Sen when he was kidnapped, in 1896, by agents of the Imperial Chinese Legation in London (Wong and Wu, 1932: 321–2; Manson-Bahr, 1962: 73–4).

An important event was the opening of Peking Union Medical College, founded by a union of several missionary societies, in 1906. Somewhat later, i.e. from 1915, this college was developed by the Rockefeller Foundation into the leading research and training centre of China. 'The objective was to place the very best that modern medical science could offer in one strategic location, with the hope that it would both help train the nucleus of a native medical leadership and serve as an example to other institutions', says Croizier (1968: 48–9).

As long as the Manchu ruled, there was just one official attempt at using Western medicine to the benefit of the state: in 1881, the viceroy Li Hung-Chang established at Tientsin a medical school for the training of doctors for the army and navy. The leading minds of the early republic, however, were utterly convinced that modern science, and accordingly science-based modern medicine, were essential for the future welfare of the nation. But the number of graduated doctors was still ridiculously small in relation to the population: about 300 in 1897, and 11,000 at most thirty-five years later.

Around the turn of the century, a new type of physician began slowly to appear: doctors trained in scientific medicine but also acquainted with traditional methods of healing (Croizier, 1968: 63).

The superiority of modern medical science became evident, even to traditionally minded observers and especially administrators, when in 1910 a dreadful epidemic of pulmonary plague broke out in Manchuria. By energetically applied sanitary measures, Dr Wu Lien-teh (1879–1959) a Cambridge graduate, succeeded in checking the spread of infection. In his own words (Wong and Wu, 1932: 431): 'The terrible epidemic . . . though it exacted a toll of 60,000 lives . . . definitely laid the foundation for systematic public health work in China'. In April 1911, on the eve of the revolution which broke out in October of the same year, an international plague conference, with Wu in the chair, convened at Mukden, in southern Manchuria, and in the following year, the Manchurian Plague Prevention Service began its work.

Japan

In old times, Japanese medicine followed mainly the Chinese teachings. But even during the two centuries of her voluntary, strict isolation, from the seventeenth to mid-nineteenth century, Japan had some contact with Dutch medicine, which was, rather picturesquely, nicknamed 'red-hair medicine' (Beukers *et al.*, 1991). The Dutch were the one Western nation was allowed to keep a foothold on Japanese territory, namely the small 'man-made' island of Deshima, in the harbour of Nagasaki. There were always a few Japanese doctors inclined to profit by the anatomical knowledge and the surgical skills of their Dutch colleagues (most of them surgeons to the Dutch East India Company).

The mission of US captain Matthew C. Perry, in 1853, was the decisive move which forced Japan to enter in commercial and diplomatic relations with the rest of the world. The Japanese resented this imperialistic intrusion no less than any other people would, but, with unprecedented vigour, they took it as a challenge to win for themselves a place among the world's leading powers. With tremendous speed and efficiency, they adopted Western technology and science, and particularly medical science. Judging that nowhere was medicine so systematically built on scientific principles as in Germany, they chose German medicine as their model. They read German journals, invited German professors, and sent their brightest young men for postgraduate training to Germany.

The most conspicuous example of such a career is Shibasaburo Kitasato (1852–1931), who in 1885 went to Berlin to study bacteriology with Koch and von Behring, was appointed professor at Berlin University, and finally became Japan's leader in the fight against infectious disease. He did outstanding research work, and just by a hair's breadth missed the discovery of the plague bacillus.

THE SCOURGE OF INFECTIOUS DISEASE

Cholera

Towards 1830, a frightening newcomer entered the global scene of deadly diseases: asiatic cholera. From India, its breeding ground, it spread to China and Africa as well as to Russia, Western Europe and America. Quarantine and military cordons – measures applied earlier with some success against the spread of plague – proved completely useless in the case of cholera, the causative agent of which, unknown at that time, is carried by water, seafood, milk, etc. This disappointing experience favoured, in medical ideology, the rise of anticontagionism: obviously, a contagious matter did not exist; poor conditions of living in filthy surroundings together with corrupted, 'miasmatic' air seemed completely sufficient to explain the outbreak of this and other epidemics. Simpler minds, however, were prone to believe in wilful poisoning of food and drink: in Paris, in 1832, a few poor wretches were even lynched on this suspicion.

But in the course of the following pandemic – i.e. an epidemic of worldwide dimensions – the London physician John Snow (1813–58) demonstrated the water-borne character of cholera (1849–55) (Snow 1849: 730–2, 745–52, 923–9). Famous is his story of the Broad Street Pump (in Soho), which dispensed heavily polluted water: when its handle was removed, the outbreak was checked, as Snow had predicted.

When another pandemic broke out in 1883, Robert Koch travelled to Egypt and to India and could, at last, isolate the responsible bacterium, *vibrio cholerae*. Some years later, Waldemar M. W. Haffkine (1860–1930), a cosmopolitan bacteriologist and immunologist of Russian origin, elaborated, at the Institut Pasteur, a first kind of cholera vaccine. The greatest benefit of all this research lay, however, in the field of public health: improvement of water supply and sewerage. With a view to this, Koch could even speak of cholera as of 'our old ally', because it helped so much to get funds for sanitary purposes.

Plague

The old foe of humankind, plague – in both its forms, bubonic and pneumonic (pulmonary) – was (and is) still alive. The last pandemic began in 1894 in South China (Canton, Hong Kong); within some years, it swept over all continents except Europe. In 1900 it was brought to San Francisco and thus, for the first time in history, to North America.

Already in June 1894, two 'microbe hunters' had set out for Hong Kong: the well-known Japanese Shibasaburo Kitasato, who met with ample official support, and Alexandre Yersin, a Swiss-born freelance microbiologist from Pasteur's school, who had to grapple with extreme difficulties. But while Kitasato searched for the plague germ in the blood of victims, Yersin sought it in the pus of the ominous groin swellings, the buboes, where he found the bacteria, as it were, in pure culture. In his honour, the plague bacillus is now called *yersinia pestis*.

In the following years, India was heavily struck by the plague, and Bombay became the centre of feverish international research activity: how did the bacilli attack man, and how were they scattered over whole cities? It became clear that plague is primarily a disease of rats (and other rodents) and that it is transmitted by fleas from rat to man, and also from man to man. Among the many contributions to the elucidation of these intricate facts, the work of the Frenchman Paul-Louis Simond (1858–1947), is especially worth remembering (Simond 1898: 625–87). Pneumonic plague, as it broke out in 1910 in Manchuria, is transmitted from man to man directly by droplet infection.

In South Africa as well as in North America, infected rats passed the disease not only to men but also to wild rodents such as, in the West of the United States, the ground squirrel. Thus, there is now a permanent plague reservoir, which sporadically gives rise to infections in humans. In a way, plague is still with us.

Yellow fever

For centuries, yellow fever had infested the tropical parts of Africa and America, and even reached out as far north as Philadelphia in 1793. The disease got its name from the jaundice it often causes in severe cases. It is an acute virus infection, and the virus is transmitted from man to man, or from ape to man, by mosquitoes.

A truly murderous epidemic of yellow fever struck, in 1802, the French expeditionary force which Napoleon had sent to Haiti in order to reconquer this island and then to invade the Mississippi valley: out of 33,000 men, 29,000 died from the fever. Which thus, in a most impressive way, justified its nickname 'the patriotic fever': as the native population was largely immune, it was spared from infection while the invaders perished. This military disaster induced Napoleon to sell, in 1803, Louisiana – then a vast and only vaguely delineated area on the west bank of the Mississippi river – to the United States.

In 1881–2, in Cuba – the island suffered much from repeated outbreaks of yellow fever – Carlos Juan Finlay (1833–1915) suggested that the disease was transmitted by mosquito bites. His hypothesis was confirmed, about twenty years later, by an American Army Board led by Walter Reed (1851–1902). Reed and his colleagues succeeded in proving that, in fact, the mosquito *aëdes aegypti* (known at that time by the name of *stegomyia fasciata*) transmits the infection provided that certain conditions are given.

This conclusive demonstration of the sinister role of the mosquito made it possible to eradicate yellow fever, in the United States and the West Indies, by destroying the insects. In this way, too, the American military surgeon William Crawford Gorgas (1854–1920) was able to remove the danger of yellow fever and malaria infections from the isthmus of Panama so that, in 1904, construction of the canal could be undertaken and safely carried out.

Malaria

In contradistinction to the three acute and epidemic infections we have so far considered, the course of malaria is chronic and its character is endemic, i.e. it occurs constantly in the countries where it is at home, and these were all more or less the warm countries of the world. On the whole, therefore, malaria has killed more people than the epidemic diseases, which, after a certain time, pass away. Its challenge to medical research was, however, quite similar: the primary points were to identify the pathogenic organism and to detect the method of infection. By the multiple efforts of physicians and biologists, this was also achieved by the turn of the century.

Malaria has, of course, several particularities. The causal agent is, in this case, not a bacterium (as in cholera and plague), nor a submicroscopic virus (as in yellow fever), but a unicellular animal, a protozoon, the *plasmodium*. This was discovered, in 1880–1, by Alphonse Laveran (1845–1922). And there is not just one plasmodium, but four species of it, which are responsible for the different clinical forms of the fever. But again, it is a mosquito – *anopheles* – which infects man. It is not the place here to describe the intricate life cycle of the plasmodia, which was elucidated in those years by Camillo Golgi, Patrick Manson, Ronald Ross, William George MacCallum, Giovanni Battista Grassi, and others. Most important is the fact that asexual forms of the parasite develop in the red blood cells of their human hosts; after regular intervals of one, two, or three days, depending on the particular species of plasmodium present, all the infected blood cells burst simultaneously, and this gives rise to the intermittent fever attacks so typical of malaria. Fortunately, a drug efficient against plasmodium was already available: quinine. In order to combat malaria on a large scale, however, the fight against the mosquitoes and the destruction of their breeding places by draining swamps was of paramount importance.

The four examples we have looked at may suffice to demonstrate the brilliant results which the scientific approach brought about in the domain of infectious diseases. Nowhere so clearly as in this field could a specific cause now be assigned to an ever growing number of morbid conditions. Doubtless, the most impressive case, for the medical profession as well as for the educated public, was Robert Koch's discovery of the 'tubercle bacillus' (now *mycobacterium tuberculosis*), in 1882 (Koch 1882: 221–30). On this occasion, Koch defined the criteria which must be fulfilled before any microorganism seen under the microscope might rightly be claimed to be the cause of a certain disease. Koch's postulates imposed a salutary discipline upon bacteriologists – there were, in fact, too many people who hoped to become rapidly famous by a microbiological discovery which soon after turned out to be a sham.

Of true discoveries, however, there were plenty. And many of them could be put to practical use almost immediately; not so much in the sense that the microbes or parasites could be killed by infallible drugs, than in terms of measures of personal hygiene, public health, or environmental sanitation directed against the transmission of the guilty microorganisms and their carriers, particularly the mosquitoes and other insects involved.

There was ample reason, in fact, to be proud of the progress in the fight against the scourge of infectious disease, under which humankind had suffered from time immemorial. This pride certainly contributed much to the enthusiastic optimism which greeted, in 1901, the beginning of a new century – an optimism justified but poorly by subsequent events.

SOME GENERAL CONSIDERATIONS

The medical profession found itself, in the course of the nineteenth century, between two conflicting aspirations: the ideal of unity and the necessity of specialization. Awareness of the comprehensive unity of all medical science was strong: every doctor was now expected first to have studied the basic sciences and then to have acquired a broad knowledge of clinical medicine in all its complexity before assuming the responsibilities of medical practice. On the other hand, the enormous increase of knowledge, and of diagnostic and therapeutic techniques and tools, made it more and more impossible to become a true master in more than a limited field.

The first branch of medicine to be organized as a speciality was psychiatry: mentally ill people obviously were a distinct category of patients and had to be cared for in separate institutions by specially trained doctors and nursing staff.

In somatic medicine, i.e. in the domain of bodily disease, ophthalmology was admired as the model of a science-based discipline after the ophthalmoscope had been invented, in 1850, by the young German physiologist Hermann von Helmholtz (1821–94), and when ophthalmic optics were developed by Helmholtz and the Dutchman Frans Cornelis Donders (1818–89).

Obstetrics, too, became a medical speciality, practised and taught by adequately trained doctors. This meant that, in the well-developed countries, the midwives lost their independent professional status and were reduced to the condition of mere auxiliaries, subordinate to the male obstetricians. This is being deplored now by some social historians, but it was an inevitable evolution, which enhanced the safety of women in labour.

On the other hand, young women fought their way to medical education and graduation. The first to do so was English-born Elizabeth Blackwell (1821–1910), who graduated in 1849, though at a rather obscure place: Geneva, in the state of New York, USA. Some years later, she founded in New York City a hospital exclusively staffed by women. The first European university to admit female medical students on equal terms with their male colleagues was Zürich in Switzerland, from 1867; this university had been founded some decades earlier in a liberal spirit, which proved to be still alive.

Medical education became a particularly harassing problem in the United States when the great rush to the West began. As doctors were urgently wanted, dubious 'medical schools' shot up which, for high fees, provided ignorants with meaningless diplomas. But in 1847, doctors who felt responsible for their profession and their patients, united in the American Medical Association, in order to strive for high scientific and moral standards in medicine. And right from its start in 1893, the Johns Hopkins Medical School at Baltimore acted as a shining model of first-rate medical education. (By the way, a group of ladies, anxious to secure an opportunity of medical training for women, raised an endowment of $500,000 to help the establishment of this school.) When at last, in 1910, Abraham Flexner (sponsored by the Carnegie Foundation) produced his report on medical education in the United States and Canada (Flexner, 1910; 1912; 1925), this was the signal for a nation-wide reform of medical teaching in the US. The two last-mentioned events laid the foundations for the rise of American medical science to its internationally leading position in the twentieth century.

Many more things might be discussed in connection with our subject, the development of medicine in the nineteenth century. Thus, for example, the beginnings of health insurance, first in 1883 in Germany, under Bismarck's sometimes enlightened despotism, and then, in 1911, in Great Britain, with Lloyd George's much opposed National Insurance Act. A great theme, too, would be the development of nursing, for which Florence Nightingale (1820–1910) did so much. Or the Red Cross and the Geneva Convention for the protection of war victims (1864) brought about by the empathic humanitarian engagement of a citizen of Geneva, Switzerland: Henry Dunant (1828–1910).

The nineteenth century was decisive for the evolution of the scientific medicine of today. Towards the turn of the century, medicine enjoyed an unprecedented esteem as a real science. Evidence for this is the Nobel Prize: in his last will, Alfred Bernhard Nobel (1833–96) put 'medicine and physiology' on the same high level as physics and chemistry, the exemplary sciences of nature.

BIBLIOGRAPHY

ACKERKNECHT, E. H. 1952. *Rudolf Virchow, Doctor–Statesman–Anthropologist.* Wise, Madison.
——. 1967. *Medicine at the Paris Hospital 1794–1848.* Baltimore, pp. 16–32.
BEUKERS, H.; LUYENDIJK-ELSHOUT, A. M.; VAN OPSTALL, M. E. (eds)1991. *Red-Hair Medicine: Dutch-Japanese Medical Relations.* Amsterdam.
CROIZIER, R. C. 1968. *Traditional Medicine in Modern China – Science, Nationalism, and the Tensions of Cultural Change.* Cambridge MA, pp. 37–49.

FISCHER, F. H. 1991. *Der Missionsarzt Rudolf Fisch und die Anfänge medizinischer Arbeit der Basler Mission an der Goldküste (Ghana).* Herzogenrath (BRD).

FLEXNER, A. 1910. *Medical Education in the United States and Canada.* New York.

——. 1912. *Medical Education in Europe.* New York.

——. 1925. *Medical Education: A Comparative Study.* New York.

JETTER, D. 1973. *Grundzüge der Hospitalgeschichte.* Darmstadt, p. 38.

——. 1977. *Grundzüge der Krankenhausgeschichte (1800–1900).* Darmstadt, p. 12ff.

KOCH, R. 1882. Die Aetiologie der Tuberkulose. In: *Berliner klin. Wochenschr,* 19, pp. 221–30.

MANSON-BAHR, P. 1962. *Patrick Manson – the Father of Tropical Medicine,* London, p. 73ff.

RÖNTGEN, W. C. 1895. Ueber: eine neue Art von Strahlen. In: *Sitzungsber physikal.-med. Ges. Würzburg,* pp. 132–41.

——. 1896. Ueber eine neue Art von Strahlen. In: *Sitzungsber physikal.-med. Ges. Würzburg,* pp. 11–19.

SIMOND, P. L. 1898. La propagation de la peste. In: *Ann. Inst. Pasteur,* 12, pp. 625–87.

SNOW, J. 1849. On the Pathology and Mode of Communication of the Cholera. In: *London-med. Gaz.,* 44, pp. 730–2, 745–52, 923–9.

VIRCHOW, R. 1858. *Die Cellularpathologie in ihrer Begründung auf physiologische und pathologische Geswebelehre.* Berlin.

——. 1894. *Morgagni und der anatomische Gedanke.* Berlin.

WONG, K. C.; WU, L. T. 1932. *History of Chinese Medicine.* Tientsin, pp. 142–431.

6

THE HUMANITIES AND SOCIAL SCIENCES

Alexander O. Chubariyan, coordinator

in collaboration with *Tatiana V. Golubkova, Igor N. Ionov,*
Marletta T. Stepaniants and *Efim B. Tchernjak*

The nineteenth century has a special place in history. It marks the end of a long phase of history: on the one hand, it seems to recapitulate a multiplicity of previous economic and political processes and, perhaps to an even greater extent, to recapitulate by creating universalist theories, what had gone before in the realm of ideas and in humankind's intellectual development; on the other hand, the end of the century saw the emergence of many new trends and phenomena, heralding the advent of a new era in technology, in the organization of economic life, and in the social and intellectual spheres.

Very few periods of human history can be compared with the nineteenth century as regards the development of philosophical, aesthetic and religious thinking or the methodology of history and economic theory, and it was in the course of that century that there began what may be called the 'technogenic' or 'machine' stage in the process of civilization.

Unlike pre-industrial civilizations, the machine civilization demanded continuous technological improvement. The dynamics of technological progress created the basis for the emergence of a new type of civilization. As compared with the past, the rate of technological progress – made possible by the close linkage between machine-based industry and a science that focused on practical aims – became much more rapid. That linkage, which had already been established in England in the later eighteenth century and was carried through to completion in the nineteenth century, created increased possibilities for improving output and satisfying material needs on an unprecedented scale. It seemed that the machine-based civilization would reduce, if not abolish entirely, human dependence on nature, human subjection to crop failures and famine, to disease and natural disasters.

In fact, human dependence on nature did not disappear but changed its character. Among the first who foresaw the new problems and dangers facing humanity was the British economist Thomas Malthus (1766–1834), whose *Essay on the Principle of Population*, written at the very end of the eighteenth century (1798), was to enjoy considerable popularity in the following two centuries, attracting many supporters and equally many opponents.

Malthus foresaw a gloomy future for humanity: generally speaking, the improvement in living standards would lead to a fall in the death rate and an increase in the birth rate but,

at a given stage, economic growth would be unable to keep up with population growth, condemning humanity to starvation and extinction due to over-population. Malthus' conclusion was that the increase in the birth rate needed to be kept in check, particularly among the 'lower orders'.

Another British economist, David Ricardo (1772–1823) considered that economic growth depended primarily on one unalterable factor – land. Both he and Malthus believed humanity would eventually come up against the limits of natural resources. These pessimistic predictions were made at a time when the future course of the Industrial Revolution was far from clear, a time when the dependence of the economy and of human existence in general upon the land was especially keenly felt, and when sources of energy were extremely limited.

Throughout the nineteenth century and in the twentieth too, the ideas and predictions of Malthus and his followers were attracting the attention of scholars and public figures. The prospects for economic growth and their mutual relationship with the problems of population had a determining influence on a particular current of thought in the social sciences, and the establishment of demography as a science, as well as the development of political economy and other disciplines, can be clearly traced back to this question.

The genesis of the machine civilization resulted in the rapid growth of commercial and political links between the countries and cultures of the world, considerably changing the situation for developments of social knowledge in general. It was a controversial process.

On the one hand, the world market and a considerable number of Asian and African countries had been divided between Western powers as their spheres of influence. By the early twentieth century the political and commercial unity of the world was greater than ever. International trade and international investments reached their peak. As a result international law and the international political system, and the terms and regulations of international trade, were increasingly based on the principles put forward by Western social sciences – created partly during the Enlightenment Age, and partly in the nineteenth century. This led to the tremendous growth of Western culture and Western worldviews' role in the world. Enlightenment ideas and positivist concepts were being absorbed by every continent. More or less successful attempts at liberal reforming were initiated in Russia, Japan and Turkey, and Enlightenment societies were created in many countries. For many countries the very term 'civilization' was associated with the Western model.

On the other hand the nineteenth century had laid the cultural and scientific foundations for the large-scale global dialogue which developed in the twentieth century. Individual publications on the history and philology of Oriental countries were replaced both in the West and in Russia by systematic anthropological, archaeological, sociological and religious studies of ancient and contemporary non-European cultures on a broad interdisciplinary basis. The methods of Western social sciences were gradually adopted in China, India, Iran and other countries, which followed Russia in creating a civilizational consciousness of their own. By the interaction of science and religion in Europe, India and Japan, a synthesis of various world cultures' spiritual experience was formed.

The eighteenth century made a profound impression on the development of world enlightenment and social thought. The ideology and culture of Enlightenment and secular philosophy took over medieval views on nature and society.

A new spirit of liberal and democratic tendencies was pervasive in the field of intellectual life and in philosophical, political and artistic fields.

Hobbes and Locke in England, Spinoza in Holland, Montesquieu, Voltaire and Rousseau in France, Lomonosov and Radischev in Russia, and many representatives of Enlightenment thought from Eastern countries, advanced new ideas, called for changes in social relations, and laid the foundations for new legal norms and notions of being human.

The ideas and culture of the eighteenth century for the most part constituted the basis for the outburst of social thought and development of culture and art in the nineteenth century.

In the realm of ideas, the end of the eighteenth century and beginning of the nineteenth were a time of turbulent intellectual activity in Europe; new ideals were in gestation, and the nineteenth century ushered in a genuine 'revolution of the spirit' that was to a large extent dependent on revolutionary changes. The upheavals occurring in France (the Napoleonic wars and the revolutions of 1830 and 1848), Italy, Germany, Russia and elsewhere had a very direct effect on public attitudes, on social thought, on the development of the social and human sciences, on literature, music and art, and on mentalities and the way they manifested themselves.

The nineteenth century will be remembered as an era of extraordinary diversity in ideas and theories. It saw a burgeoning of philosophical and historical thought and the emergence of sociology, anthropology and political economy. A theoretical evolution, 'a revolution of the mind', also occurred in the aesthetic field, that of art and literature.

Change had begun to be clearly perceptible in the last quarter of the eighteenth century, the period that has come to be known as the Age of Enlightenment, the age of the *philosophes*. The ideas of the Enlightenment had a fertilizing effect in various areas of intellectual life, influencing philosophy, literature and art alike. 'Rationalism' predominated both in science and in culture, taking its cue from the metaphysical conceptions of Descartes, Leibniz

and Spinoza. The idea of 'experiment' held sway in the minds of both thinkers and men of action.

The *encyclopédistes* and Rousseau exerted a great influence. The theory of the social contract and the democratic ideas widespread in pre-Revolutionary France and throughout Europe represented the apogee of the Age of Enlightenment, but at the same time they carried within them seeds of a new world outlook, testifying to the approaching decline of the ideology and aesthetics of the Enlightenment. In place of the Enlightenment, for whose proponents the realities of life constituted a field of action where plans that had been drawn up could be put into effect, there came a new age with different values and a different correlation of ideals and reality: the Age of Enlightenment opened the way to romanticism.

In general terms the origins of romanticism are closely connected to the French Revolution, which, on the one hand, demonstrated greater complexity and greater contradictions in historical development and in the greatness of humankind, striving to transform the world in all its diversity. On the other hand, the outcome of the Revolution and the experience of the post-revolutionary period proved the limitations of human powers and potential, and resulted in a general disenchantment as regards the possibility of achieving the ideals and dreams of the pre-revolutionary and revolutionary periods.

INTELLECTUAL LIFE

German classical philosophy (rationalism)

The basic factor that determined the specific characteristics of nineteenth-century intellectual life was the greater attention paid, as a result of the modernization that was under way, to the processes underlying people's lives. The Industrial Revolution and the liberalization of social and political institutions, in spite of all controversies, made it impossible to ignore the temporal component of existence. As a result, there came into being an historical consciousness that interpreted the processes of secularization and rationalization of scientific thought in its own particular way. The desire to represent the whole richness of being on the basis of a single conception was combined with an increased attention to the process of becoming. The philosophy of history and the history of philosophy to a large extent supplemented logic and ethics as the basic themes of philosophical thought. History as a subject of study was transformed from the description of events in consecutive order into the systemic characterization of the processes of society formation. The world changing over time was perceived as the field of human activity. Evolutionism, the doctrine of the inherently orderly phenomena of improvement in nature and society, penetrated the most diverse areas of knowledge. 'Historical' genres flourished in literature and art – in social and historical novels, realist painting, opera, etc.

At the same time, life was being revealed in its contradictions: contradictions which provided a basis for both optimistic and pessimistic interpretations of events and of history as a whole. Against this background, the harmonious image of the world that had characterized the Age of Enlightenment began to fall apart: the critique of reason begun by Hume and Kant took on extreme forms, even spilling over into irrationalism; and attempts to 'flee' from the present into the future (Utopianism) or into the past (romanticism) became widespread. Debate ranged widely over human nature and the prevalence therein of good and evil, and over ways of resolving contradictions.

One substantial result of the changes that were taking place was the emergence of national cultures in Central and Eastern Europe and the development of a free human personality, of human self-consciousness. In this context, increasing attention was paid to national values and national traditions, thus shattering the universalism of the Age of Enlightenment; but this same emphasis on values yielded to pressure from the rapidly changing interests of individuals and groups. A crisis of values, of differences of opinion over the ideals of truth, justice and beauty, arose. Individualism developed, placing the individual at the centre of the universe and regarding individual perception and thought as the only possible criteria. Relativism took hold in the spheres of values and cognition, leading by the end of the nineteenth century to an epistemological crisis. Modern literature and art concentrated increasingly on individual perceptions.

Rationalism remained the nineteenth century's most influential intellectual current, especially in Western Europe, but the forms in which it manifested itself changed. The collapse of metaphysics resulted in the demolition of an integral system of knowledge: the previously unified image of the world was split into the world of nature and the world of man. The question of truth was likewise placed in a historical context. The strict division of knowledge into scientific and non-scientific gave way to the idea that knowledge grows gradually out of preconceptions. All this made rationalism potentially more flexible but also weakened its hand in the combat with irrationalism. These contradictions found their fullest expression in German philosophy, which became the most remarkable manifestation of nineteenth-century intellectual life.

All the philosophical constructs of the nineteenth century bore the stamp of the ideas of Emmanuel Kant (1724–1804). Although Kant wrote and published his main works in the latter half of the eighteenth century, it is no exaggeration to say that his thinking influenced the whole of nineteenth-century theory and philosophy. The celebrated Russian philosopher Vladimir Solovyev (1853–1900) believed Kant's 'philosophical criticism' to be 'the principal turning-point in the history of human thought, so that the whole development of philosophy, if not in content then in relation to thought, may be divided into two periods: the pre-critical (or pre-Kantian) and the post-critical (or post-Kantian)'.

Kant's philosophy transcended the previous rationalist philosophy of the Enlightenment, and in his early works he criticized formal logic and metaphysics.

The principal teaching in Kantian philosophy concerns cognition. Cognition had a strong influence on thinkers of that period, who concentrated their attention on the specific features of the process of cognition, those features constituting the chief meaning and purpose of any philosophical theory. According to Kant, the primary properties of such qualities as time, duration, space or causality, previously regarded as being inherent in things-in-themselves, independently of those attempting to ascertain them, were determined by the enquiring mind in its transcendentality.

In his opinion, science should concern itself chiefly with the study of the *a priori* forms of knowledge, not-so-called experiential knowledge. In his *Prolegomena* he writes: 'Things are given to us as objects of our senses outside ourselves, but of what they may be in themselves we know nothing, knowing only their phenomena, that is, the representations they produce in us by acting upon our senses'.

At the stage of the 'immediate perceptions' of the senses, a determining role is played, according to Kant, by space and time, which are those very *a priori* forms that order sensory experience in certain relations. Thanks to this *a priori*-synthetic nature of time and space, mathematics developed as true knowledge formed from synthetic *a priori* judgements.

Kant's theory of consciousness and categories made up his 'transcendental analytics', which, together with his 'transcendental aesthetics', represented an integral system. Kant himself referred to this system as transcendental philosophy or true metaphysics, whose mission it was to replace the false metaphysics which he believed should be demolished. It exerted a great influence on all subsequent philosophical thought. His teachings were of great significance for the critique of so-called rational theology.

Kant also worked out a moral doctrine, rejecting a sham morality based on the instincts and feelings in favour of imperatives which he himself formulated and of which he established a detailed classification. The will of every reasonable being is a manifestation of the universal law-giving will. As in his teachings on cognition, Kant paid great attention to the universal laws of nature.

Kant's philosophy as a whole constitutes an integral, complex system that embraces virtually all the main philosophical and epistemological trends and also ethics, politics, law, religion and art. He liberated theory from the old, dogmatic metaphysics while asserting the dialectical perception of the major categories of philosophy.

Kantianism engendered many philosophical theories but, in accordance with the laws of dialectics, it paved the way for Kantianism itself to be transcended.

The fullest expression of the classical German philosophy of the nineteenth century is to be found in the works of Georg Wilhelm Friedrich Hegel (1770–1831), who on the one hand continues, so to speak, along the lines started by Kant, Schelling and Fichte but, on the other, goes beyond them and in many respects parts company with them.

While taking up some of Descartes' ideas, in particular those dealing with the influence of mechanical motion on all the phenomena of the external world and that of rational self-consciousness upon the internal, spiritual world, and analyzing Kant's ideas concerning antinomies and the dialectical confrontation of opposing principles, Hegel approached the problems of consciousness from a different standpoint.

According to Hegel, the spirit achieves true freedom not by standing aloof from objects but by getting to know them in their true nature. The truth is not to be found in things themselves and is not created by things themselves, but it is revealed in the living process of the absolute idea, which includes the diverse forms of objective and subjective being, and which reaches the stage of full self-consciousness in the human spirit. Hegel had a very broad view of the essence of truth, which in his opinion was inherent both in ourselves and in objects.

The concept of the absolute idea lies at the heart of Hegelian philosophy. It is based upon the idea of the dialectical development 'from itself' into a complete and coherent system. It was Hegel who is given credit for elaborating the fullest expression of the dialectical method. The true dialectical method sets off 'intellektuelle Anschauung' against rational thought: it is the reason that divides the living whole into parts and initiates the thinking process.

The initial stage of the method, at which a given concept is confirmed in its limited state as positive or true, is followed by a second stage, that of the self-negation of the concept because of its internally contradictory nature – as Hegel puts it, the dialectical contradiction of 'thesis and antithesis'.

Hegel considers the real, true expression of the dialectic to be contained in the concept of the 'absolute' itself. The true character and essence of the absolute is expressed in its self-negation, and its opposite is its own reflection, the upshot being that the absolute finds itself and returns to itself as the fulfilled unity of itself and its opposite; and since the 'absolute' is that which is in everything, then a similar process constitutes a universal law. In Hegel's view, individual phenomena constantly proceed from one to others and return to themselves in a new, renewed form. The whole meaning and truth of all that exists is contained in this all-penetrating and all-forming movement. Physical and spiritual phenomena are joined together and are organically linked with the absolute idea, which simply does not exist as something separate.

The Hegelian dialectical method was thus closely linked with content: both constituted self-developing categories, one taking the form of method and the other being content itself. Content and form are shown to be inseparable one from the other.

The Hegelian system was of great significance not only for philosophy but also for the natural sciences. The same absolute idea, in Hegel's view, also finds expression in natural philosophy, in mechanics, physics and biology. Mechanics relates to the categories of space, time, motion and matter, and at a subsequent stage it includes within itself the laws of gravitation, the solar system and the laws governing the motion of celestial bodies. Physics for its part deals with objects – light, heat, electricity, magnetism and so on, while biology, where the absolute idea likewise prevails, covers the plant and animal kingdoms and the various organic phenomena and processes.

Hegel was much concerned with other forms of being as well, with the sciences in particular. Of particular relevance in this connection is his philosophy of spirit, and the so-called phenomenology of the spirit was a kind of introduction to his whole philosophical system.

Ethics, law, morals and history are all organically integrated into the Hegelian system and into Hegel's general theory: according to him, for instance, the state is the supreme manifestation of the objective spirit, the embodiment of reason in human life, a kind of absolute end in itself.

The doctrine of the absolute and the dialectical method which lie at the heart of Hegelian philosophy had a powerful influence on the development of philosophy and the human sciences in the first half of the nineteenth century.

Hegel found his principles expressed both in society and in history. In his view, the family, an undivided, integral social entity, is transformed by a process of division into civil society, which, in turn, overcoming its internal contradictions, forms a new integral whole, the nation, the integrating force of which is the national spirit and whose form of existence is the state. The nations of history and the (states) created by them in their turn pass through a number of stages connected with the realization of the spirit's striving for freedom. At a first stage, in the despotisms of the ancient Orient, freedom existed for only one; at a second stage, in Antiquity, it existed for the few; at a third stage, in the Germanic world, it was realized that every human being is free. Thus, the growing realization of freedom becomes the criterion of progress, and the pattern of historical development assumes the character of a spiral moving towards a determined goal – the German limited monarchy, in which history culminates.

Hegel's views and the Hegelian system are a kind of a summation of the development of German philosophy: the consistent line running through to him from Kant, Schelling and Fichte enabled Hegel to work out a new method and a new system. It was German philosophy of the late eighteenth and early nineteenth centuries that bequeathed to later philosophical theories a prepared system of views concerning the subjective and the objective and the process and method of cognition.

After Hegel's death a school was established that developed, extended and modified his teaching and that was to influence theoretical thinking throughout the nineteenth century.

ROMANTICISM AND IRRATIONALISM

The intellectual tradition of the Enlightenment also encountered opposition from the romantic philosophers, who could not accept the ideas of historical progress and of the rational nature and potential omnipotence of humanity. The attention of the romantics and irrationalists was focused on the shortcomings of the modernization process, the inadequacy of logical forms for coherent cognition of universal harmony, and humankind's need for God. Whereas nineteenth-century rationalism rested primarily upon the Western European intellectual tradition, irrationalism rested on the Central European tradition. Its development was linked with the slow process of modernization and secularization in Germany, where the Reformation helped to open the way for rationalism and individuation without breaking with the traditions of the Christian faith.

Irrationalism as a philosophical trend is closely connected to the romantic direction in literature and art, and in culture as a whole. Romanticism was a specific world outlook that manifested itself in politics, economics, history, literature, art, music and poetry. The romantics laid claim to universality, and strove to integrate all human knowledge, to achieve a new understanding of the world in its unity and its diversity.

Although in many respects the ideas of romanticism arose from the expectations created by the age of revolutions, they were themselves influenced by the unfulfilled hopes and by the contradiction between fine theories and harsh reality. Classical romanticism is, as a result, characterized by a split between ideals and reality; as a rule, however, the romantics regarded the ideal as superior to the real.

Speaking of the impression created by the victory of the French Revolution, Hegel wrote: 'it was a magnificent sunrise ... A lofty sense of rapture prevailed at that time, and the whole world was imbued with an enthusiasm of the spirit, as if a reconciliation of the Divine principle with the world had for the first time occurred'. Very soon, however, these hopes of a sunrise, of the victory of the 'forces of reason', turned in the minds of many thinkers into pessimism and a deep sense of disappointment. It was to a great extent out of this bitter historical experience, out of yearning for an ideal, that romanticism was born.

One of romanticism's characteristic features is the way it turned to the ideals and heritage of Antiquity and the Middle Ages. The Renaissance period was also, as we know, interested in the legacy of Antiquity, but the romantics' attitude thereto was quite different: for them, it was, as distinct from modern times, a pristine age, a time of integrity and purity. 'The turning towards Antiquity', wrote the German philosopher Friedrich Schlegel, 'was prompted by a desire to escape from the depressing circumstances of the age', while Jakob Grimm considered that 'there was more greatness, purity and sanctity than in us in people in ancient times, the glow of the Divine source still shone upon them'.

The ideas of the pre-romantic period were already clearly discernible in the aesthetics of Jean-Jacques Rousseau and Johann Gottfried Herder. Herder was one of the sources of inspiration of the literary movement known as 'Sturm und Drang', which strongly advocated the ideas of *Humanität* and national identity. Herder's philosophy was imbued with the ideas of historicism. Pre-romantic tendencies are also to be observed in the art of 'sentimentalism', in some works of Mozart and Beethoven and of the young Heine and Schiller.

In philosophy, romanticism was linked primarily, in Germany, with the names of Schelling and Fichte. Friedrich Schelling (1775–1854), is associated with the dissemination of the achievements of natural science. His *Naturphilosophie* was an attempted philosophical explanation of the successes attained in the development of electricity and its connections with chemical processes. On this basis, Schelling attempted to investigate the interaction of nature and humanity. He saw nature as a stage preceding self-consciousness, and he understood the common character of nature and consciousness as in some way representing their identity – the Ego and the non-Ego.

Working along the lines of the Kantian methodology, Schelling also sought to find in both nature and consciousness real opposites. In inorganic nature, such opposites were represented by magnetism (the opposite poles), electricity (positive and negative charges) and chemical substances (alkalis and acids), in the organic world by sensitivity and excitability, and in the realm of consciousness by the subjective and the objective. Central to his philosophy was his understanding of the dialectic of nature, and even when he subsequently developed the idea of some kind of absolute or divinity in which opposites met, the idea of opposites (both the clash of opposites and their reconciliation) nevertheless runs through many of his works. His teachings on the dialectical interaction of opposites were based on advances in physics, chemistry and biology, and for that reason his views were popular both among philosophers and among natural scientists.

Schelling's irrationalism manifested itself most clearly in his 'positive philosophy', starting from his work *Philosophy and Religion*, published in 1804.

Schelling also dealt directly with the problems of cognition, his view being that so-called rational cognition was determined not by deduction and proof but by intellectual intuition.

Schelling paid considerable attention to interpretation of the historical process of the development of society. He believed that a law of unity of freedom and necessity (which was later to become one of the central postulates of Hegelian philosophy) operated in society, but here again he made the problem of intellectual intuition and freedom the cornerstone of his thinking.

Schelling's views, in particular his critique of reason, followed the mainstream of German romanticism's ideas. He endeavoured to replace the simple, empirical explanation of phenomena by some kind of supersensory, super-empirical intellectual world. Schelling put forward the idea of religion penetrating into all areas of the state's activity, and he believed that the alliance of the nations should be sealed in the universal convictions of faith. In this respect, he was clearly moving in the same direction as Kant, with his ideas of perpetual peace and the universal alliance of nations.

Schelling also dealt with purely historical phenomena and with the philosophy of history in particular. In his early works he drew a picture of the gradual embodiment of God in history through the periods of the rule of fate (the ancient Orient and Greece), of nature (Rome and Europe) and of Providence (in times to come), but in later works, in keeping with the romantic approach to history, he transferred his ideal from the future to the past.

Another German philosopher expressing ideas to replace the old Enlightenment philosophy was Johann Gottlieb Fichte (1762–1814). Like several other philosophers, he 'rejected' many of Kant's teachings and adopted a more consistently idealist position. Fichte attempted to deduce all the diversity of the forms of reality, which he regarded not as an inert but as an active substance, from the action of some absolute 'Ego'. He also tried to raise and resolve the problem of transcending the dualism of object and subject, of nature and consciousness. In his opinion, practical activity exerts an influence on theoretical capacity. Reason, as he interprets it, is also fully practical.

Thus Fichte, like Schelling, was swayed by the same ideas as were raised by Kant. He developed the idea of opposites and he also inclined towards a dialectical understanding of the process of cognition, endeavouring to resolve the eternal dualism of theory and practice, of object and subject.

Fichte's philosophy started to take irrationalist shape in 1800, when he attributed divine qualities to the absolute 'Ego'.

Fichte devoted much attention to questions of law, government, commerce and property. In his *Addresses to the German Nation*, he set out his system of views on education. He advocated a new system of education to bring about a moral rebirth of humankind. This system foresaw several stages in children's education: contemplation of the child's own activity and sensations; contemplation of spatial objects; the free movement of the body, physical exercises and the development of 'bodily strength'. Taken together, these were to form the basis for German national education.

Fichte also wrote about civic and religious education. He advanced a somewhat Utopian idea of educational communes, all the members of which should follow general rules, subordinating themselves entirely to the tasks of German nation. He tried to link education with the development of reasoning and character.

Fichte thus in some respects was in the mainstream of German romanticism, dreaming of some ideal or other, while on the other hand he was trying to combine Kantian ideas with a new empiricism. He broadened the horizons of the German school of philosophy and enlarged the range of problems it dealt with, combining analysis of the process of cognition with practical ideas in ethics, morals and education. His writings had a significant influence on the development of nineteenth-century German educational thinking.

It should be observed that romanticism was also productive in the matter of developing historical methodology. Whereas the rationalists made a gift of source criticism to history, the romantics gave it hermeneutics, the science of interpretation of historical texts. One of the forerunners of hermeneutics was the German philosopher and philologist Wilhelm von Humboldt (1767–1835), who, although he considered the historical process to be irrational, was nevertheless not deterred from seeking to ascertain the driving forces of history. According to him, this principal force is culture, which determines the individuality of the historical subject and which he considered to be embodied in language, which consolidates the specific features of the world outlook. It is possible to ascertain the history of nations that have already pursued their path from maturity to degeneracy because of the fact that their ethical ideas and their values are preserved in the language, which binds together in a single whole our fragmentary knowledge of history. Humboldt was the first to propose 'reading' and comprehending the cultures of the nations of history as if they were a particular kind of text, instead of explaining the march of history by reference to speculatively proclaimed aims and laws.

The romantics thus centred their attention on cultural values and their decisive role in the formation of society and its history. They saw the *homo economicus* of rationalism, actuated by the logic of satisfaction of his needs, not as the symbol of progress but as the symbol of the degeneration and collapse of the primal ideals. They put forward their own model of the historical process, in opposition to the positivists' linear model.

The romantics' ideas on the philosophy of history were extremely fruitful, and linked up with the ideas of the rationalists. This synthesis enabled the French historian Edgar Quinet to establish the basis for a systemic model of society; in this model, an integrating role was played by religious values, which gave rise to specific kinds of political institutions, social communities and philosophical ideas. The idea of religious values as the basis of society made it possible to rethink the concept, introduced into the philosophy of history in the middle of the eighteenth century, of civilization and the theory of civilization as a whole. The idea of civilization as a universal process of development of culture, way of life and economy was replaced by that of local civilizations as mutually independent *socio-cultural* communities, or 'monads', as they were described by the French philosopher Charles-Bernard Renouvier (1815–1903).

Renouvier introduced the first classification of civilizations, dividing them into primary (arising out of the clan and tribe structure), secondary (assimilating the experience of their cultural predecessors), and tertiary (having a deep cultural background and being capable of looking back at the experience of the past and assimilating it in a process of repeated 'rebirths').

These theories were developed to the utmost by the German historian Heinrich Rickert, who set forth the idea of the 'relatively eternal' existence of cultural-historical types, as he called local civilizations, and created a model of the multilinear development of history, only later taken over by the positivists. Rickert demonstrated that civilizations are capable of responding only to those cultural impulses that are akin to their inner intentions.

The influence of romanticism on historical thinking contributed to the weakening of Eurocentrism, which remained the dominant tendency among rationalists until the very end of the nineteenth century. The gradual recognition of the equal rights of the cultural values of various countries made it possible for the Eastern European nations, including the Russian nation, to enter the European dialogue; and for the first time, it was not simply a case of copying and trying to improve on Western European thinking (Russia had some eminent 'Westernizer' philosophers such as Alexander Herzen (1812–70), Nikolai Chernyshevsky (1828–89), Nikolai Mikhailovsky (1842–1904), Boris Chicherin (1828–1904) and others, who mostly developed Hegelian and positivist ideas) but of creating a philosophical system reflecting the specificity of the national culture, its values and its attitude to the object and process of cognition.

Such a system was established by the 'Slavophile' philosophers Aleksey Khomyakov and Ivan Kireyevsky, whose ideas were close to those of the German romantics, and were further developed at the end of the nineteenth century by Vladimir Solovyev. Central to this system were the ideas of 'unitotality' (*vseedinstvo*) and 'living knowledge' (*zhivoznanie*). 'Unitotality' in Solovyev's works means the absolute, the integral whole, the only framework within which to understand individual phenomena and arrive at the truth. Its integrating force is God, and for that reason cognition is not possible through the reason alone. Cognition involves the human being as a whole, human reason, feelings and will, and involves love, the outcome of the synthesis of interconnected empirical, rational and mystical experience.

The philosophy of history, and in particular the interpretation of Russia's place in history, loomed very large in nineteenth-century Russian philosophy. Whilst the 'Westernizers' took a sceptical view of its historical role, the Slavophiles and their followers endeavoured to show that Russia was a potential leader of Europe and the rest of the world, a sleeping giant who would soon awake. These ideas received their fullest expression at the end of the 1860s in the work of the Pan-Slavist Nikolay Danilevsky (1822–85). Borrowing Rickert's ideas of cultural-historical types and local civilizations and also their four 'bases' (those of religion, science, forms of authority and socio-economic forms), he presented Russia as the embryo of a Pan-Slav federation, which would become the most advanced among local civilizations and would for the first time fully develop all four 'bases'. Although Danilevsky interpreted Rickert's ideas in a positivist light, he completely rejected the possibility of a universal civilization and universal ideals. It should be said that by no means everyone agreed with Danilevsky: Dostoevsky and Vladimir Solovyev, who dreamed of a reconciliation between East and West and of universal harmony, were among those who criticized him.

The nineteenth-century Russian philosophy of history thus paved the way for thinkers in a number of other countries which in the twentieth century entered upon the process of modernization – India, China, the Arab world, Africa. As a rule, they began by trying to present the values of their own culture and their own social norms as superior to those of the West, by the West's own standards (cf. the apologia for Indian individualism and rationalism), and then aimed to work out their own, non-Western standards, exploring the idea of the equality of cultures.

Romanticism was in certain respects superior to rationalism as it assimilated and developed the Christian idea of the limitations of human potential, an idea neglected by the rationalists. It was more sensitive towards non-Western cultures and had less of the cultural imperialism that was typical of rationalism. It took a more holistic approach to the cognition process and had a less schematic view of the human role in that process, one that did not reduce it to a function of the reason. For these qualities to bear fruit, however, moderation was called for. The development of pessimistic tendencies veered in the direction of crisis. What got lost along the way was the Christian idea of salvation.

The preconditions for increasing pessimism were created by the crisis of values that accompanied the process of modernization. This made it impossible to place any serious hope in the traditional values of religion such as the romantics relied upon. It was in reaction to this process that the philosophy of pessimism associated with the name of the German philosopher Arthur Schopenhauer (1788–1860) was to develop. He finds the deep-seated premise of being in the 'will to life', a striving after absolute domination, the presence of which turns the existence of the world into universal enmity, an enmity which in society is only partly held in check by the state.

The universal 'will' occupies an important place in Schopenhauer's concept. By his definition, science was an activity aimed not at knowledge but at the affirmation of the will. It was the principle of will that influenced practice. In Schopenhauer's view, contemplative cognition, which is inaccessible to science, can be understood and revealed on the basis of intuition, which he saw as belonging, in its highest form, to geniuses. Schopenhauer's attitude to the significance of the human will and intuition subsequently had a considerable influence on Nietzsche and Bergson.

Schopenhauer's ethical views are well known, and were also rather pessimistic. He believed suffering to be the basis of human existence. Human beings can find no satisfaction in anything, including religion. Here again, pride of place goes to geniuses, who are able to ascertain the universal will, but this is followed by dissatisfaction and by asceticism, which helps to overcome suffering. Schopenhauer's ideas were extremely popular at the beginning of the twentieth century, when intellectuals in many countries were subject to profound pessimism and loss of faith in human capabilities.

Nineteenth-century philosophers sought various ways out of the impasse of pessimism. One of these was to postulate 'eternal values' as the basis of historical knowledge. On the other hand, the German philosopher Friedrich Nietzsche (1844–1900) formulated a critique of the values of the society of his times, seeking ways of overcoming pessimism within the situation of a crisis of values. Having proclaimed his aim as being a critique of all values, Nietzsche proceeded to place at the centre of his philosophy the concept of life, defined primarily as a striving for self-assertion and might – the will to power. The life process is one of continuous creation, a struggle between strong and weak wills, in which there can be no rules or absolutes. Life's perpetual becoming implies a moral relativism and a relativism of values, but for Nietzsche becoming is not an ascending, progressive process but an 'eternal recurrence', cyclical transitions from the domination of the 'aristocratic', creative will of the strong to that of the 'democratic', degenerate will of the weak, the extreme manifestation of which is socialism, in which life denies itself and cuts off its own roots.

Like Schopenhauer, Nietzsche asserted that the determining force in both nature and society is the 'will'. The course of history, in his view, depends on the will of single individuals, and the driving force of history derives, precisely, from the 'will to power'.

The partial surmounting of pessimism in a 'philosophy of life' was quick to produce positive results. The writings of the French philosopher Henri Bergson (1859–1941), present a particular view of the phenomena of life (as distinct from those of non-living nature) that influenced many twentieth-century thinkers. In particular, Bergson presents life as a genuine, primary reality, representing an integral whole wherein the manifestations of both matter and spirit are mingled and where there is no place for the opposition of the subject and object of cognition, since both are aspects of life's understanding of itself. Only 'dead things' are susceptible of rational cognition. The essence of life is ascertainable with the aid of intuition, which penetrates direct into the object, merging with its individual nature. It is not difficult to see why Bergson's ideas were congenial to Russian philosophers.

In Bergson, intuition represents a particular, specific kind of cognition that makes it possible to ascertain the truth 'directly', outside of the process of sense and reason. Bergson regarded the source from which intuition derives as being the 'creative' or 'vital impulse' (élan vital) from which everything springs. Bergson's name is also associated with a much exaggerated, hypertrophic interpretation of the mystical principle. The rather amorphous concept of élan vital and the theory of intuition go together in Bergson with an inflated view of the importance of 'vital', primeval human instincts and of the role of religion.

Bergson's views were highly popular among the advocates of modernism in the early twentieth century. In particular, symbolism, with its exaggerated emphasis on the 'deeper bases' of human consciousness and the unconscious, was exceptionally attuned to the Bergsonian theory of intuition.

The 'philosophy of life' as a whole introduced a number of fresh ideas into the nineteenth-century intellectual world. Human beings began to be regarded not as rational or social beings, as they were seen in rationalist philosophies, and not as cultural beings or believers, as the romantics saw them, i.e. not in terms of their needs or their values, but as and for themselves, in the actual process of living. This was the beginning of the establishment of philosophical anthropology, which was fully to take shape in the twentieth century.

The impetus for the move towards philosophical anthropology came, in the nineteenth century, from both the rationalists and the irrationalists. The best-known representative of anthropological materialism was the German philosopher Andreas Feuerbach (1804–72), whose aim, as it was for the romantics, was the use of all human qualities in cognition. He saw the truth as lying, not in knowledge as such, but in the fullness of human life, and he took into account not only the individuality of human beings, but also their generic essence, their need for personal contacts and love.

Another tendency in the move towards anthropology is linked with the name of the Danish philosopher Sören Kierkegaard (1813–55). Kierkegaard set himself the task of defining the ontological nature of human reality in relation to the other principles of the universe, to nature and to God.

At the end of eighteenth century and during the first third of the nineteenth century, the ideological and political climate in Spanish America and Brazil was determined in many respects by the influence of the European philosophy of Enlightenment and the results of the French Revolution. Liberalism and romanticism gradually took possession of the minds of the intellectual and political elite. The liberal constitution adopted in Cadiz in 1812 was significant in the War for Independence of 1810–26.

The total refusal of everything connected with the historical past of the Spanish colonies and a complete denial of the positive contribution of Spain to the history of the peoples of American continent were characteristic of the liberally oriented thinkers and politicians of Latin America. After the declaration in 1823 by the renowned Venezuelan thinker Andres Bello (1781–1865) of the intellectual independence of the former Spanish colonies of America, all these tendencies were refracted in the historico-philosophical and literary works of Latin America romanticism.

This trend was widespread in Latin America in the period 1830–1870. It proclaimed the originality of each national culture and, following from this principle, declared the necessity of careful study of the historico-cultural past of the peoples of the New World. Most vividly and completely, romanticism showed itself in Argentina in the works of Jose Esteban Echeverria (1805–51), Juan Bautista Alberdi (1810–84), Vicente Fidel Lopez (1815–1903) and Bartolome Mitre (1821–1906). The last two were not only great thinkers, but also presidents of the country.

POSITIVISM

Positivism was perhaps one of the most outstanding phenomena in nineteenth-century intellectual life, exerting an exceptionally strong influence on the development of history and philosophy, sociology and other social and human sciences. It is associated primarily with the names of the eminent French thinker Auguste Comte (1798–1857) and the British philosopher Herbert Spencer (1820–1903).

The critical and historical approaches were developed more coherently in positivist philosophy. The positivists rejected any attempt to get to know the essence and purpose of phenomena, and confined themselves to discovering the laws of succession and resemblance in nature and society. They based themselves more or less systematically on the ideas of the agnostic philosophers of the eighteenth century. They regarded scientific, positive knowledge as only one of the stages in the development of the human mind, of which there were three: the theological, the metaphysical and the positive. At the last of these stages, the human mind has abandoned speculative ideas and explains phenomena only in terms of principles already established by science. As a result, the positivists put forward the theory of reductionism, i.e. explanation of phenomena of a given (usually higher) order by stereotypes of the functioning of phenomena of another (lower) order. Comte's reductionism is physical in character, while that of Spencer is biological and evolutionist.

Positivism as a world outlook was the most complete reflection of a new vision of the historical process. Comte himself, a mathematician and philosopher, and a pupil of

Saint-Simon, came under the influence of rationalism and Utopian socialism. In the years 1830–52 he published his celebrated six volumes of sixty lectures, the *Cours de philosophie positive*. *Le catéchisme positiviste* appeared in 1852, and *Le système de politique positive* in 1853–54.

Whereas Saint-Simon affirmed that knowledge of the human being, which he regarded as 'extended' (organic and social) physiology, was possible, Comte advanced the idea of knowledge of society (the so-called 'social physics'), which he understood as being the eternal unity of the social and the organic. He defined this new field of knowledge as 'sociology'.

According to Comte, sociology is the 'positive study of the functional laws of actual social phenomena'. Such knowledge presupposes the existence of two types of laws, 'static laws', which conserve and preserve society, and 'dynamic laws', which move it forward. The static guarantees order in society, and the dynamic its progress.

Comte also studied the development of the human intellect and the total knowledge accumulated by it. He discovered what he considered to be a 'fundamental' law, according to which this knowledge went through three states or stages: fictitious or theological knowledge; metaphysical or abstract knowledge; and scientific or positive knowledge.

At the *theological* stage, in a context of polytheism and theocracy, the dominant activity, in Comte's view, is not economic but military, and a slave-owning form of society thus prevails. With the establishment of monotheism, however, the role of slave labour diminishes while there is a growth in the role of dependent peasants and of intellectuals, who exert a moral influence on society. The *metaphysical* stage is a watershed: industrial production makes its appearance, and military action is harnessed to the task of defending economic interests. Such a society is not, however, without its contradictions, such as economic crises, inequalities in the distribution of income, or class struggles. To resolve these contradictions is the aim of society at the *positive* stage of development, using for that purpose the resources of science. Comte depicts this stage in Utopian colours, and he planned to found a religion whose saints would be the heroes of science and progress.

Comte rules out the idea of absolute knowledge and proposes to seek the origin of phenomena and to determine their innermost causes. In order to explain facts, he proposes to establish the linkage between various facts and, chiefly, to single out the basic facts which determine other phenomena. In his view, the progress of human knowledge consists in the generalization of facts.

Comte's positivism is in reality in line with the recognition of objective laws governing historical development. He regarded the law of the so-called 'three stages' as the main law of historical development linked to the structure of human knowledge and the chronology of knowledge (or cognition process).

He added the sixth science – sociology – to the outline of five basic sciences (mathematics, astronomy, physics, chemistry and biology).

Comte saw the Middle Ages as an age of theology and religious authority. The Renaissance and Enlightenment were a new era where the metaphysical spirit prevailed and critical thinking developed, including critical thinking about the social order; but this criticism was based on such abstract categories as law, man or the constitutional system. European society in the nineteenth century became an industrial society, and a positive scientific spirit developed along with the development of knowledge and technology. Society's ideal was a new social order wherein power would be shared between philosopher-scientists and industrialists. Comte looked for the main arguments in support of the law of the three stages in the development of the human individual, claiming that each of us is a theologian in childhood, a metaphysician in our youth, and a physicist in our maturity.

Having founded sociology, Comte sought to discover the laws of politics and to create a sociology of the *modus operandi*. The positivist method as a whole encompassed knowledge in the fields of mathematics, astronomy, physics, biology and chemistry (with references to Newton, Laplace, Lavoisier *et al.*). Comte was not, however, exempt, from the human tendency to elevate one's knowledge to the status of the absolute. He declared his philosophy to be 'the new religion of humanity', with its acts of worship, mysticism, sacraments and prayers. The 'Society of Positivists', which he set up in 1848, became a sort of religious sect on the lines of Catholicism, with claims to universality and control over science and culture. His 'religion' was based upon the trinity of *le Grand Milieu* (Space), *le Grand Fétiche* (the Earth), and *le Grand Etre* (Humanity).

Positivism as a philosophical current was born in France and became a new methodology, in the framework of which the desire to set history on a scientific basis was most fully expressed. It very quickly ceased to be a purely national school. It spread widely in England in the second half of the century, thanks to the work of Herbert Spencer, Hippolyte Taine and John Stuart Mill. The positivists wanted to change history from storytelling and an art into a science. They typically broadened the range of topics, turned their attention to monetarism, sought empirical methods and made use of sources, paying attention to their practical interpretation.

On a European scale, positivism left its mark on the development of history as a science: in Germany and Russia, where the emphasis was predominantly conservative, in the 1850s–1870s, and in Britain and France in the 1860s, where however, it quickly declined in importance.

Positivism's historical models changed as it developed. Comte saw history as a linear, stage-by-stage process (with the reservation that he regarded order as a value, as well as progress). Spencer criticized Comte for his theological inclinations and his unrestrained optimism. Such a state of equilibrium is short-lived and usually ends by collapsing into decadence. Progression and regression are for Spencer equally valid sides of the process of evolution. The French sociologist Emile Durkheim (1858–1917) laid increased emphasis on this, pointing out, as had the romantics, the multilinear nature of the historical process, this multilinearity being based on the different ways of meeting people's needs in different parts of the world.

As it developed, positivism thus shifted from a view of man as a being whose nature is characterized by reason to the model of *homo economicus*, whose nature is primarily characterized by needs and interests. This latter model received wide attention in the positivist philosophy of history and in particular in the works of the British historian Henry Thomas Buckle. He pointed out that the course of the historical process is determined by the relationship between man and nature, which in turn depends on the pattern of human needs. In temperate climates, the need for proteins and meat, warm clothing and expensive housing raises the cost of manpower, forcing the capitalists to take account of the workers' opinions and the rulers to take into account the views of the people, narrowing income differentials and differences in rights, and guaranteeing the dignity of the individual, which leads to an increase in knowledge and man's transformation of nature, i.e. to progress. Conversely, in hot climates people need only a starchy vegetarian (and thus cheaper) diet and can do without warm clothing and housing; manpower is thus very cheap, no one takes any notice of people's needs and rights or of their dignity, the personality remains undeveloped, and it is not man but nature that determines the character of the historical process, which is slow-moving or cyclical.

In Buckle's concept the positivists came closest to the idea of *homo economicus*, even attempting to derive cultural values from the means of satisfying human needs. It should, however, be pointed out that this was not typical of positivist sociology as a whole; the positivists held to the idea of a multiplicity of factors and considered 'monistic' theories as being metaphysical.

The rigidity of the views of the Hegelians and positivists on the philosophy of history and the sharp distinction they drew between the deductively arrived-at 'meaning' of history and the historical facts, led to a demarcation being sharply drawn between the philosophy of history and the emergent science of history. Since it was postulated that it was impossible for historians (but not philosophers or sociologists) independently to ascertain the meaning of history, historians concentrated on 'artisanal' tasks, like source criticism and bringing to light reliable information about the past, such as were performed, in particular, by the founder of this school, the German historian Barthold Niebuhr. His compatriot Leopold von Ranke, though he was a Hegelian, nevertheless considered that integral historical knowledge was possible only in the realm of the divine and that the practical task of the historian was to reconstruct the past 'as it really was'. The fact that historians turned to narrative, especially political narrative, caused them to disengage with the theory of social development, slowing down the progress of historical knowledge.

Positivism as a whole constituted a broad, amorphous current of opinion, embracing a large number of different outlooks. The positivists tried to find some third way, beyond idealism and materialism. The principal effect of positivism on history was to affirm a complex understanding of the process of development and a way out of the impasses of speculation.

By the end of the nineteenth century, positivism had gradually become less attractive, and different philosophical concepts and a new value system were established; the methods of studying and understanding human beings changed radically.

The ideas of positivism were widespread in Latin America in the last third of the nineteenth century and at the beginning of the twentieth. The most adherent followers of this doctrine were Mexican mathematician and philosopher Gabino Barreda (1818–81) and Brazilian philosopher Luis Pereira Barreto (1840–1923). These countries were characterized by the actual state support of positivism. In Mexico, Barreda received all possible support from the president of the country, Juarez, and in Brazil the active supporter and propagandist of positivism was one of the founders of the Republic, Benjamin Constant Botelho de Magalhaes (1838–91).

THE SOCIAL SCIENCES

A greater number of fundamental scientific discoveries were made in the nineteenth century than in any preceding period. Scientific progress was accompanied by rapid technological advances, which were changing the face of the 'civilized world' at an increasing rate. By 1900, European industry had grown approximately sixfold compared with the level at the beginning of the previous century. The face of the civilized world, which had changed relatively slowly in the first decades of the Industrial Revolution, was radically altered in the course of the century, although the 'age of steam' differed incomparably less from the preceding period, that of the early Industrial Revolution, than it differs from the age of electronics and atomic energy.

The social sciences, whose only standard of comparison was the era of the early Industrial Revolution, were unable to assess correctly the significance of many social and economic phenomena, and either defended and justified them or, on the contrary, attempted to discern therein evidence of the imminent end of a new order that was as yet still in the process of formation.

In the 1820s and 1830s, Europe and America entered the era of statistics. The developing economy demanded, in addition to the previously required data on the dynamics of, and trends in, external trade, information on the scale of domestic industrial and agricultural output and trade, for which only fragmentary and inaccurate data had, as a rule, been hitherto available; furthermore, such data had not been made generally available by the state.

The founding father of modern statistics, Lambert Quételet, in his 1835 study *Sur l'homme* (published in English as *A Treatise on Man and the Development of his Faculties* and later republished in French as *Physique sociale*), emphasized that, unlike the actions of individuals, the activities of significant masses of people conform to certain laws, and the task of science is not only to investigate the causal connection between the actions of groups of people but also to predict, on that basis, how they will behave in various circumstances. The rapid development of statistics provided a factual basis for sociology, which was at that time taking shape as an independent science.

THE IDEAS OF LIBERALISM

In Western Europe and North America, the leading positions in economics were, to an increasing extent, held in the nineteenth century by the ideology of free trade, or the 'Manchester school', led by the radical British politicians Richard Cobden and John Bright. Free trade was the most coherent embodiment of the principles of non-intervention by the state in economic affairs.

The consolidation of free trade as the economic doctrine of liberalism reflected the specific situation in a part of the most advanced region, namely Britain, where the trends in world development revealed themselves in a relatively 'pure' or 'classical' form, and which, having overtaken other countries, was able for about a quarter of a century to maintain a hegemony in five crucial areas (industry, trade, finance, colonial and maritime affairs). In the sphere of relations between labour and capital, the age of free trade was a time of transition from the economic control and social legislation of feudal countries to the social policy of the twentieth century.

Economic liberalism was linked with political liberalism, the defence of the principles of representative government, equality before the law, political freedoms and human rights. The free trade school's economic and political liberalism may be regarded as integral parts of a single overall doctrine, but at the same time the linkage between these parts was not a strict one. The acknowledged mastermind of liberal Europe, Herbert Spencer, gave the following list of characteristic features of political liberalism in his book *The Man versus the State*: constitutionalism; participation by the people in the affairs of state; universal suffrage; autonomy of local government; equal rights for women; trial by jury; even distribution of taxation (income tax); freedom of speech, assembly and conscience; freedom of scientific research, without hindrance from the temporal or spiritual authorities; limitation of the state's power to a minimum (to the role of 'night watchman'). However, the doctrine of economic liberalism largely remained a simple wish-list: not only were scarcely half of its demands put into effect, but no start was even made on meeting them during the period of industrial development in the nineteenth century.

Over a long period, various ideologies – the Reformation, the Enlightenment, nineteenth-century liberalism – succeeded one another. The successor doctrine replaced its predecessor, borrowing a great deal from it and incorporating the borrowed elements into a basically different system of views. There is no doubt as to the 'revolutionary nature', for their times, of the first two of these doctrines. In the nineteenth century, socialism – linked to them precisely by its 'revolutionary nature' – was for a long time regarded in certain quarters as their heir. This led to a distorted idea of liberalism as an allegedly covert reactionary theory (particularly as there were increasing attempts to give a conservative interpretation of liberal doctrine and of liberal interpretations of the basics of the conservative world outlook). Liberalism aimed to achieve its purpose by way of reforms and compromises with the old ruling strata and political circles.

The Enlightenment had two nineteenth-century heirs. One of them inherited the zeal for the rejection of feudal society and carried it over into a criticism of the 'reign of harmony' whose approach was heralded by the Enlightenment philosophers. Liberalism, on the other hand, built upon, and gave practical form to, the positive part of the political thought of the Enlightenment, inheriting the Utopian hope that the implementation of that programme in a new, updated form would ultimately lead to social harmony.

Despite all the harsh implications of economic liberalism, it did contain elements that reflected reasonably well the realities of its times. Its proponents managed to feel their way to discovering some of the laws actually governing the economic system as it then was. It is true that they hastily declared them to be eternal laws, corresponding with human nature, whereas activists in the workers' movement firmly believed that they were only the laws of capitalist economics. The truth was more complicated, as the experience of the twentieth century has shown: some of these laws really did have a solid linkage with human psychology (especially those concerning market relations, the direct relationship between the remuneration of employees and the efficiency of their work, etc.).

One of the characteristics of liberal ideology was its demand for freedom in the establishment and functioning of political parties, although parties in the modern form of mass political organizations, as distinct from shapeless social movements and loose parliamentary alliances, made their appearance only in the 1870s and 1880s.

Usually associated with nineteenth-century liberalism is the attempt to put into practice the idea of a law-based state. Essentially, this idea means simply the 'rule of law', with no indication as to which laws should be strictly observed. It is an idea that goes back to Antiquity, was resurrected by the Enlightenment thinkers, beginning with Montesquieu, and was even taken up by the ideologists of enlightened absolutism, who regarded the rule of law as the feature that distinguished enlightened monarchies from despotisms. The theoreticians of enlightened absolutism held that although monarchs themselves retained their role as the fountainhead of laws, in their capacity as 'first servants of the state' they acted according to the logic of existing legislation and general interests of society. Some of the thinkers of the Enlightenment went further, and their ideas were developed during the French Revolution; they considered that the idea of the rule of law was directly connected with that of freedom and participation by the people in the affairs of state. Here again, liberalism was only continuing and 'codifying' Enlightenment ideas, incorporating the whole complex of liberties that typifies the parliamentary system into a vague concept of political freedom.

Historians frequently refer to the crisis of liberal ideology at the end of the nineteenth century, an argument that may be accepted only with a reservation that radically alters the significance of this crisis: it was not a case of the decline of liberalism but of liberalism taking on a new form corresponding to a new stage of development. The crisis took the form of liberalism rejecting many elements of *laissez-faire* doctrine and gradually working out a social policy. Whilst the crisis of 'old' liberalism in this sense was a fact, the associated idea of a crisis of political democracy in the last thirty years of the nineteenth century is clearly unsubstantiated.

The liberals thought they discerned the features of the harmonious society imagined by the thinkers of the Enlightenment in the early bourgeois system. The father of utilitarianism, the British jurist and philosopher Jeremy Bentham (1748–1832), reworking the idea of enlightened self-interest – according to which the interests of individuals, correctly understood, coincide with those of society – thought that satisfaction of the self-interest of individuals was the way to achieve 'the greatest happiness of the greatest number'.

Liberal thinking traditionally saw the reduction of the influence of the military on social and political life as one of the factors contributing to progress. Comte wrote about the antagonism between militarism and the spirit of industry, while Buckle believed that, with the development of civilized society, social strata were formed which had an interest in preserving peace and whose combined significance was such as to prevail over the influence of other strata whose interest lay in making war.

At the century's end, this confidence was shaken by the rapid growth of military technology, and there was much talk of militarism, although in fact expenditure on armies and navies absorbed much the same proportion of countries' gross national product as in preceding decades.

Together with the gradual breakdown of class barriers and the establishment of civil and political equality went an increase in social and economic inequality. In the nineteenth century, in the culminating phase of the transition to a mature bourgeois society, the question of the liquidation of the new order was already on the agenda of the social sciences, and many suggested solutions were clearly Utopian. This situation left a strong imprint on the development of political economy, which acquired special prestige among the social sciences and in which argument raged between the adherents of the Adam Smith/David Ricardo theory of labour value and those supporting the theory of 'factors of production'. Underlying the differences of opinion among economists was the old dispute – continuing in the new circumstances created by the Industrial Revolution – as to which social groups' activity was productive and whether those groups created, or participated in the creation of, social wealth and were thus entitled to a maximum share of material goods. Ricardo's ideas, as set out in his *Principles of Political Economy and Taxation* (1817), particularly in view of his admission of the conflict of interests between social classes, was rebutted by economists such as Jean-Baptiste Say (1767–1832), who stated that the three factors of production – labour, capital and land – were the source of value. Attempts were made to interpret the theory of labour value too in this sense. In the latter half of the nineteenth century, many elements of the theory of factors of production were reproduced in the works of economists of the historical school (Wilhelm Roscher, Bruno Hildebrandt and Gustav von Schmoller) and of those who idealized small-scale commodity production (Jean-Charles-Léonard Sismondi, Pierre-Joseph Proudhon).

In the 1890s, counterbalancing the theory of labour value, the so-called Austrian school (Eugen von Böhm-Bawerk, Karl Menger, Friedrich von Wieser) put forward the theory of marginal utility, according to which value is determined not by labour costs but ultimately by the subjective assessment of the utility of that quantity of a given commodity which is capable of satisfying the least urgent of the individual's needs.

SOCIAL UTOPIAS: MARXISM

The nineteenth century witnessed the spread of socialist ideas. The best known and most widespread of these was Marxism, but even before its appearance socialist ideas and views were finding their adepts in various European countries, the most celebrated of whom were the Briton Robert Owen (1771–1858) and the Frenchmen Charles Fourier (1772–1837) and Henri Saint-Simon (1760–1825).

Each had his own specific views and ideas but they had a common programme and similar principles. They were united in their strong criticism of the existing social system and their outright rejection of the new order and the new phenomena that had established themselves in Europe in the late eighteenth and early nineteenth centuries. They were severely critical of the new industrial bourgeoisie, declaring themselves to be the defenders of the dispossessed. Criticism of social inequalities was one of the planks in their platform. Owen, for instance, spoke out strongly against the system of private property and competition, which he saw as leading to poverty and pauperization. He described bourgeois society as an irrational social system, and he blamed the introduction of machines for the worsening situation of the workers.

Owen's contemporary Charles Fourier endeavoured to set out his views in a more philosophical form. He believed that there were three basic factors at work in the universe: God, matter and mathematics. Matter is inert, and it is God who sets the world in motion with the aid of mathematics. He divided history into several stages: savagery, the patriarchal and matriarchal systems, and civilization. Harmony could be achieved by humanity at the stage of civilization, but inequality and the division of the world into rich and poor stood in the way of that harmony. The decline in the living standards of the population was attributable to profound social inequality, which in turn was the result of a defective social system.

At about the same time, another French philosopher, Saint-Simon, also strongly criticized capitalism and in particular the 'industrial system'. He sympathized openly with the ideas of the French Revolution and was even for a time a supporter of the Jacobins.

United in their criticism of contemporary society, all three philosophers put forward theories and schemes for improving the situation and for radical changes.

According to Saint-Simon, the transition from feudalism to the industrial system necessitated a transition from the theological phase in the development of reason to the metaphysical phase, and from the latter to the positive (scientific) phase. He regarded reason as the principal driving force and cause of historical progress.

Attributing supreme importance to the industrial system, Saint-Simon advanced the idea of the unity of science and industry, of scientists and 'industrialists', who should work together to control industry for the benefit of the people as a whole. He criticized the 'parasitical' character of the rich and argued that everyone should work and be remunerated in accordance with their work. In fact, Saint-Simon was the founder of the idea of the new 'social Christianity'. Owen also called for the progress of human reason and, like Saint-Simon, he spoke of socialism as a redemptive phase in human development and advocated the 'rational organization' of society.

The development of Russian socialism needs also be considered in the context of the history of European socialist ideas. It embraces a wide variety of different elements. Herzen's ideas of social (*obshchinny*) socialism, Chernyshevsky's attempts to find a rational society, and the Russian anarchism of the latter half of the century, most fully represented in the writings and activities of Mikhail Bakunin (1814–76) and Pyotr Kropotkin (1842–1921), all brought the Russian liberation movement and Russian socialism closer to the development of European socialist thinking as a whole.

In the mid-century, the social theorists Karl Marx (1818–83) and Friedrich Engels (1820–95), advanced a theory that was to have a great influence on subsequent developments. According to Marx's sociological theory, the basis for social development lies in the replacement of one mode of production by another. In the framework of these modes of production, a struggle develops between the 'exploiting' and 'exploited' classes. The increasing discrepancy between the emergent productive forces and the existing 'production relations' causes an aggravation of 'class antagonism and social revolution', leading to the breakdown of the old mode of production and the social and political system built thereon, and to the forming of a new social order. The replacement of modes of production and their superstructure of social and economic systems should, in Marx's view, culminate in a 'proletarian revolution, as a result of which power will pass into the hands of the working class'.

Political economy plays a paradigmatic, structuring role in Marxism. Marx's and Engels' reflections were inspired by an image of Europe in the age of the Industrial Revolution, wherein social priorities were determined not by spiritual, but by material factors and by knowledge gained in the natural sciences. It was therefore no coincidence that they endeavoured to give Hegel's dialectic a materialist character. The laws of the Hegelian dialectic were reinterpreted as laws of nature. Matter was proclaimed as the primary, everlasting and endless reality, which engenders consciousness. Consciousness and cognitive activity were, for Marx and his followers, entirely mediated by matter and praxis.

Rejecting Hegel's teleologism and Comte's positivism, Marx created his own version of Utopia in the form of socialism, a system where 'man's good nature will be liberated from the oppression of the exploitative relationships that distort it'. The image of socialism in Marx was eschatological in character. Against the background of Marx's fundamental atheism, this meant that Marxism, like positivism, would aim to fill God's vacant place and to resolve in its own way the problem of the origin of evil that had always vexed theologians.

Marxism declared all contemporary economic and social theories, including socialist Utopias, to be unscientific, as reflecting the interests of ruling classes who were unconcerned with seeking out the scientific truth (justificatory 'vulgar' political economy, the ideas of free trade, and so on). And yet, trying to claim support from its predecessors, the founders of Marxism often referred to Hegel and his disciples, the French thinkers of the Enlightenment and historians of the Restoration period, Utopian socialists such as Owen, the authors of anarchist theories, and representatives of the Smith/Ricardo British school of political economy.

NEW BRANCHES OF SCIENCE

Among the natural sciences having a direct influence on the study of society, an important place was occupied by anthropology, which emerged as a separate discipline studying man's origins, his place among other beings, the distinguishing features of various races, and human growth and physical development. Debates as to whether species evolved or were unchanging, and whether man was descended from one or several points of origin, exerted an influence on attempts to enumerate and classify races and to determine the possibility of their cross-breeding and acclimatization, and on the problem of ascertaining how old the genus *homo* was.

The mid-century saw the emergence of ethnology (ethnography), which, by studying life styles and customs, tried to provide a theoretical explanation of the various periods in the development of traditional societies (Edward Tylor, Lewis Henry Morgan, James Frazer). The development of anthropology and ethnography was one of the nineteenth century's contributions to the establishment of the complex science of human being, which belongs to the following century.

Alongside new approaches to the analysis of the social and political structure, considerable attention was paid to the study of international relations, primarily relations between states. In the development of social studies and, in particular, in the works of such leaders of liberation movements as Giuseppe Mazzini in Italy and Lajos Kossuth in Hungary, much attention was devoted to national problems.

In the last three decades of the century, the national idea, interpreted in nationalistic terms, became the official policy of the authorities in several countries, merging with a state nationalism that consisted in extolling one's own state and its actions, including expansionist foreign policy. Many research works were published, examining the various aspects and possible results of this policy and providing a basis for the idea of the nation (as a territorial, ethnic, social, linguistic and cultural entity).

HISTORICAL METHOD AND HISTORICAL SCIENCE

The predominant influence in Germany was that of the school of Leopold von Ranke (1795–1886). Its main fields of research were political history and the history of law. Ranke was the pupil and follower of Barthold Georg Niebuhr, who had been the first historian to establish the task of separating truth from fiction by source criticism and to lay the foundation of source studies. Ranke continued the development of methods for receiving objective knowledge of the past, which formed the basis of history as a science and which to some extent remain actual even now, in spite of all the changes in the theory of history.

Ranke made objectivism the slogan of his school. According to him, historian's main task was to receive unbiased information on the events of the past, free from party preferences: 'How had it really happened?' In this he went further than Niebuhr, separating not only fact from fiction, but also fact from opinion, from politically influenced estimates of events. Unbiased truth, in his opinion, could only be found in documents whose origins prevented the author from distorting it – like the correspondence of statesmen or reports by ambassadors, etc. Everything absent from the documents was non-existent for a historian. The documents themselves, however, were subject to historical criticism: the establishment of their correct date, the level of their authenticity, how well informed the author was and what political preferences he had. On this basis Ranke criticized contemporary historiography and created a large number of original studies, which became classic for his time: the history of the papacy and the Reformation, the history of Prussia, and of inter-state relations. He started the large-scale publication of sources.

Ranke's ideas were adopted and implemented by his pupils, the students of the Berlin University who later became distinguished historians: F. W. Giesebrecht, Georg Waitz, Heinrich von Sybel, Hans Gottlieb Delbrück, Wilhelm Georg Friedrich Roscher and others. They established the leading position of the German historical school in nineteenth-century historical science.

Ranke was developing his ideas in his polemics with another distinguished German historian, Friedrich Christoff Schlosser (1776–1861), who regarded the moral assessment of past events as the main task of historical science and accepted the influence of the historian's subjectivism on the interpretation of history. The victory of Ranke's school was a great step forward for historical knowledge. In the second half of the nineteenth century, however, in the works by the outstanding history theoretician Johann Gustav Droysen, the confrontation of these two schools was interpreted as

a special problem of scientific cognition of history. Droysen showed that the controversies between the restoration of the objective truth about the past and its subjective assessment are inevitable. These are dialectic controversies rooted in the very structure of historical science, which has to fulfil the parallel tasks of criticism and interpretation of historical sources, as well as that of the artistic exposition of the knowledge acquired.

In France the development of historical science was connected to the severe criticism of the Enlightenment 'philosophical history'. It was initiated by romantic historians like François René Chateaubriand and Joseph de Maistre, who, rejecting the rationalist view of history, stressed the anti-historical character of this approach to the Middle Ages and accused it of aiming to eliminate the individuality of national identities, to measure them all by the same standard, and depicted the development of society as a slow, organic process whereby the 'national spirit' took flesh. Conservative conceptions were opposed during the Restoration period by a distinguished group of French liberal historians: Augustin Thierry (1795–1856), François Guizot (1787–1874), and Adolphe Thiers (1797–1877), in whose works a central place was occupied by the history of the rise of the Third Estate in the struggle against feudal nobility.

Romantic and positivist historiography laid the scientific basis for the study of the history of Antiquity and the Middle Ages. Prominent here were Theodor Mommsen (1817–1903), Georg Maurer (1790–1872), Jacob Burckhardt (1818–97), Fustel de Coulanges and others.

The study of national problems proceeded against the background of the considerable successes achieved, particularly in the second half of the century, by the science of history. The writings of J. R. Green and Karl Lamprecht made a great contribution to historiography. The positivist historiography of this period is distinguished by its refusal to present history as a story of statesmen and politicians, its attention to economic and social history, its adherence to the idea of social evolution, the existence of objective social laws and their scientific study, and its belief in progress.

The major philosophical systems and theories, such as German classical philosophy, romanticism, liberalism, etc., had a direct influence on the understanding of history. Whereas in the case of Kant and Hegel, Schelling and Fichte this influence was exerted through their views on object and subject or consciousness and cognition, Schopenhauer's idea of 'chosen' men and geniuses had a very direct bearing on history and historiography.

Schopenhauer's views were very close to those expressed by the British historian, philosopher and writer on matters of public interest, Thomas Carlyle (1795–1881), who was also regarded as a follower of German classical philosophy and romanticism. Pursuing the Hegelian ideas of an everlasting and absolute divinity, Carlyle developed the so-called 'philosophy of clothes', according to which society, state and religion are the temporary and constantly changing 'clothes' of an everlasting divine essence.

Extending Fichte's idea of the active subject as the world's creative principle and sharing Schopenhauer's interpretation of the role of geniuses in history, Carlyle set out his theory of hero-worship in his work *On Heroes, Hero-Worship, and the Heroic in History* (1841). This theory states that heroic leaders are the principal driving force in history, whilst the masses for the most part play only a passive role. In the spirit of this general attitude, Carlyle idealized a variety of historical figures, even if they were on opposite political sides. A principal figure was Cromwell, to whom he devoted a work of apologetics, *Oliver Cromwell's Letters and Speeches*. He was also captivated by such personalities as Danton, whom he regarded as the hero of the French Revolution. In the 1870s, the German 'Iron Chancellor' Bismarck became one of his heroes. Carlyle's historical views, which gave scientific currency to many new issues and facts, had a significant influence on nineteenth-century historians.

Historiography made substantial advances in Russia. Nikolay Karamzin (1766–1826), who was an eye-witness of the French Revolution, used the ideas of the Enlightenment, in particular rationalism, the theory of progress and the idea of the decisive role of great men in history, as a basis for his thinking on the subject of the central role of the state and its leaders in Russian history. Karamzin succeeded in creating the first genuinely scientific concept, based on wide use of chronicles, of the history of Russia.

Under the influence of the French historians of the Restoration period, interest grew in Russia in the history of social relations. This movement was headed by specialists in European history, in particular the mediaevalist Timofey Granovsky (1813–55), a prominent liberal and Populist and an advocate of a European path of development for his country.

At the beginning of the latter half of the century, the predominant school in historiography was the 'state' school, which focused its attention on the history of the state and took only a partial interest in that of society. Most of the 'Westernizer' liberals belonged to this school, believing as they did in the leading role of the autocracy in the progressive changes in Russia, from Peter the Great to Alexander II, the father of the liberal reforms of the middle of the century.

The views of Sergey Solovyev (1820–79) enjoyed great authority at this time. Following in the footsteps of German historians, Solovyev was the first to offer an 'organic' approach to Russian history as a natural and necessary process, governed by the conditions existing in the country, and he criticized the views of Karamzin and the Slavophiles as being subjectivist and anti-historical. He was primarily interested in the internal causes of historical phenomena, not external influences such as those of the Normans or the Tartars. Drawing general inferences from the disputes between Westernizers and Slavophiles, Solovyev put forward the idea of Russia's 'intermediate' position between East and West and of the struggle for Russia by heterogeneous forces. Whereas until the sixteenth century pressure had come mainly from the East, thereafter Russia itself went over to the offensive against the East, in so doing becoming the vector of Western influences. This idea was repeatedly reworked by historians and writers on public affairs in the nineteenth and twentieth centuries.

The leading Russian historian of the late nineteenth century was Vasily Klyuchevsky (1841–1911), who derived general conclusions both from the achievements of the 'state' school and from the researches of the Populists or Narodniki. Influenced by the ideas of positivism, he explained the evolution of Russian society in terms of the specific features of the country's natural environment and national character. His historical researches centred on the Russian colonization of new territories and the concomitant process of the emergence of social strata and the reconciling of their contradictions by the state.

A particular feature of the nineteenth century was the increasing extent to which the historians of the Western Hemisphere became involved in scientific research.

The development of nineteenth-century scientific and social thought in the United States followed in the general mainstream, passing through the stage of 'early' romanticism, which was succeeded, as in Europe, by positivism. Like their European counterparts, American scholars adhered to the idea of the linkage between natural and human sciences. Many of them were educated in European universities, mostly in Germany and Britain, where they assimilated European philosophical, historical and sociological ideas, but whereas old and well-established traditions existed in Europe, human sciences were only just beginning to develop in the United States. In fact, only at the end of the century did many significant works begin to appear there in the fields of social and human sciences.

Research was concentrated on the colonial period in American history and on the War of Independence. Herbert Adams, Herbert Osgood, George Beer, James Ford Rhodes and others considered various problems of American history and philosophy.

The distinguishing features of American historiography are its achievements in the fields of economics and economic history. A lot of attention was paid to the settlement of the American West as the principal driving force in the country's history. This was the theme of works by one of the most eminent representatives of the economic school, Frederick Turner. He stressed the influence of the new natural circumstances in which the settlers found themselves and which transformed the old European ideas, traditions and institutions into American ones. He wrote that democracy was not imported into Virginia aboard the *Sarah Constant* or into Plymouth on the *Mayflower*, but emerged 'from the American forest'.

'Economic theories' received a complete development in the works of Charles Austin Beard, who at the turn of the century actively studied the economic factors and conditions of the United States' political history.

A number of independent states appeared on the political map of Latin America in the first quarter of the nineteenth century. Simultaneously, the long and complex process of the emergence of national cultures, the establishment of social thinking and of the social and human sciences started. Up to the War of Independence (1810–26), the defining ideas in the ideology of *americanismo*, which had taken shape in the latter half of the eighteenth century and which was essentially anti-colonial, were those of equality and sovereignty; but it was now the desire to grasp the nature of Latin American identity and comprehend the Latin American nations' role in the history of the Western Hemisphere and the world as a whole, to determine the most acceptable path for the newly-formed states' social, political and economic development, that came to the fore.

Anti-colonial theories, associated to a large extent with the name of Simón Bolívar, were developed in many Latin-American countries.

As statehood and social thinking took shape, increasing attention was paid to seeking the most acceptable model for the social, political and economic development of Latin American states.

The Argentinian thinker and politician Domingo Faustino Sarmiento (1811–88) turned his attention to a wide range of issues relating to the past, present and future of the peoples of Latin America. In his book *Facundo* (1845), he analysed the interaction of the two phenomena of 'barbarism and civilization'. In Sarmiento's view, this historical and philosophical conception which the Venezuelan writer Juan Liscano called a 'specifically Latin American theory', provided the answer to many questions, in particular those relating to the causes of Latin America's cultural and economic backwardness. Sarmiento saw the realities of national life in Argentina and indeed the whole of Latin America as 'pure barbarism', and he equated progress in the region with its Europeanization and the transplanting of the achievements of European civilization into Latin American soil. The United States was his ideal of a state system.

An opposite concept of Latin America's future was held by Bolívar's teacher, the celebrated philosopher Simón Rodríguez (1771–1854), who advocated the establishment in Latin America of a 'social civilization', distinct in every respect from the 'individualistic' and 'exploitative' civilization of Europe. He idealized the future of his continent, not its past: 'America should become the model of the beautiful society'.

The sincere faith that many of Latin America's men of learning held in America's historic mission came up against a tangle of political, economic, social, ethical and cultural problems, each with its specific features in different countries. A number of scholars and publicists in Venezuela, Mexico, Peru, Cuba, Brazil and Chile, including Andrès Bello (Venezuela), Manuel González Prada (Peru), Rui Barbosa (Brazil) and Justo Sierra (Mexico) were trying in their works to find answers to a number of complex philosophical and social questions.

In the course of its development, Latin American social thinking naturally came under strong European influence. In the first half of the nineteenth century, it was Hegelianism and then positivism that seemed most attractive, while in the last three decades of the century the influence of Marxism was felt in some intellectual circles, although by no means all the theoretical constructs of these historical and philosophical movements were taken on faith by New World thinkers.

At the end of the nineteenth century and the beginning of the twentieth, scholars were concentrating their research on the origins of the Latin American identity and the problems of *indianismo*, while increasing attention was at the same time paid to the synthesis of the spiritual values and cultural traditions of America, Europe and Africa upon which Latin American culture was based.

THE SOCIAL SCIENCES IN THE COUNTRIES OF THE EAST

The nineteenth century has a special place in the history of the countries of the East, which had, in the preceding period, been to a considerable extent isolated from the outside world in their intellectual development. Peoples from different civilizations that had previously each been developing its own traditions in accordance with the logic of its own evolution found themselves, essentially for the first time, in a situation in which their fate became indissolubly linked, and in which the nature of social trends was largely identical.

There were two decisive factors, one internal, the manifestation of which was the crisis of traditional systems, feudal monarchies for the most part, and the other external, the unprecedented expansion on the part of the West.

The nineteenth century and the early years of the twentieth century are often described as the era of 'the awakening of Asia', having regard to the universally apparent stirrings of social thought, especially in the social and political, economic and religious and philosophical areas. Intellectual effort was directed towards the solution of problems of great moment that amounted, in their totality, to the search for a simultaneous way out of the situation of stagnation conditioned by the burden of outmoded traditions, and a means of overcoming age-old backwardness without the loss of national independence and cultural identity. In a word, social thought was being directed, in the final analysis, towards the formulation of the dominant Eastern nineteenth-century nationalist ideology.

Comparison of the historical experience of the prosperous West with the state of affairs that had developed in the East prompted the conclusion that the upsurge and progress in nineteenth-century Europe and throughout the world stemmed from nationalism. Such was the conclusion of Liang Zi-Chao (1873–1929), one of the leading Chinese theoreticians of the period. He took nationalism to be

> the uniting of people of the same race, language, religion and customs, and of fraternal peoples around the ideas of the struggle for independence and self rule, and for the creation of an ideal State with the aim of achieving social prosperity and strength for protection against external enemies.

Awareness of the need for such a rallying could be achieved only through the education of the people. 'Education is the basis of cultural progress' wrote Ahmad Riza, an eminent member of the Young Turk movement. 'Education ensures the wealth and flourishing of the country, the greatness and future of the State, and the rights, life and property of the people'.

Educational movements became a main feature of social life in the countries of the East in the initial stage of the establishment of a nationalist ideology. The educational societies that were created everywhere had an effect not only on the cultural, but also on the political atmosphere. That this was so is convincingly demonstrated by the activity of the Indian Brahmo Samaj (founded in 1828), the Syrian Society of the Sciences and Arts (1847–52), the Burmese Sasanadara (founded in 1897), the Guandun Science Society in China (1898), and other societies.

The eradication of illiteracy and the development of schooling were the priorities of the educators. The organization of education on a secular basis, following the European model, was often attempted. Such establishments included, for example, the Dar-al-Funun (Palace of Sciences) in Tehran, that was regarded as a kind of Persian Eton (1850), the National School opened in Beirut in 1863 by the Arab educationist al-Bustani, the Dunwen school opened in China in 1867, and the Burmese Sam Buddha Ghosha school (1897).

Great hopes were placed on the press as a possible means of social enlightenment. The first newspapers and journals printed in local Eastern languages, which appeared in the nineteenth century, became 'beacons of knowledge'. As was noted in the first issue of one such publication, the Malaysian journal *Al-Munir*, published in Singapore at the beginning of the century by Muhammad Tahir b. Jalal al-Din al-Azhari and modelled on the Cairo *Al-Munir*, its aims were 'to educate Malayans, to arouse those who had fallen asleep, and who had forgotten their duty, to indicate the path to those who had strayed, and to support the wise'.

The educationists assumed justifiably that the national language and literature should be the main educational tool. The press played an immense part in 'restoring the rights' of Eastern languages and in the formation of a new literature in the countries of the region. As has been justifiably commented by the eminent Russian orientalist I. P. Minaev, 'the press in India did for the language what had been done in Italy by Dante and in Germany by Luther'.

Writers and poets were true exponents of the thoughts and aspirations of their peoples. It is difficult to overestimate their contribution to social thought, bearing in mind that, in the absence of the social sciences in the countries of the East (in the modern sense of objective knowledge independent of religious teachings) it was they who were frequently the first to express the ideas from which the social concepts and theories that were to win the minds of their fellow countrymen were shortly to take shape. Such notables included, for example, the Persian poet Abu Nasr Fath Allah Seinai, the father of modern Bengali prose Ram Mohan Roy, the Ceylonese scholar and linguist James de Alvis, the 'first poet' of Nepal, Bhanubhakta, the founder of the new Malaysian literature Abdullahah bin Abdul Kadir Munshi, and the Javanese poet Ronggawarsita.

It is noteworthy that those educationists who were men of letters frequently emerged as the exponents of advanced social and political ideas. For example, it may justifiably be asserted that the creativity and the activity of the Turkish poet and writer Namik Kemal, one of the leading ideologists of secret political organization 'The Young Ottomans' (established in 1865), prepared the ground for the proclamation of the first Turkish Constitution (23 December 1876). The popular political writings of Namik Kemal reflected views on the origin and causes of the collapse of the state, the nature of the law, the principles of the social order and problems of economic development. In the main, he and his comrades-in-arms supported a parliamentary constitutional monarchy that would assert the principle of national government and be incompatible with arbitrary rule.

Similarly, the creative writing of the Egyptian author Qasim Amin was distinguished by a clearly expressed social trend. He ventured to raise the question of the emancipation of women (in his books *The Liberated Woman* and *The New Woman*), and in so doing was demanding that the precepts of the Muslim Shariat concerning family law be re-examined.

The aim that the educationalists were pursuing in their activity was simultaneously to arouse the interest of their fellow countrymen in the national cultural heritage and to acquaint them with the achievements of Western culture. In the historical situation that had arisen, the problem that was uppermost in public discussion was that of the relationship between national traditions and the Western ideals and values that were equated with modernism. Those taking part in the discussion were split into two camps, depending on which of the two diametrically opposed viewpoints they supported.

In the one instance, there was a noticeable rejection of everything Western and an idealization of one's own traditions, which, like the social order based on them, were regarded as not being open to radical change. Conversely, the monarchical (and frequently theocratic) system of rule, the pre-capitalist (most often feudal) forms of economic life and the medieval moral precepts were regarded as meriting preservation. In that context, ideas of social progress as a forward-looking movement were considered to be in contradiction with the traditionally accepted outlook, which was customarily associated with a particular religious doctrine.

Thus, supporters of the status quo in Muslim countries justified their apologetically conservative positions by references to the doctrine of what was termed the finiteness of the prophecy of Muhammad. The *sura* of the Qur'an that proclaims 'he is the Messenger of Allah and the Seal of the Prophets' (33:40) was interpreted by them as evidence of the perfection of the homilies of the Muslim prophet, which could neither be added to nor amended. In precisely the same way, there was no need to improve upon the socio-legal order hallowed by Islam: it was both ideal and universal.

The idea of social progress being consequent upon collective efforts was also represented as incompatible with the fatalistic outlook of Islam; was there any need to talk of social progress if the fate of individuals and their behaviour were predetermined by God's will? Absolute acceptance of the principle of transcendental teleology admitted of the interpretation of progress only as a process of the realization of God's previously established purpose.

References to the appropriate tenets of their doctrines were also used by the adherents of other Eastern religions to justify opposition to radical social changes. For Buddhists and Hindus, for example, the principles of *samsara* and *karma* that were among their basic tenets, meant that the ideal was conceived of not as a higher stage of social development (therefore the improvement of society did not arise in the main), but as a higher stage in the next incarnation, dependent on individual behaviour and conduct, on one's *karma*.

The idea of progressive development was also rejected in accordance with the concept that the movement of society was not an ascent, but a descent. According to the Buddhist tradition, developed in the fifth century by Buddhaghosa, there are five stages of degradation with one millennium between each of them.

Given such an interpretation of tradition, social progress was naturally seen as something that was not predetermined and was, moreover, illusory; contrasted to it were individual efforts aimed at achieving personal salvation that, if not *nirvana*, would at least be a higher status in a new existence or birth in the 'Pure Land' where Buddha Amitabha rules.

The apologetic argument was widely used as a justification for what has been termed the ideology of feudal nationalism, which expressed the attitude of those strata of the population who opposed colonialism, and who laid the blame for all the burdens of life exclusively on foreigners. Monarchs and courtiers, landed gentry and feudal aristocracy, peasants who had suffered from the land-taxing policy of the colonial authorities, tradesmen ruined by the destruction of craft industries, and the local clergy, dissatisfied with the activity of Christian missionaries and the spread of secular ideas, together made up the varied body of those prepared to accept the ideological platform of feudal nationalism. The slogans of that nationalism in India in the period of the Sepoy movement called for restoration of the power of the Great Mogul and the formation of *mulk-i padishah* (the land of the *padishah*, the Mogul ruler); in Indonesia Muhammad Samman and his supporters declared a 'holy war' in 1881 against the 'infidel' foreigners, and were able gain a victory for a while, create a military-theocratic state and seize a large part of the territory of Great Aceh; in

Burma the anti-colonial peasant movement of the 1880s–1890s, headed by feudal lords and Buddhist monks, advocated restoration of the monarchy, supporting the claims to the throne not only of the princes of the Konbaung dynasty, but also of the pretenders claiming to be Sadja Mina, rulers and precursors of the Maitreya Buddha of the future kingdom of order and justice.

The diametrically opposed attitude towards tradition was expressed in a negative stance, sometimes extending as far as total rejection of it as being totally outmoded and unsuited to the conditions of the new times. At the same time there was excessive idealization of Western ideals, values and institutions. Paradoxical as it may seem, the modernist and pro-Westerners were able to call upon the same doctrines as the conservatives to justify their point of view, but they arrived at opposite conclusions, saying that if some Eastern religion makes no call for change and is even opposed to change, it must be rejected as a regulator of social relations, and one must arm oneself with the values of the bourgeois world that are capable of ensuring progress and prosperity. The modernization of Eastern society was seen to lie along the path of its secularization – separation of religion from the state, development of secular education, introduction of secular legislation, etc.

An example of such an approach was clearly exhibited by the representatives of *egaju*, the Japanese school of 'Western science'. One of the founders of this trend was Yamagata Banto (1746–1821), author of *In Place of Dreams* (*Yume no shiro*) – a work that has an important place in the history of Japanese social thought; he persistently persuaded his fellow countrymen that 'There is nothing to worry about in the mastery of the West, it is necessary to follow it and to trust warmly in it', because when it comes to the recognition of nature and understanding the processes of creation 'the only true way is Western science relying on experimentation'.

By way of opposition to the supporters of the *kokugaku*, the school of 'national science' (first and foremost in the person of such a thinker as Hirata Atsutane, 1776–1843) and to followers of the movements 'for the expulsion of foreigners' (for example, Sato Nobuhiro, 1769–1850), who called for the 'closing' of Japan, the strengthening of imperial power and a strong, centralized military and feudal state, the Japanese modernists advanced the slogans 'Eastern morals, Western skills' (Sakuma Shozen, 1811–64) or 'We shall take technology and science from them, but our morals and dedication are our own' (Hashimoto Sanai, executed in 1859).

The position of one of the leaders of the Chinese reform movement of 1898, the poet and philosopher Tan Sitong (1865–98), was largely similar. As was the custom in China, he combined his work as a fairly high-ranking civil servant with scientific work and teaching. Tan Sitong took part in the organization of the 'Southern Educational Society' (Nan Xiuehuei), and published a newspaper and a journal. In 1898 he was nominated as one of the four secretaries (they were known as the 'Supreme Councillors') of the Supreme Imperial Council in Beijing for the purpose of preparing and carrying out reforms. Shortly, however, in connection with a *coup d'état*, all four were declared to be criminals and were executed.

Although Tan Sitong acknowledged the high authority of Confucius, he nevertheless deemed it necessary to 'transform his teaching to the modern manner'. He was also critical of Lao-zi, considering that his ideas taught his fellow countrymen passivity and an attitude of reconciliation to

what was going on around them. He had an even more adverse opinion of Xun-zi, as the person responsible for the strengthening of authoritarian rule. Tan Sitong was the author of the *Study of Altruism*, which was published posthumously. He emerged in it as a radical opponent of the traditions that were the basis for the social order existing in China. He wrote: 'Above all it is essential to lose patience with the network of scholastic sciences'. Then to pierce the network of world social doctrines, the network of the Heavens, the network of world religion. Lastly, to pierce the network of Buddhist laws, Tan Sitong permitted himself to refer to monarchs as 'great bandits' and to their apologists among the so-called wise men as 'deceivers and sycophants'. He made inroads into the age-old precepts of the absolute submission of subjects to the ruler, children to their parents and women to men, asserting that such an order was contrary to natural justice. Tan Sitong called for changes in the Confucian examination system for posts in the civil service, a thorough overhaul of the administration, the institution of a parliament, education in the practical sciences, and so on.

A programme of political, social and economic reforms was advocated by Tan Sitong on the basis of premises stemming from a view of the world according to which the origin of all that exists in the universe is a single substance – ether (*itai*). Events in the world are the essence of its manifestation. Changes, combinations, stratifications, inceptions, disappearances and other forms of interaction between things are an all-embracing process, which Tan Sitong called *Zhen* ('altruism').

As seen by Tan Sitong, reforms of laws and moral precepts should serve for the rejuvenation of China and the prosperity of its people. He saw no point in mass demonstrations against foreigners, and he regarded a hostile attitude towards Christian missionaries as harmful and unjustified, since he assumed that the Chinese themselves, by upholding outmoded traditions, were to blame for the calamitous situation of the country. The general trend of Tan Sitong's views may be gauged from the fact that he attempted to convince his fellow countrymen of the need for the transformation of Chinese society by comparing the activity of Confucius with that of the reforming zeal of Martin Luther.

Neither the apologetic nor the nihilistic attitude to the country's traditions became a dominant feature in the social thought of the countries of the East. It was the reformist approach that prevailed as more realistic and promising and most in accord with the interests of the rising national bourgeoisie and the new generation of intelligentsia.

The word 'reformation' (Latin: transformation, correction) is used in both a narrow and a broad sense. In the first case the reference is to the Reformation (with a capital R) as an anti-Catholic movement in sixteenth-century Europe, which led to a split in the Christian church. In the second, it covers a more extended process started by the heresies, including such early reform movements as Lollardism, and continued until the seventeenth century – a process aiming at the transformation of traditional society into a liberal, modern one. It was an extremely complex process, especially in the sixteenth century; it is no accident that the latter has been called 'the age of reformation (or of reformations, in the plural), not just of the Reformation' (*The Encyclopaedia of Philosophy*, 1972, vol. 7, p. 99). The socio-economic and political developments in the countries of the East, as compared to Europe, were mostly delayed by three centuries. Hence, it was not before the nineteenth and the twentieth centuries that traditional Oriental religions and societies started to undergo processes of the kind that took place in Christianity and in many Western countries. There are many features of the religious reform movements of the East which are comparable with those that had taken place in the West; however, it will be more suitable to apply the term 'reformation' to this region in its broader sense.

On the epistemological plane, as Hegel believed, the Christian Reformation was caused by the separation of the objective and the subjective. The view of the sacred as something external in regard of the believer necessitated the introduction of a connective link, a mediator. The church, which assumed the role of the mediator, taught that one could be saved from divine punishment through formal actions: going to mass, assuming vows, going on pilgrimages, etc. Moreover, it was permitted to impose these actions on others by buying some of the excessive good deeds ascribed to saints and thus achieving salvation.

Luther rejected the concept of grace as a blasphemous haggling with God, and opposed to it the idea of salvation through faith, thereby superseding formal, *external* religiosity by making religiosity the *inner* substance of human being.

In the Oriental religions, the reformative process also involved an attempt to eliminate the separation of the objective and the subjective, to bring the believer closer to God. Each religion substituted internal religiosity for the external one in its own fashion.

Thus Devendranath Tagore (1817–1905) introduced a pledge that bound the members of the reformation movement he headed, the Brahma Samaj, not to participate in idol worship, and worship God only through deeds pleasing to Him. Since the power of the Brahmans in Hinduism is sanctioned by the caste system, reformers stressed the injustice of the privileges by birthright and fought against caste discrimination. The Brahmans' monopoly right to a knowledge of sacred texts and their role as mediators was rejected; reformers like Tagore held services for all castes, handed over the Brahmans' sacred cord to the untouchables (*Arya Samaj*), and so on.

In Islam, there is no category of persons belonging to the priestly estate by birth or official ordination. Here, the functions of the clergy are performed by the *mullahs*, the *qadis*, but above all by the *ulemas* – theologians versed in law who have the right to interpret divine texts and law. It is not surprising that the Islamic reformation put forward as one of its principal slogans the 'opening of the door of *idjtihad*', i.e. a rejection of the duty to follow a *taqlid* (the principles of the four legal schools, or *mazhabs*) and giving every believer the right of independent judgement (*idjtihad*).

It was common for the religious reformers in the East to recognize a high degree of the freedom of will, thus not only justifying the independence of human efforts aimed at a transformation of earthly life, but also raising them to the level of a moral and religious duty. The main ethical principal of religious reformers was effective participation in the struggle for the transformation of society on a new basis (more humanist than the previous one), rather than a renunciation of the world, asceticism and the search for individual salvation.

The concepts of *karma, maya, nirvana, mukti* and others were revised in Buddhism and Hinduism. The degree of radicalism in this revision varied, of course. Rammohan Roy (1772–1833) and Devendranath Tagore rejected them

out of hand, regarding them as logically unsubstantiated. Ramakrishna Paramahamsa (1836–86) and his followers saw individual enlightenment, or *mukti*, as a necessary stage in the salvation of others (just as the cars of a train can only reach their destination if drawn by a locomotive).

The attitude to religious asceticism, to monasticism, also changed. Previously, an *anagarika* (lit. 'homeless'), a wondering ascetic, was seen by Buddhists in Ceylon as a saint because of his complete renunciation of worldly affairs. However, according to the interpretation offered by the reformers, an *anagarika* was a person occupying an intermediate position between the monk and the layman, one that not only strictly observed all the injunctions of the Buddhist canon but also spared no effort in public activities (above all in the propaganda of Buddhism). Moreover, even Buddhist monks, traditionally forbidden to interfere in politics, were said to have the right to participate in the life of society.

It was natural for the reformers to aspire to put an end to medieval law and order, and to clear the way to social progress obstructed by the traditional way of life and the colonial regime. Nationalism mostly appeared in a religious guise, just as in medieval Europe. Nationalism and religion were even sometimes directly identified, so that every religious person could be enjoined to serve the cause of national liberation. Nationalism, said Aurobindo Ghosh (1872–1950), was a religion sent by God. He described the nation as an embodiment of one of the aspects of the divinity; he identified love of the native country with worshipping God; India with the Kali goddess, the divine maternal force; in the name of saving India from the 'vampire' – colonialism – one had to struggle and shed one's blood.

In an attempt to make the ideas of nationalism more accessible to the people, reformers secularized religious concepts, so that *maya* was perceived as a liberal illusion about the role of the British in India; boycott of British goods was termed *yajna*; the 'Bande mataram' national song became a *mantra; shakti* a desire for the national liberation. More than any other, the concept of *ahimsa*, fundamental to Buddhism, Jainism and Hinduism, was transformed. Though the fundamental permissibility and even inevitability of violent methods of struggle was recognized, both by Aurobindo Ghosh and Bala Gangadhara Tilak (1856–1920), leader of the left wing of the Indian National Congress, nevertheless a more moderate Gandhist interpretation of *ahimsa* later became the political platform of the anti-colonial movement in India.

In the Muslim countries, reformers sought for a moral substantiation of the struggle against colonialism in the concept of *jihad*. Thus Mohammed Ahmad (in 1844–5), leader and ideologue of Sudanese Mahdism, even raised the 'holy war' to the rank of one of the six basic obligations for any Muslim. The Babi movement in Iran in the 1840s and 1850s against feudal lords and foreigners was also run on the lines of *jihad*.

Thus, in general, the reformers' approach combined respect for the national cultural heritage with a sharply critical assessment of outmoded traditions, an anti-imperialist disposition with a recognition of the undoubted achievements of Western civilization, and a steadfast religious faith with an understanding of the need to be familiar with the achievements of modern science and technology. The complexity of reformist thought, its contradictions and its dramatic quality, are demonstrated by the most outstanding representatives of Eastern cultures in the nineteenth century, Kang Youwei, Swami Vivekananda and Jamal al-Din al-Afghani.

Kang Youwei (1858–1927) was the leader of the reformist movement in China around the turn of the century. As the son of a family that had produced thirty generations of scholars, and having himself gained the highest academic degree, *jinshi*, he had a profound knowledge of the cultural history of his country, for which he felt the deepest respect. Nevertheless, the defeats suffered by China in the wars with France and Japan, and the obvious backwardness of the country in relation to the countries of the Western world, convinced Kang Youwei of the need for profound reforms. He repeatedly set out his views in this regard in petitions to the emperor Guang Sui. It is noteworthy that Kang Youwei recommended that the emperor examine and, insofar as possible, follow the experience of the Meiji Restoration in Japan and the reforming activity of Peter I in Russia. Ultimately (in June 1898) the emperor accepted Kang Youwei's proposals and decreed the application of a new approach to state policy. However, the reform period lasted no more than 100 days before it was ended by a palace coup. Those carrying out the reforms were executed. Kang Youwei succeeded in avoiding their fate by fleeing to Hong Kong. Subsequently he was obliged to live abroad. While in exile he converted his 'Society for the Protection of the State' into a 'Society for the Protection of the Emperor', which had branches in Japan, the United States of America, Latin America and South East Asia. In Canada he founded the Chinese Reform Association.

The guiding idea behind all of this Chinese reformer's activity and creativity was the thesis: 'Change is the way [*Dao*] of Heaven'. He asserted that the prevailing ideology on China was fallacious because it was based on classical texts falsified during the rule of the usurper Wang Mang. He devoted a special work, *Studies on the Falsified Classical Canons of the Xing School*, to proving that the canons had been falsified.

In order to justify a critical review of existing law and order and traditional moral precepts, Kang Youwei appealed to the authority of Confucius, whom he presented as the greatest reformer. In *Studies on the Teaching of Confucius on Reform of the Machinery of State* he asserted that Confucius had been a convinced supporter of periodic changes in the system of government.

The reform programme that Kang Youwei himself devised envisaged the scrapping of the old examination system, the creation of a university in Beijing and of educational establishments on the Western model in the provinces, modernization of the army and navy, 'the enrichment of the country' by the improvement of agriculture (the spreading of knowledge on scientific farming and the use of agricultural machinery), encouragement for industrial development and the expansion of trade (including the granting of licences to private individuals to build and operate steam-ships, railways and mines), and a complete reform of the entire administrative system. While advocating assimilation of the achievements of Western science and technology, the creation of high schools to teach science and technology and other educational establishments for the exact sciences, Kang Youwei at the same time decisively opposed the activity of the Christian missionaries and the spread of Western ideology in China. He proposed wider promotion of Confucianism, the building of Confucian temples abroad and the sending of Confucian missionaries to other countries and, in so doing, 'to use against the foe those means that he employs against us'.

Kang Youwei's main theoretical work was *The Book of the Great Uniformity (Da tung shu)*, written between 1884 and 1902 and published posthumously. In it he set out the view of a reformer on historical development and his concept of the ideal society. Kang Youwei made use of the division of the history of society into three parts accepted in the Confucian canon *Li Zi'*, which he identified as the era of Chaos, the era of Coming into Being and the era of the Great Unity or Great Uniformity. The most remarkable thing is that, in contrast to the accepted Chinese tradition of turning to the past as an ideal 'golden age', Kang Youwei's social ideal was directed towards the future. He asserted that the China of his day was still in the first stage, i.e. in the era of Chaos, and he therefore recommended the development of a struggle for transition to the era of Coming into Being or the Lesser Well-being, so that the ideal of the Great Uniformity might be realized in the future.

The Great Uniformity presupposed a society free of any public, racial, national, class, social, religious or even sexual division. Kang Youwei saw the creation of a single global state as coming about by passing through a stage of the 'absorption' of small states by the great powers: he assumed, for example, that the United States would swallow up the American continent, and that Germany would absorb Europe. It seemed to him that racial differences could be evened out by a change of geographical scene and by the institution of mixed marriages. He proposed replacement of the family by temporary marriage contracts in order to eliminate sexual inequality. He expected that all creeds would gradually disappear from the world scene, giving way to the Buddhism, the religion of the future. Consequently, the Great Uniformity was conceived of as nothing other than a Utopia, the image of which would be made up of heterogeneous and, most often, incompatible elements borrowed both from his own Chinese culture and from Western cultures.

Swami Vivekananda (1863–1902) was one of the best-known public figures in India in the nineteenth century; he was the founder of a religious and social organization, the Ramakrishna Mission (which remains active both within and outside India).

Narendranath Datta (such was Vivekananda's real name) was the son of a highly educated and liberal minded Indian lawyer; he received a good education, including the elements of European philosophy and sociology, and became socially active quite early on. After an initial period, in which he was associated with the Brahmo Samaj movement, he subsequently distanced himself from it and became a Freemason for a time. In 1881 Vivekananda, having become acquainted with Ramakrishna, a priest at the Kali Temple near Calcutta, accepted his teaching, and after Ramakrishna's death he headed the company of his disciples and monks. Vivekananda came to wider public attention in connection with his attendance at the World Parliament of Religion in Chicago (1896). The address by the Indian *swami* (holy man) was a great success. He was immediately invited to lecture on Indian spiritual culture – mainly on Vedanta – in many cities in the United States of America, and later in Britain, France, Switzerland and Italy. On his return home Vivekananda was given a triumphant greeting by his fellow countrymen. It was then that he founded the Ramakrishna Mission and became an active preacher.

Vivekananda's creative writing and activity pursued the aim of arousing India, and awakening simultaneous feelings of pride and shame in his fellow countrymen. Pride for the wealth of their cultural heritage (in that sense Vivekananda was disgusted by what he regarded as the excessively critical attitude of Indian educationalists, modernizers and many reformers). Shame for the calamitous situation of a great country and its population of many millions. In his opinion there were two main reasons for the 'degradation of the nation'. First, there was the indifference of the property-owning classes to the needs of the people. In one interview he referred to disregard of the masses as 'a great national crime'. Second, there was the passivity of the Indians, their unwillingness and inability to oppose evil in its social manifestations.

Vivekananda was convinced that the situation in India could be changed for the better only through the religious feelings of the people. In his words, the Indians were capable of understanding politics and sociology only through religion, which was 'the theme, while all the rest was merely the variations on the national melody of life'.

Vivekananda interpreted the meaning of religious duty and service in a fundamentally different manner from that traditionally accepted in Hinduism. He asserted that man must believe, above all, in himself. 'Losing faith in one's self means losing faith in God' (Vivekananda, 1994: 195). This faith presupposed recognition of the supreme status of a human being in the universe and hence of service to him. In answer to the question, where to go to seek God, Vivekananda answered: 'Are not all the poor, the miserable, the weak, Gods? Why not worship them first?' (1964: vol. 5, p. 51).

The Indian reformer rejected the egoistic interpretation of *mukti* as the obtaining of personal salvation. In his interpretation, personal salvation was achievable only through service to the people: 'It is only by doing good to others that one attains the one's own good' (1994: 107). It is only by leading others to *mukti* that one attains it oneself.

Jamal al-Din al-Afghani (1839–97) has a very special place among the reformers of the East, since his activities and views were not confined within a national framework, but were models for the multi-ethnic Muslim world as a whole, with all its diversity of states; the inception of the ideology of pan-Islamicism and its development are associated with his name.

One of the *ayats* of the *Qur'an* that Afghani most loved and most frequently quoted was *ayat* 12 (*sura* 13): 'Surely, Allah would not withdraw a favour that He has conferred upon a people, until they change their own attitude towards Him'. He assumed that the need for a fundamental reform of Muslim society must begin with changes in the frame of mind of people and above all of spiritual teachers: 'No reform can be carried out', he declared, 'until religious leaders attempt to reform their own minds, until they comprehend the utility of science and culture' (Pakdaman, 1969: 246). The main thing that Afghani attempted to instil into his fellow believers was that material prosperity was directly dependent on the ability of the people to make use of scientific achievements. His explanation for the causes of the calamitous situation of the countries of the East was that they were unaware, to use his own words, 'of the noble and important role of scholars'. In addressing a conference on the progress of science and the professions in the new Dar al-Funun university in Istanbul (December 1870), Afghani likened the scholar to a prophet, declaring

that prophesy was as much a profession (*sina'a*) as medicine, philosophy, mathematics and so on. The difference between them was that prophetic truth was the fruit of inspiration, whereas scientific truth was the product of reason. The precepts of the prophets changed with the times and with conditions. Scientific truth, on the other hand, was universal. He even asserted that prophesy was not a requisite for all epochs, but that 'scientific guidance that is capable of raising humankind out of the bog of obscurantism and flailing around onto the path of progress and prosperity is always needed' (Pakdaman, 1969: 47). This address was denounced as heretical and Afghani was obliged to leave Istanbul on the pretext of a pilgrimage to Mecca.

Jamal-al-Din drew certain conclusions for himself from this event: it strengthened him in thinking that positive changes in the Islamic world were impossible without making an appeal to religious feelings and arguing that reforms were in line with the basic tenets of the faith. Thereafter he constantly made use of religious slogans for the achievement of political aims, chief among which was the renaissance of the Muslim peoples.

It is common knowledge that nationalism as an ideology asserting that national unity is the foundation of statehood is in principle in opposition to the precepts of Islam. Nationalism is here identified with *asabiyya* ('love of one's own'), traditionally condemned by the prophet Muhammad, who regarded it as group solidarity, loyalty exclusively to one's own tribe, one's people, and thus excluding union in the *umma* – the Muslim community that does not recognize racial, ethnic and other differences. On that basis, but most importantly understanding that the Muslim people, when once united, would be more readily able to withstand the imperialist onslaught, Afghani advanced a pan-Islamic programme, in which national solidarity was contrasted to the solidarity of co-religionists: 'Muslims know no other true nationality apart from their religion'.

The newspaper *Al-Urwa al-Wuthqa* ('The Fast Knot'), which Afghani began to publish with Muhammad 'Abduh in March 1884, became the mouthpiece for pan-Islamic propaganda. Despite the fact that it appeared for only eight months, it had a very great influence on pan-Islamic attitudes. The nature of the material published by the newspaper is illustrated, for example, by the article 'Muslim Unity', in which it was said that

> European states justify the humiliation to which they subject the countries of the East by the backwardness of those countries. Those same states are attempting by every means at their disposal, even by war, to prevent any attempts at reforms or the rebirth of the Muslim peoples. That makes it necessary for the Muslim peoples to unite in a great defensive alliance to save themselves from destruction. They must master the achievements of science and technology and learn the secrets of European power.
> (*A History of Muslim Philosophy*, 1963–66, vol. 2, p. 1487)

Projects for an alliance of the Muslim countries were repeatedly drawn up. Afghani appealed at various times to the Khedive of Egypt, the Mahdi of Sudan, the Shah of Persia and, lastly, the Sultan of the Ottoman Empire. Monarchy was not a political ideal for Afghani, as is convincingly demonstrated by what he did for the establishment of parliamentary democracy in Egypt, and by his conviction that it was permissible to overthrow an 'unjust' monarch. Because, however, he saw eradication of foreign domination as the most immediate task, he relegated the question of the nature of political power to the background.

Afghani sought support not only from Eastern monarchs, but also from the ruling circles of various European powers, in an attempt to play upon inter-imperialist contradictions. However, neither the Eastern monarchs nor the Western governments were interested in carrying out pan-Islamic projects. It was only shortly before his death that Jamal al-Din acknowledged the error of his calculations, when he wrote to a Persian friend:

> Might it not have been better if I had sown the seeds of my ideas in the fertile soil of popular thought, rather than in the barren ground of royal courts? Everything grows and flourishes in the first, and everything withers in the second.
>
> (Pakdaman, 1969: 326)

The foundations of nationalist ideology in the countries of the East laid by the social thought of the nineteenth century were subsequently to be built upon in the twentieth century, which heralded in practical realization of the ideological and political machinery for the achievement of state sovereignty. A range of new problems appeared on the agenda: how to find the most effective models of national development, and the search for ways of acquiring the status of a subject of world politics with equal rights for those who had previously been deprived of those rights.

THE LINK BETWEEN THE HUMAN AND NATURAL SCIENCES

The large number of fundamental discoveries made in the natural sciences greatly surpassed the more modest achievements of the social sciences, which as a rule and by their very nature do not lend themselves to experimental verification. Attempts were therefore made to apply the methods of the natural sciences to the social sciences. The mechanical identification of biological phenomena with social phenomena was clearly evident in so-called 'Social Darwinism', in attempts to equate the functioning of biological and social structures (Spencer), and in the drawing of an artificial analogy between society and the animal or human organism (Paul von Lilienfeld, Albert Schäffle, René Worms), out of which arose the racial and anthropological theories of Gobineau, Houston Chamberlain and others.

The actual movement that was known as Social Darwinism and which carried over the biological laws discovered by Darwin into social life came into being in the latter half of the nineteenth century. The theory of the evolution of living nature first set forth by Darwin in 1859 in his great work *On the Origin of Species by Means of Natural Selection* of course contained a proposition concerning the constant variability and evolution of species. Variability and natural selection were taken by the proponents of Social Darwinism as being the driving force behind development as well. Social Darwinism was also closely allied with Malthusianism, in which the ideas of natural selection were likewise given wide circulation.

Benjamin Kidd, in his *Social Evolution* (1894), replaced Spencer's 'survival of the fittest' within a given state with the idea of a struggle for survival by nations and races, and tried to prove that religion, by promoting altruism, was the instrument which softened the impact of the harsh laws of social development. 'Social biologism' emphasized the biological components of social processes.

The famous physiologist Claude Bernard dismissed as unscientific the theory of a special 'life force', distinguishing organic from inorganic nature, and urged that research should seek the directly material causes of the phenomena under study. Attempts to derive psychological phenomena in a mechanical fashion from physical ones did not, however, produce positive results. The representatives of so-called 'physiological materialism' held that thought was a secretion of the brain and that the content of individual and social consciousness was directly determined by physiological processes dependent on diet, climate and other natural factors.

The aforementioned works of Nietzsche expressed revulsion against the limitations of the 'liberal herd' and 'socialist egalitarianism'. Nietzsche demanded a 'revaluation of all values', of political and ethical norms, in the name of strengthening the will to power and the domination of the masses by *Übermenschen*. Sigmund Freud's theory of psychoanalysis, which was formulated around the turn of the century, ties in with Nietzsche's philosophy, as well as with the widely held belief in analogies between social and biological systems. This theory rested on the idea that the principal role in human behaviour is played by unconscious animal instincts that are rooted in the sexual impulses experienced in childhood. Civilization's role is primarily to curb these instincts with the help of religion and morality.

The French school of sociology (Durkheim), which included aspects of anthropology and psychology and which was positivist in its basic approach, also had an international following at the end of the century. Durkheim was of the view that sociology should concentrate on social factors that were independent of individuals and that had a compelling effect on them, especially changes in population density and the growth of social contacts, which led to a transition from 'mechanical' to 'organic' solidarity, In the mass, imitation thus transformed 'thousands of people who have congregated together into a single animal, a nameless, monstrous beast'. One of the authors of the 'theory of imitation' declared that it provided the key to understanding of social processes.

The progress of statistics made it possible to place empirical research into the causes and roots of crime on a firm basis. Until the early nineteenth century, the notion of crime as the product of malign will predominated in criminology. Supplementary evidence later showed the impact of social causes on the crime rate and the nature of crimes and the composition, by sex and age, of the criminal community. In the last decades of the century, the anthropological school whose acknowledged leader was Cesare Lombroso laid claim to predominance. Lombroso put forward the idea of born criminals, preordained by their physical and psychological peculiarities to enter and remain on the path of crime. (In the twentieth century, Lombroso's ideas, to which his contemporaries objected strongly, served to encourage research into the genetic and hormonal basis of criminality.) The dispute between the social and anthropological tendencies was not confined to criminology, but spread to many other branches of social studies.

The process of secularization of social life and of state and political structures, with the church maintaining its position for the most part on the level of everyday life only, continued during the nineteenth century. This gave rise to a tendency towards a reconciliation between religion and the doctrines of liberalism as well as social Utopias. The confrontation between science and religion that characterized the preceding age of Enlightenment decreased considerably, which, however, did not prevent the development of critical research into the origins of Christianity. As a result, it was not the confrontation of science and religion but their alienation one from the other that prevailed, although it did spill over into confrontation at the time when the papacy was pressing claims, as formulated by the Vatican Council (1869–70), amounting to a demand for the church's control over science and social and political thought. The American historian John William Draper, the author of a widely known *History of the Conflict between Religion and Science* (1872), referred to these claims as a revolt against modern civilization.

Both the natural and social sciences generally tried to exclude the relationship between science and religion from consideration as being a problem outside their purview, while science itself began to lay claims to a monopoly of the truth. Claims that were, at least at the level of development science had then reached, unfounded.

The nineteenth century was on the whole an age of optimism, of a belief in the goodness of human nature and in the great potentialities of science, a belief that science had come close to solving the enigma of the origins of humanity and of some of the mysteries of life and death.

SOCIAL THINKING AND HUMAN SCIENCES AT THE TURN OF THE NINETEENTH CENTURY

The end of the nineteenth century was to a large extent the period of revision of the classical philosophical model – its transformation or rejection – and the genesis of non-classical philosophy. The classical model itself was pregnant with ideas that made it possible to create non-classical philosophy. Kant's idea of reason's limited capabilities (the incognoscibility of the 'thing-in-itself') led to the development of positive philosophy, utilitarianism and pragmatism, while Schelling's idea of the significance of irrational forms of cognition brought to life Kierkegaard's and Schopenhauer's irrationalism, as well as the 'philosophy of life' and intuitivism.

Richard Avenarius (1843–96) and Ernst Mach (1838–1916) were the most outstanding representatives of philosophical thinking of the period. Their principal field of interest was the problem of cognitive value of human knowledge. According to them, the solutions to traditional philosophical problems – those of existence, the objectivity of cognition, values – cannot be regarded as scientific, as they all are the problems of essence, which, from the view of human cognition, is the eternal 'thing-in-itself', and – thus – incomprehensible. Only cognition dealing with phenomena, based on experience, can be of value, and empirical description of facts is the principal form of knowledge. According to this approach a single science – the natural one – is the model of positive (correct) cognition. While early positivism (that of Auguste Comte and Herbert Spencer) was characterized primarily by the genetic (psychological) approach to experience (meaning that cognition originates from experience), the methodological approach became dominant later (i.e. cognition is tested and controlled by experience). The substance, however, remained the same: for both approaches experience was the criterion dividing scientific and empirical knowledge. Therefore, description and systematization of facts was the

only task of science. The research process itself was reduced to watching, the collection of data, and then to their transformation into scientific theories and laws. The development of science, therefore, is a purely cumulative process – that of the permanent addition of new terms and laws to a group of theses.

This methodological approach formed the basis of empiriocriticism, represented by Avenarius and Mach; in the field of psychology positivism developed into John Stuart Mill's utilitarianism and William James' pragmatism; in the social sciences it was reflected in the philosophical and sociological concepts of Max Weber.

The philosophical ideas of the Austrian philosopher and physicist Ernst Mach are based on Kant's thesis that only the phenomena of things, but not their essence, are susceptible of cognition. But, unlike Kant, Mach denies the existence of objective reality, the 'things-in-themselves'. Science does not reflect objective reality, it is the manifestation of the adaptive biological function of the human organism (in accordance with Darwin's theory of evolution). Taking this thesis as a point of departure, Mach created the so called 'biological-economic cognition theory' with the 'economy of thought' as its basic principle. Both natural laws and scientific notions do not reflect any objective links between things. They are just products of the human spirit, created to satisfy the needs of the cognizing individual and having no meaning without the man. Therefore, Mach argues, the question of objective substance of a scientific theory is meaningless on the whole. What philosophers regard as objective reality, as a body, are in fact only 'logical symbols' of the complexes of our sensations.

The construction of these logical symbols in thinking is similar to the stenographic recording of a speech. The atom, the molecule, the mass, etc., according to Mach, are not objective realities, but only symbols in the economical description of sensations. In Mach's system the principle of economy of thought leads to the thesis of 'description' as the ideal of science.

Almost simultaneously, and independently from Mach, the Swiss philosopher Richard Avenarius elaborated his principal theory, according to which economy of force is the cornerstone of theoretical thinking. Avenarius regarded philosophy as the analysis of a complex of empirical data under the principle of minimal waste of force. Every science, including philosophy, should reject all speculative notions exceeding the bounds of experience. The laws of cognition are by their very nature absolutely different from the recognized norms of logic and the demands of pure reason; their significance is biological, not logical. Science should restore the natural outlook towards the world, instead of obscuring it by metaphysical constructions. In his famous theory of introection, Avenarius gave an explanation to the genesis of metaphysical and dualistic prejudices.

In essence this theory stated that joint human activities are based on a proposition that other people are the same kind of beings as myself, i.e. their feelings, thoughts and experience are similar to my own. So it is necessary to distinguish my picture of the world from the other one, to discern different aspects of the surrounding reality. Thus the perception of the dualistic opposition between the inner and the outer world, between the subjective phenomenon and objective reality is formed. This is called introection. It occurs when we are not satisfied with mere description of the things we perceive and those other people perceive. We try to find these perceptions either within ourselves, or within the people around us. Introection, Avenarius argued, is the 'reduplication of the world', the creation of an illusion that apart from the world of objects given to us directly in our experience, there is a world of perceptions, existing somewhere within our soul or consciousness. The introection formula is a short manifestation of a long row of dualist oppositions, and therefore, according to the philosopher, it should be eliminated. This is the elimination of the metaphysical opposition of spirit and matter, and, therefore, of subjectivism, agnosticism, spiritualist and materialist metaphysics.

The founders of empiriocriticism did not create a 'school' in the strict sense. But some aspects of their pure experience theories influenced many outstanding philosophers and psychologists of their time.

The principal ideas of empiriocriticism have much in common with the 'immanent philosophy' of the late nineteenth century, represented by the Neokantian Marburg and Baden schools.

The 'immanent philosophy', probably more than any other school of that period, accepts the idea that everything real is immanent to Ego, i.e. existence is immanent to consciousness (is contained in that consciousness). The 'immanent philosophy' in essence was limiting itself to the boundaries of our consciousness, to the data of our experience. The German philosophers Wilhelm Schuppe, M. Kauffmann, Johannes Rehmke and others belonged to this trend. In accordance with Kant's theory these philosophers thought that the world of objects is not given to us directly, but is constructed by our consciousness.

The Neokantian schools (those of Marburg and Baden), which took shape in Germany at the turn of the century, also had much in common with the philosophy of empiriocriticism. The initial point of these Neokantian schools, i.e. rejection of the 'thing-in-itself' and the possibility of cognition going beyond the limits of consciousness phenomena, links them both with empiriocriticism and the 'immanent philosophy'.

The Marburg Neokantian school was founded by Hermann Cohen (1842–1918). The school also included Paul Natorp, Ernst Cassirer, Rudolf Stammler and others. Its followers saw their task in the reorientation and amplification of the subject of philosophy. They rejected philosophy in the sense of a science dealing with the world as sheer metaphysics. Only the process of scientific cognition is the subject of philosophy. Primarily, philosophy is a science dealing with science, with cognition itself. Along these lines they interpreted Kant's teachings too.

For the representatives of the Baden (Freiburg) Neokantian school, Wilhelm Windelband (1848–1915) and Heinrich Rickert (1863–1936), philosophy meant the very analysis of the logical structure of knowledge, the scientific methodology. The school's principal problem was the creation of a methodology of history. Historical science, in their opinion, should collect and describe individual events, not pretending to discover any laws in history. Any reality, including the historical one, is an individual clear notion. And, as individual phenomena and reality as a whole is an endless, multi-faceted and inexhaustible row, cognition using concepts with any kind of logical links cannot reflect it adequately. At best it would always simplify, or, in the worst case, transform the materials of notions about reality. Reality manifests itself only in the particular and individual, so it is impossible to construct it from general elements.

The concept of historical laws, according to Rickert, is meaningless. Historical sciences should deal with individual events in their unique originality. Historical development is a row of these unique events. 'He who speaks about "history" in general, always thinks about a single individual course of events'. The idea of historical development excludes the concept of historical law. The only principle of selection and systematization of historical events is their attribution to cultural values.

Empiriocriticism, however, enjoyed its greatest success in Russia (Vladimir V. Lesevich (1837–1905), Aleksandr A. Bogdanov (1873–1928); S. S. Yushkevich) and in the USA, where it was represented by the pragmatism and instrumentalism (often called 'businessman's philosophy') of William James (1842–1910). In his theories James used the above-mentioned principles defining the meaning of philosophy through the individual's activity and world outlook. For this reason his ideas can be regarded as part of the same philosophical tradition, based on the thesis: 'there is no object without a subject'.

The Latin word *pragma* means 'action' and according to this meaning the philosophy of pragmatism is the philosophy of human activity and practice. All abstract and speculative constructions of no connection with human practice are discarded by James immediately like 'useless old rags'.

Reality itself has a vast number of forms; free human activity creates a polyphonic picture of the world; so, James argues, there are as many philosophies as there are men. Every man has his own unique philosophy. To philosophize means to perceive life in an individual way, and philosophical tendency depends only on the person's innate temperament. Philosophy for everybody, from this point of view, is the method of settling philosophical disputes, the method based on practical consequences of human activity.

James's pragmatic theory of cognition was connected to a broader philosophical world outlook, which he himself called radical empiriocriticism or pluralism. In the philosopher's opinion, faith was the crucial feature of this worldview; he gave faith highest priority and actively defended it from the attacks of theoretical reason. Theoretical reason, with all its diverse approaches, cannot fully satisfy the spiritual needs of an individual, and therefore cannot eliminate the significance and competence of faith. James elaborated his religious teaching in a course of lectures entitled *The Variety of Religious Experience*, where he interpreted religious problems using the psychological method. Religiosity as such is defined by James as a permanent and stable reaction of an individual to the integral cosmos. Reconciling conflicts, this reaction introduces harmony into the very system of human life.

The problem of regulating, systemizing empirical material in the field of sociology constituted an important trend in the theories of Max Weber (1864–1920), a well-known German philosopher and historian of the turn of the century. His views developed under the direct influence of positivism and especially Neokantianism. Weber's famous theory of 'ideal types' was in essence a continuation of Rickert's attempt to interpret empirical material by constructing special schemes or images of the analysed phenomena where the most important features of these phenomena are, on the one hand, singled out depending on the researcher's particular interest, and, on the other, are taken in the ideal form, cleared from the layers of real life. In fact, empirical material is generalized in the form of ideal types by exposing repetitions in the individual cultural-historical phenomena.

Selecting the principles of creating (constructing) historical-cultural phenomena, Weber does not give priority to material or spiritual premises. He prefers to speak of 'adequacy', an 'internal relationship' between different phenomena of material and spiritual kind. Weber's 'ideal type' is not taken from empirical reality – it is created as a theoretical construction. The more one-sided and determined this construction is, the more alien 'ideal types' are to the real world. Weber, however, is well aware that it is impossible to avoid a certain structural rigidity in these constructions. This rigidity can be avoided only if an 'ideal type' is not an end in itself, but just a conventional instrument of historical knowledge. An ideal construction makes it possible not only to organize historical material, but also to single out deviations, to fix different variants of historical development. Therefore it can facilitate cognition of history in its imperative and regular character, as well as in its individuality and local variety.

The latter argument is especially important, as Weber, like Wilhelm Dilthey before him, was developing the cognitional strategy of 'understanding', of hermetic interpretation of social and historical phenomena, oriented towards the individual, and opposed to the strategy of 'explanation', borrowed from the natural sciences and oriented towards the general, the regular, the imperative. In fact these strategies intertwined in his works, but subjectively Weber tried to overcome the narrowness of the 'explaining', law-giving models in sociology.

Like his methodology, the subject of Weber's studies also became more and more non-classical. While most scholars before him directed their attention to the rational and functional (correct) behaviour, distinguishing it from the irrational and dysfunctional (incorrect) kind, Weber was the first to introduce gradation of behavioural rationality, determined, apart from the motivation of an individual, also by his social orientation towards the 'other' ('others'). Besides the traditional purpose-rational activity, using means adequate to achieve the purpose, he singled out the value-rational activity, when the means are adequate not to the goal, but to the values of an individual, as well as the affectional and traditional behaviour (i.e. action when the means are adequate correspondingly to the emotional state of an individual and to historical tradition). Actions in this connection can be regarded not as rational or irrational ones, but as the manifestations of rationality's various forms, which radically changes the approach to the problem. New topics appear within its framework, for instance that of the role of value-oriented behaviour in the genesis of purpose-rational activity.

In his famous work *Protestant Ethics and the Spirit of Capitalism* (1904) Weber tried to answer this question for the first time. In his opinion, the origins of European capitalism are primarily connected to the formation of a special psychological type of personality under the influence of the Reformation, rather than to economic development itself. Thus the purpose-rational type of activity, which is characteristic of modern society, is not a 'natural' one, but is based on a special interpretation of the predestination concept in Protestantism, i.e. on a certain value orientation. Unlike Islam, where the concept of totally predetermined existence led to fatalism, Protestantism limited the notion of predetermination to life after death, where only the 'chosen' are saved. But the 'choosing' itself is not completely hidden in Divine Providence, it is manifested in the success of the individual's professional activity, regarded as a form of 'divine vocation', and therefore sacralized. Thus the daily life of a Protestant becomes spiritually rich, transforming into a form of serving God, into a test of a person's selectiveness.

This elevates systematical and honest labour to a form of religious duty, connecting the achievement of economic goals to the highest goal – salvation. As a result, purpose-rational activity receives justification by values, and then by tradition. Labour is torn away from its immediate goal – satisfaction of routine needs. As a result, a Protestant starts working more persistently and systematically than a Muslim, or even a Catholic. Economic success does not stop him, but acts as a stimulus for further, even more active work. This is the basis of the Western civilization's dynamic development, bringing capitalism in its wake. In the subsequent process of intellectual secularization, Protestant beliefs received their secular equivalents. The idea of selectiveness, for instance, is connected to the notion of creditability. Purpose-rational activity finally takes shape as an individual type, as opposed to the value-rational one.

Returning to the thesis of the significance of irrational forms of cognition (faith, intuition) for the genesis of non-classical philosophy, we should emphasize that in the late nineteenth century these forms of cognition were studied most actively by the so called 'philosophy of life', incited by Schopenhauer's ideas. Above we have already studied the views of Schopenhauer, Nietzsche and Bergson. But here we are returning to these theories in connection with the 'philosophy of life', which became prevalent at the turn of the century.

Will, not reason or soul, is the basis of the world according to Schopenhauer; the world itself is our perception of it, and the man's life forces are the reason of existence. Therefore it is the acting man, instead of God, or spirit, or idea, who becomes the initial point of thought. Essentially, it was an attempt to explain the world on the basis of human existence, human values. That was why the problems of anthropology, culturology, philosophical interpretation of life and creativity became central to the 'philosophy of life', with 'life' and 'will' as its main categories, practically substituting the category of being.

The 'philosophy of life' itself took shape in Germany and France in the second half of the nineteenth century, and Friedrich Nietzsche is sometimes regarded as its founder. This philosophical trend was represented by Wilhelm Dilthey, Henri Bergson, Georg Simmel and many other philosophers.

This approach interprets 'life' itself as a primary reality, an integral process, which undergoes subsequent differentiation, producing all the variety of phenomena and events. One should also note a certain vagueness of the category of 'life' in this philosophical system. Numerous variants of its interpretation are possible: Nietzsche, for instance, regards 'life' as the will to power, Bergson as *élan vital*, Simmel as a 'stream of feelings'.

The dominating feature of the 'philosophy of life', its guiding principle, is the priority of life over truth. Hence its initial tendency for critical reappraisal of previous philosophy (as there is no absolutely valuable truth, there are no absolutely true values either). Truth here is an instrument, a stage in the process of creating various values by our will. Just an instrument, not the goal (in contrast to the previous philosophical tradition). Life itself, created by will, is the only goal.

Another feature characteristic of this trend in general is its attitude to life as a creative process, constantly destroying stability. Life is an endless coming-to-be, so its adequate cognition is absolutely impossible. The essence of life can be grasped by intuition, by irrational insight, by symbolizing, rather than logical speculations. To cognize life means not to explain, but to feel it, being a part of its changes and becoming.

The world, too, is an absolute, endless coming-to-be. It is a certain chaos, lacking integrity, order, logic and expediency. The becoming of the world is the struggle of wills, equally striving for domination, and this process has no tendency to stability. It can only strive for permanent growth, as every 'will centre' tries to encompass all surrounding space with its force. The strongest one wins, creating his own system of forces, including the universe, humankind and the human being.

These features and peculiarities of the 'philosophy of life' reflected the tragedy of the transition period's culture. Within the great variety of topics of Nietzschean philosophy, the problem of human adaptation to crises of life occupies a special place. Culture, in Nietzsche's opinion, is the principal way of adaptation. Primarily, he argues, the human being is a 'weak animal', which uses its intellect, rather than force, to adapt to the environment. But this rational approach is also pregnant with destruction, as the perceptions of life are formed to a large extent by the use of logical laws and language, which cannot express the whole richness of life. Knowledge systems and language, no matter how perfect they are, are torn from reality. Rather, logic and language are constructing new life, lacking initial integrity. Moreover, language and intellect are creating conditions which suppress the instinctive will to live, leading to the degradation of personality. Only a creative attitude towards life, manifesting itself through art, can grasp its integral essence, produce its adequate reflection in feelings and images.

It was from this argument that Nietzsche's major idea followed, the idea of a two-way human adaptive orientation through culture. The first type of adaptation is the rationalist, 'Apollonian culture', aimed at the rationalization of the world even at the price of its simplification and sketchiness (which finally leads to its negation). This type, developed to the utmost in speculative philosophy and Christianity, leads to a stereotyped culture, to the loss of self-consciousness as a value, to manipulation of individuals lacking will, to the 'cult of mediocrities'. The second type – the 'Dionysian culture' – on the contrary, is connected with a creative attitude towards life, the manifestation of all possible human features. This type of adaptation demands the development of individuality and strong will. It is based on the emotional 'grasp' of reality, of universal harmony.

It presumes the existence of a super-personality. The most complete grasp of life's essence, therefore, is the domain and result of the activity of the elite human being, possessing the will to live and free from pre-established morals. This Nietzschean 'superman' is an absolutely free individual, consciously taking responsibility for his acts. He creates instead of consuming, builds instead of destroying. In Nietzsche's philosophical system the 'superman' acts in two ways – as an ideal of humankind's development and as a real phenomenon of history, personified by outstanding figures (Alexander of Macedonia, Julius Caesar, Napoleon,

etc.). But in any case, life is the supreme value for the superman. Will is manifested as a norm in his culture, introducing harmony into the world of chaos.

This theme was continued by Wilhelm Dilthey (1833–1911), one of the most outstanding representatives of the 'philosophy of life'. He defined life primarily as a cultural-historical phenomenon. Hence his aspiration to penetrate deeply into spiritual life, to overcome the tendency for a natural science approach in the sphere of the humanities.

The 'understanding', hermeneutic methodology in studying all phenomena of life is the basis of Dilthey's theory. Life in general, the philosopher argues, is something absolutely inexplicable from without; every event in our life is a complex mix of instincts, feelings, environment and fate. That is why the precise formulae of natural sciences are absolutely inapplicable here. Life is the inner state of the soul. Life is the only trustworthy thing for us, the only thing which cannot transform into illusion. Therefore life can be understood only from within. For Dilthey, hermeneutics is the very art of understanding the manifestations of life, the direct comprehension of an integral emotion connected with a certain object.

Dilthey saw his principal task in the critique of historical reason on the basis of a subject's internal experience, retaining the strict scientific approach at the same time. In his main work, *The Introduction to the Sciences of the Spirit*, the philosopher formulated a general theory of humanitarian sciences, which in his opinion included primarily history, philology and their common basis – 'descriptive psychology'. This descriptive psychology he distinguished from the explanatory one. The latter, according to Dilthey, has an impossible task – that of causal interpretation of psychological phenomena. But if we take into account the ambivalent polyphonic character of human spiritual life, any cause explaining a psychological phenomenon has to be chosen arbitrarily, to be enforced by an outsider. Thus any hypothesis about the causes of psychological phenomena will remain a speculative one, unable to stand the test of experience. Therefore, the philosopher argues, psychology can only be descriptive, as only this kind of psychology ensures a direct emotional interpretation of inner life's facts, which is the only way to approach comprehension of a certain spiritual entity.

The topic of intuitive penetration of the essence of life was developed by the aforementioned Henri Bergson, the most outstanding representative of the 'philosophy of life' and 'intuitivism'. Life as becoming, in the philosopher's opinion, starts as a result of an initial explosion of *élan vital*. It acts as a stream of qualitative changes, undergoing evolution from the appearance of forms of life and cognition like intellect and intuition, to their mutual estrangement and acquisition of opposite characteristics. While initially *élan vital* is a powerful, integral stream, it then gradually loses its tension and disintegrates, and in this process life produces spirit and matter. But the original, initial integrity of life can be 'grasped' only intuitively. Life cognizes itself, absolutely disregarding the opposition of subject and object, the cognizable and the cognizing. This kind of intuition is immanent to man, as the path of *élan vital* goes through him also. This feature provides man with an ability to create, linked with irrational intuition.

But the ability to create is a divine gift, given only to those chosen. Therefore Begson's concept of culture and creativity, like Nietzsche's, is an elitist one. He accepts two types of society and two types of morals – the 'closed morals', which satisfies the necessities of preserving humankind as a whole (while the individual and truth are sacrificed to the group) and the 'open morals', giving the creative activity of a free individual priority over the preservation of human race.

Finally, we should say that philosophical thought of the turn of the century became a turning point in the history of philosophy and science. In this period a new type of philosophy, with its methodology and problems, took shape; the models of future philosophical systems and methodologies of the twentieth century were forming. Philosophy and humanitarian knowledge were abandoning the narrow, mostly rationalist approach, science was overcoming positivist, experimental-inductive learning. This process facilitated the resolution of the crisis in science, the genesis of the new, particularly non-classical quantum-relativist physics, which accepted the 'non-classical' thesis that the world will answer our questions only if it is included into the sphere of our activity, and these answers are integrally connected to the questions' character. The new physics, as we know, had abandoned the strategy of collecting and generalizing experimental data, putting forward the idea that theory can be initiated by experience, but does not result from its analysis. And, finally, it took into account the possible plurality of formulations of a single theory. These theses later formed the basis of the work of Niels Bohr, Werner Heisenberg and Albert Einstein. Different philosophical schools and trends were turning to polyphonic, tolerant philosophy, generating common approaches and concepts, which in the twentieth century developed into phenomenology, the philosophy of dialogue, the philosophy of language, into the progress of esoteric knowledge and the principle of creative intuition.

Thus, the development of philosophical theories and humanities in general reached a completely new level, simultaneously exerting a considerable influence on the progress of the natural and exact sciences.

CONCLUSION

In the 1890s, the contradictions that had accumulated as the century drew to a close became more and more evident in the human and social sciences. They were manifested in the decline of classical liberalism and the crisis affecting many of the ideas and conceptions that had been advanced in the age of romanticism; positivist theories made serious ground. The interaction between the social and natural sciences gained strength.

Social development and the *fin de siècle* mood (a term that came to be widely used) clearly reflected the deep-seated national, social, religious and ideological contradictions which led to the world wars of the next century. Dissenting voices became louder behind the generally optimistic tone of scientific thought. Public opinion was quick to pick up ideas put forward by the social sciences about the biological causes of criminality, racial inequality and the right of the strong to leadership. The idea was actively promulgated that the social sciences, unlike the natural sciences, should study only the characteristics of individual phenomena, not the general laws of social development.

The human and social sciences in general made great headway in the nineteenth century, mainly on the basis of the positivist methodology. The great advances made in social psychology and the great step forward taken in the intellectual and cultural development of humanity, which together changed conceptions of the meaning of life and of the rights of individuals in their relationship with society, caused increased attention to be paid to spirituality. They made it possible to re-interpret the problems and contradictions of being and rethink moral imperatives, and to subject the violation of individual human rights to severe criticism. It was inevitable that the new *fin-de-siècle* spiritual quest consequent upon the development of the natural, social and human sciences, together with the increasing public interest in the most varied aspects of the development of the individual and, at the same time, in the substantiation of ideals and values common to all humanity, should assume new forms in keeping with the standards and conceptions of contemporary society.

The important scientific achievements of the nineteenth century, together with radical changes in ideas about the world and about humanity resulting from developments in all branches of knowledge, prepared the ground for the basic changes in the spiritual life of humanity that began at the turn of the twentieth century.

BIBLIOGRAPHY

A HISTORY OF MUSLIM PHILOSOPHY, 1963–66. Vol. 2. Edn Muhammad Sharif, Wiesbaden, p. 1487.

ALTHAUS, H. 1992. *Hegel und die heroishen Jahre der Philosophie*. Munich/Vienna.

ASSOUN, P. L. 1980. *Freud et Nietzsche*. Presse Universitaire Française, Paris.

BARRY, N. P. 1986. *On Classical Liberalism and Libertarianism*. Macmillan, Basingstoke.

BENTLEY, M. 1987. *The Climax of Liberal Politics: British Liberalism in Theory and Practice, 1868–1918*. Arnold, London.

BIBLER, V. S. 1991. *Kant-Galilée- Kant: (Razum novogo vremeni v paradoksah samoobosnovaniya)*. [Reason of new time in paradoxs of self-substantiation]. Misl, Moscow.

BIKOVA, M. F. 1990. *Gegelevskoe ponimanie mishlenia* [Hegel's understanding of thinking]. Nauka, Moscow.

BOCOK, R. 1983. *Sigmund Freud*. Horwood, Chinchester.

BRUSH, S. C. 1978. *The Temperature of History: Phases of Science and Culture in the Nineteenth Century*. Burt, Franklin & Co., New York.

BRYANT, CH. G. A. 1985. *Positivism in Social Theory and Research*. Macmillan, Basingstoke.

COLLINS, I. 1957. *Liberalism in Nineteenth Century Europe*. Routledge and Kegan Paul, London.

CRAMPE-CASNABET, M. 1989. *Kant: Une révolution philosophique*. Bordas, Paris.

DICKEY, L. 1987. *Hegel: Religion, Economics, and the Politics of Spirit, 1770–1807*. Cambridge University Press, Cambridge.

ELEY, L. 1995. *Fichte, Schelling, Hegel: Operative Denkwege im 'deutschen Idealism'*. Ars Una, Neuried.

GAIDENKO, P. P. 1970. *Tragedia estetizma. Opit harakteriski mirosozertsania Sorena Kierkegaarda*. [The tragedy of aestheticism. Experience of characteristics of the world outlook of Sören Kierkegaard]. Iskusstvo, Moscow.

GANDER, H.-H. 1988. *Positivismus als Metaphisik: Voraussetzungen und Grundstrukturen von Grundlegung der Geisteswiss*. Alber, Freiburg, Munich.

GLOY, K. 1990. *Studien zur theoretischen Philosophie Kants*. Koenigshausen and Neumann, Würzburg.

GULIGA, A. V. (ed.) 1994. *Hegel*. 2nd edn, Tovarischestvo Soratnik, Moscow.

——. 1994. *Kant: K dvuhsotletiu izbrania Kanta russkim akademikom*. [On the bicentennial election of Kant as a Russian academician]. Tovarischestvo Soratnik, Moscow.

HALFPENNY, P. 1982. *Positivism and Sociology: Explaining Social Life*. Allen & Unwin, London.

HAMLYN, D. H. 1980. *Schopenhauer*. Routledge and Kegan Paul, London.

HANS, J. S. 1989. *The Question of Value: Thinking through Nietzsche, Heidegger and Freud*. Southern Illinois University Press, Carbondale.

HEIDEGGER, M. 1994. *Hegel's Phenomenology of Spirit*. Indiana University Press, Bloomington.

JANKELEVITCH, V. 1989. *Henri Bergson*. Presse Universitaire Française, Paris.

JARDIN, A. 1984. *Alexis de Tocqueville, 1805–1859*. Hachette, Paris.

JARVIE, I. CH. 1984. *Rationality and Relativism: In Search of a Philosophy and History of Anthropology*. Routledge and Kegan Paul, London.

KELLNER, M. 1988. *Feuerbachs Religionskritik*. ISP-Verlag, Frankfurt a.M.

KREMER-MARIETTI, A. 1983. *Le concept de science positive: ses tenants et ses aboutissants dans les structures anthropologiques du positivisme*. Klincksieck, Paris.

LACEY, A. R. 1993. *Bergson*. Routledge and Kegan Paul, London/New York.

LAZAREV, V. V. 1991. *Rau I. A. Hegel i philosophskie diskussii ego vremeni*. Nauka, Moscow.

Le XIXe siècle et l'histoire: Le cas Fustel de Coulanges. Presse Universitaire Française, Paris.

LOSEV, A. F. (ed.) 1994. *Vladimir Soloviev*. 2nd additional edn, Misl, Moscow.

LOTHMAN, Y. M. 1987. *Sotvorenie Karamzina* [The creation of Karamzin]. Kniga, Moscow.

LÜTKEHAUS, L. 1980. *Schopenhauer: Metaphysischer Pessimismus und 'soziale Frage'*. Bouvier Verlag (Grundmann), Bonn.

MACKAY, N. 1989. *Motivation and Explanation: an Essay on Freud's Philosophy of Science*. International University Press, Madison CT.

Malthus and his time. 1986. Ed. M. Turner. Macmillan, Basingstoke.

MANET, P. 1987. *Histoire intellectuelle du libéralisme: Dix Leçons*. Calmann-Lévy, Paris.

MANQUARD, O. 1987. *Transzendentaler Idealism, Romantische, Naturphilosophie, Psyhoanalyse*. Verlag für Philosophie Jürgen Dinter, Cologne.

MARQUET, J. F. 1973. *Liberté et existence. Etude sur la formation de la philosophie de Schelling*. Gallimard, Paris.

MOTROSHILOVA, N. V. 1984. *Put Hegelya k 'Nauke logike': Formirovanie printzipov sistemnosti i istorizma* [Hegel's road to a 'Science of logics': Formation of principles of systematization and historical method]. Nauka, Moscow.

OIZERMAN, T. I. 1991. *Narskii I. S. Teoria poznania Kanta* [I. S. Narskii's. Theory of Knowledge of Kant]. Nauka, Moscow.

OTTOMAN, H. 1987. *Philosophie und Polik bei Nietzsche*. de Gruyter, Berlin/New York.

PAKDAMAN, H. 1969. *Djamal-ed-din Assad Abadi dit Afghani*, Paris, p. 246.

PESCH, E. 1985. *Freud*. Bordas, Paris.

RENAULT, A. 1986. *Le système du droit: Philosophie et droit dans la pensée de Fichte*. Presse Universitaire Française, Paris.

RILEY, J. 1988. *Liberal Utilitarianism: Social Choice Theory and J. S. Mill's Philosophy*. Cambridge University Press, Cambridge.

ROSENBERG, J. D. 1985. *Carlyle and the Burden of History*. Harvard University Press, Cambridge MA.

ROSSET, C. 1989. *L'esthétique de Schopenhauer*. Quadrige. Presse Universitaire Française, Paris.

Schopenhauer. 1988. Schroedel, Hanover.

STADLER, F. 1982. *Vom Positivismus zur 'Wissenschaftlichen Weltauffassung': Am Beispiel der Wirkungsgeschichte von Ernest Mach in Österreich von 1895 bis 1934*. Löcker, Vienna/Munich.

SUTTON, J. 1988. *The Religious Philosophy of Vladimir Solovyov: Towards a Reassessment*. Macmillan Press, Basingstoke.

The Common Bases of Hinduism. 1994. In: Swami Vivekananda. *An Anthology*. Delhi, p. 195.

The Encyclopaedia of Philosophy, 1972. Vol. 7, New York/London, p. 99.

VIVEKANANDA. 1964. *The Complete Works*. Vol. 5, Calcutta, p. 51.

———. 1994. Washing the Living God. In: *An Anthology*. Delhi, p. 107.

WARREN, M. E. 1988. *Nietzsche and Political Thought*. MIT Press, Cambridge MA.

WARTOSFKY, M. W. 1977. *Feuerbach*. Cambridge University Press. Cambridge.

WINCH, D. 1987. *Malthus*. Oxford University Press, Oxford and New York.

Zigmund Freud, psihoanalyz i russkai misl [Zigmund Freud, Psychoanalysis and Russian thought]. Leibinia V. M. Respublika, Moscow.

7

EDUCATION AND RESEARCH

Bernadette Bensaude-Vincent, coordinator

with contributions from *Christine Blondel, Conrad Grau, Leoncio López-Ocón, Françoise Mayeur, Maria-Luisa Ortega-Gálvez, Anne Rasmussen, Brigitte Schroeder-Gudehus* and *Iba Der Thiam*

In the realm of education and research, it was during the period from 1789 to 1914 that most of the structures that make up our modern world were put in place. Despite differing national and cultural traditions the education system steadily became institutionalized and opened its doors to ever-wider segments of the population. Research, which had still been a leisure activity during the Enlightenment, gradually became a profession.

How was this process shaped? Where, in what circumstances and under what pressures did the institutional setting emerge that moulded and fashioned our modern culture?

This chapter begins by describing the various stages in the organization of education, from the elementary school to the most advanced university levels. The general trends in the organization of research are then highlighted: professionalization, specialization and internationalization. Finally we trace the development of a means of spreading knowledge, namely popularization, that first appeared in the nineteenth century, counter-pointing the directions taken by research.

In these three areas, as in many others during the nineteenth century, the industrialized countries of Europe tended to impose their systems. With the spread of information and the increasing ease and speed of communications, the world became a smaller place. Migrants flocked from the country to the newly industrialized cities, and also from the 'old continent' of Europe to America and, to a lesser extent, to Africa once colonial culture began to establish itself there. In the course of this chapter we shall attempt to see whether and to what extent this amounted to the worldwide spread of European industrial culture through the standardization of structures.

EDUCATION

In the industrialized countries the nineteenth century was the 'century of the school'. The school was regarded as a panacea for all social and political ills. The gradual introduction of universal suffrage, prompted by liberal leanings and aspirations to democracy, required a minimum of culture and information if all citizens were to exercise their rights in a truly enlightened manner. Other factors, too, militated in favour of universal schooling, such as religious proselytization in England, where it was stirred up by rivalry between sects, or the desire to be assimilated into society and acquire citizenship, as in the United States; also at play was the urge to improve the moral tone of the lower classes. Universal schooling, it was thought, would put an end to poverty and the instability of the 'dangerous classes'.

Since the last third of the eighteenth century there had been a gradual expansion of state intervention in education, which accelerated in the late nineteenth century with the rise of nationalism. This was a long and complex process, which finally resulted in relieving the churches and religious communities of their responsibility for education. If in no other way, the state intervened by carrying out inspections, conducting surveys and publishing official reports that influenced lawmaking. It sometimes granted subsidies, and although it did not usually take over the task of training teachers, it did exercise control over their qualifications. It often handed over responsibility to religious organizations or establishments. Lastly, in such countries as France and Italy, a state education system was introduced alongside private education. While this did not put an end to the influence of religious institutions over education systems, it generally meant that these had to operate under the authority of the state.

By the start of the First World War, the general trend had become established for education to be placed, as a secular institution, under state control nearly everywhere, although there was a persistent gap between the principle and its actual application. The size of the gap varied with the period, place and level of instruction – primary, secondary or university. Depending on the political situation, the influence in particular of the clergy (which should not be confused with the religious basis of the educational content) took different forms.

At the beginning of the nineteenth century education was not entirely the responsibility of the school. More significant than rates of school enrolment, which was patchy and incomplete, are comparative literacy rates and progress in different countries. By the 1830s, by contrast, the school reigned supreme with the development of compulsory schooling. Secondary and higher education, however, remained the preserve of an elite.

Literacy

The spread of literacy advanced towards completion, in the industrialized countries at any rate, by the turn of the nineteenth century in ways that varied widely with social background and particularly sex.

A key cause of unevenness in the spread of literacy was geographical location. In European countries, rural areas, which tended to be sparsely inhabited, mountainous or wooded, took longer to become literate than urban areas. Since living in groups was strongly conducive to learning to read and write, towns were usually ahead of country areas. Nevertheless, the severe conditions of industrial work (with a ten-hour working day in France in the late nineteenth century) prevented most workers from acquiring any further education. Children from working-class areas were sent to the shop floor far too young and soon forgot (or never managed to acquire) even the rudiments of reading and writing, until compulsory education or changes in the labour laws forced families to send them to school. The same was sometimes true of country areas, where truancy was common until mechanization became widespread, rendering child labour superfluous.

By contrast, inequality between the sexes in regard to literacy gradually faded away. At the beginning of the century women everywhere had been less literate than men, and girls lagged far behind boys in becoming literate. The rate at which they caught up in certain countries during the nineteenth century was therefore all the more spectacular. In France, for example, women reached the same literacy rate as men towards 1900, and thereafter soon overtook them. This positive result was secured not only through generalized school-level education, but also through training on the job in post-schooling professional life.

Independently of the rise of schools, social, family, religious and professional groups continued to play a leading role both before and after schooling itself, or even at the same time. Results might be contradictory. Much literacy was imparted out of school altogether, notably in the family, where, indeed, the process always began. Lessons in reading might also be given by devout persons, as through the Sunday schools of the Protestant countries. But reading might also be taught in the army, as in the regimental schools of France. Finally, adult evening classes might be organized by various philanthropic societies, such as the Société pour l'Instruction Elémentaire, founded in Paris in 1815 along the lines of many similar English groups, some of them very long established indeed. In Athens, a Society for the Friends of Education was set up in 1836.

Elite circles, in which philanthropists, practising Christians and liberals rubbed shoulders, now made education a subject of public debate, and the often-lively discussions were formed by a desire to convey more than the catechism and the 'three Rs'.

While the overall number of persons able to read and write continued to rise, literacy rates remained modest. The countries of southern Europe at this time were dragging their feet: a census carried out in Portugal in 1900 estimated the number of illiterates over the age of seven at 4 million out of a population of little over 5 million, with a marked difference between the sexes. In Spain, 60 per cent of the population was illiterate around 1850, and the illiteracy rate still remained high at the end of the century. In the Italian states the situation was very uneven: the north was more literate than the south, but in both cases the education of girls generally remained a mainly family and private affair.

In Africa, Western-style education spread from the coast towards the interior, in line with the rapid pace at which missions were established, and developed most widely in South and West Africa. Despite the expansion of Islam in the nineteenth century in certain regions, and the importance of Koranic schools, Western influence continued to gain ground. In Senegal, for example, a 'mutual instruction' school founded in Saint-Louis in 1816 had eighty male pupils enrolled by the following year. In 1822, Mother Javouhey opened a school for girls in Saint-Louis and a second school in Gorée. In 1841, the first secondary-level boarding schools were established there. Towards the end of the century, by which time over a dozen secondary schools were operating throughout the French colony of Senegal, a training school for primary teachers was opened in Saint-Louis in 1903. There thus came into being, in Senegal as in other African countries, a small elite of a few thousand Westernized, Christianized Africans, who in very many cases enjoyed a privileged status thanks to their participation in administrative and commercial affairs. Even if this elite, trained according to Western traditions, remained numerically very small in relation to Africa's black population as a whole, the growing ascendancy of literacy constituted a potential threat to African cultures, which were essentially oral. In communities where integration into the group took the form of ritual initiation – varying from one ethnic group to another, but always in step with the individual's stage-by-stage development from childhood to adulthood – the spread of writing loosened the hold of myth, legend and story-telling, and weakened the power of the spoken word with its accompanying moments of silence and gesture, all of which had been so significant in traditional African cultures. Some missionaries, more intent on spreading the Gospel than on territorial expansion, did try to adjust to local conditions by studying the prevailing vernaculars and customs, but mission schools remained modelled on schools in the mother country, mainly England or France. The process of Westernization was fostered above all by the Protestant missions, which spread Christianity as a cultural whole including everything from education, morals and customs, to attitudes towards economics and politics.

In the Islamic East, contacts with the West were stepped up in line with the reformist policy initiated by Selim III (1789–1807). The spirit of reform spread from Istanbul to other provinces of the Ottoman Empire, such as Egypt and Syria. However, in contrast to what happened in West and South Africa, the establishment of new education systems and the new receptivity to Western culture did not at first threaten traditional Islamic education. Instead of replacing the local Koranic schools, where the teacher dinned into his pupils, at no matter what cost and mainly by rote, the letter, if not the spirit, of the Koran, the European schools offered a parallel development, setting as their main target the provision of a literary, technical, scientific or administrative training for an elite. Nevertheless, this reformist current did encroach upon the power of the 'ulamā' (Muslim theologians), who hitherto had been the sole authorities in matters of education.

A special problem arose in the United States of America as a result of the waves of adult immigrants arriving throughout the nineteenth century. School here was often the only means available for instructing and educating these uprooted adults. As a result, the East Coast states, which had enjoyed high, European-style levels of school enrolment, underwent a decline in literacy at the end of the century with the arrival of hordes of poor immigrants from Central and Southern Europe. In the West, where settlers were pushing the frontier forward, literacy levels were even more uncertain.

As regards the countries of Latin America, most of which had loosened their ties with the home countries of the Iberian Peninsula between 1810 and 1825, they had been stymied in their educational drive by a dispute between the conservatives and the liberals, eager to counter the cultural hegemony of the Catholic church which during the colonial era had been solely responsible for all educational work. The task was, given the very low school enrolment rates, a Herculean one. According to the first school census undertaken in the Chilean Republic in 1813, the capital, Santiago, whose population then totalled 50,000 inhabitants, boasted no more than seven schools, with a total enrolment of 664 students. It was only during the last third of the nineteenth century that schooling developed on a massive scale.

Elementary schooling

Everywhere in Europe, except Russia, primary education was made legally compulsory before the outbreak of the First World War. But by no stretch of the imagination can this be taken to mean that schooling followed a set pattern. From the point of view of its schools, Europe in the nineteenth century was more like a mosaic of differing systems, each of them reflecting the situation in a particular country.

In the United Kingdom, for example, schools developed against a backdrop of religious rivalries. In England, Scotland and Wales, the schools that existed in 1800 were left to private or local initiative. As industrialization spread, the system prevailing in rural Calvinist Scotland began to fall apart. Throughout Great Britain the most widely attended schools – the Sunday schools – prided themselves on providing not only religious instruction but also the rudiments of reading and writing. The results were not encouraging. The emerging middle class, 'partly Protestant, partly industrialist, passionately philanthropic', was pressing for the creation of schools. Two rival societies – a clear sign of religious tension – championed mutual education. By the beginning of the twentieth century the multiplicity of sects and the presence of Catholics had resulted in a neutral, though not secular, school system. Lessons were preceded and followed by readings from the Bible and prayers. After the passage of the Forester Act of 1870, the primary school system was run by school boards elected by the taxpayer, which were replaced in 1902 by local education authorities. The number of schools doubled between 1876 and 1900, and the school-leaving age – 10 in 1876 – was raised to 14 in 1900.

Schools in the United States were municipal. Primary education was made free and secular in about 1830; and from an early stage it was also compulsory from 6 to 14. But habits proved harder to change than laws; only 49 per cent of children regularly attended school in 1876, and although the rate was higher by 1900, it had still not reached 80 per cent. The chief difference with the old continent, noted Tocqueville, was that schooling here was co-educational: 'a democratic education is necessary to protect women from the dangers with which the institutions and customs of democracy surround them'. English-speaking Canada followed the American model closely, whereas the French province of Quebec attempted to preserve its originality by giving the Catholic church responsibility for the (separate) education of girls and boys.

Towards the end of the nineteenth century, this initial patchwork was beginning to be replaced by the existence of extensive areas in which the preponderance of certain models had produced uniform education systems. This phenomenon was particularly marked in the German sphere of influence. In Prussia, the regulations of 1763 and 1765, together with the *Allgemeine Landrecht* of 1794, which had declared schools and universities to be state institutions, governed all subsequent developments. The reform of the education system adopted after the collapse of Prussia and during the Napoleonic Wars, heavily influenced by the personality of Wilhelm von Humboldt, resulted in the establishment in 1817 of a Ministry of Worship, Education and Medical Affairs at the highest administrative level. It nevertheless proved impossible, both in Prussia in 1819, and later in Bavaria in 1867–9, to enact uniform legislation on primary education, and so schools were subject to special laws adopted on a case-by-case basis. After the creation of the German Empire in 1871, the jurisdiction of states over culture and education was, in principle, guaranteed. However, Prussian predominance in education was constantly gaining ground. Placed under anti-liberal, clerically oriented control in 1854, as was the Bavarian system in 1857, the Prussian education system obtained a new lease of life from the school inspection laws promulgated in Prussia in 1872, which laid down in fundamental and more effective terms the principle of the separation of school and church. While the efforts made in the early 1890s to introduce laws standardizing the entire education system throughout the German Empire failed, standardization eventually came about through the imposition of the Prussian system on the whole of Germany and even on Austria-Hungary after the 1867 *Ausgleich*. In Austria, an imperial primary school law, making school attendance compulsory between the ages of 6 and 14 (or 12) was passed in 1869. It should be noted, however, that while school enrolment rates tended to even out in the German sphere of influence, literacy levels showed considerable variation, ranging from 60 per cent to 25 per cent, for instance, in different regions of Austria-Hungary at the beginning of the twentieth century.

In the Russian sphere of influence, compulsory education was unknown until the collapse of the tsarist regime. In spite of the wide-ranging reforms introduced after defeat in the Crimean War, such as the abolition of serfdom in 1861, and the statutory recognition of elementary schools in 1864, there were only 90,000 schools, attended by some 4 million children (out of a total population of 110 million), when the first census was carried out in 1897. Some 60 per cent of the population over 15 years of age was illiterate in 1915, and only half of the 8–11 age group had an elementary school to go to.

It would be foolhardy to attempt to sum up compulsory education policy in the nineteenth century. Nevertheless, some general trends common to the countries of Europe can be singled out.

First, the implementation of legislative measures encountered a series of obstacles of a political or religious nature. The development of popular education – the *raison d'être* of compulsory schooling – was held back by the manifest fear of conservatives in all countries that it would break down class barriers. Only a few countries, notably Germany and certain states of Austria-Hungary, attained the goal of eight years of primary education. The development of elementary schooling was strongly influenced by the tension between liberal and conservative tendencies, and so there was no steady line of growth but an irregular curve fluctuating between periods of rapid growth and relative stagnation. The conservative influence, although not always prejudicial to education, made itself felt in educational content both through the stress laid on monarchist and Christian values for the training of loyal citizens, and in the protection of access to culture through material and financial requirements that restricted such access for the broad masses of the population. The European revolutions of 1848–9 had at first seemed to offer an opportunity for more liberal concepts of education to flourish, but with the defeat of the revolutionary movements, conservative ideas temporarily regained the upper hand. Eventually it was as a result of industrial development and social transformation, often with a political intent – such as the Russian reforms of 1860, the Austro-Hungarian *Ausgleich* of 1867, economic development under the Second Empire in France, the advent of the Third Republic, and the creation of the German Empire in 1871 – that educational reorganization became a necessity. Fluctuations were particularly noticeable in France. The attempt made during the 1789 Revolution to bring education under state control did not prevent the school from reverting to its former status: it was in the hands of local communities. The Guizot law of 1833 extended supervision over education to mayors and local dignitaries, acting in agreement with the religious authorities, while the Falloux law of 1850 strengthened the hold of the Catholic church on public schools, subject to state inspection. Private schools, which were sometimes run by 'unauthorized' religious orders, remained in existence. The Restoration notwithstanding, French schools had undergone far-reaching changes since 1815. However humble, they had more pupils and better-trained masters and were more closely supervised by the administrative machinery of state through a body of inspectors and directors of education appointed by a single ministry of public education. These authorities were not enough to eliminate the wide educational disparities between regions, but they did help to mitigate them. As the state take-over of education spread, the primary school was to give rise to serious conflict, in a number of European countries such as France, England and Belgium, over the place of religion in education. Bitter controversy between the champions of secular and religious schools divided public opinion over a long period. In France, where free primary education had been introduced virtually everywhere before the Third Republic, republicans, acting in the belief that denominational schools were a cause of national strife, had laws passed in 1882, making education and the secularization of its content compulsory, followed by a further law in 1886 under which the teaching staff was to be secularized following a transitional period, during which orders of nuns continued to teach for many years until secular schoolmistresses were available to take

their place. Anti-clerical policies came to a head in 1904, when Emile Combes, the prime minister, prohibited teaching by members of religious orders, who had thitherto been authorized to teach, and expelled them from schools, thereby making public education entirely secular. Many members of these orders thereupon became secular teachers in private schools.

Belgium included freedom of education in the constitution of the kingdom that was born of the scission with the Netherlands in 1830. Between 1842 and 1879, all communes were obliged to have at least one public school with compulsory religious instruction, but were allowed to 'adopt' private schools in place of public schools. The so-called 'wretched' law, passed by the Liberals in 1879, obliged the communes to establish a non-denominational, secular school, prohibited the adoption of denominational schools and abolished religious instruction during school hours. Public education was subject to the civil authorities, while denominational education, which had to be self-supporting, was subject only to the religious authorities. When the Catholics returned to power, which they held until 1914, they repealed the 1879 law. In 1884, the so-called 'revenge' law empowered communes to adopt private schools with religious instruction or to maintain official non-denominational schools. Only the private schools adopted were subsidized, but a system of adoption became the rule, especially in Flemish-speaking areas. This marked the reign of communal autonomy. In 1914, education was made compulsory for children between the ages of 6 and 14. In the Netherlands, freedom of instruction was upheld in principle, although the law of 1878 was inspired more by religious than by political considerations. Protestants of various persuasions and Catholics from the south of the country formed a coalition that obtained government grants subject to certain conditions. Schools in Italy were governed by the Casati law of 1859, which gradually spread out from Piedmont to cover the entire peninsula. This moderate liberal compromise respected the interests of both the secular state and the Catholic church; it oversaw private education only as regards qualifications and morality. The Casati law was to remain in place virtually unchanged until the fascist reforms of 1923.

The second general trend was that the development of elementary education led to inequality between girls and boys. Nothing was compulsory at girls' schools, and so there were few schoolmistresses. Many families considered that family education was sufficient, since girls were destined to stay at home. In the country, girls attended co-educational schools, whereas in town they were brought up mainly 'on the Church's lap'. The female teaching orders expanded rapidly.

A third trend was that the application of official measures to extend public primary education often came up against material difficulties, as regards financing and staffing problems due to the general shortage of qualified teachers. In France, for example, the state took over the training of teachers in the *écoles normales*, but further measures were required to enable them to practise their profession. In 1833, the Guizot law made it compulsory for municipalities to provide lodgings for the teacher and a minimum salary over and above the fee paid for each child by the family. In effect, elementary education made the institutionalization of teacher training inevitable. This process, which took different forms in different countries, ultimately led to the emergence of a whole new profession – that of schoolteacher – and a whole new branch of knowledge – educational science – that replaced the old-style teachers' skills and know-how.

As for the *contents* of elementary education, it became clear during the nineteenth century that the school's mission, parallel to that of religious instruction, extended well beyond the three basic learning skills, taught successively rather than simultaneously: reading, writing and arithmetic. In the United States, the authorities, concerned to foster whatever constituted a factor of integration, placed special emphasis on the teaching of language and history, together with practical courses on civic rights and duties. American primary schools were also notable for the prominence given to sport.

In France, the law of 1833 provided that, in addition to basic skills, elementary education should include not only 'moral and religious instruction', but also knowledge of the legal system of weights and measures, and the metric system which had been introduced by the Revolution at the end of the eighteenth century, but was still not in current use by the mid-nineteenth century.

In England at the same time, the School Boards were providing grants for certain primary continuation courses. But in neither country was there anything comparable to the sharing of responsibility for technical training, between the industrial and academic worlds then taking place in Germany.

So far we have stressed the diversity of the constraints that determined both the *structures* of education, and the *contents* of elementary schooling in various countries. But what of the *methods* of education? It was impossible to carry out the task of increasing the school population and absorbing ever-wider segments of society without seriously revising teaching practices. Consequently, questions of method were a subject of much debate throughout the nineteenth century. Such questions arose in practical terms in France from the early years of the century, because the Revolution had cut off the pedagogical legacy of the religious orders whose custom it had been to train their members to be teachers. The method used by the Christian School Brothers, a movement founded by Saint-Jean-Baptiste de La Salle in the early eighteenth century, had consisted in grouping together pupils of the same level, so that all of them could be given the same instruction at the same time: hence the name 'simultaneous instruction' applied to this method. But such a method could be used only if there were enough teachers and pupils, and this was rare outside urban areas. Textbooks, however, were the same for everybody. Elsewhere the 'individual' or 'traditional' method, criticized by all educators, was in use: the children took turns at 'reading to the master', while the others kept themselves busy. The standard practice, incidentally, was to teach pupils how to read before teaching them how to write.

Nineteenth-century pedagogical thought was mainly a legacy of the Enlightenment, and remained very much under the influence of two eighteenth-century Swiss thinkers. Thus the nineteenth century's diminishing tendency to regard children as mere 'imperfect adults' owed, essentially, to Jean-Jacques Rousseau; while the importance attached to practical and progressive teaching derived, for the most part, from Johann Heinrich Pestalozzi. In the course of the nineteenth century, Central Europe became the intellectual source of ideas that resulted in education becoming a separate discipline, Father Girard (1765–1850), a Franciscan Recollect from Fribourg, became a leading figure and his town a place of pedagogical pilgrimage that attracted educators of all nationalities. Following the Danish example (the Statutes of 1814 organizing public education) and under the influence of Pestalozzi, he advocated the cultivation of the entire personality through use of the mother tongue and progression from the concrete to the abstract. Above all, he called upon teachers to instil a love of education 'by instilling love for what they taught'. By the end of the nineteenth century educational reform movements were developing, in conjunction with social and political conflicts that fostered the emergence of new cultural contents and even wider differences, in all domains, between education systems.

Teaching methods in nineteenth-century schools had long been shaped as much by pragmatic considerations as by ideas and ideals. At the beginning of the century popular education everywhere in Europe lacked resources. As a result, English philanthropists, like their French opposite numbers in 1815, became virtually infatuated with a method designed to instruct a large number of children with only limited means: this was the 'Lancasterian' system, also referred to as 'mutual instruction'. This method consisted in entrusting the more advanced pupils with the task of acting as 'monitors' or tutors, working with small groups of fellow pupils in between general lessons by the teacher. Several schools of this type were active in England, under the guidance of a Quaker, Joseph Lancaster (1778–1838), and with the support of the National Society, the 'high' Anglican church, and the British and Foreign School Society. French liberals used such 'mutual instruction' as a weapon in their battle against the 'ultras' and religious education. Having thus become a sectarian issue, the method was the target of violent attacks. As time went by, a mixed system of education, combining the practices of 'mutual instruction' with those of simultaneous education was introduced in France around 1840. Public primary education gradually gave up the 'mutual' method, which continued, however, to be used in nurseries and some missionary schools. The training of teachers at *écoles normales*, already standard practice for boys before the law of 1833, encouraged educational innovations, such as grouping students according to their level of knowledge into their relevant 'courses' or 'divisions'. As the system of educational organization adopted for the department of the Seine in 1868 spread throughout the country, levels in French primary education gradually became uniform both within and between schools during the 1880s.

Primary education in the United States, where it varied widely from region to region, was shaped by a different set of local constraints. In a world where books were few and far between, people learned to read from the Bible. The function of schools, which were always co-educational in the public sector and usually run by women (who seem to have remained spinsters by vocation), was to create a single language and culture. Towards the end of the century methods derived from the ideas of John Dewey (1859–1952), began to appear in the major East Coast cities; from here, the system of active schools and teaching based on 'centres of interest' spread outwards.

In Latin America, primary schooling constituted the strong point of the programme of the liberals, who advocated principally the Lancasterian system. Schooling developed in the urban centres. In Mexico, for example, where the first Lancasterian schools opened in 1822, there were already 1,310 schools, with a total enrolment of some 60,000 schoolchildren, by 1835. Towards the end of the century, the expansion of 'positivism' – the philosophical

Table 13 The situation of education in different countries around 1900.

Country	Enrolment rate per 1,000 inhabitants
United States	186.0
Prussia	186.0
Switzerland	177.0
France	148.0
England	144.0
Queensland	120.5
Victoria (Australia)	120.2
South Australia	119.5
New South Wales	118.5
Spain	116.2
Italy	116.0
Japan	103.5
Costa Rica	62.7
Argentina	62.6
Uruguay	47.9
Australia (West)	46.0
Guatemala	44.2
Venezuela	43.7
Ecuador	41.9
Nicaragua	41.8
Portugal	40.9
Mexico	40.6
Paraguay	34.6
Chile	33.5
El Salvador	25.7
Colombia	19.8
Brazil	18.2
India	17.0
Peru	14.0

Source: L. López-Ocón, Centre of History Studies, CSIC, Madrid, 1900.

system originated by Auguste Comte which advocates the expansion of scientific or 'positivist' thought to the social and political spheres, and its extension to all the peoples of the earth – throughout the countries of Latin America, had the effect of encouraging educational efforts. The number of educational establishments thereafter increased rapidly. By 1870, Mexico boasted 4,000 schools, and more than double that number five years later, with a total enrolment of 300,000 children. These schools were financed largely (67 per cent) by the municipalities concerned, with a 7 per cent contribution by the federal government, the remainder being provided by private individuals. However, it would be wrong to speak of a 'take-off' in the matter of school enrolment on the Latin American continent. Overall, the duration of schooling did not exceed two or three years, and primary-level enrolment rates remained well below those of most European countries. Table 13, outlining the situation around 1900, shows, first, that the highest enrolment rates were situated between 10 and 20 per cent; and second, that the geographical distribution of these countries covers several continents.

Education for the elite

Secondary education in the nineteenth century remained the preserve of the elite. Whether the establishments in which it was imparted were public or private, secular or religious, it was usually fee-paying. Even in the United States, where it was provided free by the municipal authorities, in 1910 only 5 per cent of primary school pupils were taking advantage of it. In other words most young people headed straight into working life or apprenticeship upon completion of their primary studies.

And yet secondary education was developing and changing in the nineteenth century. In Great Britain, the long-established 'public schools' emerged from their torpor, following the introduction of a series of reforms by Thomas Arnold, headmaster of Rugby school from 1828 to 1842. Other schools were founded on the same principles: they were boarding schools; the pupils were divided into small groups in separate houses; there was a basis of mutual trust; and the older boys had authority over the younger ones. The purpose of the education that was given, with a strong bias towards classical languages and character training, was to form 'Christian gentlemen'. For the population at large, secondary education, which was entirely unregulated, came in all shapes and sizes.

This was a far cry from the French *lycée*, a state institution established by Napoleon, where the boarders lived collectively under strict military discipline. The course of studies, which had to be paid for, was of seven years duration and led to the *baccalauréat*. After 1815, the *lycées*, rechristened 'royal colleges', once again accorded classical studies the pride of place they had lost during the revolutionary period, although they continued to function like barracks. The organization of studies remained highly centralized and bureaucratic. As a result, many families turned instead to the religious colleges. The girls' *lycées* and *collèges*, established by law in 1880, provided a form of instruction that was considered more appropriate for women, with no Latin or philosophy, and not too much science; even so, by 1900, they had still not yet outnumbered the convent schools to which families traditionally entrusted their daughters for an education that was usually briefer than that given to boys. Taken as a whole, French secondary education, with the many reforms of content it underwent during the nineteenth century, was a distinguishing feature of French bourgeois life. Republicans nevertheless regarded it as a means of 'democratization' in that the *lycée* could, on the basis of a competitive examination, award places to scholarship-holders, who might be the children of minor civil servants or even occasionally of workers, such as Victor Duruy, who became Minister of Public Education in 1863.

In most European secondary schools the course concluded with a final examination, the prerequisite for entry to university. In France, for example, it was the *baccalauréat*; in the German *Gymnasium*, it was the *Abitur or Matura*; in the United States, as in Europe, an examination was held at the end of four years of high school (which was divided into two parts). In France, the *lycée* offered *baccalauréat*-holders work as supervisors or monitors. The training of teachers was the main function of the universities, leading to the *licence* or the *agrégation*. The latter, a competitive examination giving access to the teaching profession, was held separately in each discipline and maintained a very high standard. By and large, secondary school teachers in the nineteenth century were university graduates.

What kind of culture was secondary education inculcating? The reply varied in accordance with the type of elite to be trained. In Europe, as a rule, it consisted initially of the classical humanities, but these gradually (but not invariably, and with many ups and downs) gave way to the scientific disciplines that, step by step, had by the end of our period gained the status of 'modern humanities'. In Germany, for example, the *Gymnasium* for many long years gave pride of place to the classical languages rather than to science. An intermediate, more vocationally oriented type of education developed, not without difficulty, alongside the secondary system, for the purpose of producing supervisory staff for the armies of workers, and training middle-grade personnel for industry and commerce. In France, the law of 1833 introduced higher primary education, with the usual aims of that level. This constituted an embryonic form of vocational education, but it only began to take off in the 1880s, when new technologies gave rise to a demand for specific types of vocational training; at that point, it started to become a serious rival of secondary education.

On the African continent, some of the missionary schools focused on religious training, such as the famous school of Mother Javouhey in Senegal, whose purpose was to train an African clergy. Most schools, however, had a much broader mission, and gradually came to cater for all levels of education: their chief task was that of spreading literacy, and some countries, such as Madagascar, thanks to the numerous schools of the Livingstone Mission established throughout the island, achieved literacy rates close to those current in Europe towards the end of the nineteenth century. Other missionary schools, such as the Lovedale Missionary Institution established in 1841, in the Cape, taught a number of practical skills (printing, tailoring, carpentry, masonry), and contributed to the training of teachers and administrators. Fourah Bay College, founded in 1827 in West Africa by the Church Missionary Society, together with similar schools established in the Cape, trained large numbers of teachers and journalists, who served as relays for the spread of Western culture. In this way, there arose a mixed culture, a culture of 'creoles', as educated people were called in Sierra Leone, and this culture produced catechist priests, teachers and doctors, as well as business managers and merchants who traded abroad. When, in the late nineteenth century, this very rich, mixed culture came up against the racist or eugenic theories developed by such Western intellectuals as Gobineau or Richard Burton and propagated by European missionaries and administrators in Africa, a number of African intellectuals responded with the religious and political nationalist movement known as Ethiopianism, developing a pan-Africanism rooted in awareness of an African identity.

In the Muslim East, primary and secondary schooling, which was traditionally provided by Islamic institutions, began to claim the attention of political leaders only towards the end of the century, with the establishment of public schools, including girls' schools. For the most part, reforms were focused chiefly on specialized education. At its highest level, the education system underwent a profound renewal during the nineteenth century. The universities inherited from the Middle Ages, in which traditional knowledge was transmitted by established methods, were reformed to meet the training needs of qualified teachers, and adapted themselves to the development of research and industry. This called for specialization, which in many countries led to the establishment of technical institutions and schools.

Such was the case in Egypt. The purpose of the schools created under the *Tanzīmāt* reforms of the early nineteenth century was essentially military. The first public school established by Muhammad Ali in 1816 was a military school, and this was followed by more specialized artillery, cavalry, naval and infantry schools. Other disciplines were taught at the Medical School (established in 1827), the Pharmacological School (1829), the Veterinary School (1827–9), and the Polytechnic School (1834). But a military-style, iron discipline was the rule everywhere. The students, mainly Turkish-speaking in the military schools and Arabic-speaking in the scientific schools, were all considered to be military recruits, and were awarded military ranks on graduation. While strongly national in emphasis, this movement had the effect of strengthening ties with Europe: at first, the teachers were French or Italian; and the translation of technical works was stimulated by the foundation in 1833 of the School of Languages, which gave rise to what is known as the *nahda*, or 'renaissance' of the Arabic language. The same military interests encouraged a new openness to Western science in Morocco: at the time of the reforms of the Moroccan state (the *Makhzan*), an engineering school was founded at Fez by the Frenchman de Saulty for the purpose of training surveyors, map-makers and artillerymen, and translations of scientific books were ordered from the Pasha of Egypt. In Syria, the system of education was developed somewhat later, around 1870, and was aimed chiefly at training civil servants.

American higher education was private to begin with. Harvard, the oldest university of the United States, was founded in the seventeenth century, followed by Princeton, also in the East. For its part, Berkeley, in California, was set up in 1856. Universities were financed by foundations or by donations from alumni, without any apparent detriment to the freedom of instruction. Tuition fees were high, but reductions were granted to outstanding students of humble origin. Towards the middle of the nineteenth century the western states established universities at which, although they functioned in much the same way as the private universities, the admission fees were by contrast very low. By the end of the century technical schools had also been established for the training of engineers and for business studies. Higher education began with four years of college, during which the students received a general education before going on to specialized studies in graduate schools. These colleges were eventually converted into universities. The first colleges for girls, such as Vassar and Wellesley in the east, appeared around 1850, whereas both sexes attended the same colleges in the west. Campuses, which were generally situated outside major conurbations, were not just places for study. The teachers lived on campus, as did the students, who joined 'fraternities' and were lodged in hostels. Sporting, cultural and charitable activities combined to create a genuine social life within the university. By 1900, American universities had attained a level of prosperity attested to by the rapid growth of the student body.

European universities, which were generally much older, did not all face up to the nineteenth century with the same vitality. In France, the 'schools' which had existed prior to the Revolution were not all replaced. Higher education, now under strict state supervision, was in part dispensed at the *grandes écoles*, set up to train engineers for the major state institutions, mining, civil engineering, etc. While schools of law and medicine were restored fairly quickly because they met society's need for lawyers and doctors, faculties of letters and sciences had few students other than those aiming to become secondary school teachers or members of the clergy, with the result that many university teachers in the provinces had to take up purely scholarly pursuits or give public lectures. The picture was different in

Paris: generously endowed with institutes of higher learning, libraries and reference material, the capital attracted the brightest students and the most gifted teachers. It was not in the faculties, however, that the most valuable and voluminous scientific work was produced. Poorly housed and lacking in resources, they rarely undertook original research, and it was only towards the end of the Second Empire, at the instigation of teachers from the *Ecole normale*, that reforms were introduced. The fact that Victor Duruy, Minister of Education from 1863 to 1869, set up the *Ecole pratique des hautes études* in order to revitalize research shows that he had little confidence in the possibility of reviving it in the faculties. When the republicans came to power they took steps to combine the faculties into universities (under the law of 1896), increased the number of university posts and created lectureships in an attempt to curtail the development of private higher education and in the hope of creating a republican elite. The student body grew considerably, mainly perhaps as a result of social change. France sought to rival the best of 'Prussian' scholarship, and the University of Paris was restored to the ranks of the great European universities. The unique feature of French higher education nevertheless remained the existence of a parallel system that siphoned off the best students, namely the *grandes écoles*, which continued to proliferate throughout the century.

In Great Britain, Oxford and Cambridge woke up in the course of the century, combining a deliberately old-fashioned approach with some startling innovations. The creation of new universities posed a challenge, and, except in Scotland, they did not become scientifically productive until the end of the century. The University of London already comprised several colleges by the time it was officially recognized. In 1895 it was joined by the London School of Economics. The major industrial towns, occasionally thanks to individual philanthropists, set up colleges, which by the turn of the century had been transformed into fully-fledged universities; two such were Birmingham and Liverpool. Located in the city centre, they broke away from the Oxonian model of classical studies through the emphasis placed on the applied sciences. The Scottish universities, even more democratic in their recruitment policies, also displayed a sort of 'institutional nationalism' that explains why state intervention, still fairly negligible at the end of the century, was considered unnecessary.

With all their traditions and their contradictions, the various education systems forged in Europe were taken as a model in the nineteenth century for countries of Asian civilization that already had cultivated elites of their own. In 1868 the transformation brought about by Mutsu-Hito in Japan ushered in the Meiji ('enlightened government') era. Primary schools on the Western pattern proliferated, and the first 'new style' university opened in Tokyo in 1877. China, on the other hand, resisted innovation, except during the episode of the Hundred Days (1898), when a handful of intellectuals joined forces with learned societies, newspapers and educated circles; whereas Vietnam came under French influence after the colonization of Tonkin (1883–4). The refusal to recognize the traditional role of the lettered classes, combined with colonial exploitation, fostered a climate of latent revolt, and educational institutions were Westernized on the surface only.

In the Muslim East, universities developed rather later than the military institutes. Two attempts at founding an Ottoman university failed, in 1863 and 1870; it was only in 1900 that the Ottoman Public University was opened, with four faculties: religion, mathematics, natural sciences and literature. In Egypt, the private university established in 1908 was made into a public university in 1925, that too with four faculties: arts, science, law and pharmacology. In other countries, it was the mission schools which led to the establishment of universities; such was the case, for instance, with the Protestant College of Syria, which later became the American University of Beirut; the University of St Joseph was founded in Beirut in 1874, by French Jesuits. In fact, the purpose of many of the reforms instigated by Istanbul and applied in such provinces as Syria was to compete with the training provided by the mission schools. Eventually, the Islamic higher education dispensed by the al-Azhar Mosque in Egypt was reformed in the 1890s.

Rivalry between different religious confessions or philosophical schools was also a factor in the education dynamic in Latin America. At the beginning of the century, the liberals, who were highly critical of the Latin-based 'Gothic education', wanted to wipe the colonial slate clean and start afresh. The existing 'vice-regal' universities, which were felt to be bastions of obscurantism, were thus closed: Mexico City in 1833, and Bogotá in 1850. New universities were founded, such as Buenos Aires in 1821, and Colombia in 1867, with a view to spreading 'enlightenment'. Other universities, such as that of Santiago de Chile, were simply renovated. Thanks to its political stability, the Republic of Chile underwent continuous educational development: the state, which took full responsibility for education, undertook to ensure the systematic transfer of European scientific and technical knowledge by appointing such professors as Andrés Bello, the jurist and linguist who found the University of Santiago, the Polish mineralogist Ignacy Domeyko, and the French naturalist Claude Gay. The University of Santiago attracted students from all over Latin America, and the National Institute, an institution of secondary and higher education, was a major centre for the training of the country's leaders. However, these highly elitist institutions had a limited intake of students: only a few dozen engineering degrees were awarded by the Faculty of Science, and no more than a few hundred students attended the National Institute. Towards the end of the century, particular efforts were made to ensure the training of teachers in Latin America. The Argentine Domingo Faustino Sarmiento (1811–88), the future President of Argentina, founded the Paraná Normal School in 1870; the Mexican Gabino Barreda, an advocate of the positivism of Comte, also in about 1870 founded the Preparatory School, a secondary and higher education institution which trained the administrative elite of the authoritarian regime of Porfirio Díaz. For the most part admirers of the educational efforts of the French Third Republic, the South American reformers held numerous educational congresses between 1880 and 1900, aimed at unifying the education systems of the various Latin American republics. Pedagogical renovation was high on the agenda with the creation of pedagogical museums and publications such as *The Reform of Elementary Schools*, a Mexican periodical launched in 1885, or *The Modern School*, established in 1889.

In Africa, the creation of universities got off to a modest start with the establishment of the School of Medicine in Dakar in 1918. On the other hand, teacher training was more substantial: the Normal School of Amanzimtote, which opened in the 1860s, was followed around the turn of the century by other schools for the training of teachers and professors.

Affected by the optimism of the Enlightenment and belief in the virtues of education, the nineteenth century undoubtedly contributed to the spread of education throughout ever-broader segments of the population. But attention must be drawn to the persistent contrast between primary education, intended for all, and secondary and higher education, which remained the preserve of a moneyed and well-born elite, only slightly enlarged by the scholarship meritocracy. Thus educational institutions helped simply to readjust the balance, without provoking social upheaval.

RESEARCH

The nineteenth century witnessed major transformations in the structures and methods of research. On the one hand, scientists began to stir themselves and form associations; on the other, the powers that be were becoming aware of the link between scientific research and its potential applications in the various sectors of production. Accordingly, they began to intervene in the organization of research and higher education. The ever closer relations, in an era of industrialization and development of communication networks, between scientific work and technical, agricultural and medical work helped to sustain a belief in progress and the possibility of bettering human life through scientific development.

In the course of the century scientific research ceased to be an individual and private activity and became professional, organized, and public. The social dynamics, institutional integration and funding of research varied from country to country, but the process of internationalization that was to lead in the twentieth century to the present system of worldwide research got under way in the early years of the nineteenth century. This process was brought about by collaboration, exchanges and emulation: the professionalization and organization of research first gained momentum in Europe and then spread throughout the world in pace with the development of higher education, and with the interest shown by governments and industrialists in research, increasingly perceived as a potential source of power and wealth.

From scholar to scientist

At the beginning of the nineteenth century research was still a pursuit of 'scholars', men of science, sometimes teachers, who pursued their interests in a private capacity in what were often their own personal laboratories. Some were still 'amateurs' in the tradition of former times. Intellectual considerations, such as the increasing specialization of scientific knowledge, and material factors, such as the increasingly technical nature of experimentation, helped gradually to reduce the scope of the amateur's activities. While an amateur with a telescope, a good microscope, a geologist's hammer or a mere herbarium could still make an original contribution in astronomy or the natural sciences, this became much less frequent in physics or chemistry. Esoteric language and advanced mathematics eliminated many former readers of scientific papers. The triumphant progress of classical mechanics – a model for the other sciences – helped to shape a positivist and even reductionist view of knowledge. Some disciplines, such as astronomy and chemistry, were quicker than others to embark upon this dual process of division of knowledge and

professionalization, but the process was none the less global. By the end of the century science had become virtually inaccessible to anyone who had not received specialized training and did not possess the necessary instruments. It is true that it was still regarded as a cultural activity, but that was due largely, as we shall see, to the rise of popular science.

The process of professionalization, which was part and parcel of the specialization of research that took over from the eighteenth-century encyclopaedic version, took the form essentially of a division of labour within the scientific community. This division took place first between disciplines and then within the disciplines themselves; for example between theoreticians on the one hand and experimenters or field workers on the other. Increasingly specialized reviews appeared in many different parts of Europe and the United States. These became the exclusive repositories of research work, while the treatise retained its function as a vehicle of official, authorized knowledge for the edification of students.

Specialization soon led to changes in the nature of relations between scientists. While professionals and amateurs still mingled with some learned societies, efforts were already being made in various places to draw up criteria for separating them, in other words professional criteria. The Gesellschaft Deutscher Naturforscher und Ärtze (Society of German Naturalists and Doctors), one of the very first associations for the advancement of science (founded in 1822), restricted membership to those who had work published, which in the minds of its founding members amounted to objective recognition of competence. Little by little, learned societies of scientists doing research in a single discipline were to supplant those that covered several disciplines. For example, chemistry societies were set up in London in 1841, Paris in 1857, Berlin in 1866, Saint Petersburg in 1868 and the United States in 1876. Local and provincial academies that had flourished during the Enlightenment fell into decline, whereas the great and famous institutions such as the Académie Royale des Sciences of Paris and the Royal Society of London retained their authority and influence, although they became less effective in steering the course of research and increasingly concerned with the distribution of honours and awards.

In Great Britain amateurs managed to retain a honourable and honoured position longer than in France and possibly Germany. Witness the crucial role played by such 'gentlemen amateurs' as the mathematician Charles Babbage, the physicist James Joule and the naturalist Charles Darwin. The Royal Institution of London, founded in 1799, which was where Michael Faraday worked, was expressly given the dual task of scientific research and popularization. Unlike the Paris Académie des Sciences, the Royal Society welcomed amateurs into its ranks. And the principal activity of the British Association for the Advancement of Science, the most active of bodies for the promotion of scientific work, was to organize annual meetings at which eminent scientists presented a summary of their work and their proposals for reform to a well-educated but non-specialist public. All these societies were characterized by the independence of their members from the authorities. It is symptomatic that the proposal made in 1872 by a member of the Royal Society to set up a ministry of science, triggered reactions of hostility on the part of the scientists that were every bit as keen as those of the politicians.

Paradoxically, it was in this very country where the 'scholar' remained an important figure in research throughout the nineteenth century that the neologism 'scientist' first appeared, around 1850, signalling the end of the period in which research was carried out by scholars working individually without official obligations. Henceforth, science was to be a profession, and research an essential element in a 'scientist's' career. Scientific research became what was essentially a professional, salaried activity, requiring prior training formally sealed by a diploma. The scientist could now cut a separate figure from those practising other professions, such as engineers, or in other socially recognized categories, such as inventors.

University research

The introduction of research into university education, the cornerstone of the process of professionalization, occurred in very different ways in different countries.

In the scientific institutions created in France under the Revolution, stress lay on the practical purpose of science. The Bureau des Longitudes, the Museum of Natural History, the Conservatoire National des Arts et Métiers, the schools of medicine and above all the Ecole Polytechnique, set up to train highly qualified engineers and officers for state service, enjoyed an intellectual and social status far superior to that of the universities. The coupling of the most advanced forms of mathematics with laboratory, workshop and technical-drawing pursuits, inaugurated a new style of scientific training. With such figures as Laplace, Monge, Berthollet, Arago, Gay-Lussac, Chaptal, Cuvier and Jussieu, early nineteenth-century Paris attracted large numbers of foreign scientists. Illustrious Germans such as Alexander von Humboldt and Liebig, Davy and Faraday from England, Oersted from Denmark, de Candole from Geneva and Ostrogradsky from Russia, spent time in the salons and laboratories of Paris. However, this outburst of scientific activity, particularly among the physicists and chemists in the entourage of Laplace and Berthollet in the Société d'Arcueil, barely outlasted the 1820s. After that date, having joined the staff of the Napoleonic university or other educational establishments, French scientists devoted themselves mainly to their teaching responsibilities, and were not averse to holding positions in several different institutions at the same time. They trained few students in the techniques of research. In Russia, as in France, research tended to be initiated and undertaken far more by the scientific societies, in particular the Academy of St Petersburg, and the large observatories, which took the lead in organizing research.

The situation evolved very differently in Germany. Under the reform of Prussian higher education introduced by Wilhelm von Humboldt early in the nineteenth century, research became an integral part of the work of universities, which were independent and competed with one another. During the first half of the century stress was placed on the fundamental sciences and the acquisition of knowledge for its own sake. The marked indifference to utilitarian concerns and to technology was due partly to institutional rigidity: science continued to be taught in the faculties of philosophy. The champions of *Naturphilosophie*, who had Romantic leanings, were critical of the arid and abstract nature of the mathematically oriented and dehumanized sort of science, as they saw it, which was practised by the disciples of Laplace. Convinced of the deep-lying harmony between humankind and nature, they refused to allow science to be reduced to a set of laws. Despite their mutual antagonism, these two opposing tendencies in European thought of the early nineteenth century shared a common belief in the need for experimentation, with greater emphasis on quality among the advocates of *Naturphilosophie* and on quantity among the disciples of Laplacian physics.

At the urging of the chemist Justus von Liebig, training in research was eventually included in German university syllabuses. Thanks to the development of a very simple apparatus, the analysis of organic substances became a routine operation in Liebig's laboratories, thus freeing hands and minds for research projects. Reacting against an approach that subordinated the scientific disciplines to professional training (for medicine, pharmacy, engineering, etc.) and eager to defend pure science, Liebig set himself the task of training future researchers through intensive, daily, laboratory work. At a time when science faculties in France were giving *ex-cathedra* training to future secondary school teachers, Liebig, who had been appointed to a chair at Giessen University in the mid-1820s, introduced laboratory instruction during which students did chemistry practical for eight hours a day. The main purpose of this was not so much to extend the applications of chemistry as to probe more deeply into the foundations of the discipline and develop the students' creativity. This method of teaching, which saw science as a process of investigation rather than a set of principles to be inculcated, was squarely in the tradition of the *wissenschaftliche Seminare* or 'scientific seminars', which were veritable nurseries of young scientists in German universities towards the end of the eighteenth century. Those seminars, in which students and professors discussed their research work, were designed to train secondary school teachers as budding researchers. The Königsberg seminar, for instance, begun by the mathematician Carl von Jacobi and continued by the physicist Franz Neumann, was to serve as a model for many other universities.

The development of laboratory training gave rise to a number of major changes in the way in which science was done. In addition to the cabinet containing the instruments used to demonstrate experiments on the lecture-room rostrum, it was necessary to fit out laboratories in which the students would learn not just how to handle the equipment, but also the habits associated with the discipline, its scientific standards, and the ways of gauging errors of measurement. This led to a change in the design of scientific instruments: not only did they have to be made in large numbers; they had to meet the criteria of reliability and ease of manipulation, regardless of aesthetic considerations.

Once it had been included among a teacher's responsibilities, research became a key requirement for university appointments in Germany and for a successful career. A corollary of this development – its unconditional supporters would say a prerequisite – was the very wide freedom of choice left to teachers regarding the subject of their research and the methods to be used. Students too were allowed great freedom: no set syllabus was imposed on them, and they were free to follow courses and work with the teacher of their choice. This system, combining constraint with flexibility, was responsible for the high repute in which German universities were held in the nineteenth century.

The tandem of teaching and research, which was to spread gradually to other countries, had repercussions on the development of science. For instance, it was while composing a treatise on general chemistry for the use of students that Mendeleyev, a professor at the University of St Petersburg, decided to classify the chemical elements and, in 1869, devised the periodic table. Treatises and textbooks, forming a bridge between research and teaching, were an essential vehicle for the spread of knowledge in the nineteenth century. A product of research, they represented a particular way of recording results that fixed and presented knowledge in a form that made it easier to understand and memorize. By so doing, they greatly helped both students and teachers to identify with a particular discipline. Textbooks, moreover, were by their very nature designed to train new recruits, whole armies of scientists, who would eventually take up appointments in academe, or in industry. They were therefore a key element in the process of professionalization typical of our period.

Just as the laboratories of Paris had lured scholars and students from all over Europe during the opening decades of the nineteenth century, so the German universities – their laboratories, research institutes and seminars – were to become the training and meeting grounds for many young foreigners wishing to complete their university education and to round it off with a doctorate. In the first quarter of the nineteenth century the Ecole Polytechnique had influenced a whole generation of scientists and served widely as a model for the organization of higher technical education. Now, in the second half of the century, it was the turn of the German university system to set the pattern in many countries for the organization of institutes of higher education, in Central and Eastern Europe to begin with, and then in the United States. A good example is Johns Hopkins University, founded in Baltimore in 1876, which made basic research the linchpin of its programme of advanced studies. It was not until the end of the century that the reforms introduced by the Third Republic in France offered universities greater resources and freedom, while fostering links with local economic forces. In Paris and London alike, the German model was cited as an example when calling upon governments to provide laboratories and funds for research.

The system of faculties, chairs and institutes peculiar to European universities gave rise to demarcation problems, and was not always well suited to the relentless pace of nineteenth-century scientific breakthroughs, which brought in their train increasing specialization and differentiation between disciplines. This is why the graduate schools, operating independently of undergraduate colleges and still a feature of the American research system today, proved to be more flexible than European universities and more likely to take up state-of-the-art or interdisciplinary research. As a result, in Europe new trends, such as the physicochemical approach to biological phenomena, or the field known as the 'industrial sciences' at the turn of the century, found it difficult to make permanent breakthroughs in the university system.

Observatories played a growing role in the organization of research. In 1832, there was not a single observatory in the United States; fifty years later there was a total of 144 observatories throughout the country. In Russia under Nicholas I, in 1839, the Ministry of Public Education established near St. Petersburg the Observatory of Pulkovo, which became the great centre of Russian astronomy, thanks to its director, Friederich Wilhelm Jakob von Struve, one of the top astronomers of the day, who secured for the observatory the most powerful telescope in the world at that time.

Regardless of the reputation of the institution, scientific research was also strongly influenced by the local stimulus of scientists of high calibre, 'big name' professors surrounded by their assistants. For instance, William Thomson, who was awarded a peerage as Lord Kelvin for his scientific work, played an essential part in Glasgow, where he set his students to work in his university laboratory on the electrical problems raised by submarine cable laying. In a similar way 'research schools' sprang up all over Europe, i.e. groups of researchers trained and assembled by a leading scientist and specializing in a particular field of investigation or research programme. Following the work of Maxwell, this was to become a tradition in the field of electricity in England; in Germany a flourishing school of physiology sprang up around Johannes Müller, du Bois-Reymond and Helmholz, attracting young students from all over Europe. Other examples are the late-nineteenth-century school of physical chemistry in Sweden with Arrhenius, Ångström and Waage, and the study of soil science in Russia under the influence of Dukushayev. Historians of science, alert to the differences between these research schools, emphasize that each had its own particular method and style of conducting research, such that knowledge and skills were learned not from books, but were acquired *in situ*, in the daily work of the laboratory. Each had its own layout and way of organizing space, its hierarchy of students and teachers within the team, and its relations with the outside world, with other members of the scientific community and with engineers, technicians or agronomists. These different 'styles' of research, which tended to be ascribed to national characteristics, are today generally regarded as local traditions stemming from the way in which the research work was organized.

It is still difficult to assess the role played by the organization of research in the scientific supremacy of France at the beginning of the century, Great Britain in the middle years, and Germany at the end. Each country followed a different path, but by the end of the century scientific research in most European countries was a field of its own, with rules laid down by peers, sharply defined study courses, and investigative activities conducted in every area of knowledge.

Pure and applied research

While university research, by and large, was devoted to science for science's sake, this principle was not applied in the same way in all countries. The mobilization of French chemists and physicists during the French Revolution at the end of the eighteenth century revealed the economic and military potential of science in the extreme situation created by a state of war. When peace was restored, physicists and chemists had no difficulty in presenting their disciplines as the inevitable prerequisites of technical development. The argument from utility – 'industry is the offspring of science' – was exploited by academics in their requests for laboratories, chairs, posts and funding. During the first half of the nineteenth century such an assertion, it must be confessed, was largely rhetorical: the leading industries, metallurgy, the steam engine, textiles and the chemistry of soda and sulphuric acid, owed little to the discoveries of academic scientists. It was when methods developed in the laboratory – analysis, control, purification and standardization – began to be used in industrial production with the chemical fertilizers developed by Liebig and others, followed by chemical dyes and electrical telegraphy during the 1840s, that the distinction between pure and applied science began to be really meaningful.

In practical terms, however, the distinction between pure and applied research was less obvious on the laboratory floor than in official pronouncements. Fundamental scientific discoveries were made in many laboratories that were conducting research on practical problems. For example, the new discipline of microbiology emerged from Pasteur's work on the fermentation of beer, chicken cholera, anthrax and rabies. Conversely, theoretical physics research, such as the study of cathode rays, led to the discovery of X-rays, which were immediately used for medical purposes. The Cavendish Laboratory provides a good example of how scientific and technical activities can support one another. It was established with private money at Cambridge University in 1872, under the direction of J. C. Maxwell, and specialized in the study of electrical phenomena. Theoretical work on electromagnetism was carried out alongside the development of instruments of the highest possible precision; the electrical characteristics of telegraph cables and similar subjects were also studied. All this research was closely interlinked, both in the understanding of the phenomena involved and in the experimental methods employed. The saga of the laying of the first transatlantic telegraph cable symbolized this alliance between science, technology and the political and commercial interests of the British Empire.

Relations between pure and applied research did not constitute a one-way process. Science benefited considerably from industrial progress, in particular through the increasingly pure chemicals that became available and the advances in precision engineering that greatly improved the technical performance of instruments.

Accordingly, a number of scientific societies – at first in chemistry, then in physics and electricity – took steps to establish close links between academics and industrial or administrative circles in order to promote exchanges of information.

Ultimately, what most clearly distinguished academic from industrial research was the manner in which the results were made known: whereas pure scientific research was widely published, the findings of industrial research were protected by patents. At the same time it should be noted that there was a continuum of methods, ranging from the simple tests and controls carried out in a factory to the most abstruse theoretical research in physics.

By the end of the nineteenth century, the age of solitary researchers working in their own studies was at an end; the increasingly complex equipment and instruments necessitated a division of labour and substantial financial backing, which was often linked to military or industrial interests. Such a situation was bound to lead to the direct involvement of the public authorities.

In the service of industry and the state

Starting in the 1820s, certain scientists, such as Charles Babbage in *Reflections on the Decline of Science and on Some of its Causes* (London, 1830), began to urge the state to subsidize research. The rationale was not so much to improve the lot of humankind as to remove the obstacles to industrial progress. In those days research required only modest resources, no more than a tiny fraction of national budgets.

Until the turn of the century, nevertheless, no public authority showed any real eagerness to finance research, other than through university budgets in those countries where higher education was financed by the state. If we take the case of Germany, regarded as a country that 'invested' very early in its scientific research, we find that between 1850 and 1914, total expenditure on science and technology by the Reich and the federal states never exceeded 1.8 per cent of the total budget, including financing for universities. Of this amount, scientific and technical expenditure outside the university rose nearly tenfold – from 1.4 per cent in 1850 to 11 per cent in 1914. In absolute terms, the 1914 total is 150 times that of 1850 (10.7 million marks as compared with 62,000). This was a substantial increase, but on the whole the budget for research remained modest. Admittedly, many of the technical advances of the eighteenth and nineteenth centuries owed nothing to the discovery of the scientific principles on which they were based, and in many cases the lapse of time between a fundamental discovery and its application was far too long to incite governments to take research under their wing. Considerations of short-term profitability were the rule in all areas recognized as being of national interest, including tropical medicine, a speciality taken up by the colonial powers.

On the other hand, industrialists were beginning to take an interest in research and to invest in long-term projects. It was in Germany and the United States at the end of the nineteenth century, that laboratories began to be set up in factories belonging to the chemical and electrical engineering sectors, that were strongly dependent on research. At Siemens, Bayer and BASF (Badische Anilin und Soda Fabrik), these were genuine research laboratories and not just testing and control centres. With new sources of funding, a new institutional basis and a new focus, a blueprint for the organization of research was beginning to take shape. Research work in these laboratories was collective and goal-oriented, and invention was programmed, as it were. At the Menlo Park laboratory set up by Thomas Edison, physicists, chemists, engineers and instrument-makers all worked together. A little later General Electric installed research laboratories in its factories. Work on incandescent light bulbs led to the discovery of the thermionic effect fundamental to the diode, which was to play an essential part in wireless telegraphy. Thus industrial research proved fruitful but involved a degree of risk, since investment was high and the waiting period sometimes very long: thirty years of painstaking research passed between the discovery of the structure of benzene in 1865, and the marketing of artificial indigo; forty years between the discovery of electromagnetic induction and the manufacture of the dynamo.

When these industrial research laboratories became widespread at the beginning of the twentieth century, they began to absorb ever increasing numbers of the graduates produced year by year by higher education establishments. For young people not interested in a university career or secondary teaching, industry offered well-paid jobs. For example, the number of qualified chemists in the mainstream German chemical industry rose from ten in 1870 (0.2 per cent of all employees) to 781 in 1913 (2.7 per cent). During the same period the number of chemists holding university or senior technical school appointments declined in relative terms: higher than that of industrial chemists in 1875 (by 74 to 29), it was lagging behind by 1890 (124 to

207), and the relative decline continued – until in 1910 there were 360 chemists in university posts as compared with 651 in industry.

As links between the university and industry developed, the great 'names' of research used the booming 'scientific' industries and their economic success as an argument to convince the state of the importance of research and the need to support it. This collaboration, which became a financial necessity for research, was equally beneficial to industry, which had need of standards, measurement and control processes and units recognized in all countries. To compare the power of two dynamos, one in Berlin and the other in Paris, there had to be standardized measuring instruments. Without measurement processes to enable long-distance comparison, the only way of comparing two machines or electric lighting systems was to install them side-by-side in the same place. Indeed, one of the main purposes of the many international exhibitions held at the end of the century was to pit the technical systems and instruments of different countries against one another. The International Bureau of Weights and Measurements was established by international convention in 1875, precisely in order to lay down laboratory standards, in particular for the measurement of length and temperature. The industrial stakes were much higher in the case of electrical standards, and no country was willing to allow any other to establish a monopoly over them. Under pressure from their scientific communities spearheaded by the physicists, Germany, England and the United States founded national physical and technical research institutes: Berlin set up the Physikalisch-Technische Reichsanstalt (National Physical and Technical Institute) in 1887, London the National Physical Laboratory in 1899, and the United States Government created the National Bureau of Standards in Washington in 1901. A similar project was proposed in Japan before the First World War and materialized in 1917 with the National Physical and Chemical Institute. The task of these bodies was to produce standards, calibrate scientific instruments and analyse materials for both university and industry, and to carry out whatever research was needed for the fulfilment of their duties. While such research was one of the means by which state bureaucracies could regulate industrial and commercial activities, it also allowed them, quite apart from their testing and analysis activities, to devote a certain portion of their efforts to basic science.

With the rapid proliferation of research areas and the high demands made on researchers, the university, by requiring its staff to spend too much time and energy on teaching duties, began to seem less and less like the ideal research environment. Patronage, private or industrial, frequently came forward to make up for what was perceived as the state's failure to act. The Institut Pasteur, founded in Paris in 1888, and the Physikalisch-Technische Reichsanstalt in Berlin, were the product of public subscription, and the generosity of Werner von Siemens, the industrialist, respectively. Ernest Solvay, a rich Belgian magnate, set up several specialized institutes and organized in Brussels beginning in 1911, a series of congresses on the most fundamental aspects of physics and chemistry. It was principally in the United States that a tradition of highly promising philanthropic foundations sprang up. The pure sciences had but one national scientific centre, the Smithsonian Institution, a private foundation established in 1846, and headed for many years by a scientist of international repute, the physicist Joseph Henry. In 1901, it was the multimillionaire

Andrew Carnegie, and not the federal government, that set up in Washington an institution devoted exclusively to research and free of all teaching duties. Immediately, influential scientific circles in Germany proposed the creation of a similar body and got their way in 1911, with the foundation of the Kaiser Wilhelm Gesellschaft (now known as the Max Planck Society). Comprising several research institutes, this body was financed by the private sector (industry and banks); even though the state provided no more than the site and the Emperor's blessing, the foundation marked an important stage on the way to recognition by the public authorities of the importance of scientific research for the nation's well-being and security. For the backers of this project, the military and science were the twin pillars of German might. Germany's rivalry with America and German strategic interests dictated that optimum conditions should be provided, failing which the fatherland risked being weakened. Nor should it be forgotten that competition was a powerful factor shaping the organization and focus of research, and one which contributed to its increasingly international nature.

The international scientific community

In the early nineteenth century, scientists showed a sense of belonging to a community that transcended national frontiers. As nationalism tightened its grip on Europe, however, new forms of international relations arose in the scientific world.

Even though French and Latin, once the common languages of science, gave way to the various national languages, the traditions of communication and collaboration between scientists were maintained throughout the nineteenth century, making good use of the technical progress that made travel and communication faster and cheaper. After years of study and research under famous teachers young graduates returned to their countries of origin not just with the knowledge they had acquired but with different ways of seeing and doing. In this way they helped to spread schools of thought and practice beyond national frontiers.

Frequent contacts of this kind and the cooperative networks that sometimes sprang up in their wake, helped the international scientific community to hold fast and defend itself at a time when growing rivalry between the great powers might have threatened it. But another factor made a more direct contribution to the internationalization of science: the division of labour within the research field and the drive for efficiency resulted in the planning of research work as a highly organized undertaking. Quite apart from the specific demands of certain disciplines – such as meteorology or astronomy, for example, which required simultaneous observations – it was the need to rationalize efforts, mobilize the best qualified researchers and reduce costs that caused the division of labour to overlap national frontiers and led to the creation of international scientific associations and congresses, whose number constantly rose – doubling every eight years – from 1860 until the eve of the First World War.

Given that uniform units of measurement, terminology and standards were perceived at the time as a major prerequisite for scientific progress, international gatherings were considered essential for reaching agreement at an international level on the appropriate terminology for each scientific discipline, as well as on research instruments and methods. The eighteenth century had already set in motion the process of international collaboration in astronomy: study of the transit of Venus across the face of the sun in 1761 and 1769, had necessitated the comparison of a large number of observations made in different parts of the world. That had been a one-off operation with no centralized organization. The study of the earth's magnetism, launched in the 1830s by the German mathematician and physicist Carl Friedrich Gauss, was far more ambitious: it involved the establishment of a long-term international network of observers, all of them taking measurements in the same way with identical instruments and dispatching their observations to the Göttingen observatory for recording and comparison. The production of a photographic map of the sky, starting in 1889, the establishment of international unions for meteorology and telegraphy, and the compilation of detailed bibliographical lists testified to this new kind of international cooperation. Some of these international scientific projects were not to survive the outbreak of the First World War.

Negotiations on occasion proved difficult. For instance, the standardization of units of electricity, begun at the first international electricity congress in 1881, took over twenty-five years and three further congresses (Chicago, 1893; St Louis, 1904; and London, 1908) before agreement was reached. In the wake of the Franco-Prussian conflict of 1870–1, many a French scientist had difficulty in reconciling the ideal of international science with his own hostility to the Germans. By declaring that science knew no boundaries, but that individual scientists had their national allegiances, Louis Pasteur found an acceptable compromise formula. Despite the obstacles of national pride and economic rivalry, research had become an international and cooperative venture with a driving force of its own, operating independently of the patriotic feelings scientists might have with regard to other nations from which their colleagues might hail.

This unity of purpose on the part of the international scientific community was nowhere better illustrated than in the Nobel prizes: instituted in 1895 by Alfred Nobel, the inventor of dynamite and a fabulously rich dealer in explosives, the Nobel prizes were awarded from 1901 onwards to those scientists who had rendered the greatest services to humankind through their researches and discoveries in physics, chemistry and medicine. Only a broad consensus on the criteria of excellence, and hence on the principles and standards of scientific research, can explain the success of the whole enterprise and the recognition and prestige it still enjoys today.

Events were soon to show that science, which prided itself on being international and peace loving, was also a weapon with a permanent place in the arsenals of national powers. The First World War would have been over by 1915, for lack of munitions, if research in organic chemistry had not freed Germany from dependence on imports of saltpetre, the basic raw material for the manufacture of explosives. In all the belligerent countries, research, and of course researchers, were mobilized for the war effort. Governments were at last to realize the strategic importance in both economic and military terms of scientific research, henceforth regarded as an affair of state.

But even before the war, science managed to achieve worldwide mobilization. How was the international cientific community, which took shape in Europe, able to extend its network all over the world? In countries such as Canada, Australia and Japan, and even the United States for some disciplines, it was the tendency of academics trained at European universities and laboratories to roam the world and settle abroad that led to the creation of research centres. These globetrotting scholars brought the traditions of the laboratories of Berlin, Edinburgh or Cambridge with them to Montreal or Tokyo. They would send their own students back to those same laboratories to complete their training and meanwhile sought to make local universities receptive to research needs. They also set up institutional structures conducive to the formation of new national scientific communities by creating doctorates, scholarships in higher education for study abroad, and scientific societies modelled on the British Association for the Advancement of Science.

In many places, these institutions participated actively in local life. This was so in the case of the Sociedad Mexicana de Historia Natural (Mexican Natural History Society) founded in 1868, and the Sociedad Geográfica de Lima (Geographical Society of Lima), created in 1888 and active from 1891 onwards. Such institutions encouraged debate on the social problems stemming from the successive waves of immigration to countries such as Argentina and Brazil, or from the difficulty of integrating the native populations, especially in Mexico and the Andean regions. Brazil stands apart in that it was through the will of a prince, Pedro II, who ruled the Brazilian Empire for nearly fifty years, that an embryonic scientific network was established. A relatively tolerant sovereign, Pedro II was a member of several international academies. Taking a keen interest in science, he sought out eminent scientists at scientific congresses, and visited scientific laboratories and research centres all over the world. His avowed objective was to raise his country to the level of scientific development of Europe. He began by reinstating inside the royal palace the Instituto Histórico e Geográfico Brasileiro (Brazilian Historical and Geographical Institute), founded in 1838, under the auspices of the Sociedade Auxiliadora da Indústria Nacional (Society for the Promotion of National Industry), endowing it generously with money, books and rare documents, and collections, not to mention the various grants and prizes awarded in order to encourage research. The Emperor participated regularly in scientific meetings, which he nearly always chaired, inviting the court to attend as well. However, it should be recognized that a monarch's passion is not sufficient for the formation of an elite or the development of a scientific tradition throughout the country.

For the most part, scientific associations established away from the centres of Western science combined the functions of research and the dissemination of Western knowledge. Such was the case, for example, of the Enjümen-i dänïsh ('Council of Learning' or 'Academy of Sciences') for the encouragement of science and literature founded at Istanbul in 1851, or the Jem'īyet-i ilmīye-i Osmānīye (Ottoman Scientific Society) established in 1861 with two objectives: to publish, translate and disseminate works of modern science, and to publish the first Turkish scientific periodical. The Egyptian Institute (al-Ma'had al-misrī), established in 1859, published a bulletin and included in its membership both Egyptians and Europeans. While the sole purpose of the Egyptian Scientific Society (al-Jam'īya al-'ilmīya al-misrīya) was the translation and dissemination of scientific texts, the Khedivial Geographical Society (al-Jam'īya al-jughrāfīya al-khidīwīya) was aimed at promoting geographical and ethnographical studies of Africa.

The Western way of perceiving and acting on the natural world was thus broadly disseminated and implanted in other civilizations simultaneously with the imposition by the European countries, as they were industrializing, of their superior economic and military power. Colonial expansion opened up a vast territory for research activities: distant lands were initially regarded as mere objects of scientific investigation in such fields as botany, zoology, geology, geography and ethnology. Only later did certain colonies develop their own teaching and subsequently research activities along metropolitan lines. A botanical garden or hospital laboratory in the colonies served both the material interests of the colonial power and the pursuit of purely intellectual goals. As an integral part of the process of colonial conquest, Western science acted as a counter-balance to the mercantile system while at the same time helping to justify the claims of European superiority. The French, German, British, Danish and American empires produced bodies of colonial scientists that varied in strength. In most of the colonized countries, the research facilities that received priority were those needed by the services responsible for making inventories of local geological, botanical and geographical resources. The *Survey of India* and the *Geological Survey of India*, for instance, were high points in the development of Indian science, but on the whole, efforts remained *ad hoc* and sporadic. Given that scientific projects were sponsored mainly at the provincial level, they tended to be in the applied sciences.

In South America, the establishment of observatories was a key element in the creation by governments of official scientific bodies, museums and institutions. The Observatory of Santiago de Chile was opened in 1852, under the direction of the German astronomer Moesta. On the other hand, the observatory that began to be established in Mexico in 1877 was not really part of a scientific body, but rather came under the Highway Inspectorate of the Ministry of Public Works.

Health was another favourite area of scientific activity outside Europe. The network of overseas Pasteur Institutes established in the late nineteenth century with the support of charitable associations comprised thirty-odd institutions, including those in Asia and Africa. However, the parent Institute in Paris appeared to grant a large degree of autonomy to its subsidiaries. A meeting of the directors of all the institutes was held once a year in one of them, and very soon there sprang up between the various establishments direct exchanges, which were not necessarily channelled through the head Institute in Paris.

Botanical gardens were another way in which scientific networks spanning the world took shape. The creation of gardens with a broader purpose than merely that of providing medicinal plants was characteristic of the eighteenth century, one celebrated example being the Grapefruit Garden on Mauritius. This trend continued throughout the nineteenth century, as witnessed, for instance, by the garden of Santiago de Chile, created in 1887, and supervised by the German-born naturalist Rudolfo Philippi. The nineteenth century also saw the establishment of natural science networks of natural history museums and botanical institutions for the exchange of specimens and the transfer and acclimatization of plants. In the colonial period, the Royal Botanic Gardens at Kew had a lively exchange and correspondence with its branches in Bombay, Madras, Calcutta, Jamaica, Australia, New Zealand, Mauritius, Natal, the Gold Coast and Victoria. Usually (particularly in India),

local botanists were restricted to the gathering of plants. In this way, colonial science observed a kind of hierarchical division of labour in which the empirical work was left to native scientists, but the theoretical work was undertaken in the major European capitals.

In all the countries on the periphery of the major European or American centres, scientific potential remained weak, except in mathematics, which requires little investment. Everywhere, development was seen in terms of the colonial mother country. At the end of the nineteenth century, scientific policies consisted essentially in undertaking the translation of the chief scientific works published in Europe. Despite several controversies between local and European scientists, such as that which arose in Mexico at the beginning of the nineteenth century over Linnaeus' binomial nomenclature, and the new chemistry, Western science all too often established itself in the colonies while rejecting or discrediting local cultures and their traditional practices.

The conquest of entire continents and various populations by science presupposed a battery of slogans hailing the many benefits of scientific and technical progress. It also presupposed active information campaigns aimed at arousing public interest, and the mechanisms needed to ensure this were also invented during the nineteenth century.

THE POPULARIZATION OF KNOWLEDGE

The professionalization of science during the course of the nineteenth century, which by the end of the century had extended to the humanities, profoundly modified the social foundations of knowledge. In the eighteenth-century science was still part of the general culture of polite society: it was followed, argued over, discussed and particularly appreciated as an entertainment in the form of spectacular experiments involving electricity or chemistry. Some noblemen, indulging their scientific curiosity, attended lectures and public demonstrations or even fitted out a study in their own homes for experiments in physics or a natural history collection. Whether they were merely curious or assiduous seekers after truth, these 'amateurs' of science, who had been a familiar feature of eighteenth-century society, were virtually extinct by the nineteenth century. Their status was recognized – as it still is today – only in certain disciplines requiring a vast store of information, such as position astronomy, the natural sciences, botany and entomology. But as we have already seen, with the concentration of scientific activity in officially recognized institutions, the individual researcher, self-taught or unpaid, acting alone or in a small local group, was marginalized if not altogether discredited.

Does this development imply that science closed in on itself in the nineteenth century? The answer is no, because a process of diffusion took place alongside that of professionalization, gradually expanding the audience for science. The few enlightened amateurs of the eighteenth century, who could be numbered in scores or possibly hundreds, were succeeded by readers of popular science books, reviews and magazines in their thousands. The new phenomenon typical of the nineteenth century was popularization, the mass distribution of knowledge. There was no end to the production of works of popular science, recreational science, science for women, science for children, science for the leisured classes, science and culture to suit every taste, every level of society and every pocket, science that could be read or skimmed through, looked at or listened to. Science and culture lovers were to become consumers of products marketed by a new occupational sector: that of popularization. We shall now look into the causes of this mass phenomenon that was to spread throughout the countries of Europe and their far-off colonies, making Pasteur a world figure and science an idol, a fetish and a commodity.

Converging interests

The rise of scientific popularization was the product of a combination of scientific, technical, social and philosophical factors. The process began in the early nineteenth century at a time when the scientific community was making an effort to broaden its social base and encourage exchanges of ideas. In Germany, for example, the dissemination of science was given a strong boost by the personality of Alexander von Humboldt, a famous and popular scientist. The Gesellschaft Deutscher Naturforscher und Ärtze (Society of German Natural Scientists and Physicians) decided to organize a gathering of scientists and doctors every year in a different place and brought out a journal, *Die Naturwissenschaften* (The Natural Sciences). So great was its success that it obtained financial support from the Prussian government. In 1831, the British Association for the Advancement of Science was set up with the following aims: to give support and more systematic guidance to scientific research; to arouse greater interest in the country for the purposes of science and remove the obstacles to its progress; and to promote mutual exchanges among those who practised science and to correspond with foreign thinkers. The Association organized week-long annual conferences in various regions and fostered the study of science by opening libraries. In France, the Académie des Sciences, the leading scientific institution embodying science in its most elitist and official form, began rather timidly to open up to the broad public. Despite the opposition of most of his colleagues, François Arago, a physicist and astronomer elected Permanent Secretary of the Mathematics Department of the Academy of Science in 1830, decided to throw open the weekly meetings to journalists, and provided a room in which they could afterwards examine the papers read at the meetings. Better still, in 1835, he decided that the Academy would henceforth publish records of its meetings. These *Comptes-rendus hebdomadaires des séances de l'Académie des sciences*, which appeared in unpolished form as quickly as the Friday following the Monday meetings, constituted the first scientific periodical using modern journalistic methods borrowed from a rapidly expanding press. Although initially deemed highly questionable by some members of the Academy, this innovation was of major significance: not only did it ensure that science became a regular topic in the daily news; it also dictated a new scientific style of publishing, in which speediness and brevity were the paramount concerns – the style of publishing that predominates today in scientific circles.

The upsurge in scientific popularization was in fact closely linked to the development of the press as a whole. Over the nineteenth century, the number of both general political and specialized newspapers grew, and their circulation rose while their price per copy went down. The second half

of the century was the golden age of the mass-circulation popular press. The development of cheap newspapers was due to technical advances involving a series of decisive improvements in printing. In the early nineteenth century, the rotary press revolutionized production. In England, *The Times* adopted a mechanical press in 1811, raising its print run to 5,000 copies; in the United States, New York witnessed the birth of the first major newspapers to increase their circulation by lowering the price to 2 cents (the equivalent of one English penny or ten French centimes). The use of rotary presses based on the cylinder-to-cylinder principle, introduced by *The Times* in 1853, became general in the second half of the nineteenth century, and made it possible to boost production rates considerably.

Popular science was very much part of the new wave of cheap printed materials of all kinds. Under the banner of the usefulness of scientific and technical knowledge, popular science began to be disseminated as early as the 1820s, in the form of collections of little booklets such as the *Encyclopédie Roret*, or the *Cabinet Cyclopaedia* published by the Englishman Dionysus Lardner containing a hundred-odd small volumes, each sold for the price of a loaf of bread. Beginning in the 1830s, daily newspapers began publishing serialized 'scientific sections', which regularly informed readers of developments in the scientific and technical world, with summaries of Academy meetings and lists of newly patented inventions. Finally, inexpensive scientific magazines set themselves the task of 'keeping the public up to date', on a weekly, monthly or yearly basis, with what was happening in the world of science and technology.

The advent of such mass-circulation publications was predicated on the existence of a readers' market created by the rise of the middle classes in a rapidly industrializing Europe, and above all by the development of education. The commercial ambitions of publishers rested on a new social foundation, which entailed a potential demand for reading matter. More specifically, this policy was based on a spectacular growth in the number of libraries, which came to be regarded as a public service. They took the place of the traditional hawking of books in country areas, which over the preceding centuries had given rise to a whole genre of popular literature: the 'Blue Series' of Troyes or the 'Yellow Series' of Japan. Following in the footsteps of Benjamin Franklin, who thought up the subscription library, the English-speaking countries developed a more general mass-reading programme. In 1850, the British parliament allowed municipal authorities to introduce a flat-rate tax, in proportion to their budgets, for the financing of public libraries. Some cities in the United States (Peterborough in 1833 and Boston in 1852) individually decided to follow the same policy. But it was due mainly to the private endowment of the American Library Association in 1876, that American libraries were to undergo major expansion, helped along by subsidies from industrial sponsors like Andrew Carnegie. The growth of libraries has to be seen in the general political context of the development of a particular concept of democracy, in which the citizen, having come of age, must acquire an education. In France, for example, with the advent of the Second Republic, the 'royal teachers' of the *ancien régime* were officially replaced by 'people's teachers', although this principle was not really put into practice until a much later date, with the introduction of the new methods, such as the public readings championed by the Société Franklin (1862) and the

Société des Bibliothèques du Haut-Rhin, which led to the establishment of the Ligue de l'Enseignement.

Popular culture became a daily concern mainly among the social strata shaken up by the Industrial Revolution. It was the purpose of a large number of bodies set up by philanthropic societies or directly affecting the working class. The first local associations founded in the late eighteenth century in the north of England to organize lectures and set up libraries were replaced by a second generation of institutes, whose task was to propagate science and the humanities among the working population. For example, the purpose of the 'mechanics institutes' opened in a number of industrial cities was to provide instruction for workers that would raise their output and help to shield them from the much-dreaded moral depravity of working-class areas. Even though industrial working hours in the early nineteenth century restricted the time available for education, these institutes were promoted by the ruling class in the hope that they would forestall social unrest and disorder.

In countries unaffected by the Industrial Revolution, books generally remained more expensive and hard to get. Nevertheless, in early nineteenth-century Japan, reading became a popular social pastime with the development of commercial lending libraries. In 1808 there were 656 such libraries in Edo (Tokyo) and some 300 in Osaka. Some of the owners of these libraries, such as Anoya Sohachi, from Nagoya, developed book lending into a highly profitable business. His company, established in 1767, survived for over a hundred years, and when he sold off his collection in 1898 it comprised 26,769 volumes. Hence the expansion of the reading habit was a fairly widespread phenomenon brought about by a vast variety of technical, commercial, social and political factors.

Popular culture was also the rallying cry of the great nineteenth-century messianic philosophies. In England, Jeremy Bentham, the founder of utilitarianism, a system partly based on the principle of the greatest good of the greatest number, was largely instrumental in drawing attention to the plight of the working classes. In France, the philosopher Auguste Comte, founder of positivism, for many years gave a free public course on popular astronomy. As he saw it, the popularization of science was not just a philosophical duty to familiarize the public with scientific and positivist thinking but a political priority designed to create the spiritual power of the future that, in his political scheme of things, would help to regenerate first the West and eventually the whole of humankind. In addition, the various socialist movements set great store by the development of popular culture. Joseph Proudhon, for instance, proclaimed the right to philosophy for all, since the social revolution could not come about until the people had developed their philosophical faculties. At the turn of the century a great many socialist ventures attempted to bring culture to all the people of Europe through such schemes as the 'People's University'.

The most notable feature was the general agreement on the importance of disseminating knowledge. In fact, the audience of the popularization campaigns varied considerably according to cultural and political traditions. On the old continent, the chief target was the ruling classes, who were most apt to exert an influence on decisions affecting science and scientists. For example, in 1873 James Joule suggested that the British Association for the Advancement of Science should choose a lord as its chairman in order 'to get the sympathy and influence of the upper ten'. In North America, where, as we have seen, private initiatives and patronage played a greater role in the funding of science, scientists were much quicker to disseminate their knowledge to the broad public: they hoped thereby to garner financial support, to secure an enhanced role for scientists in the nation, and at the same time to attract fresh talent to the field of science. Whatever the objective, a multiplicity of commercial, political and philosophical interests converged to underscore the importance of broad dissemination. In every case, the cause of the dissemination of knowledge was pursued with a militant enthusiasm, which conferred on it something of the aura of a latter-day crusade.

A multiplicity of means

And so, with the enthusiastic efforts of a handful of 'apostles', knowledge was spread far and wide by all available means. Science and culture, using every possible vehicle from the most traditional to the most up to date, gradually extended into every corner of society.

Throughout the nineteenth century, oral communication remained a favourite means of disseminating knowledge. Three categories can be singled out: first, elementary courses providing literacy training or rudimentary education, frequently provided free of charge by associations; second, popular courses in science, literature or philosophy, involving some degree of specialization and intended for adults outside the conventional education system. The courses organized by the mechanics institutes, for example, were designed essentially to deliver useful information from which all religious or political content had been carefully filtered out to avoid controversy. By contrast, the courses offered by the Conservatoire National des Arts et Métiers, launched in Paris in 1819, included economic subjects. In 1830, a group of teachers broke away from the Ecole Polytechnique and founded the Association Polytechnique. Camille Flammarion, eulogist of popular astronomy, was a student and subsequently a teacher in the association, which was sometimes referred to as 'the Sorbonne of the workers'. In the 1830s, in the United States, a new and relatively unstructured society, a new dynamic came into being with the Lyceum popular culture movement offering free public lectures, in which a large part was devoted to science. These lectures – of a somewhat paternalist and moralizing nature – were offered to young Americans as a means of getting on in life. The best-known ones, at the John Lowell Institute of Boston, set up for the purpose in 1839 with money left by a rich lover of knowledge to promote both science and Christianity, were given by such prominent educators as Benjamin Silliman, Charles Lyell and Asa Gray.

A third form of oral transmission of knowledge, more spectacular though less earnest, developed alongside such free regular courses, which were really no more than extensions of the education system. This was the society lecture – an event that was often theatrical and striking and for which an entry fee was charged. A typical venue was the Royal Institution of London, founded in 1799, where famous scientists taught. Humphrey Davy and Michael Faraday recounted their latest discoveries in chemistry and electricity at the Institution, while Samuel Taylor Coleridge introduced his audience to the charms of poetry and philosophy. In the United States, the Swiss-American Louis

Agassiz, a polymath naturalist with a keen interest in such subjects as palaeontology and geology, was a popular figure in the middle of the century. In 1860, on the strength of his reputation as a lecturer, Agassiz accomplished a long-cherished ambition by opening the Museum of Comparative Zoology at Harvard. The astronomer Ormsby MacKnight Mitchel had previously managed to exploit his popular success in the same way by founding the observatory of Cincinnati in 1845 without government assistance. In Paris, the Athénée lectures and at a later date those of the Boulevard des Capucines were such a hit that in 1864, the Sorbonne followed suit by organizing 'scientific and literary evenings', which proved so popular that they often took the place of an evening at the theatre. Science and literature were presented to the public through demonstrations and slides. On the other hand, the scientific dramas, which the famous popularizer Louis Figuier tried his hand at, were a spectacular flop. The Paris public preferred the stage adaptations of Jules Verne's novels, with all their magic and fantasy, to the serious, didactic tone of Figuier's dramatizations of the lives of the great inventors.

Those who were unable to attend public lectures had access to science and culture privately, in their own homes, through reading. The mass production of popular scientific works was a feature of the late nineteenth century. From the early part of the century there had been a number of individual practical handbooks and even whole series, but popularization had not yet become a commercial strategy. In the 1840s, the American book trade discovered the enormous profits to be made out of popular science, with the success of *Botany and Philosophy* by Mrs Almira Phelps. During the 1860s, works of popular science rapidly became a lucrative business, adroitly managed by prosperous publishers. By 1870, the first work by Camille Flammarion, *La pluralité des mondes habités*, was in its fifteenth edition and had been translated into fifteen languages. In 1889, 200,000 copies of the French translation of Brewer's *A Guide to the Scientific Knowledge of Things Familiar* were in circulation, whereas Tom Tit's *La science amusante* – the precursor of the 'do-it-yourself' manual – went through forty-six editions between 1889 and 1912. Instead of bringing out separate volumes, publishers encouraged regular readership by publishing series of volumes, available in either an economy or a deluxe edition. In 1864, for instance, Louis Hachette, in collaboration with Edouard Charton, launched the 'Bibliothèque des Merveilles', a series comprising over 100 titles, many of which were reissued, translated into Spanish and Portuguese or adapted for the American market by Scribners. Although popular science works were never the centrepiece of publishing policy they helped a few major publishers, such as Larousse and Flammarion, to get off the ground while others contrived to raise their circulation by also publishing newspapers.

The dictionary, that most characteristic work of the nineteenth century, was a venture in which the interests of the publishers were most happily wed to the ideal of 'science in the service of humankind'. The 'century of the dictionary' was marked by two great names: Emile Littré, whose dictionary was published by Hachette from 1863 to 1873, and Pierre Larousse, who brought out his *Grand dictionnaire universel* in instalments from 1864 to 1876. These monumental works, soon to become classics, were still explicitly addressed to the elite. It was not until 1905, with the birth of Claude Augé's *Petit Larousse*, that dictionaries

achieved a wide circulation among the general public, in the form of compendiums designed to enlighten 'the school and the nation': 200,000 copies were sold in a single year, at 5 francs each.

The rapid development of public lectures and books on science was closely bound up with that of the popular scientific press. The various media reinforced one another through advertising and exchange of information and, above all, through the existence of a small number of successful popular science writers who gave lectures, published books and contributed to periodicals. One after the other, the writers of the weekly science sections founded their own popular science reviews, and there thus arose a new category of writers and journalists who did not yet have an established professional status, but who were none the less clearly identifiable. It was chiefly this group that was responsible for the increase in the number of scientific periodicals in France during the second half of the nineteenth century. In 1865, in Paris alone, there were fifteen such journals. The lifespan of these periodicals varied widely. Some lasted no more than several months, while others, such as *Cosmos*, produced by the Abbé Moigno, survived with ups and downs, quarrels and reconciliations, until 1935. In England or the United States, successful scientific magazines were most often the fruit of an alliance between a celebrated scientist and a well-established publisher, as was the case with the English weekly *Nature*, founded in 1869 by the astronomer Norman Lockyer and the publisher Macmillan. The record for longevity would seem to be held by the New York weekly *Scientific American*, founded in 1845, and which continues to appear. Thanks to exchanges of information and printing plates, compilations and translations, these manifold reviews tended to form an international and formidably powerful parallel network to those of professionals in the sciences and the humanities. Many journals encouraged the formation of networks of amateurs: the French review *La Nature* organized scientific excursions for its readers. When launching an astronomy review, Camille Flammarion appealed for subscriptions for the installation of a proper observatory near Paris, at Juvisy. With apparatus every bit as good as that of public institutions financed by the state, this private observatory enabled amateur astronomers to take part in professional scientific activities and eventually led to the creation of an international network when further Flammarion observatories were built in other parts of the world. In Germany, too, amateur astronomy flourished as a result of private enterprise. In 1888 an association entirely devoted to popular science, set up with the support of the scientist Helmholz and the industrialist Siemens, established the Urania in Berlin, where microscopes, telescopes and a scientific theatre were made available to the general public. With the Urania serving as a model for similar institutions in Vienna and Belgium, astronomy was a field which remained open to amateur endeavours in the closing years of the nineteenth century. These amateurs, who were very active and occasionally proved their mettle by making a number of astronomical discoveries, were the embodiment of what Camille Flammarion called 'free science'.

Scientific journalists and their networks of admirers were not content merely to relay what was happening in the scientific world. Occasionally journalists took part in scientific controversies, and did not hesitate to criticize the academic world. The controversies aroused by Pasteur's work triggered a fair amount of dissidence, which in some cases went as far as dreaming of a free, popular and alternative science. This phenomenon, which was particularly strong in the case of the French press, ever ready to cry out against the monopoly of the Academy of Sciences, was also present in other countries. In Brazil, for example, the microbiologist Oswaldo Cruz was vigorously attacked by the newspapers for his Pasteur-like management of hygiene and public health in Rio de Janeiro between 1903 and 1906. Cruz, in turn, chose to counter-attack by publishing his 'Advice to the People' in the mass-circulation press. The ensuing scientific controversy which filled the newspapers claimed the attention of increasing numbers of people; the polemic was taken up by the 'Positivist Apostolate' (which held that obligatory vaccination was an infringement of the freedom of the individual), various groups of opposition to the government, and even merchants, whose businesses were perturbed by the constant revision of health regulations.

It should be stressed that the great upsurge in popular science at the end of the nineteenth century was not limited to countries with a strong scientific potential or in which professional scientific research was already well established. Scientific publishing and journalism developed practically on all continents, although in some cases it is difficult to make a clear distinction between specialized and popular periodicals. Scientific journalism and publishing flourished particularly in Egypt, which over the nineteenth century became a major intellectual centre for the Islamic East. In the Arab world, the first scientific monthly in Arabic, al-Muqtataf (The Selection), founded in Beirut in 1876, was an important channel for the dissemination of scientific knowledge throughout the Middle East. It is worth noting that scientific reviews and magazines sprang up and prospered even when the number of readers was limited. In the middle of the century Portugal, for instance, had some fifty-odd scientific magazines for a population of no more than 3.5 million, a majority of whom were illiterate; towards the end of the century, Brazil saw a sharp rise in popular science publishing, despite a very high illiteracy rate.

In the early twentieth century, when the widespread use of photographs was radically altering the style of newspapers, popular science books and reviews appeared to go into a slight decline. But in its heyday at the end of the nineteenth century, the press that glorified and magnified scientific and technical progress wielded real power, which was feared and courted. Witness Edison, who made a point of maintaining good relations with the journalists of the New York Tribune, the New York Herald and the New York Times – in particular Uriah Painter – who played a decisive part in ensuring the success of his phonograph, which Edison had presented in 1878. Similarly, to promote another of his inventions – the incandescent light bulb – at the electricity exhibition of 1881, Edison made no bones about 'buying' the support of the journalists of the leading French reviews. The mass-circulation press undoubtedly played a major role at the time in spreading a scientific culture. Following the creation of the Nobel prizes in 1901, it was the press that helped to launch the names of the great scientific stars such as Madame Curie or Marconi. But the press also served as a forum for the great controversy in the 1890s in France over the bankruptcy of science, which opposed scientists and republicans against the literary establishment, who on this occasion allied themselves with the Catholic church.

Of all the flourishing nineteenth-century means of telling the world about something, there was one of great originality that embodied in spectacular fashion the ideals of the age: namely, the Great Exhibition. The first of these was staged at the mid-point of the century, in 1851, in that industrious and already imperial land of Great Britain. Entitled the Great Exhibition, it followed a long line of industrial exhibitions that until then had been national in France and regional in England. Such exhibitions were held in a number of countries (Great Britain, France, Austria, the United States, Belgium, Italy, etc.), and functioned as showcases for the various Western societies. While the line of great exhibitions did not altogether die out in 1914, they subsequently became much rarer and underwent a change, losing most of their Utopian dimension. Whether as international exhibitions open to all countries, or as universal exhibitions presenting every facet of production and knowledge, these major undertakings ushered in the era of 'mass culture'. Their novelty lay in their unparalleled drawing power: in 1851, 6 million visitors came to the Crystal Palace, 16M to the 1878 exhibition, 27M to the Chicago exhibition of 1893, and 50M to the great Paris exhibition of 1900. These visitors were a very mixed bag. For six months industrialists and workers, scientists and amateurs, specialists and sightseers rubbed shoulders. With so varied an audience, the promoters of these great fairs took pains to give them a meaning that everyone could understand. A hymn to the glory of progress was the basic message to all visitors, and it was uniformly and tirelessly repeated from one exhibition to the next. But quite apart from the industrial and commercial operations of direct concern to producers on the lookout for rewards and dividends, apart from the peaceful vying of nations competing directly with each other through the system of prizes, above and beyond the political manipulation aimed at bringing about wholesale social integration by offering workers cheap tickets to visit the exhibitions, and beyond the exotic displays to the glory of colonial conquest, could these exhibitions in any way be said to serve as a useful means of disseminating knowledge?

In the first place, the exhibitions functioned as gigantic theatres of progress, where the wonders of technology and industry were put on show. This emerged clearly from the huge engine rooms, which grew bigger and loftier every time, reaching their peak in the 1860s, when banks of ever more powerful machines were shown at work, generating the power needed to run the exhibition. The spectacle of working machinery could, of course, be regarded as a kind of technical education in itself, but the purpose was not really to instruct. The 1500hp Corliss motor – powerful for its time – activated by President Grant in Philadelphia in 1876, and the enormous Le Creusot power hammer exhibited in Paris in 1878, were intended to appeal to the imagination, to impress the public with the miraculous progress of industry, rather than to give a practical demonstration of how things worked. 'The intelligent visitor could readily understand that all these applications spring from pure science, the single and inexhaustible source of all progress', remarked one commentator in 1900. In fact, the aim was more to captivate the public than to provide serious explanations. The craze for panoramas at universal exhibitions is a remarkable illustration of the two different levels – emotional and rational – at which they functioned. Preceding the invention of the cinematography, these scenes painted on canvas, so typical of nineteenth-century aesthetics, always combined the goal of entertainment with the desire to give instruction on history, geography or science and technology. The panorama illustrating the 'journey to the centre of the earth' in 1889 procured the same emotions among the spectators as reading Jules Verne's novel did, and relied on the same effects. The large sections devoted to the colonies also mingled instruction and entertainment. On the one hand, an ethnological approach approved by prominent anthropologists showed the colonized peoples in their usual working and living surroundings, as presented in the Tonkin village of 1889 and the Filipino reserve of 1904, while, on the other, public curiosity was titillated by the exotic reconstitution of a 'Cairo street scene' at the foot of the Eiffel Tower in Paris, where folklore blended with national stereotypes.

With the technological breakthroughs that occurred at the end of the century, the public taste for spectacle and extravaganza easily outweighed the urge for education. The telephone, photography, cinematography and above all electricity were a pretext for entertainment, for lavish spectacle. The austere and monumental banks of machinery, like a row of technical encyclopaedias, were a thing of the past. In 1900 the 'palace of machines' was turned into a funfair. Out with celebrations of progress and industrial might: technology was now used to work magic. Electricity was the 'fairy' that cast a spell on the public at the 1900 exhibition. The *Cinéorama* evoked visions of far-off places, and science itself was used to manufacture illusion: the biggest telescope ever made was displayed in Paris in 1900, with the enticing caption 'the moon in close-up'. This expensive device, a technical marvel designed especially for the exhibition, was never able to be put to practical use in scientific research.

Nevertheless, the universal exhibitions manifest a genuine attempt to spread knowledge by highly elaborate means. This can be seen in the way in which the goods on display were classified, which grew more complicated with each exhibition, embracing not only the different sectors of industrial production but also the entire field of knowledge, from the pure to the social sciences and from the fine to the applied arts. These classification systems, which were initially intended as both a geographical and intellectual guide to the exhibition, soon took on a more ambitious role to the extent that they constituted a survey or orderly synopsis of the whole field of contemporary knowledge; according to their compilers, they were meant to form an 'encyclopaedia of civilization'. The concentric exhibition hall designed for the 1867 exhibition by Frédéric Le Play, the French engineer who was a disciple of Saint-Simon, was a masterpiece of its kind. Visitors proceeding from the periphery of the hall towards its centre traversed the whole range of civilization, from the lowest material level to the highest spiritual peak, from basic agricultural and industrial products to the supreme artistic achievements of the human mind. By strolling round the circular galleries, they took in the entire world, since the exhibits were arranged radially by nation. Each group or class was presented according to a logical progression, which led for instance from the raw material to the manufactured product, or from the physical needs of the human race to its spiritual needs. Starting in 1862, each section contained a display of 'materials, processes and methods' intended to explain and clarify the processes of manufacture, thus providing 'models that any producer could imitate' to quote the introduction to the section on the history of labour in 1867.

Finally, the universal exhibitions contributed indirectly to the dissemination of knowledge. International congresses were held in conjunction with each exhibition, in accordance with its classification system, whose declared purpose was 'to represent all human knowledge', 'to classify, order and summarise all the sciences' and 'to discuss all new discoveries'. As 'exhibitions of thought' held alongside the exhibitions of products, these international congresses reproduced the encyclopaedic discourse on offer to the broad public, adapting it to the now neatly partitioned world of scientific disciplines. There were even public lectures given at the exhibitions as a popular counterpart to the more scholarly gatherings. At the end of these events, the findings of the congresses, the deliberations of the juries and the assessments made by the exhibition organizers were recorded in lengthy reports that were printed and widely circulated. Even if those thousands of pages were perused only by scholars or specialists, they nevertheless constituted a weighty collection that bore witness to the contribution made by nineteenth-century exhibitions to the task of popularization.

Personal observation – the nineteenth century's preferred mode of spreading knowledge – was encouraged in many places besides exhibition halls. Observatories, zoological gardens and museums also relied on the link between education and entertainment. In the observatory, training of the eye provided a necessary basis for an understanding of the workings of the universe; in a zoo, the exhibition of living animals was thought to be an agreeable way of propagating an interest in and knowledge of natural history; and the display of objects in a museum was meant to familiarize the public with technology. Astronomy, which lends itself easily to the dramatization of the skies, became the showpiece of popular science in the nineteenth century, as demonstrated by the popularity of such authors as François Arago, R. A. Proctor and Camille Flammarion, not to mention the proliferation of observatories.

Most of the great modern zoological gardens were also founded in the nineteenth century. Until then there had been only princely menageries containing captive wild animals, in such places as Asia and Africa, where they were meant to display the wealth of their owners or to be used for hunting. The zoo as a means of education was invented in Great Britain with the establishment of the Zoological Society of London in 1826. With a special interest in natural history and the East, it was the first body set up to foster establishments conducive to the advancement of natural history and popular recreation, and in 1827, it took the initiative of opening the London Zoo. This example was copied directly by Dublin in 1830, Amsterdam in 1838, Antwerp in 1843, Berlin in 1844, and, in the United States, Philadelphia in 1874, Cincinnati in 1875, and New York in 1898. The European pattern also spread to the colonies, resulting in the transformation of the old-style menageries, including the famous zoological gardens of Bombay, which were linked with the Victoria and Albert Museum, those of Nāser od-Dīn, Shah of Persia, founded in Tehran in 1894, and those of Manila, Batavia and Wellington. Zoos aroused great public interest in connection with such widely reported events as the arrival in London, in 1850, of the first hippopotamus seen in Europe since the time of the emperor Commodus, and the first live gorilla in 1869. Like the great exhibitions, zoos were based on the principle of the object lesson and learning from life: the Jardin d'Acclimatation, opened in Paris in 1860, put on public display a model apiary, a fish farm and a silkworm factory, where the educational value was enhanced through public demonstrations and scientific lectures given by members of learned societies.

Museums in this period assumed highly specific functions. The display of collections – a long-standing tradition with the dual role of conservation and instruction – underwent far-reaching changes in the course of the nineteenth century. By vocation as well as by the nature of the objects on display and their heterogeneous public, museums developed by extending their range from a purely Western tradition to the entire world, via the colonial territories. The model handed down from the eighteenth century was that of the British Museum (1759), and the Louvre, which garnered the artistic works and basic historical collections of the nation, covering archaeology and natural history. Until then, all objects relating to industry or science had been confined to cabinets of curiosities, princely patrimonies or the collections of academies and learned societies. As the gap between the fine arts and the practical arts widened during the nineteenth century the aristocracy shunned the latter as being too middle class. At the national level, however, there was a growing awareness of the important part this testimony to middle-class activity could play in both maintaining social cohesion and enhancing national prestige. Hence in 1799, Napoleon ordered the products of economic activity to be exhibited at the Conservatoire National des Arts et Métiers in Paris, while in Great Britain, following the Great Exhibition of 1851 and to provide a home for the exhibits, the South Kensington Museum was opened, in 1857, with the aim of bringing science, the arts and industry closer together. In the closing years of the century the unified German Empire founded a whole series of often highly specialized museums to celebrate its industrial progress: the Postal Museum set up in Berlin in 1872, the Museum of Public Health in 1886, the Museum of the Protection of Labour in 1899, followed by the Museum of Architecture and Transport and the Maritime Museum in 1905. An even more ambitious project, Oskar von Miller's Deutsches Museum, founded in Munich in 1903, managed to combine an educational purpose inspired by the movement for popular education with a middle-class cultural ideal involving the emulation of famous scientists and engineers. With a wider variety of exhibits, it was hoped to attract a wider variety of visitors. The first museums of folk art, which resulted from a major expansion in the study of ethnology, illustrate this development. At the close of the century in Sweden, for example, there was a lengthy controversy among ethnologists over their approach to the museum: some were in favour of museums that displayed objects in their natural setting, showing them as they actually were in their own surroundings, while others preferred to select types of object, remove them from their context and display them according to an abstract classification system. The Skansen museum, inaugurated in Stockholm in 1891, was based on the first method and was the first example of an open-air museum; it was followed by the biology museum containing the whole of Scandinavian fauna in its natural setting. Unlike the natural history museums that exhibited systematically classified stuffed animals in glass cases, this new type of museum used natural history as an excuse to please and amuse the public. All in all, the number of museums increased considerably in the last quarter of the century: some 100 museums were opened in Great Britain, while fifty or so appeared in Germany between 1876

and 1880. And, like education, the practice of collecting spread throughout the world under European colonial influence. In Jakarta the collections of the Batavia Society of Arts and Science formed the core of the Central Museum of Indonesian Culture; in Calcutta the Indian Museum emerged from the Asiatic Society of Bengal; and in Sydney the naturalist Macleay founded the Australian Museum, in 1827. Latin America went through two great phases of museum creation: in Buenos Aires, Rio, Bogotá, Santiago and Montevideo in the opening decades of the century, followed by a series of provincial museums at the end of the period in Lima, São Paulo and Tigre (Argentina). By the outbreak of the First World War no continent had entirely escaped the museum craze.

Ambitions and illusions

What was the social and cultural impact of this febrile, militant and ambitious effort to disseminate knowledge, which extended over the entire period, reaching a crescendo towards the end of the century? The arguments advanced in support of the innumerable popularization schemes undertaken during the nineteenth century show remarkable consistency: 'to put science within everybody's reach', 'to satisfy public curiosity', 'to respond to the thirst for knowledge', 'to keep abreast of rapid progress' or 'to adjust to the innovations in daily or professional life'. Were these phrases – repeated *ad nauseam* in magazine editorials, prefaces to handbooks and exhibition guides – mere rhetoric? Or did the nineteenth-century popularizing zeal, often inspired by noble and generous intentions and borne aloft by Utopian impulses, genuinely transform society's relationship to knowledge? Given that popularization activities went hand-in-hand with a considerable increase in the number of schools and educational institutions, it is extremely difficult to assess their specific contribution. It is equally difficult to evaluate with any degree of accuracy the number of people actually reached. There are practically no reliable data on attendance at public lectures, and the figures given by publishers are sometimes misleading since they tended to exaggerate the size of their own print runs. It would appear from certain local surveys that in the 1880s – a time of great prosperity for popular-science publishing in France – the average print run of a book was around 10,000 copies, which is close to the average for general works of literature. But this average conceals wide disparities between a minority of best sellers and a majority of works that sold less well. Furthermore, the success of works of popularization has to be seen in the light of the fact that they often enough had a captive audience. Considered both useful and right thinking, works of popularization enjoyed wide distribution as school prizes or Christmas presents and in public libraries and philanthropic societies. A critical study is also needed to assess the social influence of public libraries, museums, observatories and zoos. In a few instances we know that the effort and investment put into the creation of such places was not always rewarded. This was the case of the Trocadéro Public Observatory, established in Paris in 1885, by French Government decree, which offered the general public the free use of telescopes and library, and organized lecture series, but which the public never really warmed to.

Furthermore, although people did flock in their millions to the universal exhibitions that periodically hit the headlines in the big capital cities, the tendency over the years, as we have seen, was to play up the magical, the spectacular: in short, everything relating to public amusement. As a result of this development, amusement parks invaded the exhibition grounds: Midway Plaisance in Chicago in 1893, and the Pike in St Louis in 1904, exemplified the switch from universal exhibition to funfair. And so the fears expressed at the very start of the universal exhibition movement by the philosopher-historian Ernest Renan were finally realized: as wary of the industrial show as of the leisure centre, he thought it a pity that 'few people came out of the *Palais de l'exposition* better than they went in'.

Even if this comment betrays the haughty contempt of the intellectual for mass culture, the fact remains that the cultural impact of most popularization activities seems dubious. Despite the plethora of similarly titled works, each new magazine, book, dictionary or series trumpeted its originality and claimed to be unique of its kind. However commonplace their intentions, all publishers professed to fill a vacant slot in the world of books, namely the middle ground between arid specialist literature, too packed with 'figures and formulas' to be accessible, and the vulgar literature of the 'traffickers in science' that beguiled without informing, cheapened science and 'failed to slake the reader's thirst. In short, works of popularization were presented as a new literary genre, both serious and easy to read, with genuine popular appeal. But it has to be admitted that with the exception of a few well-known titles and a handful of prominent authors this ambition was rarely fulfilled. Taken as a whole, nineteenth-century works of popularization are a hybrid genre, half fact and half fiction, that constantly makes use of the same old narrative methods as a teaching device, i.e. the interview, the fireside talk, the exchange of question and answer, and the adventures or journey of some everyday object such as a drop of water or a crust of bread. The fact is that this type of literature was never really recognized as constituting a genre of its own. It had letters patent in the form of famous writers, such as Flammarion, but as literature it was looked down upon.

The same ambiguity clouded the status of popular science authors. Professional scientists who took up popularization activities were often regarded as marginal and their reputation suffered as a result. Professional popularizers, even if they generally had a university background equivalent to that of professional scientists, were regarded as non-conformists who might even pose a threat to the integrity and ethical values of the academic world. Although it was considered essential, their work, designated in the Romance languages by variations of the pejorative term 'vulgarization', which suggests vulgarity, was often perceived with a certain degree of distaste and condescension. Like the 'Vulgate' of Saint Jerome in former times, it was a necessary evil in a period that fervently celebrated scientific and technical progress and sought to make a religion of science.

While critics were not lacking, the fact remains that popular science represented a radical new departure in the history of the thought and culture of the nineteenth century. For the very first time the desire to broadcast knowledge and break down the barriers between scientists, intellectuals, artists and the general public became a common goal. In the West these efforts began to bear fruit – to varying degrees – at a time when philosophers, social reformers and politicians were developing an interest in the collectivity, the greatest number or the masses, convinced as they were that the 'age of the common man' was beginning.

In the rest of the world, a scientific culture was being disseminated in the wake of the expansion of Western science, often with little concern for the ordinary public. The fact that as a result of an abundance of popular works, Humboldt, Pasteur and Jules Verne became great heroes in such countries as India and Turkey seems perfectly normal, indeed quite ordinary and even rather progressive. However, this prestige enjoyed by Western science was not devoid of consequences. By spreading scientific culture throughout their colonial empires, with all sorts of philanthropic arguments, the European countries skilfully delayed the emancipation of the colonized peoples. While it may be true that the European countries made use of their science and technology to redress the balance of trade with their colonies to their advantage, they dominated them even more lastingly by propagating the cult of science and the great scientists by all available means of popularization. All too often, scientific culture in the non-Western world developed as a result of imitation, dependency and fascination.

Thus the nineteenth century made an active contribution to the renewal and creation of educational and research structures all over the planet. Intent on spreading knowledge as widely as possible by the introduction of compulsory schooling and multiplication of the means of dissemination, it provided large segments of the population with access to knowledge and culture.

While more pronounced in the industrialized countries, if in many cases limited to the acquisition of the ability to read, this broad dissemination led to social and cultural changes of significance to humankind as a whole. By building more schools and research centres, the nineteenth century undoubtedly extended the range of culture, but with a marked tendency to uniformity which was detrimental to the diversity of cultural identities. A colourful and variegated tapestry of many different cultures was replaced by an orderly diagram of knowledge increasingly dominated and regulated by Western scientific rationality.

BIBLIOGRAPHY

ADE AJAYI, J. F. (ed.) 1989. *General History of Africa, Vol. 6: Africa in the Nineteenth Century until the 1880s*. UNESCO, Paris.

ALBERTINI, P. 1992. *L'école en France, IXe et XXe siècles: De la maternelle à l'université*. Hachette, Paris.

ANON. 1983. 'La diffusion du savoir de 1610 à nos jours', *Congrès national des sociétés savantes*. La documentation française, Paris.

——. 1983. *Le Livre des expositions universelles (1851–1889)*. Edition des Arts Décoratifs. Herscher, Paris.

BEN DAVID, J. 1971, 1984. *The Scientist's Role in Society: A Comparative Study*. University of Chicago Press, Chicago.

BENSAUDE-VINCENT, B.; RASMUSSEN, A. (eds) 1997. *Sciences à lire: L'édition et la presse de science populaire en perspective historique*. CNRS, Paris.

BOAHEN, A. A. (ed.) 1985. *General History of Africa*, Vol. 7: *Africa Under Colonial Domination, 1880–1935*. UNESCO, Paris.

BOUCHE, D. 1975. 'L'enseignement dans les territoires de l'Afrique Occidentale de 1817 à 1920: Mission civilisatrice ou formation d'une élite?'. Thesis, University of Paris I.

BROCKWAY, L. H. 1989. *Science and Colonial Expansion: The Role of the British Royal Botanic Gardens*. Academic Press, London/New York.

CHAMBRES, R. L. (ed.) 1968. *Beginnings of Modernization in the Middle East in the Nineteenth Century.* Chicago.

COHEN, Y; DROUIN, J. M. (eds) 1989. 'Les amateurs de science et de technique'. *Cahiers d'Histoire et de philosophie des sciences*, No. 27.

CRAWFORD, E. 1984. *The Beginning of the Nobel Institution: The Science Prizes, 1901–1915.* Cambridge University Press, Cambridge/Maison des sciences de l'homme, Paris.

CUETO, M. 1989. *Excelencia Científica en la Periferia: Actividades Científicas e Investigación Biomédica en el Perú, 1890–1950.* Grade-Concutec, Lima.

DELANOUE, G. 1982. 'Réflexions et questions sur la politique scolaire des vice-rois réformateurs'. *L'Egypte au XIXe siècle.* CNRS, Paris.

FOX, R.; WEISZ, G. (eds) 1980. *The Organization of Science and Technology in France, 1808–1914.* Cambridge University Press, Cambridge.

FRUTON, J. S. 1990. *Contrasts in Scientific Style: Research Groups in the Chemical and Biochemical Sciences.* American Philosophical Society, Philadelphia.

FURET, F.; OZOUF, J. 1977. *Lire et écrire*, 2 vols. Editions de Minuit, Paris.

HEYWORTH-DUNNE, J. 1968. *An Introduction to the History of Education in Modern Egypt.* Frank Cass, London.

KUMAR, D. (ed.) 1990. *Science and Empire.* NISTADS, New Delhi.

LAFUENTE, A.; ELENA, A.; ORTEGA, M. L. (eds) 1993. *Mundialización de la Ciencia y Cultura Nacional.* Doce Calles, Madrid.

LAFUENTE, A.; SALA CATALA, J. (eds) 1992. *Ciencia Colonial en América.* Alianza University, Madrid.

MARQUES, A. S. 1992. 'L'école primaire au Mozambique, XVIIe-XXe siècle'. DEA thesis, educational sciences. University of Paris V.

MAYEUR, F. (ed.) 1981. *Histoire générale de l'enseignement et de l'éducation.* Vol. 3. Nouvelle Librairie de France, Paris.

MORANGE, M. (ed.) 1991. *L'Institut Pasteur: Contributions à son histoire.* La Découverte, Paris.

ORDOÑEZ, J.; ELENA, A. (eds) 1990. *La Ciencia y su Público: Perspectivas Históricas.* Consejo Superior de Investigaciones Científicas, Madrid.

PAUL, H. W. 1986. *The Rise of the Science Empire in France, 1860–1939: From Knowledge to Power.* New York.

PETITJEAN, P.; JAMI, C.; MOULIN, A. M. (eds) 1992. *Science and Empires.* Kluwer Academic. Dordrecht, Boston/London.

PYENSON, L. (ed.) 1988. 'Macondo Científico: Instituciones Científicas en América Latina a Principios del Siglo XX'. In: Sanchez Ron, J. M. 1907–1987: *La Junta para Ampliación de Estudios e Investigaciones Científicas 80 Años Después.* Vol. 1, CSIC, Madrid, pp. 229–49.

REINGOLD, N.; ROTHENBERG, M. (eds) 1987. *Scientific Colonialism: A Cross-Cultural Comparison.* Smithsonian Institution Press, Washington DC.

SCHROEDER-GUDEHUS, B. S.; RASMUSSEN, A. (eds) 1992. *Les fastes du progrès: Le guide des expositions universelles (1851–1992).* Flammarion, Paris.

VERGER, J. (ed.) 1986. *Histoire des universités en France.* Privat, Paris.

VEYSEY, L. R. 1965. *The Emergence of the American University.* University of Chicago Press, Chicago.

8

CULTURAL DEVELOPMENT, ARTS AND ARCHITECTURE

8.1

THE WESTERN WORLD

Raymond Vervliet, coordinator

INTELLECTUAL, PHILOSOPHICAL AND AESTHETIC TRENDS

From enlightened self-consciousness to modern crisis consciousness

If we reconstruct the most important traditions in discourse during the nineteenth century, we can distinguish two basic attitudes: one of enlightened self-consciousness, and another of crisis consciousness. The first attitude was inherited from modern Cartesian philosophy and the thinkers of the Enlightenment; in the foreground here, we find the idea that problems can be mastered by reason. The idealist philosophers (Kant, Fichte, Schelling, Hegel, Herder, De Maistre, De Bonald) and the followers of empiricism (the positivists and naturalists such as A. Comte, H. Spencer, T. Buckle, H. Taine, F. Brunetière and K. Lamprecht, as well as the utilitarian-minded middle class) all had a common pattern of thought, i.e. that problems could in principle be mastered by reason. The second attitude on the other hand was a relatively new one, i.e. that reality confronted the thinker with obstacles that were almost insurmountable and which required a radical alternative. This attitude is often portrayed as being radically opposed to the products of the first: the prophets of doom versus the believers in progress. This dichotomous portrayal of events is too simple, however. The products of the second way of thinking are also based on a vision of progress, but differ from the first in that they simultaneously undermine it. Another equally schematic view of the situation presents these two basic ways of thinking as being phases in the evolution of nineteenth-century thought. The traditional view sees the belief in the future as being a state of mind that reached its zenith during positivism and naturalism and which was then challenged by another attitude, i.e. that of decadentism. Though the latter was dominant during the late nineteenth century, manifestations of it were already to

be found early on in the century, whilst on the other hand, the belief in progress still had its adherents and the end of the century. The two attitudes outlined above should not be considered as phases in a development, therefore, but should rather be seen as the poles of a field of nineteenth century cultural force.

Idealist aesthetics

The foundations for the vision of idealist aesthetics were laid by Johann G. Herder (1744–1803). His ideas lived on in romantic aesthetics but also in intercultural discourse. He influenced many nineteenth-century artists, both true-blooded romantics and later post-romantic (realist, impressionist, symbolist) artists. The main difference between these two groups of artists lies in the fact that one cannot accept the spontaneity of historic processes as applying to the second. Post-romantic artists can be shown to have possessed a crisis consciousness.

In his *Philosophie der Geschichte zur Bildung der Menschheit* (1774) and *Ideen zur Philosophie der Geschichte der Menschheit* (1784–91), Herder developed the thesis that each culture is a phase in the development of humanity. In keeping with the design of creation, humanity is striving to realize its immanent goal, i.e. the bringing about of *Humanität*. Culture is therefore not only a phase, but also a goal in itself: each culture expresses humanity in its own, albeit incomplete, way. This further explains the notion of *Volksgeist*, which is the particular cultural situation of a people at a certain moment in history. To Herder, the spirit of the people is the living and tangible source of all the poetry and religion that animates a particular community. For this reason he began, to collect folk songs in his *Volkslieder* (1778–9). In 1807 J. von Müller entitled the second edition *Stimmen der Völker in Liedern*. He considered folk songs as a form of primordial poetry and as the spontaneous expression of a creative collective unity.

Another important facet of romantic aesthetics is its attitude towards classical art. The distinction already made by Herder between classical and post-classical art was further elaborated upon, particularly by August W. Schlegel (1767–1845), in his *Vorlesungen über schöne Literatur und Kunst* which he held in Berlin in 1801 and 1802, as well as in *Vorlesungen über dramatische Kunst und Literatur* which were held in Vienna between 1808 and 1811. Classical art, which aimed at obtaining a perfect balance between idea and form, was now contrasted with a modern (romantic) form of art, which was based on the awareness that it was impossible for an idea to be expressed adequately in form. This distinction was adopted by Hegel, but mainly became common property through Mme de Staël's study on differences between France and Germany in her *De l'Allemagne* (1810).

Positivist aesthetics

A positivist attitude was to be found in France among people like Charles-Augustin Sainte-Beuve (1804–69) who used analogies of science in his historical and biographical literary criticism. It was his student, Hippolyte A. Taine (1828–93), in particular who made use of positivist methods in his literary historiography (*Histoire de la littérature anglaise*, 1863–4), in which he developed his *théorie du milieu*. In this way, literary history took on the characteristics of a social science, which later contributed to the development of literary sociology. His opinion that a novel contributed towards our scientific understanding of human nature was later shared by Zola. Taine also applied the same determinism and empiricism in his psychological studies, of which neuro-physiological and psycho-pathological research took up an important part.

In following the path taken by Taine, his student, Ferdinand Brunetière (1849–1903), made use of the Darwinian doctrine of evolution in his study of the origin, rise and decline of a literary genre. This can be found in his *L'évolution des genres dans l'histoire de la littérature* (1890) and in *L'évolution de la poésie lyrique en France au dix-neuvième siècle* (2 vols, 1894).

We can find many followers of Comte and Spencer among German philosophers of culture. The most original among them was Karl Lamprecht (1856–1915), who became acquainted with positivism through reading Buckle's work. As the author of the monumental *Deutsche Geschichte* (12 vols, 1891–1909), and as a lecturer in universal history at the University of Leipzig, he was of great influence both inside and outside Germany. In his *Die kulturhistorische Methode* (1900), Lamprecht attempted to ascribe the power of explanation to subjective factors. He designed a system of concepts that was broad enough to outline whole series of historical facts. Central to this was his socio-psychological notion of *Kultur*, which he defined as the psychic state that permeated and determined the whole of life and all extant phenomena at a particular moment. Culture was therefore the causal factor *par excellence*. It was synonymous with the *Kollektiv Seele*. In this way, Lamprecht's notion of culture is related to Comte's *le sens commun*. He saw a similar tendency towards individualism in other domains. Lamprecht himself laid much stress on the striking parallel between this

evolution towards the increasingly intensive psychic development in collective consciousness through external stimuli and that of the development of the organic species. Paul Lacombe (1848–1921) also used an analogous inductive method and put forward a causal vision of history in his *De l'histoire considérée comme science* (1894).

The belief in progress had already been undermined by these positivist cultural historians, though they did create room for possible regeneration: cultures grew spontaneously towards higher levels of intensity, though in some cases they did die out. Ultimately they continued to believe that the materials of history could be assessed and explained rationally. Nevertheless, *fin de siècle* intellectuals who were close to them at the time no longer held this belief, or at least not to the same extent. Essayists like Oswald Spengler (1880–1936, the author of *Der Untergang der Abendlandes*, 1918–22), placed a lot of emphasis on points of decadentist theory. The reason for this was that they never adopted the methods of positivism.

Modern crisis consciousness

The philosophy of German idealism was extremely influential in the first half of the nineteenth century, but gradually lost its key position. Hippolyte Taine distanced himself from his master Hegel, and Marx too was to criticize him. The materialist belief in progress seemed to provide a temporary response to this crisis. But even this alternative became subject to a second form of scepticism, i.e. distrust in progress itself. It had already been manifest in Lamprecht's work. This tone of distrust began to dominate all philosophical discourse in the third quarter of the nineteenth century, although it was latently present throughout the whole of the century. It expressed itself in the rejection of the metaphysical philosophy of history. The negative elements in the history of humankind became emphasized and were considered as being serious obstacles to progress. And so alienation became the point of departure for a radically critical form of diagnosis.

Alienation as such was a problem that was already presented by Hegel as being a necessary element in the dynamics of *Aufhebung*. The mind had to alienate itself – become lost in the other, in nature – in order to re-emerge strengthened by the battle. Alienation was necessary for the growth of self-consciousness. Things were somewhat different during the *fin de siècle*: alienation seemed to be insurmountable and could only be healed by means of professional or technical action. Psychiatrists developed therapies – often little more that speculations – in order to tackle psychic alienation. Marxists tried to install a rational organization of the economy in order to remove this alienation. The anarchists saw private property as being the cause of social (and sometimes psychic) alienation and wanted to remove it through revolution. Artists tried to make a virtue of aesthetic alienation through the professionalization and the increasing autonomy of the artistic field.

The diagnoses of decadence made recourse to a number of 'positivist' disciplines. It is often the case that materialist theories of progress lie hidden beneath the various theories of alienation: medical, sociological and politico-economic diagnoses provided the arguments in the discussion on alienation.

Issues of politico-philosophical or social alienation

The 'philosophical' works or so-called *Frühschriften* (writings from before 1847, including *Ökonomisch-philosophische Manuskripte* (1844), which was only published posthumously in 1932) of the young Marx belong to the earliest forms of systematic reflection on the issues of alienation examined from the point of view of crisis consciousness.

Contrary to the idealism of the tradition of right-wing Hegelianism and the common materialism of left-wing Hegelians like Feuerbach, Stirner, Proudhon, etc., Marx showed that man had to be considered as a component in the social structure and part of a historical process generated by the various structures in society. He thereby subjected middle-class self-consciousness in the nineteenth century to a critical analysis: modern man allows himself to be misguided by economic prejudice (private property) and by the existing relationships of power (relationships of production), which lie at their foundation. He concluded that the existing division of labour would unavoidably lead to a class struggle, and that the concentration of capital would also unavoidably lead to *Verelendung*. The nucleus of his criticism focused on the desire for private property that lay at the root of an alienating social structure. He therefore saw work as an active involvement by humans in nature, which would result in the flourishing of both. In the capitalist system, however, man was a slave of his work: the worker was there for the production process and not the opposite. Mankind could no longer develop in thought and action but was in service to something that in fact was alien to him. This pessimism did, however, go together with a vision of regeneration: class struggle would lead to revolution and to a phase in which the oppressed classes would begin to determine the course of history. The collective ownership of the means of production was the remedy for humankind in changing the process of social structuralization.

Marx's doctrine cannot be merely reduced to the issues of alienation, but this part of it was of great influence upon intellectuals in the latter half of the nineteenth century. Moreover, it provides proof of his own crisis consciousness. To Marx, history was no flawless process but a Via Dolorosa in which the capitalist production system was perhaps its bitterest stage. Contrary to the self-conscious modernists, Marx considered the negative side as playing an important role in history.

The anarchists also contributed heavily to the strengthened crisis consciousness of the last decades of the nineteenth century, though contrary to the Marxists, they did not construct any systematic, philosophically founded doctrine. Their roots stretched back to the 1840s and to the proto-anarchic ideas of Proudhon. Anarchism only became influential in the 1860s, and reached its zenith in Europe and America between 1880 and 1914. The international character of the movement can be credited to two leading figures, each of whom represented an aspect of anarchism: the Russian emigrant Michael Bakunin (1814–76), and the prophet of revolutionary anarchism and Russian prince Piotr Alexejevich Kropotkin (1842–1921), who also escaped from prison and fled his country, and who during his time in Switzerland, France and England became the spokesman of individualist anarchists.

Bakunin, who was educated in the tradition of left-wing Hegelianism, stressed the negative side of the dialectic process: 'The passion for destruction is a creative passion, too!' The only way to equality and justice lay, according to him, in the eradication of all traces of authority and, following that, in the building of a society without government in which man would be free to create the happiness he was capable of. In the same way as Proudhon, he preached a belief in small cooperative groups of tradespeople instead of dehumanizing factories. That is why this form of anarchism attracted so many small self-employed tradesmen and the uprooted in the cities who dreamed of their rural or small town origins, as well as those in areas on the brink of industrial development. This explains the temporary success of revolutionary anarchism among the Swiss watchmakers of the 'Jura Federation', among Italian workers, among Catalan tradespeople and workers and Andalusian farm labourers in Spain. The movement in Catalonia even attempted to set up an anarchist model of a cooperative society during the Spanish Republic of 1873–4, under the enthusiastic leadership of F. Pi y Margall (1824–1901).

As far as his theories are concerned, Kropotkin was the most fruitful intellectual source of the *fin de siècle*. Books like *Paroles d'un révolté* (1885) and *La conquête du pain* (1892) were *livres de chevet* (bedside reading) for many artists and writers. According to Kropotkin, the most important principle in anarchism was the spirit of cooperation. He was of the opinion that a society could be changed by cooperation into a civilization that could reach higher than the level attained by struggle and conflict. Though he issued a bitter and hefty criticism of corruption and exploitation in society, his works are still permeated by an intense optimism when it comes to humankind and its possibilities. At the basis of his individualist anarchism lay the belief that the individual, once freed from outside pressure and traditional prejudice, could lead a happy and enlightened life. The individualist anarchists adopted Max Stirner (pseudonym of Johann Caspar Schmidt, 1806–56), one of the most negative left-wing Hegelians, as their prophet. In his *Der Einzige und sein Eigentum* (1845, Universalbibliothek edn 1892), he propagated a form of extreme individualism: the highest ideal according to him was 'being oneself' at the expense of the state, the family or just 'the others', any means or act used to achieve this form of egoism being justified, be it insurrection or crime. This individualism had the advantage that its anarchist ideas could be put into practice straight away without having to wait for the great revolution: 'free marriage', refusing military service, living on the margins of society and beyond its laws, birth control, and women's emancipation. Its goals were moral independence and free and independent thought based on reason and without prejudice. Such a form of peaceful and liberating anarchism was often preached by anarchists who had previously received a religious education at an earlier stage of their lives, e.g. the French anarchists Sébastien Fauré and Emile Armand and the American Samuel Fielden.

Issues of psychic alienation

In the last quarter of the nineteenth century, medical science got involved in the debate on alienation. Popular works on medicine and discourses on psychiatry in particular were turned into an instrument for making diagnoses of culture. The nineteenth century was not only a golden era of scientific, technological and industrial progress, it was also a chronic period for diseases of the central and peripheral nervous systems. 'Degeneracy', 'nervous disorder', 'exhaustion of the nervous system' were not only terms used in neurological diagnosis but also in more general discourse on 'modern nervousness', which was seen as a syndrome of the culture of an industrial era that was focused on expansion and progress. The abnormal (with which one could became acquainted through the studies in psychology of Claude Bernard) became an artistic theme in naturalism: nervous disease functioned as an illustration of determinist theory. The problem of nervousness even became a principle of aesthetics, a new means of looking at things to be found both in naturalism and in impressionism. But besides the forms of discourse on the problems of nervousness inspired by psychiatry, there was a second important discussion in progress on psychic alienation: the quasi-sociological discourse on the decline in mass psychology.

This crisis came about as a result of a negative relationship with the positivists. It often happened that the tenets of positivism were adopted and then reformulated. Though the philosophies of culture were pessimistic, their founder thinkers were 'positivists' who believed in a form of professional therapy that could cure the illnesses of the age.

The publication in 1880 of a study called *Nervous Exhaustion and Neurasthenia* by George Beard, a New York doctor and a specialist in neuropathology and electrotherapy, led to the setting up of a discussion and publication forum that would soon spread beyond the borders of medicine. The term 'nervousness' in particular (a less clinical term than 'neurasthenia') was very fashionable at the time. The problem of nervousness became especially prevalent in the more general discussion on cultural criticism, as a result of the study by Wilhelm Heinrich ERB called *Über die wachsende Nervosität unserer Zeit* (1893). He considered the rising need for luxury, modern means of transport, the lightning speed of communications networks since the introduction of the telephone and the telegraph, and more generally by life in the big cities, as the main causes for the threat to which the individual nervous system had become exposed to. This thesis was further explored by Willy Hellpach (1877–1955), a student of Lamprecht's, in his *Nervosität und Kultur* (1902) and by the sociologist Georg Simmel (1858–1918) in *Die Grossstädte und das Geistesleben* (1903). At the end of the nineteenth century therefore, nervousness was a term used to express a zeitgeist that was dominated by a sense of decadence.

But the middle classes were also plagued by another historical trauma, i.e. the threat of the rising working class. This feeling of anxiety had been present ever since the great revolts and the insurrection of the Paris Commune. It became even more intense with the growth of the masses in the suburbs of industrial cities and towns, the lightning strikes, the rise of mass media and the demand for general suffrage, plus anarchist terrorism in the anonymity of the metropolises. Before these times mass insurrections had only occurred occasionally, but now they had become the rule. This is how Gustave Le Bon (1842–1931) began his analysis in *Psychologie des Foules* (1895). Besides these social problems, political problems too were a motif of his thought. Le Bon examined parliamentary democracy in France, believing that it was going through a crisis. His political preferences were certainly not for the *ancien régime* but for the individualist patrician democracy of England. His diagnosis was neither historical nor economic, but psychological. He defined the masses as a conglomerate of individuals who lose their individuality (i.e. their educational, cultural, personal and class-related characteristics). Anyone, be they aristocrat, intellectual or working class,

could effectively lose their intellectual capacities by joining the masses. This loss was compensated by the characteristics of mass soul: its driving force, effects and goals. All the catastrophes of the past and all the problems of the present are the result of the actions of mass soul. Mass hypnosis became a new possibility in politics. To Le Bon however, the present form of parliamentary democracy was diametrically opposed to these laws of psychology. It was a form of political culture that took no account of the sensitivity of a crowd to suggestion once it was incited. A new form of political thinking was needed to put an end to the illusion of rational political culture.

This last statement by Le Bon clearly indicates that he was a representative of late nineteenth-century cultural pessimism (the masses were unpredictable and ungovernable), but that he did not give up his belief in regeneration where charismatic leaders could guide the soul of the masses and steer it along good lines.

Aesthetic alienation

Modern culture in general, and the changed notion of time which Karl Lamprecht and Georg Simmel linked to the technological era and to the capitalist economy of money and which Gustave Le Bon had already associated with the process of 'massification', had already been diagnosed as such in advance by circles of intellectuals and artists. Such diagnoses can be found in Wordsworth's introduction to his *Lyrical Ballads* for example, or in the meta-literary writings of Baudelaire. The American poet and essayist Ralph Waldo Emerson (1803–82) derived a doctrine of intuition and aesthetic pantheism from these diagnoses (see *Essays*, 1841–4), as did the British historian and essayist Thomas Carlyle (1795–1881) in *On Heroes and Hero Worship* (1841).

Besides these, there were others who were fascinated by modernity. There was also awareness that a certain progress was taking place in culture (undoubtedly under the influence of the optimism of the Saint-Simonists). It was characteristic of the nineteenth century that the intellectual community held continual discussions on its own rules and identity, and here the notion of 'culture' became increasingly central.

The concept of culture in the mid-nineteenth century formed the central motif in the discussions about the nature of art and of its relationship to society. Its roots lay in the romantic notions of art and the artistic role in society, which had dominated literary circles in the first half of that century (Johnson, 1979: 199).

Seen from the point of view of sociological developments in intellectual activities – the growing autonomy of intellectual praxis from the practical workings of other groups in society – this interest in culture can be considered as the direct result of the new self-image of the intellectual: he was now an independent mediator and the minder of cultural values. In his essay *Culture and Anarchy* (1869), Matthew Arnold (1822–88) defined culture as 'a pursuit of our total perfection by means of getting to know, on all matters which most concern us, the best which has been said in the world' (p. 7). This definition was the starting point for a whole series of related positions on cultural theory to be found among Arnold's contemporaries. John Ruskin (1819–1900) and William Morris (1834–96) in particular put forward the idea that art should be in the service of moral values and that it could be a lever for improvement in society both in written form as in practice. Here the idea of the perfect development of the individual and of a perfect order in society formed the foundation for a belief in regeneration.

From Baudelaire onwards, psychopathological terms were given an aesthetic significance and began to be used as categories in cultural philosophy. In *fin de siècle* art, the theme of *le mal du siècle* or *maladie du siècle* came to the foreground. Popularized works on medical science became a great source of inspiration for some writers. Nineteenth-century cultural theory, both in its neo-classical and its romantic form, is very idealistic. It is a theory of values and especially a theory in search of absolute values: unselfish enjoyment, insight into the perfection of the world, insight into human emotions. Cultural behaviour was considered as consisting of the formulating of values and the achieving of those values. This could be done in two ways: through education and through artistic activities. Because of the strong identification of culture with the arts, it was obvious that there would be a tendency to make a strict separation between the notion of culture and those social habits that only concern momentary survival. These aspects were included under the term 'civilization', a term that possessed connotations of bourgeois utilitarianism and industrialization.

Until the nineteenth century art had been in the service of the church and state, and reflections on culture were almost always linked to considerations of usefulness. Now the middle-class criteria of usefulness were seen as a threat. Those people who only paid attention to the requirements of social usefulness in their cultural behaviour were now catalogued under the term 'philistine'. Utilitarianism reduced the individual to a functional component in a mechanical whole and reduced individual to masses. Artists no longer felt at home in a society that only created masses of middle-class consumers and masses of proletarians for industry.

This also explains Friedrich Nietzsche's aesthetic revolt. Already in his early writings, Nietzsche had elaborated upon this modern contradiction by using the dichotomous notions of Apollo and Dionysus. The first stands for the apparent beauty of the visible world (the 'little reason'). The second represents the life-affirming forces ('the great reason'). Following Schopenhauer, Wagner and the aesthetics were to preach too that art could bring about a liberating negation of the will.

In his later writings on the philosophy of culture, Nietzsche was to distance himself from this Schopenhauerian vision of aesthetics. To him the negation of the will was a form of 'priestly asceticism' that did injustice to reality. He decided that modern society was 'at the doorstep of nihilism' and that culture was degenerating. A decadent culture was a culture of the 'final man', of the individual who denied the creative powers and allowed himself to be led by the abstractions of cultural traditions. The present culture was characterized by its slavish morality, a morality of the oppressed that confirmed the oppressing forces (which were the enemies of life). Even worse, this slavish morality cultivated a hatred of life-affirming forces and all those who stood for them. This is clearly visible in the ascetic ideals of the 'priest' character. Nietzsche's famous adage 'God is dead' should be seen in this context: he did not so much mean that religion was dead but that life-hating abstractions (including morality, religion, metaphysics, etc.) were no longer of any value for the *Übermensch*. The

conclusion that God was dead led to praxis of life that was 'beyond good and evil': the subject had set aside his idealistic ballast. But European culture had lost its self-confidence as well as its belief in Graeco-Judaic Christian culture. Given that these values were illusions to Nietzsche anyway, he considered the time ripe for regenerating forces. He therefore formulated the theory of 'Eternal Return': despite all attempts by the subject to systematize reality, the continual renewal of forces made it impossible for him to know reality. The only thing that could really be known was that these forces and their effects returned continuously, finding new ways to express themselves each time. This certitude is the only thing that the knowing subject can hold on to. Nietzsche therefore called this theory of Eternal Return his only consolation. For Nietzsche, aesthetic alienation meant that humankind had lost the artistic élan of the *Übermensch* and had become the victim of a nihilistic culture that was hostile to life. This sharply formulated criticism of culture, but more particularly, this optimistic philosophy of history based on the vitality of life can be heard resounding in the late nineteenth-century literature of the symbolists and aesthetics and is clearly visible in that vitalist art form *par excellence*, art nouveau.

TRENDS IN ARCHITECTURE AND THE PLASTIC AND VISUAL ARTS

Introduction: the birth of the cultural market

The developments specific to the various art forms in the nineteenth century can be typified by three key concepts: secularization, the rise of the middle classes and autonomization.

Until around the beginning of the nineteenth century, artists worked in the service of the church, a sovereign or a nobleman and as a result the works of art produced served a function in those upper levels of society, which also set the taste and conventions of the day. Both art production and consumption were determined by a small closed circle of people. In the nineteenth century however, the church and the royal palaces no longer formed the centre of artistic life. A middle-class art audience, which had already come into existence in the eighteenth century, consolidated itself and replaced the church and the aristocracy in their role as art patrons: growing economic and political power allowed the well-to-do bourgeoisie to become interested in and to commission works of art. This expansion and diversification of the art audience greatly stimulated art production.

In this new century of industry and trade, the capital cities of Europe replaced the churches and royal courts as the centres of art. Potential patrons, buyers and enthusiasts were already living and working in the hearts of these great cities. Artists were able to come into contact with a widening and increasingly anonymous art public through art exhibitions, which, as the century progressed, became less and less limited to the official salons. Paris, which had already been the centre of the fashion and literature since the seventeenth century, now became the capital city of art and took over the leading role which had until then been played by Florence and Rome. Rome nevertheless, remained *the* place of pilgrimage for those who wished to study the tradition of ancient culture, while Paris became a magnet for those who wished to stay abreast of all that was new and innovative in art. Moreover, in these large municipal areas, new art schools were founded to provide training in the arts, which would destroy the monopoly of the elitist national academies, and large national museums were opened which would make the works of great masters available to everyone: already in 1792, it was decided by the Convention (government) of Paris that a museum should be founded at the Louvre; the construction of the Glyptothek was begun in Munich in 1816 and with the Anti-kensammlung in 1838, whereas the Altes Museum was founded in Berlin in 1818; the British Museum in London was built in 1823; and in 1834, the National Archaeological Museum was opened in Athens, which had then become the capital of Greece. These examples were followed in all the major cities of Europe throughout the nineteenth century. This permitted young artists to study the great works of classical art daily and copy them in completion of the tasks set by their teachers at the nearby workshops.

As a result of these institutional changes in the world of art, the status and way of life of the artist also changed. With the severing of the old links with the aristocracy and the church, the artist had to increasingly rely upon his own wits and became spiritually liberated as an individual. This further resulted in artists rethinking their position in society and history, more particularly their position with respect to tradition and the present. Because an artist could no longer address one particular community or one homogeneous audience that set standards of taste and convention in the arts – as was the case during the *ancien régime* – he was forced to increasingly seek points of support within himself. The expression of the ideals, standards and values of a particular social system was now replaced by self-expression. Both the everyday world and the past had now become purely a basis for individual confrontation. Strictly regulated imitation now had to give way to the freedom of *creatio*. This led to what at first seemed to be a chaotic confusion of styles and neo-styles: an artist who was no longer bound by authority could now either experiment with new ways and means of expression or use his personal affinity to reach back to former styles and adapt them freely to suit his own vision and the new demands of nineteenth-century society. This created continuous tension both within the highly differentiated art world and among its highly varied audiences.

The romantic and post-romantic artist was a loner. Even though he might have been an enthusiastic member of a particular school, movement or contemporary circle of like souls, once he returned to his workshop to paint, to sculpt or to compose, he was alone and felt alone. In this way, he came to the conclusion that he differed tragically though giftedly from his fellow man. This difference was to find its expression in eccentric and unusual hairstyles, clothes and ways of life, and from this too stemmed the gap between the artistic bohemian and the philistine or utilitarian citizen.

The other side of the coin, as far as this newly won independence and artistic freedom is concerned, was that, once he left his workshop with a newly completed work of art, he was confronted with an art world that was subject to the same market forces of competition and of supply and demand as the liberal economy of the society of the day. There was a clear need therefore to form sales networks. Production, distribution and consumption had now become totally separated. More and more independent exhibitions (*salons des indépendants* and *Sezessionen*) were being held outside the official salons; the first galleries and specialized art dealers began to appear, while symphony and solo concerts turned into the production apparatus

of composers – a difference now being created between the composer himself and his specialized interpreters (the conductors and solo virtuosos).

The growing trend towards organization, division of labour and specialization in the art world during the course of the nineteenth century led to the birth of different circuits, thereby increasing the tension and even bringing about schisms between artists. On the one hand, we find artists who, because of their temperament, conviction or for reasons of opportunity and material gain, were willing to go along with generally accepted conventions in taste and to meet the demands of their middle-class patrons and buyers; and on the other hand, there were the artists who would only listen to their inner creative urges and who strove to create a unique and original work of art, even at the cost of becoming isolated, unrecognized and sometimes even impoverished. This explains the success of neo-styles and eclecticism up until the end of the nineteenth century, while at the same time, wave after wave of innovation followed each other and would result in the radical avant-garde art of the beginning of the twentieth century. Further industrialization, the decline of crafts and the rise of a middle class which had little or no intellectual or artistic baggage, would drastically widen the gap between cheap, mass and often machine-made kitsch masquerading as art and limited, ergo unique and innovative, aesthetic products. A similar divide between professionalism and dilettantism, between original aesthetic work and mass-produced commercial products, also took place in music: aesthetically qualitative and innovative music became the reserve of virtuosos, whilst the production of lighter salon and genre pieces, which continued the tradition of eighteenth-century sentimentalism, was set in motion to cater for amateur middle-class consumption.

To gain insight into this overview of the massive amount of art produced in the nineteenth century, one must first be aware of the continual tension between tradition and innovation. Because of the urbanization of art, the sumptuous examples of neo-styles and of eclecticism continued to remain the most prominently visible. They can prevent us from seeing the revolutionary innovation that was going on at the same time. It was within this chaotic production of art that the notion of modernity, which lay at the root of modern art, was first to be posited. This difficult battle of liberating oneself from the grips of tradition paved the way for twentieth-century modernism and the avant-garde. The real point of rupture with tradition lies in the nineteenth century.

The struggle for liberation from the grip of tradition

Architecture

At first, the dominant style in architecture in Europe and America was neo-classical and had been most prominent since the French Revolution in 1789. The playfully elegant and individualist rococo was rejected as being typically aristocratic. It was believed that revolutionary ideology could be given more prominence by allowing architecture to follow the classical ideals of beauty found during the time of the Roman and Greek republics. The use of the antique formal language found in the solemn grandeur and sober rectilinearity of their temples was designed to impress the masses at the time. So the *directoire* style of the period following the French Revolution (1795–9) was followed by a neo-classical variant or 'empire' style (1804–15). Under Emperor Napoleon I, this classical formal language was used with an austerity and severity that bordered on the megalomaniac. Court architects like Pierre François Fontaine (1762–1853) and Charles Percier (1764–1838) played an important role in this trend. The reference book *Recueil de décorations intérieures* (compiled in 1812) would have a deep and prolonged influence on nineteenth-century architecture.

Till today the centres of most major Western cities are marked by works of original seventeenth-century classicism as well as those of neo-classicism. Victory arches, city gates, museums, theatres and parliament buildings were all built in this style. It was during the period of Napoleonic rule that the centre of Paris was given its monumental look through the many important works of architecture that were erected at the time: the renovation of the northern wing of the Louvre and the design of the Rue de Rivoli (plans by Percier and Fontaine); the Bourse, begun in 1808 by Alexandre Brongniart (1770–1847); La Madeleine, built by Bartholémy Vignon by order of the emperor as a Temple de la Gloire for the continual honour and glory of his army and later turned into a Roman catholic church by order of Louis XVIII in 1864; the Arc de Triomphe de L'Etoile, a 50m high arch inspired by the Titus Archway at the Forum Romanum and designed by Jean François Chalgrin (1739–1811); the Arc de Triomphe du Carrousel (1805–6), an imitation of the Septimus Severus arch, the plans for which were drawn by Percier and Fontaine; and the column of Austerlitz on the Place Vendôme.

In Great Britain, the classical tradition of the previous century had already drawn its inspiration from the buildings and drawings of the late Renaissance architect Andrea Palladio. This nineteenth-century neo-classicism reached its height between 1825 and 1847, with the construction of the British Museum by Robert Smirke (1780–1867). A number of striking pieces of architecture in neo-classical style which were built at the time would continue to characterize the centre of London to this day: the Bank of England, designed in 1788 by Sir John Soane (1753–1837), the most important English architect at the turn of the century; and Regent Street, the National Gallery, Marble Arch and Buckingham Palace, all built by the London urban architect John Nash (1752–1835).

It was also obvious that this neo-classical style would be used in Italy and Greece, the countries of origin of classical art. Along with its National Archaeological Museum, numerous other buildings in the same style were built in Athens, in order to place extra stress on its status as the new capital. The new wave in classical design was less apparent in the Italian capital, Rome, however, and was more visible in Naples and Milan where numerous neo-classical castles and palaces were built.

Given his megalomaniacal vision and a similar urge to radiate power and authority, Ludwig I of Bavaria had Leo Van Klenze (1784–1864) construct a colossal temple on the banks of the Danube near Regensburg between 1831 and 1843. The temple was erected in honour of all the important men of the fatherland and was called Valhalla – an allusion to the heaven of the Germanic peoples where only heros who had fallen in battle could enter. This German architect was to carry out some very important works, especially in Munich, like the Ludwigstrasse, the Brienerstrasse, the grandiose Königplatz, the Old Pinakothek and the

Glyptothek, for example. Karl Friedrich Schinkel (1781–1841) mainly worked in Berlin. We can already see from his greatest creations, like the Neue Wache at Unter den Linden, the Altes Museum and the Königliches Schauspielhaus, for example that he dealt with this rational, classical style more romantically and with more emotion by using a gothic approach.

Theoreticians propagated neo-classicism by claiming it was a universal language of form that was accessible to everyone. This message was also received in more marginal areas of influence like Scandinavia and Russia. The style reached a level of international acclaim in Sweden with the construction of the Adolf-Frederik church in Stockholm and the university buildings in Uppsala for example, whilst the Danish architects, Christian Frederik Hansen (1756–1845) and T. E. Von Hansen (1803–91), also acquired international renown. Initially, there was an understandable reaction against this originally French style in Russia; and yet their architects succeeded in developing a Russian variant. This was expressed in the monumental construction works carried out by I. E. Starow (1743–1808) and his contemporaries along the banks of the Neva in St Petersburg, as well as in the rebuilding of Moscow after the fire of 1812. The more pompous style in which the Bolshoi Theatre was built would remain in vogue well into the twentieth century and would be used for all official edifices. This was not the case in North America, where new building materials and techniques led to a radical innovation in style from the second half of the century onwards, even though neo-classicism dominated especially as far as state buildings were concerned – as can be seen from the Capitol in Washington, which was built between 1793 and 1824.

Contrary to the rationally ordered neo-classicism of the eighteenth century, whose works were faithful imitations of the classical Greek idea of beauty, the nineteenth-century variant stemmed from a freer, more emotional notion that matched the individual temperament of each architect and was more suited to the new functional demands of the middle-class society of the day. Not only did they make recourse to the classical and Hellenistic periods in Greek culture as well as to classical Roman culture, they also adapted these styles to their own national traditions. With the rise of national self-esteem, they drew their inspiration from the building styles which had been developed during the Renaissance in their own countries. This is clearly visible in the extensions made to the Louvre after 1852, during the reign of Napoleon III: the styles of sixteenth and seventeenth-century architects were taken as a point of departure, even though the extension built by Louis Visconti (1791–1853) and Hector Lefuel (1810–81) during the nineteenth century was more pompous in character. The main part of the sixteenth-century Hôtel de Ville facing the eastern facade of the Louvre would also receive extensions on both sides in the same neo-Renaissance style. Nineteenth-century architects were to make recourse to local works of Renaissance architecture, particularly for the building of city halls.

Gothic would prove to be the main source of inspiration for the more emotional works of nineteenth-century architecture. The most illustrious and influential work in this style would be the Houses of Parliament in London (1836–52), which was built by the architects, Charles Barry (1795–1860) and Augustus Welby Pugin (1812–52). They were requested to base the work on the gothic or Tudor style. Barry, who had a clear preference for works from the

Italian Renaissance, is responsible for the overall neo-gothic style with its Renaissance undertones, whereas Pugin saw to all the gothic details both on the inside and on the outside of the building. Pugin saw the application of this gothic style as his moral duty as a Christian, as can be gathered from his *Apology for Christian Architecture* (1833).

Pugin's moralistic ideas on architecture became known to a larger audience through the works of one of the greatest critics of nineteenth-century industrial society, John Ruskin (1819–1900), works like *Seven Lamps of Architecture* (1848) and *Lectures on Architecture* (1853) for example. As a result, this preference for neo-gothic spread further to non-religious circles, for not only were churches built in this style but railway stations too and textile mills, museums and court houses.

This rebirth of medieval architecture found in modern gothic was not purely limited to Great Britain. It also manifested itself in all countries where this medieval pointed-arch style had once reached a high point, particularly in those countries where the Catholic church still exercised considerable influence. In France, the country of massive gothic cathedrals *par excellence*, a new understanding of medieval monuments was already beginning to emerge at the start of the nineteenth century. This rebirth was brought about by the appearance of a standard work (published in 1800) on French monuments by the art expert Alexander Marie Lenoir (1761–1889), an apology called *Génie du Christianisme* by the writer René de Chateaubriand (1768–1848) and the in-depth studies on medieval sculpture and gothic architecture by Emeric-David (1755–1839). It became clear, from 1820 onwards, that the romantic movement, with its strong sense of nationalism and its preference for the pre-Renaissance period, could no longer be stopped and that it would destroy the monopoly held by neo-classicism, even though those in power were to continue to rely on the latter till the end of the century. The neo-gothic too was to be given a new lease of life in the second half of the century through E. Emmanuel Violet Le Duc (1814–79) who wrote a ten-volume *Dictionnaire raisonné de l'architecture française de XIe au XVIe siècle* between 1854 and 1868, and who also did much work in the restoration of gothic buildings.

In Germany, Goethe had already shown his preference for gothic as early as 1772, particularly through his *Von deutscher Baukunst*, characterizing gothic as a specifically German style of architecture. The generations that followed were spurred on in this cult of medieval architecture by the cultural philosopher Friedrich Von Schlegel (1772–1829) and his *Grundzüge der gothischen Baukunst; auf einer Reise durch die Niederlande, Rheingegenden, die Schweiz und ein Teil von Frankreich in den Jahren 1804 und 1805*. This general interest in gothic during the first half of the nineteenth century led to the initiative of completing the cathedral in Cologne. It would prove to be an inspiring initiative, which would lead in turn to the construction in 1856, of the neo-gothic Votivkirche in Vienna by Heinrich Von Ferstel (1828–83). Even following the division of the Danube monarchy into the Austrian Empire and the Kingdom of Hungary, neo-gothic buildings would continue to be erected alongside one another in neo-styles, as can be seen from the Rathaus (1873–83), which was designed by Friedrich Schmidt (1825–91). Between 1885 and 1905, the Hungarian city of Pest (now Budapest), the new seat of parliament since 1867, saw the construction of an enormous parliament building in neo-gothic style on the banks of the Danube. The building did have certain Renaissance elements to it, however. As elsewhere during the same period, neo-gothic churches and even other forms of buildings began to appear in the Netherlands, and in still strongly Catholic Flanders.

In the latter half of the nineteenth century, the ostentation of the new middle-class rulers and particularly that of the 'nouveaux riches' also resulted in a wave of neo-baroque alongside all the other neo-styles. The monumentality of this style and its use (or imitation) of expensive raw materials perfectly mirrors the desires of those whose status had been gained from material possessions. It is significant therefore that stock exchanges were quite often designed in the baroque style. It is even less of a coincidence that, following the defeat of France by the Germans in 1871, and the unification of Germany, the Reichstag, built in the capital Berlin (1884–94), was also designed in this style. All the operas – the most favoured places of relaxation for the middle classes – built at the time were in neo-baroque style, the most illustrious examples being the Théatre de L'Opéra in Paris (1861–74), designed by Charles Garnier (1825–98) and the Staatopera (1861–9) in Vienna, which along with the Ringstrasse, the Neue Hofburg and the Hofburg Theatre were also designed in the same neo-baroque style by the architects Gottfried Semper (1803–79) and Karl Hasenauer (1833–94), who joined forces for the project. This proclivity for extravagant representation led to showy eclecticism once elements from other neo-styles began to be integrated into neo-baroque. This neo-baroque eclecticism reached its zenith with the construction, between 1866 and 1883, of the Palace of Justice in Brussels, the plans of which were designed by urban architect Joseph Poelaert (1817–79). It is mainly because of this late nineteenth-century eclecticism that later generations would comment disdainfully on the lack of stylistic unity in nineteenth-century architecture.

Sculpture

Sculpture, like architecture, underwent a slow development in its fight to free itself from the grips of tradition. Here too, neoclassicism was to remain at the forefront, even though most artists were motivated by feeling and were romantic in their approach. Like the architect, the sculptor was also highly dependent on orders, more so than other artists. The nature of the materials used and their high price curbed the desire for innovation and experiment. Another impediment was the authority of the academies and the power of the salons. Throughout the whole of the nineteenth century, the academies were to uphold the classical vision as the sole and unquestionable vision of beauty. The juries at the salons were all chosen from the academies and other traditional environments. Being selected for participation meant being recognized and consequently receiving orders from official bodies and rich patrons. And finally, the very function of nineteenth-century sculpture also retarded the desire for change and innovation. The major part of the enormous amount of sculpture produced was practically always destined for the public sector. As a result of the quick expansion of municipalities and the often sizeable replanning of old city centres, impressive buildings began to shoot up along the new long, wide avenues and moreover space was cleared for squares and parks, which meant there was more room for monuments in sculpture. This love of monuments stemmed from the romantic passion for giving a solid form to one's own national self-esteem, and was expressed in reliefs, busts, crests, statues and grave monuments. Graeco-Roman sculpture served as the ideal model for all these works, and Rome therefore became the artistic Mecca of all apprentice sculptors.

Neo-classical romantic sculpture was determined to a very large extent by two sculptors, the Italian Antonio Canova (1757–1822) and the Dane Bertel Thorvaldsen (1768–1844), each a paragon in the Latin and in the Germanic world respectively. Canova was the first to sculpt that 'petrified human body' that is so typical of the nineteenth century, and in so doing strove towards classical design (including togas, drapes and classical hairstyles), the stress here being less on providing a true-to-life representation than on providing a well arranged and perfectly balanced basic form. Thorvaldsen, too, totally subjected his creative urge to the classical idea of beauty. His *Jason and the Golden Fleece* (1803–28), made him famous overnight and orders flowed in from every corner of Europe. The idealized beauty, strict simplicity, harmonious arrangement of line and monumental heroics of his work were a perfect reply to the desires and wishes of the amateurs of neo-classical art at the time. And yet, despite their exceptional skill and technique and their strong powers of composition, the works of these two artists strike us as cold and distant, as being frozen statues. These positive and negative qualities also belong to the work of their followers in the second half of the century: the Swiss sculptor Jean-Jacques Pradier (1790–1852), the creator of the *Twelve Victoriae* for Napoleon's tomb at the Dôme des Invalides in Paris; the German sculptors Johann Gottfried Schadow (1764–1850), Johan Von Dannecker (1758–1841) and Adolf Von Hildebrandt (1847–1921), who sculpted the *Wittelbacherbrunnen* in Munich; and the Englishman John Flaxman (1755–1826), who was also a designer of Wedgwood porcelain.

The most famous and also the most monumental example of this rather strict, controlled neo-classical romantic style of sculpture is the 46m-high Statue of Liberty in New York, which was created between 1871 and 1874 and unveiled in 1886, after having been donated to the people of the United States by France in honour of a century of independence. The work was created by Frédéric A. Bartholdi (1834–1904). It consists of 300 moulded copper plates placed around a inner steel skeleton, which was made by the engineer Alexandre G. Eiffel (1832–1923). The idea of liberty was given the form of a classical-looking goddess wearing a crown and holding a torch aloft in her right hand, all of which symbolized freedom, dignity and authority.

Yet at the same time, there were artists who strove from the very beginning to develop a more dynamic, emotionally charged and dramatic language of sculpture. A type of sculpture that did use these dynamic and dramatic effects can be seen in the relief on the Arc de Triomphe de l'Etoile, which was created by François Rude (1784–1855) and entitled *La Marseillaise* or *Le depart des volontaires de 1792* (1835–6). This more romantic vision is in striking contrast with another relief on the same arch, i.e. *Le Triomphe de 1810 célébrant la paix de Vienne*, by Jean Pierre Cortot (1787–1843), its more static and strictly geometrical representation clearly showing his more classical approach.

Action and the suggestion of movement are central to sculptors who were oriented towards feeling and the romantic, which often leaves us with an impression of disorder, crowdedness and emotion. This seems to be the case with the large, often architectural works of Pierre J. David (1788–1856), also known as David d'Angers, and especially in the exuberantly vitalist work of Jean-Baptiste Carpeaux (1827–75), which nevertheless shows his sharp observation of the physiognomy of his models and which is further enlivened by the play of light on his sculptures. The fact that sculptors were becoming more and more fascinated by close observation of living models, and were more given to creating true-to-life representations of reality, can be seen in the animal sculptures of Antoine L. Barye (1796–1875), whose studies were all made in the Jardin des Plantes. Even though his work combined a sense of reality with the romantic urge for dramatic effect, it was still greeted with criticism by the adherents of the academic tradition.

This careful observation of everyday reality and its true-to-life representation also extended the number of themes: from the second half of the century onwards sculptors began to depict the world of workers and the oppressed. This *verismo* is clearly visible in *The Victims of Labour* (1883), a relief created by the Italian sculptor Vincenzo Vela (1820–91) on his own initiative. The work is a realistic and tragic depiction of a worker (who had been killed while working in the St Gothard Tunnel in Switzerland) being carried away by his mates. The Belgian Constantin Meunier (1831–1905) created another form of sculptural realism in his studies of workers in the Borinage, a mining district in Wallonia. This tendency towards the heroic is not found in the work of the French sculptor Jules Dalou (1838–1902), who was himself from the working classes. But his depiction of workers, of women reading or knitting and of mothers with their children, is strictly factual.

Painting

As was the case in the other art forms, neo-classicism, whether it was rational and romantic, continued to set the trend for a long time, this being the result of the style being supported and propagated by the academies, the salons and by official bodies. The person who served as a model here was Jacques L. David (1748–1825), whose great painting *Oath of the Horatii* earned him the position of 'official' painter to the republican government – a position he was to keep during the First Empire. His strict neo-classical style with its moralistic themes, cold light, sharp outline of character, smooth brush work and restrained use of palette was continued by his students Pascal S. Gerard (1770–1837), Anne Louis Girodet (1767–1824), Antoine Jean Gros (1771–1835) and Jean Auguste D. Ingres (1780–1867). Being painters who enjoyed the favour of those in power, they dominated painting and determined academic style during the first half of the century.

Neo-classicism was also the dominant style in Germany during the first half of the century, as can be seen from the work of Jakob A. Carstens (1754–98), Gottlieb Schick (1776–1812) and Joseph Anton Koch (1760–1839), though here the individualistic subjective vision of the romantics did supplant the objectivism of the classicists sooner than in did in France. The romantic variety of neo-classicism set the trend in English high society. Its main exponents were Thomas Lawrence (1769–1830) and Lawrence Alma-Tadema (1836–1912), who were both knighted for their work. In the United States of America the official portrait of its first president George Washington was commissioned from Gilbert Stuart (1755–1828) a portrait artist who worked in the same neo-classical style as David.

And yet at this time, there were painters in many countries who broke with the formal severity and classical themes of neo-classicism. The oeuvre of David's contemporaries, like the Spanish painter and engraver Francisco J. Goya Y Lucientes (1746–1828), the English poet, graphic artist and painter William Blake (1757–1827) and the German landscape artist Caspar D. Friedrich (1774–1840) contained visible signs of a new, more open and spontaneous type of painting. These three painters lit the way towards innovation in nineteenth-century painting. Goya, an impulsive lover of freedom, expressed his social awareness through a form of merciless objectivism that would become highly caricatural in form and would use strong contrasts of colour and passionate brush work. The misery he saw about him and his own inner sufferings were expressed in emotionally poignant paintings (like *The Execution of the Rebels on 3 May 1808*, dating from 1814) and a series of hallucinatory etchings on suffering and injustice (*Los Caprichos*, 1799), war (*Los desastres de la guerra*, 1810–18) and bestiality (*Tauromaquia*, 1808–18). His themes anticipated realism and social awareness in art, and his style of painting anticipated impressionism. By using line as his main means of expression and by illustrating his own mystic and visionary poems, William Blake already anticipated art nouveau.

In France, the main rupture with neo-classicism was to occur after the 1824 Paris Salon, which exhibited a number of prominent English landscape artists like John Constable (1776–1837) and the gifted Richard P. Bonington (1801–29), who unfortunately died very young. The intensity with which they focused on nature in their work echoes Rousseau's notion of the *retour à la nature*. Adverse to the rules of classical models, they portrayed the purity of the air, the intensity of light and natural colour. The rendition of light in the work of Constables's contemporary Joseph M. William Turner (1775–1851) is so intense that the forms progressively dissolved into pure pictorial fantasies. These works were like a revelation to French painters like Théodore Géricault (1791–1824) and Eugène Delacroix (1798–1863). Géricault's *The Raft of the Medusa* (1829) and Delacroix's *Freedom Leads the People* (1830), superb, dramatic works full of contrast, movement and intensity of colour as well as expressive true-to-life characters, were the first acts of pictorial revolution in French painting. Thanks to the support of Adolphe Thiers, who was initially a journalist and an art critic and later an historian, politician and government minister, the rebellious Delacroix was at last able to obtain some important commissions (the Salon du Roi at the Palais Bourbon, the dome of the library at the Luxembourg, the Apollo gallery at the Louvre, the Chapel des Saint-Anges at the Saint-Sulpice). Following the annexation of Algeria by France in 1832, Delacroix was sent as member of a diplomatic mission to the sultan of Morocco, where he was deeply impressed by the multi-coloured world of North Africa. This would increase the intensity of colour in his work.

In the forties, a painter's front began to form, which was against the classical credo of the often dictatorial academies. In France for example a number of painters founded the 'Barbizon School': Théodore Rousseau (1812–67), Charles-François Daubigny (1817–78), Narcisse-Virgile Diaz (1808–76), Jules Dupré (1811–89) and Constant Troyon (1810–65) moved to the village of Barbizon. Their common goals were creating true-to-life depictions of nature and painting *en plein air*, particularly in the forest of Fontainebleau. A number of young German artists, who were tired of copying plaster casts and engravings of classical masterpieces, left their academies and settled at the disused monastery of San Isodoro on the Pincio in Rome. In contrast to the many others who moved to Rome to study the language of classical form, they went in search of the spirit of medieval Christian painters, with the intention of breathing new life into Christian art. Because of this, they were dubbed the Nazarenes. They mainly painted frescos using clear carefully balanced colours. They painted a number of frescos collectively at the Casa Bartholdy and the Casa Massimo. Except for Johann F. Overbeck (1789–1869) who remained in Rome, they all returned to Germany where they exerted considerable influence as a result of the important positions they acquired in the art world: Wilhelm Von Schadow (1789–1862), first in Vienna and later as the director of the Düsseldorf Academy, Julius S. Von Carlsfeld (1794–1872) and Peter Von Cornelius (1783–1867) in Munich, Philipp Veit (1793–1877) as director of the Academy of Frankfurt, Franz Pforr (1788–1812) in Vienna. Though their romantic craving for medieval art resembled an over-enthusiastic dream, they did succeed in bringing about an invigorating liberation from the classical tradition. This period is otherwise dominated by Biedermeier and its middle-class indolence, family cosiness and sentimentality. Their preference for detail, like that found in the work of the romantic painter Philip O. Runge (1770–1820), resulted in the depiction of household and idyllic country scenes and fairy tales. The two most prominent Biedermeier painters were Ludwig Richter (1803–84), who made woodcarvings of H. C. Andersen's and the Grimm brothers' tales, and Carl Spitzweg (1808–85), who in his painting moved away from attention to detail towards a more pictorial, almost impressionistic style.

With the 1855 World Fair in Paris the romantic way of painting was finally to gain recognition: this time a room was set aside for Delacroix (as well as for his neo-classical rival Ingres) in which thirty-five of his most important works could be exhibited. On this occasion, the victim of the jury was Gustave Courbet (1819–77), whose three paintings were rejected. In protest against the decision, he set up his own pavilion near the World Fair and above the entrance he placed a sign that read 'Pavillon du Réalisme'.

For about seven years, Courbet was to be the leader of *la bataille réaliste*, the second wave of innovation that caused uproar in academic and middle-class circles. He was the first and most significant presenter in painting of a realistic chronicle of everyday life among farm labourers in Franche-Comté, his region of origin. In works like *Les casseurs de pierres*, *L'Enterrement à Ormans* and *Les paysans de Flagey revenant de la foire* (which was exhibited during the 1850–1 Salon) he broke away from the dominant conventions and shocked his self-satisfied middle-class audience.

Even more brave and committed in his criticism of society was the illustrator and caricaturist Honoré Daumier (1808–79), for which he paid with a prison sentence. His deep sense of humanitarianism and justice caused him to mercilessly lambast hypocrisy and other social injustices in his caricatures in *Le Charivari* and *La Caricature*, as well as in his satirical lithographs and paintings.

The work of Jean-François Millet (1814–75) was a third variant of realism. From 1849 onwards, when he first settled in Barbizon, he dedicated himself to depicting farmers with their wives and children at their daily work in the unspoiled though hard countryside. His skilled work raised these farm labourers to the level of heroes and heroines. These scenes from country life are captured in clear, balanced compositions using harmonious colours. Millet's mystic and sentimental approach made this realistic way of painting accessible to a wider audience. Moreover, by using figures such as the farmer, the sower and the shepherd, he built up an iconography that was to remain in place till the time of Van Gogh and expressionism. His influence was considerable, particularly in the Netherlands (the Hague School, including Jozef Israëls, Jacobus Maris and Anton Mauve); in Belgium (the Brussels group who founded the *Société libre des beaux-arts* in 1868, and later in 1871 issued a magazine called *L'Art Libre* led by Louis Dubois, a student of Courbet's, in cooperation with Charles De Groux among others, the first to paint the working classes of the city); and in Germany (with the moderate but tasteful realism of von Menzel and the so-called Leibl school).

In Italy and in Florence in particular, a somewhat different form of realism was propagated in the 1860s by a group of painters known as the *Macchioioli* (Giovanni Fattori, Giuseppe Abbatie, Rafael Sernesi, Silvestiro Lega and Vito d'Ancona), who were mainly involved with the depiction of light and built their paintings up in simplified surfaces by using abstract-looking contrasts. Their experiments are interesting because they already anticipate the spiritual climate and stylization that was particular to symbolism.

Realism was also to develop along different lines in England, where the Pre-Raphaelite Brotherhood was founded in 1848 by William Holman Hunt (1829–1910), John Everett Millais (1829–96) and Dante Gabriel Rossetti (1827–1910). Rejecting the cliches of the neo-classical romantic style of painting still being propagated by the art academies of the day, they strove for a new style of painting that was honest, fresh and unconventional in its radical attempt at rendering reality as closely as possible. They sought their inspiration in a time before there were academies, i.e. in Italian art before the era of Rafael (1483–1520). The result of this return to the source was a detailed form of realism that was meticulous, razor sharp, variegated and brightly coloured and that reminded one of the old Italian and Flemish masters. They did wish to give their work a contemporary touch, however. They carried their preference for simple, unadulterated everyday reality through to religious, mythological and historical subjects, which inevitably caused scandal in Victorian society. One of the characteristics that also made them realists was their social commitment. They were messianic in their determination to restore culture and protect it against decadence and the lack of taste of an industrialized society, their antidote being the creation of beauty in everyday life and, particularly through extolling handicrafts, raising work to the level of art. In this way they were laying the ground for the spiritual climate of future practitioners of art nouveau.

At the time that Courbet's influence was contributing towards the development of realism outside France, he had already been supplanted by a third wave of innovation, which of course was the cause of further scandal and uproar. In 1863, the reaction of the artists against the decisions of the jury at the yearly Salon was so strong that they decided to set up their own exhibition and show the work of the artists that had been rejected. This *Salon des Refusés* was tremendously popular, though many thought this was merely because of the scandal it caused. One of the works considered to be so shocking at the time was *Le déjeuner sur l'herbe* by Edouard Manet (1832–83). The painter based his work on a composition by Rafael but replaced the gods and goddesses with Parisians enjoying a rest in the countryside. The fact that one of the female figures in the painting is completely naked was not considered as shocking, nakedness being common in painting since time immemorial. The problem facing this nineteenth-century art audience was that the figure was no longer a depiction of some untouchable creature from a higher sphere but that of an ordinary woman who had simply taken her clothes off.

This originally notorious and now famous painting shows that Manet was both an iconoclast and a standard-bearer of that great tradition in painting common to artists such as Velasquez, Hals and Goya. Here, for the very first and the very last time, we can witness a synthesis of tradition and innovation.

Music

Technically speaking, the emergence of romanticism in music is less typified by the introduction of new forms than by a gradual disintegration of the forms inherited from classicism. Nevertheless, there was a sea change in the world of music, which was brought about by the increased independence of the composer and the emergence of a new middle-class audience. Self-assertion turned the work of composing into an exercise of freedom. The process of composing was used consciously to change reality and as an act of revolution against the established hierarchy.

This was most clearly expressed in the battle between the religious and increasingly profane music. Compositions for mass became estranged from their liturgical function and became personal expressions of an awareness of a set of existential problems, and at times went against the demands and even the requirements of the liturgy (like Beethoven's *Missa Solemnis* or Berlioz's *Requiem*, for example). This even led to provocatively blasphemous parts in the score of Schumann's *Manfred Ouverture* and in Berlioz's *Faust*.

Thematically speaking, some of the most spectacular changes took place in opera, the most ideally middle-class of music genres. And composers dealt with themes that the middle classes could identify with in their struggle for emancipation. Ordinary people had already been given a role in eighteenth-century *opera buffa*, but now these ordinary people were presented as heros in 'grand opera', e. g. the hero from the folk tale (see Weber's *Der Freischütz*), the national hero (Rossini's *William Tell*), and even the heroic artist (Berlioz's *Benevenuto Cellini*). The repertory of romantic opera also contains political and historical themes (Beethoven's *Fidelio*, Meyerbeer's *Les Hugenots*) and fairy tales (Weber's *Oberon*). For the first time in history, the king could be presented as a historical or popular character (Lortzing's *Zar und Zimmerman*) and royal authority could even be undermined by the people (this was demonstrated by Daniel Auber (1782–1871), who worked together with the popular serial writer Eugène Scribe in creating his magnum opus *La Muette de Portici* (1828) which, when performed in Brussels in 1830, was to spark off the struggle for independence).

The spectacular character of grand opera was further strengthened by the introduction of ballet episodes. Ballet developed into a fully independent genre during the course of the nineteenth century, particularly in France. The great romantic ballets such as *La Sylphide* (1832), *Le diable Boîteux* (1836), *Giselle* (1841) and *La Péri* (1843) were known for their grace and for the virtuosity of their dance styles as well as the fairy tale atmosphere they invoked during performance. The popularity of this *ballet blanc* and its white *tutus* would remain unthreatened for the whole century. The new techniques such as the *pointe* (dancing on the tip of one's toes) and the *saut périlleux* (swan dive) required almost acrobatic virtuosity but gave the dancers that light, fleeting even ethereal character they needed to perform these *ballets fantastiques*.

The predominance of German composers in the first half of the nineteenth century is particularly striking. In contrast with the other arts, German romantic music was the trend setter in Europe. The fault line between classicism and romanticism was struck by Ludwig Van Beethoven (1770–1827). Even his earlier work from around 1790 is quite distinct from the dominant Viennese classicism of Haydn and Mozart. He was the first to express the music of modern critical self-consciousness, the music of a signifying and productive human being who wishes to positively influence and change the course of history and the society he belongs to. For him music was no longer there to serve or decorate but was a means for expressing personal feelings and ideas, which is why Beethoven did not merely adopt and imitate the standard forms which had been handed down but transformed them to fit his own individual way of thinking. Beethoven's innovative composition techniques can be characterized by the evolutive way they build upon a theme through the increasing integration of major motifs, their use of forms of melody as the raw material for creating numerous works built around the same idea, the dramatic dialectics he uses in the development of the sonata, and the principle of cyclical form found in all his major works after the third symphony. Beethoven's innovations and changes to the means of musical expression were closely related to his belief that humanity could be perfected and society transformed – all ideas which had been inspired by the French Revolution. The literary references in his major works all allude to man's revolt against tyranny (Prometheus against the gods; Egmont against Spanish oppression; Fidelio against his unjust imprisonment) or to the glorification of a brotherhood of man (the ninth symphony). Moreover, all the works in which the idea of human heroism is central (the *Coriolan* overture; symphony no. 3, the *Eroica*; and the fifth and seventh symphonies) use motifs such as revolutionary choral pieces, marches, songs and elements taken from folk music.

In this process of emancipation whereby music became an ideal self-contained implement and sound an independent means of expression, in this liberation from formal compulsion that allowed new and innovative explorations for the musical forms needed to express the ideals of freedom, solidarity and progress, Beethoven stands like a lighthouse pointing the way towards modern times.

Beethoven's era not only ushered in the collapse of the divisions between the various musical genres, but also that of the borderlines drawn between the arts themselves, particularly between music and literature, between the language of words and the play of sounds. An important contributor to this process was Franz Schubert (1797–1828), who created the romantic *Lied*, a dual form for solo singer and piano in which the vocal and instrumental parts were equally rated. He also gave a definitive form to *Lieder* cycles: cycles of songs that formed a stylistic and thematic whole. This form reached its zenith of expression in his *Winterreise* cycle, which was based on the poems of Willem Müller and

which he himself termed as 'Ein Kranz schauerlicher Lieder'. This merging of verbal and musical texts became even more intense in the work of Robert Schumann (1810–56), voice and piano often flowing into each other or the voice rising up out of the piano parts. He too composed musical cycles for the poems of Friedrich Rückert, Joseph Von Eichendorff, Adelbert Von Chamisso and Heinrich Heine. The passionate use of the voice in his chamber music added extra power to the overall sound, which thereby acquired almost symphonic proportions. Carl M. Von Weber (1786–1826) was also to gain renown through his compositions for songs taken from Körner's *Leier und Schwert*, but became more famous in Europe for his operas *Der Freischütz* (1817), *Euryanthe* (1823) and *Oberon* (1826). These works were innovative in their use of spoken dialogue, their dramatically balanced distribution of recited passages, arias, duets and finales, and their use of leitmotif and orchestration in underpinning the romantic ideal of synaesthesia and unity of colour, image and sound. A similar form of romantic orchestration, which was used to invoke the moods of nature, can also be found in the *Italian* and *Scottish* symphonies of Felix Mendelssohn-Bartholdy (1809–47), as well as in his *Overture for the Hebrides* and *Fingal's Cave*, though he did show more interest in the music of his predecessors than in that of his contemporaries.

The ideals of the French Revolution provided the impulse for many German composers to break through to romanticism quite early in the day. Paradoxically, the Revolution led to a strengthening of the classical tradition in France, resulting in the solemn stately music of choirs and grand operas designed to reflect the outer majesty of the new order of state. Composers like François J. Gossec (1734–1829), Luigi Cherubini (1760–1845) and Etienne N. Mehul (1763–1817) drew on traditional French music for the elements of grandeur and stateliness common to the former kingships, in order to put them to use for the triumphant revolution and eventually for the Restoration after 1815. This music fulfilled the same function as neo-classical architecture, sculpture and painting, and would continue to be played on state occasions far into the nineteenth century. Spectacular grand operas would also continue to be played and remain popular thanks to the work of Giacomo Meyerbeer (1791–1864) and Fromental Halevy (1799–1862). It was only in 1830 that romanticism would manage to break through with the work of Hector Berlioz (1803–69). He was unmatched in his mastery of instruments, and succeeded in deploying a monumental array of sound that mirrored the schizoid mood of the romantic as fallen angel or the dark romanticism of decadence and devil worship (as in the *Symphonie Funèbre et Triomphale*). In doing so, he drew inspiration from the literary idols of his day (Shakespeare, Goethe, Byron, Scott, Hugo and Gautier) as well as from his own passions, which he rendered in the form of romanticized auto-psychological stories (as in the *Symphonie Fantastique*).

Romanticism emerged even later in other countries. In Italy, which had dominated the eighteenth-century music scene, the important tradition of opera continued in the work of Vincenzo Bellini (1801–35), Gaetano Donizetti (1797–1848) and Gioacchino Rossini (1792–1868). Music in England did become more middle class, but this change did not bring about any major renewals. This was the case however, in Eastern Europe, particularly in Poland and Russia, which maintained intensive cultural relations with Western Europe at the time. Frédéric Chopin (1810–49), who hailed from Warsaw, was unequalled in the brilliance with which he made the soul of romanticism resound in the stormy and flighty moods of his compositions for piano. He was the romantic composer *par excellence*, relying exclusively upon his own subjective states of mind for his creations. Only in his waltzes, polonaises and mazurkas do we recognize borrowings from the dance rhythms and folk music of his native Poland. The nationalism and social insurrection common to the romantic movement formed the basis for the operas of Michael Glinka (1804–57), who broke with the dominant Italianesque style of his day in Russia. He made use of folk instruments and melodies, and was the first to stage Russian country folk in his operas: see *A Life for the Tzar* (1836) and his *Russia and Ludmilla*, an adaptation of one of Pushkin's works. In this way, he paved the way for a tradition of Russian romanticism that would produce composers such as Modest Musorgsky (1839–81), Alexander Borodin (1833–87), Pyotr I. Tchaikovsky (1840–93) and Nikolai Rimsky-Korsakow (1844–1908).

The romantic style would continue to dominate music throughout the whole of the nineteenth century, which was not the case in the other arts. This does not mean, however, that romantic composers dominated the entire music scene, for much of their innovations were greeted with protest and incomprehension by middle-class audiences. As a result, many of them often experienced financial problems and even lived in poverty. The fact that many of these early romantic composers were also *Frühvollendeter*, gave rise to the equally romantic myth of the gifted composer who was rejected by society and forced to live a marginal life as a bohemian artist – a myth that was strongly reinforced by the opera *La Bohème* by Giacomo Puccini (1858–1924).

The middle classes still considered stately neo-classical music to be the most appropriate music for official occasions. For purposes of relaxation they went to the spectacular grand opera, *ballets blancs* and *ballets fantastiques*, and in the second half of the century began to enjoy operettas. A continuation of *opera buffa* and vaudeville, operettas were the only lighthearted, playful and gracious genre of the period. Like the earlier pastorals, the genre was a world in itself and formed a buffer against the romantic art of contestation. It was a typical product of the era of *laissez faire, laissez passer*, of a world in which everyone could do what they liked as long as it did not threaten the system. The same government that brought Baudelaire and Flaubert to court tolerated the operas of Jacques Offenbach (1819–80), the 'Mozart of the Champs Elysées', and their satirical gossip columns listing the scandals of the prominent people of the day. They tolerated the humorous criticism that was levelled at the court, the army and the administration, because this form of joking did not undermine authority and was mainly meant for a limited audience whose loyalty was beyond question. In fact, such subdued, good-humoured satires as *Ventilsitte* only corroborated the system.

Given the growth of the commercial circuit in 'light' musical genres, which now included revues, cabarets, *cafés chantants*, etc., composers of 'serious' music reacted by becoming more and more professional. They made their compositions deliberately difficult, both technically and in content. These works could now only be performed by virtuosos at concert halls and only appreciated by educated audiences. The intention of a virtuoso soloist and composer like Nicolo Paganini (1782–1840) for example was to use his virtuosity and *épater le bourgeois*, but for most romantic composers the degree of difficulty of the piece was also an expression of the artist's inner complexity. As a result, programme music gained in importance. In the second half of the century, romantic music became more realistic in character.

As a rule, the term realism is not used in books on the history of music. There is one exception, however. The Italian movement known as *Verismo*, a group of opera composers including Amilcare Ponchielli (1834–56), Umberto Giordano (1867–1948), Pietro Mascagni (1863–1945) and Ruggiero Leoncavallo (1888–1919) did consciously strive after dramatic authenticity. The period 1850–80 is usually termed the (main) high romantic period. The musical works produced in these years continue the trend set in the previous decades and even reach a zenith. Moreover, given the abstractness of the musical language involved, it can hardly be termed a realistic art form. Nevertheless, there are a number of indications of the composers' concern for everyday reality as well as their adding a more realistic colouring to their romantic approach to music. The main difference between early and high romantic music is their fundamental difference in view on function. Music was no longer considered as a balm to be applied to the wound of disillusionment or as a means of escape from the disappointments of life. Musicians now felt called upon to use their music as a means of expression for confronting reality as they experienced it and for determining their own position within it.

These intentions are clearly visible in their explicit preference for programme music and for descriptive music. It is also symptomatic of the time that the classical symphony was transformed into the symphonic poem, Franz Liszt (1811–86) setting the example with his *Faust* symphony (1854), which was later followed by Camille Saint-Saëns (1835–1921) and Richard Strauss (1825–99). Other composers of instrumental pieces working outside the sphere of programme music, like Johannes Brahms (1833–97), Anton Bruckner (1824–96) and César Franck (1822–90) among others, also included realistic elements in their symphonies.

This sharpened attention to what was going on in the world can also be heard in the music itself: sounds from the everyday environment and from nature were inserted into the works or were imitated by the instruments. The depictions in sound of elements from nature, which had already been introduced by the early romantics, were further developed in rhythm, melody and musical imagery (e.g. the Moldau in the symphonic poem of the same name by Frederik Smetana (1824–84) or the vastness of the Steppes in Borodin's *In the Steppes of the Middle East*). Real sounds could be heard too, like the cannon in Tchaikovsky's *Feast Overture* or the bells in *Carmen* (1875), the opera by Georges Bizet (1875–1938), which was already very popular at the time. In fact, the setting for the action of this opera was the world of soldiers, factory workers, gypsies and smugglers. These characters were no longer cast in minor roles but had become the main protagonists, thereby enhancing the social relevance of the work. If rulers were cast, it was only to show their cruelty, as did the Italian composer Giuseppe Verdi (1813–1901) in his operas *Nabucco, Rigoletto* and *Don Carlos*. Insurrection against oppression or foreign rule had become a musical theme in this time of growing social awareness and nationalism. The interest for folk music and folk songs is also typical of both these tendencies.

The romantic movement reached its end and its zenith in the work of Richard Wagner (1813–83). The transition in

1849 to the notion of music as a revolutionary deed and the further idealization of music as an aesthetic religion were at their most absolute in Wagner's work. In 1849, he fought as a revolutionary on the barricades in Dresden. The ideas of Proudhon and his friend Bakunin are mirrored in his own manifesto *Die Kunst und die Revolution* (1849). After 1850, he developed the idea that humanity could be regenerated by the sublime nature of poetry and music in his theoretical works on music and *Gesamtkunstwerk*, as well as in his great musical dramas *Tristan und Isolde, Die Meistersinger von Nürnberg, Der Ring des Nibelungen* and *Parsifal*. In order to counter the cultural and social decadence of his day, he proposed the 'human purity' of timeless myth; to counter the inner dividedness of humanity he posited the total person in which thought and feeling formed one harmonious whole. This synthetic vision was given artistic form in the liberating unity of language, music and visual expression of the *Gesamtkunstwerk* of musical drama. Music was there to give concrete shape to thoughts, which could be experienced directly as part of one's immediate perceptions. Wagner's synthetic approach was to pave the way for the *fin de siècle*.

The rupture with tradition

Architecture

At the basis of modern architecture – of a style of building freed from every type of neo-ism – lay two drastically new factors: the use of the new materials of iron, steel and concrete, and the need for urban planning in large cities.

The new construction possibilities offered by steel and glass were first shown at an overwhelming display in Hyde Park during the Great Exhibition in London in 1851. In less than a year, the engineer Sir Joseph Paxton (1801–65) built the Crystal Palace, an exhibition hall 563m in length with a barrel-vaulted ceiling along its central aisle, in cooperation with Charles Barry, Robert Stephenson and Isambard Kingdom Brunel. This new style of building was based on principles such as clarity, efficiency, convenience and the systematic logic of its planning. They formed the opposite pole to the architectural principles of all 'neo' building styles. Many considered that this new building did not deserve to be called a palace. Originally, these new materials had ostensibly only been used in the construction of buildings that were mainly considered to have no representative function, such as bridges, railway viaducts, stations, factories, market halls and exhibition areas erected at the following World Fair in Paris in 1889, where the iron Eiffel Tower was erected as a monument to the 'art of engineering'.

Architects were highly reluctant to show these new materials in representative buildings and did what they could to camouflage them. Henri Labrouste (1801–75) used cast iron for the reading room at the Bibliothèque Sainte-Geneviève in Paris (1843–50). This large hall is divided down the middle by a row of slender iron pillars and vaulted by a barrel vault that contains ornate open transverse arches, also in iron. The exterior of the library is in sandstone, which gives the whole building the appearance of a renaissance palazzo. John Nash also used iron in a similar way for the Royal Arcade in 1816 and later for the Burlington Arcade in London in 1819. This led to the passages and streets covered with steel and glass roofs that

were a familiar sight in all large cities in the nineteenth century. The facades of the shops in these passageways were built in a uniform 'neo' style, however, in order to stress their exclusive character. This resulted in the Galerie d'Orléans in Paris (1830), the Galerie Saint-Hubert in Brussels, the Galleria Victoria Emmanuelle II in Milan (1863–7) and the Passage in the Hague (1884), all looking like parts of a palace from the *cinquecento*.

Iron was to be used as a visible element in facades in North America from about 1850 onwards. John Wilkinson (1728–1808), an iron founder, adviser for the first cast-iron bridge in 1779, was the first great advocate of this new uncomplicated style of building and the new materials involved. When large areas of Chicago were destroyed by fire in 1871, a solution to the problem had to be found very quickly. The solution was high-rise buildings. Initially traditional approaches were opted for, as can be seen in the work of Henry H. Richardson (1838–86), even though these buildings already looked very modern because of their regularity, symmetry, similarity of form and minimal amount of decoration involved. William Le Baron Jenney (1832–1907) was the first to design a building in which an inner metal frame supported its brick shell. Louis Sullivan (1886–1924) then designed the Carson Pirie Scott Company's department store (1889) and the Gage building (1898) in Chicago, the Wainwright building (1890) in St Louis and the Bayard building (1895) in New York, and ushered in the idea that the outside of a building should mirror its interior both in form and function. His motto 'form follows function' was further propagated and continued to be used by his disciple Frank Lloyd Wright (1867–1959) even though it went against the trend of 'boarding-school gothic' of the day. He pointed the way towards the new pragmatism that was to appear in Europe along with the first creations of the architects of the Bauhaus movement.

Another stimulus towards a renewal in building styles arose from the need to redevelop large cities following the growth of industry and their enormous expansion during the first half of the nineteenth century. The population of Paris rose from 548,000 to 1,050,000 between 1800 and 1846 and to 1,800,000 by 1866. This massing together of the industrial working classes in urban areas led to cholera epidemics that ravaged Europe in 1832 and 1848. Socialist theoreticians were the first to recognize the problem. During the cholera epidemic of 1832, the Saint-Simonians had already pointed out that the only way to combat cholera efficiently was to redevelop the old neighbourhoods, provide running water and to lay drains. Finally Napoleon III appointed Georges Haussmann (1809–91), prefect of the Department of Seine, to redevelop Paris. This decision was, of course, not motivated by socialist principles but rather by a desire to display and consolidate power. His new designs for the capital were meant to radiate prestige, and the large avenues were designed to facilitate military action and to prevent the building of barricades during popular insurrections. Medieval Paris was torn down between 1853 and 1870. Slums, shanties and narrow lanes were replaced by 'thoroughfares' in the form of wide boulevards, parks and large buildings. Haussmann's drastic change to the layout of the city was imitated in most other large European cities as well as in the building of many cities in North America. His concept of urban development was further expanded upon in influential theoretical works on the problems of city planning by Tony Garnier (*La cité industrielle*, 1901), by the

Berlin architect J. Stübben (*Städtebau*, 1880), by the Viennese urban developer Camillo Sitte (*Der Städtebau*, 1889), whilst the English architect Ebenezer Howard developed the idea of the garden city in *Tomorrow: A Peaceful Path to Real Reform* (1898).

So during the last decades of the nineteenth century, the whole of Europe underwent a flurry of demolition and rebuilding. Progressive young architects were also given the chance to develop a completely new style of building: art nouveau or *Jugendstil*, which was the rage all over Europe from 1890 to 1914. They foregrounded the new materials, but combined the austere simplicity of functionalism with flowing organic and at times excessive floral ornamentation in the metalwork. The Brussels architects, Henry van de Velde (1863–1957) with his home Bloemenwerf (1895) and Victor Horta (1861–1947) and his design for the Maison du Peuple (1893), which was commissioned by the Socialist Party of Belgium, were the mentors of art nouveau architecture. The French architect Hector Guimard (1867–1942) used organic ornamentation in a highly decorative and exuberant way in his designs for the entrances to Paris Métro stations, as did the Spanish architect Antonio Gaudi (1852–1926) in designing the Guël house (1885–9) and the still unfinished cathedral of the Sagrada Familia (begun in 1882) in Barcelona.

This initially excessive ornamentation would become more refined in time. The founders, Horta and van de Velde, also developed a more refined, pragmatic and functional style of building that would dominate the twentieth century.

Sculpture after 1879

As a result of the urbanization of culture, nineteenth-century sculpture became more public and monumental in function. This stimulated the massive production of sculptures on the one hand, but had a dampening effect on experiment and renewal, on the other. As the years went by, it seemed like many sculptors were being denied access to the road towards renewal. These innovative impulses were set in motion by painters who had turned their back on the academic tradition in their attempts to render all the various aspects of the world around them in a liberating play of colour, line, surface and especially light.

And yet even before 1874, when the impressionist painters first made their appearance as a group at a collective exhibition, one can already see a leaning in sculpture towards another vision of the world and the environment and another form than that recognized in official art circles at the time. It is very striking in fact that this rupture with traditional sculpture was first made by mainly graphic artists and painters, who did create three-dimensional work but not for its own sake: both Honoré Daumier (1808–79) and Edgar Degas (1834–1917) considered their sculptures as models or studies for their lithographs and paintings, and had no intention of exhibiting them to the public. Their wax models were only cast in bronze much later. Both artists strongly rejected the notion of the sculpture as a 'frozen monument' and always sought directness and spontaneity in their work.

The real renewers among the 'full-blooded' sculptors during the last quarter of the century were the Italian artist Medardo Rosso (1858–1928) and the exceptionally prolific Frenchman Auguste Rodin (1840–1917). Rosso was convincingly successful in conveying the impressionist perspective through his sculptures. His volatilization of form and sensitive surface movements that enhance the play of light and shadow are typical of all his work, be it figures, busts or portraits. His use of colour in the wax gave his sculptures a surprising sense of abstract immateriality. Rosso's impressionist figures ushered in a process of abstraction that would lead to full abstraction and even non-figuration in the twentieth century.

This was not the case with Rodin, who was the figurative artist *par excellence*. Because of his powers of deep psychological introspection, because of his capacity to visualize the essence of life forces and currents, Rodin was the one within the world of monumental figurative works in plaster, marble and bronze to end the stagnation in which sculpture found itself at the time. Like many other great artists, he cannot be cited as belonging to one particular 'ism', style or movement. His efforts to render light and movement in sculpture made him an impressionist, whilst his way of incorporating spiritual intensity gave his sculptures a symbolist bent and yet at the same time, the vitality mirrored and stressed in the contorted forms of his final works (particularly his monumental *Balzac*, 1898) already anticipates expressionism. Rodin reached the height of his creativity in the large works that were commissioned during the 1880s. In 1880, the French Ministry for Fine Arts requested him to make the entrance to the new Musée des Arts Décoratifs in Paris. He continued to work on his *Porte de l'Enfer* – which was inspired by Dante's *Inferno* – for the rest of his life without ever managing to complete it. He did finish some of the statues from the original design, like *Le Penseur* (1880) for example, which was originally meant to be a depiction of Dante, but which later grew to become an image of the archetypical poet-thinker. In 1884, following a request for entries for a competition set by the city of Calais, he was commissioned to design a monument in honour of Eustace de Saint Pierre. *Les Citoyens de Calais*, his invocation of the emotion experienced following the drama of having to surrender the city to the king of England in 1347, was so passionate in its use of clay, in its differences of depth and its play of light and shadow, that the resulting set of statues is clearly expressionist in its intensity. By transforming visible reality in order to depict ideas, Rodin in his own way also set the process of abstraction in motion in sculpture.

The road to abstraction was further paved by Paul Gauguin (1848–1903), who was inspired in his style and his use of line by Polynesian art, which contributed to the appreciation in Europe of non-Western folk art. The oeuvre of the Flemish sculptor Georges Minne (1866–1941), is linked to the organic vine-like forms of art nouveau and the spiritualism of the Pre-Raphaelites. Minne was also fascinated by the literary symbolism of his friend Maurice Maeterlinck. Works such as *Mother and Child, The Kneeling Youths* and *The Relic Carriers* all invoke the same introverted, melancholic and subdued atmosphere. Many of the sculptors who were moved by the ideas of the art nouveau movement often put their sculpting skills to practice in the applied arts by designing and creating jewellery and works in glass, ceramics or wrought iron.

The work of Aristide Maillol (1861–1944) was to have an even more profound effect on the development of sculpture, even though he only began to sculpt towards the end of the century. The work entitled *Méditerranée*, which he created in 1902, already expressed his vision of sculpture, which he saw as being an architectural balancing of forms.

Maillol liberated sculpture from the merely decorative function it was threatened with acquiring in the *Gesamtkunstwerk* of the *fin de siècle*. This opened the way for an autonomous language of form that was free of all pictorial and literary references.

Painting after 1874

The third and most shocking wave of renewal was caused by a group of thirty painters, who on 15 April 1874 (a few weeks before the opening of the official Salon), put 165 paintings on display at the studio of the photographer, Nadar, on the Boulevard des Capucines in Paris. One of the paintings at the exhibition was a view of the Boulevard des Capucines seen from Nadar's studio painted by Claude Monet. On seeing this somewhat sketchy though exceptionally warm and poetic painting, the outraged audience wondered whether they really did look like loose bits of paint when seen walking along the boulevard. The exhibition also contained another painting by the same painter of a view of a harbour at dawn, called *Impression, soleil levant* (1872), in which all the figurative elements seemed to be dissolved in colour. Hardly ten days after the opening of the exhibition, a scathing article was published by Louis Leroy, who found the title of the painting so ridiculous that he insultingly named the whole group of painters 'les impressionistes'. In so doing, he wished to show that all these painters had flaunted the principles and conventions of academic painting in order to use a web of brush strokes and unmixed touches of paint to turn a momentary impression into a painting. The painters would continue to use the nickname as the official name of the group for the next eight collective exhibitions up to 1886.

Of the original group of thirty painters, only a small nucleus would continue to apply and develop the impressionist style of painting, to ever increasing renown: Claude Monet (1840–1926), Pierre A. Renoir (1841–1919), Camille Jacob Pisarro (1830–1903), Alfred Sisley (1839–99), Edgar Degas (1834–1917), Paul Cézanne (1839–1906), Jean-Baptiste Guillaumin (1841–1927) and Berthe Morisot (1841–95). Throughout their lives, they continued to be criticized by the general public and by the established critics within the academic tradition.

Impressionism broke away from the academic tradition both thematically as well as in technique. It is first of all an urban style, because its practitioners discovered the cityscape, which had never been put on canvas till then: boulevards, squares, terraces, parks caught in the silence and first light of dawn or awash with afternoon sunlight and the bustle of anonymous crowds; or then again seen under the glow of lanterns and festive lights during *bals populaires*, the glare of cafes and bars, opera chandeliers or the footlights of variety shows. And not only did they portray the elegant, epicurean and expensive world of the *beau monde*, but also that of ordinary people or the outcasts of society: nighthawks, prostitutes and artists from the opera, ballet or popular revues. Not only did they record the happy bustle of amusement, but also fatigue, exploitation and inner shallowness – mainly things for which the painter Henri de Toulouse-Lautrec (1864–1901) had such a sharp eye. Even when the Impressionists abandoned the city and went to paint *en plein air*, their landscapes were those of city painters: elusive, sketchy, fragmented images of landscape seen through the eyes of the urbane in search of distraction in the countryside, in the Bois de Boulogne, on the banks of the Seine or at the coast along the English Channel.

Impressionism is the urban art form *par excellence* because it indicates a new type of sharpened sensitivity and a petulance of the senses. This *prima vista* painting is characterized by its changing nervous rhythm, and by impressions that vary from the sudden and strong to the volatile and elusive. The supremacy of the here and now over the universal and timeless, that Herculean feeling that everything is flowing, that reality is not being but becoming, that each phenomenon forms a unique fleeting constellation, can be considered as being the basic notion underlying the impressionist approach. It is an attempt to render in painting what Baudelaire termed 'fugitive beauty'.

Impressionist techniques also added to the shock felt by the spectators of the day. Till then objects had been depicted in art by means of iconographic signs; now they were being depicted by means of their components, the parts of the materials of which they were made. Impressionism further reduced the elements of representation to the purely visible. Visual forms in space were reduced to images on a two-dimensional plane, and furthermore these images were now also even contourless surfaces. The approach distanced itself from space as well as from linearity. And to top it all, its practitioners had their own use of palette: they painted on white canvas, and instead of applying their oils in layers they loosely placed spots of raw colour next to each other. The spectator was therefore obliged to look at the painting from a certain distance in order to let all the surfaces merge and form the right colours. This technique was applied to the extreme by Monet in his later works, where the elements of representation (the water lilies in the pond and the flowers in the garden in Giverny) become pure surfaces of colour that reduce reference to a minimum.

Impressionism underwent drastic changes in the work of Georges Seurat (1859–91), Paul Cézanne (1839–1906), Vincent Van Gogh (1853–90) and Paul Gauguin (1848–1903). They were therefore known as post-impressionists. For them impressionism was no longer a goal but a point of departure for further renewal. Seurat took colour division to an extreme in his 'pointillism', as can be seen in *Un Dimanche à la Grande Jatte* (1884–6), the much talked about painting at the impressionists' last group exhibition in 1886. The painting was made up of dots of primary and secondary colours, which only formed an optical whole of colour nuances and recognizable forms when looked at from a distance. The lines and contours trace tense decorative outlines. The painting radiates peace and harmony but also something unreal: a metamorphosis of a robot-like world in which science and technology appear as muses. Just like Seurat, Cézanne explored the building blocks of pictorial form and reassembled them to create a new language. This resulted in a totally different method known as 'cloisonnism'. Contrary to the impressionists who tried to weaken all form and even ignore it, Cézanne strove for stability and solidity of form and always sought basic form in depicting his Provence landscapes (particularly Mont Sainte-Victoire), still-lifes and characters. This gave rise to the rendering of objects as geometric shapes and to pictorial closeness. His painting consisted of a set of hermetically sealed horizontal, vertical and diagonal fields of colour that decreased in intensity as one went from top to bottom. Here the things suggested or invoked by the composition became more important than the reality they depicted. This approach would only be exploited in full in the twentieth century in cubism. It was as if Cézanne wished to overcome factors of chance, chaos and the unnecessary in what he saw by creating a pure pictorial world of balance and order.

The intense passion with which the Dutchman Vincent Van Gogh painted his works mirrors only disharmony and restlessness. Like Cézanne, he was not interested in depicting the outer appearances of reality but in expressing his tormented soul. Even in his early realistic paintings like *De wevers* (*The Weavers*, 1884) and *De aardappeleters* (*The Potato Eaters*, 1885), his urge for expression emerges in the exaggerations and distortions as well as in the way he applied the paint in rough, undulating strokes. After seeing the countryside of southern France and being influenced by the work of Toulouse-Lautrec, Gaugin and Japanese prints, he would create a form of impressionism that was dramatic expressionist in style. His intensely coloured palette, and the way he applied paint in wavy lines, strips and dots, attracted more attention than the things he painted. The very act of painting acquired an expressive value in itself. His temporary though much admired friend, Paul Gauguin, was to use impressionism as a point of departure in arriving at a completely opposite approach. Fleeing the civilized world of Paris, he began to lead a simple life in Pont-Aven, a fishing village in Brittany (1886) and rejected the realistic use of palette. Contrary to the impressionists, he did not consider colour as a means of depicting natural reality but allowed it through its intensity, complementary contrast and *cloisonnism* to contribute to the rendition of immaterial values such as unambiguity and unaffectedness. Particularly when he settled for good among the Maoris on the Marquise Islands in the Pacific Ocean in 1895, Gauguin began painting exotic paradise-like pictures of these mysterious natives, using bright warm colours in simplified decorative forms without shadow. So by presenting his paintings as symbolic signs, Gauguin broke away from the Western pictorial tradition.

During his stay in Pont-Aven, Gauguin worked together with Emile Bernard (1868–1941) on his doctrine of synthetism, which would inspire a group of young Parisian painters who later called themselves the 'Nabis' (Hebrew for 'prophets'): Paul Serusier (1863–1927), Pierre Bonnard (1867–1947), Paul Ranson (1864–1909), Maurice Denis (1870–1943), Edouard Vuillard (1868–1940), Xavier Roussel (1867–1944) and Felix Vallotton (1865–1925), who was from Switzerland. The work of these painters was defined by critics as being a manifestation of art that was subjective, synthetic, symbolist and ideational all at the same time. This is proof of a total victory over tradition, a liberation of art from its old chains, the end of an evolution in the depiction of reality which had begun in the Middle Ages and reached a climax in impressionism.

That impressionism and post-impressionism were exponents of a new urban culture could be seen by the fact that they were not limited to being a temporary phenomenon in the capital of art, Paris, but acquired adepts in all European and American centres of art. Moreover, the impressionist style would continue to be practised till the end of the nineteenth and far into the twentieth century, until it eventually became *salonfähig*. The Italian Impressionist Giovanni Boldini (1845–1931) for example, became *the* portraitist of the upper classes, and the Swedish impressionist Anders Zorn (1860–1920) was awarded a prize at the World Fair in Paris in 1900 for his painting *Midsummer Dance* (1897).

The English Pre-Raphaelites, Gauguin and the Nabis can be seen as striving towards an art form that wished to show deeper levels of reality than those observed with the naked eye. This gave rise to European symbolism in the *fin de siècle*, as was also the case in literature. Symbolism is more of a spiritual climate than a well-defined movement or style. It was a way of feeling or anticipating, an orientation that could be expressed in more than one way. This explains the eclectic approach of the symbolists. In order to feel or uncover the mysteries of life, they sought inspiration in the fantastic events of sagas and legends from the past or in untouched non-Western civilizations. Desirous of this inspiration, many sought contact with the occult, sects, and ritual; and in this way, dreams, ecstasy and trance became ideal states for opening oneself to the mysterious. The theoreticians of the day were Joris-Karl Huysmans and the eccentric Joséphin Péladan, who called himself Sar Péladan and held the famous Salons de la Rose Croix for symbolist painters from 1892 onwards.

Their predecessor and master was Pierre Puvis de Chavannes (1824–98) and his abstract-like, austerely elegant and simplified level compositions. Another inspiration was Gustave Moreau (1826–92), a painter who worked in solitude on sinister and disturbing allegories, which were composed in an eclectic style. As they were liberated from the past, the paintings and especially the graphics of Odilon Redon (1840–1916) were even more daring and more modern. They expressed the feelings of restlessness, angst and alienation that are so typical of the *fin de siècle*. Like the Belgian writer Maurice Maeterlinck (*La Vie des Abeilles*), he was fascinated by microscopic organic life forms (insects, crustaceans, mosses, etc.). By using his feeling for strange colours and materials and mysterious use of shadow he succeeded in visualizing the mystery of life in highly simplified, almost trivial representations.

In England, symbolism found a highly fertile seed bed among the Pre-Raphaelites, which led to highly refined aesthetics. Some of its high points were reached in the work of Edward Burne-Jones (1833–98) with his slender, melancholic female figures in soft pastels, and that of the book illustrator Aubrey Beardsley (1872–98) whose female figures rose up out of the elegantly undulating play of lines that typified the 'modern style'. Both drew their themes from Greek and Biblical mythology, sagas and legends, as well as from literature of the day. Their art fits perfectly into the vision that Oscar Wilde presented in his aphorism 'art is at once surface and symbolism'.

The most prominent representatives of this movement in Germany were the illustrator Max Klinger (1857–1920), Hans Von Marees (1837–87) with his antique-like style and Arnold Boecklin (1827–1901) with his fabulous and 'unheimliche' landscapes. Woman is central to the work of the Austrian Gustav Klimt (1826–1918), which is strongly erotic in tone and further captured within the lusciously decorative patterns of the *Jugendstil*. The paintings of the Swiss Ferdinand Hodler (1835–1918) acquired an allure of symbolist mysticism through their use of austere, symmetrically constructed compositions that alternately made use of straight and wavy lines.

The French innovations were quickly assimilated by an independent progressive circle of artists in Brussels called *Les Vingt* (1883) and as a result, symbolism and art nouveau flowered in the city and became internationally renowned. Two founders of the circle, Fernand Khnopff (1858–1921) and James Ensor (1860–1949) were its most original contributors. Khnopff's alienating art was in complete accord with the spirit of decadence in literature. This alienation resulted in a unique combination of photographic realism and the haziness and transparency of symbolism, both in his views of dead cities (with their clear references to medieval Bruges and the work of George Rodenbach) as in his sphinx-like portraits of women. The work of James Ensor is just as alienating but for completely different reasons. Rejecting his already highly original interiors, portraits, still-lifes and seascapes, which were painted with breathtaking skill in realist-impressionist styles, he set about creating his own symbolist means of expression. He became a rebel painter who loved pouring ridicule or making sarcastic or amusing sneers at all the seemliness of *la belle époque*. In so doing, Ensor pointed the way towards the liberation from function of the means of expression in painting.

The work of the Norwegian Edvard Munch (1863–1944) was important and highly influential internationally. This work shows us a synthesis of the cramped world of the *fin de siècle*, both in its themes and technique. What is even more drastic here is the movement away from portraying the visible outside world towards an inner world of feeling, which can only be represented in its most abstract form through colour and linear rhythm. This is a psychoanalytical sounding of the depths of human experience: loneliness, angst, torment, Eros and Thanatos, are all depicted through archetypes that he metamorphosed into his own highly original symbolic language. These paintings are modern infernos, like the dramas of the Swedish writer August Strindberg in which woman plays the dominant role of threatening *femme fatale*. Be it in his paintings, lithographs or woodcuts, Munch visualizes the ominous world of the psyche through simplified synthetic (colour) surfaces by using the dynamic line and whiplash style that was so characteristic of art nouveau. His powerfully expressive style, like that of Van Gogh and Ensor, anticipated expressionism.

So as we have seen, all the components of the various twentieth-century avant-garde styles were already to be found in the movements of last decades of the nineteenth century.

Photography

During our outline of painting during the last quarter of the nineteenth century, we have made repeated references to photographic perception, particularly its sharpness and fragmentation. In fact, many painters and sculptors turned to photography and began using photos instead of sketches for studies.

The whole technique of photography ranging from daguerro- and calotype, to the development of collodium plates and rolls of film, was developed during the nineteenth century in answer to the positivist desire to provide an objective representation of reality. Press and portrait photography were an immediate success among the general public. The French portrait photographer Nadar (pseudonym of Gaspard Félix Tournechon, 1820–1910) became famous throughout Europe. He was the first to make aerial photographs from a hot-air balloon, which inspired impressionist painters to work from this perspective.

Despite its popularity and the fact that it was used by painters, photography would not attain the status of an independent form of artistic expression during the nineteenth century. However, it did lead to the making of 'composite prints', which were obtained by placing a number of negatives together and which were one of the first forms of art photography. The pioneer of art photography through photo-montages was Henry Paul Robinson (1830–1905). Exhibitions of his work were held all over Europe and his book *Pictorial Effect in Photography* (1869) was a worldwide success. His ideas on art photography influenced the aesthetics of photography well into the twentieth century.

The invention of photography undoubtedly contributed towards liberating the 'fine arts' from the grip of the tradition of realistic representation.

The applied arts

Along with associations of artists like the German Nazarenes and the English Pre-Raphaelites, came early forms of protest against the spirit of mechanization and utilitarianism in the new industrial society. In their protest against the decline in good taste brought about by merchandising and commercialization, they first sought salvation in the soundness of the hand-crafted work of medieval guilds, in which form, function and decoration formed a natural whole. The plan of John Ruskin (1819–1900) to transform industrial society into one based on medieval guilds was soon regarded as utopian.

The cooperative workshops set up by William Morris (1834–96) and Arthur Heygate Mackmurdo (1851–1942) in 1861 and 1882 respectively, were much more realistic in their approach. Contrary to the Pre-Raphaelites, they decided that salvation could not be expected from art as such. Being of a socialist persuasion, they set about trying to change society in work and in deed. Art could only play a role in this if it were accessible to everyone, which is why they wanted art to be part of everything for everyone. They designed simple furniture, wallpaper and curtain materials for their companies, which were run as craft shops. Their ideas became more popular from 1884 onwards when they founded the Art Workers' Guild. There were other members of this group besides Morris and Mackmurdo who wished to promote the applied arts: Charles Voysey (1857–1941), Walter Crane (1845–1915), Charles Ashbee (1863–1942) and William Lethaby (1857–1931). The strong influence that emanated from this group was mainly due to the fact that most of its members were lecturers at or directors of prominent art schools. In 1888, Ashbee founded the Guild of Handicraft, where his staff were trained; a limited degree of mechanization was also carried out for certain products, which were sold on the open market. The Central School of Arts and Crafts, founded by the City of London in 1896 and led by Lethaby, provided further training in arts and handicrafts for tradesmen employed in industry.

That the Arts and Crafts movement enjoyed such a high degree of prestige at the end of the nineteenth century can be seen from the appointment of William Lethaby as the first professor of design at the Royal College of Art. Moreover, Arts and Crafts also formed the point of departure for the art nouveau style of the Glasgow School. The designs of Charles Rennie Mackintosh (1868–1928), Herbert McNair (1870–1945), Margaret Macdonald (1865–1933) and Frances Macdonald (1874–1921) were all characterized by their preference for austere geometric patterns, frames and stylized motifs, as well as by their sensitive use of pastel tints.

In strong contrast to this simplicity and austerity was the exuberant floral ornamentation and the opulent use of materials of art nouveau practitioners on the continent. Many of these artists also followed the example of the Arts and Crafts movement in using their skills in service of the applied arts. The ideas of the Arts and Crafts movement were mainly spread on the continent through the annual art exhibitions run by *Les Vingt* and later by *La Libre Esthétique*. A key figure in the promotion of applied arts in art nouveau style was Henri van de Velde (1863–1957), who left his impressionist pointillist painting behind forever in 1893 and turned to architecture and to graphic and industrial design. Applying the Wagnerian idea of *Gesamtkunstwerk* to architecture, he set about designing his own home from the exterior to the smallest detail of the interior, including everyday utensils, etc. The furniture designs of Gustave Serrurier-Bovy (1859–1910) remained closer to the simpler rustic designs of the Arts and Crafts movement.

The strongest stimulator of the applied arts in France was Samuel Siegfried Bing, an art dealer from Hamburg, who in 1896 opened a shop for new art objects in the Rue de Provence in Paris named 'Art Nouveau'. The trend in this area was, nevertheless, set by the school of Nancy, which included the glass designers Emile Galle (1846–1904), the brothers Auguste (1853–1909) and Antonin Daum (1864–1930), the furniture and wrought iron designer Louis Majorelle (1859–1926) and the jewel designer René Lalique (1860–1945). Contrary to the Arts and Crafts movement which only used traditional or local materials, these art nouveau artists did not reject the use of new materials like glass or iron, nor that of exclusive materials like exotic woods, ivory, silver or gold. This meant that art nouveau became exclusive in character and could only be afforded by those from the well-off liberal middle classes who were open to changes in art.

In German-speaking regions, the term used to indicate this new modern wave of applied arts was *Jugendstil*, from the magazine *Die Jugend*, which was set up in Munich in 1896. Both the German and the Austrian variants of *Jugendstil* are closer in their more austere geometric designs to the Glasgow school of the Arts and Crafts movement, than their more floral art nouveau counterparts in the Franco-Belgian cultural region. Following the example set in England, the Germans set up cooperative enterprises in Leipzig, Dresden and Darmstadt. As far as the applied arts were concerned, however, Munich remained the centre of *Jugendstil* and attracted artists such as August Endell (1871–1925), Herman Obrist (1863–1927), Bernard Pankok (1872–1943), Bruno Paul (1874–1968) and Richard Riemerschmid (1868–1957). In 1896, a group called the Vienna Secessionists broke away from mainstream conventions: Otto Wagner (1841–1918), Josef Hoffman (1870–1956), Joseph Olbrich (1867–1908), Koloman Moser (1868–1918) and Gustav Klimt (1862–1918). The work of the Vienna Secessionists was striking in the way it reduced surface decoration to a few geometric forms (small circles and squares) which were reminiscent of basic Byzantine and Egyptian patterns.

Similar to symbolism in painting, art nouveau grew to become a Europe-wide movement in the applied arts. Hence it was also found in urban areas in the North, East and Southern Europe. It is worth noting that the further this style moved from its points of origin, the more specifically nationalist it became in character as a result of the use of decorative elements taken from the traditions and folk art of each country concerned.

Apart from its use in posters, which brought this art movement to the streets, art nouveau in the applied arts largely remained a concern of the elite. This new style was ground-breaking, however, in that it succeeded in raising the status of the applied arts to that of the 'fine arts', which now no longer comprised the classical triad of architecture, sculpture and painting. This paved the way for the integration of graphics and industrial design into the training programmes of art academies in the twentieth century.

Music after 1880

As was the case in painting, musical impressionism would react strongly against tradition, and this became clearly apparent after 1880. This style of music would quickly reach its zenith, however: Debussy was hardly followed. Moreover, the style remained limited geographically to its country of origin, France, and only had a few significant exponents in Italy and Spain. That France was the seed bed of this new style resulted from the fact that the romantic tradition had not developed there to the same extent as it had in Germany and Austria. Romanticism flowered again in these countries in the final quarter of the nineteenth century, and from 1905 onwards expressionism would begin to manifest there both as a reaction to and as a continuation of late romanticism.

Late romantic composers continued in the tradition of high romanticism by further individualizing programmatic music. They composed pieces which provided answers to the great questions in life and which held a message for the listener. The desire to condense all the problems of existence into one composition led to hour-long performances by gigantic orchestras. The titles of these works alone show that they were founded upon philosophical ideas: Gustav Mahler (1860–1911) gave the name *Titan* to his first symphony and *Auferstehung* to his second, and called the synthesis of all his musical, philosophical and aesthetic ideas *Das Lied von der Erde*; Richard Strauss (1864–1949) composed philosophical symphonic poems which bore names such as *Tod und Erklärung* and *Also Sprach Zarathustra*; the mystical Russian composer Alexander Skrjabin (1877–1915) named his great symphonic works *Le Poème divin, Le Poème de l'extase* and *Prométhée: le Poème du Feu*. Like their predecessors they drew on literature in order to transpose the themes with which they felt affinity in music: Mahler's work varied from poems which he wrote himself for *Lieder eines fahrenden Gesellen* and folk poetry for *Des Knaben Wunderhorn* to Rückert's poems, which he used for *Kindertotenlieder*, and Chinese poetry for *Das Lied von der Erde*; Richard Strauss dedicated symphonic poems to the themes of *Till Eulenspiegel, Don Juan* and *Don Quichotte*; Arnold Schoenberg (1874–1951) used mythological sagas for his *Gurrelieder*; Hugo Wolf (1860–1903) continued the *Lied* tradition by writing scores for the poetry of Mörike, Eichendorff, Goethe, and Michelango; the Finnish composer Jean Sibelius (1865–1957) drew on themes from the Finnish epic *Kalevala* for his symphonic poems.

And yet these latter-day romantics, and the numerous profound musical changes they brought about, are all part of a transitional period that already anticipates twentieth-century music, which would continue to explore and deepen the innovations of this style. Mahler, Strauss and Wolf made their orchestration more supple, which brought about an impressionist refinement of sound. Mahler's and Skrjabin's explorations of the chromatic scale would lead to the atonal sounds found in Schoenberg's works from 1909 onwards.

Impressionist composers transposed the individualism of the romantics to the level of observation. They no longer stressed the subject to be dealt with but rather the state of that particular subject at any given time. Like the impressionist painters, they chose moments subjectively and expressed them in music, plucking them from the continuous flux of things. Music, being an art form that develops in time, is ideal for representing a series of things in movement. This is why the composers of the day preferred using subjects which already contained movement: elements like water, sea, clouds, or the depiction of a story in which the feelings of the characters become forms of movement. This also explains why we no longer find any integration of theme or motif, any development of melody or rhythm, any underlying philosophical idea or pathos in their work. Everything here has become subject to expressing movement, which also is rendered through subtle syncopations of sound and timbre. The form is no longer planned but fragmented: melodies become varied patches of sound. This was all quite demanding of the musician, who now was expected to become expert in rendering series of subtle changes and nuances. He or she was also expected to master their instrument in order to allow its timbre to melt into that of the other instruments, thereby creating a new set of tonal colours. The harp was the ideal instrument for this purpose, and the piano became the impressionist instrument *par excellence* because of its vastly improved hammers and pedal systems, which were used to maximum effect.

The latter-day romantic composer was usually an introverted and retiring artist who mainly worked alone. Impressionist composers on the other hand were enjoyers of life, for whom the sensual pleasure of sound was all important. They lived intensely along with poets, writers and painters in the cafes of Montmartre in Paris. This explains why their sung pieces mainly drew on the work of the symbolist writers of the day, for whom sonority was so important for the creation of atmosphere. Early impressionist composers such as Henri Duparc (1848–1933) and Gabriel Fauré (1845–1924) put the poetry of Baudelaire, Gautier, Leconte de Lisle, Verlaine (*La bonne Chanson*), Charles van Lerberghe (*La Chanson d'Eve*) to music. The interaction between literature and music was extremely intense in the work of Claude Debussy (1862–1928). The most important writers whose texts were integrated into his compositions were Mallarmé (*Trois poèmes de Mallarmé*), Verlaine (*Ariettes oubliées, Fêtes galantes*), Baudelaire (*Cinque poèmes de Baudelaire*), Pierre Louys (*La Flûte de Pan*, from *Chansons de Billitis*) and the opera *Pelléas et Mélisande* which was based on the similarly titled play by the Belgian writer Maurice Maeterlinck. The opera composed by Paul Dukas (1865–1935), *Ariane et Barbe-Blue*, was also based on a work by Maeterlinck, though it was unjustly less popular than his symphonic scherzo *L'Apprenti Sorcier*, a transposition in music of Goethe's ballad *Der Zauberlehrling*.

Impressionism in France ended the hegemony over French music of the German romantics and of Wagner in particular. Debussy continued a tradition in French piano playing which had already been set by Couperin, though he did change it drastically. His ground-breaking work did influence French composers such as Albert Roussel (1869–1937), Florent Schmitt (1870–1958) and Maurice Ravel (1875–1937), though only temporarily. Following a

short stay among the impressionists they moved on to expressionism and neo-classicism. Ravel's impressionist works (*Jeux d'eau, Pavane pour une infante défunte, Sonatine, Miroirs*) are strikingly different from those of Debussy in that they keep to the one though subtly nuanced set of tonal colours, whereas Debussy used a rich palette of varying colours. Eric Satie (1866–1925), a highly original, critical and sarcastic character, fell under the influence of Debussy's impressionist piano compositions out of reaction to romantic pathos, but from 1910 onwards turned against impressionism and begun exploring a 'new pragmatic' form of music.

Outside France, French impressionism was only of brief influence upon the Spanish composers Manuel De Falla (1877–1946) and Joaquin Turina (1882–1949) for their respective works *Noches en los jardines des España* (1925) and *Procesión del Rocio*. This was also the case for a few Italian composers (e.g. Malipiero and Casella) who then quickly evolved towards expressionism and neo-classicism. The exception to the rule was the Bolognese composer Ottarino Respighi (1879–1936), whose attractive impressionist symphonic poems *Fontane di Roma* (1917) and *Pini di Roma* (1924) were international successes.

Though various impressionist composers (Debussy, Dukas, Satie, Roussel and Ravel in particular) wrote music for ballet, they did not succeed in countering the process of fossilization then being experienced in French and Italian ballet. At that time, the centre of this world had shifted from Paris to St Petersburg. French and Italian dancers and choreographers such as Marius Petipa and Enrico Cechetti enjoyed enormous success there. They perfected ballet by approaching it systematically and in minute detail. Their Russian students soon went beyond the example set by their West European masters and went on to become international stars. One of these was Sergei Diaghilev (1872–1929) who performed with Les Ballets Russes in Paris from 1909 onwards.

To conclude, Afro-American music also caused a wave of innovation at the end of the nineteenth century. Though slavery had been abolished in the United States of America in 1865, the black population still lived in misery on the plantations and in the cities. They expressed their dejection, sorrow and hope through the blues. Having moved to the cities, they were influenced by the popular music of brass and dance bands and operettas. While continually improvising, they adapted these tunes to their own complex rhythms and created ragtime. The first ragtime composer was a black pianist, Scott Joplin (1868–1917), who published his *Maple Leaf Rag* in St Louis in 1896. Through ragtime, the piano became a permanent feature of jazz bands. From 1905 onwards, these jazz orchestras enjoyed enormous success in New Orleans, and were imitated by white musicians who then created the so-called Dixieland style. The end of the nineteenth century therefore marked the start of a new form of music that would become highly popular and known throughout the world during the twentieth.

LITERARY CURRENTS

Introduction: the birth of an autonomous literary field

Literary developments in the nineteenth century ran strikingly parallel with those in the other arts. Early nineteenth-century literature is also characterized by its struggle to liberate itself from the dual patronage of church and aristocracy, as well as from the normative poetics of classicism. Already in the eighteenth century the rise of a new culture of sentiment, which rejected poetics ruled by reason, now formed the basis at the beginning of the nineteenth century for the emancipatory movement of romanticism, which would spread throughout Europe and the New World. The power and sheer scale of this movement is closely interwoven with the rise to power of the middle classes and the growth of a national consciousness that would result in the struggle for independence of many nations. The new middle-class rulers and new nation states saw romantic literature as a symbolical means of consolidating their power. This explains why they would take over the role of patrons from the church and the aristocracy. The literary codes of romanticism would therefore be propagated and supported by officialdom throughout the whole of the nineteenth century. What once began as a casting off of old garments now became a new straightjacket for writers. Writers rose in rebellion against this appropriation of a once emancipatory movement in literature, which had begun with all the *élan* of a revolution, and now made efforts to safeguard the autonomy of the literary field.

This autonomy was gradually achieved over different periods of time in the various countries of Europe. It would bring about profound changes in the relationships between the production, distribution and consumption of symbolic goods. Writers were aided economically, socially and ideologically by three developments taking place at the time:

1 the growth of a socially diverse public of virtual consumers resulting from increased levels of socialization, particularly in the second half of the nineteenth century;
2 the emergence of a body of producers who in turn would become increasingly professional;
3 the multiplication of the number of points of recognition and distribution which also became increasingly specialized.

In this way, the literary field became populated by specialized independent *littérateurs*, who set their own codes and determined their own rules of work and behaviour.

A historical fault line has been clearly indicated and shown to have taken place around the 1850s in French literature – still one of the most influential of its time – in studies conducted by Jean-Paul Sartre ('Qu'est-ce que la littérature', in *Situations II*, 1947), Roland Barthes (*Le dégré zéro de la littérature*, 1972) and Pierre Bourdieu ('Eléments d'une théorie sociologique de la perception artistique', 1968; 'Le marché des biens symboliques', 1971). Sartre explains the origin of an autonomous literary field, as resulting from an ideological rupture between writers and the utilitarian middle classes, who wished to appropriate the literature of the time in order to consolidate their position of power. Roland Barthes shows this fault line by pointing to the use of a certain type of language and the ritualization of the signs in a literary text. With the creation of the mystique of the trade of the artisan writer and of their high-handed style of writing, writers wished to replace the user-value of literature by its value as an autonomous labour. The cultural sociologist Bourdieu points to the increasing differentiation among nineteenth-century readers which would result in an internal antagonism between the various

means of literary production: on the one hand, a quasi mass-produced series of literary works destined for an enormous and ever-growing public that was experiencing its first ever contact with literary culture (e.g. in the form of serial cliff-hangers, melodrama and vaudeville) and on the other hand, a type of literature that was purposely against any form of industrial mercantilism or utilitarianism, in which symbolism, significance and aesthetics superseded economic value.

Their headstrong isolation within their own autonomous literary field out of protest against the utilitarianism and materialism of industrialized society, explains the increasingly programmatic and polemic character of their writing. Writers began to join *cénacles* – groups – which were founded on the poetic programme of one central figure (as in the literary salons of Leconte de Lisle and Mallarmé). As a result, they began publishing their own independent magazines, which were often short-lived. They presented themselves as a group in anthologies or at literary events, and had their work published by expressly 'literary' publishing houses. They addressed a particular audience of lettered *aficionados* and especially their fellow believers, who shared their dream of a new society and of a new aesthetics. Their protest against the middle-class way of life was often expressed through adopting a bohemian stance. This protest would become more aesthetically radical during the *fin de siècle*, and take on forms such as dandyism and decadentism. The self-consciousness acquired by writers during the romantic period would also further develop into crisis consciousness, thereby replacing a belief in progress by that of decline.

Literature caught between continuity and rebellion

Romanticism

A new world was born at the end of the eighteenth century. Mechanization and the rationalization of production processes had reached a crucial stage, and led to the establishment of an industrialized society. This would eliminate the last remaining traces of feudalism. From this moment on, the unbridgeable gap between capital and labour meant the end of a system that divided society according to a system of trades. The new society, which was now based on class, brought with it a new way of life. Whereas, the aristocracy stood alongside the middle classes in occupying all the prominent positions in eighteenth-century society, nineteenth-century society was to be completely dominated by the middle classes. This century is also often portrayed as one, in which middle-class culture triumphed. This typology needs some further explanation, however, especially to banish the false impression that as a carrier of culture it formed one homogeneous whole. The truth is that it was made up of many different fractions. It not only included sections of the population who felt attached to conservative and even reactionary credos, and others who sympathized with more progressive and even revolutionary views; it also contained an uprooted intelligentsia which flirted alternately with the upper, and then with the lower classes, and as a result defended anti-revolutionary romanticism in its fight against the Enlightenment on the one hand, as well as a form of romanticism that stood for revolutionary liberation, on the other. In the second half of the nineteenth century in particular, this intelligentsia would develop an anti-middle class ethos and aloofness, and would call the durability of the existing social order into question.

The internal opposition at the heart of the romantic view on life was first expressed in the principled individualist programme of its writers. The *laissez faire* principle of economic liberalism, of free competition and the right to personal initiative, is mirrored in the writer's desire to express personal feeling, to allow his own personality to come to the fore and make the reader an immediate witness of his own intimate feelings and inner conflicts. Nevertheless, this individualism is not only a reflection in literature of the principles of economic liberalism that formed a reaction to the absolutism of the *ancien régime*, it is also a result of the protest against the levelling, mechanization and depersonalization of life that was an immediate consequence of that very economic liberalism. The militant character of romanticism stems from its expression of ideals of personal individualism through process and protest. Its strong cult of feeling is also a reflection of anti-classical and anti-aristocratic states of mind. They proclaimed and focused upon their feelings not because they began to feel things more strongly or more intensely than those who came before them, but because they wished to put forward a way of life that was opposite to the aristocratic ethos of self-control and aloofness. The expression of feeling, therefore, became an important artistic means of expressing a changed reality in which the middle classes were developing their own self-awareness. The historic rise to power of the middle classes and their new position as bearers of culture also explains the process of 're-puritanization' that would distinguish them from the libertine frivolity and extravagance of court circles during the *ancien régime*. Uprightness of mind also became fashionable alongside sentimentality. This further explains the high level of censorship and prohibition of publication and performance, and even prosecution when writers went beyond the mores and customs of the day.

Even though these tendencies towards individualism, sentimentality and moralism can be considered as inherent to the middle-class frame of mind, other qualities emerged which were strange for the initially optimistic mind set of this upwardly-mobile class: their tendency towards melancholy which had already become apparent in the pre-romantic period, the elegiac atmosphere of *Weltschmertz* and *Sehnsucht* that would turn into blatant cultural pessimism by the second half of the century. Moreover, by that time, members of the lower middle class, or *petite bourgeoisie*, emerged who had no previous contact with the earlier culture of the aristocracy and who had even less reason to be optimistic than the economically privileged upper middle classes. And yet even the latter's trust and self-confidence began to pale under pressure from increasing business risks, sharper competition and the threat of social unrest among the multitudinous urban working classes who were then living in utter misery. This led on the one hand to a form of literature focused on social realities and an intensification of feelings of anxiety, sympathy and revolt; and on the other to a form of escape from an unsatisfying present towards an idealized past or away from culture and civilization, towards an unoppressive state of primitive naturalness. Here, we can discover attempts at flight towards an ideal past or future or utopia. It is also characteristic of romanticism that both conservative, reactionary visions on life as well as their revolutionary counterparts were all arrived at by way of irrational idealism. Decisive in both attempts at escape, is a fear of the here and now and for the imminent destruction of the world. Romanticism is an ideology of a new society and of a generation that no longer uphold any value without first reflecting on its historical specificity. The idea that our spiritual life is in fact a dynamic evolutionary process and, being an expression of life, is therefore transient, is a discovery made by the romantics, and forms their most important contribution to our modern vision of the world.

This new development reached completion in Western Europe in a number of ways. German romanticism evolved from its originally revolutionary stance towards the reactionary, which was a result of compromise and moderation, whereas in other countries the movement evolved in quite the opposite direction, i.e. from a legitimately conservative point of view towards a frame of mind that was progressively liberal and revolutionary.

After the revolution of *Sturm Und Drang*, its greatest and most influential writers, like Goethe, Friedrich Schiller (1759–1805) and Friedrich Hölderlin (1770–1843), now began to write in the same style as the neo-classicist, J. J. Winckelmann. Nevertheless, some of their works were to provide an important impetus to the romantic movement: Goethe's *Bildungsroman* ('novel of development', usually tracing the protagonist's path from childhood to adulthood) *Wilhelm Meisters Lehrjahre*, 1795–6; *Wanderjahre*, 1829; his version of the Faust myth which was to become a symbol of the romantic quest (*Urfaust*, 1773–5; *Faust, ein Fragment*, 1790; and *Faust, eine Tragödie* (1808), the second part of which was published posthumously in 1832) and his desire for the exotic in *West-österlicher Divan* (1820); we can discover *Selige Sehnsucht* in the work of the romantic classicist Hölderlin (see his odes and hymns, *Der Archipelagus*, 1800 and his epistolary novel *Hyperion*, 1796–9); whilst Schiller pleaded for individual freedom in his plays *Don Carlos* (1787), the *Wallenstein* trilogy (1799), *Wilhelm Tell* (1804) and *Die Jungfrau von Orleans* (1801).

German romanticism was not only typified by its various phases but also by the groups which were formed in its university cities. Firstly there was the Berlin of Ludwig Tieck (1773–1853) who printed his *Volksmärchen* (1797), even began to write fairy stories, and who published an epistolary novel, *William Lovell* (1795–6) about the breaking of the ossified norms of rationalism; and of Wilhelm Heinrich Wackenroder (1773–98) who in his outpourings on the rediscovery of the beauty of medieval art (*Herzensergiessungen eines Klosterbruders*, 1797), pleaded for an appreciation of art based on feeling. This first centre was soon replaced by Jena. There a number of writers worked together for the magazine *Athenaeum* (1798–1800), these writers being more interested in speculative philosophy and not of a creative literary temperament. Wholly in keeping with the idealistic philosophy of Fichte, Schelling and Schleiermacher, the basic principles of romantic aesthetics were formulated by the brothers August Wilhelm (1767–1845) and Friedrich (1772–1829) Schlegel. To them, romanticism was a type of giant existential revaluation that would poeticize the whole world ('progressive universal poetry') and which was further based on the primacy of subjective imagination and original creative genius, and was full of a transcendental desire for the unattainable unearthly. We can find practical developments of their theories in Friedrich Schlegel's love story *Lucinde* (1799) and particularly in the lyrical prose found in *Hymnen an die Nacht* (1800) and in *Heinrich von Ofterdingen* (1802) by Novalis (i.e. Friedrich Leopold Freiherr von Hardenburg, 1772–1801) who explored the themes of love, dream and death in mystical terms and who created the *blaue Blume* as the symbol of *Sehnsucht* – a desire for harmony in the eternal that was never to be satisfied in this life.

A second group of a younger generation of German romantics was centred in Heidelberg and was more productive from a literary point of view. Belonging to this group were the brothers Jakob (1785–1863) and Wilhelm (1786–1859) Grimm, the compilers of the famous collection of fairy tales; Frederick Creuzer (1771–1858), who attempted to systematize religious myths in his *Symbolik und Mythologie der alten Völker*; Johan Joseph von Görres (1776–1848), who provides us with an overview of books of dreams, cures, riddles and predictions, weather legends and tales (including Faust, Ahasuerus, Eulenspiegel) in *Die teutschen Volksbücher*, as well as a number of poets such as Arnim, Brentano, and Eichendorff. Achim von Arnim (1781–1831) and Clemens von Brentano (1778–1842) collected and reworked old folk songs in their *Des Knaben Wunderhorn* (1805–8), while Joseph von Eichendorff (1788–1857) popularized the romantic world of feeling through the almost naive simplicity both of his prose and of his lyric work (particularly his novella *Aus dem Leben eines Taugenichts*, 1826).

Outside these groups there were other gifted writers who contributed to the influence of German romanticism. The sensitive descriptions of nature and of the soul set down in a completely new style in the novels of Jean Paul (i.e. Johann Paul Friedrich Richter, 1763–1825) were much loved, as was the fantastic fairy tale in novella form, *Peter Schlemils wundersame Geschichte* (1814) by Adalbert von Chamisso (1781–1838), *Udine* (1811), a fairy tale by Friedrich de la Motte-Fouqe (1777–1843), and the bizarrely fantastic stories of Ernst Theodor A. Hoffmann (1776–1822), such as *Die Elixiere des Teufels* (1815–16) and *Lebensansichten des Katers Murr* (1820). The zenith of romantic drama was reached with the publication of the four great tragedies (*Penthesilea*, 1807; *Das Kätchen von Heilbronn*, 1808; *Prinz Friedrich von Homburg*, 1810; and *Die Hermannsschlacht*, 1821) by Heinrich W. von Kleist (1771–1811), all of which explore the theme of conflict between a pure individual with extremely high ideals and a corrupt society.

The process that had begun in England earlier on in the eighteenth century was further developed in Germany and even taken to the extreme. If there was any lagging behind in England in the years immediately proceeding and following the *Lyrical Ballads* of Wordsworth (1798), it was largely made up for in the two decades that followed – a time in which romanticism blossomed in England.

No matter how great Coleridge's fire was in his role as the most important ambassador between German and English letters and of the philosophy of his day; and no matter how great his efforts were at receiving and assimilating contemporary German literature, literary theory and philosophical speculation into his work, the models set by his German forebears were not decisive for English romanticism on the whole, which in fact set off on its own highly varied course. The English romantics felt that they were the bearers of their own great tradition. They did not wage such an intense war on the defenders of the literary status quo as their fellow romantics did at a later stage in France. Moreover, there is little or no sign of particular schools, dogma, poetical programmes or manifestos, as was the case in Germany. The preface to the second edition of the *Lyrical Ballads* (1800), Coleridge's *Biographica Literaria* (1817) and Shelley's *Defence of Poetry* (1821) were all individual manifestos presenting each author's own ideas on

poetics. It is also striking to note that the explosions of patriotically tinted, mythical lyricism practised by the poets of the German *Hochromantik* during the first quarter of the nineteenth century, was practically non-existent in England. There is also a notable difference in their use of poetic language. In contrast to the lofty German lyricism found in their ballads, or the often exalted rhetorical tone of French poetry, the English romantics made use of a 'selection of language really used by men' in order to depict 'incidents and situations from common life'. Romantic lyricism reached its zenith of expression in England.

The first generation of English romantics combined their expressly aesthetic frame of mind with a strong sense of ethics. Initially, they were totally liberal, but their experience of the Reign of Terror following the French Revolution and the war against Napoleon forced them to adopt a conservative, anti-revolutionary stance. The movement, nevertheless, remained democratic to a certain extent and tried to popularize literature. This can be seen not only in their simplified use of poetic language but also in there approach to literature, e. g. their desire to achieve 'joy in widest communality spread'. Convinced that country people were still incorrupt and that 'the essential passions of the heart' could be found in their purest form in the countryside, a group moved to the Lake District, formed deep friendships, worked together closely and experienced their most creative period of their lives as poets. As a result, they entered literary history as the Lake Poets, though each maintained their own poetic individuality, even after a mutual exposition by Wordsworth and Coleridge of their views on romantic literature in the second edition of *Lyrical Ballads*. While further developing Locke's theories on perception and association and upholding certain humanitarian principles gleaned from the Enlightenment movement on the one hand, and reacting to elitist neo-classicism on the other, they saw poetry as 'emotion recollected in tranquility' even though its origins lay in a 'spontaneous overflow of powerful feelings'. What they wanted to voice was the 'still, sad music of humanity'. Poetry had to bring together the unique rapture of the poet and an undifferentiated openness in the public. They hoped in this way to teach their readers 'to see, to feel and to think' and thereby 'become more actively and securely virtuous'.

What is striking in this programmatic democratization of poetry is the way the two poets shared their work. William Wordsworth (1770–1850) wished to show the charm of the new in everyday things and that of the supernatural in the ordinary; Samuel Taylor Coleridge (1772–1834) wished to devote himself to the opposite. To a large extent, Wordsworth succeeded in his task by creating such beautiful poems as *Tintern Abbey*, the touching *Lucy Poems*, and his colourful descriptions of nature in *The Prelude* (1807), *Intimations of Immortality from Recollections of Early Childhood* (1807), *The Excursion* (1814) and his skilfully fashioned sonnets. His nature poetry is original in that it is not just description but also deals with himself in nature as well as his highly personal perceptions of nature. But Wordsworth wrote 'alas too many' poems, and as a result fell into a type of sonorous, moralizing simplicity, especially in his later work. This cannot be said of the less expansive but deeper and more mysterious poetry of Coleridge, whose poems such as *The Ancient Mariner* (1798), *Christabel* (1816) and *Kubla Khan* (1826) provided us with the first taste of *poésie pure*. His critical writings, such as *Biographia Litteraria* and *Notes and Lectures on Shakespeare*, also broke new ground.

This cannot be said of Robert Southey (1774–1843), a writer of long epic poems and a popular biography, *The Life of Nelson* (1813). As Poet Laureate, he had more authority than real original poetic talent.

The next generation of young romantic poets were more radical in their humanism. Their unconventional lifestyles, aggressive atheism and liberation from moral prejudice were their various ways of protesting against the politics of exploitation and oppression of the day. Notwithstanding their undeniable poetic talent, their desire for renewal and innovation was not appreciated by the readers of the day. This explains their feeling of being without a nation, and their search for solace in the strange and the foreign.

Percy Bysshe Shelley (1792–1822) was a born rebel who regarded everything legitimate, constitutional and conventional as the work of some despotic will. Kings, the ruling classes and the churches all formed one single compact power that was responsible for oppression, exploitation, violence, stupidity, ugliness and lies. His atheism, which was set out in his pamphlet *The Necessity of Atheism* (1811), is more of a revolt against God than a denial of his existence; he was battling against some oppressor or tyrant. In *Prometheus Unbound* (1820) and *Epipsychidion* (1821) he idealized free unselfish love, which to him was the only way to liberation for humankind. His now famous poems, like *Ode to the West Wind*, *To a Skylark*, *The Sensitive Plant*, *The Cloud* and *Lines Written among the Euganean Hills* are all inspired by the beauty of the landscape in Italy, to where he emigrated, and where all too soon he met his death in a storm in the bay of Spezia. It was in Italy, too, that John Keats (1795–1821) was to die at a very early age. During his short life, he taught himself how to write poetry. Graced with a wonderful gift for sound and colour and with a great power of aesthetic perception, he finally succeeded in controlling his tendency towards excessive ornamentation in his long mythical poems *Endymion* (1818) and *Hyperion* (1818–19). He achieved a classical harmony of form, idea and word in his *Odes* (1819–20). The poet to exert the most profound and widespread influence, however, was George Gordon, Lord Byron (1788–1824). He became famous for *Childe Harold's Pilgrimage* (1812–16), which was written in Spenserian stanzas, and the long, though uncompleted, witty satirical poem *Don Juan* (1818–24). The 'Byronic hero' – a proud headstrong cynic, a lonely rebel with a strong sense of freedom and a passionate lover – became a model in romantic literature throughout the whole of Europe. Sir Walter Scott (1771–1832) was equally influential as a result of his historical novels about Scotland (*Waverly*, 1814; *The Heart of Midlothian*, 1818), England (*Ivanhoe*, 1819; *Kenilworth*, 1821) and about the continent (*Quentin Durward*, 1823). His refined artistry and the precision with which he handled his historical material and characters made him as popular as writers of horror stories and sensational potboilers.

The essay also reached artistic heights at the time through the work of Thomas de Quincey, Charles Lamb, William Hazlitt and Leigh Hunt. The fact that romanticism was late in getting off the ground in France stemmed from Napoleon's adventures in dictatorial cultural policy during the Empire, as well as from the strength of the neo-classical tradition. One cannot imagine France as part of the European movement of romanticism without also thinking of the extremely strong impulses it needed to achieve this status. Next to the strong influence of English writers, which was already there in the eighteenth century (often through emigrants), German literature and aesthetics was also of major importance. The definitive breakthrough and ensuing period of bloom was prepared by 'Empire Romantics' who belonged more to the eighteenth century, like Mme de Staël, Benjamin Constant, François R. de Chateaubriand, Séancour and Ballanche. It was mainly the publication of *De L'Allemagne* (1813), by Mme De Staël (1766–1817), a friend and admirer of A. W. Schlegel, in which she provided a one-sided and at times incorrect though nonetheless impressive image of contemporary German literary thought, that formed a milestone on the road towards the liberation of romantic ideas in France. Through its 'openness' (which also implied an awareness of history and the cosmopolitan), romanticism was placed in opposition to the 'closed' system of classicism. While many romantics who had been won over to the ideas of liberalism were turning away from the church and its dogmatic articles of faith, François R. de Chateaubriand (1768–1848) saw Christianity as the highest expression of the romantic spirit (*Le Génie du Christianisme*, 1802). But it was mainly through his touching love stories, *Atala* (1801) and *René* (1805), that he introduced the feeling of *mal du siècle* in the wake of Goethe's *Werther*.

Other signs of this profound change in the world of literature were the publication of *Méditations poétiques* (1820) by the poet-politician Alphonse de Lamartine (1790–1869), the foundation of the magazines *La Muse Française* (1823–4) and *Le Globe* (1824–32), and the opening of the new salons by Sainte-Beuve and Hugo in 1827 (*le Cénacle*). It is also striking to note that this breakthrough first occurred in lyric poetry. Having initially written highly personal, elegiac, lyrical work of a sentimental type, Lamartine moved on to produce more humanitarian and religious lyric poetry. Being averse to all expressions of personal emotion, the 'ivory-tower' poet Alfred de Vigny (1797–1863) aired his highly atheistic and stoic view of life in tightly knit works like *Poèmes* (1822) *Poèmes antiques et modernes* (1826) and his long lyric poem *Eloa, ou la soeur des anges* (1824). Also to appear in the 1820s were the collections *Odes* (1822), *Odes et Ballades* (1826) and *Les Orientales* (1828) by Victor Hugo (1802–85), who became the most prominent defender of French romanticism. As a writer, he made a conscious effort to be the prophet and sound-board of his time. With his work, French romantic literature took on a political, revolutionary character, which at times led to rhetorical bombast and a tendency towards the monumental. The manner in which he moulded abstract ideas into the language of image, and the exceptional dynamism of his imagination are all manifestations of his poetic virtuosity and are particularly visible in the collection *Les Contemplations* (1856) and his cyclical poem *La Légende des Siècles* (1839–83). Alfred de Musset (1810–57) was also a true romantic lyric poet and a faithful habitué of Charles Nodier's literary salon at the Bibliothèque de l'Arsenal. As he was averse to all romantic bombast, however, his poetry is characterized by its naturalness, spiritual elegance and simplicity. In the first place, his lyrical work is an intimate expression of things that well up from the depths of the psyche. His own love affairs (with George Sand, among others) as well as the cult of pain, often give his work a melancholic and elegiac tone (especially the four long poems *Les Nuits* in *Poésies Nouvelles*, 1836–1852 (1852). The work of Gérard de Nerval (1808–55), the *poète maudit* of romanticism, is one long romanticized autobiography. The main theme in his work is his obsessional adoration of a dreamlike woman who takes on various forms such as Isis, the Madonna and particularly the Queen of Sheba, not to mention the mysterious Aurélie from the work of the same name (published posthumously in 1855), the last pages of which were found in his pocket following his suicide. The magic of the words in some of his sonnets (especially the twelve sonnets in *Les Chimères*), his poetical short stories (*Sylvie*, 1854) and his travelogues, prove him to be a linking figure between romanticism and symbolism.

Spurred on by Victor Hugo and his *Préface de Cromwell* (1827), French drama flourished. Romantic drama broke away from the unities of space, time and action and followed Shakespeare in mixing the tragic with the comic and the trivial with the sublime. The desire was to render reality in its totality, though nevertheless transform it into art. Next to Hugo's tremendous success with plays like *Hernani* (1830) and *Ruy Blas* (1838), romantic theatre was further developed by de Vigny, Alexandre Dumas and Alfred de Musset, whose *Lorenzaccio* (1834) was the most Shakespearean of all romantic drama and whose comedies show a subtle mixture of feeling and fantasy, of dream and reality.

Novel writing at the time was also profuse and many-faceted: sentimental novels in the eighteenth-century tradition, *romans noirs* based on English and German models, historical novels (the most important being de Vigny's *Cinq Mars* (1826) and Hugo's *Notre-Dame de Paris* (1831)), serial novels by Eugène Sue (1804–57) and adventure stories by Alexandre Dumas (1824–95). However, the most valuable and long-lasting work was written by the 'romantic realists' who had been shown the way by Hugo and his *Les Misérables* (1862). A romantic in his visionary powers of imagination, a realist through his powers of observation and in his scientific intentions, Honoré de Balzac (1799–1850) transformed a whole era, which was marked by the unstoppable rise of liberal capitalism, into a universe of fiction in his monumental *Comédie Humaine* (1842–6). *Le Rouge et le Noir* (1831) and *La Chartreuse de Parme* (1839), the two main novels by Stendhal (i.e. Henri Beyle, 1783–1842), constitute a clear and easy to read critique of French society during the Restoration as well as a criticism of Europe as a whole during the Holy Alliance. Stendhal used his romantic feeling of 'egotism' and his powers of rationalistic critical observation in setting out an individualistic way of life, the modernity of which would not be understood until after 1880. Sober and sceptical of mind, Prosper Merimée (1803–70) was another writer who also strove for austerity. As an independent writer who found himself outside the literary movements and *cénacles* of the time, he was particularly wary of romantic exaggeration. His novels and short stories (including *Colomba*, 1840; and *Carmen*, 1845), show his preference for short, intensive scenes, which take place in another country and in another time. The transition from a romantic vision on life to a more sober view of reality based on utopian socialism also occurred in the work of George Sand (i.e. Amandine Aurore Lucile Dupin, 1804–76). When we compare her romantic autobiographical novel *Lélia* (1832) with *La petite Fadette* (1848), which provides us with an intensely detailed sketch of country life, we can see, in the space of fifteen years, just how important that change was.

The romantic movement spread out from these three literatures to the whole of Europe, Scott and Byron being the most influential of its representatives. In Italy, Alessandro Manzoni (1785–1873) would acquire a popularity that was to spread beyond his country's borders for his historical novel *I Promessi Sposi, storia milanese del secolo XVII* (*The Betrothed*, 1827), while the poet of *Weltschmerz*, Giacomo Leopardi (1798–1837) acquired a fame that would last until the era of symbolism. Following the trend set by Byron and Scott, in Spain the poet Duque de Rivas (i.e. Angel de Saavedra Ramírez de Baquedano, 1791–1865) wrote *Romances históricos* (1841), and *El estudiante de Salamanca* (1839); and Gustavo Adolfo Becquer (1836–70) composed love poetry in his *Rimas*, while historical novels were written by Mariano J. de Larra (1809–37 – *El doncel de Enrique el Doliente*), Enrique Gil Y Carrasco (1815–46 – *El Señor de Bembibre*, 1844), and Francisco M. de La Rosa (1787–1862 – *Dona Isabel de Solis, reina de Granada*, 1837). These models of romanticism were also followed in the North. The Fleming, Hendrik Conscience, wrote *De Leeuw van Vlaanderen* (*The Lion of Flanders*, 1838) and the Dutchman Jacob van Lennep wrote *De roos van Dekama* (*The Rose of Dekama*, 1836). In the Scandinavian literatures, the main figures of romanticism were the Danish writers Adam Oehlenschlager (1779–1850) and Nikolaj F. Severin Gruntvig (1783–1872), who drew on foreign influences and mixed them with national elements taken from old Norse literature, whilst Bernard S. Ingemann (1789–1862) and Carsten Hauch (1790–1872) began to write historical novels. In Sweden, the romantic movement was mainly located at the university towns of Uppsala and Lund, where the literary society 'Auroraförbundet' was founded, its leading figure being the poet Per Daniel Atterbom (1790–1855). The main figure in the 'Götiska Förbundet' in the capital, Stockholm was the poet Esaias Tegner (1782–1846) who wrote the lyric epic poems *Frithiofs saga* (1820–25), *Nattvardsbarnen* (*Feast of Whitsun*, 1820) and *Axel* (1821). The greatest romantic poet of them all was Erik J. Stagnelius (1793–1823), known for his collection *Liljor i Saron* (*Lilies from Saron*, 1821–2). The first major writer of Norwegian letters was the romantic poet Hendrik Wergeland (1808–45), known for his ecstatic and visionary epic poetry and his nature and confessional lyric work.

During the romantic period, Eastern Europe opened itself to the West. Here the romantic movement not only grew out of a conflict between generations but also out of a desire for insurrection and liberation. This explains the great success of Byron's narrative poems and their influence upon the Polish poets, Antoni Malczewski (1793–1826), Adam Mickiewicz (1798–1855, particularly his lyric epic *Pan Tandeusz*, 1834), Juliusz Slowacki (1809–49, and his heroic epic *Beniowski*, 1841) and Zygmunt Krasinski (1812–93, and his *Nie-boska Komedia* (*The Non-divine Comedy*), 1835); and upon the Czech poet Karel H. Macha (1810–36) and his lyric epic poem, *Maj* (*May*), 1836, as well as on the Hungarian Mihàly Vörösmarty (1800–55), and his lyric epic *Zalan futasa* (*Zalan's Retreat*), 1825).

Byron's poetry was received as a revelation by the Russians round about 1820. His *Oriental Tales* unleashed much passionate emotion and were immediately translated and imitated. Over a period of twenty years almost 200 Byronic lyrical epic poems were written. And yet, Pushkin and Lermontov were the only true creators of lyric epic poetry. Alexander S. Pushkin (1799–1837) proved how he had completely assimilated Byron's narrative style in his three great romantic poems, *Kavkazski Plennik* (*Prisoner in Caucasia*, 1822), *Bakshisarayski Fontan* (*The Fountain of Bakshisarayski*, 1824) and *Tzygany* (*The Gypsies*, 1827), but these poems are further characterized by their laconic style, their limited use of metaphoric imagery and the remarkable precision with which they depict character and natural scenes. Even though it was inspired by Byron's *Don Juan*, his novel in verse, *Yevgeniy Onegin* (1833), which tells the tale of the unhappy love affair of a young dandy from the St Petersburg aristocracy, was truly an original creation. Though Michail Y. Lermontov (1814–41) admired Pushkin, his style contrasted with the latter in being more passionate in character, which led to an abundance of emotional epithets, sharp antitheses, philosophical comparisons, oratorical questions and pathetic expression. In his lyric epic poem *Demon* (*The Demon*, 1828–41) in particular, he is clearly preoccupied by the more satanic aspects of the 'Byronic hero'.

As elsewhere in Europe, the dramatic works of Goethe, Schiller and Shakespeare were also admired. They certainly inspired Pushkin when writing his historical tragedy *Boris Godunov* (1831). Inspiration from German romantic poetry can also be traced in the Russian poetry of that time, especially in the ballads of V. A. Zhukovsky (1793–1852) and in the poetic descriptions of nature by F. I. Thatched (1803–73).

A similar evolution can be traced in North American literature, which was still exceptionally receptive to European movements in literature during the nineteenth century, as we can see from the historical novels by Washington Irving (1783–1859), the lyric epics (*Evangeline*, 1847; *The Song of Hiawatha*, 1855) by Henry W. Longfellow (1807–82) and the critical essays of Sarah M. Fuller (1810–50). During this period, which was still under the sway of romanticism, a few American authors began to emerge who did not follow the dominant European models and who soon became popular in Europe. This was true of James Fennimore Cooper (1780–1851), who introduced the theme of the Native American in his *Leatherstocking Tales*. This was also certainly the case with Edgar Allan Poe (1809–49), whose grotesque 'tales of horror' (*The Fall of the House of Usher*) and 'tales of ratiocination' (the predecessors of the modern detective story, e. g. *The Murders in the Rue Morgue*), as well as his poetry (*The Raven and other Poems*, 1845), and views on 'pure poetry' (*The Philosophy of Composition*, 1846; *The Poetic Principle*, 1849; *The Rational of Verse*, 1848) were of tremendous influence on the European continent, Poe also being considered as the forefather of symbolism. His rational analyses and detailed descriptions already paved the way for the realist style of writing.

Realism

The term 'realism' was first mentioned in a theoretical discussion on literary aesthetics in the French magazine *Mercure française du XIXe Siècle* (1826), which described it as 'the imitation not of traditional works of art but of the original presented by nature'. Nineteenth-century realists were characterized by their desire to depict as accurately and as objectively as possible people from all levels of society, their everyday problems, relations and daily events. The writers of the 1830s began their literary careers by stating that the structure of society had changed totally. They believed that romantic idealization obscured present-day reality far too much. Realism therefore, was not merely focused on reality, not even on 'nature' or 'life' in general but on social existence, i.e. on a new, changed society and the consequences this entailed for all its various strata. The social awareness of the generation of the 1830s turned its writers into creators of the social novel and of realistic writing.

These writers' main source of realistic aesthetics was in fact the political events of 1848: the failure of the revolution, the suppression of the June Uprising and the seizure of power by Louis Napoleon, plus the foundation of the Second Empire. The disappointment of the democrats and the rude awakening felt by all as a result of these events found its expression as 'scientism', an austere, business-like vision based on exact science, which placed its trust only in empirical experience. Following the failure of ideals and utopias, one could only trust the facts and nothing else but the facts. The political foundations upon which realism is based give it its anti-romantic and moral characteristics: the rejection of any flight from reality and a demand for unconditional honesty when telling the facts; its effort to remain impersonal and unfeeling thus guaranteeing objectivity and social solidarity; an attitude of activism not only in depicting reality as it stood but also in wishing to change it; an awareness of time or era, a knowledge of the needs and significance of the moment, which had already come about during romanticism and now completely dominated the minds of artists; and finally the 'everyday' and the 'popular' both as themes and as point of departure i.e. a desire to reach the widest audience possible, which explains their preference for the novel and the theatre.

Next to this stimulus from the world of politics, progress in the field of science also contributed to the growth of realism. Whilst the romantic ideals of liberation and social improvement had only resulted in disappointment, scientists had continued to work in peace and in fact had really begun to change the world. It is understandable therefore, that writers became convinced that they would have more chance of success if they adopted the methods of these scientists. Therefore, these important developments in science are reflected in literature. The work of three men in particular was of vital importance for the development of realist poetics: the positivist philosophy of August Comte, which paved the way for sociological analyses of society, Charles Darwin's doctrine of evolution, which stressed heredity and environment as determining factors of human character and behaviour, and Karl Marx's economic theories and materialist philosophy, which pointed out that blind economic and political forces determined events in the world, and could not be stopped by any one person.

The real breakthrough of realism in French literature, i.e. its general recognition as a specific movement in art, can be situated after 1850. Initially propagated by a group of very obscure authors and depicters of petit-bourgeois circles such as Champfleury (*Le Réalisme*, a collection of essays from 1857), Murger and Duranty (the magazine *Réalisme*, 1856–7), realism gained in significance thanks to the heated debate on the realistic paintings of Courbet and his followers. The support offered by authoritative critics like Sainte-Beuve and Taine, who opted for this new movement from 1855 on, as well as the furore created by the success of Flaubert's *Madame Bovary* (1857) also helped in its establishment.

Realism's progress towards recognition can be divided into a number of phases.

THE YOUNG EUROPEANS

Following the Napoleonic Wars, an even greater depth of disappointment was reached during the Holy Alliance (1815–48) under the leadership of the Austrian foreign minister Prince Metternich and his oppression of subjected states, national minorities and democratic hopes in general. In their attempt to escape, most latter-day romantics left this disappointing reality behind for the beauty of nature (Eichendorff), for bizarre fantasy (E. T. A. Hoffmann), and preached passivity and even slavish subjugation (Grillparzer). The reaction against oppression in Austria and Germany was not led by the romantics, but voiced by the so-called *Junges Deutschland*. One cannot speak here of an organized movement however, as this group of young writers were only linked by their ideas. They were against Metternich's notions of state, the political powerlessness of the ordinary citizen, censorship, and the subordinate position of women and Jews, as well as all forms of moral and social convention, dogmatism and orthodoxy. In their literature, they rejected the unrealistic escapism of the romantics; considering reality as the basis of art, they used literature mainly to express their ideas; they desired the day-to-day and not *belles-lettres* purely for the sake of beauty. Their means of expression were the serial magazine, the thesis novel and critical travelogues; their weapons were caustic sarcasm and sharp ironic reflection. Karl Gutzkow, Ludolf Wienborg, Heinrich Laube and Theodor Mundt were some of their representatives. Their great mentors were Ludwig Börne (1786–1837, see *Briefe aus Paris*, 1832–4) and Heinrich Heine (1797–1856), both of whom emigrated to Paris. Heine was the more talented of the two and proved it by attaining worldwide literary fame with his *Reisebilder* (1826–31) and *Buch der Lieder* (1827), all original works of refined irony on romantic sentimentalism. His small epic in verse *Deutschland, ein Wintermärchen* (1844) is a masterpiece of satire against absolute monarchy, the dominant clericalism of the day, and the middle classes who were all too ready to subjugate themselves to Metternich's restoration, and stands as an expression of the author's hope for a free and democratic Germany.

About 1830, a literary movement that was based in reality began to develop in a number of other European countries, its goal being political freedom and social reform: *La Giovine Italia*, founded by Mazzini, *La Jeune France* in France and *Das Junge Europa* in Switzerland. In these three countries the line of distinction between them and the romantics was less sharp, and romantic writers also committed themselves to self-expression, personal freedom and the national desire for democracy. Victor Hugo, for example, belongs to this movement, as can be seen from his indictment of despotism under Napoleon II (*Napoléon le Petit*, 1852; *L'Histoire d'un crime*, 1852; and *Les Châtiments*, 1853); as does the poet Jean Pierre Béranger, a writer of political satires. In Spain too, as well as in Greece and the oppressed East European countries, romantic writers often ignited the flame of national consciousness and of resistance against the oppressor.

In North America the problem at hand was not freedom as such, but one of unity as opposed to separation, of anti-slavery against slavery, of the North against the South. Here, too, writers took the initiative in the struggle for emancipation and for a new and better world: the 'transcendentalists', Ralph Waldo Emerson and Henry David Thoreau, the poets John G. Whittier and Longfellow, and the prose writers James Russell Lowell (*The Biglow Papers*, 1848) and Harriet Beecher Stowe (*Uncle Tom's Cabin*, 1852).

In fact, the struggle against oppression grew and turned into a struggle against all forms of discrimination based on race or gender. Auerbach's *Spinoza* (1837) and Gutzkow's *Uriel Acosta* (1847) were rejections of anti-semitism.

Madame de Staël broke a lance for women's liberation in her epistolary novel *Delphine* (1802), and pleaded for a greater role for women in society. From this time on, women writers began to occupy a prominent position in the world of literature, as can be seen from Jane Austen, Charlotte and Emily Brontë and George Eliot (i.e. Mary Anne Evans) in England, Annette von Droste-Hülshoff in Germany, George Sand (i.e Amandine Aurore Lucile) in France and Harriet Beecher Stowe in America.

Though the literary quality of the work of many representatives of 'Young Europe' often suffered from their obvious tendency towards the polemic, from the point of view of literary history they form the first important step taken in the evolution from romanticism to realism.

THE *BIEDERMEIER* OR TAMED ROMANTICISM

Alongside this highly progressive political attitude that characterized *Junges Deutschland*, a second, more passive and conservative state of mind grew among the middle classes in German-speaking countries. This was fed on the one hand by feelings of disappointment, powerlessness and fatigue, and on the other by an effort to find satisfaction in simplicity, measure and humility. The term *Biedermeier* is in fact the name given to a caricature of a petit bourgeois depicted in *Gedichte des schwäbischen Schullehrers Gottlieb Biedermaier und seines Freundes Horatius Treuherz*, which was published by Adolf Kusmaul and Ludwig Eichrodt in the *Münchener Fliegende Blätter* (1855–7). In the first place, it applied to middle-class life style and home decoration in the period dating from 1815 to 1848, and how all this was rendered in genre paintings, like those by Spitzweg, for example.

In literature, *Biedermeier* signified a reaction by latter-day romantics against extravagance and exalted forms of passion, demonism and heroism. They sought quieter forms of happiness in peace of mind and in order both within and beyond the individual, in the control of passion and exaggerated daydreaming. The ideal environment for attaining all this was the family circle and the home, the village, life in a small town or in one's own (rural) area. These rather passive characters learned, sometimes through disappointment, to live in harmony with their own social and natural environments. They preached respect for the existing hierarchy instead of revolutionary insurrection. This tempered romantic vision on life was lived out in literature. There was a preference for lesser forms of epic like the idyll, the fairy tale, the anecdote, the sketch, the short story and the tale. In lyric poetry, there was a preference for epic genres like the ballad and stories in verse. The tone used was simple and even didactic, as in folk literature. In the theatre, there was a tremendous flowering of tragi-comedy.

The most clear expression of the *Biedermeier* attitude to life, 'das sanfte Gezetz' (the law of love, tenderness and clemency), can be found in the foreword to the collection of short stories, *Bunte Steine* (1853), by the Austrian writer Adalbert Stifter (1805–68). His short stories and *Bildungsromane, Ein Nachsommer* (1857) and *Witiko* (1856–7) point to the lofty ethos found in a small world and to the moral courage and truthfulness of simple lives. The *Biedermeier* way of life found its strongest expression in Austrian literature, Vienna being its centre. Self-control and contentment were also key words in the plays and stories (*Der arme*

Spielmann, 1831–46) of Franz Grillparzer (1791–1872). The *Biedermeier* way of life can also be found in the work of Bauernfeld, Raimund, Nestroy, Halm and Von Saar. As an antidote to modern radicalism, the Swiss democrat Gottfried Keller (1819–90) propagated a sense of citizenship in his short stories and especially in his apprenticeship novel, *Der grüne Heinrich*. Some aspects of the *Biedermeier* atmosphere can also be found in Germany in the work of Annette von Droste-Hulshoff, Wilhelm Raabe and Theodor Storm.

In fact, one can also find expressions of *Biedermeier* outside German literature in all European countries, where they served as a transitional phase between romanticism and realism.

In English literature, one not only finds signs of it in the work of a whole range of lesser authors in the 1820s and 1830s, but also in the early work of Dickens and Thackeray, in the grotesque satire *Sartor Resartus* (1838) by Thomas De Quincey, in *Crochet Castle* (1831) by Thomas Love Peacock, and in the novels of Jane Austen. In French literature, it can be found in the long poems (*Monsieur Jean, Maître d'école; A Madame la C. de T. . ., & A mon Ami Boulanger*) by Sainte-Beuve, and in *Adolphe* (1816), a novel by Benjamin Constant. One can also find aspects of *Biedermeier* in the work of the Italian writer Manzoni, as well as in the Spanish movement called *costumbrismo* (Mesonero Romanos, Estabanez Calderón).

In the East European literature, one can find forms of tempered romanticism that emulate *Biedermeier* in the historical scenes of the Romanian writers Costache Negruzzi and Alexandru Odobescu, in the idyllic descriptive genre poetry of the Hungarian poet Sandor Petöfi, and in the fairy tale-like musical plays of the Czech author Josef Kajetán Tyl, as well as in stories by Božena Němcová (*Babicka*, 'Granny', 1855) and Jan Neruda's *Malonstranské povídky* (*Small Side Stories*, 1878), elements of the style being also visible in the work of the Polish authors Mickiewiez and Slowacki. One can find *Biedermeier* in Russian literature in Pushkin's later work, especially *Kapitanskaya Dochka* (*The Captain's Daughter*, 1836) and *Medny Vsadnik* (*The Bronze Horseman*, 1837), and in the early work of Nikolay Gogol, e.g. *Hanz Küchelgarten*, 1829; *Arabeski*, 1835; and *Revizor* (*The Inspector General*), 1836.

All these various versions of *Biedermeier* can be considered as attempts to reconcile the ideals of romanticism with reality.

ARTISTIC REALISM

The most radical form of realism was to be found in France, where it was also sharply formulated theoretically. Its expressions in other countries, if not wholly based on their French counterpart, were certainly influenced by the French model. For nineteenth-century readers, *Madame Bovary* (1856), a novel by Gustave Flaubert (1821–80) broke totally new ground and signified the final severance with romantic literary codes. The court case initiated in January 1857 to prevent the novel's publication was a reaction against its realistic themes and style of writing, which itself was a manifestation of ideological dissent. On the one hand, Flaubert would continue his romantic fascination for the strange, the exotic and the fantastic, which was present in his earlier work, by writing evocations of the historical like *Salammbô* (1862), *Hérodias* (1877), *La Tentation de Saint Antoine* (1874); and on the other hand, he would use his realistic approach in works like *L'éducation sentimentale* (1869), *Un coeur simple* (1877) and the uncompleted *Bouvard et Pécuchet* (1881). Flaubert's oeuvre, which was innovative both in style and in theme, and his reflections on style in his abundant correspondence turned him into the figurehead of a legion of realistic novelists in France, including the Goncourt brothers, Edmond (1822–96) and Jules (1830–70), Anatole France (1844–1924), Pierre Loti (1850–1923), Jules Romains (1885–1972) and François Mauriac (1885–1970).

As English romanticism already contained a strong element of realism, realist reaction to it was not as excessive as in other countries. Moreover, the puritan morals of Victorian society put a brake on the radical realistic exposure of social injustice. Realist themes were tempered by elements which were romantic in origin, such as paternalistic sympathy, poetic imagination and well-meaning humour. This is visible in the work of the highly popular Charles Dickens (1812–70), particularly in the novels he published from 1849, like *David Copperfield, Bleak House, Hard Times, Little Dorrit, Great Expectations* and *Our Mutual Friend*, in which he presents us with psychologically realistic images of various sections of Victorian society along with their weaknesses. A disgust at and yet a shirking of excessive condemnation of Victorian institutions can also be found in the work of Elizabeth C. Gaskell (1810–65), the action of whose novels is set in the highly industrialized North (*North and South*, 1855); as in that of the ambiguous William M. Thackeray (1811–63), who wished to expose the ills of contemporary society (e.g. *The Book of Snobs*, 1846–7; *Vanity Fair*, 1848), but who nevertheless kept to the dictates of reserve and decency; in that of Anthony Trollope (1815–88) and his descriptions of clerical life (*Barchester Towers*, 1857; *The Last Chronicle of Barset*, 1867); in that of George Eliot (i.e. Mary Ann Evans, 1819–80), who depicted country life in all its detail (see *Scenes of Clerical Life*, 1857; *Adam Bede*, 1859; *The Mill on the Floss*, 1860; and *Middlemarch*, 1872); as well as in the work of the Brontë sisters, Charlotte (1816–55), who wrote *Jane Eyre* (1847), and Emily (1818–48), whose *Wuthering Heights* (1847) provides us with a psychologically realistic analysis of the great passions.

In Germany, very few writers escaped the atmosphere of resignation instilled by the *Biedermeier*; themes of regionalism and romantic sentimentalism mark the novels of Wilhelm Raabe (1831–1910) and Theodore Storm (1817–88). Theodor Fontane (1819–98) was the sole writer to provide us with objective descriptions of Prussian society. His humour is tinged with the tragic in its reaction to the oppression of the era. The central themes of his work are those of impossible love between young people of different social classes (*Irrungen Wirrungen*, 1887) and middle-class marriage (*Effi Briest*, 1895) – a theme which links him to writers like Flaubert, Ibsen and Tolstoy.

Russian literature made an important contribution to the development of the art of realist novel writing. Here realism is situated in the framework of growing criticism of the tsarist regime following the failure of the Decembrist uprising in 1825. Both Slavophile writers and those in favour of the West wrote socially engaged literature. Though no trace of unease at the social and political conditions in his country can be found in his work, Nickolay V. Gogol (1809–52) had already given realistic descriptions of life in the Russian countryside, including the degradation of serfdom, in his grotesque picaresque novel *Priklyucheniya*

Chichikova ili myortvye dushi (*The Adventures of Chichikov or Dead Souls*, 1842 – part II not completed, part III destroyed by the author). However, it was through the radical criticism of the critic Vissarion Belinsky (1811–48) and his plea for modern literature that realistic literature was given an important stimulus. From then on, contemporary social problems became the main theme. Ivan S. Turgenev (1818–83) was the first to provide us with an outraged depiction of the human tragedy of serfdom in a book that was also a poetic evocation of the Russian countryside: *Zapiski ochotnika* (*Tales of a Hunter*), 1847–51. In his novels *Rudin* (1856), *Dvoryanskoe gnezdo* (*A Nest of Gentlefolk*, 1855) *Ottsy i deti* (*Fathers and Sons*, 1862), *Dym* (*Smoke*, 1867) and *Nov'* (*Virgin Soil*, 1876), he was the chronicler of the progressive liberal intelligentsia, but also the prosecutor of revolutionary fanaticism. An even more radical indictment of serfdom and the apathy of the landed gentry can be found in the novel by Ivan A. Goncharov (1812–92), *Oblomov* (1850), the term *Oblomovism*, which was coined by the critic Dobrolyubov, thereby entering the language as signifying the lethargy of the landed gentry in a country that was still feudal in structure.

The greatest influence on literature, both in his own country and in the West, was exercised by Fedor M. Dostoevsky (1821–81) an exponent of 'Slavism' who nevertheless attempted to reconcile the conflicting tendencies. His whole *oeuvre* is built upon his own bitter experiences, as a result of which he was able to provide penetrating realistic analyses of various facets of life and the human psyche. His most important works – *Dvoynik* (*The Double*, 1846), *Zapiski iz podpol'ya* (*Letters from the Underworld*, 1864), *Prestuplenie i nakazanie* (*Crime and Punishment*, 1866), *Idiot* (*The Idiot*, 1868–9), *Besy* (*The Possessed*, 1871–2) *Brat'ya Karamazovy* (*The Brothers Karamazov*, 1879–80) – are all layered works: they are not just well-written and exciting thrillers, adventure stories and crime novels, they are also psychological, philosophical and religious books. Dostoevsky was the first writer to capture intellectual events so clearly and depict them as immediate sensory experiences, thereby exploring areas of the mind which no one had dared enter before.

The influence of Count L. Tolstoy (1828–1910) was twofold: his artistic contribution to novel writing techniques and his contribution to spirituality, which stemmed from his reaction against the materialism and utilitarianism of the late nineteenth century. With his great novels *Voyna i mir* (*War and Peace*, 1865–9) and *Anna Karenina* (1873–7) he showed that the novel was an art form that could equal the classical epic, for in these novels, the complex flux of life in a particular era was given form through the intertwined lives of numerous ordinary people, each character being representative of movements in history. These works contain the most important philosophical questions of the century: the role of the individual in the collective fate of a nation and the historical dimension of human existence. As a spiritual leader, he pleaded for the spiritual rebirth of humankind, for a return to patriarchal and idyllic goodness in the style of Rousseau and the Christian saints, and gave form to this in the character of Levin in *Anna Karenina*. As a committed reformer, he saw art as being nothing more than the pastime of the rich. He said goodbye to it, and from then on only wrote to illustrate man's mortality, for example in *Smert' Ivana Il'icha* (*The Death of Ivan Illich*, 1886); to lambast the deceits of marriage, in *Kreytserova Sonata* (*The Kreuzer Sonata*, 1891); to indict the legal,

criminal justice, political, administrative and religious systems which he saw as only protecting the privileged, in *Voskresenie* (*Resurrection*, 1899), or to issue a call for conversion to a life of the spirit, in *Chozain i rabotnik* (*Master and Servant*, 1895); and *Otets Sergey* (*Father Sergey*, 1911).

Regional realism blossomed profusely at this time in the whole of Europe, both in East European literatures (Jan Neruda, Karolina Svetla, Paul Gyulai, Laza Lazarevic, Svetozar Marcovic, Sandor Djalski) as in the Southern European literatures of Spain (Pedro Antonio de Alorcon, Juan Valera, José Maria de Pereda), Italy (Giovanni Verga) and Greece (Yeorios Vizyinos). In Scandinavia the struggle for modern ideas soon became the prerogative of women, who joined together to form one of the earliest feminist movements. Criticism of the exploitation of women in a society dominated by men full of prejudice was aired by the Dane Mathilde Fibiger in her *Clara Raphaël, Tolv Breve* (*Clara Raphaël, Twelve Letters*, 1851), by the Swedish writer Frederika Bremer in *Hertha eller En själs historia* (*Hertha or the History of a Soul*, 1856) and the Norwegian Camilla Collet in *Amtmandens Doettre* (*The Daughters of the Prefect*, 1855).

French and Russian models formed the basis for realism in North America, which at that time was becoming aware of its own specific character as a country, of its morals and customs as well as of its own problems. In *The Scarlet Letter* (1850) and *Moby Dick* (1851), by Nathaniel Hawthorne (1804–64) and Herman Melville (1819–91) respectively, the behaviour of man in society is central, the writers thereby already paving the way for realistic novels about society. The most prominent figure to propagate realism was William D. Howells (1837–1920), a professor of literature at Harvard. In his own literary work, he followed in Tolstoy's footsteps by rebelling against capitalism, and provided a heavily documented and detailed image of American society in the final decades of the nineteenth century (*Annie Kilburn*, 1889; *Hazard of New Fortunes*, 1890). His friend Mark Twain (i.e. Samuel Langhorne Clemens, 1835–1910) was the first to map out frontier civilization on the Mississippi in realistic and poetic terms (*The Adventures of Huckleberry Finn*, 1885; *Life on the Mississippi*, 1883). The greatest innovator in the art of the novel was Henry James (1843–1916), who as a cosmopolitan formed the link between America, England and France, and who explored these themes from the point of view of the expatriate in his psychologically realistic novels that provide subtle analyses of conflicts within the well-to-do middle classes (*Daisy Miller*, 1879; *The Portrait of a Lady*, 1881; *The Bostonians*, 1886; *The Ambassadors*, 1903; and *The Golden Bowl*, 1904). 'Art deals with what we see' was the credo of this sharp observer and psychoanalyst, who contributed greatly to the artistic development of the novel as a genre.

NATURALISM

During the second half of the nineteenth century the chasm between the well-off middle classes and impoverished working classes widened and deepened. The fundamental injustice of this dualistic society was indicted by anarchist and socialist alike. Influenced by their ideas, the working classes became increasingly aware of their plight and began to struggle for the protection of their rights and interests by forming trade unions and by organizing strikes. The first Workers International was held in 1846.

The enormous progress in the natural sciences in the first half of the century was followed by spectacular leaps forward mainly in the fields of biology and medicine. The works that left the deepest impression on the world were those by Charles Darwin on the doctrine of evolution *(On the Origin of the Species by Means of Natural Selection, or the Preservation of Favoured Races in the Struggle for Life, 1859; The Descent of Man, 1871)*; by the French physiologist Claude Bernard *(Introduction à l'étude de la médecine expérimentale, 1865)*, by the Italian psychiatrist and criminologist Cesare Lombroso *(L'uomo delinquente, 1876)*, by P. Lucas on heredity *(Hérédité naturelle, 1847)* and by Benédict Auguste Morel on the phenomenon of degeneration *(Traité de dégénérescences physiques, intellectuelles et morales de l'espèce humaine, 1857)*. The scientific insight they provided was used by Hippolyte Taine in his study of the arts and literature, *Introduction à l'histoire de la littérature anglaise* (1863–4).

The following year, the Goncourt brothers, Edmond and Jules, published their novel *Germinie Lacerteux* (1865). In its equally famous foreword, they stated that they were living in a time of universal suffrage, democracy and liberalism and that, as a result, ordinary people should not be excluded from being the subject of works of literature. The novel was the most apt means of portraying these people because of its increased size and significance, it being now a serious, passionate and lively means of literary study and social enquiry. Thanks to the analyses and psychological research it contained, it had become an *histoire morale contemporaine*. Novel writing was now compared with scientific work – here the Goncourt brothers were undoubtedly thinking of methods used in experimental biology. Their novel illustrated the two fundamental characteristics of naturalism for the very first time: the heroine is a serving girl from the lowest class of society and her behaviour is studied and analysed with an unprejudiced, almost clinical, precision. As far as the Goncourt brothers were concerned, it was more a matter of the aesthetic appeal of the ugly and the pathological.

Nevertheless, this novel inspired Emile Zola (1840–1902), the real founder of naturalism, to write his novel *Thérèse Raquin* (1867). It is the way the action and the characters of the novel are developed and interpreted which is naturalistic and not the plot, however: the characters are seen as being driven by blind urges, as being dominated by their 'nerves and their blood, without any free will'. In *Le Roman expérimental* (1880) and *Les romanciers naturalistes* (1881), Zola formulated theoretical principles that explained how the novelist was to be both an observer and an experimenter. This experimental method consisted in how the writer 'intervenes directly in placing his character in situations' that illustrate the mechanisms of passion and confirms his initial hypothesis: 'In the end one acquires knowledge of mankind, scientific knowledge of his individual and social behaviour'.

Zola applied his ideas rigorously and unswervingly in a cycle of twenty novels: *Les Rougon-Macquart. Histoire naturelle et sociale d'une famille sous le Second Empire* (1871–93). He traces the becoming and development of all its members at all social levels across five generations: *La Fortune des Rougon* (1871), *L'Assommoir* (1877), *Nana* (1880), *Germinal* (1885), *La Terre* (1887), *La Bête Humaine* (1890) and *Le Docteur Pascal* (1893). In doing so he also broke the taboos of the day, which resulted in heavy opposition from conservative circles who branded his novels as immoral and subversive. Following the publication of *Germinal*, and especially that of *J'Accuse* (in *L'Aurore*, January 1898) – his indictment of the sentencing of the Jewish army captain, Alfred Dreyfus – he became the symbol of the left in Europe, who saw in his work the spirit of reformist and emancipatory enlightenment.

Zola was tremendously influential in France and in the rest of Europe for a number of decades. Nevertheless, only a few French writers would achieve recognition as naturalists. One of them was Guy de Maupassant (1850–93), who followed the themes and the naturalism laid down by Zola in his objective renditions of the lives of Norman farmers, the daily life of the lower middle classes – mainly that of office clerks – as well as the world of prostitution. For his concise and sober style he owes more to his mentor, Flaubert, who was a friend of the family. He had a clear preference for the short story and the *conte* (tale), of which he became a true master, writing almost 260 of them over a period of ten years. Of his six novels, which mainly take place in fashionable and sophisticated circles, only *Une Vie* (*A Life*, 1883) and *Bel Ami* (1885) reach the level of excellence of his short stories. Alphonse Daudet (1840–97) also acquired recognition for the tempered naturalism of his picturesque and anecdotic stories about his native Provence, for example *Lettres de mon Moulin* (*Letters from My Mill*, 1868) and his novels, 'tranches de vie' in which he provides satirical sketches of the mores of the day.

Victorian England and Orthodox Russia proved to be no seedbed for Naturalism, most probably for the same reasons that the forms of realism they produced were morally and philanthropically tinted. Only George Moore (1852–1933) and George Gissing (1857–1903) made attempts to popularize the naturalistic novel.

In contrast to this, and out of reaction to the tempered 'poetic' realism of the *Biedermeier*, German naturalism proved to be the most extreme and implacable form of naturalism in Europe. A group of young writers gathered around a nucleus of older writers like Heinrich and Julius Hart, Arno Holz, Gerhard Hauptmann and Hermann Sudermann, broadening and radicalizing naturalist theory, which was clearly expressed in Holz's formula 'art = nature − x', the factor x being the artist's subjectivity. Arno Holz and Johannes Schlaf invented the *Sekundenstil*, in which the distance between the world of the novel and the narrator is eliminated and in which narrative time coincides with that of the events narrated. The three short stories in their collection, *Papa Hamlet* (1889) are the most typical of this technique.

Many writers from Southern Europe also took a leaf from Zola's book. In Italy, Luigi Capuana (1839–1915) was one of the first to show interest in French naturalism, which there was dubbed *verismo*. A cutting critic, polemicist and artist, Capuana strove for impersonality of presentation and for clinical, scientific analyses. He used the naturalist approach throughout in presenting pathological cases in his novels *Giacinta* (*Hyacinth*, 1879, dedicated to Zola) and *Profumo* (*Perfume*, 1899). Under his influence, Giovanni Verga (1840–1922) evolved towards *verismo*, particularly in his Sicilian novels *I Malavoglia* (*The House by the Medlar Tree*, 1881) and *Maestro Don Gesualdo* (1899), with their strong contrast between the lives of impoverished fishermen and farmers and those of the rich middle classes and decadent aristocracy. Other writers to come under the sway of naturalism were Federico de Roberto (1861–1927), especially in his novel *I Vicerè* (*The Viceroys*, 1864) and the *engagé* journalist and novelist, Matilde Serao (1850–1927), who wrote about degradation in Naples (*Il Ventre di Napoli* or *The Belly of Naples*, 1884, enlarged edn 1906), whilst Grazia Deledda (1871–1936), despite her naturalistic descriptions of country life in Sardinia, occupied a special position because of her mysticism, which later led her to embrace symbolism and decadentism.

Naturalism was introduced into Spanish literature through *La desheredada* (*The Disinherited*, 1881), a novel by Benito Perez-Galdos (1843–1920) in which the heroine's schizophrenia is shown to be hereditary. It was mainly Leopoldo E. Garcia De Alas Y Urena (1852–1901), better known under his pen name Clarin, who introduced Zola's work to Spain through his writings and criticism. He also wrote novels and short stories in the naturalistic style (*La Regenta*, or *The Governess*, 2 vols, 1884), though he did distance himself from Zola's all too rigid determinism. The Portuguese naturalist novelist José M. Eça de Quieros (1845–1900) would take a similar stance, even though his earlier novels, *O Crime de Padre Amaro* (*The Crime of Padre Amaro*, 1875) and *O Primo Basilio* (*Nephew Basilio*, 1878) were faithful to his mentor's set of rules.

Naturalism initially met with heavy opposition in Greece, so much so that the serial publication of *Nana* (1879) had to be stopped. The following year, it was published in its entirety in book form and contained an enthusiastic introduction by Zola. Another important innovative step both linguistically and in terms of literature was taken by Yannis Psycharis (1834–1929), whose novel *To daxidhi mou* (*My Journey*, 1888) was the first to be completely written in *dhimotiki* a written language based on spoken language instead of the archaic written form that was still used at the time. The use of this expressive language contributed to the blossoming of naturalism, which attained its purest expression in the novels and stories of Andréas Karkavitsas (1865–1922) and Alexandros Papadhiamandis (1851–1911).

Naturalism also found fertile soil in Northern European countries. Belgium was, of course, one of them, as it was a neighbour to the birthplace of naturalism and also offered possibilities for publication to French naturalists who had been rejected in their own country. The French-speaking Belgian, Camille Lemonnier (1844–1913) was a defender and follower of Zola's and became famous and infamous for his courageous depictions of impoverished and brutalized peasants and workers in *Un Mâle* (*A Big Bloke*, 1880), *L'Hystérique* (*An Hysterical Woman*, 1885), *Happe-Chair* (1886) and *La Fin des Bourgeois* (*The End of the Bourgeoisie*, 1893), a family epic along the lines of the Rougon-Macquart. The most important Belgian writer in the Dutch language at the time was Cyriel Buysse (1859–1932), who made his debut with the novel *De biezenstekker* (*The Bastard*, 1890), in which he applied Zola's experimental approach. In his other novels, he dealt with the fate of agricultural labourers who, as victims of social injustice, lived in miserable animal-like circumstances: *Het recht van de sterkste* (*The Right of the Fittest*, 1893); *Het leven van Rozeke van Dalen* (*The Life of Rozeke van Dalen*, 1906). Marcellus Emants (1848–1923) was the defender of Zola's ideas in Holland and wrote a number of naturalist novels which also betray the influence of Gogol and Dostoevsky. Louis Couperus (1863–1923) combined the naturalist approach with elements of decadentism and aestheticism (*Eline Vere*, 1889; *Noodlot*, or *Footsteps of Fate*, 1891).

In Scandinavia, the Danish literary historian Georg Brandes (1842–1927) broke a lance for naturalism in his *Hovedstrømninger i det nittende Aarhundredes Literatur* (*Main Currents in the Literature of the Nineteenth Century*, 6 vols, 1871–90). His fellow countryman Herman Bang (1857–1912) put it into practice in his novel *Haablose Slaegter* (*The Decline of the Family*, 1880) and in his short stories (*Stille Eksistenser*, or *Hidden Lives*, 1886), in which he uses a dazzling impressionistic style to describe the fate of ordinary though isolated and forgotten people whose lives seem idyllic but who are in fact undergoing inner tragedy; while the novels of the Norwegian Amalie Skram (i.e. Berthe Amalie Alver, 1846–1905) and the Swede E. Ahlgren (i.e. Viktoria Benedictsson, 1850–88) broke taboos in discussing the psychiatric care of women from broken marriages, for example. The naturalist literature of Norwegian novelists like Bjørnsterne Bjørnson (1892–1910) and Alexander L. Kielland (1849–1906) developed into a *nyttepoesi* ('problem literature'), which expressed their outrage at the injustices in the society of their day.

Zola's naturalistic approach also caught on in Eastern Europe. With the breakthrough of positivism, a strong anti-romantic movement came into existence in Poland, its goal being to create literature in the service of social usefulness. Initially this led to highly moralistic, didactic literature. Moreover, the work of Boleslaw Prus (1845–1912) and Eliza Orzeskowa (1841–1910) is merely naturalistic in its themes. In his short stories and novel *Lalka* (*The Doll*, 1900), Prus depicted the sombre blocks of flats in the poor quarters of Warsaw where his characters wage a daily war against hunger. Orzeskowa describes the harshness of life in small country towns and villages, exposes the oppression of women and of the Jewish minority and expresses her sympathy for her little heroes in a style that is often poetic and lyrical. Among the writers who were faithful to Zola's ideas were Antoni Sygietynski (1850–1923), Arthur Gruszecki (1835–1929), Gabriela Zapolska (1860–1911), who worked as an actress for Antoine's Théatre Libre in Paris for about five years, and Adolf Dygasinski (1839–1902) who was renowned for his true-to-life novels, even though they do suffer from his tendency for excessive description.

In Bohemia, the social problems that were caused by industrialization form the core of the novels written by Jakob Arbes (1840–1914), whilst Alois Mrstik (1861–1925), a faithful follower of Zola's, portrayed the economic and moral decline of the peasantry. The naturalistic vision on life in Slovakia can be found in the novels and stories of Svetozar H. Vajansky (1857–1916) and Martin Kukucin (1860–1928), respectively. Croatian naturalism, which was strongly influenced by Russian realism and Italian *verismo* alike, was furthermore highly romantic and nationalistic in character. Evgeni Kumicic (1850–1940) for example, wrote a type of Rougon-Macquart cycle, but the history of its characters was set to a pattern that was sentimental and romantic. In following more closely the naturalistic approach, Vjenceslav Novak (1859–1905) made studies of the urban proletariat and Ante Kovacic (1854–89) of the impoverishment of the peasantry.

Naturalism not only contributed to rendering the novel more popular as a literary genre, it also provided an important stimulus for innovation in the theatre. This innovation did not only limit itself to themes but also affected technique. Naturalistic playwrights found it necessary to invent new solutions for decor, structure and lines of dramatic tension as a result of which, for example, they began to provide retrospective portrayals of the pasts of their characters in *tranches de vie* (slices of life) that continued to influence their lives in the present. Moreover, they modernized stage settings, realistic representations of interiors being an important element in creating the right atmosphere.

The development of naturalistic drama was favoured by the setting up of independent theatre companies. There seemed to be no room for this new form of drama within the official circle of national theatres, while commercial theatres only seemed interested in crowd-pullers and farces. The romantic dream world encased by the gilded framework of the stage was replaced by reconstructions of contemporary reality now staged in small halls, often for a closed circle of theatre buffs who were open to innovation and experimentation. These new theatres shot up all over Europe, thus providing naturalist writers with the opportunity to stage their work: André Antoine's Théâtre Libre, founded in Paris in 1887; the Freie Buhne, set up in Berlin in 1889 by Otto Brahm, Maximilian Harden and P. Schlenther; the Independent Theatre, founded by Jack Grein in London in 1891, and the Nederlandsche Tooneelver-eniging (Dutch Theatre Company), founded by Herman Heyermans in Amsterdam in 1893.

Although the Théâtre Libre was initially founded to stage *Les Corbeaux* (*The Ravens*, 1882) a naturalistic play by Henry Becque (1837–99), the playwrights that were to set the trend in naturalistic drama throughout Europe came mainly from Scandinavia and Germany. The Norwegian Henrik Ibsen (1828–1906), in particular, was to dominate the scene. Following a promising start with plays that were written in the spirit of romantic nationalism (the best being *Brand*, 1865 and *Peer Gynt*, 1867), he left his native land and went into voluntary exile for twenty-seven years where he wrote works on issues of great social importance: *Samfundets støtter* (*Pillars of Society*, 1877), *Et dukkehjem* (*The Doll's House*, 1879), *Gengare* (*Ghosts*, 1881) and *En Folk-efiende* (*An Enemy of the People*, 1882). From *Vildanden* (*The Wild Duck*, 1884) on, he turned away from engaged social drama in an attempt to portray the inner conflicts of mankind in works that were increasingly symbolic in form. Of course his highly committed compatriot, Bjørnsterne Bjørnson (1832–1910) also joined the ranks of naturalist dramatists and wrote plays on the world of business and the press, such as *En Fallit* (*A Bankrupt*, 1875); *Radaktoren* (*The Editor*, 1875), and works on the new society that caused public outcry, for example *Kongen* (*The King*, 1877) and *Det ny system* (*The New System*, 1878) as well as works on women's emancipation (*Leonarda*, 1879; *En Hanske*, or *A Glove*, 1882). The central theme of the Swedish writer August Strindberg (1849–1912) was his pessimistic outlook on relationships between the sexes, which can be found in four plays written between 1886 and 1888: *Kamraterna* (*The Comrades*), *Fadren* (*The Father*), *Fröken Julie* (*Miss Julie*) and *Fordringsägare* (*The Creditors*). Following his 'Inferno crisis', Strindberg's work evolved towards symbolism and expressionism.

Gerhard Hauptmann (1862–1946) became the leading figure among German naturalistic writers, and attained worldwide acclaim for his first play *Vor Sonnenaufgang* (*Before Dawn*, 1889), which would cause also public outrage. What is striking about this work is that it not only exposes the circumstances in which people live, but also denounces the shortcomings of reformist ideals. Moreover, he also places the action second, in focusing on visually

portraying, as realistically as possible, each character, his/her environment and the moments of fate they are going through. That he considers environment and heredity as equally determining factors can be clearly seen from the plays that followed like *Das Friedensfest* (*The Reconciliation*, 1890), *Einsame Menschen* (*Lonely Lives*, 1891) and his masterpiece *Die Weber* (*The Weavers*, 1892), which deals with the revolt of hungry self-employed Silesian weavers against the capitalist entrepreneur Dreissiger and in which, in his desire for authenticity, he allows the weavers to speak their own dialect. Like Ibsen, he gradually evolved from naturalism towards symbolism by breaking the rules of naturalism and introducing the world of dream and fairy tale to his work (*Hanneles Himmelfahrt*, 1893 and *Die versunkene Glocke*, 1887).

Following in Ibsen's footsteps, Hermann Sudermann (1857–1928) showed that battle between truth and convention particularly in the field of sexual mores, both among the capitalists and the proletariat, for example in *Die Ehre* (*Honour*, 1889). Frank Wedekind (1864–1918) provoked the middle classes and criticized their hypocritical mores in his cynically satirical plays. Opposition to conventional rigidity, he upheld the enchantment of physical beauty, as in *Frülings Erwachen. Ein Kindertragödie* (*Spring Awakening: A Children's Tragedy*, 1891). Like Strindberg, he evolved towards expressionism.

The Dutch naturalistic playwright Herman Heijermans (1864–1924) was another who acquired international fame. Influenced by Ibsen and Hauptmann, he wrote three naturalistic plays during 1898 and 1899: *Puntje* (*The Point*); *Ghetto*; and *Het zevende gebod* (*The Seventh Commandment*), all of which contain the main themes of his complete dramatic oeuvre: the miserable lot of the lower classes, ghetto mentality and the hypocritical mores of middle-class decency. All these themes are also found in his most famous and most representative play *Op hoop van zegen* (*In Good Hope*, 1900), a work located among fishermen and dealing with a floating coffin that the owner sends to sea purely for profit.

Despite the important contributions to European theatre brought about through naturalism, real and more profound innovation would only take place when naturalism was later combined with symbolism in the work of Ibsen, Strindberg and, later, Chekhov.

IMPRESSIONISM

Already in 1879, i.e. hardly five years after Monet exhibited his painting *Impression. Soleil levant*, the French critic Ferdinand Brunetière dedicated an essay in the *Revue des deux mondes* to 'L'impressionisme dans le roman' ('Impressionism in the Novel'). He believed he could identify a number of characteristics that were directly related to pictorial impressionism in *Les Rois en exil* (1879) by Alphonse Daudet.

This fifth and final phase of realism in literature came about at the same time as naturalism and developed parallel to it. It formed a third path, which ran halfway between the extremes of naturalism on the one hand and the severe reactions against it on the other. It consisted in an intensification and an extension of the artistic implications of realism in the direction of impressionism. This explains why it is often difficult to distinguish an impressionistic literary work from the major symbolist ones or those belonging to artistic realism. Literary impressionism mainly consists in a particular style of writing and viewpoint or an *écriture artiste* which was held and practised by (some) realists, naturalists and symbolists. When one looks more closely however, one does notice clear differences: impressionism is more materialistic and more sensual, even if the reality described is less prominent than the mental impression of the observer of that reality; symbolism on the other hand is more idealistic and spiritual, even though this immaterial ideal world is nothing more than a sublimation of the world experienced through the senses.

Literary impressionism reached its zenith between 1880 and 1900, a time when contacts and exchanges between artists and writers were exceptionally intense. Like painters, writers wished to capture their rapidly changing impressions of a reality experienced through the senses. Chronology and the diachronic were replaced by the simultaneous and the synchronous. According to impressionism, facts and objects that happen or are experienced next to each other can form part of a whole.

In the same way that painters developed and perfected special techniques for evoking a *Gesamtbild*, writers too invented a new style of writing that would express their impressionist sensitivity. In order to transform the juxtaposition or simultaneity of observable fact in continuous syntax, they not only had to change word order, they had to intensify the very nucleus of the sentence, i.e. the word, to convey their personal impressions and achieve or evoke the desired effect. This explains why the impressionist style of writing contains altered syntax, word-pairing or grouping, a multitude of neologisms, onomatopoeia and highly visual word usage, all of which went towards intensifying the sensual effect. Furthermore, impressionist writers used the various tropes of synesthesis in combining various types of sensation, thus creating an overall atmosphere. The story itself was limited exclusively to situations, action to lyrical scenes and characterization to the portrayal of mood(s). Drama, too, tended towards the psychological and the lyrical, which led to *Entfabelung*, to the avoidance of a completed story, to a replacement of outer by inner movement and of action by visions of life and the world.

Outside France, the characteristics of impressionism were more frequently found in literature than those of symbolism. The passivity of the aesthetic subject, which was much feared by Wordsworth and Kant, was now chosen as a 'heroic' point of departure. The impressionism practised by the Viennese, the Germans, the Italians and the Russians – Arthur Schnitzler, Hugo von Hofmannsthal, Stefan George, the young Rainer M. Rilke, Gabriele d'Annunzio and Anton Chekhov being its main representatives – expressed a world view grounded in passivity, one of total surrender to sensory impressions from the outside world and unopposed surrender to the whim of the moment. As outer events were experienced as meaninglessness, insignificant and fragmented, this led to a sense of estrangement and solitude, to feelings of *ennui* and boredom with life.

Artistic realism reached its zenith and ended in impressionism. Maxim Gorki realised this totally and wrote a letter to Chekhov in 1900 stating: 'Do you know what you're doing? You're destroying Realism. . . . After reading one of your stories, no matter how unimportant it is, everything seems so rough, as if it had been written with a bludgeon and not with a pen'.

Literature as an autonomous creation

Art for art's sake, or Parnassian literature

Particularly after the revolution and the revolutionary upheavals of 1848, literary realism had been divided into two sharply outlined factions: social realism and aesthetic realism. Until 1848 most of the more important works of art belonged to the former more active one, whereas after 1848 they belonged to the latter, more quietist one.

In contrast to those aiming at developing an art form of social emancipation, one of 'vague humanism held by realist Proudonians and the supporters of social art' (Bourdieu, 1992: 120), a second group turned away towards *détachement esthète* (aesthetic detachment). This difference led to the forming of different groups, each with its own completely separate lifestyle, and ultimately resulted in a schism. The failure of the philosophical utopias propounded by the Saint-Simonists, the Fourierists and the Proudonians had brought discredit upon socially engaged literature. Now the new lyric rejected both the individualism of the romantics and the literature of ideas of the realists and retreated into the more esoteric stances of the theory of *l'art pour l'art* ('art for art's sake').

It was no accident that the literary poetics drawn up after literary autonomy had become institutionalized all stressed the importance of aesthetic disposition. Works of art and their interpretation had to demonstrate this independent aesthetic disposition, to show a dispassionate interest in the aesthetic qualities of a literary work and of the world. This point of view was adopted by prominent critics like Gustave Planche, Jean-Marie Nisard and Victor Cousin. Cousin, in particular, resuscitated the Kantian idea of *Interesselosigkeit* in art and placed it in the contemporary context of an increasing tendency towards specialization in capitalist society. 'Art for art's sake', therefore, was an expression of the growing tendency towards specialization in industrialized society on the one hand, and as a sort of means of resistance against the threat of industrialized and mechanized lifestyles on the other. In keeping with Cousin's *Ecole du bon sens* and his *Esthétique du juste milieu*, poets retired to the splendid isolation of their ivory towers, 'jenseits von Gut und Böse'. Romantic passion and realist revolt were exchanged for social immobility and aloofness. This isolation from society led to the world being replaced by a total cosmos that was complete in itself and furthermore created the illusion of a self-enclosed world of words.

The theoretic basis for this aesthetic movement was laid by the painter, writer and critic Théophile Gautier (1811–72). In his introduction to his novel *Mademoiselle de Maupin* (1835), he formulated the basic principles of autonomous art as follows: 'l'art pour l'art est sans but, tout but dénature l'art'. Art therefore did not need an aim or to be socially or morally committed; the artist could form his own aesthetic aims, beyond involvement with the world. Gautier, too, though he had worn his well-known red coat in 1830 and sat in the front row during the battle for *Hernani* by the Comédie Française, would apply these principles in his own work. He introduced a new form of poetry with his book *Emaux et Camées* (1852), at the same time sounding the death knell of romantic poetry. In contrast to the emotionally charged baroque wordplay and swollen oratory and extrapolation of the romantic poets, he wrote short verse in short meter that was pure and elegant in style and had few changes of rhythm. This beauty of form could only be achieved through strenuous work akin to that of a sculptor. The principles of art for art's sake were adopted and new rules promulgated by 'les Parnassiens' (the Parnassians), a group of young Gautier supporters who gathered together to publish a magazine called *Le Parnasse Contemporain* (three series of which were issued from 1866 to 1876). They did not form a school as such, but considered themselves an *amitié*. They met at the Parisian cafes, Le Divan, Le Peletier and Le Paris, and particularly in the *cénacle* of Charles M. Leconte de Lisle (1818–1894), the pivotal figure and *cher Maître* of the Parnassians who gave form to Parnassian ideals in three books of poetry (*Poèmes antiques*, 1852; *Poésies barbares*, 1862; and *Poèmes tragiques*, 1884). Young and old alike joined together in supporting the ideal of literary beauty that was like a sculpted form in which artistic notions of controlled fantasy, refined style and creative power lay hidden. Their models were drawn from Greek and Hellenic culture and the work of the sixteenth-century Pléiade poets. Nevertheless they remained close to the spirit of positivism of their own time by consciously attempting to merge science and poetry. Théodore de Banville (1823–91) laid down the Parnassian code in his *Petit Traité de versification française*. His own poetry (*Ode funambulesque*, 1857; and *Rondels*, 1875) is perfectionist in its form and displays an evocative virtuosity, although it can be rhetorical at times. The performance in 1869 of the play *Le Passant* by François Coppée (1842–1908), with Sarah Bernhardt in the leading role, was as notorious as Hugo's *Hernani* in 1830 and contributed towards consolidating the Parnassian movement as such.

Next to its founders, there were two more poets who contributed towards this movement's popularity among the public at large: José M. Hérédia (1842–1902), who only wrote one book of poetry (*Les Trophées*, 1893), a colourful history of Greece and Rome and of the Middle Ages and the Renaissance in a formally perfect though cool artistic style that betrays a pessimistic attitude towards life in which only those who serve the cause of beauty can survive; and Sully Prudhomme (1839–1907), the most productive and philosophically minded of the Parnassians, whose most noteworthy works of poetry (*Les solitudes*, 1869; *Les vaines Tendresses*, 1875) are very melancholic and meditative in content. He was awarded the Nobel Prize in 1901 for the formal perfection of his morally and intellectually excellent work. The work of Baudelaire, Verlaine and Mallarmé in particular was along the lines of this new movement, though they were only associated with *Le Parnasse Contemporain* sporadically.

Leconte de Lisle and his faithful follower Léon Dierx (*Poèmes et Poésies*, 1864) were both born on the island of Réunion. This made their work particularly popular in Spanish and Portuguese-speaking countries. Once the Coimbra school had rejected romanticism – the new prose style reaching a high point in the work of Eça de Queiros – poetry came to the forefront in Portugal after 1880. Matters of aesthetics became the focal point of interest and the cause for many a polemic. Among the poets, it was particularly Concalves Crespo (1846–83) who was most influenced by Parnassian poetics, as can be seen from his two works, *Miniaturos* (1870) and *Nocturnos* (1882). One can also notice Parnassian influence on the Spanish movement, *Modernismo*, e.g. on poets like Villaespesa and Marquina, but especially on its guiding light, the Nicaraguan poet Ruben Dario (1867–1916), who spent a lot of time in Madrid and Paris

and whose *Prosas profanas* (1896) and *Cantos de vida y esperanza* (1905) show symbolist leanings.

In 1880, the new Athens school liberated Greek poetry from the swollen rhetoric that was typical of romanticism and joined the ranks of the Parnassians. Here, the most prominent poet of the time was Kostis Palamas (1859–1943). His enormous poetic oeuvre was composed over half a century and contains more than twenty works, including *Ta tragoúdhia tis patridhos mou* (*Songs of my Fatherland*, 1886), *Ta matia tis psichis mou* (*The Eyes of my Soul*, 1892), *Iamvi ke Anápesti* (*Iambs and Anapests*, 1897) and *I Asálefti Zoi* (*Life without movement*, 1904). The focal point of this meditative poetry is the unity between ancient Byzantium and modern Greece.

The Italian Giosuè Carducci (1835–1907) led the movement of change in Italy against the dominance of romantic taste. He wanted to breath new life into the great literary tradition of the classics through the use of involved metrics. His *Rime Nuove* (*New Poetry*, 1877) and his *Odi Bàrbare* (*Barbaric Odes*, 1877, 1882, 1889) were new and fresh descriptions of nature in itself and in its relation to humans in which a new humanity seemed to be celebrating life in harmony with nature.

Though they were still deeply involved in romanticism, prominent poets like Alfred Tennyson (1809–92) and Robert Browning (1812–89) did show some connection with the adepts of art for art's sake through the importance they attached to aesthetic beauty, for which they drew upon ancient Greece for their inspiration. The poetry of the Pre-Raphaelites Dante G. Rossetti (1828–82), his sister Christina Rossetti (1830–84), and William Morris (1834–96) was more closely related to Parnassianism. The ideas on *l'art pour l'art* aesthetics propagated by Algernon C. Swinburne (1837–1909) in his controversial and at times shockingly sensual verse in *Poems and Ballads* (1866), as well as those put forward by Walter Pater (1839–94), whose philosophical novel *Marius the Epicurian* (1885) became an aesthetic manifesto for the younger generation, who crowned him the 'prophet of beauty', were both clear and uncomplicated. One of the latter's admirers was Oscar Wilde (1854–1900), who carried the banner forward to decadentism.

Parnassianism spread to Poland, where Adam Asnyk (1838–97) wrote highly stylized philosophical poetry, for example in *Nad Glebiami* (*Above the Abysses*, 1868), that was similar in style and theme to the work of Sully Prudhomme. Jaroslav Vrchlicky (1853–1912) introduced Parnassianism into Czech literature along with a complete repertoire of exotic new verse forms. The poetry of this particularly prolific poet is both highly lyrical and meditative. The Yugoslavian translator of Henrik Ibsen's work, Milan Begovic (1876–1948) was equally taken by Parnassian perfectionism in his verse. The most representative among the Parnassians of Swedish letters was the Swedish count, diplomat and poet Carl Snoilsky (1841–1903) who expressed his liberal ideas in his coolly controlled yet elegantly stylised *Sonnetter* (1871).

Russian imagism also contained parallels with French Parnassianism. Those concerned were a group of poets who adhered to Belinsky's theory, which held that composing poetry was 'thinking in images'. This implied a preference for objects, which were conducive to visual description. The most representative of the group was Apollon N. Maykov, whose work *Dva mira* (*Two Worlds*, 1881) describes the clash between Christian and pagan Rome. Like Leconte de Lisle, his sympathies went to the pagans.

Later Russian imagism (1919–25) as well as the English and American imagist schools (1908–17), focused on the word as image and also manifested some similarity of form with the Parnassian poets.

The Parnassian movement continued to be influential even long after symbolism had acquired a dominant position in France. There is more similarity between both movements than the battle for dominance would allow. Many symbolists began as Parnassians; others united both schools in their poetry, though in a subdued form.

Clearing the way for symbolism

A triad of French poets, each of whom had begun by upholding the Parnassian ideal of aesthetic beauty and whose roots can be traced to literary tradition in general, gradually evolved towards symbolist poetics. Strictly speaking, none of the three belong to the symbolist movement, but they are considered by the founders of the movement and its followers all over the world as its predecessors and even as its founders.

A major sea change in the development of nineteenth-century poetry undoubtedly occurred with the nonetheless limited oeuvre of Charles Baudelaire (1821–67). His critical work (Curiosités esthétiques, 1868 and L'art romantique, 1868) was written in the classical and romantic vein, to which he gave a new twist, however. Being a great admirer of Gautier and particularly under his influence, he linked the primacy of artistic imagination with the principles of l'art pour l'art poetics. It was through this very demand for unlimited artistic independence that Baudelaire was to lay the foundation for renewal in literature. He introduced modern urban discourse into literature in his creative writing, his collection of poetry Les Fleurs du Mal (1857), and in his poetic musical prose, Le Spleen de Paris (originally published in 1869 as Petits poèmes en prose). Many of his contemporaries considered his work as too radical and it was experienced as a Chock-Erlebnis (to use Walter Benjamin's terms). Because of its supposed 'immorality', Les Fleurs du Mal was seized by the police commissioner upon release, the poet and the publisher were fined, and moreover six poems had to be deleted from the collection. Its theme, which can be characterized as ambivalent, was considered objectionable: dissatisfied with reality and having vainly sought hope in les Paradis artificiels (1860) of drunkenness, inebriation caused by opium and hashish, and unbridled sex, the poet reflects on the eternal powers of attraction of evil, on the despair in which he leaves humankind and at the same time on an incurable longing for the purity and beauty of the lost paradise of childhood. Baudelaire was an intellectual and sensual poet, and in this way is fundamentally different from his romantic contemporaries. He saw the sensual world as forming a set of 'correspondences between the moods of the self and the symbols of the world outside'. Because he used everyday words and images from modern life in his poetry as well as 'cenesthetic' figures of style, his language had an estranging effect on his contemporaries. It was because of this and nevertheless despite his links with traditional literature that Baudelaire is considered as a precursor of symbolism.

It was rather duality and not ambiguity that characterized the work of Paul Verlaine (1844–96), a rake and a Catholic in whose poetry 'angel' and 'wearied beast' attempted 'to cohabit'. Though he repeatedly rejected symbolism (more particularly in the survey conducted by Jules Huret in 1891), he was still one of its precursors. Verlaine's first works (Poèmes saturniens, 1866; Fêtes galantes, 1869; La bonne chanson, 1870) are at first sight quite traditional and draw on the Parnassian school, and yet contrast with the formal rigidity and aloofness of Parnassian style in presenting poetry that was already sensitive and delicate and based on supple meter. Romantic nostalgia as well as weariness and ennui are all portrayed in forms of verse that are both musical and rhythmic. He professed to be engaged in a type of musical language ('De la musique avant toute chose') that must reflect the flow of ideas and feelings in a programmatic poem called 'Art Poétique' (from Jadis et Naguère, 1884 though he had conceived of and had been working with the notion since 1874).

Following his meeting and stormy homosexual relationship with the younger poet Arthur Rimbaud, his poetry (particularly Romances sans paroles, 1874; Sagesse, 1881; and Parallèlement, 1889), clearly shows his divided psyche: exuberant joy and mental and sensual inebriation alternated with unease, bitterness and regret. Out of this confessional poetry, which was cast in images and musical verse, grew the myth of the fallen and degenerate artist who was nonetheless gifted with godly inspiration and as damned as the poets over whom he was to write a study which he titled Les poètes maudits (1883).

Because of his connections with Verlaine, Arthur Rimbaud (1854–91) is also often unjustly listed as being one of the sources of inspiration for symbolism. The symbolists of the 1880s only knew him, however, for his reputation as an enfant terrible and poète maudit, as a non-conformist and adventurer, as a smuggler of weapons and a mystic, but were subject to no direct influence from his work. In his famous letter to Paul Demeny dated 15 May 1871, he spoke about the need to revise the cult of the ego and to arrive at a new vision regarding the role of the unconscious, dreams and euphoria. This letter was only published in 1912, and would serve as a manifesto for the surrealists. Neither his poems (Le Bâteau ivre, 1871; Poésies complètes, 1895), his spiritual autobiography in prose, nor his free verse and poems in prose (Une Saison en Enfer, 1873; Les Illuminations, 1886) were appreciated by his contemporaries but were much valued by the surrealists, however. They recognized their aims in his work and considered him as a visionary in a trance, cataloguing his obsessions without regard for the logic of language and reality and without bothering to be comprehensible.

The Parisian poet and teacher of English, Stéphane Mallarmé (1842–98), can be considered as the founder of symbolism, or at least as the spiritual mentor of the cénacle of young poets that gathered round him on Tuesday evenings at the rue de Rome: Paul Bourget, Gustave Kahn and Jules Laforgue, and then René Ghil, Henri de Régnier Viélé-Griffin, and then later on, Paul Claudel, André Gide, Pièrre Louys, Camille Mauclair, Marcel Schwob and Paul Valéry, his youngest and most important apostle.

Mallarmé told his disciples that poetry should be suggestive and work unconsciously upon the reader. By being thorough-going in one's use of the intellect and by using all the musical and magical powers of language, the poet should be able to transform reality into his own poetical universe of symbols. In his essays on literature and aesthetics (Pages, 1891; La musique et les lettres, 1894; Divagations, 1897) he makes a difference between everyday communicative language ('la parole immédiate') and poetic language ('la parole essentielle'). This intellectualization did not concern the content of the poem but its form or construction, which was to be based on calculation, in the same way as a musical composition follows a mathematical code. One makes a poem with words and not with ideas, was his conclusion in *Divagations*.

In this way Mallarmé's poetry evolved from the Baudelarian and Parnassian style of his first poems – the high point of which was *Hériodade* (1871) – to the symbolism of his great poems *L'après-midi d'un faune* (1876, put to music by Claude Debussy) and *Prose pour Des Esseintes*, 1885; as well as the hermetic *poésie pure* of *Un coup de dés jamais n'abolira le hasard* (1897). Mallarmé's poetry transcends the symbolism of his followers and already sets the tone for decadentism and the experiments of the modernists.

Symbolism

Though the term and the idea were not so new, their origins extending back as far as Kant, Goethe and Schelling, one could say it was Baudelaire's poem *Correspondences* and its image of 'des fôrets de symboles' (forests of symbols) that undoubtedly exerted the greatest influence on those who were to form the school or movement of symbolism in the 1880s in France. The term 'movement' is more apt here because of the degree of difference among its adepts – not to mention the various directions within the movement itself.

The founding principles of symbolism as a movement were laid by Jean Moréas (1856–1910, the pen name of Papadiamantopoulos) in his *Manifeste du Symbolisme* (published in *Le Figaro*, 18.09.1886). In 1886, Moréas also founded the magazine *Le Symboliste* together with Gustave Kahn (1859–1936) and Paul Adam (1862–1920). Then together with René Ghil (i.e. René Guilbert, 1862–1920), Khan further developed the poetics of symbolism along with the prosody of symbolist poetry: Ghil published a dissertation called *Traité du verbe* (1886, foreword by Mallarmé) and Kahn made a synthesis of this new vision on verse in *Le vers libre* (1912). The symbolists of the 1880s aired their views on poetry in magazines such as *La Revue Indépendante, La Revue wagnérienne, La Vogue, La Décadence, Les Écrits pour L'art, La Revue Blanche, La Mercure de France*, etc. French-language magazines in Belgium such as *La Jeune Belgique* and *La Wallonie* in particular also contributed to the spreading of these new views on literature. Because it was outspokenly lyrical, symbolist theatre did not reach great heights of popularity, but it was staged on an alternative theatre circuit, through the founding of the Théâtre d'Art by Paul Fort in 1890 – which was taken over by Aurélien Lugné-Poe in 1892 and renamed the Théâtre de l'Oeuvre.

From a cultural and historical perspective, symbolism can be considered as a reaction against rationalist positivist thought as well as against scientism and the capitalistic structure of French middle-class society. In contrast to all this, the symbolists constructed a vision of life and of the world in which art served as the highest value. This view was heavily inspired by German philosophical idealism and by Schopenhauer's pessimistic vision of life. They desired to go beyond the frontiers of the here and now and explore the metaphysical in search of the idea that underscored and united all perceivable phenomena in the visible world.

Seen within the history of literature, symbolism is a rejection of all forms of realism and particularly of the materialistic and determinist vision of naturalism. Moreover, even though the roots of symbolism lay in the autonomous poetics of *l'art pour l'art*, during the 1870s

symbolists turned away from the 'sculpted', highly pictorial design art of the Parnassians. Of primal importance to symbolism is its affinity with music, particularly with the symphonic music of German composers and the musical dramas of Richard Wagner. The fact that in 1876, both Verlaine and Mallarmé were no longer considered acceptable for the third edition of *Parnasse contemporaine* by its board of editors, is striking in this respect.

In following in the footsteps of the movement's founders, symbolist writers wished to explore the universal, to transcend the frontiers of sensual perception in order to discover correspondences with the spiritual world that lay beyond it and thereby reach the pure core or essence of things. This explains the ambiguity found in symbolist literature: on the one hand, symbolism usually refers to everything that is absolute, eternal, without end and unutterable, yet on the other hand it was bound to empirical reality through its focus on language. This form of literature and its poetry in particular did not wish to translate reality as such, but rather to create or evoke an inner world through the suggestive potency or potential of language. Because of its highly personal use of language, its surprising new imagery and its preference for rhythm over prosody, this poetry became quite hermetic in character and was only accessible to a small group of initiated readers.

In its land of origin, symbolism was the most influential literary movement of the *fin de siècle*, and reached its zenith in the 1880s. Many writers took part in it. Next to its founders, whom we have already mentioned above, there were others who gained long lasting renown, like Jules Laforgue, Villiers de l'Isle Adam, Henri de Régnier, Sturat Merrill, and Vielé-Griffin. In the 1890s, new members such as Francis Jammes, Alfred Samain, Charles Guérin, Pierre Louijs, André Gide, Paul Claudel and Paul Valéry joined the movement.

Though symbolism as such (i.e. as a coherent movement) was short-lived, it attracted a great number of people from outside France to Paris in search of a deeper knowledge of its principles. Thanks to these go-betweens, who introduced symbolist poetics to their own respective countries, the movement became known worldwide. Nevertheless, French symbolism was adapted to suit national taste and to fit the literary tradition of the country concerned.

As a result of their intensive exchanges and cooperation, the work of the French-speaking Belgian writers is closest to French symbolism. As a poet, Maurice Maeterlinck (1862–1949) evolved from being a 'Christian decadent' and writer of classical rhyme to an agnostic humanist and composer of free verse (*Serres chaudes*, 1889). It was mainly through his static symbolist plays on death, happiness and the human condition (*La Princesse Maleine*, 1889; *L'Intruse and Les Aveugles*, 1890; *Pelléas et Mélisande*, 1893; *Aglavaine et Sélysette*, 1896) that he attained worldwide fame in the 1890s, and later his play *L'Oiseau Bleu* was even performed at Stanislavski's Moscow Arts Theatre in 1908. He was awarded the Nobel Prize for Literature in 1911 for his voluminous and multifaceted oeuvre (which also includes essays on philosophy and aesthetics and popular scientific works). A fellow citizen from the city of Ghent, Charles van Lerberghe (1861–1907) also attained renown in Paris for his symbolist plays (*Les Flaireurs*, 1889; *Pan*, 1906) and his subtle suggestive poetry (*Les Entrevisions*, 1898; *La chanson d'Eve*, 1904). Georges Rodenbach (1855–98), who settled in Paris in 1888, modelled himself on Verlaine for his works of poetry *L'hiver mondain* (1884) and *La Jeunesse blanche* (1886), but is better known for his melancholic poetic novel *Bruges la Morte* (1892). Though Emile Verhaeren (1855–1916) was in close contact with the French poets Mallarmé, Ghil, Villiers de l'Isle Adam and Moréas during his stay in France from 1898 till 1913, he was not that strongly influenced by French symbolism. Though his poetic trilogy (*Les Soirs, Les Débâcles*, 1888 and *Flambeaux noirs*, 1891) clearly shows his rejection of Parnassian aesthetics (in the first two works) and his embracing of symbolist poetics, he went his own way in creating humanitarian and socially engaged poetry (*Les Campagnes hallucinées*, 1893; *Les Villes tentaculaires*, 1895; *Les Forces tumultueuses*, 1902; and *Toutes la Flandre*, in five parts, 1904–11) as well as his intimate love poetry (the trilogy *Les Heures*, 1896–1911) made him famous throughout the world.

Dutch-language literature in Flanders was mainly influenced by the symbolism of Charles Morice and his *La Littérature de tout à l'heure* (1889), which inspired the foundation of the literary magazine *Van Nu en Straks*, though only the poet Karel van de Woestijne (1878–1929) transformed it into a personal vision in his poetic oeuvre, which can be considered as a type of symbolized autobiography. One cannot really speak of a Dutch school of symbolism like the one in France, though the then prominent magazines *De Nieuwe Gids* and *De Kroniek* did introduce the movement to the Netherlands. Only the work of later poets like Pieter C. Boutens (1870–1943) and Adriaan Roland-Holst (1888–1976) can be termed symbolist.

Arthur Symons (1865–1954) functioned as an ambassador for symbolism in English literature with his study on *The Symbolist Movement in Literature* (1899). During the 1890s he was in close contact with Charles Morice, Paul Verlaine and Stéphane Mallarmé, and introduced Yeats to Mallarmé personally. Symons' poetry is clearly influenced by the French movement; examples are *London Nights*, 1895; and *Images of Good and Evil*, 1899. Though the spirit of French symbolism was further propagated in England through magazines like *The Yellow Book* (published in 1894 by the graphic artist Aubrey Beardsley and the writer Henry Harland) and *The Savoy* (founded by Symons in 1896), symbolism in the true sense of the word was less influential in England than the decadent movement. There, the most important and most original poet and playwright of the time was the Irishman William B. Yeats (1865–1939). His skill as a poet and his use of the Irish literary tradition allowed him to create a highly individual form of symbolism that was tinted with mysticism. During the 1890s his poetry (*The Wanderings of Oisin and other Poems*, 1889; *Various Legends and Lyrics*, 1892; *The Wind Among the Reeds*, 1899) and his drama (*The Shadowy Waters*, 1900) was much influenced by the French symbolists and by Villiers de l'Isle Adam in particular. Afterwards, Yeats' artistic vision evolved towards a greater complexity as a result of his experiences with spiritualism, which allowed him to develop a whole new system of metaphor and symbols that formed part of his visionary poetry, its high point being *A Vision*, (1925).

In Germany, Stefan George (1868–1933) established a solid relationship with the French symbolists, whom he got to know personally during his visits to Paris from 1889 onwards, introducing their word to the German public through translations and articles. The main theme of his works of poetry (*Hymnen*, 1880; *Pilgerfahrten*, 1891; *Algabal*, 1892) is the conflict between passion and control, between reality and ideals. His *Der Teppich des Lebens* (1900) marked a new period in his work characterized by its prophetic style and a return to realistic imagery.

From 1892 onwards, George gathered a number of fellow thinkers around him and published the magazine *Die Blätter für die Kunst*. Thanks to him, the Austrian poet Hugo von Hofmannsthal (1874–1929) discovered the work of Mallarmé and crossed symbolism with the Viennese spirit of *fin de siècle*. His lyrical plays (*Gestern*, 1891; *Der Tod des Tizian*, 1892; *Der Tor und der Tod*, 1900) merged impressionism, symbolism and decadentism.

Symbolism also influenced Scandinavian literature, though it did not attain a position of prominence in the region at the end of the nineteenth century, as the dominant movement at the time was neo-romanticism. Only the work of the Norwegian poet Sigbjørn Obstfelder (1866–1900) can be considered as that of a convinced symbolist, the atmosphere of his *Digte* (*Poems*, 1893) being clearly related to the paintings and graphics of his friend Edvard Munch. Vilhelm Ekelund (1880–1949) can be considered as occupying a somewhat special position in Swedish letters because of his adherence to the symbolist ideal of beauty in his suggestive nature poetry and atmospheric lyrics in *Syner* (*Visions*, 1901) and *Melodier i skymning* (*Melodies in Twilight*, 1902). Symbolism had a greater impact on Danish literature, the magazine *Taarnet* (*The Tower*) playing an important role there. This new poetics mainly took form in the work in the early work of the poets Johannes Jorgensen (1866–1956), Viggo Stuckenberg (1863–1905) and Sophus Claussen (1865–1931).

The response to symbolism was quicker and more widespread in the Latin countries of Southern Europe than in the North. Of course adventurous eclectic spirits like the Italian poet, novelist and dramatist Gabriele d'Annunzio (1863–1938) considered both symbolism and decadentism as ideal sources of sound. One can also find a similar mixture of symbolist style and decadent theme in the most representative Spanish writer of the day, Ramon del Valle-Inclan (1866–1936), whose highly erotic work is a flashpoint of influences. He shaped these influences into a clearly personalised *oeuvre*, however. His novella *La lámpara maravillosa* (1916) which he himself subtitled 'Spiritual Exercises' formulates the poetics of Spanish symbolism. The precious refinement and sensuality of his *Sonatas* (1902–5) make them the highest expressions of *Modernismo* in the Spanish art of prose. Real change occurred in Portugal with the breakthrough of the symbolist *Nefelibatas*, a group of poets who characterized themselves as 'people who live in the clouds'. The work *Oaristos* (1890) by Eugénio de Castro e Almeida (1869–1944) functioned as a manifesto for the new style of poetry and he himself reached the summit of his creative powers in *Constança* (1900), an epic poem in seven songs. The mentally tormented poet Antonio Nobre (1867–1900) and Camilo Pessanha (1867–1926) also belonged to the international group who met at the offices of *Arte*, a magazine founded by Castro e Almedia. Innovation here was more a matter of form than content, for much like realistic and Parnassian poetry, the main themes were love and melancholy.

Symbolism also reached the Slavic world, but somewhat later than the countries of Western Europe beyond France. This late arrival (1905–10) characteristically coincided with the arrival of other movements like Parnassianism, impressionism, *Jugenstil* and a form of neo-classicism. This resulted in it being adapted to local literary traditions in a more radical way than elsewhere, and furthermore being mixed with elements of national folklore. This literary movement was mainly introduced by literary groups formed by young people who were in the process of bringing about a renaissance in literature.

Russia assimilated symbolism quite quickly because its reaction against positivism and social convention and the dominance of reason corresponded to Russians' own wishes, which already had been expressed in the work of Dostoevsky and Tolstoy. They therefore remained close to French symbolism in their attempts to build a new vision of reality through new poetry and a suggestive use of language. In fact, the first symbolists to gather at the offices of *Vesy* magazine (*The Scales*, 1904–9) were strongly influenced by the poetry of Baudelaire, Verlaine and Mallarmé. Those who prepared the way were Valeri J. Brjusov (1873–1924), Konstantin Balmont (1867–1942), Fjodor Sologub (i.e. Fjodor Kuzmitsy Tetérnikov, 1863–1927). From a formal point of view, they belong to the symbolists but from the point of view of their themes of hopeless pessimism, despair, ennui and metaphysical emptiness, they are in fact closer to the decadents. Their extreme individualism, cult of beauty and disgust at social and moral values led to a widening gap between artists and people.

In order to escape this deadlock, a number of poets went in search of new values, a synthesis of aesthetics, philosophy and religion. This second phase was ushered in by Dimitri S. Meresjkovsky (1865–1941), who founded the Religious Philosophical Association together with his wife, the poetess Zinaida Hippius, in 1902. He tried to arrive at a synthesis of Greek and Christian civilization in his own work. Convinced of the imminent destruction of Western culture, he referred constantly to the messianic role to be played by 'Holy Russia'. This form of symbolist poetry therefore took on a strongly mystical and esoteric character, the result being that the gap between literature and political and social reality grew even wider. Nevertheless, a number of poets in Meresjkovsky's circle did develop into important literary figures, principally Alexander Block (1880–1921), Andrej Bely (1880–1934) and Vyatsheslov I. Ivanov (1866–1949).

Though it was heavily influenced by French symbolism at the beginning, Russian symbolism drew more on national sources during its second phase. Metaphysical approaches were less common than in the West and were closely related to the religious and national aspirations of the Russian people. The pessimism found in the first phase was now replaced by a strong belief in the role of a Russia renewed by the revolution. After 1910, their influence faded, however, as the futurists and imagists rejected the idea that the world was a 'forest of symbols'.

Symbolism manifested itself for the first time in Baltic literature in 1905. Knowledge of this Western European movement arrived there via Scandinavian, German and Russian sources. Here too the ground breakers were groups of modern young poets with an individualistic bent who were interested in existential and metaphysical themes. The movement was introduced to Estonia by the *Noor-Eesti* (New Estonia) movement, whose leading figures were G. Suits, F. Tuglas and J. Oks. In Lithuania it was introduced by the *Dzelme* (*The Gulf*, 1906–7) magazine and by the modernist almanac *Pirmasai baras* (*First Landmark*, 1915), its most prominent symbolist being the critic, poet and playwright Balys Sruoga (1896–1947).

Those Central European countries which had strong, century-old links with West European culture, especially Poland and Czechoslovakia, proved to be a fertile seed bed for symbolism. It was presented and propagated within the heterogeneous group called Mloda Polska (Young Poland) from 1898 onwards by critics and poets like Antoni Lange (1861–1929), Zenon M. Przesmycki (1861–1944) and Stanislan Przybyszewski (1868–1927). Przybyszewski in particular cleared the way with his manifesto *Confiteor* (1899) as well as by founding *Chimera* magazine (1901–7). Their reading of the French, French-speaking Belgian and German symbolist poets led to a new blossoming of Polish lyricism, particularly among poets like Kazimierz Tetmayer-Przerwa (1865–1940), Jan Kasprowicz (1860–1926) Waclaw Rolitz-Lieder (1866–1912) and Leopold Staff (1878–1937). Their characteristically pessimistic view of the world and their apocalyptic imagery stems from the strong influence upon them of the philosophies of Schopenhauer and Nietzsche. Their most representative symbolist poet is Boleslaw Lesmian (1877–1937) who nonetheless published his most important work between the two World Wars. A follower of the Bergson school of philosophy, he wrote evocative poetry, which shows his great powers of innovation in language. Symbolism also contributed to changes in the theatre. Tadeusz Ritter (1876–1921) and the poet and painter Stanislaw Wyspiansky (1869–1907) began working along the lines of Maeterlinck. The greatest innovator in the genre of prose was the novelist Waclaw Berent (1873–1940) and Stefan Zeromski (1864–1925), mainly for his 'rhapsodies', typical Polish stories written in poetic, rhythmical language in which description is more important than plot.

Czechoslovakia, which by 1880s had become less exclusively dependent upon German culture and which had wished to belong to the new movements of change arriving from Paris during the 1890s, became acquainted with symbolism in 1895 though the manifesto of *Czech Modern Poetry*, its foremost representatives being the critic František Xaver Salda (1864–1925) and the poets Otokar Brezina (1868–1929) and Antonin Sova (1864–1920).

Contact with French symbolist poetry also led to renewal in Hungarian literature. Patriotic fire had lessened, and the poets became more individualistic and began looking abroad. In 1850 *A Hét* magazine (*The Week*) declared itself cosmopolitan. *Uj versek* by Endre Ady (1877–1919) drew on Baudelaire and Verlaine for its inspiration. The magazine *Nyagat* (*The West*, 1908) played an important role as a gathering place for forward-looking poets who had been formed by French symbolism, like Dezsö Koztolanyi (1885–1936), Mihàly Babits (1883–1936) and Arpád Toth (1886–1928). A similar type of renewal – though two decades after French symbolism – ushered symbolism into Bulgarian literature, and from 1905 onwards the magazine *Misal* (*Thought*) became a centre for individualism in philosophy and modernism in literature. The new style gained in strength with the publication of *Insomnia* (1907) by Péioe K. Yavarov (i.e. Kratchalov, 1878–1914). In Serbian literature the strong influence of Baudelaire and Verlaine was responsible for a mixture of Parnassianism and symbolism in the poetry of Jovan Ducie (1871–1943), Milan Rakic (1876–1938) and Stevan Lukovic (1877–1902). The most authentic and original poetry is to be found in *Drowned Souls* (1911) by the poet and bohemian Vladisla Pekovic Dis (1880–1916).

Though one of the founders of symbolism, Jean Moréas, was of Greek origin, the movement only achieved a modest standing in Greece around the year 1892 with the publication of *Sonatas* by Stephanos Spephanou (1868–1944).

In Greek literature symbolism was associated with elegiac and neo-romanticism, as can be clearly seen from the poetry of Costas Hatzopoulos (1868–1920).

Nor did American literature have its own symbolist school or movement, though Stuart Merill, one of the most important figures of French symbolism, did succeed in spreading appreciation and renown for the French movement through his reports in *The Chap Book*. The readings by Henri de Régnier during his visits to New York and Boston in 1900 were of great influence upon young undergraduate poets, though only Wallace Stevens (1879–1955) assimilated the new poetic style to any degree of permanence. The relationship between reality and imagination is a major theme in the poetry he wrote at a more mature age: *Harmonium*, 1923; *Ideas of Order*, 1935; *The Man with the Blue Guitar and Other Poems*, 1937; *Notes Towards a Supreme Fiction*, 1942; and *Esthétique du Mal*, 1945.

Symbolism was on the wane as a movement in most countries by 1910, and had been superseded by other visions of literature which were diametrically opposed to introverted, individualistic literature. Nevertheless, its influence was to be felt far into the twentieth century, the work of the latter-day or neo-symbolists even outliving that of their predecessors.

As a result of this, perhaps the most important French symbolist poet was a young adept of Mallarmé, Paul Valery (1871–1945). Though he had made his debut in 1889 with symbolist poetry, his most important works did not appear until twenty years later (*La jeune Parque*, 1917; and *Charmes*, 1922). His poetry is a wonderful fusion of sensuality, intelligence and music. He wrote down his theories in prose form: *Introduction à la méthode de Leonardo da Vinci* (1895), *La soirée avec M. Teste* (1896), *Variété* (in 5 vols, 1924–5), *Regards sur le monde intellectuel* (1931–45), *Tel Quel* (2 vols, 1941) and *Cahiers* (29 vols, 1957–61, published in facsimile). In these works, he asserts that reason is the only source of knowledge, both scientific and artistic. So for him literature was a form of work, a construction that transformed language.

The work of Paul Claudel (1868–1955) also stems from symbolism. His reading of Rimbaud's *Illuminations* caused his faith in scientism to waver and in 1890 he joined the Roman Catholic church. From then on he bore witness to his new faith in his verse. His poetry is that of cosmic vision full of symbolism and metaphysical ideas set in an austere, rhymeless form, which is rich in imagery and assonance, all in keeping with the rules of his *Art poétique* (1907).

Symbolism continued to exert influence in prose through the work of André Gide (1869–1951) and Marcel Proust (1871–1922). During his symbolist period, the former wished to be the Verlaine of prose and in so doing unravel painful conflicts of conscience, the whole time being torn between sensuality and ascetics (*Les cahiers d'André Walter*, 1891; *Le traité de Narcisse*, 1891; *Le voyage d'Urien*, 1893). Following his discovery of Nietzsche's philosophy of life, he became a total individualist and began writing his analytical psychological novels, in which he developed his 'Gidism' which was synonymous with 'révolte, libre examen, émancipation de l'esprit, exigence envers soi-même' (*Les nourritures terrestres*, 1857; *L'immoraliste*, 1902; *La porte étroite*, 1909). After World War I he became *le maître à penser* of a new generation, that of dadaism and surrealism. His theory of *l'acte gratuit*, or impulsive unmotivated action, received a wide response. Marcel Proust on the other hand was possessed of a subtle form of aesthetic dilettantism that was characteristic of the *fin-de-siècle*, as can be seen from his very

first collection of essays, stories and poems (*Les Plaisirs et les Jours*, 1856). Continuously hurt by life, he developed a form of sensitivity that permitted fruitful introspection. Proust succeeded in creating a masterful synthesis of poetry and reality, of vision and observation, of analysis and impression in evoking *la belle époque* and the lives of the *beau monde* in Paris about 1900, in his seven-part novel *A la Recherche du Temps Perdu* (1913–27). He drew on each instant as though time stood still and by using his associative trope of *monologue intérieur* and his art of minute description, he delved deep into the human soul. Proust's *oeuvre* therefore is a synthesis of realism, naturalism and symbolism, though his style is more markedly symbolist that anything else.

Rainer M. Rilke (1875–1926) can be considered as belonging to the European neo-symbolists of German literature. His early poetry is still playfully impressionistic and is written in a refined *fin de siècle* spirit full of dark moods and passionate longing for the life of great and noble hero (*Larenopfer*, 1895; *Traumgekrönt*, 1897; and *Die Weise von Liebe und Tod des Cornets Christoph Rilke* in lyrical prose, 1906). Influenced by Hofmannsthal, Stefan George and especially the Dane, Jens P. Jacobsen, his work evolved towards symbolism: *Das Buch der Bilder* (1902) and *Das Stundenbuch* (1905). Inspired by Rodin's work in Paris, he wrote the two volumes of his *Neue Gedichte* (1907–8) in which he leaves the world of abstractions behind for the world of concrete things. His later works of poetry (*Die Duineser Elegien*, 1923; *Die Sonette an Orpheus*, 1923) are hymns to modern man and to his 'bejahende' (confirmative) view on life and on the world.

The American poet Thomas Stearns Eliot (1888–1965) created a synthesis of symbolism and modernism, settling in England in 1927 and later becoming a British subject. His early poetry (*Prufrock and other Observations*, 1917) is strongly influenced by the French symbolists, particularly by the ironic style of Jules Laforgue – a form of irony that allowed the poet to reveal his deepest thoughts and feelings while at the same time being able to analyse them critically and objectively. This style was used sublimely in his cyclical poem *The Waste Land* (1922), in which he provides a critical cultural analysis of the chaos and infertility of present day civilization, expressing it all in symbolical terms. His later poetry (*Four Quartets*, 1943) is a poetical meditation on time, which is religious and philosophical in approach.

These latter-day symbolists left their mark on the literature of the period between the two world wars; they explored the potential of symbolist poetic language to its very limits, and in so doing laid the foundations for twentieth-century modernist poetics.

Decadentism

Decadentism, which is closely related to symbolism and is therefore sometimes difficult to tell apart, is a movement found throughout the whole of *fin de siècle* literature. Moreover, because both styles are similar in origin they are even harder to distinguish.

Both movements are in fact anti-movements born out of reaction to positivism, materialism, utilitarianism and the banality of daily life in an industrialized bourgeois society. Stylistically speaking, they also distanced themselves from the ordinary utilitarian language of communication and wished to place language totally in the service of aesthetic expression. Their language was characterized by its vagueness and multiplicity of meaning and not by its denotation and precision. Both symbolist and decadent literature is full of neologisms, typically fashionable words, witty puns, twists of syntax, esoteric ambiguity and conscious obscurity.

Despite these similarities, decadent literature takes place at a different semantic level: whereas symbolism manifests its specific nature at a linguistic or poetic level, decadentism differs from it in its stance towards life and society, which mainly manifested itself through aspects of content, i.e. motif, theme and character. The main feature of this stance is its rejection of the industrial society of the day, which resulted in a loss of faith in progress and led to a radical break with the past. The prophecy of doom that replaced it did not necessarily lead to fundamental pessimism, however. Paradoxically enough, the decadents saw beauty in this loss of civilization (one often finds references to Byzantium and the latter-day Roman Empire), for decay was a necessary step towards regeneration and new life in a better and especially more beautiful society. Modern man was a neurotic creature, and the only thing that could please him was to dance atop the volcano and so escape the banality of the day-to-day. The decadent therefore consciously chose aesthetic and aristocratic isolation in Baudelaire's 'paradis artificiels'. Provocative dandyism, hyperaesthetic refinement, hypersensitivity, sexual deviance and the cult of artificiality were the outward signs of decadent lifestyle and expressed its stance against a hostile world of philistines. The urge for spiritual depth pushed many into a religious life – there were a striking number of conversions to Catholicism – and towards many forms of mysticism, the occult and satanism.

Like symbolism, decadentism also first appeared in France. The first signs of a decadentist approach to life and its aesthetics are to be found in Baudelaire's poems in *Les Fleur du Mal*. Explicit references to it can be found in *Notes nouvelles sur Edgar Allen Poe* (1867) which served as a foreword to the second part of his translation of Poe's stories. Théophile Gautier was the first to refer to the decadent elements in his (Baudelaire's) poetics in his *Notice* to the posthumous reissue of Baudelaire's poetry in 1868: in a complex inventive style that is full of nuance and variety of register. This loss of faith in progress, which had already been characterized by Baudelaire as: 'cette grand hérésie de la décrépitude' ('that great heresy of decrepitude') and the unavoidable prophecy of doom that went along with it would be generalized and strengthened in France after that country's defeat in the Franco-Prussian war of 1870.

Decadentism became a true literary movement in the 1880s. Paul Bourget (1852–1935) was the first to explain the theory of decadentism in a chapter on Baudelaire in *Essais de psychologie contemporaine* (1883) – the article had been previously published by Juliette Adam in 1881 in *Nouvelle Revue* magazine. The term became known generally through the famous first verse of Paul Verlaine's sonnet *Langueur* (1883): 'Je suis l'Empire à la fin de la décadence'. The term was first used to denote a movement in literature by Maurice Barrès (1867–1923) in a magazine titled *Les taches d'encre* (1884), a one-man operation, whilst the journalist Anatole Baju drew up a manifesto for the movement in the magazine *Le Décadent* (1886–9), of which he was the publisher.

The decadent lifestyle became known to readers in general through the novel *A Rebours* (*Against the Grain*) by Joris-Karl Huysmans (1848–1907). The work was dubbed 'l'un des plus décadents de ce siècle de décadence' in a review by Barbey d'Aurevilly. The book was considered by some to be the bible of decadentism and by others as a provocation, which led to severe criticism and much parody.

Many notable adepts joined the movement in France during the 1880s. Paul Bourget (1862–1935) used his theoretic tracts on modern psychology in his novels (*Cruelle énigme*, 1884; *Un crime d'amour*, 1886) in which he unravelled the neuroses of his characters set against the backdrop of the mundane. The sceptical aesthete and dilettante Maurice Barrès (1862–1923) was continually in search of new sensations and deeply involved with the development of individuality, which led to his trilogy on *Le culte du moi* (*Sous l'oeil des barbares*, 1888; *Un homme libre*, 1889 and *Le jardin de Bérénice*, 1891). He mainly excelled in his analyses of tormented souls and in his descriptions of desolate landscapes. The cult of adoration of Richard Wagner is an essential aspect of French decadentism, which even resulted in the founding of the *Revue Wagnérienne* (1885–8). This also explains their fascination for the eccentric dandy Ludwig II, king of Bavaria and close friend of Wagner's who was used as a model for the characters in *Le crépuscule des dieux* by Elémir Bourges (1852–1925) and *Luscignole* by Catulle Mendès (1843–1909). The search for a deeper form of spirituality led others among them to mysticism and the occult. Joséphin Péladan (1859–1918), who as founder of the High Council of the Rosicrucians styled himself Sar Péladan, strove for the sublimation of man through magic (*Le Vice suprême*, 1884; *L'androgyne*, 1891). Influenced by the work of Poe and Wagner and the German philosophers Hegel and Schopenhauer, Villiers de l'Isle Adam (1838–89) built an occult world out of elements of romantic horror (*Contes cruels*, 1883; *Histoires insolites*, 1888) and science fiction, as can be seen in the novel *L'Eve Future* (1886) which featured the typically decadent theme of the *femme fatale* or *belle dame sans merci*.

The most important innovator of language and prose among the decadents was Jules Laforgue (1860–87), who evolved towards decadentism after reading the philosophical works of Hartmann and Schopenhauer. As a 'mystic pessimist', he was an ironic observer of the vanity of life. His cosmic visions, sarcastic views, complaints and fears are all spiced with irony and humour in the same way as Heine's, and formulated in a type of free verse that is close to popular song and colloquial language (*Complaintes*, 1885; *L'Imitation de Notre Dame de la Lune*, 1886; *Les Fleurs de bonne volonté*, 1886). In his new 'Marseillaise' he calls the middle class to arms for the fierce battle against cold reason. In so doing Laforgue not only announced the demise of French positivist thought, he also heralded the arrival of modernist thinking. Laforgue's influence remained strong throughout Europe way into the twentieth century.

The Italian poet, novelist and playwright Gabriele d'annunzio (1863–1938) proved a fine receptacle for the spirit and style of decadentism, and he later became known as one of the most phenomenal decadents in Europe also because of his exuberant and eccentric lifestyle. During his stay in Rome in the 1880s and 1890s in particular, he became one of the most notorious representatives of *decadenza* with the publication of his works of poetry *Intermezzo di rime* and *L'Isottèo e la Chimera* (1889) and his novel *Il piacere* (*The Child of Pleasure*, 1889), its main character Sperelli being an Italian Des Esseintes. The novels which followed – *L'innocente* (1892), *Giovanni Episcopo* (1892), *Il triomfo della morte* (1894) and *Il fuoco* (*The Great Fire*, 1900) – are dominated by a sense of extreme aestheticism and by a hedonistic glorification of life in Nietzschean style.

Laforgue's influence continued to be felt in Italy in the poetry of Guido Gozzana (1883–1916) and Sergio Corazzini (1887–1907) and the early work of Aldo Palazzeschi (1885–1974).

The most important Spanish writer to treat the themes of decadentism was Ramón del Valle-Inclan (1869–1936). In what is considered as one of his masterpieces, the *Sonata de primavera* (in *Sonatas – Memorias del Marquès de Bradomin*, 1902–7) he creates a magical atmosphere that is a typical combination of the sacred and the profane and of desire and death. The influence of d'Annunzio and E. T. A. Hoffmann can be clearly seen here.

Decadentism found no trouble gaining acceptance in England, where it was linked to the literature of the Pre-Raphaelites and Walter Pater's Aesthetic Movement, all of whom can be considered as its precursors. Between 1893 and 1897, there was a literary circle in the West End of London that called itself the Decadent Movement. They were clearly inspired by the French movement, which also can be seen from their use of a provocative yellow cover for their magazine *The Yellow Book* (1894) – famous for its drawings by Aubrey Beardsley: the covers of *A Rebours* and *Le Décadent* were also yellow.

French decadentism was first introduced into England by Arthur Symons (1865–1954) in 1893, through an article titled 'The Decadent Movement' in *Harper's New Monthly*. He clearly followed the path set by Baudelaire and Verlaine in his own poetry (*London Nights*, 1895; *Images of Good and Evil*, 1899). Nevertheless, Algernon Charles Swinburne (1837–1909) had already been inspired by French poetry in writing his *Poems and Ballads* (1866), and the painter and writer George Moore (1852–1933) used his stay in Paris as the basis for *Confessions of a Young Man* (1888) a work that also exudes an atmosphere of Huysmansian decadence.

The movement's key figure in England was Oscar Wilde (1854–1900), a charismatic and exuberant dandy whose behaviour and writing shocked the Victorian society of the day. He became famous internationally for his light-hearted satirical dramas such as *Lady Windermere's Fan* (1892); *A Woman of No Importance* (1893); *An Ideal Husband* (1895) and *The Importance of Being Ernest* (1895), that excited audiences with their funny and (at the time) challenging dialogue and their absurd sense of situation. He came more to the fore as a decadent writer in his novel *The Picture of Dorian Gray* (1891), which was inspired by Huysmans' *A Rebours*. This horrific and at the same time *precious* story relates the tale of a person with a split personality who is torn between good and evil, the whole style of the book being hyper-aesthetic and extremely sensual. This sultry sensuality and refined evocative language is also to be found in his play *Salomé* (the French version dating from 1893 and the English version from 1894); its public performance was prohibited by the British censor, however. The scandal caused by Wilde being tried and sent to prison for a homosexual relationship (1895) not only meant the end of his career as a writer but also of the popularity of a movement that was known in Victorian England as 'the art of shocking'.

Decadentism was introduced into German letters by Hermann Bahr and his *Studien Zur Kritik Der Moderne* (1890, a collection of articles that had already been published in 1888), which included a negative evaluation of its escapism. The spirit and style of decadentism did attract a group of young writers of 'Das Junge Wien', the main figure being Hugo von Hoffmannsthal (1874–1929), the German equivalent of Wilde and d'Annunzio. The central theme of his work is the fool (*der Tor*), the eternal playful aesthete who enjoys beauty and life: when death arrives, he realizes that he has not known real life.

A lighter side of *fin de siècle* that was playful in its exposure and ironically sceptical in its eroticism can be seen in the plays of Arthur Schnitzler (1862–1931) such as *Liebelei* (*Flirt*, 1895), *Der grüne Kakadu* (*The Green Cockatoo*, 1899) and *Reigen* (*Choral Dance*, 1900). The plays of Frank Wedekind (1864–1918) are more critical and even cynical in their exposure of the hypocrisy of middle-class morals. In opposition to this he upheld the enchantment of physical beauty and the liberating power of sexuality in works such as *Frülings Erwachen* (*Spring Awakening*, 1891); *Der Erdgeist* (*Earth Spirit*, 1895); and *Die Büchse der Pandora* (*Pandora's Box*, 1904). The social issues of the *fin de siècle* and in particular his criticism of the bourgeois tendency in society that would automatically lead to cultural decay, form a central theme in the novels of Heinrich Mann (1871–1950). These are found especially in his earlier works like the three volumes of the *Die Göttinnen* (*The Goddesses*, 1902–3), which describe the decadence of opulent Renaissance life, and *Professor Unrat* (1905) upon which the film *The Blue Angel* is based. The earlier work of his brother Thomas Mann (1875–1955) is also written in the spirit of Schopenhauer's cultural pessimism: aesthetes who withdraw from the vulgarity of modern life and who experience this either as doom or liberation (*Die Buddenbrooks*, 1901; *Tonio Kröger* and *Tristan*, 1903; *Der Tod in Venedig* (*Death in Venice*, 1913).

Writers throughout the whole of Europe were all caught up in the spirit of decadence at the turn of the century. In some countries it failed to become a fully-fledged literary movement, but it did definitely influence individual writers, then again only during particular phases of their careers. This was the case for the Dutch writer and novelist Louis Couperus (1863–1923) whose historical novels occur in a culture doomed with decline or decadence, as in the melancholic poetry of the Flemish poet Karel Van de Woestijne (1878–1929). One can find traces of decadentism in Scandinavian letters among writers such as the Swedes H. Söderberg (1869–1941) and Bo Bergman (1869–1967), the Norwegian author Tryggve Andersen (1866–1920) and the Danish poet Johannes Jorgensen (1866–1956), as well as the poet, novelist and dramatist Helge Rode (1870–1937). One can also find decadent tendencies in Slavic literature, for example in the work of the Polish writer Stanislaw Przybyszewski (1868–1927) and the Czech author Julius Zeyer (1841–1901).

Decadent literature brought about a radical break with the past and closed off the nineteenth century. Following this literature of cultural doom, a new form of activist literature was to emerge: in 1909, Filippo Marinetti's *Manifeste du futurisme* was published, and in 1910 *Der Sturm* magazine ushered in expressionism. With them arrived the twentieth century avant-garde, who began the struggle for a new culture.

BIBLIOGRAPHY

ABRAMS, M. H. 1953. *The Mirror and the Lamp*. Oxford.

ANDREWS, K. 1964. *The Nazarenes: A Brotherhood of German Painters in Rome*. Oxford.

AUERBACH, E. 1946. *Mimesis. Dargestellte Wirklichkeit in der abendländischen Literatur*. Bern.

AUSTIN, L. 1956. *L'Univers poétique de Baudelaire*. Paris.

BAGULEY, D. 1990. *Naturalist Fiction. The Entropic Vision*. Cambridge.

BAIER, W. 1964. *Quellendarstellungen zur Geschichte der Photographie*. Halle.

BALAKIAN, A. (ed.) 1977. *The Symbolist Movement*. New York.

——. 1982. *The Symbolist Movement in the Literature of European Languages*. (A Comparative History of Literatures in European Languages, ICLA, Vol. 2). Budapest.

BÄR, N. 1991. *Beeldende kunsten in de 19de eeuw*. Utrecht.

BAUER, R. 1986. 'Grösse und Verfall der Decadence'. In: DROST W., *Fortschrittsglaube und Dekadenzbewusstsein im Europa des 19. Jahrhunderts*, pp. 31–4. Heidelberg.

BAUMGART, F. 1975. *Idealismus und Realismus 1830–1880. Die Malerei der bürgerlichen Gesellschaft*. Cologne.

BECKER, G. J. 1963. *Documents of Modern Literary Realism*. Princeton.

BENAMOU, M. 1972. *Wallace Stevens and the Symbolist Imagination*. Princeton.

BENEDITE, L. 1910. *Great Painters of the XIXth Century and their Paintings*. London.

BENEVOLO, L. 1971. *Die Soziale Ursprünge des modernen Städtebaus*. Gütersloh.

——. 1984. *Geschichte der Architektur des 19. und 20. Jahrhunderts*. (Deutscher Taschenbuch Verlag) Band 1–2, Munich.

BERNBAUM, E. 1949. *Guide through the Romantic Movement*. New York.

BINI, W. 1936. *La Poetica del decadentismo*. Florence.

BORNECQUE, J. H.; COGAN, P. 1958. *Réalisme et naturalisme*. Paris.

BOTTOMORE, T. 1983. *A Dictionary of Marxist Thought*. Oxford.

BOURDIEU, P. 1992. *Les règles de l'art*. Editions du Seuil, Paris.

BOWRA, M. 1943. *The Heritage of Symbolism*. London.

——. 1949. *The Creative Experiment*. London.

——. 1961. *The Romantic Imagination*. London.

BRAET, H. 1867. *L'Accueil fait au Symbolisme en Belgique 1885–1900: Contribution à l'étude du mouvement et de la critique symbolistes*. Brussels.

BRINCKMANN, R. (ed.) 1969. *Begriffsbestimmung des literarischen Realismus*. Tübingen.

BRION, M. 1966. *Art of the Romantic Era*. London.

BRUMFIELD, W. C. 1993. *A History of Russian Architecture*. Cambridge.

CARTER, A. E. 1958. *The Idea of Decadence in French Literature. 1830–1900*. Toronto.

CAZAMIAN, L. 1947. *Symbolisme et poésie: l'exemple anglais*. Neuchatel.

ČELEBONOVIC, A. 1974. *The Heyday of Salon Painting: Masterpieces of Bourgeois Realism*. London.

CHADWICK, C. 1971. *Symbolism*. (Series: The Critical Idiom) London.

CHARLESWORTH, B. 1965. *Dark Passages: The Decadent Consciousness in Victorian Literature*. Madison.

CHEVREL, Y. (ed.) 1982 [1993] *Le naturalisme. Etude d'un mouvement littéraire international*. Paris.

——.1983. *Le Naturalisme dans les littératures de langues européennes*. University of Nantes.

——. 1986. *Le Naturalisme en question*. Paris.

CLARK, K. 1973. *The Romantic Rebellion*. London and New York.

CLARK, T. J. 1973 *The Absolute Bourgeois. Artists and Politics in France 1848–1851*. London.

COLLINS, P. 1965. *Changing Ideals of Architecture, 1750–1950*. London.

CORNELL, K. 1951. *The Symbolist Movement*. New Haven.

——. 1958. *The Post-Symbolist Period*. New Haven.

DANIELS, M. 1953. *The French Drama of the Unspoken*. Edinburgh.

DECAUDIN, M. 1951. *La crise des valeurs symbolistes : vingt ans de poésie française, 1895–1914*. Paris.

DONCHIN, G. 1958. *The Influence of French Symbolism on Russian Poetry*. The Hague.

DROST, W. 1986. *Fortschrittsglaube und Dekadenzbewusstsein im Europa des 19. Jahrhunderts, Literatur- Kunst- Kulturgeschichte*. Heidelberg.

DUMESNIL, R. 1945. *L'époque réaliste et naturaliste*. Paris.

DUTHIE, E. L. 1933. *L'Influence du symbolisme français dans le renouveau poétique de l'Allemagne: Les 'Blätter für die Kunst' de 1892 à 1900*. Paris.

EAGLETON, T. 1990. *The Ideology of the Aesthetic*. Oxford.

EITNER, L. (ed.) 1970. *Neoclassicism and Romanticism, 1750–1850*. (Sources and Documents in the History of Art), 2 vols. London and Englewood Cliffs NJ.

ETTLINGER, M. 1924. *Geschichte der Philosophie von der Romantik bis zur Gegenwart*. Munich.

FARMER, A. J. 1931. *Le mouvement esthétique et 'décadent' en Angleterre (1873–1900)*. Paris.

FOCILLON, H. 1927–8. *La peinture au XIXe siècle*. 2 vols. Paris.

FOUCAULT, M. 1966. *Les Mots et les choses*. Paris.

——. 1969. *L'Archéologie du savoir*. Paris.

FRIEDRICH, H. 1956. *Die Struktur der modernen Lyrik. Von Baudelaire bis zur Gegenwart*. Hamburg.

FIRST, LORD. 1969. *Romanticism in Perspective*. London.

——. 1969. *Romanticism*. London.

——. 1980. *European Romanticism. Self-Definition*. London.

——. 1992. *Realism*. London and New York.

GAUNT, W. 1945. *The Aesthetic Adventure*. London.

GAY, P. 1984, *The Bourgeois Experience. Vol. 1: Education of the Senses*. New York and London.

GILSOUL, R. 1936. *La théorie de l'art pour l'art chez les écrivains belges de 1830 à nos jours*. Brussels.

GRAFF, G. 1979. 'The Myth of the Post-modern Breakthrough'. In: Graff, G., *Literature Against Itself*. Chicago, pp. 31–62.

GRAÑA, C. 1964. *Bohemian versus Bourgeois. French Society and the French Man of Letters in the Nineteenth Century*. New York and London.

GRANT, D. 1970. *Realism*. (Series: The Critical Idiom) London.

GRISEBACH, A. 1916. *Die Baukunst im 19. Jahrhundert. Handbuch der Kunstwissenschaft*. Berlin-Neudelsberg.

GRODEN, M.; KREISWIRTH, M. (eds) 1994. *The Johns Hopkins Guide to Literary Theory and Criticism*. Baltimore and London.

GSTEIGER, M. 1972. *Französische Symbolisten in der deutschen Literatur der Jahrhundertwende (1869–1914)*. Berne and Munich.

HAJEK, E. 1971. *Literarischer Jugendstil. Vergleichende Studien zur Dichtung und Malerei um 1900*. Düsseldorf.

HALSTED, J. B. (ed.) 1965. *Romanticism: Definition, Explanation and Evaluation*. Boston MA.

HAMILTON, GUHA. 1970. *Nineteenth and Ttwentieth Century Art*. New York.

HAUSER, A. 1951. *The Social History of Art*. Vols 3 and 4. New York.

HEMMINGS, F. (ed.) 1974. *The Age of Realism*. Harmondsworth.

HIELMEYER, A. 1921. *Die Plastik seit Beginn des 19. Jahrhunderts*. Leipzig.

HINTERHAUSER, H. 1978. *Jahrhundertende – Jahrhundertwende II*. (*Neues Handbuch der Literaturwissenschaft*, Band 19). Wiesbaden.

HITCHLOCK, H. R. 1963. *Architecture: The Nineteenth and Twentieth Centuries*. Pelican History of Art, Harmondsworth.

HOBSBAWM, E. J. 1975. *The Age of Capitalism. 1848–1875*. London.

HOFMANN, W. 1961. *The Early Paradise: Art in the Nineteenth Century*. New York and London.

HOLT, E. G. (ed.) 1966. *From the Classicists to the Impressionists: A Documentary History of Art and Architecture in the Nineteenth Century*. New York.

——. 1979. *The Triumph of Art for the Public: The Emerging Role of Exhibitions and Critics*. New York.

——. 1981. *The Art of All Nations, 1850–1873: The Emerging Role of Artists and Critics*. Princeton.

HOUSE, J.; STEVENS, M. A. 1979. *Post-Impressionism. Cross Currents in European Painting*. London.

JACKSON, H. 1913 [1976]. *The Eighteen Nineties: A Review of Art and Ideas at the Close of the Nineteenth Century*. London.

JANSON, H. W. 1985. *Nineteenth-Century Sculpture*. London.

JOHNSON, L. 1979. *The Cultural Critics. From Matthew Arnold to Raymond Williams*. London and Boston MA.

KEARNS, K. 1996. *Nineteenth-Century Literary Realism. Through the Looking-Glass*. Cambridge.

KERMODE, F. 1957. *The Romantic Image*. London.

KOPPEN, E. 1973. *Dekadenter Wagnerismus: Studien zur europäischen Literatur des Fin de Siècle*. Berlin.

KOSMIKIES, R. 1968. *Der nordische Dekadent: Eine vergleichende Literaturstudie*. Helsinki.

KRENZLIN, N. 1992. *Zwischen Angstmetapher und Terminus. Theorien der Massenkultur seit Nietzsche*. Berlin.

KREUZER, H. 1968. *Die Boheme. Beiträge zu ihrer Beschreibung*. Stuttgart.

——. 1976. *Jahrhundertende – Jahrhundertwende I*. (*Neues Handbuch der Literaturwissenschaft*, Band 18). Wiesbaden.

LACAPRA, D.; KAPLAN, S. C. (eds) 1982. 'Modern European Intellectual History'. In: *Reappraisals and Perspectives*. Ithaca NY.

LANKHEIT, K. 1966. *Classicisme, Romantiek, Realisme*. Amsterdam.

LARKIN, M. 1977. *Man and Society in Nineteenth-Century Realism Determinism and Literature*. London.

LAWLER, J. R. 1969. *The Language of French Symbolism*. Princeton.

LEHMANN, A. G. 1950 [1968]. *The Symbolist Aesthetic in France 1885–1895*. Oxford.

LEMAIRE, H. 1965. *La Poésie depuis Baudelaire*. Paris.

LETHEVE, J. 1959. *Impressionistes et Symbolistes devant la Presse*. Paris.

LEVINE, G. 1981. *The Realistic Imagination: English Fiction from Frankenstein to Lady Chatterley*. Chicago.

LEVITINE, G. 1978. *The Dawn of Bohemianism: The Barbu Rebellion and Primitivism in Neoclassical France*. University Park PA.

LINK-HEER, U. 1986. '"Le Mal a marché trop vite". Fortschrittsglaube und Dekadenzbewußtsein im Spiegel des Nervositäts-Syndroms'. In: Drost, W. *Fortschrittsglaube und Dekadenzbewußtsein des 19. Jahhunderts*. Heidelberg, pp. 13–30.

LOWE, D. M. 1982. *History of Bourgeois Perception*. Chicago.

LUKÁCS, G. 1948. *Essays über den Realismus*. Berlin.

——. 1955. *Probleme des Realismus*. Berlin.

LYON MIX, K. 1960. *A Study in Yellow. 'The Yellow Book' and its Contributors*. London.

MAAG, G. 1986. 'Fortschrittsidee und Historismus bei Saint-Simon und Comte'. In: *W. Drost, Fortschrittsglaube und Dekadenzbewußtsein im 19. Jahrhundert*. Heidelberg, pp. 35–43.

MARTINO, P. 1925 [1967]. *Parnasse et Symbolisme*. Paris.

——. 1951. *Le naturalisme français (1870–1895)*. Paris.

MARZOT, G. 1971. *Il decadentismo italiano*. Bologna.

MATTHEWS, A. J. 1947. *'La Wallonie' 1886–1892: The Symbolist Movement in Belgium*. New York.

MERCIER, A. 1969 and 1974. *Les Sources ésotériques et occultes de la poésie Symboliste 1870–1914*. Vols. 1 and 2. Paris.

MEYER, H. 1949. *Geschichte der abendländischen Weltanschaung*. Wurzburg.

MICHAUD, G. (ed.) 1947. *La Doctrine Symboliste : Documents*. Paris.

——. 1947 [1 vol. edn 1968] *Message Poétique du Symbolisme*. 3 vols. Paris.

MIDDLETON, R.; WATKIN, D. J. 1977. *Architektur der Neuzeit* (Weltgeschichte der Architektur). Stuttgart.

MIGNOT, C. 1983. *L'architecture au XIXe siècle*. Fribourg.

MILNER, A. 1991. *Contemporary Cultural Criticism. An Introduction*. Sydney.

MITTERAND, H. 1987. *Le Regard et le signe. Poétique du roman réaliste et naturaliste*. Paris.

MORIER, H. 1961. *Dictionnaire de Poétique et de Rhétorique*. Paris.

MOSCOVICI, S. (ed.) 1981. *L'âge des foules*. Paris.

MÜLLER, L. 1987. 'Modernität, Nervosität und Sachlichkeit. Das Berlin der Jahrhundertwende als Hauptstadt der "neuen Zeit"'. In: U. Bahr, *Mythos Berlin. Zur Wahrnehmungsgeschichte einer industriellen Metropole*. Berlin.

MUTHER, R. 1907. *The History of Modern Painting*. 4 vols. New York.

NELSON, B. (ED.) 1992. *Naturalism in the European Novel. New Critical Perspectives*. New York and Oxford.

NEMOIANU, V. 1984. *The Taming of Romanticism. European Literature and the Age of Biedermeier*. Cambridge MA.

NEUSCHÄFER, H. J. 1976. 'Der Naturalismus in der Romania'. In: H. Kreuzer (ed.) *Neues Handbuch der Literaturwissenschaft*. Vol. XVII. Frankfurt, pp. 33–68.

NOCHLIN, L. (ED.) 1966. *Realism and Tradition in Art, 1848–1900*. (Sources and Documents in the History of Art). Englewood Cliffs NJ.

——. 1971. *Realism*. Harmondsworth and Baltimore.

NORMAN, G. 1977. *Nineteenth Century Painters and Painting. A Dictionary*. Berkeley and Los Angeles.

NOVOTNY, F. 1960 [1970]. *Painting and Sculpture in Europe, 1780–1880*. Pelican History of Art, 2nd. edn. Harmondsworth and Baltimore.

PECKHAM, M. 1970. *The Triumph of Romanticism*. New York.

PELLES, G. 1963. *Art, Artists and Society: Painting in England and France, 1750–1850*. New York.

PEVSNER, N. 1984. *Architektur und Design von der Romantik zur Sachlichkeit*. Munich.

PINTO, V. DE S. 1961. *Crisis in English Poetry 1880–1940*. London.

PIPPIN, R. B. 1991. *Modernism as a Philosophical Problem*, Oxford and Cambridge MA.

PIZER, D. 1967. *Realism and Naturalism in Nineteenth-Century American Literature*. Carbondale.

PRAZ, M. 1933. *The Romantic Agony*. Oxford.

RAYMOND, M. 1952. *De Baudelaire au Surréalisme*. Paris.

RHEIMS, M. 1972. *La Sculpture au XIXe Siècle*. Arts et métiers graphiques. Paris.

RICHARD, N. 1961. *A l'aube du symbolisme*. Paris.

——. 1968. *Le mouvement décadent*. Paris.

RICHARDSON, E. P. 1939. *The Way of Western Art, 1776–1914*. Cambridge MA.

ROBICHEZ, J. 1957. *Le Symbolisme au théâtre*. Paris.

ROSENBLUM, R.; JANSON, H. W. 1984. *Art of the Nineteenth Century. Painting and Sculpture*. London.

SCHEMANN, L. 1938. *Die Rasse in den Geisteswissenschaften. Studien zur Geschichte des Rassengedankens*. Munich.

SCHMIDT, A. M. 1942 [1955]. *La Littérature Symboliste*. Paris.

SCHORSKE, C. 1981. *Fin de Siècle Vienna. Politics and Culture*. New York.

SCHULTZE, J. 1970. *De negentiende eeuw. Kunst in beeld*. Amsterdam and Brussels.

SIEBENMANN, G. 1965. *Die moderne Lyrik in Spanien*. Stuttgart.

SIMMONS, E. G. 1967. *Introduction to Russian Realism*. Dallas.

SHRINE, P. N. 1971. *Naturalism*. (Series: The Critical Idiom). London.

STARKIE, E. 1960. *From Gautier to Eliot*. London.

STERNER, G. 1975. *Jugendstil. Kunstformen zwischen Individualismus und Massengesellschaft*. Cologne.

SYMONS, A. 1899. *The Symbolist Movement in Literature*. London.

TAUPIN, R. 1929. *L'Influence du Symbolisme français sur la poésie américaine*. Paris.

TSUDI MADSEN, S. 1967. *Art Nouveau*. Milan.

VALKHOFF, P. 1918. *L'Influence de la littérature française dans les Pays-Bas*. Leiden.

VAN TIEGHEM, P. 1948. *Le romantisme dans la littérature européenne*. Paris.

——. 1951. *Le Romantisme français*. Paris.

VAUGHAN, W. 1978. *Romantic Art*. London and New York.

WATKIN, D. 1986. *A History of Western Architecture*. London.

WEINTRAUB, S. 1964. *'The Yellow Book': Quintessence of the Nineties*. New York.

WELLEK, R. 1955. *A History of Modern Criticism, Vol. 2: The Romantic Age*. London.

WEST, J. 1970. *Russian Symbolism*. London.

216

WILLIAMS, R. 1958 [1961, 1977]. *Culture and Society. 1780–1950.* Penguin Books, London.

——. 1961 [1965, 1971]. *The Long Revolution.* Pelican Books, London.

WILLOUGHBY, L. A. 1930. *The Romantic Movement in Germany.* Oxford.

WILSON, E. 1935. *Axel's Castle: A Study in the Imaginative Literature of 1870–1930.* New York.

WHITE, H. 1973. *Metahistory. The Historical Imagination in Nineteenth-Century Europe.* Baltimore.

WOOD, C. 1981. *The Pre-Raphaelites.* London and New York.

ZEITLER, R. S. D. 1937. *Die Kunst des 19. Jahrhunderts.* Propyläen Kunstgeschichte. Band XI, Berlin.

ZMEGAC, V. 1991. *Der europäische Roman. Geschichte seiner Poetik.* Tübingen.

8.2

LATIN AMERICA AND THE CARIBBEAN

Patrick Collard

INTELLECTUAL, PHILOSOPHICAL AND ARTISTIC TRENDS

During the romantic period and even down to the second quarter of the nineteenth century, philosophical activity in Latin America was mainly defined and determined by a few leading names in French thought. Even so, Pierre Royer-Collard, Victor Cousin, Auguste Comte, and others, must not cause us to forget the attraction also enjoyed by Herder's notion of the *Volksgeist* in fledgling nations, where representatives of the intellectual elite – many of whom were then still receiving part of their training in Europe – were themselves seeking features by which to define their identity.

Regarding the first half of the century, a special place of virtually pan-American scope must be set aside for the brilliant, literally magisterial figure of the Venezuelan Andrés Bello (1781–1865), a true child of the Enlightenment, a companion to Alexander von Humboldt in his expeditions, and at once a statesman, philosopher, poet, philologist, grammarian, translator, educator, and all-around writer of truly encyclopaedic culture (see plate section). While sensitive to Walter Scott, Byron, Chateaubriand, and Victor Hugo, Bello nevertheless continued to show firm commitment to such neo-classical principles as order and harmony. Some have regarded him as a humanist of the stature of Goethe, while his *Gramatica de la lengua castellana al uso de los Americanos*, or *Grammar of the Castilian Language for the Use of Americans* (1847), has remained a prestigious model, much quoted in works on Spanish linguistics. Bello spent nearly twenty years in London (to where he travelled in 1810 with Simón Bolívar), and more than thirty years in Chile, where he served as Finance Minister and Rector of the University, and where he also drafted the Civil Code. He made his mark in the field of philosophy through an unfinished work, *Filosofía del entendimiento*, or *Philosophy of Understanding*, only published, however, in 1881. Alain Guy writes (1997: 20–1): 'This is an imposing synthesis – reminiscent of Leibnitz – of Cousin's and Jouffroy's moderate sensualism, ideology, and eclecticism, the whole steeped in Kant's critical approach'. Particular attention should be called, in the first part or 'Psicología mental', to Bello's largely linguistic theory of ideas as signs; this portion of his work deals with the perception of ideas and the relations between them, as well as with acts of memory and manifestations of attentiveness. The second part of his work, 'Lógica', addresses the soundness in proceedings of rational argumentation. But Bello never came around to writing a portion on practical philosophy ('Filosofía moral'), which

was to have included a section on moral psychology ('Psicología moral') and another on ethics ('Etica'). His whole system was thus at once psychological and logical, since the 'science of human understanding' amounted, in Bello's eyes, to the very pivot of all philosophical speculation: no thorough study of metaphysics, for example, might be undertaken except on the basis of sound examination of the faculties of understanding.

In Chile, Bello clashed with another leading figure in the intellectual life of the time: José Joaquín Mora (1783–1864), a Spanish liberal as it were doomed to a life of constant exile. Mora had fled the Spain of Ferdinand VII and then settled for a spell in London before moving to Argentina and thence to Chile. In Chile, Mora taught at the Liceo, and published for the purposes a *Curso de lógica y ética* (a course on logic and ethics), which followed the tenets of the Scottish school of philosophy (the 'philosophy of common sense'). But Mora's teaching activities were questioned by Bello, whereupon he went on the move again, his exile now taking him to Peru and Bolivia before he finally returned to Europe.

In Brazilian Catholic circles, the eclectic spiritualism of Victor Cousin, whose teachings have occasionally been described as rather facile and superficial, nevertheless found a ready echo with the Capuchin preacher Francisco de Mont'Alverne (1785–1859), a driving force behind the reception of such ideas and the author of a *Compendio de filosofia* (*Syllabus of Philosophy*) published in 1869. Mont'Alverne's disciples at the seminary in Rio de Janeiro included Domingo José Gonçalves de Magalhães (1811–82), author of *Os fatos do espírito humano* (*Facts of the Human Spirit*), 1858; *A alma e o cérebro* (*The Soul and the Brain*), 1876; and *Comentarios e pensamentos* (*Comments and Thoughts*), 1880. Cousin again influenced the *Compendio de filosofia* of one of his own translators from the French, José, Maria de Morais Valle (1824–86), while the religious spiritualism of both Cousin and Maine de Biran pervaded the *Investigaçoes de psicologia* (*Investigations in Psychology*), 1854, of Eduardo Ferreira Franca (1809–57). All three of these men, Gonçalves de Magalhães, Morais Valle and Ferreira Franca, were physicians.

While it is a difficult and extremely sensitive matter – not to say unfair – to have to deal so selectively with the fertile growth of Spanish-American thought before the impact of positivism, at least three outstanding personalities deserve special mention here: the two Argentines Esteban Echeverría (1805–51) and Domingo Faustino Sarmiento (1811–88), and the Ecuadorian Juan Montalvo (1832–89). Echeverría and Sarmiento were members of what came to be widely known as the political and literary generation of the 'banned', on account of their opposition to the long dictatorship (1835–52) of Juan Manuel de Rosas; both spent much of their lives abroad.

Echeverría discovered romanticism through direct contact, that is, in Paris itself, where he lived between 1825 and 1830, and read Musset, Vigny, Saint-Simon, Leroux, Cousin, Goethe, Herder, Scott, and Byron. On his return to America, he became a beacon to an entire generation. To quote José Miguel Oviedo's words, Echeverría's project 'was political, ideological, and literary; its instruments were liberalism, Utopian socialism and romanticism' (Oviedo, 1997: 24). After founding the Asociación de la Joven Generación Argentina (Association for the Young Argentine Generation: later to become the Asociación de Mayo or Association of the Month of May), Echeverría, with two other writers from the group of the 'banned', Juan María Gutiérrez (1809–78) and Juan Bautista Alberdi (1810–84), drafted the text known by the title of *Dogma Socialista*, published in 1846, in Montevideo, where Echeverría spent time in exile. The *Dogma Socialista* is a basic text for our knowledge of what the generation inspired by Echeverría hoped for. The *Dogma* was written, in fact, as a document containing 'the principles making up the social faith of the Argentine Republic'. Such principles included a stand on behalf of America's cultural emancipation, belief in progress, respect for Christian morality (Echeverría also wrote a *Manual de enseñanza moral* or *Handbook of Moral Instruction*), and commitment to democratic rights for the individual. We shall see more of Echeverría below, in the section dealing with literature.

Sarmiento underwent a long period of exile in Chile, where he championed romanticism in a memorable dispute with Andrés Bello. He then travelled to Europe and the United States, before taking office as President of the Argentine Republic (1868–74). Sarmiento's direct observation of life in Argentina, to begin with, but also his readings of Cousin and of Montesquieu, Michelet, Tocqueville, and other European thinkers, nourished the pages of one of the most important books of the entire Spanish-American nineteenth century: *Civilización y barbarie. Vida de Juan Facundo Quiroga* (*Civilization and Barbarism: The Life of Juan Facundo Quiroga*), 1845. Known as Sarmiento's *Facundo* for short, the book takes its title from the given name of the novel's main character, one of the many *caudillos* or local chiefs who usurped all legal authority and dominated vast territories and even whole provinces. Sarmiento denounced, in such *caudillismo*, one of the main ills from which the young republic then suffered; and to a large extent, *Facundo* was a valid prophecy for all Latin America. Among other things, the book was a violent pamphlet against Rosas, the real target of Sarmiento's attack through the character Facundo. Sarmiento proposed the urban civilization of Europe and North America as the model for the moral, political, and social development of his own country, as opposed to the savage spirit – to be checked and uprooted – of the *gaucho* and *caudillo* of the immense Pampa, who in Sarmiento's eyes represented barbarism, an obstacle to progress, a permanent threat to central government and freedom. The author's views must, of course, be set within the context of his own age, the first half of the nineteenth century, which witnessed such sharp contrast between Buenos Aires and most other Latin American capital cities, as isolated centres of European-influenced culture, and their surrounding deserts, forests or rural areas dominated by traditional and archaic structures. Sarmiento saw the solution to his country's problems in intensive campaigns for education, in encouraging European immigration, and in founding cities. What Sarmiento preached he put into practice once in office, in turn as provincial governor, cabinet minister, and finally President. *Facundo*, in this sense, became truly a seminal text in the history of Latin American thought; its author was one of the moulders of modern Argentina. The contrast between civilization and barbarism drawn by Sarmiento had considerable impact; his novel made no little contribution to determining lines of literary creativity and to fuelling the ongoing political, cultural and social debate of Spanish America.

The life and works of Juan Montalvo were also closely linked to the history of a nation whose construction was in full swing. In Ecuador, Montalvo represented the strong voice of a civic, moral, and liberal conscience under two dictatorships: Gabriel García Moreno's ultra-Catholic rule (1860–75), then that of Ignacio Veintimilla (1875–82). In prose unanimously acknowledged as brilliant, Montalvo attacked Veintimilla in twelve celebrated *Catilinarias* (*Catiline Orations*) between 1880 and 1882. Equally sparkling were his *Capítulos que se le olvidaron a Cervantes* (*The Chapters that Cervantes Forgot*), published in 1895, his *Geometría moral* (*Moral Geometry*), which came out in 1902, and his *Libro de las pasiones* (*Books of Passions*). In his *Los siete tratados* (*Seven Treatises*), 1882–3, first written in French but soon translated into Spanish, Italian, and German, Montalvo meditated as a moralist and essayist along the lines of Montaigne on such diverse themes as nobility, genius, heroism, and beauty perceived as the supreme aesthetic, cultural, and spiritual category. Montalvo was stirred by his reading of Plutarch, and remained fascinated by the examples of moral and heroic behaviour to be found in Greek and Latin Antiquity; he affirmed his own faith in individual heroism as a driving force in history, and celebrated those men whom he considered major models for his own, modern times: Washington, Bolívar and Napoleon, among others.

Positivism made its appearance in about 1870, and as accurately observed by Oviedo (1997: 142–3), tended very soon to become a virtual repertory of formulae for government and social and economic organization, derived from the ideas of Auguste Comte, John Stuart Mill, Charles Darwin, Herbert Spencer, and others. As regards thought, the change here was spectacular indeed, since a form of materialism and a rage for empirical science and planning now took the place of what had been liberalism's spiritual component. In every country of the continent, there henceforth circulated various versions of scientific-minded positivism. The main ideas aimed to subject all social activity to a prosperous order of affairs that might be verified and quantified. Such a line of thought seemed capable of embracing all aspects of social life, including education, artistic creativity, the economic order and political organization. Positivism propounded an ideal of unlimited rational progress, subject only to universal laws. In other words, this was the new Utopia, through which the middle class saw its own role and mission confirmed as an agent for progress and modernization in America. The fact that freemasonry took hold among many members of this middle class, in a number of Latin American countries, probably had something to do with the new craze for positivism's ideals.

In many places, the new order of the day became, precisely, 'order and progress': hardly a surprising aspiration in countries which had suffered wars of independence and had just gone through, or were still experiencing, painful bouts of either dictatorship – the sort of *caudillismo* denounced by Sarmiento and others – or outright political anarchy. Nor was it owing to chance if Brazil's motto, in 1889, became the very words 'ordem e progresso'. Brazil was one of the two countries, Mexico being the other, where the whole movement first took root. Comte's teachings were openly professed by Brazil's future President, Benjamin Constant Botelho de Magalhães, when still lecturing at Rio de Janeiro's military academy. Indeed, two alumni of this institution are regarded as initiators of the whole movement: Miguel Lemos (1854–1917) and Raimundo Teixeira Mendes (1855–1927), twin founders of Rio de Janeiro's Positivist Society. Later in life, Teixeira Mendes would inaugurate, in Paris, a 'Temple of Humankind' ('Temple de l'Humanité'), while Lemos, in Brazil, set up an Apostolado Positivista do Brasil: a 'Positivist Mission of Brazil'. Among other publications, both men, together, brought out the *Circulares anuales do Apostolado Positivista do Brasil* (*Annual Bulletins of the Positivist Mission of Brazil*), as well as *A nossa iniciaço no Positivismo* (*Our Introduction to Positivism*), in 1889.

In Mexico, in 1867, the physician and educator Gabino Barreda (1818–81), as dean of the National Preparatory School, pronounced an *oración cívica* (public address) in vibrant defence of Auguste Comte's ideas, which he had heard in Paris. Barreda sought to apply to Mexico's development the three stages of Comte's historical pattern: the theological, the metaphysical, and finally the positive, which Barreda intended to bring about in Mexico himself. President Benito Juárez commissioned Barreda to reorganize the country's educational curricula on a scientific basis. After the liberal presidency of Juárez, the Porfirio Díaz dictatorship was also able to count on support from a number of positivist thinkers within the ruler's inner circle ('los cientificos': 'the scientists'). One of these advisers was the historian and educator Justo Sierra (1848–1912), author of *Evolución política del pueblo mexicano* (*The Political Evolution of the Mexican People*), 1902. Positivism's fundamental criticism of liberal individualism helps explains the attraction for supporters of positivism of authoritarian regimes concerned with law and order.

In Argentina, the palaeontologist Florentino Ameghino (1854–1911), on returning from Europe, in turn defended Darwin's theories, and sought to apply them to his own research both in his *La antigüedad del hombre en el Plata* (*Man's Antiquity in the River Plate Region*), and in his *Filogenia paleontológica argentina* (*Palaeontological Philogenetics in Argentina*), 1884.

In Chile, the three Lagarrigue brothers were active: Jorge (1854–94), inspired by Comte, founded the Sociedad de la Ilustracion (Society for Enlightenment), and further adhered to the second stage in Comte's philosophical development; Juan Enrique (1869–1927) organized a Positivist Church; and this was continued by Luis (1857–1949). Also noteworthy was the novelist, essayist and historian Victorino Lastarria (1817–88), who published his *Lecciones de política positivista* (*Lessons in Positivist Policy*) in 1874. Lastarria combined his own liberalism with Comte's ideas, in a kind of synthesis, which draped his own metaphysical conceptions of freedom in positivism's mantle.

In Peru, the brilliant and formidable political pamphleteer Manuel González Prada (1844–1918), a poet,

a defender of the Indians' cause (*Nuestros Indios*, or *Our Indians*, 1904), an anarchist, and a bitter foe of the church, also claimed positivist ideas which, he argued, offered the necessary scientific basis for the country's reconstruction after the disastrous War of the Pacific (1879–83). Another Peruvian writer who shared in the positivist outlook was Javier Prado Ugarteche (1871–1921), author of *El genio* (*The Genius*) in 1890, and *La evolución de la idea filosófica* (*The Evolution of the Philosophical Idea*) in 1891.

The philosopher Enrique José Varona (1849–1933) fought in Cuba's war of liberation and became his country's Vice-President (1913–17). His *Conferencias filosóficas*, the texts of his open lectures at Havana's Academy of Sciences between 1880 and 1888, rank among the most important monuments to positivism in the Americas. The *Conferencias* follow positivism's general evolutionary line: Varona expresses reservations regarding Comte's thought, but shows considerable affinity with the English school of John Stuart Mill and Herbert Spencer. Salvador Bueno points out that by so observing the coincidence between positivism's guiding principles, and the development projects of Cuba's own middle class, Varona applied the doctrine of evolution to philosophical speculation, and to an analysis of his country's own colonial situation, in the most progessive way which the cultural environment of his day could possibly allow. (See here Salvador Bueno, *Enrique José, Varona: esquema de su vida y obra* [*An Outline of His Life and Works*], in Iñigo Madrigal, 1987: 488.)

We cannot take leave of positivism here without further mentioning the literary and political activities of the Puerto Rican sociologist, novelist and patriot Eugenio María de Hostos (1839–1903), author of a 'Moral Treatise' ('Tratado de moral') in 1888, who dreamt of a Spanish Caribbean Federation that would include Cuba, Santo Domingo and Puerto Rico.

This only goes to show that positivism was everywhere a driving force in Latin American social and political thought at the end of the nineteenth century.

But we should bear in mind that in the same period, the teachings of the German philosopher Karl Christian Friedrich Krause (1781–1832) also attracted many thinkers in Latin America, although to a lesser extent than in contemporary Spain. The main proponents of Krause's thought in the Americas were Argentina's Julián Barraquero (1856–1935), President Hipólito Yrigoyen (1852–1933), and Wenceslao Escalante (1852–1912); Cuba's Teófilo Martín de Escobar; and Brazil's Pedro Américo de Figueiredo Mello (1843–1905). Krause's thought made headway in Latin America not only through the works of his Spanish followers such as Julián Sanz del Río (1814–69) and Francisco Giner de los Ríos (1839–1915), but also through direct familiarity with Krause's own writings: as well as with the books of two of Krause's most enthusiastic disciples, the German Heinrich Ahrens (1808–74), and the Belgian Guillaume Tiberghien (1819–1901). Krause's influence made itself most felt in the philosophy of law and also, of course, through such experiences as those of 'harmonious education'. Educators like Argentina's Carlos Norberto Vergara (1857–1928), took their cue from Spain's Institución Libre de Ensenanza (Free Institution for Teaching) and the founding principles of the Free University of Brussels.

We will dwell below, in the section on literature, on the major influence enjoyed by the thoughts of Cuba's José Martí.

THE VISUAL ARTS AND ARCHITECTURE

Architecture

Europe's rejection of the baroque found an echo in America. Such a reaction, which Castedo (1986: 282, 284) has even qualified as a form of iconoclasm because of the trend to replace or transform churches' reredos screens, was not quite so violent in Central America as in Brazil or in Mexico. A number of architects who championed the cause of a triumphant neo-classicism even showed undeniable gifts. The mid-nineteenth century saw the rise of eclecticism, however, which remained characteristic of the rest of the century and of the early twentieth century.

Neo-classicism held sway to differing degrees, and at very different times, throughout the various Latin American lands.

In Mexico, neo-classicism's triumph found expression in the work of Damián Ortiz de Castro and Francisco Eduardo Tresguerras. The latter, indeed, waged an outright crusade against the baroque. The cathedral in Mexico City owes its towers and final modifications to Ortiz de Castro, but Tresguerras' masterpiece is the church of El Carmen in Celaya. So far as secular architecture is concerned, neo-classicism's supreme monument in Mexico stands in Puebla: this is the imposing Palacio de Minería (Palace of the Mining Industry), designed by the Valencian Manuel Tolsá (1757–1816), who also made his contribution to the cathedral in Mexico City.

In Guatemala, a new capital was laid out, Nueva Guatemala de la Asunción, after a final major earthquake ravaged the old capital, Santiago de los Caballeros, in 1773. The new cathedral, consecrated in 1815, and completed by the architects Santiago Marqui and Pedro García Aguirre, who modified the original plans by Marcos Ibáñez, remains the most prestigious example of neo-classicism in Central America.

In the Caribbean, Puerto Rico and Cuba can boast a few, mainly secular, buildings, characteristic of the style, but plummeting population and economic decadence account for the obstacles faced by neo-classicism in the Dominican Republic.

In Venezuela, neo-classicism came late and mingled with the neo-Gothic and the neo-baroque. In Colombia, however, numerous buildings bear witness to the vitality of the style, as at Popayán, with its cathedral of Saint Francis (finished only in 1906), its church of Saint Augustine and its monastery of the Camillan Fathers of the Good Death. Bogotá boasts its National Capitol.

Ecuador is a case apart: the baroque here was so vigorous and splendid that neo-classicism was powerless to dislodge it and only made its presence rather discreetly felt in a few adjustments to accommodate the age's prevailing taste. The cathedral of Guayaquil, repeatedly mutilated and restored in the wake of tremors, is a curious jumble of mannerist, neo-Gothic, neo-Romanesque, and neo-Byzantine styles. Nevertheless, the architect Thomas Reed did manage to leave his neo-classical stamp on a few monuments, including the Government Palace in Quito.

In Peru, the Basque-born architect, painter and sculptor Matías Maestro, another sworn enemy of the baroque and the author of a small book called *Orden sacra*, built or altered several religious structures in Lima. He was also responsible for Lima's San Fernando College of Medicine, and drew up

the plans for the capital's General Cemetery. But the most important Peruvian neo-classical monument stands in Arequipa. Again, earthquakes and even a fire dictated the story of Arequipa Cathedral's reconstruction, begun in 1844 and completed three years later under the architect Lucas Poblete. In the Peruvian capital itself, the first building considered truly modern was the Penitenciaría, or Penitentiary, a stark fortress so designed as to allow the wardens to see – without being seen – into every cell. The plans were drafted by Maximiliano Mimey. Still in Lima, but in an entirely different, and rather exuberant and Italianate style, Antonio Leonardi and Manuel Anastasio Fuentes began construction of an exhibition palace (now the Museum of Fine Arts), completed in 1872, with a particularly light and functional inner space.

In Bolivia, neo-classicism was best represented by the Franciscan monk and architect Manuel Sanahuja, responsible, among other buildings, for the cathedrals of Potosí and La Paz. The exterior of the former (built 1809–38) echoes Spanish baroque and rococo; the interior, however, is more distinctly neo-classical.

Historical circumstances in Argentina, like the tardy creation of the Viceroyalty of the Río de la Plata in 1776, and the paucity of funds and materials, along with the sobriety of a local provincial architectural tradition of Andalusian origin, favoured the adoption of neo-classicism as early as the first half and middle of the eighteenth century, at a time when the baroque was still at its zenith in other parts of the colonial empire. Towards the mid-nineteenth century, Argentine architecture, which was mostly secular, saw its eclectic, European-style, and particularly Italianate trends increasingly confirmed. The main names here were Francesco Tamburini and Juan Antonio Buschiazzo. Tamburini built the Casa Rosada, or 'Pink House', the Presidential Palace; the Central Military Hospital; and the Higher School of Medicine. Buschiazzo was responsible for many structures and played a major role in the urban history of Buenos Aires, by planning the layout of both the Avenida de Mayo (May Avenue) and the square of the same name.

Neo-classicism's role in Paraguay was literally unique, insofar as this was the only religious and secular architectural style available to build on top of ruins: those created by the destruction of the Jesuit missions, and then those wrought by the anti-baroque, that is to say, anti-Spanish, fury of dictator Gaspar Rodríguez de Francia, the notorious 'Doctor Francia' (1814–40). The Carlos Antonio López dictatorship (1844–62) was thus faced with a *tabula rasa*, which the Italian architect Alessandro Ravizza filled by building in Asunción the most important secular structures of the period, beginning with what is now the Pantheon of Heroes, but was originally a church (the Oratorio de Nuestra Señora de Asunción) raised along lines similar to the Hospice des Invalides in Paris. Between 1854 and 1861, British engineers laid down the first railway in Paraguay; oddly enough, it is not known who designed the very attractive railway station in Asunción, one of the first in the Americas: perhaps the very same engineers?

Three builders were the main initiators of the neo-classical style in Uruguay, whose capital, Montevideo, was founded only in 1723: a Portuguese military engineer, José Custodio de Sá y Faría, drew up the plans for the cathedral of Montevideo in 1784, which was then built by Del Pozo y Demarchi. Toribio was responsible for many works, including the Cabildo (House of City Guilds) in 1804–11, regarded as the most remarkable neo-classical structure in the River Plate region.

At the end of the eighteenth century, the Italian Joaquín Toesca y Richi (1745–99) had been the outstanding neo-classical builder in Chile. Toesca made a decisive and lasting alteration to the appearance of the capital, Santiago, with his work on the cathedral, the Palace of the Mint (Palacio de la Moneda, the current presidential palace: see plate section), the prison, the San Juan de Dios Hospital, and other buildings. He also built in other parts of the country. After his death, the legacy of his untiring labour was pursued, along neo-classical lines, by architects trained by Toesca himself: builders such as Juan José de Goycolea y Zañartu or Agustín Caballero. French taste became more pronounced after 1850, with the arrival of the architect C. F. Brunet de Baines (1799–1855), who founded the first school of architecture in Chile; with him came the models of the French Restoration and Louis-Philippe styles. Brunet's most important project was the luxurious Municipal Theatre, destroyed by fire, however, in 1870. After 1857, Brunet's work was continued by his fellow-countryman Lucien Ambroise Henault, who not only constructed family mansions, but also planned and implemented a public building programme with such structures as the National Congress and the University of Chile, which were landmarks of Santiago's urban landscape in the second half of the century. Yet even before the middle of the century, José Gandarillas (1810–53) had already introduced the neo-Gothic manner in Chile. This style, and also the related historical eclectic style, spawned a number of rather hybrid structures. Most representative of this trend around 1870 were Fermín Vivaceta and Manuel Aldunate Avaria. By way of illustration of such tendencies, Vivaceta designed a fire station with a minaret, and Aldunate built a sort of imitation of the Alhambra in Granada for a wealthy mine-owner. Budding modernism, however, was mirrored in the central market's conception of space and in its metallic structure, a joint work by both architects. A new stage began in 1872, when Santiago's city centre was embellished under the supervision of Director of Public Works Benjamín Vicuña Mackenna (1831–86), 'Chile's Haussmann', who began by converting the hill of Santa Lucía into a public park. Again in Chile's capital, the French architect Paul Lathoud ensured continuity with classical taste (stressing horizontal lines, the Tuscan arch, and Greek temple fronts), while in Valparaíso, the German Theodor Burchard followed the neo-Gothic fashion. One of the most remarkable structures of late nineteenth-century Santiago unfortunately no longer exists: the San Carlos Gallery, designed by Ricardo Brown, was a brilliant example of architecture in metal and glass.

In Brazil, French neo-classical taste was the absolute rule, at any rate for official architecture, with a few adaptations to the conditions of a tropical climate, such as spaces for ventilation. King João VI had fled France's invasion of Portugal in 1807 and removed to Rio de Janeiro, where he remained until 1821; as early as 1816, he called on Labreton to direct a large team of French architects, painters and sculptors. Auguste Henri Victor Grandjean de Montigny became the first professor of architecture at Brazil's Imperial School. His lasting works in the country include the market and the customs house in Rio de Janeiro; he also drew up the project for the Imperial Academy of Fine Arts. To be sure, alongside such official commissions and projects, the construction of private homes continued very much to draw upon the traditions of colonial architecture. Indeed the time-honoured *azulejo*, or enamelled wall-tile, continued to be used everywhere, even in structures of neo-classical design.

The visual arts

In the visual arts, painting became the main expression of Latin American feeling in the romantic period, even though neo-classical taste survived for a long time in many countries, while many European painters dictated fashion or were officially appointed to academic posts. Such was the case with the Catalan, Pelegrín Clavé (1810–80), at the Mexico City Academy; of Raymond Quincac Monvoisin (1790–1870), in Chile; of the French Savoyard, Carlos Enrique Pellegrini (1800–75), in Argentina; and of Nicolas Antoine de Taunay, in Brazil. As mentioned above in the section on architecture, Brazil – at any rate the Brazil of official circles and the imperial court – was strongly influenced by French artistic taste in the first half of the nineteenth century. A typical case here is that of the romantic painter Victor Meireles (1832–1902), who studied in Rome and Paris and found success in Brazil as a student of Delacroix: whose influence is obvious in such paintings by Meireles inspired by local history as *The First Mass Celebrated in Brazil* or *The Second Battle of Guarapes*.

Nor should we forget the cultural importance of what one might call the return journey, that is, romantic enthusiasm in Europe for America's imposing and exotic natural landscapes, so much of which then still remained unexplored. Travel books and other reports from explorers, along with their illustrations, did not fail to attract to the Americas many artists looking for original themes and motifs.

In Mexico, so-called 'popular' or 'primitive' anti-academic painting was a particularly significant expression of Creole sensibility. Mexican 'primitives' cultivated portraiture, religious scenes, and historical subjects. The names of most of the artists belonging to this trend remain unknown, but several have been identified: notably José María Estrada in Guadalajara, and Hermenegildo Bustos in Guanajuato.

In Venezuela, Martín Tovar y Tovar (1828–1902), who was trained in Paris and illustrated mainly patriotic themes (*The Battle of Carabobo; Signing the Declaration of Independence*, etc.), was a typical representative of neo-classicism, while the major names associated with romanticism are those of Cristóbal Rojas (1858–90) and Arturo Michelena (1870–1900). Rojas is best known for his mastery of chiaroscuro and for the social themes in his paintings; Michelena was distinguished for his effects in shadow and light.

Two specific traits in painting and drawing mark out the art of nineteenth-century Colombia: these were the miniature portraits, notably practised by the widely gifted artist Ramón Torres Méndez; and the illustrations to the labours of the Geographical Commission established in 1850, under the supervision of the geographer and artist Agostino Codazzi (1793–1859). After exploring every nook and cranny of Colombia, the Commission illustrated its panoramic descriptions with a remarkable album of more than 152 drawings.

Two mulatto painters dominated the artistic scene in Peru. The best-known examples of the work of José Gil de Castro (1788–1835), 'el Mulato Gil', who actually did most of his painting in Chile, are his official portraits of the 'Liberators' Bolívar, San Martín (see plate section) and O'Higgins. Pancho Fierro, in his paintings, blended popular, anti-academic primitivism with a tendency to caricature, and depicted a society frozen in time – as if forever lost in dreamy nostalgia for its long-gone splendour. In Bolivia, Melchor María Mercado's naive style was somewhat reminiscent of Fierro's.

The most original and 'American' personality, in the period under consideration, was the Bavarian painter Juan Mauricio (Johann Moritz) Rugendas (1802–58). Rugendas had been a friend of Alexander von Humboldt, had taken part in France in the Revolution of 1830, and had then spent more than twenty-five years in the Americas, travelling through Brazil, Mexico, Chile, Peru, Bolivia and Argentina, often dwelling for several years at a stretch in one or the other country. Much of his work, part of which remains unpublished, is a faithful and very precisely rendered image of American realities directly observed, amounting to thousands of paintings in oils or water colours, drawings and engravings (see plate section).

In the River Plate region, several Argentine painters, such as Carlos Morel (1813–54) and Prilidiano Pueyrredón (1823–70), gave masterly renditions of their society; in Uruguay, the same was done by Juan Manuel Blanes (1830–1901), who was gifted, in Castedo's words (1986: 304),

> with flawless professionalism; he assumed the varied functions of a chronicler, in visual form, of the stirring deeds of independence; of a portraitist; and of a painter of mores and customs....With Velasco and Pueyrredón, Blanes is part of the representative trilogy of Spanish-American painting in the nineteenth century.

Castedo refers here to the Mexican artist, José María Velasco (1840–1912), who emerged from somewhat academic beginnings to become one of the great impressionist landscape painters, as evinced by his eight versions of the *Valley of Mexico City*. A few more painters from the end of the nineteenth century who represented impressionism, or showed its influence, should be mentioned here: in Mexico, Joaquín Clausell; in Chile, Juan Francisco González; in Uruguay, Pedro Figari; and in Argentina, Martín Malharro.

LITERATURE

The first three decades of the nineteenth century were marked, politically, by the epic struggle for independence and by the stormy emergence of the young nations; from a literary point of view, this was an age of transition between neo-classicism and romanticism.

The newspapers welcomed social and political satire. Journalism and prose pamphlets were in the ascendant. Prevailing literary themes can be identified as dealing with progress and civilization; philanthropy; morals; the relations between the individual and society, or with nature; pastoral and love scenes in the anacreontic vein; and fables in the highly appreciated tradition of La Fontaine and Samaniego. Horace, Virgil, Ovid, the Spaniard Juan Meléndez Valdés (1754–1817), and Chateaubriand, frequently served as leading models. In various countries, the indigenous world began arousing interest, whence the later *indianista* current: for example, the Peruvian Mariano Melgar (1791–1815), who was executed by a royalist firing squad, owes his

literary reputation to ten poems entitled *Yaravíes*, apparently inspired by Inca oral tradition.

The honour of publishing the first novel of independent Spanish America is traditionally attributed to the Mexican José Joaquín Fernández de Lizardi (1776–1827): *El Periquillo Sarniento* (literally, 'The Mangy Little Parrot', a pun on the name of the book's main character), a work in the picaresque vein with the hero's multiple adventures presented autobiographically (1816–31). The novel's many moral digressions reflect a democratic middle-class ideal based on hard work and effort, values completely alien to the aristocratic social parasites of Mexico's colonial days.

Ecuador's diplomat and political leader José Joaquín de Olmedo (1780–1847), Venezuela's Andrés Bello (see also the section above on intellectual trends), and Cuba's José María de Heredia (1803–69), were the three leading poets in this age.

The reputation of Olmedo, author of nearly one hundred poems, is based mainly on one of these, the ode to *La victoria de Junín o Canto a Bolívar* (*The Victory at Junín, or an Ode to Bolívar*), 1825.

Bello's strictly literary work is not abundant, but his sylvan ode *Alocución a la poesía* (*Address to Poesy*), 1823, in which he invites the poetic muse to quit the Old World for America, and his *A la agricultura de la zona tórrida* (*To Agriculture in the Torrid Zone*), 1826, a descriptive and didactic poem, offer something else besides their intrinsic poetic qualities: they amount to outright declarations of American cultural emancipation from Europe.

Heredia, a supporter of Cuban independence, spent more than fifteen years in exile in the United States and Mexico; he is generally regarded as the main spokesman for Latin American romanticism. Nostalgia and love for his native country run through his poetic work, mostly known for the poems *En el teocalli de Cholula* (*Upon the Aztec Pyramid at Cholula*), and *Niágara* (the latter piece much influenced by Chateaubriand's epilogue to *Atala*).

In Latin America, the age of romanticism lasted more or less from 1830 to 1875; it thus covers several generations and displays a wide variety of trends. Its sources are mainly French and Spanish, but fascination with the grand landscapes of the New World, along with the sense of a strong need to consolidate emancipation and affirm national identity, lend a character of its own to American romanticism.

The romantic movement was truly launched around 1830 by Argentina's Esteban Echeverría (see also the above section on intellectual trends). In 1837, Echeverría published, in his *Rimas* (*Rymes*), a long poem, *La Cautiva*, or *The Captive Woman*. Here he celebrated nature in Argentina, while telling the tale of a couple taken captive by Indians. The freedom of the verse and metre, the juxtaposition of various tones and styles, and the presence of a specifically American vocabulary, all contributed to the text's success. Echeverría's prose work, *El matadero* (*The Slaughterhouse*), discovered only after his death, is of equal significance: the writing of novels in the River Plate region began with this violent protest against the Rosas regime. Major romantic Spanish-American poets who should be mentioned here include: José Mármol (Argentina, 1817–71, *Cantos del peregrino*, or *Pilgrim's Songs; Armonía*, or *Harmony*); José Eusebio Caro (Colombia, 1817–53, *Poesías*); Gregorio Gutiérrez González (Colombia, 1826–72, *Memoria sobre el cultivo del maíz en Antioquia*, or *Memoir on the Farming of Maize in Antioquia*); Juan Antonio Pérez Bonalde (1846–92), *Estrofas*

(*Stanzas*); Julio Zaldumbide (Ecuador, 1833–81); Ricardo José Bustamante (Bolivia, 1821–86, *Hispano-América liberta-da*, or *Spanish America Liberated*); Alejandro Tapia y Rivera (Puerto Rico, 1826–82); Olegario Victor Andrade (Argentina, 1839–82, *Prometeo*).

In Brazil, the first great typically romantic poet was Antonio Gonçalves Dias (1823–64), whose literary career began in 1846 with his *Primeiros cantos* (*First Odes*), in praise of his homeland and the Indians; he also compiled an important dictionary of the Tupi language. Brazilian romantic poetry is dominated by the work of Antonio de Castro Alves (1847–71), author of *As Espumas Fluctuantes* (*The Foaming Waves*), an admirer of Victor Hugo, and an anti-slavery activist.

So-called *gauchesca* literature is closely linked to the spirit of romanticism and concerns at once Uruguay, Argentina, and Brazil; it evokes the world of the gauchos, the rural dwellers of the pampa, crack horsemen, always on the move, tending their cattle. In poetry, this genre in its own right appeared in the second half of the eighteenth century, as a specific narrative form. By the romantic age, the image of the gaucho had tended to become that of a popular hero, the symbol of a natural, wild freedom, a man alone, rebellious, with a touch of the thief, and quick with the knife. Gaucho poetry owed most of its prestige and appeal to a Uruguayan, Antonio Lussich (1848–1928), and to three Argentines, Hilario Ascasubi (1807–75), Estanislao del Campo (1834–80), and José Hernández (1843–86), author of the uncontested masterpiece of the genre, *Martín Fierro* (Part I, 1872; Part II, 1879). A foe to Sarmiento (see the above section on intellectual trends), Hernández explicitly set out to denounce the abuse and discrimination of which the gauchos, unfairly branded as barbarians, were the victims.

Novels in the romantic period were classified by Benito Varela Jácome according to the theme in his 'Evolución de la novela hispanoamericana' ('The Evolution of the Spanish-American Novel') (in Iñigo Madrigal, 1987: 91–134). The following list is based on this approach, but also includes Brazil. Five major trends appear, each illustrated by one or more particularly representative examples. They include:

- The Indian-centred novel: *Cumandá* (1871) by Ecuador's Juan León Mera; *O indio Afonso* (*Afonso the Indian*, 1873) by Brazil's Bernardo Guimarães (1825–84);
- The abolitionist or anti-slavery novel: *Cecilia Valdés* (first part, 1839; final edition, 1882), by Cuba's Cirilo Villaverde (1812–94); *Sab* (1841), by Cuba's Gertrudis Gómez de Avellaneda (1814–73); *A escrava Isaura* (*Isaura the Slave*, 1875), by Bernardo Guimarães;
- The historical or pirate novel: *Enriquillo* (first part, 1874; final edition, 1882), by Santo Domingo's Manuel de Jesús Galván (1834–1910); *O Guaraní* (*The Guarani*, 1857), by Brazil's José de Alencar (1829–77); *Los piratas del Golfo* (The Gulf Pirates, 1869), by Mexico's Vicente Riva Palacio (1832–96);
- The political novel: Amalia (1855), by Argentina's José Mármol (1817–71);
- The sentimental novel: *María* (1867), by Colombia's Jorge Isaacs (1837–95). *María* became a best-seller, running through no fewer than fifty editions before 1900, and is now a classic of the Spanish language and doubtless its best novel of the romantic period.

Peru's Ricardo Palma (1833–1919) enjoys a unique place in the age's narrative literature: a distant heir to the 'Chroniclers of the Indies' in the sixteenth and seventeenth centuries, Palma created his own genre, which he labelled *tradicionismo* ('traditionism'), and described, not without sardonic wit, the greater and lesser travails of the colonial age in his *Tradiciones peruanas* (*Traditions of Peru*, in six series, 1872–83).

Drama, too, from the dawn of the age of independence, became another means by which to express one's national identity and will for cultural emancipation: writers for the theatre drew on the native and colonial past, on the struggles for independence, and on the civil wars. In Argentina, the Rosas dictatorship sparked political drama just as it gave rise to novels and essays. Pretty much everywhere, a popular drama, usually satirizing customs and mores, came into being; in this connection, Cuba's *Teatro Bufo* deserves special mention. In general, Cuba's Gertrudis Gómez de Avellaneda is usually considered to be the outstanding Latin American dramatist of her day. She wrote both historical plays like *El príncipe de Viana* (*The Prince of Viana*), and comedies such as *Errores del corazón* (*Errors of the Heart*).

A realistic trend developed towards 1860, with the discovery of what is conventionally qualified as 'objective reality'. This was based on the depiction of customs, which was traditional, but also showed the impact of positivism in Latin America as well as the influence of four successful and admired European masters: Balzac, Stendhal, Dickens, and Flaubert.

Chile's Alberto Blest Gana (1830–1920) was one of the first Spanish-American realistic novelists. He wrote his *Martín Rivas* (1862), *El ideal de un calavera* (*A Madcap's Ideal*, 1863); *Durante la Reconquista* (*During the Reconquest*, 1897), and other stories. Blest Gana expressed interest in the historical process, in minute studies of social classes and the individual, and in his country's changes as seen through its middle class. The development and decline of liberalism in Chile formed the ideological core of his work.

In Brazil, the novel was dominated by the narrative art of Joaquim Maria Machado de Assis (1839–1908). His *Memórias póstumas de Brás Cubas* (*The Posthumous Memoirs of Bras Cubas*, 1881), *Quincas Borba* (1892), *Dom Casmurro* (1900), and other novels, are noted for their wit, shrewd analysis of detail, discreet eroticism, and such themes as power and money. The technical possibilities of the novel are explored, notably regarding temporal structure and the use of monologues (see plate section).

Debate on Darwinism, along with the popularity in the Americas of the novels of the brothers Goncourt and of Emile Zola, not to mention Zola's own ideas on the experimental novel itself, encouraged the appearance of novels more or less strongly imbued with naturalism. A certain time lag, however, not only regarding Europe, but even among the various Latin American countries themselves, sometimes makes it difficult convincingly to draw too sharp lines between romanticism and realism, and then between realism and naturalism, for the latter two coexisted and often tended to become fused, as in the decade of the 1890s. After all, might not naturalism, whose life was prolonged in Latin America well into the 1920s, be considered a radicalization of realism itself? Naturalist influences may thus be detected in Uruguay's Eduardo Acevedo Díaz (1851–1921), as in Peru's Clorinda Matto de Turner (1852–1909), who pleaded for education for the Indians in her problem novel, *Aves sin nido* (*Nestless Birds*, 1889). With Argentina's Eugenio Cambaceres (1843–89), who belonged to the so-called 'generation of 1880', naturalism took a rough, even sordid and brutal turn, in such novels as *Música sentimental* (*Sentimental Music*), 1884, *En la sangre* (*In the Blood*), 1887, and especially *Sin Rumbo* (*Aimless*), 1885.

Modernism, which chronologically ran parallel with naturalism, proved itself to be Spanish America's most truly original and indeed radically renovating movement. Modernism made an incipient appearance towards 1875 in certain texts by Cuba's José Martí (1853–95) and Mexico's Manuel Gutiérrez Nájera (1859–95), reached its peak between 1888 and 1916, and lasted down to about 1920. Coinciding as it did with Brazilian symbolism, modernism was represented in most Spanish American countries and, through the work of Nicaragua's Rubén Darío (1867–1916), exerted, in turn, a profound influence on the literature of Spain herself – particularly on such writers as Antonio Machado, Juan Ramón Jiménez, and Ramón del Valle-Inclán. The modernist age was one of turbulent cultural and social metamorphosis; the struggle for independence was seen as one that needed to be consolidated by securing ideological and cultural autonomy. R. Gutiérrez Girardot (1983) cites the secularization of society, and the hypersensitivity and intellectualism of urban life, as driving forces in the great change observable by about 1880. Modern middle-class society now recognized the secular value of life on this earth, a life progressing not towards some metaphysical otherworldly dimension but towards an identifiable historical future. To put it differently, large sectors of social and cultural life now finally escaped the hold of religious institutions and symbols. Not that these altogether disappeared: on the contrary, one often notes, in modernist poetry, a sort of sacralization of the profane. Religious symbols and content were used to put across a secular content: thus one spoke of a 'religion' and a 'cult' of art, while poetic imagery was enriched by drawing on religious images and notions even to express love and eroticism. In this regard, the very title of one of the great collections of modernist poetry, Rubén Darío's *Prosas profanas* (*Secular Proses*, 1896 – despite the noun, these are poems), is highly significant (see plate section).

Modernism's notorious cosmopolitanism was no mere flight from reality; on the contrary, it corresponded to the actual reality of the larger Latin American cities themselves, by the end of the nineteenth century. Urban life and the very appearance of the cities had changed profoundly. The small community now gave way to the megalopolis, and the megalopolis in turn spawned new impressions and sensations, which implied a renewed life of the mind, and heightened both the classic opposition between town and country and the intellectualism and hypersensitivity of the artist. The artist now created works within such an urban environment. Nature itself became virtually a mere symbolic dimension, something more like a piece of the Graeco-Roman heritage, unlike the very real American urban spatial dimension in which the artist lived.

During this same period, the artist now became an 'intellectual'. The precarious economic situation of the man of letters now impelled him to find some more or less official employment (often after having sowed his youthful wild oats by shocking the bourgeoisie). The writer became a civil servant or diplomat, and also a philosopher of history, producing works which purported to reflect upon the problems of the present and the future – and this at a very period which was lending itself less and less to a pause for thought and reflection. By so doing, the modernists actively participated in the major process of dignifying literature and

the writer's trade, a prelude which rendered possible the prestige and splendour of Latin American letters in the second half of the twentieth century. We should take note, however, that Latin America owes its most lucid, prophetic, and brilliant reflections on its own future to a writer who eschewed the paths outlined above, but instead spent nearly all his life in exile, and who always combined thought and action, art and political involvement: José Martí (1853–95), poet, thinker, freemason, and freedom fighter, who wrote *Nuestra América* (*Our America*, 1894), only four years before falling in Cuba's war against the Spanish. Unlike other modernists, Martí simultaneously lived out both his literary Utopia and his citizen's Utopia.

One will note at least one common attitude among the wide range of stances taken by modernist writers: theirs was an appetite to know all foreign literatures and absorb every artistic trend, whence a syncretizing form of thought which often played host to very different literary modes. Modernism thus welcomed romanticism, the influence of the French Parnasse, symbolism, impressionism, and even naturalism. In poetry, José Martí's brief and surprising collection, *Ismaelillo* (1882), is usually regarded as heralding the birth of modernism, while Rubén Darío's *Azul* (*Azure*, 1888), which contains sections in prose, along with his *Prosas profanas*, are recognized as emblematic of the movement at its zenith. Indeed, the formal and thematic traits of both these works of Darío are often taken to represent the very identifying characteristics of modernism itself. The whole movement is far too rich and complex, however, to be reduced to even these two writings. Still, Darío's distinguishing traits must be borne in mind: these were a search for intimacy and self knowledge; melancholy and nostalgia; cosmopolitanism and the evocation of exotic worlds; eroticism and mysticism in ambiguous relation to one another; a cult of form and beauty; mythological themes; the sheer music of verse and prose; and a play on simultaneous perceptions. To summarize, through his sensualism and formal refinement, the poet set out to react against materialism and everything vulgar and prosaic in reality. Such traits – or at least a few – also appear in the modernist novel, although the novel, on the whole, is probably much less representative of this general trend in letters (see D. Shaw, 'La novela modernista' ('The Modernist Novel'), in Iñigo Madrigal, 1987: 507–13). In such novels, the hero is typically a post-romantic; he is an intelligent and alienated individual, unsatisfied, wrapped in dreams, and unable to adapt; he is thus a man of lost illusions in search of new values, new ideals. In the context of these writings, women appear more as symbols of ideal beauty, even as virtual goddesses, than as creatures of flesh and blood. Humanity seemed to be split between a grossly materialist common horde, and a small circle of chosen friends, a happy few surrounding the protagonist, sharing in his aesthetic approach, and discoursing with exquisite elegance upon the beautiful and the good.

Taken all in all, Latin America's balance-sheet is an impressive one. Fundamentally, the modernist writers achieved four things:

1 Through these writers, the literature of the Hispanic world broke out of its isolation, and actively entered the main stream of modern letters;
2 These writers gave articulate literary expression to the political and historical legacy of the *Libertadores*, and in so

doing, they contributed to a Latin American continental sense of unity;

3 With their sensitive, tormented outlooks, victims of the tension between their ideals and reality, these writers offered a brilliant example of a certain concept of the writer's trade itself: to wit, the search for form and style, in conscious, craftsman-like labour, to purify the language;

4 These writers opened a new world of sensations to literature in the Spanish language, and by ushering in the reign of creative fantasy, they blazed the trail for all those to come: Borges, García Márquez, Cortázar, and the like.

In addition to the names quoted above (Martí, Darío, Gutiérrez Nájera), one ought to mention a few more important modernist writers, such as the Bolivian-born Argentine Ricardo Jaimes Freyre (1868–1933); Mexico's Salvador Díaz Mirón (1853–1928) and Amado Nervo (1870–1919); Bolivia's José Asunción Silva (1865–96); Uruguay's Julio Herrera y Reissig (1875–1910); Cuba's Julián del Casal (1863–93); and Argentina's Leopoldo Lugones (1874–1938). Active in Brazil were the symbolists João da Cruz e Sousa (1861–98) and Alphonsus de Guimaraens (1870–1921).

BIBLIOGRAPHY

BOSI, A. 1982. *Historia concisa de la literatura brasileña (A Concise History of Brazilian Literature)*. Spanish translation by Marcos Lara. Fondo de Cultura Económica, Mexico City.

CASTEDO, L. (ed.) 1986. 'La arquitectura, siglos XIX y XX' ('Nineteenth- and Twentieth-century Architecture'), and 'Las artes plásticas, siglos XIX y XX' ('The Nineteenth- and Twentieth-century Fine Arts'). In: Bonet Correa (ed.) *Gran enciclopedia de Espāna y América*, GELA, Espasa Calpe/Argantonio, Madrid.

FERRATER MORA, J. (ed.) 1990. *Diccionario de Filosofía*. Alianza Editorial, 7th edn, Madrid.

GUTIERREZ GIRARDOT, R. 1983. *Modernismo*. Montesinos, Barcelona.

GUY, A. 1997. *La Philosophie en Amérique Latine*. Presses Universitaires de France (Que sais-je? series), Paris.

HENRIQUEZ UREÑA, P. (ed.) 1969. *Las corrientes literarias en la América Hispánica (Literary Trends in Spanish America)*. Fondo de Cultura Económica, 3rd edn, Mexico City.

IÑIGO MADRIGAL, L. (ed.) 1987. *Historia de la Literatura hispanoamericana (A History of Spanish American Literature)*, Vol. 2: *Del Neoclasicismo al Modernismo (From Neo-Classicism to Modernism)*. Ediciones Cátedra (Crítica y Estudios Literarios), Madrid.

OVIEDO, J. M. 1997. *Historia de la literatura hispanoamericana (A History of Spanish American Literature)*, Vol. 2: *Del Romanticismo al Modernismo (From Romanticism to Modernism)*. Alianza Editorial (Universidad Textos), Madrid.

RAMA, Á. 1984. *La ciudad letrada (The Literate City)*. Ediciones del Norte, Hanover.

ROMERO, J. L. (ed.) 1984. *Latinoamérica: las ciudades y las ideas (Latin America: Cities and Ideals)*. Siglo Veintiuno, 3rd edn, Mexico City/Madrid/Bogotá.

SHIMOSE, P. 1989. *Historia de la literatura latinoamericana (A History of Latin American Literature)*. Editorial Playor, Madrid.

ZEA, L. 1980. *Pensamiento positivista latinoamericano (Latin American Positivist Thought)*. Biblioteca Ayacucho, 2 vols, Caracas.

8.3

WESTERN ASIA AND ARAB LANDS

Stephen Vernoit

INTELLECTUAL, PHILOSOPHICAL AND ARTISTIC TRENDS

The period from 1789 to 1914 in Western Asia and North Africa was one of considerable transition, largely under the influence of European culture. News of the French Revolution in 1789 had an impact in several Muslim circles and marked the beginning of a greater awareness of European secular thought. During the nineteenth century, European states became increasingly influential in the region through economic expansion and colonization. The French occupied Egypt from 1798 to 1801, colonized Algeria from 1830, Tunisia from 1881, and Morocco from 1912, while the Spanish governed the north of that country. Britain, meanwhile, invaded Egypt in 1882 and then occupied Sudan, and Italy invaded Libya in 1911. The outbreak of the First World War in 1914 had further repercussions, and led to the occupation by British and French forces of other Arab lands in the Middle East.

Throughout the nineteenth century European states opposed the attempts of Muslim rulers to maintain monopolies over trade, and they pressed for the right of their merchants to travel and trade without restrictions. During this period the widespread importation of European manufactures into Western Asia and the Arab lands undermined indigenous craft traditions and the traditional practices of craft guilds. By the late nineteenth century most Muslim rulers had also borrowed heavily from Europe and fallen into debt. In addition, European states intervened to protect the minority Christian communities. Some of these communities had been among the first to assimilate ideas coming from Europe. In Lebanon, for example, the Maronite church had developed close contacts with the Roman Catholic church and was acquainted with some aspects of European culture prior to the nineteenth century.

Many Muslim rulers felt a need to implement European-style reforms. In Istanbul the Ottoman sultan Selim III (r. 1789–1807) tried to carry out military reforms with the help of European officers and technicians, but he met with conservative opposition and was deposed. Mahmud II (r. 1808–39) was also aware of the need to move in this direction, but he waited twenty years before introducing his policies. After destroying the power of the Janissary corps in 1826, he created new military and medical colleges, sent Turkish students to study in Europe, and implemented military and civilian dress reforms based on European norms. Mahmud II also broke with tradition by ordering that his portrait be hung in government offices and military barracks. In 1839, at the start of the reign of Abdülmecid I

(r. 1839–61), a royal decree was issued proclaiming the sultan's intention to reform the mechanism of government itself. This marked the beginning of the so-called *Tanzimat* (reorganization) era. From the mid-nineteenth century the spread of European ideas and values among the Turks was further encouraged by the rise of a new Turkish literature, which differed both in form and content from classical Ottoman writings. French literature, in particular, began to replace the Persian classics as a major source of inspiration and the model for imitation.

The first region of the Arab world where substantial reforms were implemented was Egypt. Muhammad 'Ali (r. 1805–48), a Turk from Macedonia who came to power in Egypt amid the confusion caused by the departure of the French in 1801, was aware that the modernization of the country was imperative. By the massacre of the Mamluks in 1811 and the confiscation of their lands, he destroyed the main obstacle to his policies. He replaced the Mamluks with a modern army, trained by French officers, and created a centralized system of administration and taxation. In the interests of his military policy he opened professional schools, sent Egyptian students to study in Europe, and required them to translate European technical works when they returned. He also established a press to print the translations, and an official newspaper to publish his decrees. The first European teachers in his schools were Italians. The Italian language was then the lingua franca of the Levant and the first European language to be taught to students. Indeed, the first Egyptian students to be sent abroad went to Italy, where they learned the art of printing. Italian, however, was soon replaced by French, and with that language the ideas of French writers became accessible. From 1826 onwards, the Egyptian student missions were sent to France.

The concern to implement reforms also reached Ottoman Tunis, especially during the reign of Ahmad Bey (r. 1837–55). Some members of the ruling group of Turks in Tunis were given a modern training, the core of a new army was formed, and direct administration and taxation were extended. In 1857, under Muhammad Bey (r. 1855–9), a proclamation of reform was issued, and in 1861 a constitution was enacted, the first in the Muslim world. By 1869, however, Tunisia's debts to European banks had become an overriding issue and an international financial commission was created to administer them. This extension of European control was the prelude to the French invasion of Tunisia in 1881.

In Algeria, the French occupation from 1830 had already wrought profound cultural changes, but of a far different nature. Before the French conquest a network of *madrasas* and schools had supported a relatively strong system of education in Algeria. The French occupation, however, led to the seizure of revenues and the destruction of mosques and schools. The traditional education system collapsed, causing a severe cultural dislocation for many Algerian Muslims.

There were also some indigenous religious and cultural movements in Muslim lands that had important consequences. In Arabia the Wahhabis made several attempts from the late eighteenth century to reinstate what they believed was the purity of early Islam. They condemned the cult of saint worship and systematically destroyed tombs. They also believed that mosques should be simple structures without minarets or decoration, and condemned the wearing of jewels, silk and precious metals for personal adornment, along with tobacco, music and the use of rosaries. A Wahhabi incursion in Iraq in 1802 resulted in the sacking of the Shi'a shrine city of Karbala and the destruction of the tomb of Imam Husayn. In 1803 and 1804, the Wahhabis destroyed tombs in Mecca and Medina, and in 1810 Wahhabi forces reached Syria and threatened the city of Damascus. Although the political power of the Wahhabis was suppressed and confined to Najd in Arabia in the years that followed, the influence of their doctrines extended far and wide.

The Wahhabis particularly opposed the influence of the Sufi orders in Muslim lands. These orders were generally housed in a network of buildings endowed by supporters, where the disciples could give themselves up to devotion, meditation and ritual exercises. In the nineteenth century the impact of the Sufi orders was quite profound. Many Ottoman craft guilds, for example, had a holy member of a Sufi order among their patron saints. Moreover, calligraphers often joined Sufi orders, perhaps because in such a milieu there was a greater awareness of the mystical qualities of the Arabic letters. In Iran the Khaksar order tended to attract members of guilds.

The hierarchies within the Sufi orders sometimes had similarities with the hierarchies within the guilds. Among the duties of the heads of guilds were to uphold guild traditions, perform ceremonies, supervise the conduct of guild members and carry out judicial functions. The guilds were guided by an ethic of altruism, and it was through this principle that the activities of a craftsman derived a religious significance. With the rise of monopolistic industries and the greater availability of European goods, however, the traditional practices of the guilds were challenged. The ideals of the guilds were weakened when craft elders ceased to function as intermediaries between craftsmen and merchants, or disappeared entirely when craftsmen were reduced to the status of wage-earning labourers.

One of the most important developments during the nineteenth century was the revival of Arabic culture, especially concerning the use of the Arabic language. Prior to the nineteenth century, traditional modes of patronage by rulers, officials and affluent families were inadequate in most Arab lands because the ruling classes were Turkish, and the language of government was Turkish. In Egypt under Muhammad 'Ali, Turkish was still the language of the ruling elite and it was difficult for Arab writers to win the support of the ruling classes. With the development of Arabic printing presses in the nineteenth century, however, Arab writers started to become more prominent and were also able to earn a livelihood. The development of printing in Arabic, together with the spread of education also encouraged Arab writers to simplify their language to appeal to a wider audience.

Education in the Arab lands was largely confined to primary schools in the early nineteenth century. High schools existed only in the large cities and the subjects taught were mainly restricted to the religious sciences and law. Books were expensive because they were handwritten, and thus only available to an affluent minority. During the eighteenth century, printing with Arabic type in the Middle East was largely in the hands of Syrian and Lebanese Christians; for Muslims the printing of the *Qur'ān* and other religious texts was forbidden. This situation began to change in the nineteenth century when some government-sponsored printing presses were established. Printing with Arabic type began in Egypt in 1822 (apart from the output of the presses of the French occupation), when the first book – an Italian-Arab dictionary by a Syrian Christian, Father Rufa'il Zakhur Rahib (d. 1831) – was printed at the state press of Muhammad 'Ali at Bulaq near Cairo. During the next twenty years, 243 books were printed at the Bulaq press, the majority of them translations. Over half of them were in Turkish, but most of the remainder in Arabic. In Beirut a printing press was established in 1834. Other presses burgeoned in the Middle East from the mid-nineteenth century onwards: at Damascus in 1855, Tunis in 1860, San'a in 1877, Khartoum in 1881, Mecca in 1883, and Medina in 1885. Presses were also established in Turkey and Iran.

Muhammad 'Ali's policy of sending students to Europe encouraged the introduction of foreign influences in Arabic literature. Foremost among the early translators was Rifa'a Rafi' al-Tahtawi (1801–73), the *imam* on the first educational mission to Paris, where he remained from 1826 to 1831. There he learned French and began to translate from it accurately. He read widely in French literature, became acquainted with scientific discoveries and, on his return to Cairo, published his *Rihla*, a description of his stay in Paris, which achieved great fame and was translated into Turkish by 1840. In Cairo he taught French at the Medical School (founded in 1827), and then worked in a military college, translating mathematical and military works into Arabic. In 1835, he was appointed director of a new School of Languages, which was established to train a new generation of teachers, officials and translators. But al-Tahtawi's most important achievement was as a translator. He translated about twenty books on such topics as geography, history, logic, engineering and metallurgy, and encouraged many more, among them histories of the ancient world, the Middle Ages, and France. When Muhammad 'Ali died, however, al-Tahtawi fell from favour. Under 'Abbas I (r. 1849–54), he was sent to open a primary school in Khartoum, where he remained for four years, and in 1851, the School of Languages in Cairo was closed. Nevertheless, when Sa'id (r. 1854–63), came to power, al-Tahtawi was able to return to Cairo and once more directed a school with an office of translation attached to it. When Sa'id was succeeded by Isma'il (r. 1863–79), al-Tahtawi remained in favour and helped to plan a new educational system. Numerous schools were opened in Egypt to encourage literacy, and cultural societies and academies were founded for scholarship.

As Muslim cities expanded during the nineteenth century or in some cases were redeveloped, European notions of urban design and architectural styles were introduced. This not only occurred in lands that were colonized by Europeans but also in those that retained a measure of political independence. Attempts were made to insert new European-style streets and buildings within the old walled cities, or new cities were developed beside the old ones and gradually sapped their vitality. Palaces, government offices, banks and company headquarters were all attracted to the newly developed areas. A large percentage of the population of the new cities or quarters was usually foreign. Around 1850, for example, there were about 3,000 Europeans living in Egypt, but from the 1860s there was a vast influx. By the late 1870s there were nearly 70,000 Europeans there, almost half of whom were Greeks, the remainder being largely Italian and French. At the turn of the century nearly 125,000 Europeans lived in Egypt. By this time Cairo consisted of two distinct communities. To the west was the modern city with European-style buildings, wide boulevards, squares and gardens, while to the east lay the old city, which was still essentially pre-industrial in its way of life.

The urban renewal of Cairo was implemented during the reign of Isma'il by the engineer, administrator and writer 'Ali Pasha Mubarak (1823–93). Medieval buildings were demolished and the European architects who were employed on the new building projects adopted a variety of styles. In 1869, Isma'il opened the Suez Canal in the presence of the Austrian emperor Franz Josef, Empress Eugénie of France, the Crown Prince of Prussia, and famous scientists, writers and artists, among them Henrik Ibsen, Théophile Gautier, Emile Zola and Eugène Fromentin. Isma'il's aim was to present Egypt as part of the civilized world of Europe, rather than as an African or Middle Eastern land. The development of Egypt, however, was soon threatened by debt and near-bankruptcy. Under Tawfiq (r. 1879–92) Western control was tightened, resulting in the British occupation in 1882.

Indigenous forms of music were also undermined by the encounter with European culture. Just as orally-based cultures were threatened by the new prominence of the written or printed word, orally-based forms of music were challenged by notation. The challenge was significant because orally-transmitted music tended to allow for improvization, while notation resulted in an essentially fixed medium. Oral transmission also entailed a prolonged contact between aspiring artists and established practitioners; without that contact an entire musical culture could disappear.

European-style music was introduced in Turkey in the military sphere after the destruction of the Janissary corps in 1826. Mahmud II required a substitute for the traditional Janissary ensembles of reed pipes, trumpets, cymbals and kettledrums and, in 1828, he invited Giuseppe Donizetti (1788–1856), the brother of the Italian opera composer Gaetano Donizetti, to Istanbul to organize a new military band and teach in the new Imperial School of Music. Donizetti was responsible for introducing European notation to Turkish music, although, prior to this, a system of notation had been employed by the Armenian musician Hamparsum Limonicyan (1768–1839), which enabled some Turkish music, mainly of the religious repertory, to be written down.

In Arab lands the encroachment of European musical culture was symbolized by the construction of the Opera House in Cairo in 1869 (destroyed by fire in 1971), and the staging there of Guiseppe Verdi's *Rigoletto* and *Aida*. In Iran, meanwhile, Nasir al-Din Shah (r. 1848–96), employed French musicians to create an imperial military band and

organize musical education. Increasingly, Iranian musicians were attracted by the idea of ensemble music, which led to the development of music with a fixed melodic and rhythmic form.

Indeed, from the mid-nineteenth century most musical traditions were being conspicuously altered. Musical compositions became lighter in character with an emphasis on simple texts and short rhythmic pieces. Folk or popular tunes became more influential. With the introduction of European notation there was a greater emphasis on composed music. The example of European orchestras inspired the use of large ensembles of musicians instead of the small groups of four or five instrumentalists that traditionally accompanied a vocalist. These large ensembles played a range of traditional and European instruments. They also shifted the emphasis from displays of individual virtuosity to collective endeavours, while the idea of a concert performed on a stage altered the intimate relationship between musicians and audience that had previously prevailed.

VISUAL AND REPRESENTATIVE ARTS

Among the visual arts, calligraphy had a high status in Muslim communities because it was associated with the dissemination of the word of God, as manifested in the *Qur'ān*. Calligraphers were employed in copying the *Qur'ān* and *Qur'ānic* phrases, along with a range of other types of manuscripts and inscriptions. In architectural settings, particularly within mosques, the names of God, the Prophet Muhammad and the Orthodox caliphs, along with quotations from the *Qur'ān* and the *Hadith* (Traditions of the Prophet), invoked a recollection of God and the contemplation of the divine.

At the Ottoman court in Istanbul, there was a vibrant calligraphic tradition. Even the sultans Mahmud II and Abdülmecid I were trained in the art, and became skilled practitioners. Ottoman calligraphy was greatly encouraged by the patronage of these and other sultans, and maintained a high level of refinement in Istanbul in the work of Mustafa Rakım (1757–1826), Mustafa İzzet (1801–76) (see plate section), Mehmed Şefik (1819–80), Mehmed Şevki (1829–87), Mehmed Sami (1838–1912), and others. Some of the Ottoman calligraphers trained in Istanbul, worked in Arab lands. In Iran, calligraphy was considered an essential element in the education of a Qajar bureaucrat, along with instruction in Persian literature, Arabic, history and accounting, and a succession of calligraphic masters received patronage at the court in Tehran.

By contrast, painting in Muslim lands tended to have a lower status than calligraphy (except in some Christian communities), but as an artistic medium it gradually became more esteemed during the course of the century, especially as European values were assimilated. The main centres where European styles of oil painting first became influential were in Lebanon and Istanbul.

In Lebanon the close relations with Europe that had developed through missionary education, stimulated the practice of art in European styles. Such Lebanese Christian artists as Moussa Dib (d. 1826), and Kenaan Dib (d. 1873) painted religious scenes and portraits of clergy. A number of young Lebanese studied in the Ottoman military colleges in Istanbul, and some were inspired by the styles of painting that developed there among Turkish soldier-painters. The influence of the latter can be felt around the mid-nineteenth century in the Lebanese 'marine' school of painting. Among the first Lebanese painters to study in Europe were Daoud Corm (1852–1930), and Habib Srour (1860–1938), both of whom studied in Rome; they gained recognition for their portraits and paintings in churches and convents. Khalil Saleeby (1870–1928) studied in Edinburgh and then in Paris under Puvis de Chavannes; he was inspired by impressionism, particularly the work of Auguste Renoir.

At the Ottoman court during the reign of Selim III, the artist Kostantin Kapıdağlı, whose native land was Greece, worked for the sultan and painted his portrait in an innovative manner. As the military colleges in Istanbul began to include drawing and painting in their curricula as a means of training officers to produce topographic and technical drawings for military purposes, European values in painting were gradually assimilated. Drawing lessons were also introduced in the military middle schools and high schools. Among the Turkish students sent to Europe to complete their education were the military painters Ahmed Ali (1841–1907), and Süleyman Seyyid (1842–1913); they travelled to France in 1864, where they attended the Ecole des Beaux-Arts in Paris. Their work consisted largely of oil paintings of landscapes and still-life subjects, but they rarely depicted the human figure.

The opening of the Imperial Academy of Fine Arts in Istanbul in 1883, directed by Osman Hamdi (1842–1910), who had himself previously studied painting in Paris, marked a turning point in the promotion of Western-style painting in Turkey. In his own work Osman Hamdi concentrated on figurative compositions inspired by European orientalist painting, adopting a detailed realistic manner for which he employed photographs to attain accuracy. The Imperial Academy of Fine Arts, which taught painting, sculpture and architecture, based itself on the academic canons of the Ecole des Beaux-Arts in Paris; at first it relied largely on European tutors. By the early twentieth century a Turkish school of orientalist painting was active in Istanbul.

In Iran, artists at the Qajar court were employed to glorify the reign of Fath 'Ali Shah (r. 1797–1834) with numerous portraits of the sovereign, including full-size oil paintings and murals. The foremost court painters active during the reign of Fath 'Ali Shah were Mirza Baba, Mihr 'Ali and 'Abdullah Khan (plate section). In a large wall painting (no longer extant) in the Nigaristan Palace, Tehran, executed by 'Abdullah Khan in 1813, Fath 'Ali Shah was depicted enthroned in state surrounded by 118 life-size figures, including his sons, courtiers, foreign envoys and guards. Other artists at the court worked in painted enamels or 'lacquer' (varnished) painting.

Around the mid-nineteenth century the foremost painter in Iran was Abu'l-Hasan Ghaffari (c.1814–66). One of his achievements was the development of a style of psychological realism in Iranian portraiture. In 1842, he was appointed court painter to Muhammad Shah (r. 1834–48), and from 1846 to 1850, he studied in Italy where he became acquainted with European styles and techniques. On returning to Iran, he became painter laureate (naqqāsh-bāshī), and supervised the illustration of a six-volume Persian translation of the *Arabian Nights* (Tehran, Gulistan Library, inv. no.12367–72). For this monumental task he led a team of thirty-four painters, and executed some of the finest paintings himself. The manuscript has a total of 1,134 pages of paintings with each page containing from two to six miniatures. In 1856, Abu'l-Hasan Ghaffari led his team on another project, a set of seven large oil panels for the Nizamiyya Palace in Tehran (Tehran, Bastan Museum). The subject of this composition was Nasir al-Din Shah enthroned in state surrounded by his sons, courtiers and foreign ambassadors. In 1860, Abu'l-Hasan Ghaffari was given the task of supervising the illustrations in a weekly government newspaper, which was printed by lithography, and he contributed many excellent portraits. The following year he received the title *Sani 'al-Mulk* ('The Painter of the Kingdom').

Qajar painting developed further towards European norms in the work of Muhammad Ghaffari (1848–1940), who was Abu'l-Hasan Ghaffari's nephew.

Muhammad Ghaffari studied painting at Dar al-Funun college in Tehran in the 1870s, and was then appointed court painter. He received the title *Kamal al-Mulk* ('The Perfection of the Kingdom'), and studied in Paris towards the end of the century, where he mastered the use of perspective and light and shade. In 1911 he opened an art school in Tehran, which he directed until 1928.

As in other lands, however, the artistic traditions of Iran did not unconditionally embrace European norms, but retained a certain vitality of their own. There were even some new developments. From the mid-nineteenth century, for example, Shi'a beliefs were expressed in Iran in a new genre of religious paintings, which were executed on canvas or adorned such items as lacquered mirror-cases. Shi'a themes were also an important element in the repertoire of folk or coffeehouse paintings.

The first Arab country to formalize art education by establishing schools for art and architecture was Egypt. Schools were founded in Cairo to promote training, such as the School of Irrigation and Architecture in 1866, and the School of Applied Arts in 1868. The Leonardo da Vinci School of Arts was founded in 1898, by the Italian Society of Dante Alighieri to train assistants for architects, but at its inception most of the students were foreigners. From 1908, however, Egyptian painters and sculptors were able to enroll at the School (later College) of Fine Arts in Cairo, which was opened by Prince Yusuf Kamal. This school was the first institution in Egypt to teach Western-style art to Egyptians. The first director was the French sculptor Guillaume Laplagne, and because of a lack of Egyptian experts in Western norms the first instructors were foreign artists. In 1909, Yusuf Kamal created a trust fund for a new building and scholarships for outstanding students to study abroad. The first students of the school comprised the nucleus of the pioneer generation of modern Egyptian artists, among them the sculptor Mahmud Mukhtar (1891–1934), and the painters Muhammad Naghi (1888–1956), Mahmud Said (1897–1964), and Raghib Ayyad (1892–1980). The first Egyptian artist to be sent to Europe on a scholarship was Mahmud Mukhtar in 1911, who continued his training at the Ecole des Beaux-Arts in Paris.

The first Tunisian artist to follow Western styles of painting, particularly in portraiture, was Ahmed Ben Osman in the late nineteenth century. Western norms were also adopted by the Tunisian artists Hedi Khayachi (1882–1948), and Abdulwahab Jilani (1890–1961). The latter was the first Tunisian artist to join the annual Tunisian Salon that was inaugurated by the French in 1894; he started to exhibit there in 1912. In Algeria there was greater segregation. A native school of arts and crafts was opened by the French at Fort Napoléon in Kabylia in 1867, but when the French created an Ecole des Beaux-Arts in Algiers in 1881, it catered for artists of European origin.

Throughout the nineteenth century many European painters worked in the Middle East and North Africa. In Istanbul such artists as Pierre Guillemet, Amadeo Preziosi and Ivan Aïvasovsky were employed by the Ottoman sultans. Egypt was visited by David Roberts, Eugène Fromentin, Adrien Dauzats, John Varley, Charles Gleyre, William Holman Hunt, Jean-Léon Gérôme and others; some painters, such as John Frederick Lewis, stayed in Cairo for many years. In 1891, the resident European orientalist painters in Egypt held what amounted to the first exhibition of paintings in the country, at the Opera House in Cairo. Among native Egyptians at that time, such work appealed only to a minority of the upper class.

European architectural styles were introduced in most of the major cities. In Istanbul several plans for the redevelopment of the city were commissioned from Europeans, and the Ottoman sultans employed the Armenian Balyan family of architects to design palaces and mosques in a style that incorporated neo-classical elements. Krikor Balyan (d. 1831), who was the first Ottoman architect to train in Europe, studied at the Ecole des Beaux-Arts in Paris and then returned to Istanbul where he designed Mahmud II's Nusretiye Mosque (1826). Krikor's son Garabed Balyan (1800–66), designed in Istanbul the large Dolmabahçe Palace (1853–5) in an overt neo-classical idiom, while the Ortaköy Mosque (1854–5), designed by Garabed with assistance from his son Nikoğos (1826–58), also incorporated neo-classical elements (plate section). By comparison the Hamidiye Mosque (1886), designed by Sarkis Balyan (1831–99), incorporated tall Gothic-style windows. By the early twentieth century there had emerged in Turkey an eclectic style of architecture in which Ottoman features were grafted on to European forms, especially in the buildings designed by Vedat Bey (1873–1942), and Kemalettin Bey (1870–1927), both of whom studied architecture in Europe.

Historicist or revivalist styles in architecture and the arts were quickly adopted in Muslim lands. The use of such styles was generally encouraged at the international exhibitions held in Europe and the United States. It was discovered that revivalist idioms could mask the structure and design of new types of secular building. In Cairo, a revivalist style of architecture was developed in which features deriving largely from the Mamluk era (1250–1517), were applied as a surface veneer to buildings. Mamluk revival features first appeared in Cairo in the design for the Jazira Palace (subsequently the Marriott Hotel) by the Austrian architect Julius Franz (1831–1915), who was engaged for the project by Isma'il in 1863. The most notable example in Cairo, however, was the royal mosque of al-Rifa'i, commissioned in 1869, by the mother of Isma'il, Khushyar Khanum (d. 1885), but not completed until 1912 (plate section). Most of the work was entrusted to the Austrian architect Max Herz (b. 1856), who arrived in Cairo in 1881. Mamluk revivalism also inspired the Italian architect Antoine Lasciac (1856–1946), who was active in Egypt from 1882 to 1936, and chief architect of the khedival palaces from 1907 to 1917; and revivalist structures were built in the Cairene suburb of Heliopolis, founded by the Belgian developer Edouard Empain in 1906. Among the Egyptian architects who came to the fore were Mahmud Fahmi (1856–1925), who designed the Ministry of Waqfs building in Cairo in a revivalist idiom, and his son Mustafa Fahmi (1886–1972), who was educated in Paris and returned to Egypt in 1912. The Mamluk revival style of architecture remained in fashion until the 1920s.

In Algeria under French rule the medina in Algiers was partly destroyed between 1830 and 1870. The French building programme was characterized at first by buildings in a neo-classical style, but this was soon replaced by an official Arab-style architecture. The French also sponsored buildings in Arab styles in Tunisia and Morocco. Some of these were fanciful pastiches, but others attempted to be faithful to what was understood to be the principles of Arab architecture, based upon the enquiries of French scholars. Buildings as diverse as railway stations, markets, law-courts, casinos, schools, post offices and private villas attracted this arabizing treatment.

The spirit of revivalism also affected the manufacture of some types of artefact. In Cairo and Damascus inlaid metalwork, and other items in the style of the Mamluks were produced in the late nineteenth and early twentieth century, often for sale to Europeans. Such revivalist work, whatever the knowledge or outlook of the artist who produced it, tended to reinforce in the political sphere the idea that there were certain styles of art with distinct characteristics that approximated modern national boundaries. Thus, some lacquer items, ceramics and metal wares made in Iran in the late nineteenth century reflected the styles associated with the Safavid era (1501–1732) or even earlier periods. Generally speaking, however, craft production in Iran was characterized by its diversity (plate section).

Among the other items produced in the Middle East, the most profitable were carpets, which satisfied local demands and also served as export commodities. They were woven in court, urban, rural and nomadic settings. Geometric designs predominated in Anatolia and the Caucasus, while in Iran the designs were usually based on floral and medallion motifs. Each of the main carpet-manufacturing centres produced distinctive types. From the late nineteenth century, when Western firms became involved in the manufacture of carpets, synthetic and substitute dyes began to replace the traditional vegetable dyes in the manufacturing process.

The Mamluk revival in art and architecture was stimulated in part by a growing movement to preserve and restore medieval buildings in Cairo in the face of urban renewal projects. Cairo was the first city in the Arab world where the issues of preservation and conservation began to be addressed. As early as 1881, a khedival decree created the Commission for the Preservation of Monuments of Arab Art, the duties of which were to inventory, preserve, repair and draw up plans of buildings, and to preserve fragments and detached objects in a new museum devoted to Arab art. This museum grew to become the Museum of Arab Art (later the Museum of Islamic Art) in Cairo.

LITERATURE

The signing of the *Tanzimat* charter by Abdülmecid I in 1839, shortly after he gained the throne, signalled a new willingness among the Ottomans to modernize society along secular lines. In the decades that followed there was a literary revival in Turkey. Prominent among the pioneers of the new literature were İbrahim Şinasi (1826–71), Ziya Pasha (1825–80), and Namık Kemal (1840–88). These writers expressed their ideas in poetry, plays, novels, historical works and articles, often publishing them in the Turkish newspapers that started to proliferate in the 1860s, both in the Ottoman Empire and Western Europe.

Literature could be used as a vehicle for communicating unfamiliar political concepts. Ahmed Vefik Pasha (1823–91), who was the Ottoman ambassador to Paris (1860), served twice as grand vizier, and was president of the first Ottoman parliament (1876), was also noted for some literary achievements. These included the first serious attempt to write a Turkish dictionary in Turkish (1876), along with translations of Abbé Fénélon's *Télémaque*, of *Gil Blas de Sentillane*, and adaptations of plays by Molière.

However, as Turkish intellectuals were generally excluded from politics and from political thought, they turned to literature or scholarship as an outlet for their talents. Ahmed Midhat (1844–1912), who was a journalist, novelist and historian, played an important role with his works of fiction in developing new tastes and interests among readers still unacquainted with Western literary forms and themes. He also wrote books about history, philosophy, science and other subjects, and by this means gave an idea of contemporary European knowledge to Turkish readers. In the field of poetry, Abdülhak Hamid (1852–1937) introduced new metres and subject matter; Tevfik Fikret (1867–1915) – who suffered at the hands of the Ottoman censors – was a leading experimenter with modern European verse forms; and Mehmed Akif (1873–1936), developed a reputation as the leading poet of pan-Islamist sentiments. In the early twentieth century, however, the Young Turk Revolution and the opening of the second constitutional period (1908–18), made room for a resurgence of political themes in literature.

In Lebanon, Syria and Egypt, meanwhile, there occurred a great revival of Arabic literature after a period of stagnation lasting from the fifteenth to the eighteenth century. In the early nineteenth century traditional forms still predominated in Arabic poetry and prose, although some writers did begin to recognize that a simplification of language and style was needed. The growth of printing in Arabic encouraged this process, as did the translation of European works into Arabic (between 1870 and 1914, about seventy French novels were translated into Arabic in Egypt, and also various novels written in English). Furthermore, from the mid-nineteenth century, the use of Arabic began to replace Turkish for the conduct of Egyptian government affairs.

In Syria and Lebanon, a significant role was played by Arab Christians who had contacts with Europe. There were four influential writers, all of whom were Christian, although one of them – Ahmad Faris al-Shidyaq – became a Muslim. The writings of Nasif al-Yaziji (1800–71) and Ahmad Faris al-Shidyaq (1804–87) were traditional in form and style, but by their brilliant use of the Arabic language they suggested a way forward. One traditional genre that was given a new lease of life was the *maqāmāt* (séances), a fictional form that features two characters, a hero and a narrator. Thus, al-Yaziji's *Majma' al-Bahrayn* (Beirut, 1856) was inspired by the great *Maqāmāt* of al-Hariri (1054–1122). Meanwhile, Marun al-Naqqash (1817–55), pioneered Arabic drama and Butrus al-Bustani (1819–83), devoted much of his energy to reviving knowledge of the Arabic language. He worked on an Arabic dictionary, an Arabic encyclopaedia, and edited periodicals, all of which contributed to the creation of modern Arabic prose, capable of expressing the concepts of modern thought. He believed that Arab culture in the Middle East could revive itself only through knowledge of contemporary European thought and discoveries.

One new literary form that appeared as a result of influence from Europe was drama. The first Arabic play produced in a European style was Marun al-Naqqash's *al-Bakhīl* (*The Mean Man*), which was inspired by Molière's *L'Avare*; it was first performed in the author's home in Beirut in 1847. Throughout the remainder of the nineteenth century, however, Arabic theatre was generally dominated by actor-managers, who themselves wrote or commissioned plays with a specific performance in mind. As such plays were not really regarded as literature, their authors or translators were sometimes not named and most of the texts were not published at the time. The first person to contribute substantially to written drama was al-Tahtawi's pupil Muhammad 'Uthman Jalal (1829–98) who, in addition to his activities in Egyptian government service as a translator, judge and minister, translated and adapted five plays by Molière and three by Racine, and was an important figure for using colloquial Egyptian Arabic.

European-style short stories and novels also began to appear, encouraged by such periodicals as al-Bustani's *al-Janān* (largely managed by his son Salim), published from 1870 to 1886. The novel as we know it today did not exist in classical Arabic literature, the nearest approach to it being popular stories that were transmitted orally. Early attempts at writing novels and short stories in Arabic, therefore, tended to be in rhymed prose.

After the mid-nineteenth century the Arabic literary revival shifted its centre of gravity from Lebanon and Syria to Egypt. Civil war in the 1850s, and the massacre of Christians in Damascus in 1860, curtailed the development of artistic life and many Lebanese and Syrians went to work in Egypt. Some others travelled further still, to Europe and America, in the latter case forming the basis of the *al-mahjar* or émigré school in Arabic literature. The acknowledged leader of the Arabic literary community in the United States was the Lebanese writer and artist Gibran Khalil Gibran (1883–1931).

By the 1860s, Arabic had replaced Turkish as the official state language of Egypt. In the following decade the polemical thought of Jamal al-Din al-Afghani (1838–97), who was in Egypt from 1871 to 1879, began to have an impact. Al-Afghani had only a rudimentary understanding of Arabic and wrote relatively little (his works were written first in Persian and then translated), but his ideas influenced the great Muslim reformer Muhammad 'Abduh (1849–1905). Although 'Abduh was not primarily a man of letters, he became a fine writer of Arabic. He aimed to improve the quality of written Arabic through his writings and by his lectures on Arabic and composition at Dar al-Ulum teachers' college in Cairo, which had opened in 1872, to train Arabic teachers for the state primary and secondary schools.

At the outset the Arabic literary revival was marked by nostalgia. However, the emergence of the press and the impact of current events induced writers to concentrate on the contemporary world. Furthermore, the growth of journalism from the mid-nineteenth century gave a great boost to the development of literature. Short stories found an outlet in journals, and many novels first appeared in serialized form or as special numbers of a periodical. With the spread of literacy and education, prose writers were encouraged to write for a wider circle of readers, who were more concerned with the problems of daily life than with the past. Although the literary form of the *maqāmāt* and its ornate style influenced various nineteenth-century Arab writers, in the long run the incongruity of this style became apparent. In an era of increasing Western influence and technological advance, Arab writers realized that a simpler style might have literary merits of its own.

By the late nineteenth century nationalism was an important theme in Egyptian literature. Although this nationalism could be pan-Arab or pan-Islamic in character (the latter displaying loyalty to the Ottoman sultan), it was frequently centred on Egypt. Around this time there developed in Egypt some outstanding neo-classical poets, notably the statesman Mahmud Sami al-Barudi (1839–1904), Ahmad Shawqi (1868–1932), and Hafiz Ibrahim (1871–1932). Shawqi, who became a court poet and commemorated public events and praised rulers, was a spokesman for Egyptian nationalism. Khalil Mutran (1871–1949), who was a Lebanese 'exile' in Egypt, retained some neo-classical features in his poetry but also introduced new elements, which made him a precursor of Arab romantic poetry. The only non-Egyptian poet to achieve much fame outside his own country was the Iraqi Ma'ruf al-Rusafi (1875–1945).

In Arabic poetry throughout the nineteenth century, a continuing interest in the Arab classical tradition far outweighed any literary influences from the West. The writing of blank verse in Arabic did not win much acceptance, although free verse was better appreciated, perhaps because classical Arabic rhymed prose made the idea seem familiar. In 1905, Amin al-Rayhani (1876–1940), experimented with writing prose-poetry in imitation of Walt Whitman. The true pioneer of free verse, however, was the Egyptian poet Ahmad Zaki Abu Shadi (1892–1955), who was deeply interested in English literature.

The first Arab to attain lasting success for writing novels was the prolific Jurji Zaydan (1861–1914), a Lebanese Christian who established himself in Egypt. After writing a romantic story in 1893, he produced no fewer than twenty-one historical romances, most of which retold episodes from Arab history, embellished with the love affairs of imaginary characters. This interest in Arab history was not unrelated to the growth of nationalism in Arab lands. However, the first novel of real merit was *Zaynab* by Muhammad Husayn Haykal (1888–1956), published in Cairo in 1913. This novel described contemporary Egyptian village life in a straightforward style; it was written by Haykal between 1910 and 1911, while he was studying law in Europe.

The Arabic newspapers, magazines and journals that were published in the late nineteenth century brought new knowledge of the outside world to Arabs and were important for changing the style of essay-writing. The best-known magazines and journals, with their dates of foundation, were *al-Muqtataf* (Beirut, 1876; Cairo from 1884 onwards); *al-Hilal* (founded by Jurji Zaydan in Cairo, 1892); *al-Mashriq* (Beirut, 1898), and *al-Diya'* (Cairo, 1898). The great master of essay writing in Egypt was Mustafa Lutfi al-Manfaluti (1876–1924), who wrote in a clear, accessible style.

In the Maghrib the situation was somewhat different. The use of the French language became increasingly necessary among Arabs as a consequence of colonization. In Algeria there was a decline in the knowledge of literary Arabic. French elementary schools were slowly extended from the 1890s onwards (although often against the wishes of the *colons*, who did not want Algerian Muslims to acquire knowledge of French and the ideas expressed in it). However, popular oral poetry continued to be composed in Algeria in Arabic and Berber languages, often in response to the French occupation and the ensuing campaign of pacification. Some of these poems were rendered into French by the ethnographers of the occupation. The fact that there were rich oral traditions in Algeria that could be captured in this way possibly indicates that much of the oral literature of other regions of nineteenth-century North Africa and the Middle East may have since been lost.

Poets in Iran received patronage primarily at the Qajar court. Under Fath 'Ali Shah, there gathered a circle of poets who emulated classical Persian poetry, the most important among them being Saba of Kashan (d. 1822/3). This cultivation of Persian classicism reached a height in the work of Qa'ani (d. 1854). He was, however, also the first Persian poet to have some knowledge of European languages. The task of reforming Persian prose was a concern of Abu'l-Qasim Farahani (1779–1835), the deputy minister of the heir apparent 'Abbas Mirza (d. 1833). With the founding of Dar al-Funun college in Tehran in 1851, there was a demand for the translation of books from European languages, which was achieved through the efforts of a team of translators. In the late nineteenth century, Persian poetry began to be written with a greater political content, and the first steps were taken towards the emergence of modern fiction.

On a more popular level, passion plays (*ta'ziya*) that commemorated the martyrdom of the Shi'a imams, particularly the death of Imam Husayn at Karbala in AD 680, were produced in abundance in Iran. At *ta'ziya* performances in the late nineteenth century, Europeans and Sunni Muslims were generally excluded. To accommodate spectators at the performances, buildings known as *takiyya*s were constructed throughout Iran, often paid for by an affluent person as a pious act. While most *takiyya*s accommodated only a few hundred persons, some were able to seat thousands of spectators. The grandest was the royal Takiyya-i Dawlat, a large, circular, brick building situated beside the Gulistan Palace in Tehran; it was in use by the early 1870s. The edifice, demolished in the 1950s, had the form of an amphitheatre and could accommodate about five thousand spectators.

BIBLIOGRAPHY

AL-ASAD, M. 1992. 'The Mosque of Muhammad 'Ali, Cairo'. In: *Muqarnas* 9 (1992), pp. 39–55.
——. 1993. 'The Mosque of al-Rifa'i in Cairo'. In: *Muqarnas* 10 (1993), pp. 108–24.
BANDAI, M. M. (ed.) 1992. *Modern Arabic Literature* (The Cambridge History of Arabic Literature). Cambridge University Press, Cambridge.
——. 1975. *A Critical Introduction to Modern Arabic Poetry*. Cambridge University Press, Cambridge.
——. 1988. *Early Arabic Drama*. Cambridge University Press, Cambridge.
——. 1993. *A Short History of Modern Arabic Literature*. Oxford.
BARILLARI, D.; GODOLI, E. 1996. *Istanbul 1900: Art Nouveau Architecture and Interiors*. New York and Florence.
BEGUIN. F. 1983. *Arabisances: Décor architectural et tracé urbain en Afrique du Nord, 1830–1950*. Paris.
BELHALFAOUI, M. 1973. *La Poésie arabe maghrébine d'expression populaire*. Maspero, Paris.
BOSWORTH, C. E.; HILLENBRAND, C. (eds) 1984. *Qajar Iran: Political, Social and Cultural Change 1800–1925*. Edinburgh.
BROWNE, E. G. 1914. *The Press and Poetry of Modern Persia*. Cambridge University Press, Cambridge.

BRUGMAN, J. 1984. *An Introduction to the History of Modern Arabic Literature in Egypt.* Brill, Leiden.

CACHIA, P. 1990. *An Overview of Modern Arabic Literature.* Edinburgh University Press, Edinburgh.

CANAL, A. 1924. *La Littérature et la presse tunisienne, de l'occupation à 1900.* La Renaissance du livre, Paris.

ÇELIK, Z. 1986. *The Remaking of Istanbul: Portrait of an Ottoman City in the Nineteenth Century.* University of Washington Press, Seattle.

——. 1992. *Displaying the Orient: Architecture of Islam at Nineteenth-Century World's Fairs.* University of California Press, Berkeley, Los Angeles and Oxford.

CHATELAIN, Y. 1937. *La Vie littéraire et intellectuelle en Tunisie, de 1900 à 1937.* Geuthner, Paris.

CHELKOWSKI, P. J. (ed.) 1979. *Ta'ziyeh: Ritual and Drama in Iran.* New York University Press, New York.

——. 1989. 'Narrative Painting and Painting Recitation in Qajar Iran'. In: *Muqarnas* 4, pp. 98–111.

DEJEUX, J. 1982. *La Poésie algérienne de 1830 à nos jours.* Editions Publisud, Paris.

GERSON-KIWI, E. 1963. *The Persian Doctrine of Dastga-Composition: A Phenomenological Study in Musical Modes.* Israel Music Institute, Tel-Aviv.

HANOTEAU, A. 1967. *Poésies populaires de la Kabylie du Jurjura.* Impr. Impériale, Paris.

HAYWOOD, J. A. 1971. *Modern Arabic Literature 1800–1970.* Lund Humphries, London.

HOURANI, A. 1962. *Arabic Thought in the Liberal Age, 1798–1939.* Oxford University Press, Oxford.

ILBERT, R. 1981. *Heliopolis: Le Caire, 1905–1922: Génese d'une ville.* Paris.

——. VOLAIT, M. 1984. 'Neo-Arabic Renaissance in Egypt, 1870–1930'. In: *Mimar* 13 (1984), pp. 26–34.

JAYYUSI, S. K. 1977. *Trends and Movements in Modern Arabic Poetry.* 2 vols. Brill, Leiden.

KHOZAI, M. A. AL-. 1984. *The Development of Early Arabic Drama 1847–1900.* Longman, London.

LONDON, 1989. *Lebanon: The Artist's View: 200 Years of Lebanese Painting.* Exhibition catalogue, British Lebanese Association, Barbican Centre, London.

MOREH, S. 1976. *Modern Arabic Poetry 1830–1970.* Brill, Leiden.

OWEN, R. 1969. 'The Cairo Building Industry and the Building Boom of 1897–1907'. In: *Coloque international sur l'histoire du Caire: Cairo, 1969*, pp. 337–50.

RAGETTE, F. 1974. *Architecture in Lebanon: The Lebanese House during the Eighteenth and Nineteenth Centuries.* Beirut.

RENDA, G.; EROL, T.; TURANI, A.; ÖZSEZGIN, K.; ASLIER, M. 1988. *A History of Turkish Painting.* Seattle and London.

ROBINSON, B. W. 1964. 'The Court Painters of Fath 'Ali Shah'. In: *Eretz Israel*, Vol. 7, pp. 94–105.

——. 1989. 'Qajar Lacquer'. In: *Muqarnas* 6, pp. 131–46.

SAID, E. 1978. *Orientalism.* Routledge and Kegan Paul, New York and London.

SCARCE, J. (eds) 1991. 'The Arts of the Eighteenth to Twentieth Centuries'. In: Avery, P.; Hambly, G.; Melville, C. (eds). *From Nadir Shah to the Islamic Republic.* Cambridge History of Iran, Vol. 7. Cambridge.

SONNECK, O. 1902–4. *Chants arabes du Maghreb. Etude sur le dialecte et la poésie populaire de l'Afrique du Nord.* 3 vols. Paris.

TUGLACI, P. 1990. *The Role of the Balian Family.* Istanbul.

VERNOIT, S. 1997. *Occidentalism: Islamic Art in the Nineteenth Century* (Nasser D. Khalili Collection of Islamic Art: Vol. 23). Azimuth Editions and Oxford University Press, London.

8.4
ASIA

8.4.1
CENTRAL ASIA, SOUTH ASIA, SOUTH EAST ASIA AND CHINA

Stephen Vernoit

INTELLECTUAL, PHILOSOPHICAL AND ARTISTIC TRENDS

The many cultural traditions that flourished in Asia in the nineteenth century were contained within the parameters of the great religious systems that held sway over the continent: Buddhism, Christianity, Confucianism, Daoism, Hinduism, Islam, Jainism, Judaism, Shintoism, Sikhism, Zoroastrianism, and also communities with animist and shamanist practices. While such systems of belief transcended political boundaries, there were in some cases strong spiritual and emotional bonds between a particular faith and the land in which that faith had developed. Adherents of Hinduism, for example, invested the river Ganges with a great religious significance.

Most of these religious systems had originated in Central, Eastern or Southern Asia, but there were three notable exceptions. These were the monotheistic religions of the Middle East – Judaism, Christianity and Islam. Perhaps the most extensive religion in a geographical sense was Islam, which stretched from the western shores of Africa to the island communities of South East Asia; it also continued to win many new adherents. By various means, especially pilgrimage to Mecca, which every Muslim aspired to perform once during a lifetime, Islam was characterized over this wide area by a considerable degree of homogeneity. Christianity had also made some inroads in Asia, in the Philippines under Spanish rule, and in the expanding Russian empire (although there was not much interest in propagating Christianity among Russian officials), while elsewhere various minority Christian communities were supported by Western colonial governments and their missionaries.

In all of these religious systems and the many cultural traditions that derived from them, the role and significance of art was often inseparable from the religious context, in that its meaning largely resided in ritual or liturgical functions. During the nineteenth century, however, this traditional outlook started to come into conflict with a new secular understanding of art that was gaining ground in Western culture.

Two trends, in fact, characterized the development of the arts in much of the Asian continent in the nineteenth century: a continuation or attempted renewal of indigenous traditions, and an assimilation of Western culture as a means of encouraging development. Some intellectuals even adopted from the Western world a new understanding of the historical growth and evolution of national cultures. In this respect the emergence in Asia of educated classes formed by new secular institutions became increasingly important for determining artistic priorities.

Indigenous cultural traditions remained strong in many regions throughout the nineteenth century; such, for example, was the situation in Central Asia. Elsewhere, Western influences had a profound impact. Much depended on the exposure of a specific community to Western values, and the extent to which traditional forms of patronage were undermined. Isolated rural or nomadic communities were, of course, more likely to retain traditional values. Western notions of urban design and architectural styles, on the other hand, were introduced in some of the major cities, particularly those under colonial rule. Urban renewal schemes often entailed the demolition of medieval buildings to create European-style city plans.

Some rulers in Asia were persuaded by the military and technical might of the European powers to embrace Western ideas and aesthetic canons as the trappings of a culture superior to their own. Intellectuals, merchant communities and religious minorities were also attracted in some instances to Western culture and lifestyles. The most extreme breakdown in traditional forms of patronage occurred in those regions that were colonized. Improvements in transport throughout Asia, however, meant that many local economies were exposed to the importation of European manufactures, which had the effect of undermining indigenous craft industries and skills.

In Muslim communities an emerging consciousness of the plight of Islam developed in response to news of the encroachment of the European colonial powers. Thus, although the political power of the Wahhabis was confined to Arabia, the influence of their doctrines extended far and wide. In India, for example, a reform movement was led by Sayyid Ahmad (1786–1831), who established a headquarters in Patna, while his followers founded a mountain retreat at Sittana beyond the Indus, which attracted those Muslims who objected to living under non-Muslim rule. With its emphasis on *jihād*, the Wahhabi movement in India was a constant source of trouble to both British and Hindu rulers.

Muslim culture, however, was also influenced by the Sufi orders, which attracted vast numbers of people throughout the world. Most of the orders were represented in Mecca, from where their tenets were disseminated. Some Sufi orders, such as the Naqshbandiyya, were prepared to confront a ruling power if the need arose, believing in such instances that the reform of government was prerequisite to the reform of society. The Naqshbandiyya, therefore, played an important role in resisting British rule in India and the Russian domination of Central Asia and the Caucasus. Like the Wahhabi movement, the Sufi orders tended to cut across political boundaries. They also sometimes generated their own distinct forms of expression, in literature, art and music.

In South East Asia there was an expansion of Islam as Muslim reformers strove to revitalize and propagate the faith through preaching, education and military conquest. Literacy in Arabic was spread over a wide area as greater numbers of people became acquainted with the *Qur'ān* and with Muslim history and science. The uniqueness of the Muslim faith was stressed, along with its incompatibility with other forms of worship. In this respect Islam often took on the role of the standard-bearer of protest against colonialism. Believing that returned pilgrims from Mecca were causing much of the social unrest, the Dutch tried from the early nineteenth century to hinder the pilgrimage from South East Asia to Mecca, although they did not suppress it altogether. Those pilgrims from South East Asia that remained in Mecca had a profound influence on the spread of Islam in their native lands, through their teachings and writings in Arabic and Malay.

Pilgrimage to sacred sites, of course, was also an important ritual in other religious systems. As with the pilgrimage of Muslims from South East Asia to Mecca, improvements in transport led to greater numbers of people participating in such rites. With the construction of railways in India from the mid-nineteenth century, for example, pilgrimage among Hindus to sacred sites and temples – traditionally the most prominent context for Hindu art – became more popular. Railways enabled pilgrims to travel throughout India with relative ease.

Cultural traditions in all regions were challenged by wars or political and social upheavals. This was particularly the case in China. In the eighteenth century China had been a great imperial power, but during the nineteenth century it suffered a series of defeats at the hands of foreign powers. These defeats threw into stark relief the military weakness of the country. The first Opium War between Britain and China, which ended with the defeat of China and the signing of the Treaty of Nanking (1842), forced the formal opening of China to Western powers. Thereafter Western influences steadily increased in cultural life. The Taiping Rebellion revealed the existence of indigenous hostility against traditional practices – a hostility which manifested itself in the destruction of temples and shrines, whether Buddhist, Confucian or Daoist. During the rebellion over 600 cities were stormed. Meanwhile, growing antagonism between Europe and China in Guangzhou (Canton), led in

1860 to an Anglo-French expedition that occupied Beijing (Peking), and looted and burned the Summer Palace. The resulting treaties of Tianjin (Tientsin) permitted the establishment of diplomatic missions at Beijing, opened more Chinese ports to foreign trade, and laid down regulations for trade with the interior. The treaties marked the apogee of European exploitation of China. At the end of the century China endured yet another major loss at the culmination of the Sino-Japanese War (1894–5). In 1900, attacks against foreigners during the Boxer Rising led to a second occupation of Beijing by European forces and further lootings from the imperial palaces.

In some regions Western colonization led to the imposition of new languages and educational policies. In India under the rule of the British East India Company, for example, Thomas Macaulay (1800–59), the president of the Committee of Public Instruction, put forward in 1835 his 'Minute on Education', which introduced a thoroughly English education system. In Macaulay's words, the new education system would create 'a class of persons, Indian in blood and colour, but English in taste, in opinion, in morals and in intellect'. In Vietnam, most French officials in the late nineteenth century were convinced that to achieve permanent colonial success, Chinese influences, including the traditional writing system, had to be suppressed. Missionaries believed that the Confucian literati were the main obstacle to a Catholic conversion of Vietnam. The elimination of the Chinese language, it was argued, would separate Vietnam from this heritage and neutralize the traditional elite. It was towards this aim that a romanized phonetic script, *quoc ngu*, was introduced. In the Philippines, meanwhile, the Spanish conquest in 1565, followed by American rule from 1898, led to the introduction of Spanish and then English as literary media.

The spread of printing throughout Asia had further cultural consequences. Literary activities were stimulated, usually to the detriment of orally-based cultures, and Western ideas became more accessible. In some areas the introduction of typography was displaced by lithography, the advantages of which were that calligraphic hands could be directly reproduced and publishers avoid expensive investment in founts. Lithography especially favoured those scripts that were difficult to reproduce typographically.

Printing and lithography had a notable impact on cultural life in China and the Indian subcontinent. In Thailand, American missionaries introduced a press and printed Christian tracts in Thai in 1836. The potential of the technology, however, was quickly recognized by the Thai monarchy, which in 1839 printed a royal decree. In 1858 the first Thai official gazette was published by the newly founded government printing press. In Vietnam, where the French instituted printing in the second half of the nineteenth century, the press played a significant role in the formation of the modern Vietnamese language and literature. New literary, philosophical and scientific terms were introduced into the language, which also became more standardized. In the Philippines, the press played an important role in the nationalist opposition to Spanish rule. A number of presses were also in operation in Malaysia by the late nineteenth century, and writings in Malay concerned with Islam became available, imported from Bombay and Mecca. In Indonesia, printing and publishing enterprises were mainly in European or Chinese hands; however, a lithographic press run by Sayyid Oesman produced a large number of Arabic and Malay booklets between 1875 and 1914.

Musical traditions throughout Asia were also modified or transformed as traditional sources of patronage were undermined. In India, for example, patronage for music was traditionally provided by the princely courts or the temples (especially in the south of the country). In central India in the early nineteenth century the musical capital was Lucknow, which attracted musicians from the declining Mughal court. Lucknow continued as a centre for music until the Indian uprising of 1857–8, but after the uprising other princely courts had to provide patronage. As the British Raj generally ignored Indian music, this court patronage served as a lifeline for musical traditions until Indian independence in 1947.

An important development in Chinese court music in the nineteenth century was the acceptance of the 'Peking opera'. Although this opera style was introduced to Beijing as early as 1790, it was scorned at the court as a vulgar form of entertainment until Xianfeng (r. 1851–61) in 1860, invited actors from the city to perform in the palaces in honour of his thirtieth birthday. His experiment was short-lived because he fled from Beijing later that year to escape the Anglo-French army. However, in 1884, the Dowager Empress Cixi again brought in actors from outside the palaces as part of the celebrations for her fiftieth birthday, and this time the practice persisted. As for Western music, it had little real influence in China before the Revolution of 1911.

In South East Asia, meanwhile, traditional music was characterized both at the royal courts and in villages by the use of gong-chime ensembles, but there was a great diversity of musical expression. Although Western music was imported to some areas with colonization, its appeal was mainly limited to a Western-educated elite in urban areas. Nevertheless, Western values and customs did start to affect some South East Asian theatre genres, from the mid-nineteenth century.

The influence of the Western ideologies of historical evolution and nationhood was also felt in Asia. These ideologies were propagated by various means, and especially at the international exhibitions held in Europe and the United States, which commenced with the Great Exhibition in London in 1851. Many countries of the world were encouraged to participate in the exhibitions by displaying artefacts and products. But the exhibitions themselves tended to serve as a forum for Western nations to disseminate their beliefs about the progress of civilization.

The assumption that there were different stages of civilization had appeared in Western thought in the eighteenth century, but it was in the nineteenth century that the idea began to be forcefully expressed. One widely-accepted theory divided the development of civilization into three stages: this approach can be found in the work of the American anthropologist Lewis Morgan who, in *Ancient Society* (1877), referred to the three stages of development as savagery, barbarism and civilization. The study of the first stage, the savage, was considered to be the domain of ethnography. The belief that art could exist at this stage was doubted, so objects were presented in museums with an emphasis on their scientific curiosity and, sometimes, on the level of their skill. The second stage, that of barbarism, which was characterized by tribal life, was believed to have commenced with the invention of pottery, and to have ended with accomplished literary composition, such as that of the Greek Homeric period. The Semitic and Aryan races, meanwhile, had brought the world to the third stage, that of civilization, but this last stage was developed by the Aryan race alone. From the political point of view this stage entailed the coalescence of tribes into nations.

But while the evolution of humankind was known to have occurred over a long period of time, the earlier stages of development – as in the Darwinian evolution of species – were believed to be still present in the world. It was within this evolutionary framework that the various Asian cultures were located either at the stage of savagery or barbarism.

In such theories of evolution there was an implicit understanding that race and nationhood could be defined through art and architecture. This meant that Asian societies found themselves confronted by the need for self-definition. The idea of establishing representative styles of architecture for the nations of the world was first raised as an issue at the Exposition Universelle of 1867 in Paris. Around the main exhibition hall were constructed national pavilions that were designed either by architects from the countries represented, or by European architects on their behalf. The intention was to project the architectural 'essence' of a particular country. In reality, however, indigenous styles of art and architecture were often manipulated by the colonizing nations to reinforce their own hegemony; the British, for example, created an Indo-Saracenic idiom to suit their political ideology in India.

It was also in the context of such notions about historical evolution that the idea of artistic 'progress' on Western lines was propagated throughout the world. The creation of works of art that could be accepted in the Western sense as 'fine' art was encouraged because 'fine' art signified a high level of progress in cultural evolution. However, opinions varied among Western commentators over the extent to which individual Asian nations could master the principles of 'fine' art.

VISUAL AND REPRESENTATIVE ARTS

In India, the growing power of the East India Company was marked by the transformation of Calcutta and Madras from commercial trading enclaves into elegant neo-classical cities. The arrival in Calcutta of Marquis Wellesley as Governor-General (r. 1798–1805), marked the beginning of a profound change in British self-awareness. Conquests in India under Wellesley more than doubled the size of the territories under the control of the East India Company, thereby stamping an imperial dimension on British rule. In architecture this change was symbolized by the erection of Government House in Calcutta in 1803 to the designs of Charles Wyatt (1758–1819); the building was modelled on Kedleston Hall in Derbyshire, England, built in the 1760s to the designs of Robert Adam. Over the years Indian merchants also adopted elements of European styles for their houses in Calcutta, and the cross-fertilization of architectural styles even affected religious architecture.

Some Indian rulers, however, retained a measure of political and economic independence. In Lucknow, the nawabs of Avadh became active patrons of architecture and a new architectural idiom developed as Hindu, Muslim and European elements interacted. While religious buildings in Lucknow tended to continue earlier Mughal traditions of architecture, secular buildings were constructed in a style that freely incorporated European features. For example, the nineteenth-century nawabi palaces in Lucknow, the Chattar Manzil (1803–27), and the Qaisarbagh (1848–50), incorporated a range of neo-classical elements, although the palaces were essentially Indian in execution.

Interaction also occurred in the visual arts as opportunities arose for East India Company employees to become patrons of painting. The result was the emergence of what has been labelled the 'Company style' in Indian painting. Indian artists working in British areas, when encouraged to adapt their style, produced paintings at low prices for European patrons. Such paintings revealed an intimate understanding of Indian life, especially when compared with the work of British artists. From the late eighteenth-century onwards, Indian artists were commissioned by Europeans to paint natural history subjects and depictions of landscapes and customs. In the early nineteenth century, especially after the East India Company occupied Delhi in 1803 and the blind Mughal emperor Shah 'Alam II (r. 1759–1806), was placed under British protection, Indian artists were commissioned to depict architectural monuments. The building most often depicted was the Taj Mahal at Agra, which for Europeans became a popular symbol of the past achievements of Mughal civilization. But the range of subject matter of Company paintings reflected the new European self-confidence in recording all aspects of the known world.

Calligraphy was in little demand among Europeans, even though it was a high form of visual expression in India. At Lucknow and other Muslim courts, however, calligraphers remained in high esteem and were among the principal recipients of royal patronage. Various other arts practised in the Indian subcontinent managed to retain some vitality. They included the manufacture of carpets, cottons, embroidery, metalwork, enamelling, jewellery, pottery, and items carved of stone, wood, ivory, horn and tortoiseshell. Carved stone and wood also had some significant architectural uses.

The architectural styles introduced by the East India Company in Calcutta and other cities quickly spread through the Indian states. Large neo-classical British residences were built at Hyderabad, Lucknow and Mysore. A neo-classical Town Hall in Bombay was designed by Thomas Cowper (1781–1825), and at Murshidabad a new palace for the nawab designed by Duncan Macleod (1780–1856) in 1837 was based on Government House in Calcutta. The British also constructed churches in India, the prototype for many being the church of St Martin-in-the-Fields in London. Some churches contained examples of funerary sculpture, which was shipped out from London. The principles of Victorian Gothic Revival architecture inspired the design for the Afghan Memorial Church (1847–58), at Colaba in Bombay. For their houses the British adopted the bungalow, an indigenous form from Bengal, embellished it with masonry, tiles, arcaded verandahs and louvered screens, and exported the form throughout the world.

In the second half of the nineteenth century the British promoted Gothic Revival architecture in India. The style was particularly prominent in Bombay, especially after Frederick Stevens (1847–1900), designed the Victoria Terminus railway station (1878–87), and the Municipal Buildings (1888–93). For the latter building, however, the Gothic Revival style mingled with the Indo-Saracenic idiom, which was considered by the British as a style that was particularly appropriate for use by the Raj. It was, in effect, a self-conscious idiom that blended Hindu, Muslim and European styles in an attempt to symbolize the harmony between the different communities. Many palaces designed in the late nineteenth century in the princely states were in the Indo-Saracenic idiom. An influential exponent of the style was Samuel Swinton Jacob (1841–1917), who worked in Ajmer, Jaipur and Rajasthan.

The designs of Indian temples and mosques, however, tended not to be affected by the Gothic Revival or Indo-Saracenic styles. This was largely because after the Indian uprising of 1857–8, the British sought to enhance any semblance of independent legitimacy that the Indian princes might possess. But as many of the princes, for a variety of reasons, chose to adopt British social habits, there occurred a corresponding change in the designs of their palaces and the manner in which they were furnished.

Art education was also encouraged by British officials, from the mid-nineteenth century onwards. In Madras in 1850, a private school of art was founded by a Dr Hunter at his own expense with the aim 'of improving the taste of the native public as regards beauty of form and finish in the articles in daily use among them'. By 1853, this school had been incorporated into a government institution called the School of Industrial Arts. The latter consisted of two departments: the artistic, which taught drawing, and the industrial, which was concerned with metalwork, jewellery, woodwork, textiles and pottery. In 1854, another School of Industrial Arts, organized on similar lines, was founded in Calcutta. In 1857, the Sir Jamsetjee Jeejeebhoy School of Art opened in Bombay, and in 1872, a fourth institution, the Mayo School of Arts, was founded in Lahore. Despite British government support for these schools of art, however, their results were soon thought to be disappointing. This outcome was perhaps not surprising in view of the fact that the four schools of art were not located in traditional centres of art in India, where they would benefit from local expertise, but in the principal cities of British administration.

The British also began to study and conserve Indian monuments and establish museums. In 1861, the Archaeological Survey of India was founded, and in 1904, the Viceroy Lord Curzon (r. 1898–1905), created a framework of statutory control with the Ancient Monuments Preservation Act. The many museums established in India by British administrators tended to reflect colonial preoccupations. In Lahore, John Lockwood Kipling (1837–1911) – father of the novelist and poet Rudyard Kipling – was both principal of the Mayo School of Arts (from 1875 to 1893), and curator of the Central Museum. Nevertheless, Lockwood Kipling was motivated by artistic rather than commercial interests, and genuinely desired to preserve indigenous traditions. He therefore introduced a new technique of art education, which involved circulating examples of Indian artefacts for use as models. In a sense, he was attempting by this policy to graft a new system of patronage on to the old.

From the late nineteenth century some Indian artists began to be inspired by the Western concept of 'fine' art. Ravi Varma (1848–1906), for example, who was one of the first Indian painters to become popular with the Westernized Indian elite, painted portraits and depicted themes from Indian legends and history. By the early twentieth century the notion of an Indian tradition of 'fine' art was being promoted on an international platform, largely in the context of the paintings produced by Abanindranath Tagore (1871–1951), and his followers in Calcutta.

Compared with many regions of the Indian subcontinent, the arts and architecture of Central Asia tended to escape Western influences – although after the Russian conquests and the building of the Caspian railway, some crafts such as metalworking declined. Since the transcontinental trade across Central Asia had been brought to a standstill by the nineteenth century, many Central Asian towns had lost their economic basis and were now isolated. The richest and most active trading centre in Central Asia was Bukhara, and the wealth of the city and the opportunities it provided for employment tended to attract artisans from throughout the region. Foremost among the urban arts was the production of metalwork, and the urban craftsmen, who were organized in guilds, produced items for both urban and rural populations. It was fortunate in this respect that, despite the Russian presence in the late nineteenth century, many of the old towns of Turkestan remained intact.

In Mongolia and Tibet, the Buddhist monasteries, along with the houses of the nobility, provided markets and employment for artisans. In Tibet there was some specialization of craft production. Thus, silversmiths worked mainly in Shigatse and goldsmiths in Lhasa; it was also generally recognized that the best workers in precious metals in Tibet were Newaris from Nepal. In eastern Tibet until recent times Derge was the foremost metalworking centre. Large Buddhist figures were made in Mongolia and Tibet by a combination of working methods, the head and hands being cast separately and the body and limbs made from sheet. The parts were then joined by pins or rivets and soldering. The foundries of Dolon-Nor in Mongolia produced bronze and brass bells, figures and religious utensils for all the Buddhist areas of Central Asia; when visited by Huc and Gabet in 1844, they had just produced a huge statue for the Dalai Lama. This statue was cast in sections and packed on six camels for transport to Lhasa, where the sections were soldered together.

Along with metal wares, the manufacture of textiles was important in Central Asia. An outstanding product of Turkestan textile handicrafts was the *ikat*, produced in a great variety of patterns. Like *batik* textiles in Southeast Asia, the method used to dye the *ikat* fabrics was the so-called 'resist' or 'reserve' technique. *Ikats* were used in households and were also popular for male and female clothing. From the late nineteenth century, however, cheap cotton printed fabrics from Russia began to supplant the products of the traditional Turkestan textile workshops, bringing them almost to a standstill.

Ceramics also tended to be manufactured locally in Central Asia, although some upper class households owned porcelain from China. Both local ceramics and Chinese porcelain, however, were increasingly replaced by items manufactured in Russia. Wood was a valuable commodity because it was scarce; it was used occasionally for architectural elements with high-quality carving, such as the doorposts of town houses. The homes of the wealthy might also be adorned with plasterwork.

In China, after the period of creativity in the visual arts during the reign of Qianlong (r. 1736–95), artists, craftsmen and patrons seemed to lose their sense of direction. The Qing court in the nineteenth century was not one of cultural distinction and its patronage often lacked inspiration. Artists and craftsmen found themselves dependent on the market or a particular patron, and there was a general tendency towards repetition or elaboration in their work.

European enthusiasm for Chinese artefacts had by this time also begun to wane, especially as Europe was now producing large amounts of porcelain from its own factories.

While the art of calligraphy remained important in China, the status of painters declined somewhat. They tended to work in a traditional style, which was characterized by heavy brushwork. Ren Bonian (1840–95), who painted bird and flower pictures in ink and colour on paper or silk, derived inspiration from the art of the Ming dynasty (1368–1644). Wu Changshi (1844–1927), developed a style of rich colour and strong calligraphy. More originality in traditional Chinese painting, however, emerged in the twentieth century in the work of Qi Baishi (1863–1957), and Huang Binhong (1864–1955).

The imperial Chinese kilns continued to produce porcelain during the nineteenth century, but did not achieve the standards of earlier times. At first there was a trend towards greater ingenuity and elaboration in the manufacture of items. While some of the wares produced during the reign of Daoguang (r. 1821–50), were of fine quality, there was in general deterioration in both the material and decoration of the porcelain. In 1853, the imperial porcelain industry suffered a blow when the manufacturing centre of Jingdezhen was sacked by the Taiping rebels. But the factory was rebuilt in 1864, during the reign of Tongzhi (r. 1862–74), and there was a gradual revival in the reign of Guangxu (r. 1875–1908). Meanwhile, in various provincial factories, the manufacture of pottery maintained some vigour.

Many precious materials were worked in China, including jade, rhinoceros horn, tortoiseshell, mother-of-pearl, gold, and silver. Ivories were made both for indigenous consumption and foreign export, the latter items coming mainly from Guangzhou (Canton). Likewise, the decoration of export porcelain took place in workshops in Guangzhou. Cloisonné enamelled vessels and carved and painted lacquer were also made for indigenous consumption and export demands, with markets in Europe, Russia and Asia. Along with the art of embroidery, a range of woollen rugs and hangings were manufactured, especially in the northern borderlands of China, and in 1860 a Buddhist priest called He Jiching started a weaving school at Baogu for the poor of Beijing. The chief centre of glass production was Boshan in Shandong, and it was this town that supplied the so-called 'Peking glass'. The technique of painting on glass ('back painting'), probably introduced to China from Europe in the eighteenth century, was popular for still-life subjects and other scenes, some of which were copied from European prints. Most of this work was also probably executed in Guangzhou for export to Europe, especially Britain, where this medium was popular in the early nineteenth century. The Chinese, however, considered such paintings to be vulgar items made for foreigners and no reference to them occurs in Chinese writings on painting.

Under the influence of Cixi, the Dowager Empress of China from 1861 to 1908 (herself an accomplished painter of birds and flowers), there was a short revival of artistic patronage at the court. It was marked by extensive palace building, notably the Summer Palace on the shore of the Beihai to the northwest of Beijing. Another late nineteenth-century building was the Jiniandian or Hall of Annual Prayers, erected near the Altar of Heaven in the southern quarter of Beijing. The revival of many arts under Cixi was in the style of the late eighteenth century, but lacked the delicacy and skill of that earlier period. On porcelain the polychrome overglaze decoration tended to have a heavy appearance. Textiles and costumes were also manufactured (plate section), although their quality could be affected by the use of recently introduced aniline dyes. After the Sino-Japanese War (1894–5) there was more interest in European and European-inspired Japanese techniques.

In Thailand (formerly Siam), after the establishment of Bangkok as the new capital in 1782, Rama I (r. 1782–1809), set about reconstructing the kingdom. He built the original Grand Palace, with the Temple of the Emerald Buddha, courts, council chambers and private residences, and he also constructed the canals around the city for defensive purposes against the Burmese. Later the liberal Rama V (Chulalongkorn) (r. 1868–1910), developed the Dusit area of the city and made changes within the old Grand Palace. Vietnam and Cambodia, meanwhile, had fallen under colonial rule. France's acquisition of Vietnam in stages had the effect of dividing the country into three parts, so that Cochinchina became a French colony in 1867, and Annam and Tonkin were proclaimed French protectorates in 1883. In 1887, the French Union Indochinoise was formed of the protectorates of Annam, Tonkin, Cambodia, Laos and the colony of Cochinchina. While many new cultural ideas arose in these lands, traditional art forms such as lacquer work, painting on silk and wood block printing also continued. In the Philippines under Spanish rule, where Roman Catholicism was responsible for inspiring new forms of art and architecture, colonization had an even more marked impact.

In South East Asia an increasingly strong focus and cultural identity for the region was provided by Islam, although many other customs and practices continued. In mosque architecture, such traditional features as square plans and tiered roofs continued in the nineteenth century, as at the Friday Mosque in Singkarak, Sumatra. Other mosque designs reflected architectural influences coming from India; mosques with domes, for example, were first built in South East Asia in the nineteenth century. One of the earliest mosques of this type was the new Masjid Baiturrachman (1881), in Aceh, with a timber-framed dome; since then the mosque has been given four more domes and two minarets (plate section). Calligraphers and illuminators, meanwhile, found patronage primarily at the royal courts. Manuscripts were usually written on imported European or Chinese paper, using a modified form of Arabic script called *jāwī*. Copies of the *Qur'ān* and other manuscripts were commissioned, some with illuminated frontispieces and colophons, while royal letters provided a further opportunity for scribes to demonstrate their skills.

Textiles, which were items of aesthetic, ritual and economic significance, were central to the cultural life of South East Asia. While garments were traditionally made up of sets of rectangular textiles, the influence of Muslim culture, which required the body to be clothed in public, especially during ceremonies and observances, led to the use of robes, coats, shirts, jackets, trousers and many smaller costume accessories. All of these items demanded tailoring skills. Head cloths of various types were also made, some of which were adorned with calligraphy.

For the decoration of textiles, the batik technique was particularly prominent. Like the *ikat* technique of Central Asia, the batik technique used a dye resist, which was usually wax. It was applied to the cloth to prevent the dye from penetrating the covered areas of the fabric, so that a pattern was created in negative. During the nineteenth century, batik production at first faced competition from the printed cotton industry established by the Dutch in Jakarta. By the mid-nineteenth century, however, the batik art of hand waxing was being replaced by a new method of waxing the cloth with a copper stamp. This revolutionized production, and was the single most important factor in the creation of a batik industry. The cities of the north coast of Java became thriving centres of batik production. Later in the nineteenth century, however, there was a threat from mass-produced European and Japanese cottons, and by the 1890s the Chinese controlled the import of cambric cloth, thus dominating the batik industry.

Some motifs and designs on textiles fell from favour in South East Asia with the spread of Islam, but others began to appear. These included the lion as the symbol of 'Ali, sometimes bearing a flag and often depicted beside the double-bladed sword, Dhu'l-faqar. Another motif was *burāq*, the mythical creature that carried the Prophet Muhammad on his night journey (*mi'rāj*). On certain Acehnese and Malay embroidered hangings were tree motifs influenced by Mughal-Persian designs, as found on prayer carpets and on painted and printed cottons from India. Under reformist Islamic influences, however, there appears to have been a deliberate rejection of scenes with human figures, while arabesque designs increasingly appeared on textiles as well as on objects of metal, wood and stone.

LITERATURE

Throughout Asia in the nineteenth century attempts were made to revitalize or re-establish a range of literary traditions. Languages were adapted to express new ideas and Western literary genres were introduced. In this context the translation of scientific and literary works from European languages had an important impact on Asian literary cultures. Western writings also furnished writers with new patterns and techniques of narration. Thus, in some instances, the writing of prose fiction in Asia passed through several stages of development – historical, romantic, realist and symbolic – in search of a modern form.

As a medium of literary expression in India, the Persian language gradually lost ground to Urdu, which had been gaining in importance since the eighteenth century. Such poets as Ghalib (1797–1869), the last great poet of the Mughal era, composed in both languages. Ghalib was associated with the Delhi court of the Mughal emperor Bahadur Shah II (r. 1837–58), who was exiled to Burma after the Indian uprising. Traditional Persian poetic forms were adapted in Urdu to express new social and ideological concerns, beginning in the work of the poet Altaf Husayn Hali (1837–1914), and continuing in the poetry of Muhammad Iqbal (1877–1938). In the poetry of Iqbal, which he wrote in both Persian and Urdu, a memory of the past achievements of Islam was combined with a plea for reform.

In Shi'a centres in India, especially at Lucknow and Hyderabad in the Deccan, *ta'ziya* dramas were popular. Lucknow was the scene of spectacular performances in which the Nawabs of Avadh participated. Buildings known in India as *imāmbāra*s, where Muharram and other religious events were celebrated, were built to the credit of the rulers. These buildings consisted of one or more halls to accommodate the large assemblies that gathered for the Muharram ceremonies, and were richly decorated and furnished. Several of them were to become tombs for the nawabs of Avadh.

In addition to Persian and Urdu, fine poetry was written in Bengali, the language spoken in Bangladesh, West Bengal, and parts of Assam, Bihar and Orissa. The greatest of all Bengali poets – and one who also achieved fame in the Western world after winning the Nobel Prize for Literature in 1913 – was Rabindranath Tagore (1861–1941). He was also a gifted painter and composer, who set numerous poems to music. The Bengali writer Bankimchandra Chatterji (1838–94), who wrote many novels, essays and short stories, may be considered the first novelist in India. In 1872, he began the journal *Bangadarsana*, in which most of his work appeared in serial form. His work was greatly influenced by British novelists, especially Walter Scott.

The first novel of any importance in Malayalam was O. Cantu Menon's *Indulekha* (1889), a story of the impact of Western ideas on an orthodox family of South Malabar. B. R. Rajam Ayyar (1872–98), was the author of one of the earliest novels in Tamil, *Kamalambal*, the story of a south Indian Brahmin family, published serially between 1893 and 1895. His unfinished novel in English, *True Greatness*, gives an impression of the humour and outlook of his Tamil work.

In lands where Western influences largely failed to penetrate, such as Central Asia, oral literatures retained great vitality. The most highly cultivated form of literature among the Turkic peoples was narrative poetry, both of a heroic and non-heroic nature, and also dramatic ritual poetry. The recitation of narrative poetry was often accompanied with stringed instruments of various types, while other instruments such as the Jew's harp, reed pipe or flute, drum and tambourine were also popular. As the most important factor in the life of the Asiatic nomad was his horse, songs and stories about horses were common. Women usually composed elegiac poetry, while shamans were responsible for spiritual and intellectual poetry.

The impact of Western civilization on Chinese literature began to be felt after the military defeat by Britain in 1841. An advanced foreign language school, the Tongwenguan, was established in 1867, for training Chinese scholars in European languages. This marked the beginning of increased activity in translating Western philosophical, scientific, political and literary writings. Plans were also made to send Chinese students abroad on government scholarships, although such policies initially had mediocre results. Wang Tao (1828–90), who wrote books based on Western sources, achieved fame as an expert on foreign affairs with his *A Record of the Franco-Prussian War* (1872; expanded version 1886). Yan Fu (1853–1921), who studied in England and joined the secretarial staff of the viceroy Zhang Zhidong (1837–1907) at Wuchang, introduced Western philosophy to China. In 1898 he rendered Thomas Huxley's *Evolution and Ethics* into classical Chinese prose; his other translations included Herbert Spencer's *Principles of Sociology*, John Stuart Mill's *On Liberty*, and Montesquieu's *L'Esprit des lois*. Lin Shu (1852–1924), also made available to Chinese readers Western novels and short stories in translation, although he was not personally familiar with any Western language and depended on assistants. In fact, some of his translations of Western texts were based on Japanese translations.

In poetry, Wang Kaiyun (1833–1916), distinguished himself by emulating the works of the great masters.

However, the next generation of poets, although steeped in tradition, was brought into closer contact with the outer world. The first signs of change appeared when a number of scholar-poets, headed by Tan Sitong (1865–98) and Xia Zengyou (1865–1924) launched a movement called 'new poetry'. They introduced new terminology – mostly transliterations of foreign words – into traditional verse and employed references to foreign literature. Among the poets that cultivated new styles, the most successful was Huang Zunxian (1848–1905). A man with a wide range of interests – he was also a scholar, folklorist, reformer and diplomat – his official duties took him to Japan, Britain, France, Malaya and the United States. He felt a need to free Chinese poetry from the conventions of the past and did not specialize in any traditional writing style, such specialization being a practice of poets of his day. In his verse he explored new subject matter and tried to avoid clichés by using a plainer medium. His indignation over the treaties that were signed with foreign nations in the late nineteenth century was expressed in poems lamenting the loss of Port Arthur and Weihaiwei. Similar feelings were expressed in poems describing the burning and looting of Beijing by Western forces during the Boxer Rising in 1900.

In fiction, Wen Kang (nom de plume: Yanbei Xianren) in *Tale of Heroic Men and Women*, originally in fifty-three chapters of which only four have been preserved, struck a new note. A superior novel of the same type was *Three Heroic Knights and Five Righters of Social Wrongs* (1879), of uncertain authorage. To reach a wide audience, the liberal scholar Kang Yuwei (1858–1927) and his pupil Liang Qichao (1873–1929) modified the literary language into a semi-classical prose style that was more satisfactory for expressing Western ideas. Meanwhile, the daily and periodical presses in China provided new opportunities for the serializing of writings. This trend, which rose to great popularity after the Sino-Japanese War, elicited a large number of novels constructed on the model of the picaresque romance. Satirical novels were written by Li Boyuan (1867–1906) and Wu Yuyao (nom de plume: Wofo Shanren) (1867–1910). The great novel written by Liu E (1857–1909), *The Travels of Lao Can*, appeared serially between 1904 and 1907; it is a realistic account, using fictitious names, of the experiences of the author and his contemporaries. Liu E was also a fine poet.

In Burma in the late eighteenth and early nineteenth century there was in literature a general movement towards liberalization, as shown in the appearance of humour and satire. They appeared first in a type of long narrative poem known as *yagan*, and then in dramas called *pya-zat*, which were based on Buddhist, Hindu and other stories. Styles of writing became freer, and many works were composed in a mixed style that combined the rhymes of verse with the cadences of prose. The early plays by U Pon-nya (c.1807–66) and U Kyin U (c.1819–53), were intended for performance before the king and provincial governors. By the 1870s, however, these gave way to plays for more popular audiences, the texts of which could be printed cheaply and in large numbers as a result of the establishment of vernacular printing presses. Such plays marked the beginning of popular literature in Burma, and were only slowly displaced in the early twentieth century by Western-style novels. After 1886, the year in which the monarchy fell from power and Burma became a province of Britain's Indian empire, a sense of national consciousness was increasingly expressed.

Burmese historical writings were written in both verse and prose. From 1829 to 1832, a committee of scholars appointed by King Ba-gyi-daw (r. 1819–37), compiled an official chronicle, named the *Glass Palace Chronicle*, after the palace hall where the scholars met. The work, which was a revised and updated version of the *Great Chronicle* by U Kala (fl. 1714–33), was compiled in thirty-eight sections covering Burmese history to 1821. A continuation of the *Glass Palace Chronicle*, in ten sections, covering the period to 1854, was compiled between 1867 and 1869 by a committee appointed by King Mindon (r. 1853–78). A further continuation up to 1886 was written in 1909 by U Tin of Mandalay.

In Thailand under Rama I (r. 1782–1809), who was himself a poet, traditional literary works were produced and a high standard of prose writing was established. The first prose fiction was written by the court poet Chao Phraya Phra Khlang (Hon). These trends continued during the reign of Rama II (r. 1809–24). The revival and rewriting of Thai classical literature, however, reached a peak during the reign of Rama III (r. 1824–51). Generally speaking, poetry was in a state of transition in Thailand as poets began to venture outside the court and observe life. The court poet Phra Sunthon Wohan (Sunthon Phu) (c.1786–c.1855), the author of the epic-romance *Phra Aphaimani*, wrote verse that retained a common touch. The best known of the mock-epics was *Poor Prince* by Phra Maha Montree Sub (fl. 1809–51). This landmark in Thai classical literature blended royal and popular elements and prepared the way for a more broadly based literature. During the nineteenth century, as the Thai reading public increased, prose writing came to predominate, although poetry, particularly dramatic poetry, remained popular.

Modern Thai prose literature is generally dated from the introduction of printing techniques, journalism and modern education, which resulted from the policies of Rama IV (Mongkut) (r. 1851–68), who opened Thailand to the Western world. The beginning of modern critical prose writing can be dated to 1858, when the Thai government began publishing the *Royal Gazette*, which informed the public about decrees, laws and other news. Non-fictional prose writing also developed through the writing of chronicles. The writing of fiction can be dated to the appearance of the Thai journal *Advice To Young Men* in 1874, which was published by Thais.

In Vietnam prior to the nineteenth century, the Vietnamese language was written in characters derived from Chinese in a system known as *chu nom*. The great period of *chu nom* literature – which in Vietnamese is synonymous with poetry – was in the eighteenth and early nineteenth centuries. Among the poets there were several women of distinction, including Ho Xuan Huong (1768–1839), whose technical ability, humour and celebration of everyday life earned her the title 'queen of *chu nom* poetry'. The Nguyen dynasty (r. 1802–1945), sought to buttress its own legitimacy by reaffirming Confucian precepts. Political and social upheavals, however, led authors to give various responses to the issue of loyalty to the ruler. The upheavals were best reflected in the greatest of all *chu nom* works, *The Tale of Kieu* by Nguyen Du (1765–1820), a 3,254-line epic poem based on a Chinese legend.

During the nineteenth century, *chu nom* in Vietnam gave way to *quoc ngu*, the romanized phonetic script in use today. This script was originally devised by Jesuit missionaries in the seventeenth century and was adopted by the French colonial authorities to encourage a severing of links with China. The introduction of *quoc ngu* also led to a break with Vietnam's past by making dynastic records and ancient literatures inaccessible to a new generation of colonized Vietnamese. Modern Vietnamese literature, therefore, began with the French colonization of the country, despite the fact that Vietnamese culture was already highly sophisticated when the French introduced Western literary concepts and techniques. The great pioneer of *quoc ngu* literature was the Vietnamese writer Truong Vinh Ky (Petrus Ky) (1837–98), who produced works ranging from folk tales and accounts of his own travels to a history of Vietnam. He also translated several works from *chu nom* into *quoc ngu*, thereby making them widely available for the first time.

In Cambodia, which became a French protectorate in 1863 and part of the French *Union Indochinoise* in 1887, there was some resistance to French religious and cultural influences. Literature in Cambodia in the nineteenth century, therefore, consisted largely of traditional-style verse and prose works, along with royal chronicles.

In the Philippines, the Spanish conquest of 1565 led to the introduction of a romanized alphabet and new literary forms. The penetration of Spanish culture in the Philippines was extensive, and the majority of the population was converted to Christianity. Spanish-style romances and Christian dramas were adapted, chiefly by Tagalog poets. The replacement of indigenous belief systems by Christianity, along with the spread of literacy, challenged traditional oral and epic narrative literature. By the nineteenth century, however, most writers were using Spanish, which became the language of Filipino nationalism. An important transitional work was *Florante at Laura*, a narrative poem in 399 quatrains, by Francisco Baltazar, better known as Balagtas (1788–1862). The first printed edition of this work dates from 1861, although it was composed as early as 1838. It is considered a masterpiece of Tagalog literature, breaking new ground in the use of Tagalog as a literary medium. Balagtas used allegory, symbolism and disguised satire to conceal from his censors his dislike of Spanish rule. Theatrical forms were also borrowed from the Spanish. The most famous Philippine novels were *Noli me tángere* (1886) and *El filibusterismo* (1891), both written in Spanish by the Philippine nationalist José Rizal (1861–96), who had studied in Spain. In this respect the contrast between Rizal's and Baltazar's work is instructive. The latter's poem was given a fabulous setting (Albania), and it mixed Spanish phrases into the Tagalog verses to heighten the grandeur of the diction. Rizal's *Noli*, on the other hand, with its contemporary, identifiable setting, was written in Spanish prose enlivened with Tagalog words for realistic, satirical or nationalistic effect. Furthermore, *Florante at Laura* was intended to be recited aloud, while *Noli* was for reading. Shortly after Rizal's death, the first Tagalog novel was serialized in 1899. By that time, however, the Philippines had passed to American rule, with another change of language. Thus, from 1898, to the Second World War, English was introduced as the official medium of instruction.

In Malaysia, both the vocabulary and the grammatical structure of the Malay language were affected by European influences in the fields of science, government and culture. Munshi Abdullah (1796–1854), who was an amanuensis and secretary to Stamford Raffles (1781–1826) in Malacca and Singapore, can be regarded as the first modern Malay author, although his work did not inspire a new literary movement in the nineteenth century. Although Abdullah wrote in a style that was often reminiscent of classical Malay writings, his works were innovative because they valued realism, presented his personal views, criticized assumptions underlying political or social behaviour, and took account of the colonial presence. Abdullah's most famous work was his long and detailed autobiography, the *Hikayat Abdullah*, completed in 1845. The fact that his writings had little influence on Malay literature during the remainder of the nineteenth century was probably because colonization inhibited the development of an indigenous literary culture. A reflection of Abdullah's work, however, can be found in the writings of his son, Muhammad Ibrahim. Novels and short stories in Malay were not written until the 1920s.

Literature in the islands of Indonesia (formerly the Dutch East Indies) entered a somewhat transitional period in the nineteenth century. The Javanese writer Ranggawarsita, although still rooted in the traditions of Javanese culture, was influenced by contact with the West. In the Malay world, the historian Raja Ali Haji (*c.*1808–*c.*1870), who was also acquainted with Arabic, introduced a new note in his *Tuhfat al-Nafis* (*Precious Gift*), begun in 1865, by criticizing the status and value of his traditional sources. A modern attitude, however, is more easily detected in the writings of Munshi Abdullah. In the second half of the nineteenth century the growth of a literary culture was closely linked with an emerging vernacular press, and news stories were sometimes presented in poetic form. The basis of the Indonesian language and its literature were laid when the Christian missions and the government of Dutch India opened Malay schools both in Malay-speaking territories and in areas with no written language of their own. The use of written Malay in these schools, and the adoption of romanized script, resulted in some Europeanization of the traditional language. Further modifications took place in the twentieth century.

BIBLIOGRAPHY

ARCHER, M.; ARCHER, W. G. 1952. *Indian Painting for the British 1770–1880.* Oxford University Press, Oxford.

BALLHATCHET, K.; TAYLOR, D. (eds) 1984. *Changing South Asia: City and Culture.* Hong Kong.

BEURDELEY, M.; RAINDRE, G. 1986. *Qing Porcelain: famille verte, famille rose.* New York.

BIRDWOOD, G. C. M. 1880. *The Industrial Arts of India.* London.

CHADWICK, N. K.; ZHIRMUNSKY, V. 1969. *Oral Epics of Central Asia.* Cambridge University Press, Cambridge.

DAVIES, P. 1985. *Splendours of the Raj: British Architecture in India, 1660–1947.* John Murray, London.

ELMAN, B. 1984. *From Philosophy to Philology: Intellectual and Social Aspects of Change in Late Imperial China.* Cambridge MA.

FORBES WATSON, J. 1866. *Collection of Specimens and Illustrations of the Textile Manufactures of India.* 18 vols. India Museum, London.

——. 1866. *The Textile Manufactures and the Costumes of the People of India.* India Museum, London.

GUHA-THAKURTA, T. 1992. *The Making of a New 'Indian' Art: Artists, Aesthetics and Nationalism in Bengal, c.1850–1920.* Cambridge University Press, Cambridge.

GÜNTHER, R. (ed.) 1973. *Musikkulturen Asiens, Afrikas und Ozeaniens im 19. Jahrhundert.* Gustav Bosse, Regensburg.

HAVELL, E. B. 1910. *Essays on Indian Art, Industry and Education.* Madras.

JASIEWICZ, Z. 1977. 'Traditional Handicrafts of Uzbekistan in the Process of Culture Changes in the Second Half of the Nineteenth and in the Twentieth centuries'. In: *Ethnologia Polona*, Vol. 3.

KALTER, J. 1984. *The Arts and Crafts of Turkestan.* Thames and Hudson, London.

MACKERRAS, C. 1972. *The Rise of the Peking Opera 1770–1870: Social Aspects of the Theatre in Manchu China.* Clarendon Press, Oxford.

——. 1975. *The Chinese Theatre in Modern Times from 1840 to the Present Day.* Thames and Hudson, London.

MAXWELL, R. J. 1990. *Textiles of South East Asia: Tradition, Trade and Transformation.* Australian National Gallery, Melbourne.

METCALF, T. R. 1989. *An Imperial Vision: Indian Architecture and Britain's Raj.* Faber and Faber, London and Boston MA.

MITTER, P. 1977. *Much Maligned Monsters: History of European Reactions to Indian Art.* Clarendon Press, Oxford.

——. 1982. 'Art and Nationalism in India'. In: *History Today*, Vol. 32, pp. 28–34.

MOSCHKOVA, W. G. 1970. *Rugs of the Peoples of Central Asia at the End of the Nineteenth and the Beginning of the Twentieth Century* (in Russian). Tashkent.

PAL, P.; DEHEJIA, V. 1986. *From Merchants to Emperors: British Artists and India, 1757–1930.* London.

SCHUYLER, E. 1876. *Notes of a Journey into Russian Turkistan, Khokand, Bukhara, and Khuldja.* 3rd edn, revised, 2 vols. London.

SHARAR, A. H. 1989. *Lucknow: The Last Phase of an Oriental Culture.* 2nd edn, translated and edited by E. S. Harcourt and F. Hussain. Oxford University Press, Delhi.

SOAME JENYNS, R. 1971. *Later Chinese Porcelain: The Ch'ing Dynasty 1644–1912.* 4th edn. Faber and Faber, London.

STRONGE, S. 1985. *Bidri Ware: Inlaid Metalwork from India.* London.

TEAGUE, K. 1990. *Metalcrafts of Central Asia.* Shire Publications Ltd, Princes Risborough.

U POK NI. 1952. *Konmara Pya Zat: An Example of Popular Burmese Drama in the Nineteenth Century.* Luzac and Company, London.

VERNOIT, S. 1997. *Occidentalism: Islamic Art in the Nineteenth Century.* (Nasser D. Khalili Collection of Islamic Art: Vol. 23). Azimuth Editions and Oxford University Press, London.

WELCH, S. C. 1978. *Room for Wonder: Indian Painting During the British Period, 1760–1880.* National Federation of the Arts, New York.

WESTPHAL-HELLBUSCH, S.; BRUNS, J. 1974. *Metallgefäße aus Buchara.* Publications of the Museum für Völkerkunde, NF 29, Berlin.

<h1>8.4.2</h1>
<h2>JAPAN</h2>

<hr>

<h1>8.4.2.1</h1>
<h2>CULTURAL DEVELOPMENT, LITERATURE AND THE ARTS</h2>

<hr>

Paul A. Akamatsu

The Tokugawa regime seemed to rest on solid foundations at the close of the eighteenth century. For almost two centuries, the emperor had delegated his political authority to the *shōgun* who administered the territory jointly with his vassals, the *daimyō*, overlords who possessed independent fiefs. The *Bakufu* – as the government of the *shōgun* was called – was responsible for decisions concerning the whole of Japan and relations with the outside world. Notwithstanding various dynastic crises, the responsibilities of the Tokugawa were confirmed by imperial mandate and the renewed vows of loyalty of the *daimyō*.

But foreign pressure began to worry Japanese patriots, first among the officers in the service of the fiefs and then among the *Bakufu*'s retainers. In a Japan whose subjects had not travelled overseas since the 1630s and which, since that time, had maintained contact only with China and the Netherlands, the opening to international trade in 1859 was to result in political upheavals and, more especially, an irruption of Western influences for which few minds were prepared.

THE REVERSAL OF IDEAS

The formation of the elite

At the end of the 1780s, which had been marked by a series of famines and natural disasters, the *Bakufu* seemed content merely to reiterate its intention of introducing reforms, and bolder minds were growing impatient with its apathy. Some believed that the *shōgun* should be subordinated to the emperor to a greater degree. When Russian ships appeared off the coasts of Japan's main islands, the more clear-sighted called for the establishment of more effective defence. But the *Bakufu* invariably responded with censure and repression to such suggestions, which were indeed justified, as future events were to demonstrate.

Nonetheless, officers and nobles of the imperial court were undeniably being subjected to more rigorous training than before. The *shōgunal* schools, which took in the sons of officers from the age of eight, forbade any teaching not based on Zhu Xi's neo-Confucianism. Moreover, officers in active service were required to sit exams in order to determine their level of general knowledge, the benchmark being classical Chinese: seventeen sessions were held, at irregular intervals, from 1792 to 1865. The *daimyō* followed the example of the *Bakufu*. True, instruction followed the Zhu Xi doctrine more closely, but the number of schools in the provinces increased and the training received by young officers improved.

Kyoto was not to be left behind. The emperors of the new branch of the dynasty, established since 1789, were also anxious to promote studies. A school, called *Gakushūin* or the Institute of Studies, was set up near the palace for the sons of the nobles serving at court. Courses were actually offered from 1847 onwards, with neo-Confucianism in pride of place. But other currents of Chinese thought were not excluded and, later, courses on Japanese literature were introduced.

Outside the official schools, teachers could profess non-official doctrines such as the neo-Confucianism of Wang Yangming, which was more suited to the critical mind, whereas that of Zhu Xi was designed more to promote respect for the established order. Other schools continued the research work begun in the seventeenth century with the aim of analysing the ancient Chinese texts on the basis of their original meanings, disregarding later commentaries. The study of ancient Japanese works reached its zenith with the works of Motoori Norinaga (1730–1801), whose successors attached ever greater importance to religious and nationalistic traditions. Among the merchant class, increasingly in the countryside, and even in the warrior class, teachings emphasizing rectitude, honesty and good conduct, based on neo-Confucianist doctrines, which accommodated the religious syncretism of the masses, became more and more popular.

The beginnings of Western studies

When the *Bakufu* resigned itself to opening Yokohama and Hakodate, in addition to Nagasaki, to foreigners, it was not entirely ignorant of Western languages and cultures. Starting in the 1720s, a few scholars, whose circle had gradually widened, were authorized to read scientific works from the Netherlands. Siebold, the Bavarian doctor who passed himself off as a Dutchman, managed to stay in Nagasaki from 1824 to 1828, introduced Japanese pupils to medicine, surgery, pharmacology, and natural history.

Accordingly, as events gained speed, more and more efforts were made to update the instruction given to those who were going to be responsible for setting up the new imperial regime. The *Bakufu* had already dispatched officers to Europe to learn languages and disciplines, which were unknown in Japan, in order to be able to teach them to Japan's military cadets.

The opening of minds

In the declaration made by the young Meiji emperor on 6 April 1868, he recommended to his subjects that they should seek all over the world the knowledge required for the establishment of the new state.

Despite the inevitable break with the past, the Meiji government inherited an infrastructure from the *shōgunate* which could be used as a basis for the creation of the educational system required to launch the modernization movement. European languages had pride of place, first of all in private schools, Dutch being followed by English, and then French and German. However, it was the former translation bureau of the *Bakufu*, which trained the first academics.

The new educational institutions

Compulsory education was instituted in 1872, and its six-year duration, as well as the principle of free education, in 1907, at which time there was an attendance rate of 97 per cent.

Tokyo Imperial University was founded in 1886, and four other imperial universities came into being under the Meiji, in Kyoto (1897), Sendai (1907) and Fukuoka (1910). At the same time, private institutions grew up which were destined to become universities too. They included Keiō-gijuku, established in Tokyo by Fukuzawa Yukichi (1835–1901), the former *Bakufu* interpreter; Waseda, also in Tokyo, by Ōkuma Shigenobu (1838–1922), a former officer of the fief of Saga and minister during the initial Meiji years; and, lastly, Dōshisha, in Kyoto, by Niijima Jō (1843–90), a Protestant pastor who had studied theology in the United States. The official status of university was granted to these private institutions in 1919.

With the assistance of other establishments, the new curricula focused on military instruction and technical, scientific and medical research, but without neglecting law, economics and political studies. The teaching of philosophy came into conflict with the concepts acquired through the reading of the Chinese classics. Western philosophies were presented and explained up to the First World War; later on they would become part of the Japanese system of thought.

LITERATURE AND THE ARTS

The old culture

The first half of the nineteenth century can be regarded as the period when literature and the arts blossomed for the second time, under the Tokugawa.

Ōta Nanpo (1749–1823), who served under the *Bakufu* almost until the end of his life, was also one of the scholars who had the greatest influence on his contemporaries. He was a prolific poet who wrote comic and satirical verse in Chinese and Japanese, and he also left behind many scholarly essays. He encouraged Santō Kyōden (1761–1816), who established a model of the popular novel, which was followed for decades. Kyōden's speciality was plots set in the forbidden quarters, and he published ten-page instalments, twice the length usual until then. The illustrations took up a large proportion of the space, and were surrounded by the simple text.

Many other authors adopted a personal approach in works, which were read by an ever wider public. Shikitei Sanba (1776–1822) excelled in the creation of lively scenes set in popular environments, for example, in a public bath house (*Ukiyoburo*, 1809–13), and at the barber's (*Ukiyodoko*, 1813–14). He holds his readers' attention from one episode to the next by increasing the number of instalments, whose publication was sometimes spread over several years. Jippensha Ikku (1765–1831) wrote *Dōchūhiza kurige* (*Shanks' Mare*, 1802–22), a work full of farcical adventures and burlesque dialogues. Alongside these works describing everyday life in realistic settings, but whose comedy often masked mordant satire, were works of the imagination, inspired by classical Japanese and Chinese works. One such example was the parody of *The tale of Genji* (*Genji monogatari*) by Ryūtei Tanehiko (1783–1842), who gave it the title of *Nise Murasaki inaka Genji* (*Bogus Murasaki, Bumpkin Genji*, 1829). He set the plot in the fourteenth century, whereas the model was written at the turn of the tenth century.

The most remarkable novelist of the period was Kyokutei Bakin (1767–1848). He left behind him the monumental story *Nansō Satomi Hakkenden* (*Satomi and the eight dogs*, 1814–42), based on the Chinese novel of the Ming period *Shuihuzhuan*. The story, written in a rather scholarly style, is based on Confucianist ethics, with primary emphasis on loyalty to the sovereign and power wielded on behalf of the weak in order to ensure the triumph of good over evil. Despite the story's rational construction, it is not without supernatural elements, with links being woven from character to character in the course of the transmigration of souls. Bakin gathered friends around him, and some of them were to continue this story-telling genre until the beginning of the Meiji period.

The influence of Tamenaga Shunsui (1790–1843) was also to continue until the end of the nineteenth century. In most cases, his plots were based on triangular and quadrangular love relationships, and his style was much appreciated by his female readers. Demand was such that he could not satisfy it single-handed, and needed to employ a whole team of writers.

A number of these authors of the first half of the nineteenth century, including Shunsui, ran into trouble with *shōgunal* censorship, in particular from the 1840s onwards. Although the change of government did not immediately produce a crop of masterpieces, it did offer reasons to seek new sources of inspiration, and relaxed the tension.

The initial Meiji years

The tradition of both Shunsui and Tanehiko was continued by writers who claimed to be inspired by them. The works were still published in instalments, but, starting in the 1870s, serialized versions began to appear in magazines and newspapers instead of coming out as individual fascicules.

The first innovation was the adoption of an atmosphere, which was intended to be Western. Kanagaki Robun (1829–94) wrote *Seiyō dōchū hizakurige* (*Western Journeys*, 1870–6), a transposition of Ikku's work, which was often clumsy because Robun himself had never left Japan.

The turning point

Translations of Western texts introduced new words, themes and modes of expression. Western works gradually came to be known, in most cases in the form of extracts, summaries and adaptations, almost exclusively translated from English. *On Liberty* by John Stuart Mill could be obtained in 1871, and *The Social Contract* by Jean-Jacques Rousseau in 1882. *Around the World in 80 Days* by Jules Verne was translated from the original French (1878–80).

Tsubouchi Shōyō (1859–1935), who had learned English in his youth, was the first to put forward a theory of the novel, *Shōsetsu Shinzui* (*The Essence of the Novel*, 1885–6), in which he advocated the use of realism to describe society as it was. A younger author, Futabatei Shimei (1864–1909), a translator of Russian who was very close to Shōyō, interpreted realism in a novel as being the 'image of reality', in his *Shōsetsu sōron* (*General Theory of the Novel*), 1886.

Shimei also belonged to the movement that pressed for the unification of the spoken and written languages. His novel *Ukigumo* (*The Drifting Clouds*, 1888–9) is said to be the first literary work in which both narrative and dialogue are written in the same style.

The newspaper *Yomiuri* (1875–) had already been printing news reports, which used the spoken language. The style used for dialogue in the plays and novels of the preceding period was adapted to produce a new literary language, and it kept pace with changes in the spoken language. When *Yomiuri* began to serialize good quality literary works, many more authors began to experiment with new styles. Kōda Rohan (1867–1947) was a devotee of literature and the arts under the Tokugawa, and used a more archaic style. The *Yomiuri* team included Shōyō himself and also Ozaki Kōyō (1867–1903) and Mori Ōgai (1862–1922).

The flowering of literature under the Meiji

At the beginning of the Meiji period, Kōyō gathered a large number of promising authors around him in a circle called *Ken.yūsha* (Friends of the inkstone). Some of them, including Yamada Bimyō (1868–1910), who was one of the theoreticians of the unified language, created their own groups. Kōyō himself tried his hand at this new prose style, with *Tajō takon* (*Much Love, Much Regret*, 1896) in which he narrated the tribulations of a misanthropist who could not come to terms with his fondness for the wife of his only friend.

The *Ken.yūsha* group deserve credit for publishing *Garakuta Bunko* (*Library of Odds and Ends*, 1885–9), the first Japanese journal devoted to literature.

Ōgai and the Shigarami sōshi

Mori Ōgai was responsible for another new development in the world of literature. Born to a family with a medical tradition, he studied in Germany, and worked as a military doctor almost all his life. He had shown a great talent for writing from a very early age, and in Europe he acquired a solid grounding in philosophy. He founded the magazine *Shigarami sōshi* (*The Weir Magazine*, 1889–94), with which to 'hold back the plentiful waters of literary currents', so as to be able to assess their worth. From 1891 to 1892, Ōgai took issue with Shōyō, criticizing the latter's inductive approach to literary criticism and instead advocating deductive criticism. Shōyō replied in the university journal *Waseda Bungaku* (*Waseda Literature*, 1891–), and while acknowledging the need to have an aesthetic standard of reference, preferred to leave the debate open. Ōgai, who had strong leanings towards romanticism, devoted himself to research on aesthetics while *Waseda Bungaku* was to become the standard-bearer of naturalism.

Other journals were breaking new ground in other areas. *Teikoku Bungaku* (*Imperial Literature*, 1895–1921), which brought together lecturers and students of Tokyo Imperial University, set out to acquaint its readers with the literature of the whole world in order to assert the individuality of Japan's own literature, according to one of its founders, Inoue Tetsujirō (1855–1944). It covered symbolism in its very first issue: Maeterlinck and Verhaeren and, later, Ibsen, George Bernard Shaw and Nietzsche.

POETRY

Inoue Tetsujirō also launched a manifesto calling for the invention of a 'new form' of poetry. With two of his friends, he produced an anthology of translations of Western poetry, interspersed with works of their own composition, which were longer than traditional poems and addressed themes not usually dealt with in a lyrical style, such as encouragement to study. Doi Bansui (1871–1952), a collaborator in the *Teikoku Bungaku*, offered the young people of his time poems which came close to the 'new form'.

But poetic inspiration assumed a wide variety of forms. The poet Higuchi Ichiyō (1872–96) remained faithful to the classical style. She praised adolescent love in her prose works, whereas the journal *Myōjō* (*Bright Star*, 1900–8), reproached the 'new form of poetry' with its cultural poverty. Its founder, Yosano Tekkan (1873–1935), who was joined by Hō Akiko (1878–1942) whom he married, launched a manifesto: 'Our poetry is pure love ... We love to read the poetry of the ancients ... Still, our poetry does not imitate their poetry. It is ours ... It is the national poetry of the Meiji'.

NATURALISM

Shimazaki Tōson (1872–1943) had expressed his romanticism in his youth, in particular in the poems, which he published in the journal *Bungakukai* (*The Literary World*, 1893–8), which he had founded with some friends. But the publication of his first prose works now revealed leanings towards naturalism. For example, *Ie* (*Household*, 1910–11), which is partially autobiographical, denounces the repressive patriarchal structure. Tayama Katai (1871–1930), a great admirer of Guy de Maupassant, composed a work with a completely different atmosphere. In *Futon* (*The Quilt*, 1907–8) he tells the story of his own affair with a young pupil, which, while remaining platonic, nevertheless has undercurrents of perversion.

The journal *Waseda Bungaku* put up a stout defence of the naturalist approach. Their literary talent aside, Tōson was reproached with the weakness of his social critique and Katai with traces of romanticism and insufficiently rigorous and objective observation.

The fine arts

At the beginning of the twentieth century, literature and the fine arts began to move together, following the trend that had developed in the West.

During Japan's period of self-isolation some artists had begun to adopt those Western techniques, which had filtered through to them. Thus, for instance, Katsushika Hokusai (1760–1849) and Andō Hiroshige (1797–1858), both of whom produced prints, had begun to take account of perspective and to centre their compositions as Western artists did. Their works naturally attracted attention after the Goncourt brothers and Manet had expressed appreciation of them. As soon as Yokohama was opened up to the outside world Japanese painters converged on it to be taught by Western artists.

Another milestone was the founding the Fine Arts Academy in Tokyo in 1887 (at the same time as the Academy of Music). From then on scholarships enabled young artists to travel to France and Italy to study. Goseda Yoshimatsu (1885–1915) and Kuroda Seiki (1866–1924), who returned from Paris in 1889 and 1893 respectively, passed on new techniques, notably portrait painting and still-lifes painted in the open air. These two painters organized exhibitions at the *Hakubakai* (White Horse Society, 1896–1910) which brought new talents to light, an example being Aoki Shigeru (1882–1911) whose painting *Umi no sachi* (*Gifts of the Sea*, 1901) was the first to show a male nude.

From 1907 onwards the Japanese Ministry of Education organized annual exhibitions with three sections: Western-style paintings, traditional Japanese paintings, and sculpture.

The traditional Japanese paintings attracted much less attention from young artists than those based on Western models. Nonetheless, E. F. Fenollosa (1853–1908), a philosopher who taught at Tokyo Imperial University, appreciated traditional Japanese painting and was able to convey his admiration for it to his pupils, the most enthusiastic of whom, Okakura Tenshin (1862–1913), helped the representatives of the Kano School to preserve the art of painting on silk. He also encouraged experimentation with new forms of expression such as the technique known as *mōrō* (soft), which did away with the continuous line formerly used to border areas of colour, and which was applied by Hishida Shunzō (1874–1911) and Yokoyama Taikan (1868–1958).

A symbiosis between Japanese sensitivity and an appreciation of the achievements of Western art occurred in literary circles where the new aspirations could be freely expressed.

The circle based on the magazine *Shirakaba* (*The White Birch*, 1910–23) had room for both Kishida Ryūsei (1891–1929), who did oil paintings of traditional subjects, and Takamura Kōtarō (1883–1956), a poet and sculptor who was a devotee of Rodin.

The Meiji legacy

Although authors like Ōgai explored avenues opened by their knowledge of Western languages and cultures, they did not relinquish their deeply ingrained Japanese characteristics. Ōgai worked on *Mita Bungaku* (*Literary Mita*, 1910–), the literary organ of Keiōgijuku University, which adopted styles other than naturalism. He also participated in the launching of *Subaru* (*The Pleiades*, 1909–13), the successor of *Myōjō* which had stopped publication as a result of internal dissensions. He published *Gan* (*Wild Goose*, 1911–13) in it. One of his last major novels, it concerns a courtesan who fails in her attempt to seduce a student, and whose fate resembles that of the wild goose which the student accidentally shoots down. But the leading light on *Subaru* was Ishikawa Takuboku (1885–1912), a brilliant, fleeting genius who created classical verse and verse written in the spoken language with equal ease. The same journal published the first works of Tanizaki Jun-ichirō (1886–1965) who was to become one of the greatest novelists of the period from the 1920s to the 1960s.

But the author who made the best transition from the Meiji period to the next was probably Natsume Sōseki (1867–1916). He was a teacher of English who made his debut in *Hototogisu* (*Cuckoo*, 1897–), a journal founded by his friends the poets Masaoka Shiki (1867–1902) and Takahama Kyoshi (1874–1959) who rehabilitated *haiku* poetry. Sōseki's first publication, *Wagahai wa neko de aru* (*I Am a Cat*, 1905–6), made fun of modernist intellectuals. This humorous piece, which was only supposed to be a single episode, was so successful that it continued in serialized form for over eighteen months. After leaving his job as lecturer at Tokyo Imperial University, Sōseki took up a post with the newspaper *Asahi* (1879–) and was put in charge of the literary section. To select his greatest masterpiece from among his novels, from *Sorekara* (*And then*, 1909) up to his last finished work, entitled *Michikusa* (*Grass on the Wayside*, 1915), would be no easy task. He analysed the difficulty of reconciling the aspirations of husband and wife and the ideal of intellectual endeavour with socio-economic interests. He oscillated between reclusive selfishness and deliverance through altruism. Illness meant that he often lived an isolated life, but he kept in contact with his friends, and in particular with the *Shirakaba* team. At the end of his life, he sought peace in meditation so as to 'be at one with the heavens on taking leave of self'.

On the eve of the First World War, Japanese literature had been enriched by the contributions of the authors who have been mentioned here, and by those of many others. The Meiji period heralded a fruitful and innovative future.

BIBLIOGRAPHY

DE BARY, WM. T. (ed.) 1964. *Sources of Japanese Tradition*. Vol. II, pp. 406. Columbia University Press, New York, London.

DORE, R. 1965. *Education in Tokugawa Japan*. 346 pp. University of California Press, Berkeley.

FUJI, J. 1958. *Outline of Japanese History in the Meiji Era*. XIII+544 pp. Ōbunsha, Tokyo.

GONCOURT, E. (ed.) 1891. *Outamaro*. 265 pp. Bibliothèque Charpentier, Paris.

——. 1896. *Hokousaï, Hokousaï*. 326 pp. Bibliothèque Charpentier, Paris.

HIRAKAWA, S. 1989. 'Japan's Turn to the West'. In: *The Cambridge History of Japan*, Vol. V, pp. 432–98. Cambridge University Press, Cambridge, New York.

JANSEN, M. B. 1989. 'Japan in the Early Nineteenth Century'. In: *The Cambridge History of Japan*. Vol. V, pp. 24–136.

KATŌ, S. 1986. *Histoire de la littérature japonaise*. Vol. II, 276 pp. Vol. III, 374 pp. Fayard, Paris.

KIMURA, K. 1957. *Japanese Literature, Manners and Customs in the Meiji Era*. XI+512 pp. Ōbunsha, Tokyo.

KŌSAKA, M. 1958. *Japanese Thought in the Meiji Era*. V+512 pp. Pan-Pacific Press, Tokyo.

LAVELLE, P. 1997. *La pensée japonaise*. 128 pp. Presses Universitaires de France, Paris.

OKAKURA, T. 1906. *The Book of Tea*. 160 pp. New York, Duffield, Tuttle, Tokyo.

——. 1963. *Le Livre du Thé*, 133 pp. [1998, Dervy, Paris, 135 pp.]

OKAZAKI, Y. 1955. *Japanese Literature in the Meija Era*. XIV+673 pp. Ōbunsha, Tokyo.

ŌKUMA, S. 1909. *Fifty Years of New Japan* (translated from the Japanese). 2 vols, XI+646 pp.; VIII+616 pp. Elder and Co., Smith, London.

PIGEOT, J.; TSCHUDIN, J. J. 1983. *La littérature japonaise*. 128 pp. Presses Universitaires de France, Paris.

SHIBUSAWA, K. 1958. *Society in the Meiji Era*. XIII+527 pp. Ōbunsha, Tokyo.

UYENO, N. 1958. *Japanese Art and Crafts in the Meiji Era*. Pan-Pacific Press, XI+223 pp. 162 full-page ills, Tokyo.

8.4.2.2

ARCHITECTURE

Nicolas Fiévé

Since the eighteenth century, the principal changes in Japanese architecture have stemmed from the growth of built-up areas. In the new, ever-expanding towns and cities, storeyed buildings became widespread, the size of gardens decreased and fire prevention measures led to the abandoning of thatched roofs and the building of many plastered storehouses. From the point of view of design, however, architecture hardly changed until the middle of the nineteenth century. The architecture was of wood and was the affair of a single corporation – that of the carpenters – which reproduced the principles established by the ancients. The richly decorated *shoin* style, with its alcoves, raised daises and coffered ceilings, was used for the dwellings of the ruling classes; the *sukiya* style, more modest and delicate, which used less sumptuous materials but with a fine finish, was to be found in the houses of certain merchants and intellectuals, as well as in the buildings set aside for entertainment. The town houses (*machiya*) were built along traditional lines, with earthen floors in one part for the service areas and raised tatami-covered flooring for the living quarters. The heavy roofs of earth and tiles were supported on very stout timbers.

CONTACT WITH THE WEST AND THE FIRST WORK OF EUROPEAN ARCHITECTS

The extraordinary change in architecture which took place during the second half of the nineteenth century was closely linked to the economic and political decisions of the Meiji government, architecture being regarded as an indissociable part of industrialization. The government also insisted that Western architecture should systematically be used for any large public building, so as to present an image of modernity to foreign nations and to make its influence in internal politics still more marked.

Three secondary factors also help to understand the reasons for the exceptionally swift architectural development, which in less than two generations, led to the assimilation of new techniques and to complete freedom of form and style among Japanese architects. First, by the end of the 1860s, half the population of Tokyo had left. The great military families were no longer obliged to live in the city and returned to the provinces; the palaces fell into ruin and many areas could be rebuilt. One of the effects of the resulting *tabula rasa* was new urban development. Second, time and space were brought up to date, in accordance with the ancestral concepts of Far Eastern cultures. The reign of the Emperor Meiji marked the start of a new era and Tokyo became the capital of Japan. The entry into the modern world thus benefited from the vigour of a cultural era with fresh potential. Third, the search for a modern identity took place in a context, which contained no trace of a colonial past. Modern architecture was not associated with the memory of a foreign occupying power. It was, in addition, reserved for the large, public buildings of the industrial age. Dwelling houses were still built along traditional lines and the users did not experience any sudden change in their age-old ways of living in them.

Prior to 1868, a number of factories and shipyards had been built with the help of European technology and from 1860 onwards, the first buildings for Western establishments (consulates, churches, residences for foreigners and commercial buildings) were adopting a neo-colonial style, in wood, with outside verandahs. This trend was to last only a few years.

After the 1870s, ministries, administrative and military buildings, banks, large commercial buildings, stations, schools and hospitals were systematically built with the help of Western technology and design (metal frames and brick or stone walls; 28,000 schools were built with parquet floors and bow sash-windows). At the request of the Japanese authorities, European architects were invited to design 'modern' buildings, the resistance of which to earthquakes and fire was also much appreciated. The British, Germans and French produced an architecture which reflected the eclecticism of the European architecture of the period – a mixture of French or Italian classical styles, Victorian Gothic, Renaissance or baroque.

THE EMANCIPATION OF ARCHITECTURE

The education policy promoted by the government led to the creation in 1877 of a 'Building Department' at the Imperial Industrial College. Here, thanks to the teaching of an Englishman, Josiah Conder (1852–1920), training was given to the first generation of architects who were very soon to master the most advanced techniques of the time. In addition, young graduates were sent abroad to expand their scientific knowledge and knowledge of style. By the end of the nineteenth century, the work of Katayama Otokuma (1853–1917) and Tatsuno Kingo (1854–1919) was reflecting the complete autonomy of modern Japanese architecture.

Katayama was the official architect of the Imperial Office of Building. His extensive works include the Nara Imperial Museum (1894), the Kyoto museum (1895) and the Akasaka Detached Palace (1909), the style of which is reminiscent of the French Second Empire. Tatsuno designed many banks, including the headquarters of the Bank of Japan (1896), the Department of Engineering building at the University of Tokyo (1888), the National Sumo Hall (1909) which could house 13,000 spectators under its vast metal dome, and Tokyo Station (1911–14), the two steel cupolas of which have now disappeared.

THE RETURN TO TRADITION IN PUBLIC ARCHITECTURE AND MODERN INFLUENCE ON PRIVATE DWELLINGS

At the beginning of the twentieth century, Japanese architecture in the modern idiom attained its full maturity and it was no longer necessary to call in Western specialists. After its victories over China and Russia, Japan became an internationally recognized power; the need to assert its power through modern buildings thus became less necessary. There followed a return to tradition and the construction of a number of public buildings such as the Nara Hotel (Tatsuno, 1909), the Industrial Exhibition Pavilion of the Prefecture of Nara (*Naraken bussanchinretsu-jo*) (1902), Nijo Station in Kyoto (1902) and Taisha Station (1924).

These elegant buildings with their wooden structures mingle traditional building techniques with modern spatial composition and decorative features. Soon the same basic principles were to be found in the work of the new generation of architects of the Taisho period (1912–26), who sought to combine traditional and modern trends in the design of private houses. Houses of a remarkable quality were designed at that time, thanks to the outstanding skill of the Japanese carpenters, preservation of the traditional use of space and an ingenious application of the health-promoting concepts of Western architecture. These extremely fine buildings in their turn influenced Western architecture during the years 1920–30.

BIBLIOGRAPHY

FUJIMORI, T. 1993. *Nihon no kindai kenchiku* (Modern Architecture in Japan). 2 vols. Iwanami Shinsho, Tokyo, pp. 308–9; Iwanami Shoten, Tokyo, pp. 257–67.

HATSUDA, T.; OGAWA, M.; FUJIYA, Y. 1992. *Kindai wafū kenchiku* (The Japanese Style of Architecture in the Modern World). Kenchikuwashoku, Tokyo, p. 325.

STEWART, D. B. 1987. *The Making of a Modern Japanese Architecture, 1868 to the Present.* Kodansha International, Tokyo/New York, p. 304.

YOSHIKAWA, S.; MIZUNO, S. (eds) 1990. *Tôkyô eki to Tatsuno Kingo* (Tokyo Station and Tatsuno Kingo). East Japan Railway Company, Tokyo, p. 176.

8.4.3

KOREA

Alain Delissen

INTELLECTUAL, PHILOSOPHICAL AND ARTISTIC TRENDS

The reform of Confucianism and Korean identity

With a cultural and political system fossilized around its literary bureaucrats, and with the country in voluntary isolation, turned towards an idealized China, the vigorous socio-economic changes occurring in eighteenth-century Korea imposed a return to Confucianism with reform as the keynote. As a reaction against a mode of thought preoccupied by abstract metaphysics and ritual order, it was appropriate for the thinkers of the time, many of whom came from the educated elites excluded from power, to return to concern for the people and their well-being.

This is what brought together a series of heterogeneous propositions under the banner of the 'science of the real' (*sirhak*), though it cannot be called a 'school'. In the work of Pak Chiwŏn (1737–1805) and Chŏng Yagyong (1762–1836), the concern for social, historical and geographical surveys resulted in proposals for specific economic and social reforms. It was less a question of declaring a new order than of returning to the original sources of a Confucianism debased by history. There also becomes apparent a wish to distinguish Korea from its Chinese model, strengthened by the major surveys of the state of the kingdom and the nation that were carried out.

Modernity, Chinese mediation and monotheism

Far from being completely cut off from the world, Korean intellectual life added to these resources of its own the influences received from the real China, where there were European missionaries, and gave birth to the 'science of the North' (*pukhak*) or 'of the West' (*sŏhak*). In addition to the scientific and literary material that gradually filtered into mission reports or translations from Beijing, ideas and views about the world, new for the peninsula, made their way across the half-closed borders of the 'hermit kingdom'. Thus the Christian idea of God as a unique, transcendental, celestial being managed, right at the beginning of the nineteenth century, to found an early Catholicism here, to spark off persecution for heterodoxy there, and elsewhere, as in the 'science of the East' (*tonghak*) of Ch'oe Cheu

(1824–64), to merge in a syncretic way with local metaphysical ideas and representations.

Openness, enlightenment and mediation from Japan

Despite its resistance throughout the nineteenth century to entering the diplomatic, commercial and cultural order of a world dominated by the ideas and practices of Western modernity, Korea was forced to open up in 1876. The intellectual revolution, characterized by 'modernity' suddenly received rather than gradually acclimatized and centred on the idea of 'openness' (*kaehwa*) or 'enlightenment' (*kyemong*), brought to the centre of the political and cultural stage a new type of educated elite, who were the heirs of the Korean reformers and acted as local intermediaries for the major intellectual, philosophical and artistic trends of the Western world.

Contrary to the general model, however, and despite the penetration of Christian missions, the greater part of the modernization movement was not accomplished under the pressure of European imperialism, but largely under the iron rule of Japan. Japan was not, therefore, the simple mediator of Western modernity in Korea. In addition to its domination, it offered it above all an initial cultural synthesis (its own) between East and West.

Nationalism and the dilemmas of modernization

With the reforms of 1894, the new ideas about the organization of modern society and government and the need for a productive industrial base as the foundation for independence, finally introduced the idea of the sovereign nation-state into the catalogue of the modernization movement. Korean nationalism, backed up by older formulations of identity, gave elites a programme for national awakening through universal education and the modern media. But their efforts were not enough to counter the thrust of Japanese imperialism, which led to the annexation of the peninsula in 1910. Intellectual life was then faced with the dilemma of either collaborating with Japan to bring about modernization or renouncing modernization in the name of the nation. As the twentieth century began

Marxists were just starting to try to resolve this debate theoretically and in practice.

THE VISUAL ARTS AND THE PERFORMING ARTS

Popular culture, seat of Korean identity

The pluralistic movement of thought that the 'science of the real' constituted had many echoes in the artistic world of the late eighteenth century. The struggle for influence between the elites in power and the elites excluded from power tended to be pitted against the former, who gained legitimacy from their orthodox mastery of Chinese artistic genres, the freer forms of a creative style consequently perceived as 'Korean' by contrast. The multiplication and freeing up of pictorial and musical genres was also echoed, in parallel with the 'social surveys', by the appearance of ordinary people as subjects in art. An example of this is the series of scenes of ordinary urban life painted by Sin Yunbok (1758–1820). In addition, surveys and pictures led to the recording of popular cultural customs and practices, which sources had previously ignored. Peasant music (*nongak*) connected with agricultural work and the agricultural year, the festive moments of village life (masked dances, *t'alch'um*) and the world of itinerant storytellers (epic and comic songs of the *p'ansori*) began to be mentioned and, no doubt as a result, more strictly codified.

Modern art under surveillance

At the other end of the nineteenth century, great changes came to all the circumstances of production of cultural forms and all the social meanings of art. Here, the appearance of new technologies and new media (the first modern newspapers in the 1880s) created new occupations; there, the demands of modernism or nationalism guided creative practices. However, this acceptance of modern Western pictorial and musical forms, which occurred chiefly at the end of the nineteenth century, took place largely under the surveillance of Japan.

The first modern theatre was opened in Seoul in 1908, but its modernity was not able to extend as far as putting on the plays of the new Korean theatre movement, which conveyed a nationalist message. Kept in check by censorship and the police, Korean creative life hesitated between an official modernity emptied of its power of revolt and protest, and fringe activities – those in which a nascent modern Korean art was trying to assert itself, and those which aimed to organize the preservation of the traditional arts in erudite works that formalized them.

East–West: the two landscapes

In fact, the new forms of modern art arrived in Korea only after a considerable lapse of time. It was not until the early years of the twentieth century that modern pictorial and musical works and modern media (e.g. photography) gained a direct foothold in Korea, and so it was only much later, in the course of the twentieth century, after a period of imitation and adaptation, that they became part of the Korean artistic landscape with national practitioners. From that time, two clearly distinct cultural worlds tended to form.

Far from making any attempt to develop a common language, painters either painted 'traditional' pictures in the Chinese style or 'modern' pictures in the Western style. Musical life too was marked by this dichotomy, which is also found in the real landscapes of architecture. In 1870, the regent, who tried to reassert royal authority, undertook the construction of the Kyŏngbok Palace in the purest Chinese style, using vernacular crafts. In 1898, the Myŏndong Cathedral in Seoul did more than set a foreign scene; it provided a symbol of modernity that preceded, at the turn of the century, the appearance of the word and of professional practices in architecture (*kŏnch'uk*), borrowed from Japan.

LITERATURE

The development of Korean literature: towards written Korean

During the eighteenth century, the cultural hierarchies defined by language, in which the culture of the elites written in classical Chinese (*hanmun*) was distinguished from a popular, oral culture in Korean, started to blur and then break up. The at first slow, then accelerated, spread of the Korean alphabet devised in the mid-fifteenth century (called *han'gŭl* in 1909), made it possible to develop a truly Korean literature.

In addition to making it possible to collect the works handed down by oral tradition, this alphabet allowed the emergence of new genres for books that were more and more widely circulated. This was true of the short, sung, poetic genre, the *sijo*, mixing the Korean alphabet and Chinese characters: after Pak Hyogwan's and An Minyŏng's great compilation was published in 1876 (*Kagok wŏllyu*), it stabilized in the form of three strictly syncopated lines, later transformed into symbols of national poetry.

The same was true of personal narratives, memoirs, journals and satirical novels which, like *The Story of a Mandarin* (*Yangban chŏn*) by Pak Chiwŏn (1737–1805), attest to the existence of a 'parallel' literature, freed from Chinese models and deliberately irreverent about established literature and government. It should, however, be noted that this new Korean literature often appeared anonymously. The fact that it owed much to women and banned writers contributed to making it an illegitimate production, unable to give birth to the modern 'author'.

Towards a national modern literature

The socio-political programme of the 'Patriotic Enlightenment' (*aeguk kyemong*) and the imperialist, then colonial, context made the education of the people a central issue of Korea's metamorphosis into a sovereign state. The national written language had to be spread through educational establishments and the new media. Literature drew fully on this modernizing, nationalistic ambition. It now gave writers in the national language the prestige of being authentic authors.

Korean literature in the late nineteenth century was, however, caught in a sort of tension, which formed the basis of its profound renewal. On the one hand, the writers of the time had to 'nationalize' the written language by standardizing it against the dialects, stabilizing spelling and setting it down in a grammar. Pressmen like Sŏ Chaep'il (1866–1951) and his daily *The Independent* (*Tongnip sinmun*, founded in 1896) played an essential role in this respect. On the other hand, works introduced from the West had to be adapted, and this ushered in a metamorphosis of written genres. Matching the strictly linguistic work of translation was a more ambitious, poetic translation of literary forms. The pioneering role of Yi Injik (1862–1916) should be mentioned here. He introduced the 'new theatre' to Korea, as well as the 'new novel' (*sin sosol*) with his *Sea of Blood* (*Hyŏr-ŭi nu*), published in 1907.

Lastly, we should mention the new importance in the institutionalization of literary life assumed at the turn of the century by literary reviews such as *Childhood* (*Sonyŏn*, founded in 1908), often intended for young people. The founding fathers of the new literature, Korean and modern, such as Ch'oe Namsŏn (1890–1957) and Yi Kwangsu (1892–?), published their first poems or prose in these reviews. Heirs of the first attempts at Korean literature in the seventeenth and eighteenth centuries, they made it blossom in the next century, bestowing on the modern *sijo*, for example, its full vitality.

8.5
SUB-SAHARAN AFRICA

Roger Somé

INTRODUCTION: DEFINITION AND HISTORICAL BACKGROUND

Despite scientific developments, technical advances and the considerable accumulation of knowledge in various fields, it is still no easy matter to write a history of Africa south of the Sahara. So it is a challenge to produce an account today of cultural developments, the arts and architecture in this part of Africa from the time of the French Revolution up to the first two decades of colonial occupation.

To view this undertaking as a challenge is to recognize that the way in which knowledge is transmitted in Africa; usually ascribed to the oral tradition, it does not, despite its positive aspects, tally with a particular conception of the preservation of cultural heritage.[1] This observation immediately suggests dividing our subject into two parts: the first on the state of culture, the arts and architecture in Sub-Saharan Africa from 1789 to 1900, that is, in the pre-colonial period; and the other from 1900 to 1914. This division is prompted by the widespread notion of a pre-colonial era marked by Africans' lack of access to Western writing, indeed to all writing, given the ideological refusal to recognize the existence of African writing, in contrast to a post-colonial era in which Africans acquired writing and thus assimilated a feature of Western civilization. It is not particularly relevant, however, as the hypothesis on which it is based is not fully verifiable. In fact, the relations established between Africa and Europe by Portuguese travellers as from the fifteenth century, followed by the introduction of trade, in particular the tragically famous 'triangular trade', led to a considerable mingling of populations, with deportation and subsequent 'export'. Thanks to, or as a result of, this phenomenon, young Africans were educated at the courts of European monarchs and, from the eighteenth century onwards, achieved distinction in letters, science and/or war. This was the case of the Ghanaian philosopher Antoine-Guillaume Amo. who, brought up at the court of the King of Prussia, presented a thesis in 1734, on 'The Impassivity of the Human Mind' at the University of Wittenberg. There was also Abraham Hanibal, who was a mathematician, and from 1758 a general in the Russian army. Although the former is not particularly well known nowadays, the latter has emerged from obscurity because of his great-grandson, Pushkin, and the recent publication of his biography (*Dieudonné Gnammankou*, 1996).

These two examples, which belong to an age preceding the one under consideration, belie the widespread notion referred to above, thus inviting us to adopt a thematic approach, and illustrate the difficulty of demonstrating cultural evolution in Sub-Saharan Africa from 1789. A fully comprehensive account of cultural development would have to be based not only on the action of Africans within their political, historical and social context, but also on their efforts on behalf of their culture of origin after acquiring outside knowledge, in this case European. From this point of view, it is clear that the identification of African intellectuals in the period under consideration and an examination of their thinking would have been of considerable interest, as it would no doubt have allowed us to gauge the extent to which they contributed to the cultural development of Africa.[2] However, given the limits of this study, work on that scale is out of the question.

Furthermore, given the major historical events that have befallen the continent, we are entitled to question whether there was any possibility of cultural evolution from 1789 to 1914, a period during which the slave trade and colonial conquest reached their height. To put it another way, how could development take place in spite of a seemingly unfavourable historical context? What is it in the *proprium Africana* that enables us to discern a development of culture during this period? Lastly, is it really possible to confirm this cultural advance, if any, without noting whatever obstacles might have reduced its effect once it was under way?

If we take culture to mean everything produced by the mind, it is a specific characteristic of human beings, depending on their inventive capacity and their ability to assimilate elements from outside their own background. Hence culture is that which enables humans to know that they are human; it is the trace of human existence in a given time and space. This trace, as a sign, may be perceived through the expression in different regions of such concepts as art, language, history, religion, science and technology. Thus, through some of these forms of expression, for instance, art, we can still today gain an insight into the existence of people who lived hundreds or even thousands of years before us. In line with this hypothesis, archaeological excavations have enabled us to acquire some knowledge of life as it was in Jenne (Mali) and in Komaland, in the north of present-day Ghana, going back as far as the fifteenth, or even the fourteenth century. Thanks to the wonders of archaeology and history, we also know that the Sao of Chad developed a style of architecture with a defensive capacity; the term 'fortress house' (*maison forteresse*) is used to designate buildings of this kind. It is a style that has been observed elsewhere, for instance in West Africa – although the buildings there are less monumental – and remains in use to this day. Indeed, in Burkina Faso this kind of fortress house is characteristic of the architecture of the Lobi and the Dagara, who have often used their houses to defend themselves against attack from outside. Built without any side openings other than small windows, these houses are equipped with a ladder to the flat roof, from where a second ladder positioned in the middle of an opening in the roof leads down to the rooms. The external ladder is pulled up every evening. Furthermore, the tops of the walls around the roofs are supplied with balls of baked clay, which can be used as projectiles in case of attack. The windows are used as observation posts; poisoned arrows could be fired from them at an enemy. During the conquest and subsequent colonial occupation, the French administration learnt this to its cost before finally managing to subjugate these peoples, in particular the Lobi, whose military strategies were highly sophisticated. A similar, almost identical style of architecture, apart from some minor differences, can still be seen today in Taberma territory in Togo.

The ruins of the Monomotapa Empire, in present-day Zimbabwe, also attest to great technical skill. According to Massudi Alabi Fassassi, the monuments of the Zambezian kingdoms were 'built in dry stone, that is with no trace of masonry, using a highly advanced technique'. This architectural civilization 'reached its peak probably in the seventeenth and eighteenth centuries' (Fassassi, 1997: 70). Reference to this style of architecture brings to mind the cultural influences exerted by population movements in the same region in the late eighteenth century. The Shona and the Venda both adopted stone building techniques, which may explain the Shona mastery of stone carving. From the eighteenth century onwards, at the end of the Mambo period, or Shona II according to the chronology established by archaeological research, they carried on a traditional form of stone sculpture until 1957, when Frank McEwen, director of the National Art Gallery in Salisbury, set up the first experimental centre, thus conferring an academic character on a traditional practice (Laude, 1990: 73–4; Willett, 1990: 22 n9, 254–6).

While this historical clarification terminates with events that are fairly recent in relation to the period of our study, we should explain why we referred to phenomena that are much older. This reference demonstrates that there is a certain continuity in cultural history, evidence of the distant origin of an evolutionary process whose results can still be observed today, sometimes in places other than the starting point; this suggests avenues for research into the spread of populations in Africa. It also raises a question that is directly linked to the whole problem of the cultural evolution of Sub-Saharan Africa. Study of the historical documents reveals that the continent has had major cultural centres. Whether in the case of Sao or Zambezian architecture, or iron-ore mining, there is ample evidence of a high level of technical skill in Africa. However, when we consider the current state of overall development and the form it takes in certain fields, we are entitled to ask ourselves why a break has occurred. Why have great architectural achievements, indicative of highly sophisticated technologies, not been further developed, despite the existence of visible masterpieces such as the Ashanti palace of Osei Bonsu in the first quarter of the nineteenth century, or Njoya's palace in Bamum in the early twentieth century? Why did Africa fail to produce the wheel when it could work iron very early on? Why does everything appear to have come to a halt, as if by choice? These questions show how problematic it is to affirm cultural developments in Sub-Saharan Africa,

particularly in the nineteenth century. Nevertheless, some elements do indeed testify to cultural advances, whilst others, on the contrary, have impeded the full flourishing of African cultural development.

ART AS EVIDENCE OF CULTURAL DEVELOPMENT

One of the key fields for the expression of African cultures has been, and still is today, art.[3] Indeed, from the fifteenth century onwards, the African art that captured the attention of so many European travellers formed part of the goods traded by the Portuguese, with the result that the curio collections of the time already contained gold weights from the Gold Coast (present-day Ghana), and ivories from Congo, Dahomey (Benin) and Nigeria.

In the field of art, development undoubtedly took place. Whether in hierarchical groups, kingdoms or lineage societies, to borrow the conventional anthropological term for societies without a centralized power structure, artistic developments occurred both as a result of factors internal to those societies and in response to events originating elsewhere.

For instance, the Dagara, who now straddle Burkina Faso and Ghana, began to develop the sculpture of ancestor figures towards the end of the nineteenth century. Displaced by warrior groups, the Zaberma in this case, and fleeing raids by slavers, they settled on either side of the river (the Black Volta, subsequently the Mouhoun) that was to become the frontier between Upper Volta (Burkina Faso) and Ghana upon independence. This forced migration obliged the populations to innovate. Accordingly, they replaced ancestor-worship based on the use of tombs, which they were unable to take away with them in their many displacements, by a form of worship that involved the use of a readily transportable symbol, the statue. Its introduction enabled religious practices to continue, slightly modified but culturally enriched. When fleeing, there was no need to take all the statues placed on the altar – taking the oldest ancestor figure sufficed. Once settled in a new home, each family reconstituted the altar by sculpting new statues representing each of the deceased family members. This artistic production still goes on and contributes to the growing diversity of African art. Today's altars, laden with statues and fairly well preserved despite various threats to the works, make it possible to reconstruct family genealogies. In addition to this example, there are the mask societies, which, through initiation, provide opportunities for education and the transmission of skills. It is within these societies that the techniques of mask making are learnt, thereby helping to perpetuate the cultures of the peoples concerned.

While these examples illustrate the diversity of the settings in which art flourished in Sub-Saharan Africa, it is more clearly observable in societies with a centralized power structure. From this point of view, royal African art is known mainly through the famous kingdoms of Ashanti, Benin, Congo and Dahomey, whose sovereigns accorded considerable importance to art in general. Changes can be observed in artistic production in Benin, which spanned four centuries, from the late sixteenth to the late nineteenth centuries. During that period, the modern era (the eighteenth and nineteenth centuries) saw the greatest production, probably because of increased imports of metal from

Europe, in particular bronze, but also no doubt owing to the foresight of some rulers. For instance, art was strongly favoured during the reign of King Agonglo, who commissioned numerous 'objects', the thrones inspired by Ashanti models being among the most famous. In addition to jewellery, he promoted the art of weaving and encouraged artists, some of whom became very well known (Preston, 1998: 108). Royal patronage was also practised elsewhere. At the beginning of the nineteenth century, King Osei Bonsu of the Ashanti offered money at certain times, usually after a victorious war, to his captains so that they could enlarge and redecorate their homes (ibid.: 128). He gave orders for the construction of a modern stone-built palace inspired by the European buildings on the coast. The palace was completed in 1822 and was used, among other things, as the royal treasure house. This borrowing from the European architectural tradition exemplifies the role of outside influences in the artistic and cultural development of Africa, which can be observed in several fields of culture. From the artistic point of view, in addition to the use of materials such as bronze, some works owe their beauty to a combination of European and African styles. For instance, the throne of Eresonyen (eighteenth century) was 'a work of great beauty, possibly inspired by a throne made by the Portuguese for his ancestor' (ibid.: 74).

The art historian Suzanne Preston Blier notes several examples of works bearing traces of European styles. These include zoomorphic vases, notably a leopard vase, that she states are 'certainly modelled on European prototypes' (Preston, 1998: 55), and the Silver Lion, symbol of King Glélé, which shares 'some stylistic features with European silverware' (ibid.: 114). While all these examples reveal possible stylistic borrowings and thus testify to long-standing economic and cultural exchanges between Europe and Africa, the importance of such influences should sometimes be qualified. Otherwise, certain remarks might appear of little relevance, or even naïve. To state, for instance, that leopard-shaped vases are 'certainly' based on European models may be true, but there is nothing to prove it. In any event, the author offers us no such proof. The implication is that without the original model there would have been nothing. Yet there were mutual influences among African cultures that Preston points out herself, including the following example. During the first half of the eighteenth century, a masquerade was introduced in the city of Benin. Its purpose was to celebrate the festival of the new yam, and it took the form of a ceremony following the yam harvest during which the sovereign demonstrated his generosity by distributing yams to his subjects. This social event led to the production of impressive and terrifying copper masks. The name for this kind of mask (Oduduwa) refers to the Yoruba god of the earth and indicates a borrowing from Yoruba culture in Ife.

Of all the sovereigns who contributed to an apparent blossoming of culture in Sub-Saharan Africa, the actions of Njoya, a young king who came to power at the age of nineteen in a small country (8,000km^2) in the mountains of Central Africa, proved decisive. He conceived and then carried out a number of innovations. He had a series of palaces built, the last of which, constructed over a five-year period (1917–22), was of dried brick, with a ground floor and two upper stories. It is 60m high and very imposing. With a rectangular ground plan, it represents a break with the traditional circular form. As to clothing, beaten bark and cotton were abandoned for clothes made from material produced in other cultural areas, for instance, the voluminous boubous worn by Muslims. Incidentally, Islamic influence went hand-in-hand with borrowings from European civilization. In agriculture, Njoya set up an experimental farm and encouraged arboriculture through the introduction of a rule that anyone who planted trees for ten years won the right to farm the land. He grew European vegetables and cereals (tomatoes, barley and wheat) but with little success. Against this background, traditional strains were widely diversified and Foumban became an oil-palm plantation.

Of all these innovations, the most surprising one for us today – given the widely accepted notion that Africa had known only oral civilization – was the invention at the end of the nineteenth century of a writing system known as the Bamum script. Njoya's active reign began some time between 1892 and 1896. The writing system, which started off with more than 500 signs, is made up of drawings, many of them corresponding to words transcribed in the form of pictographs. The system flourished and evolved until an alphabet was devised, whose final revision, the sixth, dates from 1918. However, it was eminently useable as from 1911, the number of signs having been considerably reduced from 500 to 80, 'including the numbering symbols'.

Texts were written down with the help of this invention, which was for the exclusive use of the royal palace. The most important of them is *Histoire et coutumes des Bamoun*, written under the direction of Sultan Njoya.[4] Another contains a description of the king's religious beliefs, under the title *Nuët Nkuëtë* (Tardits, 1977: 287). In this text, King Njoya explains his religious ideas, which involve a particular form of syncretism, freely blending Islam and Christianity. This combination reflects two influences: Muslim (Fulani) and Christian (German, through the activities of the Basel mission). This syncretism is already apparent in the writing system, which contains Roman characters (A, H, T, Y, etc.) – some of them reversed in transcription – Greek characters (α, Y, Δ), Muslim symbols and African pictographs. However, the sovereign did not try to eradicate all Bamum values. Even though his philosophy did reject some customary elements – for instance, he renounced his role of 'ancestor priest' (ibid.: 287–8) – it had to be taught in the Bamum language. This syncretism, which reveals a desire to open up to the outside world without surrendering all authentic values, makes of Njoya a precursor of the political culture embodied in Kwame N'Krumah who, through his concept of consciencism, sought to promote African development based on intrinsic African values and hence capable of integrating and assimilating external elements.

In that respect, Sultan Njoya was a man of his time. As a result of the efforts of missionaries, who founded primary and secondary schools, an intellectual elite sprang up. By taking over a religious movement known as 'Ethiopianism', African intellectuals were to promote the notions of African dignity, the defence of African peoples, African solidarity and above all African unity. In so doing, they pioneered the emergence of consciencism as a political movement. In addition to the Bamum sovereign, these pioneers include: James Africanus Harton (1835–83), born in Sierra Leone of Ibo parents; Edward Wilmot Blyden (1832–1912), a West Indian who emigrated to Liberia; and James Johnson (1836–1917), born of Yoruba parents in Sierra Leone (Ade Ajayi, 1997: 53–6).

The invention of the Bamum script led to the establishment in the palace of a 'book house' and royal schools where this writing was taught, such as, for example, the 'Bamum Schule des Häuptling Ndscoya in Fumban'. In 1918, the French recorded some twenty of these schools. The existence of writing led to the invention of a printing press, which was unfortunately never used. Claude Tardits lays the responsibility for this on the French administration: 'in 1920 the press was ready but Njoya, who was being harassed at that time by the French administration, in his rage had the characters melted down' (1977: 283).

Historically speaking, this was not the only writing system in Sub-Saharan Africa. Other systems preceded it, but unfortunately they no longer existed by the nineteenth century, for reasons that are not really known. They include scripts for Basa and Mende (Sierra Leone, Liberia), Nsidibi (eastern Nigeria), Vai (Sierra Leone) and Vili (Republic of the Congo, Democratic Republic of the Congo) (Balogun et al., 1977: 141–212). The Bamum script finally disappeared in the twentieth century, unable to hold out against the writing systems imposed by Europeans.

More generally, Africa south of the Sahara went through a period of intellectual ferment partly brought on by Arab influence, which in certain instances led to the appearance of the Ajami script. In other instances the use of Arabic resulted in the introduction of scientific knowledge as a political principle. It was against this background that Sultan Ousman Dan Fodio and his successors caused 250 books to be produced. Their interest in matters intellectual became more widely known when the English explorer Claperton, who encountered Ousman Dan Fodio's son, Mohamed Bello, reported that the latter knew Euclidian geometry from a work he possessed in Arabic, subsequently destroyed in a fire (Ki-Zerbo, 1972: 365–6).

The events described here hint at the introduction of innovations which are partly due to external factors, in particular the European presence in Africa. In some instances this involves the arrival of missionaries prior to the installation of the colonial administration, as in the case of the London Missionary Society in South Africa. Imbued with the civilizing ideology of the Gospels, these religious institutions helped to transform culture in Africa by spreading new knowledge and new skills. The arrival of the London Missionary Society in Madagascar in 1820 led to the opening of the first schools. Subsequently the mission's activities resulted in the production of a Malagasy grammar as early as 1825, i.e. after a mere five years' presence, although the manuscript was never published. Some religious works were produced in the Malagasy language, however, and distributed two years later in 1827 (Bah, 1992: 69–90).

In South Africa (from where the London Missionary Society probably left for Madagascar) the presence of this and other missions – such as the Methodists in Thaba Nchu in 1833, the Paris Evangelical Missionary in Lesotho in the same year and the American Board Missionary in Ndebeleland, Tswanaland and Mosegaland in 1835 and Zululand in 1836 – had the same effect. Ngwabi Bhebe confirms this:

in the process they (missionaries) became vehicles for transmitting Western education and Western industrial habits. Thus mission stations, missionaries and their African helpers found themselves performing several functions, such as literary teaching, preaching and training people in agriculture, carpentry, building and many other crafts. They also learned African languages into which they translated the Bible and other religious texts.

(Bhebe, Chapter 15.6, this volume)

Today, it is established that the principal objective of these missions was not philanthropic; they provided an infrastructure which the colonial powers made use of to extend their sovereignty over the conquered territories. Furthermore, their innovatory impact on African civilizations had side effects, which gave the missions a bitter-sweet image. This is true, up to a point, of all European influence in Africa.

BITTER HONEY

While European influence in Africa contributed to a marked transformation in the way culture was perceived, and in some cases led to significant developments, it was also, paradoxically, an obstacle difficult to overcome, with effects that linger today. In an effort to determine the nature of that bipolar influence, we have borrowed – out of context – a title from the Burkinabe novelist Jean-Baptiste Somé, who died only recently. The point we are trying to make is illustrated by missionary activity and its impact on the African psyche.

The Christian missions in black Africa, with the laudable intention of promoting social development in the name of divine love and charity, undertook various activities ranging from the teaching of trades (builder, joiner, carpenter, farmer) to literacy and education of a Western kind. While those activities have an intrinsically constructive element that can still be observed today – the African elite that was to assume responsibility for the continent's destiny after independence was largely a product of the Christian schools – they also had the paradoxical effect in practice of alienating Africans from their culture.

Evangelism involves the dissemination of the Christian virtues with a view to bringing civilization to indigenous peoples, or even to making them fully human.[5] This task of transformation entails a process of destructuring that undermines the notion of cultural development in Sub-Saharan Africa during the period under consideration.

In so far as it was Western education based on Christian principles that was introduced, the teaching did not serve to promote African culture. Moreover, being a Christian at that time meant giving up traditional religious practices, the main field of expression of African cultures. It was clearly understood that every time an African was converted, an auto da fé of the 'objects' testifying to the existence of the gods previously worshipped would follow – unless, of course, a member of the family was in a position to recover them. As a result, a considerable part of the African artistic heritage went up in flames at the hands of God's missionaries, although it is true that this tendency was modified in spite of certain zealous priests who continued the practices of the early missionaries. Other priests were able on occasion to save works of art.

Against this background, it would be difficult to agree with Boahen that 'in the cultural field, the impact of colonialism was relatively speaking neither profound nor permanent' (Boahen, 1984). While it may be true that the changes introduced into African cultures did not directly affect every population or every section of the various populations, it is wrong to think that the impact of these changes on cultures was 'neither profound nor permanent'. The qualification introduced by Boahen through the term 'relatively speaking' does not bear examination when the issue is considered from a standpoint beyond the immediately temporal, for the lack of depth and durability is only apparent. True enough, in the early years of the establishment of the colonial system, i.e. during the nineteenth century, the impact was not a deep one, but that was purely for reasons of time and space. In other words, the significance of the effect of these actions depended on how long it took to carry them out and where they occurred. Obviously, the peoples who were most affected were those living on the coast and in the towns where the Europeans settled.

In the long run, depth and permanence, which are the decisive factors in this process, are easy to detect. Ever since the colonial period, Africa has been a continent of two extremes: the countryside – the 'bush' – and the town, relatively large agglomerations, even though some of them, such as Nairobi, founded in 1896, were a creation of the colonial system (Boahen, 1984). Contrary to popular belief, these two entities, which appear to exist in isolation, are only relatively independent of one another. If this independence seemed more marked in the nineteenth century, owing to very poor means of communication in the broadest sense of the term, it has become less and less important over time as a result of technical progress and consequent improvements in the infrastructure. Today, for instance, it is almost non-existent, since the African 'bush' lives at the same tempo as the towns, albeit without the latter's structures and amenities. Like city dwellers, rural Africans who have never left the countryside could watch *Dallas*, for instance, or *Les feux de l'amour*. Young people returning from the towns, and secondary school pupils and students going back to their villages during the holidays, have urban lifestyles and pass on ways of life and thinking that individuals of all age groups who have remained in the village imitate, with no knowledge of the background and no control over the means. We also know that, without reaching an advanced level of study, people who have attended Western schools usually consider ancestral customs to be backward. Some African intellectuals, including philosophers, claim that there is no African philosophy on the grounds that a critique of knowledge is impossible unless thought is written down, the condition which enables a critique to be made. On this basis they even reject the African past as a possible starting point for a philosophy in their sense of the term. This is the viewpoint of Paulin Jidenu Hountondji. Accordingly, the lack of permanence referred to by Boahen does not seem to us to be well founded, since we can now see how long it has lasted. From where else would the perennial condemnation of African cultures come, if not from an oft-made comparison with Western culture?

Far from being a digression, this lengthy investigation lies at the very heart of our subject, showing how difficult it is to talk of cultural development in Sub-Saharan Africa at a time when this part of the continent was no longer responsible for its political choices. It is true, as J. F. Ade Ajayi hoped, that an understanding of African history has to be built up on elements that are internal to Africa so as to avoid certain myths according to which African societies underwent no change prior to the colonial system. Or alternatively, when changes did occur, they were said to be the result of events external to Africa, in particular the Western invasion. But how could we fail to take the external element into account? How could we ignore the impact of the colonial system on cultural development, art and architecture in Sub-Saharan Africa when we know that certain colonial structures, such as the missions, had a considerable influence on African religions, through which cultures arose and spread? How could we not take account of the effects of the slave trade, for instance, whose haemorrhaging of the population reached new heights in the eighteenth and nineteenth centuries? This latter example offers a fascinating field for investigation in its relation to cultural development. Despite the enormity of the phenomenon, its effect on African societies had certain 'positive' as well as disastrous aspects.

In view of the emergence of a cultural efflorescence in Africa south of the Sahara in the nineteenth century, we are justified in thinking that certain elements of this development had their origins in a previous period. Accordingly, this development could be the culmination of a process that had begun earlier. As it happens, some of the phenomena that emerged during the period of our study, such as writing systems, did not survive. We are entitled to ask why. Was it simply because Africans were unable to develop their own invention? Was it due to colonial influence? Although we have nothing to go on in the case of the earlier scripts, we know that the inventor of the Bamum writing system saw his power and authority destroyed by the French colonial administration, which deported him, and placed him under house arrest in Yaoundé, where he died in 1933.

CONCLUSION

The history of Africa was written with Africans – that much is clear. However, it was made with Europeans too. Today, while retaining its own specific character, it forms part of the history of Europe and vice-versa. For that reason, it is impossible to consider cultural developments in Africa in the nineteenth century without taking the colonial system into account. This consideration, however, requires a critical approach, since the encounter between Africa and Europe took place amidst such violence that the momentum of African progress was interrupted.

Although new cultural achievements can be observed in the nineteenth century, it should be noted that these initiatives did not come to full fruition. So there was no genuine cultural development in the nineteenth century, despite the examples described in this study. The century was, as Ade Ajayi put it so well, 'the African Age of Improvement'. However, Europeans were able to use the desire for change to consolidate their own positions, ending up by imposing a colonial regime and stifling internal pressures for reform and development. True development has still to be attained, and to get there, Africa must build on its own foundations if it is to assimilate fully the external elements, which now form part of its everyday environment.

NOTES

1 The notion of cultural heritage deserves a closer look, since what is for the West an item of the cultural heritage and therefore to be conserved, is not necessarily considered as such in the African context. Embarking on such an

analysis here would, however, divert us from the core of our subject. We will therefore accept the Western concept of culture as it relates to the heritage, that is, as the full range of intellectual aspects of a civilization, which, in their expression, leave evidence behind and should therefore be preserved.

2 We by no means support the idea that the cultural development of a people depends on its possession of writing, particularly in view of the fact that the term has semantic variations which cast doubt on the very idea of 'societies without writing', to use the classical terminology of anthropology, since in cases where no writing system is discernible, it might be due to the existence of a different system of alphabetical writing that cannot be deciphered by someone who does not possess the key to its interpretation. Accordingly, mention here of writing refers on the one hand to what it actually is, i.e. a cultural phenomenon, and on the other to its relationship with the preservation of the constitutive elements of a culture which can be immediately accessible today. A knowledge of events in Africa in the late eighteenth century and throughout the nineteenth century can only be had, at the present time, through mainly Arabic and European sources or through lengthy fieldwork which, in any event, could not be done without consulting the writings of contemporary travellers. On the other hand – and this seems indisputable to us – the emergence of alphabetic or near-alphabetic scripts in some parts of Africa is necessarily a manifestation of cultural development. In this event, contrary to what one might think, it is not writing that leads to cultural development; writing, as we shall see, is one of the forms of expression of this development.

3 This concept of art cannot be applied uncritically to African masks and statues, since these 'objects' in specific circumstances, in particular in Africa, are not illustrative of the concept of art. Even in the West, where the concept arose historically and geographically, it has not always been understood in the same way throughout history, and even today it is still undergoing semantic shifts as contemporary art evolves. Consequently, we will use it here in its primary meaning of the creative activity of the mind based on a command of a series of activities, as opposed to instinctual behaviour. Regarding the different meanings attached to the concept in various periods and geographical contexts, we refer the reader to our work: *Art africain et esthétique occidentale* (*African Art and Western Esthetics*), L'Harmattan, Paris, 1998.

4 Translated into French by Pastor Henri Martin. In: *Série populations*, no. 5, Mémoire de l'IFAN, Centre du Cameroun, 1952.

5 Two centuries earlier, in the time of the legal dinosaurs who sought to legitimize the trade in Africans (the slave trade), evangelism was the means of bestowing humanity on that particular kind of merchandise, which would thus acquire a soul (Articles 2–14 of the French *Code Noir*). What did it matter whether this being was endowed with a moving principle (i.e. a soul), to employ an Aristotelian concept, since it was capable of movement without a force external to itself? And how could it be otherwise, since these were 'objects' or 'things', not living creatures, much less human beings?

BIBLIOGRAPHY

ADE AJAYI, J. F. 1989. Africa at the Beginning of the Nineteenth Century: issues and Prospects. In: *The General History of Africa*, Vol. 4, Africa in the Nineteenth Century until the 1880s, pp. 1–22. Heinemann, California, UNESCO, pp. 861ff.

AGUESSY, H. 1997. *'Visions et perceptions traditionelles': Introduction à la culture africaine.* Rowman and Littlefield, Lanham MD, pp. 243–64.

ANQUANDAH, J.; VAN HAM, L. n.d. *Discovering the Forgotten 'Civilization' of Komaland, Northern Ghana.* Accra and Rotterdam, pp. 48ff.

BAH, T. 1992. Construction, reconstruction et modernisation: L'Ethiopie et Madagascar. In: Elikia M'Bokolo, *Afrique noire-Histoire et civilisation*, Vol. 2, Hatier-AUPELF, Paris, pp. 69–90.

BALOGUN, O.; AGUESSY, H.; DIAGNE, P. 1977. *Introduction à la culture africaine.* Prolégomènes par Alpha I. Sow. UNESCO, Paris, pp. 316ff.

BOAHEN, A. A. 1984. The Colonial Heritage. *UNESCO Courier*, no. 5, May, Paris, pp. 33–8.

——. 1989. New Trends and Processes in Africa in the Nineteenth Century. In: *The General History of Africa, Vol. 4: Africa in the Nineteenth Century until the 1880s*, pp. 40–63. Heinemann, California. UNESCO, pp. 861ff.

ECHARD, N. 1983. (texts collected by) Métallurgies africaines, Société des Africanistes (*Mémoires de la Société des Africanistes*, 9), Paris, pp. 339ff.

FASSASSI, M. A. (ed.) 1997. *l'Architecture en afrique noire.* l'Harmattan, Paris, pp. 185ff. 1st edn, François Maspero, Paris, 1978.

GNAMMANKOU, D. 1996. *Abraham Hanibal, l'aïeul noir de Pouchkine.* Présence africaine, Paris, pp. 251ff.

HOLAS, B. 1972. *La pensée africaine.* Geuthner, Paris, pp. 495ff.

HOUNTONDJI, P. J. 1970. Remarques sur la philosophie africaine contemporaine. *Diogène*, No. 71, Gallimard, Paris, pp. 120–40.

——. 1980 [1976] Sur la *'philosophie africaine'. Critique de l'ethnophilosophie.* François Maspero, Paris.

KAMBOU, J.-M. 1993. *Peuples voltaïques et conquête coloniale 1885–1914, Burkina Faso.* Preface by Joseph Ki-Zerbo. ACCT/L'Harmattan (Racines du présent), Paris, pp. 476ff.

KI-ZERBO, J. 1972. *Histoire de l'Afrique Noire.* With photographs. Hatier, Paris, pp. 702ff.

LAUDE, J. 1990. *Les arts de l'Afrique noire.* Librairie générale de France, Paris, pp. 383ff.

PERROT, C.-H.; VAN DANTZIG, A. 1994. *Marie-Joseph Bonnat et les Ashanti, Journal (1869–1874).* Société des Africanistes (Mémoires de la Société des Africanistes), Paris, pp. 672ff.

PRESTON, B. S. 1998. *L'art africain.* Flammarion, Paris, pp. 271ff.

SOME, R. 1998. *Art africain et Esthétique occidentale (Etudes africaines).* L'Harmattan, Paris, pp. 347ff.

——. 1993. Afrique: une ruine d'âme. In: *Cesure, No. 4, Revue de la convention psychanalytique.* Paris, pp. 225–48.

TARDITS, C. N. (ed.) 1977. (c.1875–1933) ou les malheurs de l'intelligence chez un sultan Bamoun. In: Charles-André Julien; Magali Morsy; Catherine Coquery-Vidrovitch; Yves Person, *Les Africains.* Vol. 9, pp. 261–95. Editions J. A., Paris, pp. 343ff.

WILLETT, F. 1990. *L'art africain.* Thames and Hudson, Paris, pp. 286ff.

9

THE PLACE OF RELIGION IN
THE CULTURES OF
THE NINETEENTH CENTURY

Emile Poulat, coordinator

with contributions from *Ok-Sung Ann-Baron, Jean-Pierre Berthon,
Isabelle Charleux, Khalifa Chater, Olivier Clément, Thierno M. Diallo,
Jacques Gadille, Vincent Goossaert, Sophie Le Callenec,
Indira Mahalingam Carr, Marie Louise Reiniche* and *Rodolfo de Roux*

INTRODUCTION

If geography is the science of space, history is the science of duration, and even, for us, of profane time as opposed to sacred time. It is primarily comprised of dates, which set and organize the unfolding of events that compose it. And yet, it fits uneasily into the chronological frameworks that we impose on it: eras, centuries, reigns or cycles. Our major reference point – the Christian era – is a late construction, six centuries after its founding event – the birth of Jesus Christ – and only accurate to within a few years. It was centuries before it became accepted as the Common Era, in universal use, and in some parts of the world it continues to coexist with other calendars.

From this viewpoint, it is undeniable that the nineteenth century began in 1815 at the Congress of Vienna, when Europe reorganized itself at the end of the revolutionary upheaval, and that it ended in 1914, with the outbreak of the First World War. It is equally undeniable that the eighteenth century ended in 1789, at the dawn of a French Revolution which was not limited to France: Jacques Godechot has spoken of an Atlantic Revolution launched with the Declaration of Independence by the British colonies in North America (1776). In between, there were forty years which shook old Christendom from the Americas to Russia, the prologue or prelude inseparable from our religious nineteenth century.

For religions, the key features of the nineteenth century can be summarized as: an internal secularization of Western societies, associated with advances in the sciences and industry in the spirit born of the Enlightenment; an unprecedented missionary expansion of Christianity; an encounter of all the religions of the world under the triple impact of this religious expansion, colonial conquests and academic curiosity about religions outside the Judaeo-Christian tradition.

This evolution can easily give the impression of an inevitable decline, heralding the end of the religious spirit and the death of the historic religions. To see things in that way is to misjudge their powers of resistance and the needs that they alone continued to satisfy. Religions had not yet run their course, but it is true to say that the time of religions changed profoundly and took a novel course. They moved from a state of peaceful possession to a challenge and questioning that launched them into a vast confrontation with the new forms of culture. For religions too, exit from the *ancien régime* proved to be a long drawn-out affair that was painful and fraught. One can understand that they should hesitate over which path to take, what price to pay, what efforts to make, what novelties to introduce. At the end of the century, in Germany, there was talk of a *Kulturkampf*: the expression may be extended and generalized to be inscribed, beyond all politics and ideology, as part of the general movement of our society.

Such a realization, easy though it is today, was less obvious in the last century, when things were less advanced, and our world was more compartmentalized. There was indeed a cultural revolution, as the plan of the present volume testifies. In it religion appears as the last of the nine topics considered, after for so long occupying the first place unquestioned, as still witness the classification scheme of the *Catalogue général* of the Bibliothèque Nationale in Paris, designed under the Second Empire.

The nineteenth century was still the era of the 'Great Powers' – essentially states in Europe and the two Americas – which alone had a say in the international concert. Much of humanity was far from living this so-called 'Western' time: the hour of globalization had not yet sounded, of which colonization was the first stage. For religion, the century had two key features: The great stability of the traditional religious domains, and the missionary expansion of Christianity. To say, that is to say that the place of religion in societies and civilizations was, first and foremost, an issue in and a result of this ongoing revolution through the conflicts or alliances that it produced, before being the object of scholarly assessment or a confession of faith. But it was indeed from Europe that the movement started which, through various and even opposing channels, has led us to the 'global village' which is henceforth our condition.

CHRISTENDOM REVOLUTIONIZED

The revolutionary upheaval

At the end of the eighteenth century, France was the most populous country and the leading power in Europe, although England had already positioned herself at the cutting edge of industrial progress. The history of the world was at that time restricted to Europe and the Ottoman Empire, thus including the Mediterranean basin. The two Americas were a colonial dependency of this world, only the thirteen British colonies on the Atlantic seaboard having declared their independence in 1776. With farthest Asia – China, India, Siam – relations were limited to diplomatic relations, trading factories and mission stations. The world population was estimated at a billion.

The borders of states were shifting, dictated by peace treaties and dynastic marriages. Europe was monarchical and confessional: Catholic in the south, Protestant in the north, Orthodox in the east, except for Catholic Poland, partitioned among its three powerful neighbours. The Swiss cantons gave an idea of what a republican regime might look like, in contrast to the absolute monarchy or enlightened despotism which prevailed everywhere else: that was the path on which the young United States embarked.

In France, Catholicism occupied a privileged and protected status. It was, constitutionally, the religion of the king, the kingdom and its inhabitants; its clergy was the first of the three estates of the nation, ahead of the nobility and the third estate; its laws were French laws, applicable to all and first and foremost to the courts. It is true that it was a Catholicism à la française, which clung to its peculiarities and its traditions: its relations with the papacy were often difficult, and it was ever ready to assert against the pope 'the liberties of the Gallican church'.

There were two exceptions to this unanimity. First, after the Reformation and the Wars of Religion, the Protestants, to whom Henri IV had granted a degree of tolerance (the Edict of Nantes, 1598), revoked by Louis XIV (1685), and restored by Louis XVI (1787). And the Jews (numbering about 40,000, chiefly in Alsace), expelled by Charles VI, who were treated as a foreign nation.

No one then dreamed of the earthquake that we have come to call the 'French Revolution' and which affected the whole of Christendom, from the Americas to Russia. Yet the tell-tale signs were there, two in particular: the spread of new ideas (deism, libertinism, the Enlightenment, the *Encyclopédie*, freemasonry, the 'philosophes') and, in North America, the revolt of the British colonies against the British Crown.

Reforms were what people wanted and revolution is what they got, in the new sense of the word (no longer the astronomical sense). The desire for reforms was expressed in the *Cahiers de doléance* prepared in France for the *Etats généraux* summoned by Louis XVI in May 1789. These soon transformed themselves into a Constituent National Assembly. This began by drafting the Declaration of the Rights of Man and the Citizen (26 August 1789), which recognized full freedom of conscience and expression for

all. In need of money, it decreed the nationalization of the property of the clergy, along with the civil and religious reorganization of the country. The church of France was provided with a 'Civil Constitution of the Clergy' which Pope Pius VI condemned in 1791 (brief *Quod Aliquantum*) as an unacceptable interference.

From then on the tragedy unfolded. A 'Constitutional church' was set up, with a self-appointed episcopate and a clergy obliged to swear the oath of loyalty that all officials had to swear. Those who refused to do so – known as the *réfractaires* – could choose only exile, imprisonment or going underground. The monarchy was abolished, the Papal States invaded and the pope imprisoned. Revolts broke out. War became general. The separation of church and state was declared. Regimes and constitutions came and went. Bonaparte imposed himself as saviour, declared that 'the Revolution is finished', proclaimed the Empire and had himself crowned by Pope Pius VII. Europe was put to fire and sword until his final defeat at Waterloo in 1815.

The French clergy suffered enormously from the Revolution: seminaries were closed, obstacles put in the way of religious practice, libraries confiscated, congregations suppressed, priests defrocked, some made martyrs (canonized or beatified, in certain cases), some exiled. Emigrant priests were to be found in almost every country in the world, as far as Russia and America. Thus, in the United States, the Sulpicians would found the first major seminary at Baltimore and several dioceses would be headed by French bishops.

At the end of this period, three models now coexisted: the historical tradition of the state religion – 'cuius religio eius religio' – dear to the Lutherans, the Anglicans and the Orthodox in Scandinavia, Britain and the Slav lands; the French tradition of rivalry between church and state to determine which was supreme; and the American tradition of religious freedom, the work of the dissenters who had fled England to escape from the state church and founded a state with no power over the churches. For its part, the Holy See continued to cling to the medieval model of Christendom, of which the modern form was the Catholic state, such as Spain and a number of Swiss cantons.

The new society

For the allied powers who had defeated Napoleon, the problem was not to finish the Revolution, but to put it behind them. This task was undertaken by the Congress of Vienna, in 1815. After bitter bargaining, it redrew the map of Europe, confirmed the partition of Poland and restored the Papal States, which were made into a monarchy. It was crowned by a mystical pact, the 'Holy Alliance', made 'in the name of the Most Holy and Indivisible Trinity' in order to defend 'the precepts of Justice, Christian Charity and Peace'. Pope Pius VII preferred not to get involved.

This restoration did not bring back the old order. France had changed too much: in the countryside, there had been a vast redistribution of land, which no one challenged; at the higher levels, there was a new society, anxious to succeed and get rich, with which the nobility had to accommodate itself. Europe was a cauldron on the boil. The whole policy of Metternich, Chancellor of Austria and the strong man of the monarchies, was aimed at keeping the lid on. Against it were ranged liberals of all stripes and secret societies (with, in the forefront, the *Carbonari*).

The 1830 Revolution marked their first victory. In France, where prosperity coexisted with poverty, it was marked by strong anticlericalism. On France's border, Belgium seized its independence from the Protestant Netherlands thanks to a short-lived alliance between liberals and Catholics. Spain was in the grips of a succession war between the Carlists (Catholic legitimists) and the liberals. Portugal had to accept the independence of Brazil. Russian-ruled Poland revolted, but unsuccessfully.

It was in this situation that an intransigent Catholicism took shape, aided and abetted by the Holy See, whose vitality manifested itself in several ways. One of the most visible forms was the foundation of numerous religious, teaching, nursing or missionary congregations, both male and especially female, along with the restoration of the great monastic orders (Benedictines, Carthusians, Dominicans, etc.).

In a Europe that was overwhelmingly rural, parish life continued at its own local pace, according to the rhythm of the days, the tasks and the seasons. Bishops saw to 'recruitment to the priesthood' with minor seminaries in which a classical education was given and major seminaries where a traditional spirit was inculcated without it being very clear what that tradition was. At any event, there was a suspicion of cities in them, for cities were the source of the new ideas whose penetration was assisted by the relative freedom of the press and the building of railways.

At any event, if something was stirring, it was indeed in the cities where the 'social question' emerged under the impact of urbanization, industrialization and proletarianization. A whole range of hopes for a solution emerged which can be grouped under two broad trends: the early socialisms – Owen, Saint-Simon, Fourier and Cabet, which Marx would judge 'utopian' – and a social Catholicism marked by a proliferation of private initiatives, of very varied inspiration, which the papacy did not yet seek to unify in an institutional and doctrinal framework. Socialists and Catholics were at least at one in calling for 'association' against the 'laissez-faire, laissez-passer' of the new economics.

Two cultures, one shaped by the church, the other emerging from the Enlightenment. Two Frances, it would soon be said: one of Joan of Arc and St Louis, one of Voltaire and Rousseau. And between them, there was war. It was not a situation peculiar to France: the Germans talked of a *Kulturkampf*, and in 1850, the Italian Jesuits launched a high-quality review (still published) called *La Civiltà cattolica*, one that points out 'the way, the truth and the life', before the laxity and error of 'modern civilization'.

The Catholics soon found the name for what was at stake between them: *naturalism*. The word designated everything that, in thought or society, in theory or in practice, led to dispensing with the 'supernatural', thereby putting into the hands of man alone the government of societies, the conduct of individuals, the explanation of history and the future of the world. It was a word of protean dimensions: the varieties and derivatives of it are without number. Pius IX set himself to list them in 1864, in his Syllabus ('System of the Principal Errors of Our Time'), eighty propositions commented on by the encyclical *Quanta cura* that accompanied them: rationalism, pantheism, indifferentism, liberalism, socialism, communism, etc. Before long, utilitarianism, positivism, scientism, democratism and others would be added to the list.

In the secular world there was a universal outcry against an attitude seen as demented and suicidal. For Catholic circles, long divided, this was make or break; the Syllabus decided firmly between those whom the pope confirmed in their doctrinal intransigence and those who continued to be sympathetic to the principles that were condemned.

These latter have passed into history by the name of liberal Catholics: a European and even international trend, known in France above all for the 'Menaissian school', grouped in 1830 around the daily *L'Avenir*, and for being twice condemned by Gregory XVI (1832, 1834). In fact, these trends went far beyond Lamennais, his friends and those grouped under this label. They included all those who gave up being 'oppositionist Catholics' and saw themselves as 'mediation Catholics'. A prefix well known to theologians since Pelagianism would cover this fluid grouping: *semi*. 'Semi-liberalism' leaves us as far from true liberalism as the German 'semi-rationalism' condemned by Gregory XVI (Hermès, Günther) is from authentic rationalism.

In North America, Protestantism reigned supreme. The United States was a WASP (White Anglo-Saxon Protestant) federal state where there was complete religious freedom for all, but a freedom which was only with difficulty extended to papists and with even more difficulty to atheists. Irish, Poles, Germans and Italians constituted well-organized Catholic minorities. Immigration and conquest led to the formation of a sort of religion of 'Americanness' in which all could communicate: newly arrived Europeans had to be integrated while at the same time the movement westward to the Pacific was in full swing. The Black problem and slavery precipitated a Civil War, the war of secession (1861–5) between North and South. To the north, Canada remained a British colony, overwhelmingly Protestant, with a French-speaking Catholic province, Quebec, where the Catholics eventually won out over the liberals.

Europe perpetuated its disputes and divisions. The 1848 Revolution represented a short-lived 'springtime of the peoples', marked by the awakening of nationalities. The year 1870 saw the meeting in Rome of the first Vatican Council, which proclaimed the dogma of papal infallibility. It was interrupted by the Franco-German war, which led to the fall of Napoleon III, the Commune (which would haunt the collective imagination for years to come) and the re-establishment of the German empire, while in Italy the Piedmontese completed the unification of the peninsula. Deprived of his states and his city (20 September 1870), Pope Pius IX regarded himself as a prisoner in the Vatican.

Europe was stabilized for forty years. It dreamed of expansion, thanks to industry and to the occupation of 'masterless lands'. The 'powers' partitioned Africa among themselves at the Berlin Conference (1884–5) after seizing for themselves the myriad islands of the Pacific. In this situation, in the Christian churches, mission went hand in hand with colonization, albeit with intense rivalries between confessions and between nations.

The social question and the intellectual crisis

The capture of Rome in 1870 marked the beginning of 'the Roman question', an apple of discord between the Holy See, strengthened in its intransigence, and the kingdom of Italy, on the side of liberalism. Its settlement had to wait sixty years. Leo XIII, elected Pope in 1878, was an elderly, sixty-eight-year-old aristocrat. He would reign for twenty-five years, winning in France the reputation of a liberal. Such was not the judgement of Italians. In fact, he was able to put a brave face on adversity: thanks to him, the Catholic church would make a spectacular comeback on the international stage.

In that sense, he was the first of the modern popes, devoted as much to St Augustine as to St Thomas. From the former he took the great sacred drama of the 'Two Cities' – the City of God and the City of the Prince of this world – with which he nourished his devotion to the rosary and St Michael the Archangel. From the latter he sought, from the very beginning of his reign (encyclical *Aeterni Patris*, 1879), an intellectual guide both for the rightness of Catholic thought and for the advent of a Christian society.

His great success was in a direction unexpected by the teachers: the 'social doctrine of the church', whose charter long remained the encyclical *Rerum novarum* (1891). It dealt with the 'condition of workers' and repeated the double condemnation: no to liberalism, no to socialism. It gave shape to what would come to be called 'the Catholic movement' or, more precisely, 'the Catholic social movement', which took a stand against the worker and peasant socialist movement as the White International against the Red International. It took different forms in different countries: in Italy, within the *Opera dei congressi*, men, women, boys and girls by diocese and parish; in Germany, a political party (the *Zentrum*), Catholic Trade Unions and a General Association (the *Volksverein*) which held regular meetings (the *Katholikentag*); in Belgium and the Netherlands, structured as a 'pillar' alongside the socialist pillar and the liberal pillar each offering a complete range of services. The German model proved to be the most stable one and Pius X imposed it on the crisis-ridden Italian movement in 1903.

The Catholic movement developed in Catholic-majority countries, but never really took root in the Anglo-Saxon countries. It was very strong in Germany, Belgium and Italy, but much less so in France. The movement was periodically wracked by crises, which it got through with more or less success. All through the nineteenth century, the Catholic church had lived on the defensive or secure in its certainties. Leo XIII set it on the offensive, to reconquer a lost world. For the old intransigents, still regretting the Papal States, social Catholicism looked like a worrying innovation. Then, at the end of Leo XIII's pontificate came the democratic rumblings of Catholic Youth (Marc Sangnier in France, Romolo Murri in Italy, both condemned by Rome), the rise in Germany of interconfessional trade unions, tensions between the Catholic hierarchy and secular leaders, and finally worker separatism in Catholic organizations.

All these developments were a source of great concern for those who disapproved of them and were reputed 'conservative' and who, under Pius X, even spoke of *social modernism*. At the time such an objection was mortal: it referred back to the intellectual modernism whose 'errors' Pius X had condemned in the encyclical *Pascendi* (1907). This crisis in high Catholic culture had been smouldering ever since Ernest Renan's *Vie de Jésus* (1863; Eng. tr., *Life of Jesus*). It erupted after two books by Alfred Loisy, *L'Evangile et l'Eglise* (1902), and *Autour d'un petit livre* (1903). At its heart was the new Biblical exegesis, based on the historical-critical method with its avowed rationalism. In reality it came from something much deeper: from the development of the natural sciences, which, since Galileo, had begun to call into question Biblical cosmology and anthropology.

In fact, this crisis was part and parcel of an intellectual movement, both philosophical and theological, in which the Protestant countries – Germany, Britain, the Netherlands – played a leading role. What Catholic, Lutheran or Reformed Orthodoxy had to confront were new 'schools' and 'systems': British empiricism, Kantian criticism, German idealism, French eclecticism and positivism, American pragmatism, Nietzschean humanism, etc. The Danish philosopher Søren Kierkegaard (1813–55), paved the way for an existential reaction to this flood of speculations that left the individual disoriented in his anxiety for his fate. This situation explains both the success of pietistic currents and the emergence of a religious rationalism known as *liberal Protestantism*, symbolized by two men as different as Auguste Sabatier (1839–1901) and Adolf Harnack (1851–1930).

In Great Britain, the Anglican church was torn between a High church tendency attracted by Rome and its ritualism (the Oxford Movement and the conversion of John Henry Newman) and a Low church tendency, Calvinist in inspiration, or even a Broad church tendency in which what came to be called a 'broad' Christianity prevailed. The United States of America was the country and the laboratory of this fragmented Christianity, in which there was room for every religious experience, and where the number of denominations was constantly rising.

From this fragmentation would emerge the idea of reversing the movement towards a unity to be rediscovered: this was *ecumenism*, the first initiative for which goes back to the Lutheran Archbishop of Uppsala (Sweden), Nathan Söderblom. This fragmentation was occurring at the same time as a phenomenon of disengagement whose impact varied from country to country. The twentieth century would inherit these problems.

THE AREA OF ORTHODOXY

Like the Latin church of Rome, the Orthodox Greek church of Byzantium-Constantinople was a historical legacy of the Roman Empire, separated since the eleventh century. Orthodoxy had come to identify itself with the Slavic peoples, less Poland, plus Greece. By the nineteenth century it was politically divided among the Ottoman Empire, exposed to independence movements, and the Russian Empire, in the process of expanding eastward into Siberia and as far as Alaska, and southward into the Caucasus. Within the two empires, it had as neighbours traditionally independent ancient churches: the Armenian and Georgian churches in the Caucasus, the Syrian churches in the Near East, and the Eastern Catholic or Uniate churches, that is those attached to Rome in the sixteenth century.

Athonite monasticism

Mount Athos – the Holy Mountain, a tiny monastic republic less than 350km^2 in area, at an altitude of 2,000m – traditionally holds a very special place in Orthodox spirituality. As a revolutionary wind was rising in France, it was the scene, for Orthodoxy, of a new religious impulse.

The eighteenth century was a period of distress for the Orthodox church. In Russia, the patriarchate was suppressed by Peter the Great in 1721, and the church made subject to a synod in which real power belonged to a senior lay official (the 'Procurator-General of the Holy Synod').

The 'enlightened' empresses, especially Catherine II, froze recruitment into monasteries and secularized church property. The French Revolution and its aftermath dragged the Russian Empire into a series of wars, and Napoleon's armies reached Moscow. The Ottoman Empire, threatened by Austria and Russia, turned persecutor: making a mockery of the patriarchate of Constantinople (48 patriarchs in 75 years), displacing Serbs (from Kosovo) and Greeks (from Attica itself) in order to give their lands to Muslim Albanian settlers. Yet a spiritual revival was getting underway with the preaching of social justice, more and more schools at all levels, female prayer groups in Russia, the revival of the hesychast tradition in Moldavia, etc.

Internal reform burst out at the end of the eighteenth century. A group of monks on Mount Athos, especially Nikodemos the Hagiorite and Makarios Notaras, breaking with an Athos which had turned its back on its educational institute and lapsed into traditionalism, rediscovered the communal sense of celebration, advocated frequent communion and developed a whole pedagogy of the faith. Nikodemos, who had learned Latin, Italian and French at the school in Smyrna, translated several spiritual authors from the West, notably a paraphrase of the *Spiritual Exercises* of Ignatius of Loyola, and rediscovered the great theological and mystical synthesis of the Byzantine middle ages. Makarios and Nikodemos's major work was the *Philokalia* – 'Love of the Beautiful', five volumes published in 1782, a vast collection of theological, ascetic and mystical writings – which summoned not only monks but also lay people to the 'prayer of the heart' and the 'Jesus Prayer', in order to feel the light and life that shine from the risen Christ: it was less a flight from the world, in the final analysis, than an effort to transfigure it. A Ukrainian *starets* settled in Moldavia, Paisii Velichkovskii, using the methods of Western scholarship, organized a great work of translating and publishing patristic texts, and enabled the Philokalic movement to move from the Greek world to the Slavic-Romanian world. The Slavonic *Philokalia* was published in Russia as early as 1793, while many monks trained by Paisii came to that country where they renewed 'spiritual fatherhood'. Similar phenomena were observable in Romania and Greece.

Ottoman Europe

In the course of the nineteenth century, the Christian populations of the Balkans liberated themselves one after the other from the Ottoman Empire. The church, which had preserved not merely the faith but also the language and culture of these nationalities, was in the forefront of the battle. It was the metropolitan of Patras, in Greece, who in 1821 raised the standard of revolt, while the patriarch of Constantinople, responsible for the Orthodox millet, was hanged by the Turks at the Phanar gate. In Serbia, one of the 'towers of skulls' formed by the occupier, at Niš, became the centre of what was in effect a shrine raised around it that was both Orthodox and national.

In each of these re-emerging nations, the church, because it was at one with its people and feared Turkish influence over the patriarchate of Constantinople, made itself autocephalous. The Greek church became autocephalous in 1823, the Bulgarian church in 1860; the Serbian church became autonomous in 1823 and autocephalous in 1879. There was a sharp debate in Greece between supporters of tradition, that is loyalty to the 'Ecumenical See', and

nationalists, modernist in varying degrees, who emerged victorious. Gradually, and not without some foot-dragging, Constantinople recognized this transformation of daughter-churches into sister-churches which, except for Greece, were erected into patriarchates. But the principle of autocephalous status was that it must be territorial and not national: when the Bulgarians demanded a national church which would include their compatriots in Constantinople, a council meeting in that city in 1872 condemned *phyletism*, religious nationalism, 'national rivalries, quarrels between peoples within the church of Christ'.

In Greece, the Bavarian dynasty imposed by the European 'powers' did not understand, indeed even ridiculed post-Byzantine civilization, and armed prophets arising from the masses led unsuccessful uprisings against it. The real response came, not from school theologians trained in Germany to intellectualism and pietism, but from the impact of the *Kollyvades* driven out of Athos and scattered all over the country. They fuelled a real cultural renaissance. Alexandros Papadiamantis above all (d. 1911) expressed in his short stories and novels the best of popular monastic spirituality, and a sort of liturgical practice of existence, even in the simplest gestures. At the beginning of the twentieth century, a visionary, Apostolos Makrakis, fought for the renewal of the episcopate, rediscovered the anthropology of the fathers and became the herald of a quasi-messianic '*Megale Idea*', a 'Great Idea', which, led, in the years after the First World War to a national disaster.

In Romania, 'paissianism', which guided monastic life both towards the 'prayer of the heart' and intellectual activity, was balanced by Saint Callinicos of Cernica through the development of social service. However, the unification of the kingdom in 1864 inaugurated a period of secularization, which led, but only after the First World War, to a new awareness of tradition once again made capable of invigorating culture. In Transylvania (then part of Hungary), the Eastern Catholics or Uniates – Byzantine-rite Catholics – played a key role in the Latinization of the language and culture. Finally, on Mount Athos, where monasteries of all nationalities lived side by side, but where what appeared to be a Russian invasion was worrying the Greeks, the hesychast tradition was given unfortunate new expression among Russian and Serbian monks, at the beginning of the twentieth century, with the movement of the 'worshippers of the Name', the 'onomatodox', which the Russian state violently rooted out.

Roman Catholicism was moving towards the proclamation of the dogma of papal infallibility (1870). The Orthodox churches opposed it from an early date in an ecumenical spirit. In 1848, in response to an appeal from Pope Pius IX, the patriarchs of Constantinople, Alexandria, Antioch and Jerusalem published a solemn encyclical to beg the pope not to introduce the dogma of infallibility but rather to repent as Peter did and to proclaim that the Truth is preserved by the whole body of the church. In Russia, this document, approved by the Russian Holy Synod, led two great lay theologians, Kireievskii and Khomiakov, to develop the notion of catholicity (*sobornost*) as free communion of faith and love. As a major dialogue developed with the 'Old Catholics' (those who rejected the new dogma in 1870), in which Volotov, the great historian of dogma, and St Nectarios of Aegina played a leading role, an encyclical from the patriarch of Constantinople in 1902 called on the Christian churches to get to know one another better and to work together for a common witness. This appeal, which was reiterated in 1920, played a considerable role in the formation of the ecumenical movement and later the Ecumenical Council of churches.

Tsarist Russia

In the nineteenth century, in order to give itself a popular base, the tsarist state sought to reinvigorate the ideal of the Orthodox empire and took as its motto 'Orthodoxy, autocracy, nationality'. This was in fact nothing more than a sort of mystical nationalism – Moscow, the third Rome – whose most remarkable representative was Pobedonostsev, procurator-general of the Holy Synod from 1880 to 1905: he attempted to hold back the spread of education in order to preserve the village religion of the *muzhik*, while extreme right-wing circles channelled popular discontent into anti-Semitism (pogroms, the 'Protocols of the Elders of Zion'). The game was lost before it started: education developed and took on a decidedly anti-Christian secularism; science, in full flood, was positivist. Salvation could only come from a free church, promoting within itself a personal and conscious faith.

The fame of St Seraphim of Sarov and the 'Philokalic' mission carried out by the disciples of Paissii, led to a new emphasis on the prophetic, charismatic ministry of the *starets* or 'spiritual father' endowed with 'spiritual discernment': not only the people but intellectuals, 'seekers of God', the great 'Slavophile' thinkers such as Kireievski and leading literary figures such as Gogol and Dostoievski and thinkers (Leontiev, Soloviev) flocked to him. The movement to translate and study patristics, inaugurated by the monasteries, was resumed and developed by the Institutes of Theology whose level reached that of the best Western universities.

This spiritual and intellectual renaissance gradually breathed new life into the clergy. Leading bishops, such as Philaret of Moscow (d. 1867), reasserted the church's independence. The closure of the priestly caste (a priest being almost always the son of a priest) was undermined not only by the revolt of numerous seminarists (Joseph Stalin being one of them) but also by this spiritual flowering. Archimandrite Alexander Bukharev (d. 1871), an emblematic figure, voluntarily and dramatically renounced a brilliant ecclesiastical career to bear witness to the 'kenosis' of the Word and detect, in the apparently anti-Christian 'dark depths of modern thought', 'the abundance of Christic light to be found there'. For the first time, there emerged from the impersonality of ritual a priestly sanctity with, at the beginning of the twentieth century, Ivan of Kronstadt who evangelized the working classes, engaged in large-scale welfare work and advocated frequent communion preceded by communal ceremonies of public confession.

This renewal cannot be separated from an ever-deeper encounter with the West, which looked down on folk religion but encouraged an inner religion. Unlike an intelligentsia, which made atheism its religion, there were those who discovered in the depths of nihilism Christ the conqueror of death and hell. So it was that Orthodoxy, archaic in many ways, harboured one of the 'fathers' of modernity, Dostoievski, as important, but in an altogether different way, as Marx, Nietzsche or Freud (who would write about him). Dostoievski's God is not the god of pietism, moralism or nationalism: he is revealed in the dislocations of man, on the edge of nothingness.

Following on from Dostoievski, between the end of the nineteenth century and the First World War, there were the great years of Russian 'religious philosophy', closely bound up with a vast scientific, artistic and literary revival, sometimes called the 'silver age' of Russian culture. Vladimir Soloviev (1853–1900) attempted a synthesis of the Western quest and Eastern contemplation, in a vision which anticipated ecumenicism. The Renaissance and the Enlightenment had liberated the human mind from clerical constraints and made possible tremendous explorations, but they threatened to end up in an empty freedom, cut off from *Sophia*, Wisdom, the mysterious femininity of God who magnetizes the cosmic future.

In the early twentieth century, the 'new religious consciousness' (Merezhkovski, Hippius, Ivanov) embarked on a spiritual reading of Nietzsche, seeking to combine Dionysianism and Christianity. The 'sophiologists', heirs to Soloviev (Florensky, Bulgakov), conceptualized the 'sacred tellurism' of the Russian soul and were already proposing a Christian ecology. Rozanov, turning Freud's interpretations on their head even before they had been formulated, showed that loving sexuality was the possible path to a fundamental religious experience. Shestov undermined the 'self-evidence of reason' with the 'revelations of death'. Nesmelov, the sole professor of theology among these adventurers of the mind who were rarely university-educated, suggested an intaglio view of the image of God by stressing that the person has no other definition than being indefinable. Berdiaev accepted the challenges and reductions of modernity: eventually, the choice came down to one between 'the death of man' or the discovery of the person, the image of God, existence in communion, synthesis of the universe.

It is remarkable that priests and bishops should have taken an interest in all this research on the meaning of the cosmos, eros and human creativity, whose aim was to invest in history and culture the effort of 'transfiguration' and 'deification' previously the preserve of monasticism. This interest led to the 'religious and philosophical meetings' where the most serious churchmen met the boldest thinkers. 'It was as if the walls of the room were going to fall away and open up endless horizons. . . . Everything seemed possible', noted Merezhkovski.

The church was calling for its institutional freedom with the restoration of the patriarchate. The summoning of a council was decided on in 1904, and a 'preconciliar commission' prepared a vast *aggiornamento*. This council, repeatedly postponed by a compulsively hesitant emperor, finally met in 1917, only to be dispersed by the Bolsheviks the following year.

LATIN AMERICA

Latin America is a term that came into use more for history than for geography. It stretches from Tierra del Fuego to Mexico. It is overwhelmingly Spanish- and Portuguese-speaking, the product of colonization by Spain and Portugal, which thereby brought it within the orbit of Catholicism. This situation changed rapidly at the beginning of the nineteenth century.

Decolonization and its religious aftermath

In 1810, the 'cry' (*el grito*) went out from Mexico, calling on the Spanish colonies to rise up for their independence, like the British colonies in North America in 1776 and Haiti, a French colony, in 1791. In 1824, the last Spanish armies in South America surrendered at Ayacucho (Peru). Two years earlier, in 1822, without any fighting, Brazil had separated itself from Portugal. There followed a difficult period for the Catholic church, the cornerstone of the old regime. But the crisis of the traditional model of Iberian-American colonial Christianity had already begun in the second half of the eighteenth century, with the 'enlightened' and 'regalist' policy of Madrid and Lisbon, which sought to strengthen royal control over the clergy. The expulsion of the Jesuits from the Portuguese dominions in 1759 and the Spanish ones in 1767, was a political demonstration of the new spirit of the Enlightenment (*las Luces*). The end result of this policy was to turn a significant part of the clergy against the crown, and hence to reinforce the opposition.

At the time of the wars of independence (1810–24), the Spanish clergy played a major role in both the loyalist and the revolutionary camps, not only because of its influence and prestige but above all because of its total integration into American society. Like that society, it was affected and divided by this great political crisis. Most of the bishops (18 out of 42 had been appointed by the king between 1814 and 1820) remained loyal to the crown, as did many religious, who included a large proportion of Spaniards. The Creole clergy, which opposed the monopoly of the 'peninsular' clergy over major posts and offices, were more likely to march with the 'patriots', and did so first in Mexico.

The wars of independence left the church extremely weakened: material damage, closure of seminaries, shortage of vocations, secularizations, victims of the fighting, repatriation to Spain of royalist clergy, etc. It has been estimated the numbers of the two clergies fell by, between 35 per cent and 60 per cent in twenty-five years, depending on the region, while the population continued to grow. In Mexico, for example, between 1810 and 1834, the secular clergy fell from 4,229 to 2,282 and the regular clergy from 3,112 to 1,726. The educational and welfare work, which gave the church its social standing, was permanently undermined.

Throughout this period, relations with Europe were intermittent and difficult. For the new states, all of which were republics (except for Brazil, which gave itself an emperor), the first problem was their stability and the second their legitimacy; the populations had to understand that it was possible to be both a good Catholic and a good republican. Furthermore, they regarded themselves as the natural heirs to the royal rights of patronage in church affairs. In Spain, the monarchy refused to recognize this emancipation achieved through force and intervened to that effect with the Holy See. All these problems held up the appointment of new bishops and explain the long vacancy of many sees: up to twenty-two years in the case of that of Buenos Aires (Argentina).

At first, Pope Pius VII had condemned the independence movement (1816, brief *Etsi longissimo*). As soon as he was elected, his successor Leo XII was concerned to restore contact as far away as Chile (Muzi mission, 1823–5, one of whose members was the future Pius IX). In 1835, the pope officially recognized the republic of New Granada (modern-day Colombia); in 1836, the republic of Mexico, and then all the other republics.

In Brazil, Article 5 of the 1824 Constitution declared that the Catholic religion would continue to be the religion of the empire (which lasted from 1822 to 1889). In 1825, Lisbon and Rome recognized the new state. There was

continuity in all areas, in total contrast to what was happening in the former Spanish empire, where conflicts soon developed with the rulers of the new republics. Rome sought to profit from the new situation to recover its full authority over Latin American Christendom – after three centuries of royal patronage. The state sought the support of the church while keeping it firmly under control; the church sought its freedom from the state while retaining its position as the religion of the nation.

Bitter rivalry then ensued between church and state. Anticlericalism was met with antiliberalism. For these liberals, children of the Enlightenment, the Catholic church was the prime obstacle to the advance of reason and virtue. It had survived the Spanish defeat but remained a hangover from the colonial system. The liberals called for the closure of monasteries denounced as useless, unproductive and, above all, dangerous because of their popular base and their subordination to the papacy, that is a foreign sovereign. They wanted to put an end to the clergy's legal privileges and to the church's economic power (all over the continent, its property was secularized, with the *desamortización* of property held in mortmain). They blamed the clergy for the illiteracy and 'fanaticism' of the masses. For them, religion was nothing more than superstitions and expensive devotions. Finally, education had to be secularized and the control of young minds taken away from the baleful influence of priests so that 'enlightenment' might dissipate ecclesiastical 'darkness'. They made a careful distinction between the church, which they were fighting, and the religion, which they respected. They invoked the Supreme Being and stressed the practical utility of religion, which they recognized as playing an important role in maintaining public order for which the state was responsible.

By the middle of the century, the church had thus become the focal point of the political struggle between 'conservatives' (*blancos*) and 'liberals' (*colorados*), who alternated in power in the various republics. Rejected by the liberals, the church found itself hostage to the conservatives. There was a gradual slide towards the violent disestablishment of the Catholic church and to support by the liberals for the Protestant churches, which for them represented progress and tolerance.

The arrival of an external Protestantism

Protestantism had first arrived with the military chaplains of the British regiments, which supported the Creoles against the Spanish forces at the time of the wars of independence. They were followed by British and German diplomats, businessmen, bankers, industrialists and technicians, and later American ones. The newcomers offered an alternative to the Catholic church and attacked its 300-year-old monopoly.

Between 1850 and 1880, the triumph of liberalism in a number of countries favoured a Protestant proselytism, which went beyond the resident foreign communities. Yet the Anglican church, the first to arrive, like the 'historical' churches that had emerged from the Reformation in the sixteenth century, regarded Latin America as a Catholic preserve and felt that missionary work could only be undertaken among the Indians unconverted by the Catholics. Furthermore, immigrants from Protestant Europe were arriving to settle in southern Brazil and the neighbouring regions of Paraguay, Uruguay and Argentina, founding large German-American Lutheran communities. In addition to these transplanted churches there were the missions of the North American 'traditional denominations': Presbyterians, Methodists, Episcopalians and Baptists.

Between 1880 and 1916 the tempo of Protestant penetration speeded up without, however, achieving significant results. It was above all a new style, which marked this Protestantism convinced of its own superiority and borne along by the drive of the North American missions. By the turn of the century, their growing activity from Mexico to Argentina, with their schools and their welfare work, clearly heralded the rising power of the United States.

In response to the 1910 World Missionary Congress in Edinburgh, dominated by the European churches, which reasserted the principle of missionary non-interference in Latin America, a Catholic continent, forty religious bodies in the United States organized the Pan-Protestant Congress of 1916 in Panama, designed to endorse and coordinate missionary activity that was already under way. At this time, the organizers counted 128,000 Protestants out of a population of some 70 million: fewer than in the English-speaking Caribbean islands alone which had 160,000 Black Protestants. The Panama Congress concluded that there had been a failure: Protestantism had not taken root in Latin America. The Pentecostals would succeed in doing so after the Second World War.

Positivist spirit and Roman spirit

By 1860 liberalism was in full flood. Regalism was giving way to positivism, which, in some countries ended up in a tolerant agnosticism and in others in a militant anti-clericalism or even, as in Brazil, which cultivated the memory of Auguste Comte, in a new cult, the 'religion of humanity'. But in America, the word 'positivism' soon took on an all-embracing meaning that went beyond the accepted meaning in Europe: it took on board Darwin's evolutionism, its application by Spencer to society and history, and Bentham's or John Stuart Mill's utilitarianism. It was a positivism experienced as a 'scientific culture' which sought to shape economics and politics. This worldview, combining 'order and progress', underpinned the action of the Protestant churches, rested on freemasonry and opposed the influence of the Catholic church. This situation created something new, which was to be decisive for the future: Latin-American Catholicism turned to Rome and became attached to the papacy. For the papacy, liberalism was both the enemy and a sin, a source of errors harmful to society, which Pius IX had denounced in his 1864 *Syllabus*.

Faced with these challenges, the church reacted in three ways. It continued to defend its traditional rights, guaranteed, where possible, by the constitution or a concordat. It relied on conservative forces and the peasant masses to thwart liberal policies. It put its faith in education, the family, the press, not to mention the evangelization of the Indians and, in Brazil (where slavery survived until 1888), of the Blacks. It saw its goal as winning over the elites without losing the people, and securing recognition of Christian principles not only by individuals but also by the state. Finally, it received decisive help from the Holy See and the European churches.

With such an approach, it was no longer enough to be Catholic: it was necessary to be Catholic as in Rome. The Latin American clergy and ecclesiastical structures must move from 'colonial Catholicism' to the 'universal Catholicism' of Rome, with all that it implied in terms of doctrinal, moral and hierarchical discipline. Two events symbolize this shift: the foundation of the Colegio Pio Latinoamericano (1858), from which twenty-six bishops and archbishops, as well as the continent's first cardinal (1906), would emerge in the space of two thirds of a century; and the first Plenary Council of Latin America, convened by Leo XIII and held in Rome in 1899. A clear institutional dynamism accompanied this movement of Romanization: there were more and more dioceses, seminaries and parishes and a rise in the numbers of both national and European clergy.

In Brazil, the bishops were the precursors of this 'Romanization'. Pedro II had taken advantage of his rights to weaken the church. After the fall of the empire (1889), the new constitution (1891) established freedom of religion, secularized civil registration and education, and excluded the clergy from teaching and religion from the curriculum. The state abolished the religious budget, ceased to recognize religious vows, renounced patronage and distanced itself from the Catholic church, which in turn distanced itself from the state. Taking advantage of this freedom, the church embarked on rapid institutional development: in thirty years, the number of dioceses rose from 12 to 58.

By the end of the nineteenth century the situation of the Catholic church varied considerably from country to country, from secular Mexico to Catholic Colombia. It retained a strong hold over civil society while continuing to be marginalized in public life. It was striking for both its religious vitality and its cultural impoverishment, in the spirit of a scholastic theology whose chief support came from the Roman universities and the diocesan seminaries. Conversely, like the liberals, it had to confront new social forces, arising from economic development and European immigration: radicals, socialists, communists and anarcho-syndicalists. These new-shared adversaries encouraged a measure of rapprochement between the Catholic church and Latin-American governments, with the notable exception of Mexico, where the revolution began in 1910, and Uruguay, held by the liberals.

DEEPEST AFRICA

Nineteenth-century Africa is too easily portrayed as the product of one major event: the settlement of Europeans on the continent, the political division of the territories and, at the end of the century, the establishment of the colonial system. This situation did indeed profoundly transform the life of Africans. Deprived of their sovereignty, they also had to change their economic behaviour and cultural reference-points, with the advance of schooling and the penetration of Western ideas. But it would be reductive to limit the history of this period to the effects of European advance: Africa was at the same time undergoing a whole series of internal upheavals, arising in particular from another, less visible, less brutal penetration, that of Islam, which made no less of a contribution to altering the traditional view of the world and things in African societies.

Tradition

Animism, totemism, ancestrism, naturism, fetishism and paganism – such are the major notions adopted by ethnologists. In the nineteenth century, 'traditional' African religions differed widely in their beliefs, rituals and values, as well as in their modes of transmission and the role assigned to them within society. But they did have a real common core. Most referred to a supreme, inaccessible being, to whom prayer was pointless. Then came numerous deities, genies and spirits, to whom offerings, sacrifices and incantations had to be addressed. The word was of the utmost importance. In addition, religious observance went through a number of stages, from initiation (the ceremony of entry into adult life) to death. Finally, African religions were present whenever order was disturbed (war, famine, epidemic, death, technical setback) to engage the process of a 'return to normality', thus becoming closely involved in everyday life.

Contrary to what was long believed and written about them, they were far from static: rather, they showed themselves to be continually changing, displaying an astonishing capacity for adaptation: permanent contacts between African societies and the oral transmission of religious knowledge, the very fact that such knowledge was not written and codified, contributed greatly to this state of affairs. In the nineteenth century, however, the increase in interactions, both among Africans themselves and with Europeans, helped to speed up this process and, through the absorption of elements of Islam or Christianity, promoted new religious forms. While, for the general history of Africa, it has been demonstrated that adaptations were a permanent feature of African religions, for the nineteenth century the pattern of such an evolution is still poorly known.

Islamization

For many centuries, Islam had been widely but gradually settled in Africa. It was, at first, an Islam of merchants, cities and chiefs, and used three methods of penetration; in the East, from Somalia down to Mozambique, as a result of maritime trade with Asia; in the North through Egypt and Libya by way of the Nile Valley to Chad; and in the West by means of trade across the Sahara with countries of the Maghrib (Morocco, Algeria and Tunisia). In the nineteenth century, the advance of Islam on the 'Black Continent' accelerated. In Central Africa, the increase in trade associated with both European and Arab demand encouraged more and more conversions among the peoples dependent on that trade, who often associated the wealth of Arab or Swahili traders with their religion, while at the same time such conversion sheltered them from being seized in slave-raiding. In the same way, in the North East of the continent, Islam benefited greatly from the advance of the Egyptian 'frontier' towards the Great Lakes region. In West Africa, what was happening was often similar, and the advance of Islam, essentially the work of Africans themselves, was associated with the commercial hegemony of certain ethnic groups. It was thus able to penetrate new regions, previously 'protected', like the forest zones, and groups or states long hostile to the religion of the Arabs, like the Mossi, the Bambara and the Asante. But this advance was essentially the work of committed groups (notably the Hausa, Fulbe and Dyula), anxious to win as many converts as possible or simply to 'cleanse' the practices of Islam among 'bad Muslims'.

This desire was reflected in the increase in the number of religious wars (*jihâd*), which were waged by several recently-created West African states, from the theocratic state of Futa Jallon, established in 1760, to the empire of Samori Ture in the second half of the nineteenth century.

While the violence that accompanied conversions led to revivals of traditional practices and, often, fear and rejection of the new religion, Islam benefited from several advantages which made its expansion much easier than that of Christianity: simplicity of conversion, which dispensed with prior instruction, 'rite of passage' or public renunciation of former religious beliefs at baptism; and tolerance of old religious practices, and even old beliefs. Above all, it did not alter the life of the new believer: polygamy, circumcision, secular integration into society, all continued as before.

Finally, Islam was paradoxically given a boost by the arrival of the Europeans and the beginnings of colonization. Those administrators who, like Faidherbe, governor of Senegal, had served in Algeria before being appointed to Black Africa, knew and respected Islam; for them, in the idea of the 'civilizing mission' which fell to Europeans, Islam represented an 'advance' compared to African 'paganisms'. Conversely, the open hostility of some Europeans to Islam made it a focus of opposition to European penetration: the conversion of Lat Dior in Senegal, driven from his throne in Kayor by the French and combining a political and a religious crusade, is a good example of this.

One of the characteristics of African Islam has to do with the existence of brotherhoods. The Moors had spread through West Africa the Qadiriyya, an ascetic and mystical brotherhood that originated in the Middle East, which generally recruited its members from among the elites. Al-Hajj 'Umar, a member of the Tijaniyya, a brotherhood originating in North Africa, helped both the spread of that brotherhood in Sub-Saharan Africa and a certain retreat of the Qadiriyya. The undeniable success of the Tijaniyya is explained by the simplicity of its 'rule', the fact that it recruited among the ordinary people and its relatively egalitarian mode of operation. Finally, the nineteenth century saw the appearance of indigenous brotherhoods, such as Muridism, founded in Senegal by Sheikh Amadu Bamba, the most striking example, both because of the deep roots it put down in society and its articulation with local cultures, and because of its success. These new brotherhoods contributed greatly to the emergence of a specifically African Islam, a 'Black Islam' (Vincent Monteil).

Certainly, through the monarchies and followers, under the influence of a certain Sufism, a Sub-Saharan Islam took root, adapted to the customs and habits of the population, as happened in the Far East, in Indonesia. It merits being better known and understood after being so long neglected.

Christianization

The nineteenth century was supremely the century of Christian penetration into Africa. It is true that Ethiopia had, since the fourth century, represented a solid bastion of Christianity; in addition, in the age of the great discoveries, the first European missionaries had landed on the coasts of Africa, in particular in Congo. But in the nineteenth century the missionary effort really took off. Everything helped to encourage it: the intensification of trading relations, mainly with the West coast of the continent; the growing settlement of Whites in South Africa; the spread of the idea of a 'civilizing mission' among Europeans; and finally, at the end of the century, colonization. Missionaries arrived in ever larger numbers up to the First World War. Also, the explorers who crisscrossed Africa contributed to the spread of Christianity: these included David Livingstone (1813–73), doctor, explorer and minister, member of the London Missionary Society; and Henry M. Stanley (1841–1904), who undertook to interest the king of Buganda, Mutesa, a Muslim recently converted for reasons of politics, in Christianity.

Every great nation and every Christian denomination contributed to this movement, even the Black American churches from Sierra Leone and Liberia, which had become homes for freed slaves. As a result, Christianization was marked by two major features: rivalry among churches and, as a consequence, religious fragmentation, and a *de facto* partition among missions, which prefigured the colonial partition. Yet the degree of penetration varied from region to region: it was significant in South Africa, where it was associated with the settlement of Cape Colony; less in West Africa, where not simply the strength of Islam but above all the living conditions discouraged many would-be efforts.

The story of Christianization in Africa is less the story of missions – which has to do rather with the story of Europeans in Africa – than that of Africans and their reactions to missionary activity. From the beginning, relations between Africans and Christianity were highly ambiguous. The missionaries, opposed to slavery and the slave trade, found a ready ear in servile groups of the population and in societies that had been victims of slave-raiding. In addition, the Christian religion was often associated with the wealth, power and prestige of Whites. Cultural, economic and religious factors were closely mixed up together. The missionaries promoted useful progress: mission kitchen gardens, small-scale craft activities, schools, medical care, etc. Finally, for many individuals ill at ease in societies undergoing rapid change, deprived of their previous prestige, suffering from the superiority of Europeans, the new religion offered the opportunity of a new status. Thus, many young catechists acquired among their associates a power and influence hitherto the preserve of elders and chiefs; attendance at mission schools, and an ability to write, quickly became the surest means of social advancement.

But Christianity was not all advantages. On many points, its message conflicted with representations of the sacred and their socialization. It rested on the written word, the Bible, whereas African cultures were essentially oral. Its doctrine was codified, its strict rules condemned polygamy and, in Catholicism, demanded celibacy of its religious personnel. Attempts to reconcile African traditions and Christian demands were few and far between: the Anglican bishop Colenso was even excluded from his church for having allowed polygamy among the Zulus in South Africa. The rituals and symbols did not sit very well with the customs of the populations. Finally, preaching was addressed to the individual and his family, who only existed by virtue of their belonging to a community. In addition, membership involved preparation, the catechumenate, and a rite, baptism, foreign to the African tradition of initiation. Thus, many new Christians felt the need to continue to worship the old deities and respect the taboos of their group.

There were two further weighty considerations. One was that these African churches continued to be led by Europeans. The 'indigenization' – of clergy, liturgy or theology – was slow and late, partial and controlled. The other was that the arrival of the new religion often appeared to be associated with the unpleasant effects of White colonization experienced on a day-to-day basis. While the first conversions were often those of isolated individuals, rejected by their own societies, in the second generation they were essentially those of whole communities. Several of these developments were associated with precise events: thus the Padhola in East Africa were converted by force by their Baganda attackers who wanted to prove their superiority and that of their religion; the Tswana, on the other hand, went over to Christianity following a military victory which they thought they owed to the Reverend Robert Moffat: Father Dorgère was able to win over the 'Dahomeyans' (Benin) by becoming interpreter and confidential agent to King Behanzin; Ranavalona II, queen of Madagascar, converted to Protestantism in 1868, calling on her subjects to follow her example. Finally, in the situation of social disintegration into which some societies were plunged in face of the European advance, and given the political uncertainties and their loss of power, many chiefs themselves turned to the missionaries.

Resistance and appropriation

The European intrusion precipitated a malaise that was so deep, and so subversive of the order of things and knowledge that many communities began to question themselves. The Bible became an instrument of understanding as well as a ferment of opposition. A succession of prophets, sorcerers, secret societies, priestesses and rain-makers made their appearance, along with myths of encounters with supernatural beings. The discourses thus produced provided different explanations for the misfortunes which seemed to be befalling Africa. In addition, these millenarian-inspired messages sought to predict an end to them. Usually, the prophets would announce the forthcoming arrival of an era of prosperity, justice and independence; power and even the fate of humanity would be in the hands of Blacks who would then rule over Whites. There were countless versions of this reversal of situation: a storm of fire would consume the Whites; all water would be transformed into blood; a saviour would arrive providentially, perhaps a man, a god, a reincarnation of Christ or a whole people coming from far away. This hope was so deep-rooted among the followers of some religions that several groups stopped all work, and destroyed crops and flocks (such as followers of mumbo in Gabon, in the early twentieth century).

These religious movements supplied anticolonial resistance with the sites and personnel necessary for it to mature and express itself. Thus the priests of the Maji-Maji movement (Tanganyika) made talismans to protect their followers from bullets in fighting with Europeans. Similarly, the 'leopard-men' secret society on the Slave Coast (Gulf of Guinea), turned itself into a small guerrilla army, which attacked Whites and sought to terrorize them.

In areas where Christianity had made little headway, the traditional religions absorbed some of those traits that had been picked up by people who had attended mission schools: monotheism (which was far from alien to African 'paganisms'), belief in the devil, the notion of good and evil, adoption of European-type morality, the idea of salvation, expectation of a 'messiah', all began to become part of many African religions. The case of Bwiti is a striking example of this, in that it skilfully combined features drawn from the Bible with the history and customary religion of the Fang (Gabon).

The religious renewal also affected Christianity and produced something that had not been seen before: the emergence of new Christian churches, in the same way as in North America and for similar reasons. The phenomenon of messianism, analysed as early as 1902 by the missionary Maurice Leenhardt for South Africa, certainly went back to the seventeenth century and the arrival of the first Portuguese missionaries. But it really took off at the end of the nineteenth century. Its origin lay above all in the attitude of the missionaries: racial segregation in the churches, the contradiction between this attitude and the life of ease of the missionaries and the message of brotherhood and poverty of Christianity. This dichotomy led to a rejection of the 'White man's religion', followed by the creation of Black churches, a return to the true religion against the message distorted by these 'bad Christians'. In addition, the religious rituals better reflected the demands of the members of these churches: purification rituals, healing sessions, litanies and trances, all deeply impregnated with the old customs.

The numerous studies of these various messianic movements led to a distinction being made among different types. In South Africa, Bengt Sundkler identified 'Ethiopian' churches, which dreamed of the land of Ham and the kingdom of Prester John as the Promised Land; and 'Zionist' churches, so-called by reference both to the 'New Jerusalem' and to Zion City (Illinois, USA) where, in 1896, one of the earliest Black churches was founded. Today, more detailed typologies provide for a variety of movements: thus, the 'Hebraist' churches preached a belief in God but not in Christ, still expecting the coming of a messiah.

Throughout Africa, these churches played a political role from the very beginning, which was part of the long process leading up to the time of independence.

CHRISTIAN EXPANSION

The new missionary spirit

Until the end of the eighteenth century, the action of European churches outside Europe was closely controlled by states. It generally did not go beyond making religious provision for Europeans. Among Catholics, the poor quality of the colonial clergy was a well-known fact, and the wealthiest settlers entrusted the education of their children to schools in the mother country. The religious, it is true, especially the Jesuits, were more independent and pursued the evangelization of the indigenes, but disputes about how to proceed in China in dealing with indigenous customs, and jealousies aroused in Paraguay by the economic and social success of their 'Reductions', caused their endeavours to be aborted and even contributed to the dissolution of the Society of Jesus in those countries.

At the same time, also during the eighteenth century, the Evangelicals were inventing new forms of missionary action of their own, with their pietistic 'revivals', in Denmark, Germany and the Anglo-Saxon countries. These groups, notably the Clapham sect in the suburbs of London, came together with members of parliament involved in the anti-slavery movement in the 1790s to return freed slaves to Sierra Leone, as the American societies did a little later in Liberia. One of these freed slaves, Samuel Crowther, born in what later became Nigeria, was to be the pioneer

of evangelization on the unhealthy coast of the Gulf of Guinea. On popular and sometimes interdenominational bases, like the London Missionary Society in 1795, missionary societies brought together personnel and funding to distribute the Bible and support the evangelization of local populations. After 1814 this movement spread to the continent, with similar societies being founded in Basel, Paris and Berlin and in Scandinavia.

Among Catholics, the movement had a similar popular character, drawing inspiration from Anglo-Saxon methods, such as Pauline Jaricot's 'Halfpenny for Propagation of the Faith' at Lyon in 1822. The link with the anti-slavery movement came later, and was less strong, but was associated with experience on the ground acquired by missionaries such as the Sisters of St Joseph of Cluny in Reunion and Senegal, led by their founder Anne-Marie Javouhey (1770–1851). A number of secular priests such as Monnet and Levavasseur had become convinced that baptism required the formation of stable families and hence the abolition of slavery. This train of thought led the convert son of a rabbi from Saverne, in Alsace, François Libermann, to launch the *Oeuvres des Noirs* in 1839, the kernel of what was to become the Congregation of the Immaculate Heart of Mary which, after its amalgamation with the Congregation of the Holy Ghost, became one of the most powerful Catholic mission societies, the Holy Ghost Fathers. At the end of the Second Empire, Charles Lavigerie (1825–92), the new archbishop of Algiers, created his congregation of the 'White Fathers', giving it the task close to his own heart of saving orphan and slave children. Twenty years later, he took the lead in an anti-slavery campaign, which led to the Brussels conference in July 1890.

By then France was the leading mission country. The pre-1789 congregations were re-established in 1816, led by the Paris Foreign Mission Society, which focused on Asia. New congregations, of both men and women, were founded, drawing recruits ever more internationally; they divided up among themselves the territories subject to the jurisdiction of the Holy See.

Evangelization strategies

All this missionary activity was carried on as close to the people as possible, with total commitment, accepting, for the most part and out of necessity, local living conditions – except for a family or community life regarded as a vital safeguard against isolation and all sorts of problems. Even after the discovery of quinine (1820), existence continued to be very precarious: in equatorial Africa, in particular, a heavy tribute was paid in the lives of young men and women, victims of yellow fever, sleeping sickness or the terrible 'haematuric fever'.

There was a sharp difference in method between the Protestant missions and the Catholic ones. The former focused principally on distributing the Bible: thus, William Carey and his two companions, established near Calcutta, translated the entire Bible into six languages, including Chinese, and the New Testament into some thirty languages or dialects. The Congregationalist structure, the most widespread form of organization among the Evangelicals, encouraged deliberative bodies, but decision-making power in them was the preserve of Europeans. Among Catholics, clerical celibacy, the parallel hierarchies (vicars or apostolic prefects, local superiors) and the prime concern of the church to found new ones set the goal of the mission: to win over populations who still clung to the traditional religions one by one, by opening dispensaries, schools or chapel-farms, in order to train catechists, who would be permanent adjuncts for European missionaries travelling out from a main station.

In the Reformed churches, especially among the Anglicans in East Africa and Nigeria, missionaries travelled over even greater distances, dispensing with fixed stations and leaving behind indigenous catechists and later clergymen: the first African bishop was Samuel Crowther who, from his consecration at Canterbury in 1864 to his death in 1890, evangelized the area around Lagos, demonstrating a remarkable respect for traditional beliefs and an openness to dialogue with Muslims.

Finally, Protestant and Catholic missions divided up territories between them, sometimes in due legal form (as in Indonesia): this had the effect of consolidating mutual ignorance between them, without eliminating competition and rivalries, especially over schools. The same problems arose among Protestant denominations or among Catholic congregations.

Like all their compatriots, missionaries sought the support of the military and administrative forces of their respective countries. As precursors of colonial occupation, they often carried out the same topographical and linguistic surveys as the explorers. Missionaries were universally patriotic and governments were fully aware of the influence they derived from protecting Christian interests, especially in Asia. It was in this spirit that the French administration turned to French Protestant missions in Oceania and Madagascar to take over control of missions established by Anglo-Saxon societies. This missionary nationalism was underpinned by a firm belief in the superiority of 'Christian civilization', whose offshoots in pagan countries made up for setbacks in the modern West.

But it would not be accurate to regard Christian missions as an aspect of colonial expansion and in the service of that expansion. Whether British or French, all administrations were suspicious of religious proselytism. For their part, the missionaries kept themselves away from the big urban centres and from a European population whose mentality and behaviour they feared. Finally, the administrations' desire for control, especially in matters of land and education, could easily turn to open hostility.

Differences in approach were apparent on the social and cultural level too. It was to the weakest and most exposed members of traditional societies that missions provided aid and protection: former slaves, girls subject to hiring contracts or forced marriages. Catholic nuns and Protestant female auxiliaries personified the social advancement of women. While the aim of missionaries was to train catechists and future clergymen, the administration saw schools as training grounds for interpreters or clerks; the attraction of the city and the European way of life also operated on pupils, encouraging them to learn the main foreign languages: sometimes the conflict could be sharp, as it was between the German colonial administration and the Bremen Mission in Togo.

As regards indigenous cultures, missions played rather a conservationist role; by preparing a variety of reports, glossaries or memoirs, they created materials that could be recycled to reconstruct local cultural identities. In this respect, the works on the Malagasy language and political and religious traditions by the French Jesuit Callet and the Norwegian Lutheran Vig, which have been highlighted by recent studies, are exemplary: thanks to their perfect knowledge of the language, they were able to conduct oral surveys among elders who had taken refuge in the countryside, and were able to put together a 'corpus', publication of which was completed only after their death, which today provides the bulk of the royal traditions and religious rituals, reconstituting the remote past of Madagascar.

In East Africa, we are indebted to the patient work of the Holy Ghost father Charles Sacleux (1856–1943), for knowledge and standardization of both the Kiswahili language and Kiswahili culture: along with a thousand-page dictionary which he continually updated from its first edition in 1891, he wrote a religious history, school textbooks and hymns which passed into everyday use in Anglican as well as Catholic missions. He also had another passion, botany: he prepared an initial classification of East African flora and left his herbals to the Muséum de Paris and the University of Montpellier.

At the same time, Maurice Leenhardt (1878–1954), a Protestant missionary, was collecting in New Caledonia the linguistic and ethnological materials that he was later to exploit on his return, after the First World War. The German Catholic missionary Father Wilhelm Schmidt (1868–1954) was surely the most famous of them: he founded the Vienna ethnological school and the journal *Anthropos* (1906), was a greater believer in surveys, and was the theoretician of 'primitive monotheism' and 'culture cycles'. Finally, mention should be made of the work of Father Charles de Foucault, the hermit of Tamanrasset in the Sahara, murdered in 1916, and in particular his *Grammaire et dictionnaire français-touareg, touareg-français* and his collection of *Poésies touarègues*.

These are but examples of a comprehensive study which remains to be made, without omitting the medical and health work, alongside official services. Father Damien de Veuster, a Belgian Picpus missionary, who died of leprosy in 1889 in the leprosarium on Molokai (Hawaii), remains the emblematic figure of this fight against the great endemic diseases.

Feedback

Europe could not remain unaffected by all this patient work on the ground. With the support of the Vienna school of religious ethnology, the first International Week of Religious Ethnology was held in Louvain in 1912, and the series continued a few years after the war: the Louvain Missiology Weeks took over from them. In France, Maurice Leenhardt continued his work in public higher education and at the Société des Océanistes, while Father Sacleux set up what was in effect a language academy at the mission seminary at Chevilly-Larue.

For many years, missionary journals directed at the faithful such as the *Annales de la propagation de la foi* (1825) were the only window on the wider world open to a popular rural readership, offering a fraternal and sympathetic opening to peoples who in those days were described as 'primitive'. But, predictably, it was on the churches themselves and on theological thought that the impact was strongest, beginning with the first tentative steps towards a rapprochement among the churches. Evidence of this is to be found in the interventions of the Indian and Chinese delegates at the great World Missionary Congress in Edinburgh in 1910, which is generally agreed to mark the beginning of the ecumenical movement among the Reformed churches. Only the war prevented the formation of an International Mission Council. Outside a few groups or journals formed around individuals such as the Lazarist Fernand Portal in France, this ecumenism did not yet have any counterpart in Catholic missionary circles. The publication, in 1912, of a thesis defended in Toulouse by a young theologian, Louis Capéran, on 'the problem of the salvation of infidels', initiated an ongoing debate inside the Roman church on this great missionary theme. Finally, at Halle, around Gustav Warneck, and later at Munster around Joseph Schmidlin – one Protestant, the other Catholic – a new discipline in theology took shape – 'missiology'.

In the receiving countries, reactions were soon forthcoming: in Southern and Eastern Africa, a host of Bantu prophetic movements appeared, from which future independent African churches would emerge. They can be seen as the religious expression of an emerging awareness of the political and cultural identity of these peoples, as shown, for example, by the recently rediscovered first writings of the first Congolese priest, Stefano Kaozé, on the traditions of his people in the early years of the twentieth century.

Even more striking examples of the reaction of local religious consciousness could be noted in Asia, such as the Brahmin who attempted to invent a Hindu version of Christian monasticism, Brahmabandhav Upadhyay (1861–1907), who would end up joining the educational movement of Rabindranath Tagore. Finally, it is well known how much the earliest leaders of the first Chinese republic, beginning with Sun Yat Sen, educated in Protestant missionary schools, were open to Western influences and were even anxious to seek out what strength Westerners had drawn from Christianity.

In the East, the Orthodox mission

The Orthodox mission, during this period, was essentially the work of the Russian church. It was identified with an often brutal attempt at Russification in the seventeenth and eighteenth centuries and had also long been associated with persecution of the 'old believers', but in the nineteenth century, and down to 1917 it became more respectful of local languages and cultures. It now based itself on a liturgical witness (in the indigenous language) and often disinterested social work. Three great missionaries – archimandrite Makarios in Western Siberia, Ivan Veniaminov and Saint Herman of Alaska in the Far East and Northern Pacific – braved a harsh and extreme environment, attempted to understand the shamans and translated the scriptures and liturgy into dialects which, in so doing, they made into written languages. By around 1900, the Kazan Academy had become a great centre of missionary studies and Islamology. It published a whole Orthodox library in fifty of the languages of Upper Asia. The Russian mission continued in Alaska and the Aleutian islands after their sale to the United States in 1867, and could thus embrace all the Orthodox immigrants arriving in the United States. There, many Uniates, from sub-Carpathia, who were looked down on by an Irish-dominated local Catholicism, voluntarily returned to Orthodoxy, a solution preferable to the forced liquidation of Uniatism in the Russian Empire, notably in 1853 under Nicholas I.

In Japan, Father Nicholas Kasatkin ensured the growth of a vigorous Orthodox community, which used only Japanese. Archimandrite Spyridon (whose admirable memoirs have been translated and published in French as *Mes missions en Sibérie*) kept company with Buddhists from the borders of Mongolia and, impressed by their deep spirituality, hesitated to baptize them, preferring to work for the time when their wise men, always portrayed with their eyes closed, would open them.

In the Middle East, the Russian church (represented in particular by the Russian Palestine Society) intervened in favour of Byzantine-rite Orthodox Arabs who were dominated by a Greek episcopate imposed by the patriarch of Constantinople, responsible for the Orthodox millet throughout the Ottoman Empire. This situation prevented the Orthodox from defending themselves effectively against the Uniates (better equipped culturally and protected by France), and against Protestant missionaries (backed by the Anglo-Saxon countries). The opposite was the case in the largest and most populous patriarchate, that of Antioch (whose seat since the Middle Ages had been at Damascus), with the long crisis (1891–1906) which, despite Constantinople and the Turkish authorities, led to the advent of an Arab patriarch and the strengthening of an equally indigenous episcopate. Orthodox Arabs then became the pioneers of the Arab renaissance, the *Nahda* (awakening), which called for the unification and independence of the Fertile Crescent in a secular society open to modernity.

THE MUSLIM WORLD

There is always a risk of forgetting that Islam is not limited to part of the Mediterranean basin, from Morocco to the Near East, including Egypt and reaching as far as the Arabian Peninsula: an Arab Islam, Arabic being the language of the Prophet and the Qur'an. Beyond this vast historical zone is Turkish-speaking Islam, extending from Asia Minor (present-day Turkey) to Central Asia (the former Soviet republics), and also Iranian Islam. Beyond that it occupies the enormous area stretching from Afghanistan to the Sunda Islands (Java, Borneo, Sumatra) in the Pacific, and the gates of Australia (which until 1788 was inhabited by only a few aboriginals). To that must be added its outposts in Black Africa and, isolated in the Balkans, Albania.

A world in ferment, a world coveted

This Islam sees itself as 'the community of believers' (*umma*), a whole both religious and political, as Christendom might be. For both, reality has never matched the dream. Religiously very diverse, as a result of history and cultures, Islam was also fractured – chiefly between Sunnis and Shiites – with its heresies, schisms and dissident groups. Politically it has never been neither unified nor even unitary. The Ottoman Empire and the British Empire in India brought together peoples of different races and religions. In the Near and Middle East, very ancient Christian churches, themselves divided, had survived the Hegira.

All this gave rise in the nineteenth century to two movements developing in different directions but tending to the same outcome. On the one hand, in the Ottoman

Empire, a desire for freedom among the Christian countries in Europe – Greece, the Balkans – as well as in the Arab regions – Egypt, Arabia, Syria. On the other, the expansionist impulse of the great powers, which affected the whole of the Islamic world, in a race to carve up the world's wealth: from the 'sphere of influence' to annexation by way of the 'protectorate'. It was the century of imperialism and colonialism: geopolitical and commercial considerations justified armed interventions.

The Ottoman Empire was the first to be threatened. Despite the reformism (*tanzîmât*) of its Sultans, it gave way on all fronts. Symbolically, 1830 saw both the independence of Greece – an example to its Balkan neighbours – and the French conquest of Algeria. Egypt followed its own path, open to French influence (Bonaparte in 1798; the Saint-Simonians; de Lesseps and the Suez Canal, inaugurated in 1869): governed by a viceroy (*khedive*) since 1805 (Muhammad 'Ali), it asserted its designs over the Sudan where the revolt of the Mahdi triumphed between 1881 and 1898, but itself fell victim to British occupation in 1882. Tunisia, Morocco, Tripolitania, Cyrenaica, Eritrea and Somalia fell one after the other under French or Italian control. Throughout the century, Arabia thought only of its independence in the name of a strict Islam (Wahhabism).

Further, East Persia and Afghanistan retained their independence, albeit under Russian and British influence. Queen Victoria was named Empress of India in 1878, ruling Muslims and Hindus as well as religious minorities such as Sikhs, Parsis and Syro-Malabar and Syro-Malankar Christians. What would later become Indonesia was under Dutch rule, and what would later become Malaysia, under British rule. The Philippines, under Spanish rule until 1898, had only a Muslim minority.

For the Muslim community, the nineteenth century was a time of trials, on the defensive, externally and internally, forcing it to react, sometimes in contradictory ways. The *dâr al-Islâm* was a world extending over a vast distance, in ferment and coveted on all sides. While there are no figures for the beginning of the century (one billion?), by the end, in 1900, the world population was estimated at 1.6 billion, of whom 200 million were Muslims, one eighth of humanity. Of this number, 175 million were Sunnites belonging to four schools or rites (Hanafites, Shafi'ites, Malikites, Hanbalites) and 25 million were Shiites (including the Alawites and Isma'ilis).

To this listing must be added, with no estimate as to numbers, three minority religious groups that emerged out of Islam: dating from very ancient times, the Druses and the Karaites; in the nineteenth century, through the episode of Babism, the Baha'i, persecuted as heretics before spreading to Europe in the years after 1890. Their founder, Bahâ' ullah, advocated a universal religion based on overcoming racial, social and religious conflicts.

Between fundamentalism and modernism

Challenged, the Muslim community reacted. Its ulemas were the first to engage in a re-reading of tradition promoting new religious attitudes and even the hope of a 'renaissance' (*nahda*). The approaches varied depending on the regional cultures and the extent of European influence. The vitality of religious life is striking, marked by struggles among schools and the development of sects and brotherhoods, as well as by the emergence of a movement to return to the early days (*Salafiyya*).

Having extended their competence and progressively consolidated their authority, the ulemas exercised a leading role in the everyday public life of Islamic society. They held a monopoly on education, led prayers as *imams* and delivered the Friday sermon (*khutba*), in which they dealt with the problems of the community. As cadis or muftis, they dispensed justice, interpreted legal documents and regulated relations among individuals. While they guided the faithful, they did not spare the rulers who, often, had to accommodate them. But they themselves suffered the effects of a crisis which affected Islamic thought itself: they clung to the language of the earliest masters without going beyond a literal exegesis. Unreserved submission to tradition (*taqlîd*) was more important than the effort of personal interpretation of the law (*ijtihâd*).

The end of the century saw a rapid expansion of the marabout movement. The main brotherhoods or *tarîqas*: the *Qadiriyya*, the *Sadat al-Uafaiiya*, the *Bakryakhalwatiya* and the *Tijaniyya*, wove networks all over the Islamic world forming solidly established communal institutions. Under the leadership of the sheikh and his *muqaddams* or lieutenants, they brought together their followers or *muridin* in *zawiyas*, where they performed their religious observances.

Is it possible to speak of an age of 'medieval obscurantism'? In the religious centres, the teaching of reading and writing ensured a degree of literacy and opened up direct access to the Qur'an. Studies could be continued in the great mosques and the madrasas (schools), but solely in religious subjects, to the exclusion of profane culture.

A movement to return to the roots appeared in the late eighteenth century in the Indian subcontinent and the Arabian Peninsula, following the example of the 'pious predecessors' (*al-salah al-salah*). This movement (*Salafiyya*) drew inspiration in India from Shah Wali Allah (1702–62), and in Arabia from Muhammad ibn 'Abd al-Wahhab (1703–92). This marked the birth of Wahhabism, a true fundamentalism, which sought to cleanse Islam of its unnecessary excrescences (cult of saints, visit to tombs, intercession of the Prophet and even the institution of the sultanate-caliphate in Constantinople). The theologian formed an alliance with emir Muhammad Ibn Saud to win power: Riyadh was taken in 1786, the Hijaz occupied in 1805, and Mecca and Medina captured. The sultan reacted and, with the help of Egyptian troops, put an end to the adventure in 1818, but without undermining the strength of the movement.

The capture of the holy places by the Wahhabites had an enormous impact in the Muslim world, thanks to pilgrims. In the Maghrib, the tradition of openness, the strength of Malikism and the rejection of violence were an obstacle to their doctrines. These influenced the Sanusiyya in Libya (founded in 1843) and, through it, Sub-Saharan Africa; they reached Yemen, and in 1821 the Punjab, where they fuelled opposition to the British after its annexation in 1849. The latter saw in it the 'most dangerous' of sects: 'Its missionaries are as numerous and zealous as the Christian missionaries. . . . They are even respected, for their austerity, by the Orthodox Muslims' (1870 report).

The modernists saw this spirit and approach as leading nowhere. To halt the decline of Islam, it was necessary on the contrary to 'borrow from the West', without hesitation and without fear. Bonaparte's expedition to Egypt (1798) had sent shock-waves throughout the Islamic lands: it was perceived as a crusade, and there was a call for *jihâd* in response. The modernization and industrialization of Egypt by Muhammad 'Ali (1769–1849) opened another path that inevitably divided the ulemas. Among them, Rifa'a al-Tahtawi (1801–73), was the prime mover among the modernists after a five-year stay in France (1826–31), from which the lessons were drawn in his book *L'Or de Paris*. He was followed in Tunisia by Mahmud Kabadu (1815–55), who paved the way for Tunisian reformers. Khereddin's book, published in Arabic in 1867, and in French in Paris in 1868 (*Réformes nécessaires aux états musulmans*), was regarded as the manifesto of this new spirit.

At odds though they were on the line to follow and how to behave, fundamentalists and modernists were at least agreed on the need for spiritual resistance to Western rule. Manifestations of this are the epic of 'Abd al-Kadir in Algeria (1842–7), and the theocratic kingdoms in Black Africa, such as the caliphate of Sokoto in Nigeria, which held out against the British until 1900, or Samori and the Sudanese Mahdists, both finally defeated in 1898, the former by the French, the latter by the British: two forms of *jihâd*.

Therein lies the explanation why the renewal of Islamic thought can be observed in these two differently but equally 'reformist' directions. This can be seen in the two periodicals, *al-Urwa al-wuthqa*, founded in 1884 by Jamal al-Din al-Afghani (1839–97) and his follower Muhammad 'Abduh (1849–1905), and the more modernizing *al-Manar*, founded in Cairo in 1898, by the latter. They shared a common certainty: Muslim backwardness was to be blamed not on Islam, but on the passivity of believers, symbolized by the traditionalists and the brotherhoods. But this awakening and renaissance faced two models: the Islamic society of the early days or the lessons of Western development. The question took on a new urgency with the European conquests: were the colonized lands to be regarded as the abode of war (*dâr al-harb*), since they were neither that of Islam (*dâr al-Islâm*), nor that of truce (*dâr al-sulh*). The new generation of reformers in the Indian peninsula followed in the footsteps of the fundamentalism of Afghani, 'Abduh and their followers.

Generally, the ulemas turned first to the powers that be to exhort them to engage in *jihâd*. When they showed little enthusiasm, they turned to the Muslim communities. Then, as a last resort they appealed to individual believers, calling on them to save Islamic law by living it in their private life: 'The Islamic community will only become prosperous again when it has resolved to apply the shari'a strictly once again and put an end to usury, false witness, theft and lust and forbid the use of musical instruments' (Fatwa of the Moroccan 'alim Jaafar Ibn Idriss, al Kattani, 18 May 1881).

The reaction of Muslim intellectuals thus took two directions, based on different approaches: on the one hand, the *Salafiyya* and fundamentalism which called for a strict reading of the shari'a, often taken literally; on the other, the modernist school which did not recoil from bold reforms. Thus the cadi Kacem Amin (1873–1908) called for the emancipation of Muslim women and abolition of the veil, *hijâb*, as early as 1898, arguing that no Qur'anic text sanctioned the practice. Far from being secular in the sense that the Kemalists in Turkey were, the modernist approach sought solutions compatible with the shari'a.

THE FAR EAST

For Westerners, Asia is above all 'the Far East' – China, Japan, Korea, India, Ceylon (Sri Lanka), Indochina – a cultural grouping in the heart of a vast geographical area which includes Siberia in the north and extends from southern Turkey to present-day Indonesia – a Muslim area – and the heavily Christianized Philippines. It is a region which testifies to the antiquity of man, the home of the earliest cultures of humanity with specific, well-demarcated religious traditions.

India and South East Asia

Ceylon (Sri Lanka) and India share influence over the countries of South East Asia. But while Hinduism broadly prevails in India, Buddhism is dominant in these countries: Mahayana (Great Vehicle) Buddhism in Viet Nam, Hinayana (Lesser Vehicle) Buddhism, in other words Theravada ('doctrine of the elders'), in the rest, where it is organized around numerous monasteries which provide the religious and educational training of the young.

Islam was the largest minority in these countries. Christianity, which accounted for as much as 10 per cent of the population in Viet Nam and Ceylon (Sri Lanka), was well established on the coasts of India as a result of successive waves, the earliest of which is said to date back to the apostle St Thomas, and the oldest for which there is evidence being the work of Nestorians in the fifth century, followed by Portuguese colonization in the sixteenth century and the French missions in the seventeenth century.

Religions were thus a major meeting-point between Europe and Asia, and an important chapter in their relations, which have been many-sided and tumultuous. India in particular was the scene of commercial activities, which, after the fall of the Mughal Empire in 1858, turned into systematic colonization by the British crown. Siam – present-day Thailand – opened up to European influence, but was able to maintain its independence. Ceylon – present-day Sri Lanka – fell under British rule in 1802. After three wars with the British, Burma was annexed to the Indian empire in 1885. In 1863, Cambodia, coveted by its Siamese and Vietnamese neighbours, placed itself under the protection of France, which also seized Laos from Siam and Cochin-china from Viet Nam, and then went on to establish a protectorate over Tonkin and Annam in 1873.

Before the British conquest, the Indian subcontinent had never been unified under a central government. The tendency to political fragmentation between Hindu and Muslim rulers was settled through alliance or war. Hindu and Sufi mystics easily found areas of understanding. Muslim rulers accommodated themselves to the caste system. Hindus incorporated the cult of Muslim saints into their pantheon.

Colonization brought about a new governmental rationality. It relied on a Westernized intelligentsia which acted as cultural middleman between the administration and the population at large. The West discovered the richness of Eastern religious thought while at the same time throwing a critical light on it, thus inciting it to self-examination.

Despite its Brahmins and ascetics, Hinduism has always been a religion without a church, inseparable from a highly hierarchical society, which identified itself by its values. The situation was different in the countries where Theravada

Buddhism prevailed: there the moral code of Buddha proclaimed itself universal; the religious way of asceticism and meditation prevailed over knowledge and power. This helps to explain why in these countries, under the impact of the economic and political situation, a religious revival emerged from the monasteries with many centres which continued to develop all through the century.

In Ceylon (Sri Lanka), for example, each sect endeavoured to show itself more canonically orthodox than the next. Educated monks opposed the English-speaking elite, but they also opposed Christian missionaries and their grip on education. In 1862, one of them founded the Society for the Propagation of Buddhism, equipped with a very active printing-house. All this activity was further fuelled by rising nationalism.

Similar revivalism was to be seen in Hinduism. Colonial reforms precipitated revolts, which, especially among the tribes, assumed religious forms with millenarian overtones, sometimes borrowing their themes from Christianity. On the other hand, sects behind a spiritual master, in Gujarat or Uttar Pradesh, demonstrated a degree of Puritanism. But a reform movement that was rather different from neo-Hindu reformism produced by the Anglicized Indian elite requires particular attention.

It was not enough for this elite to attack customs that were deemed to be barbarous in Europe (immolation or non-remarriage of widows, child marriage). The clash of cultures called for in-depth religious analysis, and in this Bengal and especially Calcutta was the first centre with the figure of Ram Mohan Roy (1774–1833). Born a Brahmin, but having studied Persian, he was thoroughly versed in Muslim culture and admired the monotheism of Islam. He learned English, joined the East India Company, became familiar with Western rationalism and the Protestant religion. He remained a Brahmin, but professed a strict monotheism, which combined the quest for salvation with social action in this world. In order to promote his reform programme, he founded a sort of religious order, the Brahmo Samaj, which set up branches in the major cities and where the British administration recruited officials for the whole of India. Among its members were D. N. Tagore, the father of the poet, and K. C. Sen.

A little later, also in Calcutta, appeared the extraordinary figure of Ramakrishna (1834–86), a mystic who experienced spectacular ecstasies and who identified with Hindu deities as well as with Christ and Muhammad. His leading disciple, Vivekananda (1862–1903), founded the Ramakrishna mission in 1897 and made his master the symbol of the universality of Hinduism, capable of embracing all religions and even the secular values of Western humanism, for the liberation of India and the salvation of the world.

During the nineteenth century India was among the select, a land of meetings and exchanges, where numerous personalities, Hindus, Muslims and even Zoroastrians were prominent. Mahatma Gandhi (1869–1948), the figure at the helm of this movement, was living in Europe. This is the environment which explains the origin in India of the Theosophical Society, founded by Helena Blavatsky (1831–91). Ideas circulate, which bring inspiration, blurring the classical borders of the great religions where life was hardly affected by them.

In widely scattered areas numerous reformist associations came into being, with a programme of moral education and social action. Faced with this sometimes syncretic modernism, conservative, even fundamentalist reactions were inevitable, to defend the social system of castes, customs and the cult of images. This reinforced the concern to present a united Hinduist front to non-Indian religions, especially when the Muslims had won the right to form a separate electoral body in 1909. It was the beginning of an age of growing tensions between the aspirations of elites and the traditions of a society which was resisting change, between the desire for a return to the pure religion of old and the reality of popular cults, attached to their gods.

China

For China, the nineteenth century, cut in two in 1840 by the first opium war, is generally regarded as a period of decline. Under the Manchu Qing dynasty (1644–1911), China suffered an ever more oppressive foreign presence, initially European and later Japanese. For traditional – and still to a large extent current – historiography, religion was not at the centre of this evolution: religious decline in China was something settled long ago. None of the three great institutionalized religions was able to incarnate the resistance of Chinese society to foreign pressure and the crises that it provoked.

Confucianism, which had become highly secularized since the Ming (1368–1644), now took the form of a domestic and personal religiosity, which rejected any public expression. Families came together around the ancestor cult, organized in the form of powerful guilds; individuals regulated their moral behaviour according to Ledgers of Merit and Demerit (*gongguo ge*) and, when they doubted, questioned the gods through 'inspired writing' which at this time underwent considerable expansion. While the literate elite continued to live their status as a partly spiritual vocation, they ceased to provide any liturgical service outside the prescribed rituals (ceremonies of passage, cults of spring and autumn), increasingly interpreted in a purely formal manner. Confucianism retained its power to set ethical norms, but detached itself from collective forms of religious life (festivals, cults, etc.). The co-optation of popular cults into the official pantheon and the rise of very popular patron divinities of war and examinations, Guandi and Wenchang, to the top of this pantheon, were not enough to bind society together around a Confucianism regarded as a national religion.

At the highest level of the Confucian religious edifice, the sacrifices of the state cult continued to be at the core of the concerns of government, despite the many other problems it had to cope with. The theological debates of the previous dynasty had died out. The end of the empire in 1911, more than the disappearance of Confucian ritual, thus implied the abandonment, already a *fait accompli* among many intellectuals, of the traditional cosmology in which all expressions of Chinese religion were articulated. By the end of the century, the innovators were turning towards the image of a 'reforming' Confucius made into a god, before going on to abandon all reference to tradition. This radicalization, following the fall of the Qing, led to the end of the official cohabitation of all the cults in an overarching system patronized by the emperor as protector of all religions.

While Confucianism failed in its task, the other two institutionalized religions were in no position to take its place. Buddhism was no longer experiencing the explosion of schools and doctrinal creativity that it had in the first millennium and even at the beginning of the second. Reformist intellectuals' interest in Buddhist philosophy, which increased sharply at the end of the century, was accompanied by a militant anticlericalism, and a rejection of collective or individual practices (meditation, devotion, etc.). As for Taoism and the vast range of cults that it embraced, its divorce from the intellectual and political world was complete, and official or foreign sources had nothing but silence or contempt for it. There were educated converts, such as Min Yide (1758–1836), in Jiangsu or Chen Minggui (1824–81), in Guangdong, who produced apologetics, albeit by endeavouring to define a purged Taoism brought closer to Confucianism, which was of interest only to a tiny elite.

Religious institutions were seized with a hardening of the arteries, which hampered their renewal. Monasteries recruited adolescents and, among adults, now attracted only those unsuited to an active or family life. The social status of the clergy had rarely been so low. Yet it continued to constitute a social group of great importance. There is little information on figures for the nineteenth century, but a 1739 census counted 350,000 monks and nuns (they were probably twice that number in reality, 85 per cent of them Buddhists and 15 per cent Taoists); by the beginning of the twentieth century, there were over 500,000 Buddhist religious. The discipline and quality of the contemplative life of the few large communities (about 5 per cent) were maintained despite increasingly difficult economic and political circumstances.

The 'sects', on the other hand, experienced unprecedented growth. These movements, which the state lumped together under the general rubric Bailian, 'White Lotus', were organized around masters who demanded of their disciples neither observance of a rule nor long initiation, but taught techniques of bodily asceticism and meditation which brought health and long life, as well as martial arts techniques. These movements also produced a devotional literature in the vernacular, the baojuan, which combined eschatological fears, the cult of a primordial goddess (unknown to the institutionalized religions) and traditional morality. Secret societies, analogous to masonic lodges, also developed among traders and artisans in the big cities such as Shanghai, at the expense of the traditional guilds and their cults. But these remained very much active up to the mid-twentieth century. Thus the majority of the population was involved in secularized religious organizations (the clergy participated in them but did not control them), whose attitudes ranged from conservatism to open protest.

Most of the sectarian movements, being underground, limited their activities to organizing fasts and communal prayers, but some, won over by predictions that the world was about to end, took up arms and rebelled against the state. Such revolts had been sporadic in the previous century, but in the nineteenth they became more numerous and broke out on a larger scale. Some kept up centres of resistance for more than ten years. While the biggest revolt in the century may have been nothing to do with the White Lotus, it was also religious in inspiration. In 1850, the young Hong Xiuquan (1813–64), who was the follower of an American Protestant missionary, declared that he was Jesus's brother and promised to transform the world. His messianic visions put him at the head of the Taiping movement. They formed the basis of a religious system, which was a mixture of a harsh Protestant-inspired Puritanism and an egalitarian utopianism drawing on ancient Chinese traditions, violently

attacking the local cults around which Chinese society was organized. For ten years the armies raised by Hong occupied the richest part of the country and founded a kingdom with its capital at Nanking: they were not defeated by the Qing until 1864.

These outbreaks of violence, largely religious in origin, contributed to the breach between an elite ever more fascinated by the West and its anti-religious discourse, and a traditional society whose liturgical bases (guilds and communities of local cults), were threatened by the economic upheavals. Despite everything, the construction of temples on local initiative continued at the same pace and even an accelerated one during the reconstruction that followed the defeat of the Taiping. The real decline of the place of the temple in society began at the beginning of the twentieth century, with the expropriations to set up schools, and later the confiscation of property.

In such circumstances, foreign religions made progress but without the mass conversions they had hoped for. Islam made advances through its Sufi networks, which had already since the sixteenth century been successfully expressing themselves in works that met the requirements of classical literature. But the demotion of Chinese Muslims (hui) and non-Chinese peoples to the status of minority was accompanied by bloody rebellions. Christianity, already present since the first Jesuits in the late sixteenth century, had suffered several persecutions; now there was a rise in the number of rival missions and denominations, but it also provoked violent reactions by its intransigence towards Chinese religiosity. The best known of these is that of the Boxers (Yihe tuan), a sect related to the White Lotus practising martial arts, whose uprising spread to much of northern China and led to the siege of Beijing in 1900.

Conversely, Lamaism, Tibetan Buddhism, had long since been welcome in China, but this welcome grew even warmer in the nineteenth century. For the Tibetans, as for the Mongols, then part of the empire, this religion was at the centre of everyday life. The Dalai Lama and the qutugtu Jebcundamba were tacitly recognized as rulers, the one of Tibet and the other of outer Mongolia, but their reincarnations were controlled by Beijing. Moreover, it found itself penalized in two ways: by the halt to imperial patronage due to the bankruptcy of the state (which in the seventeenth and eighteenth centuries had funded a large number of monasteries, especially in the Mongol areas); and by rising hostility towards the economic stranglehold of a theocracy which controlled almost half the national wealth of the two countries and made between a third and a half of the male population immobile in its monasteries. The Gelugpa school was able to impose its complete domination and no new development appeared in the fields of doctrine, ritual or art: in the nineteenth century, Tibetan-Mongol Buddhism was taken up with writing its own history.

Thus the tragic entry of China into modernity had only limited effects on traditional religions. Their institutions lost power and influence, but their values continued to inform society, and their literature, whether in the form of novels, dramas or morality books (shanshu) remained in the forefront of reading and public recitation. While Confucianism was permanently radicalized, hostile to religious reforms, Buddhist intellectuals, especially around Yang Wenhui (1838–1911), advocated a committed secular religiosity, and a Buddhist press, publishing house and schools made their appearance, designed to train men of action for a more moral society. This movement, partly nationalist in inspiration, was also encouraged by an international Buddhist modernism, active in Japan and South Asia, supported by sympathetic Europeans. Among the Taoists, who did not have similar international backers, although they early on aroused keen interest among Japanese scholars, there was also, belatedly and timidly, the creation around Cheng Yingning (1880–1969) in Shanghai, of groups of seekers after 'inner alchemy' (*neidan*). The practice of such methods of immortality is very old, but here it was based more than ever on a synthesis of various religious traditions, and it attracted numerous intellectuals, some of them Western-educated, who wanted to rediscover their Chineseness. The nineteenth-century fashion for popular *neidan* handbooks, as opposed to an older and less accessible output, which met with great success among the middle classes, prefigured the great qigong movement, which was to be one of the key features of Chinese religious modernity in our times.

Japan

For Japan, the Tokugawa dynasty (1603–1868) – fifteen generations – was both the 'Era of Great Peace' and a long period of being closed in on itself. With the Meiji Restoration (1868), the country embarked on the path of rapid modernization. Confronted with this transformation, the traditional religions – Shinto and Buddhism – reacted differently, while new religious movements made their appearance.

Putting an end to the endemic warfare which afflicted medieval Japan, the Tokugawa had built a strong, well-administered state, which promoted the development of a commercial economy while keeping the population alive to its duties. Buddhism, treated more or less as the state religion, occupied a special position, strengthened by the ban on Christianity imposed in 1612, and the requirement imposed on everyone to put his name on the register of a Buddhist monastery on pain of being charged with being a Christian. It rested on the family and the ancestor cult, which, in its popular manifestation, became its major characteristic.

Confucianism had profoundly permeated the country's moral conceptions, impelling people more to action than to resignation. Every favour received from the deity committed the beneficiary to a reciprocal action, which could never be enough and left him in debt. The relationship of every individual to his parents, elders and superiors was analogous to those linking men to the deities. Whence the importance of filial piety and, with it, loyalty, the supreme Japanese virtue.

Shinto was loosely structured around three ritual poles: the cult of the imperial family, a few big national shrines, and finally, in the villages, the cult of the local deity which watched over people and harvests. It thereby expressed the harmonious relations which throughout life ought to prevail between men, nature and the gods. Birth and fertility were at the core of its concerns.

The modernization of Japan came at a price. It did not benefit all equally: it produced some who were dissatisfied and some losers; it marginalized part of the population. New religions made their appearance, which, for the most part, advocated a return to the age of the gods, associated with a future just ahead which would see the establishment on earth of a new kingdom of plenty. These movements – among others, Kurozumi-kyô, Tenri-kyô, Kontô-kyô,

Maruyama-kyô and Omoto – proved to be popular expressions of protest. The enemies were at one and the same time, and ambiguously, foreigners and the government. The saving figure of Miroku – Maitreya, the 'Future Buddha' – was often present in those movements (as in the case of Omato) in which the messianic hope was strongest. In addition to that there were sometimes other figures from the Japanese pantheon, often minor deities, updated, who were entrusted with a mission of healing or moral recovery (the figure of Konjin, taken from Taoism, in the Konkô-kyô movement). This 'expectant messianism' was also accompanied by intense proselytism, something absent from the traditional religions.

The old territorial base of Buddhism and Shinto, which had for centuries defined the twin religious allegiances of the Japanese through lineage (ancestors, family, even the nation) and place (of birth, residence), had difficulty withstanding industrialization, mass urbanization and the gradual disappearance of peasant society and the traditional extended family (*ie*), which was at once a domestic, an economic and a symbolic unit. It was this freed space that the 'new religions' came to fill.

The restoration of imperial power marked the end of an era during which three different knowledge systems had coexisted: national studies, in the service of Japanese identity; the neo-Confucian intellectual school, nurtured on Chinese traditions; and more recently, the contribution of Western science. It also marked the intervention of the state in the religious life of the country, designed to forge a new national consciousness around the figure of the emperor.

A rescript 'separating Buddhism and Shinto' (*jinbutsu bunri-rei*) was promulgated in March 1868. Buddhism, henceforth regarded as a foreign religion, saw many of its monasteries, cult objects and sacred writings destroyed. After having been invited to register with a Buddhist monastery during the Edo period, the Japanese population now had the duty to unite behind a hierarchy of countless shrines, served by a zealous clergy whose chief activity would be to assert the links between Shinto and the state. This policy of religious construction found concrete expression in the Great Teaching movement (*Taikyô senpu*), which was elaborated in the years following 1870. Missionaries sent by the government crisscrossed the country and taught the population 'respect for the Shinto deities and love of country'.

In 1882, in order to meet a legitimate desire for religious freedom on the part of the population at large, as well as other religious organizations, the government launched the artificial concept of 'shrine Shinto' (*jinja Shintô*), a civil religion which was now distinct from the religious form of Shinto known as 'sect Shinto' (*kyôha shintô*), embracing thirteen movements, with a variety of origins, which were gradually granted official recognition. In order to mark a clear distinction between these two categories, 'shrine Shinto' was placed under the Ministry of the Interior and 'sect Shinto' under the Ministry of Education. What followed was a manipulation of historic Shinto: the government launched more and more official ceremonies and festivals designed to popularize imperial authority and the emperor's divine character. Among the popular religions calling for social reforms, those that did not belong to 'sect Shinto' were regarded, like Christianity in seventeenth-century Japan, as 'heretical' (*jakyô*) and were, in consequence, persecuted.

During this period, Buddhism allied itself with Shinto against Christianity, which had finally been granted toleration, under pressure from the Western countries, in 1873. Faced with the collapse of its old privileges and the slow erosion of village civilization, Buddhism appeared to be a religion in crisis fearing that Christianity, currently associated by a section of the population with the emergence of a modern and Westernized Japan and democratic ideas, might conduct missionary work at its expense. The Buddhist movements thus tended to associate with the nationalist tendencies of Shinto and the defence of national cultural identity.

For the first time in their history, the end of the nineteenth century saw Japanese religions present on foreign soil. This trend, initially a small-scale affair because of the culturally specific features of Shinto and Japanese Buddhism, proved to be lasting and assumed unforeseen dimensions thanks to the proselytism of the new religious movements, independent of the old territorial and family ties.

The first religions to move abroad were Buddhist schools of thought which, calling on the ancient concept of 'religion protecting the nation', accompanied the Japanese army into continental China, Formosa (Taiwan) and Korea. The other presence, a more peaceful one, was in the service of Japanese emigrants who, at the end of the nineteenth century, went and settled in Hawaii and the United States, and in South America (particularly Brazil). Their Buddhism and Shinto were in the service of Japanese communities, which were preserving abroad their cultural and religious identity.

Korea

Korean culture is heavily influenced by two major events: in the fourth century, the introduction of two Asian religions, Confucianism, of Chinese origin, and a sanitized Buddhism, of Indian origin; and, in the nineteenth century, the penetration of Christianity, the agent of profound transformations.

In the eighteenth and nineteenth centuries, Korea experienced a collapse of the hierarchical society based on neo-Confucian doctrine. A series of large-scale social reforms led to the birth of the so-called 'Practical Learning' (*Sirhak*) school, a pragmatic philosophy. Faced with this decay, a group of scholars called for a 'return to the practical' which would overcome the formalism of religious rituals and contempt for technical activities. They ran up against the hostility of the country's authorities, who criticized them for allowing themselves to be influenced by

Western culture. Most converted to Catholicism, perceived as another path to modernization.

It was at the same time and for the same reason that the Korean aristocracy discovered Catholicism. Clashing with the Confucian conception of the social order, the new religion was persecuted during the first half of the nineteenth century, but enjoyed rapid popular success because of its religious message and its reformist action.

The nineteenth century saw the emergence of a truly Korean thought: 'Eastern Learning', as opposed to the 'Western Learning' which designated the whole of Western culture. Unlike the Practical Learning of the first Catholics, it emerged in the countryside; the doctrine was founded by Ch'oe Cheu (1824–64), a reformer removed from central power, who developed the notion of national identity in reaction against the West. He sought to free society from the ultraconservative spirit of the neo-Confucianism of the time, by going back to the sources of Korean tradition. He taught that men are equal and preached the adoration of the 'Lord of Heaven' (*Ch'onju*). This religious monotheism, a modernization of the idea of the heavenly being (*Hanunim*) present in ancient popular beliefs, was in fact an amalgam of three religions – Confucianism, Buddhism and Taoism – and ancient indigenous beliefs. Like the Catholics it was repressed by the government. This syncretic popular religion underwent a change of name; it became the 'School of the Heavenly Way' (*Ch'ondo-gyo*). At the end of the nineteenth century its followers started a peasant revolution.

At the beginning of the second half of the nineteenth century, American Protestant missionaries were very active. Addressing rural Koreans, workers from the lowest classes and women, they preached equality of the sexes, monogamy and the elimination of concubinage. They notably helped to reform the educational system, to found numerous schools, and to develop social work and medical care. It was their good fortune to arrive in Korea just as the country was opening up to the West: the Royal Government signed a treaty of friendship and trade with the United States in 1882, and with France in 1886. In 1910, the Japanese occupation began: Eastern Learning, Buddhists and foreign missionaries would all support the return to independence.

A new century was about to begin which, with these sorts of exactions and the rivalries that they provoked between states, would precipitate two world wars, developing an unprecedented degree of death and enslavement. Reduced to a minor influence, as in Japan, or peripheral as in the West, religions proved themselves to be powerless to influence the course of events: this was now a *modern* situation, which would compel them to look into themselves to rethink and find new paths for their tradition.

C

REGIONAL SECTION

IO

EUROPE

IO.I

WESTERN EUROPE

IO.I.I

THE FRENCH REVOLUTION AND
THE TWENTY-THREE YEARS WAR (1789–1815)

François Crouzet, coordinator

WESTERN EUROPE IN THE 1780s

When we read the accounts of travellers – such as the English agronomist Arthur Young – who wandered over Western Europe during the 1780s, their judgements and impressions confirm the quantitative estimates by Paul Bairoch, showing that per capita income disparities were not big from one country to another (approximately 1 to 1.5 or 1.6); indeed, they appear to have varied more sharply between regions in the same state, as each state had its own very poor areas. And yet there was a clear pecking order: England, the United Provinces, present-day Belgium and Switzerland headed the list for living standards, France stood at the European average level and was followed by 'Germany', the Scandinavian countries and Italy. At the bottom of the scale, Spain and Portugal were noteworthy for their almost universal poverty.

In fact, the eighteenth century had been a period of 'prosperity', economic expansion and even growth in per capita income – despite a sharply rising population in certain regions. The great majority of people made a living from farming, but the 'agricultural revolution' had as yet affected only a few pioneering areas such as Flanders, Holland, England and the Po Valley. Almost everywhere, however, some moderate progress had been made (such as the introduction or extension of new crops like maize or potatoes). Although poor harvests continued to mean hard times for ordinary people, they were no longer followed by famines, epidemics or falls in population levels. The bad harvest of 1788 and the rise in the price of bread hastened the fall of the *ancien régime* in France, but people did not starve to death in 1789.

The non-agricultural sectors were the ones that had expanded the most. Cottage industries were to be found in many country areas; for example, from Brittany to Silesia, a long swath of woollen and linen workers girdled Europe. But centralized forms of production – printed calico factories, for example – had also progressed. In Great Britain there had recently emerged a system of production, based upon machinery, factories, the use of coal and of steam engines, technological innovation. Although industry on the continent generally remained faithful to traditional practices, the British inventions started to make inroads, often, admittedly, as a result of government action (particularly in France) rather than of private initiative. But the continentals also had their inventions, including dramatic ones such as the hot air balloon (1783).

A spectacular development in the eighteenth century had been the rapid expansion of commerce and especially overseas trade with 'the two Indies', that is, North and South America and South and East Asia. Its expansion benefited the 'colonial' powers – Great Britain, the United Provinces, France, Spain and Portugal (although the last two gained little from it) – but not only these, since it created a demand for products from the countries of Northern Europe (wood for shipbuilding, hemp, flax, copper, iron and tar) and a re-export trade in colonial produce to countries without colonies (although Denmark and Sweden had their own 'East India companies'). All this resulted in an active coastal traffic along all the coasts of Europe. From Leghorn to Barcelona, from Bordeaux to Liverpool, from London to Amsterdam and Hamburg, the major ports of Europe expanded considerably as business and urban centres in the eighteenth century. They were linked by sophisticated financial networks – based on the circulation of bills of exchange – and a truly international capital market. But the population of cities in general had grown, a trend not without political consequences; in paintings and engravings we can see a family resemblance between the major cities of Europe, nearly all of which were paved and lit up at night.

In the 1780s, Western Europe was therefore 'prosperous', the word being placed in quotes because, by present-day criteria, the standard of living of the great majority of Europeans was very low indeed. But the inventories of possessions drawn up after death show more moveable property – in the broad sense – in poor households than at the beginning of the century. The consumption of coffee or tea (depending on the country) had become widespread in the cities.

This prosperous Europe was also 'enlightened'. Admittedly, only the elite had read the works of the 'philosophers' and others who spoke for the Enlightenment. But literacy had made progress in the eighteenth century, not only in the Protestant countries, of course, but also in Catholic countries such as France, and glimmers of the new ideas filtered through to the 'lower' classes.

In any case, many European governments in the second half of the eighteenth century had been 'enlightened', i.e. had sought to carry out reforms aimed at strengthening the state by rationalizing institutions and stimulating economic development, although such reforms also owed something to the dominant ideology (hence certain 'anti-clerical' policies). Admittedly, between 1786 and 1790 the most famous of the enlightened despots – Frederick II, Joseph II, and Charles III of Spain – died one after the other, leaving Catherine II as the sole survivor until 1796. Indeed, according to an old joke that captures the ambiguity of the concept, they were more despotic than enlightened. None the less, the 'enlightened' side of their achievements was not insignificant, and there were also the efforts of the rulers of smaller states such as Tuscany, Bavaria, Denmark and a number of others. Even in France, Louis XVI was an enlightened king, though only by fits and starts; although he had a heavy turnover of reforming ministers, their work produced at least some results (for example, tolerance for Protestants). If he had died in 1786 or 1787, it would have been amid praise and lamentations.

In Great Britain there was no question of despotism, but George III had finally managed to drive out the cliques of Whig aristocrats who had long held a monopoly of power, and to place in Downing Street a man of his own, the Younger Pitt (1783). But Pitt set about introducing numerous reforms, particularly in the financial field; he succeeded in restoring the equilibrium of public finances, left in a parlous state at the close of the American War of Independence, an achievement beyond the capacity of the ministers of Louis XVI. It is true that Great Britain had its Parliament, whose approval legitimized the taxes imposed, however harsh they might be. As was said by some historians, what France lacked was a House of Commons.

This idyllic picture, in the style of Greuze, of Europe in the 1780s should be, however, severely qualified. The Enlightenment created all sorts of aspirations which were left unsatisfied. These were compounded by certain economic and social problems, which together caused tension and even 'revolutions'. In Geneva in 1782, in the United Provinces in 1786–7, in the Austrian Low Countries and in Liège in 1789, 'patriots' (let us cautiously call them democrats) challenged the sway of traditional oligarchies or – in Belgium – of a distant authoritarian power. Admittedly these rebellions, taking place in small states, were repressed without difficulty by the military intervention of a great power or (in Belgium) of the ruler. But this would not be the case when revolution broke out in the most populated state in Europe, France, where visible signs of a crisis in the regime had become apparent in 1787, with the Assembly of Notables and the fall of Calonne, and even more so in 1788, when serious disturbances (sometimes referred to as the 'pre-Revolution') broke out here and there. Even in Great Britain there emerged a 'radical' movement calling for the reform of Parliament, which was considered to be corrupt and unrepresentative.

R. Palmer linked these disruptions to the American Revolution, which had occurred earlier but had been crowned with success, and launched the concept of 'Atlantic Revolutions'. His idea was rejected by those who maintained that France was a case apart; they stressed how much more radical and inventive the French Revolution was in comparison with the others, including the American one. And yet all these revolutions broke out in countries or cities that were economically and socially advanced, with close ties to overseas trade and international finance. Nevertheless, the French Revolution was indeed something new, not to say unprecedented, with the possible exception of the English Revolution of the 1640s. It epitomized both the culmination and the failure of the Enlightenment.

REVOLUTION IN FRANCE

The French Revolution, with its consequences in France and abroad, the wars that came in its wake and the subsequent Napoleonic Wars, engendered an enormous volume of source material, both handwritten and printed, and later a colossal number of historical studies. It is difficult to be sure of one's ground, because every conceivable claim and counter-claim has been made about the Revolution, and because the passions it aroused among its protagonists and among onlookers have continued to thrive – and even gain in intensity – among historians. This was confirmed by the 1989 bicentenary, despite the predominance of a mollifying consensus of approval.

The first step in the Revolution was the fall of the *ancien régime*, which was very rapid – from May to October 1789; we could even narrow this down to the period from June to August, but absolute monarchy had in fact already come to an end when Louis XVI, on 8 August 1788, convened the Estates-General, which had not met since 1614. The collapse also took place without hindrance: no force capable of halting it pitted itself against the revolutionary process.

A collapse of this magnitude makes it tempting to take the view that the whole structure was moth-eaten and needed only a few gentle knocks to bring it tumbling down. Traditionally, historians distinguish between underlying causes and immediate causes but, depending on whether they give pride of place to the former or to the latter, the collapse is seen as inevitable or as the product of circumstances or even of a set of coincidences.

We are not trying here to find the 'roots' of the French Revolution. We need only say that the French political system had long been suffering from numerous dysfunctions, which had been brought to light in particular by the disasters of the Seven Years War. In addition, the relentless opposition of the *Parlements* was undermining the authority of the monarchy, and paralysing its action. Towards the end of his life, Louis XV had in fact abolished them, but they were reinstated by Louis XVI; intelligent people deplore this error, but it was committed. That said, the *ancien régime* was an inextricable web of privileges, by no means confined to the first two orders, but which generated resentment among all those with lesser privileges or no privileges at all. Many of the numerous and well-educated bourgeoisie were displeased, not so much those enriched by the economic expansion and 'rise of capitalism' as the lower bourgeoisie of lawyers and minor intellectuals, who were deeply influenced by the Enlightenment and from among whom most of the Revolution's leaders would be recruited. It is clear that absolutism, along with other institutions and practices of the *ancien régime*, was no longer accepted by the elite, including a large proportion of the nobility (one is reminded of Chateaubriand's famous remark: 'The Revolution was started by the patricians'). The elite wanted a share of power, a say in decisions, a measure of control. 'Revolutionary discourse' had gained a foothold long before 1789 (on the subject of equal taxation, for example, in the 1760s).

For their part, the 'people' were predominantly rural but with large urban groups whose position gave them considerable political influence; their behaviour in 1789 and subsequent years showed them to be strongly hostile to the established order, with the peasants in particular rejecting feudalism and the burdens it placed upon them. Events would show that this 'populace' was also profoundly credulous, believing in the arrival of 'brigands' during the Great Fear of 1789, in 'aristocratic plots' and in treachery, haunted by ancestral fears (especially of famine) and containing within itself individuals who were full of envy and hatred, prepared to commit violence and take the law into their own hands.

The web of privileges seems to have slowed down economic progress, especially in agriculture, but the most obvious and most dangerous failure of the *ancien régime* lay in the field of public finances. It was here that the terminal crisis began. It is true that the French monarchy was not the only one with budget deficits, very heavy debts and unfair taxation. What is more, recent research has revealed that it was only during the 1780s that the situation deteriorated to a dangerous extent: the loans raised during the American War had to be followed up by fresh loans raised in peacetime – a wholly unprecedented step – with the result that increasing interest payments aggravated the deficit year by year; it could no longer be made good unless new resources were created.

Relatively speaking, the French were less heavily taxed than the British or the Dutch, but they themselves were convinced that they were crushed by taxes, especially in view of a blatantly unfair distribution and of the partial exemptions enjoyed by the 'privileged'. The financial crisis was one of the 'underlying' causes of the Revolution in that it arose from the inability of the *ancien régime* to solve problems such as tax privileges and from its propensity to wage costly wars. But it was also a direct cause or trigger in that, during the summer of 1788, the state could no longer find any lenders and was forced into mini-bankruptcy, obliging the King to call for Necker – the pro-reform minister whom he had dismissed seven years earlier – and convene the Estates-General.

The elections were influenced by debating societies so won over to the new ideas that, when the Estates-General met in Versailles on 5 May 1789, men of the Enlightenment were in the majority. In addition, the 1788 harvest had been poor, and during the months that followed an 'old-style crisis', characterized by rising prices for staple foods and by unemployment, had ripened; its main victims were the underclasses in the cities, whose real incomes dropped sharply and who, frightened by the possibility of real famine, blamed their hardships on court intrigues. Financial crisis, political crisis, economic crisis: it was an explosive mixture. The personalities of the King and Queen were to make matters worse: faced with growing unrest, Louis XVI accepted too late the plans for reform, and vacillated between spasms of resistance (even recourse to force) and complete capitulation. In less than four years, his incompetence would lead him to the scaffold.

The Estates-General were immediately blocked by a procedural issue – the verification of credentials, a problem which in fact raised the fundamental issue of orders and privileges – on which public opinion had been divided since the summer of 1788. The Third Estate, by its refusal to carry out this operation, blocked the proceedings and then, in a truly revolutionary gesture, arrogated to itself the constituent authority and even outright sovereignty, proclaimed itself a national assembly and promised to give France a constitution (17 and 20 June). At a stroke a major political revolution had been accomplished.

The Court tried to react: Necker was dismissed again and a government to fight the issue was set up. But it lasted only a hundred hours. Paris rose up in arms and a city council and national guard were constituted. The storming of the Bastille by the citizens in revolt was in itself a minor incident but it had a tremendous impact. The army could not be relied upon and Louis XVI had no choice but to give way.

But that was not the end of the matter. Throughout the country, the 'municipal revolution' created new authorities in the cities, while the royal administration and tax collecting system collapsed. Above all, the 'Great Fear' spread through the countryside, setting off an immense peasants' revolt that forced the seigneurs to renounce their 'feudal' rights.

Threatened with general anarchy, the Constituent Assembly sought to recapture the initiative: during the night of 4 August, all privileges were sacrificed. Despite the delay in bringing out the implementing decrees, which introduced certain restrictions, such as the obligation for peasants to buy back certain rights, an immense revolution that was at once institutional and social had been accomplished. The *ancien régime* had been destroyed, once and for all. There was never again any question of re-establishing the provincial Estates, the tax privileges of the nobility and clergy or the sale of offices. On 26 August, the Constituent Assembly voted the Declaration of the Rights of Man and of the Citizen.

A last spasm of resistance from the Court triggered an offensive by the Paris revolutionaries: the national guard and the 'populace' marched on Versailles, whence the King, his family and the Constituent Assembly were brought back to Paris, not quite as prisoners but kept under close watch (5–6 October).

June, July, August and October 1789: in four stages, the *ancien régime* had been crushed.

The task now was to build a new polity. The Constituent Assembly worked assiduously with its characteristic slightly messianic zeal, its faith in reason and logic and its tendency to promote standardization. Its impressive output in legislation included the so-called 1791 Constitution. It was able to set about this work in a relatively calm atmosphere, for 1790 has been described as the 'happy year' of the Revolution: there were no major disturbances and, thanks to a good harvest, the prices of basic foodstuffs dropped sharply. On 14 July 1790, the *Fête de la Fédération* expressed a spectacular reconciliation between Monarchy and Nation.

But the period of calm did not last. The botched flight of the King to Varennes (20 June 1791) shattered the fragile consensus that seemed to have been established – although it had already been compromised by a religious split – and brought a republican movement into the open. The Constituent Assembly gave way to the Legislative Assembly, which, though elected on a property qualification system, was distinctly more radical. One might even say more 'left wing', since the classification into right wing and left wing dates from the Constituent Assembly. The new chamber soon came into conflict with the King, who vetoed certain decrees it had voted.

However, an almost universal consensus emerged at the beginning of 1792 among political forces, from the King to the democrats (although naturally for different reasons) in favour of war against Austria, which was accused by the patriots of working to support counter-revolutionary intrigues. This war, declared with a 'light heart' on 20 April 1792, would weigh heavily on the destiny of the Revolution, and almost at once provoked a second major revolutionary crisis. As the French army was not ready, the war began with a series of defeats, which angered and frightened many supporters of the Revolution, particularly in Paris. Moreover, a poor harvest and the issue in increasing numbers of the paper money *assignats*, which had been created in December 1789, had pushed up prices and rekindled popular unrest.

The well-organized and victorious insurrection of 10 August 1792 was followed by the abolition of the monarchy and the establishment of the Republic (21 September). With the September massacres, blood flowed in abundance for the first time. The Legislative Assembly gave way to a new assembly, the Convention, elected by a fifth of the citizens, and once again distinctly more left-wing than the body that had preceded it. Some have seen the events of the summer of 1792 as a 'second French Revolution', while others have regarded them as a violent deflection of the Revolution from its true course.

After the French armies had driven back the invaders beyond the national frontiers, there was a lull for consolidation under the aegis of the Brissotins or Girondins, the dominant faction at the beginning of the Convention (although this did not prevent the execution of Louis XVI). But radicalization was to be given fresh impetus in the spring of 1793, by military defeats, the coalition of almost all the states of Europe against France, and the uprising in Vendée. To overcome their Girondin foes and impose the radical public-safety measures they considered necessary, the Montagnards joined forces with the Parisian *sans-culottes*; their forcible take over on 2 June 1793 drove the leaders of the right from the Convention at the cost of violation of national representation.

Further disasters (Toulon and its fleet surrendered to the English on 27 August) and the pressure exerted on it by the *sans-culottes* and extremists (riots of 4 and 5 September) forced the Convention to accept a series of revolutionary measures: mass conscription, mustering of revolutionary armies, the law of suspects, freezing of prices and wages, official proclamation of the Terror and a declaration that the government would be revolutionary (i.e. dictatorial and centralized) until peace was restored.

In certain respects, the Revolution reached its climax at the end of 1793 (or beginning of 1794), with the bloody repression of the 'federalist' uprisings in the provinces (particularly in Lyon) and the de-Christianization campaign (on 22 November 1793, all Paris churches were closed). Soon the most radical revolutionaries would fall victim to a Revolution that devoured its own offspring: on 24 March 1794, Hébert and his friends were guillotined (on 5 April Danton and the 'Indulgents' suffered the same fate) and on 27 March the revolutionary armies were abolished. For certain historians, this repression of the 'popular' movement marked a decisive turning-point and even the end of the Revolution proper, more so than 9 Thermidor, which was, moreover, facilitated by the demobilization of the *sans-culottes*. However, the months following the 'fall of the factions' were the months of Robespierre's 'dictatorship' and an attempt to impose Virtue by Terror. The feast of the Supreme Being (8 June), the finest of the civic feast days so adored by the Revolution, was accompanied by an effort to liquidate the enemies of the Revolution; it is difficult not to see the law of 22 Prairial (10 June 1794) and the 'great terror of Messidor' that followed as the peak of the revolutionary process.

In short, the history of the Revolution from May 1789 to July 1794 emerges as a series of sudden 'skids', the one in the summer of 1792 being the most important. There was a general trend towards radicalization, which was only briefly suspended, in particular during the 'happy year' of 1790 (despite the fact that the Constituent Assembly adopted during that year the Civil Constitution of the Clergy, a radical measure if there ever was one).

Why this shift to the left? It may be viewed as inherent in the key ideas that inspired the revolutionaries, or at least the key ideas derived from Jean-Jacques Rousseau, especially the concept of the general will. Rousseauism is intolerant, totalitarian: no freedom for the enemies of freedom. Moreover, the theatrical rhetoric of revolutionary discourse in the mouths of men raised on Livy and Plutarch lent itself to deflection towards extremes and ended up as an endlessly repeated dramatization of conflict. It has also been observed that the Terror was present, both in the language used and in reality, from the summer of 1789, although its victims at the time were few: in the language used, for example, by Marat's campaign in the *Ami du Peuple* and, in actual practice, in the lynching of officials of dignitaries of the *ancien régime* such as Launay, Foulon and Berthier. And did not the decisions of the Constituent Assembly drift leftward as the year 1789 progressed? Seen like this, the radicalization of the Revolution was a natural trend and any attempt to stop it was bound to fail and even to be counter-productive, since it led to the political or physical liquidation of those involved. Furthermore, this radicalization was supported by the 'people' of Paris, by the *sans-culottes*, an ill-defined but well organized and armed group that recruited from both the *petite bourgeoisie* and manual workers and was the spearhead of the revolutionary movement. Until March 1794, its pressure on the Assemblies, particularly during the 'Journées', had a marked impact on the course of the Revolution.

It may be acknowledged that a terrorist potential was inherent in the Revolution, but as to why it developed and triumphed as it did the old, 'theory of circumstances' remains the best explanation of what caused the revolutionary process to 'veer out of control' and usher in the Terror.

We should not forget to include among such circumstances the signal blunders of the royal couple, who adopted a *politique du pire* and actively sought war; or the later ineptitude of the Brissotins during their heyday at the beginning of the Convention. But a greater impact was produced by inflation, which started to rise at the end of 1791 as a result of poor harvests and other supply problems and the increasingly numerous issues of *assignats*, which were the only means of resolving a disastrous budget deficit in the absence of fiscal measures that were never attempted. As in 1789, price rises stirred up strong feelings among the people and triggered demands for authoritarian measures to halt them; but such measures – which culminated in the 'Maximum' (i.e. the blocking of prices and wages) – were counter-productive and aggravated the shortages, thus setting in motion a vicious circle which contributed to radicalization.

But the most powerful and decisive of the factors that speeded up the Revolution was the war, and more particularly the defeats that marked its beginning and were experienced again in 1793, and the cases of treachery (La Fayette, Dumouriez, the defection of Toulon). The civil war – the Vendée uprising and the federalist movements also – roused passionate feelings. It was in this siege atmosphere that the 'first terror' of 1792 took place, and that the Reign of Terror was decided upon and launched a year later. True, it was France that declared war on Austria on 20 April 1792 and on Great Britain on 1 February 1793. With only a few exceptions, the revolutionary leaders wanted war, which of course they relied upon to be short and victorious; subsequently there was an escalation of provocations (annexing of territories, the doctrine of 'natural frontiers', attempts at a propaganda war) calculated to unite almost the whole of Europe in a coalition against France.

The Jacobin – or Montagnard – Terror was the central episode of the Revolution (not, however, for those who see its end as the end of the Revolution) and the most controversial one. Long held in almost universal horror, it was subsequently rehabilitated and even glorified by politicians (from Georges Clemenceau to François Mitterrand, for whom 'the French Revolution is one and indivisible') and by the 'Jacobin' school of historians. The latter saw it as the apogee and even the essence of the Revolution, as the Revolution's 'popular' and 'democratic' phase and as an episode that foreshadowed democracy and socialism (while many Jacobins were haunted by the model of Sparta and republican Rome).

Politically, it heralded the future, because the Constitution of Year II (which was never implemented) introduced universal suffrage (for men), because there reigned a kind of direct democracy within the clubs, sections and people's societies, and because, for the first time, men of lowly birth and position acceded to posts of responsibility. And yet it seems paradoxical to speak of a democratic phase of the Revolution when the Convention was elected by a minority of citizens and when the revolutionary government was a dictatorship run by a very small minority, who terrorized the great majority of French people. In point of fact, the true mass movements of the day, in France and abroad, were anti-revolutionary movements!

On the economic front, some have seen the first signs of socialism in the interventionist system of Year II: freezing of prices and wages, control of foreign trade and exchange, requisitioning of goods, forced loans from the wealthy, rationing, state-run factories to manufacture arms, uniforms, etc. In fact, almost all the Montagnards were orthodox liberals who agreed to such measures only under the pressure of the *sans-culottes*, themselves wedded to an out-of-date anti-capitalist 'moral economy', and under the pressure of circumstances, especially the need to supply the armies and major cities. This objective was on the whole achieved, but the interventionist approach did not work well and turned out to be counter-productive by bringing about a drop in agricultural production and severe food shortages during the winter of 1794–5. As for its foreshadowing a 'social republic', caring for the poor and the weak and eager to educate the people, such aims were more in the nature of vague impulses and declarations of principle.

The Terror itself – a police state based on denunciations and numerous executions after a summary trial or even no trial at all – has embarrassed the majority of Jacobin historians (except a few, who, carried away by class hatred, have eulogized it), who have attempted to minimize or to justify it.

Certainly, we need to take a more balanced view of the most spectacular episode: the guillotine on what used to be Place Louis XV and subsequently became Place de la Concorde. Famous heads rolled there, from those of Louis XVI and Marie-Antoinette to the heads of Danton, Vergniaud, André Chénier and Lavoisier, but so did those of a majority of obscure individuals; and the total number of executions in Paris during the Terror was 2,639, including 1,515 in the two months of June and July 1794. Far more numerous were the victims of repression following insurrections in the provinces – by drowning in Nantes and gunfire in Lyon for example – making a probable total of 30,000 deaths in all, including 16,000 by guillotine. Above all, there was the repression in Vendée where, on the express orders of the Committee of Public Safety, not only were the 'brigands' captured in possession of weapons massacred, but women and children, too. The maximum estimate is 300,000 dead, or 1 per cent of the population of France, by no means an insignificant number, especially as the Terror strictly speaking lasted less than a year (and hundreds of thousands of suspects were imprisoned). The Terror was not systematic, except after the law of Prairial; it struck at random, a fact which made it all the more effective: fear silenced opponents, made the interventionist system work after a fashion and incited the generals to win victories.

In the nineteenth century, it is true, the memory of the guillotine was used as a deterrent in the hands of conservatives and did a lasting disservice to the cause of the Republic, with which the Terror appeared to be indissolubly linked. At the same time, on the other hand, a myth was created, the myth of a heroic nation, resisting the assaults of a coalition of tyrants and mercilessly punishing traitors and the half-hearted; of a social democracy, which failed only because of the tactical error of Robespierre on 9 Thermidor. The 'ephemeral and prophetic Year II was seen as a beacon of light that illuminated the whole of the nineteenth century' (E. Labrousse) and as an inspiration for numerous political activists and revolutionary movements (even its violence attracted those who dreamed of sending their enemies to their deaths).

All in all, the Jacobin school has blackened the Revolution by assimilating it to the ephemeral domination of bloodthirsty Utopians and by disguising the fact that it was above all a revolution of freedom, which sowed in France – and elsewhere – the seeds of twentieth-century democracy. In the short run, however, in their desire to found the reign of Virtue on a mountain of guillotined heads, Robespierre and Saint-Just discredited both terror and virtue and left behind them a dismal trail of chaos and instability.

Paradoxically, the 'dictator' Robespierre depended on the confidence of the Convention. Isolated in his Utopia and paranoia, at odds with his colleagues on the Committee of Public Safety, at a time when military victories seemed to be making the Terror unnecessary, he fell victim, on 9 Thermidor (27 July 1794), to the manoeuvrings of a few extreme terrorists who felt that their own heads were under threat: given little support by the Parisian *sans-culottes*, he was guillotined the next day.

In theory nothing had altered, but in fact everything was poised to change, and Thermidor was, for the French, a liberation. The executions stopped; in order to avoid a new dictatorship, the Convention dismantled the revolutionary government; the interventionist approach collapsed and the 'maximum' was abolished; a few notorious terrorists were executed in their turn while others in the provinces fell prey to a spontaneous 'white terror'. The club of the Jacobins was closed down and the last two revolutionary 'days', in Germinal and Prairial of Year III (1 and 2 April, 20–23 May 1795) saw the crushing of the insurgents. The *sans-culottes* vanished from history into the realm of myth.

Thermidor was a turning-point of the utmost importance: utopianism, which had proved that it could turn into bloodthirsty despotism, was abandoned and human hopes were pitched lower. The Revolution returned to its sources, to its original tendency, namely economic and political liberalism, with the subtle balance of powers that the Constitution of Year III was to establish. The Republic also returned to its bourgeois sources as the bourgeoisie now held a monopoly of power.

A return to sources? Yet it was impossible to erase the wounds of the Terror, to put a rapid end to the war, or to halt the hyperinflation that wreaked havoc in 1795 and early 1796, with rates of 30 to 50 per cent *per month*, and disrupted the workings of the economy.

At the same time, through a perfectly normal swing of the pendulum, many French people among both the elite and the masses had reverted to monarchism, and a restoration like that after the English Revolution in the seventeenth century might have been a solution. The 1797 elections to the Councils, the only 'free' elections during this period, gave a powerful majority to the royalists. And yet the restoration did not happen: the unfortunate Louis XVII died at the Temple; his uncle, who proclaimed himself Louis XVIII, proved to be a reactionary unlikely to rally the support of moderates, even royalist ones; armed attacks from abroad (the Quiberon landing) or within the country (the rising of 13 Vendémiaire in Paris) made the republicans dig in their heels; lastly, the question of conquests and natural frontiers, which the republicans and generals were not willing to give up, proved a decisive obstacle both to the restoration of the monarchy and to peace. But the 'bourgeois' republic was also being threatened on its left, by pressure from neo-Jacobins. Gracchus Babeuf's 'conspiracy of equals', it is true, was not really dangerous, but his proto-communism made him famous.

Sitting on the fence between the Jacobins and the Royalists, the Thermidor regime and the subsequent Directory survived solely by force, the latter by violating its own legality and staging a series of coups, especially that of 18 Fructidor (4 September 1797), which eliminated the royalists. The Thermidorians had had no programme except to save their own heads by bringing down Robespierre and then to hang on to power. The Directory was no different, and it is no easy task to find any positive elements to its action, that herald the achievements of the Consulate. The politicians who survived the heat of the Terror were not in general the most brilliant or the most ideologically committed: many would serve subsequent regimes, one after another, up to Louis Philippe and even Napoleon III! The result was a mediocre and corrupt regime. Moreover, although the French economy took a turn for the better after the very severe depression of 1795–6, the recovery was slow and jerky. True, the paper money had been abolished and coins circulated again; but the public finances were in a sorry state. Government kept going only by not paying its creditors, namely, fund holders (two thirds of the national debt was cancelled), army contractors, and soldiers, who compensated themselves by plundering. Some have called the post-Thermidorian period a 'period of consolidation', but such consolidation was very insecure until the Consulate.

The main reason for this was the war, which was still going on. Admittedly, peace had been made in 1795 with Prussia and Spain; then Bonaparte's lightning campaign in Northern Italy forced Austria to sue for peace in its turn. But the Directory's intransigence led to failure of the negotiations to which England, isolated and weary, was resigned, and attempts at diversionary strategy in Ireland and in Egypt failed. The provocative policy of annexations and expansion practised by the Directory quickly prompted a second coalition involving England, Austria and Russia, which immediately won some major successes. For the Republic, the danger – both external and internal, since Chouans and Royalists had taken up arms again – was perhaps greater in 1799 than in 1792 or 1793. But the French armies had regained the upper hand when the last of the Directory's *coups d'état* – that of 18 Brumaire (9–10 November 1799) – gave supreme power to Bonaparte.

REVOLUTION, WAR AND OTHERS

So far this chapter has mentioned the role of the war in the unfolding of the French Revolution, but we must now return to a phenomenon which in fact continued well beyond the Revolution itself, what the French have traditionally described as the wars 'of the Revolution and Empire' and the English as the ' French' or Napoleonic Wars. We could speak of the 'twenty-three years war', since war raged in Europe – between France and one or more other powers – from April 1792 to June 1815, except for two brief periods of respite represented by the Peace of Amiens (14 months) and the First Restoration (9 months). The contrast with the century that followed (1815–1914), during which there was no general war, is striking. War, or more accurately a series of wars, actually had a more powerful impact on men and women of the period than did the French Revolution; people lived more in the shadow of war than in that of the guillotine. These wars swept across almost the whole of Europe: there was fighting from Cadiz to Moscow, from Calabria to Finland, and few were the regions – like Great Britain and Sweden – which altogether escaped military operations, invasions, foreign occupations or civil disturbances. Everywhere else there was the repeated ebb and flow of armies, especially for people living in the traditional theatres of warfare such as Belgium, the Rhineland and Northern Italy. Apart from London, Stockholm and Saint Petersburg, there was not a single European capital that escaped enemy occupation.

The point is often made that these wars were of a new type, different from the 'lace-collar' wars of the Age of Enlightenment. It is true that, from 1792 onwards for the French and a little later for their enemies, the war took on a 'national' and 'patriotic' character, which had been virtually absent from the armies of mercenaries in previous conflicts. As early as 1791, the Constituent Assembly decided to raise 100,000 volunteers; in August 1793, the Convention ordered the *levée en masse* – mass enrolment – but that was an exceptional measure; in 1798, on the other hand, conscription was introduced, that is, the principle whereby all young citizens could be called up for military service (several states imposed other forms of compulsory service). In the same year, the British government came up with another invention, also destined for a bright future – income tax. The war also took on an ideological and social colouring: the French boldly claimed to be liberating other peoples (while making them share in the cost of the operation) and they declared 'war on castles, peace to cottages'. Brigades of *emigrés* fought with the armies of the coalitions and legions of foreign 'patriots' served in those of the Republic.

However, it would be overstating the case to regard the twenty-three years war as foreshadowing the 'total war' that would rage during the twentieth century. The practice of warfare was not significantly more barbaric than it had been during the Enlightenment: prisoners were not killed (except renegades caught in possession of weapons, who were executed), the wounded were not finished off, and civilian populations were not massacred (with some exceptions, as we shall see). Nevertheless, the civilian populations suffered, especially from looting, forced contributions to the war coffers, quartering of troops and other exactions. The French armies, often poverty-stricken, lived off the land; in 1814 and in 1815, the allied armies sacked part of France.

And yet relations between the occupying forces and the occupied were not necessarily tense. The occupiers were sometimes even welcomed, at least when the two sides had some ideological sympathies; 'enemy' officers were thus admitted to the best society.

Nevertheless, there were atrocities, or 'war crimes' as we should say today, but these chiefly occurred in unusual circumstances, when popular insurrections clashed with regular armies. There were two types: the first was civil war (the Vendée uprising; the Chouan revolt throughout the west of France; the federalist movements of 1793; and, on the other side, the Irish insurrection of 1798), while the second consisted of popular uprisings against a foreign occupier – in fact against the French occupying forces and their local allies (the 'peasants' war' in Flanders in 1798–9; the peasants' uprising in Italy in 1799; the counter-revolution in the Kingdom of Naples against the Parthenopean Republic; the revolt of Andreas Hofer's Tyrolians in 1809; and above all guerrilla warfare during the Spanish War of Independence). In all cases, repression was pitiless: the summary execution for 'brigands' and *guerilleros*, the

burning of villages, the taking and execution of hostages. In Vendée, the violence of the Republican 'devil's columns', which burned and massacred everything in their path, including women (especially when pregnant) and children, are an extreme example of the violence directed against movements in which Catholic peasants rose up against 'enlightened' regimes.

Another new feature of the twenty-three years war was the confrontation of human masses on an unprecedented scale: in early 1794, the revolutionary government succeeded in mobilizing more than a million men and, in 1812, it was with 900,000 men that Napoleon invaded Russia. There were also innovations in tactics and in strategy. The Republic's armies, with their many inexperienced volunteers, were ill-suited to the subtle manoeuvres perfected by eighteenth-century generals. The French generals abandoned them for repeated mass attacks without worrying about casualties. They also abandoned siege warfare in favour of full-blooded offensives, rapid manoeuvres, attempts at decisive blows and the destruction of the opposing army.

These wars were nonetheless bloody: a major battle left tens of thousands of dead and wounded, with many of the latter doomed to die owing to the inadequacy of medicine in those days and the frightful conditions that reigned in military hospitals. But disease killed even more soldiers than did weapons. It is estimated that the wars of Napoleon caused a million deaths in the French armies (including soldiers from countries annexed to France) and that the Revolution and its wars accounted for a similar number of victims. Hence a total of 2 million dead, probably balanced by a similar figure for France's adversaries; in short, the wars cost some 4 million lives over a period of more than twenty years, representing an average of about 200,000 victims per year for Europe as a whole.

Why this series of unending wars when at the outset both sides had expected the issue to be decided rapidly? The first reason is that the Revolution was not defeated and crushed in 1792 or in 1793, as the 'aristocrats', émigrés and leaders of the coalition countries hoped it would be. It may, indeed, be wondered whether such a defeat was possible: if the Prussians had been victorious at Valmy, had taken Paris and subjected it to the 'military execution' announced in the Brunswick Manifesto, would that have put an end to the Revolution? The fact remains that the armies of the Republic halted and then drove back that invasion, crushed the Vendéens and other rebels and then, from 1794 to 1796, achieved some major conquests.

These successes are easy to explain. With 28 million inhabitants in 1789, France was the most populated country in Europe; the energy of the revolutionary government (and particularly of the Committee of Public Safety) enabled it to mobilize and equip, as we have seen, a million men; this gave it numerical superiority over the rather modest forces that the coalition partners enlisted. We need not fall for the 'soldiers of Year II' myth, but they were clearly often under the spell of patriotic enthusiasm. To command them there emerged, in G. Lefebvre's words, an 'extraordinary generation of war leaders', many of them very young, like the most brilliant of all, Bonaparte. All in all, the Republic forged a new and effective military weapon, which, though not invincible, would dominate European battlefields for two decades. Napoleon inherited it and, thanks to his own genius, for a long time led it from victory to victory.

Besides, the weaknesses and mistakes of France's enemies contributed quite substantially to the military triumphs of the Revolution – and of Napoleon. Until 1813, none of the coalitions against France managed to unite on the battlefield the three great military monarchies in Europe: Russia was absent from the first coalition, Prussia from the second and third, etc. As for Britain, leader and banker of the coalitions, for a long time it practised a peripheral strategy, which had no impact on the main conflict. Incomplete, unable to coordinate their actions or take advantage of opportunities, the coalitions were also torn apart by dissension, in particular because of the partitions of Poland (1793 and 1795), whose misfortune possibly saved the Revolution. Lastly, in the field, the allied armies were often commanded by mediocre leaders more concerned with capturing cities and seizing negotiable advantages than with destroying the enemy.

Thus the Revolution survived and started on the trail of conquest; but at the same time we find all the ingredients of a 'perpetual war'. The renunciation of their conquests was unacceptable to the French political and military leaders, while the expansion of a greater France, with its 'natural frontiers' and satellite republics, was unacceptable to the major European powers, which resigned themselves to peace only under duress and were determined to take their revenge at the earliest opportunity. Moreover, Great Britain was unvanquished; the French navy had been disorganized at the start of the Revolution, and neither the Republic nor Napoleon was able to turn it into an instrument capable of affronting the formidable Royal Navy; each encounter with it was disastrous for the French squadrons and France's Spanish and Dutch allies. Each advance of French hegemony on the Continent made it increasingly unacceptable to Britain. This produced a vicious circle that would continue to turn until 1812: coalition, French victories and conquests, another coalition and so on. Nevertheless, the French victories and conquests had the effect of spreading around the principles and institutions of the French Revolution.

The 'Revolution in France', as Edmund Burke, its virulent opponent, termed it, was an essentially French phenomenon, which seriously affected the rest of Europe only when it triggered war. Certainly, in its early phase, it had admirers in 'enlightened' circles throughout Europe; the dawn of a new era and the triumph of freedom over despotism aroused enthusiastic responses such as the well known reactions of the Englishmen Charles James Fox and William Wordsworth. But the Revolution's violent excesses, the September massacres, the deaths of Louis XVI and Marie-Antoinette, the Terror, the fear of social upheaval, and later the expansion of a now more aggressive Republic, plus active counter-revolutionary propaganda, gradually thinned the ranks of Revolutionary sympathizers and swelled those of its enemies. To sum up, the most striking fact is that the French Revolution, in itself, had few emulators.

Admittedly, there existed English, Scottish, Batavian, German, Swiss, Italian and Austrian 'Jacobins', but they were never more than tiny minorities – a few noble men and enlightened bourgeois; the same circles had produced the leaders of 1789 but, unlike the latter, they remained generals without soldiers, for they lacked the popular support that had been decisive in the summer of 1789. Sometimes they were even hated by the people: the republicans of Naples and the *afrancesados* in Spain, for example, and before them the non-conformist ministers, intellectuals and businessmen, who in England had been the warmest supporters of the Revolution in its early stages became victims of the King and Church Mobs. And yet it was in Great Britain that the Jacobin movement, which was in fact moderate, developed most successfully; with his *Rights of Man*, Thomas Paine produced for it one of the classics of revolutionary thought, which long remained influential, and organizations such as the London Corresponding Society had successes in poorer quarters that were reminiscent of the *sans-culottes*. By the late 1790s, the 'united' societies were truly revolutionary, but their real strength was insignificant, except in Ireland.

These 'Jacobins' terrified certain governments and were the target of harsh repression, but the number of victims was generally – and for good reasons – small, except in the case of Ireland, where the 1798 revolt of the 'United Irishmen' ended in a bloodbath (30,000 dead in three months) reminiscent of the Vendée genocide. But everywhere else the 'Jacobins' were too few in number and too weak to constitute a serious threat to the established order and conquer power on their own. It was only the French victories and conquests that brought some of these small groups to power, mainly when a 'sister republic' was set up. Whereas Belgium, the left bank of the Rhine, Savoy, the Comté of Nice, Mulhouse and Geneva were quite simply annexed to France, the United Provinces became the Batavian Republic (1795); in Italy there appeared in succession the Cispadane Republic, the Cisalpine Republic, the Ligurian Republic (1797), the Roman and Parthenopean Republics (1798 and 1799), while, after French invasion, the Swiss Cantons became the Helvetic Republic (1798). Although some of these republics did not last long, Napoleon later reduced various other states to vassal status. The ex-Jacobins or patriots were often useful collaborators with the occupying forces, but the French intervened shamelessly in the affairs of their satellites, which they exploited without restraint, thus undermining the popularity of the new regimes. In short, the principles and institutions of the Revolution were exported by 'missionaries in uniform'. This process was to be extended and intensified when the 'great nation' became Napoleon's Grand Empire.

THE TRIUMPHANT REVOLUTION UNDER NAPOLEON

As First Consul, then as Emperor (1804), Napoleon Bonaparte was sole master – and an increasingly absolute master – of France and of a part of Europe from 1799 to 1814. While his personality may be repulsive to some and seductive to others, it is impossible to deny his intelligence, his ceaseless activity and his ability to grasp and solve the most complex problems or his military genius. He was the son of the Revolution – without it his meteoric rise to power would have been inconceivable – but he was also its heir and perpetuator. His regime constituted the triumph of the Revolution and thus of the Enlightenment. Napoleon may be regarded as the last and greatest of the enlightened despots; in particular, he consolidated irreversibly some of the 'conquests' and 'achievements' of the Revolution, but left his own mark on them. The Napoleonic state was authoritarian, bureaucratic, centralizing, one might even say 'despotic', and certainly much stronger than the absolute monarchy had been. Despotism was almost inescapable given the anarchy that prevailed at the end of the Directory, but it implied that the optimism of the Enlightenment and of the early days of Revolution had faded. Bonaparte immediately and with some brutality re-established order in France and his regime, then moved gradually in the direction of a police state, with censorship and state political prisoners (admittedly, he had to forestall plots against him fomented from abroad).

The authoritarian trend was apparent in all areas. For example, Napoleon used the new administrative divisions into département, arrondissement, etc., introduced by the Constituent Assembly, but placed in authority over each area no longer an elected council but a single official – prefect or sub-prefect – appointed by the government (the mayors of communes were also appointed). Similarly, magistrates were no longer elected but appointed by the government. Napoleon retained legislative assemblies, but they came more and more under his control and their members were in fact appointed. In education, the lycées, established in 1802, were a cross between convent and barracks, and the Imperial University was in theory given the monopoly of education. Where finances were concerned, Napoleon strengthened the administration of direct taxes set up by the Directory to improve tax collection, but he reintroduced indirect taxes on consumption (1804), which the Constituent Assembly had abolished. The Banque de France was one of his long-lasting initiatives (1800) but he lost no time in bringing it under his control.

Admittedly, the imperial bureaucracy, although more numerous than in the days of the monarchy, was much smaller than in recent times; but it was far removed from the minimal and liberal state, the decentralized self-government which the Constituent Assembly had sought to introduce and, of course, even farther from the sans-culottes' dreams of direct democracy. As we know, subsequent French regimes carefully maintained the authoritarian and bureaucratic model handed down to them by Napoleon.

At the same time, Napoleon wished to 'complete' the Revolution by achieving the reconciliation of the French people. By means of the Concordat (1801) with Pope Pius VII, he ended the schism within the French church and won the support of the Catholics, whom the anti-religious policy of the Revolution had antagonized; but he also brought the church under his control, with its bishops appointed by government (Protestants and Jews were similarly controlled). He succeeded in winning over the majority of ex-revolutionaries and a proportion of the former nobility; in 1808, he created an imperial nobility, which he regarded as a pool of the most eminent talents and of his own servants.

The Napoleonic system was therefore a combination of institutions established by the Revolution and of other elements (such as the Council of State), which came from the ancien régime, but they were all suffused with authoritarianism. For example, the Civil Code or Code Napoléon of 1804 is based on customary law, roman law, the work of the revolutionary assemblies and the spirit of the Enlightenment.

In spite of its authoritarian approach and the continuing war, the imperial regime won the support of the great majority of French people thanks to the Emperor's prestige (one of the first examples of personal rather than dynastic power), to his victories, to the order which prevailed and to the prosperity that reigned until 1810.

Although Napoleon consolidated, while at the same time he distorted, the work of the Revolution in France, he also exported it to Europe, continuing and reinforcing the work begun during the Revolution (especially through the creation of 'sister republics') and by himself in Italy in 1796–7: he has been called 'Robespierre on horseback'. Following the pattern mentioned earlier, France's expansion gave rise to coalitions that were defeated owing to the quality of the French armies and the military genius of Napoleon; but these victories and conquests engendered fresh coalitions and hence, until 1812, further conquests. Thrice victor over Austria (excluding his campaigns in 1796–7), he crushed Prussia in 1806, became reconciled with and an ally of the Tsar at Tilsit (1807), and came to dominate a large part of Europe, stretching as far as present-day Croatia and Poland, by ruling through a variety of systems, rather like concentric circles. In the centre lay the French Empire itself, enlarged by successive annexations and eventually including 130 départements from Bouches-du-Tibre (Rome) to Bouches-de-la Trave (Lübeck). Then came the satellite states, governed by relatives or agents of Napoleon: the kingdoms of Holland, Westphalia, Italy and Naples, the Grand Duchy of Berg and, from 1808, part of Spain. The next circle was composed of vassal countries, especially the German states grouped into the Rhineland Confederation (1806), of which Napoleon was Protector. The last one comprised allied countries of sometimes doubtful loyalty, such as Prussia, Austria, Russia, Denmark and Sweden.

The political map of Europe was, in fact, radically simplified by Napoleon and the number of states reduced (changes which his victors would to a large extent ratify). In particular, the Recez of 1803 abolished hundreds of tiny sovereign lands within the Holy Roman Empire (which itself ceased to exist in 1806). They were abolished in favour of large- and medium-sized states that were given linear borders less confused and complex than before. Subsequent annexations and adjustments imposed by Napoleon further simplified the map. In the end, Italy was reduced to two political entities, not counting the parts annexed by France.

At the same time, the new French system of institutions set up by the revolutionary legislation as revised and adjusted by Napoleon was imposed in full in areas annexed by France. But many of its features, such as the administrative divisions, the legal hierarchy and the tax system, were introduced into satellite states and even into certain vassal countries. Lastly, in the 'independent' states, certain governments – especially that of Prussia after the disaster of 1806 – contemplated resuming the struggle against France, and thought that they would be better prepared for this eventuality by introducing reforms based to some extent on the French model but also owing something to a local tradition of enlightened despotism. However, the importance of the reforms in non-annexed countries should not be overestimated, especially in social matters, since the nobility had to be handled with care.

There was nevertheless a trend towards the harmonization of institutions; a number that were typical of the ancien régime, such as serfdom, the feudal system, guilds and various economic regulations, were widely abolished. The most striking example was the introduction of the Code Napoléon into many states, including the kingdoms of Italy and Naples (but not Bavaria or Saxony) and the grand duchies of Baden, Berg, Frankfurt and Warsaw. In some of them it remained in force after the fall of Napoleon.

There was thus a degree of European integration (which also embraced foreign policy and defence), but that integration was of an 'hegemonic' kind, in which one country – even one man – dominated, on the basis of unequal relations: supremacy for the French and subordination for France's vassals or allies.

There was also a certain amount of economic integration, through the Continental System. By means of this system, Napoleon hoped to unite European states in an economic war – the Continental Blockade – against Great Britain, principally by keeping that country out of continental markets. There was something quite new in forcing almost the entire continent to adopt a common economic policy, even though this policy boiled down to a series of measures directed against the trading activities of an external enemy. But Napoleon did not seek to construct the economic unity of Europe, the 'continental trading confederation' that some of his advisers proposed. Although he had established a European Empire, he was unable to see that Empire as an economic entity; he contemplated its problems from an egocentric point of view, in relation solely to France, whose interests always came before those of its vassals. He set an example of extreme protectionism, and the lesson was not lost on post-1815 governments, which thought they had found in it the key to economic development. Napoleonic Europe was never an economic community sharing interests that would have consolidated it. Only with a great many qualifications can the Continental System be seen as the earliest forerunner of the European Union!

Nevertheless, a large part of Europe was borne along by shared economic destiny. The maritime war with England and the Continental Blockade (although the latter lasted only seven years) had important long-term economic consequences and contributed to the establishment of new structures.

Some of these changes were not for the better. In particular, the maritime blockade, to which Great Britain, through its mastery of the seas, subjected the Continent, caused the collapse of maritime trade, which had been the most dynamic sector of the economy up to 1793; the major ports were paralysed from 1807 and their industries and hinterlands, closely reliant on trading by sea, grew weaker, while some regions such as Western France suffered de-industrialization. Indeed, the Atlantic sector of the European economy did not regain its prosperity after the wars were over, mainly because the British had seized the opportunity to monopolize overseas markets. The loss of its empire, triggered by the events of 1808, was a major reason why nineteenth-century Spain became so sluggish and marginal.

On the other hand, the Continental Blockade functioned actually as an ultra-protectionist system that protected the industries most exposed to English competition and stimulated their growth. The leading example is the cotton industry (especially machine spinning) in France, Switzerland, Saxony and elsewhere. Although this industry was not competitive and suffered sorely after the end of the wars, its development and the growth of industry between 1800 and 1810 in several parts of Europe laid the foundations for Europe's industrialization in the nineteenth century. Moreover, some major and lasting changes were taking place in the economic geography of Europe: coastal regions were in decline, while the industrial and business centres of the interior were expanding, particularly in a vast area between the Seine and the Elbe. The hub of the continent's economy shifted from the Atlantic seaboard to the Rhine.

The Continental System helped bring into being a new European economy in which the differences with Britain were pronounced; Britain looked towards the oceans and had truly global interests, while the Continent was more inward looking, concentrating on exchanges among neighbours. It was furthermore weakened by the treaties of 1814–15: the territorial and political division imposed by the British government to ensure the 'containment' of France and a balance of power in Europe led to economic fragmentation.

On 20 March 1811, Napoleon's second wife, daughter of the Emperor of Austria, gave him the heir so long desired, who was immediately proclaimed King of Rome. Three years later (6 April 1814), the Emperor abdicated.

At the origins of this reversal of fortune was the tenacious resistance of Britain. Protected from invasion by its invincible fleet, it also succeeded, though not without moments of hardship, in withstanding the economic warfare of the Continental Blockade. Quite apart from anything else, this resistance undermined the Great Empire, weakened its economy and damaged its prestige. In addition, the financial and maritime power of Britain enabled it to help the enemies of Napoleon and, from 1808 onwards, it succeeded in maintaining a small but excellent army in the Iberian Peninsula, which made a decisive contribution to keeping open the abscess that Napoleon had unwisely created on the southern flank of his Empire.

By dethroning the Spanish Bourbons and replacing them with one of his brothers, Napoleon had sought to revitalize to his own advantage a country whose potential he, like many others, overestimated. What he actually achieved was to spark off an immense Vendée, the uprising of an entire Catholic people, with its wounded faith and wounded pride, led by its clergy and nobility; but the country's resistance was backed up by the regular Spanish army and by the troops of Wellington. The Spanish or Peninsular War lasted for six years; the French, unable to wear down Spanish resistance, suffered heavy losses, and gradually lost ground, until Wellington eventually invaded south-west France at the end of 1813.

Although the Spanish nation was the first to stand up to Napoleon, there was growing hostility to French domination in Germany as well as in the Low Countries and in Italy. Although in many cases the French armies had met with a not unfriendly welcome at the outset, the prolonged foreign occupation exacerbated by extortionate demands aroused national sentiment. The subjects of European rulers feared and hated the French more than their own masters: in 1809, 150,000 volunteers enrolled in the Austrian army.

In 1810, a widespread economic crisis broke out, which was not unjustifiably blamed on the Continental Blockade and the arbitrariness and brutality with which it was enforced; the crisis was followed by a long recession, which caused serious discontent in business circles throughout Europe, including France. Moreover, the conflict between the Emperor and the Pope once again alienated large numbers of Catholics, and there were rumblings among French royalists. A growing number of young men eluded conscription.

From 1808 onwards, cracks had therefore begun to appear in the imposing Napoleonic edifice, which was now based solely on force and victory. Nevertheless, it might have endured had not the Emperor thrown himself into an attack on Russia, which nothing obliged him to do, even though his alliance with Alexander I had broken down. The rest is well known: Russian distances, the Russian winter, the Russian resistance and disease destroyed the Grand Army. Napoleon was able to muster a new army and win some further victories in the spring of 1813, but he had to deal simultaneously with Russia, Prussia and Austria as well as with the uprisings of subject peoples. The Battle of the Nations at Leipzig (16–19 October 1813) was an irreparable disaster. During the 1814 campaign in France, Napoleon had only a few tens of thousands of men against the hundreds of thousands of the Coalition, whose union was held together by the diplomacy and subsidies of England. If he had been more conciliatory in the negotiations that were going on at the same time, he might just have kept his throne, but the fall of Paris and the betrayal of state dignitaries who owed everything to him forced him to abdicate. The following year, the 'Flight of the Eagle' from the island of Elba to Paris, the Hundred Days, and the Battle of Waterloo – so dear to the British ego – marked an episode of high drama, certainly, but of limited importance. Napoleon spent six painful years at St Helena but won the halo of a martyr. 'What a story my life has been!' he is supposed to have said; it was a story that would feed the aspirations of many an ambitious leader, and the Napoleonic legend was not without influence on the history of the nineteenth century. But the brother of Louis XVI had returned to the Tuileries: surely this was the end of the revolutionary and imperial interlude?

TENTATIVE ASSESSMENT

The 'restoration' carried out by the victors in Europe in 1814 and 1815 was far from complete. True, a number of legitimate dethroned monarchs – starting with the Bourbons – were restored to power, and several states which had been wiped off the map, reappeared. But the *ancien régime* was not resurrected wherever it had been abolished, in France or indeed elsewhere. Neither feudal rights nor *Parlements* were re-established in France, and nor were the princelings and ecclesiastical principalities reinstated in Germany or the republics of Genoa and Venice in Italy.

Admittedly, the treaties of Paris and of Vienna established a new equilibrium in Europe that was not favourable to the principles of 1789 and was even designed to abolish them. France, the source of those dangerous ideas and regarded as a smouldering fuse ready to explode and to take up arms again, was deprived of all its conquests and surrounded by a solid barrier to contain it should it be tempted to re-expand: in the north was the Kingdom of the Netherlands, the cherished offspring of English diplomacy, and in the Rhineland Prussia received large territories. At the same time, by forcing on France a dynasty, which soon became unpopular, France's victors – without realizing it – had condemned the country to political instability. Destabilized by the Revolution, split into warring factions, France became prey to a state of latent (and sometimes not so latent) but ongoing civil war, which has lasted to the present day. The Revolution was the founding event of modern France, but on a sort of *tabula rasa*: it cut France off completely from its past, from its memory; for France, it was *the* most important turning point in its history. What is more, the trend towards voluntary birth control, which had appeared in France before 1789, grew stronger during the Revolution and the Empire; French population now increased more slowly, and then stagnated from the middle

of the nineteenth century onwards, while the populations of other European countries were expanding rapidly. From all points of view, France was demoted and started a long decline. Much of its monumental and artistic heritage – the richest in Europe after Italy – had been destroyed. Yet for a long time the French continued to see themselves as 'the great nation'.

On the other hand, the major military monarchies had become larger and stronger – Prussia, Austria (which dominated Italy) and Russia, this last to all appearances the chief victor, although the real victor was, as we shall see, Great Britain. The dangers that had threatened them made their leaders more vigilant in regard to subversion and their regimes more authoritarian and police-dominated. Post-1815 Europe was fundamentally monarchic and aristocratic, and Britain and France, where large landowners were still the ruling class, were no exception.

Did the 'reaction' win on all counts? No, it did not; it would be by-passed, so to speak, by two underlying movements which were more powerful than the armies of the Holy Alliance, the union of Napoleon's victors set up to maintain the order they had re-established.

First, the 'principles of 1789', those proclaimed in the Declaration of the Rights of Man and of the Citizen, remained an inspiration for many people in France, Europe and beyond the seas (for example in the countries of Latin America which were in the process of winning their independence). Let us therefore give a brief outline of this ideology.

If the men of 1789, and all those subsequently inspired by the Revolution, had been asked to sum up in one word their ideal, they would have replied: freedom. The French Revolution was fundamentally liberal, although this quality has been disguised by its excesses and by certain historians. It liberated the individual by abolishing serfdom and condemning arbitrary arrest; it affirmed freedom of conscience and of thought, including in religious matters, and freedom of expression, and hence freedom of the press. As for slavery in the colonies, the Constituent Assembly had done nothing: it was the slaves' revolt in Santo Domingo that prompted the Convention to vote for its abolition (14 February 1794). But Bonaparte re-established it in 1802 and it lasted in the French colonies until 1848 (whereas the British had abolished slavery in their colonies in 1833, having prohibited the slave trade in 1807). The Revolution also freed the land: the abolition of 'feudalism' meant that ownership of the land ceased to be shared between lord and tenant but became 'quiritarian', that is to say, appertaining to a single person.

Second, the Revolution was profoundly hostile to the *corps* typical of the *ancien régime* and closely bound up with privileges. These bodies – clergy, religious orders, *parlements*, guilds, universities, academies, and so forth – were systematically abolished. The notion of organized political parties was alien to the Revolution's philosophy, which saw such groupings as mere factions. There should be no intermediary between the citizen and the state. But the 'intermediary corps' had guaranteed *freedoms*, in the plural; the optimism of 1789, made people overlook the danger which the state might come to represent for *freedom*.

Equality, of course, is the second great revolutionary principle (fraternity made only a brief appearance in 1793–4), but it is also ambiguous and open to differing interpretations. And yet the members of the Constituent Assembly had been explicit: 'men are born free and equal in *right'*. Hence equality before the law, which is the same for everyone, equality in taxation, equality of opportunity: careers opened up to the talented – and this was no hollow concept in the armies of the Revolution and of Napoleon. But where political rights were concerned, the Constitution of Year II – never brought into force – was the only one to make provision for universal adult male suffrage; the Constitutions of 1791 and 1795 – and still more the Constitutions imposed by Bonaparte – reserved participation in political life for citizens who possessed a certain amount of property. However, the principle of equality could be interpreted broadly to include political rights, and the French Revolution contained a 'democratic option' that would gradually gain the upper hand in the course of the nineteenth century.

In any case, political rights were for men only, even though women were active both in the Revolution and in the anti-revolutionary movements, and a few feminists spoke up for the rights of women. But revolutionaries of all persuasions were utterly against any political role for women (owing in part to memories of royal favourites and the hatred felt for the Austrian Marie-Antoinette). The function of women was to be wives and mothers, to raise children for the fatherland. On 30 October 1793, the Convention prohibited all women's organizations, and the feminist leader, Olympe de Gouges, was guillotined. As for Napoleon's own views, they were no different and he introduced into his Code some clauses prejudicial to women.

On the other hand, equal rights and citizenship were granted to the Jewish minority – then a very small group of people in France – although not without some hesitation and delay (Decree of 27 September 1791). This did not prevent them from suffering the consequences of the anti-religious campaigns of 1793–5, but Napoleon would later both strengthen their position and at the same time bring them under his control. This emancipation was extended to annexed and satellite countries and progress towards it was made in other countries such as Prussia. The rise of the Rothschild family during the wars of the Empire may be seen as symbolic.

Except for the *enragés* and the Babouvists, equality was never understood by the revolutionaries as egalitarianism or a levelling of wealth and living conditions. It is too often forgotten that the Declaration of Rights places property alongside freedom and equality as one of man's inalienable rights. Indeed, the ideas of freedom and property joined forces in the abolition of feudalism and in the freedom of enterprise, which, if we discount the fleeting aberrations of the Year II, was one of the great 'achievements' of the Revolution. Monopolies, corporations, guilds, and privileged companies were abolished. Combinations of wage-earners or of employers were forbidden. In rural areas, freedom of cultivation and freedom of enclosure were proclaimed – but in fact not often practised. The French Revolution was therefore liberal in its leanings, quite the opposite of socialism: in March 1793, the Convention decreed the death penalty for any proponents of an agrarian law, which would redistribute land.

Last, the Constituent Assembly had proclaimed the sovereignty of the nation and the right – even the duty – to resist oppression. This did not prevent minorities, especially the Jacobins, and later an individual, Napoleon, from seizing that sovereignty, though they did so in the name of the people as a whole. In 1814, Louis XVIII would introduce

a 'Constitutional Charter' establishing an elected chamber, admittedly based on highly restrictive voter qualifications, but whose powers were far from negligible. Although, after the fall of Napoleon, a stronger form of absolutism held wide sway in many countries, the ideas of a written constitution and of a representative regime remained influential. During the nineteenth century, there were fewer and fewer regimes which rejected such ideas completely and made no attempt to base their legitimacy on elections.

The eclipse of the 1789 principles, due to the fall of their champion, Napoleon, was therefore only temporary; the ideology of the French Revolution would eventually triumph and conquer most of the world – in much the same way as the metric system of weights and measures, a typical example of standardizing rationalism and the scientific outlook, was to do, although it was based on an inaccurate calculation of the earth's meridian. As early as 1820–1, 'revolutions' in Spain and in Italy showed that the revolutionary hydra was not dead. In fact, as soon as a revolution – the first of the modern breed – had taken place and had succeeded in France, the idea that it was both possible and just to overthrow an established order was bound to spread, and with it the image – non-existent prior to 1789 – of the revolutionary as a person consciously preparing the way for a revolution.

However, it must also be recognized that the ideal of the Enlightenment, which had inspired the Revolution, had at least partially failed, and not just as a result of the restorations in 1814 and 1815. The optimism of 1789 had been severely tested by the traumatic events of the next quarter of a century, and there would be little further sign of it until 1848. It was clear that reason and good intentions were not enough to change the human lot; hopes, as we have seen, were set lower and realism – even cynicism – pervaded the minds of those who had survived the Terror and other political convulsions.

What is more, the spirit of the Enlightenment was no longer the only ideology, as it had been in the eighteenth century, when the 'philosophers' had had a free hand and their rare adversaries had been ignored. The Enlightenment had been hostile to revealed religions and, aided by circumstances, the French revolutionaries tried at first to bring the French church under control by the Civil Constitution of the Clergy, and then threw themselves into de-Christianization, persecution of those still faithful to the old religion, and the promotion of deism and secular cults. But this sparked violent opposition from people loyal to the traditional religion, and insurrections like the one in Vendée. Although Napoleon re-established religious peace, France remained at least partly de-Christianized, but things were different in the rest of Europe. Indeed, in certain countries such as England, with its Methodist movement, and Germany, with its Pietism, a religious revival had begun before the Revolution and had been strengthened by reactions against the Revolution's anti-religious zeal. By 1815, churches had been revitalized by the ordeal and purged of eighteenth-century laxism, but they had also become more rigid in their intransigent opposition to the principles of 1789 and to liberalism, and they sought an alliance of Throne and Altar to combat irreligion and anti-clericalism.

The Revolution also engendered a counter-revolutionary body of thought, a self-conscious conservatism, which had not existed in the eighteenth century. As early as 1790, Edmund Burke published his *Reflections*, which would become the sourcebook for all ideologies hostile to the French Revolution. The counter-offensive was continued by Joseph de Maistre, Bonald, Chateaubriand and Gentz. In fact, part of the 'intelligentsia' – if such a term is appropriate – shifted from Enlightenment to conservatism and in so doing created a lasting split. Moreover, German romanticism, and French romanticism likewise at first, were openly hostile to the Revolution.

As we have already noted, the wars gave a powerful boost to nationalism. First of all in France, where *Vive la Nation* (Long live the Nation) was one of the earliest and most popular slogans of the Revolution: the French were proud of being the 'country of freedom', of having resisted the coalition of 'tyrants' and gone from victory to victory, and modestly referred to themselves as 'the great nation'. For a long time, national sentiment and the principles of 1789 would be indissolubly linked in their eyes. But to people who suffered from occupation and exactions on the part of French armies, the necessary alliance between an awakening and increasingly strident national sentiment and liberalism seemed less obvious: during the nineteenth century, nationalism and liberalism often advanced together, but in the end they went their separate ways. In any case, cosmopolitanism, which had been such a powerful movement in the eighteenth century, was destroyed by the wars of the Revolution and Empire, which also damaged the general spirit of the Enlightenment and its optimism. It could be argued that the terrible thirty-year civil war in Europe from 1914 to 1945 had its roots beyond the intervening century of peace, in the twenty-three years war of 1792–1815.

Be that as it may, the legacy of the French Revolution was not the sole threat to the re-established order in 1815. By a remarkable paradox, subversion would come from a country which had been the most constant and implacable enemy of revolutionary and imperial France, Great Britain, whose special status should be emphasized. As the only undefeated country, the only country never invaded by the French armies, it was the major victor of the French wars and it would become the sole superpower of the nineteenth century. Although it had harshly whipped into line its own Jacobins and Irish Republicans, it had maintained throughout the wars its parliamentary and liberal regime, which was now the sole alternative to the bureaucratic absolutism of continental monarchies, and a model regarded with admiration and envy by foreign liberals.

Still more important, however, is the fact that England had invented modern economic growth. The Industrial Revolution, which began in about the mid-eighteenth century, continued during the wars against France in spite of their enormous cost (England's economic progress was one of the reasons for its resistance and ultimate victory), and then accelerated with the return of peace. Major changes in other sectors, including agriculture, transport and finance, had preceded or accompanied the transformation of industry. Thanks to gains in productivity derived from technical inventions, Britain avoided the age-old Malthusian trap: for the first time in history, population increased rapidly without a long-term fall in real wages.

The Industrial Revolution acted like a solvent on the old order, for it created two new classes – the industrial middle class and the working class – which were antagonists yet drawn to band together against the domination of large landowners. Without revolution, but not without disturbances, the English middle class managed to win from

the aristocracy a series of concessions for the sharing of political power.

During the nineteenth century, similar types of power sharing would occur in several continental states. The Industrial Revolution was contagious: the formidable competition of the British was forcing the continentals to modernize along the same lines. This process, which started to take shape between 1780 and 1790, gathered strength during the Empire and especially after 1815, but mainly in north-western Europe, with the result that the latter region came to contrast more and more sharply with the rest of the continent.

The Industrial Revolution therefore breathed new life into the liberal ideology, which in 1815 appeared to be threatened by the forces of 'reaction'. Although the French Revolution and the Napoleonic legend were the founding myths of the nineteenth century, the Industrial Revolution represented a powerful force for change. Each of the two hereditary enemies, Britain and France, had invented its own revolution, and it was the combination of those two revolutions – one economic, the other political – that created nineteenth-century civilization.

BIBLIOGRAPHY

AFTALION, F. 1987. *L'Economie de la Révolution française.* Paris, Hachette [Engl. trans. 1990. *The French Revolution. An Economic Interpretation.* Cambridge University Press, Cambridge].

BERDING, H., FRANCOIS, E.; ULLMANN, H.-P. 1989. *La Révolution, la France et l'Allemagne.* Editions de la Maison des Sciences de l'Homme, Paris.

BERGERON, L., LOVIE, J.; PALUEL, A. 1972. *L'épisode napoléonien (1799–1815).* 2 vols. Editions du Seuil, Paris [Engl. trans. Vol. 1. Bergeron, L. 1981. *France under Napoleon.* Princeton University Press, Princeton].

BLANNING, T. C. W. 1983. *The French Revolution in Germany: Occupation and Resistance in the Rhineland. 1792–1802.* Oxford University Press, Oxford.

COBB, R. 1987. *The People's Armies.* Yale University Press, London.

CONNELLY, O. 1965. *Napoleon's Satellite Kingdoms.* The Free Press, New York.

CORVISIER, A., MEYER, J.; POUSSOU, J.-P. 1991. *La Révolution française.* 2 vols. Presses Universitaires de France, Paris (Covers not only France, but Europe as a whole).

CROUZET, F. (ed.) 1987. *L'Economie britannique et le Blocus Continental.* 2nd edn. Economica, Paris.

——. 1993. *La grande inflation. La monnaie française de Louis XVI à Napoléon.* Fayard, Paris.

DICKINSON, H. T. (ed.) 1989. *Britain and the French Revolution 1789–1815.* Macmillan, Basingstoke.

DOYLE, W. (ed.) 1988. *Origins of the French Revolution.* 2nd edn, Oxford University Press, Oxford.

——. 1990. *The Oxford History of the French Revolution.* Oxford University Press, Oxford.

EHRMAN, J. 1969–96. *The Younger Pitt.* 3 vols. London.

ELLIOTT, M. 1982. *Partners in Revolution: The United Irishmen and France.* Yale University Press, New Haven.

ELLIS, G. 1991. *The Napoleonic Empire.* Macmillan, Basingstoke.

EMSLEY, C. 1979. *British Society and the French Wars, 1793–1815.* Macmillan, Basingstoke.

FURET, F. 1978. *Penser la Révolution française.* Paris, Gallimard [Engl. trans. 1991. *Interpreting the French Revolution.* Cambridge University Press, Cambridge].

FURET, F.; OZOUF, M. 1988. *Dictionnaire critique de la Révolution française.* Flammarion, Paris.

FURET, F.; RICHET, D. (eds) 1965. *La Révolution française.* 2 vols. Hachette, Paris. 2nd edn, 1973, 1 vol. Fayard, Paris.

[Abridged Engl. trans. 1970. *The French Revolution*. Weidenfeld and Nicolson, London] (The founding stone of the 'revisionist' school).

GODECHOT, J. (ed.) 1956. *La Grande Nation: l'expansion révolutionnaire de la France dans le monde de 1789 à 1799*. 2 vols, 2nd edn, 1983. Aubier, Paris.

HUFTON, O. H. 1992. *Women and the Limits of Citizenship in the French Revolution*. Toronto University Press, Toronto.

KAFKER, F. A.; LAUX, J. M. (eds) 1989. *The French Revolution: Conflicting Interpretations*. R. E. Krueger, Malabar FL.

——. (ed.) 1989. *Napoleon and His Times: Selected Interpretations*. R. E. Krueger, Malabar FL.

LEFEBVRE, G. (ed.) 1935. *Napoléon*. Presses Universitaires de France, Paris. 6th edn revised, 1969. A classic general history of the 1799–1815 period [Engl. trans. 1969. *Napoleon*. Columbia University Press, New York].

——. 1951. *La Révolution Française*. Presses Universitaires de France, Paris (A classic, somewhat obsolete, but not limited to France).

SCHAMA, S. 1977. *Patriots and Liberators: Revolution in the Netherlands 1780–1813*. Knopf, New York.

SOBOUL, A. 1974. *The French Revolution*. 2 vols, London (The Jacobin School at its extreme).

SUTHERLAND, D. M. G. 1985. *France 1789–1815: Revolution and Counter-Revolution*. Oxford University Press, Oxford.

TARLÉ, E. (ed.) 1966. *Napoleon*. 3rd edn. Editions en Langues Etrangères, Moscow.

WOOLF, S. 1990. *Napoléon et la conquête de l'Europe*. Flammarion, Paris (French translation).

10.1.2
PEACE AND EXPANSION (1815–1914)

Theo C. Barker

PRELIMINARY SURVEY OF THE YEARS 1815–1914

The period between the close of the Twenty-Three Years War in 1815 and the outbreak of the First World War in 1914 has a certain unity in that, unlike the century before 1789, it saw no major European conflict: The campaigns for German and Italian unification were brief, although French republican zeal prolonged the Franco-Prussian War by six months. The Crimean War was a brief, mid-century punctuation of peace and the colonial alarms and excursions were no more than the European powers' bids for hitherto unclaimed parts of the world, especially in Africa. The Boer War was significant in demonstrating the military weakness of economically powerful Britain. The other countries of Europe were delighted to see the humbling of the greater by a small and proud nation of farmers.

How are we to explain this remarkable Century of European Peace? It is clearly related to the other outstanding feature of these years: the wholesale exodus from Europe of young people, many of whom left the ports of entry and pressed on inland, to inhabit the open spaces of the rest of the world, to till the virgin soil, raise cattle or supply services to the new migrant agriculturalists. For many it was a hard, frontier-like existence, in the American case often vividly recalled by twentieth-century Hollywood. It was shared by men and women alike. They raised families often with a great struggle. They had to start from scratch building their homes with next to no resources, often in fairly lawless conditions and having to ward off not only envious competitors but also any remaining evicted natives. It is reasonable to suggest that such struggles to survive and make good absorbed the excess energies of the young and channelled any natural aggressiveness into peaceful and productive pursuits. The numbers involved were considerable: 600,000 European immigrants per year crossed to the United States alone by the 1880s and over 1,200,000 just before 1914. Many others moved abroad to join their fellow countrymen elsewhere in the world: Italians, Spanish and Portuguese to Latin America, for instance, Scots to Canada and many from Great Britain to Australia and New Zealand, a more frequent destination for them than the United States.

During the Century of Peace the population of Western Europe, as defined in Table 1 (see Chapter 1), roughly doubled. Because of the differing dates at which each country took its earlier censuses, the first grand total of population, about 116,000,000, is very much an estimate

and not so reliable as the second, taken just before 1914: 241,000,000.

The populations of countries with rapid economic growth, notably Germany and Great Britain (England, Wales and Scotland), grew above the norm. Others, including Belgium and Switzerland, below it. Ireland's population actually fell and its Malthusian crisis will be discussed later. The most interesting case of all is that of geographically large France, considerably more than twice the population of Great Britain at the outset but of the same order of magnitude – a little larger if Alsace-Lorraine is added – just before 1914. The remarkably rapid growth of Western Europe as a whole was due, of course, to the excess of fertility over mortality with inevitable fluctuations in each over short periods. Birth rates per thousand populations, however, varied considerably between nations. At the outset they ranged form the high 30s in the territory of the future German Empire and Finland to the low 30s in France and Norway. Death rates stretched from the mid-20s (France and Germany) to 19 or less in healthy Norway, with Sweden nearer the former than the latter. By 1913, the last full year of peace, birth rates had fallen much further than death rates. They ranged from Germany with 27.5 (birth rate) and 15.0 (death rate) and Belgium with 22.3 (birth rate) and 14.2 (death rate) – similar to that of Great Britain – to France, still unusual with 18.8 (birth rate) and 17.7 (death rate). Mortality had fallen impressively and fertility had followed it down for reasons, which will be discussed later.

More of this greater population came to live in large towns. At the beginning of the nineteenth century there were only eighteen in Western Europe with populations over 100,000: Amsterdam (201,000), Barcelona (115,000), Berlin (172,000), Copenhagen (101,000), Dublin (165,000), Hamburg (130,000), Lisbon (180,000), Lyon (110,000), Madrid (160,000), Marseilles (110,000), Milan (135,000), Naples (427,000), Palermo (139,000), Paris (547,000), Rome (163,000), Valencia (100,000), Venice (134,000) and, towering above them all, London (1,117,000). By 1910/11 the number had grown to fifty-nine, with twenty-one of these over 500,000: Amsterdam (574,000), Barcelona (387,000), Berlin (2,071,000), Birmingham (840,000), Brussels (720,000), Cologne (517,000), Copenhagen (559,000), Dresden (548,000), Glasgow (1,000,000), Hamburg (931,000), Leipzig (590,000), Liverpool (753,000), Madrid (600,000), Manchester (714,000), Marseilles (551,000), Milan (579,000), and London, still by far the largest of them all (7,256,000). Dublin, Lisbon, Palermo, Lyon, Valencia and Venice on the first list are missing from the second; and nine are newcomers: Brussels plus – most significant if we correlate megalopolitan and economic growth – four German and four British cities.

These statistics, derived from national sources, are helpful in gathering a rough and ready impression of the remarkable changes which occurred in Western Europe during these years; but they depend, of course, on where the urban boundary is set. The national totals, too, can be misleading, for they are averages, which can conceal quite wide differences within countries. Even in highly urbanized England, for instance, there were remote areas, which saw relatively little development. Oral history interviews carried out some time ago in rural parts of East Anglia, for instance, showed that social attitudes changed little before 1914, despite the spread of schools and, from the later nineteenth century, newspapers. It was an inward-looking area and few of its inhabitants ventured far before the First World War. Other nations, particularly those with a geographically larger land area, no doubt had similar islands of tradition of which we shall get to know more only after a number of careful national studies have been made.

It is often said that people were not long-lived in this period, and especially in the earlier part of it. Some writers, keen to emphasize the unhealthiness of growing towns, sometimes claim that the expectancy of life at birth in this or that place may have been, say, thirty-nine in the year 1840. Such statements are, however, very misleading. It is important to note that the death rate everywhere was highest among infants and young children; but those who were able to run this gauntlet of early death often had a long working life ahead of them. Work started when they were very young, often at home as part of a family engaged in outwork manufacture, in weaving, for instance, or in domestic service in someone else's home. Many jobs involved hard physical work, unaided by mechanical power of any sort: digging, manhandling, carrying, loading and unloading, or pushing laden handcarts. The working time of life was a hard struggle. Numbers succumbed to illness or accident. But others went on to live to a ripe old age. A surprising number lived to be over eighty. Old age is no modern phenomenon, though more of us now survive to experience it. Possibly the tough survivors of earlier generations enjoyed their old age more than present-day old people, many of whom were weaklings kept alive by modern medicine and always prone to suffer from serious ailments of one sort or another.

Demographic statistics show the extent of human survival in different nations. The Scandinavian countries provide this information for the earliest part of the century. For Sweden, indeed, we have details from 1810. In a population of 2,396,000 in 1810, 532,000 of whom were then under 10 years of age, 421,000 were over 50 years old and of these 12,000 were over 80. By 1860, if we may ignore national immigration or emigration, of the ten-year cohort of 1810, no fewer than 285,000 had survived. 20,000 were then over 80. Or take Belgium, a highly urbanized country for which we have age statistics for 1846. The total population was then 4,337,000 and of these 971,000 were under 10 and 727,000 over 50. Here, 33,000 had survived to be over 80. The comparable figures for England and Wales with a population of 15,914,000 and even more urbanized by 1841 when the earliest age breakdown is available, are: 4,010,000 under 10, and 2,171,000 over 50, of whom 102,000 were over 80.

These survival rates become more thought provoking when they are compared by sex. In the two youngest age groups (0–4 and 5–10) the number of boys almost always exceeded that of girls (Finland 1825 and England and Wales 1841 being the exceptions) though there was little difference in number between the two at those ages. They both survived the gauntlet of death with equal fortitude or fortune. Thereafter the position was reversed, sometimes remarkably soon and always eventually on a considerable scale. There were more females than males in the age groups 15–20 and 21–25 from the earliest available age breakdown returns in Denmark, Finland, Germany, Ireland, Italy (from 1881), Netherlands, Norway, Portugal, Spain, Sweden, Switzerland, England/Wales, and Scotland. In Belgium and France, however, the numbers of women began to exceed that of men only from the ages of 45–50. Elsewhere, however, the excess of women below age 50 was rarely more than a few thousand apart from Germany, Spain and Portugal where it was greater, sometimes reaching 100,000 in certain age groups. From the age of 50 or thereabouts many more women than men survived at all ages throughout Western Europe.

The longer survival of women throughout Western Europe is all the more surprising when the number of conceptions was much higher than today and childbirth, without the benefits of modern medicine and hospital care, was much more dangerous as well as more frequent.

Apart from the hazards of childbirth, it cannot be said that the lot of females was at any stage in their lives easier than that of males. The general opinion at the time was that men were the masters and that it was women's duty to obey. This came with the religious upbringing in a world in which this counted for more than it does today. Much has been written about drunken husbands who returned home after carousing and thought that they had every right to beat their wives. On the other hand, it seems reasonable to suppose that in all marriages the stronger and more intelligent partner was often the wife, then as now. Whatever the legal position may have been regarding property rights – and in the case of poor people who owned no property this did not count at all – or the prevailing opinion on the deference of women, it seems highly likely that quicker-witted wives were always able to have the last word. It was they who, more often than not, handled the family income and decided on day-to-day purchases.

The lot of women in the poorer classes – often accurately described, especially when living in towns, as 'the labouring poor' – was hard from the time they were children. As daughters they had special responsibilities at home, assisting mothers to clean and look after any younger children. Before spinning became a factory industry, they were the spinsters; the name still remains. So long as manufacturing was carried on at home as part of the system whereby raw materials were 'put out' and the finished produced carried to market (and the 'putting-out' system survived longer on the Continent), women played their part in the family unit. With the spread of power-driven factories, they went out to work for long hours tending the machines, though it is important to remember that this transition from home to factory happened relatively slowly during the nineteenth century, even in textiles. It occurred even later in dressmaking. There was still much scope throughout the period for individual skills. And in agricultural communities women played their part on the farms as well as in the farmhouses.

Domestic service, living in the homes of the better-off and working from morn till night with very little free time, was the main occupation for girls from the countryside who could no longer live in the limited rural accommodation as families grew in size. Marriage was an escape but, as has been seen, merely exchanged one sort of hardship for another. Many wives took in small outwork jobs to eke out the family income. Some wives went out to work before they had children, or afterwards if they could leave them with nearby relatives. A husband who could afford to keep his wife at home instead of sending her out to work was considered by the wives in those days (unlike today) to be bestowing a great benefit upon them. It certainly gave them social superiority among other wives, just as the sort of house or neighbourhood in which they lived also managed to do. There were various gradations among the working classes, even among 'the labouring poor'. Those who went out to work found jobs as dressmakers and milliners or in markets, shops or places selling food or drink – often alcoholic – on the premises. The hours in retailing were long, especially at the end of the week when men's wages were paid.

The lot of the more fortunate, middle-class woman was less arduous but no more enviable, as some of the advocates of women's emancipation such as Mary Wollstonecraft had been quick to point out. Other able women writers made this clear enough in their novels. The range of respectable jobs open to them was much more limited. Young ladies were expected to learn the pianoforte, sit at home, look beautiful and wait for a suitable proposal of marriage. They could become governesses in private homes or teachers in private schools, though to be teachers in the growing number of church or charity schools was considered rather below their station in life. The spread of the telephone, the typewriter and the modern company office eventually started to widen the range of opportunities towards the end of the nineteenth century. Nursing, exceptionally spartan and pitifully paid, but distinctly superior to the tasks of the poor skivvies who cleaned the hospitals, was another possibility. The chances of training as a doctor was made difficult by the men students, afraid of the competition. Unpaid charitable work was always prestigious.

All in all, it is surprising that more women than men survived longer in those more difficult days. They have never been 'the weaker sex'.

The hardships which many working-class people still endured during the Century of Peace were offset to some extent by increased purchasing power after mid-century and certainly after 1870, as the spread of new technology and new scientific ideas paid off. The opening up of primary producing areas abroad, in which European emigrants played their part, together with railways there and in Europe, and cheaper sea freight, brought down the cost of living. This benefited everyone and especially poorer people, most of whose income was spent of foodstuffs. Farmers in Europe adjusted to the new competition, producing more perishables like milk and fruit, or bulky goods of low value such as vegetables, in which they still enjoyed the advantage of proximity to the market. Free trade Britain, which already enjoyed the highest annual income per head by 1860 (estimated at £33, compared to £21 in France and £13 in Germany) gained most from the subsequent increase in imports. Her unprotected farmers had to make more extensive readjustments than those on the Continent where agriculture still loomed the most important part of national economies. Farmers could therefore continue to bring political pressure to bear to secure an element of protection.

But everywhere the price fall was considerable between 1874 and 1896. Thereafter demand caught up with supply. Some prices may have risen somewhat; but little of the earlier gain was lost.

These material advances were influenced by movements in the trade cycle, the alternating booms and slumps. On the upswing, wages rose as more labour was recruited. Longer hours were worked. On the downswing earnings were cut and short-time working returned. The remarkable fact about these years, however, was that the larger labour force produced by population growth could be absorbed by Western Europe's growing economies. Trade cycles, lasting perhaps seven years from peak to peak, were comparatively short and frequent.

The Century of Peace can conveniently be divided into three periods, and to these we must now turn.

THE AFTERMATH OF THE TWENTY-THREE YEARS WAR, 1815–30

When the smaller population and more limited resources are taken into account, the Twenty-Three Years War, stretching, as has been noted, from Cadiz to Moscow and from Calabria to Finland, resulted in human and material losses comparable to those of the other Great War, which ended this Century of Peace. And the earlier conflict lasted not for four but for twenty-three weary years. The nations emerged much poorer than they would otherwise have been. Even Great Britain, which had escaped any serious fighting on its own soil, emerged laden with debt. This had risen from £243,000,000 in 1792 to £745,000,000 in 1815. It went on rising in the depressed and discontented post-war years to £844,000,000 in 1819.

Great Britain, a little offshore island with a small population, was already established as the world's leading industrial nation well before the French Revolution. It managed to maintain its position in wartime, thanks to the Royal Navy's continued command of the seas. Commerce with other continents was continued, as well as a certain amount of trade with the rest of Europe. The continental blockade, however, as has been noted, gave continental industry a certain amount of protection against British competition, and this encouraged its growth in some areas.

The post-war settlement gave potential advantages to two countries: Prussia (with its newly-acquired territories in the Rhineland and Westphalia) and the Netherlands (with its Belgian provinces). They had been set up by the Congress of Vienna as a bulwark against any future attempt of France to burst out from its frontiers. The Belgian provinces included coalfields in the valleys of the Sambre and the Meuse and Prussia in the Ruhr. This enabled the Belgian provinces, which became the separate state of Belgium in 1830, to become the most industrialized part of Western Europe. It was some time longer, however, before Prussia seized its opportunity.

England's earlier ascendancy, despite its small population, originally depended upon its remarkable increase in foreign trade through London and good communication from London both by road and by water (coastal shipping connecting with rivers inland) with the rest of the country. These advantages were already starting to be exploited effectively in the sixteenth and seventeenth centuries. Britain also gained from the good fortune of possessing geographically widely scattered coalfields. The reverberatory furnace, developed from 1610 onwards to use coal or coke to melt ores and minerals to make a variety of products (glass, copper and eventually iron), the puddling of iron and the steam engine all depended on abundant coal supplies. The earlier spinning and weaving machines were small, depended upon human energy and increased labour productivity little; but they became important from the later eighteenth century when, after further development, they became power driven, by water and increasingly by steam. Spinning went into the factory first, thus swelling the ranks of hand loom weavers. These earlier developments, which had established Britain's lead in certain key industries well before 1815, were taken further after that, particularly when weaving went into the factories after the mid-1820s, bringing misfortune and misery to the expanding army of workers at hand looms. British governments used legal means to try to forbid the export of the new machines and to prevent those who had the know-how to make them from leaving the country; but even when the new owners on the Continent managed to produce saleable output, they could not always sell their production in competition with imports from Britain.

This, however, was by no means a one-way process. For many of her purchases customers in Britain depended not upon the relatively narrow range of power-produced goods but on those which had been traditionally imported from the Continent (linens and silks, for instance) or which Britain did not produce in sufficient quantity herself (such as wool or grain). For exotic consumables – tea, coffee, sugar – she had long been reliant on imports, and for the raw material essential to feed her new machines: cotton. Trade is always a two-way business benefiting supplier and customer alike.

Scientists and inventors met together on both sides of the English Channel. The major centres of Western Europe all had their centres of scholarship. Their learned societies published transactions for all to read, then as now. All these countries were relatively advanced, possessed 'ingenious men' and skilled craftsmen capable of making scientific apparatus or mock-ups of machines. Far from being looked up to as industrial leaders, the British were often looked down upon as money-making mass producers. Yet it was those capable of producing basic goods on a large scale who drove down the price and benefited men and women everywhere.

There was one industry in particular in which the British came to depend particularly on the superior scientific knowledge of the French and to depend on Continental superiority. This was the chemical industry. Nicholas Leblanc in France had developed a means of decomposing salt to make soda as a synthetic substitute for the natural barilla and kelp. Leblanc soda came to be manufactured in England from 1815 on the Tyne and then, more extensively, on Merseyside to make soap, needed to scour and clean cloth, the bleaching of which had been greatly speeded with the use of chlorine. Glass manufacture was another industry in which the British lagged behind the Continent. St Gobain produced high-quality plate glass for a century before attempts were made in the 1770s to produce it in Britain with the aid of French artisans. Not until the 1790s could this be achieved with economic success. Another form of flat glass, accurately called German sheet glass, more advanced than the sort then produced in Britain, was not introduced until the early 1830s.

We now know that the view of France lagging in its industrialization far behind Britain is quite mistaken. From the mid-eighteenth century its industrial sector grew, but in a more traditional way, depending more on skilled craftsmen, spreading more widely over the country as a whole and catering for more locally based markets and using traditional methods, not coal-based production in which it was at a disadvantage. France did not experience urbanization at the same pace as Britain. By 1830 only a quarter of its population lived in towns of any size, compared with a third in Britain. France's slower population growth, already stressed, meant the spread of material advantage over fewer people. More was available per head. Even so, because of Frances's larger population (30,462,000 in 1821 and 32,569,000 in 1831) the increase in the decade was larger in absolute numbers than in England and Wales (12,106,000 in 1821 and 13,994,000 in 1831).

Germany already had a good reputation for scientific enquiry and concern for higher education; but, despite Prussia's newly acquired territories, it was still a motley collection of states, many of them small. It consisted of villages, medieval towns, castles and impressive religious houses. Knowledge of the great growth to come should not blind us that for many years after 1815 divided Germany lagged well behind the unitary nation of France. The potential of the Ruhr and other coalfields lay ahead. In the 1820s iron working was still a handicraft industry using charcoal. Siegerland consisted of small metal working establishments, and in the Solingen district to the north the owners of furnaces and timber and the miners operated together but lived on their own small estates. Germany was basically still a peasant society engaged in manufacture. The Prussian government, however, was already taking wise fiscal decisions. Its 1818 tariff, applying to all its scattered territories, admitted raw materials free and charged manufactured imports 10 per cent, while making more from exotic imports like coffee and sugar with 20–30 per cent duties and making a killing on non-Prussian German goods which inevitably had to pass through its territories. There were strong reasons for moves to join the Prussian customs system before Prussia, having built a number of strategic roads through some of the acceding states, was able to set up a *Zollverein* in 1834, which covered a population of 23,500,000.

The years after 1815 saw a continued interest in the spread of literacy, by which is meant an ability to read if not to write. The authorities were coming to realise that economic growth called increasingly for information to be spread by signs, notices, hand-written and printed papers, not just by word of mouth. Sermons from pulpits were no longer enough. At the same time the authorities were concerned lest, by the spread of literacy, ordinary people should start to get ideas above their station and try to exercise political influence. If the property-less, the overwhelming majority in all countries, should use their superiority in numbers to take action against the propertied minority and use the printed word on a large scale to achieve this objective, in that direction lay radical change, which most of the establishment of the day, whatever their differences among themselves, united to oppose. For them, growth should not be at the expense of stability.

On the whole, however, the dangers of the spread of literacy were more than offset by the advantages. Political newspapers, like the *Allgemeine Zeitung* and *The Times*, both dating from the later eighteenth century, had a cover price far too high for wage earners to afford even if they had time to read a daily paper. Yet that did not prevent other printed matter from circulating cheaply among them, using simpler language they could understand, brief and to the point. They could start to create a climate of opinion. Day by day at work, and especially in the evenings at the local inn, new ideas were discussed, and notions of stability began to be challenged. Such gatherings were easier in towns, increasing in size and number. But in the Western Europe of this period farming communities still predominated, even in Britain.

Religious and secular organizations sprang up to help the young and others to read (if not to write) and to calculate. Church schools had a long tradition of religious instruction and this led to the three Rs (reading, writing and arithmetic). Such schools catered mainly for the middle classes, but by means of scholarships, which paid all, or part of the fees, they also included the underprivileged. The objective of these schools, however, was mainly to prepare their girls and boys for some form of further education, usually with a post in the professions as the ultimate goal. The idea of teaching literacy to those entering *ordinary working jobs*, as an addition to skills taught on the job by apprenticeship and by learning from older people with much practical experience, was something new. Charitable bodies with this laudable aim, however, often had little difficulty in obtaining support from others, often among the well-to-do, who wished to encourage this attempt to enable those who wished to do so to better themselves and their children. Municipal and even national authorities also often chipped in. In France, for instance, it is said that about half of the communes possessed some sort of school by 1830. A larger fraction was true of England and Wales; and Scotland had an even longer and stronger educational tradition. In Britain many people came to learn to read at special classes held in churches on a Sunday as part of a Sunday School movement dating from the later eighteenth century. A reliable estimate puts the number of the working classes in England and Wales who could read simple texts in 1840 at between two thirds and three quarters.

What has subsequently come to be called 'adult education' also spread. Movements like the Mechanics Institutes in Britain held meetings in the evening, again essentially an urban phenomenon, though their membership was by no means confined to engineers nor their topics and courses to engineering subjects. At the top of the education ladder came new and reinvigorated universities. The new University of Berlin (1809–10) recruited lively minds from various institutions in that city as teachers, and developed new courses. London got its two first university colleges in the later 1820s. Three former high schools in the Netherlands were reorganized as state universities in 1815; and in its Belgian provinces in 1817 universities were opened at Ghent, Louvain and Liège. France led the way, benefiting enormously form its elitist educational system: the Ecole Normale for teacher training and the Ecole Polytechnique, which provided for the best grounding in Europe in the practical sciences. At the other end of the scale, however, and despite the spread of schools in half France's communes, 60 per cent of army conscripts in 1827 could not read.

Towns, and particularly the larger ones, were the key to all these developments. Throughout Western Europe life was very different for the majority of the population who still lived in the countryside. Life in the countryside was more traditional and deferential. It was dominated by the weather, the size of the harvest or the health of animals. It was a world of seasons. Springtime welcomed longer and brighter days and hopes for a good summer. Later in the year came thanksgiving for the harvest and fairs at which clothes, or the materials from which they could be made, were bought. In the cold winter weather more work was undertaken inside in tasks such as threshing grain by hand. Standards of living in the countryside depended on so many variables: the hilliness of the terrain, for instance, the quality of the soil, the type of tenure and the size of holding. The extent of change at this time depended upon whether there were large landowners (as in East Prussia) bent on adopting modern methods, including enclosure, or whether good access to growing urban populations made investment and innovation worthwhile. Sometimes the state took a determined lead, as in Denmark, where half of the farms had already been enclosed by 1807. In England, a suitably compact country, change and improvements on the land and agricultural specialization had been occurring for centuries in response to the growth of London and, in the previous hundred years, to the rise of provincial centres like Manchester, Liverpool or Birmingham as well as many smaller places. Where landowners and farmers benefited, their labourers stood to benefit too. And in the countryside it was usually possible to fall back on an element of subsistence cultivation on little plots of land. It is always argued that country life was healthier than that in towns and population statistics generally support this view. Yet country folk had to endure the cold and the damp and often needed to travel, usually on foot, for considerable distances in all weathers. The local inn might have its attractions and the local church or chapel its consolations; but the regular seasonal routine and the same old familiar faces could be boring.

This was especially true for younger people growing up into this traditional world at a time when families were large and there was not enough work to go round. Non-agricultural jobs in the nearest town had their attractions and there were certainly new people to meet, not least of all the opposite sex. The bigger cities exercised an even greater appeal. The lights might not, in the 1820s, have been so bright as they were later to become; but there were certainly more of them.

Concentrations of populations engaged in industry and commerce and in providing services of all sorts had much to commend them, even though towns were less healthy. Here public services could eventually be provided in a way that was never possible in the scattered countryside: water supplies, for instance, and gas lighting. Waste disposal was a great problem as towns grew; but the increasing population was able to band together to form a local authority, which levied a local tax in order to remove the worst nuisances. They possessed hospitals for those who were taken ill, and medical people to attend them. The fact that, as we shall see, there was general ignorance about how illness spread does not detract from the importance of these facilities, for recovery, as we now know, often depends on rest, care and attention. Charities, supported by the better-off in towns, enabled poorer people to go to hospital, the better-off being themselves more often than not looked after when ill not in such institutions but in their own homes. In any case, the rapidly-growing populations of towns at this time consisted of an unusually large proportion of immigrants, strong young men and women better able to withstand illness and recover from disease.

Urban jobs could afford to pay higher wages than elsewhere and offer better promotion prospects. Many employers had risen from the ranks, and while they were proud of their own superior positions, they often did not have the same rigid love of stability or devotion to deference. Nor did employment in towns vary with the seasons. It depended on fairly predictable cycles, not on the unpredictable weather. In towns the proverbial 'rainy day' could be catered for by private saving and salesman's credit. Competition between market traders provided lower prices and a range of goods available throughout the year – unheard of in the countryside. Food might not have been picked that day but it was cheaper and in better supply; and there were shops for those who could afford them. Towns were places, too, where professional people, legal and medical (whether quacks or not) lived and worked. There was not one local inn with limited amusement but hundreds of hostelries with any amount of entertainment, respectable or otherwise. Codes of behaviour in towns were less rigid than those in the countryside, though those arriving from the countryside brought the moral training of their upbringing. And many rural customs and traditions, such as fairs and visiting circuses, were carried over to the growing towns.

The largest – and usually the capital – cities offered special opportunities to groups of specialists to form groups devoted to this or that subject. Cities also offered better access to reading matter of all kinds. Theatres, concert halls and opera houses had long been established. New organizations, still surviving, date from this time; for instance, the Royal Philharmonic Society, London (1813), the Philharmonische Gesellschaft, Berlin (1826) and the Société des Concerts du Conservatoire, Paris (1828). Some of the most famous composers flourished at that time too. Although Beethoven and Schubert lived in Vienna, their influence certainly extended to the whole of Western Europe. Both died in 1828, having composed their last masterpieces in the Austrian capital, while elsewhere Mendelssohn (born 1809) and Chopin and Schumann (both born in 1810) were writing their earlier pieces. The prolific composer who compressed almost all of his writing into this period before taking early retirement in 1829 was Rossini (born in 1792). He first made a name for himself by composing *Tancredi* at the age of twenty-one in 1813. Already established two years later as director of the Carlo Theatre in Naples, he wrote *The Barber of Seville* there in 1816, then contracted with La Scala to write two operas a year for them and did, in fact, manage to write 36 operas in 19 years. In 1823 he moved to Paris as director of the Théatre Italien. His last success, *William Tell*, was produced in Paris in 1829 – after, which aged thirty-seven, he decided to retire, and lived in retirement until 1868. Meanwhile in Germany, Weber (born in 1786) wrote *Der Freischutz*, first performed in Berlin in 1821.

England had no part in this musical flowering; but London used its wealth to commission Weber to write *Oberon* for Covent Garden and to come and conduct it there in 1826. The infant prodigy Mendelssohn, who had composed five symphonies in 1821, spent some time in London in 1829 during which, *inter alia*, he presented the first performance of his overture to *A Midsummer Night's Dream*. Rossini's earlier visit to London in 1823, between leaving Italy and moving to Paris, was the most profitable. In five months he earned £7,000.

To the Continental Europeans who produced the musical giants of this period, England must have seemed a very uncultivated land, a place which concentrated on making money, not music. This, however, is not quite true. As we have seen, Londoners respected the superiority of Continental Europe and England had the performers to play that music. There were music festivals elsewhere in the country. More fundamentally, there was already in Britain a well-established tradition of choral singing. Provincial towns, as well as London, had their choral concerts in which the mass of the people took an active part. In the North of England there was already great interest in brass band music and many amateur brass band players. As in so much else, Britain and the British were different. But it is the Continent's great contribution to music at this time, which remains.

LAYING THE MATERIAL AND SCIENTIFIC FOUNDATIONS: THE DIFFICULT YEARS, 1830–74

From the later 1820s Britain consolidated and built upon her earlier power-driven lead. In textiles, cotton weaving became power-driven, first for coarser cloth and then for the finer qualities. Flax spinning also followed cotton from the mid-1820s, strengthening Northern Ireland's position in the linen industry. Wool, more fragile than cotton, was being spun on power-driven machines by mid-century and subsequently woven. The hosiery industry brought up the rear from the late 1860s. Even so, many women continued to knit for themselves.

Water had vied with steam as the main power source; but after about 1840 with the beginnings of what can be properly called precision engineering, steam engines worked more reliably and became the preferred alternative in Britain with its abundant and well distributed sources of coal. They were more efficient in fuel use as higher pressures became practicable. The steam engine was also put on wheels. Earlier locomotive development at collieries, where steam pumps were already familiar and coal was dirt cheap, by George Stephenson and other able craftsmen, had by the 1820s reached the point where a longer colliery mineral line, the so-called Stockton and Darlington Railway, which connected with east coast shipping at Stockton but then ran westwards not just to Darlington but many miles further inland to the Auckland coalfield, first demonstrated the possibilities of the steam railway. It also owed its success to a new iron rail, invented at nearby Morpeth. This was a most important feature, for, as experimenters in and around London discovered, the power-to-weight ratio of steam engines was not then sufficient to allow them to operate over ordinary rough roads as distinct from smooth, load-bearing rail roads. George Stephenson's Stockton and Darlington initiative attracted the attention of promoters of a much more important venture, the first intercity railway which ran from the port of Liverpool to the cotton textile centre, Manchester. Originally intended, like the Stockton and Darlington, only to carry heavy freight at slow speed, it proved an even greater success for the carriage of passengers, mails and higher-value items when George Stephenson's son, Robert, managed to produce, just before the line's opening, a locomotive with a multitubular boiler capable of averaging a previously unheard-of *average* speed of 20 miles per hour, twice as fast as any relay of horses could gallop over such a distance. Britain now led Western Europe in land transport as well as mechanized factories. This quite brief period of unchallenged dominance was marked by the mounting in London in 1851 of the first international exhibition, known as the Great Exhibition. It was held in an impressive building built of metal and glass, which came to be called the Crystal Palace. Employers gave their workmen several days off to go to London by cheap excursion train to view the industrial achievements, and at the same time bring back any ideas for the improvement of their own particular business.

The Liverpool and Manchester Railway yielded good dividends to its shareholders and encouraged further speculation to link the other main British centres of population. This came in two great bursts (so-called railway manias), in the mid-1830s and mid-1840s. All but one of the main rail routes was completed by the early 1850s. On the Continent, however, it was a different story. Capital was not so plentiful and proposed routes were not likely to carry much remunerative traffic. Governments often had to guarantee minimum returns in order to attract investors; and lines were not so generously built, with single instead of double tracks, which moved around the contours instead of tunnelling along the shortest route. By 1850 Britain already had nearly 10,000km of railway open and France under 3,000km. Germany (within the future imperial boundary) could, however, boast nearly twice that length. By 1871 Germany, with nearly 19,000km, had almost caught up with Britain, which in the previous twenty years had been adding branch and less important lines, while France, with 15,500km, lagged considerably behind them both. By 1870 Belgium, a much smaller country, had 2,900km to its credit and the Netherlands just over 1,400km.

Despite Germany's faster progress, by 1871 France continued to grow slowly and steadily. Its metal working facilities at Le Creuzot developed as well as Belgium's at Seraing, which also possessed coal and iron in close proximity. In the Mulhouse area was built up a most progressive textile industry. At the Paris Exhibition of 1867, the showing of French, as of German, products was superior to their showing in London in 1851 and this apparently increasing competition became a cause of anxiety in Britain. Living standards in France continued to gain from its slow population growth, from 32 million in 1830 to 38M in 1870. Germany's, then 41M, had grown quickly from 27M in 1830. Great Britain's was still smaller than both (26M, having increased quickly from 16M in 1830) although it was more urbanized. Half of Britain's population was living in towns by 1850. This degree of urbanization was not reached in Germany until towards the end of the century and in France until after the First World War. Not all those who worked in the country were engaged in agriculture, however; about a quarter of the British rural labour force, for instance.

The rapidity of urbanization and persistence of agricultural employment carried important social implications. Heavy fixed investment in railways, factories and the urban infrastructure would bring improved living conditions in the future but produced slow immediate returns. And, at the same time, quickly-growing towns attracted labour from the surrounding countryside and the resulting labour scarcity encouraged the earlier introduction of labour-saving methods there. The threshing of grain, for instance, saw the arrival of peripatetic steam threshing machines by about mid-century in England. In France and Germany where agricultural labour remained plentiful, there was no such incentive to innovate. Investment in drainage, however, paid off by bringing more land into cultivation in the coastal

regions of Holland and Germany and other watery places. In England the practice spread in order to grow more grain on existing acres. But everywhere the returning of minerals to the soil was a much faster way of increasing yields. Horse droppings from the growing towns were recycled and, as artificial fertilizers became available, these, too, had the same result: higher returns within the year.

Urbanization involved internal movement within countries, for towns could not grow fast by natural increase alone. Once uprooted from the countryside and having taken the decision to move townward, the migrant felt footloose enough to move further and perhaps to emigrate. England benefited considerably from such movements, especially from the arrival of better trained specialists from the Continent who wished to take advantage of her superior economic possibilities, in, for instance, the chemical industry, where Andrew Kurtz, having fled from his native Wurtemberg in the time of Napoleon, had learned his chemistry in Paris and became one of the founders of the British chemical industry after 1815. Better known is Ludwig Mond, born in Cassel and educated at Marburg and Heidelberg, who came to England for the first time in 1862 and eventually joined forces with Henry Brunner to develop the ammonia soda process. In textiles many Germans were involved in worsted merchanting in Bradford – Schlesinger, Behrens, Albrecht and others – and formed a distinct community, sending their sons to fight for the Fatherland when need be. Across the Pennines it was a foreign, and again largely German, community in Manchester who led the artistic life of that city. Charles Hallé, born in Westphalia, settled among this community in 1848 and started the famous orchestra which still bears his name. Even better known perhaps is Friedrich Engels, son of a businessman of Barmen, near Düsseldorf, who in 1838 became partner with Peter Ermen in a spinning and bleaching firm there. Ermen already owned Victoria Mills at Seedley, just outside Manchester, and it was into the Manchester office of this business that young Friedrich was sent in 1842 at the age of twenty-two.

Engels (born 1820) wanted to be a writer, but his father insisted that, at the age of sixteen, he go into the business, and two years later packed him off to an office in Bremen to continue his training. A highly intelligent young man, he read voraciously and started to write newspaper articles. He developed opinions of his own, liberal in religion and radical in politics. Leaving Bremen in April 1841 and, after six months back in Barmen, he volunteered for the Guards Foot Artillery as his year of military service. This took him to Berlin, where he was strongly influenced by the Young Hegelian movement, then very much in vogue, and by the humanist views of Feuerbach. Well indoctrinated by October 1842 when he completed his year's service, his outlook became even more radical after a visit to the *Rheinische Zeitung* in Cologne, which propagated extreme views, including those of the Young Hegelians. He jumped at his father's proposal that he should continue his training at Ermen and Engels, Manchester, seeing in this posting an opportunity to study what he saw as the evils of capitalism at its very heart. He called again at the *Rheinische Zeitung* on the way, met there one of its editors, the legally trained Dr Karl Marx, only two years his senior, and arrived in wintry Manchester at the end of 1842 right in the midst of the worst trade depression of the entire nineteenth century.

For the next twenty months this observant and already politically committed young man had every opportunity to see rapidly growing 'Cottonpolis' and some other parts of England at their very worst. Large numbers of immigrants were crowded into inadequate accommodation before the local authority had made much progress in urban improvement. There was much unemployment during the trade depression. Engels was convivial and sociable, upright in stature (his Guards training) and always well turned out. He seems to have picked up English quickly, and on a businessman's income could move in all sorts of company, though he later claimed, and we have no reason to doubt his word, that he 'forsook the port wine and champagne of the middle classes' and devoted his leisure hours 'almost exclusively to intercourse with plain working men'. He certainly took a working-class mistress, Mary Burns, an ex-cotton operative to whom he remained attached after he returned to Manchester years later. He also had the advantage of press coverage, particularly in the Chartist *Northern Star*, and evidence in volumes of helpful parliamentary papers of the worst social evils collected from different parts of the country – at the request of progressive reformers keen to put an end to them and to better the conditions of working people.

In the autumn of 1844 Engels was back in Barmen sorting out the notes he had taken in England and poring over his volumes of parliamentary papers he had taken home with him. From these he published in German for the benefit of German readers, *Die Lage der arbeitenden Klasse in England*, now universally known in English translation as *The Condition of the Working Class in England*. As he told Marx in a letter written on 19 November 1844:

> I am buried up to the neck in English newspapers and books... I shall present the English with a fine bill of indictment. I accuse the English bourgeoisie before the entire world of murder, robbery and all sorts of other crimes on a mass scale.

He went on to underline the fact that, although the book was to be about the English, it was intended for the German middle class 'of whom I say clearly enough that it is just as bad as the English'. He wrote at speed and his book was published in Leipzig in 1845. Significantly there was no English translation until a very poor one appeared in New York in 1887 and a better version in London in 1892. By then not many English readers had personal knowledge of what living conditions were really like in the early 1840s depression, but increasing numbers were then becoming interested in left-wing collectivist views. They lapped it up. The German version, however, had long established Engels's reputation among communists. As a polemic it was a remarkable achievement for a young man of twenty-four. Engels became Marx's closest associate.

Marx became another immigrant to England. After the failures of the 1848 revolutions, he settled in the country, living first in considerable poverty in central London but was soon able to move out to a healthy house in the suburbs after his wife received a small legacy and to a second and larger one after she received another. He took advantage of the fruits and freedom of capitalism, not least in the extensive library of the British Museum, to plot and forecast capitalism's downfall. Engels, too, who must have had an unusually tolerant capitalist father, returned to the Manchester firm in 1850, lived the life of a successful businessman, drinking champagne and riding to hounds with the Cheshire Hunt. He supported the earnest Marx financially until Marx's death in London in 1883. The jovial Engels retired to London in 1870, and, twenty-three years later, celebrated his seventieth birthday in style – 'we kept it up until half-past-three in the morning and drank, besides claret, 16 bottles of champagne'. He died five years afterwards. The revolution which he had so confidently predicted had still not arrived, for there was no such thing as a working class to fight a class war; only gradations of the working classes, unskilled and skilled, who had opportunities to move up the social scale into the equally variegated middle classes.

By the middle of the nineteenth century, as schools spread – the state being more supportive on the Continent than in England – more parents of the working classes came to appreciate the importance of education if their sons were to get the better jobs and move up in the world. Adult education became more popular, too, and more affordable. New libraries appeared. Improved printing methods saw more journals and books published. An illustrated periodical press emerged, led by the *Illustrated London News* (1842) and quickly followed, a year later, by *L'Illustration* in Paris and *Illustrierte Zeitung* in Leipzig. With the spread of the electronic telegraph, to be considered later, news agencies emerged, notably those of Havas in France, Wolff in Germany and Reuter, another German immigrant, in England. National and regional newspaper circulations increased rapidly and more local papers, usually claiming no particular political affiliation, were published after taxation on the papers themselves and the advertisements which appeared in them were reduced and removed. Readership spread to the more serious, literate section of the working classes. If they had a day off, Sunday newspapers proved particularly popular among them and enjoyed larger circulations than the dailies, even in the mid-nineteenth century. Knowledge and ideas spread more rapidly and widely through this great outpouring of the printed word. Marx's articles were brought together in pamphlet form, for instance; and in 1867 appeared the first volume of *Das Kapital*. Every other conceivable political opinion found printed form, though the title of none is so well known.

The challenge of accepted concepts and attempts to learn more about the physical and human world and to improve living conditions was fostered during these years by what may be called the beginnings of the dawn of modern science. Before 1830 most technical improvements had been the work of ingenious craftsmen like Watt or the Stephensons, not the result of any real understanding of the scientific principles involved. This was to change as specialists defined, counted and experimented in laboratories. Instruments – like the far better achromatic microscope, invented about 1830, and an improved atmospheric burner, further improved in 1855 when Bunsen's version of it was installed in his new laboratory at Heidelberg – helped the new experimenters. The British Association for the Advancement of Science held its first meeting in 1831 in an attempt to encourage the English to pay more attention to fundamental research. Germany was certainly doing this. Liebig, for instance, back from studies with Gay-Lussac in Paris, opened the first part of his soon-famous laboratory in Giessen in 1826. Investigators in all countries made their contribution to scientific discovery and, when successful, published and circulated their results. Those who lagged behind in any area did their best to recruit specialists from other countries who were in the lead as happened, as we have seen, in the British chemical industry. The German consort Prince Albert brought the promising young German chemist A. W. Hoffman, to start the Royal College of

Chemistry in London in 1845. Many students were trained there to work in British industry and it was there that, in 1853, W. H. Perkin, attempting to synthesize quinine, stumbled upon the first aniline dye, maurine mauviene. Other artificial means were discovered of replacing natural sources by synthetics to the considerable advantage of people in all walks of life. The substitutes were more consistent and reliable, could be made stronger and, when produced on a large scale, cheaper.

All this emphasis on the merits of scientific enquiry, however, had disturbing social consequences well fore-shadowed in the writings of the French philosopher August Comte (1798–1857), a natural rebel against existing authority. His *Course of Positive Philosophy*, the first volume of which appeared in 1830, argued that scientific ideas should apply as much to the organization of society as to physics or chemistry. A religious or metaphysically-based nation was merely a prelude to what should become a modern, positivist, science-based state. J. S. Mill, a regular correspondent of Comte, while he was writing the further volumes of his book over the following twelve years, also favoured a more science-based, materialist world. So did Jeremy Bentham and his followers in advocating the *summum bonum* to be 'the greatest happiness of the greatest number'. A climate was being created among opinion formers, which would be more receptive to ideas of evolution. These were advanced by George Lyell in his *Principles of Geology* (1830–3). Naturalists were soon discussing it everywhere; but it was Charles Darwin (1809–82) who, after much con-templation, was, in 1859, to supply the explanation of human evolution in *On the Origin of Species by Means of Natural Selection, or the Preservation of Favoured Races in the Struggle for Life.*

Charles Robert Darwin was born in Shrewsbury, the son of a medical man with a large practice who had married the daughter of Josiah Wedgwood, the Staffordshire pottery entrepreneur. He grew up in a conventional religious home, and indeed, when he reached Cambridge after abandoning medicine at Edinburgh, was intended to take holy orders; but here chance intervened with remarkable results. He had been much influenced in favour of natural history by reading Humboldt's *Personal Narrative*, and after taking his degree – tenth in the list of those who did not seek honours, nothing to write home about – and having two further term's residence to keep, he went on a field course after which, through John Henslow, Professor of Botany, who had befriended him, he was offered the position of non-salaried naturalist on the 235-ton, 10-gun brig *Beagle* about to set out on a long surveying expedition to South America. With strong support from his uncle, the second Josiah Wedgwood, if not from his father, he agreed and was out of the country from December 1831 to October 1836. As they sailed south, the observant young man noticed slight differences between the same breed of creature in one place and another, farther on but divided by sea. He also saw, particularly in the Galapagos archipelago, just south of the equator off the western coast of South America, differences between the same creature and fossi-lized remains of its ancestors. This caused him to ponder the religious teaching about human nature as distinct from his scientific observations. After his return to England there was no longer any thought of his entering the church, though he continued for the rest of his life to have many Anglican friends and to support the church's charitable and social objectives.

From 1838 to 1841 Darwin served as secretary to the Geological Society and saw a great deal of Lyell: but, although he had previously been hale and hearty, his health collapsed completely while in London. He went to live in the country at Down, a small village in Kent, sixteen miles south-east of London, where he and his wife, daughter of his uncle Josiah Wedgwood, lived off an income from the family, keeping a regular, well-organized regime which involved walks, much reading and a few hours work a day. His was the life of a semi-invalid, one long struggle against sickness, and he only very rarely left Down to appear at conferences, especially after the mid-1850s when he stop-ped going even to those of the British Association. He corresponded regularly with friends, however, and in 1844 he could write to Joseph Hocker, the best of them: 'At last gleams of light have come and I am almost convinced (contrary to the opinion I started with) that species are not (it is like confessing a murder) immutable'. He went on pondering over this in his country retreat, and a decade later Lyell urged him to prepare a paper lest someone else got in and published his ideas before he did. He had, in fact, drafted much of his study when, out of the blue, in June 1858, the naturalist Alfred Russell Wallace (1823–1913), who had, like Darwin been much influenced by Malthus, wrote from the remote Moroccas, sending him an essay for his opinion which, quite independently, expressed Darwin's own views on natural selection. With Lyell's help, Darwin then moved very fast indeed, presenting a joint paper to the Linnean Society, read on 1 July 1858 and subsequently published in the Society's *Transactions* for that year. Darwin then completed his *Origin of Species*, all 1,250 copies of which were sold on the day of publication, 24 November 1859. Science had struck a vital blow for logic against faith as was clear from the famous, heated debate between T. H. Huxley, the scientist, and Samuel Wilberforce, Bishop of Oxford, at the British Association's meeting in that city the following year. Darwin, too delicate to stray far from Down, went on publishing books, including *The Descent of Man* (1871). Many honours were bestowed on him, especially from France, Germany, Italy and his own country. He received one of the greatest distinctions of all: burial in Westminster Abbey.

Epoch-making though Darwin's findings undoubtedly were, many good honest folk found them deeply disturb-ing. The church was made to stand for clerical exclusiveness and intellectual stagnation. Progress lay with science and material things. The dignity of man was under challenge and so was the authenticity of the Bible. True and forward-looking though they were, the opinions of Darwin and other scientists did not add to the greatest happiness of the greatest number.

The work of the Frenchman, Louis Pasteur, on the other hand, brought nothing but benefit to the human race.

Louis Pasteur (1822–95), born in the Jura, the son of a tanner, grew up and went to school in Arbois, which he looked upon as an oasis of peace to which he always liked to return when he could. He did not distinguish himself par-ticularly at school but his capacity to work ferociously hard at, and become very enthusiastic about, anything that really interested him became evident and he was encouraged to train as a teacher. After an unsuccessful attempt to obtain further preliminary training in Paris (like Darwin his health broke down, though not permanently), he went to the Royal College in Besançon where he obtained a bacca-laureate in science, and, after another year's hard study, entered the Ecole Normale Supérieure in Paris in 1843. After obtaining the aggregation (1846), he stayed on to take a doctorate (1847). He worked as assistant in one of the laboratories of the Lecturer in Chemistry at the Ecole, A. J. Balard, and first attracted the attention of other scientists as the result of a typically obsessive interest in crystals. Always well read in the published work of others, he realized that crystallographers, and especially the elderly and much respected J. B. Biot, had been unable to explain why tartrate and paratartrate crystals reacted differently to a beam of polarized light, one moving the beam to the right, the other to the left. Pasteur spent many long hours seeking a physical explanation. Eventually he succeeded and convinced Biot – who then became Pasteur's champion. Through his influence the young and enthusiastic Trojan was appointed to an assistantship in Chemistry in 1849 at Strasbourg Academy, the first rung on the academic ladder. There he impressed all those who came to inspect his work. He further enhanced his reputation by transforming tartaric into racemic acid (1853), for which he was made a member of the Legion of Honour and received a 1,500F prize. The following year, aged thirty-two, he was appointed Professor of Chemistry and dean of a new faculty of science at Lille, a town which, as the Minister of Public Instruction pointed out, was 'the richest centre of industrial activity in the north of France'. It was made very clear to Pasteur that he was expected to liaise with local industry and assist them with his scientific knowledge. This he did with his usual dedication, taking groups of students round many of the works in the area. There his interest in fermentation was first aroused when a manufacturer of alcohol from beet juice sought his help when the process started making lactic acid instead. In 1857 Pasteur published a paper on lactic fermentation, which secured him the appointment in Paris as Director of Scientific Studies at the Ecole Normale Supérieure. His diligence and enthusiasm were paying off – and the wide reading of the work of others which they had not followed up. 'In the fields of observation', he believed, 'chance only favours those who are prepared'.

He continued to study alcoholic fermentation and came to realize that ferments were living organisms, each responsible for a particular fermentation, each coming from parents similar to themselves, born from living germs. In 1863 he showed that, to make wine stable, it could be heated slowly to 55°C and then allowed to cool. This was a process which could be applied to other liquids, and came to be known as pasteurization. Then, working in various breweries, he showed that his fermentation theories applied also to beer. In 1871 he patented a means of fermentation which avoided contact with the atmosphere. He came to London that year to visit the British Patent Office and to offer his advice, microscope in hand, to several London brewers, including the largest of them all, Whitbread, which produced 500,000 hectolitres a year. J. C. Jakobsen, a great admirer of Pasteur, was encouraged to set up an impressive laboratory at his Carlsberg brewery in Copenhagen later in the 1870s, and other progressive businesses, like Heineken of Rotterdam, followed suit.

Pasteur's germ theories were first applied to the saving of human life by Joseph Lister (1827–1912), who had been appointed surgeon to Glasgow Infirmary in 1860. Chloroform, discovered in 1831, had, from 1847, encouraged surgeons to put patients to sleep and operate on all occasions, more often than not with deadly results from septic infection. Lister, who specialized in the treatment of fractures and wounds, knew that exposure to the air explained this high mortality and also came to realize that it was not the gases in the air itself that were the cause but something they carried with them and which he could not understand. In 1865 the Professor of Chemistry at Glasgow University drew his attention to Pasteur's work, which encouraged him to use carbolic acid, discovered as long ago as 1834, and already known to him as an antiseptic. The remarkable fall in mortality was reported in the *Lancet* in 1867. Here, thanks to Pasteur as much as to Lister, were the beginnings of modern medicine. The identification of particular germs as the carriers of specific diseases followed. But this must await consideration in our next section, as must Pasteur's own experiments with animals leading to a cure for human hydrophobia. The Institut Pasteur, established in 1888 and located near the Ecole Normale in Paris, came to cure thousands of men and women bitten by rabid dogs. When Pasteur died, in 1895, already loaded with honours, he too, received a state funeral, at Notre Dame.

The years between 1830 and the mid-1870s did not see any marked advance in living standards for the majority of people in Western Europe, though generalization is difficult. Those who worked in the new power-driven industries may have had monotonous jobs and long hours of work; but they enjoyed higher earnings, and employees in other jobs in which the higher earners spent their wages were better off then they would otherwise have been. On the other hand, those who found themselves stranded in formerly skilled occupations subjected to the new competition, like the handloom weavers, were certainly worse off as they struggled to survive. Men who worked on the new railways as they stretched through the countryside may not have been paid much; but they were better off than other rural dwellers financially and they enjoyed regular employment: the trains ran whatever the state of the trade cycle. Agricultural workers fared better if they were on farms near to, or well connected with, growing towns than if they worked in remoter areas. Again, environmental conditions in the growing towns were slow to improve before the middle years of the century. Paving, draining, sewering and more adequate supplies of water were slow to catch up with the urban population's growing needs. And outbreaks of cholera and other diseases could not be tackled, despite urban improvement, without knowledge of germs and how they spread.

The rewards for the sacrifice, struggle and scientific enquiry of these years came after the mid-1870s. This is to be seen particularly in the results of the spread of steam at sea. The early steamboats, from 1815 onwards, were so inefficient and consumed so much fuel that they were profitable only on short journeys along the coast, up estuaries or on lakes. With the development of higher-pressure engines, however, steamships could operate profitably over longer distances. By the 1850s some of them could operate profitably across the Atlantic. (The Cunarders of the 1840s depended upon the subsidy of the mail contract.) A great breakthrough came in the mid-1860s when Alfred Holt of Liverpool started to run 2,000-ton vessels powered by compound engines profitably between England and China, a voyage greatly shortened after the opening of the Suez Canal in 1869 which saved the long voyage round the Cape of Good Hope. Owners of some sailing vessels responded with faster, clipper ships, on the one hand, and, on the other, by carrying bulkier cargoes in existing vessels where lower cost was more important than speed and reliable timekeeping. And all captains learned more about where to catch following winds. The tonnage of sail, as well as steam, went on growing for years at time when railways in other continents brought increasing amounts of more cheaply produced food and raw materials at ever lower cost to ports aboard. Investment before the mid-1870s and the application of new, reasoned, scientific ideas, may have bestowed only limited social benefits; but they laid the foundations for unprecedented social improvement thereafter.

Those who may still doubt these pre-1870 achievements should not forget the disaster which befell the Irish population, or more precisely the population of western Ireland, in the 1840s. Here was a truly Malthusian crisis. The Irish population had shot up from an estimated total of about 4,750,000 in 1790 to an enumerated 8,178,000 at the time of the 1841 census; and 4,000,000 of them survived almost entirely upon potatoes. The potato disease, no newcomer, reached southern England in the summer of 1845 and had spread to Ireland by the following October. The crop of 1846 began well but by the end of July was completely blighted. Three out of every four acres of potatoes were ruined. The disease vanished quickly and the 1847 crop was good; but by then the people, weakened by hunger, fell victim to fevers and other illnesses. More died after than during the 1846 famine year. Many of the survivors emigrated first across the Irish Sea, and then many of them to the United States. The total emigration exceeded 100,000 in 1846, rose to above 200,000 in 1847 and then after falling a little in 1848, remained above 200,000 in 1849, 1850 and 1851. At the time of the 1851 census Ireland's population had fallen to 6,554,000 and by 1871 to 5,412,000. Here was the awful warning of what could happen if population growth, of the sort experienced elsewhere in Western Europe, was not accompanied by economic change – and when other nations which experienced such economic change, Britain in this case, were unable or unwilling to come to the rescue and accept the further responsibility of trying to induce change in western Ireland, as they were already doing elsewhere in that country, by their purchases of food, brought across the Irish sea by steamboat, to help feed the urban population of north-west England.

THE YEARS OF REWARD, 1874–1914

The opening up of lower-cost areas elsewhere in the world and the associated development in steam-powered transport on land and sea to carry the cheaper food to Europe – not to mention the stimulating effect of this competition on European agriculture – greatly increased the quantity and range of foodstuffs available for Europe's customers. After the mid-1870s prices fell dramatically until the mid-1890s and the ensuing slight raise thereafter until 1914 had hardly any effect on the earlier fall in food costs. The fall in wholesale prices was often further increased by more efficient methods of retailing, by bulk buying and distributing in the growing towns through chains of attractive, well-lit, specialist retail shops with plate glass windows and much larger-lettered advertising, rightly described as a retailing revolution. These developments particularly benefited poorer people, who spent 60 per cent or so of the family income on food and non-alcoholic drink. A more varied and healthier diet now came within the reach of everyone.

Imports of cheaper raw materials changed the cost structure of industry and encouraged greater competition among manufacturers. This, in turn, led to production of consumer durables on a larger scale and, for instance, cut the price of shoes and clothing. Chains of shoe shops began to appear, through their benefits did not penetrate so far down the social scale as specialist food multiples; and in dress-making and the manufacture of items of men's wear labour costs were cut by the influx of those escaping from the eastern European pogroms, before they could move on to better jobs. The 'downs' as well as the 'ups' of the trade cycle have, however, to be taken into account, some of the former, especially that of the later 1870s, being very severe. It has nevertheless been estimated that in free trade Britain, where prices fell most because import duties were at a minimum, average real earnings per head were slightly over 75 per cent higher in 1896 than they had been in 1874; they had risen more than six times faster than in the third quarter of the century. Elsewhere in Western Europe, where heavy investment in railways, docks and the urban infrastructure continued for longer, and stronger rural pressure group activity obtained a higher degree of protection, the social advantages were relatively less. In France, for instance, it has been estimated that real earnings in the last quarter of the nineteenth century were only double that of the third quarter. In German, too, per capita real incomes lagged far behind Britain's, rising only about a third in the last quarter of the nineteenth century. But, all in all, the years 1874–96 were far from being the 'great depression' that they are often said to have been. Some of the better off, however, had to get used to more difficult times as interest rates fell; and less efficient businesses found greater competition and lower profit margins hard going. But the more enterprising did well and flourished as never before.

Many interrelated developments, as well as the upward movement of real earnings, also need to be taken into account in explaining the social progress of these years. Consider, for instance, the improvements in public health, which led to the greater longevity to which attention was drawn in our introductory survey. Towns had long been notoriously unhealthy places, and in the most congested centres more people died than were born. This was still true in the worst parts of city centres; but the creation of local authorities, empowered to levy taxes on the townsmen in order to bring about the physical improvement of these places, prevented overall urban death rates from rising, despite very rapid growth in the second half of the century. Yet periodical outbreaks of cholera and other diseases could not be prevented until medical men came to understand how these diseases spread.

We have seen that it was in the middle of the 1860s that medical light had still to dawn. Nobody had yet identified the carrier of any specific disease, until a remarkable German, Robert Koch (1843–1910), educated at Göttingen and just starting his working life as a physician in a little town in East Prussia, in 1876 identified the particular germ which caused anthrax, principally a disease of sheep. Three years after Pasteur began investigating chicken cholera, extracting the killer organism from the head of a diseased bird and making a culture (chicken broth) in order to produce more of these germs so that he could continue his experiments with them. He happened to be away for a period, leaving the broth exposed to the air. On his return he was astonished to find that the germs were no longer deadly but had been attenuated and gave healthy birds a mild form of the illness, which, after recovery, provided further immunity. Lister, from 1877 Professor at King's College, London, summarized these continental achievements at the International Medical Congress held in London in 1881 at which both Pasteur and Koch were present, and at which Pasteur spoke, using the words 'vaccine' and 'vaccination' in homage, as he put it, 'to one of the greatest men of England, your Jenner' who, in 1796, had used the mild cowpox to inoculate against the more virulent smallpox. Koch used Pasteur's process of attenuation to inoculate against anthrax in 1883. Soon after that, Pasteur himself produced a rabies vaccine for animals and then, as we have seen, as a cure for hydrophobia for humans bitten by mad dogs. Like Pasteur, the other two members of the triumvirate received well-deserved public recognition. Koch, appointed to a chair at Berlin University and as Director of the German Institute of Health in 1885, received the Nobel Prize for Medicine in 1905. Lister got a baronetcy in 1883, became President of the Royal Society from 1894 to 1900, in the course of which he was made a baron (1897), and received the Order of Merit in 1902. By then modern medicine had fully dawned. The bacteria causing a whole range of illnesses, including diphtheria, pneumonia, meningitis, tetanus, plague, cholera and dysentery, had been identified, ultimately a far greater contribution to public health than anything that had gone before.

These important medical developments became effective after, rather than before 1900, and death rates accordingly fell more rapidly. Before that the main killers, responsible for the overwhelming majority of deaths of those over one year of age (infant mortality rates did not then fall), were tuberculosis, typhus and scarlet fever. In the case of tuberculosis and typhus, improvement in the diet was still of paramount importance for it increased the ability of the human body to resist disease.

These were the years of demographic transition in Western Europe, even in France where, as we have seen, lower birth and death rates were already being experienced. As death rates fell, birth rates began to fall, too, in sympathy: otherwise family size would have been larger than ever. Although artificial means of contraception had been known and publicized from the 1830s, if not before, and were given further publicity by reformers after the mid-1870s, it is clear that *coitus interruptus*, the withdrawal method which depended upon the action of the male, was still the preferred means. Contraception was practised least in the poorer families, who stood to benefit most from not having to bring up such a large number of children, although in the short run the situation changed as the children started to contribute to the family income before they themselves married and brought up their own families. Families not practising contraception raised families of five or more; those who did came to bring up five or fewer.

There was no shortage of competition for the greater disposable incomes which cheaper food had made available from the 1870s. Some better working-class cottage property was built when costs of building materials fell. Rents were adjusted accordingly. Cheaper supplies of gas became available in towns for lighting and then for cooking. Furniture became cheaper and a second-hand market developed. In relatively prosperous Britain many of the better-off working classes could afford a piano, often imported from Germany and bought on hire purchase. Higher disposable incomes were sometimes used to buy a little more leisure. In Britain a half-day holiday on Saturday afternoons became general and with it the growth of organized spectator sport (shopkeepers took their time off on other half days,

standardized for each town). Bicycles, expensive at first, came down rapidly in price, especially from the middle 1890s when a brisk second-hand trade in them developed. They were popular among women as well as among men. They became, in fact, the first form of private transport to be owned by most people. The railways, which had run excursion trains at low fares almost from the outset on holidays, now ran many more of them and advertised them widely. Newspaper proprietors, taking advantage of cheaper newsprint and technical advances in typesetting and newspaper production, cut their cover prices and boosted circulation among readers of more modest means, especially on Sundays when they had more time to read them. Book publishers brought out cheaper volumes, including the forerunners of paperbacks. Schooling went on longer, often compulsorily, and there was more higher and further education. Urban entertainment proliferated, catering increasingly for working-class audiences, often in specially-built theatres. And, as we shall see, from the mid-1890s moving pictures succeeded public magic lantern shows as a completely new fascination, and gramophones and gramophone records became available. All in all, Western Europe was beginning to develop a distinctly modern aspect.

The pace at which this happened depended upon the extent of economic change in different national regions, and here we are up against the problem of the impossibility of desegregating the national statistics to which we have already referred. A further difficulty is that for purposes of international comparisons those employed in agriculture, forestry and fishing are lumped together. The figures do, however, show the sharp difference between Great Britain (England, Wales and Scotland) and the leading Continental nations. In Britain the numbers employed in agriculture etc., peaked with 1,824,000 males and 230,000 females in a total population of 17,926,000 early as 1851, when we know that half the population was still described as living as outside towns. The relation of agriculture etc., to total population may nevertheless be taken as a rough and ready indication, though a diminishing one, of the proportion still in traditional forms of employment, even though agriculture etc. did not employ most of them. By 1901 the number of males employed had fallen to 1,390,000 and females to 86,000 in a total population of 37,000,000 after which, with increased demand for home-produced food and British trawlers' catches of fish, totals grew slightly, to 1,489,000 and 117,000 respectively by the census of 1911, but by then Britain's total population had grown by nearly 4,000,000 to 40,831,000.

The numbers employed in agriculture etc. in France, excluding Alsace-Lorraine, by contrast, peaked only in 1901, at 8,245,000 (5,581,000 males and 2,604,000 females) when total population stood at 38,451,000. In 1866 when comparable figures first become available on an international basis for France – again for our purposes excluding Alsace-Lorraine – the comparable totals were 7,495,000 (5,248,000 males, 2,237,000 females) in a total, which by 1872 stood at 36,103,000. By 1911 the number of males had fallen slightly but still numbered 5,331,000 in a total population of 39,192,000, but that of females had risen to 3,241,000. France still remained a conservative, peasant society.

The German statistics show a different pattern. They start for agriculture etc. only in 1882. The male total, 5,702,000, may have been at or around itsr peak (5,702,000 in a population, including Alsace-Lorraine, which already stood at 45,234,000 in 1880), fell to only 5,540,000 in 1895, and to 5,284,000 in 1907, the last pre-war return in the published international series. Female employment kept going up, however, slowly at first, from 2,535,000 in 1882 to 2,753,000 in 1895; then it shot up to 4,599,000 in 1907. Germany's total population by 1910 had long surpassed that of all other Western European nations and reached 64,926,000.

These statistics show the pace at which Britain had shed its traditional sector as its total population had at last caught up with that of France, geographically a far larger country. Both France and Germany each still had over 5,000,000 males in their traditional sector just before 1914; but whereas France's total population had grown only from 36,000,000 to 39,000,000 since the early 1870s, Germany's had grown by nearly 24,000,000. The extensive acres of rural France remained more traditional. In Germany many men still worked in the countryside – 40 per cent of the total in 1913 – but many of them were employed on larger farms feeding a vastly increased non-agricultural population.

Coal production, a major source of energy and supplier of fuel and power, is a good indicator of economic change, the other side of the rural coin. Output in Britain grew from 118,000,000 tons in 1871 to 292,000,000 tons in 1913. Output (including lignite) in Germany grew much more impressively, from a much lower initial base: 37,000,000 tons (1871) to 278,000,000 tons (1913). France's output, by contrast, increased only from 23,000,000 tons to 41,000,000 tons in the same period. (By 1913 this was only about as much as Silesia alone). In Germany the Ruhr became the great coal source and by 1913 Germany was exporting 20,000,000 tons altogether, mainly to other parts of the Continent. Britain shipped overseas a quarter of its production in 1913, including its high-quality steam coal from South Wales. Germany's collieries, unlike Britain's, were not well situated for shipment overseas; indeed, in 1913 Britain supplied the coastal regions of Holland and Germany with 11,000,000 tons of coal.

After 1880, thanks to the Thomas and Gilchrist (British) invention of a method of making steel with phosphoric ore, available in abundance in Lorraine and Luxembourg, Germany surpassed Britain in steel production and also caught up, just before 1914, in pig iron production, too. In 1880 Germany produced about 1,500,000 tons of steel to Britain's 3,700,000 tons, and over 2,700,000 tons of pig iron to Britain's 7,800,000 tons; but Germany overhauled Britain in steel in the 1890s, and by 1910 produced 13,000,000 tons to Britain's 10,000,000 tons. By then Germany was producing nearly 15,000,000 tons of pig iron to Britain's 10,000,000 tons. Germany came to excel in all sorts of iron and steel goods and machinery, heavy and light, just as Britain continued to excel in textiles of all kinds, both high quality and mass produced; exports never did so well as in the years just before 1914. Britain's exports of textile machinery also continued to thrive.

In chemicals Germany continued to benefit from her long-established laboratory tradition and university education. German specialization in dyestuffs enabled the British to import them to dye their more valuable textiles more cheaply than would otherwise have been possible. Germany also built up a heavy chemical industry, the products of which were mainly consumed at home, especially to fertilize the soil. Heavy chemicals did well in Britain, too. The scene was being set by mergers before 1914, which were to result, in the mid-1920s, in the creation of I. G. Farben and,

in response, Imperial Chemical Industries. France lost her earlier technical lead in industrial chemistry, and was not helped by the inconvenient location of raw materials nor by the lack of abundant supplies of coal tar, but she was not so disadvantaged in fine chemicals. France did play a leading part, however, in the beginnings of two new industries which were to have important social consequences.

Although Daimler and Benz are rightly remembered for producing the first petrol-driven, horseless vehicles in south-west Germany in the mid-1880s, they did not manage to develop them at this stage to the point at which they could find buyers. This was achieved by French entrepreneurs, notably Peugeot, and Panhard and Levassor, using German patents, in the early 1890s. France remained the main producers of *automobiles* in Western Europe before 1914. Ownership spread much more rapidly in the United States, where a larger population and higher disposable incomes enabled Henry Ford and others to increase production greatly, reduce unit costs and cut prices; but on this side of the Atlantic where motor cars still remained expensive, the spread of much less costly motorcycles, with Britain to the fore, enabled more of the middle classes to move up from their pedalled vehicles. More important, the introduction of a satisfactory motorbus in European towns in the years just before 1914 at last replaced the slow and costly horse, which had to be fed even when not working. Vehicle size grew, speed increased and routes were lengthened. The working classes, who could rarely afford horse-bus fares, could now afford to travel by the many new motorbuses. Together with the electric tramcar, which we shall next consider, the motorbus made it much easier for people in all walks of life to get about in towns. In many ways the motorbus and electric tramcar complemented each other and are often overlooked when standards of living are considered.

The electricity industry, like that of internal combustion, originated in Europe many years before the 1880s, and in several parts of Europe, as may be seen from the names of some of the pioneers: Galvani and Volta (Italy), Oersted (Denmark), and Ampère (France). The relationship between electricity and magnetism had been established by 1831 when an Englishman, Faraday, used the interaction of electric and magnetic fields to produce mechanical motion. This was the essence of an electric motor which, when reversed, became a dynamo. Faraday showed how mechanical could be converted into electric power and vice-versa, though half a century was to pass before this fact was exploited commercially. For the time being electricity was to be provided on a small scale from primary cells, already known and being improved from the beginning of the nineteenth century. Further improvements were made for use when only small currents were required, especially by the Frenchman Leclanché in 1868.

The combination of electricity and magnetism was first applied commercially in the electric telegraph. Baron Schilling, a German attached to the Russian Embassy in Munich, produced the first needle telegraph in 1832, and two other Germans, Gauss and Weber, were able to operate a needle instrument at Göttingen in the following year. Its possibilities for the rapid transmission of information were slow to be perceived, however, even by the new railways then being built. In 1837 two Englishmen, Wheatstone and Cooke, the latter having been to Germany, demonstrated to one of Britain's railway companies the effectiveness of the needle telegraph over a two-mile distance, but it was turned down. Another British company did start to use it over a 13-mile stretch of line out of London, but was slow to extend it. Meanwhile Samuel Morse, an American painter who had heard about electro-magnetism before leaving the United States to study the old masters in Europe (1829–32), thereafter suffered abject poverty for a decade or so before he could persuade enough customers to adopt his Morse Code and the apparatus he developed which printed out the dots and dashes on to paper tape. Until the middle of the nineteenth century the electric telegraph was used, without any great enthusiasm or wish to exploit it, mainly by the railways themselves. Commercial exploitation was developed by private companies in Britain and undertaken by governments abroad, notably by Prussia, whose authorities instructed Ernst Werner Siemens in 1848, when he was an army officer in charge of the defence of Kiel, to build the first telegraph line from Berlin to Frankfurt. In 1851 a submarine cable was laid on the bed of the English Channel to link the English and French railways and London with Paris. More cabling soon followed. In 1866, after several unsuccessful attempts, a transatlantic cable came into use and by the 1870s Europe was in telegraphic contact with China and Australia. Messages could then be sent to almost any city in the world in hours instead of weeks and answers received with an equivalent saving of time. There had never been such a rapid speeding up in communication either before or since, though the price per word was very high and messages had to be succinct.

The telegraph, with the development of batteries, cables, repeaters and the rest prepared the way for the telephone, but the telephone did not have anything like the same impact. To converse over several miles instead of face-to-face, or even between towns in the same country, was a relatively trivial saving compared to being able to communicate all over the whole world, even if only one way at a time. Although the principle of the telephone had been demonstrated in Germany in the early 1860s, it was Alexander Graham Bell, born in Edinburgh, who first drew attention to its possibilities. The son of a specialist in the mechanism of speech who had moved south and became a professor in the subject at University College London, he himself followed in his father's footsteps. In 1870 the family moved to Canada and in 1873, at the age of twenty-six, he was Professor of Vocal Physiology at Boston University. The following year he became a naturalized American citizen. He started to experiment with the transmission of sound by a short length of cable using tuning forks. In 1875 he patented his invention and soon incorporated an electromagnetic microphone in his system. The idea of a telephone exchange to permit more than a pair of instruments followed in 1878. By this time the American Western Union Company, seeing the telephone's commercial possibilities, brought in Edison to provide improved versions of the Bell system without infringing Bell's patents.

By the 1870s attention began to switch from small-current telegraphy to high-tension dynamo generation and electric lighting and traction. In Germany Werner Siemens, who was in partnership with George Halske to develop the telegraph system, had become more interested in electricity generation. Well supported by German banks, Siemens and Halske and others (including from 1883 German Edison, later and better known as the Allgemeine Elektrizitats Gesellschaft: AEG), built central power stations to supply current for lighting and then for traction. Siemens produced his own improved dynamo and so did pioneers in the

electric power industry in other countries, including Gramme, Crompton, Ferranti and Wenstrom. Some central streets were better lit by powerful arc lights; and the filament lamps of Edison and Swan brought electric light into private homes. By 1882 Edison was supplying 1,000 electric lights in central London. The new source of illumination, supplied from central power stations, became available in all European towns, although in those places which already had a good supply of gas lighting, the impact was limited, especially as gas responded to the competition with gas mantles. Country houses also installed electricity if they could afford their own generator.

Electric lighting, both outdoor and indoor (where it could be switched on and off by the flick of a switch) was a welcome arrival; but the coming of the electric tramcar was of far greater social significance before 1914.

Horse-drawn tramways had spread from America to Europe during the 1860s. Because horses could pull larger vehicles and carry more passengers over smooth rails than along rough road surfaces, they had always been able to charge lower fares than the horse buses which, as has been seen, were middle-class vehicles. From the outset horse trams carried some of the working classes, especially by early morning services which carried them to work. But, as we saw with the motorization of the horse bus, the substitution of horse by mechanical traction offered rich rewards. Siemens and Halske demonstrated electric traction's possibilities on a small-scale tramway at the Berlin Trade Fair in 1879 and at the Electromechanical Exhibition in Paris two years later. Other pioneers experimented elsewhere in Europe; but the real breakthrough came in America. An American naval officer, Frank Sprague, had become interested in the subject on a visit to the British Electrical Exhibition in London in 1882. He had then resigned his commission, worked with Edison for a time and then set up his own company. Using the overhead trolley and series/parallel controller, he demonstrated that many vehicles could be run at the same time on the tramway system, at Richmond, Virginia, in 1888. As happened with the petrol car later, a few American firms started to produce tramway equipment on a larger scale, thereby cutting costs. America's tramways were electrified and new ones built. Then American firms took the lead in electrifying Europe's tramways and extending them. Local authorities and private companies in Western Europe's fast-growing cities rebuilt existing horse tramways, electrified them, often using lower-cost American equipment, and supplied them with new, larger and faster cars. This ushered in a completely new era in public transport, which had very important social consequences.

Fares were cut, journey times were reduced, and more people could afford to live farther from their place of work. This outward movement, which had started with workmen's steam trains in the 1860s, was now vastly accelerated. More poorer people than ever were enabled to follow the better-off to the suburbs. They moved from congested central accommodation where rent per square foot was high to more pleasant and airier sites where they could find somewhere to live at lower cost. The new electric tramcar provided the fast, comfortable mode of travel, well lit on dark days and at night, virtually unknown for horse-drawn travellers. And as horses began to be banished from urban streets, so these thoroughfares became cleaner and less disease-ridden as the flies had fewer droppings to feed upon. Tramways, however, had the disadvantage of having to run along fixed tracks; but the motorbus, which arrived a few years later as we have seen, filled urban gaps, provided onward services from tramway termini and appeared in places not large enough to justify the heavier fixed investment of tram track.

Electrification of the heavier steam trains, over- or underground, and the building of new urban railway systems also followed, if it did not coincide with, the building of electric tramways in the largest cities. In the years before 1914 the rapidly increasing numbers served by a public transport system of electric trams, train and motorbus were to become the envy of their successors. It was certainly much easier, cheaper and hassle-free to get about in towns in those days than it has subsequently become.

The development of wireless telegraphy and the application of internal combustion to flying need not detain us for long. Although in the longer run they have become of great concern, in the earlier years of the twentieth century, just before 1914, they were as yet of little social significance, but highly newsworthy.

The transmission of electromagnetic waves through space had been forecast mathematically in 1873 by the Scot, Clerk-Maxwell, the first Professor of Experimental Physics at Cambridge University. The idea was tested experimentally in 1886 by Hertz, a professor at Karlsruhe, still known to all as the measurer of the length of electromagnetic waves. It was, however, the Italian-born Marconi, another significant immigrant scientist gain to Britain, who first transmitted the Morse letter 'S' across the Atlantic from Cornwall to Newfoundland in December 1901. Wireless telegraphy was used to a strictly limited extent at sea before 1914. Wireless telephony (to be known generally as wireless or radio) lay in the future.

Physical movement through the air – powered flight – was also in its infancy before 1914. Although the Wright Brothers were first to get a powered machine off the ground at Kill Devil Sands, North Carolina at the end of 1903, even more credit is due to them for their subsequent, and highly secret, development work in 1904 and 1905, in which latter year they offered a machine to the US War Department; but they did not receive the encouragement of a contract – and this only for a single machine, until 1907. In Europe the Frenchman Santos-Dumont and the Dane, Ellehamer, flew short hops in 1906 and Ellehamer accomplished the first flight on German soil, at Kiel in June 1908. By then France had become the main centre of activity in Europe as it had with motorcars. Wilbur Wright's visit there in 1908 – he was in the air on one occasion for one and a half hours and flew 55 miles – encouraged greater European effort and further progress was made. In June 1909 Louis Blériot won a newspaper prize and created a great stir by flying the English Channel, which he only managed to do because a fortunate shower of rain cooled his overheated engine, which had never before covered such a distance. Much progress was made in Britain and Germany, as well as France, before 1914; but commercial flying did not start – and then very fitfully – until 1919.

The French also took the lead in another new invention. This was cinematography which, though also much more important after the First World War, already brought much pleasure to many millions before the war.

Magic lantern shows, by which still photographs on glass were projected on to a large screen by a strong beam of electric light through a magnifying lens, became increasingly popular during the 1880s. To make the still image

move was the next step forward. The persistence of human vision had been known for centuries as a means of producing this illusion of movement. To flick pieces of paper on which a succession of slightly different lines had been drawn was already a well-known method of deceiving the human eye. In October 1888 a French physiologist, Etienne Jules Marey, read a paper to the French Academy of Sciences which explained the principles of what was to become a cine-camera, using a ribbon of photographic paper and a shutter which cut off the light every time the paper was moved forward from one spool to another. Enterprising men elsewhere were soon attempting to improve on this idea and to make it marketable. The versatile Edison, who saw Marey's work in Paris in 1889, in 1891 used 35mm celluloid film in place of photographic paper. His main interest then, however, was in the mechanical reproduction of sound and the sale of his patented phonograph, which reproduced sound from a revolving cylinder, the output being modified mechanically through a large horn. He saw the moving image as an adjunct to this, and not as something which was highly marketable on its own, thereby anticipating the arrival of the talking film, but not appreciating how long this would take because of the difficulty in synchronizing sight and sound. He failed to exploit his kinescope, but it was exhibited in various places, including a fair at Vincennes, just outside Paris, where two enterprising brothers, Charles and Emile Pathé, decided to use it to attract customers to their *bar américain* near the Place Pigalle. Some customers decided that they would like a projector for themselves and by 1894 the Pathé were soon making and selling their own *Phonographes Pathé* and cylinders. They established the industry in the Paris suburb of Chatou.

In the meantime two other enterprising French brothers, Louis and August Lumière, photographic manufacturers of Lyon, designed a cine-camera and projector, which were an improvement on Edison's. Having filed their patent in February 1895, in the following June they filmed delegates of the French Photographic Society arriving at their annual congress and projected it to them 48 hours later. Before the year was out they opened a public cinema in the basement of a Paris café, which was soon attracting an audience of 2,000 a night. They showed brief, outdoor scenes of which 'The Arrival of a Train' has since become a classic. By then R. W. Paul in London and C. F. Jenkins in Washington DC were also concerned with the cinematograph. Cameramen were soon shooting other short sequences: the advance of Kitchener's army in the Sudan, for instance. Films were copied and distributed far and wide. Longer films began to be made, of specially acted episodes as well as outdoor scenes. Many countries started their little film studios.

At the end of the 1880s the phonograph, which the Pathé brothers had been so successful in marketing, was eclipsed by the gramophone, the invention of a German immigrant to America, Emile Berlin, who used disc instead of cylinder. London became its European centre and the Gramophone Company later became famous with its slogan 'His Master's Voice' and the image of a dog sitting up appreciatively to listen to the sounds emerging from the wind-up gramophone's huge horn. So in 1901, the Pathés went into films and by 1908 had become the world's largest filmmakers with branches throughout the world. Before 1914 they were marketing a weekly *Pathé Gazette*. Small picture houses emerged in towns large and small and attracted sizeable audiences; employing a projectionist and few staff, entry was much cheaper than to the live theatre. By 1913, to give two English examples, Bradford, with a population of under 300,000, claimed a daily attendance of 30,000 at its thirty cinemas; and in the following year Manchester (700,000) reported a cinema seat for every eight inhabitants. Britain as a whole then boasted at least 3,500 cinemas.

We noticed earlier when the spread of literacy and political awareness was being discussed, that the property owners of Europe were concerned about the dangers which would arise if ordinary people were to get ideas above their station and seek political power for themselves. This certainly came to pass in the years after 1870. It accompanied the general improvement of living standards, growing urbanization and what has been called 'the contagion of numbers'. Dissatisfaction with the political *status quo* arises not when people are poor but when they become less impoverished and want to speed up the process. Living together in towns, the discontented can be more readily organized into movements to press for political change.

Wage earners took advantage of cooperative movements and friendly societies, which encouraged prudent expenditure and thrift. When friendly societies were confined to a particular craft, they took on the appearance of trade unions, though so long as trade unions were confined to the skilled, they were usually, though not always, more concerned with friendly society activity – insurance against sickness and accident and the cost of burial – than with bringing pressure to bear upon their employers. In any case, numerous employers had once been wage-earning trade unionists who had got on in a world open to talent. When the lower paid unskilled – the 'have-nots' of labour – joined or formed trade unions, however, more radical political ideas started to prevail. Although the majority of wage earners never belonged to trade unions, the growth in union membership reflects the arrival of these more radical new unionists. From 1886 membership grew from 1,250,000 to 2,000,000 (1900) and 4,000,000 (1913) in Britain, more powerfully from 300,000 to 850,000 (1900) and 3,000,000 (1913) in Germany, and from 50,000 to 250,000 (1900) and 1,000,000 (1913) in France. The rate of increase was far greater in Germany and France; the absolute totals greater in Britain.

That the new popular forces exerted greater political influence throughout Western Europe before 1914 is without question, but the differences between the various nations is so great that generalization is extremely difficult. We can, for instance, consider the extension of the franchise. Universal male suffrage was allowed in the German Empire from its outset in 1871; but the German constitution denied the Reichstag, for which German males over twenty-one voted, any real power. In Britain, where many urban males had the vote from 1867 for a House of Commons which did have some powers, there was universal male suffrage from 1884, but many property owners continued to have more than one vote, sometimes many more. In Italy only 7 per cent of the population could vote in 1882, and universal suffrage did not arrive until 1912. No women had a national vote in Europe before 1914 apart from those in Norway and Finland, who received it in 1907. Throughout Europe, nevertheless, new left-wing parties emerged and some older ones moved leftwards.

In Germany the Marxist Social Democrats became a unified party after the Gotha Congress (1875). They gradually increased their vote, and by 1912 had 28 per cent of the seats in the Reichstag. The French equivalent had also been growing at the same time and in 1893 returned

40–50 'Socialist' Deputies. In Britain the Socialist Federation (1880), later the Social Democratic Federation, had few followers and was not very socialist; but more radical opinion began to grow. It was centred upon the Independent Labour Party (1893), but the Labour Representation Committee (1900, some trade unions, the Fabian Society and the ILP/SDF), which became the Labour Party in 1906, was certainly not Marxist. More important was the leftward lurch of the Liberal Party, then in government. No revolutions were experienced anywhere in Europe. This is explained by the considerable improvement in living standards and by the greater opportunities for the able, hardworking (and lucky) to scale the social ladder. In local government, in which property-owning women sometimes participated, some success was achieved in the municipalization of private utilities ('gas and water socialism'). Finally, the establishment in power, often in its own defence, started to show consideration for wage earners' needs.

Here the lead was taken in Germany by Bismarck, who perceived wage earners' inevitable impoverishment if they lost earnings because of accident, sickness or when they became too old to work. Responsibility for accidents at work, if it were not the worker's fault, was put upon the employer from 1871 and became a state responsibility from 1884. Sickness had been covered by state insurance the year before, and old age and invalidity insurance followed in 1888. By 1911 German state insurance schemes covered nearly 9,000,000 Germans.

Britain eventually followed Germany's example, the more radical Liberal government bringing in non-contributory old age pensions in 1909 and sickness insurance by an Act of 1911. They went even further than Germany by including in that Act sections providing insurance to cover unemployment; but this was brought in first of all only in 1913 and then applied only to less vulnerable occupations. By then there were state-encouraged insurance schemes of one sort or another in France, Belgium, Holland, Italy, Denmark, Norway, Sweden and Switzerland. The welfare state had not yet arrived; but it was being foreshadowed.

RETROSPECT AND PROSPECT

By the middle of 1914 anyone who took the trouble to look back over the Century of Peace had every reason for satisfaction.

During its first 50 years, mechanical power had gradually augmented human effort at work, making it possible for the nations of Western Europe to prove Malthus, the clever mathematician, wrong. Powered machines were able to provide enough employment to sustain their growing populations, few of whom were yet the direct beneficiaries of the new power but who benefited from the expenditures of the factory workers, the other jobs created by industrialization and the growth of imports paid for by their manufactured exports. More people came to live in towns, the heart of these economic and commercial developments, although (apart from in Britain after 1850) townspeople were still in a minority. Rapid inward urban migration created great social problems which local authorities battled hard to offset by physical improvements; but they lacked the medical knowledge to achieve much.

Steam power was also applied to transport – railways and ships – over gradually greater distances. As a result, increased, improved, cheaper and more reliable services made travel easier for those who could afford the fares, often without prior booking. Equally important was the ability to carry higher-value goods and mails with greater speed and reliability. Yet, just as more power at work had generated more jobs outside power-driven factories, so the spread of steam transport resulted in further growth of transport in its traditional form. Greater sailing tonnage carried bulkier, low-value cargoes; and horse-drawn traffic by road continued to grow in towns and on many routes unserved by railways. Commerce with, and between, nations grew, further encouraged by customs unions where internal free trade did not exist already. Import duties from other nations were reduced or abolished, to the advantage of customers everywhere. The spirit of empirical enquiry, built upon past experience, began to be supplemented by more scientific research, which looked to the future.

All this considerable investment produced rich results in the second 50 years. Western Europe became part of a global world in a completely new sense. Mounting waves of emigrants moved abroad. International specialization brought cheaper food and raw materials from afar, often from different climates and hemispheres on a scale hitherto unknown. The electric telegraph flashed early warning of their availability and voyages could be more carefully planned. Cheaper raw material inputs stimulated competition among manufacturers and the creation of larger, more efficient industrial units. Improved methods of distribution passed these gains on to the consumer and advertised the fact by billboard and in the increasing number of local newspapers. Working-class living standards grew as never before.

Towns became healthier places partly because of the continuation of earlier improvements, but also because of greater medical knowledge about germs and disease. Medical officers of health issued regular reports. Electric traction allowed poorer people to follow the better off into the more salubrious suburbs. Motorbuses soon afterwards made travel cheaper and easier along roads where the fixed route tramways did not run. Greater disposable income and easier mobility – helped by cheaper safety bicycles – saws the emergence in towns of spectator sports, theatrical entertainments and the new craze, the cinema. The importance of education, both at school and beyond, came to be more widely appreciated and working-class movements started to make themselves felt. The establishment, however, parried their efforts – often anticipating them – by state insurance schemes. In 1914, men and women who had gained so much had every reason to expect social improvement, by then so well established, to go on uninterruptedly forever and ever.

Yet progress is always accompanied by the possibility of setback. Industry and science, which had made economic and social advances possible, had also made possible more fearful warfare with equal efficiency, capable of inflicting pain, suffering and impoverishment beyond the wildest imagination of the previous beneficiaries. The results went far beyond the enormous losses as thousands and thousands of enthusiastic young men were sent over the top to be mown down by machine guns, or the physical destruction of property. They went far beyond the sufferings of the greater number who were disabled, or the grief of the families of the dead and wounded. The results lasted long after the war ended in other ways too. The 1917 Revolution would not have occurred if the Russians had not been defeated; in which case there would have been no Stalin and

no Cold War in more recent times. If, during the war, resources had not been switched from goods exported to the manufacture of armaments, the course of multilateral systems of trading would not have been destroyed. In Britain's case, markets in South America would not have been lost to the United States nor in the Far East to the Japanese. In the end, real peace and progress never returned, even to America which, after the 'roaring twenties', suffered the Wall Street Crash and impoverishment in the 1930s on a scale unknown even in Europe, where the indebted nations never returned to the pre-1914 'normalcy' but suffered from chronic unemployment on a scale previously unknown. The rise of dictatorship in economically distressed Germany persuaded another generation of enthusiastic youth that amends needed to be made for the defeat of 1918. To that extent the First World War led to the Second, after which pre-1914 'normalcy' still did not return.

No doubt the continued spread of labour-saving machines in factories, leading more recently to labour saving in the office with the coming of computers, would have given rise to present-day problems sooner or later, war or no war; but if the peace had not been shattered in 1914, such problems could have been given top priority, unhindered by more immediate distractions. Time would have been available to have considered the possibilities of, for instance, a shorter working week and work sharing in a world where nations continued to compete commercially and not militarily, as they have come to do with the Cold War and the arms race since the 1950s.

The great mistake of 1914, which so abruptly ended the Century of Peace, has had very protracted consequences. The possibilities in July 1914 were so great. The realities of July 1914 have been so far reaching.

BIBLIOGRAPHY

BRIGGS, A.; SNOWMAN, D. (eds) 1996. *Fins de siècle. How Centuries End, 1400–2000.* For the 1790s (Roy Porter) and 1890s (Asa Briggs). Yale University Press, New Haven.

COLE, W. A.; DEANE, P. (eds) 1965. 'The growth of national incomes'. In: Habakkuk, H. J.; Postan, M. M. *The Cambridge Economic History of Europe, Vol. 6.* Cambridge University Press, Cambridge.

DARMON, P. 1996. *Pasteur.* Paris.

DARWIN, F. 1887. *The Life and Letters of Charles Darwin,* including autobiographical chapter. Appleton & Co., New York.

DOVRING, F. (ed.) 1965. 'The transformation of European agriculture'. In: Habakkuk, H. J.; Postan, M. M. *The Cambridge Economic History of Europe, Vol. 6.* Cambridge University Press, Cambridge.

GILLE, B. (ed.) 1973. 'Banking and industrialization in Europe 1730–1914'. In: Cipolla, C. M. *Fontana Economic History of Europe. The Industrial Revolution.* London.

GLASS, D. V.; GREBENIK, E. (eds) 1965. 'World population 1800–1950'. In: Habakkuk, H. J.; Postan, M. M. *The Cambridge Economic History of Europe, Vol. 6.* Cambridge University Press, Cambridge.

HARTWELL, R. M. (ed.) 1973. 'The service revolution 1700–1914'. In: Cipolla, C. M. *Fontana Economic History of Europe. The Industrial Revolution.* London.

HENDERSON, W. O. 1969. *The Industrialization of Europe, 1780–1914.* Thames & Hudson, London.

KENWOOD, A. G.; LOUGHEED, A. L. 1983. *The Growth of the International Economy 1820–1980. An Introductory Text.* Allen & Unwin, London.

LANDES, D. S. (ed.) 1965. 'Technological change and Development in Western Europe 1750–1914'. In: Habakkuk, H. J.; Postan, M. M. *The Cambridge Economic History of Europe, Vol. 6.* Cambridge University Press, Cambridge.

MATHIAS, P.; POSTAN, M. M. (eds) 1978. *The Cambridge Economic History of Europe, Vol. 8.* Cambridge University Press, Cambridge.

MILWARD, A. S.; SAUL, S. B. 1973. *The Economic Development of Continental Europe, 1780–1870.* Allen & Unwin, London.

MINCHINTON, W. (ed.) 1973. 'Pattern of demand 1750–1914'. In: Cipolla, C. M. *Fontana Economic History of Europe. The Industrial Revolution.* London.

POLLARD, S. 1981. *Peaceful Conquest. Industrialization of Europe 1760–1970.* Oxford University Press, Oxford.

POULTON, E. P. (ed.) 1910. 'Charles Darwin'. In: *Encyclopaedia Britannica.* 11th Edn.

STEPHEN, L. (ed.) 1975. 'Charles Darwin'. In: *The Compact Edition of the Dictionary of National Biography.* A completely revised edition is in active preparation. Oxford University Press, Oxford.

SUPPLE, B. (ed.) 1973. 'The state and the industrial revolution 1700–1914'. In: Cipolla, C. M. *Fontana Economic History of Europe. The Industrial Revolution.* London.

10.2

CENTRAL, EASTERN AND SOUTH EASTERN EUROPE

Nikolaï Todorov, coordinator

10.2.1

THE HABSBURG MONARCHY

Jean Béranger and Charles Kecskeméti

The Habsburg Monarchy, Habsburg Empire or Austro-Hungarian Monarchy was a multinational, multicultural and multiconfessional state. In 1815, the Habsburg Empire stood as a challenge to the ideas propagated by the French Revolution, opposing both German nationalism and Hungarian separatism. Would it succeed in leading its many peoples to a prosperous economy and a blooming culture while sustaining its supranational tradition? That was the question the 'decisive nineteenth century' had to answer.

In 1789, the Monarchy included territories belonging to the Holy Roman Empire (hereditary provinces, Bohemia, possessions in Northern Italy and in the Netherlands) as well as territories which had never been part of it: the countries of St Stephen's Crown (Hungary, Croatia, Transylvania) and the former Polish provinces of Galicia and Lodomeria. In order to make governable this vast and heterogeneous complex, the Pragmatic Sanction of 1713 had imposed a regime of personal union, which reconfirmed also the internal autonomy of each land. In 1804, Emperor Francis took a decision fraught with serious consequences for the future of Europe, when he proclaimed himself Emperor of Austria and then declared the Holy Roman Empire dissolved. A unitary, although not centralized, state was thus born. It existed until the constitutional reorganization of 1867.

Lower Austria, with its capital Vienna and the neighbouring kingdom of Bohemia, constituted the nucleus of the Monarchy. The other hereditary provinces extending from Lake Constance to the Pannonian plain enjoyed larger autonomy. Following the French Wars, the Habsburgs renounced their Rhine area estate, the Breisgau and the Austrian Netherlands, but consolidated their position in Northern Italy. The Austrian hegemony in the peninsula was secured by the creation of the Lombard-Venetian kingdom, composed of the duchy of Milan and the territories of the Venetian Republic, annexed in 1797.

The historical kingdom of Hungary represented a territory of 325,000km^2 with a population of 12 million at the time of the Vienna Congress. Notwithstanding the complaints of the Hungarian political class, the territorial integrity of the kingdom was not restored. The autonomous Principality of Transylvania was considered as a possession *per se* of the dynasty. The Military Frontier, an innovative creation of the sixteenth-century opposite to Turkish Bosnia, was governed directly from Vienna. It became, after 1740, the breeding ground of the regular army. Its population composed of Serbs and Croats escaped from seigniorial rule.

Leopold II reinstated, in 1791, the special status of Hungary and of the associate kingdom of Croatia, disregarded by Joseph II. The administration of the kingdom was delegated to the palatine (a Habsburg archduke from 1790 on) who resided in Buda and was assisted by a lord lieutenancy. Close to rebellion in 1789, Hungary remained loyal to the dynasty throughout the two decades of the French Wars. The political class of noblemen did not want to risk a social revolution.

Finally, in 1772, when Poland was first partitioned, Austria received Galicia and Lodomeria. Bukovina, also beyond the Carpathians, was annexed in 1775. These provinces were kept after 1815.

Travellers might have got the impression of visiting a German-speaking Catholic country, but in fact, the Empire lacked linguistic and religious unity. As in these parts, the languages spoken by the various peoples were traditionally respected and as the Habsburgs had never indulged in trying to acculturate their subjects, the Austrian Empire was a genuine Babel, where co-existed German and Hungarian with Slavonic and Latin languages. German, which served as a common cultural language, was not the mother tongue of the majority of the subjects. The population was German-speaking in the hereditary provinces, in parts of Bohemia and Moravia, and also in Hungary, in the medieval 'Saxon' districts of Upper Hungary (Slovakia) and Transylvania, in commercial and mining towns and the eighteenth-century settlements in the Plain.

Hungarian, the only non-Indo-European language of the Monarchy, belongs to the Finno-Ugrian group. It was spoken in the central area of the Kingdom and in parts of Transylvania. Regulation of the spelling started only in the sixteenth century. Latin served as administrative and legal language until 1843, a convenient arrangement in a multi-lingual country.

Slavonic languages had different statuses. In Bohemia-Moravia, Czech became a written language as early as the fourteenth century. The country was bilingual; the position of German strengthened from the 1620s to the 1780s, when there began a Czech 'renaissance'. Polish served as the official language in Galicia and Lodomeria. The efforts made by Joseph II to impose German as the administrative language fell short. Only the Jews of the *Shtetl* spoke among themselves the German-based Yiddish, brought to Eastern Europe by medieval migrations and written in Hebrew script. The Polish provinces had one major linguistic problem: the rural masses east of Lvov spoke Ukrainian, while Polish remained the language of the elite.

The population of Upper Hungary spoke Slovak, closely linked to Czech and Polish. Until the linguistic awakening of the 1780s, written Slovak was hardly used outside pious Catholic books and private correspondence. Administration was expedited in Latin, and the Lutheran church conserved Czech for writing.

The South-Slavonic Slovene had a status similar to that of Slovak. It was spoken by the rural population of the mountainous regions of Carniola, Carinthia and Styria, while German served for writing, administration and higher culture.

Orthodox Serbs and Catholic Croats spoke the same language but used different scripts, Cyrillic and Latin respectively. Their history differed too. The Croatian kingdom, founded in the early tenth century, while retaining self-government, accepted union with Hungary in 1102. The Habsburgs recognized the rights of Croatia, governed by the *ban*, the third highest secular dignitary of Hungary. The Serbs, who had built successively two Empires in the Middle Ages, came under Ottoman rule after the battle of Mohacs in 1526. Migration to Hungary had begun in the fifteenth century. In the 1690s, the entire Serb population of Kosovo, led by the patriarch, sought refuge under the protection of the Austrian Emperor in newly reconquered Southern Hungary. The Serbs supplied the majority of the population in the Military Frontier and in four counties of the kingdom. They also established commercial settlements northwards, along the Danube.

Finally, two of the languages spoken in the Monarchy, Italian and Romanian, belonged to the Latin family. Vienna never questioned the status of Italian as language of culture and government. Romanian, on the other hand, was not given formal recognition, neither in Transylvania nor in Bukovina, where it was the language of the majority, nor in Eastern and Southern Hungary.

Populating the western (Austrian) half of the Empire, from Milan and Innsbrück to Prague and Graz, Italians, Germans, Slovenes and Czechs were Catholic, the latter brought back to the church by the Counter-Reformation after 1620. Protestantism survived only in some Styrian valleys. Taking advantage of the Patent of Toleration promulgated by Joseph II in 1781, which authorized all non-Catholic faiths with minor restrictions only, a few dissidents reconstituted Calvinist communities in Bohemia and Moravia.

On the other hand, the religious map of the Hungarian part of the Monarchy was even more variegated than the linguistic map, except in homogeneously Catholic Croatia. In spite of the persistent efforts of the dynasty, the Counter-Reformation achieved only partial success. One third of the Hungarians in the kingdom and the greater part in Transylvania remained Protestant, mainly Calvinist, with Lutheran and Unitarian (Socinian) pockets. A significant percentage of the Slovaks and of the old German communities belonged to the Lutheran church. This is the background which explains, on the one hand, the massive settlement, after 1720, of non-rebellious Catholic Germans, known as 'Swabians', in the depopulated territories, and the enthusiastic reaction of the Hungarians to the Patent of Toleration on the other hand.

The government succeeded in attracting the Ruthenians and almost half of the Romanians to the Uniat church, which conserved the Orthodox ritual and admitted marriage of the low clergy, but recognized the authority of the pope. The Serbs, privileged by Leopold I, stayed faithful to Orthodoxy, their patriarch and their bishops.

The population of Galicia and Lodomeria was composed of Catholic Poles, Uniat Ukrainians and Jews.

The emerging national awareness and confrontations can hardly be understood without taking into account the nineteenth-century concept of 'historical nation'. The term designated those groups which entered the Habsburg Empire with their constitutional law and institutions rooted in a medieval statehood: Croats, Czechs, Hungarians, Italians and Poles. Austro-Germans were in a more ambiguous position. Subjects of the Holy Roman Empire and faithful to the dynasty, they were also strongly attached to their small provincial fatherland. They shared no collective Austrian national awareness.

Slovaks, Slovenes, Ukrainians and Romanians, integrated in one of the historical entities and destitute of specific institutions, turned to a faraway past when looking for historical rights that would justify their claim to nationhood.

At the time of Joseph II, only German, Italian and Polish (the majority of the speakers of these three languages lived outside the Habsburg Empire) had an administrative, literary and scholarly status corresponding to the West European standard. Between 1770 and 1790, movements emerged within all other communities, for renovating and polishing the native language, so as to make it apt to convey contemporary culture and science. Dictionaries, grammars and national histories were compiled, periodicals launched, translation encouraged, reading clubs and theatres organized. Poets and writers, among them clerics of all denominations, became respected public figures. The names which follow illustrate the simultaneity of the linguistic awakening throughout the Monarchy: Josef Dobrovsky (1753–1829), Czech Jesuit, author of a dictionary and Vaclav Matej Kramerius (1753–1808), founder of Czech journalism; two Slovak priests, Anton Bernolak (1762–1813), author of a dictionary and Jura Palkovic (1763–1835), translator of the Bible; Valentin Vodnik (1758–1819), Slovene poet, translator of the Bible; the Hungarian György Bessenyei (1747–1811), philosopher and playwright, Ferenc Kazinczy (1759–1831), poet, translator, organizer of literary events, both Calvinists, and Miklos Révai (1749–1807), Piarist, founder of the first Hungarian newspaper, grammarian; three Romanian Uniat priests, linguists and historians, Gheorghe Sincai (1754–1816), Samuel Klein (1742–1806) and Petru Maior (1751–1821); Matija Rjelkovic (1732–1798), Croatian officer, poet; and Dositej Obradovic (1739–1811) Serb educator, translator of Chrysostom. The University Press of Pest played a paramount role in the national awakening of the peoples of the Monarchy. From 1777 to 1848, out of a total production of 1,490 titles, it published 558 books in the languages of the non-Magyar nationalities.

The Monarchy comprised three economic zones. The richest and best- performing Italian provinces would be lost after 1860. As to the two other zones, a customs-barrier separated, until 1851, the more urbanized hereditary provinces and Bohemia from rural Hungary, a protected market, together with Galicia, for the industry of the western provinces. In return, Hungary could sell its agricultural surplus to Austria and Bohemia. From the late eighteenth century on, Hungarian opponents as well as foreign observers and, following them, generations of historians, employed the adjective 'colonial' to qualify this system. Two American historians, David Good and John Komlos, have recently questioned the 'colonial' conception.

Development of transport became, already before 1848, the decisive lever of the Empire's economic progress. Railways attracted interest quite early on. On the eve of the revolution of 1848, the Austrian network comprised 1,622km of active railways. At the same time, the Hungarian network was only 150km. By 1857, Vienna was connected with Prague, Cracow and Budapest, and also with Trieste, by the spectacular Semmering line climbing up to 900m. The construction of this first mountain railway in the world was conducted by the Italian born engineer Karl von Ghega. Baron Wilhelm Engerth, engineer, developed a special articulated five-axle locomotive. Thanks to perfect adhesion to the track, it could negotiate sharp curves. In 1914, the total network approached 46,000km with c.24,000km in Austria and 22,000km in Hungary.

Besides the free flow of goods and persons enabled by the railway, two other factors were instrumental in achieving economic progress and integration: the postal and tele-communication service and the banking system. From the 1870s, postal traffic grew at an annual rate of 8–10 per cent. It attained in 1912 a volume of three and half billion items (letters, parcels, etc.), close to the relevant figure of France. Post offices numbering 17,000 operated in the Monarchy, most of them serving also as telegraph offices. The telegraph network was developed parallel to that of the railways and roads. Daily national papers could instantly publish reports from their correspondents of sensational events of interest to their readership. Press cables benefited from a 50 per cent discount. The first telephone exchange was opened in 1881. By 1918, all localities of some importance were connected to the telephone network.

The organization of a modern banking system started in 1855, when the Rothschilds, in association with several representatives of the old aristocracy, created their great merchant bank, the Creditanstalt. In both parts of the Monarchy, the rapid expansion of banks was stopped for several years by the 'Black Friday' of 9 May 1873. When the economy recovered, a more cautious policy permitted the development up of safe money markets in Vienna and Budapest controlled by some ten banks of major importance.

At the beginning of the twentieth century, the Monarchy's economic integration was practically achieved. The major part of the exchange was made within the common market constituted by the two halves of the Monarchy, and dependence from foreign products and markets was not too heavy. Until the war, the Monarchy exported primarily agricultural products and raw materials and imported, in return, industrial goods. In 1913, both Austria and Hungary felt, all in all, satisfied with the *Ausgleich*. The thesis of Hungarian under-development maintained by Austrian capitalists taking advantage of the customs union, as well as that of the general backwardness of the Austro-Hungarian economy, could hardly be upheld anymore.

The Monarchy benefited from a steady growth all through the nineteenth century, with a spectacular boom in the years following the *Ausgleich*. The stock-exchange crisis of 1873, which ruined thousands of small investors, had lasting effects on society and turned Austrian opinion away from liberalism, but had no long-term economic consequences. Like France, Austria-Hungary was, in 1914, a predominantly rural country equipped with a modern industry. Economic progress was evidenced by the success of the monetary reform of 1892, when the Monarchy, following the example of all developed countries, passed to the gold standard and adopted a new currency, the crown (*Krone* in German) worth 1.25 francs in parity with the German mark.

The Monarchy's strength was based on a fairly large population: 47 million in 1900, 51.4 million registered by the last census in 1910, including Bosnia-Herzegovina's 2 million inhabitants. Population density reached 95 per km^2 in Cisleithania and 62 per km^2 in Hungary, from respectively 67 and 48 in 1869. The annual growth of the population was higher in Austria (0.82) than in Hungary (0.74). Hungary's weaker demographic record was due partly to the emigration overseas of nearly 2 million persons, mainly landless peasants from the northern and eastern regions whom industry could not absorb.

The Austro-Hungarian economy was blooming, and heading towards greater prosperity, provided that the unity of the Monarchy was not broken. Nobility, clergy and privileged bodies dominated Austrian society until the conquests of 1848. Even more than in Western Europe, property in land alone conferred wealth and prestige. Peasants did possess hereditary tenures, the *Rustical*, but only by right of use and were subject to all kinds of dues, *Robot*, rent, tithes and state taxes. Outside Galicia, nobility did not mean a uniform status. Tradition as well as public law made a distinction between ordinary gentlemen and aristocrats. The lesser landed nobility carried no significant weight in Austria and Bohemia. The aristocracy comprised several hundred families in the Empire. They owned the land (up to 80 per cent in Bohemia), and thus concentrated in their hands the economic power (many manufactures located in rural areas belonged to them) and the political power in the provinces and in the Vienna government offices.

From the reign of Maria Theresa on, monarchs ennobled commoner civil servants and army officers at the end of their career. Aristocrats and gentlemen of the old nobility, the 'First Society' might well snub this service nobility, but the system had the merit of keeping ambitious commoners content. Instead of dreaming of revolutions, they committed themselves to their duty in the army or in the bureaucracy in order to obtain a higher social position. They formed the 'Second Society', a specifically Austrian grouping, devoted to the state and loyal to the dynasty. Long after the democratic enthusiasm of March 1848, power and prestige remained attached to aristocratic titles and property in land.

The Hungarian society of the *ancien régime* differed sharply from the West European pattern. Nobility, a conglomerate, united only by the common privileges of tax exemption, right to landed property and participation in public life, comprising fabulously rich aristocrats and well-to-do gentlemen, as well as tens of thousands of penniless peasant-nobles, journeymen and clerks, made up between 5 and 6 per cent of the population. The urban middle class of the privileged cities and boroughs, together with the peasants of the free districts, represented a comparable percentage. The peasantry, i.e. 90 per cent of the population, lived in rural settlements under seigniorial authority. In economic terms, the overwhelming majority of the population made its living from agriculture and husbandry.

The revolution of 1848 ended the age of seigniorial rule in both parts of the Monarchy. Peasants became free owners of their former holdings, totalling close to 50 per cent of the cultivated land. In Hungary, more than half of the peasantry, cotters and servants, had not possessed land except as tiny plots, gardens or vineyards. They were to form a large rural proletariat, supplying industrial manpower, immigrants to the US and the troops of agrarian socialism at the end of the nineteenth century. Aristocracy and gentry, however, retained their wealth and even, if short of wealth, their influence.

The traditional bourgeoisie of the Hungarian cities, few in number, lacked both capital and organizing capability to take the lead in building up a modern economy, based on competition and entrepreneurship. This role was assumed by the Jewish community, which grew from 100,000 in 1800 (1 per cent of the inhabitants) to 640,000 (4.6 per cent) in 1880, which saw the end of large-scale immigration, and to 940,000 (5 per cent) in 1910. The Hungarian political class welcomed the Jewish immigration because it gave the country a bourgeoisie of merchants, bankers and industrialists, and because the Jewish community became rapidly Hungarian-speaking. The Jewish religion received, in 1895, the 'legally admitted' status equal to that of the six Christian denominations of the country.

Until 1914, the dynasty constituted the only bond that united all subjects of the Empire, who were expected to be emotionally attached and faithful to the Emperor, the gracious and righteous father of his peoples. Francis I considered this bond more important than a strong, centralized, Josephist State or an Austrian national consciousness as dreamed of by his brother, archduke John.

The French Wars reinforced the dynasty's prestige. Emperor Francis, who acceded to the throne in 1792, some weeks before the declaration of war, braved all defeats until the final victory over Napoleon. His brother, archduke Charles, proved to be a great general and a remarkable organizer of the imperial army. The legitimacy of the House of Austria was questioned by none; its states had either belonged for centuries to the family's patrimony, like the alpine lands and the Duchy of Milan, or had freely elected a Habsburg king, as Bohemia and Hungary had done in 1526. Doubts were raised by the recent acquisitions only, because they were based on conquest (Galicia in 1772, Venice in 1797).

The people of Vienna genuinely liked Francis, being charmed by his simplicity and good nature. While the reign of Francis means for us government by censorship and political police, his subjects were satisfied with the image of a paternal and conservative Empire, consistent with their political culture. The splendour of the court enchanted them and the festivities organized for the Vienna Congress gave them the impression that they were living in the capital of Europe, restored and appeased thanks to twenty-five years of self-sacrificing efforts. In fact, Viennese burghers

and provincial peasants had hardly any interest in politics; they willingly left this field to aristocrats and civil servants. The Emperor governed with the assistance of some ministers. The most illustrious among them, Prince Metternich, was chancellor from 1809 to 1848. Until the end of the *ancien régime*, no genuine cabinet was formed in spite of Metternich's efforts to confer this status to the State Conference. The monarch, first bureaucrat of the Empire, reads and annotates the reports, undisturbed in his study – that is the way Francis Joseph conceived his mission throughout his reign, which lasted almost seventy years.

No Austrian national consciousness transcended the particular Bohemian, Styrian or Tyrolean sense of identity. After 1806, archduke John endeavoured with the help of baron Hormayr, to arouse an all-Austrian national awareness that would eclipse and federate provincial patriotisms and fortify fidelity to the monarch. The enterprise failed because the Emperor was not inclined to appeal to popular sentiment. One was contented with common symbols, such as the black and gold flag adorned with the two-headed eagle, inherited from the Holy Roman Empire, and the imperial anthem *Gott erhalte den Kaiser* (God save the Emperor), composed in 1797, on the English model by Joseph Haydn, and intended to become the 'anti-Marseillaise'.

Although Joseph II had reshaped its relations with the state, the Catholic church remained the most solid pillar of the House of Austria. In Hungary, the bishops, appointed by the king, rarely departed from a loyal subservience to the dynasty. From the reign of Joseph II on, the Hungarian practice of the *placetum regium* was extended to the whole Empire: bishops were forbidden to correspond directly with the Holy See or the papal nuncio in Vienna; seminars and faculties of theology were placed under government control.

Bishops and parish priests considered themselves as servants of the state. The church was in charge of elementary and secondary education. Many priests and friars taught in colleges. In Hungary and Galicia, the Order of Piarists (*Patres scholarum piarum*) pioneered modern education, giving an important place to natural sciences.

The army was placed under the direct and exclusive authority of the Emperor. In the multilingual and multiconfessional Empire, the officer corps represented a unique melting pot. Commoners could easily join it; they supplied the large majority of officers in the 'learned arms' (artillery, engineering, medicine). The proportion of noble officers was high only in the cavalry and in some prestigious *Jäger* (Light infantry) regiments. In principle, military service was universal. After 1867, all conscripts served three years in the joint army. The political and strategic importance of the militia, called *Landwehr* in Austria and *honvédség* in Hungary, was gradually growing. Until the end of the Monarchy, German served as common language of command. In each regiment, recruited within a given territory, the ranks were addressed in their mother tongue.

The two halves of the Monarchy came to the *Ausgleich* with quite different legislative and administrative traditions. In Cisleithania, each province had had its diet since the fifteenth century. Suspended by Joseph II, restored by Leopold II, they progressively lost their role in lawmaking and financial competency. In 1811, the Emperor promulgated the new Civil Code without consulting the diets, and their consent was no longer needed for levying new taxes. Local administration and justice, traditionally dispensed by the seigneury (*Herrschaft*), passed under state control in the eighteenth century. The reforms of Maria Theresa and Joseph II laid the foundations of Austria's famous bureaucracy: a smoothly operating machine, unbiased, honest, not too dynamic, not eager to assume responsibilities but capable of keeping together the country by the effoprts of its personnel, its language and its methods. Hungary preserved, except during the Josephist and neo-absolutist interregnums, its representative institutions. Its bicameral Diet adopted the laws, voted the taxes and submitted the grievances of the nation to the monarch. The upper house, composed of prelates and magnates loyal to the dynasty, was the stronghold of conservatism. The lower house, elected from the nobility of the forty-nine counties, was often in conflict with the Court. The four last sessions of the Diet, in 1832–6, 1839–40, 1843–4 and 1847–8, forged the strongest liberal movement in Central Europe, and prepared the 'lawful revolution' of 1848.

From 1825, when he founded the Academy of Sciences, until the revolution of 1848, count Istvan Széchenyi (1791–1860), a liberal aristocrat, inspired and conducted the effort for fighting under-development. In three books, *Credit, Light* and *Stadium*, published between 1830 and 1833, he advocated immediate measures that would make progress possible. His main achievement was the construction between Buda and Pest of the Chain Bridge, overseen by two British engineers, Adam Clark and William Tierney Clark.

Because of an overcautious censorship, until the 1840s, political journalism was limited to scholarly or literary periodicals. The first high-quality and influential newspaper, the *Pesti Hirlap* (Gazette of Pest) was edited by Lajos Kossuth (1802–94), the charismatic leader of the liberal opposition and of revolutionary Hungary. The press grew and diversified rapidly.

A group of young writers and scholars undertook, in the 1840s to outline the institutional reforms needed to enter modernity. They received the nickname of 'centralists' because they demonstrated that no progress towards democracy was possible without getting rid of the nobiliary county. Baron Joseph Eötvös (1812–71), a liberal statesman and thinker, akin to Alexis de Tocqueville, directed the 'centralist' campaign. The author of numerous essays (on the emancipation of the Jews, prison reform, etc.), he published in exile his classic treatise on the *Influence on the State of the Principal Ideas of the Nineteenth Century*.

No state service operated in pre-1848 Hungary at the lower levels. Field administration was in the hands of the elected county officers, noblemen by definition, who were also supposed to implement the orders and instructions of the Lord Lieutenancy, representing the royal power. The tradition proved to be ineradicable. Long after the Compromise and the establishment of a parliamentary system, repeated government attempts to nationalize the administration were rebuffed. The election of county officers, although no longer necessarily nobles, lasted until the end of Austria-Hungary.

Freemasonry, forbidden in 1796 in the whole Monarchy, was restored in Hungary after 1867. In 1913, 95 lodges operated in 55 towns of Hungary and Croatia. They were deeply involved in the campaign for universal suffrage, and conducted extensive poor-relief activities. As the prohibition was not lifted in Austria, several German-speaking lodges were created near the border and the journal of the Grand Lodge was also published in German.

In implementing the Compromise with Hungary, Francis Joseph operated a constitutional reform introducing ministerial responsibility in Austria. Because of the extremely complex national question, the embittered conflict between Czechs and Germans and an increasingly enraged and influential anti-Semitic propaganda, the parliament was often paralysed. Nevertheless, Austria was on its way to democracy. Universal (male) suffrage was introduced in 1907. The Austrian Social Democrats became a major parliamentary party and developed an original doctrine of 'Austro-Marxism' aimed at resolving the national problem without destroying the Monarchy. They proposed to confer equal status on all national-linguistic communities, independently of their territorial distribution.

The Hungarian political class, obsessed by the danger of losing Magyar supremacy and by the prospect of socialists dominating the parliament, resisted to the end the electoral reform. Voting rights remained restricted to no more than a fifth of the adult male population. In spite of a democratic deficit in political life, the principles of nineteenth-century liberalism and the rule of law were observed in the Monarchy. The press was free, hundreds of periodicals were published in all languages, and even middle-range provincial towns could have two or three daily papers. In 1883, an allegation of ritual murder against the Jews of Tiszaeszlar was firmly rejected by the judicial and political authorities, and those accused were acquitted. Courts gave nationalist and socialist 'agitators' fair treatment; most actions against 'subversion' ended with acquittal or the early release of those sentenced to imprisonment.

For posterity, Vienna from the 1780s to the 1820s means Music with a capital M. The four greatest composers of the time, Haydn, Mozart, Beethoven and Schubert, lived in or near Vienna. The Viennese public, conservative in its musical tastes, kept its attachment to the Italian opera. Rossini had many successes after 1820, while Beethoven's *Fidelio* was a total fiasco. After the death of Beethoven and Schubert, Vienna continued to be a metropolis of music, although no great composer chose it for residence until the 1870s.

Vienna of the time of the Holy Alliance developed the Biedermeier style, corresponding to the taste of a well-to-do bourgeoisie. The furniture and decoration of this period, less cold than Empire style and more elegant than Louis-Philippe, is functional and cosy. People in Vienna, even if poor, were light-hearted, frequented inns in the suburbs and, above all, theatres and balls. One danced in Vienna for forgetting one's troubles or just for pleasure. The waltz, developed from the Tyrolean *Ländler*, appeared around 1815. It brought a revolution. In contrast to the solemn and chaste court dances, couples danced entwined, scandalizing the moralists. Two orchestras shared between them the public's favour, that, more gentle, of Joseph Lanner, and that of Johann Strauss the elder, more flamboyant.

Franz Grillparzer (1791–1872), major dramatist of the Biedermeier period, benefited from a sinecure as director of the Treasury archives. His tragedies exalting the history of the House of Habsburg were staged in the Burgtheater, dedicated since Joseph II's time to hosting the German-language repertoire. Many popular stages, like the famous Leopoldstadt theatre, performed plays in Viennese dialect. They are now forgotten, except for those of Ferdinand Raimund (1790–1836) and Johann Nepomuk Nestroy (1801–62), which are still acted. Plays were produced in impressive quantities. Each author had to supply at least ten pieces per year in order to satisfy a public eager for novelty. Nestroy, who made egotism the motive behind his dramatic action, professed a disenchanted vision of the world disguised beneath humour. His plays suited the temper of the Viennese burgher, frivolous in appearance, pessimist and anxious in fact.

Similar features characterized the way of life of the upper classes. Balls were organized in the aristocratic palaces, especially in carnival time. Cafés served already for socializing, but public theatres remained the favourite meeting places of high society: the Theater an der Wien, the Opera and the Burgtheater.

The imperial capital had no cultural monopoly. As in the time of the Enlightenment, the Czech national movement, focusing on a cultural and linguistic programme, had for driving forces artists and scholars. The Bohemian aristocracy had created the Theatre of the Estates in Prague in 1782. A generation later, an bilingual nobility took an active part in the foundation of the Royal Scientific Society, the Prague Conservatoire and the National Museum created in 1818. These institutions were soon to become tools in the fight for national revival and centres for the dissemination of Slav culture. A first task consisted in restoring the literary reputation of the Czech language, because scholars like the linguist Josef Dobrovsky or the historian Frantisek Palacky (1798–1876) published their works in Latin or German. Joseph Jungmann (1773–1847), made an outstanding contribution to the national cultural renaissance by publishing, between 1835 and 1839, his great Czech-German dictionary.

In Hungary too, poetry and scholarship, linguistics and history were intimately associated with the 'awakening' of the nation and the advent of liberal political thought. The age of Enlightenment began in Hungary with the discovery that classical metric prosody was compatible with the Magyar language. After two generations of language renovators, Mihaly Vörösmarty (1800–55) inaugurated the age of national classicism. Born into a Catholic family of the petty nobility, he was the creator of a Hungarian mythology, the author of philosophic and lyric poems acclaimed by the public. Editor of various periodicals, he founded the review *Athenaeum*. He translated Shakespeare and admired Victor Hugo.

Two poets of popular origin, Sandor Petöfi (1823–49) and Janos Arany (1817–82) brought the national classicism to its plenitude. Petöfi, Lutheran by religion, the son of a South Slav innkeeper and a Slovak servant, was the first Hungarian lyricist to achieve immediate praise abroad. Nationalist and revolutionary in his poetry and in his action, he was the leader of 'Young Hungary', the circle of radical intellectuals. The revolution of 15 March 1848 began with Petöfi declaiming his *Rise, Hungarian!* to the crowd. Aide-de-camp to General Bem, he disappeared in the battle of Sighisoara on 31 July 1849. His close friend, Janos Arany, from a Calvinist peasant family, is still considered as the unequalled master of the Hungarian language. He wrote epic poems and ballads, translated Aristophanes and Shakespeare, and presided over the most prestigious literary society of the country. He was after 1865 the secretary general of the Hungarian Academy.

The Croats also formulated their political and cultural claims. The nobility requested a greater autonomy for the Diet and the union of all Southern Slavs. Metternich regarded this 'Illyrian' movement, born under the short-lived French administration (1809–13), with favour. Influenced by the distinguished Slovene linguist and Court Librarian Bartholomaeus Kopitar (1780–1844), he viewed 'Illyrism' as a counterweight to the Hungarian pressure. Ljudevit Gaj (1809–71), writer and editor of the journal *Novine Hrvatske*, undertook to coin a South Slav literary language based on the Dalmatian *Stokav* dialect rather than on his native Croatian mother tongue. Gaj proposed a South Slav union under Habsburg authority, intended to contain pro-Russian pan-slavism. After the conclusion of the Hungaro-Croatian compromise of 1868, Josip Juraj Strossmayer (1815–1905), bishop of Djakovo, became the leading personality of the Illyrian movement. He advocated a political and cultural union of Southern Slavs and, together with the historian Franjo Racki (1829–94), he was instrumental in founding the Yugoslav Academy of Sciences in Zagreb and in promoting the unification of the Serbo-Croatian literary language.

After ten years of struggle, the Croatian diet obtained a university in Zagreb, intended to raise the cultural level of all South Slav lands. At first the university comprised three faculties only: theology, law and arts. Sciences and medicine were added after 1900. The opening of the university in 1874 symbolized nevertheless the integration of Croatia into learned Europe. Developments in academia and the reform of primary education were significant indicators of progress.

Lutheran intellectuals took over the leadership of the Slovak national movement in the 1820s. While Jan Kollar (1793–1852), minister and poet, and Josef Safarik (1795–1861), historian and Librarian of Prague University, called for Slav reciprocity and close ties between Czechs and Slovaks, L'judevit Stur (1816–56) editor of the *Slovenskie Narodné Noviny*, fought for the recognition of a distinct Slovak identity. Slovak efforts at obtaining political autonomy were severely handicapped by the fact that the Slovak elite, in particular the Slovak-speaking nobility, accepted linguistic assimilation in the dominant Hungarian nation.

The rise of Vienna as a modern metropolis dates from 25 December 1858. The *Wiener Zeitung* of that day gazetted a rescript of Francis Joseph ordering the demolition of the useless fortifications (they could not prevent the occupation of the city by Napoleon in 1805 and 1809) and authorizing the Treasury to sell the land between the ramparts and the suburbs. The Ringstrasse was thus born under neo-absolutism. Along the Ringstrasse, prestigious apartment houses, characterized by impressive staircases, were let to the well-to-do, government officials, businessmen and professionals. The Ringstrasse was also the site of private mansions and public buildings.

Prominent architects, like the Dane Theophil Hansen, architect of the Parliament and the Viennese Siccardsburg, and van der Null, who built the Opera, endeavoured to make the best use of the extremely expensive ground. For aesthetic reasons they also harmonized their projects, copying styles of the past in the spirit of historicism. Monumental buildings, constructed between 1870 and 1900, accentuated the majestic appearance of the Ring. The Opera was constructed in a style inspired by the Italian Renaissance. Semper and Hasenauer added a neo-baroque wing to the Burg, constructed the new Burgtheater and, facing the Hofburg, two museums (the Kunsthistorisches Museum and the Naturhistorisches Museum). Further north on the Ring, various architectural styles were adopted according to the vocation of the building: Flemish gothic for the City Hall, Italian Renaissance for the University, Grecian for the Parliament.

As soon as they came to power, the liberals were determined to reshape Vienna. The municipality concentrated on the creation of parks, the regulation of the Danube, water supply and public health. The main epidemic diseases disappeared after 1880, except tuberculosis. Slums were removed to the periphery and, in the districts around the Ring, many huge tenement houses (*Mietkasernen*) were constructed, but the housing shortage could not be overcome before the First World War.

During the Metternich era, from 1808 to 1848, study directors appointed by the government kept higher education under close watch. They had also to supervise rectors and faculty deans commissioned to control the texts of the lectures, which professors had to submit in advance. If they discarded the official programme they could be suspended, as happened to the philosopher Bolzano.

Few universities existed then (Prague, Cracow, Lemberg/Lwow, Buda, Graz and Innsbruck) besides that of Vienna, uncommonly apathetic because of the well established practice of appointing docile professors towards the end of their career. As universities were supposed to educate obedient subjects, the reforms carried out in Berlin by Alexander von Humboldt and adopted also by universities in Northern Germany were disregarded in Vienna. The faculty of arts remained dormant until 1848 because higher education served exclusively vocational purposes. Universities had to train priests, civil servants, professors and physicians. Higher technical education was therefore favoured. In 1815, a Polytechnic School opened in Vienna. It produced well qualified engineers and played a role similar to that of its Paris model. Johann-Joseph Prechtl, who paid close attention to the progress of science and technology, directed the School for thirty years. But despite their limitations, Austrian universities were remarkably successful. The faculty of law of Vienna increased fivefold the number of its students between 1810 and 1848, contributing thus to the growth of bureaucracy. Besides young aristocrats and sons of civil servants, the University recruited also poor students, who paid for their studies by giving lessons.

During the neo-absolutist era, surveillance of universities became tougher. In 1850, after the publication of the third volume of his *History of the Czech Nation*, Palacky was silenced and two years later discharged from his office at the National Museum. In 1851, the philosopher Alfred Smetana was deprived of his chair at Prague University, at the request of the Catholic church, because he did not hide his sympathy for Hegel. The Minister of Public Education and Cults, count Leo Thun, a Catholic conservative, refused, however, to put higher education under church control in order to prevent the Austrian university becoming an intellectual ghetto. He adopted the Prussian model and granted autonomy to the universities, against the commitment that they would recruit Catholic professors only and ban those books which had been put on the Index. He suppressed the two preparatory years at the faculty of arts. Universities underwent forced Germanization, except that of Cracow, where Polish was maintained, while German was used in Lwow/Lemberg. In 1882, Prague University was split into two, a Czech and a German university. The latter had 2,200 students; as the oldest academic establishment in Central Europe, it attracted professors from Germany and thus could preserve a high standards in law, medicine and the arts.

With a view to promote consciousness of a common history, count Thun founded at Vienna University, on the model of the French Ecole des Chartes, the Institut für Österreichische Geschichtsforschung (Institute for Austrian Historical Research), intended to bypass the national approaches to history. This objective could not be achieved because Czechs and Hungarians refused to reappraise their national history from the standpoint of the *Gesamtmonarchie*. Under the direction of Theodor von Sickel, from 1868 to 1883, the Institute became one of the leading centres in Europe for medieval history, auxiliary sciences and archival studies.

Count Thun fostered also the development of the Austrian Academy of Sciences, founded on the eve of the revolution of 1848, after a century and half of procrastination and twenty-three years after the founding of the Hungarian Academy of Sciences. Yet intellectual life was paralysed by the intolerance of the authorities. Austria could not fully benefit from these new institutions until the era of dualism. Scholarship then achieved significant results in a wide range of disciplines, and university professors lacked neither time nor spirit to engage in research.

The Monarchy had a particularly remarkable record in historical sciences. The Sickel Institute and the fabulously rich public archives in Vienna provided solid foundations for historical research in all parts of the Monarchy. Some names, chosen at random, will illustrate the riches and vitality of the Monarchy in this field: Alfred von Arneth (1819–97), director of the State Archives, author of a monumental history of Maria-Theresa; Franz von Krones (1835–1902), author of a General History of Austria in five volumes; and Alfred Francis Pribram (1859–1942), specialist in the seventeenth-century – in Austria; Arpad Karolyi (1853–1940), the first Hungarian student of Sickel, archivist and then director of the State Archives from 1877 to 1909, specialist in Austro-Hungarian relations; Henrik Marczali (1856–1940), and Laszlo Fejérpataky (1857–1923), who introduced modern research methods at Budapest university – in Hungary; Antonin Gindely (1829–92), director of the National Archives of Prague, specialist in the Czech Brethren; Jaroslav Goll (1846–1929), master of methodology and author of *Bohemia and Prussia in the Middle Ages*; and Josef Pekar (1870–1937), disciple of Goll and editor of the *Cesky Historicky Casopis*, all three professors at Prague University – in Bohemia.

In medicine, the Vienna school, founded by Karl Rokitansky (1804–78) acquired an international reputation with Ignace Semmelweis (1818–65), 'the saviour of mothers'; Ferdinand Hebra (1816–80), founder of scientific dermatology; and many other outstanding physicians. In 1914, Robert Barany (1876–1936), otologist, received the Nobel Prize for Medicine.

During the liberal era, Johannes Brahms, born in Hamburg, was Vienna's greatest composer. The public adopted him and so did the formidable critic, Eduard Hanslick, who praised his symphonic compositions as well as his chamber music (*Lieder* and quartets). Billroth, the great surgeon, reviving the tradition of early nineteenth-century aristocrats, offered soirées in his honour. Anton Bruckner, composer and Court Organist, and Hugo Wolf represented an anti-rationalist tendency. Hanslick fiercely opposed Richard Wagner, but could not prevent his success, supported obstinately by the conductor Hans Richter. The Opera, funded by the privy purse of Francis Joseph, regained its full splendour after 1869, under the direction of Wilhelm Jahn. Gustav Mahler, brilliant conductor and composer of genius, became director in 1897.

Musical life had, besides the Opera, other prestigious centres, such as the Musikverein (Society of the Friends of Music), which constantly gained importance from Schubert's time onwards.

Vienna did not give up light music. The Vienna operetta gently eclipsed Offenbach. Johann Strauss the younger (1825–99), the 'Waltz King' (*The Blue Danube, Tales from the Vienna Woods, Kaiserwalzer*, etc.) was also a master in lyric composition (e.g. *Die Fledermaus* and *Zigeunerbaron*). Franz Lehar revived the tradition of the Vienna operetta in the early 1900s.

Popular music, so important in Vienna's cultural life, contributed to glorifying the myth of the *Wiener Gemütlichkeit*, the charming conviviality of the imperial capital. Christian socialists contrived to make of it the credo of the petty bourgeoisie and popular circles.

Musical life was rich in all parts of the Monarchy. Bedrich Smetana (1824–84) and Antonin Dvořák (1841–1904) attracted worldwide attention to Czech music. Franz Liszt (1811–86) travelled all over Europe but kept in contact with his native country. In 1875, he accepted the presidency of the newly founded Budapest Academy of Music.

Hugo von Hofmannsthal belonged also to the generation of 'Vienna 1900', disappointed with liberalism and tormented by a rising anti-Semitism and the militant comeback of clerical conservatism. An intellectual elite of Jewish descent, assimilated and more or less detached from religion, dominated the Second Society, breeding ground of Austrian creativity and refuge for frustrated ambitions. Sons of successful industrialists determined not to pursue the family business were excluded from top government and diplomatic posts, reserved for the aristocracy, while they had free access to medicine, art, journalism and literature. Some of them, like Victor Adler and Otto Bauer, found a shelter in the social democratic ideal, while others fled to the cult of *l'art pour l'art* and invented modernity. Hugo von Hoffmanstahl (1874–1929) admired in his early youth as a master of lyric poetry, made a career as a playwright. He revived the baroque theatre through translations and his taste for medieval mystery plays. He supplied libretti to Richard Strauss, in particular that of the *Rosenkavalier*, a double evocation of the Court of the eighteenth century and of Vienna 1900. Hofmannsathl's œuvre expresses the subtle style of Vienna society.

Arthur Schnitzler (1862–1931), equally important as a playwright, had a much more caustic mind. A neurologist, he affects towards humankind a deeply pessimistic tolerance. His comedies, frivolous in appearance, unmask Viennese society, criticize its codes and denounce its foibles. The conventional amorous intrigues of his plays could actually be misapprehended and staged in a way that missed the social satire inherent in them. Schnitzler's comedies, interspersed with sayings in Viennese dialect, had a tremendous success and a wide audience. In *Liebelei*, he presented the theme of the young girl from the suburbs (*das süsse Mädel*), who becomes an easy prey for the young gentleman. In the story *Leutnant Güstl* (1900), he showed the absurdity of duelling. The text caused a scandal and Schnitzler was deprived, in 1904, of his rank of medical reserve officer. In his novel *Der Weg ins Frei*, set in the famous Café Griensteindl, he raised the issue of the place of the Jews in the Viennese society. His play *Professor Bernhardi*

features a Jewish doctor who refuses to frighten his seriously ill patient by calling a priest to give the last rites.

The new generation of writers of the Young Vienna group had not much in common, except the will to challenge bourgeois culture and its moralizing. They chose for their leader Hermann Bahr, who had lived in Paris and Berlin and whose ideas were superior to the plays he wrote. As a drama critic he supported Schnitzler, opposed the scenery style of Makart, frowned on pompous declamation, and defended unpretentious staging. Franz Werfel from Prague and the Viennese Stefan Zweig and Robert Musil, somewhat younger, revealed already in this period their talents as novelists and essayists. They would write their main works after 1918.

Nevertheless, in conformity with the tradition, Vienna 1900 achieved more in music and in the fine arts than in literature. The generation of 1900 turned resolutely against the aesthetic rules professed by Hanslick and illustrated by Johannes Brahms, although the innovations of the young Arnold Schönberg and the symphonies of Gustav Mahler left the music-loving public unmoved. Schönberg was carrying out a musical revolution, rejecting the traditional tonal system and introducing dodecaphonism, or the twelve-tone or 'atonal' system, which required a complete re-education of the ear. It took fifty years before atonality, developed in the 1910s, was accepted by audiences. Nevertheless, the fact is that Schönberg, with Alban Berg and Anton von Webern, made a revolutionary contribution to twentieth-century Western music with the creation of what musicologists call the Second Vienna School.

Young artists drew inspiration from French impressionism, Belgian naturalism, English Pre-Raphaelitism and German *Jugendstil*. They all agreed to reject realism, and they undertook a quest for the essence of modern man. This was the Vienna Secession movement, with Gustav Klimt as its most gifted painter. Architecture went through a complete renewal with Otto Wagner, who, at the age of seventy, constructed the first building in concrete. It happened to be the *Sezession* house. Adolf Loos provoked a scandal when he designed for Michaelerplatz, opposite the Hofburg, the Savings Bank, the first modern building with an unadorned façade. This building, in its classical simplicity, constitutes a landmark in the history of twentieth-century architecture.

The most famous figure of Vienna 1900 is Sigmund Freud, a perfect representative of the Viennese intellectual. He was born in a totally assimilated Jewish family originating from Bohemia. After brilliant success in his medical studies, he went to Paris for an internship in the neurologist Charcot's department at the Salpetrière Hospital. Frustrations in his own life helped him to develop his method of the interpretation of dreams, to explore the subconscious and, eventually, to create the psychoanalytic therapeutic procedure, in which, after lengthy sessions, the patient comes to reveal the hidden aspects of her or his personality. He was convinced that the experiences of infancy acted on the adult's behaviour. He proposed to explain the personality with reference to early emotional relations with the mother and to the Oedipus complex, which Freud held to be the subconscious desire of the son to kill his father in order to liberate himself. In a sense, the Oedipus complex affected all Viennese intellectuals of his generation. 'Psychoanalysis' attracted a prodigious following, first in Vienna, then in Central Europe (the Hungarian Psychoanalytical Society was created in 1913) and finally all over the world. The disaster of 1918 did not interrupt Freud's activities. It was only the later *Anschluss* with Nazi Germany that forced him to seek refuge in England in 1938.

The evolution of Budapest runs parallel to that of Vienna, although with some peculiar features. It became a genuine capital in 1867 only, but it succeeded in building up, at an impressive pace, infrastructures in administration, education, economy, public health and communications necessary to govern a country rapidly approaching 20 million inhabitants.

Like Vienna, which Germanized its immigrants from all over the Empire, Budapest became the Magyarizing melting pot. It assimilated the German-speaking part of the population (as much as 56 per cent in 1850) comprising old-established burghers as well as workers and engineers from Cisleithania and Jewish immigrants of German or Yiddish mother tongue. Budapest was the country's only city with a million inhabitants by 1914. The University of Budapest lost its monopoly when Cluj (1872) and Zagreb (1874) received their universities, but continued to accommodate three quarters of teaching staff and students. The universities of Pressburg and Debrecen only began operating in 1914. All major publishers, learned societies, museums, libraries and periodicals were headquartered in Budapest, which represented 60 per cent of the printing capacity of the country. By 1900, the number of books published per year passed 5,000, and Hungary had its first comprehensive encyclopaedia, the eighteen-volume *Pallas Lexikon*.

The splendour of the city and the progress of the nation were celebrated, in 1896, by the self-admiring festivities of the Millennium (the thousandth anniversary of the conquest of the country by the confederation of Magyar tribes), a National Fair, the inauguration of the first metro line of the continent, and the Millenary Monument closing the perspective of the city's main avenue. With the construction of three road- and two railway bridges, the embankments, boulevards and avenues, and the completion of the Royal Palace, Budapest received its current urban and architectural aspect. Miklos Ybl (1812–96) planned the Opera, the new wing of the Royal Palace and the High Court, as well as churches, thermal baths, banks and aristocratic mansions. The gigantic Parliament on the riverbank, reminiscent of the Westminster Parliament, cradle of the parliamentary system, due to Imre Steindl (1839–1902), became the emblem of the city. Ödön Lechner (1845–1914), architect of the Museum of Applied Arts and also of the town halls in Szeged and Kecskemét, and Zsigmond Quittner (1857–1918) architect of the Gresham Palace, facing the Chain Bridge on the Pest side, pioneered art nouveau in Hungary.

Jozsef Kiss (1843–1921), creator of a Hungarian-Jewish poetry, opened his literary journal *A Hét* (The Week) to the new generation, pioneering the aesthetic revolution and democratic thought. The new intellectual elite broke abruptly with the comfortable self-complacency of its elders, a complacency still intoxicated with the glory of 1848, the success of 1867, the liberal deceit and an aggressive nationalism. By a striking coincidence, the leading talents of the generation of 1900 in art, literature and scholarship were born between 1875 and 1885: the poets Endre Ady (1877–1919), Mihaly Babits (1883–1941) and Dezsö Kosztolanyi (1885–1936); the novelists Gyula Krudy (1878–1933), Ferenc Mora (1879–1934) and Zsigmond Moricz (1879–1942); the composers Ernö Dohnanyi (1877–1960), Béla Bartok (1881–1945) and Zoltan Kodály (1882–1967); the

mathematicians Lipot Fejér (1880–1959) and Frigyes Riesz (1880–1956); the sociologist Oszkar Jaszi (1875–1957), the philosopher György Lukács (1885–1971), the historian Gyula Szekfü (1883–1955) and the critic and essayist Dezsö Szabo(1879–1945).

In its lifestyle, Budapest resembled Vienna. In both capitals, the 1900s were the golden age of cafés (Budapest had some 600 of them) and of journalism. Columnists, poets and critics gathered, wrote and discussed in their habitual cafés. Readership of the old liberal papers (*Pesti Naplo, Pesti Hirlap* and *Budapesti Hirlap*) was declining. Penny papers appeared in 1896, and the some twenty other daily papers tended to politicize and to side with one or another party or group, ranging from the ultramontane and anti-Semitic right to the radical and social-democratic left.

For John Lukács, the exceptional quality of secondary education, rather than the universities, was the origin of the cultural blooming of the 1900s. It explains also the impressive careers of many expatriate scientists, like Philipp Leonard, the German Nobel laureate (1905) in physics. According to Gyula Szekfü, disciple of Marczali, the most influential historian after 1918, the assimilated Jewish bourgeoisie and professionals played a decisive role in producing and nurturing new sensibilities, new curiosities and new trends.

In fact a significant proportion of prominent intellectuals were of Jewish descent: Marczali, Fejér, Riesz, Lukács and Jaszi among those mentioned above; Imre Kalman (1882–1953) composer of operettas, Ervin Szabo (1877–1918) historian and translator of Marx, and Ferenc Molnar (1878–1952), novelist and playwright, one of the rare Hungarian writers who could overcome linguistic isolation.

The first decade of the century also saw a restructured periodical press. Two literary journals acquired national readership, the conservative *Uj Idök* (New Times) edited by the novelist Ferenc Herczeg (1853–1954) and favoured by the genteel society, and the progressive *Nyugat* (Occident) edited by the critic Ignotus (Hugo Veigelsberg, 1869–1949). Ady, whose volume *Uj Versek* (New Poems) made a tremendous impact on the literary life of the country, joined the *Nyugat* staff. Continuing the long literary tradition of drawing inspiration from France, Ady shared his time between Paris and Budapest. As a journalist and as a poet he raged against the governing politicians, who refused to understand that Hungary had no future without passing to democracy. Babits, less engaged in politics than Ady, belonged also from the beginning to the *Nyugat* team. He would become, after the First World War, editor of the journal and the leading personality of Hungarian letters, and in the 1930s was to translate Dante's *Divine Comedy*.

The two great romantic writers and storytellers of the nineteenth century, Mor Jokai and Kalman Mikszath, died in 1905 and 1910 respectively. The new prose followed other directions: naturalism with Moricz, novelist of peasant tragedies, and impressionism with Krudy, who invented a new way of writing with no plot, nor events, but only images, memories, dreams and nostalgia.

The education offered by the Academy of Music of Budapest attained a level comparable to that given in the Vienna conservatoire. Like Schönberg and Alban Berg in Vienna, Bartok endeavoured, with the help of Kodály, to break the tonal system, but with a different approach. He conducted extensive research on the folk music of the peoples of Hungary and Transylvania (Hungarians, Slovaks, Romanians) first, and then of Turkey and North Africa. He created a new musical language based on the ancestral legacy outshone in the nineteenth century by the Gypsy music which inspired Brahms. Bartok, one of the most important composers of the twentieth century, obtained public recognition in 1916, when his ballet *The Wooden Prince* was produced at the Budapest Opera. The major part of his instrumental œuvre was composed after the First World War.

Czech literature of the 1900s was as rich as that of Hungary in talent, with writers such as the poets Viktor Dyk and Karel Toman, the novelists Jakub Deml, a priest, Stanislav K. Neumann, an anarchist, Jaroslav Hašek, author of *Infanterist Svejk* (*The Good Soldier Schweik*), Frana Sramek, and Karel Sezima, all of whom were born around 1880. And yet, overshadowed by Vienna, Prague appeared to be a capital in decline.

The German press (*Bohemia* and *Prager Tagblatt*), distributed throughout the kingdom, retained its quality and remained faithful to the liberal tradition. German-speaking Prague gave birth to brilliant writers, most of them bilingual. When Rainer Maria Rilke (1875–1926) left his home town, he did not opt for Vienna, but for Paris, where he met with fame. The other prominent writers who would continue to produce after 1918, Franz Kafka (1883–1924), Max Brod (1884–1968) and Franz Werfel (1890–1945), belonged to the wealthy Jewish bourgeoisie which, unlike that of Budapest, adopted German and not the national language. They formed small literary circles in contact with Berlin, Vienna and Paris. Beyond their attachment to their milieu, they participated in a multinational European culture.

The history of the Monarchy comes to an end in 1918. *Finis Austriae* began seven decades of unprecedented suffering for all the nations which succeeded the Empire. More than once they were to lose their intellectual elite, killed, banned or forced into exile. Composers like Bartok and Schönberg, painters, conductors, film directors and scientists, including all the Austrian and Hungarian Nobel laureates of the 1920s and 1930s, left their country and went to enrich the art and science of happier nations. The descendants of the subjects of Francis Joseph now live in twelve different states. All these nations retain the signs of Habsburg times in the architecture of their towns and cities, from Ljubljana to L'viv and from Plzen to Brasov, as well as in their approach to artistic and scholarly values. They share a common European cultural heritage.

BIBLIOGRAPHY

BARANY, G. 1968. *Stephen Szechényi and the awakening of the Hungarian Nationalism 1791–1841*. Princeton University Press, Princeton.

BAREA, I. 1966. *Vienna. Legend and Reality*. London.

BÉRENGER, J. 1976. *L'Europe danubienne de 1848 à 1970*, Coll. 'Le fil des Temps', p. 266. Presses Universitaires de France, Paris.

——. 1978. *Lexique historique de l'Europe danubienne*. Lexique U. A. Colin, Paris.

——. 1978. *La Tchécoslovaquie*. 'Que Sais-je?', no. 1726, p. 128. Presses Universitaires de France, Paris.

——. 1994. Histoire de l'Autriche. Coll. Que Sais-je ? no. 222, p. 128. Presses Universitaires de France, Paris.

——. 1997. *A History of the Habsburg Empire 1700–1918*. p. 342. Longman, London.

DE BERTIER DE SAUVIGNY, G. 1982. *Metternich*. Fayard, Paris.

BLED, J.-P. 1987. *François-Joseph*. Fayard, Paris.

——. 1988. *Les fondements du conservatisme autrichien 1859–1879*. Publications de la Sorbonne, Paris.

——. 1984–1992. *Etudes danubiennes*. (Periodical). Rédacteur en chef, Strasbourg.

BRIX, E. 1982. *Die Umgangsprachen in Altösterreich zwischen Agitation und Assimilation. Die Sprachenstatistik in den zisleithanischen Volkszählungen 1880 bis 1910* [The Spoken Languages in Ancient Austria between Agitation and Assimilation]. Böhlau, Vienna.

BRUSATTI, A. 1973. (ed.) *Die Habsburgermonarchie 1848–1918. In: Die wirtschaftliche Entwicklung* [The Habsburg Monarchy I: The Econommic Development]. Akademie Verlag, Vienna.

DEAK, I. 1979. *The lawful revolution. Louis Kossuth and the Hungarians (1848–1849)*. Columbia University Press, New York.

——. 1990. *Beyond Nationalism. A Social and Political History of the Habsburg Officer Corps, 1848–1918*. Oxford University Press, New York.

FILLITZ, H. 1996. *Der Traum von Glück. Die Kunst des Historismus in Europa* [Gluck's Dream. The Art of Historicism in Eurpe. Exhibition catalogue]. 2 vols, p. 706. Vienna.

GOOD, D. F. 1984. *The Economic Rise of the Habsburg Empire 1750–1914*. California University Press, Berkeley.

HAMANN, B. 1985. *Elisabeth Impératrice d'Autriche*. Fayard. Paris.

——. 1988. (ed.) *Die Habsburger. Ein biographisches Lexikon* [The Habsburgs. A Biographical Dictionary]. Vienna.

——. 1996. *Hitlers Wien. Lehrjahre eines Diktators* [Hitler's Vienna. Apprenticeship of a Dictator]. Piper, Munich.

HANTSCH, H. 1956. *Geschichte Oesterreichs* [History of Austria]. 2 vols. Graz and Vienna.

——. 1954. *Die Nationalitätenfrage im alten Oesterreich* [The National Question in Ancient Austria]. Vienna.

HOENSCH, J. K. 1987. *Geschichte Böhmens. Von der slawischen Landnahme bis ins 2O. Jahrhundert* [History of Bohemia from the Slav Conquest to the Late Twentieth Century]. Beck, Munich.

——. 1988. *Modern Hungary 1867–1986*. Longman, London/ New York.

HOREL, C. 1995. *Les Juifs de Hongrie (1825–1849)*. Problèmes d'assimilation et d'intégration. Strasbourg.

JANOS, A. C. 1982. *The Politics of Backwardness in Hungary, 1825–1945*. Princeton University Press, Princeton.

JASZI, O. 1971. *The Dissolution of the Habsburg Monarchy*. University of Chicago Press, Chicago.

JELAVICH, B. 1983. *History of the Balkans: The Twentieth Century*. Cambridge University Press, Cambridge.

KANN, R. A. 1974. *A History of the Habsburg Empire 1526–1918*. California University Press, London.

KECSKEMÉTI, K. 1989. *La Hongrie et le réformisme libéral. Problèmes politiques et sociaux (1790–1848)*. Il Centro di Ricerca, Roma.

KÖPECZI, B. 1992. (sous la direction de). *Histoire de la Transylvanie*. Budapest.

KOMLOS, J. 1993. *The Habsburg Monarchy as a Customs Union. Economic Development in Austria-Hungary in the Nineteenth Century*. Princeton University Press.

LE RIDER, J. 1990. *Modernité viennoise et crises de l'identité*. Presses Universitaires de France, Paris.

LUKACS, J. 1990. *Budapest 1900. Portrait historique d'une ville et de sa culture*. Paris.

McCAGG, W. O. 1989. *A History of the Habsburg Jews 1670–1918*. Indiana University Press, Bloomington.

——. 1986. *Jewish Nobles and Geniuses in Modern Hungary*. Boulder and New York.

MICHEL, B. 1976. *Banques et banquiers en Autriche au début du XXème siècle*. Paris.

——. 1986. *La mémoire de Prague. Conscience nationale et intelligentsia dans l'histoire tchèque et slovaque*. Perrin, Paris.

——. 1991. *La chute de l'Empire austro-hongrois*. Robert Laffont. Paris.

——. 1995. *Nations et nationalismes en Europe centrale XIXe–XXe siècle*. Aubier, Paris.

MIKOLETZKY, H. L. 1972. *Österreich, das entscheidende 19. Jahrhundert. Gescichte, Kultur und Wirtschaft* [Austria, the Decisive Nineteenth Century. History, Culture, Economy]. Austria-Edition, Vienna.

NOUZILLE, J. 1991. *Histoire de frontières: la frontière militaire austro-turque.* Berg International, Paris.

OKEY, R. 1986. *Eastern Europe 1740–1985. Feudalism to Communism.* University of Minnesota Press, Minneapolis.

PAMLÉNYI, E. 1974. (sous la direction de). *Histoire de la Hongrie.* Horvath, Roanne.

PIETRI, N.; MICHEL, B.; BUFFET, C. 1992. *Villes et sociétés urbaines dans les pays germaniques 1815–1914.* SEDES, Paris.

RANKI, G.; BEREND, I. 1974. *Economic Development in Eastern Central Europe in the nineteenth and twentieth Centuries.* New York.

RENOUVIN, P. 1955. *Histoire des relations internationales, de 1871 à 1914. L'apogée de l' Europe.* Vol. VI/2, Hachette. Paris.

SCHORSKE, C. 1961. *Fin-de-siècle Vienna.* New York.

SEIBT, F. 1993. *Deutschland und die Tschechen. Geschichte einer Nachbarschaft in der Mitte Europas* [Germany and the Czechs. History of a Neighbourhood in the Middle of Europe]. Piper, Munich.

TAYLOR, A. J. P. 1970. *The Habsburg Monarchy 1809–1918. A History of the Austrian Empire and Austria-Hungary.* Penguin Books, London.

VALIANI, L. 1966. *La dissoluzione dell'Austria-Ungheria.* Milan.

WANDRUSZKA, A.; URBANITSCH, P. 1976. *Die Habsburgermonarchie 1848–1918, III: Die Völker des Reiches* [The Habsburg Monarchy III: The Peoples of the Empire]. 2 vols. Akademie Verlag, Vienna.

ZOELLNER, E. 1965. *Histoire de l'Autriche.* Horvath, Roanne.

10.2.2

POLAND

Hanna Dilagowa

Between 1788 and 1792, the 'Four Years Sejm' took on the task of reforming a state in decline. The Constitution adopted on 3 May 1791 established a modern system of political organization. The lost war with Russia in 1792 and the crushing of the anti-Russian insurrection of Kosciuszko in 1794 led to successive partitions of Poland between Russia and Prussia in 1793 and between Russia, Austria and Prussia in 1795. There was thus no time for the reform of the state to be implemented. Those in the independence movement, who had fled abroad, sought help from outside the country. From 1794 they joined up with revolutionary France and with Napoleon, to whom they remained loyal up to the end. For a short while they won back for themselves a little country – the Grand Duchy of Warsaw (1807–13), which was under the thumb of Napoleon – and, which represented 21 per cent of pre-partition Poland. Other ways of regaining independence by establishing links with one of the occupying powers were not supported by the people. After haggling between the members of the victorious coalition against Napoleon, a Kingdom of Poland (with 17 per cent of the pre-partition territory) was set up at the Congress of Vienna and linked to Russia in the person of the ruler. This relative independence was effectively brought to an end in 1831, when an anti-Russian insurrection was put down.

Throughout the occupation and up to the regaining of independence in 1918, the activities of Poles conscious of their national identity and citizenship had two objectives. One group felt a duty to fight to regain their national independence, and they acted with great determination, organizing a series of insurrections (1794, 1806, 1830–1, 1846, 1848, 1863–4). The other group sought to preserve all that they could of the former splendour of their state and to develop public education, science and culture. There were also wide divergences within each camp. Sometimes their activities overlapped, notably in their efforts to win over large sectors of the population, in one case to regain their independence and in the other to enjoy the benefits of public education, culture and civic rights. Education was an important item in the programmes of various groups in the first half of the nineteenth century. The initial aim was to provide instruction for peasant children. The pre-partition *Rzeczypospolita* was a country of farmland, and it remained so throughout the nineteenth century. At the end of the eighteenth and beginning of the nineteenth century only the nobility, barely 8 per cent of the population at the time, were able to read and write. The peasants, who formed 70 per cent of the population, were almost without exception illiterate. The Jews had their own schools attended in principle by all Jewish children. The country towns were like urban farming settlements. After partition, the work started by the Committee for National Education, set up in 1773, continued, with the emphasis on elementary schools. The failure of the anti-Russian insurrections of 1830–1 and 1863–4 led to the use of Russian in the schools. The provision of education in Polish for the children of peasants and workers during the period of positivism was regarded as a civic duty by educated Polish women. But the percentage of persons unable to read or write remained highest – 70 per cent – on land under Russian occupation.

In all the schools on Prussian-occupied territory German became the compulsory teaching language. Education was universal and illiteracy prior to the First World War was barely 0.5 per cent. In these zones education in Polish was supported by social organizations such as the People's Education Society and the Poznań Association of People's Reading Rooms.

In the areas under Austrian occupation (in Galicia) and as a result of the autonomy obtained by the Poles, schools took to using Polish from the 1860s. Primary education was made available to a greater number of children, bringing the illiteracy rate down to 56 per cent towards the end of the nineteenth century.

Advances in primary education played an important part in making possible the subsequent training of children from peasant or worker families. The children of wealthy families often used to study at home. As a result, the role of private tutors developed considerably. These families also employed foreigners to give lessons in other languages, especially French; English was only just coming into fashion.

Secondary schools developed in different ways under each of the three occupiers, but in general maintained quite a high standard. The lycées awarded a baccalaureate that enabled pupils to continue their studies in institutions of higher education. Under Russian occupation, where Russian became the teaching language, a large-scale self-education movement emerged. It recruited young people from the secondary schools, who created an extensive underground educational network. A 'Flying University' was set up in Warsaw in 1885 with courses being given in different places to avoid detection by the Russian police. After the Russian Revolution of 1905 the Flying University was made legal and carried out its activities as the 'Society for Scientific Courses'.

After 1795, Polish science lay in ruins but the scientific approach was not dead. During the first three decades of the nineteenth century, science was still dominated by the ideas of the Enlightenment. Mathematics and the natural sciences were gaining ground at places like the University of Vilna, where Polish scientists such as Jan Sniadecki, mathematician and astronomer, and his brother Jedrzej, a chemist, were active. The Polish nobility and intellectuals usually used their own language.

In 1800, the Society of Friends of Science was founded in Warsaw and was open to men of science from all three annexed territories. The University of Warsaw, founded in 1816, was closed down by the Russian authorities after the insurrection of 1830–1. In 1832, as part of the post-insurrection repression, the University of Vilna was also closed and the Society of Friends of Science dissolved. After their defeat in the Crimean War (1853–6), the Russians adopted a slightly more liberal stance in the Polish lands occupied by them. In 1862, a Polish university called the 'Main School' opened in Warsaw and functioned until 1869, when it was turned into a Russian university. It brought together and trained a group of competent scholars for science in Poland and introduced the philosophy of Auguste Comte, which was current in Europe at the time. Benedykt Dybowski, in the natural sciences, Jakub Natanson in chemistry and Jósef Mianowski and Tytus Chalubinski in medicine became known in this way and Jan Baudouin de Courtenay began his career in the humanities there. After the abolition of the Main School, academic activities in the exact sciences were continued thanks to the 'social initiatives' of the Museum of Industry and Agriculture (1875) and by the Mianowski Fund in the humanities. The latter financed a great many publications, including some of an encyclopaedic nature such as the *Geographical Dictionary of the Kingdom of Poland*, which is still an irreplaceable tool for the historical geography of the entire territory of the pre-partition *Rzeczypospolita*. The publication from 1857 to 1890 of a multi-volume work by Oskar Kolberg entitled *Lud* (The People) was a major event which laid the foundations for advances in Polish ethnography. These two publications were as important as the *Dictionary of the Polish Language* by Samuel Bogumiłł Linde published 1807–14. Even though there was no Polish institute of advanced studies, a group that came to be known as the Warsaw School of History (Władysław Smoleński, Tadeusz Korzon, Adolf Pawiłski) developed in the capital.

In Prussian-occupied territory (Poznania and Pomerania) there was no Polish-language university. The young studied in German universities. Nevertheless, efforts were made to popularize the results of scientific research. Large private foundations were set up, such as the Raczyński Libraries in Poznań and the Dzialyński Library in Kórnik. In the 1840s, Poznań was a ferment of activity in the pedagogical sciences (Ewaryst Estkowski, Bronisław Trentowski) and philosophy (August Cieszkowski, Bronisław Trentowski and Karol Libelt). In 1875 the Poznań Society of Friends of Science, the leading scientific institution in the area annexed by Prussia, was founded.

From the 1870s, conditions for the development of science were most favourable in the areas annexed by Austria, which had just obtained their autonomy. The Universities of Lwów and Cracow (Jagielloński) were made Polish. As a result, some men of science were able to work in their own country and achieved results recognized throughout the world. In 1883, for example, Zygmunt Wróblewski and Karol Olszewski liquefied air and Marian Smoluchowski

made advances in kinetic-molecular theory. In the medical sciences, important advances were made in Cracow by Józef Dietl and Napoleon Cybulski, founder of the Cracow Faculty of Physiology. The Cracow Faculty of History (Józef Szujski, Walerian Kalinka, Michał Bobrzyński) developed a unified interpretation of pre-partition Polish history and the reasons for Poland's downfall. Unlike the 'optimistic' Warsaw Faculty, it was regarded as pessimistic as it pointed to failings in the Polish regime as the cause of partition. In Cracow, Karol Estreicher prepared his *Polish Bibliography*, based on the collections of the Jagiellons Library, and it was published in several volumes in 1870. In Lwów, Ksawery Liske set up the Polish Historical Society (1866), which became a forum for historians from all parts of Poland, organized general congresses of Polish historians and published a scientific journal, the *Kwartalnik Historyczny* (Historical Quarterly). Other academic associations with their own journals also came into being. From 1817 there existed in Lwów a 'Science Establishment', which was a private foundation belonging to Józef Maksymilian Ossoliński, who financed the library and scientific research as well as publications. In 1873, the Cracow Academy of Learning was founded and served the whole of Poland.

Polish men of science from the three annexed territories were often regarded internationally as representatives of Russian, Austrian or German science. Some of them were forced to flee Poland to escape prison or deportation to the Russian interior. Others were unable to find employment in the few Polish institutes of advanced studies; the occupying powers were not interested in promoting Polish science. A few of these scholars found ways of pursuing their activities outside Poland and made their contribution to world science in this way (Ignacy Domeyko in Chile, Józef Babiński and Maria Skłodowska-Curie in France, among others). Between 1795 and 1914, the perseverance of Polish scientists not only kept Polish science alive but helped it to score significant successes.

The nineteenth century was an important period for Polish letters. The leading poets were Adam Mickiewicz, Juliusz Słowacki and Zygmunt Krasiński, who were recognized as the great national poets. Abandoning the rationalism and empiricism of the Enlightenment, they attached much greater importance to spiritual elements and drew on popular and national sources. Polish romanticism was infused with the hope of a new pattern of relations in Europe and of Poland regaining its independence. The period of great romantic poetry was brought to a close by Cyprian Kamil Norwid. Novels and short stories marked the positivist movement in Poland: writers of the time such as Eliza Orzeszkowa, Bolesław Prus, Henryk Sienkiewicz (Nobel Prize in 1906) and Maria Konopnicka portrayed characters struggling with the vicissitudes of fortune. One major theme was patriotism – the duty to resist the occupying forces and to engage in 'organic work' to remedy Poland's cultural backwardness. Historical novels by writers such as Józef Ignacy Kraszewski and Henryk Sienkiewicz described the past splendour of Poland and awakened hopes for the future.

Writers at the turn of the century (known as Młoda Polska or Young Poland) shared the awareness of a crisis in the life of ideas and systems that was emerging in Europe at that time. Influenced by the philosophy of Schopenhauer and Nietzsche and led by Stanisław Przybyszewski, their battle cry was 'art for art's sake'. In general they distanced themselves from the civic and social themes of Polish letters during the partitions, although a number of Young Poland prose writers such as Stefan Zeromski and Władysław Reymont (Nobel Prize in 1924) remained faithful to them. The outstanding dramatist was Stanisław Wyspiański, author of plays such as *Wesele* (The Wedding) that are still staged today and who adopted a new approach to the theatre. The literature produced by the Young Poland movement continued the idea of a community of Poles transcending the Partitions. The press played a major role: newspapers printed the novels of established writers and the weeklies published articles on cultural and social subjects. Newspapers and periodicals were widely read, and their circulation increased considerably in the second half of the nineteenth century. In country areas, books and periodicals were less common; they were bought by teachers, priests and the nobility. But as a result of the social initiative of teachers, some women of the nobility and a few priests, more country people were introduced to reading books and periodicals. Censorship by the occupying powers, very strict at certain periods, was avoided by the use of metaphor or by setting stories in the far distant past. Books and periodicals printed abroad were also ordered.

Literature and the press were then the only means of communication. Drama, music and painting were accessible to a more restricted circle, but that of Polish origin had a crucial impact on the development of Polish culture. Polish theatres of a high standard, established in the second half of the nineteenth century, were to be found in Warsaw, Cracow, Lwów and Poznań. The greatest figure of the national stage was Wojciech Bogusławski, author, actor and director. Despite their problems, these theatres had at their disposal actors well up to European standards (Helena Modrzejewska, Irena Solska, Ludwik Solski) and some good playwrights in addition to the major national writers Aleksander Fredro and Stanisław Wyspiański. It was Wyspiański who introduced a modern approach to play writing and directing. Before the First World War a modern building for the Polish Theatre, with a revolving stage, was built in Warsaw and it was there that plays from the national repertory were performed.

Conditions in the annexed territories did not encourage musical activities either. However, it was quite common for the children and young members of noble and educated families to be taught the piano, and this helped to make people in general more sensitive to music. In the first half of the nineteenth century, the best-known musician was Fryderyk Chopin, whose compositions – especially his mazurkas and polonaises – were recognized in Poland as national music. Another national composer was Stanisław Moniuszko (1819–72), who wrote the best-known Polish operas, including *Halka* and *Straszny Dwór* (The Haunted Manor), and over 300 songs and ballads which were sung not only by professional soloists but also by amateur singers and at family gatherings. Moniuszko had a profound influence on musical creativity in Poland. Towards the end of the nineteenth century, musicians belonging to the Young Poland movement, such as Mieczysław Karłowicz and Ludomir Różycki, broke with this tradition. It was at that point that a number of celebrated virtuosos, composers, conductors and singers (Ignacy Paderewski, Karol Szymanowski, Emil Młynarski, Ewa Bandrowska-Turska, and so on) launched their careers. Interest in music gradually increased as choirs were formed to sing both religious and secular music and musical activities were organized in people's homes.

Painting took pride of place among the arts in nineteenth-century Poland. Patriotic themes, reflecting the country's political situation, can be discerned throughout the period. Paintings of battles or of historical events were produced in classical (Aleksander Orłowski) or romantic (Piotr Michałowski, Juliusz Kossak, Artur Grottger) style. The most famous historical painter was Jan Matejko. There were also realist paintings depicting for example, the situation of various social groups, genre paintings and landscapes (Józef Chełmoński, Julian Fałat, Aleksander i Maksymilian Gierymski, Wojciech Kossak). Polish painters studied in Rome, Munich or Paris, where they became acquainted with new trends in the arts.

The other arts, such as architecture, reflected contemporary European trends. After some major building projects in the classical style (generally in the cities), architects began to build in the neo-gothic style, especially churches. At the turn of the century, a great number of bourgeois apartment blocks in the Austrian *sezession* style were constructed in the cities.

Culture in a very general sense was nevertheless the preserve of the elite. Country areas remained faithful to the traditional culture based on the seasons and religious holidays. Ordinary buildings, costumes and customs remained practically the same up to 1914. The parish was the normal point of reference, as the Catholic church played an important role in Poland, and the pulpit was sometimes the only medium of mass communication. The growing secularization of intellectuals, who had taken over the leadership role from the nobility, was not yet strong enough to have a marked impact on life in the countryside in this respect.

The Jews formed a distinct group in Polish society. In some cities they represented as much as 50 per cent of the population. They usually constituted close-knit communities distinguished from the rest of the population by their style of dress, their religion and their culture. Only a few individuals accepted assimilation and these generally joined the ranks of the intellectuals and made an important contribution to progress in Polish science and culture.

The nineteenth century was a period of vast social and economic transformations, which affected living standards throughout the country. The major cities were provided with water supply networks. The country's population almost doubled and in cities such as Warsaw and Łódź the expansion was much greater. In addition to their own natural population increase, the cities absorbed those leaving overpopulated villages to meet the needs of industry and services. Peasants who could not find a job in the cities or rural communities emigrated. The construction and expansion of the railways encouraged closer social cohesion in Poland, despite the frontiers separating the annexed territories. On the eve of the First World War, there were already a number of social factors that fostered a pooling of efforts to win back and safeguard Polish independence.

BIBLIOGRAPHY

BRÜCKNER, A. 1991. *Dzieje kultury polskiej. Dzieje Polski porozbiorowej 1795/1772/1914* (History of Polish culture. History of Poland after Partition). Wiedza Powszechna, Warsaw.

DAVIS, N. 1982. *God's Playground. A History of Poland. Vol. 2: 1795 to the Present*. Oxford University Press, Oxford.

DUBY, G. 1987. *Atlas historique – l'histoire du monde en 317 cartes*. p. 165. Larousse, Paris.

——. 1987. *Historia nauki polskiej* (History of Polish Science). Vol. 3: 1795–1862. 1977; Vol. 4: 1863–1918. Ed. J. Michalski. Ossolineum, Warsaw.

——. 1987. *Histoire religieuse de la Pologne*. Sous la direction de Jeozy Kloczowski. Le Centurion, Paris.

——. 1987. *Polska, Jej dzieje i kultura* (Poland: its History and Culture). Vol. 3: 1795–1930. Trzaska Evert i Michalski, Warsaw.

WANDYCZ, P. 1993. *The Lands of Partioned Poland 1795–1918*. University of Washington Press, Seattle and London.

10.2.3
RUSSIA

Igor N. Ionov and Alexei N. Tsamutali

The situation in which Russian culture and science developed in the nineteenth century was the result of large-scale reforms in the spheres of government, social life, economy and culture, initiated by Tsar Peter I at the turn of the seventeenth century. They put an end to the Orthodox church's absolute domination in Russia's cultural life and led to the creation of a secular state; the foundations of secular education and science were laid; technical, administrative, cultural achievements were borrowed from Europe on a broad scale (while the autocratic political system was left intact and serfdom strengthened). These changes, however, were accompanied by the sharpening of controversies within society. From the aspect of cultural development, the destruction of Russian society's cultural unity was of special importance. With the gentry imitating the clothes, customs and even the language of West European nations, the traditions, ideals and values of the ruling elite and the majority of the population were coming into conflict.

At the turn of the eighteenth century the cultural split in society reached a dangerous level. The gentry and the peasantry were refusing to see each other as representatives of the same culture. The names which the labouring classes used to identify themselves – *krestiane* (meaning peasants, but also very close to the word *khristiane* (Christians) and *narod* (the people, which can be also interpreted as 'those born') – reflected their ambitions for a monopoly in the spheres of correct faith and human status. The nobles in their turn often used pejorative nicknames for peasants. All this resulted in mutual incomprehension and growing social conflict. The paradox of the situation was that both the peasants and the gentry regarded the tsar as the main exponent of their interests. While the gentry had every reason to think so, for the peasants this world outlook was Utopian. Still, it survived throughout the whole nineteenth century.

The sharpening of social and cultural conflicts in society raised the significance of social thinking and ideology in Russian culture, making educated people pay more attention in the sphere of learning to the problems of morality and social order, rather than to those of theology or natural sciences. Thus, as had been the case in traditional Russian culture, ethical aspects remained dominant, and *belles lettres* determied the shape and principal directions of spiritual strivings. Art, science, and theology were only gradually winning a place of their own within the system of culture. In the course of the development of the educated part of the population as a social stratum, these peculiarities manifested

themselves in its consciousness. Their concentration on ethical problems and social improvement projects enabled Russian intellectuals to oppose themselves, at least to some extent, to their counterparts in Europe, who were dealing with problems closer to everyday practices, being more rational and bourgeois. Russian educated circles found their self-esteem primarily in their moral and psychological sensitivity, in their ability to sympathize with the sufferings of the people, in their readiness to sacrifice themselves for a better future. These features formed the definition of the term *intelligentsia*, which by the mid-nineteenth century became the Russian intellectuals' own name for themselves (it was first introduced in 1863 by the writer Pyotr D. Boborykin).

Various social forces – the state, the church, the intellectuals – were trying to restore society's cultural unity. The idea of a completely secular, Europeanized state, which could be hardly understood by the majority of the people, already by the reign of Catherine II (1762–96) was partly superseded by the imperial idea of restoring a universal Orthodox state, the creation of a Greek Empire under the Russian patriarchy on the territories which had formerly belonged to the Byzantine Empire. Catherine wanted to see her grandson Konstantin, named in the honour of the last Byzantine emperor Constantine XI Paleologue, on its throne. And though this idea was never put into practice, it gained the support of the peasantry, and Konstantin, even after his death, remained a personified legend among the people. The idea of Russia's mission to expand Orthodoxy and legal authority (legitimism) was repeatedly revitalized in the autocratic ideology during the nineteenth century and used in the efforts to bring the people and the authorities together during the reigns of Emperors Alexander I (1801–25), Nicolas I (1825–55) and Alexander III (1881–94). It received its most complete reflection in the 1830s and 1840s in the slogan 'Orthodoxy, autocracy, populism' (*Pravoslavie, samoderzhavie, narodnost'*), which became the basis for the policy of 'official populism', paternalism and traditionalism, limiting the Europeanization and modernization projects of Russian tsars. We must note, however, that though the role of the state in cultural development (especially in education) remained significant throughout the century, it was diminishing constantly. The authorities were losing their active position *vis-à-vis* society, where radicals became more and more important. Thus the government project for a cultural synthesis was never completely realized.

Religion and the church constituted an important aspect of the cultural life of Russia's peoples. The general influence of the church was, by the end of the eighteenth century, seriously undermined by three factors: the liquidation of the church's authonomy, when it was subordinated to the government institution – the Holy Synod; policing functions imposed on the priests by the authorities, infringing the secrecy of confession; the limitation, and then secularization, of monastic property. As a result, the intellectual level of priests was reduced, they were losing their status as popular intellectuals, and the monasteries were no more regarded by the population as a model of social organization. The clergy and especially the monks reacted by trying to renew deep spiritual strivings at a certain distance from the state. This movement was called the *starchestvo*.

In pre-Revolutionary Russia every person had to profess a certain religion. It was religion (not nationality) that was included in official identity papers – passports, service records, etc. Legally, it was impossible to be an atheist. The Orthodox church was governed by the aforementioned Holy Synod, consisting of several Metropolitans and bishops. The *Ober-Procurator* (not a member of the clergy, but a high-ranking official appointed by the Emperor) was at the head of the Synod. The Metropolitan of Petersburg or Moscow was his deputy (*Pervoprisutstvoyushchii*). He had the right to address the Emperor directly on church affairs. The church's subordination to the state was further emphasized at the end of the reign of Alexander I, in 1817, by the founding of the Ministry of Church Affairs and Education, instead of the former Ministry of Education. The new ministry lasted until 1824.

Up to the 1860s the Orthodox clergy was an exclusive caste, with hereditary transfer of rights and duties. It was very difficult for persons from other social strata to join the clergy in the first half of the nineteenth century. A special law broke this exclusiveness only in 1869 and liberated the children of clergymen from the obligation to remain within the caste. It also allowed every member of the Orthodox church to become a priest. The representatives of duty-bound estates (*podatnye sosloviia* – peasants and lower-class urban dwellers), however, needed the governor's permission for this. The law of 1869, on one hand, liquidated the exclusiveness of the clergy. On the other hand, clergymen were made exempt from corporal punishment, duties, taxes and conscription, that is they received a number of important privileges similar to those enjoyed by the gentry.

Apart from those professing Orthodoxy there were representatives of other Christian confessions in Russia – Catholics and Protestants. Part of the population was Moslem. The Jews were subject to the most severe limitations on religious grounds – they could live only in the Pale, which included present-day Ukraine, Belorussia and the Polish territories belonging to Russia.

Intellectuals played the most important part in the process of overcoming the cultural opposition between educated strata and the people. The degradation of Russian, which by the late eighteenth century had been pushed to the cultural periphery, was not overlooked by the Russian Academy: in the early nineteenth century it published the *Dictionary of the Russian Academy* – the first Russian dictionary. The interaction between colloquial Russian, Old Church Slavonic and slang, incorporating concepts identified in European culture, formed the basis for the genesis of literary Russian. The historian and writer Nikolai M. Karamzin (1766–1826) and the great Russian poet Aleksandr Pushkin (1799–1837) played a major part in its creation. The collection of Russian folk ballads, historical and lyrical songs, the consolidation of

literary Russian's norms at the linguistic faculties of the universities, contributed to the process substantially.

In the second half of the nineteenth century the role of radicals increased in the dialogue between the people and intellectuals. They were using popular Utopian ideas of the possibility of the state as a system of autonomous egalitarian communes, based on social justice without legalized violence and taxes. This dialogue and the cultural synthesis of populist Utopian ideas and socialism, however, led to a deepening split between the people and the ruling classes, between the nation and the authorities. It raised the prospect of overcoming the cultural divide by humiliating and pushing aside a part of society. Still this direction of cultural striving had a considerable power and was gradually winning widespread support.

In this situation, orientation to the European model played a controversial role for Russia. On one hand, this orientation facilitated the appreciation of European achievements in science, literature, art and education. But on the other, the period of revolutions in Europe from 1789 till 1871 made Russian society regard revolutionary movements and revolutionary ideology as a universal law of development. Westernism (*Zapadnichestvo*), the European orientation of Russian culture during the nineteenth century, was gradually merging with revolutionary democratism and socialism (and, to a much lesser extent, with liberalism). The attempts to resist this tendency, to create a national ideology and culture, differing from the European, were inevitably leading to nationalist criticism of the European cultural experience in general, emphasizing the peculiarities of the Russian state, society and culture, which opened the perspective of cultural self-isolation. This perspective was as dangerous as that of a destructive revolution.

From 1789 to 1914, i.e. the period between the French Revolution and the eve of the First World War, Russians and other nations populating the territory of European Russia went through a complicated process of cultural development. The cultural and scientific life of Russia's peoples in the aforementioned period can, in its turn, be divided into three stages. The first stage started in 1789 and ended in 1861, with the abolition of serfdom. The second, from 1861 to the end of the nineteenth century, was manifested by the economic boom after the reforms of 1860s and early 1870s. The third stage, between the turn of the century and 1914, bore the imprint of the first Russian revolution of 1905–7.

In the late eighteenth and early nineteenth century Russian culture developed under the influence of Enlightenment ideology. Simultaneously, Russia and its peoples were becoming more and more actively involved in the general progress of humanity. Contacts with other countries, primarily with Western Europe, were increasing, both in trade and cultural exchange. Educated Russians were following West European cultural life closely. It was the gentry, which, by its social status, constituted that part of the Russian society where the achievements of science and culture were understood. Most of them mastered French. Many of those who worked in the Academy of Sciences, or were teaching at the universities and gymnasiums, had a good command of German. All this facilitated their acquaintance with the latest innovations in the intellectual, scientific and cultural life of other countries.

In the late eighteenth and first half of the nineteenth century, many educated Russians were influenced by the Enlightenment, the ideas of Voltaire, Diderot, Helvetius and Holbach. The progress of the French Revolution was closely followed in Russia. Initially revolutionary developments in France met with a positive reaction in educated society. Many regarded this as a way to the consolidation of civic dignity, the triumph of virtue, to the equality of estates. This part of Russian educated society was correlating the results of the French Revolution with their own ideal – 'enlightened monarchy'. However, as more information about the actions of French peasants and the urban poor reached Russia, these sympathies began to turn into anxiety and even hostility. After the overthrow and execution of the king and the establishment of the Jacobin dictatorship, the Revolution's adversaries increased substantially in number. The government of Catherine II definitely turned towards reaction. The writer Aleksandr N. Radishchev, whose book *Journey from St Petersburg to Moscow*, condemning serfdom, had been printed in the very days when the rebels in Paris were taking the Bastille, was exiled to Siberia. At the same time the Secret Expedition (secret police) monitored conversations in St Petersburg, where people were suggesting that Russia follow the French example and get rid of the 'tyranny'.

Emperor Alexander I, who came to the throne in 1801 after his father, Emperor Pavel I, had been killed during a palace coup, understood the necessity of reform, but was not resolute and consistent enough when it came to implementing it. Reformist projects were discussed during the first years of his reign. Of special significance among them were the projects elaborated by Mikhail M. Speransky, who dared not propose the immediate abolition of serfdom, but drafted a plan of gradual transformation of Russia's system of government. According to Speransky's draft proposals, Russia could acquire the features of a West European constitutional monarchy. A body resembling a parliament – the State Duma – should be established. His system also included the election of local authorities and the separation of legislative, executive and judicial powers. Speransky's reforms were carried out on a limited scale. Russia did not receive its State Duma. The only practical result was the improvement of government institutions. In 1812 Speransky himself was forced to resign.

Alexander's indecisiveness, the strict secrecy surrounding the discussions of reforms and the strengthening of reactionary tendencies in government policy, led to the creation of secret societies of reformists, and their attempt to carry out these reforms via an armed rebellion, which took place on 14 December 1825. On that day the most progressive and educated people in Russia threw down a challenge to autocracy and the system it was supporting. Emperor Nicolas I managed to suppress the rebellion, and its participants were subjected to severe reprisals. 'The events of December 14, 1825 swept Russia's best intellectual forces from the scene, and a different era began', wrote the historian Vassilii Ya. Bogucharsky.

Among the results of the Enlightenment ideology's influence was the formation of the Russian educational system. In 1803 a statute on the system of educational institutions was adopted. They were divided into four categories: the parish, the district, the provincial and the universities. At that time universities existed in Moscow, Vilno (Vilnius) and Derpt (Tartu). It was decided to establish three additional ones: in Kazan (opened in 1804), in Kharkov (opened in 1804) and in St Petersburg. In St Petersburg the Pedagogical Institute was initially established in 1804 (in 1816 it was renamed the Main

Pedagogical Institute), which was transformed into the University of St Petersburg in February 1819. The publicist Nikolai V. Shelgunov, paying tribute to the role of Russian universities in the first half of the nineteenth century, wrote that 'the universities brought much of light into Russian life and substantially cleared and prepared the way for all the subsequent intellectual movements of the sixties'. Progressive professors, in addition to arousing students' interest in science, introduced a certain liberal spirit into the university atmosphere.

Along with universities, institutions to train engineers were organized. The Institute of Communications Engineers (1810), the Technological Institute (1828) and the Institute of Civil Engineers were founded in St Petersburg. Lyceums – privileged high schools – played an important part in the development of education in Russia. In 1811 the Lyceum at Tsarskoye Selo was opened, and Aleksandr Pushkin graduated from its first class. In 1805 the Demidov Lyceum was established in Jaroslavl (the Jaroslavl School of High Sciences). In 1817 the Richelieu Lyceum was opened in Odessa. In 1820 the Prince Bezborodko Gymnasium of High Sciences of was founded in the city of Nezhin. The writer Nikolai V. Gogol studied there.

The number of students increased in the first quarter of the nineteenth century. In 1808 there were about 77,000 students in the educational institutions of the Ministry of Popular Education and Orthodox church schools. By 1824 their number had increased to 115,000. In 1834 there were 134,000 students in the aforementioned institutions. Another 245,000 studied in institutions belonging to other ministries, including the War Ministry. By that time Russia had a population of 51 million. Thus there was one student for every 200 persons. In the cities the number of students per 100 persons was higher than in the countryside. In St Petersburg, with its population of 441,000 there were 22,116 students, i.e. 5 students per 100 persons. In Moscow there were 9,642 students in a population of 316,000, i.e. 3.1 students per 100.

As we can see, those having access to education remained a thin layer in Russian society. During the reign of Nicolas I the increase in student numbers slowed down. In 1827 the law against peasants entering higher school barred the way to education for people of common origin.

In the period of reaction, the Enlightenment ideas, intellectuals, professors and teachers were subject to persecution by the authorities. The first wave of repressions took place immediately after the beginning of the French Revolution. Practically the whole first generation of intellectuals, brought up at Moscow University, was persecuted for 'free thinking'. The second wave of persecution started in the early 1820s. Emperor Alexander's reactionary ideas were of a nationalist character. Nationalists like Alexei A. Arakcheev, Aleksander S. Shishkov, Archimandrite Fotii, and M. L. Magnitsky were very influental in higher government circles. This was the time when the policy of 'official popularity' began to take shape; it was finalized in the 1830s, at the peak of the third wave of reaction, by Sergei S. Uvarov. By that time the ideals of the Enlightenment had been discarded by the government.

In this controversial situation the most important of cultural processes in nineteenth-century Russia – the genesis of the national culture – was developing. The Patriotic War of 1812 and the subsequent campaign against Napoleon in Europe were accompanied by considerable enthusiasm in Russian society and the rise of national consciousness. For the first time Russians looked at Europe not as its pupils, but as its rescuers. This was the background for the abrupt rise in the Russian gentry's self-esteem. The verses of the poets from the gentry (Gavrila R. Derzhavin, Vassilii A. Zhukovsky), which had been always loyal to the throne, now often displayed liberal or lyrical tendencies, glorifying beauty and world harmony. This was the birth of the 'golden age' of Russian poetry – its grandeur was determined by Aleksander Pushkin and the poets from his milieu: Evgenii A. Baratynsky, Pyotr A. Vyazemsky, Nikolai M. Yazykov and others. Their poetry was genuinely national both in its language and motifs. Pushkin was greatly interested in folklore and national history, which provided the themes for his famous tales, the poem *Rouslan and Ljudmila*, the tragedy *Boris Godunov*, etc. However, it was the life and feelings of an educated nobleman of his time that constituted the poet's central topic (as in the poetic novel *Evgenii Onegin*). The dialogue with folk culture and self-knowledge was developing, with an indissoluble connection with European culture, and in reinterpretation of its themes (for example in *Small Tragedies*).

National culture in Russia, as in other Central and East European countries, was taking shape as the wave of enthusiasm for romanticism. The period of its domination, however, was short. In the works of Mikhail Yu. Lermontov (1814–41) and Nikolai V. Gogol (1809–52) we can already see the transition to realism, which gradually acquired a sharp critical spirit, demonizing the bearers of evil and striving for a social ideal. It was the beginning of the tendency which would later be named 'critical realism'. The subject of the writers' interest was also changing. While Lermontov was still concentrating on the problems of the gentry (as in his novel *The Hero of Our Time*), Gogol went all the way from an interest in folk culture to the theme of penetrating sympathy for 'the small man', the common urban dweller, and attempts to understand his problems and psychology.

The aesthetic principle which characterized the works of Pushkin and his milieu gradually gave way to the ethical principle, the theme of compassion and sermonizing. By the mid-nineteenth century this theme was powerfully manifested in the works of such young writers and poets as Ivan A. Goncharov (1812–91), Ivan S. Turgenev (1818–83), Fyodor M. Dostoyevsky (1821–81), and Nikolai A. Nekrasov (1821–77). The interest in folk culture was reflected in the expansion of the sphere of folklore studies. The work of Vladimir I. Dahl (1801–72) was of paramount significance in this connection: starting with essays on the life of peasants, he later published the classic *Explanatory Dictionary of Contemporary Russian*, and the collection of *Proverbs of the Russian People*.

This was also the period when Russian national theatre emerged. The plays of Aleksandr S. Griboyedov (1795–1829), Nikolai Gogol, and Aleksandr N. Ostrovsky (1823–86) gave a vivid picture of Russian life and national character. Quotations from these plays contributed to the treasury of national humour, and their characters became archetypes. Realism on stage was becoming a national tradition. Its emergence was related to the activities of the great actor Mikhail S. Shchepkin (1788–1863). In the process of developing the realistic tendency of Russian theatre, the Malyi Theatre in Moscow, founded in 1824, became the centre of national theatre tradition.

By the mid-nineteenth century Europe discovered Russian literature for the first time. Thanks to Prosper Merimée's initiative, the first translations of Pushkin into French were made, followed by those of Lermontov, Gogol, Turgenev. Gogol's play *The Inspector*, a satire on relations between Russian society and the authorities, was staged in Paris. Wilhelm K. Kuchelbecker and Adam Mickiewicz began academic discussion and teaching of the history of Russian culture in France. The cultural exchange between Russia and Europe, which for a long time had been a one-way process, was becoming a mutual interchange.

In the same period Russian classical music was born, the composer Mikhail I. Glinka (1804–57), who made an important contribution to many musical genres, being its founder. He created a Russian national opera, national instrumental music, and the national romantic genre, which received their full development in the nineteenth century. The Bolshoi Theatre, dedicated to opera and ballet performances, which had opened in Moscow in 1825, was playing an increasing role.

Russian architects were also elaborating a special national style. Following the tradition of classicism, they were improving its forms. This tendency was manifested especially in the creation of new buildings and whole complexes in St Petersburg. The Admiralty building, designed by Andrian D. Zakharov, is regarded as the model example of Russian Empire style, which was characterized by simplicity, grandeur and sense of proportion. These features were reflected in the work of Karl I. Rossi, who was responsible for several developments in the centre of St Petersburg – Palace Square with the General Staff building, the Senate and Synod building, and the Alexandrine Theatre complex were among them.

Auguste A. Montferrand worked in a different manner, but his monumental and immense buildings, though some art historians regarded them as a manifestation of the crisis of classicism, supplemented and completed successfully the complexes built by Zakharov and Rossi. St Isaac's Cathedral is Montferrand's most significant creation. He also designed the Alexandre Column in the centre of Palace Square.

Osip I. Bovet was developing the Empire style in Moscow. He designed the new facade of the shopping centre (*Torgovye Ryady*) completing the Red Square complex, and the Theatre Square complex with the Bolshoi Theatre at its centre. Domenico I. Gilliardi built Moscow University in the classical style. Among the buildings constructed in Moscow in the mid-nineteenth century one should also note those designed by Konstantin A. Ton, especially the great Kremlin Palace and the cathedral of Christ the Saviour.

Mid-nineteenth-century Russian architecture tended towards grandeur and immensity, which was to a large extent due to the fact that the architects were working on government buildings and other constructions which were of interest to the authorities. Another sphere of art – painting – was, however, displaying the same features that were manifested in literature. The paintings of Alexei G. Venezianov and the portraiture of Orest A. Kiprensky and Vassilii A. Tropinin combined exquisite colouring with deep penetration into their characters' psychology, humanist ideas and romanticism. Some pictures by Russian painters, like Karl P. Brullow's *The Destruction of Pompei* were popular not only in Russia, but in Western Europe too. Brullow's idea provoked many disputes in Russia, France, Italy. The majority regarded *The Destruction of Pompei* as an allegory of the drama of humankind. The idea of Aleksander A. Ivanov's *Appearance of Christ Before the People*, with its moral and even social motifs, also went far beyond topics concerning only the Russian public. By the mid-nineteenth century, Russian painting showed a strong tendency for depicting daily life. In this connection the works of Pavel A. Fedotov, who was gradually turning to the realistic style, were attracting public attention.

The creation of the fundamentals of Russian national culture in the first half of the nineteenth century was the result of a synthesis of noble and popular culture. But a parallel process was taking place too – the culture of the progressive gentry was estranging itself from the official culture. The creators of national consciousness were trying to distance themselves from the ideologues of 'official popularity'. Liberal nationalism was trying to oppose itself to *étatiste* nationalism. Faced with severe censorship and police surveillance of the activists of public organizations, the exponents of new ideas were developing them within small semi-underground groups, which became a characteristic Russian form of contact between intellectuals. This situation led to a great diversity of opinions on Russia's place in the world. In the extreme form this idea was formulated by Pyotr Ya. Chaadayev (1794–1856) in his *Philosophical Letter*, published in 1836. He condemned the national cultural tradition sharply as a negative phenomenon in world history, having only an edifying significance, and supported the values of European Catholicism against those of Russian Orthodoxy. Later, however, he admitted that a great future was possible for Russia, but only because it lacked a positive cultural tradition of its own.

In the 1830s-1850s many thinkers, both nationalist and Westernized, tried to answer the problem formulated by Chaadayev. Nationalist Slavophiles Alexei S. Khomyakov, Ivan V. Kireevsky, Konstantin S. Aksakov and Yuri F. Samarin were defending the importance of national values – Orthodoxy and folk culture (communal collectivism, informal family relations, the role of faith and intuition in the process of cognition) – in spite of their critique of autocracy (Aksakov) and serfdom. 'Progressivist' Westernists Timofei N. Granovsky, Sergei M. Solovyev, Boris N. Chicherin and Konstantin D. Kavelin supported European values and emphasized the significance of Peter the Great's reforms, which had dragged Russia out of cultural stagnation and made it a great European power. They criticized the Russian peasant commune, patriarchal family relations, the arbitrariness of Russian authorities and the lack of a developed rationalist tradition in Russian philosophy. They were European-type liberals, though of a rather conservative kind; for instance, they argued for the abolition of serfdom, but never attacked autocracy. There was, however, a radical, democratic group among the Westernists.

The philosophical systems of Kant, Fichte, Schelling and Hegel attracted a lot of attention in this intellectual atmosphere. Schelling's *Naturphilosophie* and aesthetics were popular among scholars specializing in natural sciences and trying to explain the world philosophically. The authorities felt that the interest in philosophy was hindering the expansion of official religion, and repeatedly resorted to repression. In 1821 professor A. I. Galich was dismissed from St Petersburg University under the accusation that he preferred the atheist philosopher Kant to Jesus Christ, and Schelling to the Holy Spirit. In spite of this persecution philosophical strivings were quite widespread. To some extent 'German philosophy . . . was a substitute religion for young men'.

The aforementioned Slavophiles Ivan Kireevsky and Alexei Khomyakov found Schelling's philosophy quite an attractive one, especially his idea of the absolute spirit laying the basis of the historical process, and the relevant idea of the national spirit as the main principle determining history. They followed the example of West European, primarily German, scholars who were actively engaged in Slavonic studies. German romanticism and enthusiasm for folk life and art also had much in common with their own views. Just as the Grimm brothers had been collecting and publishing German folk tales, Ivan Kireevsky and his brother Pyotr collected Russian folk songs and ballads. Advocates of Schelling regarded Hegel's philosophy critically; it was too rationalist for them. Hegel, however, was quite popular in Russia. The philosopher Nikolai V. Stankiewich, the historian Timofei Granovsky and the anarchist theoretician Mikhail A. Bakunin were Hegelians. The literary critic Vissarion G. Belinsky, a well-known figure in Russia, was initially influenced by the views of Schelling and Fichte, but later turned to Hegel's dialectics after a complicated evolution. Finally Belinsky created a philosophical system of his own, characterized by his adoption of materialist principles.

The materialist tendency was important for the ideology of the liberation movement. Aleksandr I. Hertzen, for instance, comparing materialism and idealism from the gnostic point of view, took the side of the former. He also accepted Hegel's dialectics, which he regarded as the 'algebra of revolution'. Hertzen was forced to emigrate; he subsequently became one of the most radical critics of autocracy and serfdom in Russia.

In spite of the difficulties caused by the government's repressive measures, Russian scholars made important progress both in human and exact sciences. Scholars specializing in the exact sciences should be given much credit for the development of Russian culture. They were closely following the achievements of European scientists and always paid attention to new trends in fields such as physics and chemistry. The physicists Vassilii V. Petrov and Emilii H. Lenz concentrated their attention on the problems of electrotechnics. Boris S. Jacobi was the first to suggest methods of calculation for electromagnets in electric motors, and designed and tested a maritime electric engine. In 1832 Pavel L. Schilling invented the electromagnetic telegraph and demonstrated it in St Petersburg. In the first half of the nineteenth century the foundations of Russian chemistry were laid. Especially important in this connection was the contribution of Nikolai N. Zinin, who was sent abroad after graduating from Kazan University, and became acquainted with the work of the most advanced laboratories of Britain, Germany and France.

Paramount attention was attributed to practical research, particularly in the metallurgical sphere, where the invention of new methods of making high-quality steel was one of the main achievements. These achievements were demonstrated by tests on an artillery piece cast under the supervision of Pavel M. Obukhov, at the London World Exhibition in 1860, where it was awarded a medal. Successes in astronomy could be attributed to Vassilii Ya. Struve, who founded the Pulkov Observatory near St Petersburg in 1839.

Apart from practical research, Russian scholars were making discoveries in the sphere of the fundamental sciences. Often they were ahead of their time and did not receive due credit immediately. For instance, Nikolai I. Lobachevsky (1792–1856), one of the greatest Russian scientists of the first half of the century, became famous as the founder of non-Euclidean geometry only after his death. Lobachevsky's discovery was later used in many branches of mathematics and natural sciences, for instance in the elaboration of the theory of relativity.

The Great Reforms of 1860s and 1870s became a turning point in the development of Russian society and culture, especially with the abolition of serfdom (1861), which facilitated economic progress and gave a start to the industrial revolution. Russia had always been a predominantly peasant country; now her urban population was growing rapidly, the capitalist and working classes were forming, and the role of urban culture was increasing. Western European influence was playing a part in all these processes, especially as it was Russia's backwardness in the economic and military spheres that became an important catalyst for the reforms.

The underdevelopment of the education system was an acute problem. By 1861 only 7 per cent of serfs were literate. In the reign of Nicolas I, which preceded the reforms, education exhibited a clear class character. The intellectuals understood that the liberation of the peasantry could not be completed while peasants remained culturally separated from the educated strata and bound to archaic traditions and ideals. The Committees for Literacy, organized in Moscow and St Petersburg, were attempting to change this situation. They saw their task as the introduction of universal primary education, the transition from utilitarian professional education to a general, stimulating, non-class-based system. The efforts of a group of pedagogues headed by Konstantin D. Ushinsky (1824–71), the founder of the national school of pedagogical thought, which consolidated itself around the Committees, resulted in the establishment of a system of non-class-based primary schools in 1864. Public organizations, in addition to the government and the church, received the right to open these schools. Under this program 40,000 three-year schools, belonging to the *zemstva* (local self-government institutions), were opened in the period from 1864 to 1914. In addition to reading, writing and arithmetic, their students were taught the fundamentals of natural sciences and history. The curriculum of the Sunday schools was also broader than in the state schools. Parish schools, however, remained the biggest category of primary schools, and the church's influence was increased there. All these measures produced certain results. The numbers of the literate grew more rapidly. By 1914 more than 30 per cent were literate. Still, the scale of primary education development in Russia remained substantially lower than in Western Europe. Rudiments of the class system survived also in secondary and higher education. They were manifested in the division of secondary schools into gymnasiums and technical schools. Graduates from the latter category were not permitted to enter universities.

Nevertheless, there was a 'golden age' in the history of higher education in Russia, when the universities gained autonomy in the period 1863–84. They turned into real centres of intellectual life, temples of knowledge, and young people entered them with reverence. Academics' prestige increased greatly. Science became more popular among the young generation, which later resulted in the emergence of a whole constellation of brilliant scientists in Russia. Among the consequences of university autonomy was the rapid spread of revolutionary ideas among students and professors. Gradually, university education came to be regarded primarily as a way of associating with the democratic ideas of the *intelligenzia*, and only secondarily as a means of learning.

During the reign of Emperor Alexander II (1855–81), when liberal ideas spread to the highest circles of society, and the *intelligenzia's* ideals began to claim the role of universal moral foundations, a new revolutionary-democratic culture was rapidly developing within Russian universities. Later this new culture would in many respects determine the country's destiny. The ideas of socialist populists (*narodniki*) like Nikolai G. Chernyshevsky, Mikhail Bakunin, Pyotr L. Lavrov and Nikolai K. Mikhailovsky were especially popular among students. Like Hertzen before them, the *narodniki* saw the future of Russia's social progress in the spread of egalitarian ideals, personified, according to them, in the Russian peasant commune, rather than in capitalist development. Under their influence, students organized a mass movement for 'mixing with the people', to appreciate the people's experience of social organization and to disseminate revolutionary ideals among them. And though in the 1870s this movement ended in failure, propagandizing to the peasantry using the materials of folk Utopias against the forces of state power and landed gentry in the early twentieth century helped the successors of the *narodniki*, the Socialist Revolutionary party, to win support among the peasantry and turn it into a revolutionary force.

This 'idolizing of the people' and the worship of communal values inevitably left its imprint on the intellectuals themselves, who became more influenced by the revolutionaries' views and opinions, regarding them as models of self-denial and moral purity. The intellectuals accepted those archaic peasant values adopted by the revolutionaries: asceticism; egalitarian collectivism; idealization of the people and those who served them; an instrumental attitude towards death; and attributing the features of omniscience and immortality to revolutionary leaders.

Populist ideas were disputed by the followers of Marx. Georgii V. Plekhanov, the author of numerous works on philosophy, history and sociology, played a major part here, beginning in the 1880s. Unlike the populists, who regarded the peasantry as the main force, Marxists primarily addressed the proletariat.

Democratic ideals exerted considerable influence on the development of the Russian national school of painting and Russian music. The critic Vladimir V. Stasov was the inspirer of this movement. In painting, democratic views were shared by the *Peredvizhnik* group of painters, organized in 1871, who were the first to choose the themes of Russian landscapes and the life and sufferings of the people as the central subject of their work. The group included Vassilii G. Perov, Ivan N. Kramskoi, Nikolai A. Yaroshenko, Ivan I. Shishkin, and Isaac I. Levitan (1860–1900). The most outstanding member of the *Peredvizhniki* was Ilya Ye. Repin (1844–1930), famous for the realistic style and deep psychological character of his paintings, combined with a powerful talent. Valentin A. Serov (1865–1911), the greatest Russian artist of the early twentieth century, was his pupil. In Serov's works, however, we can clearly see that the painter was returning to aestheticism, abandoning the pretentiousness and bookishness characteristic of some *Peredvizhniki*.

Russia was quickly reacting to new artistic tendencies in Western Europe. Konstantin A. Korovin's style was close to impressionism. The works of Mikhail A. Vrubel manifested the emergence of new directions in painting. From 1892 the

Tretyakov Gallery in Moscow became a real treasury of national painting.

In the sphere of music, democratic views consolidated a group of composers calling themselves 'The Mighty Handful'. Their works became classics of the Russian opera, and they included Modest P. Musorgsky (1839–81), Nikolai A. Rimsky-Korsakov (1844–1908), Aleksandr P. Borodin, Milii A. Balakirev, and Ceasar A. Kui. They saw their principal task in creating folk musical dramas on epic historical topics. Their work reflected the Russian people's spiritual power and patriotism.

Pyotr I. Tchaikovsky occupies a special place in world music. The creations of this genius combined realism with romanticism, linking the Russian musical tradition with the world's musical legacy.

Still, it was the development of national consciousness and national culture, rather than democratic ideas, that made it possible for a number of aspects of Russia's culture in the second half of the century to become classical. In literature great Russian novelists, not writers of the populist type, determined the main trend. Their works gained high esteem in Europe and throughout the world. Russian literature reached maturity in the prose of Ivan S. Turgenev, whose novels were devoted to the gentry's psychological problems. Fyodor M. Dostoyevsky and Lev N. Tolstoi raised deep philosophical problems in their books. The problems of good and evil, the quest for God, relations between God and man, the problem of freedom, and the question of the compatibility of evil with divine omniscience were central to their reflections. In his novels *Crime and Punishment, The Demons*, and *The Brothers Karamazov*, Dostoyevsky for the first time tried to explore the unconscious, the 'underground' features of a human being, exploring a new theme which was to become central to modern literature. The poetry of Fyodor I. Tjutchev (1803–73), philosophical in its essence and crystal clear in its language, stood apart in poetic lyricism.

In the 1880s the playwright Anton P. Chekhov entered the realm of literature, to receive worldwide fame in the years to come.

The rise of literature was accompanied by the successes of the theatre, where Aleksander Ostrovsky's plays should be noted especially.

The image of post-reform Russia changed significantly. Russian science achieved important successes. The Russian school of mathematics took shape, headed by Pafnutii L. Chebyshev and his pupils Andrei A. Markov and Aleksandr M. Lyapunov. Sofia V. Kovalevskaya became the first woman professor; she taught mathematics in the University of Stockholm, and her works received wide recognition. Many scientists took part in the re-equiping of the Russian army, improving its artillery. Ivan A. Vyshnegradsky was the author of important works on the theory of automatic regulation and machine construction; N. V. Maievsky on ballistics; and Axel V. Gadolin on the theory of extensibility and the calculation of the strength of materials.

The emergence of the Russian school of physics included both theoretical and practical studies. Russian physicists paid special attention to new scientific trends. Aleksandr G. Stoletov elaborated the methods of calculating the work of electrical machines. Pavel N. Yablochkov invented the electric candle – the first type of electric light source practically applicable for illumination. Aleksander S. Popov, developing the ideas of the German physicist Heinrich Hertz, designed and demonstrated in 1895 a device he called

the storm meter, which was in fact the world's first radio receiver. In 1896 Popov created a device which he used to transmit the first radio message in history, consisting of two words: 'Heinrich Hertz'. Popov's discovery, like many other Russian inventions, received no support or proper appreciation in tsarist Russia. Yet the achievements of Russian scientists were receiving world recognition. The work of the chemist Aleksander M. Butlerov was well known abroad. He created the theory of chemical structure, which became fundamental to modern chemistry. Dmitrii I. Mendeleyev, another scientist of worldwide fame, worked in many spheres, primarily in chemistry, and discovered in 1869 the periodic law of chemical elements.

While the exact sciences were closely connected with the development of technology, production and other practical tasks, the natural ones were often related to philosophical discussions, and influenced the formation of a worldview, as knowledge of nature's secrets forced scientists to make a choice between the rationalist, materialist interpretation of the problems in question and explanations based on idealistic theories. Therefore, discoveries in the sphere of natural science in Russia often became phenomena of public life as well. That was the case with the work of the physiologist Ivan M. Sechenov. His book *The Reflexes of the Brain* attracted the attention both of specialists and public. Sechenov's claim that physiological processes form the basis of human psychological phenomena was regarded by the supporters of the materialist interpretation of natural sciences as a significant success in their dispute with idealists. Sechenov's subsequent studies of the human central nervous system attracted wide scientific attention in Russia and abroad. The young Sigmund Freud, who was only starting his research into human psychological activity in the external environment, was among those who studied the works of Sechenov, who founded the Russian physiological school; Ivan P. Pavlov was one of his pupils. Even at an early stage of his career he demonstrated the qualities of an independently thinking scholar.

Ivan I. Mechnikov, whose most important discoveries were in the sphere of embryology and microbiology, was also in close contact with foreign, as well as Russian, research institutions. From 1888 he worked in Paris at the Pasteur Institute, but stayed in touch with Russian scientists. Charles Darwin's theory of evolution enjoyed considerable popularity in the Russian academic community. Besides Mechnikov and Sechenov, Klimentii A. Timiryazev, the founder of plant physiology as a discipline, and the Kovalevsky brothers were the most prominent Russian supporters of evolution theory. Aleksandr O. Kovalevsky was working in the spheres of embryology and histology, and his brother Vladimir became the founder of evolutionary palaeontology as an independent discipline.

The tendency for philosophical interpretation of research data was characteristic of specialists in the human sciences too. Under the influence of Auguste Comte's theories, the positivists tried to reconsider the history of mankind, applying the laws of natural science to their studies. They attributed much significance to the influence of environment on the evolution of human relations. The factor of geography occupied an important place in the theoretical constructions of the historian Sergei Solovyev, author of the multi-volume *History of Russia from the Ancient Times*. Russian historians paid much attention to the history of other countries.

At the turn of the nineteenth century Russia's territory stretched for 4,676 kilometres from north to south and 10,732km from East to West. In 1897 this great country had a population of 129 million. European Russia (excepting Finland and Poland) had 103 million inhabitants in 1897, and 142 million in 1914. The Asian part of the country was populated rather sparsely. Peasants constituted the majority of the population. In European Russia in 1908–1914, the urban population reached 14.4 per cent only, and the remaining 85.6 per cent lived in the countryside. When we compare the urban and agrarian populations of Russia with the countries of Western Europe, great differences become obvious. In the same period in Britain 78 per cent lived in the cities, and in Germany, 56 per cent. In 1897, 32.6 per cent of Russian men and 13.6 per cent of women were literate. In the Caucasus the number of literate persons was even lower: 18 per cent of men and 6 per cent of women. When we take this level of literacy into account, it is quite understandable that the church still occupied an important place in Russian culture.

At the turn of the nineteenth century every Russian was still obliged to profess some kind of religion, at least from the official point of view. In 1900, 91 million were considered to be Orthodox (72.6 per cent of the population). In addition, there were 12 million Catholics (9.2 per cent) and 2 million Protestants (1.8 per cent). Christians, therefore, constituted a majority. Muslems numbered 14 million (11.2 per cent) and Jews, 5 million (4.2 per cent). Thus we can roughly estimate that the majority of European Russia's population was Christian, and among these members of Orthodox confession dominated. The Orthodox church retained its leading position and still played an important role in the public, daily and cultural life of citizens, who, in addition to Russians, Ukrainians, Belorussians, Georgians, Armenians, Karelians and Greeks – the nations traditionally professing Orthodoxy – included representatives of other nations as well.

Behind its seemingly unshakeable facade, the Orthodox church was undergoing a serious crisis. Significant changes taking place in the country, especially in the spheres of economics, social structure, and scientific and technical progress, put the reform of the church on the agenda. There were plans to summon the Land Assembly (*Pomestnyi Sobor*) and elect the Patriarch there; Nicolas II promised to summon the Assembly, but did not keep his word.

Due to its inseparable link with the monarchy, the church suffered moral setbacks as the prestige of the monarchy declined. Clergymen began to lose their authority and found it hard to oppose infringements of their standards of morality. The official church was subject to criticism in various forms. Philosophers, writers and publicists debated religious problems. Relations between the church and the writer Lev Tolstoi became a complicated problem for the former. Tolstoi considered himself a follower of Christ, but rejected the dogma of Christ's divinity and resurrection and was against the official church, which he regarded as a political organization devoid of any Christian essence. In 1901 the Synod excommunicated him. The religious strivings of the writer Dmitrii S. Merezhkovsky and the poetess Zinaida N. Gippius went parallel with their condemnation of the church's official status and their fears that Christianity had exhausted itself. The religious-philosophical essays of Nikolai A. Berdyaev, Pyotr B. Struve, Semyon L. Frank, Sergei N. Bulgakov and others, published in 1909 in the book *Vekhi* (Milestones), began

a critique of the Russian intelligentsia's atheism, emphasizing its responsibility for the dissemination of anarchism and other revolutionary theories. Even some representatives of the revolutionary camp joined the ranks of 'God-seekers' and 'God-builders'; the Social Democrats Aleksandr A. Bogdanov and Aleksandr V. Lunacharsky, for instance, and the writer Maxim Gorky, who expressed similar ideas. Vladimir I. Lenin and Georgii V. Plekhanov became their uncompromising opponents – these latter of course staunchly supported materialist philosophy.

The development of exact sciences in the early twentieth century was characterized by the emergence of schools and trends headed by gifted scholars, which created the theoretical basis for the advance of most progressive technologies. In mathematics Vladimir A. Steklov, who specialized in mathematical analysis, extensibility theory and hydrodynamics, founded a school of mathematical physics. A. N. Krylov carried out important research both in mathematical analysis and the problems of ship stability, buoyancy and unsinkability. The school of theoretical aerodynamics took shape under the guidance of Nikolai E. Zhukovsky; Sergei A. Chaplygin was his most promising pupil. This school illustrates well the fact that Russian scientists' theoretical achievements often progressed far ahead of the development of national industry. The first aeroplanes, created by Russian designers, were produced by the St Petersburg Russian-Baltic factory only in 1913. The designs of Igor I. Sikorsky were especially innovative – his multi-engine planes *Russian Warrior* and *Ilya Muromets* had no match in their payload, range and equipment.

The ideas of Konstantin E. Tsiolkovsky were directed to the distant future. He designed an all-metal dirigible, wrote a book on the theory of flight and created a model wind tunnel. In 1903 Tsiolkovsky published the book, *The Exploration of Global Spaces by Jet Devices*, where he formulated the theory of rocket propulsion and proved a number of theorems on jet propulsion.

Many Russian scientists worked on problems which later were related to the most important discoveries of the twentieth century. The physicist Pyotr N. Lebedev created the basis for further research in electromagnetic light theory and the estimation of mass and energy, which determined nuclear processes. Experiments performed by the brilliant experimental physicist Dmitrii S. Rozhdestvensky contributed directly to Niels Bohr's nuclear theory. Research by Russian chemists was also at a high level. Alexei E. Favorsky created the independent Russian school of organic chemistry. A member of this school, Sergei V. Lebedev, obtained the first sample of synthetic rubber in 1910. The new discipline of petrochemistry was the domain of Nikolai D. Zelinsky. Vladimir I. Vernadsky and his pupil Aleksandr E. Fersman founded geological chemistry. Apart from his practical studies, Vernadsky paid much attention to the theoretical interpretation of relations between man and the environment.

International attention attracted by the works of Russian physiologists was an example of Russian science becoming an integral part of the world scientific process. In 1903 Ivan Pavlov gave a highly successful report on the conditioned reflexes at the XIV International Congress of physiologists in Madrid. In 1904 he was awarded the Nobel Prize for his works on digestion physiology. Pavlov was the first Russian scholar to receive this award.

While the activities of Russian scholars and inventors, connected with the general progress of science and technology, were marked by purposefulness and confidence in the future, the spiritual life, literature, art, and even music was permeated, apart from some optimistic motifs, by a mood of disappointment and pessimism. This mood was to a large extent influenced by dissatisfaction with the situation in Russia, where the struggle against the existing system was gathering strength, leading to the revolution of 1905–7, and by growing tension in the wider world, especially in Western Europe with the threat of war, which was initially envisaged as a European conflict, but in reality was to become the First World War. This complex situation led to the characteristic diversity of artistic trends and directions in every sphere of Russian culture in the early twentieth century.

The realistic tradition was still strong in Russian literature of the early twentieth century. Realists like Lev Tolstoi and Anton Chekhov were very influential and to a considerable extent determined the preferences of the reading public. After their deaths (Chekhov in 1904, Tolstoi in 1910) realism remained a dominant trend in Russian literature, mostly thanks to the talents of Aleksandr I. Kuprin, Ivan A. Bunin, Vladimir G. Korolenko, and Maxim Gorky (i.e. Alexei M. Peshkov). Gorky's early works were marked by revolutionary romanticism, but at a later stage he gradually turned to realism, and his books were especially popular in circles sympathetic to revolutionary ideas. Many works of the talented writer Leonid N. Andreev combined a realistic style with mysticism and pessimistic philosophical reflections on the purpose of life and human imperfection.

Trends in modernist literature (symbolism and perfectionism (acmeism)) were also developing, aimed at the transformation of life on the basis of the aesthetic ideal. The first generation of Russian symbolists included poets Konstantin D. Balmont and Valerii Ya. Brusov. Their writings, as well as those of the younger poet Aleksandr A. Blok, reflected complex religious, philosophical and aesthetic strivings. 'Acmeism' was founded by the poet Nikolai S. Gumilev, who regarded the symbolists as his predecessors, but rejected their mysticism, proclaiming the triumph of the *élan vital*, the cult of a strong personality, seeking trials and adventures. Anna A. Akhmatova, whose verses were full of exquisite sensual lyrics, and Osip E. Mandelstam also belonged to the acmeists. The literary life of the early twentieth century was full of heated disputes.

Russian theatre, like literature, in the early twentieth century saw both the successes of realists and bold, innovative experiments. The Moscow Art Theatre, opened in 1898 under the directorship of Konstantin S. Stanislavsky and Vladimir I. Nemirovich-Danchenko, staged modern plays – by Chekhov, Gorky, Ibsen, Hauptmann, Maeterlinck – and classic plays – primarily Shakespeare – with equal success. Stanislavsky himself, together with Vassilii I. Kachalov, Ivan M. Moskvin, Olga L. Knipper-Chekhova and other brilliant actors, created an outstanding gallery of characters in their roles. The actors of the Alexandrine Theatre in St Petersburg – Vladimir N. Davydov, Maria G. Savina, Konstantin A. Varlamov, and Yuri M. Yuriev – followed the realistic tradition. Vera F. Komissarzhevskaya's brilliant talent reflected itself, apart from her excellent roles, in the activities of the theatre which she created in St Petersburg in 1904. Vsevolod E. Meyerhold, whose bold modernist innovations provoked many disputes, had made his first steps as theatre director together with Stanislavsky and Komissarzhevskaya.

Russia's musical culture was also full of creative strivings. The deceased composers had worthy successors: Sergei I. Taneev was Tchaikovsky's pupil, Aleksandr K. Glazunov and Igor F. Stravinsky were taught by Rimsky-Korsakov. Three of the youngest generation of composers – Sergei V. Rakhmaninov, Aleksandr N. Skriabin and Sergei S. Prokofiev – occupied a special place in Russian music. Each was a figure of strong artistic individuality, differing from the others in his outlook and creative manner, but they had something in common – their music reflected the dynamic, complex and tragic character of the early twentieth century, as it was seen by the Russians and other nations of the world. The achievements of Russian theatre and musical culture were interacting more and more with world art, especially with West European culture. The names of the opera singer Fyodor I. Shalyapin, and the ballet dancers Anna P. Pavlova and Vazlav F. Nizhinsky, were known worldwide. Ballet connoisseurs were closely watching the reforms of Russian ballet-masters Aleksandr A. Gorsky and Mikhail M. Fokin. Sergei P. Dyagilev had done a great deal to promote Russian ballet and Russian art abroad, thus contributing to the links between Russian and world culture.

There were many innovative tendencies in the development of Russian painting in the beginning of the twentieth century. Painters specializing in graphics, stage decorations and costumes, and – which was most important – attributing a special significance to skill and seeking new forms of artistic creativity – formed in 1898 the 'World of Art' circle, headed by Aleksandr N. Benois. Diversity of styles prevailed in Russian painting. The position of realism, represented primarily by Repin and Serov, was still strong. New trends, however, were finding their followers in Russia at the beginning of the century. In 1907 Nikolai K. Chiurlenis created real symphonies of colours, lines and shapes. The painter Yuri P. Annenkov considered Chiurlenis the pioneer and the prophet of abstract painting. Vassilii V. Kandinsky and Kazimir S. Malevich became masters of abstract painting. Vladimir E. Tatlin was the first Russian constructivist. In his works he tried to reflect the development of industry and technology, to create an aesthetic of mechanical progress.

Marc Z. Chagall was one of the most original Russian painters. Lev S. Bakst and Mstislav V. Dobuzhinsky, prominent members of the World of Art circle, were his teachers, but he elaborated a style of his own. Chagall's paintings combined fantasy with reality, reflecting the most delicate nuances of romantic and lyrical mood in an original way.

New trends in architecture were represented, together with *Art Moderne* (Fyodor O. Schechtel, 1859–1926), by the neo-Russian style, which was developing the 'national style' of the late nineteenth century. Many beautiful buildings in Moscow, including the Historical Museum and the City Duma, were designed in this manner.

Former revolutionaries began to show interest in the idea of a spiritual and aesthetic transformation of the world, as opposed to change by way of revolution. This idea found its supporters especially among those intellectuals who had left the revolutionary movement but retained their liberal views and were not attracted by the reactionary *étatiste* propaganda. They wrote articles for, and subscribed to, the so-called 'thick magazines', which played a special part in Russia's public life and culture in the second half of the nineteenth and in the early twentieth century. *Vestnik Evropy* (The European Courier), edited from 1866 by

Mikhail M. Stasiulevich, was one of the most well known. The interests of this part of the intelligentsia in the early twentieth century were evolving from social problems to religious and psychological ones, from national and class solutions to those of a cosmic dimension. Vladimir S. Solovyev (1853–1900) was the scholar who managed to turn Russian philosophy from positivism and Hegelianism to religious themes. He spared no effort in developing the idea of the national ('Sophian' – i.e. intuitive and self-absorbed) style of thinking, outlined first by the Slavophiles, in studying the problems of goodness and freedom. These directions were later further developed by Nikolai Berdyaev, Sergei Bulgakov, Semyon Frank and Pavel A. Florensky. Nikolai F. Fyodorov founded the Russian philosophy of anthropocosmism. Tsiolkovsky and Vernadsky became its supporters.

The Russian Empire was a multinational state. Apart from Russians, dozens of other nationalities lived on its territory. They were developing their own culture and national consciousness. And at the same time a constant dialogue of cultures was taking place in the country, giving them common features. In the nineteenth century the international and interconfessional dialogue was especially active. From the levels of traditional folk culture and the political culture of the élite, it expanded to the level of artistic culture, literature and education. Because of this, many nations made their contribution to Russian culture.

This review of Russia's cultural life would be incomplete without mentioning the development of non-Russian and non-Orthodox cultures, the complex cultural interactions which determined the unique character of Russian civilization.

The development of the cultures of the nations populating Russia was meeting with serious difficulties throughout the nineteenth and early twentieth centuries. Teaching in the native language was subject to persecution in the Ukraine and Belorussia. In the early twentieth century about three quarters of the Ukranian and Belorussian population were illiterate. For Belorussia the figure was even higher – 78 per cent. Schools had 226,000 students, which amounted only to one fifth of school-age children. The most gifted students usually studed in Russian gymnasiums, and then entered the universities of St Petersburg, Moscow, Kiev, Kharkov, or Odessa. The University of St Vladimir in Kiev, the Novorossiisky University in Odessa, and the University of Kharkov were officially regarded as Russian institutions, though they were situated in the Ukraine. Courses were taught in Russian there. Informally, however, they were centres of interest in the revival of the national culture as well as in scientific advance. In this situation many scholars made important contributions to the studies of Ukranian geography, history and other relevant topics. The activities of scientific societies attached to the universities were especially fruitful in this connection. The historical society of Nestor the Annalist was to be found at Kiev University, in which both Russian and Ukranian historians participated, notably Vladimir S. Ikonnikov, Mikhail F. Vladimirsky-Budanov, Mitrofan V. Dovnar-Zapolsky, and Vladimir B. Antonovich.

Historical studies of the Kiev Rus period, for instance, were contributing both to Russian and Ukranian cultures. Nevertheless, many Ukranian scholars, especially those studying and working in St Petersburg, Moscow and other Russian academic centres, while their achievements were recognized on the Russian, and even the world stage,

became separated from the national Ukranian tradition. In this connection the role of writers, actors and painters in preserving and developing national culture was especially significant. Ivan Franko, Lessya Ukrainka (Larissa Kosach), Mikhail M. Kotsjubinsky, and Marko Vovchok (Maria A. Vilenskaya-Markovich), following the example of Taras G. Shevchenko, were writing in Ukranian. It is worth mentioning that some of them lived on Ukranian territory belonging to Russia, while others, like Ivan Franko, in Galicia (West Ukraine). This fact demonstrated the integrity of Ukranian national culture. The work of several talented theatre companies contributed to the preservation and dissemination of Ukranian culture and language. As in Russia, there were whole families devoted to the theatre in the Ukraine. In this connection we can mention the talented and famous actors, the brothers P. K., M. K. and I. K. Tobilevich, known under their stage names Saksagalsky, Sadovsky, Karpenko-Seryi.

The second half of the nineteenth century and the early twentieth century witnessed the growth of Ukranian national consciousness. Ukranian discontent was aggravated by the fact that Ukranian was not accepted as an independent language in contemporary Russia, and there were practically no publications in this language. At the beginning of the twentieth century the historian Mikhail S. Grushevsky reconsidered the problem of the common origin of Russians and Ukranians, starting from the Middle Ages. Belorussian national folklore inspired the classics of Belorussian literature. The poets Janka Kupala (Ivan D. Lutsevich) and Jakub Kolas (Konstantin M. Mickiewicz) were most prominent.

Literature also helped to preserve the cultural traditions of the North Caucasian and Transcaucasian nations. At the beginning of the twentieth century the Georgian writers Ilya Chavchavadze and Akakii Tsereteli were still working. They found worthy successors in V. Pshavela and Aleksandr Kazbegi. The Ossetian poet Kosta Khetagurov was writing both in his native Ossetian and Russian. In the early twentieth century the Caucasus was closely linked to Russia, both in economic and cultural life. National diversity was characteristic of the cultural life of the region. In Tiflis (Tbilisi) papers and magazines were published in Georgian, Armenian and Russian; in Baku, in Azerbaijani, Armenian and Russian. Many persons of Caucasian origin were closely connected with Russian cultural centres. The career of the Orbeli brothers is a good example here. Leon A. Orbeli was trained at the Military Medical Academy in St Petersburg and became one of Ivan Pavlov's closest disciples. Joseph A. Orbeli graduated from St Petersburg University and became a prominent Orientalist, archaeologist and cultural historian. The work of composers from the Caucasus was interconnected with that of Russian composers. The Georgian Meliton A. Balanchivadze and the Armenian Aleksandr A. Spendiarov studied at the St Petersburg Conservatory under the supervision of Rimsky-Korsakov; the Georgian Zakharii P. Paliashvili was Taneev's student at the Moscow Conservatory. The Azerbaijanian Uzeir A. Gadzhibekov studied musical theory in St Petersburg and Moscow. These composers laid the basis for the genesis and development of modern musical culture in Georgia, Armenia and Azerbaijan. The Russian composer Mikhail M. Ippolitov-Ivanov for a long period was the head of the Tiflis musical school, which played an important part in musical education in the Caucasus. Some cultural figures representing non-Russian nations, whose links with Russian culture were especially strong, became an integral part of its history. The Georgian actor and director Aleksandr I. Sumbatashvili-Yuzhin, better known in Russia as Sumbatov-Yuzhin, headed the Malyi Theatre in Moscow for several years.

The contribution of Russia's various nations facilitated an influx of the best talents into Russian science and culture. However, in tsarist Russia some of them were not able to participate in the progress of the national culture to which they belonged.

The achievements of numerous painters, composers and scientists, especially those who pioneered innovations, contributed to universal culture in its broad definition – reflecting both national peculiarities and those traits belonging to humankind as a whole. The Armenian painter Martiros Sarian received his training at the Moscow School of Painting, Sculpture and Architecture, being the pupil of Valentin Serov. Sarian's strong and original talent attracted the attention of painters and connoisseurs far beyond the borders of Armenia and Russia. Another outstanding Armenian, the writer Hachatur Abovian, graduated from Derpt (Tartu) University, far from his motherland, but made a great contribution to Armenian culture by preserving national traditions and carrying out a reform which made the integration of colloquial language and literature possible.

In the late nineteenth and early twentieth centuries Derpt University remained a significant academic centre, working in close cooperation with Russian scholars, especially those from St Petersburg. The development of the Estonian, Latvian and Lithuanian cultures, however, faced the same difficulties as other national cultures. Even so, these peoples' national traditions were growing stronger in the first years of the twentieth century. Poets and writers helped to preserve national languages and also worked to reconstruct the cultural legacy of the past. In Estonia, Friedrich R. Kreizwald compiled and published the folk epic *Kalevipoeg*. Latvia produced a whole constellation of writers and poets, including Krishjanis Baron, Janis Rainis and Andrei Upit. The talented painter Julius Fedders depicted Latvian landscapes in his works. The Lithuanian Chiurlenis was a great innovator, both in music and painting. The writer Julia A. Zhemayte occupied a prominent place in Lithuanian literature.

One should not overlook the links between the Moslem and Christian cultures in the Russian Empire. In the nineteenth century Russian troops were often used to suppress Moslem uprisings. Nevertheless, cultural dialogue was also developing; from 1800 Moslem literature was published without constraints, and Russia was becoming one of the world's biggest publishers of the Koran. This process was facilitated by the creation of the academic school of Islamic studies, which included Viktor R. Rosen, Vassilii V. Bartold, V. F. Girgas, and M. A. at-Tantavi. By 1859 the Kazan printing house had published more than 82,000 copies of books on Islam, which became well known both in Russia and abroad. In the early twentieth century the Moslem modernizers, the *Jadides*, headed by I. Gasprinsky, even regarded the Russian modernization experience as a kind of ideal, more suitable for Moslems than the European model. The *Jadides* thought that the incorporation of Moslem nations into the Russian Empire had been a historical necessity, providing them with the opportunity to become an integral part of the world community.

That many nations found it impossible to develop their culture within the Russian Empire was a serious infringement of their rights and dignity. The position of Russian Jews was difficult. A percentage quota existed for those Jews who wished to enter high school and many other secondary education institutions, especially those controlled by the government. Many talented Jews living in Russia were integrated into Russian culture and regarded as its representatives. The paintings of Isaac Levitan, Lev Bakst and Marc Chagall, and the sculptures of Mark M. Antokolsky, are recognized as masterpieces of Russian art. Some Jews found it expedient to change religion and became Christians. The physicist Abram F. Ioffe, for instance, joined the Lutheran church. Jewish writers to a larger extent managed to reflect the originality of Russian Jewish culture. Sholom Aleihem (the pen name of Sholom N. Rabinovich) was the most famous among them.

The struggle for national equality gradually became an integral part of the political struggle in Russia. The representatives of radical and liberal parties alike were engaged in various forms of protest against national oppression. The political struggle in Russia also left its imprint on cultural life. Russian writers, scientists and painters raised their voice in protest against the actions of the tsarist government, especially during the revolution of 1905–7. Political struggle, in its turn, was reflected in various spheres of cultural life. The revolutionary camp was represented by several political parties. These included the Social Democrats, and the Socialist Revolutionaries headed by Viktor M. Chernov. The former split into the Bolshevik Party, headed by Lenin, and the Mensheviks, headed by Plekhanov and Julii O. Martov. Liberal opposition was represented by the Constitutional Democratic Party, with the prominent historian Pavel N. Muliukov among its leaders. Miliukov belonged to the so-called 'Moscow' historical school, headed by Vassilii O. Kliuchevsky.

The outstanding achievements of Russian scholars, actors, musicians, and painters facilitated Russia's cultural progress. Yet a large part of its population, especially the peasantry, was still suffering a great deal of hardship. Discontent was growing in the country, and political parties calling for transformation by way of revolution received strong support.

Only under the influence of the first Russian revolution of 1905–7 did the tsarist government make some concessions. Nevertheless, even after the establishment of the State Duma, the Code of Principal Laws declared that 'supreme autocratic power' belonged to the Emperor. The last Russian Emperor, Nicolas II, stubbornly tried to preserve the autocratic character of his position. This policy was becoming an obstacle to the peaceful evolution of the political system: it hindered badly needed reforms, making the threat of revolution imminent, and it was leading Russia and its culture into a period of crisis.

BIBLIOGRAPHY

AKHIEZER, A. S. 1991. *Rossiya: kritika istoritcheskogo opita*. [Russia: Criticism of Historical Experience]. Vols. 1–3. Moscow.

BESANÇON, A. 1974. *Education et société en Russie dans le second tiers du XIXe siècle*. La Haye, Paris.

BESSONOV, B. N. 1993. *Sudba Rossii: vzglyad russkikh mysliteley*. [Russia's Destiny: Russian Thinkers' Point of View]. Moscow.

CONFINO, M. 1991. *Société et mentalité: collectives en Russie sous l'Ancien Régime*. Paris.

DMITRIEV, S. S. 1985. *Otcherki russkoy kultury natchala XX veka*. [Essays on Russian Culture at the Beginning of the Twentieth Century]. Moscow.

EIMONTOVA, R. T. 1985. *Russkyi universitet na grani dvukh epokh (ot Rossii krepostnoy k Rossii kapitalistitcheskoy)*. Moscow.

EKLOF, B.; FRANK, S. (eds) 1990. *The World of the Russian Peasant*. Boston MA.

GRAHAM, L. R. 1993. *Science in Russia and the Soviet Union. A Short History*. Cambridge.

HINGLEY, R. 1967. *Russian Writers and Society. 1825–1901*. New York and Toronto.

POZNANSKIY, V. V. 1975. *Otcherk formirivanya russkoy natsionalnoy kultury. Pervaya polovina XIX veka*. [Essay on the Development of Russian National Culture. The First Half of the Nineteenth Century]. Moscow.

——. 1994. *Puty i miragy russkoy kultury*. [Paths and Mirages of Russian Culture]. St Petersburg.

SHTCHERBINA, V. R. (ed.) 1987. *Mirovoye znatcheniye russkoy literatury XIX veka*. [The Global Importance of Nineteenth-century Russian Literature]. Moscow.

SOBOLEVA, E. V. 1983. *Organizatsiya nauky v poreformennoy Rosii*. [The Organization of Science in Russia after the Reforms]. Moscow.

VOLINKIN, N. M. 1976. *Otcherky istoryi russkoy kultury vtoroy poloviny XIX veka*. [Essays on the History of Russian Culture in the Second Half of the Nineteenth Century]. Moscow.

WILLIAMS, R. C. 1997. *Russia imagined: Art, Culture and National Identity. 1840–1995*. Frankfurt a.M.

YAKOVKINA, N. I. 1989. *Otcherki russkoy kultury pervoy poloviny XIX veka*. [Essays on Russian Culture in the First Half of the Nineteenth Century]. Moscow.

10.2.4

SOUTH EASTERN EUROPE

10.2.4.1

OVERVIEW

Nikolaï Todorov

NATIONS WITHOUT STATE

The period after 1789 was one of intensive political and cultural transformation in the Balkans. Social and cultural changes that had been gradually unfolding in the broader eighteenth century, now reached their climax. The French encyclopaedists' views, Voltaire's satires, the principles of popular sovereignty proclaimed by Rousseau and especially the slogan of the French Revolution 'Liberty, Equality, Fraternity', and the nation-state, found a receptive audience in the Balkans, primarily among groups of Orthodox merchants and intellectuals in the urban centres of the Ottoman Empire. These ideas were linked with the ideal of national independence, and imbued the struggles for liberation that broke out among all Balkan peoples during the nineteenth century, with a romantic and revolutionary pathos.[1]

The international environment meanwhile was not favourable for actions of this kind. In 1815, in Vienna, the Holy Alliance was signed declaring the principles of conservatism and legitimacy of empires to be the dominant political principle in Europe. While the Ottomans were not invited as co-signatories, the principle was extended to comprise the Ottoman Empire as well. Any attempt at overthrowing foreign domination was to be considered an act of terrorism. Already, back in 1798, Rhigas Velestinlis (c.1757–98) had been detained by the Austrian authorities and handed over to the Ottomans, who promptly executed him. At that point, however, nothing could stop the appeals for armed resistance and revolt by the oppressed peoples. Secret revolutionary committees and organizations were set up which gradually spread over the whole territory of the Balkan Peninsula. Solidarity between the Balkan peoples became the rule as representatives of neighbouring ethnic communities joined in the liberation efforts of a Balkan nation.

The Serbs were the first to succeed, already at the beginning of the nineteenth century, in gradually winning autonomy within the bounds of the Pashalik of Belgrade. Bulgarians and Greeks hurried to their aid. Two decades later, the Greeks also rose in an epic ten-year war against

foreign oppression. Volunteers from all over the Balkans poured into the Danubian principalities and the Peloponnese, the two centres of the Greek uprising. The European powers began to question the viability of the legitimacy principle, which they themselves had imposed. The circumstances were favourable for the Russo-Turkish war of 1828–9, as a result of which Greece gained independence, albeit as a rump state with only a quarter of the Greeks under Ottoman rule. In fact, state- and nation- building in the European provinces of the Ottoman Empire constituted the most revolutionary development in nineteenth-century Balkan history.

Throughout this century the Balkan peoples persisted in their efforts at throwing off Ottoman domination with variable success. During the 1870s, the South Slavs waged an uncompromising fight for liberation: Serbs and Montenegrins in Bosnia and Herzegovina, Bulgarians to the north and south of the Balkan range. International indignation at the cruel suppression of the April 1876 uprising in Bulgarian lands provided Russia with the grounds for another armed intervention against the Ottoman Empire. As a result, by 1878, the *de facto* independence of Bulgaria was also won, and Montenegro and Serbia were recognized as independent states. Romania, which took part in the war, revoked its vassal status, and also received independence. Thus, the new states emerged out of a series of revolutionary outbursts, and their territorial aspirations were realized through a long process of irredentist upheavals against Ottoman rule. The irredentist claims became the major theme of the respective foreign policies of the newly emerged states *vis-à-vis* the Ottomans, the great powers and each other.

Significant portions of the Balkans, however, still remained under the rule of the Ottoman Empire, whose subject populations carried on their revolutionary struggle with the support of their co-nationals in the newly established Balkan states. The recognition of the political independence of Serbs, Greeks, Romanians, and Bulgarians precipitated adjustments in the great European powers' strategy in South Eastern Europe. Along with the traditional interests of Great Britain, France, Russia and the Habsburgs, who had long been competing with each other for influence in the Balkans, a new distribution of power was underway. Austria-Hungary gained a solid footing in the western and central parts of the peninsula, while Germany made her voice ever more loudly heard in the European power chorus. Each power pursued its interests in the Eastern Mediterranean, striving to secure a firm political foothold in the Balkans, and promoting its cultural influence as well.

There were typological differences in the growth of national consciousness among the peoples under Habsburg and Ottoman rule. The former were not generally dragged into confessional conflict with either the state authority or the dominant church, within a framework of shared Christianity. The situation of the Balkan peoples ruled by the Ottomans, on the other hand, was quite different. With the dominance of Islam as the state religion, the struggle of the Balkan peoples, Christian in their majority, for the overthrow of Ottoman domination had commonly taken the form of a struggle of the Cross against the Crescent. This explains the frequent concerted actions of participants in the liberation movements of neighbouring countries. Gradually, however, religious pathos as the central characteristic of the nation receded to a secondary position. Controversies, which were setting at odds the Balkan Orthodox churches, especially the Greek and the Bulgarian, were now aroused not over the pre-eminence of the institution but over the territorial scope of the nation.

NATIONAL REVIVAL

The nineteenth century saw the transformation, even if not concurrently, of the economic role of entire strata of the Balkan populations. Their increased self-esteem was projected on all spheres of public life. It was first among the Greeks that an influential commercial and entrepreneurial stratum was formed. Its power and prominence owed much to the large Greek diaspora in nearly all the Mediterranean trade centres, in Central Europe and in Russia. They had accumulated wealth by virtue of a middleman's role in the Levantine trade of the European states, benefiting from the changing political climate in Europe in the last decades of the eighteenth and the beginning of the nineteenth century. With the opening of the port of Odessa, the Greeks who had settled in Russia took over the biggest share of Black Sea commerce. By mid-century, the Greek merchant fleet had reached a capacity of 300,000 tons. Over half of the ships along the Danube were sailing under the Greek flag. Since it was dispersed all over the Balkan Peninsula, the Greek bourgeoisie came to be regarded by contemporary observers as the Balkan middle class.

The material progress of the Greek middle class enabled it to undermine the traditional dominance of the Greek notables and big landowners, whose position had been enhanced by the support of the Ottoman authorities who recruited from among their ranks high dignitaries and the *hospodars* of the principalities of Moldavia and Wallachia. The contest for precedence between the two groups was particularly fierce in the sphere of education, where new secular subjects related to the natural sciences began to be introduced. The modern and progressive ideas coming from the West were adopted and spread, and there were efforts to elevate the vernacular to the status of a literary language. However, consensus within the Greek intellectual world was not achieved. One pole coalesced around the champions of the 'Megali Idea', which fully crystallized around the middle of the nineteenth century. It was based on the assumption of an unbroken continuity between modern Greece and its classical and medieval past, and the resurrection of the Byzantine Empire in terms of its cultural mission and within its territorial limits.

It was only during the latter part of the nineteenth century that moderate nationalists, inspired by the so-called Ionian school, made their influence felt. The School had been headed by Dionyssios Solomos (1798–1857), a poet who argued in favour of the spoken language to be adopted as the literary idiom, and extolled the revolutionary achievements of the Greek War of Independence. Moderate patriotism, whose most outstanding spokesman in the second half of the nineteenth century was Kostis Palamas (1859–1943), made gradual but major inroads in the intellectual sphere, and finally triumphed.

Throughout the nineteenth century, while Athens continued to build its reputation as the spiritual site of Hellenism, the economic capital of the Greeks was Constantinople. This was enhanced by the Tanzimat reform movement in the Ottoman Empire, which guaranteed equal civil rights to Muslims and Christians. The Greeks got the best out of these reforms: they became the bankers of Constantinople and took up one third of the commerce in Alexandria.

In independent Greece itself, under the governments of Trikoupis (1832–96), impressive public works were carried out, the Corinth Canal was built, and at the beginning of the twentieth century the Greek maritime fleet reached a freight capacity of nearly one million tons. Urban dwellers amounted already to 30 per cent of the total population. But these diverse activities swelled the state's foreign debt, and Prime Minister Trikoupis was forced to declare bankruptcy. Agriculture was a problem area, with nearly three quarters of all arable land in the hands of large estate owners, engendering strong resentment and frequent unrest among the small landholders and the landless poor. The advent of Eleftherios Venizelos (1864–1936) to power, after his effective display of political skill during the revolts on his native island of Crete, ushered a new period in Greek history. Venizelos undertook the reorganization of Greece's state institutions and, at the same time, launched a series of Balkan foreign policy initiatives.

The national revival among the Romanians ran its separate course. The two Danubian principalities were not entirely incorporated into the Ottoman system. They had preserved their social structure and a relative autonomy as vassal principalities in return for a fixed annual tribute to the Porte. Owing to their geographical location, however, Wallachia and Moldavia had been continually involved, not only in the Balkan political arena, but in the expansionist policies of Austria and Russia in the Danubian basin as well. Until the beginning of the eighteenth century, the principalities had been ruled by Romanian princes and a *boyar's* council. Implicated in Russian or Austrian intrigues, the local princes lost the support of the Sublime Porte, which put control of the principalities into the hands of the Greek Phanariots. In the course of the eighteenth and the beginning of the nineteenth century, the Phanariot *hospodars* secured the domination of the Porte and the hegemony of the Greek Phanariot establishment in the Balkans.

As the 1821 uprising broke out, volunteers from all Balkan peoples, responding to the appeals for liberation, poured in large numbers into Wallachia. The Romanian insurgents were led by Tudor Vladimirescu (c.1780–1821) whose programme, with its social components and anti-Phanariot edge, deviated from the priorities of the Greek uprising. Besides, the Romanian insurgent leaders soon began to falter in the face of Russia's negative attitude and the imminent invasion of Ottoman troops concentrated in northern Bulgaria. Despite its failure, the uprising has been generally considered as the beginning of Romania's modern history. Moreover, in the aftermath of these events, Russia assumed the role of an avowed protector of the Danubian principalities. The temporary Russian administration initiated not only a reorganization of the political structure of the principalities but also of their economic and social life. During the revolutionary events of 1848 in Europe, Wallachia and Moldavia became the scene of revolutionary agitation of the part of young liberals, most prominent among them Nicolae Balcescu (1819–52) who had taken part in the events in Paris. They came up with demands for political rights and agrarian reform. Under pressure from the joint armed intervention of Russian and Ottoman troops, the revolutionary forces were crushed, while the situation of the overwhelming majority of the population – the peasantry – began to deteriorate progressively. Brighter prospects for the Danubian principalities dawned after the Crimean war (1853–6), when a number of encouraging changes were effected, and freedom of navigation on the Danube was affirmed. The one question that remained unsolved was that of the Romanians of Transylvania. Following the Hungarian revolution, the Habsburgs turned this region into a separate province under the direct rule of Vienna, and strengthened the German presence there.

Beginning in 1859 and throughout the 1860s, during the reign of the native prince Alexandru Cuza (1820–73), the Romanians managed to achieve de facto unification. Under the premiership of Miliail Kogalniceanu (1817–91), far-reaching reforms were carried out, such as the secularization of church properties outside the country and agrarian reform, abolishing forced labour and allowing the purchase of land, which the peasants had cultivated until then.

The state formally adopted the name Romania under Carol I Hohenzollern, who had ascended the princely throne in 1866. All formal dependence on the Porte was lifted after Romania's participation in the Russo-Turkish war of 1877–8, and Carol proclaimed himself king in 1881. Two major problems attracted the attention of king, government and public in the half-century preceding World War I: the condition of the peasantry and the fate of the Transylvanian Romanians. Large estates remained predominant in Romania: several thousand big landowners possessed over half of the arable land, while an army of millions of landless peasants and small landholders was inexorably controlled and exploited by both landed magnates and the state. Protests, isolated clashes, and suppression were frequent occurrences in the countryside. In 1907, the grievances culminated in a mass peasant revolt whose leading slogan was 'We want land', and which was crushed with the utmost violence. Public opinion and political parties were unanimous in their attitude to the fate of their co-nationals in Transylvania. Romania's temporary orientation towards Austria made possible the establishment in Transylvania of an autocephalous Romanian church, as well as parity for the Romanian language alongside German and Hungarian. After the promulgation of the Dual Monarchy of Austria-Hungary in 1867, however, Hungarians re-established their privileged position in the province.

The Serbs entered the nineteenth century with considerable cultural credit owing to the intellectual activity of the Habsburg Serbs of Vojvodina. As in Novi Sad, book printing and higher education gained solid ground and the city became known as the 'Serbian Athens'. The 'Omladina', a cultural and educational society, began its activities there. Dositej Obradovic (c.1739–1811), an advocate of the Enlightenment, was the first to endorse the idea of the unity of all Serbs, which was based on the notion of their distinct tribal and linguistic community. After Serbia's liberation, Belgrade became the second centre of Serbian culture, where Vuk Karadzic (1787–1864), the progenitor of the modern Serb literary language, conducted his cultural activities. For the rise of national consciousness and a sense of unity among the Serbian people, the role of Peter II Njegos (1830–51), the bishop of Montenegro and a prominent poet, was also of the utmost importance.

By the middle of the nineteenth century, the population of the Serbian principality numbered about one million, most of them small and middle-sized landholders, with a thin layer of large estate owners, and a commercial and money-making middle class. The first upsurge of industrial development, mainly in the mining sphere, came at the turn of the century. Serbia's political history before World War I was permeated by the corrosive rivalry between the two Serbian dynasties, the Karageorgievic and the Obrenovic. In 1844, the Serbian statesman Ilija Garasanin (1812–74) presented a plan – 'Nacertanj' – charting the course, which Serbia would have to follow in her foreign policy in the future. Imbued with a mission to make Serbia the Piedmont of the Balkans, it envisaged the creation of a large South Slav state under the aegis of the Serbian dynasty. Subversive activities were undertaken for the realization of this Greater Serbian programme in the Slav-inhabited provinces of both the Habsburg and the Ottoman empires. Links were established with G. S. Rakovski, the Bulgarian intellectual and revolutionary, who founded a Bulgarian military school in Belgrade, and joined the campaign for the destruction of the Belgrade fortress, which was still occupied by an Ottoman garrison. Between 1817 and 1878, Serbia doubled its territory. During the last decades of the nineteenth century, Serbia sank into economic and financial dependence on Austria. Against the repressive royal regime a liberal opposition crystallized, as well as a revolutionary democratic movement led by Svetozar Markovic (1846–75), which later evolved into a social democratic one.

Bosnia and Herzegovina occupies a special place in the history of the Serbs. Local lords who converted to Islam managed to retain a relative autonomy throughout the centuries of Ottoman domination. Relations with the central government grew strained during the Tanzimat period of reforms. In the course of several decades, a real war was fought with varied success between the local landlords and the Sultan's troops. It ended only after substantial losses and when the landlords' resistance was suppressed in 1851. Hereditary prerogatives were abolished, and the two regions were united in a single province whose capital was moved from Travnik to Sarajevo. A year later, the Christians of Herzegovina staged a revolt against the central government's decision to disarm the population. Montenegro intervened in support of the insurgents. Following a stubborn and protracted struggle, in 1862 a compromise was reached. A new revolt in Bosnia and Herzegovina erupted in 1875 that set the stage for the great Eastern Crisis (1875–8). The occupation of Bosnia and

Herzegovina by Austria-Hungary in the aftermath of the Congress of Berlin, their subsequent annexation in 1908, the accompanying persecution of Serbs and the settlement of German colonists, all contributed to making this region one of the potentially most explosive areas in the Balkans.

Throughout the nineteenth century, the aspirations of the South Slavs within the confines of the Habsburg Empire also evolved from cultural demands for broad internal autonomy to complete independence. The creation of the Illyrian provinces by Napoleon, and their short-lived but radical transformation, abolishing serfdom and introducing liberal reforms, had a particularly strong impact on the Croats. In the 1830s and 1840s Illyrianism as the ideology unifying Serbs and Croats on a common platform promoting national culture was highly influential. Headed by Ljudevit Gaj (1809–72), the movement scored numerous cultural achievements, most prominently the promotion of Serbo-Croat as the common language of the South Slavs. During the revolution of 1848, Hungary's rejection of Zagreb's demands for the creation of a unified Croatia with extended internal autonomy, prompted the Croats to join forces with the Austrians in the suppression of the Hungarian revolution. While a strongly integrationist Croatian nationalism developed in parallel with pro-Hungarian and pro-Austrian factions within the nobility and the elites, the 1860s saw the strengthening of the Yugoslavism of Bishop Joseph Strossmajer, that together with other manifestations of South Slav solidarity, paved the way for the creation of the Yugoslav state in the aftermath of World War I.

The Bulgarians, who were inhabiting the eastern parts of the Balkan Peninsula, had been the first to come under Ottoman rule. Deprived of their own nobility, which was either annihilated, had emigrated or became assimilated, for centuries they had remained a predominantly agrarian population at the top of which was a thin layer of village leaders (chorbadzhii). Bulgarian villages, made up of small peasant proprietors and sharecroppers, suffered mostly from the arbitrary treatment of tax-farmers and the shortage of land. Social tension was endemic and peasant subversion was periodically recorded. Widely reported in Europe were the riots of the 1830s and 1840s in the north-western parts of the country, so much so that an international commission of inquiry was sent to report on the situation.

During the first half of the nineteenth century, Bulgarian society underwent a major transformation, at the roots of which was the emergence of a middle class that positively affected the welfare of entire groups of the urban and rural population. The geographical proximity to the imperial capital with its huge consumption capacity enabled some Bulgarian retailers to take full control of the supply of sheep, and other entrepreneurs to organize the production and delivery of cloth and braid for the uniforms of the reorganized Ottoman army. The most significant effect of this social ferment was the rise to prosperity of the towns along the southern foothills of the Balkan mountains, which developed manufacturing production for distant markets. It was not accidental, therefore, that the first textile factories with European equipment in the Ottoman Empire – one state-owned, the other private – appeared in Bulgarian lands around the mid-nineteenth century. Bulgarians could not draw on a diaspora of the kind the Greeks and the Serbs had in the neighbouring and more distant countries. The Bulgarian middle class was concentrated inside the country and in Constantinople. In the imperial capital, the 1840s saw the beginnings of the Bulgarian periodical press. The

determined effort to secure church services in the Bulgarian language, and to achieve an autocephalous status for the Bulgarian church, was crowned with success in 1870, when the Porte recognized a separate *Bulzar millet* and the institution of the Bulgarian Exarchate, although at the expense of a schism with the Constantinople Patriarchate. Another centre was Bucharest, where the liberal opposition, as well as the revolutionary and democratic movement, were concentrated.

By mid-century, preparations for revolutionary action began in earnest. During the Crimean war, Bulgarian volunteers formed separate units attached to the Russian army, where they received proper training. The population at large joined in conspiratorial activities for stirring up local riots. Well-armed bands were transferred across the border from Serbia and Romania into Bulgaria. The leader behind this campaign was Georgi S. Rakovski (1821–67), the first Bulgarian proponent of coordinated and united Balkan action for national liberation.

Drawing on the experience of the other Balkan independence movements, as well as on European revolutionary ideas that were penetrating the Balkans in the 1860s and 1870s, the Bulgarian movement for national liberation entered a new stage. A Central Revolutionary Committee was formed in Bucharest that set itself the task of covering the whole country with a network of secret committees. Alongside Lyuben Karavelov (1834–78) and Kliristo Botev (1848–76), the most prominent figure of the Bulgarian national revolution was Vasil Levski (1837–73).

The brutal suppression of the April uprising of 1876 focused the attention of foreign public opinion on the unbearable condition of the Bulgarians, and a fresh aggravation of the notorious 'Eastern Question' ended in a war of Russia against the Ottoman Empire, in which Serbia and Romania took an active part. With the revocation of the short-lived Treaty of San-Stefano, which had created a Greater Bulgaria within the borders of the Bulgarian Exarchate, i.e. based on an ethnic criterion, the Congress of Berlin recognized a rump Bulgarian Principality in northern Bulgaria under formal Ottoman suzerainty, and the creation of the autonomous province of Eastern Rumelia in southern Bulgaria under a Bulgarian governor appointed by the Porte. The other territories (most notably Macedonia) were returned to the direct and unconditional rule of the Porte. In 1885, with great popular enthusiasm, the unification of the Principality with Eastern Rumelia was carried out. It prompted the ill-reasoned decision of King Milan of Serbia to attack Bulgaria. The war ended in Serbia's defeat, but left deep traces of mistrust between the two neighbouring nations.

Bulgaria thus became the largest among the newly liberated states and, despite various difficulties, made considerable progress in its economic and social development. In the political domain, on the other hand, the country became the arena of bitter clashes between political parties and leaders over the issue of who would best safeguard Bulgarian interests, chief among them the issue of the Bulgarian irredenta in Macedonia: Russia or the Western powers? In their battle for dominance, both camps resorted to political assassination. For a decade at the end of the century, the most crucial role in the political life of the country was played by Stefan Stambolov, who fell victim to a conflict with the monarch. Prince Ferdinand (who became King after the proclamation of independence in 1908) concentrated thereafter all power in his hands, and pursued an active policy among the Bulgarian population in Macedonia that was still under Ottoman rule.

The Albanians with their tribal structure, linguistic (*Tosk* and *Gheg*), and religious divisions (70 per cent Muslim, 20 per cent Orthodox, 10 per cent Catholic) had to overcome serious obstacles on the road to national unification. Whatever schooling existed was conducted in the languages of the dominant religious establishments: Turkish and Arabic for the Muslims, Greek for the Orthodox, Italian and Latin for the Catholics. At the beginning of the nineteenth century, *ayans* of Albanian origin like Ali Pasha of Ioannina and Mustafa Pasha Bushati of Slikoder, established virtually independent territories in central and southern Albania, opposed to the centralizing policy during the period of reforms.

The Albanian revival (*Rilindja*) began after mid-century, with the publication of textbooks in Albanian and, above all, focused on the efforts to create a separate Albanian alphabet. Of great significance was the literary contribution of the Albanian colonies in Italy who were inspired by the ideas of the Italian Risorgimento. Set up in the aftermath of the Congress of Berlin, the Albanian or Prizren League (1878) opposed any attempt to annex Albanian territories and aimed at achieving autonomy within the Ottoman Empire. Especially crucial was the role of the numerous members of the Frasheri family, among them Abdul (1839–92), the leader of the Prizren League, his brother Naim (1846–1900), the most prominent Albanian poet of the period, and many others. Resistance to the Ottomans was widespread but the Porte succeeded in putting it down. In the United States, Fan Noli (1882–1965) founded an Albanian Orthodox church under the jurisdiction of the Russian Patriarch, which became an important centre of national consciousness and agitation.

The Albanians rose en masse in 1912. At the height of the Balkan states' preparations for a war against the Ottoman Empire, the Turkish government was unable to commit adequate forces against the Albanians. It was forced to recognize the independence that the Albanians had proclaimed at the meeting of their National Assembly in Valona, led by Ismail Kemal Bey (1844–1919). The Albanian provisional government carried out a general mobilization and took vital diplomatic steps for its international recognition in Vienna, Rome and London. Thus Albania was ready to take a firm position in safeguarding its integrity and independence in the course of the Balkan wars of 1912–13.

The last among the Balkan ethnic groups to develop a national consciousness were the Turks, the dominant group in the Ottoman Empire. Most of them demurred at the introduction of Europeanizing reforms, which they considered to run counter to their religious customs and identity. The benefits which the reforms provided for the general condition and self-confidence of the subject Christian population, engendered further resentment. An ambivalent situation thus emerged during the nineteenth century: on the one hand, the Turks still considered themselves masters over all the inhabitants of the huge empire and, on the other hand, they felt exposed to semi-colonial exploitation on the part of the great powers, and threatened by the upward economic and social mobility of the subject Christian nations.

The reign of Abdul Hamid II was marked by internal repression and intensified national struggles: the Greeks of Crete rose, followed by a Greek-Turkish war; a mass revolt broke out among the Armenians in Anatolia, and later among the Bulgarians in Macedonia and Eastern Thrace; even co-religionist Albanians were radicalized. Retaliation against the participants in these revolutionary campaigns was brutal and, particularly in the case of the Armenians, presaged the catastrophic genocidal events of World War I. The great powers, who on the whole had been upholding the Ottoman state for decades through international protection and heavy investment, made a shift in their policy. A readjustment of interests took place. Great Britain and Russia, having settled their disputes in other areas of the world, adopted a new Balkan policy, to which France soon acceded. Germany remained the one staunch supporter of the Ottoman Empire.

In the Ottoman state itself, in the second half of the nineteenth century, a liberal opposition coalesced among the so-called 'Young Ottomans'. They saw a solution to the internal dissensions which were weakening the empire in the adoption of a constitution. But their experiment with the institution of a more liberal regime was short-lived: Abdul Hamid II revoked the constitution and disposed of its author, the great Ottoman reformer Midhat Pasha. Around the beginning of the twentieth century, new groups and societies arose, in the empire and abroad, known under the common denomination of 'Union and Progress'. This movement laid the beginnings of the 'Young Turk' opposition as a national Turkish organization, which sought to modernize the state. Their platform included the introduction of a parliamentary regime and representation for all nationalities linked by a common loyalty to a unified state. The right of self-determination and independence was flatly discarded. Yet, despite some reservations about the ultimate intentions of the Young Turks, the coup which the latter carried out in 1908 aroused general support and great hopes that the regime would be liberalized. Elections to the new Ottoman parliament returned 147 Turks, 60 Arabs, 27 Albanians, 26 Greeks, 14 Armenians, 10 Bulgarians, and 4 Jews.

This multinational representation notwithstanding, various restrictions on national schools and other national activities soon followed. The authorities set about disarming the population, and Muslims from Bosnia and Herzegovina were settled in Macedonia. Pan-Turkism began to be espoused as the official ideology, and the appellation 'Turk' came to be used with respect to all subjects. The young Balkan states took the campaign against the Christians in the empire as an overt challenge to them. The idea of joining their forces together for combined military operations against the Ottoman Empire was increasingly gaining ground, not without substantial backing from the interested powers of the Entente. Within a short time the Balkan governments' diplomatic endeavours met with success: an alliance was concluded in 1912 between Bulgaria, Greece, Serbia and Montenegro for the final expulsion of the Ottomans from Europe, and the partitioning of their possessions among the four Balkan states.

In the first Balkan war of 1912, the Ottoman Empire was totally defeated. The victorious Balkan states, however, proved unable to reach an agreement about the division of the newly liberated territories. The principle of autonomy for Macedonia was abandoned. Moreover, the aspirations of the Albanians for independence were totally disregarded. Disputes among the Balkan allies led to collisions and finally to a new war in 1913, this time against Bulgaria, with Romania and the Ottomans joining in. This war, in which

Bulgaria was the loser, determined strained relations between the Balkan states for decades until World War II, with an irredentist Bulgaria and the winners determined to defend the newly acquired status quo.

The Balkan nations had emerged from the centuries-old Ottoman autocracy, but found themselves drawn into the orbit of rival great powers. Austria-Hungary was the only such power with possessions in the Balkans, and a numerous South Slav population within its borders. In the summer of 1914, therefore, it was thus not at all surprising that a war should be sparked off there, by the unresolved national question of the South Slavs. In the meantime, the Balkan wars had determined the major divisions between the Balkan states as adherents to the two rival great-power military alliances, with Greece, Serbia, and Romania on the side of the Entente, and Bulgaria and the disintegrating Ottoman Empire on the side of the Central powers.

NOTE

1 On the subject of the influence which the French Revolution had on the Balkans, and on the formation of a national consciousness in the people of the Balkans, see the works of Paschalis M. Kitromilides: *I Galiki Epanastasi kai i Notioanatoliki Evropi* [The French Revolution and Southeastern Europe], 1990, Athens; and *Enlightment, Nationalism,*

Orthodoxy: Studies in the Culture and Political Thought of Southeastern Europe, 1990, Variorum, London.

BIBLIOGRAPHY

CASTELLAN, G. 1991. *Histoire des Balkans, XIV–XX siècle*. Presses Universitaires de France, Paris. (See also Presses Universitaires de France's collection of histories of the Balkan peoples by the same author.)
DIMITROV, S.; MANCHEV, K. 1971. [*History of the Balkan Peoples*]. Vol. 1. Sofia.
——. 1975. [*History of the Balkan Peoples*]. Vol. 2. Sofia.
IORGA, N. 1936–39. *La place des Roumains dans l'histoire universelle*. Vols. 1–3. Bucharest.
——. 1985–91. [*History of Bulgaria*]. Vols 5–7. Sofia.
——. 1975–7. [*History of the Greek Nation*]. Vols 11–14. Athens.
JELAVICH, B. 1983. *History of the Balkans. The Eighteenth, Nineteenth and Twentieth Centuries*. Vols 1–2. New York.
KARAL, E. 1970. [*Ottoman History*]. Ankara.
——. 1970. *Les Lumières et la formation de la conscience nationale chez les peuples du Sud-Est Européen*. Bucharest.
MILLER, A. 1975. *Mustapha Pacha Bairaktar*. Bucharest.
PETROVICH, M. 1976. *A History of Modern Serbia, 1804–1918*. Vols 1–2. New York.
POLLO, S.; PUTO, A. 1977. *Histoire de l'Albanie des origines à nos jours*. Rouanne.
SVORONOS, N. 1956. *Le commerce de Salonique au XVIIIs*. Paris.
TODOROV, N. 1983. *The Balkan City, 1400–1900*. Seattle.
TRAIKOV, V. 1978. [*Ideological Programs and Trends in the National Liberation Struggles of the Balkan Peoples*]. Sofia.

10.2.4.2

THE ARTS

Remus Niculescu

The nineteenth century was a particularly significant period in the art of the peoples of South-Eastern Europe. Caught up in a general drive for modernization and emancipation, these ethnic and cultural communities sought to integrate themselves with the artistic movements on the continent and, at the same time, to create forms of expression that would reflect a new era of their sensibility and spiritual life. This process, while accelerated or delayed by local historical circumstances and marked by the specific characteristics and traditions of each people, followed, with some exceptions, similar stages of development. In several countries of the region the start of the modern period witnessed a remarkable flourishing of neo-classicism. The dominant genre in painting was initially the portrait, which manifested a new vision of the human personality in the spirit of the Enlightenment. The romantics discovered the power that the evocation of great figures and events from the past could have in arousing national awareness. Early monumental sculpture fulfilled the same function. Academism spread a fairly uniform set of techniques and established a false hierarchy of genres. But the attention of the artists was increasingly captured by everyday, especially rural life. This trend coincided with the taste for landscape and, at times, with the practice of *plein-air* painting. In the work of painters and sculptors was revealed, in various ways, the liberating effects of impressionism. Towards 1900 and in the following years, independent artists emerged and academic conventions were progressively abandoned. These facts contributed to a growing interest in vernacular art and in the ancestral sources of artistic creation.

ARCHITECTURE

One of the most original features of the architecture of South-Eastern Europe in the nineteenth century was the urban housing inspired by local traditions. From a few fundamental types a wide range of building styles was developed; using, in their design and decoration, motifs borrowed from the Islamic East and also from Central Europe, from the late baroque to neo-classicism. Particularly well-preserved examples of this kind of domestic architecture, the style of which is strongly marked by national traditions, can be found in Bulgaria (especially in Plovdiv, the museum-town of Koprivštića, and Turnovo), northern Greece and Albania. The work of the Bulgarian architect Nikola Fichev (1800–81), a self-taught, prolific and inventive master-builder, was at the centre of this cultural renaissance. The caravanserai of Manouk-Bey

(1808) in Bucharest offers a wide array of traditional motifs. The *konak* (town house) of Miloš Obrenović, built from 1831 to 1834 in Belgrade by Hadzi Nikola Živković, illustrates the transition from a Balkan to a Central European style in Serbian urban architecture. The Albanian buildings of this period include seraglios of the pashas, houses with porch and balcony, and fortified dwelling towers.

In the Romanian principalities, the influence of neo-classicism in religious architecture of the Byzantine tradition can be seen mainly in the decorative elements and, occasionally, in the plan of the building itself (the Round Church, Lețcani, c.1795). Neo-classicism was more widely developed in secular architecture. The reigning prince's palace (1806) and the residence of the boyar Nicolae Rosnovanu (1832) in Iași, both built by the Viennese Johann Freywald, as well as that of prince Grigore Ghica IV in Bucharest (1822), reflect the aspirations of Romanian society of that time. The principal Romanian neo-classical architects were Alexandru Orăscu (1817–94), who studied at the Munich Academy and designed the Bucharest University building (1857–69), and Ștefan Emilian (1819–99), trained in Vienna, who made his debut with the building of the Andrei Șaguna high school in Brașov (1851–6) and crowned his career with the Institute of Anatomy in Iași (1890–94).

The neo-classicism of Munich found its way to Greece, the very homeland of Mediterranean classicism, after the accession of King Otto in 1832. The former Royal Palace in Athens (now the Parliament Building), designed by Friedrich von Gärtner of Munich, was completed in 1841. The Danish brothers Christian and Theophilus Hansen also contributed to this movement. Christian Hansen was the architect of Athens University (1837–64), while his brother designed the Academy of Sciences (1859–87) and the National Library (1859–91). The Greek architect Lysandros Kaftanzoglou (1811–86), who studied in Rome and France, built the National Technical University (1861–76). Despite their archaeological inspiration, these buildings left a characteristic mark on nineteenth-century Athens.

In Turkish architecture, the presence of the baroque continued to be felt in association with neo-classical elements. The Dolmabahçe Palace in Istanbul (1853) was built in that composite style by Karabet Balyan. The minarets of the Dolmabahçe mosque (1854) took the shape of Corinthian columns. A purer form of the baroque style can be seen in some memorial buildings, such as the tomb of Nakshidil Sultan, the wife of Abdulhamid I (1818), as well as in the Küçük Effendi mosque at Yediküle, dating from 1825 and forming an architectural complex with a library and a fountain.

The neo-gothic style appeared in the Romanian principalities during the romantic period. In 1837 a contemporary writer admired the gothic home of the Sturdza family at Miclăuşani in Moldavia. At a later date, the architect Ion Berindei (1871–1928) adopted the gothic style for his masterwork, a vast edifice which is now the Cultural Palace of Iaşi (1907–26). Many buildings were designed in an eclectic style that combined Renaissance elements with a modernized baroque. These were often the work of French architects, such as Albert Galleron (the Romanian Athenaeum, Bucharest, 1888), or Central European architects such as the Czechs J. V. Hrasky and A. J. Hruby (the Opera of Ljubljana, 1892) and Ferdinand Fellner and Hermann Helmer of Vienna (the Opera of Zagreb, 1895; the National Theatres of Iaşi, 1896, and Sofia, 1906). The former Royal Palace of Belgrade (now the National Theatre), was designed in a similar eclectic style by the Serbian architect Aleksandar Bugarski (1835–91). In Sarajevo, the National Museum was built in 1913 by Karlo Pražik (1857–1942) in a neo-Renaissance style. By 1914, sumptuous private mansions, designed according to the French taste of the eighteenth century by Romanian architects educated in Paris, dominated the centre of Bucharest.

Some architects reacted against eclecticism. Ion Mincu (1852–1912) dedicated his life to the creation of a new Romanian style based on the forms of peasant and old religious architecture (the Central School for Girls, 1890–4, Bucharest). Many architects, including Cristofi Cerkez (1872–1955) and Petre Antonescu (1873–1965), followed his example. A return to local traditions can also be seen in the work of Svetozar Ivačković (1844–1925), whose monumental Church of the Transfiguration (Pančevo, 1873–7) was inspired by medieval Serbian architecture, and in the St Blaise church (Zagreb, 1912), built by the Croatian Viktor Kovačić (1874–1924), recalling Dalmatian and Byzantine constructive principles. The Turkish architect Kemalettin (1870–1927), designed in an Ottoman revivalist style the Mausoleum of Mahmud Schevket Pasha in Istanbul (1909).

SCULPTURE

The development of sculpture, which Orthodox dogma and Islamic doctrine had permitted only in the form of non-figurative decoration, was much delayed in most of South-Eastern Europe. A pioneer of Turkish sculpture was Yervant Oscan (1855–1914), who studied in Rome and afterwards became a professor in the Art Academy of Istanbul. Albanian sculpure seems not to have started until 1899, with a bust of Skanderbeg by Murat Toptani (1865–1918). Even in Greece, notwithstanding its precious heritage of ancient monuments, the first modern sculpture by local artists appeared relatively late. The statue of Rigas Ferraios (1871) is the work of Ioannis Kossos (1822–73), a pupil of Christian Heinrich Siegel (1808–83) at the Art Academy of Athens. Neo-classicism dominated Greek sculpture until the end of the nineteenth century. Educated in Munich, Leonidas Drossis (1834–82) decorated with statues the Academy of Sciences building in Athens. Working in a more realist spirit, Demetrios Philippotis

(1839–1919) choose subjects from daily life. Yannoulis Halepas (1851–1938), trained at first with Drossis, then, like his master, studied in Munich (1873–76). After his returning to Greece, he produced his celebrated *Sleeping Girl* (1878), a classicist funerary monument.

Modern Serbian sculpture set out under the auspices of Munich eclecticism with Petar Ubavkić (1852–1910), who also studied in Rome, and Simeon Roksandić (1874–1943), as well as of French academic realism with Djordje Iovanović (1861–1953). The ascendency of Rodin manifested itself in the works of the Croatian Rudolf Valdec (1872–1929). Ivan Meštrović (1883–1962) attained an international reputation. His studies in Vienna (1901–5) revealed his latent affinities with the Secession style. He, too, discovered the aesthetic world of Rodin, reflected in one of his first major works, *The Fountain of Life* (Zagreb, 1905). Afterwards he exhibited the model of the *Temple of Vidovdan*, which was to be erected on the site of the Battle of Kossovopolje. He never completed this vast project, for which he destined the statutes of the heroes *Miloš Obilić*, *Kraljević Marko*, and *Banović Strahinja* (1908–10), typical examples of his pathetic and tumultuous art.

In Bulgaria the first sculptors were the portraitists Jeko Spiridonov (1867–1945) and Martin Vassiliev (1867–1931). The leading Bulgarian master in this field, Andrey Nikolov (1878–1959), who returned from Paris in 1907, also showed in his work hints from the art of Rodin. During the Balkan Wars, Ivan Lazarov (1889–1952), a graduate from the Art Academy of Sofia (1912), sculpted small statues representing Bulgarian soldiers. In the following years he produced peasant figures and groups vigorously stylized.

The most complex Romanian sculptor of the second half of the nineteenth century, Ion Georgescu (1856–98), studied in Bucharest under the neo-classicist Karl Storck (1826–87) and later in France, where he admired the works of Carpeaux and his late eighteenth-century forerunners. He was an excellent portraitist (*Mihail Pascaly*, 1882) and a master of monumental sculpture (*Gheorghe Asachi*, Iaşi, 1890). The anxious romanticism of certain works by Ştefan Ionescu-Valbudea (1856–1918) seems to foreshadow expressionism. After the turn of the century, Dimitrie Paciurea (1875–1932) was noted for the impetus of his *Giant* (1906) and his bold attempt to create in his sculpture a stylistic equivalent of the Byzantine icon (*The Dormition of the Virgin*, 1912). In his portraits can be discerned features of both impressionism and symbolism. Constantin Brâncuşi (1876–1957), the founder of the modern tradition in twentieth-century sculpture, underwent thorough professional training in Craïova (1893–8), in Bucharest (1898–1902) and finally in Paris (1905–7). During his Rodinian period he modelled studies of children (1906–7) and *The Sleep* (1908), but with *The Prayer*, a figure destined for a funerary monument in Buzău (1907–10), *The Kiss* (1907–9) and *The Wisdom of Earth* (1908), he discovered his own style, shaping essential forms with deep symbolic meaning. In the *Maiastra* (1910–12) a sculpture embodying a mythical being inspired by a Romanian folk legend, he created one of his masterpieces. To this theme he returned in the subsequent years, in increasingly spare and spiritualized versions. By 1917–1918 Brâncuşi was already working in his Paris studio on a preliminary model of the *Endless Column*, which was eventually erected in 1937–8 as a part of Târgu-Jiu ensemble consecrated to the Romanian fallen in World War I.

PAINTING

Forerunners

Before 1800 the Ionian islands, for several centuries under the rule of Venice and sheltered from Ottoman domination, offered a favourable climate for the development of easel painting. Two artists native to Zante, Nikolaos Koutouzis (1741–1813), who trained in Venice, probably under Giambattista Tiepolo, and his disciple, Nikolaos Kantounis (1768–1834), painted not only religious subjects but also remarkably realistic portraits. The artistic output of the Ionian school remained, however, an isolated phenomenon whose influence did not even extend to the Greek mainland.

The impact of neo-classical Vienna on the painters of South-Eastern Europe can be seen principally in portraiture and iconostasis decoration. It is present in the work of such masters of Serbian classicism as Arsenije Teodorović (1767–1826) and Pavel Djurković (1772–1830). Some of Teodorović's works are still close to the baroque tradition, which gives them greater breadth and monumentality. With their sharp outlines and minute detail, the portraits painted by Djurković form a vivid gallery of contemporary physiognomies. The Slovene Franc Cavčić (1762–1828), an author of learned and well balanced classical compositions, taught at the Academy of Vienna and eventually became its director (1820).

Eustatie Altini (c.1772–1815) was sent from Iaşi to study at the Academy in Vienna in 1789. After his return he greatly contributed to the spread of neo-classicism in Moldavia, where he painted a number of iconostases and refined portraits. In his composition consecrated to an episode in the life of Metropolitan Veniamin Costachi (1813) he showed a romantic sensibility. An early romantic note is also detectable in certain canvases by Mihail Töpler, the portraitist of the Bucharest aristocracy under the last years of the Phanariot regime. Nicolae Polcovnicul (1788–1842), a religious painter traditionally trained, but belonging by his style to the same innovative current, also produced portraits, including that of the Manu family recently removed from the church of Leurdeni (1825).

The renaissance of Bulgarian painting is closely tied up with the activity of several religious artists and with their fresh and personal vein. The most talented among them was Zahari Zograf (1810–53), youngest son of Khristo Dimitrov, the founder of the Samokov school, who had been trained in icon painting at Mount Athos and had also travelled in Austria. Zograf was Bulgaria's first important easel portraitist. His gift for observation and colour, his sense of humour and his taste for the fantastic are displayed in the murals of the Bachkovo monastery (1841). The spirit of the Samokov school and its distinctive popular character endured to the end of the nineteenth century in the work of Nikola Obrazopisov (1828–1915).

Biedermeier, romanticism and realism

Affinities with the Viennese Biedermeier are evident in the work of such foremost Serbian portraitists as Constantin Daniel (1798–1873), who also excelled in religious and still life painting, Katarina Ivanović (1811–82) and Dimitrije Avramović (1815–95). The first master of modern Croatian painting, Vjekoslav Karas (1821–58), developed his delicate sense of form in Rome (1841–7), under the influence of the Nazarenes. At times the Serbian romantics turned for their inspiration to legend and history. Novak Radonić (1826–90) illustrated a ballad published by Vuk Karadžić, *The Death of Kraljević Marko* (1857). The writer and painter Djura Jakšić (1832–78) gave his portraits a lively and personal touch and, in some historical compositions, chiaroscuro effects. Trained in Munich, Djordje Kristić (1851–1907), who chiefly owes his place in Serbian art to his realistic rural types and scenes, painted also iconostases, portraits and landscapes.

The Romanian Constantin Lecca (1807–87), a classicist portrait painter and church decorator, Mihail Lapaty (1828–62), an admirer of Géricault, and Theodor Aman (1831–91) devoted compositions to the life of Michael the Brave, the forerunner, at the end of the sixteenth century, of the unity of his people. Aman, who exhibited at the Paris Salon as early as 1853, was also an excellent portraitist and, in his genre scenes, an elegant intimist. Gheorghe Panaiteanu (1816–1900), who studied, and then lived, in Munich for many years, was a typical representative of Biedermeier taste. Noteworthy among the Romanian portraitists of this period were also Ion Negulici (1812–51), Barbu Iscovescu (1816–54) and Constantin David Rosenthal (1820–51), who all took part in the 1848 revolution in Wallachia. Iscovescu portrayed several leaders of the Romanian revolutionary movement in Transylvania. Rosenthal painted a symbolic image of *Romania* (1851), whose romantic affiliation can be traced back to Delacroix. A different aspect of romanticism is that of the watercolours of Carol Popp de Szathmari (1812–88), an indefatigable traveller interested not only in local types and landscapes, but also in the exotic world of the Middle East.

Greek painters began to look towards Munich, where many of them studied. Theodoros Vrysakis (1819–78) returned to Greece only to gather material for his compositions of the war of independence (*Lord Byron at Missolonghi*, 1862). Nikiforos Lytras (1832–1904) and Nikolaos Gysis (1842–1901), both disciples of Karl Piloty in Munich, belong to a later period. They painted scenes with Greek themes, especially young peasant women and children, of whom they made authentic symbols of the nation. The realism of Lytras' works as well as that of Polychronis Lembessis (1849–1913), at first supported by museum tradition, evolved towards *plein-air*. Konstantinos Volanakis (1837–1907), who in his seascapes generally recalled the Dutch masters of the seventeenth century, knew also how to capture, in his most personal canvases, the impression of life and the quality of light. Gysis became in his turn a teacher at the Munich Academy (1882). His subsequent evolution led to the decorative, idealistic style of his last compositions and allegorical figures (the poster *Historia*, 1891).

The first noteworthy Turkish painters of the modern period were Scheker Achmet Pasha (1841–1906), and Süleyman Seyyit (1842–1913), who went to France and developed their visual sensibility and technical skill in academic studies. These early masters, as well as Hüsseyin Zekaï Pasha (1860–1919), preferred landscape and still life to portrait painting. The human figure was central to the work of Osman Hamdi (1842–1910). In his descriptive canvases he also gave special prominence to his country's ancient furniture, rugs and ceramics.

The painters of the Bulgarian renaissance, who worked for the liberation of their country, continued to concentrate on portraiture. Returning home in 1856 after studies in

Moscow and St Petersburg, Stanislav Dospevksi (1823–79) painted Bulgaria's leading intellectuals, endowing them with strongly accentuated features. The portraits by Khristo Tzokev (1847–83), another artist who studied in Russia, are more intimate and more conspicuous for their pictorial quality. Nikolay Pavlović (1835–94), who completed his studies in Vienna and Munich, also represented historic episodes (*Asparuch on his way to the Danube*, 1867–9).

Modern Albanian painting began with historical subjects and depictions of contemporary types and manners. Skanderbeg, champion of the fifteenth-century Albanian struggle against Ottoman domination, attracted several artists. He is the principal figure of a composition by Simon Rrota (1887–1961), *Skanderbeg in the Battle* (1915). Kol Idromeno (1860–1939) trained in Venice (1875–8) and produced realistic religious murals as well as scenes, landscapes and penetrating portraits. Ndoc Martini (1871–1916) studied at the School of Arts and Crafts in Shkodër, in Italy and then in France (1904–9). He was a portraitist and also painted frescoes for the Chambre des Députés in Paris.

Plein-air painting, impressionism and symbolism

With Nicolae Grigorescu (1838–1907), one of the pioneers of *plein-air* painting in European art, the Romanian school of painting reached its maturity. He studied in Paris and among the Barbizon masters (1861–9), returned afterwards to France at various intervals and took a keen interest in the discoveries of the impressionists. From the War of Independence (1877–8), which he witnessed from the frontline, he brought hundreds of drawings and a series of paintings conceived in the same modern spirit. His lyrical mood found equally successful expressions in portraits and landscape. Towards the end of his life he dedicated the main part of his work to the Romanian village, of which he was the most appealing and profound interpreter. Several of his compatriots owed to his art the revelation of their own talent. Such was the case of Ion Andreescu (1850–82) whose canvases, notwithstanding certain affinities with the impressionists (especially Pissarro and Sisley), retained their originality, residing in a grave and almost tragic vision of nature, people and things. After studying in Bucharest and Munich, Ştefan Luchian (1868–1916) found in Paris, in the paintings of Manet, Degas and Gauguin, a favourable ambiance for his development (1891–2). In his portraits, landscapes and flower paintings, the synthesis of form and the quality of colour convey an elevated spiritual message. Gheorghe Petraşcu (1872–1949) assimilated the European tradition from the Venetians and Rembrandt to the impressionists, and used a rich and dense pictorial matter to create the concentrated world of his motifs (landscapes, figure studies and, above all, interiors and still-lifes). After his beginnings in the symbolist climate, Theodor Pallady (1871–1956) developed an art voluptuously clear and calm, with subtly orchestrated tones. Other painters also enriched Romanian art after 1900: Camil Ressu (1880–1962), known for his austere vision of peasant life and his rigorous concept of style; Josef Iser (1881–1958), whose wide experience of satirical drawing led to his monumental interpretation of human forms, and Nicolae Dărăscu (1883–1959), whose luminous landscapes belong to the heritage of impressionism.

In the works of Périclès Pantazis (1849–84) Greek painting met modern conceptions of light and colour. The facts of having left the Munich Academy, to go to Paris

(1872) and of having frequented Manet's circle, reveal the artist's preferences. His seascapes, painted in Belgium, where he became a founding member of the 'Groupe des XX' (1883), show evident connections with impressionism. Such contacts are also apparent in the landscapes and joyous *plein air* scenes of Symeon Savvidis (1869–1927). Konstantinos Parthenis (1878–1967) experienced the Secessionist movement in Vienna and later post-impressionism and symbolism in Paris (1909–11). In his stylized religious and allegorical compositions this independent and influential master aimed to incorporate Greek antiquity and Byzantine tradition into an ideal vision of Hellenism.

Historical painting was still present in Serbian art, as exemplified by the vast canvases of Paja Jovanović (1859–1957), author of *The Coronation of Emperor Dušan* (1900). In Croatia two different trends can be discerned. While Vlaho Bukovac (1855–1922), a pupil of Alexandre Cabanel in Paris, was a skilled follower of academism, Miroslav Kraljević (1885–1913), who studied in Munich and also worked in Paris, based his works on the contrast of clear colour planes. Many artists benefited from the liberal spirit that prevailed in the private academy founded in Munich by the Slovenian painter Anton Ažbè (1862–1905). Among them were his compatriots Rihard Jakopić (1869–1943) and Ivan Grohar (1867–1911), who both became adepts of impressionism. By 1900 some of their works were shown in Ljublana. Among the principal Serbian painters belonging to the modern trend were Milan Milovanović (1876–1946), an exponent of divisionism who left Munich for Paris, and Kosta Miličević (1877–1920) who adopted the *pointillist* technique. A brilliant palette expressed the poetic symbolism of Leon Kojen (1860–1934). But the leading figure in Serbian painting of these years was Nadežda Petrović (1873–1915). Her development went through an impressionist period followed by a series of *avant-garde* experiments akin to those of the Fauves.

Towards the end of the nineteenth century Bulgarian painting was revitalized by a generation of artists mainly interested in peasant life. The genre canvases of Ivan Mârkvička (1856–1938), a native of Bohemia, faithfully depicted Bulgarian villagers and their customs. In the works of Anton Mitov (1862–1930) landscape plays a more prominent role, as well as in those of Iaroslav Vešin (1860–1915), another Czech established in Bulgaria, whose outlook is more dramatic, especially in his compositions inspired by the Balkan War of 1912. Ivan Angelov (1864–1924) painted peasants at work in sunlit fields. After 1900 the leading Bulgarian painters, at times receptive to the suggestions of impressionism, distinguished themselves either in the psychological portrait, as Elena Karamihailova (1875–1961) and Tseno Todorov (1877–1953), or in pure landscape, as Nikola Petrov (1881–1916).

During the same period *plein-air* painting was spreading among Turkish artists, some of whom were still studying in France. Ali Riza Effendi (1858–1930), whose landscapes are at times reminiscent of the Barbizon School, and Halil Pasha (1856–1939), who painted interiors inhabited by magnificently dressed figures, also evoked ancient streets, the neighbourhoods and outskirts of Istanbul. The painters of the following generation, including Nazmi Ziya Güran (1881–1937) and Hüsseyin Avni Lifij (1889–1927), equally found their motifs in these surroundings, which they depicted with a clear palette and coloured shadows.

BIBLIOGRAPHY

ARAPOGLU, E. 1996. 'Greece: Painting'. In: *The Dictionary of Art*, XIII. Macmillan, London, pp. 351–3.

——. 1978. *Artet figurative Shqiptare* [Albanian figurative art]. Tirana.

ASLANAPA, O. 1971. *Turkish Art and Architecture*. London.

CEVC, E. 1966. *Slovenska umetnost* [Slovenian art]. Ljubljana.

——. 1967. *Slovenačko slikarstvo 19. veka iz zbirke Narodne Galerije Ljubljana* [Slovenian Painting of the Nineteenth Century in the Collections of the National Gallery, Ljubljana]. Belgrade.

CHRISTOU, C.; KOUMVAKALI, M.; ANASSASIADI, B. 1982. *Modern Greek Sculpture, 1800–1941*. Athens.

DEMOSTHENOPOLOU, E. 1970. *Öffentliche Bauten unter König Otto in Athen*. Munich.

DHAMO, D.; KUQALI, A. 1996. 'Albania: Painting and Graphic Arts'. In: *The Dictionary of Art*, I. Macmillan, London, pp. 540–1.

Entsiklopediya Na Izobrazitenite Izkustva V Bălgariva. 1980–7. [Encyclopedia of the fine arts in Bulgaria]. 2 vols. Sofia.

EROL, T. 1988. 'Painting in Turkey in the XIXth and early XXth Century'. In: *A History of Turkish Painting*. Seattle/London.

FILIPOVIĆ, M. (ed.) 1987. *The Art of Bosnia and Herzegovina*. Sarajevo.

FRASHËRI, G. 1996. 'Albania: Architecture'. In: *The Dictionary of Art*, I. Macmillan, London, p. 539.

FRUNZETTI, I.; POPESCU, M. 1958. *Scurtă istorie a artelor plastice în R.P.R.* [A Short History of Fine Arts in the Romanian People's Republic], Vol. II. Bucharest.

GIANNOUDAKI, T. P.; ARAPOGLU, E. 1996. 'Greece: Sculpture'. In: *The Dictionary of Art*, XIII. Macmillan, London, pp. 353–5.

GOODWIN, G. 1971. *A History of Ottoman Architecture*. London.

IONESCU, G. 1982. *Arhitectura pe teritoriul României de-a lungul veacurilor* [Architecture in Romania through the Centuries]. Bucharest.

ISPIR, M. 1984. *Clasicismul în arta românească* [Classicism in Romanian art]. Bucharest.

——. 1975. *Jugoslavenska skulptura 1880–1950.* [Yugoslavian sculpture 1880–1950]. 1975. Belgrade.

KATZAROVA, V. 1996. 'Bulgaria: Architecture after 1878'. In: *The Dictionary of Art*, V. Macmillan, London, pp. 149–50.

KOŠČEVIĆ, Z. 1996. 'Croatia: Painting, Graphic Arts and Sculpture (1800 and after)'. In: *The Dictionary of Art*, VIII. Macmillan, London, pp. 178–80.

KOLARIĆ, M. 1965. *Le classicisme serbe, 1790–1848*. Belgrade.

KOUTAMANIS, A. 1996. 'Greece: Architecture c.1830–1900'. In: *The Dictionary of Art*, XIII. Macmillan, London, pp. 348–9.

LYDAKIS, S. 1972. *Geschichte der griechischen Malerei des 19. Jahrunderts*. Munich.

MAVRODINOV, N. 1957. *Izkustvoto na Bălgarskoto Natsionalno Văzrazhdane* [Art of the Bulgarian National Revival]. Sofia.

MEDAKOVIĆ, D. 1981. *Srpska umetnost u XIX veku* [Nineteenth-century Serbian Art]. Belgrade.

MIHALCHEVA, I. 1977. *Osnovni ideino-hudojestveni nasoki v bălgarskata jivopis 1900–1918* [Fundamental Ideological and Artistic Trends in Bulgarian Painting, 1900–1918]. Sofia.

MLADENOVIĆ, L. 1982. *Gradjansko slikarstvo u Bosni i Hercegovini u XIX veku* [Painting in Bosnia and Herzegovina in the Nineteenth Century]. Sarajevo.

MOLE, V. 1965. *Umetnost južnih slovanov* [Art of the South-Slavs]. Ljubljana.

Monumente të arkitekturës në Shkipëri. [Architectural Monuments in Albania]. 1973. Tirana.

MUCENIC, C. 1996. 'Romania: Architecture after 1800'. In: *The Dictionary of Art*, XXVI. Macmillan, London, pp. 708–9.

NEDEVA-WEGENER, J. 1996. 'Bulgaria: Painting and Sculpture (after 1878)'. In: *The Dictionary of Art*, V. Macmillan, London, pp. 154–5.

NICULESCU, R. 1996. 'Romania: Painting, Graphic Arts and Sculpture (c.1780–1890). In: *The Dictionary of Art*, XXVI. Macmillan, London, pp. 713–15.

OPRESCU, G. 1943. *Pictura românească în secolul al XIX-lea* [Romanian painting in the nineteenth century]. 2nd edn. Bucharest.

——. 1964. *Sculptura statuară românească* [Romanian Statuary Scultpure]. 2nd edn. Bucharest.

——. 1961. *Slikarstvo XIX. stoljeća u Hrvatskoj.* [Nineteenth-century Painting in Croatia]. Zagreb (exh. cat.).

TVRTKOVIĆ, P. 1996. 'Croatia: Architecture'. In: *The Dictionary of Art*, VIII. Macmillan, London, pp. 176–7.

VLASIU, I. 1996. 'Romania: Painting, Graphic Arts and Sculpture after 1890'. In: *The Dictionary of Art*, XXVI. Macmillan, London, pp. 715–16.

ZITKO, S. 1989. *Historizem v kiparstvu 19. stoletja na Slovenskem* [Historicism in Slovenian Sculpture of the Nineteenth Century]. Ljubljana.

ŽIVKOVIĆ, S. 1996. 'Serbia: Sculpture'. In: *The Dictionary of Art*, XXVIII. Macmillan, London. 453–4.

——. 1994. *Srpski impressionisti* [Serbian Impressionists]. Belgrade.

——; DJORDJEVIĆ, M. 1996. 'Serbia: Painting and Graphic Arts after 1800'. In: *The Dictionary of Art*, XXVIII. Macmillan, London, pp. 450–2.

11

NORTH AMERICA

Peter N. Stearns

THE UNITED STATES IN THE EARLY NINETEENTH CENTURY: GENERAL FEATURES

United States history in the nineteenth century is often divided according to major presidencies or other political markers, but a less superficial periodization is also common. The most important event of the century was the Civil War, 1861–5, and this frequently serves as a divider in the rendering of the nation's history; or a division is identified slightly later, in the 1870s, as the Civil War's aftermath became clearer and as the United States began to emerge as a major industrial economy. For the decades prior to the Civil War, there is increasing agreement that major changes began to reshape the American experience around 1800, setting the framework not only for this initial nineteenth-century period but for several more durable national characteristics.

Two sets of factors dominated the history of the new nation after the 1780s. The first involved the formation of the political institutions of the American republic, plus the rhetoric and expectations surrounding United States independence and the establishment of extensive political rights. Political culture, in other words, shares a billing with specific constitutional issues. A subset of the political challenge involved efforts to define and implement a distinctive national culture, in contact but also in competition with the dominant styles of Europe. An American intellectual life began to emerge. The second set of influences revolved around the increasing commercialization of the American economy, both rural and urban, along with the establishment of early factory centers. Growing involvement in a money economy promoted new linkages for transportation and communication. The impact spilled over into family patterns such as birth rates and family ideals. The institution of slavery was altered and deepened by the growing commercial importance of cotton production. Obviously, additional ingredients played a role in shaping American history during this initial nineteenth-century period. Particularly by the 1830s, new complexities included renewed European immigration, a new set of reform concerns including anti-slavery movements and early feminism, and accelerated westward expansion.

The relationship between patterns of history in the United States and Western Europe included important new complexities during the decades around 1800. Several distinctive features persisted: the institution of slavery was

one, as was the continued involvement with a frontier experience. The absence of an aristocracy colored the development of the United States in many ways, both before and after the Revolution. Specific features of American religion, such as recurrent Protestant revival meetings, had begun to take shape during the colonial period and continued in the early nineteenth century. Other American characteristics were newer, including a considerable commitment, on the part of cultural leaders, to an effort to define national differences from what was sometimes referred to as the 'old world'. The existence of a republic and a partial democracy differed from European patterns before 1848. An American commitment to a belief in social mobility, in the importance of urging people to try to improve their station in life, emerged more clearly in the 1820s and 1830s, in contrast to greater European hesitation about encouraging new personal expectations. Relatedly, a concern for mass education took shape, except in the American South, more rapidly than in most parts of Europe. European visitors to the United States, while often commenting on vulgar habits and the lack of cultural amenities, also typically noted some unusual features of American family life, including opportunities for women and children to speak their minds. On another front: when leading American cities formed police forces in the 1830s, they explicitly decided that the police should be armed, in direct contrast to the policy determined in the same period in Britain. Racial and ethnic tensions in the United States, plus the importance of weapons in frontier tradition, determined a different national pattern. Features of this sort, both carryovers from the colonial experience, and new markers, have led many historians of the United States to emphasize American exceptionalism, the national differences from European trajectories despite many points in common; indeed, some have argued that a separate American civilization was emerging in the United States during the early nineteenth century.

On the other hand, some aspects of the United States were coming to resemble European patterns more closely. Population density on the Atlantic seaboard, including the growth of cities, brought new concerns about crowding and began to yield a larger propertyless laboring class. The birth rate began to drop, though it still exceeded European averages as a result of greater per capita resources, including the availability of land on the frontier. Attempts to develop a more formal culture led to new exchanges with Europe, such as the importation of the romantic movement. While American racial diversity was distinctive, policies that drove most Indians to vacant lands in the West reduced the Indian presence in mainstream American life. Early industrialization depended on extensive borrowing of European inventions and capital, and it created additional economic and social similarities as well as contacts. A new middle class emerged eager to develop more formal manners, often in emulation of European modes. Family advice literature, including standards recommended for middle-class women, came from European as well as American sources. The comparative framework for analyzing American history in this period becomes if anything more complex, as the nation experienced a variety of fundamental new developments.

Politics and culture

The formation of United States political structure in the decades after the Revolution created a number of durable institutions and several larger themes in the nation's political life. The Articles of Confederation, adopted during the revolutionary war, in 1777, did not function well, in leaving predominant power to the states. The absence of effective national government was noted in diplomatic affairs, as it proved impossible to force Britain to live up to its agreement to vacate American territory after the revolutionary settlement. The lack of national tax power was compounded by heavy indebtedness by the individual states, while negotiations with various Indian tribes, toward pressing them to vacate additional territory, broke down, leading to a new round of Indian wars that peaked in the early 1790s. Renewed social unrest pitted hard-pressed farmers against state taxing agencies. These various pressures produced growing support for a constitutional convention in 1787, and for the resulting document.

The new Constitution grappled successfully with several issues. Profound suspicion of a strong executive, based on the experience with the British monarchy, was addressed through the separation of powers among the legislative, executive and judicial branches. Insistence by the states on preserving substantial authority ran counter to the demands by leading federalists for a stronger central agency. Compromise involved the establishment of a federal system, with powers divided between state and national levels, both of which were responsible to popular sovereignty. A more specific negotiation created two national legislative houses; in the Senate, each state would be equally represented, while allocation of seats in the House of Representatives would correspond to population size. Protection of states' rights also allowed the framers of the Constitution largely to sidestep the issue of slavery, even though many Northern states were moving toward its abolition. Concern about abusive government was further assuaged by the passage of an initial ten amendments that constituted the Bill of Rights, protecting rights to freedom of speech, freedom of religion, jury trial and so on. The election of George Washington, the planter and revolutionary general, as first president added prestige and careful leadership to the new government.

During Washington's eight-year presidency and beyond (Washington refused to serve more than two terms, which added another, informal protection against undue presidential authority), a pattern of disputes continued to divide supporters of strong national government, the Federalists, from those urging a small state and a strong independent citizenry, the Republicans. Though the drafters of the Constitution had cautioned against a political party system, hoping that legislators would serve the whole citizenry, in fact an informal, two-party arrangement emerged quite quickly. Federalists initially had the upper hand, and enacted a national bank and a national tariff policy. The new government was also active in securing control over territory between the Appalachian mountains and the Mississippi river, in prosecuting the Indian wars, and in establishing a more effective foreign policy aimed at neutrality during the conflicts of the French Revolution. The bitterly-contested election of Thomas Jefferson, the leading Republican in 1800, and his successful accession to office, confirmed the capacity of the American electorate to accept changes in party leadership within the system.

Issues of government scope continued to define American politics. Despite Jefferson's firm views about the importance of limited state action, his presidency saw major initiatives in the purchase of the vast Louisiana territory from Napoleon (1803), which constituted a huge extension west of the Mississippi; Jefferson also commissioned the Lewis and Clark expedition to explore to the Pacific (1803–6). Subsequently, in 1819, the government successfully negotiated the acquisition of Florida, after informal raids on the Spanish. The national government also established new functions in improving rivers and harbours, particularly during the 1820s. The leading judicial authority, the Supreme Court, under its first Chief Justice John Marshall, established its right to review the constitutionality of congressional laws, by a decision in 1803, and also that of state courts (1821); here were important implementations both of division of powers at the national level and of the balances within the federal system. An 1824 decision established the power of Congress to regulate interstate commerce, which was crucial in developing an untrammelled national market.

The first thirty-five years of the new government's operation, though filled with significant disputes and debates in principle, were remarkably free from the kinds of paralyzing divisions that often afflict new nations, that were at this very time affecting some of the newly-independent states of Latin America. Extensive agreement on the compromises embedded in the Constitution, plus the existence of relatively experienced political leadership forged initially in colonial legislatures and then during the Revolution, account for this stability. In 1814, as renewed war with Britain went badly, New England states threatened to secede, but the war's successful conclusion ended that movement. During the 1820s and beyond, Southern states, eager to export cotton and other agricultural goods, struggled bitterly with Northern states that sought tariff protection for infant industries, but again the disputes remained within the system. It is also important to realize that during this formative political period the national government exercised very modest authority, by the standards of most European states. Defence and diplomacy (with, however, a very small standing army), territorial acquisition and pressure on the Indian tribes to move further westward, and some rudimentary economic and infrastructure policies described most activity, though individual states, responsible for policies toward the poor, prisons, and (often) schools added to the list of functions in the overall federal system. The United States remained a small-government society in many ways until the 1930s, with a strong tradition of suspicion toward any assumption of additional functions.

During the 1820s, a movement to extend manhood suffrage introduced several new themes to American politics. The trend toward democracy began in some newly-admitted frontier states, such as Ohio, which in their initial state constitutions offered the vote to all adult white males. Initially, most states had confined the vote to a minority of property-owners, despite considerable reference to popular sovereignty. Older states now joined the democratic trend (defined, however, to exclude not only women and slaves, but also, in most states, free black men) if only to live up to prior rhetoric and to prevent further migration of farmers and artisans toward the West. Popular interest in politics, including belief in the political rights of working men, grew rapidly in the 1820s and 1830s, along with the new voting systems. In 1824, 27 per cent of all adult white males were voting, compared to 58 per cent in 1828 and 80 per cent by 1840.

The more democratic political climate fed support for Andrew Jackson, elected president in 1828, and a wave of populism that somewhat revised the two-party system. Now, Democrats wielded the small-government heritage of the old Jeffersonian Republicans, while adding a commitment to populist rhetoric directed toward the interests of workers and farmers. This Jacksonian party drew among urban groups in the North, both workers and small merchants, and widely in the South and West, among planters and farmers hostile to undue industrial growth. The Democrats also appealed to new German and Irish immigrants. The second party was the Whigs, drawing from wealthier classes in all regions, favourable to rapid commercial development, and from native-born Protestants suspicious of growing immigration and its Catholic components. Whigs and Democrats competed during a series of undistinguished presidencies after Jackson. Their rivalry continued into the 1840s and 1850s, even as new disputes over Southern slavery began to produce ultimately unmanageable tensions at the national political level.

The formation of national political institutions and both early versions of the two-party system was accompanied by a variety of popular rituals designed to solidify loyalty to the system and to values, such as democracy and limited government, for which it seemed to stand. School readers by the 1820s and 1830s were emphasizing a heroic version of the nation's history, including hymns to the sterling character of George Washington. National festivals, notably 4 July as Independence Day, won widespread public participation. Jacksonian democracy did relatively little specifically to aid rural and working-class supporters, but a sense of commitment to the democratic process was widespread. It was crucial that American workers gained voting rights in advance of extensive industrialization, which helps explain why their ultimate political reactions to industrial pressures were relatively mild. A short-lived Workingmen's Party arose in the 1830s, committed to attacks on advancing American capitalism but also to the political rights they associated with republicanism. The party made only modest gains, but confirmed the eager participation of many workers in democratic rhetoric.

Developing a formal American culture was more difficult, the process more amorphous, than establishing political institutions and a political style. In 1820 an English wit quipped: 'In the four quarters of the globe, who reads an American book? Or goes to an American play? Or looks at an American picture or statue?' The presumably negative answer was doubtless accurate: American cultural expressions had not been extensively developed. Even in science, where many colonial Americans had participated extensively in empirical observations and where leading doctors, like the

Philadelphian Benjamin Rush, were active researchers, most work was derivative of Europe. In the 1830s, the few American doctors who sought formal scientific training, as opposed to often crude apprenticeships, went to Edinburgh or Paris. American intellectual life more generally developed in the shadow of European superiority.

Yet a number of distinctive American writers emerged in the early nineteenth century. James Fenimore Cooper, in the 1820s, rates as the nation's first great novelist, dealing with themes of westward expansion and interactions with Indians. His character, Natty Bumppo, independent but naturally good, was an attempt to sum up national qualities held superior to those of European-influenced cities and industrial society. Nathaniel Hawthorne wrote more critically of American traditions such as narrow-minded Puritanism. European romanticism influenced slightly later writers, such as the poet Walt Whitman, whose work celebrated democracy and individualism. Herman Melville, whose *Moby Dick* was published in 1851, emphasized the focus on achievement and individual striving characteristic of American middle-class culture more generally. A group of New England philosophers, the transcendentalists, also incorporated romantic themes, particularly in celebrating communion with nature. From the transcendentalist group in turn came a number of American thinkers and writers, including Utopian theorists and anti-slavery campaigners. American activity developed more slowly in the arts; most formal painting, for instance, was still done in a primitivist style, emphasizing bucolic scenes but in little contact with the level of activity in Europe.

Educational developments complemented the emergence of more formal American culture, but they had contradictory implications. White Americans had the highest literacy rate in the world in the late eighteenth century. Many states voiced a commitment to extensive education in their new constitutions, but there was little practical result. During the first decades of the nineteenth century emphasis lay on private academies, designed to provide moral training and exposure to elite, European-derived culture for the growing middle class. The number of universities expanded also, as prosperous Americans proved willing to pay for schooling that would distinguish their sons from the masses. During the 1830s, however, a new generation of educational reformers, headed by Horace Mann, returned to the charge of developing widespread public education, as a means of providing the training essential to a democratic electorate. Massachusetts instituted a state Board of Education in 1837; the principle of public support for education became widespread, and some states instituted attendance requirements. Democratic impulse mixed with a desire to use education to install middle-class habits and national loyalty. In this general movement Southern states lagged, however, with continued resistance to providing any kind of formal schooling, including literacy, to the slave population. Women, however, benefited considerably from the new educational surge, gaining high rates of literacy; and some universities began to open doors to women during the 1830s. By 1861, 94 per cent of the Northern population and 83 per cent of the white population of the South (58 per cent of the total) were literate. These were unusually high figures on a comparative basis. They reflected the fact that American education had developed particular emphasis on democratic access to primary training, whereas facilities for the elite, though present, were more haphazard. While training in science and engineering was available, the first engineering facility opened as part of the West Point academy for army officers, a firm tradition of higher schools had yet to develop. Educational democracy became deeply rooted in American values, helping to convince many that opportunities were available for all; the society that provided schools was fulfilling its obligations to social justice. The racial exception to this stance, in segregating or excluding most blacks, would also long remain part of the nation's development.

Religion formed another distinctive feature of American culture. By the 1790s, an important popular revival movement, called the Second Great Awakening, opened in American Protestantism, in response to Enlightenment-style rationalism. Highly emotional camp meetings developed among Methodists and Baptists, particularly in the South. As in England, religious fervour also responded to some of the stresses of early industrialization; but in the United States the movement incorporated unusually large numbers of women and also spread to religious enthusiasms among African Americans and Indians. Religious fervour underlay the formation of several of the Utopian communities, such as the Shakers (a sect imported from England) who sought to undo traditional gender divisions. Other new religions were formed in this enthusiastic atmosphere. The Church of Jesus Christ of Latter Day Saints (Mormons) was established in 1831, forming communities in several areas before settling in Utah after local hostilities forced them further West. Also in the 1830s William Miller anticipated the end of the world, and when it did not materialize some of his followers organized the sect called Seventh Day Adventists. Deep religious emotions and recurrent innovation became part of the nation's cultural history, alongside the more sedate Protestant churches and a growing Catholic population.

Commercialization and its consequences

Formation of national political and cultural characteristics was accompanied by a fundamental transformation of the American economy, toward more active market involvement, with huge attendant social consequences. The colonial economy had featured considerable merchant presence and some manufacturing, plus of course the export agriculture of the South. But much agriculture was geared toward local subsistence; cities were small; and many people were not extensively involved with commercial motives or mechanisms. Barter was more common than sales for money in many areas, with people exchanging work service for craft goods or additional food. One elderly New England farmer, as late as 1828, maintained his land by making shoes for his neighbors, in return for their help with planting and harvest.

This situation began to change rapidly around 1800. Several factors entered in. British industrial imports cut into some local manufacturing. Sheer crowding reduced access to the land, creating a growing group of landless laborers and many farmers eager at least to supplement their subsistence efforts. American population grew from 5.3 million to 9.6 million in the two decades after 1800. New needs prompted more initial change than did dramatic entrepreneurial spirit. But there were growing opportunities, as commercial production expanded, and soon an interest in profits, improved living standards and upward mobility entered into the mix.

As in cases of growing commercialization in other societies, complex cultural shifts accompanied economic change. As late as 1852 a rural magazine was still writing: 'As a general rule it is better that the farmer should produce what he needs for home consumption. He may obtain more money from tobacco, hops or broom corn, than from breadstuff, but taking all things into consideration will he be better off?' Many farmers continued to cling to plots of land long after they had ceased to be really profitable, because the way of life was more important than material ease. Resentment of profit-seekers was widespread, as economic inequalities grew along with market transactions. Recurrent slumps, as in 1837, convinced many people that the new economic system was misguided. The Workingmen's Party blasted the powers of the capitalists over individual liberty. Individuals filled their diaries with laments: 'Many of the distinctions and inequalities among men come from the selfishness, the avarice and ambition of those who call themselves upper classes'. The growth of new religious sects, like the Mormons, was fed by people displaced or threatened by change. Other movements picked up the discontent. Sylvester Graham advocated sexual restraint and a healthy diet based on home-processed grains, in explicit protest against the rise of commercial products and city ways; his movement drew support from many people, particularly male artisans.

Yet new ideas did gain ground. Farmers began combining traditional virtues like hard work and frugality with a desire for greater wealth: 'Though riches are not the chief good, it is desirable to have the comforts of life, and be in some respects independent', one young farmer wrote to his fiancée. Crucial in the American context was an unusual emphasis on the possibility of social mobility. Newspapers by the 1830s trumpeted the notion of advancement, and its accessibility to anyone willing to work hard. By contrast, poverty was the result of personal fault. By mid-century, rags-to-riches stories by Horatio Alger and others were common fare. Beliefs of this sort, often associated with insistence on the availability of basic education, were staples in middle-class history in many places during this period, but they were more widely disseminated, less frequently qualified in the United States. Here lay the origins of particular American reliance on the idea of social mobility, a pronounced tendency to exaggerate its frequency and a greater-than-average tendency to blame poverty on the habits of the poor.

Growth of the market economy initially involved the expansion of household work to include extra farm products, like eggs or butter, or craft work done by wives and children. Increasing agricultural specialization also entered in. Many New England farmers began to raise meat for sale in Boston or other growing cities, greatly increasing their output during the early decades of the century. Clothing was store-bought, rather than homemade. In general, market-oriented agriculture remained a vital staple of the American economy and society, despite many worries about new motivations and vulnerabilities. Commercial farming was enhanced by the continued availability of new land. Pressed by population growth but also new opportunities, New England farmers moved into western New York State, and thence to the rich lands of the Midwest. Specialization and movement were not the only responses of the farming population. Landowners were among the first groups in many areas to reduce their birth-rate, along with the urban middle class whose ideas they often shared. They wanted to preserve land and commercial opportunities for their offspring. Here was another contrast with the reactions of more traditional peasant populations in places like Western Europe, and with the outlook of landless rural laborers in these same regions of the United States, where birth-rates remained high and signs of new outlook less visible.

Commercialization caused rapid improvements in transportation, and these improvements facilitated further change. Americans took a lead in developing steamboats for use in river shipping. Oliver Evans created a lighter steam engine toward this end, and Robert Fulton, using an English-built engine, introduced the *Clermont* on the Hudson River in 1807. By 1811, steamboats were beginning to run down the Ohio and Mississippi Rivers. Road-building also expanded, initially under private auspices and then with government backing. Important routes that cut through the Appalachian Mountains were expanded. Then in the 1820s, canal building began in earnest, particularly important in connecting the rich farms of the Midwest to the growing cities of the East. New York State sponsored the Erie Canal, connecting the Hudson River with the Great Lake chain, with completion in 1825. Traffic was so heavy that tolls repaid the entire construction costs within seven years. Ventures of this sort encouraged migration westward, both by native farmers and by immigrants from Europe, and vastly increased the commercial exchange of agricultural and manufactured goods. These same functions encouraged rapid American adoption of the railroad, with an initial track opened as early as 1830. By the 1840s, expanding railroad systems were taking over the lead in transportation, with mileage tripling during this decade and again in the decade following, particularly in the Northeast. By 1850, the federal government began to encourage development by granting huge amounts of public land to subsidize the private companies – one of the great examples of government economic support in the nineteenth century. During this period also, from 1844 onward, Americans introduced the telegraph, stringing more than 50,000 miles of wire by 1860 and, a year later, connecting San Francisco and New York.

The initial stages of industrialization accompanied this overall surge in commerce. The nation's easy contacts with Britain, despite revolution and war, facilitated the borrowing of technology. As early as 1790 a British machine builder, Samuel Slater, had set up a spinning mill for a Rhode Island merchant. While technological imitation played an ongoing role in the nation's industrial revolution, along with massive infusions of British capital, American inventors were active as well. Eli Whitney invented the cotton gin in 1793, to remove seeds from cotton. Other inventors worked to improve European innovations such as interchangeable parts. An 'American system of manufacture' became known for its reliance on interchangeable parts to facilitate the standardized production of equipment. American industry benefitted greatly from the Napoleonic Wars, which interrupted European competition; even inexperienced owners and workers could profit from new factories. Between 1807 and 1815, the number of mechanized cotton spindles increased more than fifteenfold. In 1813, the power loom was introduced by the Boston merchant Francis Lowell, who improved on a British prototype. Factories, based primarily on water power, and whole industrial towns began to proliferate in New England. Technical innovation and abundant resources spurred rapid growth in productivity and national income.

Initial industrial labor was recruited mainly from the rural population. Much of it was female, with farm families sending daughters to work to help fund the family farm and provide a nest egg for ultimate marriage. Labor conditions were initially fairly good, though the work was strenuous. Labor shortage, given the availability of land for agriculture, helped assure moderately good wages; employers were careful to supervise the housing and moral conditions of their employees. Skilled male workers also won relatively high wages and enjoyed some real bargaining power with their employers.

By the 1840s the factory system spread and with it the use of steam engines. Factory owners began to displace more traditional merchant capitalists. The value of manufactured goods quintupled between 1840 and 1860, with the industrial center located in the Northeast and in a few Midwestern cities. By this point urban growth was accelerating as well. The population of leading cities on the Atlantic coast tripled in the two decades before the Civil War, with New York's figure surpassing a million. Whereas only 14 per cent of the Northeastern population was urban in 1840, a full 26 per cent was living in towns or cities by 1860, in contrast to the 10 per cent figure in the South.

Commercial growth and early industrialization heightened economic and social inequalities in the United States. Most entrepreneurial families had earlier merchant roots. While social mobility was possible, the bulk of the elite in the growing cities were not new-rich, so much as richer than before. By 1860 5 per cent of the American population controlled 50 per cent of the wealth. Beneath this group an expanding middle class operated smaller business establishments and filled the growing ranks of lawyers, doctors and other professionals. This urban middle class began to articulate a distinctive culture that combined older values, such as a strong emphasis on hard work and thrift, with more elaborated manners and styles. It was in the 1830s, for example, that European fashions began to serve as models for female elegance. Etiquette books, some authored by Europeans, taught Americans how to smooth out the rough edges of frontier behavior. Elaborated protocols were established for greeting strangers, receiving friends, or maneuvering through the many courses of the new French-style restaurants. Middle-class families began to sport consumer items like watches or clocks, initially less to tell time than to display wealth and modern awareness.

Social stratification and typical ambivalence about money and industrial life helped propel a new domestic ideology in the urban middle class. The home became a refuge, women and children pure beings to be kept free from the taint of commerce. An elaborated family advice literature urged that women had a purity that men lacked, particularly in their more restrained sexual appetites and great maternal feeling. This was a vital ingredient in the growing need to limit birth rates, mainly by periods of sexual abstinence. Women were also schooled in refinements such as piano playing, as these instruments became standard furnishings in the middle-class home. To women also were entrusted the care of often elaborated households and the raising of young children. Middle-class households often employed at least one live-in maid, a branch of work that, as in European cities, soon became the largest single category of urban employment for working-class women.

The new middle-class culture embraced more than manners or gender relations. It included growing emphasis on guilt, as a principle of childrearing and social remediation, as opposed to colonial reliance on shame. Older forms of punishment, including spanking children or publicly chastizing offenders, seemed increasingly barbaric. Urban conditions, with growing populations of relative strangers, required new family efforts to internalize good behavior. Emphasis on character development, backed by strong maternal love and a great reliance on feelings of guilt, provided one of the markers of this sweeping middle-class outlook on life.

New tensions

Pressures of early industrial life and growing economic and gender inequality did not produce massive unrest. Riots and strikes, though present, were surprisingly scattered. For some men, the existence of political outlets helped ease strain, though few government measures attacked industrial conditions directly; only a few states, for example, passed even weak measures against child labor. For some workers and small businessmen, opportunities to move westward, in search of land, provided a vital safety valve. While social mobility was not spectacularly high, geographical mobility was extensive. Many towns saw a majority of inhabitants arrive and leave in the same decade, though ironically it was the stable minority that often prospered the most economically. Even migration was not the only recourse for social uneasiness. New forms of religion picked up crucial tensions that could not be directly expressed. The existence of market-minded farm families, that shared some of the habits and values of the middle class, further complicated social resentments.

By the 1830s, however, there were additional signs of strain. Various industries sought to reduce wages, as competition increased and economic slumps created new anxieties. Women workers in the New England mills struck against wage cuts on several occasions, and ventured short-lived unions. While a court ruling in 1842 legalized unions for the first time, and some craft unions formed, this was not yet a powerful movement. Massive immigration from Ireland and Germany provided a growing source of low-cost labor, which reduced the potential for protest even as factory conditions worsened. During the 1840s and 1850s various nativist parties arose to protest the immigrant surge, with some impact on regional political life, but the tide was unstoppable. Between 1840 and 1860, over 4 million Europeans arrived in the United States, most of them settling in Northern and Midwestern cities.

Northern industrialization, and particular technologies such as the cotton gin, increased the dependent status of the Southern states and deepened the hold of slavery. Older Southern states, where crops like tobacco were declining, saw economic power shift to newer areas like Alabama and Mississippi, where cotton could be grown. States like Virginia shipped large numbers of slaves to these new regions. Manufacturing and trade, including massive imports from the North and Britain, largely revolved around this renewed slave economy. Slave conditions remained less severe than in the Caribbean and Latin America; the need for slaves, if nothing else, dictated material conditions adequate to maintain the population. But conditions varied greatly, and cruelty was frequent, along with division of families through the slave trade. Slave revolts were rare, but frequent enough to create elaborated laws regulating assembly and even religious life. Slaves' escapes were even

more frequent, and an 'underground railroad' developed, guided by escaped slaves and sympathetic whites, to transport slaves to the North. More informal resistance, including subtly defiant songs, theft, and destruction of equipment, was also common. Many slaves, and free blacks, also relied heavily on a separate network of Christian churches. Southern slaves and free blacks were closely interconnected with the white population, and mutual influence and occasional affection developed, but a partially distinct culture was created as well. This included a particularly important role for black women, whose labor was vital for plantation fields and households but who also served as the center of the African American family structure.

Along with various forms of unrest from slaves and urban workers, other new currents reflected the growing complexity of American life. A whole variety of reform movements burst into view by the 1830s. Individual reformers reported on appalling conditions in insane asylums and poor houses. Growing landless populations had overwhelmed local systems of informal assistance to the poor and infirm by 1800. Everywhere, cities tried to ship out unwanted transients. The insane, often cared for by families in the colonial period, were often now sent to custodial institutions. Poor farms, their populations composed disproportionately of women and the elderly, also suffered deteriorating conditions through a combination of deliberate desire to weed out the undeserving poor and a tight-fisted approach by state legislatures. New prisons, though heralded as centers for the reform of criminals through guilt and rehabilitation, increasingly became storehouses for unwanted people, disproportionately immigrant. The reform movement picked up on these growing problem areas, but without great effect.

The reform spirit also applied to the conditions of women. American feminism developed earlier than formal movements in Europe for several reasons, though it long had little impact. The strong democratic rhetoric of American political life contrasted vividly with women's unequal conditions. Relatively high levels of female literacy facilitated communication and also heightened some women's awareness of the limitations of the domestic role. Women's rights agitation also paralleled the development of movements against Southern slavery. An initial women's rights convention was held in Seneca Falls, New York, in 1848, after several decades of feminist writings against legal limitations. Individual women also pressed forward on other reform fronts. Harriet Beecher Stowe's novel, *Uncle Tom's Cabin*, roused great sympathy for African American slaves. Other women, though in small numbers, became Protestant ministers or doctors.

The most portentous reform interest centered on slavery. Here was the greatest contrast between American political rhetoric and social reality. Northern reformers, from about 1817 onward, focused increasingly on the evils of slavery, inspired often by intense religious conviction. William Lloyd Garrison, in 1831, founded a newspaper, the *Liberator*, in a relentless crusade against the institution, and a host of antislavery societies sprang up. Free blacks like Frederick Douglass, an escaped slave, presented damning portraits of slave life. While several articulate Southerners spoke in defence of slavery, arguing among other things (rather like Russian defenders of serfdom) that slaves could not manage on their own, the propaganda barrage continued. Stowe's novel sold 300,000 copies within a year of its publication in 1852. Insistence on national political action grew – as did Southern resistance.

The conflict over slavery was the dramatic focus of an even wider set of issues in American society as it took shape after 1800. Democratic commitments were widespread, and the nation led in expanding the suffrage. Many observers also noted a certain informal democracy, in the ability of women and children to speak up in family settings, or the ease of communication and fuzziness of ranks in frontier settlements. At the same time, economic and gender equalities in many ways expanded, and the entrenchment of plantation slavery vividly demonstrated the contradictions between American racial policies and any democratic values. Efforts to develop more formal manners and cultural outlets, including elite secondary schools, showed a vigorous reaction against democracy even in white society. These tensions pitted groups against each other, but they also warred within individuals, unsure of their own balance between equality of rights and an admiration for wealth and privilege.

The crisis of the Civil War

Tensions over slavery and serfdom were common elements of nineteenth-century history in several areas of the world, but only in the United States did they lead to civil war. The reasons are several. To a degree, the American conflict was a belated outcropping of the kinds of disagreements common in the formation of new nations, when different groups and regions bring different assumptions to the political process. Slavery had been fairly explicitly sidestepped during the constitutional process, when the South was allowed to count each slave as 3/5 of a census person for purposes of legislative allocations. Later compromises, when new states like Missouri were brought into the union, attempted to trade off slave and free states (Missouri was paired with non-slave Maine). But ultimately the issues could not be avoided.

Arguments common in other societies, that the coercive labor system was increasingly uneconomical, were harder to sustain in the United States. The growing importance of cotton production in the deep South, and the unusually extensive internal slave trading arrangements that benefitted other parts of the region, made the system pay. Tragically, cotton's importance deepened the institution's roots just as humanitarian concern about slavery intensified in other quarters. Humanitarian and practical arguments against Russian serfdom, in contrast, played against a labor system that was less clearly profitable.

Anti-slavery forces, while echoing humanitarian sentiments common in other parts of the Americas and Europe, were unquestionably strong. Strong Protestant convictions, on the part of groups like the Quakers convinced of the equality of souls, joined with genuine democratic political commitments, in the North and among some individuals in the South. Wider regional conflicts enhanced the specific dispute. Historians continue to explore the issue of how different the two sections of the country were. The economic systems contrasted increasingly, with the industrial North juxtaposed to the South's export-dependent plantation economy. Southern defenders of slavery delighted in pointing out the hypocrisy of Northern abolitionists who ignored the miseries of their own factory workers. Elements of Southern culture were also highly distinctive. Plantation owners liked to fancy themselves an aristocracy of sorts, with a commitment to passionate defence of honor, as opposed to the puritanical or commercially-minded North. Violence and fighting were more common recreational outlets in the South. Northerners paid more attention to a rhetoric of individual opportunity and access to economic growth. On the other hand, many white Southern families read the same materials as their Northern counterparts, and many planters were clever capitalists. Gender distinctions were similar except in the slave population, where the position of women was more central. However great the cultural overlap, enough general differences existed to allow partisans of each region to go beyond attacks on or defences of slavery, to a broader portrait of systems in conflict. Each region was convinced it was defending a way of life. This wider debate, along with beliefs in the inferiority of blacks, helps explain why the majority of Southern whites, though not slave owners themselves, ultimately aligned with the regional cause.

In the context of mounting abolitionism alongside the economic success of the plantation system, the specific precipitant of growing conflict involved the steady westward expansion of the United States. As the nation added territory, representatives from the slave and free states became increasingly embroiled in quarrels over the spoils. The old principle of division, with one new state slave for every new state free, became increasingly untenable, given the abolitionist passions of the North combined with the fact that more people and economic power emanated from that region. The South, worried that a disproportion between slave and free might lead to political attacks on the institution of slavery, became increasingly defensive.

General consensus supported the principle of expansion itself, by the 1840s. The demographic and industrial growth of the United States made territorial growth attractive. European powers continued to prove willing to negotiate the surrender of loosely-held territory – as with British holdings in the Northwest in 1846 (the current states of Washington and Oregon), though there were some border skirmishes with Canada. The opposition of other occupants, Mexico in the case of Texas and areas of the Southwest, and American Indians generally, could be overcome by military force. Publicists and politicians trumpeted the nationalist notion of 'manifest destiny', that the United States should control the continent, or at least the continent south of Canada, from Atlantic to Pacific. American settlers in Texas proclaimed independence from Mexico in 1836, and concern that the new republic might form a rival continental empire prompted admission to statehood in 1845 despite the fact that Northern leaders resented its slaveholding status. Mexico went to war in protest against this as well as the increasing infiltration of American settlers into California and the Southwest, and the United States victory in the Mexican-American War led to a huge territorial acquisition in the region.

Compromises permitted the admission of new states from the West, but the political process grew increasingly strained. The Whig party was destroyed by dispute, as the Democrats came increasingly to represent interests either favourable to slaveholding or concerned about the growing dominance of Northern industrialism. Replacing the Whigs, from 1854 onward, was a new Republican party devoted to blocking slavery in newly-settled territories such as Kansas. Specific attempts of Southern states to pass laws against fugitive slaves in the North, and a Supreme Court ruling in 1856 that supported the constitutional right to slavery, fanned the flames of dispute. Abolitionists staged a raid on the South in 1859, hoping to spark a slave rebellion. Southern leaders grew increasingly fearful that their interests could not be protected in the existing nation. The presidential election of 1860, won by the Republican candidate Abraham Lincoln, was the last straw. Lincoln was morally opposed to slavery and to its expansion to new territory, though he was not in fact an abolitionist. Southerners, convinced that their position in the Union was hopeless, began to vote withdrawal, and the seceding states formed a separate Confederacy. All efforts at compromise failed, and war between the North and South began effectively in January 1861, with the firing on a federal fort in South Carolina.

The Civil War is often billed as the world's first industrial war, and in terms of the use of factory-generated equipment, including mass-produced weaponry, plus the role of railroads and steamships in troop movements, this is an accurate description. Huge economic and population advantages lay with the North, which account for its ultimate victory. However, the rural South, fighting a largely defensive war on its own territory, held its own for a surprisingly long time. The South also benefitted from considerable division in the North about carrying the war forward, including some major urban riots against military service and against blacks; and the Confederacy won diplomatic support from nations like Great Britain, eager to protect their cotton supply and not unwilling to humiliate the United States. The result was a prolonged, immensely bloody clash, in which more American lives were lost than in any other military conflict in the nation's history, before or since.

Northern naval superiority limited maritime fighting, but skirmishes occurred in various parts of the continent. Small forces battled in portions of the Western territories. A major Northern force closed the Mississippi at its mouth in the Gulf of Mexico, conquering New Orleans. Subsequent campaigns worked down the river from the North. Larger battles occurred in Virginia, with some Confederate forays into Pennsylvania; here, particularly, is where results long alternated, with many Southern victories. A final set of campaigns began in 1864, with Union forces attacking in Virginia while a large army laid waste from Tennessee to Georgia, and on to the coast. The Confederacy surrendered in April 1865, and President Lincoln, who had marshaled the war effort and now planned a conciliatory peace settlement, was assassinated by a Southern actor just a few days later.

Not surprisingly, the war had massive results. Its shock effect reverberated for decades. As late as the 1890s, Union army veterans continued to rouse massive crowds during annual parades. War stories crowded the pages of boys' magazines. No single event has so influenced the national memory, even into the late twentieth century. Yet the war was not a historical watershed. It encouraged certain trends and briefly launched other innovations that were, however, soon modified. It did end slavery, after some hesitations on Lincoln's part, but it did not manage to restructure race relations or to alter the dependent economic status of the South.

The War encouraged industrial growth, but the basic process was already well underway. To fuel expanding factories, coal mining increased by 20 per cent in the North; mechanization accelerated, which along with heightened immigration helped keep wages low, while the railroad network grew. Women gained new functions with men at the front, and though there was no permanent shift in gender relations Southern women acquired some novel organizational experience while the ranks of nurses durably expanded through the entry of women. American armaments production soared, and after the war the nation became an international military supplier for the first time, sending surplus weapons for example to contending factions

of samurai in Japan. At the same time, the importance of agriculture in the United States was confirmed. The Homestead Act, passed in 1862, granted 160 acres of public lands to Western settlers who lived on the property for five years and paid a small fee. This was an aggressive national policy designed to confirm territorial expansion beyond the Mississippi and promote the ideal of commercially-oriented family farms.

Political developments had more novel implications. The War's results confirmed the longstanding party division between Republicans and Democrats, with the latter long a minority with a disproportionately Southern base. Equally important was the War's role in strengthening American government, adding significantly to its functions. Early in the conflict Congress passed the Morrill Act (1862), which granted public lands to state governments, to provide a basis for funding state-sponsored education. This act led to the formation of many state universities, the so-called land-grant institutions. Though the educational role of the federal government remained limited, states now played an active role, not only expanding university access but creating institutions that were particularly linked to popular needs for research and training in agriculture, engineering and other practical fields in addition to the conventional liberal arts. At the federal level itself, tariffs increased to the highest level ever, becoming in the process a major source of tax revenue as well as protecting industry.

The war also spawned a host of temporary measures, including the first national draft law (1863) which roused so much popular resistance. Lincoln gained special authority under a War Powers act, though he used it sparingly. Taxes increased, and for a time a modest income tax was imposed, again amid massive constraints from popular opposition. National banking activity increased, and Congress also pressed for a transcontinental railway, granting massive public lands to the companies involved; the Union Pacific line was completed in 1869, far ahead of transcontinental systems in most other regions. Overall, however, there was no durable breakthrough in the role of government in American society, though the alignment with industrial interests grew more pronounced. Important precedents were established – both for new systems and for popular hostility to them. Specific measures in the economy and in education had genuine impact. Some permanent growth occurred in the federal bureaucracy; by the 1870s civil service measures were being discussed, while government offices provided unusually early opportunities for white-collar employment for women. Also important was the system of benefits for Union veterans established after the War, and steadily expanded as a politically popular measure in ensuing decades. By 1900 most surviving veterans were receiving pensions, in what became the first durable welfare program in American history. Yet the United States remained a loosely-governed society, compared to its counterparts in Western Europe, with fairly limited scope for government functions; a long series of relatively weak and undistinguished presidencies after Lincoln's assassination, lasting until the early twentieth century, both reflected and confirmed this pattern.

The War's impact on race was, along with the preservation of national territory, its most important effect, though here too the effects must not be exaggerated. Northerners, including Lincoln himself, were very ambivalent about race and about how to treat slavery and the South. Even many abolitionists, though unambiguous in condemning slavery, had patronizing views of blacks themselves. Amid divisions, Southern white leaders were able to regain considerable influence surprisingly quickly after the War's end.

Support for ending slavery increased as the War continued, for only this goal would seem to justify the tremendous sacrifices involved. Lincoln issued the Emancipation Proclamation on 1 January 1863, though slaves in border states that had not left the Union were not affected. As Union armies seized Confederate territory, actual liberation occurred, with tens of thousands of former slaves joining the war effort. A constitutional amendment in 1865 abolished the institution throughout the nation. Only in a few cases were former slaves granted any land by the Union army; economically, American emancipation was far less generous than its counterpart two years before in Russia. At the War's end, with much of the South devastated and 4 million blacks virtually without possessions, many planters hoped to reinstate a modified form of slavery, but the federal government, and its occupying army, prevented this result. A Freedman's Bureau offered various protections and food assistance to blacks, plus some encouragement to the acquisition of land.

The years after the War, until 1877, are known as the Reconstruction period, filled with debates over federal policy toward the South. Immediately after Lincoln's death, Congress was dominated by radical Republicans from the North, who sought a harsh Southern policy backed by military force and the political exclusion of many Confederate sympathizers. Their motives included concerns about racial issues, but they also embraced a desire to keep Southern Democrats at bay in order to preserve policies, like high tariffs, favorable to Northern industry. Hasty post-war efforts in Southern states to enact Black Codes, to limit the freedom of blacks, for example through heavy fines for vagrancy, spurred Republican zeal. Blacks were declared citizens of the United States, and two new constitutional amendments (14 and 15) granted adult black males voting rights and equal protection of the law. For a time, black politicians gained active roles in the Southern states – which increased the resentment of many Southern whites, convinced that Congress was forcing corrupt governments upon them.

During this phase of Reconstruction, Southern blacks began to develop new economic activities, purchasing a fair amount of land in small holdings. About 20 per cent of all blacks in the South owned land by the 1870s. With some aid from Northern philanthropists, including many women teachers, educational gains spread rapidly. By 1870 over 4,000 schools were in operation, educating about 12 per cent of the total freed black population of relevant age. By 1876, about 40 per cent of all black children were in school, and a network of black academies, soon colleges, was providing more advanced training. Independent black churches also gained ground, providing a new leadership group through the often inspirational Protestant ministers.

Change was limited in important respects. Most blacks worked as sharecroppers for white landowners, in an adaptation of the old cotton-growing plantations. Unlike their white counterparts, black women even in the cities usually continued to work, often as domestic servants, throughout their lives. This facilitated considerable stabilization of black families, but on a distinctive basis. More important, by the 1870s black political and legal gains began to be rolled back in the Southern states, as federal controls eased and the army was withdrawn. New secret societies, like the Ku Klux Klan,

were formed to intimidate black voters, and many acts of violence and murder occurred. White Democrats regained control of the Southern states, and the traditional ruling class was restored, commanding political support from poorer whites in an atmosphere of racial division. Banks and employers discriminated against black workers. Ironically, even in the North urban blacks often lost ground to new waves of immigrant workers from Europe.

Race relations had changed in the United States, with some real gains for blacks. But the racial problem had been redefined, not resolved. The federal government had not been willing to press attacks on Southern property owners, and ongoing beliefs in the inherent inferiority of blacks persisted. By the end of the nineteenth century a welter of Jim Crow laws segregated blacks in the South, denying for example equal access to schools and public facilities. Poll taxes and literacy tests were used to restrict black voting. Informal violence against blacks, including lynchings, increased, with an average of 187 per year during the 1890s. Imprisonment of blacks increased disproportionately, as did their use on chain gangs for road work and other heavy labor. Novel but limited industrialization, in mill towns that competed through the use of cheap, non-union black and white labor, altered the economic profile of the South but only to a modest degree, as the region lagged well behind the North by all standard indicators of per capita health, education and income. Here too, change was important but circumscribed.

In race as in other areas, the United States was not the same in the aftermath of the Civil War as it had been before. Yet to a surprising extent, the tumult of the War confirmed patterns – like limited government and the federal system – or furthered pre-existing trends, more than it caused radical new departures. Even novel developments, like the new racial violence in the South, perpetuated older differences in regional cultures in new ways. Northerners, tired of their exertions, seemed content to let the South go its own way. Congress and the Supreme Court, after Reconstruction, largely sanctioned the Jim Crow legislation. The Civil War confirmed the union, belatedly ending any major possibility of territorial realignments or secession. It demonstrated the effectiveness of existing political institutions, which could respond to extreme demands of war without yielding to authoritarian forms. It maintained, though with novel specifics, the deep tension between democratic rhetoric and racial reality, which had been born with the nation itself.

CANADA

From 1780 to 1867

The decades around 1800, extending in many ways to the British North America Act of 1867, constituted a formative period for Canadian politics and indeed for the emergence of the nation itself. It was during these decades also that the dominant comparative characteristics of Canada took shape. As a frontier society, increasingly focused on commercial agriculture and exports, challenged by rapid immigration, Canada in many respects resembled the United States. Both domestic and foreign observers noted the development of cultural features and personal motivations that seemed very similar to those south of the border. But Canada, if different from Europe, also differed from the United States. It was not a revolutionary society. Its religious culture was much more substantially shaped by established churches – Anglican in most regions, Catholic in Quebec and a few other French settlements. Canadian politics was less quickly democratic than those of the United States, and the ties to the British monarchy remained quite real. Social rhetoric was less fiercely egalitarian. As the Canadian nation developed, and as American power became ever more obvious, efforts to insist on a distinct Canadian identity increased, relying heavily on the factors that had separated the two nations during the gestation of their political institutions.

Development during and after the American Revolution confirmed some of the political, as well as territorial, distinctions between Canada and the United States. As the large American forces tied to the British crown went down in defeat, about 40,000 loyalists migrated to Canada, into Ontario, the Maritime Provinces and Quebec as well. They brought with them a vigorous attachment to the crown and to British ways, and a hostility to the institutions of the new republic to the south. At the same time, the British government became more careful in its treatment of the principal provinces. Quebec, particularly, was granted considerable autonomy; this did not attach French Canadians to British rule, but it did persuade them that they would benefit from continued independence from the United States, so that their province could manage to go its own way.

In 1791 a Constitutional Act set up elective legislatures in Upper Canada in the west, and Lower (French) Canada in the east. (The term Canada, from an Indian word, was first used at this point). Separate provincial governments also persisted in the eastern Maritime Provinces. These governments had significant, though advisory, parliamentary powers, with a reasonably extensive manhood suffrage; the executive branch flowed from colonial governors appointed by Britain. The result, in Quebec, was a perpetual struggle between the British-appointed governor and his executive, and the French-dominated assembly; politics of cultural division were shaped early in this province. The policy of provincial autonomy, here and in other areas, plus the very real linguistic and cultural differences among the provinces, created the basis for much more serious provincial politics in Canada than in the federal system of United States, and in the end for a more genuine balance between provincial and national government functions.

The War of 1812 brought renewed conflict with the United States. American settlers had been pouring into Upper Canada, a few because of British sympathy but more because of available land. Clashes with Indians and trappers were frequent. Leading American politicians predicted annexation as a result of the war with Britain, and several badly-organized invasion attempts occurred. French Canadians largely avoided the fray, but British loyalists in Canada were eager to avenge earlier wrongs, and along with British troops maintained the frontier despite several battles north of Niagara. While a hint of Canadian nationalism resulted from this successful struggle, government remained resolutely provincial and the larger message involved an ongoing desire to differ from the United States – not to be American, rather than attempting positively to define what it was to be Canadian. From a diplomatic standpoint, relations improved from this point onward. By 1818 a treaty regulated armaments on the Great Lakes and established an agreed-upon boundary to the Rocky Mountains, and then in 1846 the Oregon Treaty extended this line to the Pacific Ocean. The two countries, though still subtly different, managed to coexist in unusual harmony, with only rare

exceptions. Neither country directed significant military planning or resources to their long mutual border.

Political debate during the first half of the nineteenth century within Canada involved steady legislative pressure against often inept colonial governors. The legislature in Upper Canada gained increasing taxing authority in this process. Radical groups headed by William Mackenzie urged the example of United States democracy, though the bulk of Canadian politicians were committed to the monarchy and to greater conservatism. Indeed, American egalitarianism encouraged an alternative formulation of Canadian political culture. Here, British parliamentary precedent and the rule of law were touted as bastions of liberty, as against the whims of mass democracy.

During the early part of the nineteenth century as much energy flowed into the sheer issue of settling middle Canada as into establishing appropriate provincial political institutions. The European population increased from 250,000 in 1791, predominantly French, to 1.6 million by 1846, with the French now a minority in that they did not receive extensive immigration. English-speaking immigrants concentrated particularly in Upper Canada (now Ontario). Most staked out subsistence farms, supplemented by hunting and trapping – much like the bulk of the inhabitants, the more established farmers in Quebec. Bartering was long more common than sales for cash. During this period also, from the 1790s onward, various expeditions explored western Canada, to the Pacific, while one small group of settlers was established in Manitoba. Particularly in Upper Canada, provincial governments gradually introduced some better, paved roads, which launched a process of growing commercialization. Some canal building in the 1820s improved connections among the Great Lakes. An initial railroad opened in 1836, though by 1850 there were only 66 miles of rail line in the whole nation. The repeal of the Corn Laws in Britain opened a much greater market for export agriculture, facilitating a major turn toward market production after the 1840s.

Though these developments lagged a few decades behind comparable expansion and commercialization in the United States, they highlighted some similar motivations. Emphasis on wealth as the measure of human achievement increased, particularly in Ontario. Immigrants worked hard to gain more land and advance their social position. Family labor, including children, was committed to the struggle for rural success; as in the United States, however, growing population prompted many farmers to begin to reduce birthrates in order to preserve property for their sons. Rates in Quebec however, remained high, in what one historian has termed 'the revenge of the cradles', in part because of the strong Catholic hold; by the 1830s, the resulting land shortage began to promote a considerable French-Canadian emigration to the United States. Geographical mobility was substantial in English Canada as well, both in search of land and to avoid the encroachment of greater crowding and 'civilization'. The successful farmers delighted in claiming that they constituted a 'new breed of man', freed from the limitations of old-world outlook. Other observers agreed that Canadians were different, thanks to frontier opportunities, but mainly by their naked acquisitiveness and materialism; Ontario thus might be described as 'bustling, noisy, pretentious, vulgar and ugly'.

Characteristics of this sort did not, however, override some differences between Canadian and United States frontiers. One measure was the treatment of Indians.

Canadian whites frequently pushed Indians off established lands, substituting European property laws for the more amorphous territoriality of hunting-and-gathering groups. Some Indians were herded directly onto reservations, again as in the United States. But there was much less warfare and violence – in general, levels of violence in Canada of all sorts were lower than those of the United States. Treaty rights with Indians were more commonly honored. Several factors account for this difference. The Indian population, at 2 percent around 1850, was somewhat larger in Canada as a percentage of the total. Rural policing, established by British colonial governors, was better established, and emphasis on the rule of law may actually have curbed Canadian greed. Some Indians lived on the northern fringes of white settlements, in territory whose climate precluded extensive agriculture and, therefore, pressing territorial demands. Culturally, Canadians seem to have developed a greater tolerance for diversity than Americans, and were less bent on acculturation programs designed to make all groups measure up to middle-class norms. Provincial distinctions helped encourage this kind of latitude, and on the whole racial attitudes were less rigid. Not only Indians, but also blacks, including escaped slaves from the United States, received relatively restrained treatment in Canada, though there were some instances of blatant discrimination against both groups. At the end of the century several laws also sought to exclude Asians; Canadian tolerance was imperfect. Indians served as relatively sympathetic (if often ill-treated) figures in Canadian literature, as opposed to their frequently villainous casting in American stories.

Some elements of formal cultural activity took shape during the early nineteenth century. Several colleges were established between 1789 and 1818, though the pressure of farm labor long constrained literacy rates in Canada as a whole, including Quebec. Several novels in English, appeared, by both male and female authors, inaugurating this strand of Canadian culture. Publications in French, established earlier, maintained a steady pace.

Major political and social tension developed in Ontario and Quebec during the mid-1830s. French Canadian resistance to British domination seemed intractable; relations between the legislature and colonial governor were perpetually tense. In Ontario, democratic agitation was heightened by the impact of minority Protestant faiths, like Baptists and Methodists, spread from the United States and hostile to the Anglican establishment. Many farmers resented rule by urban oligarchies. The situation had overtones of the American Revolution of 1776, and a new democratic newspaper, the *Constitution*, launched in 1836 on the 60th anniversary of the Declaration of Independence, specifically urged revolt. Leaders began to organize paramilitary troops, and some clashes with British troops occurred in the autumn of 1837. But the numbers involved were small, and the government quickly put down the risings. Even most French Canadians remained aloof, and the Catholic church pointedly refused its support to protest, having no enthusiasm for a republic. A radical attack on Toronto failed, and the United States, despite a few tense hesitations, declined to support rebellion.

Britain reacted swiftly, despite the ease of repression; it had no desire to see North American history repeat itself. The rebels were treated leniently. A new report, by Lord Durham, blasted the corruption of colonial officials and urged self-government under imperial control. Against French Canadian objections, Upper and Lower Canada were united with a single governor and legislature; the English language was to be preferred, though French was allowed. The Union Act (1840) did reduce French isolation, while expanding legislative power. While governors were still to be appointed, there was growing recognition that they must be closely monitored and the wishes of the legislature informally considered. During the 1840s, considerable jockeying continued over the real source of control over the executive, with the British increasingly realizing the need to grant fundamental authority to elected legislatures. This right of responsible government was granted in the Maritime Provinces beginning in 1847, and then in 1849 it was established in United Canada as well, when the governor accepted a bill against his own judgment, simply because it had passed the legislature. While this issue was resolved, the thorny question of fusion between French Canadians and English Canadians was not. The former bitterly resented forced union, all the more as their relative numbers declined steadily thanks to British immigration, despite the high birth-rates of rural Quebec.

By mid-century, political developments began to be overshadowed by Canada's massive economic development and westward expansion. The 1850s was a decade of rapid railroad construction, most of it financed by British capital and backed, after 1849, by government guarantees of interest on debts. In 1854 a major line opened in Ontario, and planning began on a connection between Montreal and Toronto. Canadian exports benefitted hugely from British needs during the Crimean War. A pattern of supplying agricultural goods, particularly wheat, plus minerals for industrial markets, was beginning to be established as the framework for the Canadian economy, and with it considerable dependence on fluctuating demands in the industrial countries. Significant industrial development took shape as well, primarily for internal markets. In Montreal Hugh Allan, President of the Board of Trade, opened extensive textile and paper mills, using a high percentage of female and child labor. Grain milling also expanded in various parts of the country. The discovery of gold in British Columbia in 1857 increased immigration to this region, by Mexicans and Chinese as well as Europeans. New policies toward Indians facilitated forcible removal from territories sought by Europeans. Larger European populations in the northwest also increased the rates of communicable disease among Indians, in a familiar pattern, which further released land for European acquisition.

Commercial and limited industrial development brought some familiar concomitants. Education expanded, and a growing urban middle class became committed to schooling for their children. British and American standards concerning gender had increasing impact in Canadian cities, with concomitant notions of the home as refuge and the wife as domestic moral agent. Social structure became more complex, after the greater openness of the frontier period. Canadian upper-class wealth and styles of life, however, remained more modest than those of the great American industrial barons, suggesting in yet another way the slightly more conservative tone of the nation.

Canada's political structure gained its more modern form in this atmosphere of economic expansion, with growing interest in encouraging but also regulating westward development. Ongoing political clashes amid French opposition in United Canada made it imperative to think about other arrangements, including a re-division of Ontario and Quebec. Democratic – and

English-speaking – reformers, eager for a more responsive parliament, pressed for voting by head, but the French, now decisively outnumbered in United Canada, resisted strongly. Political action seemed stalemated by the later 1850s. The final propellant to restructuring was the American Civil War. Apparent British sympathy for the South roused American nationalist resentment, and Canada might be a target. Irish immigrants in the United States had already conducted raids on Canada, as a means of attacking British oppression of their country. Now, responsible officials in Lincoln's government began talking of the inevitability of annexing Canada, as part of the United States' 'Manifest destiny'. And the fact was that the North for a time boasted the largest army in the world. In this context, British officials joined Canadian politicians, including the French-Canadian leader Georges Cartier, in a major restructuring of Canada and the granting of the first Dominion, or self-governing status. (The idea of a Kingdom of Canada was rejected lest it offend republican sentiment in the United States.)

Under the British North America Act of 1867, New Brunswick and Nova Scotia joined Ontario and Quebec, now separated as provinces once again, in a confederated Dominion of Canada. Improved transportation made this link with the Atlantic coastal provinces feasible. The federal government – each province also had its own government – consisted of a two-house parliament, with the upper house consisting of equal membership from Ontario and Quebec with a third segment representing the Maritimes, and an elected lower house which was the more important legislative body. The British continued to appoint a governor-general for the whole country, as representative of the monarchy; a premier, however, was now selected by parliament to run the executive branch directly. John Macdonald was first chosen for this position.

Canadian expansion, 1867–1914

The new federal government was soon complemented by a vigorous opening of the Canadian West, capped by a national railroad, which decisively shaped Canada's enhanced position in the world economy during the final decades of the nineteenth century. In a very broad sense, Canadian and United States history share a certain periodization. During the first two thirds of the long nineteenth century, both were preoccupied with establishing a viable and durable political structure (at which both succeeded admirably after some often costly false starts), with setting some broader cultural characteristics in relation to politics, and with establishing an increasingly commercial economy. During the final portion of the nineteenth century, a different crop of economic and social issues came to the fore, superseding explicitly political manoeuverings, joined by new pressures and opportunities created by heightened immigration and westward growth.

Two major political parties, Liberal and Conservative, contested Canadian elections into the twentieth century. Liberals tended to be more hostile to arrangements favoring religious education and there were disputes over tariff policies. But the split between the parties was not profound; as in the United States, a considerable consensus prevailed. A number of reforms completed the new political system; notably, in 1882, the Canadian government installed civil service procedures for selection of federal officials. Modelled on British policies, the initial measure was a compromise venture, with relatively easy examinations for appointments in which political considerations continued to play a significant role.

Westward expansion focused political and economic attention alike. The territory between Ontario and British Columbia (still administered as a separate colony) was historically ruled by the Hudson Bay Company. The Company, eager for fur trade profits, positively discouraged settlement and agriculture, and promoted intermarriage between whites and Indians toward a mixed population that would continue trapping. Only the one settlement on the Red River, established as a refuge for discontented Scottish Highlanders, in present-day Manitoba, qualified this policy, and even it encountered constant harassment from the Company. In 1867, the Red River valley had a population of 12,000, over half of whom were mixed French and Indian families known as *métis*.

Government interest in this area included concern that lack of action might open the way for illegal American settlement, for westward expansion in the United States recurrently produced statements about the untapped riches of the Canadian plains. The first step – and the first major act of the new Dominion government – involved negotiations with Britain to extinguish the Hudson Bay Company's title. The government bought out the Company's interest, reserving some territory for it, which still allowed it to maintain a lucrative fur trade. Canada, in turn, acquired about 2,500,000 square miles of territory, with a total population of 175,000. The trappers were intensely aggrieved at the prospect of agricultural settlement, and they were not consulted as government surveyors laid out rectangular plots for putative farms. Louis Riel, a French Canadian with some Indian blood and a former student for the priesthood, became the leader of the protest group. Riel and his colleagues formed a separate government in 1869, in what became known as the Red River rebellion. A Canadian was killed, and the government sent an armed force to put down the rebels. Riel was exiled, but other residents were placated by the granting of provincial status to Manitoba in 1870. Immigration expanded quickly, with settlers taking up the rich lands and converting them to wheat growing. With a population of 181,000 in 1881, Manitoba boasted a quarter-million a decade later.

Territory west of Manitoba was controled directly by the Dominion government in Ottawa. In 1874, the Royal Mounted Police were organized to keep order in the West. The force became as stereotypic a part of Canada's westward expansion as the shoot'em up cowboy was in the United States. The difference was not merely symbolic. Canadian westward expansion involved relatively little violence, thanks to a strong cultural commitment to order and the visible presence of national law enforcement. Even mining camps, in subsequent gold discoveries, maintained consistent discipline. The great Klondike strike of the 1890s drew a large number of American 'thugs' (as one Canadian put it), but the Mounties held firm. Elsewhere, Canadians retained a more deeply internalized need to conform to rules, even when the police were not actively present. Here was another difference in values, involving respect for law, that many observers argue continues to distinguish the two cultures.

Settlement involved more than policing, of course. By the 1870s, the national government was spending considerable sums to attract immigration, while imitating the United States policy of granting homesteads to active farmers. National policy also began to address Indian affairs for the first time, with measures in the late 1860s aiming to extinguish Indian titles to Western lands in return for reservations, schools and farming equipment. The resultant treaties were scrupulously enforced, and after 1879, as the buffalo herds diminished, the government provided additional temporary funding. In 1885 a final rebellion of the *métis* was put down (the Northwest Rebellion), and Riel, who had re-emerged as its leader, this time was executed.

The giant step in Western settlement involved the creation of a railroad to the Pacific. The government chartered a company in 1881, with a huge grant of money and land to the Canadian Pacific. The railway was completed in 1885 and opened in 1887. The result was rapid expansion of agricultural and mining production, and substantial immigration from the British Isles, Germany and especially Slavic regions of Eastern Europe. Approximately 60,000 immigrants arrived annually by the 1890s, though some of them quickly left for the more industrial United States, and at one point economic stagnation actually reduced population levels. Even so, the Western population had risen to 400,000. British Columbia had been attracted to the confederation, by negotiations in 1870, and soon after 1900 Alberta and Saskatchewan entered as well. Disappointed that development was less rapid than hoped, for the economy lagged badly at several points in the later nineteenth century, the government sweetened the homestead deal in 1901, drawing over 200,000 new settlers annually, from the United States, now, as well as Europe. By 1900 the Canadian West housed 1,300,000 people.

Along with attentive government policy, American technology and farming methods plus British capital helped open this huge wheat growing area and some attendant mines. Canadian farmers endured great hardships in carving out the breadbasket so quickly, but they used advanced machinery rather than more traditional, labor-intensive methods. The result, as in the United States, was an industrial version of agriculture that allowed high export production and a reasonably advanced standard of living. Though Canadian industrialization proceeded less rapidly than that of its southern neighbor, with greater dependence on imports of factory products and equipment, material conditions resembled those of an industrial country.

The peopling of the West had political as well as economic implications. Canada's homesteading policy was similar to that of the United States, for the simple reason that Mackenzie and other leaders realized that anything less generous would not attract immigrants, who would have the readily available alternative south of the border. The result was a network of family-owned but commercial farms, with immigrants who quickly moved toward citizenship. The contrast with the laborer-status of the settlers of the Argentine pampas, in precisely the same turn-of-the-century period, was marked. Canada's Western farmers quickly formed vigorous cooperatives and successfully pressed the government to regulate railroad rates in their favor – in this respect, passing their American cousins in political success. The land system flowed from and reinforced a democratic political structure.

New sources of immigration also highlighted Canada's tradition of considerable tolerance for regional and group diversity. Canadians spoke of their expanding population as a mosaic, in contrast to the melting pot image used by the more assimilationist Americans around 1900. Several religious groups, like the Hutterites, were able to operate in virtually complete freedom from interference, while East Europeans – headed by Ukrainians, the largest single group – re-established folk customs quite quickly.

Success boosted Canadian nationalism, by 1900, long held in some check by fears and resentments about American gigantism. Speeches hailing the twentieth century as 'the Canadian century' were not uncommon, though they proved somewhat hyperbolic. It was after 1900 also that the Canadian government, after many tensions and false starts, tried to complete a reciprocal trade agreement with the United States. This aimed at increasing Canadian food and raw materials exports to the United States, beginning a process that would tie the two economies together closely. At the same time, American references to the ultimate absorption of Canada, and a general belittling of Canadian nationhood, encouraged further reflex nationalism, including (outside of Quebec) a passionate attachment to symbols of the British monarchy. The tariff rhetoric forced out Wilfried Laurier, the nation's first premier of French-Canadian origin, along with objections to his plans to build a navy. At the same time the attachment to British interests remained a bedrock of national diplomacy. Not without some debate, Canada contributed a noticeable force to the British side during the Boer War, and participated without hesitation (except for ardent French Canadian opposition) when Britain entered World War I in 1914.

Canadian urban development followed from commercial and population growth. Paper mills and other factory activity took advantage of natural resources. A substantial metallurgical industry had developed by 1900, backed by substantial Canadian corporations. The growth of a working class spurred labor organizations, with a National Congress formed in 1883. An estimated 155,000 Canadians belonged to unions by 1914. Provincial governments took on new activities in regulating health and working conditions. Middle-class structure became increasingly complex. A National Retail Merchants Association helped define a loose rhetoric of entrepreneurship, even as corporate organization and a white-collar sector gained greater prominence. Expansion of the middle class and education set the basis for a considerable feminist movement, including a National Council of Women. Canada also participated in the Western-wide surge of popular leisure activities. Cities like Toronto developed 'red light' districts where entertainment and prostitution intermingled. On another leisure front: in 1890 professional hockey was inaugurated by the formation of the Ontario Hockey Association.

Cultural developments paralleled economic and social institutions. Few Canadian artists achieved international status, but their contribution to discussions of Canadian identity, or of subcultures within Canada, was important. Both French- and English-language authors stressed themes of nature and the frontier, plus Canada's position in the world. French writers worked to preserve separate institutions and culture, while English-language authors fought against suffocation by the larger American presence to the south.

French work became increasingly self-conscious in its focus on distinctive heritage. 'Our institutions, our language and our law' was the motto of a Quebec journal of 1822. Historical work and religious writings loomed large, along with romantic poems and novels.

Literary production in English intensified after 1867. Women writers like Isabella Crawford dealt with pioneer life, while poets, including the Indian Emily Johnson, wrote of Indian themes. Here too, a lingering romantic aura persisted until after 1900, underlying for example the internationally popular series *Anne of Green Gables*, set on Prince Edward Island.

Formal cultural production embraced some of the modesty Canadian spokespeople both praised and lamented as part of the tenor of national life. America was credited with greater boisterousness and drive to success, Canadians with a more stable placidity; yet Canadians, a few Anglophiles aside, did not claim to be European either, with French-Canadians particularly separate from cultural currents in France. Some observers pointed not only to Canada's distinctive political culture and a somewhat constrained economy, tied heavily to exports to more successful industrializers, but to the moderating impact of a northern climate as causal factors in the ways Canadians thought of themselves. The unusual amount of emigration to the United States, particularly before 1900, also complicated the picture. Individuals, like the Scottish-born inventor of the telephone, Alexander Graham Bell, might choose to move to the United States to provide a larger field of endeavor, though other migrants, like the French Canadians who pressed into New England, long hoped to preserve values initially shaped in Canada itself, seeing the move simply in terms of relief from overcrowding. Within Canada, the effort to blend British and American traits, outside Quebec, without surrendering to either culture entirely, continued to shape a subtle set of identities and cultural tensions.

THE UNITED STATES, 1870–1914

Industrial expansion

The dominant force in the United States in the final decades of the long nineteenth century involved its accelerating industrialization, which propelled it to a position of major world influence. American industrialization offered a few distinctive features, some of which soon began to affect other societies. The accession to greater military as well as economic power in the world generated significant adjustments and tensions. These were not decades of dramatic shifts in political patterns, though there were some significant new movements. Advancing industrialization and unprecedented rates of immigration redefined some of the tensions within the nation's democracy. American participation in high culture continued to be largely derivative, as exchanges with Europe intensified. At the level of popular culture, however, the United States began to take a lead in shaping a new kind of consumer economy.

Industrial growth was extremely rapid, propelling the United States into the top rank of world manufacturing societies well before 1900. As early as the 1870s American firms like Singer Sewing Machine were setting up major branches abroad; the two biggest companies in Russia in that decade were American affiliates.

Abundant raw materials and a huge internal market combined with a growing labor force and increasingly aggressive entrepreneurs to generate this massive industrial surge. Encouragement from the federal government played a supporting role. The United States continued to borrow from European capitalists, remaining a debtor nation until World War I, and dependence on European technology remained substantial, particularly in metallurgy and in certain new industries like chemicals. Adaptations of European steel-making processes were fundamental to the rapid expansion of heavy industry, particularly in Pittsburgh and the Midwest. But the list of basic American inventions grew, with a huge increase in the number of patents granted. Developments such as the telephone, the cash register, and electricity transformed communications and office work. American experiments with oil also set the basis for a growing petroleum industry. Contributions to the development of automobiles also created a major manufacturing branch by 1910, with 5 million cars on the nation's highways by 1917.

New or imported technology joined with growing commitments to corporations and business combinations. Individual states had passed laws facilitating corporate formation through limited liability, in the 1830s and 1840s – early, compared to Western Europe – and use of this ownership form swelled after the Civil War. Railroads moved first, but in the 1870s, Andrew Carnegie employed corporate finance to begin to create his massive steel empire, vertically integrated with extensive holdings in coal mines. Corporations reduced the role of the entrepreneur, at some real cost to American middle-class imagery. Banker participation in industrial finance soared beyond the corporation to the creation of trusts, linking various units within an industry toward control of supplies and prices. Corporations and trusts were utilized to limit competition in several key industries, including oil, where the Rockefeller family parlayed Standard Oil into a position of dominance. By 1900, 1 per cent of all corporations controlled a third of American manufacturing.

American industrial growth resembled patterns in Europe, particularly in Germany, in many ways, though the sheer rate of expansion was unusual. As in Europe, advancing industrialization brought continued growth of cities, and particularly the larger centers; by 1920, the nation would pass the 50 per cent urbanization mark. Rapid extension of white-collar work followed from the growth of corporate bureaucracies and also the expansion of the teaching corps. New consumer outlets, notably the department store, followed from a generally rising standard of living and some increases in leisure time both for middle-class managers and for factory workers, particularly after 1900. There were some distinctive features, relating both to American culture and to the huge size of the American market as population growth and westward settlement created a continental unit. Expansion of retailing included huge mail-order operations, with catalogs stocked with eye-catching goods sent to farm and small-town families who could indulge consumer tastes even if unable to get to the big city. The United States also pioneered in the development of chain stores, taking advantage of wholesale acquisitions of goods to permit lower prices, plus mass advertising in the popular press. Woolworth's '5 and 10 cent' stores began to expand after 1879, reaching 1,000 outlets in the United States and Canada by 1919. New leisure sites included the amusement park. Derived from a European fair tradition, the amusement park, which drew huge throngs from the lower middle and working classes, featured also an American delight in new, fear-producing technologies such as the Ferris wheel.

Basic organizational developments were fundamental American contributions to the industrial economy of the late nineteenth century. Giant corporations, taking advantage of the huge national market and of steady advances in productivity, gradually developed new systems of bureaucratic specialization and substantial market control, while amassing great wealth. Several of the innovations in retailing, such as chain stores and the development of professional advertising firms, would also be imitated subsequently in other industrial societies. At the same time, some features seemed distinctively American. The amusement park was not fully taken up elsewhere, as a response to mass leisure needs. The great wealth of the corporate leaders – aptly dubbed as robber barons – led to a luxurious life style but also to unprecedented philanthropy. Many American cities gained symphony orchestras, art galleries and new libraries from the conscience money of the plutocrats, relying on private initiatives for institutions more commonly under public sponsorship elsewhere.

Far more than in Europe, United States industrialization included an ongoing commitment to agriculture, itself organized on somewhat industrial lines with technology rather than labor intensity producing high outputs. Rich farms in the Midwest continued to generate extensive production of grains and meats. Cities like Chicago prospered as centers of agricultural exchange and credit, and also housed massive stockyards where meat processing itself became big business. Thanks to the Homestead Act and a growing railroad network, agricultural settlement of the Western states proceeded rapidly after the Civil War. Cattlemen and farmers vied for territory, with some violent clashes. More important was the final wave of warfare against the Indians. Advancing white settlement not only pressed Indian territorial holdings but also their game supply, particularly the buffalo, which white hunters slaughtered relentlessly. Warfare continued into the 1890s, but gradually the Indians were pressed onto reservations, the bulk of the territory seized by whites. Here too, new technologies, such as mechanical plows and reapers, allowed small numbers of farmers to cultivate large stretches of land.

With massive land and efficient agriculture, American farmers began to export not only cotton, as had long been the case, but also grains and meats. Improvements in oceanic shipping and refrigeration allowed American farmers to compete favorably in European markets, to the detriment of the European peasantry. While commercial, export-oriented agriculture remained an unusually important part of the United States economy – making the nation a competitor of Canada and Argentina, on the agricultural side, even as it could rival Britain and Germany in industry – a host of tensions resulted. Industry and big business, including the great railroad companies, wielded more influence than agriculture. Farmers themselves recurrently expanded too rapidly, resulting in plunging prices and many failures. In the South, small farmers, white and black, frequently owed massive debts to banks and company stores, keeping them in perpetual poverty. Even in the West, tenancy increased, and agriculture's role relative to industry declined steadily.

Problems in agriculture were all the more poignant, by the end of the nineteenth century, in that so much American mythology was invested in the idea of the independent family farm. A number of novels and essays addressed the moral threat to the nation, when sturdy farmers gave way to big capitalists, while politicians often capitalized on this theme in appealing for rural votes. By the end of the nineteenth century also, the American frontier had vanished; available land had been occupied. Frontier imagery lingered, and it is not clear how much the change really mattered. Some historians have argued that the decline of this traditional safety valve inevitably increased urban social tensions, while others have cited the additional challenge to the nation's conventional self-identity.

Along with a distinctive agricultural segment, the American industrial surge was also wrapped up in an unprecedented wave of immigration. Twenty-five million immigrants reached the United States between 1865 and 1915, over four times the number who had come in the previous fifty years. Some immigrants originated in areas long linked to the migration process, like Germany and the British Isles, whose assimilation into the American economy, as skilled workers for example, was relatively unproblematic. But after the 1880s, the bulk of the immigrants came from new centers, notably in Southern and Eastern Europe, and often from a more traditional peasant background. There was also important immigration from East Asia on the West Coast, with workers brought in among other things to help construct the railroads. In terms of education, language and economic experience, the new immigrants seemed to clash with established American patterns. City life itself was new to most of these people, and yet opportunities for establishment as farmers were rapidly declining.

The new surge of immigration brought a host of tensions in its wake. Immigrants themselves, mostly non-Protestant, found themselves in an alien and critical cultural environment. Urban conditions were deplorable, with crowded tenements and poor sanitary facilities. Many immigrant workers encountered ethnic prejudice from the native born and also from other immigrant groups. Not surprisingly, immigrants often stuck together, creating ethnic enclaves in most American cities. Extended family ties were reconstructed. Catholics often tightened their attachment to religion – Italians, for example, might become more devoted in the new environment than they had been back home – one reason for the continued importance of religion in American life. Even in these successful adaptations, there was change. New arrivals often had to adjust to unfamiliar versions of their religion; Polish and Italian Catholics often quarrelled with the predominantly Irish and German American hierarchy. Jews from Eastern Europe were aided by an established German Jewish community, but this community also looked down on the newcomers and urged them to adopt new habits such as rigorous birth control. Italians gained from their ability to form ethnic fraternal societies like the Sons of Italy – but most immigrants, from Southern Italy, had never thought in Italian terms before, so even this refuge was new.

Immigrant adjustment was always complicated, during the decades around 1900, by intensely ambivalent reactions from established American institutions. Most American leaders looked down on the immigrants as inferior. Their arrival and initially high birth-rates sparked eugenicist comment, pointing to the disparity between the immigrants and the low birth-rates of America's 'superior' races. In one crucial instance, actual legislation moved to restrict the immigrant flow: hostility to Chinese Americans, as an inferior race and a source of unfair competition with American labor, sparked an 1882 exclusion law. At the same time, many established Americans believed that immigrant problems could be resolved through an aggressive campaign to convert this new population to established middle-class values. Even among the Chinese, Protestant mission groups undertook to teach women principles of female self-respect and sexual control, along with useful domestic skills, with some real results (along with consolidation in the Chinese-American centers themselves) in altering gender traditions. Public schools and other agencies were aggressively touted as centers for training in American values, from nationalist loyalty to proper personal hygiene.

Immigration obviously facilitated the industrialization process, by providing abundant, cheap labor. But this labor was also unskilled and unfamiliar with industrial norms; and it was viewed as inherently inferior stock by American industrialists. An enduring result was an unusual effort to discipline the labor force severely. American corporations established company police forces and spies to inhibit protest. More important still were attempts to use organizational measures to reduce worker initiative on the job. The United States became the world pioneer in industrial engineering and efficiency schemes, from the 1890s onward. Engineers examined worker behavior, through time and motion studies, with an eye to creating inflexible work systems that would maximize productivity. After 1900, Frederick Taylor instituted scientific management to subdivide tasks and speed up the whole process. These developments, widely copied in other industrial societies as part of the 'American system', set the groundwork for Henry Ford's institution of the assembly line, in 1914, with the avowed aim of making each worker as machine-like as possible. The size of American factories plus the real or imagined needs of shaping an inexperienced labor force created vital innovations in the regimentation of workers – and a new source of tension with the democratic principles American leaders continued to profess. This impulse toward organizational manipulation, along with the distinctive agricultural sector, continued to identify the American version of mature industrial society.

Emergence as a world power

A vital result of industrial, demographic and agricultural growth, including the completion of the basic settlement of the West, was a great increase in the international importance of the United States and the need for new foreign policies within the nation itself. American industrial and agricultural exports inevitably carved a new world role. Exports, for example, more than tripled between 1870 and 1900, reaching $1.4 billion annually. Giant corporations, extending their organizational scope, began to set up production facilities as well as marketing operations abroad, foreshadowing the 'multinationals' of the twentieth century. Not only Singer sewing machines but also several agricultural equipment manufacturers were early leaders in this area. At the same time, energies and nationalist fervor that had previously focused on continental growth now tended to turn outward, into a more venturesome international policy. Proponents of manifest destiny readily moved into an imperialist mode, seeing the United States as a vital contributor to the spread of civilization to lesser peoples, particularly as the domestic frontier closed.

The United States had long proclaimed its hostility to European interference in the Americas, with the Monroe doctrine of 1823. Only in the 1880s, however, did the nation begin to take a systematic interest in Latin America as a whole, at one point confronting Britain with a threat of war over a dispute in Venezuela. Expansion in the Pacific surged as well, with a treaty with Samoa in 1878, leading

ultimately to a share in the outright division of the islands, in 1899. Growing contacts with Hawaii led to discussion of annexation, which occurred in 1898. The biggest venture in outright imperialism occurred as a result of a war with Spain, also in 1898, over conflicts in the Spanish colony of Cuba. Nationalist agitation reached a fever pitch over alleged Spanish insults and atrocities. Many Americans viewed the resultant war as a splendid exercise in national manliness. Not without some bitter fighting, the United States conquered Cuba, which gained independence under American supervision, and also Puerto Rico; successful naval operations in the Pacific also brought Guam and the Philippines – the latter acquisition, however, hotly debated within the United States, which was reluctant to move so far into the imperialist camp. Conquest of the Philippines after Spanish withdrawal proved an extensive undertaking, which led to significant updating of the American military.

American imperialism continued after 1900, with frequent military interventions in the Caribbean and Central America to assure regimes friendly to American business interests. President Theodore Roosevelt's policy, 'speak softly but carry a big stick', was classic aggressive imperialism. The height of this phase of American policy occurred in the sponsoring of the Panama Canal and then manipulation of a rebellion that broke the surrounding territory away from Colombia, creating a small Panamanian nation under close American supervision, with direct United States control of the Canal itself once it opened in 1914.

Yet American imperialism was not the whole story of the United States entry into great power politics. In the first place, the United States joined the imperialist game late, when most of the colonial spoils were taken. This helped motivate some distinctive policy gambits, such as the 'Open Door' effort in China; fearful of great-power acquisitions in China, American diplomats pleaded in vain for a more general opportunity to trade in Asia. American leaders also harbored some belief that the United States, with its own firm democracy and colonial past, could stay free of the sordid entanglements of Old World powers. This motivated a special effort, particularly under Theodore Roosevelt, to mediate imperialist disputes involving others. Roosevelt negotiated the final settlement to the Russo-Japanese war (1905), helping to cut back Japanese gains in the interests of American power in the Pacific, and also mediated French-German disputes in Morocco. The strain of idealism in American policy coexisted uneasily with brash imperialism, but it remained an important complexity.

Protest and progressivism

Developments in American domestic politics, during the decades around 1900, were far less striking than those surrounding industrial growth, immigration and the attainment of great-power status. Government initiatives lagged behind changes in other sectors, which pleased many Americans, wedded to traditional liberal or free market views. Particularly during the 'Gilded Age' of the 1880s, big capitalists and their luxurious wealth seemed to rule the nation. State governments, particularly in the industrial North, did increase inspections of working and housing conditions. State support for education increased. A few states introduced modest social insurance measures. At the federal level, major public uproar over abuses in food and drug processing led to the passage of the Pure Food and

Drug Act, in 1906. Government also began to set aside public lands for national parks, in the first clear commitment to environmental concerns. The most striking federal response to growing industrialization, however, involved efforts to regulate big business, as in the Interstate Commerce Act of 1887, which monitored railroad rates to a modest degree, and particularly in legislation against monopolies. Strong middle-class beliefs in competition, espoused in principle even by big business magnates like Andrew Carnegie, supported the idea that the main purpose of government was not to pass social legislation but to make sure no one business acquired enough power to distort the operation of market forces. The Sherman Antitrust Act of 1890 allowed the government to sue to break up monopolistic businesses. The law was not widely successful, but a few signal cases – for example, against Rockefeller's Standard Oil – did produce results. This free market approach may certainly have defused other efforts to deal with some of the less desirable results of industrial advance. The federal government also maintained a high tariff policy, with the McKinley tariff (1898) among the steepest in the world, and a testimony to the harmony of interests between Republicans and industrial leaders.

American politics in this age of massive economic change were surprisingly quiet. Republicans predominated, but national Democratic victories occurred occasionally. In many big cities, machines run by powerful bosses and backed by considerable immigrant support and patronage offerings defined the political process. While a small socialist movement emerged, there was no massive challenge. The weakness of American socialism, compared to patterns in Western Europe, had several roots. In the first place, many workers were comfortable with the existing political process, since they had won the vote so early. Disagreements among immigrants and native workers, including outright language barriers, inhibited class solidarity. American standards of living may have been higher than average, despite massive poverty. Certainly a strong middle-class rhetoric directed towards individual self-improvement, and hostile to socialism as a foreign import, had a deterrent effect; so did the strong industrial policing of the giant corporations.

Protest movements did arise, however. A strong rural populist movement swept many sections of the country in the 1880s and 1890s, excoriating the power of big business over the ordinary farmer. Measures like the Interstate Commerce Act responded to this movement, which was not ideological but which reflected deep beliefs in the importance of individual farms and in the evils of excessive capitalism. At times, populist sentiments even crossed racial boundaries, with black and white small farmers collaborating in the South.

A strong trade-union and strike movement arose as well. In this area, the United States witnessed at least as much violent conflict and solid organizational development as did many European countries, even though the socialist political concomitant was largely lacking. Indeed, the number of clashes with police and strike-breakers, and the work hours lost in strikes, exceeded those in Western Europe in the same period. An initial national union movement emerged with the Knights of Labor, from 1869 onward. The Knights stood for a system of cooperation, rather than capitalism, and urged specific reforms such as the abolition of child labor. A series of failed strikes in the 1880s brought their downfall, after a peak claimed membership of 700,000 workers. In 1881, the American Federation of Labor was formed, emphasizing a respectable craft union approach that shunned unskilled factory workers. Despite the AFL approach, but tainting it in middle-class opinion, a wave of violent strikes broke out in the 1890s, with pitched battles against company police in various mining and metallurgical areas and on the railroads; government troops were mobilized to put the strikers down. A final burst of labor organization, with strong syndicalist overtones, emerged with the Industrial Workers of the World (IWW), or Wobblies, after 1900. Under the leadership of 'Big Bill' Heywood, a tireless organizer, the IWW advocated one big union for all workers, including the unskilled, hoping to use a massive general strike as a means of attacking the wage labor system. IWW organizers participated in several massive strikes, including some involving both men and women in the textile industry; they were also accused of acts of terrorism on the railroads. The bitter atmosphere of American industry persisted, though without many labor victories and without much explicit political result.

Other protest movements also surfaced around 1900, in addition to the populist and labor currents. Anarchism commanded some support, and it was an anarchist who assassinated President McKinley in 1901. Important stirrings developed among African Americans, though there was no large new movement. Various leaders protested against the increasingly severe Jim Crow laws of the South. Booker T. Washington, a leading educator, advocated self-help measures that would allow economic progress and preparation for equality, rather than political action directly. William Edward Burghardt (W. E. B.) Du Bois, the first African American to earn a Ph.D., attacked segregation and mere self-help solutions, urging restoration of full civil rights. Under his guidance the National Association for the Advancement of Colored People (NAACP) formed in 1909, and by 1915 was attacking segregation laws in the federal courts.

The most striking additional protest current featured the strong surge of American feminism, gaining support and much more political focus after its earlier beginnings. With men's political rights affirmed in principle after the Civil War, with growing levels of education for women including definite if difficult entry into major professions, and with a declining birth-rate, conditions were ripe for attacks on women's exclusion from political rights. Women became increasingly active in a variety of reform causes from the 1870s onward, including temperance, education and settlement house work. Several successful efforts focused on legal rights for women as property owners and in divorce law. A growing network of clubs, often with reform goals, provided organizational experience. Leaders like Elizabeth Cady Stanton, from the 1890s onward, began to press for full suffrage rights – hence a somewhat derisive term, suffragettes, for this phase of feminism. Arguments stressed both human equality and women's special moral virtues in describing the good that would result from this huge reform. The National Woman's Suffrage Association, with 13,000 members in 1893, boasted over 2 million by 1917. As early as 1867, a number of Western territories had granted women's suffrage, but now the pace picked up, with Washington State providing the vote in 1910, Illinois the first state east of the Mississippi to join in 1913.

Amid the welter of activities for protest and reform, mainstream politics changed slowly. The Democratic Party picked up some of the farmers' populist rhetoric, which helped cool the movement itself. The American Federation of Labor was able to work on the state level for some work reforms, including shorter hours. The principal political innovation came late, however, in the emergence of the Progressive movement, cutting across party lines, from 1900 onward.

Progressive reformers and politicians were predominantly middle- and upper-class. They believed that government should be used to correct industrial abuses; their outlook combined sincere if somewhat patronizing humanitarianism and a belief in government rationalization and the power of expertise. While they attacked aspects of big business, using terms like 'robber barons', they also disliked the patronage politics of some of the big-city bosses, and they sought to wrest control of major cities away from immigrant voters by revising city charters. In many cities, trained managers were hired as a buffer between policymaking and actual voters. Similarly, Progressives sponsored greater bureaucratic control over school systems, to reduce local variation and make sure that immigrant students were exposed to standard curricula. While eager for social justice through more government action, they had no interest in toppling the basic economic or social system. Expansion of government-sponsored welfare programs was limited, operating mainly at the state level and focusing distinctively on support for impoverished mothers.

The range of reform interests was wide. Many Progressives supported the prohibition of the public sale of alcohol, boosting this movement in American politics. Some began to agree with proponents of laws restricting immigration. At the same time, under Theodore Roosevelt's Progressive presidency, politicians put forward measures to regulate meat inspection, to compensate victims of industrial accidents, and to impose an eight-hour day. Not all these measures passed, and Roosevelt was replaced by a more moderate president in 1908. In 1912, the Democrat Woodrow Wilson won the presidency and took over the mantle of Progressivism. Though relying heavily on tighter laws against monopolies, Wilson also came to advocate federal action to prevent child labor, significant banking reform, and other unprecedented measures.

Progressivism did not create a powerful American government. Some of its greatest successes in expanding political functions came at the state and local level, rather than in federal action. For all its hesitation and ambiguities, however, Progressivism did succeed in convincing many voters that reformist political action could deal with the nation's leading problems; this in turn reduced the attractiveness of alternative political movements such as socialism. Many historians also believe that in the Progressive approach and precedent lay the seeds of the much more decisive turn to an American version of a limited welfare state, that would be enacted by politicians raised in the Progressive era, when they came to power in the 1930s.

The rise of a consumer society

Americans in the late nineteenth century were more adept at innovations in basic styles of life than they were in politics. The turn of the century decades saw vital developments in American popular culture. Some of these, like the rise of sports or new forms of urban theater, paralleled patterns in Europe, where novel forms of leisure began to add to the attributes of industrial society. As in with other cultural and institutional patterns, however, the United States introduced some distinctive variants, some of which, in turn, would later affect not only American behavior but also popular culture elsewhere.

Developments in high culture remained somewhat limited. A number of significant novelists emerged, some of them dealing with urban squalor, an important component of the Progressive movement. One of the best known writers, Henry James, spent much of his adult life in England, his novels reflecting ambivalence about the merits of American versus European culture. Several artists also worked in Europe, from which impressionism was imported to the United States. Architecture, however, was a different story. Use of industrial materials and new design concepts promoted major innovations in bridge design and also, soon after 1900, the introduction of the skyscraper, in Chicago. American science and social science made a considerable mark as well. Intellectuals and religious leaders vigorously debated Darwinian evolution; Social Darwinism, arguing for the importance of struggle in human progress, won wider acceptance among American businessmen, as a justification of their view of economic life, than among their European counterparts. Several Americans made significant contributions to economics, psychology and anthropology. At the end of the century leading universities, such as Johns Hopkins in Baltimore, began to convert to a German-derived model where research and specialized teaching would be emphasized over a more generalized moral education. Even earlier, in 1865, the establishment of the Massachusetts Institute of Technology signaled a new commitment to formal engineering training and industrial research. As university enrollments and professional training advanced, this enhanced the role of science in areas such as medicine.

American innovations in the area of popular beliefs and expressions were more considerable. The high school began to advance as the dominant center for secondary education. While most Americans still ended their education with primary school – in the South, primary schools were only generalized in the years after 1900 – high school training advanced for the middle class, both male and female, and for a growing minority of working-class youth. Entrance examinations persisted, but increasingly school systems emphasized wide recruitment. While some high schools stressed classical subjects and college preparation, the dominant tone of the high school was practical. New courses for secretaries or accountants opened new mobility opportunities into the lower middle class. Although some prestigious private academies persisted, the United States did not develop as clear a secondary school hierarchy as was common in most other industrial countries.

American high schools and colleges also developed an unusual focus on sports and other extracurricular activities. Sports, particularly for men, were held to build character, in a competitive American version of masculinity that required new outlets now that middle-class work was becoming more bureaucratic than before. High school and college rivalries, in distinctive American sports variants such as football and baseball, gained growing public attention. Along with professional sports activities, in baseball (where the first professional team formed in 1869), boxing and the like, the new role of spectator sports in leisure helped create growing numbers of 'fans' – the word was introduced around 1900, presumably derived from fanatic – who depended heavily on athletics for vicarious satisfactions.

Sports, amusement parks, plus a popular theater (called vaudeville in the United States) that began after 1900 to migrate into early forms of motion pictures all contributed to a growing emphasis on leisure and consumption. These were the decades when department stores began to become standard urban outlets, with concomitants such as a growing rate of kleptomania.

As in Western Europe, mass consumerism challenged conventional gender arrangements. While some leisure was highly segregated – like the most popular team sports, including the newly-invented game of basketball – some sports encouraged a new level of activity, and appropriately looser costumes, among women. The bicycle craze of the 1880s and 1890s, in the American middle class gave young women and men a newly-shared pastime. Tennis was another shared sport. While men and women still spent much of the leisure time separately – the popularity of male lodges, for example, gaining momentum before 1850, continued to run strong – new connections were beginning to develop. With co-education spreading at all levels, with middle-class women beginning to work as teachers, clerks and secretaries, it was small wonder that boundaries dividing previously separate spheres began to break down. But it was a shared interest in consumerism and in leisure settings such as amusements parks that would complete this social reorientation. Among urban workers by 1900, among middle-class youth by the 1910s, common consumer activities – what would soon be called 'dating' – began to replace more conventional courtship.

A growing interest in pleasure also affected sexuality. More middle-class men began to use prostitutes, at least before marriage, in a clear demonstration of a sexual double standard. 'Red light' districts emerged in the large cities to cater to this kind of trade. At the same time, middle-class women born after about 1870 had distinctly more interest in sexual pleasure than their mothers had manifested, though the definition of love still stressed the greater importance of higher, more ethereal goals.

The development of mass leisure and consumption in the United States also featured important disputes between the native-born middle class and many immigrant working-class groups. The temperance movement was a middle-class attempt to curb ethnic drinking. Efforts to curb rowdy behavior in parks focused another set of disputes. These conflicts had not ended by 1914, and diverse patterns of recreation persisted, reflecting ethnic identities and also different living standards. But there is some evidence of increasing homogeneity and orderliness in public leisure by 1914. The advent of the movie, played in a darkened theater where middle-class rules of quiet and decorum increasingly prevailed, was a major step in this direction. Increased schooling, factory discipline and policing also curbed the amount of random street violence; the United States continued to have high per capita crime rates by European standards, but the per capita rates of certain crimes were going down by 1900.

Growing indulgence in consumerism showed in many ways. It was in the 1890s that advertisements for goods began to shift from factual descriptions of price and quality to more alluring, emotionally-charged terms. Thus according to mass newspaper notices, a certain store's silk should be purchased because it made the wearer 'enticing' and 'more youthful'. During the 1890s also, middle-class Americans began to buy Christmas gifts, rather than make them by hand; and the cost of appropriate gifts began to go up. Children started to receive allowances, to help teach them the value of money, now that they were not earning wages, but also to give them the basis for learning how to be consumers in their own right.

The United States had not served as the center of the initial phases of modern consumerism, but it was ideally suited to take a lead in elaborating a new stage of the phenomenon. The nation had a huge market; commitment to capitalist values was widespread. The new ardours of work – factory regimens for peasant immigrants, bureaucratic routine for would-be middle-class entrepreneurs – cried out for some compensation, and consumer pleasures could meet these needs. While class divisions were pronounced, American commitment to democracy and the absence of an aristocratic tradition made it harder to criticize mass taste than was the case in Europe. Even women were subject to less derision for their leadership in certain consumer activities than was true in Europe. Anti-consumerist movements, attached to socialism or anti-Semitism or simply stated independently, a prominent feature in turn-of-the-century France, Germany, and Russia, were largely absent in the United States.

To be sure, cultural tensions accompanied the construction of a new consumer society. The work ethic was still valued. Americans could justify their new appetites in several ways. Vacations, for example, could be touted because they helped prepare for a return to work. Middle-class Americans were treated to expert discussions of a new disease, neurasthenia, in the 1880s; for middle-class men, the disease resulted from a national orgy of overwork, which could be cured by greater attention to constructive leisure and to exercise. Health and hygiene concerns also helped justify new purchases of bathing equipment, soaps and even cosmetics. Middle-class Americans also adopted a new concern for dieting, amid growing hostility to body fat from the 1890s onward, as a moral antidote to too much unadulterated hedonism. The United States thus began building an unusually elaborate consumer apparatus, that would serve as the basis of such developments as Hollywood's dominance of the international commercial motion picture industry after World War I. By 1914, the nation already led the world in the purchase of hygiene products and household appliances such as sewing machines and vacuum cleaners, and also in the use of consumer credit as personal savings rates declined. At the same time, Americans also constructed a number of new behaviors and rationales to reconcile their quiet revolution with older values such as restraint and hard work.

Consumerism, along with more general urban and industrial growth, also had an impact on family life. With children's work declining and schools taking over many training functions, families increasingly became emotional and consumer units above all. Birth-rates were dropping, but the emotional attention devoted to individual children increased. Ironically, a rising divorce rate resulted from some of the changes in family functions. Divorce rates were unusually high in the United States by the 1870s, compared to those of Western Europe, and the nation had its first public discussion of a divorce crisis in the 1890s, even though the phenomenon remained fairly rare. Divorce law changed in many states, for example to allow couples to dissolve a marriage on grounds of 'emotional cruelty' – reflecting new criteria for family success. Rates were higher in the urban working classes than among other groups, and disputes over the family standard of living – over whether the husband was living up to a more demanding role as provider – played a role in this process. Here was another trend that would continue to describe important aspects of American social life in the twentieth century.

Most components of American history in the later nineteenth century, including consumer satisfactions, seemed to support a mood of confidence. Contrary voices existed, but they were not easily heard. Certainly, when Americans spoke for the record as they greeted a new century in 1900, they spoke in terms of progress. Whereas the English might worry about growing international tensions, Americans for the most part looked at the trends around them and found them good. Democracy, education and prosperity had all advanced during the preceding decades. The nation's power in the world, and the good uses to which it could be put in civilizing backward peoples, were advancing. The coming decades might indeed be hailed as 'the American century'. Banquets by labor organizations were more critical of existing problems, but they too struck an optimistic note: through democracy and solidarity, the warts on American capitalism could be removed. Women's groups saw their cause advancing, and African American comment was not recorded. Official confidence was one of the powerful and durable products of the nation's history in the long nineteenth century – a century that had opened with a distinct sense of inferiority toward Europe, and a nervous attempt to shore up a host of novel political institutions.

BIBLIOGRAPHY

AHLSTROM, S. E. 1972. *A Religious History of the American People.* xvi. Yale University Press, New Haven, pp. 1158ff.

APPLEBY, J. 1984. *Capitalism and a New Social Order: The Republican Vision of the 1790s.* New York University Press, New York, pp. 110ff.

BEISNER, R. 1975. *From the Old Diplomacy to the New, 1865–1900.* Crowell, New York, pp. 162ff.

BENSON, S. 1986. *Counter Cultures: Saleswomen, Managers and Customers in American Department Stores, 1890–1940.* University of Illinois Press, Urbana, pp. 322ff.

BERLIN, I.; REIDY, J. P.; ROWLAND, L. S. (eds) 1982. *Freedom: A Documentary History.* Cambridge University Press, New York, pp. 852ff.

BLEWETT, M. H. 1988. *Men, Women, and Work: Class, Gender, and Protest in the New England Shoe Industry, 1780–1910.* University of Illinois Press, Urbana, pp. 444ff.

BLUMIN, S. 1989. *The Emergence of the Middle Class: Social Experience in the American City, 1760–1900.* Cambridge University Press, New York, pp. 434ff.

BODNAR, J. 1985. *The Transplanted: A History of Immigrants in Urban America.* Indiana University Press, Bloomington, pp. 294ff.

——. 1987. *The Patriot Game: Canada and the Canadian Question Revisited.* Stanford CA, Hoover Institution Press, pp. 310ff.

BUMSTEAD, J. M. (ed.) 1979. *Canadian History Before Confederation: Essays and Interpretations.* Irwin-Dursey, Georgetown, Ont, pp. 542ff.

BURTON, O. V.; McMATH JR, R. C. (eds) 1982. *Toward a New South?: Studies in Post-Civil War Southern Communities.* Greenwood Press, Westport CT, pp. 319ff.

CHANDLER, A. 1977. *The Visible Hand: the Managerial Revolution in American Business.* Belknap Press, Cambridge MA, pp. 608ff.

CLARK, C. 1990. *The Roots of Rural Capitalism: Western Massachusetts, 1780–1860.* Cornell University Press, Ithaca NY, pp. 339ff.

COTT, N. F. 1977. *The Bonds of Womanhood: 'Woman's Sphere' in New England, 1780–1835.* Yale University Press, New Haven, pp. 225ff.

CREMIN, L. 1980. *American Education, the National Experience, 1783–1876.* Harper and Row, New York, pp. 607ff.

D'EMILIO, J.; FREEDMAN, E. B. 1988. *Intimate Matters: A History of Sexuality in America.* Harper and Row, New York, pp. 428ff.

FARAGHER, J. 1979. *Women and Men on the Overland Trail.* Yale University Press, New Haven, pp. 281ff.

FOGEL, R. 1964. *Railroads and American Economic Growth: Essays in Econometric History.* Johns Hopkins University Press, Baltimore, pp. 296ff.

FONER, E. 1983. *Nothing but Freedom: Emancipation and its Legacy.* Louisiana State University Press, Baton Rouge, pp. 142ff.

——. 1988. *Reconstruction: America's Unfinished Revolution, 1863–1877.* Harper and Row, New York, pp. 690ff.

FORSEY, E. 1982. *Trade Unions in Canada, 1812–1902.* University of Toronto Press, Toronto, pp. 600ff.

FOX-GENOVESE, E. 1988. *Within the Plantation Household: Black and White Women of the Old South.* University of North Carolina Press, Chapel Hill, pp. 544ff.

FREDERICKSON, G. 1972. *The Black Image in the White Mind: The Debate on Afro-American Character and Destiny, 1817–1914.* Harper and Row, New York, pp. 343ff.

GENOVESE, E. 1969. *The World the Slaveholders Made: Two Essays in Interpretation.* Pantheon Books, New York, pp. 274ff.

——. 1974. *Roll, Jordan, Roll: The World the Slaves made.* Pantheon Books, New York, pp. 823ff.

GIBBS, E. 1951. *Democracy in the Canadas.* Oxford University Press, Toronto, pp. 217ff.

——. 1967. *Racism or Responsible Government: The French Canadian Dilemma of the 1840's.* (Issues in Canadian History). Copp Clark Pub. Co., Toronto, pp. 184ff.

GLATTHAAR, J. 1990. *Forged in Battle: The Civil War Alliance of Black Soldiers and White Officers.* Free Press, New York, pp. 370ff.

GUTMAN, H. G. 1976. *The Black Family in Slavery and Freedom, 1750–1925.* Pantheon Books, New York, pp. 664ff.

GUTTMANN, A. 1988. *A Whole New Ball Game: An Interpretation of American Sports.* University of North Carolina Press, Chapel Hill, pp. 253ff.

HARDY, W. G. 1960. *From Sea unto Sea: Canada – 1850 to 1910: The Road to Nationhood.* Doubleday, Garden City NY, pp. 528ff.

HENRETTA, J; NOBLE, G. H. 1987. *Evolution and Revolution: American Society, 1600–1820.* D. C. Heath, Lexington MA, pp. 283ff.

HODGINS, B.; PAGE, R. (eds) 1972. *Canadian History Since Confederation: Essays and Interpretations.* Irwin-Dorsey, Georgetown, Ont., pp. 607ff.

HOUNSHELL, D. 1984. *From the American System to Mass Production, 1800–1932: The Development of Manufacturing Technology in the United States.* Johns Hopkins University Press, Baltimore, pp. 411ff.

JENSEN, M. 1981. *The New Nation: A History of the United States During the Confederation, 1781–1789.* Northeastern University Press, Boston, pp. 433ff.

KASSON, J. 1990. *Rudeness and Civility: Manners in Nineteenth-Century Urban America.* Hill and Wang, New York, pp. 305ff.

KESSLER-HARRIS, A. 1982. *Out to Work: A History of Wage-earning Women in the United States.* Oxford University Press, New York, pp. 400ff.

LEVY, L. 1985. *Emergence of a Free Press.* Oxford University Press, New York, pp. 383ff.

LEWIS, J. 1983. *The Pursuit of Happiness: Family and Values in Jefferson's Virginia.* Cambridge University Press, New York, pp. 290ff.

LIENESCH, M. 1988. *New Order of the Ages: Time, the Constitution and the Making of Modern American Political Thought.* Princeton University Press, Princeton NJ, pp. 235ff.

LINDERMAN, G. 1987. *Embattled Courage: The Experience of Combat in the American Civil War*. Free Press, New York, pp. 357ff.

LIPSET, S. 1990. *Continental Divide: The Values and Institutions of the United States and Canada*. Routledge, New York, pp. 337ff.

MAY, H. 1976. *The Enlightenment in America*. Oxford University Press, New York, pp. 419ff.

MIDDLEKAUFF, R. 1982. *The Glorious Cause: The American Revolution, 1763–1789* (the Oxford History of the United States series). Oxford University Press, New York, pp. 696ff.

MINTZ, S.; KELLOGG, S. 1988. *Domestic Revolutions: A Social History of American Family Life*. Collier Macmillan, London, pp. 316ff.

MONTGOMERY, D. 1989. *The Fall of the House of Labor: The Workplace, the State and American Labor Activism, 1865–1925*. Cambridge University Press, New York, pp. 494ff.

MORAWSKA, E. 1985. *For Bread with Butter: The Life-Worlds of East Central Europeans in Johnstown, Pennsylvania, 1890–1940*. Cambridge University Press, New York, pp. 429ff.

MORTON, W. L. 1964. *The Critical Years: The Union of British North America, 1857–1873*. McClelland and Stewart, Toronto; Oxford University Press, New York, pp. 322ff.

NORTON, M. B. 1996. *Founding Mothers and Fathers: Gendered Power and the Forming of American Society*. Alfred A. Knopf, New York, pp. 496ff.

PALUDAN, P. 1988. *A People's Contest, the Union and Civil War, 1861–1865*. Harper and Row, New York, pp. 468ff.

PEISS, K. 1986. *Cheap Amusements: Working Women and Leisure in Turn-of-the-century New York*. Temple University Press, Philadelphia, pp. 244ff.

PESSEN, E. 1978. *Jacksonian America: Society, Personality and Politics*. Dorsey Press, Homewood IL, pp. 379ff.

RADDALL, T. 1957. *The Path of Destiny: Canada from the British Conquest to Home Rule, 1763–1850*. Doubleday, Toronto, pp. 468ff.

RODGERS, D. 1978. *The Work Ethic in Industrial America, 1850–1920*. University of Chicago Press, Chicago, pp. 300ff.

RYAN, M. 1981. *Cradle of the Middle Class: The Family in Oneida County, New York, 1790–1865*. Cambridge University Press, New York, pp. 321ff.

RYERSON, S. 1973. *Unequal Union: Roots of Crisis in the Canadas, 1815–1873*. Progress Books, Toronto, pp. 477ff.

SILVER, A. I. 1982. *The French-Canadian Idea of Confederation, 1864–1900*. University of Toronto Press, Toronto; Buffalo, pp. 257ff.

STANSELL, C. 1986. *City of Women: Sex and Class in New York, 1789–1860*. A. A. Knopf, New York, pp. 301ff.

STEARNS, P. N. 1994. *American Cool: Constructing a Twentieth-Century Emotional Style*. New York University Press, New York, pp. 368ff.

TROTTER, J. W. 1985. *Black Milwaukee: The Making of an Industrial Proletariat, 1915–45*. University of Illinois Press, Urbana, pp. 302ff.

ULRICH, L. T. 1990. *A Midwife's Tale*. A. A. Knopf, New York, pp. 444ff.

VERNEY, D. 1986. *Three Civilizations, Two Cultures, One State: Canada's Political Traditions*. Duke University Press, Durham NC, pp. 454ff.

VINOVSKIS, M. (ed.) 1990. *Toward a Social History of the American Civil War: Explanatory Essays*. Cambridge University Press, New York, pp. 201ff.

WHITE, R. 1983. *The Roots of Dependency: Subsistence, Environment and Social Change among the Choctaws, Pawnees and Navajos*. University of Nebraska Press, Lincoln, pp. 433ff.

WIEBE, R. H. 1967. *The Search for Order, 1877–1920*. Hill and Wang, New York, pp. 333ff.

WILENTZ, S. 1984. *Chants Democratic: New York City and the Rise of the American Working Class, 1788–1850*. Oxford University Press, New York, pp. 446ff.

WILLIAMSON, J. 1984. *The Crucible of Race: Black/White Relations in the American South since Emancipation*. Oxford University Press, New York, pp. 561ff.

WOOD, G. S. 1992. *The Radicalism of the American Revolution*. A. A. Knopf, New York, pp. 447ff.

ZUNZ, O. 1990. *Making America Corporate, 1870–1920*. University of Chicago Press, Chicago, pp. 267ff.

I2

LATIN AMERICA AND THE CARIBBEAN

I2.I
OVERVIEW

Germán Carrera Damas, coordinator

INTRODUCTION

Although this in no way diminishes their overall validity, the dates which set the boundaries of this chapter do not coincide with important historical landmarks in the context of Latin America and the Caribbean. The independence of the British colonies of North America is probably of greater significance, for this event set a precedent for the successful rebellion of subject colonies against the metropolis and the crown, with the imprudent aid of other crowns and metropolises, or the onset in 1810–11, in the form of a political crisis, of the structural crisis which the implanted Spanish American colonial societies had been suffering for almost half a century. This combination of events set the scene where the crisis of the European monarchies, which began in France in 1789, was to be felt. With regard to the date which brings this period to a close, perhaps in the Latin American context 1929–31 would be more relevant, on account of the effects of the Great Depression, in view of the already significant and dominant presence of the United States of America there. The landmarks of 1789 and 1914 are specifically linked to the development of Western Europe, despite the 'worldwide' repercussions of these events as they developed. This historical variation is important if we are to appreciate the scientific and cultural development of Latin America during the nineteenth century.

GENERAL HISTORICAL OUTLINE OF LATIN AMERICA AND THE CARIBBEAN DURING THE TRANSITION FROM THE EIGHTEENTH TO THE NINETEENTH CENTURY

This period was distinguished by the severance of the colonial link and the establishment of sovereign republican states, based on national projects, which were launched in the course of the nineteenth century. Mexico, which retained the monarchy, was an exception to the general

trend, and the French colony of Santo Domingo preceded this rupture by establishing the Republic of Haiti and abolishing slavery at the same time. In two of the island colonies of the Spanish crown, Cuba and Puerto Rico, the colonial link was strengthened within the context of inter-colonial confrontation with the United States of America, until it was finally broken at the end of the century. Brazil followed its own peculiar path.

Continuity and change during the period 1789–1914

The new impetus felt by the majority of the Creole societies towards the end of this period accentuated the complex nature of this historical period. The most significant event of this juncture in the scientific and cultural development of these societies was that they began to participate in the process of scientific, cultural and technological change taking place in the most dynamic centres of Western Europe.

In the Spanish colonies the nineteenth century began with a political and social crisis distinguished by two consecutive circumstances. The first of these was that the coming of age of some of the colonial societies, such as Venezuela and Argentina, coincided with the onset of the structural crisis which, to a greater or lesser degree, affected all the colonies. This crisis was due to the fact that the dynamic elements which had propelled the colonial process from its beginnings in the sixteenth century, began to run out of steam or stagnate. The second factor was the crisis of monarchy as a form of government, which began with the republican insurrection in the British colonies of North America, was aggravated by the crisis of the French and Spanish crowns, continued with the Napoleonic Wars and reached its peak with the restoration of absolutism in France and Spain. The abolition of the monarchy in America dealt a fatal blow to the absolute monarchies of Europe, from which they never recovered.

The doctrinaire political antagonism which followed between the restored monarchies in Europe and the surviving republics in the newly created states, was the greatest cause of international friction until the middle of this period. The birth and development of modern colonialism and the abolition of the monarchy in France changed the course of this confrontation once and for all.

Though tardy, the repercussions of the first industrial revolution and the expansion of international trade upset the economic model of the colonies, although this was not significantly changed. Change began to occur – in some places with great intensity – during the second industrial revolution during the latter third of this period.

The process of liberalizing and modernizing most of the implanted societies, which were deeply disturbed by the wars of independence and affected by the aftermath of civil strife, overwhelmed the second half of this period. The manifestations of this process in the social structure, cultural life and scientific and technological development gave rise to movements which were basically similar to their European counterparts.

Regional divisions

Any study of scientific and cultural development in Latin America and the Caribbean necessitates dividing the area into different regions.

If severance of the colonial link is taken as the criterion, three broad regions emerge: the French colony of Santo Domingo and the continental Spanish colonies coincided in the political crisis of severing their links with the metropolis, although each followed its own particular course; the Portuguese-American area followed its own path; the Spanish Caribbean islands – with the exception of the Spanish part of Santo Domingo – and the Caribbean islands which did not belong to Spain remained on the sidelines of the general trend of breaking the colonial link. Brazil followed its own route, which took it from an independent empire to a republic.

If socio-economic structures are taken as our criterion, different divisions must be made on the basis of the main economic activities (mining, agriculture and cattle-raising), the socio-cultural mix of the population (a strong indigenous base and the presence of numerous African slaves), and the degree of socio-political integration (societies which matured early, such as the vice-royalties of New Spain and Peru and societies which developed later such as the Captaincy General of Venezuela and the Vice-Royalty of the River Plate). Since these criteria are generally interlinked, regional divisions tend not to coincide with political-administrative, imperial and republican divisions.

As the nineteenth century advanced, the boom of economic activities which had not played a significant role during the colonial period, such as the production of coffee, wool, meat and wheat, emerged as a differentiating factor. This development went hand-in-hand with the expansion of international trade and the introduction of new technology, particularly in the field of navigation.

General and common factors

In the Spanish colonies of mainland America the political crisis was expressed as an aspiration towards autonomous government, which led to the severance of colonial links. The socio-political crisis was expressed by the abolition of the monarchy, which was replaced by republics. The joint effect of both these crises was the collapse of the internal power structure of the new societies formed within the colonial nexus. The virtually bloodless abolition of slavery in the second half of the nineteenth century, marked the culmination of this process of disintegration. Brazil followed.

From the scientific and cultural point of view, the most important general consequence of this process, both on account of its far-reaching significance and its prolonged effect, was the breakdown in international relations. The latter had been developing since the middle of the eighteenth century, albeit with some difficulty. One period of almost total disruption occurred between 1810 and 1824 as a result of the wars of independence. The other relative breakdown in relations as a result of the political 'embargo' imposed by the Holy Alliance, Spain's delay in recognizing the independence of its former colonies, and the rout and stagnation of society and economy in the newly emancipated states, lasted until more than halfway through the century.

The consequences of this situation in the scientific and cultural fields in the implanted societies were serious and enduring, since it meant that they were unable to play an active role in the first industrial revolution. Apart from Argentina, stimulated by the boom in wool exports, and some mining areas, the rest remained trapped by the survival of the traditional economy based on trade in raw agricultural materials and lacking in the products required in vast quantities by industry in the process of revolution. By the middle of the nineteenth century this lag in the technological and scientific fields – except in some aspects of university teaching – in relation to the most advanced European centres, which already existed at the end of the eighteenth century, had become an apparently unbridgeable gulf.

In most of the implanted societies of Latin America, full-blown contact with the new international economy occurred towards the end of this period, prompted by the second industrial revolution, but in circumstances dominated by their backlog of scientific and technological backwardness.

THE NATIONAL AND CULTURAL MAKE-UP OF THE REGIONS

By espousing the nation as the basis of the socio-political order, the differences in the cultural structure, which had developed during the process of the inter-cultural domination of the Conquest and perfected throughout the colonial period, were consolidated. This was crucial as far as the indigenous societies were concerned, but it also affected the population of black African descent.

A plurality of cultures and cultural traditions

The fact that the relative homogeneity of the Spanish-American Creole culture stands in marked contrast to the cultural heterogeneity of even the most developed indigenous cultures, is extremely significant. Ethnic and cultural mixing gave rise to new cultural patterns within the framework of which Euro-Creole and indigenous cultures converged on a selective basis. The latter reflected the process of cultural diversification to some degree, even when they were marginalized in either territorial or social terms. The situation in areas where the cultural gap between the

Creoles and the indigenous population was unbridgeable, was quite different. This was and is still the case in the Orinoco-Amazon area, and in areas which were already marginalized in relation to the great indigenous centres of civilization.

Relations between the Creole and indigenous cultures and the black African cultures were governed by the slavery regulations and, above all, by their strongly discriminatory racial and cultural content.

A COMMON TECHNOLOGICAL AND SCIENTIFIC TRADITION

In order to understand the convergence which occurred between the technology and scientific knowledge of the Southern Europeans and the contribution made by the indigenous societies, the disparities evident in the latter must be taken into consideration. In certain areas and fields the black African contribution must also be taken into account.

In the field of technology, the symbiotic development of Creole technology ensured the survival and, to some extent, the development of indigenous technology, which gradually adopted the use of iron and the wheel, as well as new animal and plant species. On the other hand, agricultural technology in the tropical forest and on the semi-desert of the *altiplano* had been resolved by the indigenous cultures, and was apparent in the almost immutable basic technology used in the cultivation and processing of maize, cassava and potatoes.

Perhaps the creativity born of the symbiotic Creole technology is most evident in the fields of clothing, housing and the preparation and conservation of foodstuffs. The predominance of Southern European technology is particularly apparent in the acclimatization of new plant and animal species, the introduction and use of new power sources, such as animal traction and wind and hydraulic power, and particularly in mining technology. The Escuela de Minería de Mexico, founded in 1792, was an advanced technology centre. However, irrigation regressed.

As far as scientific development is concerned, towards the middle of the period under review the traditional community began to favour the Northern European contribution. This was not the case in the period from the sixteenth to the eighteenth centuries, although the indigenous contribution was regarded as witchcraft or at best 'pre-scientific'.

Growing rejection of the 'pre-scientific' knowledge amassed by the indigenous societies is evident in the attitude of the Creoles towards indigenous medicine, which grew increasingly unacceptable until it was relegated both in social and territorial terms, being condemned in the name of science. However, indigenous knowledge of the environment, as well as their use of plant and animal species, was rapidly and effectively assimilated by the Creoles, together with their practical meteorological knowledge.

The attitude of the Southern Europeans towards science and technology and their aptitude for them is a hotly debated subject. The backwardness of the Creole societies in these fields is generally attributed to the introduction and persistence of scholasticism, which, by the end of the seventeenth century, was already regarded as outmoded in the main cultural and scientific centres of Northern Europe. Nevertheless, the importance of the institutes for science and fine arts founded in the last two decades of the eighteenth century in Mexico, Guatemala, Bogotá and

Buenos Aires should not be underestimated. However, severance of the colonial link was regarded by the American Creoles as the gateway to a radical change in the fields of culture and science.

The political, economic and social context

The period 1789–1914 is essentially one of the setting up of sovereign republics once the colonial links had been severed, the start – and in some cases development – of a process of economic realignment and, subsequently, the modernization of the Creole societies.

The road towards the constitution of sovereign republics was a long and arduous one, spanning the period from the initial severance of the colonial link to the failure of the last attempts to increase or rescue the European colonial presence in America, including the cautious admission of the sovereign republics to the international order. The significance of these circumstances in the slow pace of scientific and cultural development has not been adequately assessed. This may be the explanation why distorted conclusions are drawn, as to the reasons for the backwardness of the Creole societies of Latin America in these fields during the nineteenth century.

The start of the process of restructuring, and in some cases developing, the economy allows us to identify characteristics and distinguish stages. Parallel to the partial dismantling of the colonial economy, persistent, though not always beneficial, attempts were made to achieve institutional liberalization of the economy. In order to achieve this, reorganization of certain economic factors was undertaken, particularly as regards credit and the availability of free labour. The abrogation of entail and the right of primogeniture, together with the suppression of indigenous guarantees in some regions, broadened the internal regime of land ownership, but the concentration of ownership remained virtually intact, although a considerable amount of untilled land was transferred and land was confiscated and handed over to the military chiefs and *caudillos*. Towards the end of the period which concerns us, links with the expanding capitalist system, which had been insistently called for, hastened the acceleration and further development of the process of economic realignment.

Modernization of the American Creole societies followed in the wake of the two circumstances outlined above. In order to form a balanced view, a number of achievements should be stressed: the bloodless abolition of slavery; the forcible absorption of the indigenous societies within the liberal republican order; the legal abolition of social or racial discrimination; the revival of the urbanization process which had been at a standstill since the end of the eighteenth century; the establishment of new waves of immigrants, and the gradual laicization of the state.

SIGNIFICANCE OF THE BROAD SCIENTIFIC AND CULTURAL TRENDS IN THE PROCESS OF SCIENTIFIC AND CULTURAL DEVELOPMENT

The scientific and cultural development of Latin America and the Caribbean during the nineteenth and the early years of the twentieth century were characterized by a confrontation between persistent late 'scholasticism' and the emerging positivist and evolutionist trends. The rise and rapid spread of romanticism in the arts and in literature, in confrontation with the so-called neo-classicism of the latter days of the colonial period, contributed to the movement of scientific and cultural renewal. As in the most advanced contemporary European centres, the debate had intense political and social, as well as ideological, repercussions.

The Enlightenment and persistent 'late scholasticism'

A study of the reasons for the scientific and technological backwardness of the Spanish metropolis at the end of the eighteenth century, does not fall within our remit. The fact is that in Spain there was no development comparable to that of chemistry in France with Antoine-Laurent Lavoisier, and in England with John Dalton. It is generally recognized that achievements in physics and chemistry dealt a mortal blow to the Aristotelian system. Around 1800, the physical sciences had defined modern methods. In turn, the main result of the scientific revolution of the seventeenth and eighteenth centuries was that Greek concepts, known only at second-hand during the Middle Ages and incorporated in scholastic doctrine, traces of which still hung on in the Hispanic world, were abandoned.

Much has been said regarding the impact of the Enlightenment on the emancipation of the Spanish colonies in America. The influence of this movement on the so-called forerunners of independence is particularly evident in Francisco de Miranda. Recent Latin American historiography, having recovered from its exacerbated enthusiasm concerning the role played by this movement, has become more cautious, starting from a more critical assessment of its real impact outside an elite circle and its repercussions in the metropolis. The testimonies of Benito Jerónimo Feijóo y Montenegro and José Cadalso, regarding the scientific backwardness of Spain, are well-known. Although there was a certain zeal for the founding of educational centres, museums and libraries, Alexander Humboldt's view of the state of science in Mexico, Havana and Caracas at the beginning of the nineteenth century is known to have been adverse. In the early days of the independent republics the colonial universities, bastions of academic and social conservatism, maintained their colonial curriculum: ecclesiastical science, jurisprudence and medicine. The criterion of 'lucrative degrees' prevailed there: the natural sciences were studied by individuals who were not only isolated but few in number, and interest in developing 'useful knowledge' met with social prejudice. The phenomenon of widespread, and above all cumulative, scientific curiosity did not occur in the former colonies as it did in France and Britain during the eighteenth century, and this situation continued into the nineteenth century. Neither did crafts develop creatively. This creative evolution of craft skills formed the basis of mechanical skills, particularly in Britain. Although the printing press was more widely used during the eighteenth century, it did not come into general use. Literary and scientific publications, which have been linked to the reinforcement of American Creole awareness, appeared in Mexico, New Granada and Peru. It is accepted that the circulation of books was severely restricted, but there is considerable evidence that the works of Locke were read, and even those of French writers proscribed by the

Inquisition. This is the reason why knowledge of the ideas of Montesquieu, Voltaire and Rousseau surfaced as soon as the political crisis which led to independence began.

An arguably exaggerated appraisal of the changes which occurred at the end of the colonial period, requires us to consider the equivalent situation in the metropolis. On the basis of the available evidence, the picture which emerges reveals even greater backwardness there in some respects. The historiographic thesis according to which independence interrupted the progress which was being made in these areas, must also be accepted with caution. These effects may be attributed above all to the civil wars which took place during the early decades of the republics.

In Brazil the Enlightenment became the driving force behind official policy, being propounded by the Marquis of Pombal in Portugal.

The ideas of the French and North American revolutions

It is common practice to establish a close, even causal, link between the so-called 'ideas of the French Revolution' and the social and political events which led to the emancipation of the Spanish colonies in America. The prevalence of this approach in historiography has meant not only that events taking place within the colonies have been underestimated, but also that the impact of the 'ideas of the North American revolution' has been overestimated.

Current Latin American and Latin Americanist historiography has redressed the balance, focusing its attention on the internal events which gave rise to the structural crisis in the implanted societies, which began towards the end of the eighteenth century. Latin America and the Caribbean was not merely a stage upon which the important events of Europe were played out and where the underlying ideologies exerted an influence. Social contradictions of varying kinds erupted and came to the surface there. Foremost among these were the indigenous rebellions, such as the one led by Tupac Amaru in 1781 and the 1771 slave uprising in Santo Domingo. The conviction gradually grew that it was not possible to confront these contradictions successfully in the context of the weakened colonial relationship and that, in order to deal with them, the example and inspiration arising from the broad ideological trends of the period should be followed.

The deep American roots of the process of severing the colonial link explain why the considerable liberalizing effort of the Cortes of Cadiz in 1812, which even decreed freedom of the press and the abolition of the Inquisition, lacked dissuasive power. The growing strength of Americanism prevented the liberalization propounded in Cadiz from yielding the desired fruits of harmony and preservation of the Empire.

In assessing the impact of the different ideologies, excessive concentration on the 'ideas of the French Revolution' and a simplistic view of their possible effects is evident. Historical analysis allows us to distinguish between a *de facto* influence, the crisis of the monarchy and the bankruptcy of the Spanish crown, and explicit rejection of the anti-monarchical, anti-religious and abolitionist ideas which French propagandists and agents tried, without success, to spread. Rather than the desire to follow such ideas, what we see is an effort to prevent contamination by them, although this does not mean that these ideas did not continue to circulate. In 1794, Antonio Nariño translated and published the Declaration of the Rights of Man as passed by the French Constituent Assembly. It was not until the middle of the century that the real impact of these ideas, stripped of their original radicalism and swathed in republican, anti-absolutist ideology, began to be felt. This also occurred in Europe around the same time.

The 'ideas of the North American revolution' were particularly important during the period when the states which had recently broken the colonial link were being organized constitutionally. The example of an ordered 'Declaration of Independence' which retained control of slavery and, with its federal doctrine, supplied a functional response to the deep-rooted aspirations to autonomy of the regions and provinces, which flared up again with renewed vigour once colonial power had been dismantled, was extremely attractive to the Latin-American Creoles, bent upon reinforcing their control over the internal power structure of colonial society. Nevertheless, two aspects of these ideas discredited them: their democratic content and the promotion of religious freedom. However, the development of the federalist doctrine was influenced by the prestigious North American example.

Romanticism and realism in literature and art

The debate on so-called 'Latin American romanticism', starting with the term itself, has been no less intense. The use of this expression aims to establish an essential difference between 'Latin American romanticism' and romanticism pure and simple, the paternity of which is disputed by the French and the Germans. At the root of the matter lies the peculiar belief that in Europe romanticism was an intellectual and sentimental attitude which passed fleetingly through the essentially rationalistic European consciousness, whereas in Latin America romanticism is a virtually insurmountable trait of the Latin American temperament.

Setting this debate to one side, it is worth observing that in Latin America literary and artistic romanticism fell upon fertile ground, heartened by the wars of independence and the task of founding the republics. The romantic content, linked to the recovery of national cultural traits and doctrinaire political nationalism, fitted in very nicely with the need of the Creole societies to assert themselves. French literary romanticism, represented by Hugo and Lamartine, wreaked havoc among Latin American poets and literary society until, after a brief spell of realism after the 1870s, it gave way to the 'modernist' movement.

National and patriotic historiography accepted romanticism willingly, since the notions of independence and freedom coincided with their own fundamental concepts and sentiments. It is difficult to link romanticism to the principles of order and discipline in the political and social fields, since it relaxed the restrictions imposed by neo-classicism.

The differences between the European and Latin American expressions of romanticism are most apparent in the role played by this trend in the development of science. Whereas in Europe romanticism inspired a current of thought, Natural Philosophy, which was part of the debate on new science, in Latin America it roused, above all, the aspiration to freedom which made the new scientific trends important factors in the ideological struggle against traditional thought.

Realism in Latin American literature was a kind of return to a social reality which romantic evasion had turned spirits away from, to the point of taking refuge in fictitious worlds where the asperities of everyday life were attenuated, and beauty took on conventional forms quite distinct from the immediate surroundings. So-called *costumbrista* works made American features the basis of their aesthetic principles to the point that they became local in nature. In painting, the realism of Arturo Michelena, Eduardo Sivori and Francisco Laso stands out.

Positivism and evolutionism

It is generally accepted that the broad trends of positivism and evolutionism, and particularly the former, did not have the same impact in Europe as in Latin America, where they sometimes became so intertwined that it was virtually impossible to distinguish clearly between them.

In the Creole societies of Latin America, positivism (the seminal work of Auguste Comte appeared in 1830–42) was the theoretical, and particularly the doctrinaire, tool which finally broke with the past, rather than with Spanish colonialism, and also sought to bring the nascent republican societies into line with the more developed European societies. The case of Mexico, where Gabino Barreda began to preach the positivist gospel in 1860, is regarded as particularly representative of this attitude, although, towards the end of the period which concerns us here, it became an instrument of oppression and even exploitation under the aegis of dictatorial political power, having been adopted as the doctrine of the so-called 'scientists'.

The impact of positivism and evolutionism is particularly evident in the decade 1860–70, when university chairs were established in Argentina, Colombia and Venezuela, barely a decade after the new science had breached the portals of British universities. This stood in marked contrast to the trends of creationist inspiration, which were still current. This confrontation was further accentuated by the arrival of Darwinian evolutionary theory. The anti-dogmatic Christian turn, which the debate took on, fanned the flames of the struggle with the Catholic church, which was already opposed to anticlerical liberalism. Dogmatic obtuseness prevented conservative ideologues from seeing the potential of positivism as a source of precepts for regulating society, an aspect which was soon to be revealed in Mexico and Brazil.

At the same time, however, and not unrelated to the struggle with the church, the repercussions of positivism and evolutionism converged in the scientific vocation of naturalists who were already drawing inspiration from the travels of European naturalists. Together they gave rise to the development and modernization of medical studies and experimental biology.

Trends in economic thought

In the early days of the socio-political process, which led to the severance of the colonial link, the colonial monopoly of trade was brandished as a basic complaint. The counter-claim was for free trade to be legalized, since widespread, frequently tolerated contraband was only a palliative. Once independence had been achieved, the urgent need to re-establish the economic base, which had been seriously affected, was addressed, as well as the relationship between this economy and the new economic trends in Europe and North America.

The search for the key to gain access to economic development naturally led to the exaltation of political economy as a major science. The names of Adam Smith and the Scottish economists of the early nineteenth century began to appear in the press and in political debate. At the beginning of the century the basic work of Adam Smith, *An Inquiry into the Nature and Causes of the Wealth of Nations*, which appeared in 1776, was circulating in Spanish and Portuguese translations, but the practice of economic liberalism came up against not only colonial economic structures, but also prevailing attitudes. Attitudes polarized. Although some accepted the criteria of the new authority without reserve, a few paused to question the professed infallibility of the new doctrines. An example of the latter is Fermín Toro in Venezuela. On the other hand, a public exchequer chronically short of funds prevented trade being opened up completely, frequently justifying high duties.

Later trends

The presence of the scientific-philosophical developments of John Stuart Mill, Herbert Spencer, and Ernst Haeckel seems to have become entangled in the circulation of, and subsequent debate surrounding the materialist viewpoint and the socialist schools of thought, particularly the French and English ones, which were present to a greater or lesser degree from the middle of the century. Trade unionism also entered the social arena, throwing off its guild and mutualist shackles.

The appearance early on of socialist doctrines in the Creole societies of Latin America was favoured by two circumstances, which are related to one another and to the ethical and moral basis of the Catholic Christian conscience, which was the cornerstone of social morality. The first was the humanitarian and even redemptive missionary dimension extolled by the doctrines of so-called Utopian Socialism. The other was the fact that the social devastation caused by the first industrial revolution soon became known. Around the middle of the century, compendia of the burgeoning socialist theory were in circulation, and these ideas were debated in the press. They were even linked to the humanitarian principles of Christianity. Nevertheless, the opposition of the Vatican to such doctrines, together with its condemnation of liberalism, drew a line which few critical spirits dared cross. In turn, the new socialist proposals linked to materialism provided the ultra-conservatives with better ammunition. The latter ended up by lumping together everything related to defence of the critical spirit in social, scientific and cultural affairs.

THE INTERACTION BETWEEN FORCES FOR SOCIO-CULTURAL CHANGE AND FORCES RESISTANT TO CHANGE

For Latin America and the Caribbean, the period under study was a particularly difficult one. Any possibility of even modest socio-cultural change was interrupted by the wars of independence, with their lingering consequences of international isolation, and the loss of human resources and cultural achievements. The close interdependence between the calamitous political and military process and the timid awakening of scientific and cultural curiosity, meant that the development of the latter was disrupted for almost the whole of the nineteenth century.

The struggle against obscurantism and credulity

During the early phase this struggle was confused with the basic socio-political debate in both of its manifestations, which were interlinked: on the one hand, the trend which set those in favour of independence against those who advocated maintaining the colonial link and, on the other hand, the champions of the monarchy against the proponents of republicanism. The struggle to break the colonial link and gain independence was fought in the ideological sphere as well as on the battlefield. There is abundant intellectual output justifying the struggle for independence in opposition to those who condemned it alleging that it was contrary to dogma. The work of Juan Germán Roscio is one of the most well rounded expressions of Catholic Christian morality. The reforming work of Benito Juárez was inspired by it. Simón Bolívar, who was excommunicated by the Bishop of Popayán, bitterly censured this manipulation of the religious conscience of the people, who were led to regard independence as the work of the devil. In the second phase, once the war was over, the struggle against credulity and superstition was also complicated by debate over the measures which should be taken to re-establish the internal power structure of society, particularly with regard to the role of the church. Liberal propaganda and democratic proposals were likened to a diabolical conspiracy against religion, virtue and the social order.

In the third phase, from the middle of the century onwards, reforming movements which favoured the secularization of the state and effective religious freedom, and championed a critical spirit and the circulation of the new philosophical and scientific ideas, were also regarded as anathema. Positivist thinking, advocating reason based on science as opposed to credulity based on metaphysics and theology, was a decisive weapon in this struggle.

The role which the church had played until that time in the internal power structure, as a factor for social control, was evident in its twofold function. On the one hand, it fostered loyalty to the crown as obedience to a divine decree. On the other hand, it sought to safeguard purity of faith and to prevent contamination by doctrines regarded as disruptive. In the latter task it could count on the legal and psychological mechanisms of the Holy Office or Inquisition. The liberalizing endeavour, both in America and the metropolis, regarded the suppression of this feared institution as a primary objective, and this aim was expressed from the outset by all the emancipating movements, while in the metropolis in 1812 the Cortes of Cadiz decreed the abolition of the Inquisition, which was briefly re-established at the Restoration.

The confrontation between the champions of independence and the defenders of the colonial link was reflected in their fear of new ideas. This was true on both sides. Abolitionism, anti-clericalism and frankly anti-religious attitudes – associated with the extremist developments of the French Revolution – exacerbated the fears stirred by Spanish liberalism present in the works of Benito Jerónimo

Feijóo y Montenegro and Pedro Rodríguez, the Count of Campomanes. The new trends in educational thinking, represented initially by Juan Bautista Picornell and Simón Rodríguez, were particularly significant.

Once the wars of independence were over, social disquiet as a result of the upheaval in the internal power structures of society found expression in a struggle between two scarcely distinguishable groups: one made up of those who wanted to see the monarchy restored as a proven system of social control, but without giving up their independence, and another consisting of those who did not rule out the possibilities of republicanism and were rather of the opinion that the prevailing social ills would disappear as societies were organized in accordance with republican principles. This was the crux of the debate on social education, i.e. education which aimed to turn subjects and serfs into citizens. Pioneers in this field were Simón Rodríguez and Fray Servando Teresa de Mier. Andrés Bello, Domingo Faustino Sarmiento and Juan Bautista Alberdi represent positions which derive from this debate in the fields of linguistic and cultural autonomy, civilizing education and constitutional thought respectively. The example of North American republican society was frequently invoked, and French and North American republican thought is evident.

The controversy regarding the re-establishment of the internal power structure of societies which were now republics, meant that the social and political role of the church restricted the ideological and socio-political impact of the reform movements and provoked impassioned conflicts which gave rise, on a number of occasions, to civil wars of a religious nature. This situation was not brought under control until the economic power of the church, which had allowed it to maintain such conflicts until that time, was destroyed, due to the intervention of the so-called victorious liberal reform movements, represented in Mexico by Benito Juárez and in Venezuela by Antonio Guzmán Blanco.

The Catholic church suffered the consequences of being the institutional representative of a variety of social forces, beliefs, interests and even popular superstitions where the church itself was undoubtedly a source of values and maxims. When, towards the end of the period which concerns us, Pope Leo XII redefined the role of the church, the liberal movement regarded the differences as settled, although other movements, both ideological and religious, kept up their belligerence in what they continued to regard as a defence of the jurisdiction of reason and science. At the same time, the sectors of society most crudely related to the exploitation of indigenous peoples and peons did not hesitate to react against the church, which they accused of abandoning them in defence of its own interests.

The infiltration of scientific thought

Although scientific thought had already made its presence felt midway through the period under study, its impact was conditioned by fear of the disruptive social effect which the new scientific and cultural proposals might have, to the extent that they might undermine religious sentiment in society and weaken the institutional prestige of the church, which were regarded as necessary if the internal power structure of society was to be re-established. But two powerful external factors also contributed to the conflict: the active resistance of the papacy to liberalism and scientific

principles and the toll which this struggle took on those societies where these new ideas had arisen.

Fear of the disruptive social effect of the new scientific and cultural ideas was understandable in societies which were recovering from a profound trauma attributed in great measure to 'the influence of the new ideas', i.e. 'the ideas of the French Revolution' with their charge of scientific and anti-religious rationalism. Evolutionism clashed with vitalist creationism, but it also came into conflict with the 'finality argument', which is one of the classic proofs of the existence of God, since this is the only explanation for the 'universal harmony' between beings and things. This contradiction seemed insurmountable, although Darwinism does not imply that God does not exist, but merely refutes one of the arguments in favour of his existence. The evolutionist developments of Darwinism sharpened this contradiction and, at the same time, so-called Social Darwinism threatened one of the mainstays of the republican order, i.e. equality, jealously claimed as the key to correct one of the most odious features of the colonial monarchist order.

The hard core of active resistance to liberalism and scientific principles was represented by papal doctrine in alliance with the restored monarchies of Europe. This coalition of conservative forces assumed a historically reactionary character evident in the church, which clung to its colonial privileges. This confrontation had two consequences of particular significance from the point of view of scientific and cultural development: intellectual and scientific life was cloistered to a degree, and the debate was diverted towards the socio-political scene. The first was the result of the respect and fear which the church hierarchy inspired, even in scientific minds, forcing them to draw back both from circulating and from cultivating the new scientific trends. The second meant the eventual use, by both sides, of measures of a political and administrative nature to reinforce their respective positions.

The impact of this struggle on societies where the new ideas were being born helped considerably to sharpen the debate in the societies of Latin America and the Caribbean. Evolution was the centre of the struggle between progress and reaction in Britain and mainland Europe. Spain retrenched in its scientific and cultural backwardness. Towards the end of the nineteenth century the Spanish Nobel laureate (1906) Santiago Ramón y Cajal (1852–1934), wrote in his *Reglas y consejos sobre investigación científica*: 'Spain is an intellectually backward country, but not decadent' and he added: 'the nations of central and northern Europe have overtaken us to an extraordinary extent. We are not simply behind, but a long way behind'. France was digesting the excesses of its Revolution and settling the Napoleonic inheritance in its relations with the rest of Europe. Britain was fighting a difficult struggle to modernize, overcoming the trepidation caused by the upheavals on mainland Europe. In order to adequately compare the Latin American and European experiences in this field, it is worth remembering that the works of Alfred Russell Wallace and Charles Darwin appeared in 1858 and 1842 respectively. *On the Origin of Species* appeared in outline in 1859. Darwin's work applying evolutionary theory to humanity, *The Descent of Man*, was published in 1871. The debate between evolutionism and orthodoxy began at a meeting of the British Association held in Oxford in 1860, immediately after the publication of *On the Origin of Species*.

This allows us to conclude that towards the end of the nineteenth century the gap between Europe and Latin America was beginning to close as far as the influence of broad scientific and philosophical trends is concerned. It should be pointed out that, as the subject of academic debate and socio-political controversy, these trends existed almost side-by-side.

The arrival of the new scientific ideas in the field of historiography was very important in the societies of Latin America. Historical awareness formed the foundations of a new political, republican consciousness, which took the place of the ancestral royalist ethos. Hence, the prime concern of historiography was to justify independence. This was all the more necessary since the results obtained during the early years of the independent republics gave rise to doubts concerning the prudence of the step which had been taken. This was successfully taken care of by patriotic histories, which were bellicose, heroic and radically anti-Spanish. After the middle of the century, when national projects had been definitively formulated, the historiographical outlook had to be changed in order to foster a national conscience. National histories, which were also bellicose, heroic and anti-Spanish but required a profound re-orientation, took care of this. Under the influence of the new scientific ideas, positivist and evo-lutionist historiographical schools arose, which tried to apply the new methodology, derived from the develop-ment of the social and biological sciences, to historio-graphy. Although there were some noteworthy results, they did not succeed in essentially altering the historical consciousness which had prevailed in Latin America throughout the nineteenth century, one which clung to a view of history and society centred around hero cults, which fired popular imagination and were used politically as a substitute for well-defined national values in line with the real structure of the new national states.

The social impact of the new science

The social impact of the new science was closely linked to the modernization process launched in a number of Latin American societies in an attempt to bring them into line with the world capitalist system bent on colonial expansion in the second half of the nineteenth century.

If, in general terms, it is recognized that the profound transformation of science during the nineteenth century was essentially linked to evolutionary theory as applied to biology – with its far-reaching ideological impact – it is understandable why biology dominated the field of research and scientific teaching in Latin America. It dealt a blow to the last bastions of late 'scholastic' thought which had become an obstacle in the path of social and political change. Furthermore, biology could be cultivated, and eventually developed, without a scientific, technological and industrial base such as had been formed in Europe by the conjunction of the so-called scientific revolution and the first industrial revolution.

In this context it can therefore be stated that, if by the end of the nineteenth century no scientific and technical development had taken place in Latin America and the Caribbean, scientific thought had indeed developed. In a number of societies attempts were made to organize 'scientists' in associations for the promotion of the sciences, just as the sociedades de amigos del país had fostered the spread of new technologies. Around 1870 science was clearly attempting to assert itself with public debate and attempts at home production.

The fact that development of scientific thought was immediately transformed into social action should be stressed. For instance, the Venezuelan Darwinian evolu-tionists, like their colleagues in other Latin American countries, did not reach the same conclusion as the fol-lowers of Spencer with regard to the role of the state. Influenced by positivism, they took the opposite route and turned the new science into an instrument for furthering social well-being, particularly in the fields of education and health care.

SOCIAL AND POLITICAL CHANGE

Any assessment of the confrontation provoked by the invasion of the new scientific and cultural trends during the second half of the nineteenth century and represented by the debate between creationists (vitalists) and Darwinists (evolutionary theorists) must take account of the particu-larly difficult historical circumstances being experienced by Latin American societies. This might be summed up as follows: once the problem of the re-establishment of the internal power structure had been resolved, however pre-cariously, the task of constructing a liberal socio-political order was raised, not, as before, within the formality of institutions designed in the constitutional texts, but as a form of government practice and, above all, as a form of social organization.

Galvanizing society

The post-independence generation grasped the need to speed up the process of breaking with the surviving relics of the colonial system in independent republican society, not merely in terms of basic liberalization but as the much desired, but always postponed, institutionalization of the liberal republic with democratic leanings, although true democracy might still be a long way off.

The need to energize society was regarded as a com-pulsory step in the development of the ruling class, a pro-duct of the colonial order, in its transformation into a modern bourgeoisie capable of providing the impetus and orientation required if the new nation was to become a liberal democratic republic. Thus, the stormy road followed by liberal ideology since its beginnings reached its climax when the baton was passed on to the most hot-headed proponents of breaking the colonial link, and not to those who had carried out that break, since the latter were more sympathetic to the conservative social programme which gave rise to the political crisis at the end of the first half of the nineteenth century. Even the early attempts at setting up more or less orthodox liberal regimes, such as Rivadavia in Buenos Aires, the pipiolos in Chile, Santander in Colombia and the 1824 Congress in Mexico, met with failure or success which was more theoretical than real. Nevertheless, the basic fact is that, whether they were reformists or conservatives, centralists or federalists, republicans or royalists, their common ideological founda-tion owed something to liberalism. The new phase involved applying liberal ideas more widely in social and political fields, and this entailed an ideological struggle in which the new philosophical and scientific trends became involved.

The modernizing effects of the liberation of labour, due to the abolition of slavery and the subsequent reabsorption of freed slaves as peons, as well as the progressive elimination of other forms of subjection of labour, were hindered due to economic stagnation and the precarious nature of the technology used in farming and cattle-raising, which were the basis of the colonial system. Important exceptions as far as technology is concerned were the Cuban sugar mills and the Brazilian coffee plantations, reconciled to slavery, and the Argentine meat-processing factories and refrigeration plants. At the same time, despite the introduction of new technology, the mining economies only recovered from their loss of impetus very late in the day. The attempts by English companies to introduce new machinery to rehabilitate the mines, which had lain abandoned for a long time in Mexico and Peru, proved fruitless.

The precarious nature of the road network and the rudimentary transportation and communications technology in use made traditional exports uncompetitive. But more serious still was the fact that the formation of a national market seemed a long way off. This was aggravated by the delay in establishing, or bringing into general use, such basic national systems as a national currency, weights and measures, credit, commercial legislation, etc.

The objective of lending momentum to the formation of a new society led to the adoption of a simplistic formula based on the opposition between civilization and barbarism. Opting for the former implied clearing the way by doing away with all social structures which might be regarded as a hindrance to progress, foremost among which were those intrinsic to indigenous society. The exploitation of new land, the settlement of immigrants and the building of roads and railways frequently meant that indigenous peoples were plundered and even exterminated. On the pampas of Argentina and Uruguay and in areas of southern Brazil and Chile, the extermination and expulsion of the indigenous peoples from their lands constitutes one of the most painful chapters in the march towards civilization undertaken by the Creole societies as they strived to occupy the land to the full. In those countries where the density of the indigenous population prevented this drastic solution to the so-called 'indigenous problem', the exploitation and social marginalization visited upon them under the aegis of the practices of domination, which had nourished the 'Creole conscience' since the sixteenth century, were no less cruel. Attempts at resistance, particularly in Mexico and Peru, were put down using extremely violent means, and huge masses of indigenous people were relegated to a brutalized state of semi-slavery on estates and plantations.

NEW INSTITUTIONALIZED POLITICAL STRUCTURES

The nineteenth century was, almost in its entirety, a difficult period for the Creole societies of Latin America. They had to reconcile the re-establishment of the internal power structure of society with a liberal republican system built on the ruins of a royalist conscience which basically belonged to the Catholic Christian camp in social matters. The role either recognized by or attributed to the church in the re-establishment of the internal power structures of republican society was disputed, because the church, which had taken part in the process of reconstruction, was regarded as a tenacious survivor of the colonial order which society sought to replace. The most lucid minds considered that, in objective terms, any weakening of the social role of the

church would be disadvantageous to the re-establishment of the internal power structure of society, but that such a step was necessary if a liberal democratic republic was to be consolidated. The Mexican Reform marked the highest point in the reduction of the global power of the Catholic church. During the latter third of the century a similar movement in Venezuela even went so far as to instigate a schism. In Peru, Chile and Argentina less radical positions prevailed. Ecuador took a strictly clerical stand.

In both the internal and the papal order, the struggle against the rejection of liberalism and the new social doctrines linked to all intents and purposes to the new scientific trends, came to be seen by liberals and those promoting the scientific spirit as a crusade of reason aimed at removing the last great obstacle hindering the establishment of a more just social order, both in Europe and in Latin America and the Caribbean. Thus, the liberals regarded their interpretation of Darwinian evolutionary theory as a weapon to challenge the sway of a reactionary church. The aim was to achieve a lay state without depriving the Catholic church of its privileged position. Political actions were implemented in the conviction that, in order to have its social and political power weakened, the church must lose its economic power and education had to be laicized.

However, it was no less important to allow ideas which were socially accessible and effective to circulate freely. It was believed that the dogmatic view of life, society and government would not stand up to scrutiny. This explains the constant battle to achieve freedom of expression. The key instruments for this should be freedom of the press and free and compulsory state primary education. This feeling gradually became more widespread in Latin America after 1879, but more as an affirmation of the state in its struggle against the church than as a practice which would reach all of society.

The new economy

Liberalization of the economy came into conflict first of all with the world of the *latifundio* and monopolistic trading tendencies, but it also came up against the worldly interests of the church, represented by its accumulation of considerable tracts of land, church ground rents, the system of tithes and first fruits, and mortmain. The *latifundio* resisted all attempts to put an end to systems of subjection of labour, particularly enforced peonage, which became widespread after slavery was abolished. In the Creole societies in those areas with a dense indigenous population, the republican status of labour meant that the ancestral relationship of domination had to be formally reassessed. Trading companies set up by foreigners, taking advantage of their access to credit and control of the export market, effectively violated free trade. The new economy also required and imposed the adoption of new techniques and the creation of national structures to facilitate free movement of goods and people for trading purposes. The need to foster a business outlook and to provide training in the new commercial and industrial techniques was also raised. This led to new specialization of the labour force in the fields of manufacturing and transport. Towards the end of this period, the founding of banks, credit companies and corporations promoted the formation of a tertiary sector in the economies of the most advanced Creole societies.

DEPENDENCY AND EMANCIPATION IN SCIENCE AND TECHNOLOGY

The characteristics of the conflict between dependency and emancipation in the course of the nineteenth century are very complex, since this entailed rejecting the Hispanic past, as was natural after such a hard struggle for independence, and replacing it with standards which found widespread acceptance, particularly since its protagonists believed that by doing so, they would be closer to achieving the first objective. At the start of the period which concerns us here, the most attractive example was that of the newly emancipated former British colonies in North America which had set off down the path of prosperity based on agriculture, manufacturing and trade. Growing mechanization, first in Europe and later in North America after the Civil War, meant the emergence of a pattern of progress based on industrial and technological development, the social consequences of which also met with rejection in Latin America.

Innovation and national aspirations

The need to reconcile innovation with national aspirations was the cause of the intellectual and spiritual agonies suffered by Simón Rodríguez, for whom the break with the past offered, above all, the opportunity to undertake autonomous, creative enquiry. On the other hand, the social emergencies which immediately came to light, giving rise to policies based on the principles of free trade, led to shortcuts being taken, such as the Lancasterian educational techniques and the imitation of consumer habits, social practices and technological processes which rapidly led to a state of dependency.

Education was regarded as the area where the difficulty of reconciling the need for innovation with national aspirations had to be addressed first and with the greatest urgency. The difficulty consisted in turning a Creole population lacking almost any kind of formal education, which had dismantled and, in certain social and cultural respects, demolished the colonial system within which they had been born and raised, into citizens. In Chile, Argentina and Uruguay respectively the figures of Andrés Bello, Domingo Faustino Sarmiento and José Pedro Varela symbolize the most outstanding attempts to organize education systems.

The free-trade relationship with international trade brought in its wake a profound crisis and even led to the disappearance of crafts and workshops using traditional Creole technology. Thus any chance of development and technological innovation in this area was curtailed.

It is generally accepted that, despite the well documented efforts of naturalists and the proponents of scientific knowledge, particularly in the universities, the nineteenth century drew to a close without a solid modern scientific movement, one with institutional support and capable of producing meaningful contributions in the various fields, having been formed in Latin America. The weak point of the causes outlined above is that they would appear to have more to do with the absence of scientific development than with causes *per se*. Thus, political, economic and social instability have been put forward as a universal explanation, forgetting that the nineteenth century was not a period of peace and stability in the Western world as a whole, except in Britain, which may have been protected by its status as an island. The existence of social values and conduct which were adverse to scientific development, has also been put forward as an argument, and the same comment applies. This is also true of the argument regarding the absence of a social demand for science, where the argument which would seem to be true for technological development, is extended to the field of science.

The critical significance of these explanations is further weakened in the light of two examples, which are surely not isolated. On 22 November 1821, when the war on the soil of the Republic of Colombia had not yet come to an end, a young French scientist, Jean Baptiste Boussingault, arrived in La Guaira, having been contracted by the government as a result of an agreement between Simón Bolívar and Baron Alexander de Humboldt to found a school of mining in Bogotá, as part of a scientific project which would be extended to Mexico. At the height of the political and military disturbances in Venezuela, the Society for Physical and Natural Sciences was founded in Caracas and operated from 1867 to 1878. Among its honorary members was Charles Darwin.

Technological change

Technological change was regarded as the rapid transformation, suppression or substitution of Creole technology and the setting up of a new relationship between Creole and indigenous technologies. In this way the technological symbiosis, which had functioned effectively throughout the colonial period, was in large measure shattered. However, the problems of basic production for the sustenance of the majority of the population were solved by Creole technology, with an indigenous base, although it had to confront the difficulties arising from technological stagnation in the fields of transport, and the preservation of perishable goods. These difficulties persisted almost until the end of the century. The introduction of railways, which occurred apace in the last third of the nineteenth century, was related to the opening up of markets to imports and the extraction of traditional products, or new ones such as wool, wheat and beef which were produced on a large scale for export.

The traditional economy inherited from the colony produced little in the way of technological advances in the area of production. This was also true for new crops, such as coffee, to the semi-processed stage. On the other hand, sugar production did feel the effects of the introduction of new power sources and new technologies, which also meant that it was virtually taken over by foreign companies.

The replacement of slave labour with free labour, as well as the suppression of the guilds, raised the question of training for work based on the new imported technologies. This was undoubtedly the most important social effect of the technological changes which occurred during the second half of the century. The scene, which, until that time had been monopolized by large landowners and peons, saw the arrival of a new actor, the genuine wage earner, with which the social fabric grew more complex and social relationships began to change.

By way of a conclusion with regard to technological change, it must be stressed that the relatively early introduction of steam, both in navigation and in railway transportation, followed shortly afterwards by gas lighting, electricity and the telegraph, owed nothing to autonomous processes of technological change and that the arrival of these advances did not promote manufacturing and industrial development in any significant way. During the third decade of the century steamships began to sail on Lake Maracaibo and on the Magdalena, Orinoco and Paraná rivers. Railway fever, which after mid-century was to become the symbol of progress and civilization, had not yet begun: the first railway was built in colonial Cuba in 1838. In general terms, these changes and innovations were an offshoot of the expanding European and North American economies, which were making raw materials available for their own industry, and opening up markets for their own products.

There was one less visible area, however, where technological change had drastic and widespread repercussions. It sowed the idea of progress, understood merely as technological modernization and ignoring the moral and ethical content, which, until that time, had been uppermost in people's minds. From this time on, governments of every persuasion based the achievement of their objectives on what has been called material progress.

FORGING NEW LINKS WITH THE INTERNATIONAL ECONOMY AND OVERCOMING THE STRUCTURAL CRISIS IN THE IMPLANTED SOCIETIES

The drive to supply the vast markets created in Europe by the drift of the population towards the towns and cities as a result of the industrial revolutions, wrought changes which were both sweeping and profound, particularly in the economy of the temperate areas facing the Atlantic Ocean. Tropical and sub-tropical areas also benefited from growth in the consumption of sugar, coffee and cocoa, but they really only began to emerge from their prolonged lethargy towards the end of the period under review as a result of oil prospecting.

This process of change was due to three sets of factors: first, the need to solve the difficulties involved in being able to transport large volumes of goods rapidly and at a reduced cost, the solutions to which were the railways and large ocean-going vessels; second, the need to solve the difficulties involved in the transportation of large quantities of perishable goods, the solution to which was the development of meat extracts and the use of refrigerated ships both for the transportation of beef and bananas; the need to compete in international markets with other production centres highlighted the necessity of applying new techniques in the production of traditional tropical produce.

In general terms, it may be said that, in the first two cases, the technological solutions were not found by the producers but by the consumers. This allowed the latter to control the most lucrative links in the economic chain, i.e. exports, transport, industrialization and commercialization, and later, with the help of conditioned credit and aided by the devastating fluctuations in prices, to extend their influence to production itself. In the third case, production improvements were introduced locally, although a similar process to that described above also occurred on a smaller scale.

At the beginning of the twentieth century some of the implanted societies of Latin America began to emerge from the structural crisis which had beset them since the end of the eighteenth century. They reacted under the influence of three dynamic external factors: the second industrial revolution with its new requirements for raw materials of mining origin and new technologies; the incipient North American presence which was beginning to be felt particularly in the Caribbean and in North and Central America; and, in the River Plate region and in parts of Brazil, the mass influx of European immigrants and the first steps in the process of industrialization.

The social and political transformation of some of the implanted societies was the result of three main factors: modernization, the revival of the process of urbanization and the on-going institutionalization of political life.

Modernization involved a series of policies, including organization of public administrations, structuring of the monetary and weights and measures systems, the formation of national armies, the development of a road and communications networks, the establishment and development of national education systems, and so forth. In all these areas technology was imported rapidly on a massive scale.

The revival of the process of migration towards the urban areas, which had virtually been at a standstill since the end of the eighteenth century and was seriously affected by the wars of independence and the subsequent civil wars, meant that the processes of relocation and adoption of new mores recommenced. Modernization played a fundamental role in this area. In the River Plate basin and in southern Brazil the importance of immigration as a force for change began to grow.

Institutionalization of the political system was still a crucial matter for most Latin American societies around the end of the period which concerns us here. The contradiction between dictatorships – whether of a modernizing ilk or not – and the aspiration to institutionalize political life was a decisive factor which conditioned cultural and scientific life.

Cultural transformation

The development of the responsibilities of the state, in accordance with the process of social and political transformation, gave rise to demands of a cultural nature, which required considerable changes to be introduced in the processes of preparing and spreading information. The most noteworthy result of this cultural transformation was that, at last, in the minds of the people, the independent republics no longer lived in the shadow of their colonial past.

The difference between urban and rural culture became decidedly marked. The former was the symbol of modernity while the latter signified backwardness. The former was open, accepting new ideas of every kind, whereas the latter was relegated as a sanctuary of traditional values, which were regarded as picturesque. This change brought about a profound and irreducible schism in the cultural conscience of many Creole societies, which still exists to this day. The adoption of new ideas was not an evolutionary development stimulated in a normal way by cultural contacts. On the contrary, traditional values were rejected a priori and new ideas were adopted in their place. One exception was what is regarded as an original American contribution in the field of literature: the modernist movement, represented by the Nicaraguan Rubén Darío in the poetic genre and the Venezuelan Manuel Díaz Rodríguez in prose, opened up a new path for literature in Spanish.

The deep cleavage separating the indigenous societies and the dominant Creole culture also widened and deepened, and the marginalization of the former, both in territorial and in social terms, became more marked. The level of illiteracy, extremely high in both groups, was almost absolute in the indigenous societies which, like the majority of the population of mixed blood, whether rural or urban, had no real access to schooling. The dominant Creole culture entered a period of transformation, linked to the process of change in consumer habits and contact with a variety of intellectual stimuli, although a mechanism of a critical substitution of authorities and an almost compassionate upsurge in Hispanism after Spain's defeat in 1898, weighed heavily.

Both cultural and scientific life as well as the education system underwent increasing and ever more rapid transformation, aided mainly by the development of the political and cultural press. Modernization of the universities was considered a necessary step if Creole society was itself to modernize and, towards the end of the period under review, a radical change was heralded in this field. Free, compulsory state primary education was extended, with the massive arrival of women in education. Sport began to develop as an alternative to social gatherings of a religious nature.

The region in the world context

It is generally recognized that, as a result of the wars of independence, the subsequent civil wars and the calamitous organization of the new states, Latin America and the Caribbean remained 'in the wings of the world stage' almost until the middle of the nineteenth century. This is regarded as true insofar as the region's ability to play an active role in the international scheme of things is concerned. It has also been pointed out that this was mainly due to the failure of the Bolívar plan for unity known as the Panama Congress, held in 1826, which was replaced by a mechanism of inter-American unity controlled by the United States, which emerged after the first Conference of American States held in 1889.

However, a quite different picture emerges if we take into account the significance of the new states for post-Napoleonic European policy, which aimed to eradicate republicanism as a form of government and even as a doctrine. The same is true in the field of economics if we evaluate the contribution of the region towards the enhancement of the expansive capacity of European and North American capitalism.

The change in the European presence was a result of the transformation which took place in Europe during the second half of the nineteenth century, represented by the struggle between absolute monarchy, constitutional monarchy and republicanism. A new road was opened up for relations with Latin America and the Caribbean, this time a relationship of modern colonialism, which replaced the aims to reconquer its American domains harboured by Spanish absolutism restored under the aegis of the Holy Alliance. However, a long series of hostile acts, wars and interventions took place between both sides, which weighed heavily against the efforts of the new American states to restructure. Mexico, the Dominican Republic, Peru, Bolivia, Uruguay, Argentina, Venezuela, Colombia – in short nearly all the new states – suffered aggressions of one kind or another. The failure of this policy in Mexico and the consolidation of the United States, once it had overcome its internal crisis in 1865, brought about a change in the European attitude.

The full emergence of the United States as the dominant continental power, a power which had been flexing its muscles in the Caribbean and Central America towards the end of this period was, in the long run, urged forward by the repercussions of the Mexican Revolution and, later, by the First World War and the Russian Revolution, which led to oil prospecting in the Caribbean basin.

The new philosophical trends began to find political expression. Nineteenth-century socialism and trade unionism, as well as the popular agrarian stands, influenced by the ideals of the Mexican Revolution, began to crystallize as socialist movements inspired by the European, and particularly the French model after the 1871 Commune.

On this note this historical period drew to a close. If we are to understand this period correctly, we must bear in mind that the Creole societies of Latin America and the Caribbean were not merely sounding boards for the new scientific, cultural and technological trends generated in Europe and the United States of America. These societies made an effort to join the new current. The results should not be assessed only on the basis of the big names or the original contributions made, but also, and perhaps primarily, on the magnitude and the on-going nature of the effort made to overcome stubborn difficulties in an extremely short historical span: a past which had lasted for centuries had to be demolished in decades, and in many cases reconstruction had to begin from the very foundations themselves.

BIBLIOGRAPHY

BABINI, J. 1963. *La ciencia en Argentina*. Eudeba, Buenos Aires.

BATEMAN, A. ET AL. 1971. *Apuntes para la ciencia en Colombia*. Colciencias, Bogotá.

BELLO, A. 1843. *Imprenta del Estado*. University of Chile Press, Santiago.

BERNAL, J. 1979. *Historia social de la ciencia*. Ediciones Península, Barcelona.

BUSHNELL, D.; MACAULEY, N. 1988. *The Emergence of Latin America in the Nineteenth Century*. Oxford University Press, New York/Oxford.

CENDES (CENTRE FOR DEVELOPMENT STUDIES). 1982. *Formación histórico-social de América Latina*. Ediciones de la Biblioteca de la Universidad Central de Venezuela, Caracas.

CORTES CONDE, R. 1974. *The First Stage of Modernization in Latin America*. Harper and Row, New York.

DE GORTARI, E. 1973. *Ciencia y Conciencia en México (1767–1883)*. Sepsetentas, Mexico.

ELLIOT, J. H. 1972. *El viejo mundo y el nuevo mundo*. Alianza Editorial, Madrid.

GRIFFIN, C. C. 1962. *El período nacional en la historia del nuevo mundo*. Instituto Panamericano de Geografía e Historia, Mexico.

HALPERIN DONGHI, T. 1969. *Historia contemporánea de América Latina*. Alianza Editorial, Madrid.

HENRIQUEZ UREÑA, P. 1947. *Historia de la cultura de la América Hispana*. Fondo de Cultura Económica, Mexico.

HULL, L. W. 1961. *Historia y filosofía de la ciencia*. Ariel, Barcelona.

IVIC (INSTITUTO VENEZOLANO DE INVESTIGACIONES CIENTIFI-CAS). 1965. *La ciencia, base de nuestro progreso*. Ediciones IVIC, Caracas.

KAPLAN, M. 1969. *Formación del Estado nacional en América Latina*. Amorrortu Editores, Buenos Aires.

KOHN DE BEKER, M. 1970. *Tendencias positivistas en Venezuela*. Ediciones de la Biblioteca de la Universidad Central de Venezuela, Caracas.

LOPEZ PIÑERO, J. M. 1969. *La introducción de la ciencia moderna en España*. Ariel, Barcelona.

LOPEZ SANCHEZ, J. 1980. 'Breve historia de la ciencia en Cuba'. In: *Revista de la Biblioteca Nacional José Martí*, No. 1, January-April.

LYNCH, J. 1987. *Hispanoamérica, 1750–1850. Ensayos sobre la sociedad y el Estado*. Universidad Nacional de Colombia, Bogotá.

MURRA, J. 1975. *Formaciones económicas y políticas del mundo andino*. Instituto de Estudios Peruanos, Lima.

ROCHE, M. 1968. *La ciencia entre nosotros y otros ensayos*. Ediciones IVIC, Caracas.

——. 1975. *Descubriendo a Prometeo*. Monte Avila, Caracas.

——. 1976. 'Factors Governing the Scientific and Technological Development of a Country'. In: *Scientia*, No. 111.

——. 1976. 'Early History of Science in Spanish America'. In: *Science*, No. 194.

RODRIGUEZ, S. 1954. *Escritos de Simón Rodriguez*. Sociedad Bolivariana de Venezuela, Caracas.

SAGASTI, F. 1978. 'Esbozo histórico de la ciencia y la tecnología en América Latina'. In: *Interciencia*, Vol. 3, No. 6.

——. 1981. *Ciencia, tecnología y desarrollo latinoamericano*. Fondo de Cultura Económica, Mexico.

12.2

MESOAMERICA

Perla Chinchilla

Three broad divisions can be made in the period under discussion, although they are clearly only approximations: 1785–1820, 1820–64 and 1864–1910.

THE FIRST STAGE (1785–1820)

This corresponds to the period generally known as the 'Enlightenment', and a combination of factors mark it as a key period in the development of 'modern science' in Mexico.

In the first place, it was at this time that 'enlightened ideas' became firmly established among the Creoles. This new outlook had been developing throughout the century in a small group of individuals who formed associations and academies in the country's main cities. From these centres the new ideas were spread through books and other publications with unprecedented speed (Trabulse, 1985: 17). It is worth pointing out that an important factor in the formation of this generation of thinkers was the educational work of the Society of Jesus, although expelled from New Spain in 1767. These Jesuits helped to spread classical humanism, which was opposed to orthodox scholasticism, and to propagate some aspects of the new philosophy, such as atomic theory, and such scientific discoveries as universal gravity, seminal generation, the size of the cosmos, etc. They were also largely responsible for the increased importance attached to the indigenous cultures, the *mestizos* and their role in the founding of Mexican society, which were major sources in the growth of Creole nationalism.

Mexican scientists at that time were primarily 'encyclopaedists' who were active in various fields of knowledge, besides being excellent popularizers of the most recent theoretical and practical scientific discoveries. In this climate, the process began of establishing an institutional framework for 'modern science' during the final years of New Spain, thereby providing the basis for the construction of a 'national science' in the following century. Among the most important institutions founded during this period were the Royal School of Surgery (1768), the Academy of the Noble Arts of San Carlos (1781) and, perhaps most important of all, the Royal College of Mining (1792–1821).

Finally, but no less influential, there were the favourable circumstances resulting from Spain's introduction of an 'enlightened' policy in its American colonies. On the whole, the results for New Spain were encouraging, since it reinforced the process, recently begun, of establishing scientific institutions. The real starting-point was the botanical expedition to New Spain in 1787, whose members included outstanding Spanish naturalists such as Sessé, Cervantes and Mociño, who was born in New Spain. This was followed in 1788 by the inauguration of the Botanical Gardens of Mexico City and the establishment of a chair of modern botany.

THE SECOND STAGE (1820–64)

This period really corresponds to the nineteenth century, which saw the further development of two trends that were to some extent conflicting. The first was the increasingly direct dependence of scientific progress on the socio-economic context in which it developed and its clear links with national interests. The second, running counter to this, was the increasing unity of science beyond national frontiers, which called for closer and more regular communication among scientists. Mexican science in the nineteenth century reflected both general trends, while also displaying its own peculiar characteristics.

Social and economic conditions in Mexico were particularly unfavourable for scientific activity during this period, since it was the time of the greatest political and financial instability of the whole of the nineteenth century. By 1821, at the end of the War of Independence, many of the productive sectors of the country had been devastated: yet the false sense of optimism engendered by the wealth of the newly emergent country, which Humboldt had sought to emphasize, was to cloud any real awareness of the situation for some time.

The development of scientific activity was affected by this situation, and indeed it was to take the country more than thirty years to recover from the blow. Very few scientific works were published during those decades, and what was published was largely the work of scientists who had made advances in their research work during the final years of colonialism. This was true of the work of Andrés Manuel del Río, the discoverer of vanadium, and the *Novorum Vegetabilium* of Lejarza and De la Lave (1824). The few periodical journals that were published, such as the *Registro Trimestre, Mosaico Mexicano* and the *Museo Mexicano*, contained little that was new and were themselves short-lived.

As early as 1822, Vicente Cervantes, the professor in charge of the Botanical Gardens of Mexico City since their foundation, had requested assistance from the emperor Iturbide for their reconstruction and extension. However, by 1824 only the botany classes, which had been suspended for two years, had started up again (Rodríguez, 1992: 141–83). In 1830, Lucas Alamán, proposed that the Botanical Gardens and the Museum of Antiquities and National History should combine, so that they might operate more effectively.

Orozco y Berra, in his *Memoria para la Carta Hidrográfica* of 1856, writes that the Minister of Development and Public Works proposed the compilation of a national atlas that would encompass the history and geography of earlier times, archaeology, zoology, botany, statistics and the geological and geodesic-topographical maps of the Mexico City valley. The wars of the reform period prevented this project from developing.

Although the actual results achieved during this period were comparatively insignificant, it was then that the foundations of 'national science' were laid. Two characteristics distinguish this period from its very beginning. First, support for the process of establishing institutions came from the government. That is understandable if we bear in mind the fact that the elite which was to govern consisted of men educated in the 'enlightened' thinking of the eighteenth century, convinced that 'enlightenment and wealth were key factors in the long-desired march of progress, and it was necessary, consequently, to find ways of developing their potential' (Rodríguez, 1992: 150). In fact, this group included many men who were also concurrently playing an active role in the political life, such as Guadalupe Victoria, the first President of the Republic and a graduate of the College of Mining; Lucas Alamán, likewise a former pupil of the College of Mining and an expert in chemistry and mineralogy, who in 1825 occupied the post of Minister of Foreign Relations and, in that same year, was appointed President of the Governing Board of the recently created Institute of Science, Literature and the Arts; and, as a final example, Melchor Ocampo, a leading figure in the reform movement and one of the outstanding botanists of the century. The development of science was a matter of interest to both liberals and conservatives, and in many cases they joined forces in the common cause. The second factor was the social context in which traditional attitudes prevailed, so that few people were interested in funding scientific research.

The marked emphasis on scientific education rather than on research as such was one feature of the new-born 'national science'. Seen from that point of view, such a preference was logical, both in view of the damage that education had suffered with the vicissitudes of war and by its very ideology. By 1822, it was generally believed that 'progress' could be achieved only through 'freedom of the press for "the encouragement and propagation of enlightenment" and the promotion of "useful knowledge" so as to "dispel the darkness of ignorance"' (Rodríguez, 1992: 143). Political reform was seen as being dependent on the education of young people and public enlightenment.

In addition, the close involvement of science with the interests of the state inclined it towards matters which concerned the state, such as acquiring information about the country, with a view to both the defence of its frontiers and exploiting its economic potential. As a result, it was mainly the natural sciences and geography that were encouraged. In fact, the work carried out by the Geographical and Statistical Society (1833) was the only

clear link between the first and second halves of the century.

THE THIRD STAGE (1867–1910)

The encouragement given to science from then until the end of the first decade of the twentieth century coincides with the consolidation of Mexico as a nation-state. Greater political and economic stability and the triumph of liberalism helped to boost the growth of scientific institutions and make way for the emergence of professional scientists.

Although in many ways there was continuity with the previous stage, certain new and characteristic features of science made their appearance during this stage, both in its exogenous aspects, in terms of the society in which it operated, and in its endogenous aspects, in relation to the paradigms shared by the various groups of Mexican scientists.

Among the former is the controversial subject of positivism and its influence on the intellectual climate of Mexico in the final decades of the century. 'Orthodox liberalism' and 'positivist neoliberalism' are merely two branches of the liberal tradition that can ultimately be traced back to the Enlightenment of the eighteenth century. Positivism represented the 'period of reconstruction' following the liberal revolution, since, according to Comte's philosophy, the development of scientific thought and such modernization was an essential objective if social stability and welfare were to be achieved.

The Enlightenment view that the 'speculative sciences' should yield precedence to the 'practical sciences' reached its apogee with positivism. The admiration for science and the optimism about science teaching that was shared by those belonging to the generation of Gabino Barreda, who introduced the positivist philosophy of Comte to Mexico, had little to distinguish it from the views prevalent during the Enlightenment (Rodríguez, 1992: 330). Positivism became the 'ideology' of the governing elite.

Apart from positivism, the main influence on science in Mexico throughout the century came from France. This connection was strengthened by the French invasion under the aegis of Napoleon III and the subsequent empire of Maximilian. The country was visited by the Comission Scientifique du Mexique (1864–9), whose activities were described in the records published in Paris between 1865 and 1869. They include Boussingault, a naturalist and chemist, Milne-Edwards, a zoologist, and Marié-Davy, an astronomer; although it was, in fact, the mineralogists and geologists who made the most significant contributions. The Mexican corresponding members also included scientists as José G. Ramírez and Velázquez de León.

Owing to the fact that it was mainly through France that Mexican scientists kept in contact with European centres of research and education, Darwinism was introduced to Mexico through French versions, although at the end of the century editions of Darwin's works in English and German circulated. *La Naturaleza*, a journal published by the Mexican Society of Natural History, represents one of the best examples of this process. This journal published a translation from the *Revue Scientifique* of Darwin's work 'The Formation of Vegetable Mould through the Action of Worms', and subsequently likewise translated from the same review the anti-Darwin article by M. Virchow, 'Darwin and Anthropology' (RM2021). In these circumstances, and given the opposition on the part of Comtean positivism, it is clear why Darwinism was late in arriving in Mexico and had comparatively little impact.

Thus, towards the end of the century the conditions existed in Mexico for a more elaborate and authentic understanding of the ideas of contemporary science. A new generation of scientists – many of whom went to study abroad, especially in France – were much better informed, confident of their own abilities and of the importance of their work. Religious and metaphysical concerns, which had existed in one form or another among even the most advanced scientists of the previous generation, were left behind and 'materialism', a basic feature of science in the nineteenth century, had been largely taken on board.

Finally, we should mention the formation of scientific societies and associations towards the end of the nineteenth century and the beginning of the twentieth and, as a result, the launching of a number of new periodicals. The rapid build-up of knowledge made it necessary to establish such institutions, which would provide channels of communication among specialists. However, we need to distinguish between two types of association: those of a strictly scientific nature, whose publications were intended for the scientific community, and second, societies which sought to popularize science as the subject to which great importance was attached in the new 'liberal-positivist' climate mentioned above. Attendance at international congresses increased, as may be seen from the reports of the *Newsletter of the Mexican Society of Geography and Statistics*.

THE SEPARATE AREAS OF SCIENTIFIC INQUIRY

Mathematics

In Mexico, as in many Western countries, including the United States, there was very little study in this field during the first half of the century, in contrast to the continuous and wide-ranging research under way in, above all, France, Germany, England and Italy.

Some original contributions were to be found, however, in textbooks, mostly in the field of the infinitesimal calculus. In pure mathematics, worth noting are the ideas of Diaz Covarrubias, Manuel Gargollo and Manuel Ramírez on the foundations of the infinitesimal calculus, and in mathematical logic the *Examination of the Infinitesimal Calculus from the Logical Point of View* by Gabino Barreda.

However, while European mathematicians were exploring such areas as 'algebraic analysis' or 'non-Euclidean geometry', the calculus based on Leibniz and Newton that was being used in Mexico already belonged to the past.

Physics

At the beginning of the century, it was still widely believed that astronomy and mechanics were the last two natural sciences to which mathematical theories were directly applicable, with the consequence that much less importance was attached to their experimental aspects. However, as the century progressed, this idea gradually changed with the development of mathematical physics and the birth of astrophysics. In these new circumstances, astronomy based on observation took on much greater importance, and this,

together with position astronomy, became the most widely practised form in Mexico. This is clearly shown by the works of Díaz Covarrubias (*New Astronomical Methods* and *Journey of the Mexican Astronomical Commission to Japan to observe the transit of Venus across the Sun*) and those carried out in the National Observatory.

Apart from such observations and determinations of astronomical position, Mexican scientists do not appear to have been fully abreast of the new developments that occurred in approximately the last quarter of the century in classical mechanics. As for the physical sciences as such, according to contemporary systems of classification, i.e. optics, acoustics, magnetism and electricity, only a few studies making vague references to such subjects are to be found. Similarly, there appears to have been little experimental work in these fields.

Chemistry

This is one of the disciplines which developed more rapidly during the century, especially with the emergence of organic chemistry and the chemical industry, while greater interest was taken in inorganic chemistry, especially as it related to mining, in view of the strong tradition in this field. In fact, the work carried out in the nineteenth century was based on the work of the College of Mining, into which the study of modern chemistry had been introduced at the end of the eighteenth century. As a result, metallurgy was one of the first industries stimulated by advances in this field, as may be seen in the article 'Application of Thermochemical Theories to the Metallurgical. Theories of the Amalgamation of Silver', by C. R. Landero. However, the study by M. M. Contreras, in which he proposes the use of the 'assaying of lumps and impurities' in the amalgamation of silver, shows how traditional methods continued to exist alongside the new discoveries.

The relationship between pharmacy and chemistry was formalized. As early as 1843 the first curriculum was devised for the study of pharmacy and included the subject of chemical analysis (Trabulse, 1985: Vol. 1, 190). Among those graduating from this course was the most outstanding Mexican chemist of the day, Leopoldo Río de la Loza. In an area where controversy was still rife – prior to the appearance of 'modern atomic theory' – he carried out research in the field of chemical analysis, principally on salts, a line of research which was continued by his disciples.

Mineralogy

Prior to this century, this term covered the whole field of knowledge related to the mineral kingdom, but separate 'earth sciences' came into being: prehistory grew up alongside geology, while palaeontology and petrography developed in parallel with mineralogy proper. The study of each of these disciplines in Mexico was rooted in the research carried out in the College of Mining, as well as in the work of Humboldt, summarized in his *Geognostic Essay on the Superimposition of Rocks in Both Hemispheres* and the important work by Andrés Manuel del Río, *Elementos de Orictognosia*.

Although no research appears to have been carried out on physical or chemical crystallography, there were at least plenty of statistical studies that provided a systematic classification of the enormous variety of minerals in Mexico.

Those statistics, together with the data obtained in the rest of the scientific world, provided the basis for the classification of crystalline forms and symmetries.

In the lithological classifications that came into being, systems and explanations were based on the observation of rocks and were organized according to their geological origins. There were, for example, the studies carried out by Santiago Ramírez, linked to research on characteristic fossils. Another field of mineralogy investigated during the nineteenth century concerned meteorites. In this field, Mexican scientists joined in the work already being carried out by their colleagues from Europe and the United States.

Finally, it is worth noting the contribution of 'mineralogical collections' to the development of mineralogy. Such collections, together with those from other countries, have not only provided an important basis for research, but have also been very useful for educational purposes.

Geology

Here, too, an attempt was made to catch up with the rapid developments that had occurred at the end of the previous century under the influence of the famous Academy of Freiberg. Work in this field was the result of the combined efforts of individual scientists. New subsidiary branches of specialization were formed, although there were still scientists who dominated vast areas of study and formulated general hypotheses.

During the nineteenth century, geology spread as a vast amount of information was collected covering the whole world. The geology of Mexico aroused the interest of foreign scholars, and most of the geological studies were carried out by members of North American, French and German expeditions. By the second half of the century, there was clear evidence of interest being taken by Mexicans themselves in the study of geology. The first task undertaken by naturalists was the establishment of the stratigraphic scale. This could be achieved only through the gradual development of 'systematic palaeontology', which was then making rapid progress. The interrelationship between these two sciences can be seen in the work of Santiago Ramírez.

During the last third of the century, with the laying of railway lines and the renewed interest in mining, there was growing enthusiasm for geological and mining research, and such explorations led to the publication of geological charts and maps, which had previously been published abroad, as a rule. In 1889, the Mexican Geological Commission (1886) prepared a 'Draft Geological Map of the Mexican Republic' for the International Exhibition in Paris. However, it was not until the beginning of the twentieth century, on the occasion of the tenth International Congress of Geology, held in Mexico in 1906, that a definitive geological map of the country was drawn up.

Geologists and palaeontologists worked together on the problem of establishing the geological eras, and also joined in the discussions on evolution during the second half of the century. As a result, developments in this field of study were closely linked with the state of 'evolutionism'.

Geography

The study of geography received considerable attention, although it never enjoyed sufficient funding. The need to carry out scientific studies and surveys of the country and its coasts, as well as the changes in the northern frontiers, led the government to take an interest in the production of various kinds of maps: atlases, collections of harbour charts, maps of the federative units, etc.

The study of geography in Mexico, with its roots in the tradition established by Humboldt, greatly benefited from the latter's dynamic influence, as in the case of the new concept of 'regional geography'. However, the almost dogmatic acceptance of the *Political Essay* meant that for a long time little attempt was made to revise the geographical, geological and statistical data provided by Humboldt.

Works such as 'The Progress of Geography in Mexico' by Eduardo Noriega, and the 'Memorandum for a Hydrographic Map of the Valley of Mexico', by Orozco y Berra, reveal the efforts made not only to produce maps, but also to develop new methods and solve geographical problems.

The Geographical and Statistical Society published its *Newsletter* between 1849 and 1865, containing geographical descriptions and data of great practical relevance for the time. Furthermore, in 1850, it produced the long-awaited *General Map of the Republic*, the first since Independence, and an *Atlas and Collection of Harbour Charts* containing forty-six maps (Trabulse, 1985: Vol. 1, 197).

However, it was not until 1877, with the establishment of the Geographical Exploration Commission, that all the previous efforts were combined and coordinated. Its plans included the production of a *General Atlas* of the country and by 1914, when the Commission was disbanded, it had published 197 maps on a scale of 1:100,000 (Trabulse, 1985: Vol. 1, 197).

Zoology

The foundations for this field of study had already been laid during the eighteenth century. From these beginnings, thanks to the accumulation of new specimens and the establishment of an increasingly intricate network of intrinsic and extrinsic relationships, scientists arrived at an evolutionist view of the animal kingdom that was undoubtedly the century's major achievement in biology.

A great many works were produced, albeit fewer than in the field of botany. Of particular importance during the first half of the century were the works of Pablo de la Llave, who had spent some time in Europe, where he was director of the Museum of Natural History in Madrid.

During the second half of the century, thanks to advances in chemistry and microscopy, a completely new field of investigation was opened up, covering such subjects as parasitology, embryology and bacteriology. There was progress towards a modern conception of biology in Mexico; but it was not until the end of the century, by which time an evolutionist approach to zoology as a whole had gained wide acceptance, that studies taking a comprehensive view of the subject appeared, as was the case with *Mexican Ornithology* by Alfonso L. Herrera.

On the frontier between biology and medicine, new problems emerged that would have to be solved from the point of view of 'comparative anatomy' and 'animal physiology' and their links with chemistry and physics. Primarily through the French ideas of 'transformism' but also under the influence of the German ideas of the 'philosophy of nature' and English Darwinism, all of which provided the foundations of the new 'life sciences', the new approaches and the new disciplines, such as the palaeontology of vertebrates, embryology, genetics, anthropology and prehistory, took root in Mexico. The studies by Riva Palacio, A. Dugés and I. Ramírez show that, at least from the bibliographical point of view, foreign works were well known in Mexico.

Botany

Clearly this is the one field of study in which Mexico has a particularly long-established and uninterrupted tradition. During the early years of the century, work in this field had little impetus of its own, but followed on from the studies carried out by naturalists active prior to Independence: Mociño, Sessé, Cervantes and Humboldt. During the years following Independence, Vicente Cervantes, his son Julian, author of a number of *Botanical Tables*, and his pupil, M. Bustamante Septién, fought for the survival of the badly damaged Botanical Gardens and the professorships in this subject. An example of that process is provided by the *Novorum Vegetabilium* (1824) by Martínez de Lejarza and De la Llave, the first botanical taxonomy produced after Independence, based on the works of Mociño. It was only towards the middle of the century that Mexican scientists, following in the footsteps of their European counterparts, began to carry out studies using a morphological approach.

Herbariums of Mexican flora, i.e. collections of botanical species, were established throughout the century by both Mexicans and foreigners, who became part of the scientific community, such as Alfredo and Eugenio Dugés, while there is a long list of Mexican naturalists who established collections of plants throughout the country. Worth noting is the work of the Geographical Exploration Commission (1879), which set up a natural history museum to house the collections that it had made. On the basis of an immense mass of data, José Ramírez published in 1902 his encyclopaedic *Popular and Scientific Synonymy of Mexican Plants* (Trabulse, 1985: Vol. 1, 177–8).

Alongside these descriptive works, by the last third of the century there is clear evidence of Mexican scientists' awareness of the latest trends in modern biology, as revealed by the studies on the 'geography of plants' by M. Bárcena, which relate the flora to the environment, the *Essay on the Medical Geography and Climatology of the Mexican Republic* by D. Orvañanos, and the studies on plant physiology that appear in *La Vie Sur Les Hauts Plateaux* by A. L. Herrera and D. Vergara Lope, which was awarded a prize by the Smithsonian Institution for its contribution to the study of the effect of atmospheric pressure on living beings and their organic evolution.

Medicine

Considerable work was carried out in this field throughout the century. The development of modern medicine in Mexico began in 1833 with the opening of the Institute of Medical Sciences, and included the discussion of current doctrines, the application of recently discovered treatments, experimental human anatomy, etc., although these obviously did not replace traditional medicine, which continued to exist alongside these new developments.

Both cause and effect of this new situation were the numerous periodicals published throughout the century, the most outstanding of which was the *Medical Gazette of Mexico*.

Despite these obvious signs of change, Mexican medicine, following in the French tradition more than any other, showed little progress in experimental physiology and laboratory research. Nevertheless, original contributions, even at the experimental level, occurred towards the second half of the century, including the reports of Dr Jiménez on the puncture of hepatic abscesses, carried out from 1840 onwards, together with his studies on the clinical distinction between typhus and typhoid fever, and his work on intestinal embolism; the sterilization practised by Montes de Oca even before Lister, the work of Lucio on leprosy and, at the very beginning of the twentieth century, the research carried out by Uribe Troncoso on bodily fluids and his discovery of the method of gonoiscopy: all of these are examples of Mexican contributions to medicine.

COSTA RICA

The story of science in Costa Rica during the second half of the nineteenth century was mainly one of foreign contributions to exploration, research and technology. For example, in 1856, in the harbour of Puntarenas, boats belonging to the Pacific Mail Company carried out oceanographic explorations, and between 1876 and 1890 a railway was constructed from one side of the country to the other (Camacho, n.d.: 126). Acting in accordance with the European scientific and imperialist interests of the time, several foreigners came to carry out investigations in hitherto unexplored parts of the country. In 1847, the Dane Andrew S. Oersted arrived to study the volcano Irazú, while between 1854 and 1869 the German Alexander von Frantzius was engaged in studying various volcanoes in the country. Between 1855 and 1878, scientists who included Francisco Kurtze, Fernando Streber and Federico Maison, arrived to carry out research in seismology and vulcanology (Camacho, n.d.: 127).

From 1886 onwards, the liberals in Costa Rica introduced educational reforms mainly directed towards the encouragement of science. In furtherance of this aim, the Escuela Normal (advanced teacher training college) was established, and it was decided to bring in teachers from abroad (Camacho, n.d.: 127–8). That same year saw the arrival of Pablo Biolley, an expert in flora and fauna, and a year later Henri Pittier arrived, a teacher of the physical and natural sciences who was to carry out studies in botany, seismology, vulcanology and meteorology (Camacho, n.d.: 128). Pittier later continued his botanical studies in Venezuela.

In the circumstances, the study of natural history flourished in Costa Rica from the 1880s onwards (Gutiérrez, 1986: 105). Of course, the study of flora and fauna initially received the most support, but at the end of the nineteenth and the beginning of the twentieth century, medicine also developed as a result of the contributions of Clodomiro Picado Twight. Having studied in France, Twight was trained in the positivist school, and he influenced this discipline through his research findings in fields such as biology, ophidia, clinical laboratory work, microbiology, pathology, and the physiology of ageing (Gutiérrez, 1986: 106).

CUBA

During the eighteenth century, the Royal and Pontifical University of Cuba trained doctors and mathematicians, although it was not the only institution engaged in this work, and we know that in 1774 the College of San Carlos was the most important centre for training mathematicians, physicists and astronomers. The Jesuits were the main force in spreading scientific knowledge during this century (Anonymous, n.d.: 169).

This period also saw a movement for economic and cultural reform in Cuba through the efforts of the 'enlightened' elite to promote the study of the natural sciences with a view to developing agriculture and the industries connected with the cultivation of sugar cane (Saldaña, 1986: 69–70). The first institutions entrusted with the task of promoting science and technology were the Patriotic Society of Havana (1793) and the Royal Consulate of Agriculture and Trade (1794), both of which were established by Field Marshal Luis de las Casas (Onorio and Gutiérrez, 1994: 20).

These developments created an interest in botany. Although attempts were made as early as 1792 to establish a botanical garden in Havana (Onorio and Gutiérrez, 1994: 26), the plans only came to fruition in 1817, with the inauguration of the Botanical Garden of Havana, whose first director was José Antonio de la Ossa. He was criticized for spending more time cataloguing plants than studying how they might be usefully employed in the agricultural development of the island (Onorio and Gutiérrez, 1994: 177). In 1827, the post of director of the Botanical Garden of Havana passed to Ramón de la Sagra, who, unlike de la Ossa, combined the duties of professor of botany with actual 'field work' in the Botanical Garden (Onorio and Gutiérrez, 1994: 78).

Alongside the development of botany, advances were also made in chemistry on account of its connection with the sugar industry (Saldaña, 1986: 71). As a result, between 1837 and 1845, the regular and systematic study of chemistry, botany and agriculture was promoted, and in 1846, a chair of 'industrial technology' was established (Saldaña, 1986: 71).

Advances also took place in medicine during the nineteenth century. In 1797, a chair of clinical medicine was established in the Military Hospital of San Ambrosio, although it was abolished in 1806. Eight years later, the course reopened, this time with a more modern syllabus and under the management of the famous anatomist Francisco de Paula Alonso, who was subsequently to found the anatomy museum of the Military Hospital of San Ambrosio (Onorio and Gutierrez, 1994: 26). As a result of the development of medicine on the island, in 1848 the Royal and Pontifical University of Cuba published a history of medicine (Anonymous, n.d.: 170).

In order to encourage more rapid development in the sciences, from the 1830s onwards the government of Cuba sought to attract foreigners who would undertake the science teaching. But the project failed for lack of interest abroad (Saldaña, 1986: 71).

In Cuba, as in other countries in the region, the study of science during the nineteenth century was anti-scholastic and favoured a positivist approach (Saldaña, 1986: 72).

It was against this background that Manuel Presas wrote 'The Natural History of Cuba', which served as an introduction to the work by Felipe Poey, *A Natural and Physical Catalogue of the Island of Cuba*. This introduction was of a general character, covering such subjects as zoology, botany, mineralogy, geology and some aspects of museography. Ramón de la Sagra wrote the *Philosophical, Political and Natural History of the Island of Cuba*, a positivist work which, besides basic facts, contains a certain amount of social, political and economic analysis (Anonymous, n.d.: 170).

BIBLIOGRAPHY

ANONYMOUS. n.d. 'El desarollo de las ciencias ilustradas en Cuba'. In: *La ilustración en América Colonial*. n.p., pp. 169ff.

CAMACHO, N. L. A. n.d. *Cultura científica en Costa Rica*. n.p., p. 126.

GORTARI, E. D. 1964. 'La ilustración y la introducción de la ciencia moderna en México'. In: *Memorias del primer coloquio mexicano de historia de la ciencia*. Vol. 2, Mexico, pp. 35–52.

GUERRA, F. X. 1988. *México, del Antiguo Régimen a la Revolución*. Vol. 1. F.C.E., Mexico.

GUTIÉRREZ, J.M. 1986. 'Algunas reflexiones sobre Clodorniro Picado Twight y su contribución al desarrollo de las ciencias médicas y naturales en Costa Rica'. In: *Revista de Filosofía de la Universidad de Costa Rica*, XXIV, p. 105.

LAFUENTE, A.; JOSE SALA CATALA (eds) 1992. *Ciencia Colonial en América*. Alianza Universidad, Madrid.

MORENO, R. 1989. *La Polémica del Darwinismo en México. Siglo XIX*. UNAM, Mexico.

ONORIO, C. N.; GUTIERREZ, T. M. (eds) 1994. *Cuba, la perla de las Antillas: actas de la Jornada sobre 'uba y su historia'*. ed. Doce Calles, Madrid, pp. 20ff.

RODRIGUEZ, L. 1992. 'Ciencia y estado en México: 1824–29'. In: Saldaña, J. J. (ed.) *Los orígenes de la ciencia nacional*. No. 4, Guadernos de Quipú, Mexico, pp. 141–83ff.

SALDAÑA, J. J. (ed.) 1986. 'Marcos conceptuales de la historia de las ciencias en Latinoamérica. Positivismo y economicismo'. In: *El perfil de la ciencia en América*. XII Congreso Interamericano de Filosofía, Cuadernos del Quipú, Guadalajara, pp. 69–70.

TRABULSE, E. 1985. *Historia de la Ciencia en México*. Vols 1, 3 and 4. FCE, Mexico.

12.3

BRAZIL

Francisco Iglesias

Brazil has distinctive features which single her out from other Latin American countries and earn her a special place in the history of the continent. This distinctiveness was more evident in the nineteenth century and far less in the previous and subsequent centuries. In their first 300 years, Brazil and the other colonies had a great deal in common. Spain and Portugal, like other colonial powers, operated similar mercantilist policies.

Brazil's difference lay in the originality of her independence, so different from the rest of South America, and the form of government that arose out of it: a monarchy in the midst of a republican continent. The Brazilian monarchy was the only successful one in this part of the world. All other attempts to establish monarchies were, when they got beyond mere pipe dreams, weak, insubstantial and irrelevant. Nineteenth-century Brazil was unique in South America while colonial rule produced very similar outcomes everywhere. In the twentieth century, the differences between Brazil – already under a republican regime – and the neighbouring republics were less marked despite differences in land areas and populations.

The nineteenth century was chronologically different. It did not run from 1801 to 1900; as pointed out in the Introduction to this volume, it ran from 1789 to 1914. For Brazil it has to be placed differently: from 1808 to 1888 or 1889, in other words, from the arrival of the Portuguese sovereign and his retinue in Rio de Janeiro until the abolition of slavery and the founding of the Republic. Thus it amounts to eighty years and not the usual 100. However, as we must stick to convention, we will cover national history from 1789 to 1914 but with special emphasis on the 1808–88 period.

COLLAPSE OF THE COLONIAL SYSTEM

The Portuguese government made its presence most felt in Brazil in the eighteenth century. Spanish, French and, *inter alia*, English greed, which could have led to the loss of this huge possession, kept the authorities on their toes and prompted them to adopt consistent administrative policies.

While from the East came fine cloths and mineral wealth, Brazil could only offer Brazil wood and plants. No gold could be found despite much prospecting urged on by the riches the Spaniards had plundered from nearby lands. They had to develop farming as a viable economic alternative. Thus the sugar cane plantations – much more than gold and

diamonds that so fired imaginations – became the biggest economic undertaking of the colonial period. The fashionable exploit was to explore the hinterlands departing from the North, the North East or São Paulo.

Trouble on the Iberian Peninsula brought on by Napoleon's expansionist ambitions weakened the Iberian thrones. The colonies took advantage of this to make a push forward. And they succeeded. Between 1810 and 1830 almost all of Latin America broke free and formed new nations. The reactionary Holy Alliance's attempted recolonization failed because of the influence of the United States and, even more, of England, who saw their way to conquer new markets unencumbered.

The New World was to supply the raw materials and an outlet for English goods. A growing awareness and will for emancipation, and European political difficulties caused by French imperialism, were to help South America shake off the ties that bound her to Spain and Portugal. New nations were born, among them Brazil. They did not prolong a flagging feudal system, but espoused the emerging capitalism. These countries were still exploited, but they began the twentieth century politically independent.

THE ARRIVAL OF THE PORTUGUESE ROYAL FAMILY

Fleeing from Napoleon's French army, the Portuguese Royal Family (prince João and his family, his mother Dona Maria (insane and removed from the throne several years earlier) and a numerous retinue, parasites with no tangible functions – more than 15,000 persons plus a further 9,000 who joined them in the course of their sojourn in Rio de Janeiro – came to Brazil. Rio de Janeiro numbered 60,000 inhabitants in 1808 and reached 130,000 in 1818. The city experienced its first spurt of development. Prince João's first move was to throw the country's doors wide open to all countries, which basically provided an opening to English trade. It had to be thus. Portugal was occupied by French forces. There was no choice.

Industrial activities had been prohibited since 1785, in keeping with the mercantilist line, whereby colonies supply raw materials and not processed goods. The ban was now lifted and the government itself promoted cloth manufacturing in the São Paulo and Minas Gerais regions.

Mining, in decline, was given a new impetus. The government took initiatives and brought in European scientists; geologists and mineralogists. An embryonic steel industry could not be sustained. The territory, hitherto closed to foreign scientists, was studied by scholars and explorers, many of whom wrote important books on what they observed or discovered. Mining advanced. Companies with English capital were launched to prospect for gold or precious stones. Not only were foreigners now allowed to enter the country, they were positively encouraged through an organized immigration service. Surprisingly, the first to arrive were the Swiss, then the Germans who headed south, initiating a movement which was to profoundly mark the nation. The Banco do Brasil was founded, again due to pressure from the trading community.

This was the time of early efforts to foster education through setting up schools and promoting higher education in medicine and in military and naval sciences (with a few engineering courses on offer), fine arts and other subjects. The country hosted a French artistic mission in 1816, with famous artists and professors who imparted a new direction in art, the classic style. The Botanical Gardens were laid out and the National Library built. All areas of activity were affected. As Prince Pedro, heir to the Portuguese throne, was married to an Austrian princess and daughter of the Emperor, he imported German-speaking scientists who contributed to the introduction of new cultural interests. Brazil, as advocated by Metternich, was elevated to the status of a united kingdom, including Portugal and the Algarves.

In 1816 Dona Maria I died and Prince João acceded to the throne as Emperor with the title Dom João VI. Napoleon had been defeated and the Portuguese disliked a situation in which they were no longer the centre of the Empire, but a mere dependency under orders from Brazil. The unrest grew and, in 1820, a so-called 'liberal' revolution broke out in Oporto. In fact, the perpetrators were seeking to recolonize: they demanded Dom João's return. They wanted to be at the centre of decision-making. They advocated the constitutionalization of the state and a constituent assembly was convened. Brazilian 'deputies' were elected to take part, but it became apparent that the climate was inimical and they were forced to back out. Dom João, a weak man, had to vote in favour of a constitution that did not as yet exist. He would have preferred to stay in Brazil, where he was happy, but he had to return and was compelled to do so. He returned in 1821. He left his son Dom Pedro in charge as regent of Brazil. This situation was to be short lived. The Brazilian Party was founded by Brazilians and Portuguese with local interests who pressured Dom Pedro. Repeated orders to go home came from Portugal. The march of liberation was becoming relentless, its ranks were growing. Dom Pedro liked power, liked Brazil, and he refused to concede. Thus there occurred a singular process of emancipation led by a Portuguese prince. This does not imply that independence was given away; on the contrary, it was achieved after a tough fight on the part of the native population, a fight which had, in fact, begun with colonization. There were armed revolts, victims to the cause, martyrs.

THE MONARCHY: LEGAL FRAMEWORK AND POLITICS

The Americas were republican. Their first free nation – the United States – became the symbol of contemporary republicanism. Several countries tried out monarchies but none were consolidated. In the New World, only Brazil enjoyed

a stable monarchy for sixty-seven years. This was clearly because of the arrival of the Portuguese Royal Family in 1808 and the regency of Prince D. Pedro from 1821 to 1822. By 1889, with the change of regime in Brazil, all the Americas were republican. On 25 March 1824, Brazil enacted a thoroughly modern constitution. The law was unitary in nature and power totally centralized. It was only partly changed in 1834, through the Additional Act, to make some concessions to decentralization, and further amended by the 1840 Act. This legislation reflected the interests of the ruling class composed of big landowners who defended large landed estates and slavery, which were not however alluded to in the Act. It remained in force until the advent of the Republic in 1889, when it was replaced by a federal concept modelled on the United States. Dom Pedro I abdicated leaving the throne to his son D. Pedro, an even younger man. This episode closed the first phase of Empire. Dom Pedro could only reign when he came of age (18 years). Until then a regent had to be appointed. This regency was overthrown in 1840 by a parliamentary coup perpetrated by the liberals, who placed the under-aged Dom Pedro on the throne, in the so-called 'Majority' campaign. This heralded the longest phase in Brazil's national history, which lasted forty-nine years, from 1840 to 1889.

The Second Reign was led by Dom Pedro II, a studious, quiet, absorbed young man, moderate in all things, unlike his impetuous father. The liberal laws were amended to bolster centralization in the Constitution. The parties, Liberal and Conservative, had already gained strength. They were to alternate in government. The federal concept remained strong but had to wait until the Republic was proclaimed in 1889 to be enacted.

With the advent of the last decade of the century, Brazil entered a new political phase. This period was more affected by social and economic change than by legal innovation. But, even more significant than 1889 was 1888, because it marked the abolition of slavery. It is believed that this event, above all others, led to the overthrow of the monarchy, for the big landowners, who were also big slave owners, resented this measure, which so harmed their interests. This certainly helped precipitate the Republic.

The Republic was born of a coup, perpetrated by an alliance of military officers and politicians who were dissatisfied with the regime. They deplored the premature ageing of Dom Pedro II and could not stomach the idea of a third reign under Princess Isabel. The politicians joined forces with officers, leading malcontents against the crown, who were spurred on by the animosity of some of the senior military. Together, they were powerful enough to work the change.

The military was the first to hold the presidency in the persons of Marshals Deodoro da Fonseca and Floriano Peixoto, who became president and vice-president respectively. There was already a new Constitution. It had been introduced in 1891, drew largely on the United States Constitution and enshrined federalism and presidentialism. In 1894, civilians took power when a São Paulo politician, Prudente de Morais, was elected.

THE ECONOMY

The group that most benefited from independence were landowners, and they organized the state in their own image. As under colonialism, monocropping, large landed estates and slavery predominated. It was a farming economy. Coffee, in increasing quantities, was the main commodity. The volumes were huge. This became one of the biggest international agricultural undertakings, and the country literally supplied the world market. The economic centre of gravity shifted from the sugar-growing North East to the Central Southern region. Policies were fairly consistent. However, they were not properly supported. The coffee-drinking habit, which was very new, soon became popular and sales rose. First cultivated in the North, it spread through the province of Rio de Janeiro and southwards thanks to vast lands and abundant slave labour. It contributed hugely to the economy and was the main export. Coffee production promoted immigration: it began to attract foreigners from 1870. By the end of the century there was a glut, which disrupted the market. The government had to intervene resolutely by taking financial measures, thus departing from the liberal philosophy of the period. It was a defining moment: in 1906, the major producing states – São Paulo, Minas Gerais and Rio – agreed to regulate production and trade. The early decades of the Republic hinged on this commodity. This meant economical and financial measures became unavoidable and had to be stepped up in the twentieth century.

Apart from coffee, we should mention the growing and processing of sugar cane, which had previously been the main crop. Under the Empire, sugar production declined because of competition from the West Indies and from sugar beet.

Industry was affected by a number of factors. Small industrial undertakings were held back for several reasons: investors preferred agriculture because they were certain to have markets; people were not cooperatively-minded and lacked enterprise; the government, whose members were associated with landownership, offered no assistance. Also, the international division of labour, a concept whereby some countries should specialize in agricultural commodities while others specialize in industrial goods, prevailed. No one cared about discrepancies in the prices of goods. Agricultural commodities suffered heavy losses. It was thought wrong for the state to interfere; this was reflected in prices. Brazil, early on, in recognition of her independence, voted for favours to be awarded to other nations in terms of low customs duties, and no support for manufacturing. The latter policy affected the few existing manufacturing industries of cloth, household goods, soap and beverages. This was a hangover from colonial times. When industrial enterprise is discouraged or even banned, as was the case in 1785, small undertakings are doomed to failure.

By 1880, the industrial sector was more aware of its rights. The Industrial Association, of a nationalistic and protectionist bent, was founded to promote the cause. From then on, more factories were built to produce what goods could be produced. Mining stagnated. Initiatives taken during the second decade failed. Later, gold-mining, in the main financed with English capital, spread. Not even pounds sterling could scale up production. Iron was still being cast in small rudimentary foundries. It was only in the last two decades of the century that the first plants of any size, using better technology, were built in Minas Gerais. This was thanks to the Escola de Minas (Mining School) founded in Ouro Preto in 1875. These were the beginnings of advanced technical training, as opposed to the small agricultural and craft schools that had existed previously.

In summary, in the 1850s there was a drive, which was curbed, only to be revived towards the end of the monarchy. Support for industry was now forthcoming in the form of a firm institutional backing, a relatively protectionist customs policy, import payment difficulties, foreign exchange crises, the emergence of a few entrepreneurs, labour disputes, and nascent nationalism. While the above factors were helpful, others were more of a hindrance, like the continuing agrarian order, import restrictions, economic liberalism, a small market, and dependence on external economies, which at times determined outcomes. Before 1888 slave labour, the arrival of foreigners, and several waves of immigrants influenced the situation.

The Republic was seen as a new order, modern and divorced from archaic values. People expected change. In addition, slavery had been abolished. There were increasing numbers of foreigners, many of whom brought with them new and better craft and industrial techniques. However, if the truth be told, the economy remained predominantly agricultural despite the change of regime. From the 1880s, many more factories were built and a trend was set. Importantly, the finance minister of the first republican government favoured industry. Minister Rui Barbosa provided incentives in the form of new methods of payment and greater opportunities for business and enterprise. Overcoming the fear of inflation, Rui spoke out and encouraged others to do so, thus leading to all sorts of factories being built. Some had weaknesses and failed. The whole endeavour was more wishful thinking than a serious attempt to promote industry. In fact, although the policy was short lived and rash, some progress was made. There was a mild shake up, a sort of trial run of novel undertakings. Before the end of the decade, the agricultural economy was back in favour and industry denigrated as being unnatural. Methods of payments were re-restricted.

Brazil had been taking African slaves from the outset to meet labour requirements and make up for the shortfall of white workers. Further, the Portuguese were always closely associated with Africa and deeply involved in the slave trade. As already stated, at the beginning of this period, blacks made up 42 per cent of the population. This trade continued apace since it was very profitable. England, the dominant power, which had prospered on slavery, was now set against it and made trouble by its naval presence. In 1810, a treaty with Portugal to end this traffic was not complied with. A new treaty was signed up to in 1826, when Brazil was already a free country, not to be fulfilled either. In 1831 Brazil joined the treaty, which remained a dead letter.

Upon abolition, the system was doomed to fade away. Abolitionist fervour took hold. Brazil was one of the last countries involved in this trade so contrary to liberal thinking. From small beginnings the movement gained momentum; journalists, writers and associations joined the drive. The first big step was the law freeing the children of slaves: the so-called *Ventre Libre* (Free Womb) Act was passed in 1871. This was the first national abolitionist campaign in which all sectors of society participated. It was the biggest such movement in the history of Brazil.

The struggle against slavery gripped the people and came to dominate politics. 13 May 1888 was Abolition Day. There had remained 723,000 slaves. This is the most significant date in Brazilian history; it completely transformed society and the economy. The monarchy lost the support of the landowners. A little over a year later it fell and the Republic was proclaimed.

Black rebelliousness and society's determination, the resolve of the whole nation more than that of her leaders, put an end to slavery. To complete this victory agrarian reform was required. When there are wages to be paid, a variety of effective methods of payment are needed. The reform was not undertaken and many former slaves flooded into the cities, creating unresolved housing problems. Poorly prepared for urban employment, they constituted a cheap labour force for the industrial boom and became an unskilled proletariat ill-fitted to cope with the new order.

The solution to labour problems is immigration. It seems odd but the government never gave any serious thought to national workers, a fact which was hardly criticized by scholars and politicians. Undeniably, immigration played a decisive role although a lesser one than in the United States and Argentina. Even though it was illegal in colonial times, there were irregular flows of incomers. This history of immigration began with the arrival of the Portugese Royal Family, and the Swiss immigrants to Nova Friburgo in 1819. This influx, like the subsequent ones from southern Germany, had little impact. The trend gradually increased until 1830, when it declined because of the unstable regency. The first phase, according to the expert, Manuel Dregues Junior, extends up to 1850, by which time 21,599 individuals had entered the country. The second phase ran from the enactment of the Slave Trade Act in 1850 to the Abolition Act in 1888.

Brazil, formerly regarded with suspicion by foreigners, became a liveable place. She became attractive thanks to the absence of slaves, improved sanitation (as from the beginning of the twentieth century) and freedom from epidemics, which were very common elsewhere. In the last decade of the century alone the immigration figure was 1,443,892. From the first immigrants up until 1914 the number of entrants amounted to 3,498,495. While the Portuguese, Italians and Spaniards kept coming, they were joined by Germans, Poles, Turks, Arabs and Japanese. The Japanese started arriving in 1908, and settled in São Paulo. Their numbers grew, and in a short time they became one of the most significant groups.

The immigrants' numbers were not nearly as important as the skills they brought with them. These newcomers were better educated and skilled in new and improved agricultural practices. They contributed to the mechanization of farming and higher standards in crafts, trades, industry and manufacturing. Apart from the impact they had on production, they influenced social organization through the dividing up of landed estates and the promotion of small farms. They settled in rural villages or in cities. More importantly, many of them, in particular Italians, Portuguese and Spaniards, who brought their trade union experience with them, made their mark on workers' attitudes. They set up trade unions and associations along anarchist lines to fight for better conditions and higher wages. At the turn of the century, most factories were either owned or staffed by foreigners. The country, conservative, felt threatened and voted for the banishment of undesirables, namely the ringleaders of strikes and similar demonstrations. Hence, their influence spread beyond the introduction of new and improved technologies. They contributed to a growing and even militant political awareness through trade unions and hitherto unknown socialist propaganda. The anarchist ideology advocated by the Spaniards, the Portuguese and the Italians bulked large (Marxism only achieved a degree of popularity in the twentieth century).

INTELLECTUAL ACTIVITIES: IDEAS AND ARTISTIC ACHIEVEMENTS

Education

Very little attention was paid to education in Brazil under the Portuguese. What meagre primary education there was was provided by the Jesuits. The population was scattered over a huge area and only small numbers could be reached. Education had neither content nor relevance. The country had a bigger black population than white, made up of resident servants and slaves who worked on the land or in the mines using rudimentary tools. The Jesuit schools promoted a Counter-Reformation mentality that shunned science and empiricism. Their aim was indoctrination. Enrolments were low since the comfortably off preferred seminaries that trained for the socially desirable priesthood. The more wealthy went to the University of Coimbra (Portugal), which in many ways eschewed modern thinking and opted for a little science and a lot of rhetoric. It trained scholars who then returned home to take up administrative posts.

This flawed system was affected by Pombal's reforms. Pombal was an enlightened if somewhat ambiguous minister. He hated the Jesuits and banished them from Portuguese possessions – metropolitan and overseas – in 1759. The poor primary schools disappeared almost altogether. Disorder reigned until the state took responsibility for education and set up the Royal Schools. Small schools were on the increase and teachers were paid, but it was still a drop in the ocean. Primary education remained woefully inadequate in quantity and quality. No doubt the most important colonial contribution was the Olinda Seminary, founded by Bishop Azeredo Coutinho in 1798 and opened in 1800.

The educational scene changed when the Royal Family arrived. Dom João founded cultural institutions like the Botanical Gardens, the National Library, the Royal Printing Press and establishments that could be likened to institutions of higher education. Social changes provided an opening for them. Although the economy had changed little – it was still agricultural, based on landed estates and slavery – there was an emergent middle class of tradesmen and manufacturers. The Royal Family prodded the country into a new lifestyle featuring business activities and urban services. This trend became more marked upon accession to independence in 1822, hence a larger and more sophisticated civil service was required.

The government set up institutions like the Naval Academies (1808) and the Military Academy (1810), which provided basic advanced technical education for engineers. Two schools of medicine and surgery were set up in Bahia and Rio de Janeiro in 1808, and later developed into modern faculties of medicine. At court, an office of chemistry was set up and an agricultural course held in Bahia. Neither endured. These subjects were not valued. There was no interest either in arts and crafts, which were seen as second-class manual occupations. There was no intellectual or professional status to be gained from them, redolent as they were of slave labour, considered demeaning.

In 1816, the French Artistic Mission visited the country, bringing classicism with it. Led by top-class artists and professors it imposed conventional aesthetics on the period. It inspired the founding of the Royal Academy of Drawing, Painting, Sculpture and Civil Architecture in 1820 – later to become the School of Fine Arts. Thus the Portuguese aristocratic approach to education that disparaged primary and secondary education (despite its usefulness in training for employment) was pursued. Independent Brazil perpetuated this approach, despite the need to train people in administrative skills. Little was actually achieved.

Indeed, the first university would have to wait until the twentieth century (outside the scope of this work). This compares poorly with Spanish-speaking America, which had had several since early colonial days. Thus higher education was patchy, the odd school here and there, but no group of institutions worthy of such a lofty title. In political, public and administrative terms, the two Faculties of Law set up by Dom Pedro I in 1827, in São Paulo and Recife, were more effectual. The task of training senior civil servants fell to them.

In 1834, the first break away from the 1824 Constitution took the form of the federalist-inspired Additional Act, whereby the provinces were empowered to legislate on education. It became a responsibility shared with central government. The authorities still did very little for schools. While there was some interest in secondary and higher education, oddly there was no understanding of the importance of primary schooling. This latter fell to the politically unstable provinces, who had no funds. There were frequent ministerial changes and no administrative continuity. This led to private establishments, particularly religious orders, taking over education. A sorry reflection of the situation was the mere 250,000 pupils enrolled in primary school in 1888, when the population already stood at 14 million. Agricultural and arts and crafts schools were small and had few pupils. They were not popular in a society that fed on aristocratic ideals. These, it will be remembered, derived from slavery and the low esteem in which manual work was held.

In the 1870s, advanced technical education did better when the Central School became the Polytechnic School and the Ouro Preto Mining School, founded on the French model, began turning out top-class professional engineers and geologists. The Republic retained the system. The 1891 Constitution still enshrined decentralization. It was federal in conception and placed responsibility for higher and secondary education in the hands of central government and primary education and primary teacher training (usually for girls) in the hands of the states (formerly the provinces). The boys went to the few not very popular technical schools. Society had become more complex; increasing industrialization and urbanization meant salaried employment. Under federalism, state governments required more sophisticated administrations. Civil servants had to be better educated, hence an improvement in secondary and higher education and a boost to primary education. A middle class began to emerge as the master-slave duality, typical of the colonial and imperial eras, was overcome. But change was slow in coming. More attention was given to education. Reforms were enacted, but the legislation remained a dead letter. Radical modernizing change would have to wait until 1930 and beyond. It was only in the second half of the century that the country truly espoused modernity.

Ideas and art

As we have noted, in the course of the nineteenth century the Brazilian population grew from 3 to 19 million inhabitants. These were small numbers for a country the size of a continent. Large stretches of land like Amazonia and the central western region were sparsely populated. Most of the population was concentrated around the capital, in the Rio de Janeiro, Minas Gerais and São Paulo provinces. The south was fairly thickly populated. The north and north-east held the indigenous and mixed blood (predominantly Indian) population of whom there were few outside these regions. There was a significant number of blacks along the seaboard stretching from the north-east to Rio de Janeiro and big settlements in the hinterlands of Bahia and Minas Gerais. In and south of São Paulo, because of the huge influx of immigrants during this period, the whites were in the majority. Brazilians are mostly of mixed blood due to intermarriage between Indians and whites, blacks and whites and, to a lesser extent, between Indians and blacks.

In Brazil it is difficult to pinpoint the origins of customs, techniques, ideas, philosophies and creativity in both artistic and scientific endeavour; it is hard to say what part the indigenous peoples, the Indian mixed-blood population, the blacks or the European immigrants played. There was so much intermingling that it is impossible to ascribe basic ideas, approaches, social or economic practices, techniques, philosophies or styles to any one group. Undoubtedly, profound change came about over those hundred years. Records attest to commendable and vigorous efforts fired by a desire and a readiness for change often hindered by a fear of the new and slavish imitation of things foreign, especially European (considered more worthwhile), whether imported or merely read about.

The realm of ideas

Brazil's contribution to philosophical thought was not very original. As a new country with no scholarly tradition and a deficient educational policy, she could not be expected to achieve excellence in philosophy. Generally, ideas came from abroad, virtually always from Europe. However, these were filtered through national specificities born of the meeting of diverse cultures. Only ideas consonant with native lifestyles were assimilated. They were adapted to native mentalities, which had originated and evolved in a different way. The distinctiveness brought to imitations was more spontaneous than deliberate. Indians and blacks have an imagination and a world of their own. Some of it rubbed off on the whites. Exchanges between the various communities fashioned the Brazilian way of life.

Quite apart from the impact on practices and customs, which has been studied in depth by historians, there are less tangible features related to beliefs and outlook. Clearly this was not explored during the colonial period before the advent of the press and books and in the absence of schools. Once the nation became free in the nineteenth century, we note a degree of intellectual curiosity. This began to emerge before 1822, after the Royal Family arrived (1808) and founded schools, a great library, museums, institutions of scholarship and the press. Portugal, the colonial power, had little to offer. She did not excel in science or technology and was even less original in philosophy. Hence her contribution, if any, was small. While Portugal was an important expansionist power in the fifteenth and sixteenth centuries and discovered new lands expanding to the known world, she failed to build on her achievements and became a second-class power in late Renaissance Europe. Distinguished authors like Antero de Quental or Antonio Sergio have fiercely criticized Portugal, in this and the past centuries, for clinging to old ways and thinking. The more lucid Portuguese shared this view. Consequently, Brazil received a paltry legacy.

In any event, if somewhat parsimoniously, the country fostered philosophic enquiry. The uneducated, the bulk of the population, because of religious influence, mainly Jesuitical, confused ideas with religious beliefs. One would have imagined that the scholastic movement was significant with the works of Thomas Aquinas. However, it was not. A fragile, inconsistent, second-hand Thomism was cultivated. The small elites claimed to be Catholics but their faith was superficial. As father Julio Maria wrote in *Catholicism in Brazil* (1900), Catholicism was mere 'ceremonies which do not edify, religious fervour devoid of spirituality, prayers bereft of sincerity, processions seen as entertainment and feast days which neither gain from nor contribute to the glory of God'.

More than scholasticism, eclecticism, which had a huge following in France, was in vogue. Now, eclecticism, which failed to produce anything worthwhile anywhere, could hardly have been expected to do better here. However, it was the most cultivated school. Its founder was friar Francisco de Mont'Alverne, a famous orator during the first half of the century. He left only one work, the *Compêndio de Filosofia* (Compendium of Philosophy) published in 1859. He followed in the footsteps of Victor Cousin, the most famous and influential French eclectic. Gonçalves de Magalhães was amongst Mont'Alverne's students in the Rio de Janeiro seminary. His best work was done in Paris.

The system was intrinsically poor, ill-conceived and lacking in clarity; it attempted to reconcile differing opinions and attitudes. It never made a place for itself in the universal history of philosophy nor in Brazil despite its popularity. This latter was probably due to it being perceived as easier and more adaptable. One can see why it prospered in a country that was just beginning to explore the possibilities of the intellect with no local tradition to draw on.

In the 1870s, a new message began to take hold: positivism, a philosophical school with mystical and scientific dimensions, that lent it greater appeal. August Comte's ideas probably gained ground in France more because of their emotional appeal and humanism, than because they were a critique of society and of established ideas. This was a new system of thought with many followers. It was only successful outside France in two South American states, Mexico and Brazil, especially the latter. Towards the end of the first half of the nineteenth century, there were courses in medicine, engineering and law. The public were being educated. The 'law of the three estates' and Comte's writing became reference works. In a country with scant education and then only rhetorical education, science, mathematics, biology and sociology elicited a keen interest in those who did not subscribe to the ideas of scholasticism or eclecticism. Criticism of theology and metaphysics, the proclamation of the advent of state positivism, convinced people and won supporters, especially at the Polytechnic School and the medical schools. This philosophy first emerged outside politics amongst medical students. Increasing reference was

made to the works and ideas of the French philosopher. The thinking spread from the scientific to the social realm in 1865 when Francisco Brandão Junior published *A escravatura no Brasil* (Slavery in Brazil). This short piece created quite a stir, almost an outrage.

That same year 1865, the São Paulo-born physician Luis Pereira Bareto, who had trained in Brussels, where he encountered and espoused positivist thinking, returned to Brazil. Shortly afterwards, in 1874, he published the first volume of his work *As Três filosofias (Filosofia Teológica)* (The Three Philosophies (Theological Philosophy)), followed, in 1876, by the second volume *Filosofia Metafísica* (Metaphysical Philosophy), in 1880 by *O Positivismo e a Teologia* (Positivism and Theology) and, in 1901, by *O seculo XX sob o ponto de vista brasileiro* (The Twentieth Century from the Brazilian Point of View). The author attempts to prise science free of formerly all-pervading Catholic thinking and offer new directions, as had been done forcefully in Europe at the end of the century. The debate spread beyond medicine and other exclusive areas to encompass criticism of society at large.

The Miguel Lomos and Teixeira Mendes duo was much more militant than the positivists had been. They were like evangelists constantly keeping the debate on national issues going. They were religious positivists. They were prolific writers, and in particular, produced the *Apostolado Positivista do Brasil* (The Brazilian Positivist Apostolate), the first issue appearing in 1881. They visited Paris, and emulated the famous Religion of Humanity through worship and debate on major national issues. They addressed all matters, mapping out the conduct to be adopted by followers of their creed. The monarchy came to an end. It was shaken by the war with Paraguay and the end of slavery and fraught with religious and military conflicts. Students of the Military School, where Professor Benjamin Constant Botelho de Magalhães taught, turned to positivism. Magalhães played a central role in establishing the Republic. Comte's teachings were important to the movement. This philosophy marked the end of the century as eclecticism, although to a lesser extent, had the first fifty years.

In the last thirty years of the century a new current emerged. The materialists believed in the theory of evolution as propounded by Darwin, Spencer and the highly regarded German, Haeckel. They generated an enthusiastic following whose writing shocked and increased their influence. (This work, on the whole, was uperficial, misconceived and peddled poorly understood concepts. Many of the authors were inferior to their European counterparts.) German works became popular and there was a fondness for things German. These were emulated by authors of questionable talent. Tobias Barreto and Silvio Romero, who taught in Recife and in Rio de Janeiro, were the better exponents.

Tobias set a fashion; he became a touchstone for many members of the new generation. Silvia's erudite output was large but he did not achieve immortality. A tireless worker, he produced texts on philosophy in Brazil. He had more of a penchant for history than for philosophy. He was passionately interested in Brazil and things Brazilian and wrote extremely useful books, the foremost of which was *Historia da literatura brasileira* (The History of Brazilian Literature). Much of his work exhibits sociological discernment. His chief mentor was Spencer, a more profitable influence than the Germans who had inspired his friend Tobias. Farias Brito also contributed with books written at the end of the nineteenth century and the beginning of the twentieth century. He was associated with the German school, as he had spent time with the Recife school authors, but showed some independent thought. While Tobias and Silvio were close to materialism, Farias Brito was a spiritualist. He was an educated, well-read man who robustly opposed contemporary Brazilian thinking. His influence made itself felt more after his death when poets and other authors were drawn to spiritualism. Farias Brito revealed the inadequacies of the intellectual climate.

Legal thinking

Until 1822, Brazil's laws were made in Portugal. Their inspiration came from the University of Coimbra where lawyers were trained. This institution turned out young Brazilians with a good technical grounding, destined to be legislators or lawyers. Despite the Marquês de Pombal's modernizing reform, outdated teachings were not all removed. Coimbra trained the Portuguese senior civil servants who continued to administer Brazil for a number of years after independence. Many politicians in government and in the legislature were Portuguese-born or Brazilians educated in the Coimbra tradition. Under Dom Pedro I, law courses had already been set up in São Paulo and Pernambuco in 1827. The standards were disappointing during the early years. However, as time went by, highly qualified graduates emerged, as can be seen from the contribution politicians, administrators and writers made to the nation. Many young people chose to read law.

The newly independent nation was in need of organization, of a legal framework. Many able people were available to complete the task. The 1823 Constitution already reflected the work of many talented individuals and scholars, as evidenced by the draft submitted by Antônio Carlos. The draft, however, got no further than a preliminary debate before it was decided to dissolve the Assembly. Nevertheless, the following year a technically sound constitution was enacted which testified to the knowledge of its framers. It was shortly followed in 1830 by the Criminal Code. While this was still in the pipeline, discussion began on the Penal Procedure Code enacted in 1832. The latter was passed at the time of the first Emperor's abdication. It was ultra-liberal and reactions were so strong that in 1841 it had to be made more conservative, even reactionary, and its very nature was changed. Another code, the Commercial Code, gave rise to much debate; the bill had its first reading in 1835, but only became law in 1850. The main code, the Civil Code, still had to be tackled. The Filipes Code of 1603 was still in force. It dated back to an epoch that upheld the liberal ideas of the sixteenth to the eighteenth centuries legitimized by the French Revolution. It was essential to discard the old laws of the kingdom still in force after independence. Legal experts produced various drafts, which were neither finalized nor processed through official channels. Under the Republic, in 1898, Clóvis Bevilacqua made a proposal, which, because of endless discussion, was only adopted in 1916. Apart from these laws, which required considerable legal knowledge, a new federalist and presidential Constitution was framed for the Republic in 1891. It drew on theoretical work done by legal experts and others, generally professors of law, from José da Silvá Lisboa to Clóvis Bevilacqua.

Economic thinking

Under Portuguese domination many studies of the economy were produced. However, most of this work was superficial. There was nothing like an in-depth economic analysis. This was only to be expected, as economics was a new science. To boot, a colony ruled by a power like Portugal (or more generally, Iberia) with no particular interest in the economy could hardly produce scientific texts worthy of the name. Some of their predecessors, it should be remembered, exhibited great powers of observation and produced edifying reference works on the economy before the nineteenth century.

Turning to the nineteenth century, quite early on in 1804, José da Silva Lisboa – the future Vicount de Cairu – published *Principios de Economia Política* (Principles of Economics), a fine piece of work on all accounts. Based on Adam Smith, on classic liberalism, it displays some originality; it was not mere repetition but showed a deep understanding of the original text. He was a prolific writer and went on to publish many more books, but never again reached the critical excellence of the 1804 text, one of the most outstanding in the Brazilian social sciences bibliography. When Silva Lisboa arrived in Brazil in 1808, he influenced the policies adopted by Regent Dom João. The prince appointed him to the economics chair. This was the first in the world (France created its first chair of economics in 1816). However, it came before its time and did not attract students. The author's other works were less important and addressed many topics. Economics got off to an early start in Brazil, but was unable to sustain any momentum before the twentieth century.

Apart from the works and authors mentioned, advanced courses in economics were of a high standard and shaped the discipline. We have already alluded to the introduction of law courses in São Paulo and Pernambuco in 1827, which offered classes in economics, and state finance and accounting. The teaching was based on the works of Adam Smith, Malthus and Ricardo, as well as Say, Sismondi and Godwin. Clearly, classical liberalism and socialistic criticism of the system prevailed in the eighteenth century, as illustrated in the work of the Swiss Sismonde de Sismondi and the Englishman Godwin. James Stuart Mill, more a classical thinker, predominated in Pernambuco.

Some of the professors became famous through their lecturing or their books. After 1889, with the advent of the Republic and federalism, new law schools were founded: in Bahia in 1891, and a little later in Minas Gerais in 1892, in Porto Alegre and Rio Grande do Sul in 1902, and in Ceara in 1903. Other sources were used, in particular the German historical school. The law curricula naturally concentrated on legal matters and paid scant attention to economics, which did not help the latter's development.

Another law school, the Rio de Janeiro Polytechnic School, developed along different lines and, from 1864, taught economics. This was a long-established school whose first professor was Jose Maria da Silva Paranhos, Viscount of Rio Branco, who taught there for thirteen years. He was professor of mathematics and a believer in classic liberalism, but one who applied it flexibly to politics. Paranhos also taught at the Military School and started a trend, which was later picked up by Vieira Souto and others who were engineers and not lawyers. They did not favour a mathematical approach to economics but used mathematics in a different way to that employed in law courses. Scholars made more systematic use of mathematics and statistics in the twentieth century.

Historiography

While history has been studied since ancient times (as shown in the discoveries of past civilizations), during the Middle Ages and into modern times it took the form of chronicles. In other words it was a descriptive exercise, which sought to record significant events. It was only in the nineteenth century that a more critical and rigorous approach emerged and the so-called subsidiary sciences, which provided the researcher with analytical tools, were also put on a strict footing. The social sciences, like politics, sociology and anthropology, gained consistency. These are the disciplines needed to construct the theories used to interpret and to sharpen criticism and comprehension. The nineteenth century is rightly known as the Century of History. This situation was, however, relatively new throughout the world and even more so in newly independent countries like Brazil. Strictly speaking, the phenomenon is contemporary, although noteworthy works were produced in the nineteenth and earlier centuries; but, as was the case throughout the world, history was generally seen as a mere record of events.

Brazilian historiography did not amount to much. There were very few titles and amongst those even fewer significant ones. The advent of independence brought no change; the chronicle mentality continued with dissertations and annals. These constituted extremely valuable source material but contained no analysis.

The setting up of the Brazilian History and Geography Institute in 1838 provided a framework for sound work to commence. As was the case in the greatest European centres like Germany, serious efforts were made to gather source material upon which to base research. The seminal work was the *Monumenta Germaniae Historica* begun in 1819 and added to throughout the century until it comprised many volumes. Erudition grew, as did the so-called subsidiary subjects; documents which had been lost through negligence were reconstituted and ancient scripts deciphered. At the outset the Institute's research could rival any other. It was utterly modern, as illustrated by its publication *Revista*, an important journal that described and analysed past and present developments. Later the Institute's influence waned somewhat.

Between 1810 and 1819, the romantic poet Robert Southey wrote a remarkable *History of Brazil* in three volumes. This was the first sensitive and critical overview of the country. It was translated and published in six volumes in Rio de Janeiro in 1862. In 1840, the Institute held a competition on the 'Right way to write the history of Brazil'. The winner was a German, Karl Friedrich Philip Von Martius, a naturalist who lived in Brazil from 1817 to 1820. He also wrote an outstanding botanical work – *Flora Brasiliensis* – and a wide-ranging travelogue, *Viagem ao Brazil* (A Journey to Brazil), in three volumes, jointly with J. Von Spix, published in Munich in 1823 and 1824.

This prize-winning text shows a fine grasp of complexity on the part of a foreigner at a time when native citizens were still ignorant. He outlined a model which departed from the then favoured chronological record and which was often copied later. It paved the way for the first highly commended major history of Brazil, penned by Varnhagen of the Institute. Indeed, Francisco Adolfo de Varnhagen, native of São Paulo and of German parentage, was the first great Brazilian historian. He was a tireless researcher, as is evident from his *História Geral do Brasil* (A General History of Brazil), published in 1854 and 1857. He was closely associated with the Institute and did most of his soundly documented work there. His *História* was for many years considered the official version and is still read today. Varnhagen was well travelled; he lived in various European countries where he raided the archives to add to his store of knowledge and he wrote more books. He unearthed some remarkable manuscripts, such as chronicles from the early centuries. He overcame his racialist and aristocratic prejudices, but his monumental contribution was as the founder of a native historiography.

Varnhagen had a number of lucid and productive followers, but the old habit of compiling chronicles persisted. We will by way of example cite a few major authors and works. Joaquim Felicio dos Santos, the country's most representative romantic historiographer, wrote the *Memórias do Distrito Diamantino*, a fine piece in many ways. Joaquim Nabuco, an erudite and dedicated man, was the author of many books and knew how to organize his material. Some of his writings, mostly produced in the last ten years of his life, dealt with historical matters. He will, however, be most remembered for his great three-volume book *Um estadista do Império* (A statesman of the Empire), published between 1897 and 1899. This thoroughly documented and admirably structured masterpiece of Brazilian political history retraces the period through a biography of the author's father, who was an influential politician and an accomplished lawyer.

During the same period – before 1914 – the prolific writers Oliveira Luma and Pandiá Calógeras penned essential works. There were still others like Manoel Bomfim, a sharp critic, whose output was original and provocative. The most significant author, even today, who began work in the nineteenth century, was Capistrano de Abreu. His main work, *Capitulos de Historia Colonial* (Chapters of Colonial History), which appeared in 1907, constituted the first in-depth account of the colony. I believe this incomplete list will suffice.

Artistic production

Literature

There was something of a literary tradition already established by the nineteenth century. In the seventeenth century important baroque works were produced by authors of great calibre like the Bahia poet Gregório de Matos or the prose writer and orator Antônio Vieira, a Portuguese who spent a lot of time in Brazil. In the eighteenth century there were still remnants of Enlightenment and Arcadian poetry, with names like Basílio de Gama, Santa Rita Durão, Cláudio Manuel da Costa, Tomás Antônio Gonzaga and Alvarenga Peixoto. They were all influenced by their Portuguese contemporaries and were the forerunners of the romantics who came several decades later. These tendencies became even stronger after Independence, when, alongside political freedom, there was a desire for New World creativity.

Romanticism, the pre-eminent school in Europe during the first half of the century, also had its exponents here. The first of them, Gonçalves de Magalhaes, published *Suspiros poéticos e saudades* (Poetical Sighs and Nostalgia) in 1836. Here we see the influence of the French authors who had knocked classicism off its pedestal by introducing new themes and lighter forms freed from rigid patterns. The same process took place in Brazil; there was much discussion on the nature of man – especially Amerindian man, less on the black man – but it was all quite superficial with no real sense of a new philosophy. The romantics were the heirs to Olympus; they spoke of other lands; they abandoned the gods for man. The list is long but we will mention a few, all of whom were poets: Gonçalves Dios, Álvares de Azevedo, Casimiro de Abreu, Fagundes Varela, Castro Alves and Sousândrade. The main exponents of romantic fiction were Manuel Antônio de Almeida, Joaquim Manuel de Macedo, José de Alencar and Bernardo Guimarães. Their books gained a wide readership and some of them, for instance Alencar's, are still read today. There were playwrights, but only a few of their works have survived. Outstanding among them was Martins Pena, who in a short life wrote many plays, in particular comedies, and whose popularity endures.

After 1850, realism gained ground. This was another French import, which was espoused by writers of fiction. Machado de Assis, the greatest of them all, wrote many stories and novels, some of which belong to Brazil's finest literature. His poetry and plays did not reach the same heights. Other important realists were Raul Pompéia, Aluísio Azevedo, Franklin Távora, Inglês de Sousa and Adolfo Caminha. They depicted regional and rural life as well as scenes from the backwoods and the towns. Around the turn of the century, their art declined as decadentism appeared in Europe.

Some authors like Macedo, Gonçalves Dios, Castro Alves, José de Alencar, Machado de Assis and Coelho Neto took an interest in drama, but they only produced a few outstanding plays. Artur Azevedo wrote abundantly for the theatre. However, Corpo-Santo, whose real name was José Joaquim de Campos Leão, was even more remarkable. His work was too modern for his epoch and has become more famous since the advent of the contemporary theatre of the absurd. Sílvio Romero, José Veríssimo and Araripe Júnior, were the main exponents of literary historiography and criticism. At the end of the nineteenth century and the beginning of the twentieth century, despondency set in. A few writers, however, like Graça Aranha, Coelho Neto and Afonso Arinos, soldiered on. The most important name was Lima Berreto, who was both prolific and highly creative. His skills lay in the world he created rather than in his artistry. Apart from Lima Berreto and Euclides da Cunha, the writers of the first twenty years compared poorly with those of the late nineteenth century. Euclides, a fine historian, is best known for his literary masterpiece *Os sertões* (The Backwoods), published in 1902. This increasingly admired work, often copied but never equalled, explores issues that are vital to Brazil, such as highway robbery and the millenarian heresy.

Poetry emulated the scintillating Parnassian school. Alberto de Oliveira, Raimundo Correin, Olavo Bilac and Vicente de Carvalho joined the ranks. Rui Barbosa, with his mastery of the language and his love of effects, espoused Parnassianism in his prose, in his journalistic and legal writings as well as in his oratory. Symbolism, couched in a different philosophy and form, also came from France. It won many enthusiasts and produced two outstanding poets: Cruz e Sousa and Alphonsus de Guimarães.

Nineteenth-century literature began with a whimper but became more robust with the advent of romanticism and later realism. In the early years of this century, the works of previous centuries lived on for a while and then faded away. The 1920s were something of a vacuum, which explains the critical effervescence and the protests which gave rise to modernism and a quest for new directions as from 1922. In summary, literary works exhibited more culture and pertinence than did philosophical writings. Sensitivity and imagination prevailed over rigorous criticism, systematic analysis, enquiry and reflection. The epoch was more creative than it was learned.

BIBLIOGRAPHY

ALMEIDA (DE), R. 1942. *História de Música Brasileira*. 2nd edn. F. Briguiet & Cia, Rio de Janeiro.

AZEVEDO (DE), F. 1943. *A cultura brasileira*. Instituto Brasileiro de Geografia a Estatística, Rio de Janeiro.

——. 1956. *As ciências no Brasil*. Edições Melhoramentos, São Paulo.

BELO, J.M. 1969. *História da República*. 6th edn. Companhia Editora Nacional, São Paulo.

BRADFORD BURNS, E. 1966. *A Documentary History of Brazil*. Alfred A. Knopf, New York.

CALMON, P. 1975. *História de D. Pedro II*. 3 vols. Editora José Olímpio, Rio de Janeiro.

CHACON, V. 1965. *História das idéias socialistas no Brasil*. Editora Civilização Brasileira, Rio de Janeiro.

COSTA, J. C. 1956. *Contribuição à História das idéias no Brasil*. Livraria José Olímpio, Rio de Janeiro.

FREIRA, G. 1945. *Brazil: An interpretation*. Alfred A. Knopf, New York.

——. 1946. *The Master And the Slaves*. Alfred A. Knopf (translated by Samuel Putman), New York.

——. 1963. *The Mansions and the Shanties*. Alfred A. Knopf (translated by Harriet de Onis), New York.

FURTADO, C. 1963. *The Economic Growth of Brazil*. University of California Press (translation Ricardo W. da Aguiaru and E. C. Drysdale), Los Angeles.

GRAHAM, R. 1968. *Britain and the Onset of Modernization in Brazil (1850–1914)*. Cambridge University Press, Cambridge.

HEITOR, L. 1956. *150 anos de música no Brasil (1800–1950)*. Livraria José Olimpio, Rio de Janiero.

JOHNSON, J. J. 1964. *The Military and Society in Latin America*. Stanford University Press, Stanford.

LEVINE, R. M. 1978. *Pernambuco in the Brazilian Federation (1899–1937)*. Stanford University Press, Stanford.

LUZ, N. V. 1961. *A luta pela industrialização do Brasil (1808–1930)*. Difusão Européia do Livro, São Paulo.

MAGALDI, S. 1962. *Panorama do Teatro Brasileiro*. Difusão Européia do Livro, São Paulo.

MANCHESTER, A. K. 1933. *British Preeminence in Brazil: Its Rise and Decline*. University of North California Press, Chapel Hill.

MARTINS, W. 1978–9. *História da Inteligência Brasileira (1550–1960)*. 7 vols. Editora Cultrix, São Paulo.

PRADO, C. (JR). 1933. *Evolução Política do Brasil*. Editora Brasiliense, São Paulo.

——. 1945. *História Econômica do Brasil*. Editora Bresiliense, São Paulo.

ROMERO, S. 1953. *História da Literatura Brasileira*. 4th edn, 5 vols. Livraria José Olímpio, Rio de Janeiro.

SKIDMORE, T. E. 1974. *Black into White: Race and Nationality in Brazilian Thought*. Oxford University Press, New York.

VERISSIMO, J. 1954. *História da Literature Brasileira*. 3rd edn. Livraria José Olímpio, Rio de Janeiro.

WIRTH, J. 1977. *Minas Gerais in the Brazilian Federation (1889–1937)*. Stanford University Press, Stanford.

12.4
THE RÍO DE LA PLATA

Luis Alberto Romero

THE VICEROYALTY OF THE RÍO DE LA PLATA, 1776–1810

The creation of the Viceroyalty of the Río de la Plata in 1776 transformed social and cultural conditions in the southernmost region of the Spanish empire in America. Most profoundly affected were Montevideo, the navy anchorage, and Buenos Aires, the capital and port of this new political and economic zone, extending to Upper Peru and its silver mines.

Buenos Aires, as the main Río de la Plata port, engaged in a considerable volume of trading that was somewhat passive until Spain's political and naval problems, apparent since 1795, afforded scope for an active and independent style of doing business. The commercial dynamism of Buenos Aires stimulated the growth of cattle ranches producing leather for export, a basic activity requiring minimum technical skills. In the interior regions of the viceroyalty, economic activities – small-scale farming, cattle-raising and crafts – were developed to meet the needs of Upper Peru.

The late eighteenth century saw a marked cultural renewal, within the confines of the established culture. This was not an abrupt shift but a steady process during which new ideas were incorporated in the scholastic tradition. The traditional centre of learning was the University of Córdoba, founded at the beginning of the seventeenth century and run by the Jesuits until their expulsion in 1767. In Córdoba theology was studied and all instruction was subject to twofold ecclesiastical and political censorship, which admitted the new ideas into the culture in moderate and measured doses. Thus, with reference to Aristotle, talk began to turn around the new physics of Descartes and Newton, if only to criticize it. In 1801 the rector decided to purchase an experimental physics 'laboratory' equipped with various 'machines'. His request for authorization was turned down by the city council, which argued that the university should teach theology, while conceding that theoretical physics could be developed. The rector did, however, find strong backing among the chief administrative authorities, including the viceroy, in favour of the teaching of experimental physics.

The gradual acceptance of the century's innovations occurred on a broader scale in Montevideo, where in 1787 a chair of philosophy was established at the Franciscan College, and above all in Buenos Aires, where efforts to establish a university began in 1771. The ecclesiastical chapter decided that the new university should teach modern physics as a subject in its own right, separate from Aristotle. Opposition from Córdoba blocked the founding of the university. Nevertheless, the Reales Estudios, for studies at the primary level, opened in 1773 and the Real Colegio de San Carlos started up in 1783, admitting a student body that included the future leaders of the revolution. But it was not there that they came into contact with the new ideas, since apart from a few additional modern features, instruction kept to the confines of scholasticism.

Beginning in 1790, the pace of the intellectual renewal accelerated, bringing expanded trade to Buenos Aires. Books and periodicals, full of fresh ideas, began arriving from Spain and a few young men, like Manuel Belgrano, went abroad to study. One sign of the times was the founding of the printing house which, in 1802, launched the *Telégrafo Mercantil*, the first newspaper in the Río de la Plata region. New ideas were circulating just as they were in the Spain of Charles III. There was nothing subversive about them. The monarchy and the church shared the concern of the educated classes for the well-being of the people and provided them with powerful backing for their ideas. Manuel Belgrano, for example, was appointed by the king in 1794 to the post of Secretary of the Consulate, from which he carried on intensive renewal activity.

Belgrano and his circle were interested less in creating new ideas than in adapting those that were fashionable in Europe. For example, according to the teaching of the physiocrats, agriculture – which represented civilization – should be promoted in order to create an alternative to the huge expansion of cattle-raising, which was already in the offing. Hipólito Vieytes expounded these ideas in the *Semanario de Agricultura*, founded in 1802, and Manuel Belgrano expanded on them in the *Correo de Comercio*, which appeared early in 1810. Trade, too, came to be associated with the opening of new horizons, the dissemination of ideas, and civilization, a theory put forth by Lavardén in his book *Nuevo aspecto del comercio en el Río de la Plata* (New Aspects of Trade in the Río de la Plata Region); the easterner Dámaso Larrañaga used much the same words in 1816 at the inauguration of the Montevideo public library. In this respect the interests of the intellectuals coincided with those of the Buenos Aires traders.

In Buenos Aires cultural and scientific issues were early associated with the more immediate needs of society: scientific knowledge was appreciated insofar as it could help resolve practical problems. In 1798 the *Protomedicato* of Buenos Aires was established to license those practising medicine, to meet public health needs, which included vaccination against smallpox, and to train new doctors. Medicine was first taught in 1801 and the first intake of doctors graduated in 1808. In 1799, on the initiative of the consulate, two schools were founded: a school of design, which closed shortly afterwards, and a naval academy where the teaching of mathematics and experimental methods was highly developed. The academy combined science teaching with navigational training; both initiatives were interrupted by the political crisis following the British invasions.

INDEPENDENCE AND CIVIL WAR, 1810–52

The early years following independence were very difficult. The war had given rise to serious economic difficulties. Wealth was being plundered both from the cattle-raising regions and from the urban centres, which were also affected by the liberalization of trade and, above all, the halt in the flow of metals from Upper Peru.

These were also years of patriotic zeal and the ebullience of new ideas: the citizens of Buenos Aires could read Rousseau's *Social Contract* in Spanish and the newspaper *La Gaceta*; a 'felicitous revolution of ideas' was taking place – from the radical thinking of Mariano Moreno and Bernado de Monteagudo to the more moderate ideas of Dean Gregorio Funes. Drawing up the new curriculum for the University of Córdoba, Funes recognized the need for greater emphasis on experimental physics and mathematics, but recommended keeping traditional scholasticism for metaphysics, Manuel Belgrano, in contrast, recommended teaching logic according to Condillac, abandoning metaphysics and building up the moral aspects of religion.

Financial difficulties led to the closing of several institutions established at the end of the colonial period. Some survived, such as the Instituto Médico Militar and the Academia de Matemática y Arte Militar, vital for the training of artillery troops, because they tied in with the new military demands. After 1815 certain projects were resumed. For example, the former Colegio de San Carlos was restored and transformed into the Colegio de la Unión del Sur, where Juan Crisóstomo Lafinur began teaching theories of ideology, earning himself censure in the most traditional circles.

Civil conflict broke out immediately after the war of independence, destroying the political unity of the viceroyalty. Some territories became independent states: Bolivia, Paraguay and the Banda Oriental, which declared its independence in 1828 following a war between the provinces of Río de la Plata and Brazil. In other cases, autonomous provincial states were formed, with scant resources and impoverished economies. On the other hand, the province of Buenos Aires experienced a period of prosperity owing to the expansion of cattle-raising, which was moving into new territory in the south.

While cattle-raising methods remained archaic, innovations were being introduced into the salteries where leather and salt beef were prepared. The need to demarcate the cattle ranches led to the establishment of the Topography Department and development of surveying, rainfall gauging and other activities calling for new engineering skills.

Many experts were brought over from Europe by Bernardino Rivadavia, counting on their need to escape political persecution and on the mythical evocation of the 'Río de la Plata'. A great many leading scientists were thus recruited to work in Buenos Aires, including the naturalist Aimé Bonpland and the physicist Fabricio Mossotti. While the going was good, scientists combined professional activities with scientific and academic work. Mossotti, for example, set up an astronomical observatory at the Convent of Santo Domingo.

In the planning stage for many years, the University of Buenos Aires was finally established in 1821. On the French model, the university administered the three levels of education. Several primary schools were created and the Lancaster method introduced. The Colegio was transformed into the Colegio de Ciencias Morales (School of Moral Sciences) and accepted scholarship students from the provinces. In addition to law, the university promoted the teaching of the experimental sciences, with the help of physicists hired abroad, and medicine. In philosophy the new theories of the *idéologues* held sway, among them Condillac, Cabanis and Destutt de Tracy, with the latter of whom Rivadavia kept up a correspondence.

This intellectual renewal affected every aspect of cultural life in Buenos Aires and even reached some towns in the interior. Buenos Aires boasted five bookshops, a considerable number of periodicals, theatre and opera productions, and literary and debating groups. But political conflict soon toppled this edifice, which had rested on flimsy foundations. When Bernardino Rivadavia stepped down from the presidency in 1827, many projects were dropped. Lack of funds led to the abandonment of others, particularly public works. Political struggles also created an increasingly seditious atmosphere, and many scientists and intellectuals emigrated or were dismissed from their posts.

The government of Juan Manuel de Rosas, installed in 1829, had by 1835 turned into a dictatorship. His power, like that of most provincial leaders, rested upon rural masses hostile to the urban educated classes. Throughout the territory rural dwellers were indeed predominantly antagonistic towards cities and urban culture.

A new generation of intellectuals sought to understand and remedy the situation. They were influenced by the eclectic philosophers and also by the romantic poets and writers, who introduced them to the ideas of Herder, and by the reverberation of the French revolution of 1830. The goal was to discover the nature of the Argentine people and, above all, to explain Rosas and the popularity he enjoyed.

The 'generation of 37' started up in the Buenos Aires of the Rosas administration; its members later emigrated to Santiago (Chile) and Montevideo, where they joined the anti-Rosas opposition. Their chief works were produced in exile: *Dogma socialista* by Esteban Echeverría, *Facundo* by Domingo Faustino Sarmiento, and *Fragmento preliminar al estudio del Derecho* by Juan Bautista Alberdi.

Rosas's enemies gathered in Montevideo: they came from Buenos Aires and the Banda Oriental. Many, including Guiseppe Garibaldi, were from Europe. These émigrés enlivened cultural life and promoted periodicals, literary debate and academic activity. The newspaper *El Iniciador* was launched in 1838; starting in 1833 various university chairs were established and by 1838 there was talk of setting up a university, although this idea did not materialize immediately. A library, a museum and archives were successively established, and in 1843 the Institute of History and Geography opened its doors. A secondary school established in 1848 was converted shortly afterwards into a national *colegio*, and the university was founded in 1849. Andrés Lamas began compiling documents on the history of Uruguay, a task similar to that undertaken in Buenos Aires by Pedro de Angelis.

ORGANIZATION AND NEW HORIZONS, 1852–80

The fall of Rosas in 1852, coinciding as it did with the beginning of the great expansion of capitalism, transformed conditions in the Río de la Plata. Both capitals, and some other cities as well, grew and modernized at a rapid pace. The states, however, did not fully come into their own until the end of this period.

Intellectuals and politicians who had been educated in exile took an active part in this process of institution-building in the two countries, proposing alternative structures based on political liberalism and economic openness. In Argentina the most outstanding figures were Juan Bautista Alberdi, whose work *Bases* served as the model for the Constitution of 1853, and Domingo Faustino Sarmiento, who became president in 1868 and was influential in many fields, especially education. In Uruguay, on the other hand, the *doctores* (intellectuals) – politically active in the two traditional parties – were unable to counter the influence of the *caudillos*.

Social renewal came from two major sources: immigration – stimulated by colonization – and education, especially primary or 'popular' education. The great propagandists and opinion leaders were Sarmiento and the Uruguayan José Pedro Varela. Initiatives were transformed almost immediately into legal instruments, which made education compulsory, free and secular. The Normal School of Paraná was founded in 1870, and it was there that Pedro Scalabrini disseminated the ideas generically labelled positivism, in particular secularism and a firm belief in science. The teachers trained in that school – known as *normalistas* – were to exert a huge influence on public education.

The ideas of rational progress and secularism were spreading rapidly, as was Darwin's theory of evolution. Progressive, liberal and anticlerical groups clashed with the Catholic church and with intellectuals combining ultramontane attitudes with a more general spiritualism. In Uruguay, liberals founded the rationalist club in 1872, where they adopted a rationalistic profession of faith that merged doctrinaire liberalism with a vigorous moral appeal.

In the field of education, other issues were resolved. In 1863 Argentina established a system of state schools intended to train a new and highly educated political elite loyal to the nation state. In accordance with those goals, the curriculum was strongly oriented towards humanism. University education was also restructured. The University of Buenos Aires recovered from the neglect it had suffered under Rosas. Its new department of exact sciences accepted its first intake of engineers in 1868. The academic community in Argentina nevertheless remained aloof from the intellectual renewal and debates of the time.

Outside the university, the sciences were developing very significantly. Argentina was making great efforts to promote scientific institutions and bring in European scientists. Noteworthy among them was Germán Burmeister, who reorganized the Buenos Aires Museum of Science; he later moved to Córdoba where, in 1870, he was instrumental in setting up the faculty of physical sciences and mathematics and the Academia of Córdoba, which in 1878 became the National Academy of Sciences. At the same time the Argentine Government established a meteorological observatory in Córdoba, making the city a second centre of scientific accomplishment. Scientific publications – such as the museum annals published by Burmeister – proliferated in Buenos Aires and Córdoba, which exchanged information with major science centres throughout the world.

In 1872 a group of teachers from the Buenos Aires faculty of exact sciences founded the Scientific Society of Argentina. In conjunction with the 1875 Industrial Exhibition, the Society organized a competition on the contributions of science to industry in Argentina and, in particular, the working of national raw materials. They were not the only scientists of the time seeking to apply theoretical knowledge to social needs; physicians were grappling with serious health problems in Buenos Aires, whose population had been decimated by yellow fever in 1871.

FROM OPTIMISM TO DOUBT, 1880–1914

In the closing decades of the century, Argentina and Uruguay were moving towards political order and unity (although Uruguay was to experience its final civil war in 1904), the consolidation and development of state institutions, and sustained economic growth. The latter was based on foreign trade, agricultural exports, capital investment and, above all, immigration, which profoundly changed the structure of society. The countryside was modernizing and the principal cities were growing, especially Buenos Aires and Montevideo.

The economic boom and the new political order gave rise to a spontaneous philosophy in which the positivist values of material progress, science and secularism were embraced in a natural and uncritical manner that owed more to conformity than to activism; besides which they reached a broad public through newspapers, reviews and books since – what with a strong education policy – literacy was on the rise. The 1890s, however, saw a shift from confidence to doubt, marked by a climate of tension and mistrust in political institutions, which began in Argentina with the revolution of 1890.

The newly created states fully endorsed the programme of 'educating the sovereign people' – providing free, secular and compulsory basic education which would, it was assumed, produce a new citizenry. This function was to be fulfilled by the primary schools and *colegios* (secondary schools), thereby giving the state control over a countryside in which neither the church nor the institutions of foreign communities could compete. The educational ideas of the normal-school movement circulated widely and were given fresh impetus with the founding in 1905 of the University of La Plata, where the focus was more on practical knowledge and experimental methods than on the humanities.

One consequence of effective state control of the country's territory was its systematic scientific exploration. A group of German scholars living in Córdoba accompanied General Roca on his 'conquest of the desert', helping to survey the territory; later a civilian professional, Francisco P. Moreno, and Commander Fontana systematically explored and described Patagonia and the Chaco region. Moreno assembled an enormous collection of objects, which went to the Museo de La Plata. The museum, which later became affiliated with the university, devoted itself to the study of natural sciences and anthropology, a model for other state-supported institutions such as the Ethnographic Museum, the La Plata Observatory, the

Darwin Museum and the botanical gardens and zoo of Buenos Aires.

Scientific progress was accompanied by intense controversy over Darwinian theory. In Montevideo the debates took place at the Ateneo, a cultural centre founded in 1877. The matter was just as hotly debated in Buenos Aires. Darwin's adversaries included the Catholic intellectuals, like José Manuel Estrada, and scientists like Germán Burmeister, who rejected the theory of evolution and defended creationism. Among the defenders of Darwin was Florentino Ameghino, the most notable Argentine scientist of the time. Appointed head of the Buenos Aires Museum in 1902, this outstanding geologist and palaeontologist, fiercely opposed by Burmeister, theorized that the human race had originated in the Americas, and more precisely in the Pampas, and formulated a basically evolutionary worldview in his work *Mi credo*.

Positivist thought dominated the University of Montevideo between 1880 and 1900. It gained acceptance more slowly in Buenos Aires; but, by the end of the century it had found its place in the faculty of philosophy and letters where, in 1904, Ernesto Quesado was appointed to the first professorship in sociology. These years were marked by sociological concern, the aim being to bring the thinking of Comte, Spencer, Taine, Le Bon, Durkheim and Simmel to bear on the new social issues. The massive influx of foreigners gave rise to reflection on race and the idea of the melting pot. The masses of people visible in every large city made it necessary to think in terms of urban management. Many in this highly heterogeneous society began to wonder about their roots, seeking them in the Spanish heritage or the Creole tradition; many others were concerned about the growing cosmopolitanism, which they tried to counter with an appeal to nationalism.

Many theoreticians switched to action, proposing social or political reforms. Noteworthy among them were José Batlle y Ordóñez in Uruguay and the more moderate Joaquín V. González in Argentina who, in 1904, proposed a labour code that was to legalize union activity. For their part, Roque Sáenz Peña and Indalecio Gómez promoted the electoral reform, which in 1912 opened the way for democracy. One way or another, all of them believed strongly in progress and in the human capacity for making and controlling progress. Towards the end of the century, however, misgivings about these values began to set in. They were to be seen in the use of positivist methods of investigating social ills, but also in the questioning of positivism itself and of the belief that associated progress with material welfare. This stance is present in the philosophical attacks on positivism made by Carlos Vaz Ferreira in Uruguay and by Rodolfo Rivarola and Coriolano Alberini in Argentina. At the same time, markedly intolerant attitudes and initiatives were emerging, typified by the residency law, adopted in Argentina in 1902, which authorized the expulsion of undesirable foreigners, or the most exacerbated forms of nationalism. Perhaps the most telling expression of this trend was the work of the Uruguayan José Enrique Rodó, whose *Ariel* (1990) came to symbolize an

aristocratic and spiritual ideology which, it was beginning to be asserted, characterized the essence of Hispanic America.

In many ways the First World War cut this process short. The acute social problems following the war shook progressive optimism to its very foundations while the world economic crisis, coupled with increasingly serious national economic woes, hindered the role of promoter of culture and science that the state had been assuming so vigorously. In the adversities of the ensuing years, the decades that preceded the Great War came to be recollected as a golden age.

BIBLIOGRAPHY

BABINI, J. 1986. *La evolución del pensamiento científico en la Argentina.* Solar, Buenos Aires.

CAMACHO, H. 1971. *Las ciencias naturales en la Universidad de Buenos Aires.* Eudeba, Buenos Aires.

CHAVEZ, F. 1973. *La cultura en la época de Rosas.* Theoría, Buenos Aires.

DE ASÚA, M. 1993. *La ciencia en la Argentina. Perspectivas históricas.* CELA, Buenos Aires.

FURLONG, G. 1953. *Historia y bibliografía de las primeras imprentas rioplatenses.* Guarania, Buenos Aires.

HALPERIN DONGHI, L. 1970. El aporte de los hombres de ciencia extranjeros que actuaron en la República Argentina en el siglos XIX. In: *Boletín de la Academia Nacional de Ciencias de Córdoba,* T. XLVIII, pp. 103–13.

HALPERIN DONGHI, T. 1962. *Historia de la Universidad de Buenos Aires.* Eudeba, Buenos Aires.

MONSERRAT, M. 1986. La presencia evolucionista en el positivismo argentino. In: *Quipu,* Vol. 3, no.1. Paidós.

PALCOS, A. 1964. Reseña histórica del pemsamiento científico. In: Academia Nacional De La Historia, *Historia argentina contemporánea, 1862–1930.* Vol. 2. El Ateneo, Buenos Aires.

PROBST, J. 1924. La educación en la República Argentina durante la época colonial: Introducción al tomo IV. In: *Documentos Para La Historia Argentina.* Instituto de Investigaciones Históricas de la Facultad de Filosofía y Letras, Buenos Aires.

ROMERO, J. L. 1965. *El desarrollo de las ideas en la sociedad argentina del siglo XX.* Fondo de Cultura Económica, Buenos Aires.

SALVADORES, A. 1941. *La instrucción primaria desde 1810 hasta la sanción de la ley 1420.* Consejo Nacionàl de Educación, Buenos Aires.

SOCIEDAD CIENTIFICA ARGENTINA. 1923–1978. *Evolución de las ciencias en la República Argentina.* Buenos Aires.

SOLER, R. 1968. *El positivismo argentino.* Buenos Aires.

TEDESCO, J. C. 1970. *Educación y sociedad en la Argentina.* Pannedille, Buenos Aires.

TORCHIA ESTRADA, J. C. 1961. *La filosofía en la Argentina.* Unión Panamericana, Washington.

TORRE REVELLO, J. 1940. *El libro, la imprenta y el periodismo en América durante la dominación española.* Facultad de Filosofía y Letras, Buenos Aires.

WEINBERG, F. 1977. *El Salón Literario de 1837.* Hachette, Buenos Aires.

WEINBERG, G. 1995. *Modelos educativos en la historia de América Latina.* 4th edn. AZ, Buenos Aires.

——. 1998. *La ciencia y la idea de progreso en América Latina, 1860–1930.* Fondo de Cultura Económica, Buenos Aires.

12.5

THE ANDEAN REGION

Margarita Guerra Martiniere

The turn of the eighteenth century brought a serious crisis to the Andean countries. When the old system of government fell, their societies were ill-equipped to take over, for even though the republic had been formally adopted as the political form of government, they had no experience of governing themselves because they had been under the Spanish yoke. They made little headway with social change, the major achievements being accomplished in the second half of the nineteenth century (abolition of the indigenous tribute and emancipation of the slaves).

At the international level, foreign powers sought trade relations with the new states only because they considered them inferior on account of the prevailing disorder. The political crisis, social stagnation and the weakness of the economy retarded scientific and cultural development because nascent industries were overwhelmed by international competition. Only raw materials required for major industries (nitrates, guano, raw cotton, wool, etc.) were marketed; no business capital was available to permit the establishment of industrial enterprises; and there was a lack of modern machinery and qualified staff to operate it.

Industrialization began in Peru, Ecuador and Bolivia at the end of the nineteenth century with the second industrial revolution, the outbreak of wars such as the Franco-Prussian War, the First World War, etc., and the immigration of skilled European workers fleeing persecution for their anarchist and trade-union connections.

Cultural development was paralysed by internal struggles that brought the new schools, colleges and universities to a standstill, although Lima was a hive of intellectual activity between 1850 and 1870, as could be seen in particular in contributions to the *Revista de Lima* (Lima Review) (1859–63). Towards the end of the century, cultural associations, academies and learned societies were established which served as a channel for new schools of thought.

ASSERTION OF NATIONAL AND CULTURAL IDENTITY IN THE REGIONS

With independence, nationalist feeling found expression in a rejection of metropolitan influences and the strengthening of the ancient and modern traditions that had underlain *mestizo* society from the beginning. That did not, however, preclude clashes between conflicting Andean, Hispanic and African interests.

Plurality of cultures and cultural traditions

When the Spaniards arrived, countries with a large autochthonous population like Bolivia, Peru and Ecuador had a highly developed culture, which strongly influenced the new forms of cultural expression.

Total acculturation of the Andean countries was not possible because of the division into three distinct regions: the coastal region much influenced by the West, the *sierra* or mountain region, which is the cradle of the highest forms of indigenous cultural expression, and the *selva* or forest region which even now, despite the work of Catholic missions, is largely impenetrable.

In both Peru and Ecuador, and to a lesser extent in Bolivia, the African contribution to the racial mix was limited, owing to the Africans' social status. In the nineteenth century, new immigrants arrived from Europe and Asia, which put the finishing touches to German Arciniegas's expression 'The continent of seven colours'.

Common technological and scientific traditions

Between 1770 and 1850, various Western innovations were brought into the Andean region. Thus, in Peru, under Abascal, a public cemetery was opened, smallpox vaccination began and, later on, steamship navigation and other innovations were introduced. Andean societies were resistant to change because the geographical features of the region cut them off to some extent from the outside world.

In agriculture, work was done on a community as well as on an individual basis; crop rotation was intensified but terracing was abandoned and it was not until the twentieth century that new irrigation methods were used to reclaim arable areas. Draught-animal ploughing was introduced, as was industrial-scale production of crops such as grapes, sugar-cane and cotton, and large-scale animal husbandry with livestock brought in by the Europeans, such as sheep, cattle, and pigs, improved breeds of livestock being imported for that purpose.

Basic clothing needs were met from native (lamoid fleece) and Western (flax) fibres, which were combined to produce blended fabrics. Similar mixed influences were to be found in housing (saddle roofing and stone walls) and food production (food preservation system). In industry, there were various experiments in the use of hydraulic energy, especially in textile manufacturing.

Scientific advances were slow to gain acceptance and some instruments were considered 'diabolical'. The use of corpses in medical practice was not easily accepted, for ethical and religious reasons. In mountain communities, indigenous or traditional medicine held out against Western or scientific medicine.

Somewhat conservative attitudes, evident in a reluctance to accept ideas and customs that seemed opposed to the Catholic faith, were inherited from Spain. Scholasticism was the filter through which modern ideas were passed on to America, with the result that young Creole champions of progressive ideas, especially the advocates of free-thinking, were viewed with distrust.

Political, economic and social context

Between 1780 and 1825 the new states broke with Spain and in the subsequent years set themselves up as autonomous, politically sovereign states with free-market economies, but they failed to fulfil social aspirations. The Andean republics inherited monarchical authoritarianism and were dazzled by the examples they saw in Europe. But Andean America had to contend with the European powers, which made it feel its political, social, economic, scientific and cultural inferiority. The economic reconstruction of the Andean region when it became part of the international economic system was based on its status as a mere supplier of raw materials. Servile labour was the rule up to this century and was provided first by the slaves, then by Asians, and, throughout, by the Indians. Wages were paid through notes that were legal tender only on the estates.

The nineteenth century saw the establishment of large-scale agricultural holdings and attempts to break up the property of indigenous communities on grounds of private ownership rights; it was not until the twentieth century that the communities were granted legal status.

Towards the second half of the nineteenth century, the volume of trade increased; banking and financial institutions developed and the Andean countries became part of the international capitalist system.

The estate-based structure of society was phased out as economic considerations came to rank more highly than skin colour. The republican society identified itself as *mestizo* and egalitarian laws were enacted, such as those providing for the abolition of titles of nobility, equality before the law, and citizenship. Commercial and industrial development, which entailed urban growth, contributed to this. Immigration, encouraged by Andean governments and by European interests, also helped to bring about these changes.

IMPORTANCE OF NEW TRENDS IN SCIENTIFIC AND CULTURAL DEVELOPMENT

Did scholasticism persist in the Andean countries?

Intellectual development in the Andean countries was fraught with contradictions. From the end of the eighteenth century educational reforms were introduced in the universities of Chuquisaca (Bolivia) and San Marcos (Peru), and also in San Carlos and in the seminaries, from which the revolutionary generations graduated.

Politically, Spain and the Inquisition were opposed to the new developments in science and technology. However, learned men like the Viceroy of Peru, Gil de Taboada y Lemus, and Friar Diego Cisneros supported newspapers like *El Mercurio Peruano* (The Peruvian Mercury) (Lima, 1791–4) and the formation of academic research societies. In Quito, Bishop José Pérez Calama exerted an influence in promoting the new ideas, especially in regard to manual occupations, such as crafts and trades, until 1809. Baron Alexander von Humboldt testified to this progress when he wrote of newspapers and educational centres that were a good match for those in Europe. At the end of the eighteenth century, these societies opened up to critical knowledge. Special interest was shown in the natural sciences and experimental knowledge, and the humanities fell from favour. The new legal provisions placed emphasis on technical occupations.

Positivism and evolutionism

The second half of the nineteenth century was marked by the combined influences of liberalism, evolutionism and positivism, which held sway until the twentieth century.

With evolutionism, immigration was seen as the 'panacea' for development and the native American as an inferior being. The Indian was considered incapable of cultural creation and the *mestizo* as the 'lowest of the low'. This resulted in many laws being passed to promote immigration while sociological, medical and biological studies concurred in recognizing the worthlessness of the indigenous Andean people and governments ignored them in their legislation.

Positivism, after Comte, directed society towards 'order and progress'. Order in politics left the way open to despotism, and progress meant improved communications, especially the railways. For this reason, Bolivia resigned itself to the conclusion of border treaties with Brazil (Petropolis 1902) and Chile (1904) under which it lost some territory but was compensated with 2 million Brazilian pesos for the territory of Acre, which it invested in building the railways linking La Paz, Oruro, Cochabamba, Potosi and Sucre; and Chile built the Arica-La Paz railway. This work was carried out under the presidency of Ismael Montes and was continued by Eliodoro Villazón.

Opposition to the involvement of the church in education arose in Bolivia (1899–1908, with José Manuel Pardo and Ismael Montes) and Ecuador (1876–83), to a greater extent than in Peru. In Ecuador, religious orders were eventually excluded from the management of state educational bodies and religious instruction was abolished (Eloy Alfaro, 1895). In Peru, despite the liberal influence of Sebastian Lorente (1841–76), the clergy maintained its position.

Later trends

As from the last three decades of the nineteenth century, new schools of thought, such as romantic socialism, anarchism, Marxist theories, German socialism, etc., appeared on the scene in the wake of immigration from Europe, triggered by political and social persecution, study tours by Spanish-Americans to Europe, and literature that entered the region through various channels.

CONFLICT BETWEEN SOCIOCULTURAL CHANGE AND RESISTANCE TO CHANGE

The struggle against tradition and religion

New ideas about man and society led to a rethinking of power relations between the church and the state, society and the state, and science and faith, and confrontation was inevitable. Rousseau's influence was noticeable in the work of Toribio Rodríguez de Mendoza, Manuel Chávez de la Rosa (Peru); Vicente Cañete y Domínguez, Saturnino Rodriguez Peña (Chuquisaca); José Pérez Calama, Bishop of Quito, Eugenio Espejo (Ecuador) and others, who put an end to the colonial influence in education. The Lancasterian system of education was introduced later.

When they broke with Spain, the new states wished to retain the privileges of royal patronage in their relations with the church. Bolivia and Peru proceeded to close down monasteries with fewer than eight friars and confiscated a large amount of church property to finance their independence. In Bolivia, some leaders used religion as a shield. Freedom of worship was encouraged in Ecuador after Garcia Moreno, but was not officially allowed in Peru until 1915.

The impact of scientific thought

Liberalism brought with it a desire to transform everything, including culture and science. In Ecuador, as Salvador Lara reports, the first mass vaccination campaign against smallpox took place around 1800. However, in matters of health the Andean societies, with the exception of the elite, maintained the old habits they had been taught. These societies were prejudiced against rationalism, free thinking and materialism, which were contrary to religion. Certain advances in medicine were seen as an attack on Catholic dogma, an example being experimental work on corpses, which was not allowed in the Peruvian vice-royalty until the anatomy department was established under Hipolito Unanue.

The influence of evolutionism was to be seen in the encouragement given to Aryan immigrants, which was belittling both to the Indians and the *mestizos*. In the words of a Bolivian, Nicomedes Antelo, a resident of Buenos Aires (1860–2), who espoused Darwinism: 'The Indian is useless. But, indeed, he represents in Bolivia a living force'. In Peru, too, between the end of the nineteenth century and the beginning of the twentieth, such theories were held, for example by Clemente Palma, who spoke of 'The future of the races in Peru' and said that the country had to improve the race through European immigration because of the incapacity of the indigenous and *mestizo* population; and an educator like Alejandro Deustua declared the Indian to be 'ineducable'. By contrast in Ecuador, José León Mera spoke of Indians as 'a cause for national pride'; Monsignor González Suárez conducted research into the great achievements of the Indians and in 1916 convened the first Catechist Congress, which gave them pride of place, and in 1922, Pio Jaramillo Alvarado published *El indio ecuatoriano* (The Ecuadorian Indian).

The new doctrines were secular, but Catholicism continued to be the state religion until the middle of the century. From 1870 on, anti-clericalism prevailed, and in Bolivia, the liberals separated the church from the state towards the end of the nineteenth century. In Ecuador, the break occurred between 1901 and 1905 but in Peru the separation between church and state was not proclaimed until 1979.

Developments in communications speeded up the inflow of new ideas, but not their practical application. Darwinism (*On the Origin of Species*) spread as from 1859 and held currency until 1920, when pro-Indian feeling came to the fore. Darwin's second work, *The Descent of Man, and Selection in Relation to Sex* (1871), which ran counter to the Bible and Andean religiosity, was accepted only by a certain intellectual elite.

The debate on evolutionary theory radicalized the advocates of secularism, with Carlos Lisson (Peru) proclaiming himself to be 'the personal enemy of Jesus Christ'.

Social implications of the new science

The new science accentuated attitudes of paternalism in the social sphere, which meant that three quarters of the population were relegated to inferior status. Scientific progress conflicted with social and racial prejudice, and biological and social studies put an end to scholasticism, but racism was still the underlying thread. Europe was admired because life there was different and it was thought that social homogeneity had been the key to progress.

Because of the delay in applying science and technology to industry, the only advances were in such disciplines as medicine, the natural sciences, geography and mathematics, with scientific debates in the press on their industrial applications.

In Peru, studies were conducted on warts (Daniel Carrión), tropical diseases (Ugo Pesce) and aspects of psychiatry (Hermilio Valdizán); research was carried out in mathematics (Federico Villarreal); and expeditions were sent into Amazonia. In Bolivia, there was little scientific progress, but support was given to studies in statistics (José Maria Dalence) and botany (Manuel Montalvo). There was more emphasis on geographic expeditions, with the participation of French scholars like Alcides D'Orbigny. Ecuador followed the same course. The complex topography of the Andean territories contributed to advances in geography, and in the second half of the nineteenth century the *Geography of Ecuador* (Manuel Villavicencio) was published. Gabriel García Moreno encouraged the study of science and technology at Central University and, as President of the Republic, promoted statistical studies, established the Polytechnic School (1870) and the School of Industrial Arts and Crafts (1871), modernized the teaching of medicine, founded the chairs of natural sciences and chemistry, hired foreign scientists, and so on.

Scientific thought was the motor of material progress, but at the same time, in the social sphere, it heightened prejudice against indigenous people and *mestizos*. In education, however, it inspired modern laws, such as those promulgated by García Moreno (Ecuador, 1869–75), Manuel Pardo (Peru, 1876) and the liberals in Bolivia at the end of the century. There were plans to eradicate illiteracy and to develop technical education, but the state lacked the resources to do so. Hospital care, orphanages, asylums and social welfare were generally left to national and foreign public charities and to the church.

SOCIAL AND POLITICAL CHANGE

After accession to independence, the pace of events quickened and the new doctrines found themselves in competition with the old ones of authoritarianism and sectarianism in political, social and intellectual life. In the political and social order, liberal policies met with resistance in the form of restrictions on freedom of expression, the isolationism of the elite, etc., owing to the radical nature of the change. The old aristocracy continued to command respect, in spite of the laws.

The national constitutions set the seal on the new liberal socio-political order, but did not respond to the realities of the day; the Conservatives, being more realistic, had the advantage.

Development of society

International relations brought the region closer to the liberal republican model, but military authoritarianism and belated participation by the people in government held back progress. Until the twentieth century, the right to vote was selective and some 70 per cent of the population remained on the sidelines. The liberal republic became a reality only when formal political parties were allowed.

A modern, business-based middle class was slow to emerge in the countries under consideration because of the inadequate level of economic development, the failure of immigrants – welcome though their presence was – to subscribe to the host countries' national projects, and conflict between traditional and modern views and interests, which delayed the emergence of the liberal democratic republic. On the labour front, traditional agriculture was characterized by slave-type labour.

Ecuador abolished slavery around 1851 (José María Urvina), and attempts were made to improve the status of Indians, but little headway was made. Peru abolished slavery in 1854 but Asian immigration, which lasted until 1874, was already under way, in conditions similar to those of slavery, and the 'indenture' of Indian labourers on coastal plantations was introduced. Similarly, in Bolivia, the system of large holdings expanded, with indigenous labour being provided practically free of charge (through various types of sharecropping).

The workforce began to receive wages when industrial techniques were introduced into agriculture (for example in producing sugar cane).

The difficult terrain of the Andean region hampered internal communications, and the major public projects concentrated on the construction of railways to boost domestic and foreign trade. The benefits of this policy were felt at the beginning of the twentieth century. In Bolivia, in addition to the Arica-La Paz line, the Oruro, Cochabamba, Potosí and Sucre railways were built. In Ecuador, García Moreno began to build 'roads suitable for traffic' and the final impetus to railway construction was given by Eloy Alfaro (1895–1900, 1906–11) with the Quito-Riobamba-Sibamba railway; highways were also planned (the Alóag-Marte and Cuenca-Molleturo-Naranjal). In Peru, Castilla, in 1851, built the Lima-Callao railway and work was continued by José Balta (1869–72) with the contactor Meiggs, and by Manuel Pardo (the Central railway and the Arequipa-Puno-Cusco line (1872–6)).

After independence, the expansion of domestic markets was impeded by the coexistence of different systems of weights and measures (British and North American) and the retention of the colonial peso, at the rate of eight reales, alongside the weak local currency. Government control of the issue of coins and notes came late. Banks were set up towards the second half of the century but there were shortcomings in the credit system.

Institutionalization of new political structures

The advent of the republican system symbolized the break with the past, but governments did not forgo certain privileges such as royal patronage, in order to consolidate their power internally.

The liberals sought to limit the power of the church. Early on, Bolívar, acting under the influence of the liberals and freemasons, had seized church property as a step towards freedom of worship. The liberal and positivist modernization programme concentrated on attacking the clergy and religion through freedom of the press and the establishment of free and compulsory public primary education.

The modern economy

The influence of British liberalism in the Andean countries affected the communities' textile workshops owing to the influx of British fabrics; affected tradespeople and small-scale national industries because of the low level of capital; and affected the church because it lacked the economic power to pursue its social work. There were few capitalists who like Francisco Quiroz in Peru risked their fortune in the years preceding the fifties or sixties, and those who did were not always successful.

Ecuador, Peru and Bolivia had an age-old textile manufacturing tradition as well as other small industries. With the end of colonial rule, the countries entered the world market, but this had dire consequences for all these small industries. Many of the skilled craftspeople returned to the countryside, with a consequent decline in social status.

There was no financial organization to speak of until the 1860s. Prior to the establishment of the banking system, there were only merchant banks for the trade in metals, but with the exploitation of the guano and nitrate deposits, the recovery of the mining industry and investment in agriculture and related industries, the establishment of banks was seen as a necessity, and branches of European banks, such as the Bank of London, Mexico and South America, were set up, later to be followed by mixed capital.

The durability of the new states had been firmly established.

The banks performed various functions ranging from the minting of money to the granting of credit. In Ecuador, under Vicente Rocafuerte (1835–9), the Agricultural Savings and Mortgage Bank was founded. Pawn and loan institutions were also established in the three countries. Other businesses included stock companies like the Compañía de Salitres (Nitrate Company) of Antofagasta, in Bolivia, set up with British and Chilean capital (as from 1870).

In the course of the century, progressive governments set about providing their people with lighting, water, sewerage and telegraph services. Gas lighting was introduced in the middle of the century and electric lighting towards the end. It took a long time to install water supply and sewerage facilities, and few capitals actually had such services. The first telegraph lines date back to the 1870s but the network was not expanded until the twentieth century.

INFLUENCE AND CONTRIBUTIONS IN SCIENCE AND TECHNOLOGY

Having broken their ties with Spain, the new countries looked to England (for industry), France (for culture) and the United States (for democracy). They turned their backs on the past as a symbol of backwardness, forgoing their originality in the process and wanting everything to be new, modern and progressive.

Innovations and national aspirations

The liberators saw education as the key to modernity, but laws, and also the foreign teachers who were hired, proved inadequate to the task, since they failed to take either the Andean reality or national aspirations into account.

The Enlightenment first of all, and then liberalism and positivism sought to bring culture to the people, but in fact emphasis was laid more on educating the elite. The idea of making citizens out of serfs came to grief because there was no proper blueprint for education. Law upon law was enacted, but to no avail. The only education most people received was in the home. Central governments and local authorities failed to cater to needs which were met, in part, by the church and private individuals.

Technological changes

New technology was not immediately applied and was difficult to reconcile with indigenous technology.

Subsistence needs were met through the communities' collective work and extensive farming on the large estates. Pre-Hispanic methods of preserving food continued to be used. Mule-drawn vehicles were still used as the main means of transport until the seventies, when the railways came into their own. Agro-industrial production began late, with the exception of sugar cane production (in Peru and Ecuador). Semi-free labour was used for cocoa, cotton and, later, rubber production, and also for mining (in Bolivia and Peru).

Liberalism and industrialization put an end to slave labour, with the emancipation of the slaves. People in traditional crafts and trades were dislodged, trade unions were banned and industrial arts and crafts schools were established.

The Andean countries and the international economy

The second industrial revolution expanded the markets for raw materials from America, Asia and Africa and asserted its economic dominance (in the form of technology and capital) in these countries. In international trade, transport was speeded up by the use of steamships and the railways to transport heavy goods, and the Andean governments readily

made the transition, although the variety of agricultural and animal products supplied by Ecuador, Peru and Bolivia for international trade made it necessary to use refrigerated ships belonging to European companies.

The Andean countries were well placed on world markets with their raw materials (guano, nitrates, rubber) but not when it came to products manufactured virtually on a cottage-industry basis.

SURMOUNTING THE STRUCTURAL CRISIS OF THE NEW SOCIETY

In the early twentieth century the Andean societies asserted their own specific identity, but had to contend with various external factors, such as migration, which affected their outlook and attitudes.

Social and political restructuring

Modernization had a considerable impact on the rural population, whose flight to the cities led to urban sprawl. Parties were admitted to political life, although they always revolved around personalities. Calls were made for the armed forces to be institutionalized.

The process of modernization was complex and difficult to direct after the streamlining of the administration in Peru (the 'practical republic') under the government of Manuel Pardo and the democrat, Nicolás de Piérola. Ecuador also experienced policy swings, from the conservative dictatorship of Gabriel García Moreno (1860–75) to the liberal policies of Alfaro (1895–1919). In Bolivia, the process of modernization came later, with the liberals José Manuel Pando, Ismael Montes, Heliodoro Villazín and José Gutiérrez Guerra (1899–1920). They all gave priority to the monetary system and adopted the gold standard. The decimal measuring system became the rule. For national defence purposes, contracts were signed with European military missions – German in Bolivia and French in Ecuador and Peru. The building of railways and the extension of the telegraph service were speeded up, but meanwhile home-grown talent was wasting away. Urbanization proceeded apace and new cities sprang up, but others declined with the change in activities.

Trade was a paramount factor in this development, but it was in the hands of foreigners and the countryside was dependent on urban expansion. The cities' appeal as cultural centres and a source of work left the smaller towns to stagnate. There were those who hankered after colonial times.

Political life was characterized by the authoritarianism of civilian and military, liberal and conservative dictatorships, but all were eager to streamline the administration, modernize communications and strengthen the congress, local government bodies and other representative institutions. The climate was conducive to educational reform. Bolivia switched from an encyclopaedist-humanist approach to education to one of total freedom. In 1871 primary education became compulsory and free and there were three universities, but the illiteracy rate was still 90 per cent. Of the scientific disciplines, botany, statistics, geography and bacteriology were promoted.

In Ecuador, after Rocafuerte (1835), education rested on a moral and scientific basis. Under García Moreno, religious orders dedicated to education, like the Jesuits, arrived, but on the former's death, the religious presence was rejected. Under Eloy Alfaro (1895–1917), the Mejía National Institute for secondary education was founded, as were the Juan Montalvo and Manuela Cañozares teacher-training colleges, at the instigation of a sizeable intellectual community and ministers enamoured of scholarships, such as Julio Andrade (the School of Fine Arts), Luis Napoleón Dillón and Manuel María Sánchez.

In Peru, San Martín y Bolívar was the first to take up the issue, but the church was the institution that made the greatest contribution through its religious orders dedicated to education (Jesuits, Sacred Heart schools for boys and girls, Saint Joseph de Cluny, Christian Brothers, etc.). Some private individuals like Domingo Elías and Nicolás Rodrigo (Guadeloupe, 1840) and clerics like Bartolomé Herrera (San Carlos, 1842) also played a role.

In the sciences, advances were made in geography, medicine, mathematics and the natural sciences, outstanding figures being Cayetano Heredia in San Feernando, Daniel Carrión, Hermilio Valdizán, Mariano Eduardo de Rivero and Antonio Raimondi. Some European travellers such as Charles Wienner and Alcides D'Orbigny carried out studies in these three countries, while other scholars took an interest in navigation (Aurelio Garcia, Federico Carrasco, etc.).

Regarding developments in technology, steam, gas lighting, daguerreotype, photography, the telegraph and other innovations were all in use but there were also pioneering experiments in Peru with the application of new inventions, examples being José M. Flores' attempted hot-air balloon flights and Pedro Ruiz Gallo's clock, brass harp, harmonic vihuela, etc.

In Bolivia, too, there were attempts at technological development, especially in mining, where new methods were tested for the mining of tin, the new mineral that was and still is one of the country's main sources of wealth.

Cultural restructuring

Culture was the key to inducing the people to adapt to the new models, but this adaptation was not easy to achieve. The new developments had the effect of widening the gap between urban and rural society. Cities were modernized but the countryside closed in more and more on itself because of the lack of communication, attachment to tradition and distrust of anything new.

With the self-affirmation of autochthonous cultures came the realization that 'modernity' was belittling to both *mestizo* and indigenous culture. The ruling classes were generally anti-Indian and pro-Western, and the greatest concession was to accept intermingling, albeit with a predominantly Western influence. The new situation precipitated cultural change in science and education. Formal education took precedence over private education. More and more boarding schools were established. Education was provided in the arts, the sciences and occupational skills. Foreign teachers were brought in but, with a few exceptions, they were confined to the capital cities.

Journalism flourished, but the focus was political, and there was little freedom of expression; even so, there were inflammatory attacks in the press. There were some cultural journals, but they were not published regularly until the middle of the century. In Lima, after the *Mercurio Peruano*

(Peruvian Mercury) of 1791, mention must be made of the *Revista de Lima* (Lima Review) (1859–63), *La Revista Peruana* (Peruvian Review) (1879–80) and the *Perú Ilustrado* (Peruvian Illustrated Review) in the 1890s. In Bolivia, there were the *Revista de Cochabamba* (Cochabamba Review) (1852), published on a non-periodical basis (187) and the *Aurora Literaria de Sucre* (Sucre Literary Aurora) (1864). In Ecuador, Juan Montalvo set the literary tone, with a markedly liberal and anti-clerical emphasis, both inside and outside the country, as from the 1860s.

From 1870 on, the universities adopted a positivist approach to medicine and law studies. The study of Latin and theology was curtailed. Administrative studies were introduced and an attempt was made to bring the university closer to the national reality, although teachers and students alike continued to belong to the elite.

Women began to be taken into account in education, but with reservations, since they had no say in politics and earned lower wages on the labour market. In the middle of the century, they made a breakthrough into literature but were admitted to universities only at the end of the century, with special congressional authorization.

Sports activities were not for the masses. Horse riding, regattas and tennis – the British influence – had no competition from ball games, which were practically unknown at the time.

The region in the world context

Only in the middle of the century, with the codification of legislation (civil, criminal and procedural codes), did the constitutions and governments reach maturity, which coincided with the emergence of the new wealth that won these countries international acceptance.

The 1848 revolutions brought drastic changes to the world. This was compounded by the strengthening of the position of the United States after the War of Secession and the affirmation of the Monroe doctrine, which to some extent caused the European countries to change their attitude towards America.

The United States began to assert its authority in these states through the Monroe doctrine (1880); the involvement of Henry Meiggs and North American firms in general in railway policy (1870) and in oil drilling (Bolivia, Ecuador and Peru) is clear evidence of the trend, and the presence of commercial and loan companies was a reflection of the economic inroads made by North America. Meanwhile, however, Peru and Bolivia felt cheated when they were excluded from the protection of the League of Nations.

The impact of the political and social thinking of the day was evident in the ideas of the new political parties that emerged from 1920 on. However, as from 1900 and even before industrial development had taken off in America, the arrival of European immigrants brought with it social unrest and anarchist trade-unionism. Underground workers' newspapers circulated and strikes were organized in support of social claims, especially the eight-hour working day. These ideas affected rural and urban areas alike. The voice of the peasants (day workers, tenant farmers, sharecroppers, Indians working on community lands, etc.) made itself heard. There were calls for land to be given to rural dwellers and for agrarian reform, in a region in which nearly 80 per cent of the population depended on agriculture for a livelihood.

In the cities, there were demands for participation by the people in political decision-making, for universal suffrage, for the right of illiterates to vote and for the establishment of communication channels to improve working conditions and access to culture. This is the climate that prevailed in Bolivia, Ecuador and Peru in the years prior to the Great Depression of 1929.

BIBLIOGRAPHY

ARGUEDAS, A. 1922. *Historia general de Bolivia* (General History of Bolivia). Arno hermanos Publishers, La Paz.

BASADRE, J. 1964. *Historia de la República del Perú* (History of the Republic of Peru). 5th edn, vols 1–8. P.L. Villanueva Publishers, Lima.

BELMONTE, J. 1971. *Historia contemporánea de Iberoamérica* (Contemporary History of Ibero-America). 3 vols. Guadarramo Publishers, Madrid.

CARDOSO, C. F. 1987. *Historia económica de América Latina* (Economic History of Latin America). Crítica Publishers, Barcelona.

CUETO, M. (ed.) 1995. *Saberes andinos. Ciencia y tecnología en Bolivia, Ecuador y Perú* (Andean Skills. Science and Technology in Bolivia, Ecuador and Peru). IEP, Lima.

CHEVALIER, F. 1963. *América Latina: de la independencia a nuestros días* (Latin America: From Independence to the Present). Labor S.A. Publishing Company, Barcelona.

ESCOBARI CUSICANQUI, J. 1975. *Historia diplomática de Bolivia* (Diplomatic History of Bolivia). Casa Municipal de la Cultura 'Franz Tamayo' Press, Bolivia.

FINOT, E.; BAPTISTA GUMUCIO, M. 1978. *Nueva Historia de Bolivia. Historia Contemporánea de Bolivia* (New History of Bolivia. Contemporary History of Bolivia). Gisbert & Cía S.A. Publishing Company, La Paz.

GUERRA MARTINIERE, M. 1984. *Historia general del Perú* (General History of Peru). Vol. 11. Carlos Milla Batres Publishers, Barcelona.

———. 1994. *Historia general del Perú* (General History of Peru). Vols 7 and 8. Brasa Publishers, Lima.

GIRARD, R. 1976. *Historia de las civilizaciones* (History of Civilizations). Vol. 3. Istmo Publishers, Madrid.

GUZMAN, A. 1981. *Historia de Bolivia* (History of Bolivia). Los Amigos del Libro Publishers.

HALPERIN DONGHI, T. 1981. *Historia contemporánea de América Latina* (Contemporary History of Latin America). Alianza Editorial Publishers, Madrid.

HERNANDEZ SANCHEZ BARBA, M. 1981. *Historia de América* (History of America). Vol. 3. Alhambra Publishing, Madrid.

———. 1986. *Historia general de América* (General History of America). Vol. 23. Caracas Academia Nacional de la Historia de Venezuela Press.

KLEIN, HERBERT S. 1992. 'Respuesta campesina ante las demandas del mercado y el problema de la tierra en Bolivia. Siglos XVIII y XIX' (Rural Response to Market Demands and the Problem of Land in Bolivia. Eighteenth and Nineteenth Centuries). In: Sanchez Albornoz, Nico lás (ed.) *Población y mano de obra en América Latina* (Population and Labour in Latin America). Alianza Editorial Publishing, Madrid.

LYNCH, J. 1988. *Historia de América. Historia contemporánea* (History of America. Contemporary History). Cátedra Publishing, Madrid.

SALVADOR LARA, J. 1995. *Breve historia contemporánea del Ecuador* (A short Contemporary History of Ecuador). FCE, Mexico City.

SANCHEZ, L. A. n.d. *Historia de América* (History of America). Vols 3 and IV. Juan Mejia Baca Publishers, Lima.

SANCHEZ ALBORNOZ, N. 1977. *La población de América Latina. Desde los tiempos precolombinos al año 2000* (The Population of Latin America. From Pre-Columbian Times to the year 2000). 2nd edn. Alianza Publishing, Madrid.

———. 1992. (ed.) *Población y mano de obra en América Latina* (Population and Labour in Latin America). Alianza América, Madrid.

VELASQUEZ, M. DEL C. 1965. *Hispanoamérica en el siglo XIX* (Spanish America in the Nineteenth Century). Promaca Publishing, Mexico City.

ZEA, L. 1986. *América Latina en sus ideas* (Latin America Through Its Ideas). Siglo XXI, Publishing, Mexico City.

———. 1965. *El pensamiento hispanoamericano* (Spanish American Thought). 2 vols. De Promaca, Mexico City.

13

ASIA

INTRODUCTION

Wang Gung Wu, coordinator

MAXIMIZING THE REACH OF MARITIME EMPIRES

At the beginning of this long century from 1789 to 1914, no one could have foreseen that the relatively new idea of progress could have dominated the lives of so many, not only in the countries which were inspired by the idea but also in areas of the world which never saw the need for it. The new faith in inexorable progress arose from the successes achieved by a small number of countries on the edge of Western Europe that built their wealth and strength from competitive trade and war. This had stimulated and supported inventiveness in technology and scientific discovery, which in turn made the commercial and military advantage of these countries irresistible during the nineteenth century. All this was built on the foundations of maritime supremacy in the great oceans of the world.

Some of the elites of South and South East Asia in the last decade of the eighteenth century probably did see that this was their fate, to be dominated by the ships of their European trading rivals. They admired the new military technology and the efficient organizations that accompanied it, but did not think that it would lead them to changes in their core values. Instead, where political institutions were concerned, the elites used the new technologies to consolidate their own control of land and peoples, or reshape the power landscapes, rather than to streamline their systems of rule. In East Asia, walls of defence had been erected in all countries, and the imperial courts of China and Japan were convinced of their invincibility from enemies who came by sea. All this was to change, by the first two decades of the nineteenth century for South and South East Asia, and the middle of that century for East Asia. After that, to the surprise of aggressors and defenders alike, the pace of economic and political transformations accelerated greatly all over the Asian continent. With the exception of Japan, the response to the Western challenges was largely too slow and too late.

This story is now familiar to students of this period of empire and Western power, and the various chapters in this volume seek to reassess the major tendencies and debates that help us evaluate the era's contribution to scientific and cultural development. Each chapter tells a special story, but those on Central Asia and the European penetration into the African and South Asian interior underline a trend that gains significance when we look at the remaining chapters on the developments in East and South East Asia. The latter emphasize a refrain that reminds us of earlier periods of victories at sea. It is the refrain of maritime profit and dominance. Again and again, throughout the nineteenth century, the navies of the British, French, Dutch, and Americans determined the fate of port cities, and the coastal regions of kingdoms and empires, and thus laid the foundations of a global chain of capitalist growth in the decades to come.

The overland expansions of the Russians into Central Asia, of the British into India and various European powers into the heart of Africa did little to change the nature of agrarian and nomadic societies. Their impact on landlocked regimes and cultures was transient The conquerors found the resistance to modern ideas and institutions, to science and technology, greater than that in the areas that were exposed to sea power. This reflects the fact that, for centuries, the great armies that invaded the Eurasian land mass, whether they came from the east or from the west, whether they were Huns, or Muslim Arabs, or Mongols and Turks, or Russians across Siberia, contributed little to scientific and cultural development.

In contrast, once the oceans were mastered, the carriage of new ideas and technologies through naval power and by long-distance ocean shipping was swift and increasingly sure. Fresh attitudes were transported quickly overseas, including the idea of free trade that flourished more readily in open and receptive ports. In earlier centuries, cities like Goa, Malacca, Macau, Manila and Batavia (Jakarta) were little more than garrison ports in splendid locations. But access by sea to faster and better-armed ships made a difference. These cities were followed by trading centres that were more open, and Calcutta, Bombay (Mumbai), Madras (Chennai) and Colombo were examples of efficient transmitters not only of goods but also of new economic and technical skills. By the period covered in this volume, there came the free ports of Penang, Singapore and then those of China, from Hong Kong to the treaty ports, best exemplified by Shanghai and Tientsin, forced open after the Opium War. It was during the nineteenth century that the volume of commercial goods far surpassed that which travelled overland in all the continental land areas of the world. It was no accident that economic wealth and political power also decisively shifted to countries with the greater navies by the end of the eighteenth century. Although it took another several decades before the new scientific culture and the products of an industrial revolution could totally overwhelm all the traditional polities of Asia, there were signs early in the nineteenth century that, for better or worse, victory was inevitable.

Why did the great empires and kingdoms not fight back more successfully? Certainly poor leadership and weaknesses in economic systems were factors. Once key cities were lost to foreign control, first in India and Java and later in Burma (Myanmar) and Vietnam, superior arms led these invaders to capture territory and impose limits on local talent. The subdued colonial populations were given few chances to learn the new knowledge. At the same time, there were also rigidities in old established cultures that rejected the challenges of science and technology and the even more radical institutions of modern economics and administration.

China was saved from subjugation partly by its size, but also because the Western powers had overreached themselves in South and South East Asia. China's mandarin leaders had the chance to change, and some even showed some willingness to learn from its mercantile enemies, but the weight of their own imperial history, particularly the alien Manchu rule at the end of a dynastic cycle, complicated their response. Thus began in China from the 1860s a new kind of historical spiral, that of reform and reaction, followed by radical reform and bitter reaction, to be succeeded eventually by revolution at the end of the long century. Once into that cycle, China continued in the twentieth century with more reform and more revolution and yet further reform.

Of all the Asian countries, only Japan responded successfully. After its enforced opening, its leaders watched China's defeats by the Western powers with increasing alarm. They absorbed the lessons of those failures, and united the elites of the country to learn directly from the new forces that had superseded the Confucian civilization they had long admired. Discarding a once powerful set of adopted values to embrace the newly powerful technologies proved to be easier in Japan than anywhere else in Asia. Their island environment helped them grasp the fundamental shift in history brought about by sea power more readily than could the Chinese mandarins who had been so thoroughly drilled in earthbound concerns. It is significant that when the best Japanese brains were concentrating on learning the science and engineering needed to build a great navy and their own heavy industry, China was engaged in debilitating land wars in a dozen provinces and in the long-drawn out conquest of Turk-Mongol territories in Xinjiang (Chinese Turkestan). That may be compared to the equally unprofitable conquests in Central Asia that engaged the Russians throughout the century. They may also be compared to the British advances into sub-continental India and the Afghan wars. At least for the nineteenth century, being sucked into the Eurasian heartland was the wrong way to go. Certainly, from the point of view of scientific and cultural development, it was maritime transport to the open port cities of Asia that brought the world together and prepared the twentieth century for the kind of modern global interdependence now being experienced.

13.1

NORTHERN AND CENTRAL ASIA

Ahmad Hasan Dani

Russia's advance towards Asia followed her historical upsurge as a Russian nation by assimilating the Slavic population of Northeastern Europe (Sturley, 1964: ch. 4) on the basis of the Greek Orthodox church. The Russians were drawn to eastward political expansion as a part of their previous history (Grousset, 1991: ch. 10) and this gave to them a chance to play a historical role in Asia. Their first advance was towards Siberia's vast forest zone in the tundra region stretching from the Urals to the Pacific Ocean, a region peopled by Turkish-speaking people who intermingled with the earlier hunting and fishing communities and were known in history as 'Siberian Tatars' (Akiner, 1983: 93–102; Jochelson). The second group of Tatars is descended from the White Horde under the command of Batu's brother Orda (Grousset, 1991: 393).

THE RUSSIAN ADVANCE INTO THE KAZAKH STEPPES

After the Russians consolidated their control over Siberia, they began to look southward to the Kazakh steppes for further expansion of their trade and political interest. The Kazakh were caught between the Russian expansion and the Chinese advance into Zungaria and Kāshgaria (see below) where the Buddhist Oirots, Zungars and Kalmuks, had made a bid for a new state taken from the old Mongol power which was now confined to eastern Mongolia. These Buddhist states were pressing westward into the Kazakh steppe. The Kazakhs themselves had broken into three groups – the Little Horde, Middle Horde and Great Horde. In order to keep their pastureland safe and get over the trouble caused by eastern raids, they were seeking new friends and alliances. It was this danger from the east that led them to make treaty relations with the Russians (Hambly, 1969: 144–8).

Pressed by the Oirots from the east, the Khān of the Kazakhs, Tauke (1680–1718), realized that Russia was his only potentially effective ally, and hence it is said that between 1680 and 1693, he sent six separate emissaries to the Russians in Siberia (Olcott, 1987: 30). On the other hand in this period Peter the Great was pursuing the policy of expanding Russian trade eastward. It is reported that: 'On 8 September 1730, Abdul Khayr, Khān of the Small Horde, sent a letter to Empress Anna Ivannovna requesting to become her subject by asking for citizenship' (Olcott, 1987: 31; Hayit, 1984). Such a report is one-sided. As explained by Olcott, the relations with the Russians meant only treaties signed first with the Small Horde on 10 October 1731, the second with the Khan of the Middle Horde in 1740 and third with Ablay Khān in 1742. The treaties were for mutual benefit: for the Russians to expand their trade and for the Hordes to provide freedom and security to graze in wider areas.

In the second half of the eighteenth century a final attempt was made by the Khān of the Middle Horde to reunite the Kazakh steppes and restore to the Kazakh Hordes something of their former greatness. Thus, Abdul Khayr (Hambly, 1969: 147) extended his authority over the Small Horde and part of the Middle Horde, attached Bashkiria, already subject to the Russians in 1737, and temporarily occupied Khiva in 1740. After his death in 1749, his son Nur Ali played a leading role but, when his successor Ablay Khān (1711–81) sought to add the Great Horde in his possession, he clashed with the Manchu rulers of China. According to Olcott, 'Ablay called himself Khān as early as 1760 and refused Russian suggestions that he be formally invested in Orenburg, left a son there as *amanat*, and received an annual pension in exchange for his support' (Olcott, 1987: 42). When Empress Catherine tried to woo him by offering him 'a diploma, naming him a Khān', he refused the offer when Catherine did not agree to confirm him as the Khān of all three hordes. Both Ablay and his son and successor Khān Vali turned to the Chinese. After the death of Ablay Khān in 1781, his son was unable to play his father's game. After Vali's death in 1819, his widow Aiganym was won over by the Russians. As a result, her son Chingis and grandson Chokhan Vali Khanov were to receive Russian schooling and later both of them were absorbed into the Russian imperial service. However, Ablay's other grandson, Kenesasy Kasimov, waged a ten-year struggle against the Russians from 1837 to 1847. The Russians counted on one branch of the family of Ablay for their advance in the Kazakh lands, and by playing the game of 'divide and rule' succeeded in extending their control over the region and eliminating Chinese influence for good (Asfendiarov, 1935).

The Russian advance into the Kazakh steppes not only introduced great political changes in the internal relationships of the Kazakh people and between them and the Russians, but had also a drastic influence on the nomadic-pastoral life of the Kazakhs. The changes can be seen in the fields of economy, society, culture, education and above all in the ethnic makeup of the population. The Kazakhs were not entirely a nomadic people. They were also settled on agricultural land in Semirechye and Syr Daryā region. On the other hand their pastoral economy needed extensive grassland for pasturage. Such land was not privately owned.

Olcott has given details of how the Russian advance brought about changes under the heading of 'Economic changes in the steppe under colonial rule'. She observes:

> The Russian land policy led to the destruction of the nomadic economy practised by the Kazakhs. By 1917, some 17 million *desiatins* of land were awarded to nearly 3 million Russian settlers in 500,000 families, and the Public Land Fund contained an additional 20 million *desiatins* of land intended for future homesteaders. This Russian settlement changed the character of life in the steppe.
>
> (Olcott, 1987: 89–90)

As far as administrative changes are concerned, the Russians managed the Kazakhs through their Sultans with centres established in the Siberian cities of Orenburg and Omsk. This system no longer held good when the Russians advanced south of the Jaxartes (Syr Daryā) and met the demands of the fully established monarchies in Transoxiana. Hence in 1882, two governor-generalships were created, those of the Steppe region with headquarter at Orenburg and of Turkestan with headquarters at Tashkent besides the western *oblasts* of Turgay and Ural'sk, which were the responsibility of the Ministry of Interior. This system lasted until 1917.

The Russian advance into the steppes also created the problem of education. In the first instance the problem was to impart instruction to the new Russian settlers. For them, purely Russian schools were opened from the beginning. In this Russian school system the Kazakhs took little interest. Hence the Tatars were encouraged to come and educate the Kazakhs in the first instance. As a result the Tatar influence increased. Hence the Russians thought of another alternative to assimilate the Kazakhs by teaching them Russian language and culture. Russification became a policy and a goal. Some orientalists tried with another scheme to introduce a new Russian programme for instruction by imparting Western-style education in the pupil's own language through native teachers. The idea was to train the Kazakhs through their own language and also prepare them for possible administrative jobs. Hence *aul* schools were established where Kazakh and Russian were both taught. From there the students could go to higher schools right up to a Russian City School.

EASTERN CENTRAL ASIA AND THE CHINESE ADVANCE

After the destruction of the Mongol state the new political developments divided the Mongols into two wings: the eastern with Khalkhas the main tribe, which tried to reunite the Mongols in this region and revive the tottering state; and the western wing that included the Oirots and Kalmuks, who not only dominated in western Mongolia and Zungaria, but also made a bid westward to seize land and power from the Kazakhs. The Manchus succeeded in establishing their protectorate over the Khalkhas in eastern Mongolia. In order to finish off the power of the Oirots the Manchus finally defeated them in 1758 and their last king, Amur-Sana, died a refugee in Russian Tobolsk. The Manchus advanced into the upper Ili valley and founded Kulja as a military post. The Oirots finally disappeared and the Manchus absorbed Zungaria and the Tarim basin as far as the Pamirs into their empire. But though there was a

Russian advance eastward, their western boundary remained ill defined.

CONQUEST OF THE KHĀNATES

The Khānate of Kokand

The Russian advance into the lands of the Kazakhs brought them face to face with the Kokand Khānate, which was expanding towards the north. This Khānate had grown out of old Farghana – the home province of Timurid Babar and still earlier a part of the Chaghatai realm. The region became separated from the Amirate of Bukhārā during the struggle for succession in the time of the Mangit rulers, and a Shaybanid prince, Shāh Rukh, founded the Min ruling dynasty of Kokand. The Khānate extended its claim over all the land on the banks of the Syr Daryā and over the province of Turkestan. In the nineteenth century it advanced towards Ura-tube, Khojend, Osh and Tashkent. Thus, on the one hand the Khānate clashed with Bukhārā Amirs and on the other it faced the Manchu rulers of China. By the end of the eighteenth century the Chinese are alleged to have supported the Khānate against the claims, of Bukhārā Amirs. Their rulers Alim Rhan (1798–1808) and Mohammad Umar (1808–21) directed their campaigns against the Kazakhs and controlled the caravan route to Kāshgar. The latter ruler built the Ak-Mechet fort on the Syr Daryā in 1817. His son Mohammad Ali (1821–42), is regarded as the greatest monarch of the dynasty. He scored a victory over the Chinese and supported Jahangir of Kāshgar and further imposed taxes on Akshu, Turfan, Kāshgar, Yangi-shahr, Yarkand and Khotan. In 1839 he had a successful encounter with the Russians and repulsed the attack of the Cossacks, but against the Bukhārā Amir Nasrullah, he failed and was finally defeated and hence accepted the sovereignty of Bukhārā and ceded Khojend. Later, in 1842, he was executed along with his two sons. This was followed by a continuous struggle between the Kokandians and Bukhārans, leading to a division of the state between east and west. Khudayar Khān (in 1845–58 and until 1875), tried to stem the tide of Russian advance. When trouble again started in Kokand, he took refuge with the Bukhārā Amir Muzaffaruddin, who in vain supported him and tried to re-establish him on the Kokandian throne. It was at this time that the Kokandian state was actually divided, the east failing to the Qipchaks and the west to Khudayar with his residence at Samarkand. When the Russians advanced towards the Syr Daryā, no united action could be taken against them. The Russian advance was from three directions along the Syr Daryā, from Semi Palatinsk, and from Vernyi. They occupied Ak-Machet, renamed as Petrovosk (and now Kyzyl-Orda) in 1853, and drove away the local governor Yakub Beg. Between 1850 and 1854 the lands south of the Ili river were occupied and gradually fell to them: Zambul, Chimkent and the entire territory occupied earlier by the Kazakhs. Amir Muzaffaruddin, the patron of Khudavar Khān, could not help him, having himself been defeated by the Russians in 1866, and hence Khudayar Khān slipped into the protection of the Russians (Hambly, 1969: chs 10, 17–19; Grousset, 1991: 502–43).

In the meantime Yakub Beg carved out a Khānate for himself in Kāshgar in 1867, by ousting the Chinese. His sudden rise was an affront both to the Russians and the Chinese. He thus became a suspect for harbouring friendly relations with the British and giving them an opportunity to exert their diplomatic influence right into Zungaria and Semirechye. It was to avert this possibility that the Russians occupied Kulja in 1871. But later in 1877, Yakub Beg was killed in a battle with the Chinese. His realm of Kāshgar crumbled and the Chinese regained mastery over the region. The Russians, being satisfied, returned Kulja to the Chinese (Holdsworth, 1959: 5–8; Pierce, 1960: 23–9, 34–7).

While these changes took place in eastern Turkestan, the Russians had already established, in 1865, the oblast of Turkestan, extending from the Arab Sea to Issyk-kul lake. In 1867 the Governor-generalship of Turkestan was formed with Tashkent as capital and General K. P. Von Kaufman as Governor-General. When Kokandians rose against the Russians and their protégé, Khudayar Khān, the Russian forces advanced to crush the resistance, took Namangan and Andijan and finally took Kokand. In 1876 the Kokand Khānate was abolished and Farghānā was incorporated into the Turkestan governor-generalship. This brought to a close the British influence in this region. The Chinese were satisfied with their possessions of Zungaria and Kāshgaria, and the Russians extended their territorial possessions to the far south into the Pamir.

The Amirate of Bukhārā

The Amirate of Bukhārā actually covers the history of three dynasties that followed the Timmurids in Transoxiana: the Shaybanids from 1500 to 1599, the Astrakhānids or Janids from 1599 to 1785, and finally the Mangits from 1785 to 1920.

Russia (Vambery, 1990: 379–82) had carried on political intercourse with Bukhārā in former centuries. The old commercial route from the heart of Asia necessitated occasional communication between the grand dukes of Russia and the Amirs of Bukhārā. However, the first diplomatic embassy sent from Russia to Bukhārā was the one conducted by M. Negri in 1820. The friendly relations with Bukhārā would have continued but for the British, who tried to bring influence on the Amirs by sending Alexander Burnes in 1832 as their envoy. As a counter-measure the Russians began sending their own envoys after 1834 and tried to secure some concessions, but the Amir was adamant. The situation did not improve even when the Afghan ruler Dost Mohammad Khān took refuge in Bukhārā (1839). The British extended their influence up to the Oxus, and the Russians sent a politico-scientific mission to Bukhārā in 1840. The Russians could not secure the desired concessions, as Amir Nasrullah's aggressive policy went against their interests. His son, Amir Muzaffaruddin, continued his father's policy and pushed his advance against Kokand, which was divided into east and west regions. Although Amir Muzaffarudin tried to create diplomatic contact with Moscow, he failed in his venture and was forced to fight a war against the Russians in 1866. After his initial victory, he was finally defeated at Yirjar on the left bank of the Syr Daryā and he accepted the Russian presence in this region. In the next round of war in 1867, the fortress of Yenghi Kurgan was taken and in the following year Samarkand was occupied. This was followed by a Russian advance towards Bukhārā. In 1868 the Amir had to sign a treaty by which a war indemnity was paid, the Zarafshan valley with Samarkand and Kette Kurgan was ceded, and the Russians gained trade concessions, including the right of trading freely throughout the Khānate, the right of free passage through the Khānate and to the neighbouring countries, and finally a limitation of the tariff on all Russian imports to 2.5 per cent of their nominal value (Allworth, 1990: 103–20).

The Khānate of Khīva

The state of Khīva, known in history under the name of Khwarizm, comprised the country formed by the lower course of the Oxus river (Āmū Daryā). It was peopled by Uzbeks, Turkmens, Karakalpaks, Kazakhs, Sart (Tājī ks) and Persians. The principal trade was with Russia and other Western countries.

An Uzbek Chieftain of the Kungrat tribe, Muhammad Amin Inak (1792–1804), founded a new dynasty. He waged constant war against the Bukhāriots and other Turkmen tribes, such as the Yomut and Teke. It was his son, Mohammad Rahim Khān (1806–25), who welcomed in Khīva Shāh Mahmud, a rival brother of the Afghan ruler Shāh Zaman. His son, Allah Quli Khān (1825–42), faced the challenge of General Petrovsky in 1839 and forced him to retreat. Several Russian prisoners were taken by the Khīvans, and until 1857, Khīva could not be conquered by the Russians.

It was only when Von Kaufman became the governor-general of Turkestan that a plan was made to move against Khīva. This was preceded by detailed survey work of the region. Ultimately advances were made from four directions under the joint command of Kaufman. Great resistance was offered by the Yomut tribesmen in the desert, who were vassals of the Khān. But ultimately Khīva was taken in 1873. The fate of the Khān of Khīva was not decided here but byan international agreement between Britain and Russia, by which the Khānate retained its entity, although the Khīvan territory on the right bank of the Oxus, together with the river Delata, was ceded to the Russians, who also gained trade and commercial concessions by way of exemption of Russian traders from customs throughout the Khānate, and they controlled the future foreign policy of the Khān and his internal administration.

This was followed by a campaign against the Yomut tribes, who were thoroughly humbled. To round off the remaining Turkmen tribes, Russian forces advanced from Krasnavodsk (now renamed as Turkmenbashi) on the Caspian Sea, where a Russian stronghold was established in the eighteenth century. The Russians now advanced eastward to annex the adjacent territory after the surrender of Khīva. It was only when international diplomacy smoothed the way that the Russians began to move against the Tekke Turkmens and continued their attacks between 1879 and 1881. When the Akal tribesmen sheltered in the fortress of Geok-tepe and made several fierce sorties to engage in hand-to-hand combat, the fortress finally fell to the Russians on 12 January 1881. Later in 1884, the fortress of Merw was occupied. The entire area was combined with the oblast of Trans-Caspia. The final agreement signed in July 1887 between Britain and Russia left Balkh to Afghanistan, free from Russian interference (Caroe, 1967: 81–6) and the Russians retained control over the territory of the Turkmens up to the outer fringes of Kopet Dag mountain. To its south lay the territory of Iran.

With this Russian expansion in Central Asia, a new administrative structure evolved. A new governor-generalship of Turkestan with headquarters at Tashkent was created in 1865. After the disappearance of the Kokand state and the subordination of Bukhārā and Khīva, this governor-generalship was strengthened. In the case of the Trans-Caspian region, administrative control was first exercised by the Trans-Caucasus governor-general until it was finally attached to Turkestan. Similarly the two Kazakh oblasts of Syr Daryā and Semirechye came under the jurisdiction of the Turkestan governor-general.

However, the greatest change occurred in the field of education. Before the coming of the Russians the educational system was based on the Muslim tradition of mektebs and madrassahs. The tsarist educational policy can be understood in two different stages: the first for the steppes and the second after the creation of Turkestan. For the steppes, some detail has been given above.

In Turkestan, where the traditional mektebs and madrassahs flourished, an attempt was made by Von Kaufman, the governor-general, to establish 'mixed schools' which were brought under a Board of Education with a Chief Inspector at Tashkent. In the next stage, Russian-vernacular schools were started by which the Russian educational system was reformed and the traditional schools brought under control. However, the greatest change came with the establishment of reformed mektebs at the initiative of the Tatar educationist Ismail Gasprinskii. As a result,

> on the eve of the 1905 revolutions Muslim education had progressed in the quantitative sense and at the same time had made an endeavour to open itself to the modern world: an endeavour most marked in the reformed Mektebs but visible too in the traditional schools.
>
> (Carrere d'Encausse, 1963: Vol. 2, 374–94)

When national sentiments grew in Turkestan after the 1908 revolution in Turkey, there was rapid growth of the reformed mektebs and also a keen desire to promote the reformist tendency in the Muslim schools as a whole. This led to the rise of Jadidism – an intellectual awakening in Turkestan, with an influx of new, modern ideas resulting mainly from contact with the Russian population and from economic change, particularly due to the increase in cotton production and the penetration of Russian capitalism. This latter factor, along with the introduction of new communications and a modern railway system, including construction of the trans-Siberian railway, completely changed the socio-economic order in Central Asia. All rail connections led westward to Moscow and other cities of European Russia. The economy materially changed with the increase in cash crops, such as cotton, and its linkage with Russian industrial growth. In the field of architecture new tendencies were seen in the building of the Sitarai-Makh khosa (Tivrikov, 1982: 67–9) palace at Bukhārā, in which we find an integration of Western style with that of traditional forms. Similarly the Chinese influence is seen at Panfilav, where the Muslim community built a mosque (Dani et al., 1991: 96–7) in 1887. However, the traditional architectural style remained in the palace of Khodavar Khān at Kokand.

AFGHANISTAN

The state of Afghanistan was founded by Ahmad Shāh Abdali in 1747 on the demise of his overlord, the Afshar ruler Nādir Shāh of Iran (Gankovsky, 1985: ch. 3). It was Nādir Shāh who had separated the territory west of the Indus river from the Mughal Empire (Caroe, 1983: 253–55)

and he also took away the Balkh region from the Amir of Bukhārā. After his death Nādir's empire collapsed and his eastern territory, dominated by the Afghan units of his army, became independent. They were led by several Khāns of the Abdali tribe, who got together in a *Jirga* (assembly) at Kandahar and, in October 1747, elected Ahmad Khān Shāh, a young military commander from the Saddozai clan (of the Popalzai branch), as the head of state. He chose for himself the simple title of *Durr-i-Durran*, i.e. 'Pearl of Pearls' (Gankovsky, 1985: 122). Hence his dynasty came to be known as the Durrani (Caroe, 1983: 256). While Ahmad Shāh Abdali was busy consolidating his Afghan state, the British were expanding in India with their own political ambitions and tsarist Russia was moving into the northern part of Central Asia. How the Afghan state emerged into the limelight is a long story of the clash of interests between the British and the Russians pursuing their imperial designs.

Ahmad Shāh began by subduing the Khānates and then conquered the different regions, including 'several small Khānates north of the Hindukush: Balkh, Shibirgan, Andhkoi, Qunduz and Maymanah' (Gankovsky, 1985: 123), Balochistan, Sindh, Multan, Lahore and Kashmir. He fixed his boundary at Sirhind beyond the eastern limits of modern Pakistan (Elphinstone, 1972). The climax of his success was reached in 1761, when he defeated the Marathas in the Third Battle of Panipat and finally ended the Maratha ambition to dominate north India. At the same time he opened the way for British expansion in India.

Ahmad Shād died in 1773 at the age of fifty and was succeeded by his son Timur Shāh, who reigned until the spring of 1791. He transferred his capital from Kandahar to Kabul and made Peshawar his winter capital. It was in the time of Timur's son and successor Shāh Zaman (1793–1800) that the Sikh Sardar, Ranjit Singh, by rendering his services to take heavy artillery beyond the Jhelam river, obtained in 1799 by royal investiture the capital of Punjab, i.e. Lahore (Caroe, 1983: 265–6). Henceforward, Punjab remained outside the Afghan state. With the death of Shāh Zaman the family quarrel among his children started, and the British took advantage of this. The first British mission was led by Monstuart Elphinstone (Elphinstone, 1972), who, in 1808, extracted favourable terms from Shāh Shuja against Napoleon's possible alliance with Indian rulers.

The family quarrel led to dynastic change and the Afghan throne passed from the hands of the Popalzai branch into those of Barakzai Sardars, but the British continued to support Shāh Shuja of the earlier branch, who was in their pay in Peshawar – a city which became a bone of contention between Ranjit Singh and the Afghan Sardars. Finally, Afghanistan lost Peshawar and the Afghan territory remained confined to the west of the Khyber Pass. However, the powerful ruler of the second dynasty, Dost Mohammad Khān (1826–63) opposed both the Sikhs and the British and sought help from Iran and Russia. A Russian representative, I. V. Vitkevich, was sent by V. A. Parovsky, the governor of Orenburg, with the open intent to develop trade between Afghanistan and Russia, but the Russian presence here and the dynastic quarrel led to the first Anglo-Afghan War (1838–42). This resulted in a great disaster for the British. Their candidate, Shāh Shuja, was killed and Alexander Burnes, who had played a leading role in the affairs of Afghanistan and Bukhārā, was murdered. However, this military defeat was turned into an advantageous diplomatic game by the British. Dost Mohammad Khān succeeded in becoming reconciled with the British, from whom he received economic help, which he used for reuniting Afghanistan. In the meanwhile the British did away with the Sikh state and ended the independence of Sindh, and thus came face to face with Afghanistan. It is pointed out by Sir Olaf Caroe (Caroe, 1983: 346) that the British 'crossed the Indus and set about the business of organizing a new frontier to a new province in a Central Asian land, which had no real affinities with India'. This advance of the British in the second half of the nineteenth century became more complicated after the death of Dost Mohammad Khān. While the British followed the 'closed border policy' to control the Pathan tribes on their western border, Dost's successor Sher 'Alī (1863–65 and 1869–78), gave preference to a Russian mission rather than to the British, which led to a second Anglo-Afghan War (1878–80). Anglo-Russian rivalry was at the root of the new developments. While Russia wanted a neutral state in Afghanistan, the British wished to control Afghanistan and secure their western imperial border. They took full advantage of the dynastic power struggle. While Sher 'Alī's son and successor, Yaqub Khān (r. 1878–9) recognized the British right to control Sibi, Pishin and the Kurram Valley and the Khyber and Michni passes, another agreement between Russia and Britain proved to be of greater importance. Gankovsky points out: 'In 1873 the tsarist government renounced its former proposal on Afghanistan's neutrality and officially assured the British that it regarded Afghanistan 'beyond the field of Russian influence'. Under an agreement between Russia and Britain the Āmū Daryā River was recognized as the northern frontier of Afghanistan (Gankovsky, 1985: 153). However, at the end of the Second Afghan War and after the death of Yaqub Khān, the Afghan throne was occupied by Abdur Rahman Khān (1881–1901), his cousin, who had spent more than ten years in Central Asia. He and his son Habibullah Khān continued to rule in Afghanistan until 1919.

Abdur Rahman Khān, who very well understood the interests of the British in India and of Russia in Central Asia, managed the internal affairs of Afghanistan in the course of time by suppressing the opposing forces and re-establishing the unity of the country. At the same time his other achievement was to determine the new boundaries of his state, first in the Northwest and then along the Durand line in the east. The British were satisfied with his cooperative attitude and his agreeing to keep a British agent at Kabul. At the same time in northern India the British managed to keep control over Gilgit, Hunza and Chitral and kept the Wakhan corridor in the hands of the Afghans, thus maintaining a distance from their own Indian possessions and that of the Russians in Pamir. Later, in the time of Habibullah Khān, the British adopted the 'forward policy' and created a new administrative pattern over the 'tribal areas' of their western frontier after establishing the new Northwestern Frontier Province (Caroe, 1983: ch. 25). By the convention of 1907 Habibullah Khān settled his independent position in Afghanistan, while Britain and Russia agreed further on their spheres of influence in Iran (Dupree, 1973: ch. 19). It was in the time of these two rulers that the real foundations of the national state of Afghanistan were laid (Dupree, 1973: ch. 18). However, it was under Sher 'Alī Khān that attempts were made to improve school education and improve the economic system. (Gankovsky, 1985: 133–55). But Dupree has rightly pointed out that 'Abdul Rahman's reign was not only

characterised by external boundary-drawing and internal imperialism, but early attempts at modernity' (Dupree, 1973: 428), by hiring many foreigners to assist in technological development.

BIBLIOGRAPHY

AKINER, S. 1983. *Islamic Peoples of the Soviet Union*. London, pp. 93–102.

ALLWORTH, E. 1975. *Soviet Asia, Bibliographies*. Praeger Publishers, Westport CT.

——. 1990. *The Modern Uzbeks*. Hoover Institution Press, Stanford, pp. 103–20.

ASFENDIAROV, S. 1935. *Istoriia Kazakhstana*. Alma Ata and Moscow.

Aziatskaia Rossiia. 1914. 3 vols. and atlas. St Petersburg.

BACON, E. 1980. *Central Asians under Russian Rule*. Cornell University Press, Ithaca NY.

BARTHOLD, V. 1984. 'Kucum Khān'. In: *Encyclopaedia of Islam*. Brill, Leiden.

——. 1927. *Istoriia Kulturnoi Zhizni Turkestana*. Leningrad.

BASIN, V. Y. 1968. *O Suskhnostic i formakh Vzaimovtnoshenii tsarskoi Rossi i Kazakhstana va XVIII*. Vece, Alma Ata.

——. 1969. *Kazakhstan V. Sisteme vneshnei politiki. Resiciv pervoi polovine XVIII veka in Kazakhstan v XV–XVIII*. Vekākh, Alma Ata.

BURNES, A. 1834. *Travels into Bukhārā*. London.

CAROE, O. 1967. *The Soviet Empire*. Macmillan, London, pp. 81–6.

——. 1983. (reprint) *The Pathans (1550 BC to 1957)*. Oxford University Press, Karachi.

CARRERE D'ENCAUSSE, H. 1963. 'Tsarist Educational Policy in Turkestan, 1867–1917'. In: *Central Asian Review*, Vol. 2, pp. 374–94.

CHUKUBAYE, V. A. A. 1957. 'The Social, Economic and Political Effects of Russian Influence in Kirgizia (1855–1917)'. In: *Central Asian Review*, Vol. 5, pp. 235–46.

COURANT, M. 1912. *L'Asie Centrale aux XVI Ie et XVIIIe siècles: empire kalmouk ou empire mantchou?* Picard, Paris.

CURZON, G. N. 1889. *Russia In Central Asia In 1889; and the Anglo-Russian Question*. London.

DANI, A. H.; ASKAROV, A. A.; GUBIN, S. P. 1991. *Rediscovery of Civilizations of Central Asia*. Islamabad, pp. 96–7.

DUPREE, L. 1973. *Afghanistan*. Princeton University Press.

ELPHINSTONE, M. 1972. *An Account of the Kingdom of Caubul*. Oxford.

GANKOVSKY, Y. V. 1985. (English translation) *A History of Afghanistan*. Moscow.

GRAHAM, S. 1916. *Through Russian Central Asia*. New York.

GROUSSET, R. 1991. *The Empire of the Steppes (A History of Central Asia)*. (English translation by Naomi Walford). Chapter 10. Rutgers University Press, New Brunswick.

HAMBLY, G. (ed.) 1969. *Central Asia*, London, pp. 144–8.

HAYIT, B. 1984. 'Some reflections on the subject of Annexation of Turkestani Kazakhstan by Russia'. In: *Central Asian Survey*, Vol. 3, No. 4, pp. 61–75.

HOLDSWORTH, M. 1959. *Turkestan in the Nineteenth Century*. London.

HOWORTH, H. H. 1876–80. *History of the Mongols*. London.

HUTTON, J. 1977. (Reprint) *Central Asia from the Aryan to the Cossack*. London. Ist edn 1875, London.

JOCHELSON, W. 1928. *Peoples of Asiatic Russia*. Amercian Museum of Natural History, New York.

KARRYYEV, A; ROSBYAKAY, A. 1958. 'Turkmenistan 1868–1917'. In: *Central Asian Review*, Vol. 6, pp. 12–142.

KENNER, R. J. 1942. *The Urge to the Sea*. University of California Press.

KHALFIN, N. A. 1956. *Tri Rasskiye Missi'č*. Tashkent.

KHAN, A. R. 1900. *The Life of Abdur Rahman, Amir of Afghanistan*. Ed. Sultan Mahomed Khān. London.

KHANOF M.; VENINKOF, V. 1865. *The Russians in Central Asia.* Trans. John and Robert Michell. London.

KRAUSSE, A. 1899. *Russia in Asia (1858–99).* London.

LANSDELL, H. 1885. *Russian Central Asia.* London/New York.

LENTZEFF, P. G. V. 1943. *Siberia in the Seventeenth Century.* California.

LIASHCHENKO, P. 1949. *History of the National Economy of Russia to the 1917 Revolution.* New York.

MARVIN, C. 1880. *The Eye-witnesses' Account of the Disastrous Russian Campaign against the Akhal Tekke Turcomans.* London.

——. 1880. *The Russians at Merv and Herat and their power of invading India.* London.

MCKENZIE KERMIT, E. 1989. 'Chokhan Valikhanov: Kazakh Princeling and Scholar'. In: *Central Asian Survey*, Vol. 8, No. 3, pp. 1–30.

MITCHELL, J.; MITCHELL, R. 1865. (translated from the Russian) *The Russians in Central Asia.* London.

Official history of the Kazakh USSR. 1957. Kazakhstan on the Eve of its Annexation to Russia, Vol. 1.

OLCOTT, M. B. 1987. *The Kazakhs,* Hoover Institution Press. Stanford, p. 30.

PIERCE, R. A. 1960. *Russian Central Asia, 1867–1917.* University of California Press, Berkeley.

RYSKULOV, T. R. 1929. *Kirgizstan.* Moscow.

SARAY, M. 1984. 'Russo-Turkmen Relations upto 1874'. In: *Central Asian Survey*, Vol. 3, No. 4, pp. 15–48.

SCHULER, E. 1876. *Turkestan.* London.

SEMENOV. 1937. *The Conquest of Scheria.* Berlin.

SOKOL, E. D. 1954. *The Revolt of 1916 in Russian Central Asia.* Baltimore.

STURLEY, D. M. 1964. *A Short History of Russia.* Longman, London, ch. 4.

TREADGOLD, D. W. 1957. *The Great Siberian Migration Government and Peasant in Resettlement from Emancipation to the First World War.* Princeton.

TIVRIKOV, V. 1982. *Bukhārā.* Moscow, pp. 67–9.

VAMBERY, A. 1990. *History of Bukhārā.* Karachi, reprint, pp. 379–82.

VIATKIN, M. P. 1947. *Batyr Srym.* Moscow.

——. 1947. *Ocherki Poistorii Kazakhskoi SSR.* Moscow.

WHEELER, G. 1964. *The Modern History of Soviet Central Asia.* London.

13.2
SOUTH ASIA

Sumit Sarkar

INTRODUCTION

The 'long' nineteenth century in South Asia, from the 1750s to the First World War, was marked most obviously by a century-long process of gradual British conquest of the sub-continent, the high noon of this empire during the decades succeeding the suppression of the rebellion of 1857, and the beginnings of the modern anti-colonial nationalist movements that would eventually make that empire untenable. Inevitably, South Asia became and remains central to debates about the nature of modern Western imperialism and its impact on the non-West, in its manifold and interrelated socio-economic, political, and cultural dimensions.

There has been a strong and partly justifiable tendency, therefore, to set all history writing about nineteenth-century South Asia within a colonial and anti-colonial polemical frame, though there are signs in recent years of important moves beyond that mould. Apologias for British rule for long sought to identify the British East India Company's expansion across the sub-continent, followed after 1858 by direct British suzerainty, unequivocally with progress and modernization. The argument was sought to be strengthened by the assumption that the earlier history of South Asia had been marked by alternate spans of 'Oriental' despotism and anarchy and an absence of fundamental change. Anti-colonial critiques, whether animated by nationalism, Marxist analysis of capitalist imperialism, or theories of development or under-development, have been inclined towards sharing a similar assumption of total rupture with the coming of British rule, though of course with values sharply reversed. The economic consequences were attacked with particular keenness: an alleged 'drain of wealth' from India to Britain, destruction of flourishing pre-colonial handicrafts like cotton textiles through Lancashire competition buttressed by unfair state policies, excessive taxes on land, a commercialization of agriculture of little benefit to peasants, hindrances to indigenous industrial growth, all contributing to making and keeping South Asia poor and backward. Nationalist assessments of the cultural aspects of the Western impact tended to be more ambiguous during the decades of actual anti-colonial struggles. There was a widespread assumption of a 'renaissance' produced by Western education among its middle-class beneficiaries, which in time led on to modern nationalism. Cultural criticism was generally characterized not by total rejection, but an emphasis upon the partial, incomplete nature of colonial modernity in terms of its reach and content. The recent, world-wide shift in analyses of the epoch of European domination from politico-economic towards culturalist criteria, however, has produced more extreme critiques of 'colonial discourse' and what are assumed to have been its 'derivatives' among the colonized literati. Such 'post-colonial' criticism at times veers towards rejections of 'Western modernity' as a (somewhat undifferentiated) whole (Chatterjee, 1986; 1994).

Erosion of assumptions of a total pre-colonial and colonial rupture began with the more defensive form of colonial apologetics that stressed continued stagnation, or at best 'growth without development', rather than dramatic improvement or progress under British rule. This was a modification rendered necessary particularly by a wave of devastating famines during the closing years of the nineteenth century. Continuing and abysmal poverty among the great majority of Indians was admitted, but sought to be traced to 'natural' factors like climate or demography, and/or to structural continuities with pre-colonial times. Emphasis shifted towards the limits, rather than the reach or efficacy, of British domination. Recent versions of 'continuity' arguments – that figure prominently in many volumes of the New Cambridge History of India series, for instance – are sometimes suspected of having a residual apologetic strain. The important contributions that these have nevertheless made at times in terms of adding richness and multi-layered complexity to historical understanding still seems difficult to deny.

Equally undeniable, however, are some key areas where the old nationalist critiques, despite undoubted crudities and exaggerations, do seem to have stood the test of time. These include, in particular, the centrality of colonial India in the structures that buttressed nineteenth-century Britain's military and economic pre-eminence, and the widening gap between British growth and prosperity and Indian poverty, through the two centuries of colonial domination.

Land revenues, extracted ultimately from South Asian peasants, enabled the maintenance of a large European-style British Indian army, that was used frequently in military adventures in many parts of the world: China, South East Asia, Africa, West Asia, ultimately during 1914–18, in the killing fields of France. Control over South Asia was equally crucial for British naval predominance. The economic gains of empire for Britain have been more controversial, but still difficult to deny. It is true that nationalist claims of a direct link between tribute or 'drain' from India and industrial revolution in Britain have found few takers, and the bulk of British capital investments went to the white settler colonies and not to the formal empire in South Asia. There have been arguments, in the colonial era as well as today, that some of the material gains of empire could have been attained at less expense without formal conquest and rule. Debates continue about the specific weight of economic considerations behind imperial expansion, as well as regarding the degree of conscious motivation or intentionality that can be discerned behind that process. Yet the reality of the material advantages to Britain appear undoubted. Remittances to Britain from Indian revenues – the so-called Home Charges – provided an indirect subsidy to the British exchequer, while their transfer through a constant and growing Indian export surplus often helped to stabilize the otherwise unfavourable British balance of trade. Famous for many centuries for its cotton handicrafts, India in the nineteenth century became a source of cheap raw materials and often semi-servile indentured labour, and a market for British manufactures, primarily Lancashire textiles. The colonial transformation of Asian economies from major centres of production and export of artisanal products to mere exporters of agricultural raw materials underlay what Chris Bayly has termed an 'epochal growth of differentials in income between Asians and Europeans'. The British East India Company's conquest of India thus provides 'one of the first and most striking examples of dependent economic relations' between the West and the non-West (Bayly, 1987: 2).

What such dependency meant for the great majority of South Asians can be glimpsed from a few aggregate statistics. In 1900, arguing against nationalist charges that British rule had immiserized India, Viceroy Lord Curzon declared that the per capita income of Indians was as high as Rs30, or £2 sterling per annum. A modern estimate places the corresponding figure that year for the United Kingdom at £52 (Bagchi, 1972: 3). The contrast cannot be explained by population pressure, for demographic growth remained very slow till 1921, with only a 30 million increase between 1871 and 1901, decades during which over 12 million deaths were officially attributed to famine. Life expectancy at birth was estimated at 24.6 in the 1870s, falling to 23.8 in the 1890s (Bhattacharya, 1989; Visaria and Visaria, 1983: 502). And British rule ended in 1947 with the subcontinental literacy rate at 16 per cent for those above 10: hardly surprising, since public spending on education had been a miserable 0.2 per cent of the national income in the nineteenth century (Kumar, 1983: 937).

Significant modifications in once-standard assumptions seem required, however, in two key respects. The interfaces between pre-colonial and colonial are turning out to have been more complicated and varied that had been thought earlier. There is a growing, though by no means universal, tendency among historians of medieval India to focus more attention on the limits of bureaucratic centralization under the Mughals, who appear in many ways to have been what they declared themselves to be, *Shah-an-Shah*, 'king of kings', claiming the loyalty of multiple layers of intermediate, semi-autonomous princes and chiefs rather than absolutist 'Oriental' despots, as once imagined. The eighteenth-century 'fall' or 'decline', consequently, may not have been that dramatic, for both the mystique of Mughal suzerainty (formally acknowledged even by the East India Company right down to 1857), and Mughal administrative practices persisted in large parts of the sub-continent well into the nineteenth century (Bayly, 1987). The theme increasingly emphasized nowadays, however, is not continuity equated with stagnation, but a spilling over of processes of change across the precolonial-colonial borders. Bayly in

particular has been emphasizing the role of upwardly-mobile intermediate groups – scribal families, revenue farmers, local gentry, merchants and bankers, who had benefited from Mughal centralization and decline alike, and then often played a crucial role in providing loans, knowledge and support to the East India Company as 'uneasy collaborators in the creation of colonial India' (Bayly, 1987: 4; 1983; Marshall, 1987).

This might occasionally appear to come perilously close to a self-justifying attribution to Indians of prime responsibility for their own subjugation. But continuity arguments have been helpful in drawing attention to questions of variations and multiple levels, breaking with tendencies towards looking at colonialism and the colonized as homogeneous blocs.

British interests in India were certainly always diverse, shifting, even contradictory: inevitably so, since the Britain which conquered and ruled India was also simultaneously going through the greatest era of transformations in its entire history. The sudden accession of a group of merchants to enormous territorial power and profits aroused considerable suspicion and resentment in British ruling and parliamentary circles. The East India Company and its employees could be at odds over matters of private trade, and there were growing pressures from 'interlopers' and free traders to open up the monopoly control over trade between Britain and India. To this was added in course of time the emerging interests of Lancashire industrialists, pressing with considerable success for high import duties on the Indian cotton goods through which the Company had been remitting much of its own and its servants' profits, and eager through a one-way 'free trade' to win the vast South Asian market for its own machine-made textiles. The result was a succession of Charter Acts (1793, 1813, 1833) through which the Company gradually lost its monopoly rights over British trade with India and then China, and in fact ceased to be a trading concern at all by the 1830s. Meanwhile wider British attitudes and assumptions concerning India and the non-West in general were also diverse and variable. These included 'Orientalist' scholarly interest and admiration for ancient cultures, paternalist fascination with 'simple' peasant life and village communities, evangelical enthusiasm about spreading Christianity among the 'heathen', and utilitarian drive for aggressive modernizing reform (Stokes, 1959; Guha, 1963; Metcalf, 1997). Elements of racial arrogance in encounters with the subjugated, never perhaps entirely absent, certainly deepened in the aftermath of the bloody suppression of the 1857 rebellion. Racism itself should not be seen as an unchanging bloc, for it has had cultural as well as biological forms, the first eager to spread Western education and enlightenment among the benighted non-whites, the second insisting on irremediable racial difference.[1]

South Asian responses and developments in the colonial era evidently demand similar – indeed, probably greater – disaggregation, in terms of times, regions, and social spaces. The expansion of British control over the sub-continent – both direct and indirect (via subordinated 'native states') – took place at widely different paces, times and conjunctures, with the major spurts occurring around 1757–65 (Bengal and Bihar, associated with Clive), 1792–1805 (under Cornwallis and particularly Wellesley), 1816–26 (Hastings and Amherst), and 1848–56 (the annexations of Dalhousie) (Fisher, 1993: ch. 1). Differential times of conquest superimposed on already existing regional variations a considerable degree of distinctiveness in colonial administrative practices and assumptions, notably for instance in matters of land revenue settlements. Always an alien tiny minority ruling a vast population, the British everywhere had to come to adjustments with indigeneous power structures and locally dominant groups – princes, landlords, peasant upper strata, merchants and bankers, high-caste Hindu and elite Muslim literati – but the precise quality of these relationships came to differ considerably over time and across regions. Thus the Bengal area was distinctive in the virtual absence of princely states, stable alliances with landlords, and a much more overwhelming economic predominance of British business interests than regions of later conquest and partly indirect control, like the interior of Bombay Presidency. And, of course, the overall apparatus of colonial rule itself underwent major changes, with the 1858 takeover of the East India Company by the crown as the most obvious, but not the only possible, dividing line.

Most crucial of all perhaps, were the differences in colonial penetration and impact across social levels. Environmental and social historians today are emphasizing long-term rhythms where the colonial presence might have been marginal or at least far from decisive. These would include the far-reaching consequences of changes in river channels as in Eastern India; the ebb and flow of epidemics; the fluctuations in the frontiers between settled peasants and nomadic, pastoral or food gathering peoples; and many aspects of religious and cultural life, of structures of family, kinship or caste. And if the extent of colonial penetration was variable, even more so was the nature of its impact and the quality of responses. The cruder kinds of nationalist assumptions of virtually total immiserization of a once-prosperous and conflict-free people, and of an eventual near-automatic, 'natural' swing into resistance to foreign rule, obviously need to be abandoned. Disaggregation here has to pay attention to dividing-lines of class, but also of gender, caste, ethnicity, and religion. Many among the subordinated did turn to anti-colonial ways, and their rally proved decisive in the eventual fall of empire and establishment of democratic structures over the major part of the sub-continent. But with regard to hierarchies of gender and caste, in particular, colonial structures and policies did seem to hold out at times resources for a degree of improvement or upward mobility for the subordinated, prospects of modifying slightly what had always been a most unequal and oppressive society. It is both impossible and retrogressive to neatly encompass everything in modern South Asian history into an unitary and homogenized colonial or nationalist frame.

c.1757–1858

The East India Company's military and commercial power expanded from the mid-eighteenth century in a political context set by the variety of successor states that were developing behind the facade of continued Mughal formal suzerainty. These included the Maratha, Sikh and Jat kingdoms, which had originated from anti-Mughal rebellions of local gentry and warrior-peasants, had some connections at times with anti-hierarchical tendencies in religion as well as with emerging regional loyalties, but became more socially conservative over time. Brahmannical orthodoxy was notably refurbished, for instance, by the rule of the Peshwas of Poona in the Maratha heartland. Petty

kingdoms emerged in many parts of the sub-continent ruled by Rajput chiefs, upwardly-mobile peasant-warriors turning into overlords, and Muslim adventurers. Among the latter, notably, were Hyder Ali and Tipu Sultan, who made Mysore quite formidable for the British in the late eighteenth century. In a third category were the imperial provinces of Awadh, Hyderabad, and Bengal, where the governors subverted the Mughal principle of separation of military and revenue authority, and established their families as hereditary rulers.

The impression of anarchy and decline that this political maze conveys is now considered exaggerated. Agricultural and commercial decline in one area could be balanced by growth in another. Decentralization helped the gentry who had served in the Mughal bureaucracy in transferable posts to get more rooted in localities as hereditary landholders, and indigenous commercial and usurious capital advanced in many areas, through the tightening of connections between trade-cum-banking and the processes of surplus-extraction from peasants. By the mid-eighteenth century, the great banking house of Jagat Seths in Murshidabad had become virtual partners of the Nawab in ruling Bengal, remitting for instance the imperial tribute by drawing bills on their Delhi agents. Well before 1757, European merchants had inserted themselves into these complex structures as important, but as yet far from dominant, players. Thus in Bengal the British, French and Dutch East India Companies had become the major purchasers of high-quality cotton and silk piecegoods for export to Europe, in return for which they had to bring in large quantities of silver: for prior to the industrial revolution in textiles Western Europe had little to offer in the way of goods to Asian countries. Meanwhile the quest of Company servants for private fortunes in addition to their salaries led to increasing participation in internal and inter-Asian trade, which further tightened the linkages between Europeans and Indian merchants and financiers.

But the revisionist argument about the eighteenth century can perhaps be pressed too far. For nearly a quarter-millenium since the coming of Vasco da Gama in 1498, the European presence and influence in the sub-continent had remained primarily coastal and commercial, with little political significance. Such marginality was surely related in part to the control exercised over the interior of the sub-continent by a powerful empire for the major part of these centuries. The weakening of centralized authority by the 1740s–50s both enabled, and seemed to necessitate, the building up of armies and political alliances by European trading companies. These were needed as insurance against interference or extortion by indigenous rulers and, even more, in the context of fierce rivalries among themselves (in particular the Anglo-French wars of 1742–8 and 1756–63). Imperial decline also became an opportunity for the British East India Company to effectively solve what had been a perennial problem for European trade with Asia. A progressive appropriation of land revenue eliminated the need to buy sub-continental goods with bullion brought from Europe, which had been clearly contrary to dominant mercantilist assumptions.

It was hardly fortuitous, therefore, that the sequence of events that culminated in the British becoming *de facto* rulers of Bengal began with Nawab Sirajuddoula's attempt to stop the Company from fortifying its trading centre of Calcutta. Within eight years of the latter's defeat at Plassey (1757) through an alliance of the many influential groups he had managed to alienate – the British (led by Clive), high officials, leading landholders, merchant-usurer capital as embodied in the house of Jagat Seth – the Company had acquired revenue-collecting rights (*diwani*) for the entire province of Bengal from the Mughal emperor. Its exports from Bengal could now be bought with money extracted as taxes from Bengal itself: the core of what would come to be called the 'drain of wealth'. Political control also enabled the servants of the Company to amass fabulous fortunes for themselves, 'presents', while making and unmaking Nawabs four times within a decade (1757, 1760, 1763, 1765), monopolies over lucrative lines of internal trade, and a progressive extension of control over inter-Asian maritime commerce and shipping. Indeed, the immediate pressure for expansion often seems to have come from such private interests rather than metropolitan economic needs or even conscious Company decisions.

Company territorial expansion beyond Bengal took place through oscillating phases of aggression and relative quiescence. From the point of view of the London authorities – the Court of Directors of the Company, and after 1784 the Board of Control set up by the government to oversee British Indian affairs – expansion might be ultimately profitable, but often a short-term liability in terms of diversion of investments of Indian revenues from commerce to military expenditure. The immediate motivations behind expansion, therefore, were often politico-military rather then economic: threat-perceptions about European rivals (France during the Revolutionary and Napoleonic Wars; tsarist Russia from the 1840s onwards), and signs that one or other Indian state might be getting impermissibly strong through adaptation of Western military and mercantilist techniques (notably the Mysore of Tipu Sultan in the 1790s). It is not accidental, therefore, that the most decisive period of expansion was between 1798 and 1805, under Wellesley (the brother, incidentally, of Wellington, of Waterloo fame), which saw the final destruction of Mysore and major gains at the expense of the Maratha states – the latter process being completed under the Marquis of Hastings in 1818. The other major spurt came in the 1840s and early 1850s, under Auckland, Ellenborough, Hardinge, and above all Dalhousie, when the frontiers towards the north-west needed to be consolidated against possible threats from Russia through annexations of Sind, Punjab, and the remnants of Awadh, and a disastrous foray was attempted into Afghanistan.

But direct economic impulses were also far from absent at times. Thus a detailed study has revealed the importance of Bombay-based private trade interests in the export of pepper from Malabar and raw cotton from Maharashtra in the extension of British control over Mysore and the Maratha interior, between 1792 and 1805.[2] (Nightingale, 1970). Beyond a point the political/economic divide becomes difficult to maintain in any case, for in large parts of the country the cutting edge of Company expansion was provided by the so-called subsidiary alliances. Indian princes who had become dependent allies had to provide money for the maintenance of a stipulated number of Company regiments in return for a British guarantee of their 'defence'. Failure to meet the heavy subsidy obligations could lead to partial or total annexation, while the system enhanced burdens on the princes' subjects, starved their administration of funds – after which complaints by Company Residents of 'misrule' could justify passage to direct control. And the revenue extracted, whether from directly-ruled

territories or client princely states, ultimately funded Company commercial investments, military and administrative expenditure, and remittances to Britain alike.

The variegated times and patterns of British expansion made for considerable differences in the extent and nature of colonial impact on Indian economy and society. So far as indigenous commerce and manufactures are concerned, the old nationalist model of near-complete subjugation and decline still appears fairly relevant for areas of early (and therefore long-continued) colonial domination, notably the Bengal region. Even there, there was an initial, late eighteenth/early nineteenth-century phase when European trading activities did require a degree of mutually profitable collaboration with indigenous merchants. Some of the latter could become fabulously rich, and one or two, notably Dwarkanath Tagore, even innovative entrepreneurs. But thereafter Bengali enterprise rapidly declined, for Calcutta became the great citadel of British capital, which controlled the bulk of overseas shipping and trade, established control over the organized money market through institutions like the Bank of Bengal (set up in 1808 with all-white directors), and benefited enormously from its racial affinity with governmental power. As for traditional manufactures, the initial expansion of exports of cotton and silk goods as major channels of Company remittances after 1757 was accompanied by oppressive forms of monopsonist control over artisans. The extent of the subsequent 'deindustrialization' through the inflow of Lancashire industrial goods has been much debated, but a considerable decline in handspinning and some adverse effects on handlooms, together with a variegated but widespread downturn in a large number of other artisanal manufactures, still appears the most plausible hypothesis. Indigenous mercantile and usurious capital survived, even flourished, but mainly as dependent agents of British export-import firms, or providers of loans to peasants and artisans. Particularly in Eastern India from around 1850 to the First World War, it had become clearly subordinated to what Amiya Bagchi has called a collective European near-monopoly over the commanding heights of business life (Bagchi, 1972: ch. 6).

Such domination obviously took longer to develop, and remained less complete, in regions of slower and uneven political penetration like the upper Ganga valley. It is such areas that have provided the evidence for recent revisionist arguments about the crucial role of Indian collaboration and continued or even enhanced prosperity of indigenous business for much of Company rule. More significant ultimately was the pattern that developed in the Bombay region. There, Parsi and Gujarati merchants had retained a toehold on shipping and external trade, while a significant part of the opium and raw cotton, which became the principal exports, were grown in areas under princely, and not direct British, control. It was here that Indian industrial capitalism would have its birth, with cotton mills in Bombay city and then Ahmedabad in the second half of the nineteenth century.

Agrarian policies in the Company era were conditioned by the often conflicting requirements of maximizing revenue, and the need to build bridges with dominant groups in the countryside for political stability. A further variable was added by the considerable differences in existing structures of land relations across regions. In Bengal, initial efforts to extract as much revenue as possible through short-term revenue farms – a policy that helped to worsen the effects of the devastating famine of 1770 – was followed in

1793 by Cornwallis' Permanent Settlement with land-holders (*zamindars*). The latter were expected to blossom into loyal and enterprising gentry of the British type through fixing their revenue-payments in perpetuity, giving them a virtually free hand in extracting rent from peasants, and in general allowing 'the magic touch of private property' to set a 'productive principle' into operation. After an initial period of much transfer of *zamindari* due to the new insistence on immediate sale if revenue was not paid with absolute punctuality, the system did help to promote loyalism among Bengal landlords. But the 'productive principle' failed to work, as the free hand *vis-à-vis* peasants (with a limited degree of protection against rack-renting and eviction being extended to some tenants only from the late 1850s) enabled *zamindars* to benefit from the growing gap between revenue and rent without need of much entrepreneurial innovation. The gap also produced much sub-infeudation of rentier interests, and helped to provide the material bases of a colonial 'middle class' of petty gentry that also took to modern education and professions: the *bhadralok* who would figure so prominently in late-colonial cultural life and nationalist politics.

Outside Eastern India, differences in rural conditions and shifts towards more anti-landlord attitudes in industrializing England led to non-permanent revenue settlements with the peasant upper stratum, either individually or with collectivities of dominant-caste villagers. The possibility everywhere of the revenue-payers leasing out their land to sub-tenants meant, however, that landlordism remained or emerged also in areas of non-*zamindari* settlement. Other important and broadly common features of colonial agrarian structures included the consolidation of hereditary and alienable private property rights to land (which in practice often came to mean indebted peasants losing their land to moneylender-traders or bigger landholders), and expansion of cultivation at the expense of forests and cultivable wastes. Colonial policies were strongly tilted against migrant pastoralists, food-gatherers and shifting cultivators, as such groups seemed to pose problems of control, and were unlikely to constitute stable markets for metropolitan goods. It has been even argued that in many areas British rule helped to virtually create the 'traditional' India of 'settled arable farming, of caste Hindus and of specialist agricultural produce, "at the cost of the" stranger, older India of forest and nomad' (Bayly, 1987: 144). By the late nineteenth century, some of these nomadic groups were being branded officially as 'criminal tribes'.

Agrarian legislation, as well as mid-century changes in laws regulating business transactions, were thus grounded on the whole in assumptions of market freedom and individual rights. But there was no unambiguous thrust in colonial law towards bourgeois modernity. It is true that in criminal jurisprudence moves were made towards the modern European notion of sovereignty embodied in the assertion of state monopoly over legitimate violence, exercised indifferently over legally equal subjects. Recent research has revealed, however, the many tensions within colonial criminal law, and the ways in which qualifications were often made to accommodate existing hierarchies of caste and gender. And so far as what came to be called 'personal' or 'family' laws are concerned, Warren Hastings in the 1770s had laid down the basic principle that 'inheritance, marriage, caste, and other religious usages' were to be administered according to Hindu or Islamic scriptural texts and in consultation with Brahman *pandits* or

Muslim *ulema*: differentially, in other words, for the two major religious communities. Superficially, this was a continuation of Mughal practice. But Mughal courts never tried to penetrate deep into lower levels of society through the kind of systematic hierarchy of appellate jurisdictions that British rule developed over time, and disputes must have been often decided at local or village level according to diverse customary standards that would have had little to do with textual principles. Colonial 'personal' law centralized, textualized, and thereby probably enhanced to a significant extent the influence of Brahmans and *ulema* over society. Debates about social reform had to take on the form of diverse interpretations of texts assumed to be sacred.[3] They developed perforce along religiously segregated lines, and helped to constitute the bases for partially distinct Hindu and Muslim public spheres: contributing greatly to what twentieth-century Indian English would term 'communalism' (Datta, 1999: ch. 3). Yet, at the same time, enough of the discourse of equal rights and citizenship that was coming to dominate Western societies reached the sub-continent to constitute possibilities of alternative kinds of potentially secular and democratic publics.[4]

Effective colonial rule demanded the progressive accumulation of what has come to be widely termed 'colonial knowledge'. This began, for obvious reasons, with collection of information about indigenous traditions of revenue and law, and quickly extended into knowledge of the terrain (indispensable for conquest) through cartography and geography, the tackling of unfamiliar diseases affecting Europeans through 'tropical medicine', botanical and geological surveys for the exploration of agrarian and mineral resources, the mastering of the Indian past by archaeology and history: to mention only some of the striking instances. Intellectual curiosity about a largely unfamiliar sub-continent suddenly opened out to the European gaze, and requirements of colonial power-knowledge, combined in varying proportions to underlie the growth of such disciplines.

The study of the implicit assumptions of colonial knowledge, enormously stimulated in recent years by the widespread influence of Edward Said's *Orientalism*, has threatened at times to become a field peculiarly open to simplifications. It is being increasingly recognized now that colonial discourses were never a homogeneous bloc, imposed entirely from outside and structured uniquely by stereotypes of Western power-knowledge constructing the Orient as its Other. The Others could have been many and changeable, including for instance groups within Britain subordinated by class or gender.[5] The values brought in by the new rulers were extremely diverse and subject to radical change. Thus the equation sometimes made between Western cultural impact and 'Enlightenment rationality' forgets that for a crucial period in the conquest of India the dominant assumptions in British ruling circles, engaged in bitter wars with Revolutionary and Napoleonic France, tended to be deeply anti-Enlightenment. Nor can Christian missionary activity be presented as an undifferentiated tool of colonialism. It was initially discouraged by the Company, and despite closer connections with sections of the administration by the mid-century and considerable religio-cultural arrogance and obtuseness, there remains much evidence of occasional tensions with other British in India. (A striking instance was the missionary criticism of atrocities committed by white indigo planters on Bengal peasants, for which Reverend Long was even sent to jail on a charge of libel in 1860, and became immortalized through a well-known Bengali ditty.) And, diverse Western importations apart, a recent major work has emphasized that, particularly in the earlier phases, inputs from indigenous informants and already-existing information networks were indispensable for the growth of colonial knowledge. Through such information, purveyed on the whole by privileged literati groups, upper-caste Hindu or elite Muslims, colonial rule helped to consolidate pre-existing indigenous forms of religious and cultural hierarchy (Bayly, 1996).

'Western' or 'English' education was of course the most evident way in which colonial knowledge sought to become an instrument of control or hegemony. Here desire was undoubted (though also with great diversity of methods, shifting from 'Orientalist' collaboration with traditional Brahman and ulema literati trained in Sanskrit and Persian to 'Anglicist' insistence on the English medium only in the 1830s) but greatly outran performance. The new English-educated 'middle class', which Macaulay in 1835 had hoped would become white in thought and culture and thus loyal bulwarks of the colonial regime, had become by the end of the century the principal bearers of anti-colonial nationalist ideology and organized politics. As so often, the question of multiple and diverse appropriations is much more important than origins and their motivations. The low financial outlay and literacy rates that have been mentioned already indicate that education could have had little to do with any hegemonic control over the peasant masses. Despite the enormous focus in cultural histories on the impact of English education, which has been alternately hailed or denounced for decades, arguably much more far-reaching was the colonial importation of the printing press. This quickly became associated, as in early modern Europe, with the development of vernacular prose writings in the many languages of India (for moveable print requires much wider markets for sustainability than scribal culture), stimulating both an impressive literary outcrop and the creation of new kinds of public spheres.

This account has emphasized the many contradictions within early colonial structures and policies. Some of these surfaced through a major economic depression in large parts of Company-ruled India from the mid-1820s until the 1840s, with prices in Madras Presidency for instance declining in 1840–5 to 50.8 per cent of the 1816–25 level. The drive towards revenue maximization, fuelled by Company military and political needs, had come to hinder widening of markets for British manufactures and development of agricultural raw materials exports, for it often imposed intolerable burdens on the peasantry. Agricultural prices declined because the heavy revenue demand, collected by the British invariably in cash, obliged the peasants to sell in such quantities as to produce gluts. Effective demand was reduced further by the disintegration of many Indian court elites, as well as by Company efforts at retrenchment from the late 1820s after years of heavy military expenditure. What has been described as 'the crisis of the North Indian political economy' was climaxed by two major famines, in 1833–4 and again in 1837–8 (Bayly, 1983: ch. 7). There were some signs of recovery and apparent stabilization from the late 1840s, with moves towards some reduction in revenue burdens and Dalhousie's encouragement of railways, road construction, and irrigation works. But other aspects of the latter's 'modernizing' policies, in particular the ruthless expansion of direct British rule, manifested in the takeover of a

number of princely states (Satara, Jhansi, Nagpur) under the so-called 'doctrine of lapse'[6] and the annexation of Awadh in 1856, contributed significantly to the great anti-British armed rebellion of 1857–9.

It is now generally accepted that violent resistance or rebellion – what the pioneer work on the subject described some forty years ago as 'civil disturbances' (Chaudhuri, 1953) constituted an endemic feature of the first century of British rule. Indeed, some of these could be more formidable than the rather rickety resistance put up by most Indian rulers against Company expansion. What were coming to be described as the 'tribal' areas proved the most troublesome, with major rebellions, for instance, by Kols (1831) and Santals (1855), to mention only two among a very large number. Here societies of food-gatherers and shifting cultivators were having their forest resources eroded by the advance of settled agriculture and British efforts to appropriate forest products for 'scientific', commercial exploitation. Tribal areas were becoming in addition centres for recruitment, often by trickery, of indentured labour to work in European plantations in Assam, as well as other British colonies. In addition, the relative absence of caste hierarchies probably contributed to a greater degree of unity and militancy. In more settled or developed regions, the heavy Company revenue pressure provoked resistance by local rural communities under their 'traditional' zamindars or petty rulers – with the latter at times engaged in bitter conflict with nouveau-riche landlords who had benefited from commercialization and stricter notions of alienable property in land. There are also some instances of urban resistance around issues of taxes or market regulations (e.g. the Benaras house tax protest of 1810–11), and conflicts over rent between peasants and landlords. The latter, however, seem to have been less visible in this period than they would become in late colonial times, for the state was still the major appropriator of agrarian surplus.

The many strands of diverse resistance came together, briefly and in the end inadequately, in 1857 following the mutiny of a very large part of the Bengal army, which had been the main instrument of the Company in conquering India. Recruited in the main from relatively higher-caste petty landholders and peasants of the Benaras-Awadh region, many of whom had been losing land under the new, more commercialized order, the sepoys had been incensed by certain military orders that seemed to insult their caste and religious beliefs. For a few months the British seemed on the point of being driven out of the upper Ganga valley, with Delhi and Kanpur lost and Lucknow beseiged, while, particularly in Awadh and the western part of Bihar there was a kind of mass uprising of peasants in support of the rebellion. But the highly differentiated nature of the early colonial impact meant that there had been many apparent beneficiaries as well as the alienated. Thus the emerging Western-educated intelligentsia of Bengal kept away from the revolt, as did the Punjab, which had just been conquered by the same army. Other loyal groups included the bulk of traders and moneylenders, and the 'new magnates' who had been benefiting from Company rule through purchase of land from gentry and peasants unable to keep up with the pressures of intensified commercialization. The rebellion, therefore, became in some ways 'a phenomenon of the backwoods' (Bayly, 1987: 193, passim). But quite often the line between rebellion and loyalism seems to have been porous, determined by local circumstances, and cutting across social divides. While some prominent princes became (or were made) the leaders of the insurrection – Bahadur Shah the last Mughal Emperor, Nana Saheb, the Rani of Jhansi – many others (Hyderabad, the Sindhias of Gwalior, the Rajput chiefs) remained loyal. The rebellion was crushed by 1859, after bitter fighting and enormous atrocities. Enraged by incidents like the massacre of white women and children at Kanpur, the victorious British tortured, hanged, shot, or blew from their guns 'tens of thousands of soldiers and village guerrillas'. Awadh and western Bihar estimates suggest a significant drop in population between 1853 and 1871 (*Ibid.*, p. 194). What was left behind was a trail of blood and racial bitterness.

c.1858–1914

The year 1857 spelled the end of the Company, with India brought directly under the crown in 1858, to be governed by the Viceroy in tandem with a Secretary of State and Council ultimately responsible to the British parliament. The immediate consequences included a drastic restructuring of the British Indian army. The proportion of white soldiers was pushed up to one third (as compared to 14 per cent before the Rebellion), artillery was made a strict European monopoly, and recruitment grounds shifted from the Awadh-Bihar region to areas like Punjab and Nepal (with groups like the Sikhs and the Gurkhas now discovered to be peculiarly 'martial races'). Divide and rule became a frankly-avowed policy. Charles Wood, Secretary of State in 1862, declared: 'I wish to have a different and rival spirit in different regiments, so that Sikh might fire into Hindoo, Goorkha into either, without any scruple in case of need'. (Sarkar, 1983a: 16). British officialdom was thus discovering great virtues in 'traditions' of caste and religion, which missionaries and utilitarians had denounced as backward or obscurantist.

The apparently conservative swing manifested itself also in efforts at building stable alliances with princes and landlords. The doctrine of lapse was abandoned, annexations virtually stopped, and until Independence about a third of the sub-continent remained a patchwork of 662 'native states' of widely varying sizes. A few of these were occasionally ruled by fairly enlightened princes, many were crudely authoritarian, but all got the protection of British 'paramountcy' provided they remained obedient to the instructions of viceregal agents (Residents) stationed in their courts. There were attempts to invent a kind of loyal aristocracy, notably through the pageantry of proclaiming Victoria 'Empress of India' in 1877. Efforts were made to conciliate landlords through a policy of 'sympathy' (particularly in Awadh where so many had joined the rebellion), and while suggestions for an extension of the Permanent Settlement beyond Bengal Presidency proved abortive, there was a gradual decline in the land tax in terms of prices and as a proportion of government revenues.[7]

Yet, as throughout, colonial structures and policies had contradictory implications, for the main post-1858 thrust was towards authoritarian colonial modernity. Railway mileage, only 432 in 1859, was nearing 25,000 by 1900. Construction, subsidized by Indian tax revenues through a system of officially guaranteed minimum profits to British private companies, was geared above all to British commercial interests. They linked up regions of exportable agricultural production to ports, though there was also a lot of construction of strategic lines in the north-west in the context of the perpetual Russian bogey. The leap in

communications brought about through the coming of print-culture and then by railways, improved roads, postal services, the telegraph and telephones, together with a submarine cable and the Suez Canal revolutionizing connections between London and British Indian authorities, all made for a Raj that was now qualitatively different from all preceding sub-continental regimes in the extent and reach of its centralized authority. It was a state uncompromisingly despotic and white underneath a thin veneer of a few nominated Indians in viceregal and provincial councils and occasional talk of a long training for self-government. Europeans in the 1880s, for instance manned all but sixteen of the 900–odd posts of the Indian Civil Service, recruited from the 1850s, by examinations held in Britain. Racist divides are generally thought to have considerably deepened in the late nineteenth century, as manifested most notably by the Ilbert Bill agitation of whites in the early 1880s, against a move to give a few Indians judicial authority in cases that might involve Europeans.

The revolution in communications helped to create for the first time a genuinely unified market in bulk commodities, as well as regional specializations in crops. Above all, there was a major spurt in the export of peasant agricultural products like raw cotton, raw jute, food-grains, and oilseeds (along with tea and coffee grown on British-owned plantations), alongside growing imports of British textiles and other manufactures which could now penetrate much deeper into the interior.[8] Export booms – like that in Western Indian raw cotton in the 1860s, when the US Civil War deprived Lancashire mills of American cotton, or jute in East Bengal in the early twentieth century – brought a measure of prosperity and chance of upward mobility to sections of peasants. The picture of uniform rural immiserization (or of commercialization as a totally 'forced' process) that was projected in cruder varieties of nationalist polemic is probably exaggerated. But the bulk of the profits clearly went to the British business houses controlling overseas trade and shipping, while Indian trader-moneylender intermediaries also cornered a secondary but substantial share. In Bombay and Ahmedabad, capital initially accumulated through *compradore* trade could become the basis for an indigeneous modern textile industry, for in this region foreign capital was less omnipresent than in Eastern India, and the British were not interested in investing in cotton mills that might compete with Lancashire. Peasant gains, however, remained patchy, highly uncertain, dependent on the vagaries of distant markets over which they had no control or even information. Thus the cotton boom of the 1860s quickly collapsed, and early twentieth-century jute-induced growth was followed by the long worldwide agricultural depression from the mid-1920s till the late 1930s. It must not be forgotten that the late nineteenth-century expansion of external trade and a regular export surplus went along with a series of devastating famines, particularly in the 1890s, across a large part of the country.

Post-1857, effective Pax Britannica did not end the narrative of popular resistance, but did significantly modify its forms. British conciliation of princes and landed elements, and the gradual decline in the earlier role of the state as principal appropriator of agrarian surplus, combined to make the earlier pattern of armed, unified resistance under traditional chiefs or *zamindars* less common. There was greater scope now for class-related anti-landlord or anti-moneylender movements, as in Pabna in East Bengal in 1873, where peasants fought back *zamindar* efforts to hike rents through predominantly peaceful, legal methods, or the disturbances in the Maharashtra Deccan in 1875, as indebtedness mounted in the wake of the collapse of the cotton boom. Violent upheavals remained more common in tribal areas that were being adversely affected more than ever by processes of commercialization and extension of state control over forests. But there too traditional chiefs were losing their hold, and resistance tended to be associated with 'revitalization' movements under messiahs of obscure origin, at times selectively appropriating elements from Christianity, Hinduism, or Islam. Such was the rebellion of Birsa Munda in South Bihar (1899–1900), or the later phases of endemic resistance in the forests and hills of the 'Rampa' region in Andhra. A rather special case is presented by the Mappillas of Malabar (Kerala), where Muslim peasant agrarian discontent against upper-caste Hindu landholders and moneylenders inextricably intermingled with militant Islamic ideology to produce no less than thirty-two violent outbreaks between 1836 and 1919, and a major rebellion in 1921. Meanwhile industrial capitalist development centred around British-owned jute mills around Calcutta and Indian textile factories in Bombay and Ahmedabad was beginning to produce sporadic strikes, as workers drawn from the countryside and still marked by community loyalties of religion and caste gradually and intermittently moved towards trade-union organization (Sarkar, 1983b: 5–24).

Such movements were often not self-consciously anti-colonial, being directed rather against immediate oppressors, almost always Indian. The distant British overlords could even be appealed to as protectors, as when the most radical demand of the Pabna peasants took the form of a plea to be 'ryots [tenants] of the Queen of England alone' (Sengupta, 1974: 42). They were, in addition, scattered and localized, with no signs as yet of countrywide or even regional consolidation. Yet, from a longer-term perspective, the most far-reaching consequence of the administrative, economic and communicational integration brought about by late-colonial structures and policies was the creation of the conditions of possibility for the development of consolidated, crystallized identities. There had certainly been distinctions earlier between, say, Hindus and Muslims, and also occasional local conflicts amidst much of everyday coexistence and commingling of practices. But the absence of modern communications networks had made formation of tight countrywide blocs seeking to iron out internal differences unlikely. It is roughly the half-century between the 1870s and the 1920s that saw the emergence, more or less simultaneously, and in inter- animating yet often conflicting ways, of solidarity projects, ideologies and organizations of 'national', 'regional', 'communal' (the Indian English term for mutually-hostile and aggressive religious identities), 'caste', 'class', and 'gender' kinds. Recent historiography has been emphasizing in this context the impact particularly of British census operations that began systematically from 1871. Enumeration required the fixing of firm boundaries (e.g. Hindu or Muslim, distinct castes and ethnic groups), and stimulated competitive number games regarding which 'community' should have what proportion of jobs or political representation – rivalries which the rulers for obvious reasons did much to encourage or even create. Yet multiple identity formations should not be reduced to a series of indigeneous responses to stimuli flowing from colonial structures, divide-and-rule policies, or discourses alone. One needs to focus also on

more 'internal' dimensions, in particular the ways in which tighter notions of community could help shore up beleaguered hierarchies of religious authority, caste, gender, or class. Otherwise we remain bound to an ultimately restrictive and unilinear nationalist framework, which has often been tempted to designate all emerging identities other than the 'Indian' (passing over sometimes into the 'Hindu') as automatically divisive, sectional, or separatist.[9]

In a country with low literacy levels, data concerning indigenous identity-formations necessarily come in the main from the writings of the colonial literati. The beneficiaries of Western education were at first male, upper-caste Hindu (who predominated among the early products of colleges and schools in Bengal, Bombay and Madras), or high-status Muslim. Often seeing themselves as an 'educated middle class', they tended to come from families that had some rentier interests in land, but which unlike, princes and big landlords, were also in need of income from professions, or jobs, mostly clerical, in the lower rungs in British administrative and business offices. As superior posts everywhere for long remained a virtual white monopoly, they were deprived of positions of command in bureaucracy, army or economy, and till late in the nineteenth century had little confidence in their capacity for effective political intervention. Literati initiatives were concentrated rather in two areas: vernacular literature, and efforts for (or against) reform of indigenous religious and social life.

Printing and its concomitants, vernacular prose and the possibility of writing about many more subjects than had been feasible in scribal culture, stimulated major developments in the many Indian languages. New literary genres like novels and short stories emerged in partial emulation of European literature, and there were significant achievements in poetry, drama, and essays. Together with vernacular journals and newspapers, these were coming to constitute a public sphere potentially far more open in theme and authorship than anything possible in pre-print literate culture. Vernacular development also enhanced sentiments of regional solidarity, while for the intelligentsia the new link-language of English facilitated country-wide, if also somewhat elitist, initiatives. Nineteenth-century achievements in the visual arts were considerably less impressive, and the structure of 'liberal' higher education set up by the British provided little support for Indian scientific and technical education or research. Some autonomous efforts were beginning, however, in these areas by the turn of the century, while in medicine there was an interesting indigenization of homoeopathy as a cheap alternative to official structures.

In ways once again not unrelated to print, developments within religious traditions tended to base themselves on what were considered the 'classical' or 'foundational' texts, now made far more accessible through print and translation. These were used in widely different ways to critique, or defend, existing beliefs and practices. Thus Rammohan Roy, the founder of the Brahmo movement in Bengal in the 1820s, appealed to the Upanishads to construct a reformist and monotheistic version of Hinduism. Later on in the century, the more successful Arya Samaj of Dayananda in northern India used the Vedas to project a more accommodative style of reform which by the early-twentieth century was building bridges fairly easily with their earlier opponents, the 'Sanatanist' defenders of conservative Hindu solidarity. Broadly similar reform or revivalist tensions and rapproachments were manifest within Indian Islam. There were the fiercely anti-Western 'Wahhabi' Muslim purists of the early-nineteenth century who sometimes fought against British rule, the later 'Aligarh' tradition founded by Sir Syed Ahmad combining modern education and a measure of reform with loyalism, and the efforts of the 'reformist' *ulema* of Deoband and other seminaries to discipline and purge Islamic society of 'innovations' and 'Hindu' importations through *fatwas*, religious education in *madrasas*, and an extensive polemical literature in Urdu.

Controversies about idolatry and monotheism apart, the major preoccupation of the nineteenth-century intelligentsia concerned themes related to family and gender. The centrality of the 'women's question' was indeed quite remarkable and unique in South Asian history. The principal 'social' issues were those of widow-immolation or *sati* (banned by Bentinck in 1829 following missionary polemics and representations by Rammohan), women's education, the marriage of Hindu widows (made legal in 1856, after Vidyasagar had skilfully manipulated ancient texts to bring out its permissibility), and questions of Hindu polygamy, child-marriage, and the age of consent. The reformers were overwhelmingly male, and severe limits were often imposed by the scriptural form of argument made obligatory by the British insistence that matters of Hindu and Muslim personal law had to be decided by reference to the *dharmasastra* or the *shariat*. The achievements, in statistical terms, were also minimal, and largely confined to a small section of upper-castes. Thus despite its newly-established legality, few widows remarried in face of continued and great social opprobrium. What social reform agitations did, however, was to problematize, compel even the most conservative to use arguments in open public debate, in place of unquestioned custom or closed confabulations among Brahman or *ulema* experts followed by command. Texts made accessible (among Hindus, it should be emphasized, there had been a strong taboo against women and low castes having access to the Vedas) became at once more influential, and open to debate and divergent readings. Through such debates in public spheres, further, one can see at times the beginnings of new notions of individual and equal rights. Such openings, however, were often immediately sought to be closed through renewed insistence on community obligations, as when a ferocious campaign was launched in 1890–1 against the proposal to raise the minimum age for sexual intercourse in marriage from ten to twelve. Colonial domination facilitated such closures, for it remained easy to brand efforts at social change as surrender of indigenous values to Western cultural domination (Sarkar, T., 1993; 1997).

If the public sphere constituted through print was at first the domain of relatively privileged males, it did begin to reach out fairly soon to include some women and lower-caste men as readers and increasingly, authors. One must not forget also the considerable heroism showed by women participating in male-initiated reforms, as they defied social taboos to learn to read and write, at times in secret, go to school, or abandon the established norm of austere widowhood. In languages like Bengali and Marathi, women's writings soon became fairly numerous, and by the early twentieth century autonomous women's initiatives were becoming visible in education, and then in demands for voting rights and legal reforms.

A few theoretical critiques and some changes in personal practices apart, high-caste reformers did little about caste oppression until close to the end of the century. Much more significant were the beginnings of autonomous intermediate and low-caste initiatives, expressed no longer through dissident forms of piety as had been the pattern earlier, but through appropriations of some of the new structures and opportunities of the colonial era. In Maharashtra, Jyotiba Phule in the 1870s developed a trenchant critique of Brahmannical domination, neatly inverting the growing 'mainstream' emphasis on the civilizing nature of ancient Aryan expansion over the sub-continent by branding upper-castes as descendants of invaders of the Maratha homeland. A similar anti-Brahman critique emerged in the South, projecting autochthonous 'Dravidian' or Tamil culture against North Indian Aryan high-caste incursions. These were mainly intermediate-caste movements, but already by the 1890s, there were signs, notably once again in Maharashtra, of stirrings among the lowest strata of untouchables or Dalits.

Most caste movements, it is true, were considerably less radical, and confined in their declared aims to claims to higher status within the established caste hierarchies in ways that anthropologists have later termed 'Sanskritization', or 'imitation' of high-caste norms and rituals. Yet even here occasional anti-hierarchical rhetoric coexisted with modest pleas for merely positional change, as can be seen in the mass of claims and counter-claims spurred into existence by the attempt by census authorities in 1901 to determine precise caste rankings for each locality. A striking feature of the early-twentieth century was, in fact, a spate of vernacular tracts produced by obscure lower-caste (as well as plebeian Muslim) villagers or small townsmen. Many of these struck a note that had been heralded already in the later writings of Phule: an 'improvement ethic' of petit-bourgeois upward mobility through the combination of enterprise and frugality, an indication perhaps of some connections with a measure of rich peasant development in some parts of the country.

Resentment and fear evoked by these early signs of affirmation of rights by women and lower-castes probably contributed as much, if not more, than growing sentiments of cultural nationalism to efforts at consolidation of tighter notions of Hindu and Muslim community. Enemy images of each other provided the best cement for such solidarity. These developed along several interacting levels. Outbursts of mass rioting around, most often, the issues of Muslims sacrificing cows and Hindus playing music in front of mosques started getting frequent from the 1890s, while at another level rivalries were deepening between Hindu and Muslim educated elites over jobs and political representation. An upper-caste Hindu demographic panic was fostered by some census figures that seemed to indicate a relative decline in Hindu numbers. Together with fears about conversion to Islam or Christianity, this 'dying Hindu' syndrome led to efforts to retain lower-castes within the Hindu fold through ameliorative reform-from-above of a Sanskritizing kind, combined with polemic against other religious communities. Muslim consolidation efforts meanwhile sought to insert into peasant improvement literature an aggressive note of puritanical Islamic solidarity (Datta, 1999; Sarkar, S., 1997: ch. 9).

Yet the consolidation of multifarious, mutually-conflicting identities was not the only dimension of turn-of-the century sub-continental history. Colonial domination could not but provoke into existence, and that to an increasing extent, platforms for united anti-colonial struggle. Early educated middle-class initiatives, typified by the formation of the Indian National Congress in 1885 – at first an annual conference for the ventilation of grievances and demands rather than an organized party – were no doubt quite limited in objectives, methods, and support-bases alike. Thus there was an evident elitism, as well as much moderation, in demands, for instance, for more jobs for Indians in civil services, or the claim to political rights – by a Congress president as late as 1905 – for the educated alone as 'natural leaders of the people'. But even such limited objectives, together with the simultaneous working-out of a systematic critique of British policies as responsible for the evident massive poverty of the country, could eventually strike much wider chords. They did focus on the key themes of alien political domination, racial oppression, and economic exploitation, and moreover sought to do so in an unifying, secular manner. For a few years around 1905, when Curzon's provocative partitioning of Bengal stimulated 'extremist' experimentation with new objectives and methods, and then, on a qualitatively different scale under Gandhi from 1919, anti-colonial nationalism was able to reach out, at its peak-points, to very wide sections of the Indian people, mobilize vast numbers of peasants, workers, traders and industrialists, lower middle classes, cut across – sometimes, and in the end only partially – barriers of caste, religion and ethnicity. Mass participation and initiatives played a key role in inscribing on the agenda of anti-colonial struggle demands for democracy and social justice. But the narrative of such developments, and the complicated and partial ways in which they sought to integrate or transcend the many conflicting tendencies we have tried to outline in these pages, must belong to another volume.

NOTES

1 Thus Macaulay's Minute of 1835 had visualized that the higher education through English that it was giving official support to would create eventually a class brown in colour but white in thought and culture. By the time of Curzon, however, the more conservative-minded officials were thinking that the whole policy of acculturation had been a mistake, for the English-educated Indians were often turning into effective anti-colonial spokesmen and agitators.

2 English private traders in another region – Awadh – may, however, have preferred the continuation of a dependent Indian state to Company takeover (see Marshall, 1975).

3 In recent years, colonial law has become one of the richest areas of historical research (Washbrook, 1981; Singha, 1998; Sarkar, T., 1993).

4 British Indian administration, laws and courts asserted principles of legal equality irrespective of caste or religious affiliations, while at the same time protecting white privileges on blatantly racist lines. This contradiction whetted the desire for equal rights.

5 For a perceptive study of the ways 'Orientalism' was conditioned by developments and conflicts within the West, (see Majeed, 1992).

6 Dalhousie grabbed princely states without direct male heirs for the Company, disallowing the widespread earlier practice of adoption.

7 The share of land revenue in gross Government of India receipts, still 43 per cent in 1880, fell to 23 per cent in 1920, while in Madras Presidency between 1860 and 1920, grain prices rose by between 120 per cent and 180 per cent but average assessment per acre went up only from Rs1.7 to Rs2.1. Washbrook, 1981: 671.

8 Indigo exports to the West and opium to China, which had been central to the Company's structure of remittances in the first half of the nineteenth century, declined in the new era. For details, see Chaudhuri, K. N., 1983, particularly pp. 842, 844, 858.

9 The Muslim-nationalist variant that eventually came to constitute the dominant ideology for Pakistan has operated in a very similar way.

BIBLIOGRAPHY

BAGCHI, A. K. 1972. *Private Investment in India 1900–1939*. Cambridge.

BAYLY, C. A. 1983. *Rulers, Townsmen and Bazaars: North Indian Society in the Age of British Expansion, 1770–1870*. Cambridge.

——. 1987. 'Indian Society and the Making of the British Empire'. In: *New Cambridge History of India*. II. 1. Cambridge.

——. 1996. *Empire and Information: Intelligence Gathering and Social Communication in India 1780–1870*. Cambridge.

BHATTACHARYA, S. 1989. *Aupanibeshik Bharater Arthaneeti, 1850–1947*. Calcutta. [in Bengali].

CHATTERJEE, P. 1986. *Nationalist Thought and the Colonial World: A Derivative Discourse?* Delhi.

——. 1994. *The Nation and Its Fragments: Colonial and Post-colonial Histories*. Delhi.

CHAUDHURI, K. N. 1983. 'Foreign Trade and Balance of Payments'. In: Kumar, D. (ed.) *Cambridge Economic History of India, Vol. 2, c.1757–c.1970*. Cambridge.

CHAUDHURI, S. B. 1953. *Civil Disturbances During Early British Rule in India, 1765–1857*. Calcutta.

DATTA, P. K. 1999. *Carving Blocs: Communal Ideology in Early-Twentieth Century Bengal*. Delhi.

FISHER, M. H. (ed.) 1993. *The Politics of the British Annexation of India, 1757–1857*. Oxford in India Readings, Delhi.

GUHA, R. 1963. *A Rule of Property for Bengal*. Paris.

KUMAR, D. 1983. 'Fiscal System'. In: *Cambridge Economic History of India, Vol. 2, c.1757–c.1970*. Cambridge.

MAJEED, J. 1992. *Ungoverned Imaginings: James Mill's History of British India and Utilitarianism*. Oxford.

MARSHALL, P. 1975. 'Economic and Political Expansion: The Case of Oudh'. In: *Modern Asian Studies*, 9, iv.

——. 1987. 'Bengal: The British Bridgehead, Eastern India 1740–1828'. In: *New Cambridge History of India*. II. 1. Cambridge.

METCALF, T. R. 1997. *Ideologies of the Raj*. Cambridge.

NIGHTINGALE, P. 1970. *Trade and Empire in Western India, 1784–1806*. Cambridge.

SARKAR, S. 1983a. *Modern India 1885–1947*. Delhi.

——. 1983b. *Popular Movements and Middle-Class Leadership in Late Colonial India: Perspectives and Problems of a 'History from Below'*. Calcutta.

——. 1997. *Writing Social History*. Delhi.

SARKAR, T. 1993. 'Rhetoric Against the Age of Consent: Resisting Colonial Reason and the Death of a Child-wife'. In: *Economic and Political Weekly,* 4 September.

——. 1997. 'Talking about Scandals: Religion, Law and Love in late Nineteenth Century Bengal'. In: *Studies in History,* XIII, 1.

SENGUPTA, K. K. 1974. *Pabna Disturbances and the Politics of Rent, 1873–1885.* New Delhi.

SINGHA, R. 1998. *A Despotism of Law: Crime and Justice in Early Colonial India.* Delhi.

STOKES, E. 1959. *The English Utilitarians and India.* Oxford.

VISARIA, L.; VISARIA, P. 1983. 'Population (1757–1947)'. In: *Cambridge Economic History of India, Vol. 2, c.1757–c.1970.* Cambridge.

WASHBROOK, D. A. 1981. 'Law, State and Agrarian Society in Colonial India'. In: *Modern Asian Studies,* 15, iii.

Shu-li Ji

China saw the most cultural conflicts in the nineteenth century. The conflicts stemmed, on the one hand, from within Sinic culture as a whole – the bifurcation of super-culture and subculture, which was frequently polarized in violent antagonism of the latter by the former. On the other hand, there was another conflict from without, a conflict with an alien culture that China had never met before. Both conflicts spurred China to modernization, at once by the external pressure to have the ancient culture Westernized, and by internal pressure to remain Sinicized. China's modernization thus unfolded through the tension between Westernization and Sinicization, and nineteenth-century China saw both an enlightenment from the West, and a renaissance of her own tradition.

The cultural conflicts were not only interwoven into an unprecedented cultural crisis but also embodied a deadly political crisis for the Qing dynasty. While the dynastic crisis had been mitigated with the efforts at restoration and reformation, and finally overcome by revolution, the cultural crisis kept going through the Sinic enlightenment and renaissance in the next century.

DECLINE AND EARLY RESTORATION (1796–1840)

The decline of the Qing dynasty

The turn of the century coincided with extremes of fortune of the great Qing dynasty: once the zenith of Qianlong's reign had passed, the dynasty went abruptly downhill. Traditional polity increasingly failed to deal with social developments, chiefly the demographic explosion and commercial growth. Correspondingly, a general demoralization emerged throughout the bureaucracy, and corruption became a legal prerogative. By the time the emperor Jiaqing came to power in 1796, central government had become dysfunctional.

Through the prosperous days of the early Qing dynasty, the population doubled from about 150 million in 1700 to 300 million in 1800; now it further increased to over

400 million in the mid-century. The explosion was a natural evolution of a family-centred society, in which it was regarded as a sacred duty to carry the family line on, and was also an investment for probationary labour and old-age insurance. Both conscience and calculation led to more births. The explosion stimulated the internal market economy, but the all-encompassing bureaucracy, founded on a small-scale peasant economy, hindered the growth through a sort of physiocracy: 'Valuing agriculture and devaluing commerce'. The government relied more on commercial dominance than *laissez-faire* trade.

The three salient maladministrations were most telling. The Grand Canal administration for feeding Peking with southern rice swelled its own ranks with sinecure appointments and the special funds allotted. Consequently, stretches of the Canal were frequently silted up. The Yellow River Conservancy, which was joined to the complex canal system at its mid-point, failed totally to regulate water levels on the Yellow and Huai rivers where the Canal crossed, seeming not to prevent floods but to keep them regular enough to justify the steady flow of funds. The idea of transport by sea by hiring merchant vessels was repeatedly put forward but repeatedly put off by the vested interests. Lastly the salt monopoly system, by which licensed merchants delivered the commodity to government depots for local distribution, became complex, thus inspiring bureaucratic sub-networks and salt smuggling. Hence, taxed salt rose so high in price with successive commission, transport charges, and official peculation, that half of the salt came to be illegally produced and distributed through difficult routes, which were too costly to prevent. The officials and smugglers thus coexisted without interfering with each other until the final privatization after the First Opium War.

The merchants, however, grew in number along with the growth of commerce. Commonly those in the same line of trade united in guilds as their commercial base. They also developed regional associations of those from the same province, or *Landsmannschaften*, which remained a shadow of the more fundamental patriarchal clan system, and complementary to, sometimes substituting for, the guilds.

Alongside patriarchal clan and secret societies, both guild and *Landsmannschaften* constituted the third greatest social organization on behalf of a middle class between official-dom and the commoners. Though not as politically opposed to the former as the latter, they were still actors unfavourable to a stability-oriented society.

The fragile equilibrium was further broken within the ruling literati-officialdom by the increase of population without commensurate provincial quotas of degree holders and official promotions. The limitation of upward mobility led to swollen staffs and job competition in the government, which induced all sorts of bribery and corruption. Personal favouritism skewed administrative procedures and patron-age networks upset the impartiality of the state examina-tions. The unemployed literati had either to serve as advisors (*mu-you*) of the governors, further swelling the staff, or simply to fall into the ranks of marginalized subversives.

Emperor Jiaqing was by no means a fatuous ruler, nor did he unintentionally alter the status quo. Upon coming to power, he ended his father's luxurious inspection tours to safeguard the national treasury and purged the patronage network headed by Heshen, the favorite of Qianlong. To revitalize the government, he encouraged a free airing of views by remitting, as an example, the death-sentence on Hong Liangji, the first scholar to warn that unchecked population growth would outrun the productive capacity of the nation. In scouting broadly for talent, the Han–Manchu ethnic distribution in the provincial officialdom began to shift subtly in favour of the Han Chinese. The celebrated reformist scholars, Ruan yuan and Tao Shu, were soon promoted to governors.

The basic imperial system seemed, however, to be incapable of recovering its vigour. The emperor's endeav-our to cleanse his empire relied more on rhetoric than on specific policies. His pleas for frugality on the part of his bureaucracy were poignant, but did little to cut costs. Heshen's network was effectively cleansed, but others soon rose to fill the vacuum. Jiaqing and his son Daoguang both promoted a Confucian purism, but did nothing substantive to counter the current troubles.

Adjustment within Sinic values

The early Qing experienced the intellectual flourishing of Han learning against Song learning, or Neo-Confucianism, as a state philosophy. The Han scholars became tired of the latter's 'idle talk' of metaphysical moralism and over-politicization, and strove to restore the former's more rea-listic mood in which faint opposition was expressed against the Manchu rule. The Han school made every effort to disclose the wrongs in the classics usually cited by Song scholars, and made contributions to this debate. In its decay, however, the school turned out to favour a hair-splitting scholasticism, burying itself more and more in textual criti-cism and keeping aloof from grim social reality. Having lived through Qing's heyday, subsequent generations became less hostile to the Manchus, worrying about the decline of the dynasty along with Sinic culture. Orthodox textual criticism thus began to be viewed as irresponsible, and Song meta-physics were reconsidered. Fine tuning within Sinic values appeared as a necessary mental preparation among the literati-officials articulate in support of cultural regeneration.

Ruan Yuan was a model for the new trend, both as a skilled statesman and master of the classics. He sought moral and intellectual regeneration through classical studies, and oriented the classes of his Academy of the Sea-of-Learning toward mastery of the classics through etymological and philological research stressing the Han commentaries. Meanwhile, the emphasis was put on 'solid learning', factual information, and the effort to apply the principles of the classics to current affairs. Ruan's eclecticism was illustrative of the transition in the scholarly climate at that time. In addition, his earlier work, *Biographies of Mathematicians* (of the Qing dynasty), included thirty-seven European mis-sionaries who had worked in China. This brought out their contributions to China's scientific development and renewed scientific interest amongst the Sinic literati. The splendid scientific tradition in ancient China, especially in mathematics, astronomy, chemistry, and medicine, had developed along an independent line from the West. Now there loomed some revitalization in science since the decline of the late Ming dynasty.

The generation after Ruan forged ahead to a new interpretation of the classics. In opposition to the versions of ancient texts written in the old 'tadpole characters' dis-covered in the Later Han dynasty, now there was the New Text Version in its current 'seal characters' script based on oral instruction in the former Han dynasty after the Qin book burning. Under the banner of Han (in fact the former Han), the New Text school concentrated on the *Gongyang commentaries* (*gongyang zhuan*) of the Confucian classic, *The Spring and Autumn Annals*, which was the only remaining classic of the New Text version. The classics provided not only a model of actual and political concern for this world, but also an idealized pattern of social evolution through three ages of chaos, ascending peace, and universal peace. The New Text thus aimed to secularize Sinic values, with some more pragmatic orientation (also intrinsic in the classical tradition), and hence provided some theoretical justification for restoration and reformation.

Gong Zizhen took the initiative to use the *Gongyang Commentaries* to criticize the decline of China in the age of chaos, an age of official corruption, the degeneration of the state examination system, unequal distribution of wealth, foot-binding and opium smoking. 'There is no ancestral code which can never be abolished', he held, 'nor any public opinion never be obsolete. What is most needed is a self-reformation'. In terms of statecraft, Lin Zexu called for the first time for people to 'open their eyes to the world' by compiling a world geography, the *Illustrated Gazetteer of the Four Continents*, in order to widen Chinese horizons. By the same token, Wei Yuan diverted his attention, in the 1820s, from Han learning to Qing's malfunctions and military affairs. He put forward the idea of 'learning from the bar-barians good skills to overcome them' as the first protracted strategy for China's modernization. On the basis of Lin's work but in further detail, he completed *Illustrated Gazetteer of the Maritime Countries*, as a means for achieving this strategy.

The new trend was displayed also in popular literature, typically in *Flowers in the Mirror*, one of China's greatest satiric novels, written during 1810–20 by Li Ruzhen, a Confucian scholar from Peking. The novel presented a 'female country' where all conventional gender roles were reversed: man must taste the life of humiliation by having his ears pierced, his feet bound, and spending hours over his make-up to please female lords. The novel represented the sense of social dis-location shared commonly by those who found it difficult to pass the examinations and find a job. Another equally sardonic novel, *The Unauthorized History of Scholars*, popular at the same time, ridiculed the world of fading Confucian literati and the system of state examinations. The author Wu Jingzi, himself once a failed examinee, experienced personally the abuses of the system. Another writer, Shen Fu, portrayed his own fate in *Six Records from a Floating Life* in a calm and poignant tone. It was written around 1807 while he wandered about the country in various roles as a scholar, merchant, and secretary. He also recorded his affectionate marriage with a gifted wife, and described how they were worn down by his failures and poverty. The author concluded by asking why society only rewarded conventional virtues with sorrows and hardships?

This trend indicated a beginning of value-reorientation, which was so significant a cultural conversion that it was subsequently referred to as a Sinic renaissance. This renaissance was encouraged by the West, through the indispensable endeavours of the missionaries in particular, yet remained in essence an indigenous cultural movement, originating at a time when missionary work in China was at a low ebb.

The bifurcation of Sinic culture

The dynastic decline further polarized the innate bifurcation of Sinicism into its literate and illiterate compartments, or elitism and populism. It was really a disparity between two cultures, superculture and subculture, and two traditions, elite and plebeian. The former was the culture of officials or would-be officials, who spoke mandarin replete with classical quotations and allusions that the populace could hardly understand. Where the elite experienced the refined and delicate manifestations of the culture as a whole, the populace presented the popularized and vulgarized one. The cultural bifurcation was embedded in officialdom and schools on the one hand, and in secret societies at the grassroots on the other.

Sinic populism, however, was by and large in parallel with elitist Confucianism. It was deeply committed sometimes to Daoist or Buddhist fanaticism, primarily to Confucian universal brotherhood or to righteousness (*yi*) as one of the Five Conventions, and loyalty (*zhong*) that bound the brethren by blood oaths to the leader as patriarch, also integral with fundamental family values. It finally took inspiration from New-Textual themes: the 'great unity' (*datong*) relating to the harmony of the community and the 'great peace' (*taiping*) as the paramount ideal of humanity. The secret societies as its embodiment, while initially organized for self-protection beyond reproach, now usually served as the only political opposition, using violence in the dynastic finale. Their activities dated back to the Former Han, grew vigorous in the early Qing with calls to 'overthrow the Qing and restore the Ming', and culminated in the late Qing.

The White Lotus Society committed to Eternal Mother, heir to Pure Land Buddhism, rioted during 1796–1804 in the mountainous South West; these disturbances were probably a direct protest against imperial malfunction. A similar protest was carried on in the North in the 1810s by one of its sects, and finally defeated in an attempted attack on the palace. Since then, the Northern societies have been generally been termed religious sects (*jiao men*) such as the typical White Lotus. They remained usually a latent force for riot, but were often loosely organized on a peaceful, semi-legal basis while disseminating their fanatical ideas. In the South, secret societies were parties (*hui dang*) generally better organized and politicized. The dominant Triads, mainly sailors and poor city dwellers, had their own blood oath with a series of arcane, nocturnal initiation ceremonies, secret symbols and passwords to ensure strict discipline. They swore not to oppose the 'heavenly mandate', nor to oppress the weak by the strong, the poor by the rich, the few by the many. Nevertheless, they engaged in criminal extortion, robbery, kidnappings, and the protection of criminals through their collusion. By the 1830s, Triad lodges were also recruiting numerous peasants and all those living on the edge of destitution, including women, who were thus were given a role in society otherwise largely denied to them.

EARLY RESPONSE TO WESTERN IMPETUS (1840–60)

The opening of the Great Wall

Heretofore only homogeneous/indigenous Buddhism had been assimilated for thousands of years, in a fundamentally peaceful process which entailed no alien cultural domination of China. Now a heterogeneous culture coming from the West by sea was presenting such a wealth of new ways to exploit human social, intellectual and physical energy, as to almost overwhelm local traditions. Moved by the desire for markets and materials and the passion for power, the new culture had become dominant wherever it had been promoted – Africa, India, the South Seas, and the Americas – before reaching China, where it was no longer restricted to the peaceful preaching of the age of Matteo Ricci, but now came in terms of new cannons and gunboats. After a traumatic two decades, the Celestial Empire was forced to open her once-closed Great Wall.

The cultural conflict was manifested first in commerce and ideology, and the relevant merchants and missionaries were either held in contempt or treated with hostility. For the merchants, there was the conflict between Western mercantilism and Sinic physiocracy, which suffocated free trade and held the former in contempt as ill-bred and barbaric. Britain came to the Far East through the East India Company. The Sino-British trade grew rapidly through Chinese exports: of rhubarb, tea, silk, and all forms of *Chinoiserie*, whereas the Western imports, either woollens and furs or clocks and tin, remained unsaleable at Canton. Eager as the Western traders were to expand their markets, they were kept penned in along a narrow strip of riverbank outside the city walls and limited to dealing with authorized *Cohong* merchants. The door was slammed in their faces again and again. They had underestimated the difficulty of their task, assuming that all mankind was after profit pure and simple; and were thus being squeezed between pressure from investors at home and the restrictions on trade in China.

As the unfavourable balance of trade grew increasingly, the British at last found a cash crop that would earn revenue through export sales. This was the opium that grew in abundance in India, and could be processed with an abundant supply of labour. Hence, a triangular opium trade developed, from India to China with a counter-flow of silver from China to Britain. And opium addiction spread as fast as the outflow, disrupting the national economy and destroying both individual and national health morally and physically. During 1836–8 a heated debate was carried on at court on the opium traffic, over whether to legalize it or ban it absolutely. An uncompromising attitude prevailed at last, and Lin Zexu was sent to Canton as imperial commissioner.

In order to ban the evil trade at once and at the same time avoid a war, Lin twice wrote to Queen Victoria appealing to morality and law. 'By what right', he questioned, 'do they use the poisonous drug to injure the Chinese people? Where is their conscience?' When no response was forthcoming, strict measures were adopted to arrest the drug traders, and to confiscate and burn the drugs. Lin overrated the West's lust for commercial profit and the appetite for Chinese goods, but underrated British resolution to defend *laissez-faire* and the interests of its Empire. Ironically, in the British parliament a heated debate took place between the hawks and the doves, similar to that at the Qing court two years before. This time, however, it was the doves, the Tory opposition, who invoked morality and justice against 'a war calculated to cover this country with permanent disgrace', while the Whigs talked of the dignity of 'a country unaccustomed to defeat, to submission or to shame' (Holt, 1964: 98–9).

Once the imperial commissioner made up his mind to ban the drug, unexpectedly, war became immediately unavoidable, and the outdated imperial army was defeated with ease. The resulting Treaty of Nanjing in 1842 and its supplement in 1843, and others with France and the United States in 1844, created a system of unequal treaties. Then Hong Kong was ceded, five ports were opened to trade and missions, and an unprecedented crack appeared in the 'Great Wall'.

This breakthrough soon provoked popular resistance. Even the walled city of Canton, the already conquered city, had successfully refused the conquerors entry even after another commissioner promised this in 1849. The opponents found that Qing troops were not to be relied on, while the British barbarians were not to be feared. The open door struggle had not ended with military victory, but only deepened the gaps between the Chinese and the Westerners, and the government and the populace, inciting a radical nationalism from then on.

On the other side, the conciliatory move proved to be inadequate in the eyes of Western merchants. Sino-Western trade did not expand as expected, the market was still limited to a few treaty ports, and the Chinese economy remained largely self-sufficient in basic necessities. In 1850 Chinese imports of British manufactures were even lower than those in 1844. In period 1840–60, the value of Chinese purchases increased less than twofold, and the lucrative opium trade remained illegal. Dissatisfied with what had been acquired through the treaties, the West tried to open the door of more ports inland. A joint paper was presented to Peking in 1854 by France, Britain and the United States, demanding a revision of the treaties, but this was completely refused by Emperor Xianfeng and his favourite, the Manchu aristocrat Shushun. Likewise, the missionaries were dissatisfied with the post-war situation. All foreigners benefited from free locations and buildings, yet no special provision was made for missionary work. France had demanded freedom of religious belief, but in vain.

The British and French were determined to impose their demands upon Peking by any means available. Under the pretext of some minor incidents, namely the arrest on piracy charges of the *Arrow*'s crew and the execution of a French

missionary in an inland area forbidden to him, they launched the Second Opium War in 1856. The allied Anglo-French army captured Canton the next year, went on an expedition northwards in 1860 to burn the famous Summer Palace, and seized and looted the capital at last. It was a catastrophe never before experienced by the imperial court, which in cowardly fashion fled to Johol. As a result, the series of treaties of 1858–60 further opened up China with the addition of eleven free ports, permission for Westerners to travel and their goods to circulate in the country, and the legalization of opium imports.

The catastrophe of 1860 gave rise to conciliationism at court to reorient national policy. On the occasion of Xianfeng's death in exile, a *coup d'état* in 1861, which decapitated Sushun and other hawks, was launched by the Empress Dowager Cixi, the newly-enthroned boy emperor's biological mother, who had assisted the late emperor with remarkable ability and personal ambition. Her chief ally, Prince Gong, the capable younger brother of the late emperor, had been left in Peking to deal with the invaders' peaceful withdrawal. Hence a new era was inaugurated.

The two Opium Wars not only narcoticized but also awakened China. She experienced a 'Copernican' revolution in her shift from 'Celestial Empire' to earthly periphery. She had no alternative but to keep on terms with the West. Subsequently, Sinic culture, in both traditions, took the hard and roundabout route in search of modernization.

The first attempt to Westernize the subculture

The God-worshipping society, the Bud of the Taiping Heaven, was markedly different from the Nians in the North. The Taipings were highly centralized rather than dispersed roving rebels; and from the Triads in the South, they no longer aimed at a return of the Ming dynasty, which was already a vanishing dream for those living in the late Qing. The new Western-Christian influence endowed them with new values, primarily the sense of transcendence, thus emboldening them to make the first attempt to Westernize Sinic subculture.

The God-worshipping theology was first created in the 1830s by Hong Xiuquan, a frustrated examinee from a Hakka family in Guangdong. He happened upon a foreign missionary and a native interpreter after his second failure in the state examination, and, in despair of ensuing failures, fell into a coma when he was vested with a 'holy book' and an 'imp-slaying sword' by God and Jesus Christ. Either as a psychopathic case or as a wanton fabrication for political purposes, the coma was really a projection of his actual meeting with two people who gave him a pamphlet, *Good Words for Exhorting the World*, and encouraged him to 'attain the highest degree'. He invoked once again the age-old myth of heavenly mandate, used in past peasant uprisings, to justify his action, only this time replaced it with the fundamentalist Protestantism that emphasized the evangelical purpose of selected verses of the Bible and the evils of all forms of idolatry. The Jehovah presented here was not the loving father of the New Testament, but the angry and jealous god of the Old Testament, who destroyed cities and punished transgressors with death. Such militant Protestant offshoots slighted the quintessence of Christ's message – the emphasis on God's love. As a militant evangelist, Hong carried his 'imp-slaying swords' and relied on that coercion and physical force that characterized all Taiping projects.

Thus Hong and some of his co-initiators, also failed examinees, bred resentment against both the Manchus and Confucianism, and inclined naturally to inherit both the effective political organization of the Triads, and the attractive religious commitment of the Nians. Other than the passivity of Daoism or the otherworldliness of Buddhism at the grassroots, Taiping theocracy galvanized myriad of the oppressed to create a 'New Heaven, New Earth, and New World'. It further imposed a moral discipline, which befriended commoners and attracted recruits by its dedication, a discipline so austerely puritanical at first as to segregate men from women. They took full advantage of their political and religious vitality during their earlier development.

The Taipings mobilized the biggest anti-Confucian movement in history. The God-worshippers destroyed the sacred tablets and temples of Confucius at the very start, and banned 'anyone who dares read or teach any Confucian classics' during the early years in Nanjing. The veterans, however, were paradoxically trained in the orthodox manner. Deeply impressed by the idea of 'Great Peace' in New-Text classics, Hong named his new dynasty the Heavenly Kingdom of Great Peace, the captured Nanjing as the Heavenly Capital, and himself the Heavenly King. The political-military system was derived from the ancient classic of the *Rituals of Zhou*, by which the army was so highly organized as to be admired by their enemy. Later in Nanjing, they moderated their early hard line to publish *The Book of Changes* (*I-Ching*) and to schedule for publication a revised edition of the classics of Confucius and Mencius, though this was never realized. It was, anyway, a landmark effort at closing the gap between Confucianism and Christianism.

To meet their political needs, Taiping Christianity was further secularized and vulgarized. Hong drew from the term *Yehehua*, the transliteration of 'Jehovah' in the first Bible in Chinese, a far-fetched analogy where the character *ye* stood for father and *hua* for 'China'. Hence Jehovah would be in the Heavenly Capital, the centre of the world. Because of the infinite productivity of the notion of Universal Fatherhood, Hong remodelled this theocracy after the patriarchal clan system, revering God as 'Heavenly Father', Jesus as 'Heavenly Big Brother', and completing the Holy Family with the assumed 'Heavenly Mother' and 'Heavenly Sister-in-law'. To reward his sworn brothers, he extended the Family to them all as God's sons. The loss of the Christian transcendence of the deity in Heaven, which was so vulgarized by this hotchpotch of numerous gods, inevitably incited the internecine struggle for power on earth. After Hong's deification in order to seize power, the ambitious military leader, Yang Xiuqing, deified himself in the same way. The pivotal role in the capture of Nanjing had brought Yang the title, 'Holy God's Wind', an ambiguous translation of the Holy Spirit from the Trinity, along with Holy Father and Holy Son in the first Chinese Bible. Now, in the name of God's Wind, Yang claimed to be God's incarnate spokesman in order to supersede Hong's authority. A protracted and brutal massacre among the Heavenly Brothers followed in 1856, when their military prestige began to decline.

History once again re-enacted the old story: the initial victory of a peasant revolt soon turned out to be a tragedy through corruption and internecine carnage, which was almost predestined by the parochialism of the petty peasantry. Having entered Nanjing, the Taipings soon set up a rigid hierarchy in which, entirely against their early egalitarianism, the princes enjoyed privilege no less than had the Mandarins. Then the King wallowed in his religious fantasy, and the princes in sensual pleasures with numerous concubines. The promulgated agrarian law to free the peasants and to share the harvests was never applied. Having won over rapidly the whole lower basin of Middle Yangzi in 1853, the rebel offensive continued westward to the Upper Yangzi to secure provisions for the capital, while their projected expedition northward against Beijing soon came to nothing but the enhancement of vested interests, an essential limitation of the immaturity of this subculture.

This parochialism invited multiple opposition. Radical Taiping anti-Confucianism caused at once a reaction at the grassroots and a rebound from orthodoxy. Zeng Guofan, as a master of the latter, organized a militia, the Hunan Army, as a well-indoctrinated new army with the mission of defending the Confucian heritage. Urged to rescue the Middle Yellow River in early 1854, he issued a public proclamation, The call to 'denounce the Guangdong Bandits', in which he accused his rivals of 'converting to Christianity, forbidding students to read Confucius, and breaking our rites and morality of thousands of years into pieces'. He trained a number of literati as courageous generals. After him, his fellow provincial and classmate, Zuo Zongtang, formed another sect of the Hunan Army, and his student Li Hongzhang, another militia in Anhui, the Huai Army, as a substitute for the Hunan Army. The trend of local paramilitary organization since the early years of the century had reached a stage where it could act as a substitute for the regular imperial troops, the corrupt Eight Banners and Green Standard Army. There followed an unusual series of military campaigns led by Confucian generals with their loyalty to Sinic values, who were determined to rescue the Qing dynasty by perpetuating the prevailing social system. The rivalry between Zeng Guofan and Hong Xiuquan was thus, other than being merely a rivalry between Qing and Taiping, a conflict between Confucianism and Christianity and superculture versus subculture. In 1861 as Zeng recovered Anqing in Anhui, the most strategic gate of the Heavenly capital, his victory was already a foregone conclusion. It was not so much a victory of the Qing over the Taipings as that of the elite tradition over the plebeian tradition.

Taiping Christianity had been approved in the earliest days by some missionaries as 'the true prophet of Christianity in China'. As time elapsed, however, they became increasingly hostile to the heresy; as a missionary in Nanjing predicted, the pope would have had the blasphemers burned if that were possible. Britain had maintained a policy of neutrality until 1860, when she saw the rebels as a threat to foreign trade, particularly to the opium trade. After the *coup d'état* of 1861, in an effort to stabilize Sino-British relations, foreign involvement took concrete forms, either directly with foreign forces, as with the famous 'Ever Victorious Army', or indirectly with the provision of modern arms and training. The former was more symbolic than practical, while the latter more historically significant for the modernization of China's army and arms industry.

In the end, Taiping Christianity also estranged its theocracy from the indigenous subculture. Its exclusive purity and uncompromising dualism hindered it from cooperating with other secret societies. The Taipings allied sporadically with the Triads and the Nians, yet no long-term alliance resulted. In particular the Nians, who were scattered gangs joined loosely by families or villages, engaged in some anti-social and anti-cultural operations. Sympathetic with the Taiping movement, in the early 1850s they rallied in mobile militia with superiority in cavalry. They created a series of flexible strategies and tactics in guerrilla warfare, attacking without warning and then retreating when confronted by the enemy. With such flexibility, they survived the Taipings for several years, but at the cost of frequent defection by some of their leaders as their beliefs collapsed.

RESTORATION UNDER EARLY WESTERNIZATION (1860–85)

Restoration through self-strengthening

The reign of Tongzhiopeneda new era of 'return to universal order', as literally implied by the boy emperor's title. Nineteenth-century history saw not only the 'second blossoming' of the dynasty, lasting for another half century, but also a restoration of the millenarian civilization which appeared to have collapsed in the confrontation with vigorous Occidentalism.

The defeat of the rebels provided a necessary condition. The Tongzhi Restoration prominently featured a pragmatistic Westernization, which coincided with a reorientation of Sinic values through the extraordinary efforts of some leaders in the 1860s. The new rulers, the Empress Dowager Cixi, Prince Gong and his talented assistant Wenxiang, began to orientate national policy of 'conciliation with the invaders'. The 'Bureau for Appeasing the Barbarians' was replaced by the newly created Foreign Ministry (*Zonyli Yamen*), symbolizing the recognition of foreigners on equal terms. A relatively peaceful phase of two decades followed the two Opium Wars.

The call for Westernization as the spirit of the times was first made by Feng Guifen, a statecraft-oriented scholar. He was early on aware of China's need for self-reliance through acknowledging her own faults, and by way of practical study of the West, besides the manufacture of ships and guns, in the more essential exploitation of human and material resources to facilitate communication between monarch and subject and the unity between rhetoric and reality. He proposed in particular a drastic remodelling of the traditional system of education and examinations, leaving room for Western science and technology, as the only way to restore the splendour of Sinicism. 'We are just now', he wrote in his famous anthology, *Straight Words from the Lodge of Bin* [Early Zhou] *Studies* (1861), 'in an interval of peaceful and harmonious relations; it is an opportunity probably given us by heaven to strengthen ourselves [*ziqiang*]', an idea from *The Book of Changes* which features a Confucian gentleman who was able to regenerate himself.

The soul of the Restoration was Zeng Guofan, not so much the great saviour of the dynasty from the Taipings and Nians as the great restorer of Confucianism, and not so much a fundamentalist Confucian as the greatest statecraft-oriented Confucian in the mid-century. He was deeply influenced by Yao Nai, the leader of the Tongcheng literary school which, like the New Text school, stressed practical statecraft and piece-meal reformation within the tradition. He perceived the completely changed situation China

faced, and pointed out two elements of the *Tao* of change – timing and context – that ran independently of human will. The only way for China was to seize the opportunity and adjust herself to the situation, as *The Book of Change* says: 'Exhaustion leads to change, and change leads to the way ahead'. All of these, however, he proceeded to bring under the moral code elaborated by Neo-Confucianism. He believed that an immoral society could only be redeemed by a few noble figures, and that the mores of the age could be shifted through their advocacy.

Li Hongzhang also perceived the changed situation. 'The defence of the border', he wrote in 1874,

> was along the West and North bounded by the Great Wall, where there was hardly difference in strength between the host and the invader. Now the border moved to the East and South along the long coastline with a great disparity in strength: the foreigners could go freely to and fro without any wall. It produced a situation unique in Millennia.

It was they, the generation of talented restorers, who reasserted the validity of Confucianism amid lengthening shadows. The Restoration had taken a new stride forward in the Sinic renaissance since the beginning of the century.

As early as the recapture of Anqing in 1861, Zeng Guofan built the first domestic arsenal and invited to it the most celebrated scientists of the time, Li Shanlan, Hua Hengfang, and Xu Shou. After a disappointing early attempt in 1864, he met Yung Wing, the first Chinese graduate from an American university, Yale, and asked him to buy machinery abroad. A chain-reaction was produced with a series of homogeneous enterprises: the famous Jiangnan, Nanjing, Fuzhou, and Tianjin arsenals founded in 1865–7. Interpreters were necessary, and the Translation Office (*tongwen guan*) was established in Peking in 1862. In its wake, similar offices appeared in Shanghai and other treaty ports, and served as technical and language schools where Western learning was taught. Meanwhile, the offices attached to the arsenals produced numerous scientific and technological works, mainly through the cooperation of the Chinese scientists with Western missionaries, and this greatly rekindled scientific enthusiasm in China.

Accompanying the expansion of Protestant missions in the mid-century, there emerged a tendency towards professionalization. The most successful cooperation was achieved by Alexander Wylie, a British missionary, and Li Shanlan, a mathematician specializing in algebra and logarithms. They collaborated, with many others, to take up the translation of Euclid's *Elements of Geometry* at the exact point (Book VII) where Matteo Ricci had left off in the early seventeenth century. Another American missionary, John Fryer, a translator at the Jiangnan arsenal for twenty-eight years, completed with the help of Hua Hengfang and Xu Shou 119 translations of work in the natural and applied sciences. He can be seen as the archetype of the so-called 'secular missionary', whose mission seemed to have attached more importance to the strengthening China by way of Western science.

The early phase of the Restoration, however, was generally restricted in scope, as Feng Guifen wrote, 'to take Sinic ethics as essential and Western appliances as supplementary'. This was later abbreviated as the 'Sinic body and Western use', which had become a formula for dealing with the clash of Sino-Occidental civilizations throughout the century. Then the restorers, as technocrats, attached in general to solid gunboats and effective cannons, opened

China primarily to Western scientific-technical culture in the early response to the impact of the West.

Further developments in the search for wealth

China's Westernization soon went its own way beyond these narrow bounds. As the Western threat shifted from the military field to the economic one, the official monopoly system became so inadequate as to close Jiangnan and Fuzhou arsenals. Li Hongzhang, getting realistic enough to seek wealth before power, enrichment before strengthening, proposed to renovate the economic structure with a new system of 'government supervision and merchant operation'. This symbolized a new phase of the Restoration.

The innovation began to commercialize some agricultural sectors, thus breaking away from rudimentary physiocracy which 'valued agriculture but devalued commerce'. The new system enabled some amassing of capital, whence came new personalities: capitalists, compradors, factory workers, and modern literati familiar with Western learning. Wang Tao, the founder of the first Chinese newspaper, the *National Evolution* (*Tsun Wan Yat Pao*) in 1873 in Hong Kong, wrote a series of editorials to advocate commercial and other practical knowledge. Instead of the traditional 'agricultural warfare' and current military confrontation, he supported 'commercial warfare', which represented the Western idea of 'creating wealth through commerce'. Zheng Guanying, a comprador and one of the first capitalists in China, called more daringly for the free development of trade and industry without official intervention. Xue Fucheng, an advisor to Zeng Guofan and Li Hongzhang, went further in claiming that only by being wealthy could a nation be strong; thus commerce was the key to the success in agriculture, industry, science, technology, and education. From this point mercantile attitudes began to replace the stubborn physiocracy, and Westernization policies began to advance from the level of technical appliances to that of social institutions.

The new generation of reformers were enlightened, on the one hand, by missionary endeavour. Having gradually become divorced from evangelical aims, Protestant missionaries secularized their work, switching their emphasis on 'saving the heathen from the sufferings of hell' to 'saving the heathen from the hell of suffering in this world' (Richard, 1916: 197). They became more and more specialized in certain fields, notably medicine and education. In medicine, they either directly educated China's first modern physicians or indirectly transmitted modern medical knowledge in mission hospitals and schools. As for missionary education, after the first general conference of Protestant missionaries in China in 1877, they made secular endeavour an active policy. The newcomers seemed to be more interested in producing professional educators than ministers. Other than general education, chiefly at the elementary level, Protestants established numerous universities, opened libraries and museums, and published newspapers and magazines with the privilege exclusive to foreigners in open ports. Since 1875 Young J. Allen had published in Shanghai *The Globe Magazine* (*wanguo gongbao*) monthly, devoted to 'the extension of knowledge relating to geography, history, civilization, politics, religion, science, art, industry, and general progress of Western countries'. Through all of these means, Protestants won less converts but gained influence in China's modernization.

Many reformers were so indebted to them as to be called 'Christian reformers'. Wang Tao was baptized in Shanghai, and spent a two-year sojourn in Europe as James Legge's translation assistant. Zheng Guanying learned English from John Fryer, and the influence of the missionaries is everywhere in his writings. If there was a Sinic Enlightenment, it was certainly they who deserved to be named as its philosophers.

While most reformers took advantage of Western resources, they had not become thoroughly Christianized as yet. Wang Tao himself had never even mentioned his Christian identity in all his writings – but word leaked out from an unpublished diary. Zheng Guanying at once advocated Occidentalism and regarded Sinicism – Confucianism, Daoism and Buddhism – as good medicine for rectifying the current malady. They never renounced the Sinic stock onto which useful Western elements could be gradually grafted. Because the challenge was also a spur to China, Wang Tao even thanked heaven for granting China this golden opportunity. He and Zheng shared the insight of 'strategic timing' derived from the cosmology of Neo-Confucianism, a naive theory of evolution that encouraged them to strive for a bright future for China. The notion of 'use' in the 'body-use' formula was broadened to cover social institutions beyond the technocratic level, but never led to outright Westernization. Wang Tao wrote in the 1870s: 'What is variable is the tool, what is invariable, is the *Tao*', where *Tao*-tool was but another expression of 'body-use'. The regeneration of China was both enlightened by the West and animated by the Sinic heritage, really a combination of the Sinic Enlightenment and the Renaissance.

Counterbalance with Sinicism

Early Westernization had been contained from the very start by orthodox Sinicism. The decision to open the Translation Office to Western learning was bitterly criticized as 'having China barbarized'. The opposition at court was led by Woren, the Grand Secretary and leading Neo-Confucian scholar, acknowledged as a moral authority at the time. He believed sincerely that 'the way to establish a nation depends on morality, not trickery; on mind, not techniques'. Ship-building and railway-construction also triggered heated debates with the fundamentalist Confucians, who regarded any step to modernity as excessive Westernization. This is, indeed, the inertia of an agricultural society against a coming commercial and industrial society.

Moreover, every step toward Westernization was inevitably complicated by steady imperialist political and economic pressure. The municipal councils of foreign concessions in treaty ports were elected by foreign residents, while only the Chinese ones were taxed. Consular courts and jurisdiction, in line with extraterritoriality, were miniature governments on Chinese territory. Operating often contrary to Chinese customs or simply based on racial discrimination, they generated constant friction. Foreign post offices were set up in the main ports to dispatch mail, but only for the foreigners. Foreign control over Chinese customs turned from a local and temporary expedient into a permanent institution, though the English inspector general, Robert Hart, made the service outstandingly efficient. In economic life, the zone of operation for foreign merchants had been considerably enlarged in the North and the interior from 1860 on. Foreign industrial concerns were founded to make use of cheap labour and raw materials for the local market.

In addition to all these humiliations, there was a vast divide between basic cultural values. As the missionaries increased – to about 600 with half a million converts for Catholicism, and to over 1,000 with 30,000 converts for Protestantism in 1885 – the friction quickly escalated. The Catholics lived in interior villages and small towns in uneasy contact with local officials and gentry. The 'right of protection for Roman Catholics' exerted by France after the 1860s treaty, sometimes wrongly enabled guilty converts to escape Chinese jurisdiction. The right to reoccupy the land they had lost caused countless quarrels with the new land-owners. In Catholic orphanages, some deaths of poor but healthy children gave rise to still darker suspicions. The newly arrived Protestants, often from small towns with less cosmopolitan interests than their Catholic brethren, held the local culture in contempt and isolated themselves from the native population. Consequently, a lot of new converts – office workers, interpreters, shopkeepers, and coolies – were mere 'rice Christians' even criminals seeking protection. Even the missionaries had not always followed Christian morality. Behaviour such as the sexual harassment of women and children, and especially homosexual relations, generated the greatest hatred. Occasional incidents of this nature were especially liable to evoke infinite exaggeration and result in bloodshed.

With the new hatred piled upon the old, both the literati-officials and the populace were provoked to radical nationalism or even wild xenophobia. Around 1860 a pamphlet appeared entitled *An Authentic Statement Designed to Eliminate Heterodoxy*, written by 'the most despairing man in the world', as the author signed himself; it was a typical xenophobic mixture of theological criticism, obscene anecdotes, denunciation of the East-West discrimination in customs, and accusations of kidnapping and sorcery. In such a hostile climate, violent religious incidents happened so frequently that hardly a year passed without a demonstration of strength by France or Britain on the Chinese coast or in the Yangzi basin. This culminated in the massacre of Tianjin in 1870, in which over fifty were killed and some missionary buildings burnt. Zeng Guofan was attacked at the resolution of the incident for his impartial judgment of the rioters, and for the humiliating compensation and apology that he offered. He was caught between being 'ashamed of pure criticism without, and guilty of conscience within'. It was also a reflection of the political impasse for the court, where its conciliationism met a new challenge from the 'purification clique' impatient at the endless concessions. Seeking to rescue national dignity and traditional values, they flaunted Sinic moral force and advocated an uncompromising stance. The young officials in high posts were as militant as Woren, though not necessarily against modernization. This was the case with Zuo Zongtang and Zhang Zhidong, both leaders of the clique and the chief Westernizers at the court.

Events unfolded under increasing foreign pressure, as the clique had predicted. At their insistence, the Ili region was finally regained through Zuo Zongtang's negotiations with Russia in 1881. When France imposed a war on China in 1883, the clique was potent enough to impose a firmer line on the court. In 1884 Zhang Zhidong, as governor-general of Canton, published an anti-French proclamation vigorously appealing to patriotism. The Sino-French war ended in China's defeat on the whole, but with partial victory in

contrast to the preceding wars, and the resulting treaty was not as severe as its predecessors. The system of unequal treaties got no worse, at least not immediately. By and large, China was not yet to be dismembered or further colonized, an outcome, as it were, partly of the puritanical Sinicization.

FROM RESTORATION TO REFORMATION (1885–1900)

Politicization of the Westernization process

The evolution of China's process of Westernization from technological to political levels was overlapped by the inner propensity of Sinicism. Zeng Guofan emphasized that the right course for an upright Confucian was from internal self-cultivation to external state-administration and world-pacification. Moving forward to *bianfa*, which means reforming institutions and legality, the Tongzhi Restoration was irresistibly politicized in the 1870s. Guo Songtao, as a typical Confucian literati-official, issued the first call for political reform when he witnessed Western civilization at first hand as the first Chinese ambassador in Britain in 1877–9. He discovered that its essence lay neither in technology nor in commerce, but in politics and law, which was embodied in parliamentary democracy.

Shocked by the Sino-French war, the reformers of the new generation began to turn seriously to political reform. He Qi, a young Hong Kong lawyer who had studied in Britain, denounced the technocratic Restoration as a disaster unless there was to be a real parliamentary system. Sun Yat-sen, in the same context, perhaps partly influenced by He, made up his mind to topple the Manchus soon after the war. Having spent most of his formative years overseas, Sun was considerably Westernized by his Western educational background, facility in the English language, and Christian conversion. In 1894 he organized in Hawaii China's first modern revolutionary society, the Society to Revive China (*xingzhong hui*), to 'drive away the Manchus, restore China, and create a republic'. The older generation strove after the same goal but more moderately. Wang Tao classified Western political institutions into three types: imperial authority, people's authority, and the joint authority of the emperor and the people. Zheng Guanying further elaborated the third type of balanced power: neither bias towards the high, nor towards the low. Guo Songtao also rejected what he perceived as democracy's inherent malady, of being susceptible to the dictates of populism. They all preferred British or Japanese-style constitutional monarchy to the more radical French or American democracy.

On the basis of this development, Zhang Zhidong, a new star who had risen to prominence in the Sino-French war, further widened the scope of Westernization to include Western 'public law' on a par with technology and science. He reinterpreted the 'body-use' stance as 'Sinic learning as internal, Western learning as external; and with the former to cultivate body and mind, and the latter to handle social affairs'. For him only ethics were invariable, as holy principles or Holy Spirit, while other matters such as crafts and legal institutions were all variable. In short, *fa* was temporal, the cultural spirit was permanent. After Chen Li's synthesis of the Han and Song schools, he tried to go further to incorporate Western learning into Sinicism, or rather, to Sinicize Occidentalism as a 'new culture'.

The reformist course was abruptly accelerated by Japan's boom. By means of its Confucian-Shinto heritage stressing independence, individual self-respect and the self-sacrificing *bushito*, the Meiji Restoration achieved success in the late 1860s, and became rapidly Europeanized, with the goal being to 'quit Asia for Europe'. With a mingled feelings of admiration for China's past with contempt for her present, Japan began to march against China in terms of her 'continental policy'. Having repeatedly clashed in the Korean peninsula, the duel of the two Asian giants in search of modernization had its final showdown in the Sino-Japanese war of 1894–5. In a naval battle in the Yellow Sea lasting a few hours, China's Northern Fleet, that had existed for ten years, was destroyed. The aftermath of the war appalled the Chinese people more than any event since 1840. The failure was not only military, but more severely, a fiasco for all the modernizing endeavours for more than a generation. What is more, it was galling to be defeated by such a small country, peripheral to China and nurtured by Confucianism, with a common writing system and racial background; galling because Japan was so close to China both in geography and culture. China had now suffered a double disaster, both internal and external, that was to blow its modernization project off course.

Kang Youwei, Yan Fu, and the radicalization of reform

Kang Youwei emerged in this stressful era as a radical both culturally and politically. Impressed by the Neo-Confucianist Lu-Wang's mentalism and by Mahayana Buddhism, from his youth he devoted himself to the salvation of the Chinese. But having experienced the brand new civilization in Hong Kong and become acquainted with Liao Ping, the head of the New Text school in the late Qing, he decisively converted to it. The school seemed to him more lively than Lu-Wang's mentalism, more useful than Buddhism, and more amenable than Occidentalism, although a factual synthesis of all these elements was in his mind. On this basis, he entirely rejected any kind of orthodox authority in his *Study of the Classics Forged during the Xin Period* of 1891, and remodelled the figure of Confucius in his *Study of Confucius' Reform of Institutions* of 1897. He testified textually that Confucius had actually composed the major classics as a sanction for institutional reform. He invoked the naive theory of evolution of the New Text classics: the Three Ages of Disorder, Approaching Peace (which phase the world now was entering), and the Great Peace. Being the last leading New Text scholar after his forerunners Gong Zizheng and Zeng Guofan, Kang became the leading reformist for carrying out Westernization, but still acted in the name of Confucius himself and fundamentalist Confucianism.

In addition to Kang, Yan Fu pioneered the vogue of cultural Westernization. Raised with a perfect grounding in Sinic classics and well read in Western learning in Britain from 1877 to 1879, he was immensely impressed by the Social Darwinism just then shaking the world. This theory expounded the necessity of the survival of the fittest in society, and hence the need for creative adaptation to avoid extinction, which seemed so lamentably relevant to China's plight. The shock of 1895 to him was new evidence to support the theory, and he expressed his own ideas in a series of essays. In the first, 'On the Extreme of Worldly

Change', he claimed that such extreme change stemmed from the forces of timing and context, forcees unpredictable even to a sage, who could not alter their course but only foresee and act in concert with them. Further, he identified the real source of Western power and wealth as 'revering the truth against the false in learning, and subordinating the private to the public in politics and law' as he summarized it. To transform the Chinese 'vision of reality', he introduced systematically the Western humanities. Amongst other influences, there was Thomas Huxley's *Evolution and Ethics*, which he introduced under the title *On Evolution*, with his own added commentary and interpretations, and in Chinese parlance more succinct and inciting. 'Things compete, Heaven selects; the superior wins, the inferior fails; the weak are the prey of the strong'. This sounded the most imminent alarm for national subjugation and genocide. This and the ensuing translations of such influential works as John Stuart Mill's *On Liberty*, Montesquieu's *De l'esprit des lois*, and Adam Smith's *Wealth of Nations*, pushed the Sinic Enlightenment forward to a new climax. Yan Fu highly praised Western culture for liberating individual potential, and denounced the Confucian stress on personal obligation to the establishment at the expense of individuality and creativity. He went on to reinterpret the 'body-use' formula as freedom being the 'body', the essential value, and democracy the 'use', the incarnation of freedom in institutions. In regard to culture, he was even more radical than Kang Youwei.

As an evolutionist, however, Yan never forgot the traditional stock onto which this advanced civilization could be grafted. He found the origin of modern science and the cream of social evolution as roughly expounded in the Sinic classics. Hence, he believed all along in gradual evolution as against the miracle of mutation, thus believing in a political gradualism rather than Kang's radicalism. Excused from arrest after the Reform of 1898, he continued to advocate 'enlightening the people's wisdom' and proposed a systematic plan of self-salvation for complementing Sinic learning with that of the West.

The Hundred-Day Reform of 1898

Kang Youwei began his political career with serial memorandums to the throne, the second of which was sent soon after the war in 1895 with Liang Qichao and the signatures of 1,300 candidates for the metropolitan examination, which he and Liang happened to take in Peking. This memorandum was the first to call for constitutional monarchy, though it never actually reached the Emperor. The next one, however, was finally read by Emperor Guangxu, and dispatched to all governors; it set off a reformist upsurge. The Society for Strengthening Study was established under Kang's support with the membership of Zhang Zhidong, Li Hongzhang, and the British and American envoys. It disseminated reformist ideas by lectures, translations, and a daily paper, the *Bulletin of China and the Foreign*.The most influential journal, the *Current Events Gazette*, was also published by Liang Qichao.

Soon impeached by officials at Peking, the centre of the movement was reluctantly transferred from Peking to Hunan, where the governor was sympathetic to it. For political reform Huang Zunxian, as a high official there, wrote *The History of Japan* based on his personal diplomatic experience abroad, the only first-hand documentation of the Meiji Restoration at the time. The local gentry, Wang Xianqian and Ye Dehui, galvanized the movement by a joint endeavour with the radicals. In 1897, they founded the South Study Society to promote the local rights of the gentry as supporters of the provincial parliament, and in addition, to establish libraries and publish the *Hunan Study Journal*, the first newspaper in Hunan.

The honeymoon between the radicals and moderates, however, soon came to an end when Liang Qichao was invited to be the general tutor at the School for Current Affairs. Liang and his colleagues, Tan Sitong and Tang Changcai, reinterpreted the Confucian classics with Western ideas of freedom and equality, and disseminated some anti-Manchu works describing the early massacres. Liang became so exasperated by the German occupation of Jiaozhou, as to urge Hunan's independence, following the example of Satmuku and Choshu in late Tokugawa Japan, the two feudal domains which led regional autonomy to the final success of the Meiji Restoration. The movement was thus suddenly radicalized beyond the tolerance of the moderates, and led to an ideological schism in the spring of 1898. Wang Xianqian initiated a learning convention against the heterodox vogue current throughout the province. Zhang Zhidong published his *Exhortation to Learning* in instalments in the *Hunan Journal*, where he emphasized that Westernization could only be attained by way of existing authority. The schism presaged the failure of the radicals, who lacked the social sanctions enjoyed by the official gentry. When a provincial staunch supporter was forced to have Kang's works burned, the dream of independence vanished completely.

There was, meanwhile, an unexpected development in Peking when Kang's fifth and sixth memorials impressed the Emperor, who was trying to establish his own authority, away from the control of the Empress. The ambitious Emperor made up his mind to stake the fate of both the Qing and himself on one throw. He issued the first reform decree on 11 June 1898 to begin the Reform, and this persuaded Kang and his disciples to reappear on the scene. A flood of some 40–50 edicts followed, dealing with administration, education, and the economy. Almost in a flash, many useless offices were closed, the subsidies for the Manchus cut, the outdated Green Standard disbanded, and the old academies and temples transformed into modern schools. As vested interests were seriously hurt by all this, grievances grew rapidly, thus estranging even the moderate reformers at court from the hasty and over-radical programme. The high-flown edicts were boycotted in the central administration and ignored by local officials, not to mention the vast indifferent masses. As the atmosphere got more and more tense in Peking, the Emperor and the Kangs, with more enthusiasm than power, had no alternative but to stage a *coup d'état* in a bid to eliminate the opposition at one stroke. But the Empress, keeping a close watch on their every move, crushed the plot easily on 21 September thanks to Yuan Shikai's betrayal. The Emperor was subsequently confined to a small island in the palace lake, Tan Sitong and five others were executed, and Kang and Liang fled abroad. The Hundred-Day Reform vanished like mist.

From cultural conflict to populist riot

The aftermath of the Sino-Japanese War touched off a scramble for concessions: Russia controlled the region by the northern Great Wall; Britain, the Yangzi valley; France, Guangdong, Guangxi and Yunnan; Germany, Shandong; and Japan, Fujian. China was threatened with imminent partition. Xenophobia became so bitter as to even submerge the innate hatred against the Manchus, thus leading to a bizarre alliance of elite and populace. Some secret societies gradually diverted their priority from 'opposing the Qing and eliminating the foreign', to 'supporting the Qing and eliminating the foreign'. The hawks at court led by Cixi fell into such impotence before the threat that they began appealing to the mob.

The missionaries were the focus of hatred, though they had contributed more to China's progress than all others: merchants, diplomats and armies, who sought exclusively their own interests. The cause of this hatred centred on the missionaries' holy mission to replace Confucianism with Christianity. They held Sinic civilization in contempt as 'rotten wood' unworkable and only to be 'wholly cut away'. Arthur H. Smith, an American missionary who had spent over forty years in China (Smith, 1894: 330) wrote in this vein. They felt generally hostile to ancestor worship, thus creating an unbridgeable gap. To Sinic sages, the *Tao* begins with husband-wife, so family values lie at the core of the Confucian value-system. 'The central idea of their cult is filial piety', as Robert Hart observed, 'reverence for seniority settles all the details of family, social, and national life' (Hart, 1901: 151). Such an obligation-oriented culture, stressing everyone's immanent obligation to family, country, and the world, was diametrically opposite to a Western philosophy based on inalienable individual rights. These latter values struck at the root of a kinship society.

Anti-foreign sentiment was highly focused on Shandong, the birthplace of Confucius, where Germany took Jiaozhou and Britain took Weihaiwei. The missions there were accused of being the source of all the untold sufferings, and Chinese converts were seen as traitors willing to be foreigners' slaves, infuriating the public even more. As the xenophobia became more and more intense, the hawks saw more and more popular patriotic emotion which could be mobilized. The 'Righteous and Harmonious Fists' (*yihequan*), known as the 'Boxers' in the West, organized at first for self-protection through Sinic martial art, now were advised to rename themselves the 'Righteous and Harmonious Militia' (*yihetuan*) by the governor, and increasingly relied on magic, with amulets and incantations, thus appearing as a vast anti-foreign movement that mixed modern patriotism with primitive sorcery. In March 1900 the Boxers moved northward, bold enough to destroy railways and telegraph lines under court patronage. By July large bodies of rampaging Boxers swarmed into the capital to burn and massacre; Peking soon became the centre of the rioting. Meanwhile the secret societies reactivated and agrarian disturbances broke out again. The whole country was in turmoil.

As another massive populist riot, the Boxers reversed the Taiping stance from pro-Christian and anti-Manchu to anti-Christian and pro-Manchu, and converted Christian monotheism into popular polytheism. Their gods included the Jade Emperor from the secularized Daoism, Sun Wukong, Zhuguo Liang and Guangong from popular novels, Xiang Yu and Huang Tianba from popular drama, and the like. They denounced all those who were connected with foreigners as 'the secondary barbarians', including Emperor Guangxu, Kang Youwei and Li Hongzhang, an extremist opposed to all supercultures either

Western or Sinic at the grassroots. The disturbances provoked the opposition of some provincial authorities, who organized the 'mutual defence of the South East' on good terms with foreign consuls. The tension between the two cultures thus intensified.

Eight foreign powers allied to mount a punitive expedition. They entered Peking in August 1900, having perpetrated a systematic slaughter and plunder comparable to the worst excesses of the Boxers. Field Marshal Count von Waldersee faithfully carried out German Emperor William II's order: 'Peking must be razed to the ground. Show no mercy! Take no prisoners!' Then the whole city was sacked, and the imperial palace was stripped of most of its treasures. Von Waldersee directed forty-six bloody punitive operations in north China, where missionaries were attacked. As a result, discord arose in the Allied camp, and, during their negotiations with Li Hongzhang, a variety of issues undermined any pretence of unity: Germany demanded stern punishment, France did not seek China's break-up, and the United States reiterated the Open Door Policy, supporting the 'Chinese territorial and administrative entity'. The eventual treaty, in 1901, included the usual severe punishments and a heavy indemnity, yet, unusually, no further territorial claims.

As the first mass movement against modern imperialism, the Boxer rebellion failed, yet forced the world powers to reconsider the partition of China. Even Waldersee acknowledged in his memoir that the militant spirit of the Chinese had not been defeated in the war. An irrational rebellion brought about a rational outcome.

FROM REFORMATION TO REVOLUTION (1900–12)

Cultural infiltration in depth

Despite this chaos, Western ideas continued to penetrate China at the dawn of the new century.

Yan Fu further promoted Western ideology by successively translating such works as Herbert Spencer's *A Study of Sociology* and S. Jevons' *Logic* in the 1900s, in an attempt to have the 'stability-oriented' culture Westernized as 'activity-oriented'. Along the same lines Wang Guowei, as an aesthete, drew upon the subjective initiatives of Kant, Schopenhauer and Nietzsche. The political trend of thought coincidently leaned towards revolution, with both outright Westernization and radical nationalism. In 1901–2 the exiled Kang Youwei wrote his most extreme *The Great Commonwealth* which, as an expression of the finale of the Three Ages of New Text classicism, completely rejected the family values upon which the entire edifice of Confucian morality was erected. It seemed to him that only if the family were abolished could the abolition of private property and a national state then follow. For this purpose, he suggested that a man and a woman should not be allowed to cohabit for more than one year, a programme even more radical than that of Karl Marx and Friedrich Engels' *Communist Manifesto*. But paradoxically, he upheld the Emperor on the grounds that the Chinese were still too immature for revolution. This formed a weird Kangian eclecticism of cultural radicalism and political moderation.

Zhang Taiyan, as a radical anti-Manchu revolutionary against Kang, refuted the so-called 'immaturity thesis' that the revolution *per se* would mature into the Chinese revolution. The young revolutionary Zhou Rong openly praised revolution in his radical treatise 'The Revolutionary Army', as a law of social evolution and a global axiom, and put forward the case for creating a Republic of China. Its publication was managed by Zhang in 1903 in the *Jiangsu Tribune*, which he edited. This resulted in the stirring '*Jiangsu Tribune* Case', in which Zhou died in jail at twenty years of age and Zhang was imprisoned for two years. The case incited great revolutionary zeal at home and abroad. Despite his radical nationalism, however, Zhang was by no means an anti-traditionalist. He rejected Yan Fu's early worship of the West by holding that evolution brings about not only good, but also evil; and likewise, that the representative system does not necessarily represent equal rights of the rich and the poor, of noble and commoner. He opposed the New Text school, especially the worship of Confucius as a reformist pope, as did Kang, but inclined towards legalist Xunzi and Mohism. Having become increasingly in favour of the positive role of Buddhism, he proposed to 'rely on oneself instead of others', to rely neither on the transcendental God of Christianity, nor on the external gods and ghosts of Daoist theology. He devoted himself finally to creating a new civilization, really a synthesis of Sinic, Western, and Indian cultures.

During 1902–5, when the fortunes of the revolution took a turn for the better, Sun Yat-sen united Huang Xing and Song Jiaoren in The Chinese United League (*tongmeng hui*) and elaborated his revolutionary programme as Three People's Principles: nationalism, democracy, and socialism, after Abraham Lincoln's expression 'of the people, by the people, and for the people', and Henry George's idea of taxing landowners on all increments in land value. Even though radical as a Westernizer, Sun did not break with tradition to the same degree as his successors. He explained his ideas comprehensively in the first issue of the *People's Tribune* in 1905: 'The principles I insist upon for revolution, are that some follow the traditional moral code, some are modelled on European theories and developments, and some are created by my own originality'. He thought 'to accomplish the political and social revolutions at one stroke', in order to realize the classical ideal of the 'Great Harmony under Heaven'.

Cultural infiltration still proliferated in popular culture. Lin Shu was the first intermediary of Western novels by translating no less than 150 titles in 12 million words. Without any knowledge of foreign languages, he grasped the spirit and mood of the original and expressed them in an elegant and vivid classical Chinese through his cooperator's oral rendition. Such noted novels as *La dame aux camelias* by Alexander Dumas, *David Copperfield* by Charles Dickens, and *Ivanhoe* by Sir Walter Scott, narrowed the gap between the new intellectuals and Occidentalism. Partly elicited by the Lin translations, there emerged a stylish trend in colloquial novels. Some, prone to modern critical realism, condemned the decadence of officialdom, the outstanding among such works being *The Revelation of the Official Circles; The Monstrosity Witnessed for Twenty Years; and Laocan's Travels*. Others disclosed the vices in certain life-styles of urbanites, although with little literary merit. The new-style drama appeared in Shanghai in 1902, first as 'civilized drama' based on foreign texts and played by foreigners. When written and played by the Chinese, they showed modern life, especially the lives of such revolutionaries as *Qiu Jin, Xu Shilin*, and *The Revolutionary Family*, in contrast to the traditional opera. The first cinema opened in 1903. The infiltration was double-edged: it Westernized the Chinese against fundamentalist Confucianism, and also revolutionized them against the West as well as the Qing.

The ten-year New Deal of the court

Thorough reform began with the Empress's decree on 8 January 1901, from her painful exile at Xian. Reluctant as it had been to keep the dynasty, it survived on the defensive. The New Deal was a genuine reform, even more daring than that of the Hundred-Day episode. At the request of the court, Zhang Zhidong and Liu Kunyi jointly presented three memoranda advising further Westernization of education and law, and of the political and economic systems. The ideas ranged from those of Feng Guifen to Kang Youwei, but were elaborated in more exhaustive detail and with more vitality for the whole period.

In 1905 the Russo-Japanese war impacted on China and ended in Japan's victory, which spurred the country further to political reform. 'The outcome of the War', Zhang Jian commented, 'is victory for constitutional monarchy and defeat for the autocratic monarchy'. Zhang Zhidong and Yuan Shikai at once personally presented memoranda calling for a constitution to the Empress, who issued an edict next year to promise its preparation. The constitutional movement suddenly caught fire and rapidly spread throughout the country. Zhang Jian, once the number-one examinee in the court and then the first modern entrepreneur in China, was most active in his special capacity as the chief of the movement. Kang Youwei, in exile, encouraged by the new trend, changed his Emperor-Protection Society into the National Constitutional Society. Still more excited, Liang Qichao organized a 'Political Information Society' and published in Japan the *Political Information Magazine* to promote responsible parliamentarism and judicial independence to show good will towards the court. He continuously advocated gradual political change under the constitutional regime through his *The New People's Miscellany*, and in a new style, mixed classical and colloquial diction, which won an immediate following among the reading public.

The New Deal realized some awaited political innovations. Cixi acknowledged that the main achievement of Western civilization lay in the sympathy between rulers and ruled rather than in mechanical arts. The edict of 1906 further approved a constitution to bring the Emperor closer to the commoners. A year later the court recommended a constitutional assembly and provincial assemblies. Limited to scholars and rich landowners as the suffrage was, the provincial assemblies immediately became the centre of opposition, while the government seemed more clumsy and insincere in response to pressure. Some provincial officials even preceded the court in this proposal to redesign the accessibility of the government to the people. Zhao Erxun in Shanxi innovated a mutual-security system, *baojia*, to reorientate the administration in favour of greater popular participation. Others established women's schools, developed the urban police system, and redirected funds from local communities to reform local government and education. The newly formed Bureau of Government Affairs officially publicized these initiatives, and formally proposed sub-county administration in 1905. Following the Japanese model, Yuan Shikai moved swiftly to set up a 'self-government bureau' to explore limited representation in local administration.

More noteworthy, the New Deal established the basis of a modern education system. Cixi admitted that the chief defect in the existing administration lay in its obsolete methods, which led to a deplorable lack of men of real talent. Zhang Zhidong declared simply that the survival of the dynasty depended on the quality of schooling. A series of measures was thus adopted to abolish the eight-part (*bagu*) essay in 1901, to transform the traditional academies into new-style schools first in Shandong by Yuan Shikai in the same year, and finally in September 1905 to abolish the traditional state examination system which had lasted over two thousand years and had become the focus of almost all abuse by officials in its last phase. The creation of the Ministry of Education and a number of education societies of the provincial elite offered further support for modern schools. Correspondingly, Zhang Zhidong strongly promoted the orders of 1901–2, to select students to study abroad, rising from 20 to 2,000 at the end of the 1900s. These students, especially those studying abroad, contributed both to the Qing dynasty and to the first Republic of China.

The interaction of constitutional reform and republican revolution

The New Deal took a step forward by transforming the ideological conflict between moderate and radical reformers into one between constitutionalists and republicans. A heated debate had been carried on in Japan 1905–7, mainly in the pages of Liang Qichao's *The New People's Miscellany* and *The People's Tribune*, the official journal of the United League. The focus, however, was not so much on the future form of government as on the urgent issue of whether it was necessary to topple Manchu rule. It was unnecessary for Liang to take a particular view, as the Manchus had begun to modify their autocracy. Among his sensitive and varied viewpoints, he insisted consistently on gradual reform rather than on the sudden destruction of the ancient traditions. Sun Yat-sen and his followers launched a powerful counter-attack arguing for the need to abolish the regime, which he held responsible for all the disasters China had suffered. They defended Sun's pro-Western attitude, akin to that of enlightened foreigners from whom he had openly sought support. Even within the same camp, Zhang Taiyan poignantly accused Sun of accepting large sums of money from foreigners, worried lest the revolution to be too foreign-oriented at the expense of China's own culture.

The new policy aroused both constitutional zeal and discontent with bureaucratic dilatoriness, both of which converged in constitutional movements. With the support of the gentry-merchants and the new bourgeoisie, the constitutionalists organized a boycott in 1905 of American goods to protest against the new immigration laws that discriminated against the Chinese, and another similar boycott took place against Japan in 1908. Mammoth demonstrations for parliamentarism broke out repeatedly in 1910, with tens of thousands in sixteen provinces involved.

As the gentry-merchants determined to defend both their economic interests against foreigners and their political privileges against the court, the campaign for withdrawing rights from foreign powers surged ahead with full force. In 1905 Zhang Zhidong managed to buy back from America the concession for building the Hankou-Canton railway for Guangdong, Hunan, and Hubei, and for developing a line from Hankou to Sichuan. But neither of the provinces proved strong enough to undertake the huge construction project. The court took the opportunity to nationalize the main railway by raising huge foreign loans, leaving only the minor or branch lines to private operation. The Provincial Assembly of Sichuan led a protest, and founded the Railway Protection League in June 1911 to circulate petitions and organize more demonstrations. Popular patriotic agitation was especially outraged by the loans, and a vast mass movement sprang up in August to demand the postponement of nationalization. A massacre and arrests on 7 September pushed the movement beyond its original defensive aim to kindle the flames of revolution. 'Domestic politics is hopeless', a League leader declared, 'The government apparently does not care for the people. To save the country, there is no other way but revolution'.

The pulse of revolution synchronously quickened. The republican revolutionaries had widened their connection with new students, the new army, and secret societies. Joining the Hong League (hongmen) and being elected generalissimo in Honolulu in 1902, Sun Yat-sen was welcomed as 'Elder Brother Sun' in the United States in 1904. After the founding of the Society to Revive China, he accelerated the pace of armed uprisings, now totalling ten during 1895–1911, and culminating in the uprising of Yellow Flower Mound at Canton in April 1911.

The final success of the Wuchang Uprising was rather a combined result of both trends than a premeditated action such as had been the case in previous revolts. The Uprising began with an accidental bomb explosion on 9 October in a peripheral organization of the United League, and then prompted a mutiny in the New Army to capture the office of the governor-general in Wuchang on 10 October. For lack of a well-known figure among the rebels, a brigade commander, Li Yuanhong, was persuaded to head the provisional military government, and a constitutionalist, Tang Hualong, was put in charge of civil administration. Most provinces were taken over within fifty days by various social forces, from constitutionalists to republicans, from opportunistic officials to secret societies. Some League leaders refused to accept the Uprising, and Sun himself saw it at the time as a 'pure accident'. Huang Xing arrived at Wuchang on 20 October, too late to dislodge the president, and then forcibly created a second centre in Nanjing and Shanghai. Hence a bitter rivalry developed in the struggle for the presidency between the two centres, until Sun Yat-sen returned from abroad to be elected as president. He was inaugurated in Nanjing on 1 January 1912, year 1 of the Republic of China.

History, however, did not end. The rapidity of the success, only eighty-three days in all, was seldom equalled by other great revolutions of the world. The ambitious Yuan Shikai seemed indispensable at the time for saving the country from civil war. He urged the Qing to issue a decree for the imperial abdication at last on 12 February 1912, and next urged the newborn Republic to appoint him to the presidency on 10 March. Then followed an era of tangled warfare among warlords, once again throwing China into chaos. The fruit of the 1911 Revolution invited second thoughts. In later explaining his Three Principles of the People, Sun Yat-sen invoked traditional 'Loyalty and Filial Devotion, then Kindness and Love, Faithfulness and Justice, then Harmony and Peace', against those who were intoxicated with wholesale Westernization. Despairing of the Revolution and, in addition, with the explosion of World War I, Yan Fu denounced Occidentalism as a culture of 'slaughter for benefiting oneself and shamelessness without the least shame', which seemed to him an inevitable result of excessive individualism. He called for continuing reliance on time-tested Sinic culture.

History was awaiting a new round of restoration, reformation, and revolution. China would continue her search of modernization under the tensions of Westernization and Sinicization, while the past century was merely a prologue to the coming century.

BIBLIOGRAPHY

BANNO, M. 1964. *China and the West, 1858–1861: The Origin of the Tsungli Yamen.* Harvard University Press, Cambridge MA.

BOARDMAN, E. 1952. *Christian Influence upon the Ideology of the Taiping Rebellion, 1851–1864.* University of Wisconsin Press, Madison.

CHEN, X. 1992. *The Social Metabolism of Modern China.* Renmin Chubanshe, Shanghai.

CHESNEAUX, J.; BASTID, M.; BERGERE, M. C. 1976. *China: From the Opium Wars to the 1911 Revolution.* Random House, New York.

COHEN, P. A. 1963. *China and Christianity: the Missionary Movement and the Growth of Chinese Antiforeignism, 1860–1870.* Harvard University Press, Cambridge MA.

——. 1973. *Between Tradition and Modernity: Wang T'ao and Reform in Late Ch'ing China.* Harvard University Press, Cambridge, MA.

FAIRBANK, J. K. (ed.) 1978. *The Cambridge History of China, Vol. 10: Late Ch'ing, 1800–1911.* Part 1. Cambridge University Press, London and Cambridge.

——; LIU, K. C. (eds) 1980. *The Cambridge History of China, Vol. 11.* Part 2. Cambridge University Press, London and Cambridge.

FENG, G. 1884. *Straight Words from the Lodge of Bin Studies.* Jiangsu, Feng family.

FEUERWERKER, A. 1968. *China's Early Industrialization: Sheng Hsuan-huai (1844–1916).* Harvard University Press, Cambridge MA.

FOLSOM, K. E. 1968. *Friends, Guests, and Colleagues: The 'mu-fu' System in the Late Ch'ing Period.* University of California Press, Berkeley.

GONG, Z. 1959. *Complete Works of Gong Zizhen.* Zhonghua Shuju, Shanghai.

HAIL, W. J. 1927. *Tseng Kuo-fan and the Taiping Rebellion.* Yale University Press, New Haven.

HART, R. 1901. 'These from the Land of Sinim'. In: *Essays on the Chinese Question.* Chapman and Hall, London.

HOLT, E. 1964. *The Opium Wars in China.* Putnam, London.

HSU, I. C. Y. 1970. *The Rise of Modern China.* Oxford University Press, New York.

JIAN, B.; XUNZHENG, S.; HUA, H. (eds) 1951. *The Boxers.* Shenzhou Guoguang She, Shanghai.

——. 1953. *The Reform of 1989.* Shenzhou Guoguang She, Shanghai.

JIAN, Y. (CHIEN YU-WEN). 1962. *Complete History of the Taiping Heavenly Kingdom*. Chien's Meng-chin Studio, Hong Kong.

JIANG, D. 1956. *A Tentative Study of Nian Army History*. Sanlian Shudian, Beijing.

KANG, Y. 1891. *A Study of the Classics Forged During the Xin Period*. Various later edns.

——. 1897. *A Study of Confucius as an Institutional Reformer*. Datong, Shanghai.

LATOURETTE, K. S. 1929. *A History of Christian Missions in China*. SPCK, London.

LEVENSON, J. R. 1953. *Liang Ch'i-ch'ao and the Mind of Modern China*. Harvard University Press, Cambridge MA.

——. 1974. *Between Tradition and Modernity: Wang T'ao and Reform in Late Ch'ing China*. Harvard University Press, Cambridge MA.

LI, H. 1905. *Complete Works of Li Wenzhong Gong*. Commercial Press, Shanghai.

LUO, E. 1937. *An Outline History of the Taiping Heavenly Kingdom*. Commercial Press, Shanghai.

QI, S.; LIN, S. (eds) 1954. *The Opium War*. 6 vols. Shenzhou Guoguang She, Shanghai.

QIAN, M. 1937. *A History of Chinese Scholarship over the Past Three Hundred Years*. Commercial Press, Shanghai.

RICHARD, T. 1916. *Forty Five Years in China*. New York.

SCHIFFLIN, H. Z. 1968. *Sun Yat-sen and the Origins of the Chinese Revolution*. University of California Press, Berkeley.

SCHWARTZ, B. 1964. *In Search of Wealth and Power: Yen Fu and the West*. Harvard University Press, Cambridge MA.

SHAO, X.; et al. (eds) 1955. *The Sino-French War*. Renmin Chubanshe, Shanghai.

——. 1956. *The Sino-Japanese War*. Xinzhishi Chubanshe, Shanghai.

SMITH, A. H. 1894. *Chinese Characteristics*. Fleming H. Revel, New York.

SPENCE, J. D. 1990. *The Search for Modernization of China*. Norton, New York.

SUN, Y. S. 1950. *The Complete Works of the National Father*. Guomindang History Commission, Taipei.

WANG, E. M. 1977. *Historical Essays on Modern Chinese Thought*. Hua-shih, Taipei.

WANG, T. 1883. *Supplementary Writings of Tao Garden*. Privately issued, Hong Kong.

WEI, Y. 1944. *Illustrated Treatise on the Maritime Kingdom*. Amplified version.

WRIGHT, M. C. 1957. *The Last Stand of Chinese Conservatism: The T'ung Chih Restoration, 1862–1874*. Stanford University Press, Stanford.

YAN, F. 1922. *Yan Fu's Poems and Essays*. Guohua Shuju, Shanghai.

——. 1931. *A Collection of Famous Yan Translations*. Commercial Press, Shanghai.

XIANG, D. et al. (eds) 1852. *The Taiping Heavenly Kingdom*. Shenzhou Guoguang She, Shanghai.

XIAO, Y. 1928. *A General History of the Qing Period*. Commercial Press, Shanghai.

ZENG, G. 1876. *Complete Works of Zeng Wenzheng Gong*. Amplified version.

ZHANG, ZHIDONG. 1928. *Complete Works of Zhang Wenxiang Gong*. Wenhua Zhai, Beiping.

ZHANG, ZHONGLI. 1955. *The Chinese Gentry*. University of Wisconsin Press, Madison.

ZHAO, E. 1928. *Draft History of the Qing Dynasty*. Qing History Office, Beiping.

ZHENG, G. 1892. *Warning to a Prosperous Age*. Reprint 1965. Ta-t'ung, Taipei.

13.3.2
JAPAN

Hiroshi Mitani

In comparative perspective, the assimilation of modern Western science in Japan had two characteristics: (1) it was accomplished by the same people who had inhibited contacts before the renewed presence of Western states in the mid-nineteenth century because they succeeded in protecting themselves from colonization by the West; (2) their concern was concentrated on the technological aspects of Western culture, especially in the early stages. Consequently, modern science caused no serious and lasting conflict with traditional culture and played the role of accelerating the movement of industrialization that had already begun before the so-called 'Western impact'.

EARLY MODERN JAPAN: A PROTO-NATION STATE AND THE DEVELOPMENT OF WESTERN LEARNING

Historians today call seventeenth- to nineteenth-century Japan 'early modern', not 'pre-modern'. This is because Japanese society had formulated some characteristics of modernity before the beginning of conscious Westernization after the Meiji Revolution: the bureaucratization of the governmental system, the spread of a market economy and the secularization of society.

The early modern Japanese state was a kind of proto-nation state. Although it did not have a clearly defined border nor close relationships between the state and the people, it was surely a prototype of a nation state. Its basic unit was the *daimyo* (major lords) state that was a kind of family-owned bureaucracy. *Samurai* (warrior rulers), who once had been local lords in the medieval era were concentrated in castle towns and became bureaucrats who were dependent on *daimyo* states. They were appointed to bureaucratic posts according to their hereditary status. Contrary to China or Korea, there was no civil examination system based on Confucianism. Therefore, the government demanded of *samurai* no specific learning or ideologies. The early modern Japanese state was a federation of some 260 daimyo states gathered around a divine emperor in Kyoto and a Tokugawa Shogunate in Yedo. In power, it was a decentralized system, while in social consciousness, it began to be thought of as a closely integrated nation during the eighteenth century. This proto-nationalism was based on the interpretation of history that asserted the eternal reign (not governance) of divine kingship. The discrepancy eased both the dissolution and the reintegration of Japanese state without disturbing the social order when Japan faced the 'Western impact' in the mid-nineteenth century.

The Tokugawa Shogunate ended the era of unceasing civil war that had lasted three centuries, expelled the Catholic Christians who had usurped Latin American states and the Philippines, and limited foreign relations as far as possible. Consequently, Japan enjoyed over 200 years of perfect peace, which saw the development of a nationwide market. The Shogunate ordered daimyos to reside in Yedo and their domains alternately. This institution promoted the development of the transportation system between their domains and three central cities, Yedo, Osaka, and Kyoto, and also the long-distance trade system. On the other hand, the Shogunate began to mint large a quantity of coins, copper, silver and gold. At first, a great deal was exported to China to import in return high-grade silk goods. However, the demand from the domestic market grew rapidly and mines reached the limit of production. The government faced a domestic price problem and decided to put a strict limitation on exports and to encourage import substitution of silk. The Japanese economy was sharply separated from the East Asian market, to which it had been closely connected during medieval times.

In this closed situation, the domestic economy continued to develop gradually. Merchants traded a variety of goods from rice to manufactured products: textile goods such as cotton and silk, processed foods such as sake (rice liquor), miso (soy-based seasoning) soy sauce and luxury goods such as tea and tobacco. Trade networks grew thicker as dealings between local regions increased in addition to those between the centre, regions and localities. The traders were city merchants, landowners in rural areas who managed not only agriculture but also commerce and manufactures and daimyo states. daimyo states issued local paper money, encouraged the 'domain production', 'the export' of their products to central cities and other domains, and import substitution in cooperation with merchants in their domain. Samurai were forbidden to engage in private commerce but they acquired the know-how of trade and currency management as bureaucrats of daimyos.

Early modern Japan experienced secularization. Medieval Japan was a society based on religion, in which Buddhist temples constituted the ruling powers along with court nobility of divine kingship and samurai. However, the Tokugawa Shogunate and daimyos who built the early modern state identified themselves as secular powers in contrast to temples who had contended for supreme power with them. They deprived temples of the right to govern people and changed them into subordinate institutions, especially to inspect the Christians. During the process, Buddhism retreated from the political arena, began to concentrate on the salvation of the people and found believers among the populace for the first time in Japanese history. People prayed to various deities worshipped by families or villages for health and prosperity, while they relied on Buddhism for individual salvation after death. They observed this complex of Shinto and Buddhism as traditional beliefs while theologically they believed in various sects of Buddhism or Confucian teachings. This pattern of ideological life is still maintained.

This situation allowed the coexistence of various worldviews or doctrines. Many old textbooks on Japanese history are wrong in their interpretation that early modern government adopted Confucianism as an official ideology. In fact, it was indifferent to any religious doctrine unless it adopted a hostile attitude or refused the rule and inspection by government, as did Catholics or a closed sect of Buddhism. Samurai did learn Confucianism. However, it was because they found a suitable teaching for officials in it and not because they wished to organize the whole of their lives by it nor desired to pass mandarin examinations as in China or Korea. Therefore, early modern Japan witnessed not only the blossoming of various schools of Confucianism along with the imported Chu Hsi school, but also the rise of 'national learning' (the study of Japanese classics) and 'Dutch learning' (the study of European scholarship through the medium of Dutch). It was common that the same person studied both. This open-mindedness and intellectual variety was based on the tradition of syncretism and backed by the goverment's indifference. That is why modern Western science caused no lasting conflict with existing traditions.

Modern Western thought came to Japan along with Christianity in the sixteenth century and was wiped out during the early seventeenth century. The Japanese turned their eyes again to Western thought in the mid-eighteenth century when they showed no concern for Christianity or political doctrines. They concentrated exclusively on pragmatic aspects of science and technologies such as medicine, natural history, astronomy, geography, military armaments and industrial technology. It was not solely due to the government's suppression. Although the ban was removed after the Meiji revolution, the number of Christians did not increase beyond I per cent of the population. It made a sharp contrast with Korea, where Christianity spread widely among its people in spite of the government's hostility.

'Dutch learning' taught the Japanese an entirely new view of the world. Sugita Genpaku, one of the founders of the school, recollected the experience as though it had been a religious conversion. One day he observed an autopsy with a Dutch book of anatomy in hand, when various organs appeared in his sight that, for him, had been meaningless lumps of flesh before. He and his comrades at once decided to translate the book, though they knew little Dutch. The discovery of Western modern science drastically changed the mode of perception and intellectual perspectives as it did everywhere in the world. Perspective drawing in pictorial arts promoted this transformation, too. However, this change of perception and the introduction of the 'modern' method of cognition did not experience severe conflict with existing worldviews. Dutch medical practice had spread widely in rural areas by the mid-nineteenth century, while traditional Chinese medicine maintained its influence until the 1880s. In Japan, modern science was easily accepted and assimilated as a variety of learning or another worldview, and then gained authority as people began to be impressed by its usefulness.

'Dutch learning' expanded its sphere to include the study of the Dutch language itself through the compilation of grammars and dictionaries. Also, it reorganized the Chinese style of botany, zoology and mineralogy and introduced geography and astronomy. After studying the mathematical explanation of time and space and the method of observation and experiment, Japanese took up the new practices. A group of astronomers of the Shogunate compiled an original calendar, and Ino Tadataka and his successors drew up the sets of maps that delineated the coastlines of the whole of Japan by actual survey, during the first half of the nineteenth century. When international tension with Russia developed in the northern region at the turn of the nineteenth century, the Japanese turned their attention to European military technology. It was already common knowledge among intellectuals that Western superiority in navigation and military technology had been demonstrated before the outbreak of the Opium War, and had caused a major change in the North East Asian international environment. A few years before the arrival of Commodore Matthew C. Perry, a United States special envoy to Japan, in 1853, the daimyo of Saga switched to cast iron artillery and the daimyo of Kagoshima began to build a Western-style ship with the approval of the Shogunate. The technology was acquired by the study of Dutch books and the models imported by way of Nagasaki.

After the opening Japan to Western states, the Tokugawa Shogunate launched a systematic programme of transplanting Western technology; opened an institute-cum-school in Yedo called The Institute for the Study of Barbarian Books, and started a technical school at Nagasaki to acquire Western navigation, shipbuilding and military technology. It invited Dutch officers as teachers for Japanese intellectuals gathered from all over the country. Subsequently the institution was renamed The Institute for the Study of Western Books and then The Institute for Research and Implementation of Civilization. Simultaneously, English, French and German languages, as well as chemistry and social sciences, were added. After the beginning of foreign trade, Japan imported many finished guns, ships and machines. However, the Japanese continued to try to transplant Western technologies and thus made energetic efforts to invite Western teachers and to send Japanese students to the West. Also, gun factories and dockyards founded by the Shogunate and daimyos brought skilled foremen and workers, who, later, were to divert their skill into other industries.

THE MEIJI REVOLUTION AND THE DEVELOPMENT OF SOCIAL INFRASTRUCTURE (MODERNIZING MODULES)

The Japanese perceived the demand of Western states to open up the country as a serious crisis. The study of Western geography and the minor confrontation in the North at the turn of the century, had taught them about the worldwide conquest movement of the West and its military superiority. They began to anticipate a future crisis, which was proved by the Opium War in China. Therefore, when the Western delegates demanded the opening of Japan backed by military threat, samurai intellectuals eagerly began to advocate a fundamental reform of Japan to overcome the crisis of colonization. They advocated 'Revere the Divine King, Expel Barbarians', whatever their daimyo states. The most critical problem lay in the discrepancy between the distribution of talent and fixed hereditary status, which they solved by adopting an indirect strategy rather than direct class struggle.

The reform movement at first sought the acquisition of Western technology for rebuilding armaments neglected during during 200 years of peace. Then came the issue of political reform to produce a 'national' effort. Some of the major daimyos who had been institutionally alienated from national decisions began to claim the right to participate. It led to an unprecedented political collapse in 1858; the Shogunate rejected the major daimyos' intervention in the choice of the Shogun's successor, and simultaneously decided on the final rejection of the seclusion policy in spite of the emperor's opposition. It punished major daimyos, their vassals, intellectuals and court nobility who openly opposed these decisions. Samurai intellectuals at once began resistance to this policy, advocating 'Revere the Divine King, Expel Barbarians', and assassinated the shogun's regent in 1860. Some major daimyos continued to demand political participation in association with the emperor's court and intellectuals. The Shogunate tried to appease them by retreating in foreign policy, which was severely rejected by the intervention of Western warships. It at last announced a major concession in power-sharing – to merge the Shogunate and the court under divine kingship, to establish a national assembly filled with some court nobility, major daimyos, their vassals and intellectuals drawn from the ranks of ordinary people and to assume the post of chairman-cum-prime minister as a 'primus inter pares'. However, the active vassals of major daimyos of Kagoshirna and Yamaguchi had a deep distrust of the Shogunate and recommended their masters to ally with each other to launch a *coup d'état* to establish the divine king's government without Tokugawa leadership. They succeeded in this coup and won a small-scale civil war in 1868.

The new Meiji government ('enlightened' government) was organized by talented personnel not only from Kagoshima and Yamaguchi but also from all over Japan, even from the ex-Tokugawa government. This policy was in alignment with the Meiji emperor's 'Charter Oath' which began with the article 'Various assemblies shall be opened and every decision should be made by public discussion'. The government set up an assembly to learn Western-style debate. In 1874, it announced preparations for the introduction of public elections and began the separation of the judicial system from the administrative sector. After the major rebellion in 1877, ex-samurai intellectuals along with leading commoners launched a strong movement demanding the opening of a 'National Diet'. Facing this pressure, the government decided to fulfil its promise and sent its leader Hirobumi Ito to Europe to make a thorough investigation into the actual workings of constitutional politics. In 1890, the National Diet was opened, where opposition parties held a majority. After eight years of resistance, the government accepted the appearance of a party cabinet and a custom evolved for an alternate organization of a bureaucrat cabinet and a party cabinet during the first quarter of the twentieth century. The 'Public Discussion' movement that had begun during the late Tokugawa era not only brought the restoration of the emperor but also found an ideal model in the West to realize constitutional politics, which was the first to succeed among non-Western countries.

The Meiji government abolished the authority of daimyo states all over Japan three and half years after the restoration coup and continued further drastic reforms which had the following characteristics: (1) It made efforts to import Western institutions as the Charter Oath announced: 'Knowledge and wisdom shall be sought among overseas countries to develop the glory of the Emperor and the country'; (2) It reorganized, not only the governmental system, but also the fundamental principles of social relations. The latter were manifested in the abolition of the hereditary status of samurai and forms of discrimination. This reform transformed the principles of social relations from the hereditary status system where rights as well as discrimination were embodied in each class, to the equality of rights and free competition of individuals. Other reforms were of the same kind: freedom of travel within Japan, freedom of occupation, freedom of marriage between aristocrats and commoners, and official authorization of property owning. These reforms of liberalization released energetic activities and promoted economic development just as the government intended. On the other hand, the people who had been protected by the early modern status system suffered much. For example, samurai were deprived of hereditary income in exchange for a small quantity of public bonds. Also, the blind lost their exclusive right to massage jobs, and exemption from taxation of their financial business. However, the Meiji Revolution experienced little resistance and thus violence was limited: the death toll from the 1850s to 1877 did not reach 30,000, while in France, whose population was about 80 per cent of Japan, over 1,000,000 people were killed in domestic conflicts during the great revolution.

These reforms became effective as various institutions were introduced from the West. In the political field these were the system of constitutional politics, civil service examinations, the board of audit, and a criminal law that operated on the principle of equality before the law regardless of status. In the economic sphere, came the integration and simplification of currency and a simplified taxation system. Civil law along with commercial law guaranteed the linkage between savings and investment. The metric system enabled the standardization of industrial goods, while the patent system protected technical innovation. As for transportation and communication, the latter preceded the former: a nationwide postal service and telegraph network was almost complete by 1890, promoted by the demand for price information in central cities and foreign trade ports. Coastal shipping, which had been a major means of freight transport, was made efficient by the introduction of steamships and price rivalry among shipping companies. As for land transportation, railways were regarded as more important than roads. The 1890s witnessed a boom in railway construction in Japan. After the nationwide railway network was completed, the government nationalized 90 per cent of them to make more effective connections.

At an early stage, the means for transplanting Western institutions and technologies was to invite Western engineers, skilled workers, management experts and teachers to set up model factories and schools. Japan also sent its nationals to the United States and European countries. The most famous case of the latter was the Iwakura Mission (1871–3), which consisted of five top leaders of the Meiji government, about thirty research officials, forty-two students (including five girls) and others. The mission later published numerous illustrated volumes of reports for the enlightenment of the nation. In addition, the government founded various schools to take the place of expatriate professionals to spread Western knowledge to ordinary people. Each college founded by the ministries of engineering, agriculture-cum-commerce, justice and education sent able graduates to Western colleges. They came back with doctoral degrees and took the place of foreign professors around 1886 when these colleges were integrated into the 'Imperial University'. The professors made great efforts to translate Western academic vocabularies into the sets of *kanji* (Chinese characters) to lecture in their own language. They also tried to reorganize the orthography of Japanese to use in elementary schools and above. This enabled Japan to link higher education to lower-level instruction and allow ordinary people to study the achievements of Western civilization themselves. Because the spread of scientific innovation was not so rapid as it is today, they were not forced to progress in academic scholarship. The Meiji government laid special stress on elementary education. The school attendance rate was close to 30 per cent on average around 1870, and steadily increased thereafter.

The private sector played an important role in transplanting and spreading Western civilization. At an early stage, most students went to private schools to be educated at the middle or higher level. They were managed by those intellectuals, both government officials and others, who had visited the West. They also published many books of instruction and some of them went on to run newspapers. The most famous personality was Yukichi Fukuzawa, who established Keio Gijuku (the present Keio University) and published *Encouragement of Learning,* in which he advocated 'Individuals' Independence, National Independence'. He meant that Japan's desire for maintaining independence would be realized only when people abandoned the traditional attitude of relying on the government and started enterprises themselves. The book became a bestseller along with Masanao Nakamura's translation of Samuel Smiles' *Self Help,* and stimulated Meiji youth's aspiration to and great concern for the West. Fukuzawa and other intellectuals also published various newspapers and magazines to introduce modern ideas on politics and society. Some of them were used to mobilize local elites with 'property and learning' in the Popular Rights Movement. Consequently the movement succeeded in pressing the government to make a final decision to open the National Diet and create strong ruling parties that would consistently maintain a working majority in the lower house.

FOREIGN TRADE AND ECONOMIC DEVELOPMENT

The economy of early modern Japan was an almost perfectly closed system. When it was forced to enter world trade, Japan faced a serious trial because the unequal treaties with low fixed customs exposed it to stiff competition. The silk industry, tea production and copper and coal mining were fortunate enough to grow rapidly by discovering strong export demands, while such industries as cotton growing contracted because of the price competition with

imported goods. However, industries such as spinning succeeded in getting over the difficulty by introducing innovations. Also, various kinds of new industry were established. The national trade balance was always in the red. Because the Meiji government was too nationalistic to accept foreign loans except for a few years, almost all capital for investment was supplied from within the country, along with the efforts to find foreign markets.

Economic development from the early Meiji era to World War I can be divided into three phases: development in agriculture and traditional industry up to the late 1880s, the rise of transplanted industries, led by spinning and shipbuilding, up to the Russo-Japanese war (1904–5) and the phase of import substitution under protectionist policies.

The growth of agriculture during the first stage was aided by the export of raw silk and the gradual rise in living standards. It was not the change in management nor the introduction of epoch-making technologies that promoted this development. The main factor was the spread of the know-how that innovative peasants had developed within traditional technology: improved seeds, the new way of selecting good seeds, and such. It was promoted by the development of transportation, communication and the efforts of the government, prefectures and regional associations. They tried to encourage the exchange of information and to sponsor industrial exhibitions. These factors also promoted the growth of traditional industries such as food processing and textile manufacture. During this phase, most of the technological innovations were of a capital-saving nature and consisted of improvements in indigenous skills and know-how: minor improvements in silk-reeling machinery (such as that from hand driven to leg driven), the imitation of Western-style boilers by traditional craft skills and the combination of the traditional loom with Key's flying shuttle, an old but borrowed technology from Europe.

Despite these efforts, the Meiji government's attempts during the 1870s to transplant new technology and industry failed. It established government-run factories and farms by importing Western machines and technologies. However, these could not survive competition from traditional or foreign industries. The government sold them off to private entrepreneurs during the 1880s, except for military arsenals and the naval dockyards. Although the factories experienced hardship from price competition and technological difficulties, some of them, such as mines and shipyards, were able to develop during the next phase by introducing the newest equipment and machinery. It is well known that copper mines grew to be a major export industry that was the second largest earner of foreign currency, but they also caused a serious pollution problem.

The second phase began with the spinning industry, to which the government gave no aid. The Osaka Spinning Mill Inc. opened in 1883, with large-scale spinning mills driven by steam engines, with capital gathered from various small investors. The company ran their mills day and night by adopting the alternate working shift system and, therefore, was successful in price competition with Indian cotton thread that had come to have major share in the Japanese market. This caused a boom in establishing large-scale spinning mills, and was followed by other innovations such as the introduction of ring spinning, the opening of East Asian markets and the technical device of blending various kinds of raw cotton. Thus, spinning became the first successful import substitution industry. Shipbuilding formed another leading transplanted industry. The naval dockyards made continuous efforts to upgrade their skill by refitting imported military and commercial ships as well as adopting various machines and equipment, while trying to build minor warships. They succeeded in building a steel warship in 1890. Their skill and know-how spun off to private shipbuilders and enabled one of them to launch a large steel trading vessel in 1899. After 1896, the industry began to be protected by subsidies and, during the next phase, achieved import substitution except for major battleships. In contrast to cotton spinning, shipbuilding contributed nothing in gaining foreign currency. However, like mining, it had workshops to repair various machines, locomotives, cars, steam engines, motors and generators, that would spin off as import substitution industries during the next stage.

To transplant modern technologies, Japanese, not only imported complete machinery or plant, but also made efforts to develop intermediate technology that combined Western technology with traditional skills and technologies. European machines were simplified in order to reduce their prices: for example, the brass frame of water-powered silk-reeling machinery was substituted by a wooden frame. As Japanese skills were upgraded and the demand for labour-saving technologies increased, complete imitation of Western machines began. Copying provided a free primary school for Japanese manufacturers in their infancy until 1899, when Japanese patent law began to cover and protect foreigners' inventions.

The third phase began with the Russo-Japanese War and ended at the beginning of World War I. Japan gained a victory over Russia and was finally released from the fear of colonization by the West that had long been an anxiety during the nineteenth century. At the same time, it annexed Korea and became a full-fledged colonial empire. During this period, Japan made a conscious effort to develop heavy industries for import substitution under the following conditions: (1) a considerable amount of money was borrowed in London that, at first, was to cover the expenditure of the

Russo-Japanese war in spite of Japan's tendency to avoid foreign dependence; (2) the unequal treaties with the West were revised to allow Japan to decide its own tariff rates. Import tariffs were raised from 2 per cent to 10 per cent average by 1906 and later the tariff rates for machinery and textile products, except cotton thread, reached over 20 per cent.

The typical industry that developed under this condition was iron and steel. In 1901, the Meiji government opened the government-run Yawata ironworks to meet domestic military and railway demands. The plant was imported from Germany and soon succeeded in steelmaking, but continued to fail in the production of pig iron from Chinese iron ore and domestic coal. The problem was solved in 1905 after replacing German engineers by Japanese, who had good experience in small-scale domestic ironworks. However, it was not until 1910 that the balance sheet went into the black. During the hard times for the company a 30 per cent tariff provided a precious advantage. The same condition supported import substitution in railway rolling stock, locomotives and motors. The success of these transplanted industries depended upon the intellectual foundation established in the early Meiji era. By 1910, the number of engineers who had graduated from domestic colleges amounted to over 5,000, and the attendance rate in primary school reached 98 per cent.

However, import substitution under protected foreign trade did not achieve the level of price or quality necessary for exports. Because Japan continued to import high technology goods, the newest technologies and plant, it suffered a trade deficit along with the burden of foreign debt. The outbreak of World War I was an unexpected piece of luck for Japan. Europeans temporarily withdrew from the East Asian market and, at the same time, gave Japanese companies large orders for ships, processed foods and other goods. Thus the Japanese economy could repay its overseas debts and gain capital and time to develop heavy industries (see Table 14).

Table 14 Statistics of major economic variables (in millions of Yen and millions).

	GNE at market prices	Agricultural production	Manufacturing production	Exports of goods and services and factor income received from abroad	Imports of goods and services and factor income paid abroad	Population	Gainful workers in agriculture and forestry	Non-agricultural
1875	–	1,259	743	–	–	34.8	15.8	5.7
1880	–	1,393	911	36.2	15.9	6	–	–
1885	3,890	1,464	878	101	124	37.9	15.9	6.5
1890	4,639	1,699	1,329	134	244	39.5	15.9	7.1
1895	5,897	1,731	1,829	232	364	41.2	15.9	7.8
1900	6,267	1,846	2,101	364	608	43.5	16.1	8.3
1905	6,868	1,760	2,182	427	1,177	46.3	16.1	8.9
1910	7,961	2,135	2,960	673	917	48.9	16.1	9.4
1915	8,735	2,579	4,029	1,141	1,151	52.4	15.3	11
1920	11,499	2,868	5,689	1,234	1,798	56	14.2	13.1
1925	12,521	2,885	7,043	1,549	2,524	59.7	13.7	14.4
1930	14,137	3,203	9,261	2,211	2,985	64.5	14.1	15.5
1935	18,382	2,957	15,094	4,259	3,951	69.3	13.9	17.3
1940	23,178	3,196	20,210	4,276	4,934	–	–	–

Note

Gross national expenditure and other variables are shown in 1934–6 prices. Population is for Japanese only (that is, excluding resident foreigners in general such as Koreans and Taiwanese).

Sources: Ohkawa, K. and Shinohara, M. (1979), Tables A3, A17, A21 and A53.

CULTURAL TRANSFORMATION AND IDENTITY

Japan's industrialization was followed by a great change in its culture. Although Westernization did not meet serious resistance from traditional culture, there still occurred friction and conflicts between them. The Japanese were forced to continue their efforts to redefine themselves, that is, to change while maintaining their identity. The ending of this problem came only when they began to be surrounded by Western-style industrial goods in daily life and, at the same time, became certain that Japan had at last succeeded in catching up with the West after the rapid economic development of the 1960s.

The effort to solve this problem was reflected in the formation of a habit of both white- and blue-collar workers who worked in modern sectors: they worked wearing Western-style clothes and shoes in their office, while they relaxed in their homes by taking off their shoes and wearing the traditional kimono. However, it was not easy for intellectuals to absorb and catch up with Western science and humanities, nor to create a new cultural identity.

Japanese were optimistic during the early stages of Westernization. Their maxim was 'Eastern Ethics, Western Arts' which meant assimilating Western science and technology while believing in the superiority of the amalgam of Confucian ethics and Japanese national character. It was this conviction that lay behind the detailed report of the Iwakura Mission, which asserted that Britain had reached the height of civilization only forty years previously and therefore Japan would easily be able to catch up with the West. However, those intellectuals who began a thorough study of Western science soon recognized the fundamental difference between traditional and Western learning, as well as the rapid development of the latter. For example, young Hantaro Nagaoka (1865–1950), a founding father of Japanese physics, who presented a Saturn-like model of the atom in Nature in 1904, in 1883 took one year's leave from Tokyo University, worried about whether Eastern people would ever be able to accomplish Western scientific research.

Despite this, there appeared some scholars who produced international-level achievements in scientific observation and experiment. The typical field was bacteriology. Shibasaburo Kitazato (1852–1931) went Germany to study in the laboratory of Robert Koch and in 1890 discovered the toxin of tetanus and later invented its serotherapy. He established an institute for research into infectious disease, where Kiyoshi Shiga (1870–1957) discovered the dysentery bacillus in 1897. On the other hand, it was more difficult for engineers to invent epoch-making industrial technologies. It was not until World War I that the Japanese Navy consisted mainly of warships and weapons made in Japan. Toyota Sakichi (1867–1930) put his automatic loom on the market in 1926. In the modern world, all countries are forced to learn from and imitate each other. Because this task was crucial for latecomers, the Japanese had to spend much time in acquiring Western knowledge. However, they steadily accumulated both intellectual and material capital and began to present original works to the outside world.

In the humanities, intellectuals faced the same difficulty as Soseki Natsume (1867–1916), who was the first Japanese professor of English literature at the Imperial University and soon resigned to become a novelist in 1911. Moreover, in this field, the problem was interconnected with the task of re-creating Japanese identity in a global context. Many Westerners maintained that Japan should adopt Christianity to reach the Western level of civilization. Although some Japanese intellectuals followed this recommendation, most of them subsequently renounced it. However, as the understanding of Western civilization was promoted, the feeling of inferiority to the West deepened and, in turn, created a desire to rebuild a respectable self-image. In modern Japan, national identity was created around the divine kingship. Since the early modern era, the Japanese began to regard the 'eternal' continuity of the Japanese dynasty as one of the few characteristics superior to foreign civilizations. The Meiji government tried to make full use of this conviction to integrate its people with the state. One of the steps was to create a national system of worship of the state by organizing various Shinto shrines around divine kingship. In principle, this state Shinto system was distinguished from religions that focused on people's salvation, while it utilized the religious custom common to them in order to develop people's loyalty to the emperor. The other system that contributed more was the state school system. The government issued to every school the 'Imperial Rescript on Education', that preached the eternal relationship between kingship and the people as well as the virtue of patriotism. It was the custom for the Chinese emperors to give moral instruction to their people, while modern Japanese kings added the demand for loyalty and utilized the effective institution of the school system to spread it among the populace.

However, the national identity of the Japanese was not stable. It was impossible for them to maintain their identity just by reorganizing the 'inherent' tradition when Japanese society was undergoing rapid change in industrialization and Westernization. One of the solutions was 'Asianism', which advocated that Japan should be the leader of 'Asia'. The Japanese before the nineteenth century had little concern with 'Asian' states and placed themselves on the periphery of the Chinese empire. However, when they faced the threat from the West, some Japanese utilized the Western dichotomy of 'Asia' and 'Europe' to prompt non-European states in the Eurasian continent to come together and start reforms under Japanese leadership. The slogan 'Asia is one' advocated by Tenshin Okakura (1862–1913) fitted well with Meiji intellectuals who had been brought up by Confucianism and Buddhism, in spite of the deep difference in social structure behind them.

Despite this, most Japanese could not accept this idea of confrontation with the West while promoting Westernization. Thus, they preferred to 'Act as a bridge between the East and the West' or to 'Merge the East and the West together', which meant that the Japanese, who were the first to succeed in assimilating Western civilization in the East, should go further to integrate Western and Eastern traditions to contribute to the integration of the world. Although it was not easy to practise, not a few intellectuals in modern Japan thought their task lay in this direction. The most famous personality was Kitaro Nishida (1870–1945). He devoted his life to philosophical thinking; starting from his own Zen Buddhist experience, he expressed his ideas in the style of contemporary Western philosophy and continued to develop new systems of philosophy. Because his works were highly integrated and not a mere mixture of West and East, many able young scholars were fascinated and gathered around him to form the 'Kyoto school'.

However, it was not until the 1980s that foreigners began to read his works, since he wrote only in Japanese.

After World War I, Japan experienced a period of disturbance just as European states did. Rapid development of industries concentrated many workers in metropolitan areas. Young intellectuals were attracted by Marxism after the Russian Revolution and tried to organize workers and peasants into various social movements. On the other hand, the emergence of Chinese nationalism began to threaten Japanese colonial interests in North East China. Perceiving this, in 1931 a group of young Japanese army officers made a bid to invade North East China and forced the government to follow up their actions and build a puppet state in Manchukuo. This territorial expansion was to solve both internal and external problems at the same time. They succeeded for a short time because the sustained effort of industrialization since the Meiji Revolution had yielded a considerable difference in power with neighbouring states. However, the invasion deepened Japan's isolation in East Asia, which had already grown with the development of the country. Therefore, Japan tried to reorganize its various ideologies to ease anxiety as well as to integrate its expanding empire. Japan also sought allies, and eventually made an alliance with Germany and Italy. This development was to victimize not only the life and the dignity of neighbouring nations but also the life and the liberty of the Japanese people.

BIBLIOGRAPHY

AKITA, G. 1967. *Foundation of Constitutional Politics in Modern Japan*. Harvard University Press, Cambridge MA.

AMANO, I. 1990. *Education and Examination in Modern Japan*. University of Tokyo Press, Tokyo.

BARTHOLOMEW, J. R. 1989. *The Formation of Science in Japan*. Yale University Press, New Haven and London.

BANNO, J. 1992. *The Establishment of Japanese Constitutional Politics*. Oxford University Press, Oxford.

DORE, R. P. 1965. *Education in Tokugawa Japan*. Routledge and Kegan Paul, London.

DUUS, P. (ed.) 1988. *The Twentieth Century* [*The Cambridge History of Japan*, Vol. 6]. Cambridge University Press, Cambridge and New York.

FUKUZAWA, Y. 1981. (originally 1899). *The Autobiography of Fukuzawa Yukichi: with Preface to the Collected Works of Fakuzawa*. Hokuseido Press, Tokyo.

GLUCK, C. 1986. *Japan's Modern Myths: Ideology in the Late Meiji Period*. Princeton University Press, Princeton.

HALL, J. W.; JANSEN, M. B. 1968. *Studies in the Institutional History of Early Modern Japan*. Princeton University Press, Princeton.

HAYASHI, T. 1990. *The Japanese Experience in Technology: From Transfer to Self-Reliance*. United Nations University, Tokyo.

JANSEN, M. B.; ROZMAN, G. (eds) 1986. *Japan in Transition: from Tokugawa to Meiji*. Princeton University Press, Princeton.

——. 1989. *The Nineteenth Century* [*The Cambridge History of Japan*, Vol. 6]. Cambridge University Press, Cambridge and New York.

JEREMY, D. J. (ed.) 1991. *International Technology Transfer: Europe, Japan and the USA: 1700–1914*. Edward Elgar, London.

KEENE, D. 1969. *The Japanese Discovery of Europe, 1720–1630*. Revised edn. Stanford University Press, Stanford.

KINMONTH, E. 1980. *Self-Made Man in Meiji Japan: From Samurai to Salary Man*. University of California Press, Berkeley and Los Angeles.

KURIYAMA, S. 1992. *Between Eye and Mind: Japanese Anatomy in the Eighteenth Century*. In: *Paths of Asian Medical Knowledge*. University of California Press, Berkeley.

LOCKWOOD, W. W. 1968. *The Economic Development of Japan: Growth and Structural Change*. Princeton University Press, Princeton.

MARUYAMA, M. 1989. (originally 1952). *Studies in the Intellectual History of Tokugawa Japan*. University of Tokyo Press, Tokyo.

MINAMI, R. 1986. *The Economic Development of Japan: A Quantitative Study*. Macmillan, London.

MORRIS-SUZUKI, T. 1994. *The Technological Transformation of Japan: From the Seventeenth Century to the Twenty-first Century*. Cambridge University Press, Cambridge.

NAJITA, T. 1967. *Hara Kei in the Politics of Compromise*. Harvard University Press, Cambridge MA.

NAKAMURA, T. 1983. *Economic Growth in Pre-war Japan*. Yale University Press, New Haven.

NAKANE, C.; OISHI, S. (eds) 1991. *Tokugawa Japan*. University of Tokyo Press, Tokyo.

NAKAYAMA, S. 1984. *Academic and Scientific Traditions in China, Japan and the West*. Tokyo University Press, Tokyo.

NISHIDA, K. 1993. *Last Writings: Nothingness and the Religious World View*. University of Hawaii Press, Honolulu.

NISHITANI, K. 1991. *Nishida Kitaro*. University of California Press, Berkeley.

OHKAWA, K.; OTSUKA, K. 1994. *Technology Diffusion, Productivity Employment, and Phase Shifts in Developing Economies*. University of Tokyo Press, Tokyo.

——. SHINOHARA, M. with LARRY MEISSNER. 1979. *Patterns of Japanese Economic Development: A Quantitative Appraisal*. Yale University Press, New Haven.

OKA, Y. 1986. *Five Political Leaders of Modern Japan*. University of Tokyo Press, Tokyo.

OKAKURA, T. 1970. (originally 1903). *The Ideals of the East: with Special Reference to the Art of Japan*. C. E. Tuttle, Tokyo.

OKITA, S. 1980. *The Developing Countries and Japan: Lessons in Growth*. Tokyo University Press, Tokyo.

OTSUKA, K.; RANIS, G.; SAXONHOUSE, G. 1988. *Comparative Technology Choice in Development: The Indian and Japanese Cotton Textile Industries*. Macmillan, London.

PASSIN, H. 1965. *Society and Education in Japan*. Columbia University Press, New York.

REISCHAUER, E. O.; KATO, I.; DORE, R. P.; HOMMA, N. (eds) 1993. *Japan: An Illustrated Encyclopedia*. Tokyo, Kodansha.

——. 1977. *The Japanese Cambridge*. Harvard University Press, Cambridge MA.

SATO, S. 1979. Difference in Modernization: Japan and Korea. In: Albert Craig (ed.) *Japan: A Comparative View*. Princeton University Press, Princeton.

SHIBUSAWA, E. 1994. *The Autobiography of Shibusawa Eiichi: from Peasant to Entrepreneur*. University of Tokyo Press, Tokyo.

SMITH, T. C. 1959. *The Agrarian Origins of Modern Japan*. Stanford University Press, Stanford.

——. 1988. *Native Sources of Japanese Industrialization, 1750–1920*. University of California Press, Berkeley and Los Angeles.

SUGIYAMA, S. 1988. *Japan's Industrialization in the World Economy, 1859–1899*. Athlone Press, London.

TITUS, D. A. 1974. *Palace and Politics in Pre-war Japan*. Columbia University, New York.

TSURUMI, E. P. 1990. *Factory Girls: Women in the Thread Mills of Japan*. Princeton University Press, Princeton.

UI, J. (ed.) 1992. *Industrial Pollution in Japan*. United Nations University, Tokyo.

YUI, T.; NAKAGAWA, K. (eds) 1989. *Japanese Management in Historical Perspective*. University of Tokyo Press, Tokyo.

13.3.3
KOREA

Seong-Rae Park

The year 1800 is a convenient dividing line between the period of exuberant and liberal *Sirhak* (practical learning) scholarship and the subsequent angry reaction to things Western – including Christianity and modern science and technology. The abrupt turning point came with the succession of a young boy as King Sunjo, at the death of King Chongjo in 1800. Throughout the eighteenth-century, Korean scholars had been free to absorb new ideas and express their opinions about the new learning and new religion from the West, then known to the Koreans as 'Western learning' (*Sohak*).

Already during the latter half of the Chosen period, Korean intellectuals were taking a more 'practical' direction, thus criticizing the traditional neo-Confucian scholarship. This 'practical' learning (Sirhak) tendency seemed to have been encouraged by the new absorption of Western knowledge in the latter half of the eighteenth century. In a memoir written towards the end of the century, Chong Yag-yong (1762–1836), a distinguished Sirhak scholar, wrote that it was 'fashionable' for his young contemporaries to read about the West.

With the advent of the new government of King Sunjo in 1800, however, such a tendency was suddenly halted. Instead, conservative reaction carried the day in Korea. The brunt of the clash was to be painfully felt by the rising number of Christians who were summarily oppressed in the early years of the new government. This intellectual Dark Age was to continue for more than half a century until the opening of the country in 1876.

Korea formally opened its door to the foreigners in 1876. For almost three centuries before official intercourse with the West, however, Koreans had been having some contacts, mostly indirectly through Korean visitors to China, with the modern West. This Western influence was particularly strong among the politically estranged scholars of the Sirhak tradition.

One of the early Sirhak scholars was Yi Ik (1682–1764), who had frankly confessed the superiority of Western science, especially astronomy. As far as astronomy and calendrical science are concerned, Confucius would have adopted Western methods over the traditional Chinese way, according to him. Yi Ik emphasized that all nations could claim themselves to be the centre of the world, because on a globe as was the earth, every point could be seen as the centre. He no longer saw China as the 'middle' kingdom. The spheroid nature of the earth had clearly served as the stimulus for Korean intellectuals towards cultural relativism, thus strongly denying the time-honoured Sino-centrism.

Then, Hong Tae-yong (1731–83), had announced, in the 1760s, the daily rotation of the earth. He can be considered as the first East Asian to clearly state this.

It was under such circumstances that Pak Chega (1750–1805), at the end of the eighteenth century, had proposed to invite Western missionaries to Korea, to learn more effectively from them about advanced Western science and technology. And Chong Yag-yong (1762–1836), remembers that one of his elder brothers successfully passed the government service examination with his answer based upon the Four Elements theory of the West in the question about the traditional Five Elements theory. In the early nineteenth century, Chong also wrote about his wish to initiate a new government bureau for the introduction of advanced science and technology from China, by sending Korean scholars there.

The reaction in 1800 was the conservative answer to the scientific and cultural awakening of Korean scholars in the Sirhak tradition. When the violent persecution of the Christians started at the beginning of the new political regime, it was a sure sign for the Sirhak scholars to keep away from Western learning. Even in this 'closed door' period and in the gloomy, suppressive atmosphere of the first half of the nineteenth century, we can find some remarkable records of Korean efforts to incorporate the new ideas and knowledge from the West.

They include the massive writings by Yi Kyugyong (fl. 1830s) and Ch'oe Han-gi (1803–77), among others. From their writings we can discern that some Japanese efforts at Westernization were being partially absorbed by the Koreans in the early nineteenth century, and many Chinese versions of Western learning were available to Ch'oe even in this period.

Though Korean efforts to introduce Western knowledge in the seventeenth century and thereafter were impressive, they were only partially successful in their ultimate modernization through the acquisition of Western science and technology. The reasons are very simple. Unlike the Japanese and the Chinese, who had constant direct contacts with visiting Westerners, Koreans did not have any chance of meeting Western men of knowledge to learn directly from them.

Thanks to the distancing of Korea from the main route of Western navigators in the sixteenth century, Western missionaries and merchants had seldom had come as far as Korea. Of course there were occasional visitors from the West, when unlucky seafarers chanced to be shipwrecked due to seasonal typhoons. So it was very natural that

Korean scholars had to learn about the West through their importation of Chinese books about the new knowledge, which they had opportunities to obtain during their annual embassy to China. Koreans' absorption of Western science in the traditional period proceeded slowly, through indirect contacts with the West, unlike the direct acquisition by the Chinese and the Japanese during the same period.

It was against this background that Koreans had to make do with piecemeal knowledge about Western science, whereas there were hundreds of books prepared in neighbouring countries. Ever since Matteo Ricci, a Jesuit father from Italy, had settled down for missionary work in Beijing in 1601, dozens of Western missionaries had come to China to teach Western science and technology to the Chinese. The first successful translation of a Western science book by Japanese scholars was The New Book of Anatomy (kaitai shinsho)translated by Sugita Gempaku and others from a Dutch text in 1774. In the mid-eighteenth century there were dozens of so-called Dutch Learning (ratgaku) scholars in Japan who had effective knowledge of Dutch, while there were no such scholars in China. Unlike in China and Japan there was no single Westerner in Korea during the whole period. Korean scholars had their first opportunity to learn a Western language only after the opening-up of their country in 1876.

Unlike Japan and China, where Western missionaries had arrived early in the mid-sixteenth century, Korea had seen her first Western missionaries in 1833, when three French Catholic missionaries had secretly entered the country. The second anti-Christian spree had erupted in 1839 when the three missionaries were arrested and beheaded, along with other Korean Christians. After the first sacrifice of about one hundred Korean believers in 1801, this was the second major persecution of Christians in Korean history. Despite such harsh suppressions, however, the number of Catholics in Korea seems to have greatly increased throughout the period – from about 4,000 in 1800, to about 100,000 in 1850.

Naturally the ever-increasing influence of foreign religion was taken by conservative Koreans as a significant threat to their national identity. Furthermore, the bad news had been pouring into the ears of ruling class Koreans about Western threats in China, particularly after the debacle of the Opium War of 1839–42. Awe-stuck, Korean leaders were further terrified by the increasing infiltration of armed ships or trading vessels from the West along the coastal areas of the peninsula. To take only two examples of such cases: three French naval vessels were dispatched in 1846 to Korea to protest about the execution of the three French missionaries in 1839. And a Prussian adventurer named Ernst Oppert had secretly landed and tried to excavate the tomb of Prince Regent Taewon-gun's father in 1866. Of course there were numerous cases when the Western powers sent their vessels and demanded trade relations with Korea.

It was under these circumstances, that the then dictator Taewon-gun had decided to shut the nation's door more firmly against Western infiltration of any kind. In fact Taewon-gun acquired political power very suddenly when the reigning king had died without a son or any other designated successor, and his twelve-year old son happened to succeed to the throne in 1863. Taewon-gun, as Prince Regent, seems to have been rather sympathetic to Christianity in his early days, for some women in his household, probably including his own wife, appear to have been Christians. But political considerations were paramount in the final analysis, and he decided within a few years to promote the continuous persecution of Christians. His closed-door policy seems to have been strengthened by the French invasion of Kanghwa Island in 1866, and the American invasion of Namyang in 1871.

Naturally the conservative minded yangban or ruling class fully supported this closed-door policy. When the power struggles among the royal families forced the old regent to abdicate in 1873, giving the helm to his son the king and his wife, the closed-door policy was doomed. And it was soon after this that the Japanese dispatched their 'black' ship to demand the opening of the 'hermit kingdom'. So the door to the outside world was opened wide in 1876.

The middle part of the nineteenth century was not very productive in the matter of learning the new things from the West. Choe Han-gi (1803–77) was one of the most distinguished scholars of the mid-nineteenth century. He was undoubtedly the most productive writer of the period, with more than twenty books from 1830 to 1867 surviving today under his name. The scope of his writings range over many topics, but most of them reflect his strong interest in Western science, particularly astronomy, physics, and medicine.

Choe is often seen as the most important transitional figure in Korean intellectual history, who served as the bridge between the Sirhak and the succeeding 'enlightenment' movement of the late nineteenth century. His works are largely based on the new knowledge about the West and modern Western science, which he had actively absorbed through those books then published in China.

He was the first Korean to write clearly about the Copernican heliocentric view of the world. In his works to 1836, Choe was still writing only about the diurnal rotation of the earth, without considering its revolution around the sun. But his view had changed with his next book in 1857, where he tries to explain four different views about the solar system, including the Copernican view, with drawings. Kepler was already mentioned in 1836, and noted repeatedly in 1857. The three laws of Kepler are well explained in his later work on astronomy in 1867.

According to Choe, sound is propagated in the form of waves, and colours and smells are also delivered to distant places by similar waves. Some basic optical knowledge was also explained in this book, such as the magnifying effects of concave glasses and the refraction of light passing through water. Telescope, thermometer and barometer are explained in his book, also for the first time in Korean history.

With another work in 1866, Choe Han-gi became the first Korean to introduce basic modern knowledge about electricity to Korea. Some of the fundamental ideas of modern chemistry after Lavoisier were first introduced to the Koreans through this book, including the new knowledge of fifty-six chemical elements. This 1866 book was basically a textbook of modern Western medicine. Not only did it mention the circulation of blood, it shows substantial knowledge of medical developments in the early nineteenth-century West.

Choe Han-gi's world of Western science was a result of direct importation from the Chinese version of it, with little creative addition of his own knowledge. The contents of his books about the new knowledge of the West were piecemeal and poor when we compare them with contemporary Japanese and Chinese accomplishments. Nevertheless, considering the state of Korea under the closed-door policy in this period, Choe's achievements can be considered as brilliant.

Korean society in the period under discussion was made up of four social classes: the ruling yangban class, the professional middle class (*chungin*), the commoners, and the lowest orders. In their intellectual orientation, we can safely say that the middle class was the only element of society familiar with matters of science and technology, while the ruling yangban would have had little to do with such things. Of course, there were exceptions, and some of the ruling class, particularly those estranged portions of it, were eager for social reforms and committed to things new. Choe Han-gi was one of the yangban, and his deep commitment to the Western science can be seen as a notable exception for a man from the ruling class.

In fact this problem of traditional social classes seem to have had an unfavourable effect on the speed of modernization in Korea. And it is a well known fact for Korean historians today that the leaders of the Enlightenment movement in the late nineteenth century were inspired by Yu Tae-ch'i and O Kyongsok, who were none other than the leaders of the chungin middle class, not the yangban. When some young yangban leaders of the 1880s, such as Kim Okkyun, Hong Yongsik and Pak Yonghyo, decided to support radical reforms for their country, it was under the influence of these chungin leaders. It shows that the role of the chungin leaders was only ideological, while their ideas and visions were to be put into practice by their young yangban followers.

The social classification typical of the latter half of the nineteenth century was sustained until it was officially decreed null and void in the 1894 reforms. The ruling yangban were never fully prepared to learn science or technology for themselves. The chungin and the lower classes were much more receptive than the yangban to foreign culture, particularly Western science and technology.

Korea's two adventures in the year 1881 demonstrate the position very well. After the opening of the 'hermit kingdom' in 1876, the Korean government decided to dispatch two missions respectively to China and Japan, ostensibly to study the Westernization processes in its two neighbours. To T'ientsin went a group of thirty-eight students recruited to learn modern science and technology for an extended period of time, whereas the other group of sixty-two sent to Japan went on an observation tour. Whereas the Japan mission was composed of high-ranking government officials and their assistants of reputable families, the China mission was barely organized thanks to a lack of enthusiasm on the part of the participants. In short, the Japan mission was composed of the yangban, and the China mission was made up of chungin and lower-class people. The crux of the matter is that the actual learning of science and technology was the job of the China mission, while the duty of the Japan mission was only a general observation of modernizing Japan.

Some of the young leaders on their return from Japan become enthusiastic protagonists for modernization in Korea. But those returned from China, now with a basic knowledge of modern science, found no positions in government in which to apply their newly gained knowledge. In fact during this period Koreans began to realize that they had more to learn from Japan. And only a few students were sent to Japan, secretly, to absorb some modern science and technology as well as military skills. For instance, a Korean student, Kim Yanghan, was ordered to remain in Japan after the 1881 mission to train himself as a shipbuilding technician at the Yokosuka shipyards. He received his

diploma after finishing his training. Later an advanced shipbuilding engineer – the first of his kind in Korea – was trained in Japan. His name was Sang Ho. He received his college degree in 1906 from the Tokyo University. He was the first Korean to graduate from a Japanese college in the field of science and technology.

Thus, Japanese influence upon the introduction of modern science in Korea had started. And according to a recent compilation, the total number of Korean science and engineering graduates from Japanese colleges up to 1945 was about 200–260 in pure sciences, and 140 in engineering. Throughout the colonial period Korean students did not develop their enthusiasm fully enough to pursue careers in science and engineering. Instead, as the Kyushu University authorities had rightly commented sometime in the 1930s, almost all the Korean students in Japan showed their main ambitions in law schools with the ultimate goal of passing the government service exam or the bar exam in colonial Korea. This was the short cut for colonial Korean students to rise to high positions in society. Just as the preceding yanghan students in the traditional period were eager to pass government service examinations, youngsters in modern colonial Korea were diligently pursuing the road to success by the way of official exams.

If the persistent later influence of Japan in the development of Korea was felt already from the 1881 Korean mission to Japan, the initial impact seemed to be only of passing impressions for the visitors, who had observed the Western-style postal system, science, education and military build-up of early Meiji Japan. To be sure all this was very impressive for the visiting Koreans, but they could not really understand the new institutions or the new science and technology these were based on, having only fleeting glances on a short visit. Unlike the high-class people visiting Japan, the humbler Koreans who were dispatched to China had received some basic training in modern science and technology. But when they finally returned to Korea, those from China had nothing to do in government to utilize what they had learnt abroad, mainly due to their lower social status.

More concrete movements towards 'enlightenment' were started in the early 1880s, in several important aspects. The first signs were to be found in the publication of the first modern newspaper and the initiation of modern schools in Korea. A typical development in the period concerning the interests and concerns of Korean men of knowledge can be deciphered from the early editions of the first modern newspaper in Korea, the *Hansong sunbo*. The newspaper began publication in every ten days from the first day of the tenth lunar month of 1883. After a brief intermission the newspaper started publication again under the slightly modified title, the *Hansong chubo,* simply to signify the change in its publication from every ten days to every week.

Throughout the whole period of its publication, which lasted more than a year, the *Hansong sunbo* had tried energetically to report on modern Western science and technology in addition to the usual news coverage of home and abroad. At first the newspaper was obviously determined to see such science and technology as the key to a modern society. Every issue was decorated with details of recent developments in these fields in the West. When the paper was restarted in 1885, it was not so interested in science and technology, but a similar ardour was now evident in its coverage of Western institutions and culture. This seems to demonstrate very well the main concerns of contemporary Korean intellectuals, which were shifting rapidly in the 1880s.

It was about this time that Koreans began to show strong interest in the introduction of Western-style education. The first significant school of its kind of these times was the so-called Royal English School, as the Western teachers there had freely named it. Unlike the English title for the school, however, it was not meant to be an English education institute in Seoul. Instead it was planned as an ordinary elementary and intermediate level school to start training selected Korean students, and eventually to upgrade the school to a college. This was the first major educational institution, and similar, much smaller, schools were established in many big cities around the country over the following decades.

For the first time in Korean history, school children began to be taught algebra, science, geography, history, etc., which was fundamentally different to reading and the writing on the Confucian classics and their related primers throughout the traditional period. This educational reform, however, could not be sustained for any meaningful period. Within a few years, the Royal English School had to face financial difficulties and suffered from lack of support from the court and the government.

In the meantime, a small group of young activists under the leadership of Kim Okkyun attempted a political coup in 1884. But the ill-prepared revolutionary adventure turned out to be a total failure, halting reform movements for the next decade. It took the Koreans exactly ten more years, until 1894, to attempt another reform effort. These have become known as the Kabo Reforms, which consisted of some 660 projects over the following two years. They included the declaration of Korea's independence from China, the separation of the court from the government, the introduction of a formal budget for the government, universal military conscription, and an ambitious national programme to send talented youngsters for foreign study.

Political developments were lamentably stagnant throughout the 'enlightenment' period in Korea. And this political stagnation was much aggravated by foreign interventions such as from Japan, China, Russia, and other Western countries. Furthermore, the financial difficulties of the government were to play a major part in all Korea's efforts to institutionalize measures of modernization. Newly 'enlightened' leaders of the country were not united in their tough struggles against the conservative wing to achieve their idea of a modern Korea. In the period of just one generation, from the opening of Korea in 1876 to the end of the nineteenth century, Korea experienced a violent mixture of all the modernization syndromes of Western countries, and those of the Chinese and Japanese in the recent past.

The result was socio-political unrest, on one hand, and the popularity of millenarianism among the general populace. On the other, it was against such a background that the Tonghak religious movement found a revitalizing momentum in 1892. Originally the Tonghak (Eastern Learning) was initiated by a religious leader, Cboe Che-u (1824–64), who was summarily executed when his followers were found to be a political threat to the government. But his followers were gearing their efforts to regain their leader's honour from the government. And in the middle of this, angry peasant followers had erupted in anger against one of the local magistrates, whose harsh dominance provided a convenient target. These peasant uprisings reached their climax in mid-1895, when the rebellious forces swept over the south-western part of the country.

The battle, however, soon went badly for the Tonghaks, who were less organized, and the insufficiently-trained peasants, while their opponents were the Korean government forces assisted by modern Japanese troops. The Japanese were firmly on Korean soil at the time, using it as a base in their struggle against China in the Sino-Japanese War. Only after the end of the Sino-Japanese War, and with the suppression of the Tonghak rebellion, did Korean leaders attempt modernization efforts with the so-called Kabo Reforms.

From the turn of the twentieth century Koreans tried to build a modern nation out of the 'hermit kingdom' through the 'Patriotic-Enlightenment' movement. Many societies were organized by the educated leaders of the nation, and they tried to encourage their fellow Koreans on the road to modernization. The outstanding phenomenon of their movement was the numerous educational institutes at all levels and the many newspapers and magazines. On the part of the Korean government, many institutional reforms were carried out in politics, education, industry, and such other fields. Railways and streetcars, electricity and the telegraph were all promoted.

One typical patriotic society towards the end of the nineteenth century was the Independence Club, led by Dr Philip Jaisohn (So Chaepil, 1864–1951), Korea's the first American college graduate, who had returned to Korea in December 1895, at the height of the government's reforms. Trained as a medical doctor in America, his main concern in his fatherland was social reform, which he tried to achieve through two channels – one through mass enlightening efforts through his new newspaper, the *Independence* (*Toknip sirmun*), and through the Independence Society. Today his newspaper is considered to be the first modern newspaper in Korean history. And the Independence Society was the first democratic institution for Korean leaders of the period.

In the final analysis, however, almost all Korean efforts at modernization in this period were ill-financed, badly planned and ineffectively executed, mostly not under the leadership of Koreans but of foreign specialists employed by the Koreans or self-employed. Slowly but steadily, foreign influences were coming more and more from Japanese specialists readily at hand.

The main encounter of world civilizations in Korea was to be fashioned under the colonial dominance of the Japanese. And in the true sense of the meeting of the civilizations of the period, Korea was most unfortunate because its people were were not easily allowed to travel abroad to learn directly from Western countries. Instead young Koreans in the colonial period flocked to their centre of civilization, which was Japan at the time, and seldom thought to send themselves to Western countries for real opportunity of meeting Western civilization head-on.

During the thirty-five years of Japanese colonial rule in Korea from 1910 to 1945, only about 200 Koreans had received formal degrees from Japanese colleges in the field of the physical sciences and engineering. It is a shocking contrast to the tens of thousands of Japanese who received the same degrees in the same period in Japan. The Japanese colonial authorities seldom allowed Korean students to go to Western countries, thus making the number of Korean college graduates from the West much smaller than those trained in Japan. Because of this, Korea's real encounter with the Western civilization had to be postponed until after the country's liberation in 1945, although the first approach occurred during the latter half of the nineteenth century.

BIBLIOGRAPHY

HAN, W. K. 1970. *The History of Korea*. Seoul.

HATADA, T. 1969. *A History of Korea*. ABC-Clio Press, Santa Barbara.

HENTHORN, W. E. 1971. *A History of Korea*. The Free Press, New York.

KIM, H. K. (ed.) 1980. *Studies on Korea: A Scholar's Guide*. University of Hawaii Press, Honolulu.

ECKERT, C. J.; LEE, K. B.; ROBINSON, M. 1990. *Korea: Old and New; A History*. Ilchogak, Seoul.

——. 1984 (trans. Wagner and Shultz). *A New History of Korea*. Ilchogak, Seoul.

PARK, S. R. 1992. 'The History of Science in Korea'. In: Korea Press Center, *Korea: Its Culture and Tradition*. (A slide programme for use in Korean studies: text and slides). Korea Press Center, Seoul.

——; HAK-SOO, K. 1996. 'Promoting the Culture of Science and Innovation'. In: Branscomb, Lewis M. and Young-Hwan Choi. *Korea at the Turning Point*. Praeger, Westport CT, pp. 109–23.

SOHN, P. K.; KIM, C.; HONG, Y. 1970. *The History of Korea*. UNESCO, Seoul.

I3.4
SOUTH EAST ASIA

Cheah Boon Kheng

South East Asia is and has always been a meeting ground of several cultural forces – from India, China, the Islamic world, and the West. However, the region did not only import ideas and institutions from outside, but also contributed its own indigenous elements. The historian Lea Williams (1976: 24) rightly observed,

> Clearly, without the requisite material and institutional infrastructure, aspects of higher cultures could not have been so successfully transplanted to the region. Nor would so much that is neither Indian nor Chinese have endured had indigenous cultures not possessed vitality and been both receptive to enrichment and able to maintain distinctiveness.

This is a point worth bearing in mind as we evaluate and summarize the history of this region during the nineteenth century, which saw the greatest impact of Western imperialism.

The autonomy of South East Asian history in the nineteenth century has, since the 1950s, attracted the attention of most historians of the region. As the colonial impact was at its greatest in this particular century, the question of how much autonomy to accord the respective countries must depend on each historian's perspective and the historical information available. For Indonesian history, the Dutch scholar J. C. Van Leur had argued that for the seventeenth and eighteenth centuries, the motive forces had come from within – in general, 'the Oriental lands continued to form active factors in the course of events as valid entities, militarily, economically and politically'. Although van Leur did not take his studies up to the nineteenth century, John Smail has argued that, even for this period, despite Indonesia coming under Dutch rule, the society of which the local elite was a part had retained its vitality. In other words, the vigorous indigenous society had remained itself, and the changes had really been mere adaptations made by that society to keep up with the times.

Most of the South East Asian states were pluralistic societies, comprising within their territories different ethnolinguistic communities, either highlanders or lowlanders. While some were assimilated, others had defied assimilation and attempted to reassert their independence. The variety of minority groups in the upland regions of South East Asia has been considerable. The separation between the upland minorities, and the lowland majorities, is a social division between the two groups. On the other hand, there has been a great majority of non-indigenous Asian minorities living in South East Asia until very recent times. The major immigrant groups involved came from China and India,

but their large-scale immigration into South East Asia is a relatively late development, dating from the nineteenth century in most cases. The cultural diversity of South East Asians was largely due to their tolerance and absorptive and adaptive facility. Old animist ways co-existed side-by-side with the Islamized, Indianized, Confucianized or the Christianized, producing a syncretic blend.

Undeniably, the Western impact caused a substantial parting of the ways for the four Theravada Buddhist states of Burma, Siam, Laos and Cambodia. In the past, despite their frequent conflicts with each other, the respective governmental and social institutions and cultural and religious values of these states had been quite similar; in some cases, they had influenced one another. 'Their sources of cultural development were very much the same, and the circumstances of their historical evolution were comparable', observed John Cady (1966: 78). 'The divine king pattern of princely authority and the Theravada Buddhist system of religion were standard everywhere'. But of the four, first, Burma fell by stages under the domination of British India, then Cambodia and Laos came under the French colonial authorities. Only Siam under the astute Chakri dynasty retained its independence right up to the decolonization of the region in the mid-1950s and 1960s.

Unlike India, China had played a minor cultural role in South East Asia. Vietnam, 'microcosm of China' (Williams, 1976: 24), was the only state which had been a Chinese colony for about a thousand years. Whereas the rest of South East Asia derived much of its culture from India, Vietnam alone derived its culture from China. The Vietnamese, however, resisted Chinese control throughout their occupation. But once the Vietnamese gained their independence in AD 939, they modelled their state after China, accepting and adapting only what they needed – the learning and the writing system of China, Confucianism and Mahayana Buddhism. The Le dynasty under its ruler Le Thanh To (1460–97) particularly organized the administrative system of his kingdom by copying Chinese methods to a great extent (Pearn, 1969: 54–6). However, from 1545 onwards, for at least 250 years, Vietnam was divided into two, and each half was ruled by separate dynasties. In 1632 the Nguyen dynasty in the south introduced the Chinese system of recruitment for government service by examinations (Buttinger, 1968: 51). In 1802 the whole of Vietnam was finally brought under the control of the Nguyen dynasty. In the eighteenth and nineteenth centuries, China's Ch'ing dynasty attempted to interfere in Vietnamese internal politics and to protect Vietnam from

French aggression. But like Cambodia and Laos, Vietnam too eventually fell under Catholic French colonial rule.

A large part of maritime South East Asia, which includes the Malay Peninsula, had been Indianized states, but had gradually come under Islamic influence. In the nineteenth century, however, different parts of the island world were invaded by Western powers. The Protestant Dutch took the Indonesian Islands and southern parts of Borneo, while the Malay Peninsula, Sarawak, Sabah, Brunei and Labuan (northern areas of Borneo) came under the Protestant British. Of the Indonesian islands occupied by the Dutch, only Bali had resisted Islamization and remained Hinduized. This identity it kept throughout Dutch rule. While the Philippine Islands were 'untouched' by idealization, their southern portion comprising Mindanao and the Sulu archipelago had come under Islamic influence, but the northern region fell to Catholic Spain.

The Western impact of the nineteenth century initiated far-reaching political, economic and demographic changes to both mainland and island South East Asia. By the end of the century, the whole region was brought within the economic sphere of the West, either as a part of a European empire or that of the United States of America. It saw the importation of large numbers of alien minorities in all the countries of the region. The Chinese were concentrated in Java, Burma, Philippines, Malaya and the Straits Settlements; the Indians in Burma and Malaya. The economic impetus also encouraged a greater movement of peoples within the region. Javanese and Sumatrans migrated to Malaya, while Vietnamese entered Cambodia.

The impetus for Western control of these countries had been the Industrial Revolution in the West, which necessitated the import of raw materials, which South East Asia could supply, and the opening up of new markets where commodities manufactured in the West could be sold. Besides a desire for an increase in trade, there was also fervent Christian missionary activity among both Europeans and Americans. But protection for these activities in the respective South East Asian countries could be ensured only by imposing Western control. The rapid growth of Europe in prosperity and power in the nineteenth century produced the Western belief that Western ways of life and government were the ideal and that all the world would benefit by adopting them.

With the exception of the kingdom of Siam, most of the South East Asian countries were not exactly impressed by the Western nations. Still steeped in their own traditions, and believing in the superiority of their own time-honoured cultures, they did not understand fully the forces of Western imperialism and capitalism, nor what the economic motivations, technological progress and military might of the Western nations were capable of achieving. Some of them persisted in dealing with these Western nations as if they were inferior vassal states. Cooperation with the West did not come easily. Most of the South East Asian states fluctuated between policies of isolationism and military expansionism. Thus, the Westernization of these states was only enforced or adopted due to colonial rule or the might of Western imperialism.

In presenting this Western impact as a clash of cultures, this chapter can do no more than discuss some of the major causes which led to Western colonial intervention in the respective countries of South East Asia.

On mainland South East Asia, Burma was the first to experience the loss of her independence. In three stages, through wars with the British in 1824–6, 1852 and 1885, her territory was absorbed into the British Empire in India. It was during the reign of King Bodawpaya (1782–1819), that repressive actions and extortionate taxes against the Mons, Karens and Arakenese of Lower Burma caused them to revolt repeatedly until eventually the Arakenese rebels, who fled to neighbouring British Bengal, precipitated a frontier quarrel between the Burmese and British authorities. The accession of Burma's ambitious King Bagydaw in 1819, upon the death of his father, stimulated Burmese aggressive actions against British Bengal. British victory and the resulting treaty of Yandabo of 1826, led to the ceding of both the Arakan and Tenasserim coastal regions and the payment of £1,000,000 sterling. Lower Burma was lost in the war with Britain of 1852, due to a minor incident involving the imposition of a levy on British ships at Rangoon. Upper Burma was annexed in 1885 following British fears that it would fall under French influence. Burma's last king Thibaw, was taken to India where he remained till his death thirty years later.

Siam, lying between the main area of British power in Lower Burma and that of French power in southern Indo-China, was able to retain her independence throughout the period of Western colonial expansion, largely by playing off Britain against France, although Upper Burma, largely as a result of Anglo-French colonial rivalry, lost her independence in 1885. Siam's wise ruler, King Mongkut (1851–68), played an important role in safeguarding the country's independence by having a more 'open' policy towards the West. His son, Chulalongkorn, continued and expanded his policies in diplomacy and modernization. Both these kings were aware of the relative military weakness of Siam in contrast to the Western powers, and made concessions of territory to both France and Britain only to safeguard Siam's sovereignty and independence. In 1904 and 1907, the French signed treaties with Siam under which Siam recognized French gains in Laos and Cambodia, while under the Anglo-Siamese Treaty of 1909, Siam transferred her suzerainty over the four northern Malay peninsular states of Kedah, Perlis, Kelantan and Terengganu to Britain. These arrangements had been achieved as a result of Anglo-French rapprochement, which permitted a redefinition of Siam's frontiers, because the British and French needed Siam as a buffer between their spheres of influence.

In Vietnam, the murders of several French missionaries in the 1840s provided France with an excuse for intervention in 1858. A joint Franco-Spanish force attacked and captured Danang. The force later went down to Cochin China, the rice bowl of the country, and seized the provincial capital of Saigon in 1859. Emperor Tu Duc agreed to a treaty in June 1862, by which he ceded to France three provinces, including Saigon, permitting freedom of worship in his kingdom and opening three ports to trade, as well as undertaking to pay a large indemnity. The Spaniards in the Philippines, who had supported the venture to end the persecution of Catholic Christians, were content with the promise of freedom of worship. In 1867, the French occupied the remaining half of Cochin China, and merged the two parts they had occupied as the colony of Cochin China.

In 1874, after further defeats at the hands of French forces, Emperor Tu Duc signed a treaty giving the French control over Vietnam's foreign relations, although Vietnam remained a vassal of China. Another treaty imposed on Vietnam in 1883 converted Annam and Tonkin into French protectorates. But in 1884, war broke out between China and France. Chinese forces sent to aid Vietnam took Tonkin, which they evacuated only in 1885, under a Sino-French treaty.

Cambodia had maintained a precarious independence by paying tribute to both Vietnam and Thailand, but the French attacks had weakened Vietnam and enabled the Thais to dominate the country. Thai domination, however, was ended by the French in 1863. King Norodom was persuaded to sign a treaty putting his kingdom under French protection, on the grounds that they had succeeded to Vietnamese rights in Cambodia. Thailand gave way by signing a Franco-Thai treaty in 1867, under which she renounced all claims to authority over Cambodia. The acquisition of Laos in 1886 was largely accomplished by French exploitation of local resentment against Thai over-lordship. In 1898 the French formed the Indo-Chinese Union comprising Cochin China, Annam, Tonkin, Cambodia and Laos.

During the nineteenth century the Dutch extended their control over the greater part of the Indonesian archipelago. Whereas at the beginning of the period they held Java, the Moluccas, and a few ports elsewhere, by the end of the century they had imposed their government over most of the archipelago, including the southern part of Borneo known as Kalimantan. The Portuguese still held a part of Timor, while parts of Borneo-Sarawak, Sabah and Brunei had come under British influence. During this period most Indonesian peasants lived quietly in their villages, unaffected by Dutch rule. The Dutch East India Company (VOC) supported and, on occasion, installed pliable princes. The considerable Chinese population in Batavia, however, came into conflict with the Dutch authorities. A Dutch massacre of Chinese mounted and assisted by Indonesians forced many in the city to flee into the interior regions, but before long the Chinese were invited to return in order to revive commerce.

In 1795, due to the Napoleonic Wars, the British seized several territories, such as the Riau Islands, and Melaka on the Malay Peninsula. In 1811 the British took Java, which they returned together with Melaka to the Dutch in 1816. The Dutch, however, lost no time to consolidate and extend their rule throughout Java and the archipelago. In 1825 in Jogjakarta a holy war broke out, led by an aristocrat, Diponegoro, who had been displaced in a dynastic dispute. He aroused the Islamic sentiments of the population to resist the Dutch. Known as the Java War, which lasted till 1829, it resulted in 15,000 Dutch troops being killed and no less than 200,000 deaths among the Javanese peasants. Aceh, which had for long resisted Dutch control, was attacked in 1873. The Aceh War lasted three decades. It ended only in 1903 when the sultan acknowledged Dutch sovereignty. By 1918 the whole Indonesian archipelago had been united under Dutch rule. Britain, which had emerged as a major political power through her East India Company in India, had encroached into Burma, supplanted the Dutch in the Indonesian islands, taken up new positions on the Straits of Malacca and was threatening French interests in Thailand. Mastery of the seas had led the British East India Company to extend its interests into the Malay island world. In 1786 the Company leased the island of Penang from the Sultan of Kedah as a naval base to check French naval expansion in the eastern seas. It was the Anglo-French rivalry stemming from the Napoleonic Wars in Europe which led the British to seize Dutch Melaka on the Malay Peninsula and Riau in

Indonesia in 1795, as Holland had come under French occupation. Sixteen years later, the British took Java.

Although Melaka and Java were reurned to the Dutch in 1816, British fears of Dutch hegemony in the area led Stamford Raffles of the East India Company to plant a factory in Singapore in 1819. The acquisition of this island broke up the Johor-Riau-Lingga-Singapore Empire into two parts, Riau-Lingga under the Dutch and Johor-Singapore under the British. This division was sealed by the Anglo-Dutch Treaty of 1824, under which the British handed over Bencoolen on the west coast of Sumatra to the Dutch and acquired Melaka. The Strait of Melaka marked the dividing line of British and Dutch spheres of influence. Once this treaty had been ratified, the British lost no time in negotiating a treaty with Siam to demarcate the northern parameters of its influence in the Malay Peninsula. The Anglo-Siamese Treaty of 1826 recognized Siamese rights over Kedah, Kelantan and Terengganu and British influence in Perak and Selangor. The British also began to consolidate their authority in the three territories of Penang, Singapore and Melaka by setting up a joint administration, known as the Straits Settlements, in 1826. Although British policy was not to intervene in the Malay states, this changed in 1874, when, owing to fears of German colonial intentions, the state of Perak was made a protectorate, followed by Selangor, Negri Sembilan and Pahang. In 1885 the state of Johor agreed to place her external relations under British control. In 1909, under the Anglo-Siamese treaty, Britain completed the process of acquisition of what became known as Malaya by bringing the four northern Malay peninsular states of Perlis, Kedah, Kelantan and Terengganu under her influence.

At the beginning of the nineteenth century the west and north-west of Borneo formed the dominions of the Sultan of Brunei, but by the end of the century these were detached as British colonial territories until the state of Brunei shrank to the size of the small enclave it is today. In 1841, a British adventurer, James Brooke, became the ruler of Sarawak, a province of Brunei, in return for his services in helping quell a local revolt. Brooke and his successors gradually seized more and more territories from the weak Brunei Sultanate, assisted in some cases by the British Royal Navy under the pretext of 'anti-piracy' operations. Efforts by James Brooke to transfer his state to Britain failed, as the latter did not see any potential gains to be accrued from it. In 1881, however, the British government approved the acquisition of Sabah (North Borneo) from both the sultans of Sulu and Brunei by granting the British North Borneo Company a royal charter, which gave the British government a right of supervision over the company's administration. Like the Brookes in Sarawak, the chartered company also attempted to seize lands from Brunei. Fearing that German, French and Italian colonial intentions might extend into Sarawak, Sabah and Brunei, the British government in 1888 made agreements with the governments of those territories by which each of these units became British protectorates. Each territory retained its independence in internal matters, but their external relations came under British control.

The nineteenth century saw the decline and final extinction of Spanish power in the Philippines. Pre-colonial Philippines lacked kings, so that the decentralized, fragmented social and political structures of the Filipinos were easily transformed by the Spaniards. They spread their rule and religion without opposition until they were halted by the Muslims of the southernmost islands. The Christianization of the lowland coastal peoples of Luzon and the Visayas was accomplished, once enough Spanish friars reached the islands. In 1762, when Spain was engaged in the Seven Years War in Europe, a British expedition occupied Manila, which was, however, given back in 1764. Soon after, the Spanish partially lifted restrictions on trade and commerce with other Asian countries besides China.

Filipino expectations of self-government were raised in 1812, when the Philippines were represented in the Spanish parliament, but this reform was short-lived. Revolts against Spain broke out. During the 1840s, Spanish control was imposed over the island of Mindanao. In the Sulu archipelago the sultan was forced in 1851 to agree to a treaty putting his dominions under the protection of Spain. But towards the end of the century a spirit of nationalism had arisen within the middle-class Filipino elite, who had received education in Spanish and who had acquired the ideas of nineteenth-century liberalism. Their demands were moderate, such as freedom of speech and of the press, and the replacement of Spanish clergy by Filipino priests. The most prominent of these reformers was Dr José Rizal (1861–96). Between 1882 and 1892, he was in Europe engaged in agitation for reform and writing novels and newspaper articles. His most well-known novel, *Noli Me Tangere,* exposed the inequities of life in colonial Philippines. In 1892 Andres Bonifacio, a self-employed worker, founded the Katipunan party to demand national independence and to organize a rebellion. When the rebellion was under way, Rizal was arrested and brought back to the Philippines, tried and executed on 30 December 1896. His death aroused Filipino fury, but before long Katipunan suffered from disunity, the rebellion collapsed and its leaders left for abroad in exile.

In 1898, war broke out between Spain and the United States of America, caused by the situation in Cuba. American forces attacked and captured Manila, and by the terms of the peace, Spain ceded the Philippines to the United States. During the American-Spanish war the United States had got in touch with the former Katipunan leader Aguinaldo and sent him back to the Philippines to raise a rebellion against Spain. He proclaimed independence, set up a government and convened a congress at Malolos to devise a constitution for a Philippine Republic. But his government refused to accept American occupation and became engaged in a war of resistance. The Muslim Moros in the southern Philippines also made their stand against the Americans. Aguilnado was eventually captured in March 1901, but the resistance continued until it was suppressed by an American army of 17,000 men.

To sum up, the result of the Western impact on South East Asia was thus a general disruption of the old ways of life and the rise of demands for self-government whereby the local people would be enabled to remedy the troubles which Western intervention had brought about.

BIBLIOGRAPHY

BUTTINGER, J. 1968. *Vietnam: A Political History.* Praeger, New York.

CADY, J. F. 1966. *Thailand, Burma, Laos and Cambodia.* Spectrum, New York.

HALL, D. G. E. 1964. *A History of South-East Asia.* Macmillan, London.

OSBORNE, M. 1991. *South East Asia: An Illustrated Introductory History.* Allen and Unwin, Sydney.

PEARN, B. R. 1969. *An Introduction to the History of South-East Asia.* Longmans, Kuala Lumpur.

SMAIL, J. R. W. 1961. 'On the Possibility of an Autonomous History of Modern South East Asia'. In: *Journal of South East Asian History,* Vol. 2, No. 2, July.

STEINBERG, D. J. (ed.) 1971. *In Search of South East Asia.* Praeger, New York.

VAN LEUR, J. C. 1955. *Indonesian Trade and Society.* The Hague and Bandung.

WILLIAMS, L. 1976. *South East Asia: A History.* Oxford University Press, New York.

I3.5
CONCLUSION

Wang Gung Wu

THE TRIUMPH OF SCIENTIFIC CULTURE

The West was triumphant in every field of science and culture at the turn of the twentieth century. But the leaders both in Asia and in Europe at the time were not yet certain how long that would last. In any case, their educated elites were small groups and their peoples knew little about one another. The Asian elites acknowledged that Western science was ahead. Their counterparts in Europe knew that well and showed supreme confidence in the inevitability of their progress, but many still outwardly showed respect for Asia's traditional cultures. If there was 'orientalism' among some European officials and merchants in parts of South and South East Asia, this did not prevent their scholars and artists from admiring the best features of the ancient civilizations they encountered. The question was whether much of their admiration was limited to artefacts, the remains of what had been great, that which belonged to museums and not that which remained strong in people's faiths.

On the other hand, if most officials and capitalists in the West had begun to despise the leaders of colonial Asia, who had failed to rejuvenate their cultures after the Western onslaught, there were a few who believed that local talent was plentiful. For these few, they recognized that the ingredients for progress were there. They could one day master the new knowledge, but not allow innovation and discovery to displace the values that remain true for their communities. The establishment of the first modern universities in India, at Calcutta, Bombay and Madras, provided a judicious mixture of the latest science with the secular political and legal culture of Britain. This was in sharp contrast to the earliest institutions of learning, which the Spanish introduced into the Philippines; the pious traditional universities focused on training for the Catholic faith and imperial service. In Hong Kong, local private initiative had led to the establishment in 1887 of a Chinese Medical College, whose first two graduates included the revolutionary leader Dr Sun Yat-Sen. When the University of Hong Kong was founded in 1911, this College became its faculty of medicine, but the university's faculty of engineering for training young Chinese was a breakthrough. This was a major step towards scientific development, but it was more a response to the demands of East Asia than an extension of the Indian initiative. For the rest, the early gestures in India were not repeated elsewhere, although there was, in the course of time, the urge on the part of governments to provide some forms of tutelage to their colonial subjects. A few technical and medical colleges were set up by colonial governments, but largely to meet immediate needs. This was in part because some locally trained clerks, school teachers and technicians were needed to run the colonies more smoothly. These governments had little interest in the scientific development of peoples whose cultural vitality was thought to have fallen too low to master new ideas. It was left to local leaders to emerge with a fresh dedication to modern education. Without this, traditional ways would have to be left to stagnate and decline at leisure.

In East Asia, the conditions for cultural maintenance were different. Without colonies, and even where they had an exceptional colony in Hong Kong, Western Europeans remained largely on the periphery. By the beginning of the twentieth century, Japan had transformed the whole of its education system and built its first modern universities. The most exceptional feature of the Japanese response to the Western challenge was that, from the start, they wanted the best they could learn, not only in the sciences but also in every field of study which they thought had helped to make the Western nations strong. The Japanese pursued quality with a fierceness not to be found elsewhere in Asia for half a century. And the clear link between that policy and the military and economic power they managed to acquire by 1895 and 1904, when they successively defeated China and Russia, was clear for all to see. In little more than a generation, they had gained an equality with the West, a feat to which modern science and cultural development had made vital contributions.

In the case of China, the early respect by Western officials for its ancient civilization had given way, by the end of the nineteenth century, to a growing scorn at the ineffectual efforts to revive classical values to strengthen themselves. Even Chinese attempts (half-hearted in comparison with the Japanese) to adopt Western paths to wealth and power did not inspire confidence. Only the energy of the new Chinese merchant classes still aroused a healthy respect. Among the few who were knowledgeable, there was some expectation that, once the Chinese realized the need for institutional changes to accompany the acquisition of modern science and technology, they would be hard to keep down. Thus the long century ended with serious doubts among the Chinese about the viability of traditional values, but a willingness to believe that they could be revived if the Chinese were prepared to follow the Japanese and open themselves to key parts of Western scientific culture.

On the eve of the First World War, there were no reasons for most of Asia to believe that their political and economic condition would improve and that science and enlightenment were about to reach them. But, for East Asia, a new factor emerged on the eastern horizon. The commercial and missionary activism of the Americans had finally begun to attract attention. Particularly in China, the Americans provided a relief from the heavy political and military interventions inflicted by the British and the French. With great enthusiasm, they built schools, colleges and hospitals and their efforts were widely welcomed. Their institutions dispensed scientific knowledge at a more popular level than any other Western outlet. There were reservations among those who thought that the United States had too young a culture to be worthy of serious study. Mandarin and samurai elites interested in scientific and cultural achievements still looked to the Old World of Western Europe. And indeed, several European nations made important contributions, notably the French with their schools and colleges in Shanghai. But American zeal for education and Christian causes was impressive, and it helped to bring the culture of modern science directly to a new generation of intellectuals. This was still but a beginning at the turn of the century. No one could have

foretold that the United States was poised to make a powerful difference to the scientific and cultural development of Asia in the decades to come.

The long century covered by this volume began with efforts to extend the idea of scientific progress to the whole world. For Western Europeans, this was successfully achieved. For most Asians who reflected on their fate during this period, it might seem that the progress was gained mainly at their expense, possibly at the cost of destroying the foundations of their ancient civilizations. The Japanese experience was the exception but it offered them a double-edged sword. Japan's deep inner ambivalence, whether to lead in liberating Asia from Western dominance or to be the masters of Asia themselves, was still unclear to most. But the lesson was there. It seemed possible for modern scientific culture to be turned to use in the preservation and even revitalization of national cultures. It was still but a glimpse of the future, but it had become conceivable that, even in Asia, progress was not a zero-sum game.

14

WESTERN ASIA AND MEDITERRANEAN AFRICA

INTRODUCTION

Abdul-Karim Rafeq, coordinator

The countries of the Middle East and North Africa underwent profound changes in the period between 1789 and 1914 as a result of accumulating internal stimuli and the impact of industrial and revolutionary Europe. The aim was to modernize the state apparatus, strengthen central authority and consequently consolidate the power of the ruling dynasty. The intellectual elite, influenced by European liberal thought, advocated wider reforms and participation in the political process. The result was the flourishing of national consciousness, which contributed to the consolidation of national identities and state formation.

The Ottoman Empire, which established its rule in the sixteenth century over most of the Arab lands in the Middle East and North Africa, was the first to introduce reforms, after the territorial losses it sustained in central Europe, the Balkans and the Crimea, and the threats it encountered on the Persian front. Semi-autonomous power groups in several Arab provinces also challenged Ottoman authority.

Ottoman reforms began with Sultan Selīm III (1789–1807) and were continued by the succeeding sultans, focusing principally on the establishment of a modern European-style army, and the creation of an infrastructure to serve its needs and the needs of a new administration. To achieve this, higher education with emphasis on technical skills to prepare cadres for the new army was introduced, student missions were sent to Europe, hospitals were built and a school of medicine was established.

While the Ottoman Empire was the dominating power in the Middle East and North Africa at the time, Persia, on the eastern flank of the Middle East, having border problems with the Ottoman Empire, was exposed to attacks and pressure by Afghans from the East, Russia from the North, and the British from the Gulf, and was also challenged by internal tribal revolts. Like the Ottomans, the Qajar rulers who governed Persia between 1796 and 1924 focused their reforms on the creation of a modern army to maintain their authority. Technical and medical education was introduced, hospitals were opened and student missions were sent to Europe. The long rule of Shāh Nāṣir al-Dīn Khān

(1848–96) enabled him to continue the work of his predecessors and implement the new reforms.

Copying the example of his superiors in Istanbul, Muhammad ʾAlī Pasha, the governor of Egypt (1805–49), established a modern army to consolidate his rule and create an empire for himself at the expense of the Ottomans. His conquests in Syria and Anatolia in the early 1830s were the most serious challenge that the Ottoman state had encountered until then. Muhammad ʾAlī opened Egypt and Syria, which he controlled between 1831 and 1840, to European influences. Using the rich resources of Egypt, Muhammad ʾAlī opened technical and medical schools, sent student missions to Europe and established a school of languages to serve the needs of the new army, which became the core of the modern state in Egypt. Muhammad ʾAlī, however, failed to industrialize Egypt as his advisors the Saint-Simonians would have wished him to do. He therefore concentrated his efforts on promoting agriculture, and withdrew from Syria in 1840 under European pressure. However, the reforms he introduced, whether in Egypt or Syria, with regard to Westernization and modernization, especially on the cultural and educational levels, helped in the emergence of an intellectual elite, who advocated more radical reforms. One of the major reforms was the education and social emancipation of women, pioneered by Rifāʾa Tahtāwī and Qāsim Amīn.

Reforms by the rulers of the Ottoman Empire, Persia and Egypt raised hopes for wider reforms advocated by the new elite. In the Ottoman Empire, the Young Ottomans, followed by the Young Turks, and the Committee of Union and Progress, succeeded in making the sultan declare a constitution in 1876, albeit for a short period. In 1909 the Committee of Union and Progress deposed the sultan and re-declared the constitution. By discarding the notion of Ottomanism, which appealed to many Arabs, and invoking instead an ethnic brand of Turkish nationalism, the new Turkish rulers alienated the Arabs, who by then constituted the majority of the population in a contracting Ottoman Empire. Arab nationalism thus stiffened its opposition to Turanian nationalism and contributed to the Arab revolt of 10 June 1916 against the Turks. The Ottoman Empire was doomed, and eventually dissolved in the wake of the First World War.

In Persia, a popular uprising, following the grant by the government of the tobacco concession to a British citizen in 1890, culminated in the constitutional revolution of 1905–7. The revolutions in both Turkey and Persia, in 1909 and 1905–7 respectively, and the flourishing of opposition parties in Egypt in 1907 against the British and the Khedive, were influenced by the defeat of Russia, a European country, by Japan, an Oriental country, in 1905.

One of the major internal threats to the Ottoman Empire came from the Arab nationalist movement in Greater Syria, which gained power in the nineteenth century. It began as an intellectual movement influenced by Western liberal thought. The establishment of a number of European educational institutions in Syria, including the Syrian Protestant College founded by the American Presbyterian missionaries in 1866 (later renamed the American University of Beirut) and the French Catholic St Joseph's university in 1873, as well as the introduction of printing presses by the American and French missionaries and also by Russia, promoted the flourishing of Arabic culture. Journals and newspapers, and literary and scientific societies were founded advocating the love of one's country (the *Watan*, the *patrie*). A number of Arab literati who studied in European schools in Syria or in Europe invoked in their writings the cultural contributions of the Arabs and urged modernization and secularism. Beirut, in fact, acted as a catalyst, bringing together, through education and commerce, the different ethnic and religious groups. Thus began what came to be known in modern Arab history as the *Nahda* (renaissance), also referred to as the age of the enlightenment (*'asr al-anwar* or *al-tanwir*).

Although heavily influenced by Western liberal thought, the Arabic renaissance of the nineteenth century had its roots in the preceding centuries.

The Wahhabi movement, which figured in the Arabian Peninsula in the eighteenth and nineteenth centuries, was essentially an Arab protest in the heartland of Islam against the extreme practices of the Sufi order, which were protected by the state at the time. The Arab renaissance of the nineteenth century thus had its antecedents, which were deeply rooted in the culture of the region.

When imperialist Europe occupied most of the Arab lands in the period between 1830 and 1920, initial Arab and Islamic reaction assumed the same pattern across the Arab lands. Opposition to European rule in both North Africa and the Middle East was first led by religious or traditional leaders based in the major mosques as well as in the countryside, such as the Al-Azhar Mosque-University, and the religious scholars who led opposition against Napoleon in 1798 and against the British occupation in 1882. Algeria, which was occupied by the French in 1830, found a staunch resistance in Prince Amir 'Abd al-Qādir al-Jaza'iri, a Sufi leader who led the struggle against the French between 1832 and 1838. Elsewhere, in Libya, Tunisia, etc., the same type of leadership led the opposition to British, French and Italian invasions.

In Syria, initial opposition to French rule, in the period between 1918 and 1927, was led by leaders in the rural regions whose power base was tribal and religious. In Iraq, too, the earliest opposition to British rule was begun by tribes in the countryside. The majority of the members of the revolutionary group which prepared for the 1905 revolt in Iran, was made up of religious scholars. Thus, whether in North Africa or the Middle East, responsibility for opposing European rule and influence fell first on the traditional forces who had tribal and religious solidarity and leadership. After the failure of these leaderships, responsibility shifted to the feudal-bourgeois political parties in the urban centres and later on to the doctrinal parties who achieved power by penetrating into the army and staging military coups. Economic, social and cultural changes accompanied the shifts from one social class and one political group to another.

14.1

THE MIDDLE EAST, TURKEY AND PERSIA

Abdul-Karim Rafeq

Prior to the impact of industrial Europe on the Middle East in the nineteenth century, mercantilist Europe coexisted with the traditional economy and society of the Middle East. Through commercial treaties, known as Capitulations, the European states obtained trade privileges and legal exemptions for their nationals trading in the lands of the Middle East. The traditional structures of Middle Eastern economies and societies, however, were to undergo profound changes in the nineteenth century as a result of their exposure to the devastating impact of capitalist Europe.

INDUSTRIAL EUROPE AND THE MIDDLE EAST IN THE NINETEENTH CENTURY: CHALLENGES AND RESPONSES

The twin revolutions in Europe, the Industrial Revolution and the French Revolution, posed major challenges to the traditional political, economic and social structures of the Middle East and, indeed, the world at large. The Middle Eastern rulers, copying the example of the enlightened monarchs of Europe in the eighteenth century, introduced reforms in a bid to strengthen their power and to placate the advocates of reform and modernization. In the process, powerful local forces emerged from below to challenge the authority of the enlightened despots.

Reform in the Ottoman Empire

The Ottoman Empire was the first country in the Middle East to introduce reforms from above under pressure from the West. Sultan Selīm III (1789–1807) established a new army (*nizām-i jedīd*) in the style of Europe. To staff his army, Selīm opened military schools, introduced conscription and sent student missions to Europe. He developed his contacts with Europe by establishing permanent Ottoman embassies there in 1792. The bicentenary commemorating the establishment of these embassies was celebrated in 1992.

Sultan Selīm antagonized by his reforms the old-style troops, the Janissaries, and the traditional religious scholars, the *'Ulamā'*, who accused him of imitating the European infidels. The conservative forces prevailed and Selīm was deposed in 1807 and killed a year later. The reforming Grand Vizier Mustafā Pasha Bayraqdār was likewise assassinated in 1808.

Sultan Mahmūd II (1808–39) succeeded in abolishing the Janissaries in 1826, accusing them of ineffectiveness during the Greek revolt of 1821. He also abolished the feudal troops and the *timār* (fief) system in 1831, but these continued unofficially until later on. A Directorate of *Waqfs* (religious endowments) was established to control the *'Ulamā'* who administered them. The *'Ulamā'* thus became salaried officials controlled by the state. To further weaken the hold of the *'Ulamā'* over the religious schools, Sultan Mahmūd created a Ministry of Education which became responsible for the administration of the schools. While the primary schools were still dominated by religious education, the state controlled the secondary schools, founded *rushdiyya* schools for adolescents and linked higher education to the needs of the newly-founded European-style army. Naval and military engineering schools were established and a school of military sciences was founded to serve as a military academy. A medical school to prepare doctors for the army was likewise established and instruction was given in both Turkish and French. The head-gear of the military, and later on of civilians, was changed from the traditional turban to the *fez*, a red felt beret of North African origin. Students were sent to Europe to specialize in the sciences that served the needs of the army. A school of foreign languages was established in Istanbul. The emphasis on spreading knowledge of foreign languages is evidenced in the issuing of a French version (*Moniteur Ottoman*) of the first newspaper to appear in the Turkish language. A postal service to facilitate communication and promote centralization was also established.

The strengthening of the authority of the central government was further consolidated when Sultan Mahmūd put an end to the rule of the powerful provincial governors, such as the Mamluk governors of Baghdād (1831), the Jalīlīs of Mosul (1834) and the Qaramānlīs of Libya (1835). But Sultan Mahmūd was unable to check the expansionism of his viceroy in Egypt Muhammad 'Alī Pasha.

The second phase of reforms, known as the *Tanzimāt* (regulations) was launched in 1839 by Sultan Abdülmejid (1839–61). These began by the promulgation of the *Hatt-i Serif Gülhane* (Noble Rescript of the Chamber of Roses) in 1839, which declared equality among all the subjects of the empire regardless of race or creed. The rescript was in fact timed to win the support of European powers, notably Britain against Muhammad 'Alī Pasha of Egypt, who had occupied Syria. The Ottoman navy defected at the time to Muhammad 'Alī. A second imperial rescript, *Hatt-i Hümayun*, promulgated in 1856, re-stated the equality of all subjects, advocated religious freedom and gave all people the right to attend schools and serve in the army. Again, the rescript was timed to placate France and Britain, the allies of

Turkey in the Crimean War (1854–6), against Russia. Sultan Abdülmejid's more durable reforms, however, were the establishment of secular courts, including commercial courts composed of Turkish and European members, and the declaration of the Land Code of 1858 which gave ownership rights to any one who had the usufruct of state land.

To encourage the advancement of science, the Ottoman government established in 1851 the Society of Knowledge (*Encümen-i Daniş*). The Society did not last long and it eventually broke up ten years later. Another society, the Ottoman Scientific Society (*Cemyet-i Ilmiyye-i Osmaniye*) was founded in 1861. This society issued the first journal of sciences (*Mecmua-i Funun*) in Turkey. The journal introduced to its readers the achievements of the sciences in Europe. In 1868 a museum was opened in Istanbul to promote Turkish art. About a decade later, a School of Fine Arts was established. An Imperial School of Music was already functioning.

A new provincial administration was established in 1864 under Sultan Abdülaziz (1861–76) with the aim of consolidating centralization and promoting government efficiency. In Lebanon, for example, the dual administration headed by a Druze and a Maronite, which was installed in 1842 at the instigation of Metternich, was replaced by one administration (*Mutassarifate*) in 1861 (later on reorganized in 1864) under a Christian Ottoman governor answerable to Istanbul. Jerusalem likewise was given autonomous status in 1873 and was attached directly to Istanbul. To demonstrate his interest in what was taking place in his empire and in Europe, Sultan Abdülaziz was the first Ottoman Sultan to pay a visit in 1863 to the Khedive of Egypt Ismā'īl since this country was conquered by the Ottomans in 1517. In the summer of 1867 he visited Paris and London, and upon his return to Istanbul he tried to introduce into Turkey, European technology, including railways.

Reforms from above reached their peak by the declaration of a constitution in 1876 by Sultan Abdülhamid II (1876–1909). The constitution was the work of the liberal Grand Vizier Midhat Pasha. Its aim was to share power with the Sultan and to conciliate local opposition. Midhat Pasha declared the constitution to be the beginning of 'a new era of enduring prosperity'. It was the culmination of a century of reforms. Elections were ordered for the first Ottoman parliament, which met in March 1877. Turkey was then required to satisfy Europe regarding a settlement in the Balkans on the eve of the Russo-Ottoman war of 1877–8. Faced with criticism in the parliament directed against his ministers, the Sultan in 1878 dissolved parliament, suspended the constitution and deposed Midhat Pasha, 'the father of the constitution'. To consolidate his power and combat the nationalists, Abdülhamid advocated Pan-Islamism and adopted the title of Caliph. The German Kaiser Wilhelm II, who twice visited Istanbul in 1889 and 1898, endorsed Abdülhamid's Islamic policy. Germany was then competing with other European states in extending its influence into Turkey in line with its declared policy of *drang nach Osten*. According to this policy, the Baghdād Railway was envisaged to link Berlin with Baghdād and eventually the Persian Gulf via Istanbul.

In addition to the introduction of railways into Turkey, there were attempts, especially under Sultan Abdülhamid, to build factories and promote industry. As in Egypt, however, the lack of work consciousness and of professional expertise among the Turkish workers hampered the proper functioning of these factories.

The reforms from above paid only lip service to equality among the subjects, but they nevertheless put Turkey on the true path of modernization. While the reforms strengthened central authority and the absolutism of the Sultan, they created, on the other hand, liberal opposition from below which challenged the autocratic rule of the Sultan.

The liberal opposition was championed by civilians and military alike who were exposed to European liberalism. The opposition included students, teachers, army officers and professionals who had studied in Europe or in European-style schools in Turkey. Turkish journalists, whether at home or in exile abroad, criticized the absolute rule of the Sultan. Foremost among them was Nāmiq Kemāl, who called for parliamentary rule and advocated Islamic modernism.

Clandestine societies emulating those of Europe began to appear, the most important of which was the Young Ottoman Society in 1865. It called for Islamic solidarity under an enlightened Sultan. Its slogans was Justice, Liberty and Homeland (but not equality). It supported the constitution of 1876. But it eventually foundered because of personal ambitions, class antagonisms and an inability to present a social and economic platform to attract the masses. It was replaced in 1889 by the Young Turk Society.

The Young Turks were mostly military and more coherent than the Young Ottomans because they were drawn from the middle and lower-middle classes. In 1896, they were accused of attempting a *coup d'état* and were persecuted and then banned. The revolutionary activity then moved to Salonica, the capital of Macedonia, where the Young Turks founded the Committee of Union and Progress (CUP). The Young Turks benefited from the fact that Macedonia was a centre of freemasonry, an international fraternity with elaborate occult views. Sephardic (Spanish) Jews in Macedonia also joined the CUP.

In 1908 the CUP forced Sultan Abdülhamid II to restore the constitution, and in 1909 deposed him. The CUP, represented by a triumvirate, ruled the Ottoman Empire from 1909 to 1918. It adopted extremist, ethnic, non-Islamic Pan-Turanian nationalism, which antagonized particularly the Arabs, who had become the majority in the Empire after the independence of the Balkans from Ottoman rule. The Arabs at first hailed the coming to power of the CUP, but later called for independence after the CUP resorted to a policy of Pan-Turanian Turkification.

The Ottoman Empire had collapsed by the end of the First World War in 1918. Mustafā Kemāl was later on to establish a Turkish Republic on the remains of the Ottoman Sultanate and Caliphate. He also de-Islamized the state and created a secular regime.

The foundation of modern Egypt

The European impact in the nineteenth century was more evident in Egypt and Syria than elsewhere in the Arab Middle East. This was due in Egypt to the policies of modernization, which were applied by Muhammad 'Alī Pasha and his dynasty. Because of this, Muhammad 'Alī Pasha is rightly described as the founder of modern Egypt. Allegedly of Albanian origin, Muhammad 'Alī, at the head of a military force, came to Egypt in the wake of its invasion by Napoleon Bonaparte in 1798 and the consequent British intervention in the country. He governed Egypt between 1804 and 1848.

Napoleon's expedition into Egypt opened the country to European influence. Despite the animosity and revolts by the Egyptians against the French, the Egyptian traditional elite, in the words of the contemporary chronicler 'Abd al-Rahmān al-Jabartī, found much to be admired in French administration and culture. Jabartī commented positively on the scientific knowledge of the French and their legal system. He particularly admired their love of learning and he spoke highly of the Institute they established in Egypt and of its library.

The French expedition paved the way for Muhammad 'Alī to emerge in Egypt and to consolidate his power against his rivals. By removing the long-time dominant Mamluk tax-farmers in Egypt, he made the peasants answerable in taxation to the state through loyal government officials. He controlled the *'Ulamā'* by depriving them from the administration of *waqfs* and making them salaried officials. He created a new class of landowners from among family members and from supportive notables by giving them large tracts of state land, known as *chiftlik*, first in usufruct, then in perpetuity and finally as freehold. The new class of landowners supported Muhammad 'Alī's dynasty, and later on the British occupation, to preserve their privileges.

Muhammad 'Alī succeeded in his agricultural reforms but not in his attempts at industrialization. He developed irrigation projects by building dams and canals for intensive cultivation. He monopolized agricultural products, especially cereals, rice and long-staple cotton, which he encouraged at great risk. He fixed the prices of these commodities and controlled the export trade. In England, home of the Industrial Revolution, the support agriculture gave to industry was a great success because increased agricultural production there fed the non-agricultural population, provided surplus workers for industry and accumulated capital for investment in industry. In Egypt, industrialization was a failure despite the reforms introduced into agriculture by Muhammad 'Alī. There was a lack of local skill and of industrial consciousness and culture. There was also a shortage of internal and external markets for industrial products. Intense European competition, on the other hand, especially after the 1838 Anglo-Ottoman trade treaty, which reduced customs duties on imported foreign manufactures, flooded the market with competitive European goods. Also, peasants in Egypt were forced to go into industry, thus damaging agriculture.

Muhammad 'Alī was influenced in his policy of industrialization by the French Saint-Simonians, who tried to apply in Egypt their experimentation with an ideal society governed by science. They considered Muhammad 'Alī an enlightened despot who suited their ideals. Being a semi-religious sect founded by French count Henri de Saint-Simon, the Saint-Simonians believed in the redemption of human society through the dignity of labour.

The major project in Egypt was the cutting of the Suez Canal. Saint-Simon died in 1825 before any concrete steps were taken towards this goal. In 1833, however, under his successor, Father Enfantin, the Saint-Simonians arrived in Egypt but were met with difficulties in achieving it. Muhammad 'Alī was more interested in the building of the Nile barrage to benefit agriculture than in cutting the canal, which would profit the European states. Composed of engineers and scientists, the Saint-Simonians in the meantime were appointed directors of the Polytechnic School, the Artillery School and the School of Medicine.

Industrialization laid the foundation of Egypt's dependence on loans and foreign debts to finance it. The vast foreign debts resulted in the control of Egypt's finances by the European states, and eventually led to Egypt's occupation by Britain in 1882. The leap taken Muhammad 'Alī from subsistence economy to mixed industrial economy had proved a failure.

The economic reforms which Muhammad 'Alī attempted to introduce into Egypt were not an end in themselves, but a means to build a strong army and consolidate the power of the dynasty internally and externally. The old factional army showed weakness in the Arabian war against the unitarian Wahhābīs in 1811 and 1818 and in the Sudan in 1820–4. Recruits for the new army, the *nizām-i jedīd*, came first from Sudan and then from among Egyptian peasants. The upper ranks of the army were drawn from the Turko-Circassian class, the lower ranks from among Egyptians, and the experts and advisors from former European military officers.

Technical schools, a school of languages, and hospitals were established to serve the interests of the army. The Department of Education itself was administered by the army until 1837. Indeed, the army laid the basis of the state in Egypt. Student missions to Europe were also linked to the army. Rifā'a Rāfi' Tahtāwī, who accompanied the student mission in 1826 to Paris in his capacity as leader in prayer (*imām*) for the Muslim students, was very much impressed by the occurrence of the 1830 revolution which he witnessed there. He was struck by the role of the press, the precedence accorded to women, the strength of the constitutional movement and the growth of Orientalism, which succeeded in deciphering the ancient hieroglyphic language of Egypt. Thus the ancient history of Egypt became known and pride in it among Egyptians brought about the creation of a consciousness of Pharaonism.

Muhammad 'Alī's foreign adventures took him to the Arabian Peninsula (1811–24), Greece (1822–8) and Syria (1831–40). He fought for the Sultan in the Arabian Peninsula, for his own interests in the Sudan, with the Sultan in Greece and against the Sultan in Syria. Of all these wars, the Syrian campaign was the most significant for both Egypt and Syria. It brought to an end Muhammad 'Alī's schemes for building an empire. It also opened Syria wide to European influence.

Between the death of Muhammad 'Alī in 1849 and the British occupation of Egypt in 1882, Egypt resorted to a market economy. A railway between Alexandria and Cairo, sponsored by the British and approved by the Ottoman Sultan in 1851, was built in 1852. The concession for the cutting of the Suez Canal was given in 1854 to Ferdinand de Lesseps, French Vice-Consul in Alexandria and also Aleppo, himself a Saint-Simonian. Work on the Canal started in 1859, the Sultan approved the concession in 1866, and the inauguration of the Canal, to enormous fanfare, took place on 17 November 1869. The Canal cost the equivalent of US$100 million, was 100 miles long, and more than halved the sea journey between Europe and the Far East.

Cotton growing was developed in Egypt during the American Civil War (1861–5). When this war ended, the price of cotton collapsed and peasant indebtedness increased. The right of land ownership was granted to the peasants in 1871 to offset their flight from the land because of heavy taxation and *corvée*.

A Consultative Council of Delegates, a quasi-parliamentary body, was established in 1866 to balance the landed aristocracy, control village headmen who made up the majority of its members, and satisfy European powers. Already the Bey of Tunis had granted his people a constitution in 1861 with a consultative council.

A school for girls was first established in 1873 after Tahtāwī had called for their education and after Qāsim Amīn had advocated the emancipation of women. An Egyptian Museum was founded and so was a National (Khedival) Library, an *Institut Egyptien*, a Geographical Society and an Opera House. A number of political papers were established, several of them by Syrian émigrés, including the important *Ahrām* newspaper owned and run by the Taqlā brothers in 1876.

The British occupation of Egypt in 1882 activated the Egyptian national movement. Three forces were on the scene. First, the Muhammad 'Alī dynasty ('Alawid dynasty), which initially introduced reforms from above, but later on sided with the British to maintain its rule. Second, the traditional leaderships, such as merchants, religious notables and big landowners, who supported the government. Third, the nationalists, who were of three types. First, the national movement representing the masses and headed by junior army officers of Egyptian stock, among whom figured Ahmad 'Arābī, which was defeated in 1882. Second, the Islamic movement, headed by Jamāl al-Dīn al-Afghānī (in Egypt from 1871 to 1879) and by Muhammad 'Abduh. It counted on Ottoman support and on Pan-Islamic solidarity against the West, but it failed to achieve results after both leaders were exiled. Third, the middle-class nationalist parties who dominated the scene. Chief among these parties were the Patriotic Party (*al-Hizb al-Watanī*) established by Mustafā Kāmil in 1907, which called for cooperation with the Ottomans and the French against the British, and the Party of the Nation (*Hizb al-Umma*) formed in 1907 by liberals, chief among whom was Ahmad Lutfī al-Sayyid, who advocated reform and moderation.

The flurry of political activity in 1907 was due to the retirement of Lord Cromer (Sir Evelyn Baring), British agent and Consul General since 1833; to Japan's victory over Russia in 1905, which found admirers in Egypt; to the 1906 revolution in Persia for constitutional reform; and to the Dinshawāy incident in 1906 when villagers were severely punished for the death of a British officer. The weakness of the nationalist parties, however, was due to the fact that they addressed themselves to a limited number of intellectuals through newspapers in a country where only about 8 per cent of the population was literate. The parties also lacked social and economic programmes to attract the masses. The Egyptian economic middle class, which was crucial for supporting the national movements, was mostly alien, Syrian, Greek and Italian, and was focused on accumulating wealth. Members of this class also controlled the majority of newspapers, which advocated reform and compromise. In 1914 Britain declared Egypt a protectorate, Ottoman sovereignty was abrogated, and the title of the ruler of Egypt was changed from Khedive to Sultan. A new phase in the history of Egypt was thus to begin on the eve of the First World War.

Looking back at Egypt's attempt to industrialize her economy in the nineteenth century, one finds that little progress was made in this area for the reasons described above. Except for a few sugar and textile factories, which did well at the time, industrialization had to wait until after the First World War. Handicrafts were weakened by the competition with European goods, but many of them kept functioning. Industrialization was not helped by the British occupation of Egypt, because the British considered industrialization here detrimental to their interests.

Intellectual life, on the other hand, flourished in Egypt in the nineteenth century. Its major theme was liberalism. This was advocated in the press, and in the work of Egyptian and Syrian writers settled in Egypt, as well as in the ideas propagated by liberal Islamists. Liberalism, however, soon changed into militant nationalism directed against British rule.

The European impact in Syria

Syria, like Egypt, was exposed to European influence in the nineteenth century. For centuries before, Aleppo was a major centre for transit and long-distance trade, especially in silk. It attracted a number of European merchants who settled and traded there. Damascus, on the other hand, was more involved in the trade that accompanied the pilgrims' caravans, which assembled there every year on their way to the Holy Cities in the Hijaz.

Under the rule of Muhammad 'Alī Pasha of Egypt, whose troops occupied Syria between 1831 and 1840, the country was wide open to European influence. Ibrāhīm Pasha, Muhammad 'Alī's son, who governed Syria at the time, allowed European consulates to be established in Damascus, where none had existed before.

Foreign missionaries of different denominations and countries, Catholic, Protestant and Anglican, freely established churches and schools in Syria. Many restrictions imposed by the Ottomans on local Christians were removed by Ibrāhīm Pasha, whose man of affairs, Yuhannā Bahrī, was a Christian. These included dress restrictions and the prevention of the restoration of churches and the building of new ones. Egyptian rule also recognized the long established, but until then outlawed Catholic communities and the new Protestant communities in Syria. The Ottomans had earlier recognized only the three traditional communities: the Greek Orthodox, the Gregorian (Old) Armenians and the Jews. When the Greek Catholic community split in 1725 from the Greek Orthodox church in Syria, it was not recognized by the Ottomans as a separate church. Persecuted by both the mother church and the Ottomans, many Greek Catholics of means emigrated to Egypt, where they constituted the core of the commercial and cultural bourgeois class.

Egyptian rule in Syria established security, promoted agriculture, warded off Bedouin attacks on settled areas and consequently extended the frontier of settlement into the desert borderlands. But Muhammad 'Alī's rule soon encountered severe local opposition. Muhammad 'Alī tried to apply in Syria the same regulations he had applied in Egypt. He alienated the Syrians by conscripting them into the army, disarming them and imposing on them forced labour (*corvée*) and heavy taxation, notably the *farda*, a capitation tax on male adults.

A series of revolts occurred against Egyptian rule in Syria between 1834 and 1838. Although Muhammad 'Alī Pasha in person managed to quell the revolts, increased European intervention in Syria eventually caused him to withdraw his troops from the country and be satisfied with the rule of Egypt. Europe, principally Britain, preferred the sick Ottoman Empire to a strong state governed by Muhammad 'Alī, which could threaten British interests in the region. Muhammad 'Alī's failure was largely due to a concerted European action against him. No war had occurred in Europe at the time to distract it from Muhammad 'Alī's expansionism. Indeed, ever since the Congress of Vienna in 1815 and up to 1914, Europe tried to avoid war by resorting to congresses and alliances to resolve differences in order to prevent internal revolutions.

The significance of Muhammad 'Alī's rule in Syria is tremendous. He impressed the Syrians with his achievements and offered them an alternative rule to that of the Ottoman Sultan. The Sultan was no longer viewed by Arabs and Muslims as invincible. Rural insurgency against Muhammad 'Alī continued under the Ottomans. But the emancipation of Christians by Muhammad 'Alī and his use of Maronite troops to suppress Muslim rebels heightened Muslim-Christian tension later on.

The opening of Syria's markets to European industrial goods eventually destabilized the country's traditional economy and society. The use of steam in transport increased the volume of European exports. Beirut seaport was expanded to receive the steamers carrying large quantities of goods. A Beirut-Damascus carriage road was built in 1863 and a railway in 1889 to facilitate the transfer of goods and passengers between the two cities. The influx of European goods into Syria was facilitated by the Anglo-Ottoman treaty of 1838, which lowered customs duties on imported goods. Competition among European exporters made the prices of their goods even cheaper, which enabled them to dominate the local markets.

The influx of European textiles into Syria was devastating to the locally produced textiles using traditional looms. European textiles were cheaper, better, appealing to local taste, and satisfied the peoples' curiosity for European fashions. Diminishing sales of local textiles were recorded at the time and traditional looms were put on sale more frequently than before. Workers' wages were decreased, layoffs and bankruptcies became common and manufacturers were unable to pay their taxes to the government. Clashes occurred within the guilds, between journeymen and masters over work and wages. The guild structure, which was the backbone of the traditional economy and society for centuries, thus began to fracture.

A new class of middlemen and entrepreneurs marketing European goods began to emerge. Christians, and also Jews, dominated this class, but not to the exclusion of Muslims. Much wealth was accumulated by the members of this class, as evidenced in the sumptuous buildings they built in both Damascus and Aleppo from the 1830s. Among the most beautiful extant buildings from that time is the house of Yūsuf 'Anbar, which was built in the late 1860s. It was made a public school in the last decade of the nineteenth century and continued to function as the major secondary school in Damascus well into the middle of the twentieth century. It was recently transformed by the government into a *Palais de Culture*. Several European royal figures who visited Damascus in the second half of the nineteenth century, such as Kaiser Wilhelm II of Germany in 1898, stayed in one or another of these sumptuous houses.

The disparity in wealth between the haves and the have-nots, who included impoverished craftsmen, resulted in socio-economic riots in Aleppo in 1850 and in Damascus in 1860. The riots were exploited by interested parties, including top Ottoman officials, who were later on executed at the orders of Turkey's foreign minister, Fuad Pasha, who headed the Commission of Inquiry. What added to communal tension were the Ottoman declaration of equality in the imperial rescripts of 1839 and 1856 and also the enforcement of conscription, which applied only to Muslims. It is significant that no similar riots had occurred in the preceding three centuries. The religious communities then were fully integrated in the traditional economic and social structures. Mercantilist Europe at the time was less aggressive than capitalist Europe in the nineteenth century. It coexisted and did business with local societies and economies.

In the rural regions of Syria, an export-oriented economy became dominant. Cash crops, such as cotton and silk, were linked to the world market. In a dependency economy, feudal lords tend to make much money at the expense of the peasants, who suffer from excessive indebtedness. A peasant revolt thus occurred in 1858-9 in the Maronite district of northern Mount Lebanon. It was led by Maronite blacksmith, Tāniyūs Shāhīn, against the Maronite feudal family of al-Khāzin. A peasant republic was set up by Shāhīn. In 1860, the revolt spread southwards to the Druze district of al-Shūf where the peasants, who were made up of Druzes and Maronites, rose in revolt against the feudal lords, who were Druzes. The revolt in al-Shūf was exploited religiously because of the mixed nature of the population. Civil war ensued. Napoleon III of France, anxious to divert attention from his internal problems, in need to curry favour with Catholic public opinion at home and abroad, and interested in promoting French economic interests overseas, sent troops to Lebanon. The crisis was defused by the arrival of Turkey's foreign minister Fuad Pasha at the head of a commission of inquiry, who took drastic measures and succeeded in controlling the chaotic situation.

Local reaction to the impact of industrial Europe and to the riots was quick to follow. Local manufacturers, in a bid to pool resources and measure up to European competition, resorted to partnerships, which cut across religious barriers. The old communal integration evidenced in the guilds was thus invoked and applied in new circumstances. Local manufacturers also tried to imitate European textiles. Jacquard looms (so-called after French inventor Joseph Marie Jacquard, 1752–1834) were imported into Syria. They wove figured patterns, which competed with European manufactures. A Damascene Muslim, Sayyid Darwīsh al-Rumānī, for example, pooled resources with a Christian, Khawāja Jurjī Māshta, and together they produced patterned cloth in imitation of a European fabric admired by local women. The women, however, preferred the European cloth as a mark of modernism. European fashions were widespread at the time. Some of the men began to wear trousers, for which they used the still current Italian word *pantalone*.

The emerging proto-bourgeoisie in Syria subscribed to the ideology of Arabism, which called for a common Arab denominator, based on a shared culture and common interests binding the religious communities together. Arab national consciousness in Syria in the nineteenth century passed through two phases: a literary phase and a political phase. The role of the printing press was vital in bringing to light the common heritage of the Arabs and their past contributions to humanity. The presses introduced into the country by the Protestant missions in 1834 and by the Jesuits in 1853 played important roles in disseminating Arab national consciousness.

A group of literati, including Butrus Bustānī, Nāsīf Yāzijī and Jurjī Zaydān, revealed in their works the importance of the Arab contribution to world culture. Secularists like Francis Marrāsh, Shiblī Shumayyil and Farah Antūn advocated in their writings the need for modernization and socialism. Literary and scientific societies flourished. Journalists called for patriotism. The newspaper *Nafīr Sūriyya* (Clarion of Syria), published in Beirut by Maronite Butrus Bustānī in 1860 at the height of the social riots, had as its motto a saying ascribed to the Prophet Muhammad which means 'love of country is an act of faith'.

Modern schools played a major role in disseminating knowledge among the people in Syria. To the traditional religious schools were added modern schools established by the Ottomans, by the local communities, and by foreign missionaries. Several secondary government schools were established by the Ottomans in the 1860s and the 1870s in the major cities of Syria. A military school was likewise established. The local Christian communities were also active in establishing schools, a few of which still survive as in the case of the Greek Orthodox and the Greek Catholic schools. Among the Catholic missionaries, the Lazarists, the Franciscans and the Jesuits were the most active in opening separate schools for boys and for girls. The Protestant schools were run mostly by American and English missionaries. The Jews also had their Alliance Israelite schools. The Arabic language was taught in all these schools alongside the liturgical languages of the local communities and also European languages.

Institutions of higher learning also played a major role in transferring modern knowledge to Arab societies. Prominent in this regard were the Syrian Protestant College, later the American University of Beirut, which was established in 1866, and the St Joseph University established by the Jesuits in Beirut in 1875. Beirut at the time served as a catalyst of cultures. A School of Medicine was established in Damascus in 1903 (chartered in 1901), which constituted, with the School of Law established in 1912, the core of the Syrian University, which was formally created in 1923.

A *Salafi* Muslim movement in Damascus, advocating a return to the purity of Islam under the early ancestors (the *salaf*), when Islam was entrusted to the Arabs in the heartland of Islam, the Arabian Peninsula, promoted the Arabs' pride in their role in Islam. Liberal Arab Muslims, like the Aleppine 'Abd al-Rahmān al-Kawākibī (1849–1903), highlighted in their writings the close connection between Arabism and Islam.

The political phase of Arabism begins with the Secret Society of Beirut, which exhorted the Arabs in 1875 to rebel against the Ottomans. Later on, when the Committee of Union and Progress in Istanbul deposed Sultan Abdülhamid II in 1909 and achieved power, moderate Arab parties began to emerge. These parties, reflecting their programmes in their names, called for reform, Arab-Ottoman brotherhood, decentralization and dual Arab-Turkish rule as in the Austro-Hungarian Empire.

The moderation of Arab political parties soon changed into extremism in reaction to the policy of Pan-Turanian nationalism and Turkification adopted by the Committee of Union and Progress. The Arabs called for complete independence. This was advocated by two secret societies: the Young Arab Society (*al-Jam'iyya al-'Arabiyya al-Fatāt*), which organized a conference in Paris in 1913 calling for independence, and the Covenant Society (*Jam'iyyat al-'Ahd*) whose members were drawn largely from among the

Arab officers in the Ottoman army. The majority of these officer-members were Syrians and Iraqis. Arab and Turkish nationalisms were then heading towards a head-on clash, which was to occur when twenty-one Arab nationalists, including Muslims and Christians, were hanged by the Young Turk government in Damascus and Beirut on 6 May 1916. A month later the Great Arab Revolt against the Turks was announced by Sharif Husayn of the Hijaz on 10 June 1916.

Ottoman centralization in Iraq

Unlike the eighteenth century, when the Ottoman authorities in Istanbul tolerated the presence of dynastic and semi-independent Mamluk rulers in Iraq and elsewhere, like the Jalīlīs in Mosul and the Georgian-recruited Mamluks, who dominated Baghdād and occasionally Basra from 1747, the nineteenth century witnessed the elimination of these provincial power groups. Sultan Mahmūd II, in his bid to strengthen the hand of the central government, terminated the rule of the Mamluks in Baghdād in 1831 and the Jalīlīs of Mosul in 1834. Later on, under the able Ottoman governor of Baghdād, Midhat Pasha (1869–72), administrative reforms were introduced, which further strengthened the authority of the central government *vis-à-vis* the nomadic and Kurdish tribes in Iraq.

A major attempt at reform, introduced by the Ottomans in Iraq in the nineteenth century under Midhat Pasha, in implementation of the Land Code of 1858, gave the right of ownership of state land through title deeds to those who had the right of usufruct in it. The aim was to help settle the tribesmen, and to encourage the peasants not to leave their land. The reform did not succeed because the tribesmen still regarded the land as belonging to the tribe as long as it could defend it. The peasants, on their part, mistrusted the title deeds and dreaded more government control, including the payment of more taxes. Thus the title deeds ended up in the hands of influential local chieftains.

Of all the European powers, Britain was the most involved in the affairs of Iraq to safeguard its commercial interests in India and its lines of communication with Europe through the Persian Gulf. Several attempts were made by the East India Company to introduce steam navigation on the Euphrates and the Tigris rivers in a bid to connect Basra with Baghdād and facilitate traffic to the Syrian coast. Several surveys of both rivers were made by British experts from the early 1830s, the most important of which was the survey conducted by Francis Chesney between 1831 and 1836. Captain Lynch of the East India Company was authorized by the Ottoman government to operate steamers in Iraq in the early 1840s. River navigation eventually prospered, linking Basra with Baghdād. The company established by the Lynch family continued well into the 1930s, despite the threat posed to it by the Baghdād railway, undertaken by Germany and Turkey, linking Berlin with Baghdād via Istanbul. The railway posed a major threat to British interests in Iraq prior to and during the First World War.

Iraq's economy in the nineteenth century was less developed than that of Egypt or Syria. It benefited, however, from the establishment of a telegraph line by the British in 1861 linking Baghdād with Istanbul and shortly afterwards with Persia and India. Exports from Basra consisted of large numbers of horses destined for India where they were in great demand by the British authorities. Horses ranked second after dates as exports. In return, Indian goods including textiles were exported to Iraq. The caravan trade linking Persia with Syria and beyond via Iraq was sensitive to security prevailing in the Syrian Desert and the adjoining Iraqi territories. The opening of the Suez Canal in 1869 damaged regional and international trade through Iraq.

As in Syria, local handicrafts in Iraq suffered from the importation of European industrial goods, notably textiles. Local traditional looms, which numbered about 12,000 in the first half of the nineteenth century, dwindled to a few hundred at the beginning of the twentieth. Also, as in Syria, European machines were imported into the country to produce goods in imitation of European goods. Imports of petroleum from America and Baku hurt the local artisanal production of petroleum. Of the many bidders, English, German and Turkish, who competed in the last decade of the nineteenth century for oil concessions in Iraq, the British d'Arcy group operating in Iran was the winner in 1909 under the name of the Anglo-Persian Oil Company.

Education in Iraq was dependent mostly on the religious schools, with advanced colleges in Najaf and Karbala for the *Shī'ī* clergy. During the last few decades of Ottoman rule, however, the Ottomans introduced secondary schools for adolescents with a budget and a director of education. Midhat Pasha is credited as being the first to open a government school in Baghdād in 1870. During his governorship an arts and crafts school was established in Baghdād. It attracted mostly the children of the poorer classes who were anxious to teach their children a craft. Western missionary schools run by both Catholics and Protestants were also established, as was the case in Syria. Among the Catholics, the most active in opening schools were the Carmelites and the Dominicans, mostly in northern Iraq in the region of Mosul, where Christian communities abounded. The first British Protestant school to operate in Baghdād opened in 1896. Native Christian communities had their schools as well. The Jews had their Alliance Israelite School established in Baghdād as early as 1864. A School of Law was established in Baghdād in 1908, four years before the establishment of the School of Law in Syria.

Although many Iraqi nationalists serving in the Ottoman army joined the Arab nationalist movement based in Syria and were active in bringing about the Great Arab Revolt of 1916, the nationalist movement in Iraq was active in opposing the Pan-Turanian policy of Turkification adopted by the Young Turks. Even the Head of the Sharīfs in Baghdād (the head of the descendants of the Prophet Muhammad through an accredited genealogy) Sayyid Abdul-Rahmān al-Kaylānī and his son were critical of the policies of the Young Turks. In Basra, Sayyid Tālib Pasha al-Naqīb (Head of the Sharīfs there) was among the principal supporters of Arabism. In Istanbul, the Iraqi deputies in the Ottoman parliament were the most vocal in calling for Arab independence. With the demise of the Ottoman Empire in 1918, the nationalist movement in Iraq, as happened in Syria, turned against the British occupation of the country.

Persia between despotism and foreign intervention

As in Turkey and Egypt, Persia under the Qājār dynasty (1794–1925) was determined to modernize its military forces to strengthen its authority internally and to measure up to threats from Russia. French and British military experts were involved in this endeavour. The peak of this effort was achieved in 1851 when a College of Arts (*Dār al-Funūn*) was established to provide officers for the new army and civil officials for the administration. But with all the efforts of the Shāh, the military forces in Persia did not reach the same level as those of the Ottoman Empire. Economic resources in Persia were not as abundant as those in the Ottoman Empire. Also, the Ottomans managed to centralize their power and eliminate several provincial power groups. The rulers of Persia, by comparison, were constantly challenged by their provincial governors, some of whom were members of the Qājār family, and by tribal groupings. One of the main weaknesses of the Persian army was the spreading of its contingents in the provinces and the lack of total control over them by the Shāh. The only powerful force was that of the royal guard. The civil administration remained mostly in its traditional form and did not undergo the same modernization as in the Ottoman Empire. The rule of the Shāh remained absolute, but he was challenged by the religious authority of the *Shī'ī 'Ulamā'*.

Although the Ottoman Empire and Persia were both Muslim states, they were kept apart by the fact that the Ottoman Empire was *Sunnī* while Persia was *Shī'ī*. Both states, however, dreaded Russian expansionism. Britain intervened militarily to prevent the collapse of the Ottoman Empire and Russia's exploitation of the situation when Muhammad 'Alī Pasha of Egypt invaded Syria and Anatolia in the 1830s. In Persia, the British were more forceful in repelling and balancing Russian encroachment to safeguard their rule in India and their lines of communication in the Persian Gulf. Thus both Russia and Britain competed for influence in Persia. France exerted some influence in the Persian court to secure its overseas commercial interests, but its overall role could not be compared with that of either Russia or Britain. Wars and treaties between Russia and Persia multiplied during the first half of the nineteenth century, leading to the weakening of the power of the Shāh and to disturbances in the provinces. British policy was to balance Russia's claims in Persia through diplomacy, intervention and occasionally war.

Despite attempts at reform and modernization from above in Persia, introduced mainly by Shāh Nāsir al-Dīn Khān (1848–96), the results were rather modest. The geography of Persia made land communications difficult. A subsistence economy predominated in most parts of the country. Silk production was no longer in great demand in Europe as it had been before the eighteenth century. The government's attempt to establish modern factories around the middle of the nineteenth century ended in failure. The majority of workers were still employed in handicrafts. However, the overall trade of Persia on the local, regional and international levels increased in the nineteenth century over previous levels. A powerful merchant class emerged which, alongside the religious class and the tribes, were to play an important role in the history of the country.

Education was not as developed in Persia as it had been in the Ottoman Empire or in Egypt and Syria. Foreign missionary activity was limited to the small Christian communities. These communities were not as important economically or culturally, as was the case in Syria and Egypt. Thus overall European cultural and social influence, unlike European economic influence, was much weaker in Persia than in the neighbouring countries.

The large tribal population in Persia constituted a major impediment to centralized reform. The monopoly which the *Shī'ī* clergy (the *mujtahids*) exercised over education limited the role of the government in spreading secular education. However, deviation from *Shī'ī* doctrine and teachings put the *mujtahids* and the government on the same side in combating dissent. This common stand occurred when Sayyid 'Alī Muhammad from Shirāz declared himself in 1844 to be the *Bāb* (Gate) of the *Mahdī*, the Hidden Twelfth Imām who disappeared in AD 873. It was through the *Bāb*, according to Bābism, that the Twelfth Imām was in touch with his followers during his seclusion. The *Bāb* declared himself the awaited *Mahdī* and that he was entrusted with the establishment of universal peace on earth. The Establishment considered Bābism a threat to public order; the *Bāb* was executed in 1850 and his followers were persecuted. The movement which survived later on in Bahā'ism was the product of intense social and spiritual tension in Persia at the time.

Popular dissatisfaction with government policies reached a high point in 1890 when the government granted the tobacco monopoly (*régie*) to a British company, the Imperial Tobacco Corporation of Persia. Russia opposed this act for obvious reasons. When the *'Ulamā'* and the merchants stepped up their opposition to the *régie*, the issue assumed national dimensions. The Shāh, unable to ignore the growing popular opposition to the *régie*, abolished the monopoly in late 1891. This was a triumph for Russia, and for those who eventually became more daring in their opposition to the government at the turn of the century.

Major upheavals were to occur in Persia in the early years of the twentieth century. Under the impact of Russia's defeat by Japan in 1905, and the occurrence of a revolution in Russia in the wake of this defeat, the liberals, supported by thousands of Tehran's *bazār* (market) merchants, by *'Ulamā'* and implicitly by Britain, prevailed on the Shāh to grant a constitution in 1906. Under Russian influence, the Shāh suspended the constitution in 1908. But the democratic opposition prevailed in the following year. The Shāh was deposed and his son, a minor, replaced him.

Russia and Britain took advantage of the troubled situation in Persia and in 1907 divided the country into zones of influence between them. Persian liberals then turned to the Germans for support. Germany at the time was trying to extend its influence in the Persian Gulf, through the Baghdād railway linking Berlin with Istanbul and Baghdād. In 1914, Persia, however, proclaimed its neutrality in the First World War.

Persian oil was already being contested by the big powers. In 1901 an oil concession for sixty years was granted to William Knox D'Arcy, a British financier supported by his government. The northern provinces under Russian influence were excluded from the concession. D'Arcy's concession was taken over by the Anglo-Persian Oil Company, which was created in 1909. In 1914, Britain controlled the Anglo-Persian Oil Company.

The nineteenth century began in the Middle East with Napoleon Bonaparte's failed expedition into Egypt and Syria, and the equally failed attempt by Britain to succeed Napoleon in Egypt. By 1914, however, all of Arab North Africa had fallen under French or British rule. Iraq, meanwhile, was being invaded by British troops from India. After the end of the First World War, Greater Syria also fell under French and British rule. A new phase of the Arab struggle against European rule was to begin. The socio-economic and cultural changes experienced by the Middle East in the nineteenth century were only the beginning of more drastic changes that were to engulf the whole region later on.

BIBLIOGRAPHY

AHMAD, F. 1969. *The Young Turks: The Committee of Union and Progress in Turkish Politics, 1908–1914*. Clarendon Press, Oxford.

ANTONIUS, G. 1955. *The Arab Awakening: The Story of the Arab Movement*. Hamish Hamilton, London.

BARBER, N. 1973. *The Sultans*. Simon and Schuster, New York.

CHEVALLIER, D. 1971. *La société du mont Liban à l'époque de la révolution industrielle en Europe*. Paul Geuthner, Paris.

FAWAZ, L. 1983. *Merchants and Migrants in Nineteenth-Century Beirut*. Harvard University Press, Cambridge MA.

——. 1994. *An Occasion for War: Civil Conflict in Lebanon and Damascus in 1860*. California University Press, California.

INALCIK, H.; QUATAERT, D. (eds) 1994. *An Economic and Social History of the Ottoman Empire, 1300–1914*. Cambridge University Press, Cambridge.

IRELAND, P. W. 1938. *Iraq: A Study in Political Development*. Macmillan, New York.

ISSAWI, C. 1966. *The Economic History of the Middle East, 1800–1914*. University of Chicago Press, Chicago.

——. 1988. *The Fertile Crescent, 1800–1914*. Oxford University Press, New York and London.

——. 1991. European Economic Penetration, 1872–1921. In: W.B. Fisher (ed.) *The Cambridge History of Iran, Vol. 7*. Cambridge University Press, Cambridge, pp. 590–607.

KEDDIE, N. 1980. *Iran: Religion, Politics and Society*. Frank Cass, London.

——. 1981. *Roots of Revolution: An Interpretive History of Modern Iran*. Yale University Press, New Haven.

KINROS, L. 1977. *The Ottoman Centuries: The Rise and Fall of the Turkish Empire*. Morrow Quill Paperbacks, New York.

LAMBTON, A. 1970. Persia: The Breakdown of Society. In: Holt, P. M., Lambton, A. and Lewis, B. (eds) *The Cambridge History of Islam, Vol. 2*. Cambridge University Press, Cambridge, pp. 430–67.

LEWIS, B. 1968. *The Emergence of Modern Turkey*. 2nd edn. Oxford University Press, New York and London.

LONGRIGG, S. H. 1925. *Four Centuries of Modern Iraq*. Oxford University Press, Oxford.

LORTET, LE DR. 1884. *La Syrie d'aujourd'hui: Voyages dans la Phenecie, le Liban et la Judée, 1875–1880*. Hachette, Paris.

MANTRAN, R. (ed.) 1989. *Histoire de l'empire Ottoman*. Fayard, Paris.

MASTERS, B. 1990. The 1850 Events in Aleppo: An Aftershock of Syria's Incorporation into the Capitalist World System. In: *International Journal of Middle East Studies*, Vol. 22, No.1, pp. 3–20.

NASHAT, G. 1982. *The Origins of Modern Reform in Iran, 1870–80*. Illinois University Press, Urbana and London.

OWEN, R. 1981. *The Middle East in the World Economy, 1800–1914*. Methuen, London and New York.

QASĀTLĪ, NU'MAN. 1879. *Al-Rawda al-Ghanna' fī Dimashq al-Fayhā'* (The Spacious Meadow of Fragrant Damascus). reprint. Dār al-Rā'id al-'Arabī (originally published Beirut, 1879), Beirut.

RAFEQ, A-K. 1983. The Impact of Europe on a Traditional Economy: The Case of Damascus, 1840–1870. In: Bacqué-Grammont, J. L. and Dumont, P. (eds) *Economie et société dans l'empire Ottoman (fin du XVIIIe-début du XXe Siècle)*. Editions du CNRS, Paris, pp. 419–32.

——. 1988. New Light on the 1860 Riots in Ottoman Damascus. In: *Die Welt des Islams*, Vol. 28, pp. 412–30.

———. 1989. The Arab States and their Ottoman Heritage. In: Majer, H. G. (ed.) *Die Staaten Sudosteuropas und die Osmanen.* Selbstverlag der Sudosteuropa-Gesellschaft, Munich, pp. 333–53.

———. 1991. Craft Organizations, Work Ethics, and the Strains of Change in Ottoman Syria. In: *Journal of the American Oriental Society*, Vol. 3, No. 3, pp. 495–511.

———. 1993. Craft Organizations and Religious Communities in Ottoman Syria (XVI–XIX Centuries). In: Accademia Nazionale Dei Lincei, *La Shi'a Nell'Impero Ottomano.* Fondazione Leone Caetani, Rome, pp. 25–56.

———. 1993. *al-'Arab wa'l-'Uthmāniyyūn* [Arabs and Ottomans] *1516–1916.* 2nd edn. Atlas, Damascus.

RAYMOND, A. 1985. *Grandes villes Arabes à l'époque Ottomane.* Sindbad, Paris.

AL-SAYYID MARSOT, A. L. 1984. *Egypt in the Reign of Muhammad Ali.* Cambridge University Press, Cambridge.

SCHONFIELD, H. J. 1969. *The Suez Canal in Peace and War, 1869–1969.* University of Miami Press, Florida.

WEIGALL, A. E. P. B. 1915. *A History of Events in Egypt from 1798–1914.* Charles Scribner's Sons, New York.

14.2

THE MAGHRIB

Azzedine Guellouz

By the eve of the First World War, all the countries of the Maghrib were to find themselves under colonial domination. After landing in Algiers in 1830, France had successively brought under its control the Regency of Tunis in 1881, the 'land of the Moors' (the future Mauritania) in 1909, and Morocco in 1912, while Italy had established a foothold in Tripolitania-Cyrenaica in 1913.

This community of political destiny has cultural ramifications.

To study them, we shall first identify the problems that, from the time of the French Revolution in 1789, had led up to and prompted the French landing in Algiers. We shall then analyse the cultural evolution of each of the countries in that decisive period of eighty-four years (1830–1914) during which one of them was already under colonial domination (Algeria) while the other four were seeking, unsuccessfully, to avert a similar fate (Tunisia, Tripolitania-Cyrenaica, Morocco and the 'land of the Moors'). These case studies will enable us to follow the line of thinking and action of each of the various Maghrib partners of European expansionism, as well as their shifts of position in keeping with their perception of the colonial threat.

1789–1830: A CONFRONTATION WAITING TO HAPPEN

Internal divisions: a common culture, different methods of administration

In contrast to the denominational diversity that characterized Egypt and the Middle East, the peoples of the five countries of the Maghrib were overwhelmingly Sunni Muslim. The only two minorities of any significance – although posing no serious cultural problems at the time – were, first, the Ibadi Kharijites in the M'zab to the south of the Regency of Algiers and in Djerba to the south of the Regency of Tunis and, second, Jews who were either native to the region or the descendants of immigrants from Spain or Leghorn (Italy). As for the rest, whether Africans of ancient Berber or black stock, or deriving from different waves of migrants of Arab, Andalusian (Morisco), Turkish or European origin, they had no cultural and educational frame of reference other than Arab Sunni Muslim. Such rivalries as might exist between the different countries, and between the different ethnic communities within them, remained within that cultural framework. From Cyrenaica to Futa Toro on the banks of the Senegal river, the school curriculum was broadly comparable. The Koranic school, *kûttab* in Tunisia, *msid* in Morocco, obviously taught the Koran. However, because these were the only schools, the rudiments of grammar, arithmetic and other subjects were dispensed sufficiently widely for the military administration of occupied Algeria to observe that, when the French arrived, the proportion of literate people in the Maghrib was greater than on the northern shore of the Mediterranean.

Beyond this primary level, there was no institutional distinction between secondary and higher education. The student (*tâlib*, seeker of knowledge) chose his teachers either from one of the region's two universities (the Zaytûna in Tunis and the Qarawiyyîn in Fez) or elsewhere (the Azhar in Cairo), or more modestly from a local madrasa (secondary school). He could decide to study for personal interest, or to obtain an *ijâza*, a 'licence' to teach in his turn, which could mean no more than reproducing the contents of a textbook in a provincial Zâwiyah or, for the elite, could lead to a university 'chair' or to a career in the judiciary or the administration.

Despite this common cultural framework, the administration of education was structured differently in each country as a result of distinctions of political status. While education was invariably provided, as in all Muslim countries, by foundations (*habous*), there were significant differences in the degree of institutional supervision exercised by the political authorities. These differences were crucial in determining the splits that developed between the principles and action of the reformists and reformers in the countries concerned.

The demarcation was not between countries dependent on the Ottoman Empire and those that escaped Ottoman domination. Crucial differences existed between the three Turkish regencies. As we have seen, the governors of the three regencies had very broad autonomy in matters concerning their territory. But in Tunis this freedom was exercised by dynasts who were primarily concerned with establishing themselves in their adopted country. Culturally there was no longer anything Turkish about them, and they championed a return to the refinement and magnificence of the Hafsid dynasty. Even instruction in the Hanafite cult, which was that of the Turkish population, was given in Arabic by Hanafites who were native to North Africa. In Algiers, on the other hand, the Turkish military oligarchy, which conferred political power by cooption on a *dey*, kept its original status, that of an occupying army, which, since it was Muslim, was certainly interested in Arab culture but was not Arabized.

The result was that, in the Regency of Tunis and in Morocco, the centralized educational structures, crowned by two universities, which had been inherited from the past, were under the control of the political authorities. In the Regency of Algiers, the segregation of the Turkish military oligarchy from the native population had the paradoxical effect of discouraging the expansion of Turkish culture and the Turkish language, since the military officers considered themselves to be 'in transit' in Algeria, and leaving the way open for a takeover of education by the religious brotherhoods, which thus obtained a strong hold over the native population. So, despite the obvious difference in their political status, the situation there was closer to that then prevailing in the 'land of the Moors' and in the Regency of Tripoli. The extreme weakness in Tripoli of the Qaramânlî dynasty, even though it was Arabized (like the Husaynides of Tunis), and the almost total absence of a central authority in the land of the Moors effectively allowed the brotherhoods a virtual monopoly when it came to political decision-making and, *a fortiori*, shaping the pattern of cultural life.

External threats: an underlying continuity

The way these differences were perceived played its part in determining the policies of the different European governments with regard to the countries of the region, and their evolution following the changes that occurred in Europe around 1789.

In France in particular, the French Admiralty, which was responsible for the French consulates in the ports of the Levant and on the Barbary Coast, had drawn the appropriate conclusions. Distancing itself from the pro-Ottoman policies inaugurated by the Capitulations, it had encouraged the efforts made by the Regency of Tunis to achieve political emancipation as well as its dynastic ambitions, and acquired substantial influence there, which it used to keep the neighbouring regencies at a respectful distance. As a natural consequence, it was British diplomacy that thereafter supported Ottoman suzerainty. This situation came to a head in 1794 when, strengthened by France's acquiescence, a Tunisian expedition to Tripoli reinstated the Qaramânlî dynasty, which had briefly been supplanted by a Turkish governor. To smooth over the 'misunderstanding', an ambassador, Yûsuf Sâhib Tâba', was sent to Istanbul. His mission was successfully accomplished thanks to the influence of the French Republic's ambassador to the Porte. The French hoped in this way to favour the accession of a 'new man' to the court of Tunis, at the expense of his predecessor who had been too closely linked to the *ancien régime*.

From then till 1815 the Tunis Regency had to distance itself from the policy followed since the 1770 war. It took greater account of renewed Ottoman solidarity and at the same time put an end to France's supremacy in trade with Tunisia, which was opened more widely to other partners. It reinforced the Turkish militia but did so by recourse to massive recruitment of Koulouglis born of mixed marriages. Four barracks of janissaries date from this era. Yûsuf Sâhib at-Tâba' also built a new complex in what was at the time an outlying quarter of Tunis (Halfâwin). This new economic centre (consisting mainly of covered souks to complement the souks in the Hafsid capital) boasted a Hanafite mosque whose architect al-Kawwâsh was visibly inspired by the work of the famous Istanbul architect Sinân. It dispensed higher education financed, like the religious activities, from the

income deriving from buildings organized as *habous*. Despite this understated approach, these were politically significant measures: this Tunisian government was taking advantage of the revolutionary interlude to arrest the spread of French influence, using renewed adherence to the Ottoman Empire, in a way that was adapted to the Tunisian situation, to do so.

The French officials of the new regime were aware of all this, as they were of the underlying continuity of French interests. As early as 1796, Talleyrand had invoked the name of Choiseul, one of the most forward-looking of the men of the *ancien régime* in favour of the resumption of colonial expansion when he mooted the idea of an expedition to Egypt at the Institut de France. The Egyptian campaign responded then not only to the views and wishes of the *philosophes*, but also to the calculations of an administration that spoke the language of the Enlightenment. The plans for French incursions into other countries in North Africa, of which the archives of the era are full, are based on the same thinking. One example, from the pen of the 'philosopher' diplomat (who was to become a key collaborator of Bonaparte, and succumb to the plague in Jaffa) Venture de Paradis, contains at one and the same time a eulogy of the Tunisian dynasty, a plan for the conquest of Egypt and another for the invasion of Algiers that designated, in 1788, the site chosen for the invasion of July 1830 – Sîdi Fraj (Sidi Ferruch).

Illustrating this continuity, the French *chargé d'affaires* in Tunis in 1814 announced the fall of the minister and the princes who had been the architects of this attempted 'restoration' of Ottoman influence as a restoration coinciding with that of the Bourbons. In fact, support for autonomist movements is written into the ideology of the Enlightenment. Texts concerning the regencies evince the same sympathy for the Moriscos, descendants of the victims of the Inquisition, as for those who fled France following the revocation of the Edict of Nantes. Like them, they are credited with the merits attributed to a 'productive' bourgeoisie. It was presumed that they would welcome those who expelled their Turkish tyrants as liberators. This style of presentation found favour with the administration, and it remained unchanged by revolutions and, even more so, changes of regime. The reactionary government of Charles X distributed a manual to the officers and men of the expeditionary force in which they were called upon to treat the Moors as allies. Concomitantly, French agents at Tunis secured a benign neutrality from the 'restored' princes. There was thus no solution of continuity between the ideology that underlay the lightning war against Tunis under the reign of Louis XV in 1770, the Egyptian expedition entrusted by the Directoire to General Bonaparte in 1798 and the invasion of Algiers decided on by Charles X in 1830. This sheds an interesting light on the first decades of the French presence in Algeria, especially with regard to the educational and cultural policies of the occupiers, and also on the reactions of the different peoples, from Cyrenaica to the land of the Moors, and on the revision of these initial reactions that subsequently became necessary.

ALGERIA FROM 1830 TO 1914

Liberal ideology, the rationale of war, colonization through settlement

Historians of colonial Algeria up to 1914 identify stages that are more or less in step with those of political life in France.

There was a period when the conquest was organized (the reign of Louis-Philippe and the Second Republic), an 'imperialist' period which corresponded to the Second Empire, when the status of Arab kingdom at the heart of a French Empire was devised for Algeria, and finally a period of 'assimilation', which corresponded to the Third Republic and made Algeria an extension of mainland France, without making all its inhabitants French citizens.

Cultural realities are not so easily compartmentalized.

A dream inherited from the Enlightenment: an Arabian *nahdha* under French tutelage

Not only the government but also the regime that had decided on the invasion fell a few days after its feat of arms. The new regime maintained the French presence in Algeria: the bureaucracy that handled this dossier continued to be dominated by the 'ideologues' who remained faithful to the economic and liberal dogma of Enlightenment philosophy.

Among the occupiers were many intellectuals who had contributed to the great reformist scheme of Muhammad 'Alî, that of the *Nahdha* or renaissance. Some of them had even been members of Bonaparte's expedition. They thought that, after ridding Algeria of its Turkish occupiers, France could help the Arabs to discover European civilization and rediscover their own. This was the cultural side of the policy of General Clauzel, a believer in 'restricted occupation', who concluded an agreement with the *bey* of Tunis in 1831 conferring the *beyliks* of Constantine and Oran on his brother and son. They would have founded there French regencies in keeping with the aspirations of both their own dynasty and the Paris chancellery. Opposition by the *bey* of Constantine (up to 1837) prevented this project from even getting off the ground, while at Oran the presence of Tunisian detachments came to nothing. Besides, the French had recently discovered an ally who was better suited to, and better armed for, such a mission – Abdelkader.

The idea of coexisting with Abdelkader stemmed from the same thinking: encourage the *Nahdha* with an Arab kingdom under the aegis of France. In 1832 'Abd al-Qâdir ibn Muhyî ad-Dîn had just been elected leader of the *Qâdiríya* brotherhood, following a victory over the militia of the former Turkish *bey* of the West.

His father, Sheikh Muhyî ad-Dîn al-Hasanî, who had had his problems with the Turkish governors, had in 1827 taken his son, aged about twenty, on a 'pilgrimage'. During that journey, which lasted two years, he had met up in Egypt and in the Middle East with theoreticians and protagonists of Muhammad 'Ali's *Nahdha*.

But the brotherhood leader organized a veritable nation-state in that part of the territory he controlled for approximately thirteen years (his *smala* was captured in 1843 and he gave himself up on 23 December 1847). This is borne out, first, by his allegiance to the Sultan of Morocco, which lasted until the defeat at Isly (1844) and made the 'suzerain' reconsider his support for his voluntary vassal (which must be seen as an alliance against a common threat), and, second, by the fact that, once the militia who so wished had been 'repatriated', the Kûruglis (who were formerly excluded from the militia) were recruited *en masse* to the Emir's army.

Education ranked at the forefront of Abdelkader's concerns. From education he sought not only training for the officers of his army, but also for the modern economy that he was putting in place (agriculture, arsenals, foundries, cloth manufacture). The peoples whom he administered were therefore obliged to maintain primary schools while the administration and centralized taxation system with which he equipped his 'government in the field' (Tagdempt, his 'capital', was a camp) bore the cost of the secondary schools, *madrasas*, which had been founded in each constituency. Contrary to what had happened under the *deys*, this former brotherhood leader did not give the brotherhoods responsibility for education. So conscious were they of their differences from him that Darqâwa and Tîjaniyya led an active campaign of denigration, denouncing in particular his treaties with the French (the so-called Desmichels Treaty in 1834 and the treaty of Tafna in 1837) and his recourse to European, often French, experts, which he raised to the level of a doctrine, as indicated by this letter to the Queen of France:

> Instead of sending your noble sons to fight against me, better that they come to help me to lay the foundations of a prosperity in my country in which you will have cooperated: you will have realized the double goal of soothing your conscience and making your subjects and mine happy.

So his French partners were not all totally naive or Machiavellian in counting on him as an ally. It was conditions on the ground that transformed coexistence into a fight to the death between him and his partner, Bugeaud, in one of the most critical events in the cultural history of Algeria and perhaps that of humanity.

Bugeaud heeded the lesson, since he figures among the supporters of the restoration of Arab culture on Algerian soil, precisely because he realized it had been a mistake to want to apply the principles of the French Revolution to the Algerian people. On 2 February 1844 (after the *smala* had been captured) he criticized the creation (in Paris!) of a secondary school for Algerian Muslims, saying: 'It was in the schools of Rome that Jugurtha was educated'. He supported the maintenance of an Algerian aristocracy, which his experience as a warrior had taught him to respect. 'It was in response to the call of this aristocracy of blood and of the spirit that led all Algeria to rise up and wage a battle against France that will be the wonder of posterity'.

The mainspring of Bugeaud's plan was the creation of a secondary school inspired by the *madrasas* that Abdelkader had founded. Furthermore he suggested that the Emir's own secretary, al-Hâjj Muhammad al-Kharrûbî, direct the institution.

Alongside these proposals someone has written, 'Never'. Two symmetrical motivations converged in the administration's (anonymous) rejection: the concern (progressive, and perhaps more precisely Saint-Simonian) to save youth from religious obscurantism when modernization was what was wanted, and (relating to security) the concern to cut short the emergence of a civilized nation in Algeria, an undesirable emulator of the 'Algerian' nation as conceived by the colonists, who were set on making Algeria a colony settled by Europeans.

The liberal de Tocqueville was one who held this belief. He wrote:

> It is . . . very much to be feared that Abdelkader is in the process of founding among the Arabs who surround us a power that is more centralized, more agile, more experienced and better

organized than any of those that have succeeded each other down the centuries in this part of the world.[1]

This genius of political 'anticipation', as revealed in the same period (1835–40) in *De la démocratie en Amérique*, envisioned the evolution of Algeria, like Prévost Paradol, in terms of the past and present of the United States. There a democracy had flourished on the basis of the extermination of the native population. Once it had been decided that the indigenous Algerians were to be dispossessed for the benefit of a nation of settlers, it was logical and necessary to exclude them from political decision-making.

Unproductive attempts to found a Franco-Arab school (1847–70)

The polemic between those who wished to extinguish Arab culture and those who supported it thus overlaid, without wholly overlapping, the debate between supporters of direct administration and supporters of imperialist domination via the intermediary of a native elite. It therefore preluded the framing of a 'policy for the Arab kingdom'. But, in the meantime, the confiscation of land by force provided the means for colonization by settlement and the complete depersonalization of native Algerians. The cultural desert of colonial propaganda was becoming a reality. When surveys by the Arab bureaus set up by the French disclosed, around 1844, that in 1830, 40 per cent of the Algerian population had been literate (which was more than in France at the same time), they also discovered that, since that date, the war had reduced the number of teachers by at least half. The situation as regards quality was worse. Those teachers who agreed to collaborate proved to be greatly inferior in quality to those who refused. Even the ability to assess ability was lacking. The 'Manual of Arabic Grammar' compiled by the first 'teacher of Arabic' at the French Arab School in Algiers, opened in 1834, speaks volumes about the author's lack of competence. Nevertheless, it was used for years before the deception was discovered and the book replaced. Meanwhile, reports of this school's rejection by indigenous families provoked astonishment. In 1874 in Algiers (a city!) only fifty native Algerians were attending school.

Yet the Franco-Arab primary and secondary schools organized by the decree of 30 September 1850 were inspired by the action taken by Muhammad 'Ali and aimed specifically to attract Algerian youth away from hostile educational institutions in the country and also in neighbouring countries, such as the Zaytuna, the Qarawiyyin and the Azhar. They fell a long way short of their target.

The indigenous peoples could not be prevailed on to distinguish the cultural activities of their conquerors from their military activities or their spoliation of the Algerian economy. For their part the 'colonists' fought against these schools in the name of the realistic use of the colony's resources. These resources were administered as the 'colonists' saw fit: since the edict of 23 March 1843 the *habous* goods and foundations, which had funded educational establishments, had been taken into the state domain, and were distributed to the settlers. The *deys* had given up all control over education by handing the *habous* to the brotherhoods by default. The French rulers went one further.

The triumph of 'colonist' thinking (1871–1914)

After the fall of the Second Empire and the open repudiation of the military administration's 'arabophilia', the Franco-Arab schools were merged with the other schools (which of course were French). Similarly the Collège Impérial Arabe Français was merged into the Lycée. From then on, concern with indigenous Algerian identity ceased to be a subject for discussion. The admission of native Algerians to educational institutions was no longer an obligation, not even a right.

For the indigenous population, the point of departure for the provision of schooling had to be the cultural wasteland to which it had been reduced by a half century of total war. The uprising led by Mokrani also had a cultural significance. It was, in fact, a backlash against the abandonment of all plans to re-establish the cultural identity of an Algeria that was dominated by the ideology of the colonizers.

From that point on, the cultural management of the colony was openly identified with the management of the interests of the foreign community. A teacher-training college existed: of the 36 students in one year-group, 26 were from mainland France, 7 were Europeans from Algeria, and there were 3 native Algerians. The proportion of indigenous recruitment to the school of engineering and the university (1909), at least until 1914, can be imagined.

TUNIS FROM 1830 TO 1914: FROM REFORMING ZEAL TO DEFENSIVE REFORMISM

The French invasion of Algeria viewed from Tunis

The French landing at Algiers was at first seen from Tunis as another 'twist' in the history of the Maghrib regencies. In 1822 the Husaynite dynasty and the 'separatist' party had just had the satisfaction of seeing the Sublime Porte preside at the signing of a peace deal between the two regencies on a basis of equality between states. Both agreed that the future in the Maghrib belonged to the 'Tunisian model'. What was happening in Algiers was judged to be the foreseeable result of the policies of an oligarchy that was as unstable as it was authoritarian.

The first reforms: ambitious and optimistic

Initially, therefore, it was believed that the Tunis Regency could participate in the solution of the conflict. The acceptance of Clauzel's proposals reflected this line of thinking. The Tunisian sovereign did not realize this was an irreversible step towards the depersonalization of Algeria, any more than Abdelkader would two years later with regard to Desmichels.

Once this plan had been abandoned, there remained the now urgent concern to equip the regency with a modern national army. That would confirm its newly acquired status as a nation-state. The treaty signed with France after the capture of Algiers was the first to be drafted in Arabic, and gave Husayn Bey the title of ruler of a kingdom. To achieve this end had been the great preoccupation of Ahmad Bey, one of the two princes whom the plan had envisaged as occupying an Algerian *beylik*.

The military academy created at Bardo in 1840 subsequently became a polytechnic institute. It was to supply the officers for the new army, and more generally managers for a modernized administration. An Italian officer versed in oriental languages who had served in the Turkish army was appointed director and, after two French successors, the post was eventually given to a Tunisian. Its syllabus included military techniques, science and technology (mathematics, physics, chemistry and natural sciences as well as an introduction to medicine, agriculture and veterinary medicine) and European languages (French, Italian, English, Turkish), together with a wide range of subjects that until then had been dispensed by the Zaytuna University: Koran, Arabic language and grammar, and theology. Mahmûd Qabâdû, a sheikh known for his open-mindedness, was entrusted with coordinating these courses. The teaching of Turkish was indicative of interest in understanding a major power, rather than a sign of enfeoffment to Turkey.

The students were recruited from all the ethnic groups represented in the country: people from the cities, the countryside and mamelukes (recent immigrants or converts) rubbed shoulders there. For many of them, teaching was extended by study trips and training abroad.

The first classes formed teams who were firmly committed to the growing effort to modernize the country. They could be seen in action around the reforming minister Khayr ad-Dîn (Khereddine).

The modernization of Zaytuna University was also linked with the modernization of the army. The *Imâms*, the *qadhîs* and the *muftîs* of the former Turkish militia (chaplains and provosts) were paid out of the army's budget. In Tunis, as mentioned earlier, they were no longer recruited from among the Eastern Turks but from among the 'native born', who were Hanafite by religion but spoke Arabic. Those of them who occupied university teaching posts had, unlike their colleagues, the status and pay of officers. The decree of 21 February 1842 extended army pay to all. The teachers at the secular university were thereby taken into the public sector. The teaching staff, originally appointed by the sovereign, was henceforth composed of fifteen Hanafite *'ulamâ'* and fifteen Malekite *'ulamâ'*, whose replacements would be co-opted following competitive examination.

These measures were crowned by political reforms. The most important were the proclamation of the *'Ahd al-Amân* (1857), literally Security Pact, guaranteeing the freedom of all the inhabitants of the regency, and that of the *Dustûr* (Constitution) in 1861.

However, it has to be noted that, even while its various committees were working, the Tunisian government refused to put its political reform under the aegis of the Turkish Tanzîmât, to avoid all suspicion of allegiance. It went further: nowhere did the text of the Constitution mention any kind of relationship with Turkey.

Khereddine's disillusionment with diplomacy and nationalism

Immediately after the proclamation of the Constitution, Khereddine undertook a diplomatic marathon through various European countries (France, Sweden, Denmark, Prussia, Holland and Belgium) in four months (June to October 1861). From it he was to draw a bitter conclusion – not one of those countries would consent to a renunciation of the Capitulations, which enabled their nationals to escape the law

of the land; not even France, though the Tunisian sovereign had presented the text to Napoleon III on his visit to Algeria in 1860, and though the French Consul-General, Léon Roches, had been involved in drafting it. It was, indeed, as the result of insistent pressure from the European powers that the Constitution had to be suspended on 1 May 1864.

The significance and cultural impact of this political disappointment were decisive, and can be measured by the shift in Khereddine's intellectual as well as political outlook from that moment on. In 1867 he published his renowned work *Aqwam al masâlik fî tasyîr al-mamâlik* (translated the following year into French under the title *Réformes nécessaires à la conduite des nations*). Its thesis was this: that Muslim states would regain their former prosperity by establishing an order founded on confidence between governors and the governed. This confidence must be the result of the institution of a sense of civic responsibility, itself the result of education, to which he devoted much space. These are obvious allusions to the Tunisian experience, although – and this is a point that is rarely made – there is no specific mention of it. Nor has attention been drawn to the reservations he expresses about European goodwill towards the Muslim nations, who should not expect salvation other than through their own efforts and their own union. Unlike Tahtâwî who, writing on the same subject, gives Egyptian patriotism pride of place, Khereddine addresses himself to the *umma*, the Muslim community. More significantly, he gives a positive assessment of the Tanzîmât in his book, and summarizes the two reforming edicts, Gülkhané's Khatt i Sharîf (1839) and Khatt i Hamâyûn (1856), after having done everything he could to avoid aligning the Tunisian reforms on Turkey's position. In addition, and above all, the lack of any reference to the political reforms introduced in Tunisia between 1857 and 1864 confirm his pessimism as regards Europe and 'diplomacy'.

But he was no less pessimistic about the patriotism and the sense of civic responsibility of his fellow citizens. This was because, contrary to the arguments of those for whom modernization and democratization were a precondition, he had learned from his experience in Tunisia that the masses do not react as enlightened minds expect them to. Had he not seen, during the 1864 revolt for example, the rebellious supporters of Ben Ghdâhum fighting for a status similar to that of Tripolitania, where Turkey had established direct rule in 1835? His insistence on obtaining an involvement on the part of the *'ulamâ'* that went beyond passive consent stems from a similar pessimism, the result of the many unsuccessful meetings at which, between April and June 1861, he had tried to talk them into in-depth reform of the centuries-old Zaytuna.

The second series of reforms: realism and pragmatism

Khereddine had to resign from his ministerial post on 23 November 1862. In October 1873, he was recalled as Prime Minister. However, in spite of this title, he applied himself this time to more modest reforms, in particular the creation of a secondary school, the Collège Sadiki (January 1875) and an administrative reform of the Zaytuna (1875).

Moreover, being a realist, he constantly worked to establish relations with the Sublime Porte, which, while protecting the rights acquired by the Husseinite dynasty, would link its fate with that of the Ottoman Empire.

The creation and the organization of the Collège Sadiki (al madrasa as-Sâdiqiyya) is an absolutely typical example of the direction that Khereddine's thoughts took after his 'time in the wilderness'. The minute attention paid to detail by one of the highest authorities in the land is striking, particularly considering that no more than a secondary school was involved. Great care was moreover taken to announce that it did not seek to rival the Lycée Imperial at Galatasarây, nor the Dar al-'Ulûm founded in Cairo in 1871. Nor, indeed, was it in competition with Zaytuna University, which was the only higher education institution remaining in the country following the closure of the Polytechnical Institute at Bardo in 1864 – a year of many disappointments.

Paradoxically, it was a habous foundation constituted from assets expropriated from the previous prime minister. It was deliberately not made a state asset in order to put it beyond the reach of the Bey and his creditors.

The décret organique of 1 January 1875 instituting the Collège Sadiki has a preamble and eighty-two articles setting out the organization of courses, the internal regulations and the administrative statutes.

The courses were divided into three sections, of which the third was the most innovative. Languages, mathematics, physical chemistry, medicine, agronomics, zoology and veterinary medicine were taught there, as at the Polytechnical Institute, all this with a view to preparing school-leavers for entry into elite higher institutions. Thus the first pupils from Tunisia were sent to preparatory classes for the French grandes écoles at the Lycée Saint Louis in Paris. The first concern of the French government, which by the Treaty of Bardo had become 'protector' of the former Turkish regency, was to return these young protégés to Tunis, claiming that they were urgently required by the protectorate's fledgling administration.

From then, and more officially after the Marsa Convention (1883) had put the administration under the control of the French Resident-General and his French directors (including Mr Machuel, an Algerian-born orientalist who, significantly, combined the functions of Director of Education and Director of the Collège Sadiki), a trial of strength ensued from which the unassuming institution eventually emerged victorious. The idea of the colonial authority had been to develop the school as an extended primary school to train middle-level personnel. The Tunisians, who were participating in the administration of the school in ever-greater numbers (even if they had to wait till 1942 to see a Tunisian Director appointed), were anxious for their part to turn it into a lycée, which would prepare its pupils for higher education. The habous status of the institution's financing made it more difficult than it otherwise would have been to effect a change of mission in conformity with the policy of the protectorate.

The year 1875 also saw a new decree reorganizing the Zaytuna University. There a step was taken towards state control. The decree confirming the direction initiated by the decree of 1 December 1842 brought into the establishment two representatives of the prime minister's adviser on education (General Husayn, who was a former pupil of the Ecole du Bardo and a friend of Khereddine). It established admission procedures in keeping with the regulations of the kuttâb, the Koranic schools which supplied its candidates. It defined the cycles leading to the final exams. It specified and diversified the arrangements for these examinations, which until then had hardly ever departed from the mould of the famous ijâza. Syllabus and curriculum were defined according to specializations classified in accordance with the summa divisio of knowledge into 'ulûm naqliyya (sciences that had been handed down) and 'ulûm 'aqliyya (rational sciences).

On the other hand, some unexpected intrusions by the text of the decree into the definition of teaching methods demonstrate the nature of the resistance to which the desire for in-depth reform had to yield.[2]

Although the new reforms followed in the wake of the first, they differed from them fundamentally: first in that they were pragmatic and free of any illusions about the traditional institutions' ability to cooperate in vigorous reformist efforts, and second in that they no longer expected the European powers to show solidarity with a modernized Tunisia. What those powers meant by reform was primarily the disappearance of the obstacles, no matter how trivial, that the old institutions placed in the way of their own economic activity.

The institutions put in place as a result of Khereddine's second series of reforms certainly did not prevent the continuation or the acceleration of foreign penetration, any more than did the reforms in which he participated as Minister and Adviser to Ahmad Bey. Moreover, and most importantly, they were not spared when colonial domination really took hold.

However, the pragmatic realism that characterized them can be credited with putting up an effective resistance to the depersonalization that Algeria underwent during this same period. The Zaytuna and the Collège Sadiki could, indeed, provide the protectorate's administration with middle-ranking cadres – this being the level of instruction to which the supporters of indirect rule wished to confine them – but the very fact of their marginalization also enabled both institutions to supply the theoreticians and the militants of the struggle to maintain and promote cultural identity.

TRIPOLITANIA AND CYRENAICA FROM 1830 TO 1914: CENTRALIZATION BY A BROTHERHOOD ON THE CONFINES OF POWER

Eclipse of the central power's authority

The effect of the fall of Algiers was felt in Tripoli, logically enough in view of the latter's close relations with the Tunis Regency. The Qaramânlî dynasty, in place in 1830, owed to the Regency of Tunis its re-establishment after an interlude of direct rule.

This situation had remained largely unchanged until the beginning of the 1830s. However, the outbreak of dynastic troubles in 1832 rekindled suspicions. There was restlessness among the local communities, even in the west of the regency. Turkey was attentive to the forceful views of the European powers, which looked askance at France establishing itself on the southern shores of the Mediterranean. Those views were supported by rumours to the effect that Tunis might repeat its intervention of 1794. Preventive measures were therefore taken: in 1835, a Turkish expeditionary force deposed the Qaramânlî and placed the country under direct administration (first a governor in Tripoli, then a second and independent governor for the East).

The newly inaugurated direct rule was scarcely reflected in any change of direction in the educational and cultural sphere. Even the modernization under way in Turkey itself had little effect on the inhabitants of the province other than through the introduction of equipment and infrastructure designed to improve the security situation (such as telegraph facilities).

Conversely, circumstances were such as to favour increased receptiveness to the influence of the brotherhoods. However, the crucial new factor was that, at practically the same moment, one of the most highly organized brotherhoods in Muslim history established itself in Cyrenaica.

The Sanûsîya brotherhood and *de facto* centralization

As it happened, the founder of this brotherhood originated from the Regency of Algiers. Born in Wâsta, near Mostaganem, Muhammad ibn Alî as-Sanûsî (1787–1859) had received a religious education in the *zawiyas* and had joined the ranks of the *Darqâwa*, which were making life difficult for the Turkish authorities. He had left in 1803 for Fez, where he had become a follower of Sheikh Ahmad ibn Idrîs al-Fâsî (1749–1832), the reformer of the Qâdiriyya brotherhood and founder of the Idrisi Qâdiriyya tendency. Twenty years later, he had travelled to Cairo, but disagreed with his Egyptian colleagues of the Azhar, and with the reforms being initiated by Muhammad 'Ali.

It was not that reform did not interest him. Later, when established at Hijâz, he and other intellectuals founded a brotherhood, which had overt political and social aims. The founders' starting point was their agreement on the inability of the Ottoman caliphs to protect the territory of Islam (the French Egyptian campaign, the loss of the Regency of Algiers) and on the inadequacy of other approaches to reform: those of Wahhâbism in Arabia, and of its opponent Muhammad 'Ali in Egypt. The conclusion reached was that action should be carried out on two fronts simultaneously: opposition to the invaders and the construction of a Muslim community that would be better equipped to embrace modernity. The structure would rest not only on independent management of administrative and judicial matters (to avoid contact with the occupying powers), but also on educating the members of the community. To avoid repeating past errors, education too should aim at practical action. An urgent priority was to find the brotherhood a location where it could escape interference from authority of the type that had driven it from Mecca. With a *fatwa* having recently anathematized his 'audacity', Muhammad ibn Alî as-Sanûsî had decided to establish his *Madrasa al Umm* (Mother School) at Al-Baydhâ, close to Barqa, where Cyrenaican *murîds* (aspirants, followers) were already in place.

The tactics adopted reflected his realism: confrontation had to be avoided. His concern to place himself beyond the reach of the authorities was such that, when in 1855 his successes earned acknowledgement from the Turkish authorities in the form of tax exemptions for the brotherhood's assets (as *habous*), he concluded that he should move as far away as possible from the covetousness of the 'black serpent' (in other words, Turkey).

This was followed by successive decisions to transfer the movement's capital first to Jaghbûb (in 1856), then to Kufra for the same reasons (1895). Nevertheless, at no time did he seek to act as a rebel against Ottoman domination after establishing himself on the territory of its dependencies. A realist, he did not proclaim an independent state until 1912, when the Turks had abandoned the province.

This realism allowed him to carry through his educational and cultural programme – which, like Abdelkader, he made the pivot of his action. If not quite a university, there was an effective management training school in operation at Jaghbûb. Practical concerns were deliberately given precedence over speculative questions. Ritual practices were learnt alongside language and mathematics, various trades and the martial arts (fencing, archery and riding). The system made it possible to educate children from backgrounds other than the privileged castes and supplied cadres for another opposition movement: the one which Umar-al-Mukhtâr led against Italian colonialism.

Priority given to mobilization against colonial threats

Comparable to Abdelkader in this respect also, the founder of the *Sanûsîyya* deferred confrontation with yesterday's Muslim adversary in order to devote all his energies to building a popular resistance that would be able to fend off more effective attacks. Ahmad ash-Sharif as-Sanûsî himself asked the Turkish governor to send a representative to Kufra when he moved there. This allowed the order to benefit from legal residency in Turkish territory and protected it from attacks that were expected from the south, where the French were carving an extension to their empire at the expense of black African kingdoms, notably the kingdom of the Wadai, in the north of present-day Chad.

In fact, the Sultans who governed that area from 1838 to 1909 were followers of the *Sanûsîyya*. The first of these, Muhammad ash-Sharîf, had met Muhammad ibn Alî as-Sanûsî at Hijaz while he was formulating his doctrine. From 1900, opposition to French penetration of Chad became the major preoccupation of the *Sanûsîyya*, under the leadership of the son of the founder, al-Mahdî as-Sanûsî, and, after his death, that of his successor Ahmad ash-Sharîf (1902).

By the same logic, when the Italians wanted their piece of Africa and landed at Tripoli in 1911, the *Sanûsîyya* sided with the Turks to repel the invader. They waited to proclaim their own nation until the Turks had renounced it. From then on there was a single united front to liberate the future Libya from the foreign occupier. At its head were the *Sanûsîyya*, whose leader from 1918 was Idrîs ibn al-Mahdî ibn Muhammad, who was proclaimed king in 1951.

The Sanusi order can therefore be credited with having laboured for the advancement of Libyan cultural identity: *de facto* as a brotherhood that, since its establishment at Jaghbûb in 1856, had had a 'government' comparable in many ways with that of Abdelkader (who was also a brotherhood leader promoted to the position of head of state); and *de jure* from 1912, strengthened by the legitimacy that the Ottoman withdrawal had conferred on them.

MOROCCO FROM 1830 TO 1914: FROM THE WILL TO REFORM TO FRIVOLOUS MODERNISM

Morocco shared hundreds of kilometres of frontier with the Regency of Algiers. This proximity had naturally given rise to a good many disputes of a cultural nature. For this reason the French invasion had initially been seen, just as it had been in Tunis, as another twist in the politics of the oligarchic Turkish regime. The first appeal for help was only heeded after some hesitation, and the enterprise quickly fizzled out. Abdelkader's proposal for an alliance, accompanied by recognition of the suzerainty of the Alawite Sultan, was another matter. The alliance lasted until the battle of Isly (1844), followed by the treaty of Tangiers (1845).

The enthusiasm for reform of Sultan Abd ar-Rahmân and Sultan Muhammad III

Nonetheless, like Abdelkader in his territory and like the Tunisian reformers and the *Sanûsîyya* in Cyrenaica at the same time, the ruler of Morocco and his son, the future Muhammad III (1859–1873), were setting about modernization in circumstances that demonstrated the urgent need for it. The military preoccupation here too was accompanied by concern for training and general education. As in Tunis, the reform of traditional institutions was on the agenda as well as the creation of new ones.

First, an engineering school was opened at Fez in 1846. The curriculum offered training in military techniques (artillery, ballistics) as well as civil engineering and the teaching of science and foreign languages. As at the Polytechnic Institute in Tunis, an introduction to Arab and Islamic humanistic studies was not overlooked. These courses were supplemented by studies abroad, the preparation for these trips being provided at an institution at Tangiers. The future Sultan Muhammad III went as far as to teach the geometry class himself. This institution provided many of the staff of the Moroccan administration, but also many of the cadres for the resistance. Bû Hmâra, who was to lead the 1901 revolt against tax reform (the *Tartîb*) had studied there in the same class as the minister responsible for this innovation.

As for the centuries-old Qarawiyyin (Karaouine) University, its reform met with opposition, even more than that of its Tunisian counterpart, the Zaytuna. By the *dhahîr* (decree) of January 1845, Mûlây Abd ar-Rahmân had placed it under state control by putting it under the authority of the *Qâdhî* (Grand Judge) of Fez and providing for a five-year curriculum. But it was not until the *dhahîr* by Mûlây Yûsuf (May 1914) that it acquired a governing board and the payment of salaries was regularized, though even then it remained impossible to impose timetables or to issue any diploma other than the traditional *ijâza*.

Its senior personnel (approximately seventeen professors), most of whom also exercised legal functions, played a key role in political life. Mûlây Abd ar-Rahmân and his successors were relying on this university to rid themselves of interference from the brotherhoods, who, in Morocco, were always on the lookout for deficiencies in the central authority.

As was the case in Tunis, political and administrative measures followed, moving towards a liberalization that was advocated, or indeed imposed, by the European partners. In this way the sultans hoped to earn the respect of Europe, and its cooperation in the task of *nahdha* (renaissance).

Sooner than in Tunis, and in reaction to the experience of Abdelkader, the Morocco of Mûlây Abd ar-Rahmân became disillusioned. Until 1856 it could at least count on the cooperation of Great Britain. But after that time, although rivals in other spheres, the European powers were

in agreement when it came to insisting upon treaties modelled on the centuries-old Capitulations from which Tunisia had been trying in vain to free itself. One example was the 1856 treaty with Britain. In a Morocco that had chosen the path to modernization, it accorded to Europeans, and to the even larger number of those enjoying 'protected' status, exemption from prosecution under Moroccan law.

After Tetouan – reformism ebbs under Hasan I and Mûlây Abd al-Azîz

Morocco found itself at war with Spain in a conflict that had been deliberately provoked (1859–60). The lesson was severe: prudence and moderation were the keywords for the second wave of reforms. Mûlây Hasan I (1873–94), following the example of Khereddine in Tunisia in the 1870s (as well as that of Abdelkader after the treaty of Tangiers), no longer hoped either that the European partners would relax their pressure for long-term modernization or that the forces of tradition would give up their opposition to it. There was no longer any question of reforming the university, or of setting up new institutions. Instead, there would be officer training for the new *nidhâmîyya* (regular) army, through missions abroad (or from abroad). And there would be no more spectacular industrialization, but arms purchases instead.

But this tendency went completely awry under the reign of Mûlây Abd al-Azîz (1894–1908), who went down in history as a colourful purchaser of gadgets rather than as an architect of significant progress.

The result was that the reforms had no tangible manifestation other than tax innovations: their opponents, some of them products of traditional education as in 1881, and some, as in 1901, from more modern educational establishments, stirred up trouble. Meanwhile, the rivalry between European nations was reaching a climax.

The 1912 protectorate

Spain and particularly Germany joined France and Britain as protagonists of the crisis of 1911. After according substantial compensations France, by the treaty of 30 March 1912, declared Morocco a protectorate. As in Tunisia, control of education and culture became the responsibility of French officials.

A period of stagnation set in, very much as it had for Bugeaud's and Napoleon III's companions: despite the more original views of people like Liautey, 'colonialist' policies won through, mitigated, as in Tunisia, by the survival of institutions set up by the reformers of the mid-nineteenth century.

MAURITANIA FROM 1830 TO 1914: THE BROTHERHOODS AS CULTURAL AUTHORITIES

France's presence restored in Senegal: a new style of neighbourhood relations (1817–54)

The first effect of the French Revolution was to give the Shanâqita (the inhabitants of the 'land of the Moors') a powerful European neighbour. The 1815 Treaty of Paris had confirmed France's rights in the zone; and the French presence in Futa Toro became effective from 1817. Faithful to the doctrines and commercial objectives of the Age of Enlightenment, the Restoration had had disagreements with the Shanâqita (more precisely with the Trârza and Brâkna, who lived to the north of the Senegal) over freedom of access to the sea for the traders in gum arabic, which was produced in the north of the country, as well as over the maintenance of relations with the brotherhoods. But concern to maintain the status quo prevailed until 1854, giving trade with France time to eliminate almost completely the more cosmopolitan commerce of Arguin and Portendick. With the treaty known as the Trârza, France inaugurated a new style of relations with the 'Moors'. In it France recognized the Trârza's right to raise a tax of 3 per cent on gum arabic but made them recognize France's territorial sovereignty to the south and east of their territory and made crossing the frontier subject to the authorization of French representatives. The decades which followed saw this arrangement extended to the whole of present-day Mauritania.

The brotherhoods and 'pacification' (1903–11)

At the turn of the century, the concern with 'pacification' began to be openly expressed. The obstacles placed by the various peoples in the way of the application of the different agreements were cited as reasons, and of course use was made of the rivalries between the different ethnic groups, and even within them, and, above all, of the progress that had been made in obtaining information on the brotherhoods by an army and an administration inspired by the work of Algeria's 'Arab bureaus'. The brotherhoods had constructed a network that covered the whole of the territory, comparable with that established in Cyrenaica and in Tripolitania, but without the unity that the Sanûsîyya had been able to impose. This was the network that the colonial enterprise targeted in order to establish itself. The year 1903 saw the occupation of the Trârza and the proclamation of a protectorate over the territories of the Moors. In 1904, it was their neighbours, the Brâkna, who were occupied and one year later Tagant fell. As a result the status of the occupation changed. A decree instituted a civil territory under the authority of the Commissioner of French West Africa (AOF). With that, expansion came to a sudden halt. The French Commissioner, Coppolani, was killed in the same year. Just as he had found allies among the brotherhoods, he found other brotherhoods against him: Sheikh Mâ' al-'Aynayn ibn Sheikh Muhammad Fâdhil al-Qalqamî, leader of a dissident wing of the Qâdiriyya, was able to hold the column in check by imposing a long siege at Tîjîkja, gateway to the last great northern province of the Adrar, where Shinqît, the town after which the Shanâqita were named, was situated. The pacification of the Adrar was not to be achieved till 1911, shortly before the death of Sheikh Mâ' al-Aynayn al-Qalqamî. But it was the brotherhoods that carried the torch of resistance right through to decolonization. Significantly, the resistance leaders came alternately from different brotherhoods, including those which, in a previous phase, had been categorized as loyal collaborators. What was happening was that here, as in Algeria in some ways, and in Tripolitania and Cyrenaica in others, the brotherhoods were the instrument that the protest movement adopted, in fact was obliged to adopt, where

no political entity existed. It had no significant impact in places where, and as long as, a legitimate state authority was recognized, such as in the Regency of Tunis and in Morocco, but also in the ephemeral kingdom of Abdelkader.

Intellectual life dominated by the brotherhoods

The history of the brotherhoods in Mauritania is typical. The country was won over to Islam at a time when governmental structures were disintegrating and were to give way to structures of a feudal type. The diversification and reinforcement of religious structures came about when these feudal structures appeared to call for a counterbalance. In a terrain that was then occupied by a single brotherhood, the Shâdhulîyya, the two brotherhoods Qâdirîya and Tîjânîya, which had appeared in the previous century, had taken up the torch of educational and cultural action. It has to be said that the conditions were right: the Shanâqita were represented and recognized throughout the intellectual community of the Arab Muslim world, in the Mashriq as well as the Maghrib. In fact the different provinces prided themselves on the presence on their territories of authorities that could stand comparison with those of other countries.

The Gebla had its poet who wrote in Arabic and in Zenâga, Muhammad Bâba ibn 'Ubayd (1771–1860), and its epic chronicler, Sheikh Muhammad Mbârak al-Lamtûnî (1773–1868). It provided the Qâdiriyya movement with its successors: Sheikh Sîdîyya al-Kabîr (1832–69) then his son Sheikh Sayyid Muhammad ibn Sheikh Sîdîyya. Wadân and Shinqît had their grammarian (Hurma ibn Abd al Jalil, 1737–1828) and their jurisconsult (Sheikh Sayyid Ahmad ibn Hammânî, who died in 1900). Lastly the Walâta had Umar al-Walî ibn Sayyid Abî Bakr as-Siddîq, a historian of intellectual life in the Takrûr (land of the Tukulors).

A characteristic of intellectual life on the confines of the Sahara is the place that women have always occupied. As well as women poets (such as Âïsha bint Sayyid al-Mukhtâr ibn Sayyid al-Amîn, wife of the founder of the Qâdiriyya, Sheikh Sayyid al-Mukhtâr al-Kuntî), there were teachers (such as Fâtima bint Abd al-Wadûd who taught the last emir of the Adrar) and Khadîja bint Muhammad al-'Aqil, called Umm al-Barahîn (the Mother of All Proofs), who taught logic.

This intellectual life equipped the country with the means to resist 'pacification' and successive forms of assimilation, and ultimately to choose its destiny in the Africa that was reconstructed after decolonization.

CONCLUSION

Whether in the case of Abdelkader or Khereddine, one finds that those to whom it fell to govern the Maghrib for a sizeable part of the nineteenth century initially regarded the attack and defeat of the Regency of Algiers by Europeans as a lesson. There were great hopes that this lesson would not be lost. The Maghrib countries could be equipped with institutions that would combine fidelity to the authentic values of Islam with the capacity to assimilate the authentic values of the West. The result would be twofold: today's European opponents and denigrators would become tomorrow's partners; compatriots who for so long had been condemned to look inwards would see that their cultural past had not barred the way to the construction of a modern society.

Disappointed on both fronts, each obviously in the conditions specific to his own country, the two reformers found themselves reduced to devoting the rest of their careers to coping with more pressing matters: for Abdelkader, this meant trying to resist a campaign of eradication by force of arms; for Khereddine, it involved checking the deliberate erosion of national sovereignty by more modest reforms and a partial re-establishment of links with Turkey.

Despite the disparity of contexts, all the leaders concerned can be seen to go through this three-stage process, even those whose position was not – and for good reason – of an institutional nature. The Sanûsîyya brotherhood in Cyrenaica, and the Qâdiriyya and Tîjânîyya in Mauritania, had performed this role in the absence of a strong central power or any that appeared likely to become one.

What is most striking is that, at the same time in Algeria, the more far-sighted occupiers were paying close attention to the dazzling career of Abdelkadar not simply from the military standpoint. It was also a focus of political analysis. In this respect, the generation of 1847 (the first officers of the 'Arab bureaus') anticipated Napoleon III and his doctrine of an Arab kingdom. But the transformations which French society was undergoing at that time, meant that the *fait accompli* of 'colonization' prevailed.

NOTES

1 Alexis de Tocqueville, *Ecrits et discours politiques*. In : *Oeuvres complètes* (III, 222–4).

2 Thus: 'No (teacher) can call into question the sources accepted from generation to generation by the experts. Nor should anyone increase contestation of the authors, because the abuse of contestation is a sign of ambiguity and confusion. On the contrary the teacher should put all his efforts into understanding the intention of these prestigious (authors) and only come to pose questions after having exhaustively considered the various aspects of the text and after having meditated on what was meant'.

BIBLIOGRAPHY

ABUN NASR, J. M. 1987. *A History of the Maghrib in the Islamic Period*. 3rd edn. Cambridge University Press, New York.

AGERON, C. R. 1972. *Politiques coloniales au Maghreb*. Paris.

——. 1968. *Les Algériens musulmans et la France (1871–1919)*. 2 vols. Paris.

AHMIDA, A. A. 1994. *The making of modern Libya. State formation, colonization and resistance*, 1830–1932. SUNY Press, Albany NY.

ALAWÏ, F. 1986. *Kitāb at-takmila fī Tārīkh (imārat al-Barākina wa t-Tarāriza* [History of Brakna and Trarza's Emirates]. Ed. Ahmad Ould Hassan. Tunis.

BEN ACHOUR, M. L. 1984. *Az-Zaytūna/al-ma 'lam wa I ma 'had* [The Zitouna: the monument and the university]. Tunis.

BROWN, L. H. 1974. *The Tunisia of Ahmad Bey, 1837–1855*. Princeton University Press, Princeton.

BURKE, E. 1976. *Prelude to Protectorate in Morocco: Pre-colonial protest and resistance*. University of Chicago Press, Chicago.

CENTRE NATIONAL DE LA RECHERCHE SCIENTIFIQUE (CNRS). 1979. *Introduction à la Mauritanie*. Paris.

DAJJANI, A. S. 1967. *Al-haraka al-sanussiya, nach'atuhā wa numūwwahā fi al-qarn al-tāsi' 'achar* [The Senussi Movement: Its Birth and Development in the Nineteenth Century] SIND.

DEVERDUN, G. Art 'Al-Karawīyīn.' In: *Encyclopaedia of Islam*. Brill, Leiden, 2000.

GANIAGE, J. 1959. *Les origines du protectorat français en Tunisie (1861–1881)*. Paris.

GERTEINY, A. 1981. *Historical Dictionary of Mauritania*. Scarecrow Press, Metuchen NJ.

GREEN, A. H. 1978. *The Tunisian Ulama, 1873–1915. Social Structure and Response to Ideological Currents*. Leiden.

GUELLOUZ, A.; MASMOUDI, A.; SMIDA, M. 1974. Les temps modernes 1574–1881. Tome 3. In: *Histoire de la Tunisie*. Société tunisienne de diffusion, Tunis.

IBN ABÏ DH-DHIYÄF, A. 1963–5. *Ithāf ahl az-zamān bi-akhbār mulūk Tūnius wa 'ahd al-'amān* [History of Princes of Tunisia and Fundamental Pact]. Vols. 4–6. Secrétariat d'Etat aux affaires culturelles et à l'information, Tunis.

IBN MAS'UD, M. 1963. *Tārīkh Lībiyā al-Hadīth* [Modern History of Libya]. Matābi' 'Dār al-Andalus, Tripoli.

JULIEN, C. A. 1964. La conquête et les débuts de la colonisation (1827–1871). In: *Histoire de l'Algérie contemporaine*. Vol. I. Paris.

——. 1978. *Histoire de l'Afrique du nord*. Vols 2 and 3. 2nd edn. Payot, Paris.

LAROUI, A. 1980. *Les origines sociales et culturelles du nationalisme marocain*. Paris.

——. *L'histoire du Maghreb. Un essai de synthèse*. Centre culturel arabe, Casablanca.

LE TOURNEAU, R. 1995. *L'histoire du Maroc moderne*. University Press of Aix-en-Provence.

AL-MANNOUNI, M. 1973. *Mazahir yaqdati I Maghrib-l-hadith* [Aspects of Revival in Modern Morocco]. Dar al-Gharb al-islāmī, Rabat.

MARTEL, A. 1991. *La Libye: 1835–1990, essai de géopolitique historique*. Collection Perspectives internationales, PUF, Paris.

MIEGE, J.-L. 1954. *Les Européens à Casablanca au XIXᵉ siècle*. Larousse, Paris.

——. *Le Maroc et l'Europe*, tome III..

NORRIS, H. T. 2000. L'Art Maures. In: *Encylopaedia of Islam*. Brill, Leiden.

——. 2000. Art Mūrītānīya. In: *Encylopaedia of Islam*. Brill, Leiden.

PARSONS, F. V. 1976. *The Origins of the Morocco Question, 1880–1900*. Duckworth, London.

REY-GOLDZEIGUER, A. 1977. *Le Royaume arabe (1861–1870)*. Paris.

ROSSI, E. 1968. *Storia di Tripoli e della Tripolitania. Della conquista araba al 1911*. Istituto per l'Oriente, Rome.

SHINKÏTÏ, A. 1961. *Al-Wasīt fī tārīkh 'ulamaā' Shinkīt* [Biographies of the Learned Men of Shinguit]. Casablanca.

SIMOU, B. 1994. *Les réformes militaires au Maroc de 1844–1912*. Université Mohammed V, Rabat.

STEWART, C. 1973. *Islam and Social Order in Mauritania*. Oxford University Press, London.

TURIN, Y. 1971. *Affrontements culturels dans l'Algérie coloniale (écoles, médecines, religions 1830–1880)*. Maspéro, Paris.

VAN KRIEKEN, G. S. 1976. *Khayr al-Din et la Tunisie*. Brill, Leiden.

ZIADEH, N. A. 1968. *Sanusiyah: A Study of a Revivalist Movement in Islam*. Brill, Leiden.

15

SUB-SAHARAN AFRICA

Iba Der Thiam, coordinator

in collaboration with *Elisée Coulibaly, Jeanne-Marie Kambou-Ferrand* and *Christophe Wondji*

15.1

AFRICA UNDER FRENCH DOMINATION

Christophe Wondji

with *Thierno Bah, Jean-Baptiste Kiéthéga* and *Djibril Tamsir Niane*

INTRODUCTION

Christophe Wondji

The region which concerns us here corresponds, on the one hand, to the territories of the present-day states of Mauritania, Senegal, Mali, Niger, Guinea, Ivory Coast, Burkina Faso and Benin, in West Africa, and on the other, to those of Gabon, Congo Brazzaville, the Central African Republic and Chad, in Central and Equatorial Africa. Carved up by colonization into French West Africa and French Equatorial Africa, it is made up of three biogeographical zones: to the north, the Sahelo-Sudan, which extends eastward from the Atlantic and the Senegal and Niger rivers to Lake Chad, and whose history has long been influenced by cultural currents filtering down from the Sahara and North Africa; to the south Guinea, the main gateway to the Atlantic slave trade and, since the fifteenth century, the hub of trade with Europe; and, to the south-east, the Congolese area, whose influence extends from the Atlantic to Lake Chad, along the Congo River and its tributaries (Likouala, Sangha and Ubangi), in which we find the same phenomena as in Guinea.

In the eighteenth century, the Sahelo-Sudan was the seat of Islamic revolutions that disrupted the traditional social structures in Futa Toro, Bundu and Futa Jallon. Guinea, taking advantage of the opportunities of trade with Europe, underwent at the end of the century a number of radical economic, social and political changes, including the emergence of hegemonies such as that of Danhômê in the Gulf of Benin. Islam and trade with Europe, which had been influential factors in the history of the earlier centuries,

played a determining role in the changes that characterized the nineteenth century.

The nineteenth century can be seen as a time of revival, marked by two spectacular events. In the political sphere, the second Islamic revolution (Usman Dan Fodio, Seku Ahmadu and al-Ḥājj 'Umar) completely changed the geopolitical scene in the Sahelo-Sudan, while in Guinea power was becoming more concentrated and sophisticated, as in the case of Danhômê under Ghezo and Glélé. Alongside these political changes, we observe the emergence of oligarchies of itinerant traders, promoters and commercial adventurers on the coast and further inland, which sought to organize these regions into effective networks for linking up Atlantic trade routes with the Sudan (for example in Samori and Rabah). The revival was also cultural, in that African societies sought to master the economic and technical instruments of modern Europe made available by the opening up to international trade: chiefs, kings and emperors made an effort to adapt to the 'licit' trade which gradually replaced the slave trade, with a view to improving their economic tools and military equipment.

However, these innovative efforts could not resist the flood tide of imperialistic expansion in the last quarter of the nineteenth century, which resulted in colonial occupation and domination at the end of the century. Vanquished, and with their structures destroyed, during the first decade of the twentieth century, African societies lost their independence and their bid to act on their own. The endogenous modernization that African leaders had sought to introduce was replaced by modernization imposed from the outside, alienating and subservient to foreign influence, under the colonial yoke. This process, and the various forms it took in different parts of the region, will be analysed in the following pages.

THE CHANGING HISTORICAL SCENE IN THE PERIOD BEFORE THE SHOCK OF COLONIZATION

After the upheavals brought about by the slave trade in previous centuries (disrupted trade routes, economic disorganization, the demographic drain, migration and political unrest, etc.) in nineteenth century in West and Central Africa efforts were made at political, economic, social and cultural reconstruction. But this revival of African societies was to be abruptly halted by colonial conquest in the last decade of the nineteenth century.

In West Africa

Christophe Wondji

Islam and Atlantic trade were the most obvious factors of renewal here in the nineteenth century. With the appearance of the new Islamic-Fulani hegemonies (the Sokoto caliphate, the Fulani (or Fulbe) empire of the Massina and the Tukuloor empire of al-Hājj 'Umar), Islam entered its second revolutionary phase and its ideology was used for the political and social reconstruction of the Sahelo-Sudan. Linked to the Industrial Revolution in Europe, the abolition of slavery and the gradual decline in the slave trade, the replacement of the black slave trade with 'licit' trade in natural products triggered renewed interest by Europeans in Africa, and economic and social changes in the coastal areas, thus helping to strengthen states directly involved with Atlantic trade.

In the second half of the nineteenth century, a third factor was added to and combined with the aforementioned factors: the rise to power of the Mande-Joola merchants, whose trading network covered the whole area of savannah between the Sahel and the forestlands, and enabled Samori Touré to build a huge empire, allying Islam, Atlantic trade and the Mande culture.[1]

Political renewal in the Sahelo-Sudan: the new Islamic revolutions

First of all, it should be noted that, by the end of the eighteenth century, the great empires that had marked the golden age of the Western Sudan had long since disappeared, leaving in their stead a political and social patchwork made up of small geopolitical entities, often corresponding to an ethnic group or strongly organized around a central ethnic group. The majority of these communities were villages with a non-centralized political structure, chiefdoms and small kingdoms, such as the Senegalese kingdoms arising from the displacement of the great Jolof (Baol, Kayoor, Siin-Saalum and Walo) or the Joola kingdoms created in the seventeenth and eighteenth centuries, in the transitional savannahs between the Sahel and the forestlands, on the seaward routes (Buna, Kong, Gwiriko and Kenedugu). In this political mosaic, contradictions, conflicts and tensions were the rule in the early nineteenth century. The village communities such as the Lobi and Dagara or the Bobo and Samo fiercely defended their independence against pressure from neighbouring states, the exaction of tribute, slave raids and the imposition of Islam.

States, for their part, were constant prey to internal divisions within their ruling classes. In the Senegalese kingdoms, for example, a politico-military oligarchy with an animistic tradition opposed the group of Muslim intellectuals or qādi. Obviously this awkward coexistence of Islam and 'pagan' traditions was unlikely to ensure cohesiveness in these kingdoms at a time when they were increasingly faced with Moorish raids from the North, Bambara pressure from the East and the presence of Europeans along the Atlantic coast to the West. The same goes for the dynastic squabbles in the Joola kingdoms that were unable to control trade routes, impose Islam on animistic autochthonous communities and to meet the challenge of expansionism from nearby hegemonies (Bambara, Mossi and Akan).

The Mossi and Bambara kingdoms, with a deeply animistic tradition, were an exception to the rule of widespread socio-political splintering in the Western Sudan. The older Mossi kingdoms (Tenkodogo, Yatenga and Ouagadougou) occupied the whole of the central part of the lands of the Upper Volta, enjoying remarkable stability until the end of the nineteenth century thanks to their centralized political organization, their trade with the countries of the Gulf of Guinea and, above all, their powerful cavalry. The Bambara of the mid-Niger Valley were organized in strong kingdoms in the eighteenth century, first around Segu and later in the Kaarta, in Upper Senegal. Bastions of animism, the Bambara kingdoms relied on a military aristocracy of soldier citizens (Tonjon) hailing from the hunter brotherhood (Ton), a fleet of boats obeying the orders of the Niger fishermen (Somono) and an infrastructure of fortified villages (Tata). In the early nineteenth century they extended their hegemony to the whole area of the Upper Senegal and Niger as far as Timbuktu in the North and the Dogon lands in the East, exerting strong fiscal pressure on farmers and stockbreeders, especially the Fulani herdsmen of the inner Niger delta.[2]

Against this background of social tensions and external pressures, what was the place and role of Islam? As for the colonial system, it would be impossible to understand its relationship with Islam without bearing in mind that, after having won power (Order of 7 September 1840) and then begun the conquest of the territory (roughly between 1854 and 1900) and subdued the labour force (Decree of 13 November 1887 setting up the administrative system for indigenous populations and forced labour), the only element missing for total domination of the colonies was control over consciences. This is what Georges Hardy called 'the moral conquest'. This job was left to the schools. In this perspective Islam, as a faith and way of life and action, emerged as a cultural screen. At first sight Islam seems to have lost ground since the revolutionary flare-ups of the eighteenth century, when the religion of Muḥammad was imposed as the solution to the crisis in Sudanese societies suffering from the turmoil created by the slave trade. At Futa Toro and Futa Jallon, bastions of Fulani Islam, dynastic in-fighting and the enrichment of the elites left little room for the propagation of the faith. In the Niger Bend, the Arma of Timbuktu, descendants of sixteenth-century Moroccan conquerors, formed tribal gangs living off military stipends and trade. In most states, Muslims (both men of letters and merchants) contented themselves with perquisites from sovereigns corrupted by 'pagan' practices, regardless of Islamic orthodoxy.

In reaction to this degenerate form of Islam, Fulani marabouts organized within reform-minded brotherhoods (Qādirīya and Tijānīya) and belonging to disadvantaged social groups waged a merciless war against 'corrupt and pagan regimes'. The signal was given by 'Uthman Dan Fodio who, from 1804 to 1812, harried Hausaland, over-threw the traditional chiefdoms and laid the foundations of a Muslim State (the Sokoto caliphate), whose influence spread throughout the Sahelo-Sudan in the first half of the nineteenth century.[3]

This revolutionary influence first made itself felt in the Massina (the inner Niger delta), where the Fulani had for long suffered from the oppressive policy of the animist Bambara. Trained at the mystical school of the Qādiriya, a brotherhood professing a return to the strict Islam of the time of Muḥammad whose followers had led the earlier revolutions at Futa Toro and Futa Jallon, several marabouts unsuccessfully attempted, between 1815 and 1818, to throw off the Bambara yoke.

However, one of them, Ahmadu Ahmadu Lobbo, was more successful: having sworn allegiance in 1816 to 'Uthman Dan Fodio, he was entrusted with the banner of the holy war (jihād), took the title of Shaikh (Sheikh), organized an army of the faithful (tālibs) and from 1818 to 1826 rid his country of Bambara tyranny. With his new title of Seku (Sheikh) Ahmadu and commander of the believers (amir al-mu'minūn), he organized the Massina into a centralized state (the Dina), whose power extended from Jenne to Timbuktu. Governed by sharī'a, the Dina was the Islamic theocracy par excellence: the members of the Grand Council, around the sheikh, and members of the councils assisting the provincial governors were chosen for their religious knowledge; the justice rendered by the qādi and the education dispensed in Koranic schools were placed under state control. The Dina was a political and cultural revolution, but not a social one: whereas Seku Ahmadu gave the Massina a new capital (Hamdallahi, or 'to the glory of God') and speeded up the Fulani change-over to a sedentary way of life by creating villages for farmers and stockbreeders alike, he did not abolish slavery or the caste system. No change took place in the social order under his successors, Ahmadu Seku (1845–53) and Ahmadu Ahmadu (1853–62), until the Massina was con-quered by another reformer, al-Hājj 'Umar.

By comparison with the past, al-Hājj 'Umar's action could be described as 'a revolution within a revolution'. In fact it formed part of the general current of renovation of African societies by Islam and the specific context of the confrontation of these societies with European expansion in the latter half of the nineteenth century. A follower of the Tijāniya, a more 'democratic' brotherhood than the Qādiriya, al-Hājj 'Umar cherished a more advanced poli-tical and social vision than his predecessors, because his studies in the holy places of Islam (Mecca and Cairo) from 1826 to 1830, and his travels across Africa (Futa Toro, Futa Jallon and Sokoto) from 1830 to 1848, had led him to realize that his mission should go beyond the homeland (Futa Toro) of his ethnic group (the Tukuloors) and his social class (the aristocracy). Consequently his aims were radical ones: social reform and fighting the foreign presence.

In the middle of the nineteenth century Islam was again in crisis. The Qādiriyya, which had provided an ideological framework for earlier revolutions, had lost its mystical inspiration and the content of its messianic message. In Futa Jallon, Futa Toro and the Massina the almamiates had become hereditary oligarchies working state land and trading in slaves. Within the brotherhood itself a rigid social hierarchy now governed relations between the Shaikh and

his ṭalib. By way of opposition al-Hājj 'Umar proposed a new approach through the Tijāniyya, whose leader he had become. This proposed new forms of behaviour: direct contact between the caliph and the ṭalib, a breakdown of the barriers between the leaders and the masses, the use of local languages and a meritocracy. As a framework for upward mobility, the new brotherhood attracted people from all walks of life and all ethnic groups; it thus became a powerful apparatus for political subversion, enabling al-Hājj 'Umar to set about conquering the Western Sudan.

This conquest began with the painstaking groundwork of setting up politico-religious and military structures from 1847 to 1852: the founding of Tijān convents at Jegunko and Dinguiraye in Futa Jallon, the writing of a book of propaganda (ar-Rimāh), missions to recruit fighters in Futa Toro, and arms and munitions purchases from European trading posts (Gambia and Senegal). It entailed three stages: from 1852 to 1859, actions in Upper Senegal, such as the destruction of the Bambara-Massassi hegemony (the taking of Nioro in 1855), despite defeats at the hands of the French in Khasso, Futa Toro and Bundu (1857, Medina; 1859, Matam); from 1859 to 1861, the destruction of the Bambara hegemony in Segou; from 1861 to 1864, victory over the Massina (the taking of Hamdallahi in 1861).

By the time of his disappearance in 1864, thanks to his multi-ethnic army of fighters for the faith (mudjahidūn), al-Hājj 'Umar had created a huge empire stretching from Timbuktu in the east to the banks of the Senegal River in the west, from the Sahara in the north to Futa Jallon (Dinguiraye) in the south. This was a decentralized empire, with provinces ruled by military governors in charge of defence and security and religious leaders overseeing Isla-mization, where justice was meted out by the qādi and the economy regulated by the classical taxation systems of Islamic states (zakāt, mudu and usuru). Society was both 'pluri-ethnic' and 'anti-feudal', in accordance with Tijān tradition, but was to be dominated by the ṭalib, who gra-dually fossilized into a politico-religious elite of conquerors whose rivalries with the sofas, a military category emerging from the vanquished peoples, would mark the history of the Empire after al-Hājj 'Umar.

King of Segu and his father's successor in 1864, Ahmadu had his work cut out with the revolt of the conquered peoples (Bambara, Fulani and Massina) and the insubordi-nation of his brothers until he himself became the com-mander of the believers in 1869 and thus acquired the necessary aura to consolidate his authority. Ahmadu's reign coincided with a period of prosperity that ended only in the 1880s, when the French began their imperialist drive.

The renewal of trading activity in the Atlantic coastal areas

From the late eighteenth to the mid-nineteenth centuries the progressive decline in the transatlantic slave trade, linked to various abolitionist measures and the dissuasive action of expeditions against clandestine slave traders, opened up new trade prospects in the coastal areas. Traders, explorers, missionaries and navigators began to frequent Africa and step up the European presence on the seaboard. The main instigators of abolition, France and Great Britain, were now committed to combating the slave trade and promoting a new strategy of relations with Black Africa. The 'shameful' trade in slaves was henceforth to be replaced by the 'licit' trade in natural products which would help to spread the enlightenment of civilization to Black peoples, teaching them farming, creating trading posts in their territories and sending them missionaries. Trade, Christianity and civilization became the three pillars of the Western mission in an Africa devastated by slavery. Expeditions abounded to the African coasts, with the powerful British navy, then the world's policeman, leading the way: the fight against the slave trade led to the creation of fortified trading posts which became the springboards for new trade and starting points for the future African colonies of a capitalist, industrial Europe.[4]

In the first half of the nineteenth century, the steady decline in exports of traditional trading products (black slaves, gold, gum, spice, ivory, etc.) triggered a deep crisis in Atlantic trade. To face this crisis the Europeans sought new substitute products by implementing a policy of agricultural colonization: from 1819 to 1831; France tried to grow cotton and indigo in Senegal; between 1841 and 1857, Britain attempted the same experiment in Nigeria. When this policy failed, the two powers turned to oil crops (groundnuts and palm oil), which were more adapted to meeting the needs of Europe's industry (domestic lighting, soap manufacture and machine lubrication).[5]

These two key products (groundnuts and palm oil) produced in two main areas (Senegambia and the Gulf of Guinea) would allow the two leading powers (France and Great Britain), with the help of the autochthonous societies, to found a new Atlantic African economy. The second half of the nineteenth century was thus characterized by the palm oil and groundnut revolution, which brought about significant changes in production and trading structures and in the organization of the economic sphere. In Senegambia and the Gulf of Guinea alike a new land-owning system came about, with private and collective forms of ownership existing side-by-side; the rudiments of a wage-earning workforce appeared, notwithstanding the employment of slave labour in some sectors; worker migration towards coastal production areas and the intensification of trade due to heavy European demand attracted more and more African producers and traders into the current of the new economy.[6]

In the Gulf of Guinea, where environmental conditions were right for oil-palm cultivation (*Elaeis guineensis*), this new trade was established without difficulty from Cape Palmas to the Bight of Biafra. It was backed up by groups of merchants emerging from lineal societies during the slave trade period, in particular along the coast of present-day Ivory Coast where Neyo, Avikam, Alladian and Essouma had set themselves up as trade brokers for the slave trading posts of Sassandra, Lahou, Jacqueville, Grand-Bassam and Assini. These brokers traded in palm oil throughout the nineteenth century.[7] But with the exception of the Akan kingdoms constituted in the hinterland between the late seventeenth and mid-eighteenth centuries (Sanvi, Ndenyan, Abron and Baoule), the Ivory Coast had no solidly structured state formations which might encourage the slave trade to the same extent as on the coast of Benin, aptly named the 'Slave Coast'. In the Gulf of Guinea the example of Danhômê (kingdom of Abomey) thus offers a perfect example of the palm-oil revolution.

At the very beginning of the nineteenth century, the Fon kingdom of the Danhômê (with its capital Abomey) faced major challenges: freeing itself from the heavy yoke of its powerful neighbour to the East, the Yoruba kingdom of Oyo; reducing the revolts of subjugated peoples to consolidate its territory; controlling the gateways to the sea in

order to procure firearms, the instruments of military might. It had a number of assets to help it achieve its aims: centralized political institutions around a sovereign leader; a strong army with several elite corps, especially the corps of women fusiliers (the famous Amazons); the presence on the coast of a group of Afro-Brazilian traders particularly active in Atlantic trade and devoted to the monarchy, such as the famous Chacha Felix de Souza in Ouidah. Further assets were the longevity of the sovereigns and their political perceptiveness: Gezo (1818–58) and Glélé (1858–89).

Gezo, who was busy waging war on the neighbouring peoples to the north, the west and the east, in particular freeing himself from domination by the Oyo, defeated once and for all in 1821, was in no hurry to give up the slave trade but was aware of the need to make fruitful contact with European trade: in 1830, for example, he founded for his kingdom the coastal port of Cotonou. At the insistence of the British and the French he involved Danhômê in the palm-oil trade from 1841 onwards. The treaty signed with France in 1843 through the agency of the Régis brothers, and renewed in 1851, included articles stipulating that King Gezo would undertake to provide 'special protection for the palm-oil trade' and 'full protection for the French missionaries'. In 1861, the fathers of the Lyon Missionary Society settled in Ouidah, and by 1865 the palm-oil trade was in full swing.[8]

By the time of his death in 1858, Gezo had thus achieved the economic reconversion of Danhômê, making it one of the bases of the palm-oil trade. The state was primarily its organizer and regulator by means of a specialized administration: alongside the minister for foreign affairs (the Yovogan, minister for White men), a minister for agriculture and land issues (the Tokpon) and a minister for trade were now responsible for production and commerce. The Tokpon oversaw the organization of the royal domain, which was divided up into huge plantations placed in the hands of dignitaries and major traders and employed numerous slaves. In addition to these large plantations, smaller ones were allocated to families who either worked the land themselves around villages or let it out to others. This led to an appropriate regulation of taxes, which increased state revenues, especially since a tax on oil (the kuzu) was levied in addition to the tax on markets, the road tax and tolls levied at the entrance to towns. The manufacture and transportation of oil led to the mobilization by groups of active middlemen of a wage-earning workforce comprising former slaves, craft workers, and pirogue boatmen.[9]

A second example of this commercial revolution was the development of groundnut cultivation in Senegambia. Imported from America and integrated into the agricultural cycle of African farmers since the sixteenth century, groundnuts offered the same advantages as palm oil for the nineteenth-century industrial revolution. Groundnuts therefore attracted the attention of the British and the French, who established coastal trading posts from Senegal to Sierra Leone. Since there was no African state in that area as mighty as the Danhômê in the Gulf of Benin, it was the colonial establishments of the European powers that dominated groundnut cultivation and trade. The British based in the Gambia introduced the trade and controlled its development. But around 1851, the British abandoned groundnuts for palm oil, and it was the French who took over, through their bases in Senegal, where colonial occupation increased from 1817 to 1855. Governor of

Senegal from 1854 to 1861, Faidherbe stimulated the production of groundnuts by involving the export houses of Bordeaux and Marseilles. Groundnuts were first grown in the Siin-Saalum before their cultivation spread into the Kayoor and the river valley; Rufisque became the centre of the groundnut trade in the second half of the nineteenth century.[10]

In Senegambia this renewal of trade coincided with significant socio-economic changes. On the one hand, migratory movements from inland areas to the coast where the production and marketing of groundnuts required a plentiful labour supply, altered the social and ethnic composition of the coastal areas and the status of the workforce: landowners were joined by seasonal workers (navetans) and permanent migrants or foreign settlers (lungtans) who were allocated land; and wages of a sort were gradually introduced. On the other hand, agrarian structures were also modified: alongside the collective village farms (manuo) used for food crops there were now individual farms (kamanyango) producing groundnuts, a cash crop; this led to two types of land ownership, one alienable (individual property) and the other inalienable (collective property). In addition, intermediary groups (Africans, Eurafricans and agents of European trading houses) liased between groundnut producers and exporters, providing services relating to the transport and recruitment of labour from inland areas.[11]

In total, while production techniques and methods changed little compared with previous centuries, this trade renewal nonetheless generated new economic and social forces whose influence was to prove decisive in the colonial period. These forces resulted not only from marked changes in production structures and social relationships within African communities, but also from the foundation of European trading posts, centres for new settlement. Examples are the trading posts in Senegambia (Saint-Louis, Gorée, Bathurst, Boké and Boffa) and Sierra Leone (Freetown), where colonies of Creoles and people of mixed blood brought with them a new culture, combining elements of African tradition with those of modern European society. These proved to be bearers of Christianity and new lifestyles when the Christian missions began to settle along the Atlantic coasts in the first half of the nineteenth century. In Senegal, Catholic missions settled as early as before 1841, at Joal and Portudal, in the hope of benefiting from the existence of an ancient Luso-African community to evangelize the local communities.[12]

But it was above all in the Gulf of Guinea, especially on the Benin coast, that significant cultural changes occurred with the return of freed slaves. Saros from Sierra Leone, and Amaros from Bahia in Brazil, Cuba and the West Indies, settling in establishments founded by Europeans (Lagos, Ouidah and Porto Novo), brought with them a new culture, in which Christianity (Catholic and Protestant) and the arts and crafts of the country where they had served as slaves were factors in introducing innovation and modernization in the coastal societies. As European expansion progressed, these Afro-Brazilians and Anglo-Africans were to become active agents of modernization.[13]

From Sudan to the Atlantic: the Dyula revolutions and the rise of Samori Touré

The renewal of Atlantic trade also had an effect on trading patterns within the continent; traditional mercantile

networks, previously reaching out to the Sahel, sought to take advantage of the opportunities offered by the coastal areas whose product range was becoming increasingly wide and diverse, as the European trading posts grew in size and number throughout the nineteenth century. Yet this gradual reversal in the traffic, towards the Atlantic, did not lead to a drying up of the trade routes towards the Sahara and North Africa. On the contrary, the rich Sudanese lands continued to supply this ancient trade, as European explorers noted in the nineteenth century. The main development at that time was the very clear and growing linkage between the Sahelo-Sudan and Atlantic trading blocs.

The diversity of products being traded and the many different kinds of trade did not escape the notice of explorers, who found that merchant cities played a leading role in organizing the trade. Trade channels from the interior towards the coast conveyed salt, local fabrics and, above all, gold and slaves; in the other direction went kola nuts, firearms and gunpowder, along with various European manufactures. Two kinds of structures in the field linked trade between the Atlantic and the Sudan: the relay system, in which products were handed over from one tribe to the next, was typical of the forestlands; and the network system, whereby products were transported over long distances by the same people throughout the journey. The latter was customary in the savannah lands, which were plied by caravans of professional traders, such as the Jaxaanke (Dyakhanke) in the Senegambia area and the Mande-Joola in the area between the Niger Bend and the Gulf of Guinea. It was from these networks, which became denser and denser as Atlantic trade grew, that military hegemonies emerged, triggering the Joola revolutions of the eighteenth and nineteenth centuries.[14]

In the Senegambia area at the end of the eighteenth century the Jaxaanke (or Dyakhanke, Sarakolle Muslim traders) tried to link up trans-Saharan trade and Atlantic trade. But in the nineteenth century they deliberately chose Atlantic trade, which had become more profitable than trans-Saharan trade. In this way they could enjoy the protection of the Fulani State of Futa Jallon, which had acquired greater power in the region and now maintained secure communications between the Upper Niger and the Southern Rivers coastline. This was not the case with the Mande Joola on the routes to the Gulf of Guinea. In these southern savannahs Mande traders had begun to move southwards after the break-up of the Mali Empire, and had created within their animist societies colonies and clusters of merchants on the north–south kola nut and salt routes, linking the Niger to the forestlands and the sea. These ethnic minorities differed from their neighbours in their occupations, culture and religion, but possessed the firearms supplied by the trade with the coast. They would overthrow the established order, and create their own states so as to avoid paying the heavy taxes imposed by the local lords, and run their own business concerns successfully.[15]

It was for this purpose that in the eighteenth century the Kong kingdom was set up by Seku Wattara in the north of present-day Ivory Coast. This first Joola revolution contributed to the consolidation of Muslim settlements in the cities of Buna and Bonduku and extended west and north the Kong kingdom's economic and political influence by the creation of more or less satellite states (the kingdoms of Bobo Dyulasso and Kenedugu). A response to the same objectives, the second revolution took shape in the first half of the nineteenth century between the Upper Niger and the Bandama, where the Mande warlords, backed by Muslim traders, created kingdoms that overlapped the present-day Ivory Coast and Guinea, namely Moriuledugu of Moriule Sise in 1820; Kabadugu of Vakaba Touré in 1830. It was in the wake of this advancing revolution that Samori Touré emerged, whose career and action fulfilled every promise of the Joola revolutions.[16]

The son of a pedlar, who himself became a travelling salesman in 1848, Samori took up soldiering under the warlords Sise and Berete from 1854 to 1861 and embarked on the creation of a huge empire, which by 1881 stretched from the Upper Niger to the lands of the Upper Volta. This empire moved gradually from west to east and north to south between 1882 and 1890, when Samori came up against the resistance of the neighbouring African kingdoms and French colonial expansion. Successive annexations to the empire included the eastern part of present-day Guinea, the west of Burkina Faso and the whole of the north of Ivory Coast, in all an area of approximately 400,000 square kilometres.

Three ideas governing the Joola revolution were basic to the establishment of the Samorian Empire. First, the protection of trade routes and traders made it necessary to create a gigantic politico-military apparatus covering such a vast area. In 1886, the Emperor had an army of 54,000 foot soldiers and 4,000 cavalry armed with muskets, and later on (by 1891), repeating rifles. The army wore uniforms like those of European troops and was commanded by trustworthy officers with territorial responsibilities and substantial political power. Second, Mandingo cultural tradition designated the emperor as the 'Fama', the supreme uncontested warlord who took the ultimate decisions, assisted by his council and private secretariat. Third, the inevitable reference to Islam was used, to give the state a spiritual base. The first step was to set up Koranic schools and include Muslims in the imperial council; Samori proclaimed himself Almamy in 1886, and in 1887 decided to govern according to sharī'a (Islamic law) and impose Islam on the peoples of the Empire; but when these peoples revolted massively in 1888, he was forced to renounce his plans for a Muslim theocracy.[17]

Samori Touré's achievements were on an epic scale. For the Mande traders, he created a protected area under firm control. With his empire he reconstituted as a whole the fragmented parts of much of western Africa, and built a state, which was to meet the shock of the French conquest with one of the most long-lasting and powerful strike forces of African resistance.

In Central and Equatorial Africa

Thierno Bah

Until the end of the nineteenth century relations between Europe and Central Africa were limited to intermittent contacts along the coast, while the interior of the continent remained practically unknown. The first contacts with Europe concerned the coasts of Gabon, Congo and Cameroon. This region, stretching from the Bight of Biafra to the mouth of the Congo River, was the principal area of the Atlantic slave trade, and between the fifteenth century and the middle of the nineteenth century it attracted numerous slave traders, missionaries and explorers from Europe. From the contact with Western civilization a new elite emerged: educated in the European style, Christianized, some of mixed blood, the offspring of intermarriage, they played a vanguard role. Control of the coast was the subject of fierce competition between the main European powers at the time, Great Britain, France and Germany.

Gabon

French settlement in Gabon resulted from a convergence of commercial and naval interests and was encouraged by the declining influence of the Loango kingdom on the Gabonese coastline in the nineteenth century. Until 1848, Gabon was one of the southern trading posts which extended French influence along the west coast of Africa from the French base in Gorée. In 1839, French supremacy in this region was confirmed by treaties of alliance or protectorate, concluded with the chiefs of clans (ogas) who controlled the estuaries. The Mpongwe chiefs, very active traders, were France's main partners and one of them, Antchuwe Kowe Rapontyombo, known as 'King Denis' (1810–76), used both cunning and diplomacy to take advantage of his special relationship with France. The commercial dynamism of the Mpongwe in the nineteenth century finally gave them political pre-eminence, just as the colonial system was being put into place.

The founding of Libreville in 1849 signalled the French desire to settle in the region. It was with this in mind that the West African mission was organized and led by the Franco-American explorer Paul Belloni Chaillu. Travelling up the Ogowe River with the aim of reaching the Congo, he founded seven major trading stations and nineteen trading posts, laying the groundwork for the area to be colonized in the future.

In his remarkable book, the Gabonese historian Ambouroué Avaro puts forward ideas in support of the existence in pre-colonial Gabon of organized societies and a coherent indigenous culture.[18] He establishes that before the eighteenth century there existed in Gabon a powerful kingdom, the Pongo, which was relatively centralized and hierarchized. Various factors, mostly external, linked to the loss of control over the sea coast, led to the dismemberment of this political entity. The different clans now emancipated themselves under the leadership of a chief (oga), and those along the coast began a frantic fight for control of the slave trade.

Just before the shock of colonization, the Gabonese hinterland was also marked by major migrations of the Fang or Pahouin peoples. The epicentre of this movement was in the Adamawa, in Cameroon; after crossing the Sanaga, most of the migrants came down from the banks of the Woleu and Ntem in the late eighteenth and early nineteenth centuries. Having invaded northern Gabon they pursued their migration southwards, slowly and in small groups. They reached the Estuary region around 1840, and the Lower Ogowe (Port-Gentil) region in 1879. Organized in lineal societies, the Fang of Gabon were culturally assimilated by the peoples with whom they came into contact.

Congo

Exactly the same happened along the Congolese coast as in Gabon, namely marginal contacts with Europeans and the effect of the Atlantic slave trade. What is remarkable is the creation throughout pre-colonial Central Africa of huge and powerful kingdoms: the kingdoms of Angola, Kongo, Loango and Tyo. Of interest to us is the Tyo kingdom. Its existence is attested by European travellers, such as Pacheco Pereira, as early as the fifteenth century. Its main features were its immense size and its diversity. The Tyo kingdom, also known as the Teke kingdom, represented more than 40 per cent of the total population of the present-day Republic of Congo. From the viewpoint of identity the terms Teke and Tyo refer to the same people, all speaking the Kiteke or Etyo language. The Tyo kingdom, a huge continental state, seems not to have been visited by missionaries and explorers until the nineteenth century.

From the late seventeenth century onwards the Tyo kingdom underwent a series of destabilizing shocks, in particular the effect of the international slave trade and the confrontation with newcomers from the collapse of the Kongo kingdom. Immediately before the shock of colonization the Tyo kingdom was known as the kingdom of Makoko, a corrupt form of the title of its sovereign, the Onko. It was still a major supplier of slaves and ivory in the latter half of the nineteenth century. This famous kingdom was the centrepiece of colonial expansion, when in 1880, the king signed with Savorgnan de Brazza what was to become the famous 'Brazza-Makoko' Treaty.

Ubangi-Shari

This old French colony, currently known as the Central African Republic, is a huge, quadrilateral territory of 623,000 km², situated at the heart of the African continent. In ancient times it was part of the splendid kingdom of Kush. For centuries its people lived in peace, but the dire effects of the Atlantic and Eastern slave trades turned the region into a major pool of human resources, resulting in socio-political disintegration and mass migration.

The Atlantic slave trade that began in the fifteenth century at first had only an indirect impact on the territory of present-day Central Africa, which began to be integrated into the circuit of the new world economy in the seventeenth century. During the second half of the eighteenth century and the nineteenth century the Atlantic slave trade intensified. Many of the slaves exported to Brazil, known as 'Congo freemen', actually came from the basins of the Sangha, Ubangi and Upper Congo.

The territory of Central Africa was for long a major pool of slaves for the Eastern trade with the Mashriq. This phenomenon probably dated back as far as the sixteenth century, and was related to the predatory activities of the Kanem-Bornu. In the mid-nineteenth century the decline in the Atlantic slave trade to Brazil was offset by an intensification of the activities of the Islamic states involved in slave raids, the ivory trade and arms trafficking, which were to have a negative effect on the history of the whole of Central Africa. The main states involved in these activities were Kanem-Bornu, Baguirmi, Wadai and Dārfūr. New politico-military formations would also be involved in these lucrative activities, for example the state of Rabah and the Fulani Emirate of Adamawa. Rabah carried out armed operations in the west from 1879 on, and spent ten years in the Ubangi-Shari launching raids against the Banda and Sara peoples.

The region of Ubangi-Shari was also the theatre of operations of the Fulani Emirate of the Adamawa. From the mid-nineteenth century, Ardo Issa of Ngaoundere undertook the conquest of the Mbum and Gbaya peoples, and

creamed off many of the slaves transported as a tribute to Yola. Kounde became an important trade and slave centre until 1880, when the autochthonous Gbaya and Mbum populations organized themselves to resist the slave raids carried out from Ngaoundere.

The eighteenth- and nineteenth-century slave raids had serious consequences: demographically, a depopulation which was disastrous for traditional society and the economy; and socially, a proliferation of inter-ethnic conflict and reciprocal animosity between Muslims and animists in the northern and north-western regions.

Against this disruptive background of extreme violence, outstanding personalities managed to adapt to the situation, acquiring wealth and power and organizing their communities. They did not shrink from imposing themselves as intermediaries in the slave trade in order to acquire firearms. By means of a strategy of incorporation they created dominant clans, and imposed their authority over a huge territory with diverse populations who gradually began to use a single language and a single system to socialize their young people. The creation of these nationalities, even more cultural than social, continued throughout the nineteenth century. Around 1800, N'Dunga founded the Bandia nation of Nzakara; in 1825, the Manjia nation took control of the whole of the territory to the north of the Ubangi; 1850, saw the heyday of the Bandia nation with the Abaya dynasty; and during the same period the Zande nation asserted itself after a process of conquest, integration and assimilation, under the Angura dynasty, founded by a warlord from a powerful clan originating in the Nilotic Sudan.

On the eve of the shock of colonization the Central African area was thus marked by a twofold process: disruption from major migratory movements towards the forestlands, to escape the slave raids by Arabs settled in their zeribas (fortified camps); and the integration and constitution of various nationalities. The colonial conquest at the beginning of the twentieth century would force these wandering peoples to settle in the lands in between the Sangha and Lobaye rivers, and involve the emerging nationalities whose rise was incompatible with colonial domination.

Chad

Lying in the midst of the African continent, at the crossroads of the Arab-Muslim and Black African worlds, Chad has been of strategic importance throughout history. Owing to its huge size and the configuration of its territory, the country has an ethnic make-up of considerable diversity. This can be roughly summed up as two major antithetical sets of peoples, in ethnic, historical, economic and religious terms. A bloc of mostly (anciently) Islamized semi-nomadic peoples in the north (the Gorans or Tubus and Arabs), is contrasted in the south with sedentary and Sudanese types of peoples devoted to ancestor-worship (Sara, Mundang, Massa, Tupuri and Mbum), straddling the borders of Cameroon and Chad itself. A third composite set of peoples is made up of the Buduma, Kotoko and Kuka groups. As a result, throughout its history Chad has been described by reference to the 'north–south dialectic'.

By the end of the eighteenth century the great empires that had dominated the area currently known as Chad, giving it both political supremacy and economy prosperity, were in all-out decline. The territory of the Kanem was the most sought after by Arab tribes, who waged fratricidal struggles and carried out raids against the peoples of the South (Kanembu and Budama). Rabah would be the uniter of these Arab tribes. The Bornu, on the other hand, was but the shadow of its former self. Limited to the north by the Manga country and Kanem, over which it no longer exercised any control, to the south by the Emirate of Kano, to the east by the Shari River and to the west by the Sultanate of Damagaram (Zinder), it would begin its renaissance at the beginning of the nineteenth century, thanks to Ahmed al-Kanemi, who put down the Muslim insurrections and preserved the monarchy. He established his capital at Kuka in 1818, took the title of Shehu and managed to counter the hegemonic tendencies of the caliphs of Sokoto. His action was hampered by the civil war of 1837–55, but the situation stabilized later under his son 'Umar, 1857–81.

There were also other political formations in Chad, in particular the Baguirmi and the Wadai. The small kingdom of Baguirmi, situated in the Middle Shari, came constantly under pressure from Bornu and Wadai until the nineteenth century. Caring little for proselytism, seeking rather to acquire military might with their famous lance-bearing horsemen, the sovereigns of Baguirmi succeeded in imposing their rule over the pagan communities of the south and establishing a remunerative trade in slaves, who were sent to the north. In the nineteenth century the Wadai Sultanate, with its capital built on a remarkable defensive site at Warra, was a powerful warrior state forever fighting its neighbours. It was also one of the major suppliers of slaves for trans-Saharan trade.

In the mid-nineteenth century the political scene in Chad was dominated by hegemonic conflicts between various states: the Kanem and Baguirmi territories were coveted by both the Wadai and the Bornu, each of which tried to stake out its position by force of arms. Rabah, the Great Captain, intelligent, courageous and energetic, would impose himself by means of victorious military campaigns and policies aimed at unifying Chad territory.

Coming from the Nilotic Sudan, Rabah Fadl-Allah joined the Khedive's army at the age of twenty. After some years spent in Cairo he was drawn towards the Bahr El Ghazal, where the Jellaba (Arab) merchants plied a highly lucrative trade in ivory and slaves. There he met the famous merchant called Zubayr, who took him into his service. A cunning strategist with victorious campaigns in Dārfūr to his credit, in 1881 Rabah headed westwards to try his luck single-handed. His first target was the Bornu. Despite their large numbers and modern weaponry (firearms and cannon) the Bornu of the 1880s were prey to political instability and succumbed to the assault of Rabah's troops. Kuka, the capital of the old empire, was besieged, occupied and abandoned for Dikoa, the new capital where Rabah had himself proclaimed Emir.

From 1882 to 1884, Rabah created numerous zeribas (fortified camps) and taught his new slaves how to handle firearms. In 1888–9 he led campaigns farther south, into the Sara lands where he took away large numbers of slaves. In 1890 he operated in the Dar Kuti before approaching the Baguirmi and routing a military coalition between the Baguirmi and the Wadai. Heading still further west, he captured a number of Kotoko principalities without meeting any resistance. His military expeditions took him as far south as the kingdom of the Mandara, which, however, held out against the assault of his troops.

On the eve of colonization Rabah was thus at the head of an enormous empire that stretched from the Wadai in the east to the Bornu in the west. As Emir he exercised a genuine military dictatorship to ensure the cohesion of this huge and varied territory. He divided it into 'fiefdoms' awarded to his best warlords; based on Koranic law, justice was meted out by Qādi Mādāni, and Rabah himself only intervened in exceptional cases. The Emir had an enormous treasury (Bait al-Māl) constituted by the profits from fruitful raids and war booty, along with tax in the form of yearly tributes paid by the sultanate and the subjugated peoples.

At that time Rabah's empire had one of the best organized and equipped armies in Sub-Saharan Africa. Its main core, made up of 3,000 fusiliers, was based at Dikoa, under Rabah's personal command. Various contingents were billeted in the main cities, especially in the strategic area of Shari. In 1898 it was estimated that Rabah had at his disposal a total of 35,000 men throughout his empire.

By the time the centre of the continent, especially the surroundings of Lake Chad, became the region most coveted by the various colonial powers, Rabah had succeeded in creating a structured state with an unprecedented military strike force. In 1899 this came to France's notice, and no fewer than three missions were dispatched to Chad (Joalland-Meynier, Foureau-Lamy and Gentil), to dislodge the Sudanese warlord.

THE SHOCK OF COLONIZATION: TRANSFORMATIONS AND CONSEQUENCES

Throughout the nineteenth century, African societies had been adapting to the post-slavery era and seeking to take advantage of the peaceful exchanges that the new world context had introduced into relations between Europe and Africa. Then, however, the continent was ravaged by the expansion of colonialism, which, within the space of two decades, shattered the reconstruction efforts of a century. From 1880 to 1900, much of West and Central Africa was overrun, conquered and occupied. The violence of the slave trade was followed by the violence of colonization, whose unilateral and overwhelming nature accounted for the bitterness of widespread popular uprisings. This entitles us to speak of the 'shock of colonization' as an introduction to this section.

In West Africa

Christophe Wondji

Conquest and creation of French West Africa

Before the shock of colonization as such, France maintained trading posts in Senegal, on the rivers of the south (Guinea), Ivory Coast, Dahomey and Gabon. Explorers increased their knowledge of the Niger River and the Sudanese lands, and Christian missionaries had already begun their work of evangelizing the Blacks.[19] So it was from positions acquired on the coast (Saint Louis since 1659), in particular in the colony of Senegal (occupied since 1817), that French expansion was to occur in two main directions: the coastal axis towards the Gulf of Guinea and Gabon, and the land axis towards Niger and Chad.

In building its West African empire, France had substantial means at its disposal in terms of manpower and equipment: regular troops, with the creation in 1857 of the Senegalese infantry corps; a corps of marines and engineers trained in the tradition of Bouët Willaumez and Faidherbe; and state-of-the-art weaponry, with rapid-firing rifles well backed up by artillery. These military resources were reinforced by diplomacy in the form of various protectorate treaties signed with African sovereigns, and agreements reached with other European powers after the Conference of Berlin (1884–5) established the charter for the partition of Africa and legitimized the occupation of spheres of influence. The French expansionist drive came up against the determination and heroic bravery of the African sovereigns, who were nevertheless disadvantaged by inferior weapons and their own internal rivalries.

From 1885 to 1900, the French followed an active strategy of military occupation, aimed at getting rid of the states obstructing the political and geographical unification of their various spheres of influence. In Senegambia, they opened up the route leading from the coast to Niger by shattering the resistance of Maaba Diaxu Bā (Almami of Rip), Lat-Joor (Damel of Kayoor) and the Sarakole Empire of marabout Mamadu Lamine Drame in 1886–7. Advancing into the Middle Niger, in 1889–91 they attacked the vast Tukuloor Empire of Ahmadu. The empire was wiped off the map and its chief exiled to Sokoto, where he died in 1898. From the Middle to the Upper Niger and in northern Ivory Coast, the Samori Empire constituted a major obstacle: after years of fighting between 1891 and 1898, Samori was finally captured and deported to Gabon in 1898, and his empire disintegrated. Meanwhile, the kingdom of Dahomey had been conquered from 1890 to 1894, the Futa Jallon chieftaincy and the Mossi kingdom of Ouagadougou subjugated in 1896, Kenedugu destroyed in 1898 and the whole of the northern Ivory Coast occupied. Put down in the same period were the popular resistance movements of the Sereres and Baol in Senegal, the Samo, Marka, Bobo and Fulani of Upper Volta, the kingdoms and chieftaincies of Lower Ivory Coast and the Bariba chieftainships in northern Dahomey.

Thus, starting with the old colony of Senegal, the military occupation of Upper Senegal-Niger (1886), and with the addition of the newly acquired colonies of French Guinea (1891), Ivory Coast (1893) and Dahomey (1894), French West Africa gradually took shape from 1895 to 1900 on the ruins of African empires and kingdoms whose sovereigns had been reduced to silence, deported or killed. From 1895 to 1904, several decrees outlined the territories of the colonies making up French West Africa and defined the Governor-General as the central figure of power in the federation: it now had a capital (Dakar), central services such as a senior military command, and its own resources; the Governor-General was assisted by a governing council attended once a year by the lieutenant-governors of the grouped colonies and the main heads of the federal services. He was also the 'sole guardian of the powers of the French Republic'.[20]

The foundations and institutions of colonial power

The colonial regime in Black Africa stemmed primarily from the doctrine formulated, with local variants, which accompanied the French expansion. Basically, this made the colonies instruments in the service of the colonial power,

which could be used in an emergency to restore and reinforce it.[21] It also stemmed from Second Empire legislation, which removed the colonies from the purview of laws passed by Parliament to that of government by imperial decree. The Senate decree of 3 May 1854, proclaimed the special status of the African colonies and gave pre-eminence to the executive and its local representatives in the administrative, social and economic management of the territories and their populations.[22] Last, the historical forms taken by the conquest gave the system a military-political colouring indicated by the list of administrative units and their chiefs: cercles, subdivisions, commanders, governors, etc. In this context, the relations between European colonizers and indigenous Africans were relations between masters and subjects, as proclaimed in the decrees of 1887, 1904 and 1924 which defined the Code of Indigenous Status: indigenous people were French subjects, not citizens.[23]

Senegal, France's spearhead colony in Sub-Saharan Africa, was the place where colonial government was tried and tested. At the end of the nineteenth century it comprised three types of institution: (a) Metropolitan, in the four municipalities of Gorée, Saint Louis, Rufisque and Dakar; (b) specifically colonial; and (c) government by protectorate, which came to an end shortly after the final conquest. In the early days of the municipalities in Senegal there were large minorities of Europeans and assimilated mulattoes in Gorée and Saint Louis, which had from the end of the eighteenth century enjoyed a special status on the fringe of colonial government. These were French citizens inhabiting their own autonomous municipalities, later followed by those of Rufisque and Dakar, who elected councils and sent representatives to the Chamber of Deputies in Paris.[24] This exceptional situation contrasted with the rest of the empire, but was to sow seeds for future claims.

In the rest of Senegal and elsewhere in French West Africa, colonial government was exercised by the all-powerful local administration, which imposed a pyramidal system to organize the subjection of African populations. The Governor-General, 'guardian of the powers of the Republic', had under his orders lieutenant-governors responsible in each colony for a hierarchical network of cercle commanders and heads of subdivisions, cantons and villages. At every level of the system, the responsible official was entrusted with the powers conferred on him by the Code of Indigenous Status, including the right to penalize subjects without recourse to a judicial body: fines, corporal punishment and prison sentences were handed out without any kind of legal scruple.[25]

Summary justice was, with the poll tax and hard labour, one of the three mainstays of the indigenat regime, devised to secure the complete submission of local populations, impose compulsory taxation for the self-financing of the colonial administration, and compel the population to supply labour for the needs of the economy.

Economy and society

Economic exploitation obviously justified the omnipotence of the colonial administration and the oppressive severity of the Code of Indigenous Status. In West Africa, economic policy was furthered on two main lines of emphasis: the introduction of communication infrastructures and the production of agricultural commodities. The building of roads, railways and ports was essential to ensure effective links between coastal areas and the hinterland. Here, railways were the first to benefit from the initial work, and most tracks were already laid by 1914.[26] The effective start of work on roads and ports was delayed until after the war.

The production of agricultural commodities necessary for the mother country's economy was carried out under an import-export system, which amplified the economic effects of the trade revival in the nineteenth century but without its advantages, when African producers had been able to choose their partners. At the beginning of the twentieth century extractive industries (rubber, palm oil, wood, gum, etc.) predominated over agricultural production (peanuts, cotton, cocoa, etc.). But viewed generally, three key products received a boost from the economy and from communication policies: rubber in Guinea and Ivory Coast; peanuts in Senegal and the Sudan; palm-oil and palm nuts in Guinea, Ivory Coast and Dahomey. In any event, cultivation methods were still rudimentary, despite various efforts to introduce new crops with the creation of botanical gardens, for example, in the Sudan where the Colonial Cotton Association strove in vain to interest African farmers in cotton cultivation.[27]

At the heart of this economic system, notable for its lack of concessionary companies, the main agents were trading houses linked to the mother country's interests, particularly the CFAO and the SCOA. The Compagnie Française de l'Afrique Occidentale (CFAO), which was set up from Marseilles, had existed since 1881 and was active in Ivory Coast and Guinea, extending its influence to the neighbouring British territories (Gold Coast, Nigeria). The Société Commerciale de l'Ouest Africain (SCOA), which was set up in 1906 with capital from Lyon and Geneva, was above all active in the French territories.[28] These trading houses were opposed to the system of concessionary companies and preferred to trade in the products worked by the Africans themselves. However, subsequent protectionist measures (1892, 1905, 1913) benefited French trade and thus strengthened the monopoly of the trading houses.

As the colonial government needed African auxiliaries to operate the administrative machinery and an able-bodied labour force to exploit natural resources, it could not dispense with education and health policies. These also formed part of the ideological objectives of Europe's 'civilizing mission' in Africa.

In the nineteenth century, Christian missionaries led the way in introducing modern education into French West Africa. With the blessing of the colonial power, the Pères du Saint-Esprit established the first schools in Senegal and Guinea; the Missions de Lyon did the same in Ivory Coast and Dahomey. In the Sudan this role was taken over by the conquerors, who were replaced later by the White Fathers, especially in Upper Volta. Despite half-hearted attempts at lay education under Faidherbe, it was not until 1903 that a genuine public education system was introduced, at three levels: elementary primary education; vocational education; and continuing primary and commercial education, plus a teacher training school in Saint Louis which was to become the Ecole Normale William Ponty in 1916, recognized as having responsibility for training African high-level executives.[29] The system, which was pyramidal, was based on rigorous selection, the cult of the mother country and total disregard for African cultures. Poorly financed, this school system[30] had been relatively rudimentary before 1914.

Another of the colonial government's concerns was to protect the health of European officials and their African auxiliaries by taking all the necessary measures to counter tropical diseases, in particular endemic diseases such as malaria, yellow fever and typhoid, which had taken their toll of the families of the pioneers in the nineteenth and early twentieth centuries.[31] Until 1905, medical action had been the monopoly of naval medical officers and colonial army doctors, who were responsible for treating army and administrative staff and later on the European colonists and their native servants. Few in number and with meagre resources, they could not cover all the indigenous population, even when sick bays or health centres were provided by the missions.

In 1905, the Assistance Médicale Indigène (AMI) was established by decree in French West Africa. This was a public health service staffed by doctors drawn from the colonial troops, to which civilian practitioners were gradually added.[32] AMI thus served as a framework for the development of a network of health education, ambulance services and health centres, which reflected the colonial government's commitment to take into account the lot of the Africans. After the First World War, this commitment was confirmed by the introduction of preventive medicine for the general public, in keeping with practical views of A. Sarraut.[33]

As a last step, the colonial administration, which had not really enforced abolition under the 1848 decree, gave consideration to the question of slavery. During the conquest the officers of the Sudan had created 'freedom villages' close to post houses or along supply routes where they grouped together slaves captured from the 'rebel' chiefs. These villages in fact constituted a pool of labour for the administration, since 'villages of military captives' did not pay tax but were subject to the *corvée*, i.e. the provision of unpaid labour. This ad hoc arrangement was designed to undermine the forces of African resistance and secure a labour force for economic development; and it was followed up by the decisions of Governor William Ponty, who prohibited masters from pursuing and taking back fugitive slaves (1901), sent to prison those guilty of acts of enslavement (1905) and invited chiefs friendly to France to release captives from the colonial wars of conquest (1908). From 1905 to 1908, the 'freedom villages' were gradually subjected to common law. This policy of half measures did nothing to abolish the institution of slavery.[34]

Consequences, reactions by the populations and the political outcome

In 1914 the results of economic and social policy were still very limited. However, they did bring notable changes in people's lifestyle through the systematic introduction of a cash economy and market crops, and also through population movements towards centres of colonization and slave trade routes. These changes benefited some traditional chiefs who found that the workings of the new government's administration suited their book. They also took advantage of the services of former coastal trade brokers who helped to form the new middle class of auxiliaries: interpreters, clerks, sales representatives, priests, teachers, etc. By contrast, the people as a whole were the main victims of colonialism, since they bore the weight of colonial pressures and extortion (taxes, forced labour and the imposition of obligatory crops). The result was that they led the sporadic and continuing uprisings up till 1914 and beyond.[35]

Also noteworthy was the attitude of certain religious groups, which, without confronting the colonial system head-on, offered African populations who did not know where to turn a number of ways of surviving which were not consonant, with the objectives of colonization. In Senegal, the Murid interpretation of Islam of Sheik Amadou Bamba, entered into conflict with the French administration because its influence on the Senegalese people undermined the power of the loyalist chiefs, who were faced with increasing disobedience. Amadou Bamba was first exiled to Gabon (1895–1902), and then to Mauritania (1903–7) on the grounds that he was the instigator of an imaginary Muslim plot, intended to expel the French from Senegal. The administration also clashed with the Liberian Protestant evangelist William Wade Harris, whose preaching aroused the religious fervour of the coastal populations of Ivory Coast from 1913 to 1916. A follower of a Christianity deeply rooted in African cultures, he preached the redemption of the Black race through the Bible and the compulsory observation of Sunday as a day of rest for his flock. This obviously displeased a colonial administration firmly believing in the White man's 'civilizing mission'; above all, it ran counter to its aims of making the best use of the indigenous labour force. Harris was therefore requested to leave Ivory Coast in 1915, but the administration continued to be suspicious of the networks of converts that he had left behind him.[36]

New forms of opposition to the injustices of the colonial system also emerged in Senegal and Dahomey, which were the two focal points of social and political unrest in French West Africa. In Senegal, the existence of republican institutions in the four municipalities (Saint Louis, Gorée, Rufisque and Dakar) gave African peoples opportunities of political progress, particularly since higher training colleges for senior officials were concentrated there. But in this context, which was an exceptional one, candidates for municipal councils, the departmental council of Senegal and the Chamber of Deputies in France, were chosen from among the White and mulatto citizens, to represent both their small groups and all the Africans born in these four municipalities. In 1909, the first breach was made in this system with the election to the departmental council of Galandou Diouf, a Wolof born in Saint Louis, who was to become in 1912 one of the founders of the movement *Jeune Senegal*.[37] This movement, which supported a number of radical demands (participation by the Senegalese in political life; equal pay for equal work; improvement in the education system; equality with the French), spearheaded the demands for equality confronted with the unjust *indigénat* system. It enabled Africans from the four municipalities to elect Blaise Diagne as Senegalese deputy in 1914, and to secure for them in 1915–16 the status of French citizens while keeping their status as Muslims. These political developments affecting the Africans of the four municipalities of Senegal had repercussions in the other colonies, particularly in Dahomey where the existence of an 'educated middle-class' elite produced from the encounter of the Afro-Brazilian clans of the nineteenth century and the first degree-holders from the higher training colleges in Dakar, created the conditions required to awaken a modern political awareness. Luis Hunkarin, founder in 1917 of an underground review *Le Recadère de Béhanzin*,[38] belonged to this class of modern intellectuals, Dahomeians and

Senegalese, open to Europe and to the Negro-American world, who were to denounce the injustices of the colonial system and play their part in calling it into question between the two wars.

Central and Equatorial Africa

Thierno Bah

Conquest and occupation by the French

In Central Africa the French, who had already gained a foothold in Gabon on the coast, would use the river system as their main means of colonization and access to the hinterland. With a lofty sense of his mission, Savorgnan de Brazza had the idea of launching a large number of steamboats and barges to go up the Congo and Chari rivers. The coastal territories were swiftly annexed but, in the hinterland, conquest was slowed down by resistance from the local populations. Soon the need for effective occupation of the land in order to claim all rights therein gave the race towards the interior a harsher note, with the establishment of military outposts and stations and the signing of treaties with local chiefs. Founded in 1849, Libreville became the hub of colonial policy in the region and the territory remained under Gorée (Senegal) until 1881. When de Brazza was appointed General Commissar of the government in June 1886, he combined this post with that of head of the Congo territory.

In the north, Ubangi-Shari constituted a key element in the French strategy. Around this vast territory, de Brazza dreamed of creating a French empire that would reach Algeria in the North and the Congo River in the South. Thus the territory of Ubangi-Shari was occupied and the outpost of Bangui established on 25 June 1899. Leopold II, King of the Belgians, quickly recognized the sovereignty of France over all the territory on the right bank of the Ubangi. But the pacification of Ubangi-Shari required a series of military campaigns, since various kinship-based societies opposed colonial domination. France, however, pushed on further and further northwards, with the aim of being the first to reach Lake Chad, another key element in the French strategy of occupying the continent of Africa; hence the inevitable conflict with Rabah, who had created a vast empire from 1875 to 1898, and whose presence in the Upper Ubangi impeded the progress of French influence towards Chad. The French decided to put a stop to him after he had prevented the advance of their units between 1890 and 1899 from the Congo right up to Lake Chad via the Ubangi River and Kouango. Defeated and killed in 1900 at the battle of Kusseri, Rabah disappeared from the scene along with his empire.

The fight against Rabah was not the only episode of the French conquest in Central Africa. It was also marked by fierce resistance from the peoples of the northern states, as well as the kinship-based societies in the south. In the coastlands and forest areas of this zone, where the pre-colonial states that had emerged in the fifteenth and sixteenth centuries (for example Luango, Congo, Anzika) had broken up into myriad chieftainships, French penetration was relatively peaceful in the nineteenth century, though it encountered some energetic resistance like that of the Fang in Gabon from 1886, led by their warlord Emane Tole. Defeated in 1902, he was deported to Grand Bassam in Ivory Coast.

*Political and administrative organization: the creation
of French Equatorial Africa*

As in West Africa, the conquest of this region was accompanied by the setting up of an administrative structure. Expansion took place from occupied outposts: Libreville (1849), Franceville (1880), Brazzaville (1883), Bangui (1889) and Fort-Lamy (1900). From 1890 to 1900, de Brazza was appointed to the first administrative structures whose purpose was to achieve the best possible exploitation of the conquered territories. This led him to make the Congo the first colony run by the French Empire, and in 1894 the new territory of Ubangi-Shari was put under its own administration. As early as 1905, however, the centralizing tendency of France resulted in the amalgamation of the four territories of Chad, Ubangi-Shari, Gabon and Congo into a single political entity under the authority of a Governor-General based in Brazzaville. A few years later, in 1910, these four French dependencies were named French Equatorial Africa. The post of Governor-General of that entity was created by a decree of 15 January 1910, investing in him all the powers of the French Republic; he thus became, in fact, a proconsul. He was assisted by a council, and each of the four colonies was headed by a lieutenant governor reporting directly to him. This clearly represented a deliberate policy of centralization, with the imposition of a single structure since the frontiers between the various colonies did not present any real barrier to the movement of persons and goods.

The main victims of centralization were the traditional political institutions. Application of the general principles of assimilation and subordination turned the chiefs of kinship-based communities into mere go-betweens for passing on orders from the colonial administration. There were a few rare exceptions, resembling the 'indirect rule' of the British. Examples were the sultanates of Chad and Ubangi-Shari, such as the Ouaddaï, which enjoyed a degree of independence. In reality, however, all the indigenous African populations were subject to the system of colonial administration (*indigénat*) developed and applied in French West Africa.

Economic exploitation: the concession system

The end of the nineteenth century and the first two decades of the twentieth century were marked by a determination to develop and exploit the natural resources. From the start, the French government, following the example of the Belgian Congo, decreed that all vacant land was *ex officio* state property. At this time, the main resources of French Equatorial Africa were timber, palm-nuts and rubber. In the Congo and in Gabon, the soil and climate were suitable for the cultivation of cocoa and coffee, and in the savannah regions of Ubangi-Shari and Chad cotton was introduced at an early stage.

In French Equatorial Africa, the organization of the colonial economy was based on a system of big concessionary companies, with monopolistic groups given preference. In 1899, for example, some forty limited companies received thirty-year concessions covering nearly 70 per cent of the Congo territory (future French Equatorial Africa). The concession document handed over to these capitalists immense tracts of land, including their natural resources and their inhabitants. In the early twentieth century the most important of these was the Société du Haut Ogoué (SHO), which diversified its activities and engaged in international

trade; but the largest was the Société des Sultanats du Haut Oubangui (140,000 km²), and the smallest the Société de la N'Kémé-N'Kénie (120,000ha).[39] The economic yield of French Equatorial Africa increased with the opening in 1912 and 1914 of gold and diamond mines in Ubangi-Shari.

Divided up between a number of companies and lacking an administration established in due form, French Equatorial Africa was, in the first decades of the twentieth century, the target of a frenzied exploitation that turned into pillage: the company agents were the real masters in the Middle Congo and the south of Ubangi-Shari. Right from the start, colonization was inevitably driven by violence and coercion. The local populations were compelled to collect rubber and ivory and subjected to forced labour for the construction of roads, especially the railway line from the Congo to the Atlantic from 1925. To this must be added the heavy colonial taxes that caused many people to emigrate, in some cases as far as the Nilotic Sudan. Sorely afflicted and under great pressure, these populations suffered from famine and various diseases, and their high death rate explains why even today the population density in vast regions of Central Africa is still so low.[40] This general situation accounts for the numerous popular uprisings that broke out all over French Equatorial Africa from 1903 to 1910, and culminated in the revolt of the Gbaya from 1928 to 1930.[41]

Education, health and social change

The very nature of the colonial system imposed in French Equatorial Africa and the greed of the concessionary companies limited the human benefits of French colonization, for example in comparison with French West Africa. However, a minimum of effort was made to ensure the very survival of the colonial system.

In regard to health, the major problem was sleeping sickness. Colonial settlements, the increasing mobility of the human population, their weakened physical state and the starvation diet on the various construction sites spread sleeping sickness and made it worse. The colonial authorities made it a point of honour to eradicate the disease: mobile health units were set up and crisscrossed the rural areas, and a research mission into sleeping sickness was established in 1906 and later transformed into a permanent annex of the Institut Pasteur in Brazzaville. The health services were diversified through the use of indigenous medical assistants and a service specializing in hygiene and preventive medicine. The efforts made were doubtless appreciable, but of very limited effect. In 1909, there were only twenty doctors for the whole of French Equatorial Africa and, apart from sleeping sickness, health protection covered only the European supervisors and their African assistants living in the towns.

Education was the second sector of investment for the colonial administration. Its objective was limited to training low-level supervisors. But financial constraints and a lack of interest in providing education left French Equatorial Africa at a disadvantage in this area, by comparison with French West Africa, which was far ahead. The first budgetary allocations under this heading were opened in 1906, in Gabon, for the establishment of the first non-religious school system. This was organized into village, regional or urban schools.[42] All in all, education in French Equatorial Africa, which from the start placed the emphasis on acculturation, did not have priority status for the colonial administration, which offloaded its obligations on to the church and private denominational schools for most teaching activities.[43]

Apart from Northern Chad, an area which had been thoroughly Islamized for centuries, the rest of French Equatorial Africa experienced a meteoric expansion of Christianity at the expense of traditional religions. Here the Holy Ghost Fathers played a dual role of evangelism and the provision of schooling. In Gabon, the Congo and Ubangi-Shari, the establishment of missions was almost immediately followed by the creation of administrative outposts. As early as 1893, Monseigneur Augouard founded a Catholic mission in Bangui. However, the spread of Christianity did not put an end to the various traditional beliefs. Rather, the two religious systems adapted to each other.

To conclude, the societies of Central Africa under French domination underwent major changes as a result of various factors, in particular schooling and Christianization, which broke down the formerly unshakeable clan structures and values. Individualism and new forms of upward social mobility tended to impose new points of reference. At the economic level, it should be noted that the transition from autarchy and a barter economy to trade, the imposition by the colonial power of cash crops (cotton, coffee, cocoa) and the obligation to pay a poll tax in cash, all acted to destroy the former system and promote a new one based on the profit motive, especially in the coastal societies. One typical example of these changes is the Gabonese coast, where the combined impact of all these factors created a new elite, with which previously unknown social interactions, going so far as intermarriage with Europeans, brought into being a community of mixed blood which soon formed a highly dynamic trading elite. It was precisely in Libreville that emerged, after the war, the first modern-style opposition to colonization, in particular through the Jeune Gabon movement that sprang up in 1920 among the 'progressives', some of whom were members of the Ligue des Droits de l'Homme.[44]

CULTURE, SCIENCE AND TECHNOLOGY

Cultural evolution

Djibril Tamsir Niane and Christophe Wondji

The conditions for cultural renewal

The countries of Sub-Saharan Africa are countries belonging to old civilizations, in which a succession of famous kingdoms, empires, and cities developed over the years. Across the Sahara in the north and via the Atlantic Ocean, these countries maintained relations with the outside world, whose influences they were able to assimilate on the basis of their ancient cultural heritage. The establishment of 'licit trade' in the nineteenth century, after the abolition of the slave trade, and the Islamic revolutions in West and Central Africa, led to changes in the structures and organization of cultural life.

Changes consisted, for example, in the establishment in West Africa of Muslim confraternities and marabout culture. A typical example is the militant Islam of al-Hājj 'Umar Tall, the propagator of the Tidjane confraternity, and a religious and war leader.[45] The chief or marabout was often honoured with the title of al-Hājj, or even Caliph,

and surrounded by disciples or talibs who were devoted to him body and soul. This devotion could go as far as the supreme sacrifice. As a charismatic leader the marabout was an object of veneration, which extended also to the members of his family. In addition, an aptitude for Koranic studies and bravery on the field of battle were decisive criteria for social advancement. Thus, in contrast to the ancient social hierarchies based on the criterion of birth, merit became the fundamental criterion, imparting a new dynamic to society, which became organized around these militant and conquering marabouts at the opposite pole from the animistic dynasties and old laxist Muslim aristocracies.

In the coastal regions and Central Africa, whose societies had already been thrown into turmoil by the slave trade, the increase in trade led to population movements and the emergence of new cultural spheres. In Gabon, trade between the Mpongwe of the Estuary and the peoples of the Middle Ogoue region brought with it the establishment of social relations (marriages) and cultural relations (blood covenants). These were conducive to the creation of a common sociocultural context characterized by the adoption of the beliefs and lifestyles of the peoples of the coast by the inland societies, which spoke the Myene language (that of the Mpongwe). This was also the case in most coastal societies, in which coastal peoples in contact with European trade were the transmitters of cultural change.[46]

In addition, changes in education systems, especially from the mid-nineteenth century onwards, had repercussions on cultural life, for example in the areas in which Islam and Christianity introduced new types of schooling. In the nineteenth century, African education had been strongly characterized by the tradition of initiation, which required each adolescent boy to withdraw to a sacred retreat in the forest, for a greater or lesser period of time, in preparation for adulthood in a society with strict rules. By contrast, Koranic and Christian teaching, based on the written word, introduced a form of individual acquisition of knowledge, preparing the ground for new forms of expression in which creative people were able to assert their personality.

Language, literature and cultural syncretism

Led by the marabouts, militant Islam gave rise to a wealth of literature, not only in the old Islamic centres (Futa-Toro, Futa Jallon, Hausa country) but also in the new states (Massina, the empire of al-Hājj 'Umar). Both a warlord and a writer, al-Hājj 'Umar left to posterity over twenty works and a well-endowed library. In the nineteenth century, many 'biographies', 'lives of saints', and poems were dedicated to the prophet Muḥammad. Nonetheless, non-religious writings had not lost their place; for example the Fulani pastoral or 'bucolic' poems. History and poetry remained popular both in the royal courts and the countryside.[47]

It should be noted that alongside this literature, often written in classical Arabic, there grew up an African literature using Arabic characters. For example, the Wolof, Fulani, Tukuloor and Hausa wrote in their own languages legendary tales, history texts and poems, and composed religious songs, which enjoyed widespread popularity. Special reference should be made to three pacifist caliphs. The first is El-Hadji Malick Sy (1853–1922), who went to Mecca in 1888, created Tivaoune Tijani Zawiya and the biggest pilgrimage of his period since 1902, a very famous school and an exceptional library; the second is marabout Cheikh Ahmadou Bamba of Senegal (1853–1927), a founder of the confraternity of Murides in Senegal; the third is Cheikh Musa Kamara, who had written an important history of Black people. They comprise three of the most famous authors of an extensive literature written in Arabic, Wolof, and Pulaar.

Islam did not, however, halt the spread of Christianity, which occurred mostly in the coastlands around the old slave trading ports inhabited by long-established Christian families. This was the case in Saint Louis and Gore in Senegal, Boffa in Guinea and Cotonou in Benin, where the White missionaries did remarkable work. The first French school was established in Senegal in 1817, and in about 1840 there were the first Senegalese clerics and priests, the best known of whom was the Abbé Boilat, the author of the *Esquisses Sénégalaises* (Senegalese Jottings) which bore witness to his mastery of the language and in-depth knowledge of the country.[48]

Although traditional religion had lost ground to the two revealed religions, it still maintained a powerful influence. This made itself felt in oral literature, which retained all its vigour, even in Muslim states, where Islamization spread only in the towns and courts. Throughout the nineteenth century, the great majority of the population knew and appreciated both founding myths and oral tales, lullabies, pastorals, and so on. Among the stories and myths, special mention should be made of Kaydara, a long Fulani initiatory poem collated and translated by Amadou Hampaté Bâ;[49] it is a splendid example of this type of literature, which was indissociable from traditional religion.

Here it is appropriate to recall the paramount place of art and the mastery of the spoken word in ancient Africa, which still exists to this day. In royal courts, sovereigns, even those of Muslim chiefs such as caliphs, had their *griots*, who were historians and specialists in the spoken word. Centres of traditional history were to be found throughout the Sudano-Sahel. Keyla (near the last capital of the Mali Empire on the Niger) and Fadama (situated on a tributary of the Niger in the present-day Republic of Guinea) were two outstanding examples.

In Central Africa, cultural change took place without any Islamic influence. Exchanges of every type influenced the lives of the peoples in this zone of dense forests. In the Congo basin, the famous 'caravan route' from Loango to lake Stanley Pool introduced the circulation not only of goods but also of ideas and lifestyles – in other words, cultural features. These were mainly transmitted by the famous *pombeiros*, former slaves who had picked up an education from European traffickers. Centres of cultural dissemination, markets and trade centres grew up along the routes used by caravans to transport both slaves and cargoes of ivory.[50]

European clothes and European food made their way into these centres. The Lower Congo was a major centre for trade and communications, and the Kikongo language spread rapidly through trade, to become a vehicular language. This was also the case for Lingala along the Congo River and its tributaries (Ubangi, Sangha, Likuala).[51]

However, it was in the field of religion that the Central African peoples showed their greatest capacity to absorb inputs from the outside. Since the end of the sixteenth century, the Christianity introduced by the Portuguese had barely spread beyond the outskirts of the capitals and *chefs-lieux* of the provinces of the coastal kingdoms. In the

nineteenth century, the peoples of the coast and estuaries, and the Mpongwe traders of Gabon, helped to spread inland not only Christianity but also its objects and instruments of worship. The cross was in exceptional demand, not as a religious symbol but as a fetish. It was thought to have extraordinary powers; and fetishists, sorcerers and other magicians of the region actively sought statuettes of saints, censers and other objects of worship, which they then used for non-Christian purposes. The end of the nineteenth century thus witnessed the birth of a syncretism in which crucifixes and statuettes, considered as mukusi or protective fetishes, were hung in an indiscriminate jumble on the walls of huts. This syncretism was deeply ingrained in people's minds. It was to give birth, as it did elsewhere in the coastal zones of the Gulf of Guinea, to 'independent national churches'. One example was the Kibanguist church in the Congo, which the priests of the Catholic church were to fiercely oppose at the beginning of the twentieth century.

Different aspects of artistic creation

Nineteenth-century artistic development is better known because the *objets d'art* concerned were removed from towns, temples and sacred forests by the European conquerors. They were carried off to Europe to enrich private collections and museums, where their artistic quality was immediately recognized. Works such as the carved doors of the Dogon of Mali, the sculpted monuments of the Baga of Guinea and the Baule masks of Ivory Coast aroused the curiosity of European artists very early on, and became a source of inspiration at the beginning of the twentieth century. In Central Africa, it was above all the reliquary figures of the kuba (Congo), the Mpongwe (Gabon) and Bulu (Cameroon), characterized by an advanced degree of abstraction, which attracted the attention of the new movements in European art, especially the cubist school.

Art was closely linked to crafts. Here again, it was the end-of-century colonial conquests which introduced into Europe African weaving, velvet, raffia, seats and vases. The finish of this craftwork belied the adjectives of 'primitive' and 'savage' which greeted its discovery.

African architecture is in a class of its own: its originality and variety are striking. In the nineteenth century Sudanese architecture produced monuments well worthy of the palaces of the emperors of Mali (fourteenth century) and Songhai (sixteenth century). Two typical examples of such architecture are Hausa houses and Fulani huts, which both have striking arabesque decoration. There is also the 'Sudanese-style' of the mosques and buildings of the inland delta of the Niger in Mali, from which numerous mosques of the marabouts or caliphs drew their inspiration.

Communication was widely practised in the two regions under review: the conquerors marvelled at the speed at which the Africans communicated, for instance in the transmission of news by drum signalling, in which the coded sign system is both an art and a science. Drumology (the science of talking drums) is now being taught in African universities. Body movements and dance are arts which are taught to children very early on. Young Africans learn to walk to the sound of the clapping of hands and the singing of women in the house.

To conclude, it has been supposed that the nineteenth century, during which Africa fell under the yoke of European domination, was a period of regression. This period nevertheless bore witness to the vitality of African culture in different domains. The misappropriation of the works of art removed from their natural settings and placed in museums, where they were revealed to the entire world, contributed to the gradual rehabilitation of the creative African genius. The manuscripts discovered in Sudanese towns prove the existence of a written literature. In the same way, the collection of founding myths and other major oral works of the nineteenth century showed that, contrary to certain generally accepted ideas, the African continent had not been falling into decline on the eve of the colonial shock.

The sciences, medicine and the pharmacopoeia

Jean-Baptiste Kiéthéga

A brief look at the state of the sciences, medicine and pharmacopoeia, necessitates a review of the organizational frameworks in which they were taught and disseminated, namely the traditional education given by way of initiatory rites, and the Koranic schools introduced by Islam. From the mid-nineteenth century until the dawn of the twentieth, the scientific and technological achievements of these two traditions grappled with the new ideas, sciences and techniques inevitably imposed by colonial rule. The old dualism (African tradition and Islam) was to be supplanted by a new dualism (Islamic African tradition and modernity), a source of confrontation between two cultures.

Ancestral knowledge was still propagated in accordance with the principle of communication between humanity and the cosmos, between the earth and nature and among human beings.[52] An educational system whose functioning was differentiated according to the gender of the child brought children progressively to active life from the age of six onwards, as they learnt history, geography, the natural sciences, mathematics and ethics through the tales and legends. The same European principles obtained in adolescence, during which individuals were integrated into the community production system and the dense network of social relations. The transition to adulthood was sanctioned by initiation rites, through which people came to master their language and their political, economic, social and cultural environment. Thus the symbiosis between upbringing and instruction, between general and vocational education, was a feature of the system created for the purpose of acquiring scientific and technical knowledge.

At the end of the nineteenth century and in the early years of the twentieth, when modern schools were spreading in Africa under French colonial rule, the need began to be felt to preserve Koranic schools, which had become grafted onto the traditional education system. Thus, in the second half of the nineteenth century, primary schooling and the opening of secondary and technical schools in Senegal still left room for this type of education. From 1906 onwards, France set up *madrasas* at Djenne and Timbuktu on the Niger bend. However, the aims pursued by these schools were more political than educational, and they ended in failure. Yet in the nineteenth century the educated elite enjoyed genuine prestige. This gave rise to envy and prompted many young people to set off on the conquest of knowledge by crossing the Sahara or the Red Sea. A survey conducted in Ivory Coast in 1920 revealed the existence of a written literature in Arabic, with books on history, languages, poetry, mathematics, logic, jurisprudence, etc.[53]

Colonial schooling in a variety of forms and frameworks was superimposed on the substratum of knowledge conveyed by traditional education, with its emphasis on nature, and by Koranic teaching, which introduced a form of individual acquisition of knowledge. In 1912, it was impossible to say whether colonial schooling in French West Africa was a success or a failure. Teaching staff were a mixed bunch and teaching standards reflected this. The enrolment rate was no more than 0.85 per cent.[54]

The duality in education and science could also be seen in medicine and the pharmacopoeia. The powerful hold of traditional health systems and the objectives of colonial medicine maintained two cultures in a state of confrontation. In 1896, a microbiology laboratory was created in Saint Louis du Senegal and, in 1913, it became the Institut Pasteur of Dakar. The struggle against endemic diseases such as malaria and trypanosomiasis, and against epidemics, especially of the newly imported smallpox, was prompted by the need to open up the interior of the continent to Europeans, since fevers made it 'the white man's grave', but also to find Black people to provide the labour essential for the exploitation of the colonies.

The introduction of modern medicine, or biomedicine, was accompanied by a drive against traditional therapies, which were identified with charlatans and witch doctors and were regarded as obstacles to scientific progress. Traditional medicine, to which justice is now being done as the value of its pharmacopoeia and skills is acknowledged, was the object of great suspicion on the part of Europeans, if it was not actually banned. Yet at the turn of the twentieth century the views of the two were not so far apart. In Europe and Africa alike the air and the climate were taken to be the main causes of disease. At the time Western medical science shared the metaphysical premises of African medicine. In the case of malaria, for example, its cause was only discovered in 1880, and mosquitos were recognized as being its vectors in 1897.[55]

How can African medicine and its pharmacopoeia in the last century be described? In the first place, the term 'traditional medicine' is still used to designate all the therapeutic knowledge and practices that are not used by what is known as modern medicine, or biomedicine. This definition embraces several different approaches, since the world of traditional medicine is highly diversified as regards its nature, the way in which its knowledge is acquired and the way in which it is exercised and operates, as well as the way in which it has developed recently.[56] The sources on which these currents have drawn and continue to draw are chiefly African magical and religious systems, Islamism (the marabout therapeutic branch), Christianity (the Protestant therapeutic branch) and also syncretic medical sources (with the marabout witch doctors using both verses from the Koran and African esoteric lore).[57]

Examination of the very first of these sources, which could be construed as being 'pure African', reveals three forms tending to reflect the different levels of professionalism. First is a type of medicine whose workings bring into play the whole magical and religious system. It is often represented by a fetish to drive away bad witch doctors and cure certain diseases. Second is a type of medicine in which healing power or practice runs in a particular family. It is a family undertaking, which provides health care based on tradition and on a minimum number of plants and medicinal formulas.[58] Third is a type of professionalized medicine carried out by specialized therapists treating particular pathologies. In these cases, the art of healing brings into play skills that are either objective (pharmacopoeia, medicinal plants) or esoteric (cases of sterility and mental illness).[59]

In African practice, there have been no significant changes so far in methods of identifying a disease. The diagnosis is made after a clinical examination, which identifies simple diseases by means of the apparent symptoms and the information provided by the sick person or his or her family circle. In severe cases, the traditional practitioner gives an opinion after consulting a geomancer or observing the resistance of the disease to the treatment prescribed. For Africans, disease is one of the five categories of hardship to which human beings are potentially subject during their earthly existence. These are misfortune, torment, poverty, death and disease. Convinced that the last-mentioned of these is often exogenous, practitioners believe that the skin suffers from the worsening state of health. As a result, it is a form of medicine which treats visible body symptoms.

A number of illnesses were treated and cured by therapists. Those of the Kingdom of Danhômê were familiar with all the forms of malaria and able to cure them. A caesarean delivery was performed by Swede Gnida under King Guezo of Danhômê in the nineteenth century. Under Glélé (1858–89), anaesthesia was used at the court. It is not known, however, whether these practices were autochthonous or were inspired by Europeans living on the coast, nor why they were abandoned. Some people hold the view that the failure of surgery to develop in Sub-Saharan Africa is bound up with mental attitudes that resist any attack on the integrity of the human body.[60] In 1887, the explorer Binger saw healthy people being vaccinated against smallpox by inoculation with poison from the blisters.[61]

It can be seen from the work on traditional medicine and the pharmacopoeia of West and Equatorial Africa carried out under the auspices of the Francophone Agency for Cultural and Technical Cooperation (ACCT) between 1978 and 1983, that there were a hundred or so ailments which therapists succeeded in curing, mainly with medicinal plants. These were used not only for their curative powers but also for preventive purposes. Some treated snake bites and provided protection against them, since they also act as snake repellents or suppress snakes' aggressivity.[62] Africans even had a remedy for leprosy, a key disease in that it attacks people's physical integrity. The bark of the roots of *Newbouldia laevis*, a slender tree with dark green leaves and pretty purple bell-shaped flowers which grows in forest areas in the vicinity of settlements was used for curative treatment.

Technology

Jean-Baptiste Kiéthéga

In Sub-Saharan Africa, there was little sign of technical progress under French rule on the eve of the First World War. It consisted mainly of the introduction of new plant species and of equipment for mining and transportation. This did not give rise to any technological revolution at local level.

This is why no change has been observed in cropping techniques in agriculture. The practice of shifting cultivation by the 'slash and burn' method was the rule, and intensive cultivation using crop rotation and manure was widespread, especially in areas of high population density, as in the *moãaga* region of Burkina Faso or among the Serer in

Senegal and in sheltered areas by mountain-dwellers such as the Dogon in Mali or the Kabre in Togo. Women also cultivated the land around their huts in this way. Irrigated crops were grown in low-lying areas after floods had subsided, but there was no real control of water resources, although Barth reported the existence of artificial irrigation channels in the Niger valley. The use of draught animals in agriculture was unknown, despite the efforts made by al-Hājj 'Umar, with the assistance of Moroccan technicians.[63] The hoe (*daba*) was the main agricultural instrument. It was suited to the types of soil and the tropical climate, and ensured adequate preparation of the land, while avoiding its deterioration or sterilization by erosion.

Europeans at the end of the nineteenth century acknowledged the skill of the farmers of the Sahel, even though the techniques they used were not very productive. It is surprising, in fact, that the techniques used in agriculture since their appearance in the Sudan 6,000 years ago should not have evolved very noticeably, as for example, by making use of the wheel, which is known to have existed in the Sahara in the fifth century before our era. Some believe that this is because population pressure on the means of subsistence was not significant and that the ample sufficiency of land was the reason for the lack of technical progress in agriculture.[64] However, this does not mean that this stagnation was connected with the country's natural prosperity, which gave the inhabitants a sense of security that did not encourage technological innovations. It should rather be considered that the environment presented challenges that were difficult to overcome.

French intervention in agriculture dates back to the beginning of the nineteenth century. From as early as 1817, agronomists and agricultural workers were sent to Senegal to grow rice, sugar cane, cotton and indigo, but fevers put an end to this venture.[65] In 1818, a development plan for export crops was drawn up by Governor Schmaltz and a crop-testing centre was set up by Richard Toll in 1831. In the forest regions, coffee and cocoa made their appearance from 1885 onwards. In Ivory Coast, coffee grew naturally before the introduction of Brazilian coffee in 1895.

French agronomists found the agricultural techniques used in Africa to be both complex and entrenched in ritual. It was with the plantation economy that the machete appeared, taking the place of an earlier tool, which the *baoulé* called *alale*, whose shorter and finer blade needed less iron in its manufacture. The *jde*, a long broad-bladed knife replaced the *alale* at the end of the nineteenth century and in the early twentieth century.[66]

Imports of increasingly large amounts of European iron in the nineteenth century contributed to the decline of local iron production. The crisis in heavy iron metallurgy, which was already acute in the coastal region, progressively affected the interior, where it was abandoned half a century later. Archinard in 1885,[67] Binger in 1887 and 1888,[68] and others observed and described a large number of facilities for smelting iron ore. Large metallurgical centres operated in Burkina Faso in the Yaatenga and in the Bwamu and Senoufo country, in Mali in the inner Niger delta, in Ivory Coast in the region of Korhogo and in Togo in the Basar country. Throughout these regions metallurgists had developed techniques for prospecting for and smelting ore which are still of interest today. This local iron industry produced the metal supplying the forges, which manufactured agricultural implements, weapons, and tools for other trades.

Like its ironworkers and blacksmiths other craftsmen in the Sudan maintained a remarkable (Sudanese) style of architecture, which is difficult to define, since neither its characteristics nor its geographical coverage are clearly defined. Its origin is also the object of controversy, even though recent archaeological discoveries suggest that it comes from somewhere between the capital of Ghana, Kumbi-Saleh, and the cities of the Niger bend, of which Djenné has provided a perfect illustration up to the present day.[69] The builders of the Sudan were known as *bari*. They formed a corporation of skilled workers and architects who had very little equipment and were paid on a daily basis. We owe to them civil, military and religious edifices, which the French copied in the neo-Sudanese style of their administrative buildings. The resistance of the military constructions to French cannons was put to the test at the time of the conquest. The architect and master builder Samba Ndiaye built ten or more formidable *tata*[70] for al-Hājj 'Umar.[71]

In textiles, the impetus given by the French to cotton production involved no technological transformations. An internal division of labour led to people specializing as spinners, weavers, dyers, and finishers. Strips of cotton fabric, from 4 to 20 cm wide, were sewn together to form loincloths of varying sizes. Dressmakers then used these to make clothes. Since dyed fabric was greatly appreciated, indigo and other plants were used to obtain various colours derived from blue, brown, and yellow. Stockbreeders also used the hair or wool of their cattle, such as camels and sheep. A local type of silk, obtained by boiling the cocoon of a caterpillar living on certain trees, was produced in the *marka* country of Burkina Faso. The thread obtained from it was used to weave loincloths and very attractive, hard-wearing blankets. The local textile trade benefited from the failure of French cotton-producing policies until 1918. Even after the war, the autochthonous textile industry managed to withstand competition thanks to the quality of its products and the weakness of communication infrastructures.

In fact, the aim of the introduction of railways in both French West- and Central Africa was economic and political, designed to open up the wealth-producing regions and centralize the administration in the federal capitals. Between 1885 and 1914, railways were built to link Dakar and Saint Louis, Kayes and Bamako, Dakar and Thies, Conakry and Kankan, Abidjan and Bouake, and Cotonou and Save. Owing to the slow development of roads, motor vehicles only made their appearance in 1898. However, the first motor vehicle transport company created in the same year, collapsed in 1900.[72]

Contrary to the widely held view that Africans were afraid of the sea, the French found a large fleet of boats on the rivers and on the seaboard, where there were many fishermen. Defying the rollers, they engaged in deep-sea fishing, using lines or nets, both for their own subsistence and for trade with the peoples of the interior.[73] With the coming of the Europeans, they carried passengers and local produce along the coast and ferried goods between European vessels and the coast. Some technical features, such as sails, were borrowed, but the canoes were still largely African-made, although they could carry up to 20 tons of fish. Among other technical acquisitions was the manufacture of gunpowder from saltpetre, charcoal and imported sulphur, the repair of barter rifles and the manufacture of gun-lock plates which, when mounted on imported cannons, formed weapons that were partly 'made in Africa'.[74]

It can be considered, therefore, that at the beginning of the present century, Africa under French control had virtually preserved its own system for exploiting its natural resources. Changes were superficial and only occurred in fields where they were consistent with African ways of thinking. For instance, farmers adopted new types of plants and livestock, but still kept the cropping and stock-raising techniques of the past. In fact it is strange that these peoples, who had been in contact with the Maghrib, Arabia and the Mediterranean basin for centuries, did not adopt the wheel, or use draught animals in agriculture, or land vehicles, until the twentieth century.

CONCLUSION

On the eve of the First World War the imposition of colonial rule by France had barely been completed; a few pockets of resistance still had to be 'pacified' in the forest-lands of French West Africa and some regions of French Equatorial Africa such as Congo and Chad.[75] However, despite inadequate equipment and finance, colonial rule seemed to be soundly established in the regions that were effectively occupied and controlled, where the population's traditional way of life was thrown into disorder by the spread of an unprecedented administrative, military and economic network.

It was against this background of subjugation to a foreign administration that the African peoples would be involved in the preparations for the First World War. At the initiative of Colonel Mangin, the theorist of the Black army, the French West African authorities organized recruitment operations as early as 1912. Volunteers were called for, but conscription was the main form of recruitment; in 1914, 30,000 Black troops were called up, a figure that would swell during the war.[76]

As a result Africans were once again dragged into the tragic cycle of war: having fought foreign invasion they now had to fight their invaders' enemies. The rigours of compulsory military service were compounded by the financial burden of a war economy, leading to a number of revolts, which were harshly repressed.[77] After the abortive attempts at renewal in the nineteenth century, the shock of colonialism meant in fact the Africans' complete loss of any historical initiative.

NOTES

1 For a more detailed account see: *General History of Africa* (UNESCO), Vols. 5 and 6; and E. MBokolo, *Afrique Noire, Histoire et Civilisations*, Tome 2, XIXe et XXe siècles, Paris, Hatier-Aupelf, 1992 (French only).

2 See K. Arhin and J. Ki-Zerbo, in *General History of Africa* (UNESCO), Vol. 6, Ch. 25, pp. 662-98.

3 On the Muslim revolutions of the nineteenth century, see Thierno Bah in E. MBokolo, *Afrique Noire, Histoire et Civilisations*, Tome 2, XIXe et XXe siècles, Paris, Hatier-Aupelf, 1992 (French only), pp. 45-58; A. Batran and M. Ly-Tall in *General History of Africa* (UNESCO), Vol. 6, Chs 21 and 23, pp. 537-54 and pp. 600-35.

4 E. MBokolo, *Afrique Noire, Histoire et Civilisations*, Tome 2, XIXe et XXe siècles, Paris, Hatier-Aupelf, 1992 (French only), 96-119.

5 *Ibid.*, pp. 120-9.

6 *Ibid.*, p. 129.

7 C. Wondji, *La Côte Ouest africaine, du Sénégal à la Côte d'Ivoire, 1500–1800*, Paris, l'Harmattan, 1985, pp. 117–37.

8 J. Ki-Zerbo, *Histoire de l'Afrique Noire*, Paris, Hatier, 1972, pp. 276–80.

9 E. MBokolo, *Afrique Noire, Histoire et Civilisations*, Tome 2, XIXe et XXe siècles, Paris, Hatier-Aupelf, 1992 (French only), pp. 129–43.

10 *Ibid.*, p. 143.

11 *Ibid.*, pp. 147–8.

12 B. Barry, *La Sénégambie du XVe au XIXe siècles*, Paris, l'Harmattan 1988, pp. 232–7.

13 A. Asiwaju, in *General History of Africa*, Vol. 6, Ch. 26, pp. 720–3.

14 E. MBokolo, *Afrique Noire, op. cit.*, pp. 151–65.

15 Y. Person, in *General History of Africa* (UNESCO), Vol. 6, Ch. 24, pp. 636–61.

16 *Ibid.*

17 T. Bah, in MBokolo, *Afrique Noire, op. cit.*, pp. 62–9.

18 J. Avaro Ambouroué, *Un peuple gabonais à l'aube de la colonisation. Le Bas Ogowé au XIXe siècle*, Paris, Karthala, 1980.

19 Examples are the explorations of Mungo Park (1790–1806), Clapperton, Denham and the Lander brothers (1826–30), René Caillé (1827–8) and Henrich Barth (1850–6); and the religious congregations of the Pères du St-Esprit (Senegal, Guinea), the Missions de Lyon (Ivory Coast, Dahomey).

20 After the decrees of 1895 and 1899 establishing the Governor-Generalship and the territorial composition of French West Africa, the decree of 1902 transferred the capital of Saint Louis to Dakar and invested the Governor-General with the powers of the Republic, previously invested in the governors of the colonies, who were now relegated to the rank of lieutenant governors. The decree of 1904 consecrated the real emergence of French West Africa, conferring independent resources and central technical services on the Governor-General (cf. A. E. Afigbo in Ajayi and Crowder, *History of West Africa*, Vol. 2, pp. 424–83).

21 See the various theorists of French imperialism from P. Leroy Beaulieu to A. Sarraut, including J. Ferry (see bibliography).

22 The Second Empire was not here breaking new ground, since this provision was in keeping with the Colonial Charter of 1814 and the edict of 1842 which stressed the special legislative status of the colonies and made the Governor of Senegal the sole agent of the central authorities (cf. M. Delafosse, l'AOF. In: G. Hanoteaux and A. Martineau, *Histoire des colonies françaises*, Vol. 4, Chs 4 and 5, pp. 77–159, Plon, Paris, 1931.

23 See A. E. Afigbo, in Ajayi and Crowder, *History of West Africa*, Vol. 2, p. 449; and J. Suret-Canale, *Afrique Noire, L'ère coloniale*, Paris: Editions Sociales, 1964, pp. 418–19.

24 See M. Delafosse, *op. cit.*; and W. Johnson in Ajayi and Crowder, *op. cit.*, pp. 542–67.

25 *Cercles* commanders and heads of subdivisions used militias to enforce these penalties.

26 A network of approximately 2,418 km of railways, intended for the transport of products from the interior (Niger) towards the coast, was constructing in 1914: Dakar-Niger, Conakry-Niger, Abidjan-Niger and Cotonou-Niger. Work on the development of Dakar as a deep-water port began in 1903. See MBokolo, *op. cit.*, pp. 320–1.

27 See Afigbo, in Ajayi and Crowder, *History of West Africa*, Vol. 2, p. 471.

28 In 1914, the CFAO had about ten main agencies and twenty-one trading posts, while the SCOA had respectively six and twenty-four. See MBokolo, *op. cit.*, p. 322.

29 The school system, defined by the decrees of 1903, was only genuinely applicable in Senegal, where all the components already existed: elementary primary education with its three types of school (the village school, the regional school and the urban school); vocational training was confined to the Ecole Pinet-Laprade (which trained foremen) and continuing primary education was mainly provided by the Lycée Faidherbe in Saint Louis. The purpose of the new Ecole Normale William Ponty was to provide primary-school teachers and top civil servants for government departments, and prepare candidates for the School of Medicine which was to be set up in 1918. See J. Suret-Canale, *op. cit.*, pp. 564–71 and E. MBokolo, *op. cit.*, pp. 44–402.

30 According to J. Suret-Canale, French West Africa earmarked annually less than 2 per cent of its funds for education from 1898 to 1908.

31 Epidemics of yellow fever that were particularly deadly struck the European populations in the large coastal cities of French West Africa: Saint Louis, Dakar and Grand-Bassam between 1878 and 1903. See J. Suret-Canale, *op. cit.*, p. 491; and especially Christophe Wondji, 'Yellow Fever in Grand-Bassam (1899–1903)', *Revue française d'Histoire d'Outre-mer*, No. 215, Vol. 59, 1972, pp. 205–39.

32 In 1905, AMI had twenty-one doctors for the entire territory of French West Africa; in 1910, it had fifty-three military and thirty-five civilian doctors in 102 centres, with three hospitals: Saint Louis, Gorée and Conakry. See J. Suret-Canale, *op. cit.*, p. 506.

33 A. Sarraut believed in the 'need to preserve and increase human capital so as to make financial capital work and yield a profit'. See J. Suret-Canale, *op. cit.* p. 507.

34 The policy of setting up 'freedom villages' was initiated by Gallieni in 1887 and continued by Grodet in 1894–5. William Ponty, who was Governor of Haut Senegal Niger until 1908, and Governor-General of French West Africa from 1908–15, continued along the same lines. See J. Suret-Canale and Afigbo, *op. cit.*

35 Uprisings took place in the forest regions of Ivory Coast (1893–1915) and Guinea (1899–1911) and among the lineal societies in the Sudanese area: the Coniagui in Guinea (1902–4) and the Dogon in the Sudan (1908–10). In addition to these sporadic armed rebellions, there was continual social resistance: acts of disobedience, the refusal of forced labour, the flight and migration of populations to remote forests or across uncontrolled border areas.

36 For Sheik Amadou Bamba, see Sheik Tidiane Sy, *La Confrérie sénégalaise des Mourides, Présence Africaine*, 1969; for W. Harris, see C. Wondji, *Le prophète Harris: Le Christ Noir des Lagunes*, Editions ABC, Paris, 1977.

37 See G. Wesley Johnson in Ajayi and Crowder, *op. cit.*, pp. 542–676.

38 See C. Coquery-Vidrovitch, *Afrique Noire, Permanences et Ruptures*, Payot, Paris, 1985, pp. 338–42.

39 See Suret-Canale, J., *Afrique noire: l'ère coloniale, op. cit.*, pp. 34ff.

40 A number of writers have borne witness to this extreme poverty of the inhabitants of Central Africa and aroused public opinion in metropolitan France; they include René

Maran in his novel *Batouala* (Goncourt Prize in 1921) and André Gide in his *Voyage au Congo*, 1927.

41 On this resistance, see in particular Nicolas Métegue N'Nah, *L'implantation au Gabon. La résistance d'un peuple*, Vol. 1 (1839–1920), Paris, l'Harmattan, 1981; and Thierno Bah, 'Kamou et l'insurrection des Gbaya, 1928–30', *Afrika Zamani*, No. 2, 1974, pp. 108–61.

42 An upper primary school for children from the four territories of French Equatorial Africa was later founded in 1936: it is the Edouard Renard School in Brazzaville.

43 In 1917, a decree forbade the use of any language of instruction other than French, even in private schools.

44 Cf. J. Suret-Canal, *Afrique Noire, op. cit.*, p. 555; and *General History of Africa* (UNESCO), Vol. 7, p. 646.

45 D. Robinson, *La Guerre Sainte d'Al Hadj Umar*, Paris, Karthala, 1988.

46 E. Mbokolo, *Afrique Noire – Histoire et Civilisations*, Tome II, XIXe–XXe siècles, Paris, Hatier 1992.

47 Institut Fondamental d'Afrique Noire (IFAN-Dakar), *Fonds vieillards: Fouta-Djalon Poèmes peuls, Cahiers* No. 48–79. Massina fables and Fulani poems – *Cahiers* No. 6–24; cf. *Catalogues des manuscrits de l'Ifan* by T. Diallo, M. Bara M'Backé, M. Trifkovic and B. Barry: *Fonds Vieillards*, Caden; Brevié, Fiagret; S. M. Camara and Cremer in the Arabic, Fulani and Volta languages. *Series Catalogues et Documents*, No. XX, IFAN, Dakar, 1966.

48 P.-D. Boila, *Esquisses Sénégalaises*, Paris, Bertrand, 1853.

49 A. Hampaté Bâ (1901–91) published *Kaydara* in 1965; *Kourmen* (other Fulani initiatory texts) was published in 1961.

50 G. Balandier, *Sociologie actuelle de l'Afrique Noire – Dynamisme sociale en Afrique centrale*. Presses Universitaires de France, Paris, 1963, pp. 43–5.

51 See MBokolo, *op. cit.*, pp. 117–80.

52 A. Salifou, 1974. *L'éducation africaine traditionnelle*, p. 4.

53 Soyinka, W. 1987. 'The Arts in Africa at the Time of Ccolonial rule', in Adu Boahen, A. *General History of Africa*, Vol. 7, pp. 539–64.

54 D. Bouche, 1974, *L'enseignement dans les territoires français de l'Afrique occidentale de 1817 à 1920*, p. 693.

55 B. Ouedraogo, 1996, *Médecine traditionnelle, médecine moderne: coupure ou continuité*, p. 5.

56 *Ibid.*, p. 1.

57 *Ibid.*

58 A. Degbelo, 1992, *Traitement de la maladie dans le royaume du Danhômé aux XVIIIe et XIXe siècles*, p. 501.

59 B. Ouedraogo, 1996, *Médecine traditionnelle, médecine moderne: coupure ou continuité*, p. 1.

60 A. Degbelo, 1992, *Traitement de la maladie dans le royaume du Danhômé au VIIIe et XIXe siècles*, p. 228.

61 L. G. Binger, 1892, *Du Niger au Golfe de Guinée par le pays de Kongo et le Mossi*, Vol. 1, p. 25.

62 R. Schnell, 1958, *Plantes employées en Afrique Occidentale pour se protéger des serpents*, pp. 205–10.

63 J. Giri, 1994, *Histoire économique du Sahel*, p. 234.

64 C. Coquery-Vidrovitch, 1992, *Afrique Noire. Permanences et ruptures*, p. 25.

65 J. Giri, 1994, *Histoire économique du Sahel*, p. 212.

66 J. P. Chauveau, 1984, *Le fer l'outil et la monnaie*, p. 472.

67 Archinard, Lieut., 1885, *La fabrication du fer au Soudan*, pp. 248–55.

68 L. G. Binger, 1892, *Du Niger au Golfe de Guinée par le pays de Kongo et le Mossi*, Vol. 1, p. 261.

69 P. Maas and G. Mommersteeg, 1993, *L'architecture dite soudanaise: le modèle de djénné*, pp. 278–81.

70 *Tata*: a Mandingo term for enclosing walls. By extension, a defensive structure made of clay or stone.

71 T. M. Bah, 1971, *Architecture militaire traditionnelle et poliorcétique dans le Soudan Occidental du XVIIe au XIXe*.

72 Y. J. Saint Martin, 1973, *Les premières automobiles sur les bords du Niger*, p. 602.

73 J. P. Chauveau, 1986, *Une histoire maritime africaine est-elle possible?* p. 199.

74 J. Giri, 1994, *Histoire économique du Sahel*, p. 236. J. Méniaud, in *Les pionniers du Soudan*, Paris, 1931, Vol. 2, p. 49, reports that Samori's metalsmiths imitated the Kropatchek repeater rifle, and could manufacture GRAS rifles and reprime old cartridges.

75 The French occupation was only really completed once the Lobi communities of Ivory Coast and Upper Volta were finally brought to heel (1928–9), along with the populations of Mauritania and the Saharan borderlands of French West Africa (1934–6), and once the Gbaya uprising in French Equatorial Africa had been stamped out (1928–31).

76 In 1917, 120,000 men aged 20–28 years were recruited; in 1918 the age range was widened to 18–35, and recruitment was extended to French Equatorial Africa and systematically organized under the aegis of the Deputy for Senegal, Blaise Diagne, 'Commissary of the Republic'. Estimates of the total number of Africans recruited for the First World War vary from 140,000 to 200,000 infantrymen, according to authors E. MBokolo, *op. cit.*, pp. 333–6 and J. Suret-Canale, *op. cit.*, pp. 177–81.

77 These revolts took place in Sudan, Upper Volta, Ivory Coast, Dahomey, Congo, Gabon and Ubangi-Shari.

BIBLIOGRAPHY

ADJANOUHOUN, E. J. 1984. *Médecine traditionnelle et pharmacopée, Contribution aux études ethnobotaniques et floristiques au Gabon*. ACCT, Paris.

——. 1980. *Médecine traditionnelle et pharmacopée. Contribution aux études ethnobotaniques et floristiques au Niger*. ACCT, Paris.

——. 1979a. *Médecine traditionnelle et pharmacopée. Contribution aux études ethnobotaniques et floristiques au Rwanda*. ACCT, Paris.

——. 1979b. *Médecine traditionnelle et pharmacopée. Contribution aux études ethnobotaniques et floristiques au Mali*. ACCT, Paris.

ADJANOUHOUN, E. J. *et al.* 1978. *Médecine traditionnelle et pharmacopée. Contribution aux études ethnobotaniques et floristiques en R.C.A.* ACCT, Paris.

AJAYI, J. F. A.; CROWDER, M. (eds) 1975. *History of West Africa*. Vol. 2, 2nd edn. Longman, London.

ALEXANDRE, P.; BINET, J. 1958. *Le groupe dit Pahouin*. Paris.

D'ALMEIDA-TOPOR, H. 1993. *L'Afrique au XXe siècle*. A. Colin, Paris.

AMBOUROUE AVARO, J. 1980. *Un peuple gabonais à l'aube de la colonisation. Le Bas-Ogowé au XIXe siècle*. Karthala, Paris.

ANDEREGGEN, A. 1994. *France's Relationship with Sub-Saharan Africa*. Praeger, Westport CT.

ARBAB DJAMA BABIKIR. 1950. *L'Empire de Rabah*. Dervy.

ARCHINARD, M. L. 1885. La fabrication du fer dans le Soudan. *Revue d'ethnologie*, Tome 3, pp. 249–55.

ASSI, L. A., *et al.* (eds) 1985. *Médecine traditionnelle et pharmacopée. Contribution aux études ethnobotaniques et floristiques en République Centrafricaine*. 4th edn. ACCT, Paris.

BAH, T. 1974. Karnou et l'insurrection des Gbaya 1928–30. In: *Afrika Zamani*, No. 2, December, pp. 106–8.

BAH, T. M. 1971. Architecture militaire traditionnelle et poliorcétique dans le Soudan occidental du XVIIe à la fin du XIXe siècle. Doctoral thesis, University of Paris I.

BALANDIER, G. 1963. *Sociologie actuelle de l'AFRIQUE NOIRE. Dynamique sociale en Afrique Centrale.* Presses Universitaires de France, Paris.

———. 1950. Aspects de l'évolution sociale chez les Fangs du Gabon. In: *Cahier international de Sociologie*, IX.

BALLARD JR, A. (ed.) 1966. Four Equatorial States. In: *National Unity and Regionalism in Eight African States.* Ed. G. Carter. Cornell University Press, Ithaca NY, pp. 231–35.

BARATIER, LIEUTENANT-COLONEL. 1912. *Au Congo, souvenirs de mission.* Marchand Fayard, Paris.

BARDON, P. 1949. *Collection des masques d'or de l'IFAN.* Dakar.

BARNES, J. F. 1992. *Gabon: Beyond the colonial legacy.* Westview Profiles, Boulder CO.

BARRY, B. 1988. *La Sénégambie du XVe au XIXe siècle.* L'Harmattan, Paris.

BAYART, J. F. 1985. *L'Etat au Cameroun.* FNSP.

BEART, C. H. 1955. *Jeux et jouets de l'Ouest africain.* Mémoire IFAN no. 42, Dakar, 2 vols.

BENOIST, J. R. DE. 1987. *Eglise et pouvoir colonial au Soudan français.* Karthala, Paris.

BINGER, L. G. (ed.) 1892. *Du Niger au Golf de Guinée par le pays Kong et le Mossi.* New edn 1980. Hachette, Paris.

BOILAT, P. D. 1853. *Esquisse sénégalaise.* Bertrand, Paris.

BONNET, D. 1989. *Approche ethnologique du paludisme.* ORSTOM, Ouagadougou.

BOSER-SARIVAXENANIS, R. 1977. Recherche sur l'histoire des textiles traditionnels tissés et teints de l'Afrique Occidentale. In: *Verhandlungen der Naturforschenden Gesellschaft in Basel*, Vol. 86, pp. 301–41.

BOUCHE, D. 1982. L'école rurale en Afrique occidentale française de 1903 à 1956. In: *Etudes africaines offertes à Henri Brunschwig.* Ecole des Hautes Etudes en Sciences Sociales, Paris, pp. 271–96.

———. 1975. *L'enseignement dans les territoires français de l'Afrique Occidentale de 1817 à 1920. Mission civilisatrice ou formation d'une élite.* Université de Lille III.

BRUNSCHWIG, H. 1991. *Le partage de l'Afrique.* Flammarion, Paris.

CATALOGUES DES MANUSCRITS DE L'IFAN. 1966. By T. Diallo, M. Bara M'Backé, M. Tinkovic and B. Barry: Fonds Vieillard, Gaden; Brevié, Figaret; S. M. Camara et Cremer en langue arabe, peule et voltaïque. Serie catalogues et documents no. XX, Dakar. (Manuscripts from Futa Jallon, Futa Toro, the Massina, Niger, Senegal, Upper Volta (Burkina Faso) and Sudan.)

CHAUVEAU, J. P. 1986. Une histoire maritime africaine est-elle possible? Histoire géographie et histoire de la navigation et de la pêche africaines à la côte occidentale depuis le XVe siècle. In: *Cahiers d'Etudes Africaines*, 101–2, XXVI, Nos. 1–2, pp. 173–236.

———. 1984. Le fer, l'outil et la monnaie. In: *Cahiers ORSTOM, Sciences Humaines*, Vol. 20, Nos. 3–4, pp. 471–84.

COFFINIERES DE NORDECK 1986. Voyage au pays des baga et du Rio Nunez. *Le tour du monde*, LI 1ère semaine. pp 273–304. Hachette, Paris.

COQUERY-VIDROVITCH, C. 1992a. *L'Afrique Occidentale aux temps des français colonisateurs et colonisés. 1860–1960.* La Découverte, Paris.

———. (ed.) 1992b. *Afrique Noire. Permanences et ruptures.* 2nd revised edn. L'Harmattan, Paris.

———. 1985. *Afrique Noire. Permanences et ruptures.* Payot, Paris.

———. 1970. Le Congo français au temps des grandes compagnies concessions 1898–1930. Doctoral thesis, Sorbonne, Paris.

———. 1969. *Brazza et la prise de possession du Congo (1883–85).* Mouton, Paris.

COQUERY-VIDROVITCH, C.; MONIOT, H. (eds) 1992. *L'Afrique noire de 1800 à nos jours.* 3rd edn. Presses Universitaires de France, Paris.

COQUERY-VIDROVITCH, C.; CABOT, J.; BOUQUET, C. 1973. *Le Tchad. Que sais-je?* Presses Universitaires de France, Paris.

CULOT, M.; THIVEAU, J. M. (DIR.) 1992. *Architectures françaises d'Outre-mer.* Mardaga. Liège.

DEGBELO-IROKO, A. 1993. Traitement de la maladie dans le royaume du Danhômê au XVIIIe-XIXe siècles. Doctoral thesis, University of Paris I.

DELAFOSSE, M. 1932. Afrique occidentale française. In: *Histoire des colonies françaises*, par Hanoteaux G. et Martineau, A., Tome 4. Plon, Paris, pp. 1–358.

DENIS, C. M. 1931. *Histoire militaire de l'A. E. F.* Imprimerie Nouvelle, Paris.

DENIS, J. 1971. *L'Afrique centrale et orientale.* Presses Universitaires de France, Paris.

DENYER, S. 1978. *African Traditional Architecture.* Heinemann, London.

DESCHAMPS, H. 1972. *Histoire de Madagascar.* 4th edn. Berger-Levrault, Paris, p. 358.

DEVISSE, J. 1989. Les Africains, la mer et les historiens. In: *Cahiers d'Etudes Africaines*, 115–16, XXIX, Nos. 3–4, pp. 397–418.

DOMIAN, S. 1989. *Architecture soudanaise. Vitalité d'une tradition urbaine et monumentale. Mali, Côte d'Ivoire, Burkina Faso, Ghana.* L'Harmattan, Paris.

ETIENNE-NUGUE, J. 1992. *Artisanats traditionnels: Togo.* I.C.A, Dakar.

———. 1990. *Artisanats traditionnels: Côte d'Ivoire.* I.C.A, Dakar.

———. 1987. *Artisanats traditionnels: Niger.* I.C.A, Dakar.

———. 1984. *Artisanats traditionnels: Bénin.* I.C.A, Dakar.

———. 1982. *Artisanats traditionnels: Haute Volta.* I.C.A, Dakar.

EWANI, F. 1996. Connaissance d'un Etat de l'Afrique centrale précoloniale: le Royaume Tyo. In: *Afrika Zamani*, Nos. 16–17, Yaoundé, pp. 36–61.

FAIZANG, S. 1986. *L'intérieur des choses: maladie, divination et reproduction sociale chez les Bisa du Burkina Faso.* L'Harmattan, Paris.

FERNANDEZ, J. C. 1961. Acculturation and Fang Witchcraft. In: *Cahier d'Etudes Africaines*, No. 6.

FERRY, J. 1893–1898. *Discours et opinions.* A. Colin, Paris.

GANIAGE, J. 1967. *L'expansion coloniale de la France sous la IIIe République.* Payot, Paris.

GAULME, F. 1972. *Le pays de Cama, un ancien Etat côtier du Gabon et ses origines.* Karthala CRA, Paris.

GIDE, A. 1927. *Voyage au Congo. Carnets de route.* Gallimard, Paris.

———. 1922. *Voyage au Congo.* Gallimard, Paris.

GIRI, J. 1994. *Histoire économique du Sahel.* Karthala, Paris.

GONIDEC, P.-F. 1970. *La République du Cameroun.* Berger-Levrault.

GUERNIER, E. 1949. Afrique Occidentale Française. *Encyclopédie mensuelle d'Outre-Mer*, Vols 1 and 2. Paris.

GUILLAUME, P. 1974. *Marché colonial: XIXe siècle.* A. Colin, Paris.

HADJ EL-, O. T. D'. Cahier No. 10. IFAN, anonymous author.

HARZO, C. 1979. Histoire et devenir social: Etude rétrospective et prospective des manuels d'histoire utilisés en Afrique de l'ouest. Thesis of 3rd cycle, Ecole des Hautes Etudes des Sciences Sociales. Paris.

———. 1971. *Histoire générale de l'Afrique noire de 1800 à nos jours.* Vol. 2. Presses Universitaires de France, Paris.

———. 1970. *Histoire générale de l'Afrique noire. Tome 1: Des origines à 1800.* Presses Universitaires de France, Paris.

Histoire Haoussa : Cahier No. 10.

IFAN DAKAR. *Institut fondamental d'Afrique noire.* Senegal.

IMBERT, J. 1982. *Le Cameroun. Que sais-je?* Presses Universitaires de France, Paris.

JOLY, V. 1994. *L'Europe et l'Afrique de 1914 aux années soixante.* Presses Universitaires de Rennes.

KALCK, P.; O'TOOLE, T. (eds) 1992. *Historical Dictionary of the Central African Republic.* 2nd edn. Scarecrow Press, New York.

KIETHEGA, J.-B. 1995. Le travail du fer au Burkina Faso à l'époque précoloniale. In: Benoit, P.; Fluzin, Ph. (eds) *Paléométallurgie du fer et cultures.* Belfort-Sevenans, pp. 131–41.

——. 1992. Le fer en Afrique depuis 4000 ans. In: *Le Grand Atlas de l'Archéologie. Encyclopaedia Universalis*, pp. 316–17.

KI-ZERBO, J. 1972. *Histoire de l'Afrique noire*. Hatier, Paris.

LANGLEY, PH.; NGOM, M.; DAVID, PH. 1978. *Technologies villageoises en Afrique de l'Ouest et du Centre*. UNICEF, Abidjan.

LEBEUF, A. 1969. *Les principautés Kotoko. Essai sur le caractère sacré de l'autorité*. Centre National de la Recherche Scientifique, Paris.

——. 1959. *Les populations du Tchad*. Presses Universitaires de France, Paris.

LEHEMBRE, B. 1984. *L'Ile Maurice*. Karthala, Paris, p. 244.

LEROY-BEAULIEU, P. (ed.) 1908. *De la colonisation chez les peuples modernes*. 6th edn. F. Alcon, Paris.

LONDRES, A. 1929. *Terre d'ébène*. Albin Michel, Paris.

MAAS, P.; MOMMERSTEEG, G. 1991. *Djenné: chef-d'œuvre architectural*. KIT Publications, Amsterdam.

MBOKOLO, E. 1992. *Afrique noire: Histoire et civilisations*. Vol. 2, XIV–XXe siècles. Hatier-Aupelf, Paris.

——. 1980. *Le continent convoité. L'Afrique au XXe siècle*. Axes, Paris.

METEGUE N'HAH, N. 1981. *L'implantation coloniale au Gabon, Résistance d'un peuple. Tome 1 (1839–1920)*. L'Harmattan, Paris.

MICHEL, M. 1970. Les plantations allemandes du Mont Cameroun 1884–1914. In: *Revue Française d'histoire d'Outre-mer*. Vol. LLVII.

MONTEIL, CH. 1932. *Une cité soudanaise. Djenné, métropole du delta central du Niger*. Société d'Editions Géographiques, Maritimes et Coloniales, Paris.

MVENG, E. 1984. *Histoire du Cameroun, Tome 2: La période coloniale*. CEPER, Yaoundé.

NDINGA MBO, A. 1984. *Introduction à l'histoire des migrations au Congo*. P. Kivougou Verlag/Editions Bantoues.

NJEUMA, M. Z. 1989. *Histoire du Cameroun XIXe siècle–début XXe siècle*. Traduit de l'anglais par J. A. Mbembe et E. Nguematcha. L'Harmattan, Paris.

——. 1978. *Fulani Hegemony in Yola (Old Adamawa) 1809–1902*. CEPER, Yaoundé.

NZABAKOMADA-YAKOMA, R. 1983. *L'Afrique centrale insurgée: La guerre du Congo Wara, 1928–31*. L'Harmattan, Paris.

O'TOOLE, T. 1986. *The Central African Republic. The Continent's Hidden Heart*. Westview Press, Boulder CO/Gower, London.

OUEDRAOGO, B. 1996. Médecine traditionnelle, médecine moderne: coupure ou continuité. Forthcoming. In: *Tradition et modernité*, Ouagadougou.

PERSON, Y. 1982. Les Manding dans l'histoire. In: *General History of Africa*. Vol. 6, Ch. 24, pp. 47–56. UNESCO, Paris.

——. 1967. Un cas de diffusion: les forgerons de Samori et la fonte à la cire perdue. In: *Revue française d'Histoire d'Outre-mer*, Vol. LIX, Nos. 194–7, pp. 219–26.

SAINT-MARTIN, Y. J. 1973. Les premières automobiles sur les bords du Niger. Félix Dubois et la Compagnie des transports par automobiles du Soudan Français, 1898–1913. In: *Revue française d'histoire d'outremer*, Vol. XL, No. 221, pp. 589–615.

SALIFOU, A. 1974. L'éducation africaine traditionnelle. In: *Présence Africaine*, No. 89, pp. 3–14

SARREAUT, A. 1923. *La mise en valeur des colonies*. Payot, Paris

SCHNELL, R. 1958. Plantes employées en Afrique Occidentale pour se protéger des serpents. In: *Bull. IFAN*, Vol. 20, B, Nos. 1–2, pp. 205–14.

SOYINKA, W. 1987. The arts in Africa at the time of colonial rule. In: Adu Boahen, A., *General History of Africa*. Vol. 7, N.E.A., pp. 539–64.

SURET-CANALE, J. 1968. *Afrique noire, géographie, civilisation, histoire*. Editions Sociales, Paris.

——. (ed.) 1964. *Afrique noire: L'ère coloniale*. Editions Sociales, Paris.

——. (ed.) 1964. Résistance et collaboration en Afrique Noire coloniale. In: *Afrique noire: L'ère coloniale*. Editions Sociales, Paris, pp. 299–331.

TALL, E. K. 1992. Anthropologues et psychiatres face aux médecins traditionnels. In: *Cahiers Sciences Humaines*, Vol. 28, No. 1, pp. 67–81.

TERRIER, A. 1931. Afrique équatoriale française. In: *Histoire des colonies françaises* par Hanoteaux G. et Martineau, A., Tome 4, Plon, Paris, pp. 359–576.

THIAM, I. B. 1983. *Histoire politique et syndicale du Sénégal colonial de 1840 à 1936*. 9 Vols. State Thesis, Paris, Sorbonne

UNESCO. *General History of Africa under the aegis of UNESCO*. Cf. Vol. 5 (1999), Vol. 6 (1996), Vol. 7 (1987). Paris.

WONDJI, C. 1985. *La Côte Ouest africaine du Sénégal à la Côte d'Ivoire (1500–1800)*. L'Harmattan, Paris.

——. 1977. *Le Prophète Harris: le Christ noir des lagunes*. ABC, Paris.

——. 1974. *Quelques Caractéristiques Des Résistances Populaires En Afrique Noire 1800–1931*. L'Harmattan, Paris, pp. 333–45.

——. 1972. La fièvre jaune à Grand-Bassam 1899–1903. *Revue française et Histoire d'Outre-mer*, N° 215, Tome 59, pp. 205–39.

15.2

COUNTRIES OF WESTERN AND CENTRAL AFRICA COLONIZED BY BRITAIN AND GERMANY

Francis Agbodeka

INTRODUCTION

The peoples of Western and Central Africa (Gambia, Sierra Leone, Gold Coast (Ghana), Togo, Nigeria and Cameroon) appear to have been living in the subregion for several thousands of years.[1] Equally ancient were their efforts to adjust scientifically and culturally to their environments. Following the Neolithic revolution marked by the Nok Culture, they acquired enough knowledge about crop and animal domestication and later about improved tool-making through the development of iron-working skills. They ensured a regular food supply, which in turn caused population increase, followed by production of surpluses, devoted to supporting people in other occupations, particularly the arts.[2] The latter, improvement in communication, was an important achievement consisting of the development of articulate spoken languages. The visual, verbal, and performing arts all developed, and so did religious and social organizations.

The development of agriculture, crafts and manufacturing went hand-in-hand with the rise of societies and the formation of states, whose apogee was attained in the fourteenth and fifteenth centuries with the great empires of the Western Sudan (Mali and Songhay). The decline of these empires left behind in Western and Central Africa a political landscape that was a mosaic of different structures: in the Sudanese part, Hausa city-states (Kano, Zaria and Katsina) and the small kingdoms of Bornu, Nupe and Igala; on the Atlantic seaboard, the migration of the Jaloff led to Senegalese statelets and the rise of the Kabu on the banks of the Gambia River; along the coast from Sierra Leone to Cameroon, village communities and centralized chiefdoms mushroomed (Temne, Gan, Ewe, Igbo and Duala); and in the hinterland, between forest and savannah, small kingdoms emerged (Akan and Yoruba), which were to reach their zenith in the seventeenth and eighteenth centuries (Asante and Uyo).

It was within this historical dynamic and on the basis of earlier advances that Western and Central Africa were to make technical, economic and scientific breakthroughs between the late eighteenth and the early twentieth centuries.

ECONOMIC DEVELOPMENT

Agriculture

It was from the Western Sudan that knowledge and practice of agriculture entered the rain forest and the Guinea Coast lands to the south. The beginning of agriculture in the Western Sudan dates to the second millennium before Christ. Sudan agriculture expanded by about the beginning of the Christian era, because of the introduction of iron-working and the use of iron hoes before the end of the pre-Christian era. This expansion is seen in the great variety of crops that came to be cultivated, beginning with cereals, millet and sorghum, and then in the southern portions close to the rain forest belt, beans and peas, okra, melon, rice, oranges, lemons, lime and yams.

The early penetration of the West African rain forest by a number of root crops strongly suggests northern savannah sources. The contact points between the savannah and the forest areas to the south were identified in the west, close to the headwaters of the Niger, in the centre and in the east of the West African savannah.[3] Favourable conditions for a subsequent vigorous pursuit of crop cultivation were widespread. They included fertile soils and a congenial climate. A number of staple crops such as rice in the Senegambia region,[4] and yams in several portions of the tropical rain forest were thus grown with comparative ease.

The most important input in the development of agriculture, however, seems to have been labour and entrepreneurship. Both in Ghana and Nigeria, entrepreneurship, the initiative in cocoa cultivation (the most important cash crop in the West African subregion for a long time), came from African farmers. The introduction of the crop into Ghana may be correctly dated to the early nineteenth century; but it was when Tetteh Quarshie, a Ghanaian blacksmith, nursed in Akwapem cocoa seeds he had brought from Fernando Po in 1879 that the cultivation of the crop picked up and within three decades transformed Ghana into the world's leading cocoa producer.[5] The zeal with which cocoa farmers in Akwapem and members of independent churches in Yorubaland pursued cocoa cultivation was only matched by their innovative exploits in the industry. First it was the Krobos, adjacent to Akwapem, who had evolved a system of 'migration by company' as a means of penetrating forest country for agricultural purposes in pre-cocoa days. Now, this system was adopted by Akwapem farmers to overcome the equatorial forest and put large tracts of land under cocoa. The Akwapem people added their own innovations to effect the rapid spread of cocoa cultivation by using both patrilineal and matrilineal systems of succession, whereby a man bought land not, as was traditional in Akwapem up till then, for either his sons or nephews, but for both.[6]

An equally important innovation on the part of Ghanaian cocoa farmers was the use of cocoyam and plantain as combined food plants for consumption and as the necessary shade plants for the young cocoa trees. In this way, the cash crop boomed but, contrary to expectation, did not cause food shortages in areas where it dominated.[7, 8]

Trade

It was agricultural and craft industrial products that created exchange conditions and started off local trade between one village and another or even within the same village. Local trade developed all over the entire West African subregion but was best seen among the Niger Delta communities.[9] Further developments brought about long-distance trade. The earliest form of long-distance trade was that from the traders, particularly those in the creeks of the Niger Delta and the Cameroons, who carried inland salt and dried fish for exchange with agricultural produce and, in places like Ghana and the Senegambia region, gold as well. The Igbo-Ukwu finds of Eastern Nigeria give evidence of wealth derived from trade with the coast organized by the Awka and Aro specialist traders of Nigeria. Another type of long-distance trade, equally ancient, was the exchange that must have taken place between Ife, Benin and Asante on one hand and the areas from which they separately acquired the brass and bronze used in their artistic works on the other.[10] Yet another interesting aspect of long-distance trade was the east–west trade along the Guinea coast, which must have largely originated from sixteenth-century Benin's exports of pepper, locally made cotton textiles, beads and ivory, westwards to Ghana.[11]

A completely different type of long-distance trade in Western and Central Africa was what is sometimes referred to as the northern traffic. This took place between the peoples of the forest belt and the Sudanic peoples who founded entrepots in a number of centres near the edge of the desert. From these entrepots, the Sudanic Muslim traders called Dyula travelled south for gold, which they supplied to the trans-Saharan caravans from North Africa. The most famous route was the Jenne-Begho one, terminating north of the Akan forest, rich in gold and kola nuts. From Begho the Dyula soon extended their activities southward and were already on the coast of Ghana when the Portuguese first arrived there in the fifteenth century.[12] One of the Sudanic entrepots, Kano, became a leading market of Central Sudan.[13] Among other activities, it received kola nuts from Asante and transmitted them northwards across the desert. The Dyula who initiated this trade on the northern traffic existed in different groups. Apart from those on the Jenne-Begho route, some other groups organized similar thrusts from the Sudan southwards through small intermediary states to the Atlantic coast at Senegambia, the Grain Coast and elsewhere. In each region, the local people consolidated their hold on the trade routes, nullifying Dyula control. This was how the last long-distance trade (i.e. with Europeans on the West African coast) evolved. This trade from the West African interior to the Guinea coast resulted in the rise of a large number of coastal trading towns, including Banjul, Freetown, Takoradi, Cape Coast, Accra, Lome, Lagos, Port Harcourt and Duala.

EARLY SCIENTIFIC AND CULTURAL DEVELOPMENT

Nok culture

Nok Culture in the Niger-Benue area of Northern Nigeria (900B–AD200) has been accredited with fine terra-cotta figurines. Nok's achievements in the area of scientific and cultural advance form part of the great Neolithic revolution in tropical Africa. To the east of Nok, Igbo-Ukwu culture also reached great heights in metallurgy. Bronze objects were found there in 1960[14] depicting Igbo craftsmen as belonging to the West African bronze-casting tradition. The accumulated body of knowledge behind cultural advances must have been acquired over a long period of time. The skills perfected by these developments led to the rise of numerous craft industries in the Niger-Benue belt and in Eastern Nigeria. By the first century AD, Nigerian tin workers were already busy on the Jos Plateau, and Igbo blacksmiths have since time immemorial been known to be adept metalworkers.

Ife and Benin

Ife, the dispersal centre of the Yorubas, is one of the best-known homes of antiquities in the world. Apart from bronze and terra-cotta heads, the finds here included terra-cotta stools, 'glazed' potsherd pavements, and glass-making crucibles for making 'glazed' pottery. There was in Ife the great glass-making industry, which spread blue glass *segi* beads across West Africa. First it was the terra-cotta heads, which were found in archaeological excavations, then later followed bronze heads in a style of naturalism adjudged to be works of art comparable to the best anywhere in the world. These Ife finds astonished the world so much that at first Europeans attributed them to visitors from outside Africa.[15] But a study of the Ife terra-cotta figures reveals stylistic affinities with those of the Nok Culture, and a close examination of the Benin bronzes, which originated from Ife, shows that they were being made before the Portuguese arrived. Briefly, therefore, Ife benefited from Nok, and Benin borrowed from Ife, developing its bronze heads to the peak of perfection. It was the acquisition of the high technical skills involved in the production of these world-famous brass-castings, which gradually transformed the small lineage-based communities into the powerful Oyo and Benin empires by the eleventh century or earlier.

In the case of Ife, its contributions to a Yoruba empire must have started with metal-using communities working to Nok's artistic styles in terra-cotta. There must have been at least two waves of invaders, one bringing the knowledge of bronze-casting and the other that of urbanization,[16] to turn the whole Yoruba territory into independent states which subsequently fell under the control of the most powerful military state, Oyo. By the sixteenth century Oyo was already an important empire in West Africa.[17] Benin also advanced from a small Edo kingdom, which was transformed by the same factors as those that enhanced Ife culture. In particular, the urbanization process engulfed the entire region of the Bight of Benin, giving rise to powerful kingdoms which owed their strength to a base of lineage relationships overlaid by northern savannah scientific and cultural influences.

Results of early development of science and culture in the traditional states

The early development of science and culture in the traditional states of Western and Central Africa generated processes and institutions, which preserve society and initiate progress.

The introduction of 'advanced' metallurgy from the northern savannah into the forest zone appears to have been quite early, predating the eleventh-century beginnings of Yoruba and Edo states. Increasing technical skills boosted development of indigenous crafts and industries. To mention but a few, the local craftsmen developed manufactures in iron, gold, silver, brass, leather, wood, cotton, matting and basketwork. Pottery was widespread and so were tools and implements for hunting, fishing and farming. The people acquired knowledge of herbs through prolonged experimentation or experience, and in a few cases through initiatives of geniuses among them. In this way they established ethno-medicine, and trained specialists in this discipline healed the sick with plant medicine often accompanied by religious camouflage.

Through continuous experimentation again, the peoples of Western and Central Africa developed life skills of different sorts. In particular they came to know the properties of various food items and over the ages prepared dishes using a combination of legumes, cereals, root crops, vegetables and fruits, as well as fish or meat, which supplied them with a balanced diet to enhance healthy growth. Over the years some communities established sound food and nutritional practices, so that they not only achieved preparations of delicious dishes but were eventually able to derive so many dishes from one item (for example, the twenty-eight dishes from cassava enjoyed by the Ewes of south-eastern Ghana).

Apart from technical matters, considerable achievements have been registered in the arts. The spoken language provided the key to the development of the arts. The languages presently spoken in the forest and coastal zones appear to have been spoken originally in the savannah to the north. It is most probable that it was the original speakers who entered the forest zone. Considerable changes have since taken place, with different dialects developing from the original language. Each region or community has developed its dialect or language, some to the point of attaining fine linguistic skills. For example, there are communities in Ghana and Nigeria whose languages have developed to the point of providing names for children born in every type of situation.[18]

Verbal arts have also been developed to fine artistic levels in several communities. Local languages have been enriched with proverbs, anecdotes and poetry. The performing arts in the form of music (singing, drumming and dancing) have been developed to induce great aesthetic pleasure. Visual arts and architecture have also received great attention, the latter both in beauty and comfort.[19]

African customary laws and legal processes have from long experience been so carefully framed and applied that traditional societies enjoyed long periods of peace and stability. Traditional religion has many facets, one of which is to do the work of a police service in preserving the peace.[20] Traditional education was development-oriented. It took the form of the child simply watching and helping his or her parents to learn important lessons of life. A special form of education has often been added whereby the youth of the same age group have been drafted into training camps under specialist tutors. In some cases the programme includes military training, so that those trained may be ready to defend their homeland. Initiation ceremonies conclude these training sessions. Even more important, traditional education taught the child the values of society, skills for various industries and an attitude to work and other family or clan issues. The system of apprenticeship inculcated not only skills but also the right attitude to work. Religion combined with education to help in this respect, and the seriousness with which both the master craftsman and the apprentice (e.g. black-gold and silver smithing) approached their work has not been equalled by the modern industrial worker.

Thus we can conclude that there were some positive aspects of early culture. The most important aspect was the fact that the entire region seemed to have enjoyed complete peace, and that there were no wars then. Several pieces of evidence point to this. Ancient rock paintings from the Negro periods at Tassili, in the Central Sahara, depicted all major activities, but there were no pictures of wars or violence of any kind.[21] Much much later, in 1794, an intelligent Mandingo ruler gave the impression that normally the interior states did not engage in wars. 'She said there had been no wars in the interior country for some time, and that wars do not happen, when slaves are not wanted'.[22] There is here some indication that wars among the African states, like so many other evils, were later developments. Neither were the early traditional rulers despots as a rule. In nearly all African kingdoms, the king ruled with the advice and consent of a council of elders or ministers who could remove him at their pleasure. In Yorubaland the Basorun, the prime minister could cause a tyrannical Alafin (king) to commit suicide. In Asante it was the 'queen mother' who was the senior political officer. She nominated a new king for the consideration of both a council of elders and an assembly of 'young men'.[23] The practice of democracy is not new in African society.

However, there were serious negative aspects to the original African culture. African achievements so far discussed took place without literacy. Non-literate societies all over the world are extremely superstitious and ignorant. Thus as soon as some new development interrupted their simple origins, their mode of thinking and behaviour became warped and distorted. They believed in witchcraft, incantations and charms. This led them to acts of cruelty and injustice,[24] the inhumanity of which did not occur to them. Thus they could, for instance, burn people at the stake for alleged witchcraft, like Joan of Arc in fifteenth-century France, without a prick of conscience. This was an extremely dangerous situation, particularly in Africa, when foreign influence from the north and the south swamped the simple animist lineage origins. It was this development which undermined much of the peaceful, moral and democratic nature of early African communities. Details of this phenomenon and its results will be discussed in the next section.

ISLAMIC AND EUROPEAN SCIENTIFIC AND CULTURAL IMPACT

Islamic impact

The headwaters of the Upper Niger have long been regarded as the source of West African cultural growth.

Increasingly it has been the source of religious revolutions in the savannah territories; and from the fourteenth century began the great Malinke dispersion from the decaying metropolitan regions of the Upper Niger. This constituted a series of movements that took the Malinke east into the Hausa country in present-day Northern Nigeria, west towards the Senegambia and south into the hinterland of the Guinea forest.[25]

Various other Islamic outbursts sent their advocates and commercial agents along the well-known trade routes in all directions. In the Futa Jalon area the Fulani, largely Muslims, came with their religion to dominate the animist agriculturists and landowners. This situation gave rise to occasional fierce revolts by the agriculturist hosts against their Fulani ruling incomers. Another aspect of the Islamic impact on local populations, particularly in the hinterland of Sierra Leone and the Grain Coast, was the increase in ignorance and superstition as the pagan communities looked up to the itinerant Malam for 'medicine' charms and amulets to protect them against evil spirits. Morality was undermined and the people's outlook on life became increasingly distorted.

European impact

Meanwhile, while Europeans came to the African coasts in the fifteenth century, on their way eastwards, they became preoccupied with the East. Asia was to become a source for manufactures and exotic trade goods. To the west, Europeans were attracted to the potential of the Americas as production centres of minerals and commercial crops. This left Africa as the source of labour for mining and plantation work in the New World.[26] The Atlantic slave trade became the lot of Africa and the era under study led the trade.

The coming of Europeans to Africa was one of the results of technological development in transport and communications. Europe's scientific and cultural development conquered the hazards of sea voyages and provided weapons of protection and aggression, and these were important factors in the European penetration of West Africa. But they did not solve all the problems of penetration. The Europeans who came for slaves and even later for palm oil had to be tough and rough to endure the hardships of these early contacts, marked by African opposition, and coastal plagues and fevers often fatal to visiting Europeans. So during the slave trade period, most of the European slave traders whom Africans had to deal with were of 'the most infamous and unprincipled description'.

Results of foreign impact on African peoples

Thus, these two influences on the African – the science and culture of Islam and of the West – did not augur well for a smooth development of the region. They led to a number of situations which developed into the inhuman Atlantic slave trade. Domestic slaves had existed in Africa before foreign influence, but they constituted labour reserves and of course could not be traded outside the region. Several African authorities (e.g. in areas as far apart as the Akan states in Ghana and Takkeda in the copper mines of the Central Sahara) developed useful labour policies whereby the so-called 'slaves' (actually serfs) were settled for agricultural or mining purposes. This might involve the movement of labour from one point to another, but could not be described as a slave trade. But now with the internal weaknesses of the African animist system, described above, coupled with unsavoury foreign intrusion, African society deteriorated in many ways.

Probably the most important event was the collapse of law and order and the lack of strong government. An ugly situation developed whereby no one, when injured, sought redress at the chief's court as before. Instead, injured families, for instance in the Upper Guinea hinterland, seized one another for slaves. Chiefs often cooked up charges of adultery and witchcraft and sold their innocent subjects, sometimes entire families, to the white slave dealers.[27] Quite often the slave traders were mulattoes, like Cleveland who, by the late eighteenth century, was operating in the hinterland of Sierra Leone, breaking up communities to catch slaves. Kidnapping was a common occurrence in the Mandingo and Sufee countries. Both Africans and mulatto slave dealers indulged in it.[28] Since Africans, like other developing races, were not fully employed, they were apt to relieve listlessness by intoxication, when they could procure the means. So the European slave traders turned the African's rude propensities for European liquor, guns and gunpowder to their own immediate profit. They supplied alcoholic liquor to the chiefs, who in their drunken moments took decisions under European pressure harmful to their people. The liquor, guns and ammunition supplied by the white traders fuelled slave wars and raids among the communities, as so often happened in Upper Guinea and the Sierra Leone hinterland. In Fanteland in Ghan, European companies – English, Dutch, Swedes, Germans and Danes – were at loggerheads with each other over trade and drew the local population into these conflicts. The captives from these armed conflicts were naturally sold into slavery.[29] In the same area, *panyarring* was common, whereby Europeans attacked and captured people for sale if an African trader hailing from their town failed to settle his debts for goods the Europeans had advanced him. In the Sierra Leone hinterland, Europeans credited African factors with goods for the interior. If they failed to return on time with the agreed number of slaves, the Europeans seized their families instead.[30] Thus from the sixteenth to the nineteenth centuries the slave trade engulfed Western and Central Africa, causing it to lose large numbers of its able-bodied men and women. From Upper Guinea, the intensity of the trade shifted eastward with the centuries, through the Senegambia and Sierra Leone coasts, to the Slave Coast, to the Niger Territories and beyond.

The period of informal empires

The slave trade was, however, neither the first nor the only trade in Afro-European relations. Gold, ivory, gum and a number of tropical products preceded slaves and continued as export trade goods throughout the centuries. In the nineteenth century, with an increasing international campaign against the slave trade, emphasis was shifting to 'legitimate' trade. What Europeans needed then was informal empires to control such trading enclaves that they had established. They had three options: (a) they could use the old European establishments in places like Banjul, Freetown, Accra, Lome, Lagos, and Duala; (b) they could seek protection for their inland trade under protective African kingdoms; (c) they could back their trade in the riverine areas with the gunboat and the services of the consul in the Bights.

Essentially it was these three methods that the Europeans adopted or tried to adopt that constituted what is referred to as the period of informal empire. The protection they needed was physical, i.e. to recover debts and settle financial disputes with the African traders. Some of the old trading settlements like Freetown could provide these. In the Niger Delta, however, it was the warship in the trading rivers which could enforce the decisions of the Afro-European 'courts of equity' presided over by a British consul.[31] The increasing influence of British consuls over Ijo affairs from the 1850s also formed part of the informal British empire to control British trade.[32] In Southern Ghana, too, the period of informal empire was marked by the rise of European judicial institutions, initiated unofficially by Maclean up to 1843.[33]

The last method, that of seeking protective kingdoms in the interior to guard their trade, was conceived because of reports of large powerful inland kingdoms which could serve this purpose. However, British attempts to penetrate through the forest to the savannah, say to the Sokoto Caliphate, did not bring the desired results.

During this period, when the European traders were seeking trade protection, they expressed no interest in imperial expansion, particularly since that would have implied paying higher taxes for that protection.[34] Indeed, this was why they preferred the method of getting African umbrella kingdoms to provide that protection to their traders in the interior.

During this period of informal empire, Europeans had tried establishing agricultural colonies and fortified trading posts. Had these plans worked, Europeans would have been launched to the threshold of colonialism and imperialism by the middle of the nineteenth century.[35] But the plantation colonies failed, as seen in Sierra Leone and Lokoja at the Niger-Benue confluence. The fortified trading posts, which were to usher in protectorates, did not materialize either, postponing colonialism until the 1890s. It was because, since the fifteenth century, Southern Ghana had fortified trading posts based on forts and castles that its 1874 Protectorate was declared, ahead of time.

In the first three quarters of the nineteenth century, many Europeans in the forefront of African affairs had the spirit of Afro-Europeans, that is, they were sympathetic to African aspirations. However, around the 1880s, changes of personnel brought in Europeans fresh from Europe dedicated to imperial expansion. From this point onwards all that was needed to take over political control of the African states was technological prowess, and that Europe already had. In the areas of communications, print, telegraph, weapons, etc., Europe's achievements made their physical conquest of African states an easy affair. So it was that between 1884 and 1914 Europeans, in this case Britain and Germany, carried out direct annexations of African territories and established protectorates. Britain consolidated its control over the Gambia, Sierra Leone, Ghana and Nigeria. Similarly, Germany occupied Togoland and the Cameroons.

INDIGENOUS CULTURAL RESPONSES

Towards abolition of the slave trade

We have seen that the slave trade was a dark period in world history. But even while it was going on, both sides in the trade now and again showed a gleam of light through the darkness. Several African kingdoms, notably Asante, Dahomey and Benin, have banned or at least restricted the trade at one time or the other. In Europe, too, Christian upbringing, coupled with Western education, inculcated kindness in individuals and promoted humanitarianism and philanthropy in the United Kingdom, Holland, Denmark, Germany and elsewhere. As early as the eighteenth century individual Europeans showed kindness to African boys such as Jacobus Captein from Ghana, and got those who were enslaved, first freed, and then educated at their own or a European trading company's expense.[36] Soon, such activities blossomed into full-scale humanitarianism and plans were made to reverse Africa's role as a labour reserve for American plantations, promoting local crop cultivation so as to develop and 'civilize' the people. This involved abolition of the slave trade and, before the eighteenth century closed, the Dutch slave trade had come to an end in 1795; Denmark abolished hers in 1802 and the United Kingdom in 1807.[37] It also meant freeing and settling those already enslaved on agricultural projects in Africa. The strongest advocate for this was Granville Sharp in the British Parliament.[38]

The rise of Western-educated Africans and Afro-Europeans

The first spectacular result of the foregoing humanitarian efforts was the establishment in 1787 of the Sierra Leone Company based in Freetown. It was to pursue the various aspects of the humanitarian programme preventing slave exports in West African waters,[39] settling the liberated Africans in Sierra Leone, Christianizing and educating them and advising them, together with the local chiefs, on improved methods of plantation cropping so as to promote legitimate trade. The company hoped that in this way it would 'lay some foundation for the future happiness of a continent, which has hitherto derived nothing but misery from its intercourse with Great Britain'.[40] The educational programme succeeded and soon Western-educated Africans from Freetown's Fourah Bay College spread to all parts of the West African subregion.[41]

In Ghana, the earliest educated Africans included those trained by European trading companies, such as Philip Quaque, who became the Anglican chaplain of Cape Coast Castle; and Jacobus Eliza Johannes Capite in 1717–47, educated in Holland to man the Elmina Castle chaplaincy for the Dutch West India Company.[42]

From the early part of the nineteenth century several missionary societies, including those of the Anglican church, the Methodist, Basel and North German missions, together with several Catholic organizations, established stations and schools all over Ghana, winning converts and training the youth in Western educational programmes. In Togoland, Nigeria and the Cameroons, too, both Catholic and Protestant missions repeated similar achievements.

Before the close of the nineteenth century, educated Africans could be seen in nearly all the commercial towns along the West African coast.

The leading Western-educated Africans permeated such groups as the Creoles in Sierra Leone, the Saro (receptive returnees to Yorubaland) in Nigeria as well as the diaspora. There were great scholars among them, like Dr J. Africanus Horton of the British Army Medical Service, who contributed research reports to British medical journals. Famous Creoles included Samuel Lewis and Edward W. Blyden. It was again educated Africans such as Mensah Sarbah and J. E. Casely-Hayford, both learned members of the Ghana Bar, that led the Aboriginesl Rights Protection Society in Ghana. There was Samuel Ajayi Crowther of the Niger territories in Nigeria who became the first African bishop of the Anglican church. We have in addition to the new African elite peoples of mixed blood – the Afro-Europeans – some of whom identified themselves with the rising elite of full-blooded Africans. An abortive alliance also took place between the Westernized Africans and the traditional Africans and authorities, including those in the interior.[43]

Cultural responses during the period of informal empire: adaptation

During the period of informal empire (1840–80) European scientific and cultural impact came, among other things, as a challenge to the Westernized Africans to develop their countries in cooperation with Europeans, using the latter's superior scientific and cultural methods. This policy of adaptation would involve them, because of their 'fitness for the climate',[44] as the main agents of humanitarian projects, not excluding even the missionary educational and training programmes supporting the agricultural, industrial and commercial schemes. This programme, dubbed 'The Bible and the Plough', was the main burden of Fowell Buxton's book *The African Slave Trade and its Remedy*. Interpretations of this theory sometimes even included complete self-determination for the Africans once they reached the stage of running their own affairs efficiently.[45] In the Fanti Confederacy (1868–73), the Fanti felt they had reached the stage to run their own affairs but since partnership with Europeans was permitted, they called upon the British administration in Cape Coast for financial support for their development programmes. This was refused and the movement collapsed. The Church Missionary Society's apparent encouragement of Bishop Crowther to work towards self-supporting and self-propagating churches on the Niger also fits in with the policy of adaptation by the educated Africans.[46]

Cultural responses and resistance to imperialism and colonialism

From the 1880s, as we have seen, the new European personnel of the Anglo-African Service, recruited largely from Oxford and Cambridge, were young, idealistic and ready to assume responsibility in foreign lands. They downgraded African culture, declaring that Europeans must not abandon their efforts to civilize Africa but must expect to 'rule the dark continent' for a long time. They also discouraged the establishment of self-supporting churches. Soon the scramble and partition occurred, to give meaning to their theories.

In the face of this provocation, the educated elite had therefore no choice but to change their approach to African development. The days of cooperation were over, and in Ghana they became very critical of British administration, particularly over taxes and racial policies. Self-determination became their goal. To achieve this they had to preserve and develop African institutions and culture and base national development on these rather than on European culture. They claimed the right to be governed directly by the kings and chiefs under these institutions.[47] Through the Aborigines Rights Protection Society, an alliance between the educated elite and the traditional authorities was effected and the Society protested against government attempts to control concessions in land through Governor William Maxwell's Land Bill of 1894. As late as 1901 they objected to Governor Nathan's removal of the chief of Awudua from the stool for 'defiance' as unwarranted government interference in local politics.[48] It was with cultural nationalism that Ghana greeted colonialism.

Unlike Ghana, where literary criticism and political ideas dominated the new response to colonialism, Nigeria's response was more down-to-earth and practically-oriented. Nigerians argued that, if European-led development was to cost them their culture, then they would take over their own development to preserve that culture. This meant that they should pursue the 'Bible and the Plough' idea in newly-established ventures like the Agbowa Industrial Mission (1895–1908) under Dr Mojola Agbedi, and J. K. Coker's Agege plantations, combining gospel propagation with cocoa cultivation in Yorubaland in the early years of the twentieth century. The establishment of independent African churches to support the industrial programmes was necessary as much in fulfilment of the time-honoured 'Bible and Plough' idea as in protest against the established missions' betrayal of the original agreed idea of self-supporting churches.

An event which emphasized the Nigerians' determination to preserve their culture in all its aspects was the establishment of the Egba United Board of Management and the Egba United Government in Abeokuta to carry out a social and political revolution without destroying the Nigerian (Egba) national character. Thus, both in socio-economic and political development Nigeria exhibited cultural nationalism.

New cultural trends

Throughout the nineteenth century the peoples of Western and Central Africa had their developmental goals gradually changed in some respects as a result of foreign impact. The new goals necessitated the adoption of new techniques. Transport and communications began to improve as the construction of roads, railways, telegraph and post offices got under way. The cultivation of new crops enriched agriculture.

The coming of Christian missions resulted in conversions from the old pagan practices to Christianity, even if in the nineteenth century the new Christians formed, as it were, a drop in the ocean of animist society. Traditional educational systems also began to be replaced by formal schooling in Western-type institutions. Health care delivery based on scientific methods without the invocation of supernatural powers came to be increasingly practised. In the domain of the arts, the influence of new musical forms, i.e. church music or school songs, initiated developments towards the creation of the popular 'high-life' style of music that the region is now noted for.[49] Verbal arts increased as new modes of performance, including oral literature and drama, came to enrich the performing arts. Visual arts, too, began to change with the coming of drawing and painting as well as clay-modelling in schools. Various crafts also began to be encouraged, as part of the school curriculum. By the close of our period in 1914, these changes had only just begun. But, even so, the efforts of the subregion's people, first to preserve their culture, and second to acquire the various techniques to sustain that culture, already showed them to be a vigorous and progressive people.

NOTES

1 C. Wrigley, 1962. 'Linguistic Clues to African History'. *Journal of African History*, London, Vol. 3, No. 2, pp. 269–72.

2 O. Davies, 1960. 'The Neolithic Revolution in Tropical Africa'. *Transactions of the Historical Society of Ghana*, Legon, Vol. 4, Part II, pp. 14–20.

3 W. B. Morgan, 1962. 'The Forest and Agriculture in West Africa'. *JAH*, London, Vol. 3, No. 2, pp. 235–39.

4 H. G. Baker, 1962. *op. cit.*

5 P. Curtin *et al.*, 1978. *op. cit.*, p. 508.

6 P. Hill, 1959. 'The History of the Migration of Ghana Cocoa Farmers'. *THSG*, Legon, Vol. 4, Part I, pp. 14–28.

7 W. B. Morgan, 1962. *op. cit.*

8 C. B. Wadstrom, 1794. *An Essay on Civilization: Particularly applied to the Western Coast of Africa with some Free Thoughts on Cultivation and Commerce*. London, David and Charles Reprints, p. 4.

9 P. Curtin *et al.*, 1978. *op. cit.*, p. 246.

10 J. D. Fage, 1978. *A History of Africa*. London, Hutchinson University Library, p. 108.

11 J. D. Fage, 1962. 'Some remarks on beads and trade in Lower Guinea in the Sixteenth and Seventeenth Centuries'. *JAH*, London, Vol. 3, No. 2, pp. 343–7.

12 I. Wilks, 1962. 'A Medieval Trade-Route from the Niger to the Gulf of Guinea'. *JAH*, London, Vol. 3, No. 2, pp. 337–41.

13 R. W. July, 1980. *op. cit.*, p. 73.

14 C. T. Shaw, 1960. 'Bronzes from Eastern Nigeria, Igbo-Ukwu Excavations'. *Journal of the Historical Society of Nigeria*, Ibadan, Vol. 2, No. 1, pp. 162–5.

15 F. Willet, 1960. 'Ife and its Archaeology'. *JAH*, London, Vol. 1, No. 2, pp. 231–48.

16 J. D. Fage, 1978. *op. cit.*, pp. 106–7.

17 I. A. Akinjogbin, 1966. 'The Oyo Empire in the Eighteenth Century: A Reassessment'. *JHSN*, Ibadan, Vol. 3, No. 3, pp. 449–60.

18 This means that from somebody's name, you can tell not just the sex and social standing, but lineage or clan, time and place of birth, and information about the family.

19 Dwelling houses in the hot savannah areas were so designed to cool naturally.

20 In South Eastern Ghana, ablution to the lineage gods to punish wrong-doers had the effect of preventing the victim from taking the law into his own hands and thus keeping the peace without a police force.

21 R. G. Armstrong, 1960. 'The development of kingdoms in Negro Africa'. *JHSN*, Ibadan, Vol. 2, No. 1, pp. 27–39.

22 C. B. Wadstrom, 1794. *op. cit.*, p. 77.

23 R. G. Armstrong, 1960. *op. cit.*

24 C. B. Wadstrom, 1794. *op. cit.*, p. 117.

25 I. Wilks, 1963. 'The Growth of Islamic Learning in Ghana'. *JHSN*, Ibadan, Vol. 2, No. 4, pp. 409–17.

26 C. B. Wadstrom, 1794. *op. cit.*, pp. 5–7; P. Curtin *et al.*, 1978, *op. cit.*, pp. 215–46.

27 C. C. Ifemesia, 1962. 'The "Civilizing" Mission of 1841: Aspects of an episode in Anglo-Nigeria Relations'. *JHSN*, Ibadan, Vol. 2, No. 3, pp. 291–310.

28 *Ibid.*, pp. 15, 77–82.

29 A. K. Datta and R. Porter, 1971. 'The Asafo System in Historical Perspective. An Inquiry into the Origin and Development of a Ghanaian Institution'. *JAH*, London, Vol. 12, No. 2, pp. 279–97.

30 C. B. Wadstrom, 1794. *op. cit.*, pp. 14, 78–93.

31 C. B. Wadstrom, 1794. *op. cit.*, pp. 14, 85–93.

32 C. B. Wadstrom, 1794. *op. cit.*, p. 382.

33 *Ibid.*

34 J. D. Hargreaves, 1960. *op. cit.*

35 C. B. Wadstrom, 1794. *op. cit.*, pp. 373.

36 F. L. Bartels, 1959. 'Jacobus Eliza Johannes Captein, 1717–1774'. *THSG*, Legon, Vol. 4, Part I, pp. 3–13; Lochner, N. 1958. 'Anton Wilhelm Amo: A Ghana Scholar in Eighteenth Century Germany', *THSG*, Achimota, Vol. 3, Part III, pp. 169–79.

37 C. B. Wadstrom, 1794. *op. cit.*, p. 175; Fyfe, Christopher, 1960, 'Peter Nicholis-Old Calabar and Freetown'. *JHSN*, Ibadan, Vol. 2, No. 1, pp. 105–14.

38 C. B. Wadstrom, 1794, *op. cit.*, pp. 3–4.

39 C. Fyfe, 1960. *op. cit.*

40 C. B. Wadstrom, 1794. *op. cit.*, p. 128.

41 *Ibid.*, p. 373.

42 F. L. Bartels, 1959. *op. cit.*

43 R. W. July, 1980. *op. cit.*, p. 420.

44 J. B. Webster. 1963. 'The Bible and the Plough'. *JHSN*, Ibadan, Vol. 2, No. 4, pp. 418–34.

45 S. S. Berry. 1963. 'Christianity and the rise of cocoa-growing in Ibadan and Ondo'. *JHSN*, Ibadan, Vol. 4, No. 3, pp. 439–51.

46 E. A. Ayandele, 1967. 'Background to the "duel" between Crowther and Goldie on the Lower Niger 1857–85'. *JHSN*, Ibadan, Vol. 4, No. 1, pp. 45–63; Ajayi, J. F. A., 1959. 'Henry Venn and the Policy of Development'. *JHSN*, Ibadan, Vol. 1, No. 4, pp. 331–42.

47 K. A. B. Jones-Quartey, 1959. 'Anglo-African Journals and Journalists in the nineteenth and early twentieth centuries'. *THSG*, Legon, Vol. 4, Part I, pp. 47–55.

48 A. P. Haydon, 1970, 'The good public servant of the state – Sir Mathew Nathan as Governor of the Gold Coast 1900–1904', *THSG*, Legon, Vol. 11, pp. 104–21.

49 I. D. Riverson, 1955, 'The Growth of Music in the Gold Coast'. *Transactions of the Gold Coast and Togoland Historical Society*, Achimota, Vol. 1, Part IV, pp. 121–32.

15.3

COUNTRIES OF CENTRAL AND EASTERN AFRICA
COLONIZED BY BELGIUM AND GERMANY

Emile Mworoha

This study is focused mainly on the geopolitical area now occupied by the states of Burundi, Rwanda, Tanzania and Zaire. This is a region which two European powers – Belgium and Germany – divided between themselves in the years following the 1885 Berlin Conference. The purpose of the study is to see how, in the course of the nineteenth century, i.e. before and then during the first decades of the colonial invasion, this region had already been integrated into the world trading system and to examine the social and cultural repercussions of this situation. We shall begin by inquiring into the nature of the political societies which developed in this immense area lying between the Indian and Atlantic oceans, part equatorial forest and part open savannah, and then consider the impact of capitalist modes of thought on these societies and the cultural changes that were already taking place.

CHANGES IN THE POLITICAL ENVIRONMENT

The impact of new trading ventures

The entire region was affected by the long-distance trade in slaves, ivory and firearms, which had already penetrated to the interior of Africa in the first half of the nineteenth century. Except for the east coast and the mouth of the Congo River, which had been involved in international trade since at least the sixteenth century, these lands were the least explored of Africa. From the political point of view, three major developments may be noted: the emergence of Zanzibar as a hub of world trade; the resistance and reshaping of formerly centralized states, particularly the kingdoms in the Great Lakes region and in the savannah and, last, the emergence of new power bases fostered by trade.

At the beginning of the nineteenth century, the Swahili coast was already politically advanced and had adopted an urban style of life. City-states, the most important of which were Kilwa, Saadani, Pangani and Tanga, had been set up there in the thirteenth century and perhaps even earlier.[1] The former influence of Kilwa, already weakened by the Portuguese in the sixteenth and seventeenth centuries, gave way to that of the Arabs when the Sultan of Oman decided in 1840 to make Zanzibar his capital and to embark on a policy of conquest along the coast and even inland to further a mercantile economy based on clove plantations and the ivory trade. This sultanate would gradually acquire a strategic hold over the entire coast and become a dominant power in East Africa. Although mainly concerned with trade, it would have an important influence on the political structures of the region. Zanzibar was recognized by the European powers, who set up consulates in the first half of the nineteenth century, with the Sultan Seyyid Said signing agreements with the United States of America (1837), Great Britain (1839), France (1844) and later with the German Hanseatic cities.[2] Zanzibar became a major trade centre, exporting not only slaves and ivory but also copal and cloves in exchange for sugar, pearls, firearms, copper-ware and cotton goods from America. This commerce was financed by Indian bankers, and caravans penetrated the hinterland as far as the Great Lakes region and even west of Lake Tanganyika as early as the 1830s. A network of trading stations was established along the Tabora-Ujiji axis, bringing urban civilization up from the east coast.

Resistance and adaptation of the former centres of authority

As Central and Eastern Africa was being buffeted by outside influences introduced by traders, and the European powers were beginning to carve the region up, a variety of political regimes were operating in the area. There were states with centralized power structures, particularly in the Great Lakes region where, in Burundi for example, the *bami* (kings) Ntare Rugamba (1800–50) and Mwezi Gisabo (1850–1908) built up a well-established state that successfully defended itself against the slave raids from Zanzibar. This was also true for the Kingdom of Rwanda, which became a powerful militarized state during the reigns of its kings Mutara Rwogera (1830–60) and Kigeri Rwabugiri (1860–95). The Haya states were also based on organized political systems.[3] These kingdoms did not change as radically as those in the Uganda region, where the rulers of Buganda and Bunyoro in particular controlled trading and firearms and reorganized their power on much more centralized lines.

The Lunda and Luba empires in the Congolese savannah reinforced their political authority while participating in the slave trade. The power of the state was consolidated under the emperor (*mwata yav*) Nawej, who made use of both traditional weapons and firearms obtained from Angola. An increasing number of caravans halted in the capital (*musumba*) of the Lunda during the reign of Muteba (1857–73). In the lands of the Luba, the military power wielded by the emperor (*mulopwe*), held in great awe during the first half of the nineteenth century, began to crumble under economic pressure, particularly during the reign of Kasongo Kalombo (1870–80). In the northern part of the Congo, two states – the well-organized, highly militarized, 'urbanized' state of the Mangbetu and that of the Zandé, a kind of confederation of neighbouring populations headed by a group of overlords (*avungara*) – mounted effective opposition against the raids into these regions conducted by slave traders from Sudan.

The forest peoples generally had chiefs and were consequently much more vulnerable to better organized and better armed adventurers, and their situation gradually became more and more precarious towards the end of the century.

Adventurers become kings

The interest in commerce stimulated by the industrial expansion of Europe reached this region, where it took the form essentially of trade in ivory and slaves, and it would, in the second half of the nineteenth century, be the cause of major political upheavals. Both political and cultural life in Central and Eastern Africa was marked by the emergence of new states created by adventurers who proclaimed themselves king, established courts and imposed their authority on various peoples, foreshadowing the reshaping of boundaries that led in the colonial period to the states we know today. Examples of this political phenomenon include Mirambo, Nyungu ya Mawe, Msiri and Tippu Tib.

The empire of Mirambo (1860–84)

Originally chief of a small territory in the west of Tanzania, Mirambo is said to have been captured and trained by Nguni warriors (part of the Zulu movement) at the time of their invasion of East Africa. In the 1860s, with a group of professional warriors wielding firearms (*ruga-ruga*), he conquered a number of neighbouring princedoms, and thus succeeded in federating the Banyamwezi, a population specializing since the beginning of the century in the ivory trade and the organization of caravans to the coast. Between 1870 and 1884, he carved out a veritable empire for himself. It was a stroke of political genius to maintain the defeated chiefs in their positions in return for payment of tribute.[4] A skilful organizer who made use of firearms, Mirambo gained control of the Tabora-Ujiji trade route, forcing Arab traders to pay tolls to him. But this empire would not survive its founder. The European conquerors would soon break up all these new political entities.

The Kimbu state of Nyungu ya Mawe (1870–84)

Another adventurer and contemporary of Mirambo, Nyungu ya Mawe, in 1870 subjugated the Kimbu, a group close to the Banyamwezi, and gained control over the Tabora-Ufipa route towards the southern end of Lake Tanganyika. Unlike Mirambo, Nyungu ya Mawe appointed his own administrators (*watwale*), each of whom was put in charge of several former chiefdoms. One of the main jobs of these *watwale* was to collect ivory. The Kimbu state built up by Nyungu ya Mawe continued to function after his death in 1884.

The Garanganze state of Msiri

Another trader who led an extraordinary life came from the east as far as the Congo basin. Msiri, whose real name was Ngalengwa, was a Sumbwa chief (north of Nyamwezi country) brought to Katanga by the accidents of trading, where he founded a new state, Garanganze. His knowledge of medicine brought him fame at the court of the king of Kazembe (of the Lunda cultures) where his vaccine against smallpox created a sensation and led the local ruler to offer him a daughter in marriage and a large number of copper ingots. After becoming a powerful Kazembe dignitary, with his guns and battle-hardened followers (the Bayeke) who specialized in hunting elephants, Msiri capitalized on his influence in Katanga and finally proclaimed himself king at Bunkeya, the capital of Garanganze. He invented a court etiquette with its own royal ceremonies and bestowed on himself the title of *mwami*. His capital became a major centre for the slave trade with links to the east coast, thronged by Swahili and Arab traders. But King Msiri, who stood in the way of King Leopold's empire, was shot in 1891 by the Belgian captain Bodson.

The empire of Tippu Tib

Tippu Tib was an Arab half-caste from a family of traders established in East Africa. He carved out for himself a veritable empire in the Manyema and Upper Zaire regions, organized by a dual network of *watwale* (chiefs), mainly responsible for the collection of ivory, and *akida* (district chiefs), who included traditional chiefs and Arab or Swahili agents. He created three economic centres, Nyangwe, Kasongo and Kisangani. Tippu Tib was so powerful that King Leopold II secured his support by appointing him governor of the Stanley Falls region,[5] despite his claim to be against the slave traders. Leopold did not drop him until after the anti-slavery conference in Brussels in 1890. Tippu Tib, who realized that his era was drawing to a close, eventually returned to his native Zanzibar to live quietly on the income from capital amassed in the heart of Africa.

Altogether, the nineteenth century was a period of major political changes in Central and Eastern Africa. Though the political and military organization of certain traditional states allowed them to resist the firepower of the foreigners for a while, other peoples suffered terrible reversals that left their societies in turmoil. The period just before the imperialist rush for Africa was thus a time of instability that enabled enterprising individuals to fulfil their ambitions.

IMPACT OF THE CAPITALIST MENTALITY ON LOCAL SOCIETIES: THE OPENING UP AND EXPLOITATION OF AFRICA

The development of international capitalism and the competition it would stimulate among European nations accounts for the all-conquering imperialism illustrated by the Berlin Conference of 1885. That conference decided the fate of Africa and set in motion the period of colonial conquests. The capitalist system, whose first law is the law of profit, had immediate repercussions of the most brutal kind. In many cases, however, the Africans took up arms to defend their independence and resist exploitation. The example of the Congo Free State, the personal property of the Belgian king, Leopold II, provides a most revealing illustration of this kind of situation.

Organized pillage and exploitation of local populations

Between 1876 and 1885, Leopold II built up for himself a colonial empire (the future Belgian Congo), managed to obtain approval for it in the wings of the Berlin Conference and organized a very efficient system of exploitation. This organized pillage consisted of declaring freedom of trade throughout the Congo and at the same time encouraging the establishment of state monopolies for ivory and rubber that operated within the system of crown ownership created in 1891 and 1892. The state declared itself to be the owner of all 'vacant' land, which became 'crown property'. All land that was not farmed or occupied by the indigenous populations was thus regarded as crown property. A system of exploitation based on forced labour was introduced, under which each native was obliged to deliver a fixed quantity of rubber every fortnight. At this time, the standing army was employed in furthering the achievement of this objective. The representatives of Leopold's Congo Free State resorted to every possible means of coercion – regular punitive expeditions, the taking of hostages, the surveillance of villages by guards, floggings, and so on.

For its exploitation of ivory and rubber, Leopold's state also awarded immense concessions to Belgian companies in return for half their profits. Jean Stengers mentions two companies that amassed colossal profits in the Congo Free State. 'Abir and Anversoise made unprecedented profits but their concessions were like hells on earth. The only law that the agents of these two companies recognized was the law of profit'.[6] In 1900, the Belgian sovereign could congratulate himself on the success of his undertaking, since the profits made were adding to Belgium's wealth and making possible, in particular, the construction of major monuments and of important public infrastructures.[7]

In German East Africa, the indigenous populations were used mainly to provide compulsory labour for the cultivation of cash crops (coffee, cotton, sisal, etc.) but also as porters and plantation workers for European owners. The colonial troops (*askari*) established by Hermann Wissmann, a former agent of Leopold II appointed governor of German East Africa in 1891, included Sudanese from Khartoum, Zulus, Nyamwezi who had once worked as porters or traders, and people from Manyema who had served under Tippu Tib. In 1913, under the Pax Germanica, there were 2,500 of them – officered by 260 Germans – for the whole of East Africa.[8] But how would African societies react to this foreign annexation of their territory and the pillage of their assets?

Popular reactions and mobilization of local resources

In both the Congo Free State and the German colonies, the local peoples offered determined resistance to imperialism. As far as Leopold's empire is concerned, it should be remembered that even in countries like Britain, which were pursuing their own colonization policies, public figures denounced the atrocities of the system of exploitation employed in the Congo Free State.[9]

But the real resistance and opposition to colonization came from the African societies themselves, which were prompt to take up arms against abuses. Revolts spread through the Belgian and German colonies, obliging the new masters to repress the local populations. In the Congo Free State, most of the revolts took place against the background of the reversal of the alliances between Belgians and Arabized chiefs following the decision by the anti-slavery conference of Brussels to wage a merciless campaign against those Arabized chiefs who had until then been allies of Leopold II. Thus, between 1892 and 1895, the Arabized chiefs were removed and replaced by what were called customary African chiefs. This new policy provoked mutinies among the mercenaries, who had hoped to get their share of the loot. In Luluabourg, after the execution of Chief Ngongo Lutete, mutinies broke out in 1895, which were organized by Swahili soldiers serving in the 'Public Forces' of the Congo Free State.

In East Africa, the German colonization process was forced through by means of widespread military repression of chiefs who defended the sovereignty of their states, and populations who rebelled against colonial exploitation. Helge Kjekshus enumerates at least fifty-four engagements between 1889 and 1896 which involved deaths, the burning of villages, and the destruction of livestock and standing crops.[10] By way of illustration, mention may be made of the revolt of Bushiri, of the Chagga, of the Hehe chiefs, of King Mwezi Gizabo of Burundi, and of the Maji-maji movement, the last named being the most extensive and the most murderous.

The stiffest resistance came from the Maji-maji movement of Tanganyika (1905–7), which was the broadest-based anti-colonial struggle in German East Africa. This movement, led by Chief Kinjikitile Ngwale, brought together about twenty ethnic groups, who all refused forced labour and compulsory enrolment in the concessions. The leader of the movement made himself famous by offering sacred water with which his supporters sprinkled themselves and which was said to make them invulnerable to bullets. The leader was hanged on 4 August 1905 and the revolt was brought to an end in 1907 by extensive repressive measures that left over 100,000 dead.[11]

These revolts had a variety of consequences. For example, the German colonizers, terrified by the revolt of 1905 and by similar movements that had broken out during the same period in South-West Africa (Namibia), adopted reforms which focused more on infrastructure, development based on monetary gain for the local populations, and social action.[12] But the African peoples' opposition to colonial domination expressed their profound attachment to freedom, and provided a foundation and historic points of reference for African nationalism and the future struggles leading to the recovery of national independence.

SCIENTIFIC AND CULTURAL CHANGES

The integration of central and eastern Africa into the global system of exchanges had repercussions of a cultural, social and scientific nature which were not really noticeable until after the First World War.

The spread of common African languages and new cultural prospects

The spread of Swahili culture

Generally speaking, the spread of Swahili culture and Islam in Central and Eastern Africa was one of the major developments of the nineteenth century. Encouraged by the expansion of trade between the coast and the interior, the Swahili language eventually became a federating influence for many of the peoples in the region. It was a culture that went hand-in-hand with urban development. The spread of Swahili culture seems to be bound up with the growing importance of Zanzibar and other urban centres along the coast.

Long-distance trade gave a considerable boost to the spread of the Swahili language (*Kiswahili*), which gained ground even more quickly than Islam. Towards 1850, Richard F. Burton reported that *Kiswahili* was 'spoken fluently by the Sagara and the Gogo'.[13] At the same time, Swahili lifestyles took hold, symbolized by the widespread wearing of the *kanzu*, a form of tunic. The European scramble for Africa gave a further boost to the expansion of *Kiswahili* thanks to the work of interpreters who accompanied explorers, missionaries and soldiers. Lastly, its systematic use in the new centres established by the colonial authorities, more particularly by traders and colonial administrators, gave it added prestige in the twentieth century and brought about its further expansion in Central, Eastern and even Southern Africa.

The spread of Lingala in the west of the Congo basin

By the beginning of the nineteenth century, the Congo basin had long been part of world trade networks. Large European trading stations were operating along the Atlantic coast and had developed flourishing exchanges with the interior.[14] Around 1850, the slave trade ceased to account for the greater part of exports to the rest of the world. Other exchanges were for a long time limited to a few major products such as salt and iron and to luxury items in copper or raffia, etc., but in the second half of the nineteenth century trade began to expand again along the lines of a 'gathering economy: ivory, wax, copal, oil, coffee'.[15] Up till then, trade had focused on the lower Congo region and the Kikongo language. The new boost given to trade along the banks of the Congo river up to north of the equator, at its junction with its tributary the Ubangi River, turned the spotlight on a community of pirogue boatmen, the Ngala, a small group of 'river people' speaking Lingala. The Ngala were almost the only group to possess and use pirogues in this region. As professional boatmen they would play a fundamental role in the transport of merchandise, especially ivory.

Around 1870, the Ngala used to transport up to 5,000 or 6,000 elephant tusks from Ubangi to the Stanley Pool region and receive in exchange such hitherto unfamiliar objects as copper rings and guns and new varieties of plants. In this context, Lingala, which started out as a language spoken only by the Ngala, developed and became the key trading language[16] for a large part of the western Congo. Lingala played an important role in the spread of fishing techniques as well as in harmonizing certain institutions. Like Kiswahili in the east, Lingala was to acquire remarkable influence and prestige, becoming the language of public authority, which meant that its use spread to other parts of the country. It would also become the language of Congolese arts and music and of the capital, Leopoldville (Kinshasa).

Little-known creative and technical achievements in Africa

Very little research on African achievements in science and culture has been focused on the nineteenth century. Some indigenous initiatives were in fact thwarted or inhibited by contact with European advances in science and technology. But one of the characteristic aspects of this period was the pillage of African art objects to fill the museums of Brussels and Berlin.

In Africa itself, despite its scientific and technological backwardness and the lack of access to information, discoveries by Africans are mentioned here and there.

Joseph Ki-Zerbo cites the example of the Chagga of Tanganyika who, from 1800, perfected a storage system for foodstuffs and shelters for their cattle. The system is said to have been invented by the Chagga chief Horombo, who was at war with the Masai and trying, as Ki-Zerbo explains, to consolidate his control over land and livestock: 'In order to protect themselves from Masai raiders, the Chagga developed an extensive network of underground living quarters with areas for their livestock, foodstores and sleeping quarters and a system of ventilation and waste water drainage'.[17]

But the technical skills and cultural genius of Africans were expressed above all in the working of iron and copper and in creative art. There were peoples who had acquired a considerable reputation for such work. The Baluba, for example, had long excelled in smelting iron and copper and in weaving raffia.[18]

Moreover, the well-known explorer David Livingstone was greatly impressed by the technical skills of Africans in the upper Zambezi region. In Manganja he describes the many bustling forges and in Katanga the smelting of copper which had been extracted from malachite and was sold in large ingots shaped like a capital 'I'.[19] The originality of the Luba masks and the delicacy of Makonde statuettes also impressed travellers, who gazed in wonder at the creative genius of the Africans.

Early innovations

The beginnings of scientific and cultural exchange

Cultural, scientific and technical exchanges between East and Central Africa on the one hand and Europe on the other were at that time only just beginning. But the descriptions left by missionaries and explorers, the adoption of new food plants, the launching of major building projects, the organization of exhibitions and the work of the first intellectuals were drawing attention to certain repercussions in science and culture.

Missionaries and explorers played a key role in the dissemination of knowledge about the history and geography of Africa. It will be remembered that the first travellers to cross East Africa were looking for the sources of the Nile, whose location had been the object of curiosity since antiquity: the celebrated Greek historian Herodotus claimed that 'the Nile flowed from the Mountains of the Moon'. Between 1858 and 1863 Richard F. Burton and

John Speke discovered Lake Tanganyika, Lake Victoria and the sources of the Nile. The English pastor and doctor David Livingstone (1813–73) spent thirty years in Africa and made people familiar with the countries and peoples of the Zambezi and Upper Congo, while Henry Morton Stanley would go down in history as the first European to set out from the Indian Ocean and descend the Congo River. He subsequently placed himself at the service of King Leopold II. In 1848, the German Rebmann was the first European to discover Mount Kilimanjaro.

Missionaries also played an important role in spreading European ideas and concepts. They taught Africans to write and themselves wrote the first books on the languages, cultures and history of Africa. Above all, they helped to ensure that Biblical concepts penetrated the societies of the African interior.

Organization of international exhibitions of African art

The organization in Europe of many national and international exhibitions of African art from this period onwards is a sign of the scale of this type of cultural exchange with Europe. There were, for example, the exhibitions organized in Belgium, and the building of the Ethnographic Museum to house the works of art amassed in the Congo.

In 1885, the Belgian port of Antwerp hosted the first international exhibition on 'The Congo Free State', which displayed ethnographic collections at the headquarters of the Geographical Society. In 1894, the second international exhibition to be held in Antwerp contained for the most part objects characteristic of the various Congolese ethnic groups.[20] In 1914, a large exhibition of cultural objects was also being mounted in Dar es Salaam.

In 1896–7, the construction of the colonial palace of the Turveren Exhibition confirmed the degree of interest in African culture, notwithstanding the predatory ambitions of imperialism. Pierre Salmon praises the quality of the works that the Belgian public admired in the colonial palace of the Tervuren Exhibition. 'Care had been taken to offer to the public gaze, not quantity but quality, not a host of different objects distracting to the eye, but a few typical forms representing the history and life of the country and its inhabitants'.[21] The inauguration of the Tervuren Museum in 1908, the year when Belgium inherited the Congo Free State, is another indication of the interest that African art and culture aroused.

Revolutions in agriculture and medicine

One of the consequences of the region's integration into world trade networks was the introduction of American plants into Central and Eastern Africa. This process had started in the sixteenth century and became widespread in the nineteenth. Crops such as manioc, maize, sweet potato, beans, etc., became common throughout the region, enriching the food-producing capacities of rural Africa and encouraging a growth in population.

At the beginning of the colonial period, in spite of the first efforts to protect health (the introduction of quinine, the first smallpox vaccinations), certain endemic diseases spread (especially sleeping sickness from the Congo basin), and the progress of epidemics (smallpox and cholera from the east coast) was more rapid.

New means of supervising territories and populations

The introduction and spread of Western ideas in Africa were assisted by the establishment of a new method of government, introduced by the colonial authorities, in which bureaucratic systems made for more effective supervision of the population (censuses, health inspections, taxation, etc.), based on geographical location.

One innovation introduced into Africa by European capitalism was the railway. The Belgian and German colonies put in place a railway system that was regarded both as an instrument of development and as a 'factor of civilization'.[22] But the Africans tended to see the railways as enormous machines for their own enslavement and exploitation, especially since thousands of Africans died building them.

In 1903, three big companies were responsible for developing this sector in the Congo Free State: the Congo Railway Company, founded in 1880 and responsible for building the line from Matadi to Leopoldville; the Railway Company of the Upper Congo to the Great Lakes region (CFL); and the Railway Company for the Lower Congo to Katanga (BCK). In German East Africa, the first line, from Tanga to Moshi, was completed in 1902. But the most important one, from Dar es Salaam to Kigoma, built with the intention of taking advantage of trade with the Belgian Congo, was inaugurated in 1914.

The first African intellectuals and the educational network of missions

During the nineteenth century one can hardly speak of intellectual trends in Central and Eastern Africa, for the simple reason that educated persons were so few and far between, if not non-existent. There were, of course, Islamic converts who could read and write, especially in German East Africa, but they had no decisive influence on social policy. However, a few educated Africans who, as yet timidly, opposed the colonial enterprise were beginning to attract attention.

Education was provided by the missionary schools, which were just being established.[23] We can give two examples for the Belgian Congo: Panda Farnana and the Abbé Stefano Kaoze. Panda Farnana (1888–1930) was the first Congolese agricultural engineer; he studied in Belgium, first at Vilvorde, which he followed up with business studies at Mons, became a colonial official in 1909, and in 1919 founded the Congolese Union. He was the first Congolese to criticize the public education and land management systems and to assert 'the right of Blacks to be heard and therefore to be represented on the administrative bodies of the colony'.[24]

Stefano Kaoze is remembered as the first Congolese to write articles in French on the 'culture shock' caused by the meeting of African and European cultures. In 1910, he published in the *Revue congolaise* an article on 'Bantu psychology' in which he expresses Blacks' view of the Whites:

> To us everything seemed white about these foreigners, their clothes as well as their skin; only their feet were black. Those feet seemed strange because, unlike ours, they had no toes; the fact was, we had never seen men wearing shoes – that was the problem. As for the people in the villages, when they saw the Whites come with their retinue from Lake Tanganyika,

they thought that those people had come out of an immense forest of water like our ancestor Kiyombe with his wives, children and the members of our six clans. The villagers placed this forest of water well beyond Lake Tanganyika, towards the Indian Ocean.

CONCLUSION

How can we sum up the state of scientific and cultural development in Central and Eastern Africa at the end of the nineteenth century? The first thing to be said is that intellectual life was still very limited. There were no educational institutions or research centres. Scarcely more than the rudiments of reading and writing were beginning to be offered in the mission schools, whose main concern was to propagate Christianity. For the colonial authorities, development was a secondary concern and their energies were directed more towards setting up the structures and instruments of colonization (restructuring of territories, organization of bureaucracies, establishment of communication systems, etc.), that is to say, means of control and exploitation that would yield maximum profits.

The major cultural event of the nineteenth century was the affirmation of Swahili culture. Though Islam had begun to take root in the interior, its progress would be slowed down in the twentieth century by the development of Christianity.

Intellectual exchanges consisted for the most part of the writings of explorers and missionaries, which made Africa a little more familiar to readers. But Europeans' knowledge and awareness of Africa was also a result of the organization of exhibitions of African art, an early foreshadowing of the vogue for 'Negro art' immediately after the First World War.

Finally, it was by the twentieth century that the first bases for study and for the technical, scientific and cultural development of the region were established in Central and Eastern Africa.

NOTES

1 A. Idha Salim, 'The East African coast and hinterland, 1800–1845', in *General History of Africa*, UNESCO, Paris, 1996, Vol. 6, p. 212.

2 E. Mworoha, *Le Consulat français de Zanzibar d'avant l'expansion européenne en Afrique centrale de 1876 à 1890*, Mémoire, University of Paris, 1970, pp. 36–61.

3 On the structures of kingdoms in the Great Lakes region, see E. Mworoha, *Peuples et rois de l'Afrique des Lacs*, Dakar, NEA, 1977, pp. 46–64.

4 I. Kimambo, 'The coast and hinterland of East Africa from 1845 to 1880', in *General History of Africa*, UNESCO, Paris, 1996, Vol. 6, p. 248.

5 E. MBokolo, *Afrique Noire, Histoire et civilisation*, Vol. 2, nineteenth to twentieth centuries, Hatier, 1995.

6 J. Stengers, *Congo, Mythes et réalitées 100 ans d'Histoire*, Editions Duculot, 1989, p. 137.

7 *Ibid.*, p. 138. These included the Fiftieth Anniversary Monument in Brussels, the Tervuren museum, the extension of the royal castle of Laeken and major public works in the port of Ostend.

8 E. MBokolo, *op. cit.*, p. 291.

9 *Ibid.*, p. 314. Examples are the Report by Roger Casement (1903), British Consul in the Congo, and the publications of Edmond Morel and his Congo Reform Association between 1904 and 1913.

10 H. Kjekshus, *Ecology Control and Economic Development in East African History*, London, 1977, pp. 148–9.

11 H. A. Mwanzi, 'African initiatives and resistance in East Africa 1880–1914', in *General History of Africa*, Vol. 7, UNESCO, Paris, 1985, pp. 149–68.

12 J. Iliffe, *A Modern History of Tanganyika*, Cambridge, 1979, pp. 168–202.

13 In 1876, there were 146 of these European trading stations: 78 between Loango and the mouth of the Congo, 33 in the estuary itself and 35 between the river and the port of Ambriz. Ahmed Idha Salim, *op. cit.*, p. 261.

14 E. MBokolo, *op. cit.*, p. 174.

15 J. L. Vellut, 'Le bassin du Congo et l'Angola', in *Histoire de l'Afrique au XIXe siècle, jusque vers les années 1880*, Vol. VI, 1989, UNESCO/Cambridge University Press, Paris, p. 341.

16 E. MBokolo, *op. cit.*, p. 180.

17 J. Ki-Zerbo, *Histoire de l'Afrique Noire*, Hatier, Paris, 1992, p. 325.

18 J. Ki-Zerbo, *op. cit.*, p. 325.

19 *Ibid.*, p. 325.

20 P. Salmon, 'Réflexion à propos du propos des arts zaïrois', in Quagebeur (ed.) *Archives du Futur: Cent ans de culture francophone en Afrique centrale (Zaïre, Rwanda et Burundi)*, Brussels, Editions Labour, 1992, p. 181.

21 *Ibid.*, p. 182.

22 J. R. Chrétien, 'Le "désenclavement" de la région des grands lacs dans les projets économiques allemands au début du XXe siècle', in *Histoire sociale de l'Afrique de l'Est au XIXe et XXe siècle*, Karthala, 1991, pp. 335–62.

23 By 1911 there were about ten missionary institutes covering the main regions of the Belgian Congo.

24 M. Quaghebeur, *Cent ans de culture francophone en Afrique centrale (Zaïre, Rwanda, Burundi)*, Brussels, Editions Labour, 1992, p. 48.

BIBLIOGRAPHY

AJAYI, J. F. A. (ed.) 1989. 'Africa in the Nineteenth Century until the 1880s'. In: *General History of Africa*. Vol. 6. UNESCO, Paris, pp. 861ff.

BENNETT, N. 1978. *A History of the Arab State of Zanzibar*. Methuen, London.

——. *Mirambo of Tanzania (ca. 1870–1884)*. Oxford University Press, London.

BERGER, I. 1981. *Religion and Resistance in East African Kingdoms in the Pre-colonial Period*. Musée Royal de l'Afrique centrale, Tervuren.

BOAHEN, A. A. 1985. 'Africa under Colonial Domination 1880–1935'. In: *General History of Africa*. Vol. 7. UNESCO, Paris, pp. 865ff.

BRUNSCHWIG, H. 1957. *L'expansion allemande outremer (du XVe à nos jours)*. Presses Universitaires de France, Paris.

BURTON, R. F. 1872. *Zanzibar: City, Island and Coast*. 2 vols. Tinsley Brothers, London.

CHRÉTIEN, J.-P. 1993. *Burundi, l'histoire retrouvée: 25 ans de métier d'historien en Afrique*. Karthala, Paris, pp. 509ff.

——. 1991. 'Le "désenclavement" de la région des grands lacs dans les projets économiques allemands au début du XIXe siècle'. In: *Histoire sociale de l'Afrique de l'Est (XIe-XXe siècles)*. Karthala, Paris, pp. 335–62.

CONSTANTIN, F. 1991. 'Communautés musulmanes et pouvoir politique en Afrique orientale (XIXe-XXe siècles)'. In: *Histoire sociale de l'Afrique de l'Est (XIXe-XXe siècles)*. Karthala, pp. 103–16.

COQUERY-VIDROVITCH, C. 1992. *Afrique Noire, Permanences et ruptures.* L'Harmattan, Paris, pp. 450ff.

COQUERY-VIDROVITCH, C.; MONIOT, H. 1974. *L'Afrique Noire de 1800 à nos jours.* Presses Universitaires de France, Paris.

FOURNIER, R. P. 1966. *Mirambo, un Chef de guerre dans l'Est Africain vers 1830–1884.* Nouvelles Editions Latines, Paris.

GANN, L. H.; DUIGNAN, P. (eds) 1969. *The History and Politics of Colonialism 1870–1960.* Vol. I. Cambridge University Press, Cambridge, pp. 532ff.

GRAY, R.; BIRMINGHAM, D. (eds) 1970. *Precolonial African Trade: Essays on Trade in Central and Eastern Africa before 1900.* Oxford University Press, London.

GUILLAIN, M. 1856. *Voyage à la côte orientale d'Afrique.* 3 vols. A. Bertrand, Paris.

HOSTELET, G. 1954. *L'œuvre civilisatrice de la Belgique au Congo, 1885–1945.* Vol. I. Mém. 33. Institut Royal Collège Belge des Sciences Morales et Politiques, Brussels.

ILIFFE, J. 1979. *A Modern History of Tanganyika.* Cambridge, pp. 616ff.

KAGAME, A. (ed.) 1972. *Un abrégé de l'éthno-histoire du Rwanda.* University of Rwanda, Butare.

KI-ZERBO, J. 1978. *Histoire de l'Afrique Noire, d'hier à demain.* Hatier, Paris, pp. 731ff.

KJEKSHUS, H. 1977. *Ecology Control and Economic Development in East African History.* Heinemann, London, pp. 215ff.

KRAPF, J. L. 1860. *Travels, Researches and Missionary Labours during an Eighteen-year Residence in Eastern Africa.* Ticknor and Fild, Boston MA.

LAGAL. 1926. *Les Azande ou Niam Niam.* Brussels.

MBOKOLO, E. 1995. *Afrique noire, histoire et civilisations, Vol. 2, XIXe–XXe siècles,* Hatier, Paris, pp. 576ff.

——. 1985. *Noirs et Blancs en Afrique équatoriale. Les sociétés et la pénétration française (ca. 1839–1874).* Editions de l'EHESS, Paris.

MOREL, E. D. 1903. *The Congo Slave Trade.* Richardson and Soris, Liverpool.

MUNONGO, A. 1955. 'Msiri'. In: *Lovania 13.* Elizabethville.

MWOROHA, E. 1977. *Peuples et rois de l'Afrique des Lacs.* Nouvelles Editions Africaines, Dakar, pp. 352ff.

——. 1987. *Histoire du Burundi: des origines à la fin du XIXe siècle.* Hatier, Paris, pp. 272ff.

——. 1991. 'L'Etat monarchique et son emprise sur la société dans la région des grands lacs au XIXe siècle'. In: *Histoire Sociale de l'Afrique orientale (XIXe–XXe siècle).* Karthala, Paris, pp. 37–58.

PRINS, A. H. J. 1961. *The Swahili-speaking people of Zanzibar and the East African Coast.* IAI, London.

QUAGHEBEUR, M. 1992. *Archives du Futur: cent ans de culture francophone en Afrique centrale (Zaïre, Rwanda and Burundi).* Editions Labour, Brussels.

RANDLES, W. G. L. 1968. *L'ancien royaume du Congo, des origines à la fin du XIXe siècle.* Paris.

STENGERS, J. 1962. 'L'impérialisme colonial de la fin de XIXe siècle: Mythe ou réalité'. In: *Journal of African History*, Vol. 3, No. 3, pp. 469–91.

TOUSSAINT, A. 1961. *Histoire de l'Océan indien.* Presses Universitaires de France, Paris.

VANSINA, J. 1962. *L'évolution du Royaume Rwanda des origines à 1900.* Brussels.

——. 1968. *Les anciens royaumes de la savane.* Léopoldville.

WELS, A. J. 1967. *An introduction to the History of Central Africa.* Oxford University Press, London.

15.4

EASTERN AFRICA

A. Buluda Itandala

Eastern Africa in this study means the region made up of the Republic of the Sudan, the countries of the Horn of Africa, namely Ethiopia, Eritrea, Djibouti and Somalia; and the countries of middle East Africa, namely Kenya, Uganda, Rwanda, Burundi, and Tanzania. Like many other parts of Africa, this region underwent some very significant socio-economic and political changes during the period under review. The following is a brief discussion of these developments in its different parts.

THE CREATION OF THE SUDAN AND ITS DEVELOPMENT TO 1899

Establishment of the Sudan by Muhammad Ali in 1820

By the early sixteenth century, all Christian communities in what is now the northern Sudan, with the exception of a few small pockets, had been Islamized and their kingdoms had been supplanted by the Muslim Sultanate of Funj based in Sennar.[1] The Funj Sultanate remained in existence till the early nineteenth century, though greatly weakened by dynastic rivalries by then. Some of its provinces such as Dongola and Kordofan, for example, had almost detached themselves from it by that time. Hence when Muhammad Ali, the then governor of the Ottoman or Turkish Empire province of Egypt, decided to invade Dongola and other northern parts of the Funj Sultanate, its rulers in Sennar were not in a position to offer effective resistance.

Muhammad Ali's main reason for invading the Northern Sudan was his wish to restore trade between Egypt and the Sudan, which had been disrupted by political disorders in the Funj Sultanate.[2] Even more important was the governor's desire to exploit the economic and human resources of the Sudan, especially gold, timber for his fleet and African slaves for his army.[3]

Having conquered the Funj Sultanate in 1820, Muhammad Ali established Khartoum as the chief administrative centre of his colony, which became known as the Sudan. He appointed governors and other officers to administer it for him, but military power was the main basis of control in the territory. Economically, the Sudan was expected to be self-supporting and to pay tribute annually to Egypt in gold, ivory, grain, cattle, timber, and slaves.

Turkish–Egyptian rule and exploitation: 1820–80

The Turkish–Egyptian government in Khartoum did not expand its authority beyond the borders of the Funj Sultanate until after the route linking the Northern Sudan to the Southern Sudan was discovered between 1831 and 1841 by Egyptian expeditions, which were looking for the sources of the White Nile.[4] After this discovery, the Governor of the Sudan dispatched from Khartoum small annual trading expeditions, which obtained ivory and other goods from people living along the river. The profits made by these expeditions aroused the interest of local and European traders in Khartoum, who immediately started organizing their own expeditions to penetrate the Southern Sudan.

As its southern riverine hinterland was opened up for economic exploitation in the 1840s and 1850s, Khartoum was already linked by caravan routes to the western territories of Kordofan and Darfur, and to the eastern territories of the Red Sea coast. Initially, the northern Muslim traders and the animist Africans of the Southern Sudan faced each other on an equal footing. This initial balance of power between the two Sudanese communities seems to have disappeared as large numbers of armed Arab and Nubian traders, popularly known as *Jellaba*, penetrated the southern interior and established fortified settlements known as *zeriba* in the 1860s and 1870s.[5] From these *zeribas*, the *Jelleba* continually raided all weak neighbouring communities for slaves, cattle, and grain.

The use of force by northern traders to obtain whatever they wanted from southerners was matched by government officials and soldiers who were posted in the region. This was the case because, as non-Muslims, the southerners were regarded by northern Muslims as savages who deserved any kind of treatment. Moreover, since government officials and soldiers were not paid their salaries regularly, they often resorted to pillaging, kidnapping and plundering in order to get something to live on and to get rich quickly.[6]

The Mahdist revolution: 1881–98

The violence and economic exploitation which accompanied the conquest of the Sudan by the Turkish–Egyptian regime, were no doubt among the main factors which led to the Mahdist uprising in 1881. Other factors which contributed significantly to the outbreak of this uprising were the failure of the Turkish–Egyptian officials in the Sudan to live according to strict Islamic rules, the employment of European Christians in important administrative positions, the anti-slave trade measures introduced by European officials, the, deposition of Khedive Ismail as ruler of Egypt in 1879, and Gordon's resignation as Governor-General of the Sudan soon after Ismail's deposition.[7] The departure of the two men from power was particularly serious because it left a vacuum in the two countries, which could not be adequately filled.

While all this was happening, a man named Muhammad Ahmad emerged as a religious reformer who wanted to purify Islam and to remove from power what he considered to be ungodly and corrupt 'Turkish' rulers and their Sudanese religious supporters. In November 1881, his supporters proclaimed him the *Mahdi* or divine leader chosen by God to purify Islam and to fill the earth with justice and fairness.[8] Having done so, they launched a *jihad* or holy war against the Turkish-Egyptian regime. Among his greatest supporters, who became generally known as Ansar, were the northern slave traders whose business had been ruined by the regime's anti-slave trade measures. That is why, when they launched their *jihad*, they intended not only to purify Islam and to remove the hated Turkish-Egyptian rulers and their European Christian supporters but also to restore their exploitative practices on the peoples of the Southern Sudan. By the late 1880s, they had conquered the whole of the Sudan and attempted to invade even Christian Ethiopia.

Establishment of Anglo-Egyptian rule in 1899

The Mahdist state in the Sudan emerged at a time when the rest of Africa was being partitioned into different European colonies.[9] Since the British had already taken over Egypt as their colony in 1882, it became imperative for them to control all areas along the Nile Valley in order to protect its interests because its survival depended on the floodwaters of the Upper Nile. The existence of a Mahdist state in the Sudan, which was hostile to Egyptian and British interests in the region, made its invasion and conquest by the British inevitable. In fact, when both the Belgians and the French showed intentions of acquiring parts of Sudanese territory from their bases in the Congo (or Zaire) River Basin in the 1890s,[10] the British responded by sending a military expedition from Egypt under the command of General H. H. Kitchener to the Sudan. Kitchener's expedition recovered first the Sudanese province of Dongola from Mahdist control in September 1896, and then forced the French to withdraw from Fashoda after defeating decisively the Mahdist forces near Omdurman in September 1898.[11] Following the collapse of the Mahdist state and the French withdrawal from Fashoda in September 1898, the British established a joint British-Egyptian administration in the Sudan in January 1899.

ETHIOPIA AND THE REST OF THE HORN OF AFRICA: 1800-1900

Unification efforts under Emperor Tewodros II: 1855-68

Imperial authority in Ethiopia had almost disappeared by the beginning of the eighteenth century, due to Oromo invasions of the empire and the constant civil wars among the provincial rulers or *rases*.[12] The emperor residing at Gondar had become merely a nominal head of the empire, while the provincial rulers had become virtually independent. That is, why the period from about 1769 to 1855 is generally referred to as *Zamana masafent* or 'the era of the princes'.[13] However, the Ethiopian state did not collapse completely during this period. The church, for example, remained a national institution. Moreover, the tradition that there should be an emperor as the ruler of all Ethiopia survived also and some of the *rases* continued to claim the imperial title and to fight for it.[14] By the early nineteenth century, three contenders were competing for it. These were the *rases* of Tigre, Amhara and Shoa.

When the *ras* of Amhara died in 1850, only those of Tigre and Shoa remained in the race for the imperial title. But it was an upstart from the Amhara frontier district of Kwara named Kassa who emerged victorious. After defeating the other two contenders militarily in 1853 and 1854, he was crowned emperor under the name Tewodros II in 1855.[15] Among the things he did after becoming emperor was to attempt to destroy the independent power of the *rases* and to reduce the privileges of the church and its leaders.[16] He also collided with the British when he imprisoned their consul and sixty other Europeans after failing to obtain diplomatic recognition for his country from them and other European powers in the 1860s. He committed suicide when they sent a military force to rescue their nationals and other imprisoned Europeans to his capital at Magdala in April 1868.[17] The British were able to accomplish this rescue mission easily because most of his subjects refused to fight for him due to his unpopularity.

But despite his unpopularity towards the end of his reign, Tewodros had succeeded significantly in restoring the prestige and authority of the imperial office by the time of his death.

Unification efforts under Yohannes IV: 1872-89

Three great rivals competed for the imperial title after the death of emperor Tewodros in 1868. They were Gobase of Amhara, Menelik of Shoa, and Kassa of Tigre. Gobase appeared to be the strongest contender at first and was crowned emperor in 1868. Four years later, however, he lost the position to Kassa of Tigre because the latter was more powerful military. This victory enabled Kassa to be crowned emperor under the name Yohannes IV in January 1872.[18]

Menelik of Shoa had also claimed the imperial title after the death of Tewodros in 1868. It was not until 1878 that emperor Yohannes was able to make him renounce it. In return for recognizing Yohannes as emperor, Menelik got a free hand to extend his territorial possessions in the southern part of Ethiopia. The relationship between the two great Ethiopian leaders was further strengthened by a marriage between two of their children in 1882 and by an agreement that succession should pass to Menelik after Yohannes's death.[19] Moreover, Yohannes gained a lot of support from the regional nobility and church leaders for abandoning the unpopular policies which had been introduced by his predecessor. With this wide support, he was able to summon a large army, which he used for repelling Egyptian invasions in 1875 and 1876 in the north.[20]

Ethiopia enjoyed a greater measure of unity and prosperity than ever before following Yohannes's repulsion of the Egyptian invaders. This prosperity was, however, short-lived because a more serious danger to its very existence was soon posed by the European powers which started scrambling for African territories in the mid-1880s. Moreover, the Mahdist state in the Sudan posed another danger to its security in the 1880s. In fact, emperor Yohannes died in battle against the Mahdist invaders at Matemma in 1889.[21]

Creation of modern Ethiopia by Menelik II: 1889–1908

When Yohannes IV died in 1889, Menelik succeeded him as emperor according to their agreement of 1878. He established his capital in the heartland of Shoa at Addis Ababa. Menelik realized that Ethiopia's chances of survival as an independent state depended on the possession of modern weapons and therefore found it convenient to cooperate with the Italians, who wanted to use him as a puppet for fulfilling their ambitions in the region. That is why the two parties concluded the Treaty of Wichale (Ucciali) in 1889 under which he received large supplies of armaments in exchange for agreeing to use Italy as his intermediary in foreign affairs.[22] The Italians exploited this treaty and informed the other European powers that they had established a protectorate over Ethiopia. Menelik, however, did not accept this interpretation of the treaty, because in the Amharic version of it the wording did not indicate any surrender of Ethiopian sovereignty to Italy. Only the Italian version suggested so.[23] Therefore, when he heard of that Italian interpretation, he vigorously protested and informed the other European powers that he had not surrendered the sovereignty of his empire to Italy.

When the Italians tried to force Menelik to accept their interpretation of the Treaty of Wichale, by invading Ethiopia militarily in 1896, their invading army was disastrously defeated by his forces at Adowa.[24] Menelik was able to achieve this victory over the Italians because they themselves had supplied him with a lot of weapons and because all the provincial rulers and their armies rallied behind him.

Menelik's victory at Adowa in 1896 enabled him to consolidate his political position in the Ethiopian Empire. Second, it saved Ethiopia from colonial conquest by the European powers in their scramble for African colonies.

Partition of the Horn of Africa: 1885–1900

The partition of the Horn of Africa started when the Italians used the coaling-station which they had acquired at Asab in 1869 as a base for establishing their colony of Eritrea in 1885. The border between Eritrea and Ethiopia was defined by the Italian-Ethiopian Treaty of Wichale of 1889.[25] Similarly, from their base at Obock which they had acquired in 1862, the French established their colony of French Somaliland (now Djibouti) in 1885.[26] The British, on the other hand, established their Somaliland Protectorate on the northern Somali coast opposite Aden, in order to ensure the safety of their merchant ships sailing to and from India through the Red Sea. The border between British Somaliland and French Somaliland was defined by an Anglo-French Agreement of 1888.[27]

Another European colony was established by the Italians in the Horn of Africa. This became known as Italian Somaliland. Its boundary with what is now Kenya was initially defined by the Anglo-Italian Protocol of 1891 and that between it and British Somaliland was defined by the Anglo-Italian Protocol of May 1894,[28] while the border between Ethiopia and British Somaliland was fixed by the Anglo-Ethiopian Treaty of 1897.[29] A provisional boundary was also established between Italian Somaliland and Ethiopia under the Italo-Ethiopian Negotiations of 1897.[30] Adjustments to this boundary as well as others were made after l900.

Although the partition of the Horn of Africa was accomplished fairly easily, perhaps no part of Africa resisted European colonial occupation as fiercely as this region did between the 1880s and 1910s. It has been suggested that the main basis of this resistance was an intense patriotism and the intense Islamic faith of its peoples.[31] However, the greatest losers in this struggle were the Somali, whose resistance was crushed by about 1920, and found themselves divided into five different territories, namely Ethiopia, French Somaliland, British Somaliland, Italian Somaliland and Kenya. It was perhaps their lack of political unity, which prevented them from retaining their independence as the Ethiopians did.

DEVELOPMENTS IN THE REST OF EASTERN AFRICA: 1800–1900

Introduction of Omani rule on the Swahili Coast: 1810–40

The ruler of Oman emerged as the new overlord of the Swahili or East African Coast after offering military help to the main coastal city-states to expel the Portuguese at the end of the seventeenth century.[32] But internal conflicts within Oman prevented him from consolidating his political power in the region before the nineteenth century.[33] It was not until Seyyid Said came to power in 1806 that Oman started asserting its overlordship over the East African Coast more seriously.

Seyyid Said assumed political power in Oman with the help of the British East India Company, which was then based in Bombay. Having helped him to consolidate his political control in Oman, the East India Company urged Seyyid Said to reassert his country's claim of overlordship of the Swahili Coast. It did so because it feared that the French, who had since the 1770s bought slaves at Kilwa and Zanzibar for their sugar-cane and coffee plantations in Mauritius and Reunion, might take over the region as a colony[34] and in so doing endanger British commercial interests in East Africa. This means that the Arabs of Oman, under the leadership of Seyyid Said, were not acting entirely on their own when they claimed their right to rule the East African coastal towns in the nineteenth century. Rather they were partly acting as agents of European capitalism.

With the help of the East India Company, Seyyid Said was able to establish his political control militarily in all important towns and offshore islands on the East African coast between 1810 and 1840. Soon after conquering all the coastal city-states in the 1830s, he transferred the seat of his government from Muscat, in Oman, to Zanzibar in 1840.[35]

The Zanzibari Sultanate thus established was confined to the coastal strip and offshore islands.

Arab-Swahili penetration of the interior: 1840–85

The creation of the Omani-Zanzibari Sultanate from 1810 to 1840 eventually led to the integration of the East African interior in the capitalist trading system operating through Zanzibar town. Among the factors which contributed to this integration were the signing of commercial treaties or agreements between Seyyid Said and representatives of American, British, French and German governments in the 1830s and 1840s, the establishment of clove plantations in Zanzibar and Pemba by Omani Arab immigrants which needed a large labour force, and the invitation of Indian merchants and money-lenders by Seyyid Said to come and facilitate the development of trade in East Africa.[36] As a result of these measures taken by Seyyid Said, there was a spectacular increase in Arab and Swahili commercial activity in the East African interior using well tried routes annually since the 1840s.

The integration of the different regional subsistence economies of East Africa into the capitalist trading system operating from its regional base in Zanzibar affected the peoples of the region economically, socially and politically. Its most notable effects were the use of many people from different parts of the interior as ivory porters and as slaves to produce cloves in Zanzibar and Pemba, the rise of professional economic groups such as elephant-hunters and merchants in some parts of the interior, the establishment of trade centres or towns in the interior, and the introduction of new food crops such as maize, cassava, sweet-potatoes and a number of varieties of fruit trees.[37] It is doubtful, however, that maize, cassava, and sweet potatoes, which were American crops, could have been introduced in the region by coastal traders. They may have reached it from the Atlantic coast via Congo-Kinshasa and other parts of Central Africa.

Other effects were the conversion of some to Islam, the spread of a language known as *Swahili* or *Kiswahili*, and the introduction of slavery and the slave trade in the interior.[38] There were also political effects such, as the use of economic and military power as the main basis for political authority rather than descent and religion as was the case before 1840, the intensification of competition for succession to kingship in many political units, the rise of military rulers or warlords and brigands in some parts of East Africa, and the fragmentation of kingdoms in north-western and north-eastern Tanzania as a result of the spread of firearms in the region in the 1870s and 1880s.[39]

Ngoni expansion and its consequences: 1840–1880s

The Ngoni expanded into Central and East Africa as refugees from the *Mfecane* wars which erupted among the Nguni-speaking peoples of northern Natal in the 1820s.[40] They are said to have reached Ufipa in south-western Tanzania in the early 1840s. The small group of refugees who left northern Natal in the 1820s is said to have incorporated people belonging to many different ethnic groups whom it had conquered on its way to Ufipa.

When their leader, Zwangendaba, died in 1848, the Ngoni in Ufipa split up into five groups, namely Tuta, Gwangara, Mpezeni, Mombera, and Ciwere. The Tuta and Gwangara remained in Tanzania, the other three groups went to Malawi and Zambia.[41] The Tuta left Ufipa in a northward direction. After harassing several communities in western Tanzania in the 1850s, they eventually settled among the Sumbwa in Kahama District. Among their main effects in western Tanzania were the adoption of their war tactics by the peoples of the region and the occasional disruption of normal life and caravan trade between Tabora and Ujiji from the 1850s to the 1890s.[42] Moreover, because they lived by plunder, the Tuta Ngoni provided a model of a life style which was imitated by rulers and robbers alike.

The Gwangara also left Ufipa after the break-up of the Ngoni community. After being led to what is now Songea District by Zulu-Gama, they clashed with another Ngoni group known as Maseko which had reached Songea earlier from Southern Malawi.[43] As a result of the clash between the two groups in Songea in the 1850s, the Maseko Ngoni were driven back across the Ruvuma River to Southern Malawi, while their remnants, who become known as Mbunga, were driven to the Kilombero River Valley.[44]

Having driven away the Maseko Ngoni and the Mbunga from Songea, the Gwangara Ngoni became the most powerful ethnic group in Southern Tanzania and established two kingdoms known as Mshope and Njelu. From these two kingdoms, they terrorized a very wide area lying between Lake Nyasa (Malawi) and the Indian Ocean in Southern Tanzania from the early 1860s to the 1880s.[45] They are said to have met very little or no resistance from many of the small segmentary communities of the region. Many areas in this region were almost depopulated by their warriors as they seized captives both for their armies and for sale to Arab and Swahili slave traders from the Kilwa coast. Only the Hehe were able to prevent them from extending their raids northwards. They were able to do so because they and their Sangu neighbours had adopted Ngoni military methods and had formed strong states in the 1860s in order to defend themselves.[46]

European activities in East Africa: colonial rule

Increased European activity in East Africa started when the French from their bases on the islands of Mauritius and Reunion started buying slaves in Kilwa and Zanzibar in the 1770s. They were joined by British, American and German traders who established branches of their commercial companies in Zanzibar town in the 1830s and 1840s.[47] Thus the first group of Europeans to become involved directly in East Africa were traders.

The second group of Europeans to be involved in East Africa in the nineteenth century were explorers. Their work began when German missionaries working for the Church Missionary Society (CMS), namely J. L. Krapf, J. Rebmann and J. Erhardt, reported from their mission station near Mombassa in the 1840s the existence of two snow-capped mountains and a big inland lake in the region.[48] In response to these reports, the Royal Geographical Society in London commissioned Richard Burton and John Speke in 1856 to find out whether indeed there were such mountains and lake or lakes in East Africa or not.[49] They were also asked to look for the source of the Nile River in this lake or lakes. Their visits to the northern Swahili Coast and to lakes Tanganyika and Victoria in 1857 and 1858 verified the missionaries' reports. Meanwhile the German traveller A. Roscher and the British missionary-explorer David Livingstone reached Lake Nyasa (Malawi) at different points in 1859.[50] What now remained to be found was the source of the Nile.

After the initial exploration by Krapf, Rebmann, Burton, Speke, Roscher and Livingstone in the 1840s and 1850s, the East African interior was visited by many more European travellers for different reasons from the 1860s to the 1880s. The most prominent among them were Livingstone, Henry M. Stanley, Charles New, and Joseph Thomson.

The penetration of the East African interior by European explorers from the 1840s to the 1880s went hand-in-hand with the occupation of the region by Christian missionaries. Missionary activity in East Africa started with the establishment of the CMS station at Rabai, near Mombasa, in 1844.[51] Following this example were the Universities Mission to Central Africa (UMCA) and the Catholic Holy Ghost Fathers, which established their stations in Zanzibar in the early 1860s and later expanded their work to the East African mainland.[52] Other missionary groups were set up in East Africa by the CMS and the Catholic White Fathers, which sent missionaries to Uganda in the late 1870s.[53] These missionary groups, as well as the UMCA and the Holy Ghost Fathers, gradually extended their activities to different parts of the region in the 1880s and 1890s. They were also joined by the London Missionary Society, which established itself at Urambo and Ujiji in Western Tanzania.

The European partition of East Africa: 1885–1900

The occupation of East Africa by European traders, explorers and missionaries eventually led to the partition of the region into European colonies immediately after the Berlin conference of 1884–5 which set the rules for the purpose.[54] The first phase of this partition was marked by the Anglo-German agreement of October 1886 which delimited the mainland territories of the Sultan of Zanzibar to a 16km-wide strip and divided the hinterland into British and German spheres.[55] Then in July 1890, the British and German governments reached an agreement which ended their bitter rivalry for what is now Uganda. As a result of the Anglo-German agreement of July 1890, Germany received the island of Heligoland in the North Sea in exchange for the evacuation of Witu (in what is now Kenya) and the recognition of Uganda as a British sphere and Zanzibar as a British Protectorate.[56] Latitude 1° south became the boundary between Uganda and German East Africa, while a line stretching from the Umba River to Lake Victoria served as the boundary between the latter and British East Africa in the north-east.

In addition, the British reached an agreement with the Italians under the Anglo-Italian protocol of March 1891 which defined the boundary between their East African sphere and Italian Somaliland in the north-east.[57] What remained then was the definition of the borders between what became the East Africa Protectorate (now Kenya) and Ethiopia and between Uganda and Anglo-Egyptian Sudan in the north, between Uganda and the Congo Free State (Republic of the Congo) in the north-west, between German East Africa and the Congo Free State in the west, and between German East Africa and Northern Rhodesia (now Zambia) and Nyasaland (now Malawi) in the south-west. These boundaries were fixed and adjusted by the colonial powers concerned as they physically occupied their newly acquired colonies in the 1890s and 1900s.

The imposition of European colonial rule was vigorously resisted in this part of Eastern Africa too, especially in German East Africa. But this resistance was not as intense as that of the Mahdists in the Sudan or that of the Somali in the Horn of Africa, presumably because religion was not used as its main basis.

CONCLUSION

It is evident, therefore, that foreign intrusion by Egyptians and Europeans in the Sudan and by Europeans and coastal Arabs and Swahili in the Horn of Africa and the rest of Eastern Africa introduced significant economic, social and political changes in the nineteenth century. These external forces caused more destruction in the Southern Sudan and in some parts of the hinterland of the East African coast.

NOTES

1 Holt, P. M., 1961, *A Modern History of the Sudan*, Weidenfeld and Nicolson, London, pp. 17–48; Kropacek, L., 1984, 'Nubia from the Funj Conquest in the Early Fifteenth Century'. In: D. T. Niane (ed.) *General History of Africa*, Vol. 6, UNESCO-Heinemann, London, pp. 398–414; Afigbo, E. A. *et al.*, 1986, *The Making of Modern Africa*, Longman, Harlow, p. 8.

2 Holt, 1961, pp. 35–6; Afigbo *et al.*, 1986, pp. 136, 140; Shillington, K., 1989, *History of Africa*, St Martin's Press, New York, pp. 279–83.

3 Holt, 1961, pp. 37, 43; Collins, R. O., 1964, *The Southern Sudan, 1883–1898*, Yale University Press, New Haven and London, p. 9; Ibrahim, H. A. and Ogot, B. A., 1989, 'The Sudan in the Nineteenth Century'. In: J. F. A. Ajayi (ed.) *General History of Africa*, Vol. 6, London, UNESCO-Heinemann, pp. 359–61.

4 Gessi, R., 1892, *Seven Years in the Sudan*, Sampson Low, Martson and Co., London, p. 1; Gray, R., 1964, *A History of the Southern Sudan, 1939–1889*, Oxford University Press, London, pp. 16–19.

5 Schweinfurth, G., 1873, *The Heart of Africa*, Vol. 1, pp. 228–9, Vol. 2, pp. 417–18, Sampson Low, Martson and Searle, London; Junker, W., 1890, *Travels in Africa during the Years 1875–1878*, Vol. 1, Chapman and Hall, London, pp. 54–149; Gray, 1964, p. 6; Holt, 1961, pp. 61–74.

6 Baker, S. W., 1866, *The Albert Nyanza*, Vol. 1, Macmillan, London, pp. 9–12; Baker, S. W., 1974, Vol. 1, Macmillan, London, pp. 5–259, and Vol. 2, Ismailia, London, pp. 482–3; Schweinfurth, 1873, Vol. 1, pp. 258–9 and 355–83; Casati, Major G., 1891, *Ten Years in Equatorial and the Return with Emin Pasha*, Vol. 1, Warne, London and New York, pp. 61–2 and 314–15; Holt, l961, pp. 68–70.

7 Ibrahim and Ogot, 1989, Vol. 6, pp. 373–4; Holt, 1961, pp. 65–72 and 77–8; Holt, P. M. and Daly, M. W., 1989, *A History of the Sudan*, Longman, London and New York, pp. 33–4 and 42.

8 Afigbo *et al.*, 1986, p. 156; Holt, 1961, pp. 78–9.

9 Holt and Daly, 1989, p. 109; Afigbo *et al.*, 1986, pp. 162–4.

10 Collins, l964, pp. 92–155; Holt, 1961, pp. 104–5.

11 Holt, 1961, pp. 104–7 and 111–12.

12 Jones, A. H. M. and Monroe, E., 1965, *A History of Ethiopia*, Clarendon Press, Oxford, pp. 120–6; Afigbo *et al.*, 1986, p. 165.

13 Abir, M., 1968, *Ethiopia: The Era of the Princes*, Longman, London; Abir, M., 1978, 'Ethiopia and the Horn of Africa'. In: R. Gray (ed.) *The Cambridge History of Africa*, Vol. 4, Cambridge, Cambridge University Press, pp. 571–7; Jones and Monroe, 1965, pp. 125–34.

14 Jones and Monroe, 1965, pp. 124–5.

15 Pankhurst, R. and Cassanelli, L. V., 1989, 'Ethiopia and Somalia'. In: J. F. A. Ajayi (ed.) *General History of Africa*, Vol. 6, London, UNESCO-Heinemann, pp. 390–L: Jones and Monroe, 1965, pp. 128–9.

16 Pankhurst and Cassanelli, 1989, pp. 393–6; Afigbo *et al.*, 1986, pp. 165–6.

17 Pankhurst and Cassanelli, 1989, 397–402; Jones and Monroe, 1965, pp. 131–4.

18 Pankhurst and Cassanelli, 1989, Vol. 6, p. 404.

19 Afigbo *et al.*, 1986, p. 169; Pankhurst and Cassanelli, 1989, Vol. 7, pp. 407–8.

20 Pankhurst and Cassanelli., 1989, pp. 404–10; Jones and Monroe, 1965, p. 35.

21 Holt, 1961, pp. 96–7; Afigbo *et al.*, 1986, p. 170.

22 Afigbo *et al.*, 1986, p. 171; Lewis, I. M., 1965, *The Modern History of Somaliland*, Weidenfeld and Nicolson, London, p. 50.

23 Lewis, 1965, pp. 50–1.

24 Afigbo *et al.*, 1986, p. 173; Lewis, 1965, p. 50.

25 Hallett, R., 1974, *Africa Since 1875*, University of Michigan Press, Ann Arbor, p. 124.

26 Lewis, 1965, p. 49; Ibrahim, H. A., 1985, 'African Initiatives and Resistance in Northeast Africa', in: A. A. Boahen (ed.) *General History of Africa*, Vol. 7, UNESCO-Heinemann, London, p. 82; Hallett, 1974, pp. 129–30.

27 Lewis, 1965, p. 49.

28 *Ibid.*, p. 55.

29 *Ibid.*, pp. 56–62.

30 *Ibid.*, pp. 88–9.

31 Ibrahim, 1985, Vol. 7, p. 86.

32 Nicholls, C. S., 1971, *The Swahili Coast*, George Allen and Unwin, London, pp. 21–3; Sherif, A., 1987, *Slaves, Spices and Ivory in Zanzibar*, James Currey, London, pp. 24–2; Salim, A. I., 1989, 'The East African Coast and Hinterland, 1800–45'. In: J. F. A. Ajayi (ed.) *General History of Africa*, Vol. 6, London, UNESCO-Heinemann, p. 211.

33 Sheriff, 1987, pp. 24–6; Coupland, R., 1938, *East Africa and its Invaders*, Clarendon Press, Oxford, pp. 69–72.

34 Nicholls, 1971, pp. 119–21 and 134–62; Coupland, 1938, pp. 73–101; Freeman-Grenville, G. S. P., 1965, *The French at Kilwa*, Clarendon Press, Oxford, p. 13.

35 Coupland, 1938, pp. 295–300.

36 Nicholls, 1971, pp. 149–62 and 324–8; Sheriff, 1987, pp. 82–101; Alpers, E. A., 1967, *The East African Slave Trade*, EAPH, Nairobi, pp. 10–11; Iliffe, J., 1971, *Agricultural Change in Modern Tanganyika*, EAPH, Nairobi, pp. 10–11.

37 Iliffe, 1971, pp. 8–9; Salim, 1989, Vol. 7, pp. 228–33. Kimambo, I. N., 1989, 'The East African Coast and Hinterland, 1845–1880'. In: J. F. A. Ajayi (ed.) *General History of Africa*, Vol. 6, London, UNESCO-Heinemann, pp. 234–44.

38 Alpers, E. A., 1969, 'The Coast and the Development of Caravan Trade'. In: I. N. Kimambo and A. J. Temu (eds) *A History of Tanzania*, EAPH, Nairobi, pp. 50–56; Salim, 1989, Vol. 6, pp. 223–8.

39 Roberts, A., 1969, 'Political Change in the Nineteenth Century'. In: Kimambo and Temu, 1969, pp. 57–84; Alpers, E. A., 1969, 'Trade, State and Society among the Yao in the Nineteenth Century'. In: *Journal of African History*, Vol. 10, No. 3, pp. 405–20; Sheriff, A. M. H., 1980, 'Tanzanian Societies at the Time of the Partition'. In: M. Y. H. Kaniki (ed.) *Tanzania Under Colonial Rule*, James Currey, London, pp. 43–44.

40 Omer-Cooper, J. D., 1974, *The Zulu Aftermath*, Longman, London, pp. 2–8 and 64–72; Roberts, 1969, pp. 68–72; Sheriff, 1980, pp. 31–3.

41 Omer-Cooper, 1974, p. 73; Sheriff, 1980, pp. 33–4; Roberts, 1969, p.68.

42 Omer-Cooper, 1974, pp. 74–5; Sheriff, 1980, p. 33.

43 Omer-Cooper, 1974, pp. 75–6; Sheriff, 1980, p. 33–4.

44 Omer-Cooper, 1974, pp. 76–8; Sheriff, 1980, p. 34.

45 Sheriff, 1980, p. 35; Roberts, 1960, pp. 68–9.

46 Redmayne, A., 1973, 'The Hehe'. In: A. Roberts (ed.) *Tanzania Before 1900*, EAPH, Nairobi, pp. 42–44; Roberts, 1960, pp. 69–71.

47 Nicholls, 1971, pp. 140–62; Salim, 1989, Vol. 6, pp. 230–2.

48 Krapf, J. L., 1980, *Travels, Researchers, and Missionary Labours During an Eighteen Years' Residence in Eastern Africa*, Trubner and Co., London, pp. 543–54.

49 Burton, R. F., 1872, *Zanzibar: City, Island and Coast*, Vol. 1, Tinsley Brothers, London; Speke, J. H., 1863, *What Led to the Discovery of the Source of the Nile*, William Blackwood and Sons, London, p. 191.

50 Coupland, R., 1939, *The Exploitation of East Africa, 1856–1890*, Faber, London, p. 109.

51 Krapf, 1860, pp. 126–86; Oliver, R., 1970, *The Missionary Factor in East Africa*, Longman, London, p.6.

52 Oliver, 1970, pp. 15–22.

53 *Ibid.*, pp. 39–49.

54 Crowe, S. E., 1942, *The Berlin West Africa Conference, 1884–85*, Longman, Green, London, esp. Part II, chs 3–6; Dawson, H., 1919, *The German Empire, 1867–1914 and the Unity Movement*, Vol. 2, Macmillan, New York, pp. 204–5.

55 Hertslet, E., 1967, *The Map of Africa by Treaty*, Vol. 3, No. 264, Frank Cass, London, pp. 882–6; Flint, J. E., 1963, 'The Wider Background to Partition and Colonial Occupation'. In: R. Oliver and G. Mathew (eds) *History of East Africa*, Vol. 1, Clarendon Press, Oxford, pp. 373–6.

56 Hertslet, 1967, Vol. 3, No. 270, pp. 899–908; Flint, 1963, pp. 382–4.

57 Flint, 1963, p. 385; Lewis, 1965, p. 55.

15.5

THE PORTUGUESE-SPEAKING COUNTRIES OF AFRICA

Maria Emelia Madeira Santos

The nineteenth century began in 'Portuguese-speaking Africa' with the emergence of new political and economic conditions which affected the colonial structures. After the independence of Brazil in 1822, Africa stood out among the Portuguese overseas territories. Given the impossibility of establishing precisely the actual periodization of the history of African societies, we shall examine the interpenetration of Africa and the outside world, through the dynamic of the relationship between the coast and the interior. Although there were elements of continuity in this dynamic, it fluctuated between periods of acceleration and regression in the hinterland (*sertão*) of Angola and Mozambique in particular. The contact zone between European and African cultures was subject to variations in the pressures exerted by both sides. The European impact on African regions was often the greater, but African influence was successfully maintained.

By the beginning of the nineteenth century, the main activity of the Portuguese in Angola was the slave trade, carried on using means that were poorly controlled by the colonial authorities. Furthermore, the contact zone was moving towards the coast, under pressure from African societies. Thus, when it came to promoting or accelerating contact with the *sertão*, long-distance trade provided the link. Until 1875, the interpenetration of cultures proceeded by way of the adaptation of the first generation of Portuguese, and then by the gradual assimilation of the *mestizos* by African societies. The power struggle worsened after 1885, when the financial and technical resources made available to Portuguese colonization approached those of other European nations. The geographical area dealt with in this subchapter does not coincide with what is now Portuguese-speaking Africa, but covered vast areas of Central and Southern Africa. The case of the archipelagos of Sao Tome and Principe, Cape Verde and Portuguese Guinea is different. Cape Verde retained much of African culture more by the fact of mixing than by resistance to European influence. Sao Tome, where living conditions were very unpleasant for the Portuguese, was a country that was difficult to dominate. Guinea remained an area administratively subordinated to Cape Verde until 1879.

THE RELATIONSHIP BETWEEN THE COAST AND THE INTERIOR: COLONIAL SOVEREIGNTY, AFRICAN POWER AND COMMERCIAL AUTONOMY

The relationship between the coast and the interior was the mechanism by which the relationship was established between the areas of European influence and African civilizations. Study of this brings out the resistance by the indigenous peoples, the welcome the Portuguese gave to their civilizations and the exchanges that flowed from that. In the *sertão* of the rivers of Guinea,[1] trade between the interior and the outside world continued to flourish. In Southern Africa, on the contrary, the penetration of Portuguese into the hinterland was more effective. The major political formations were in the interior of the continent, but the sea never hampered trade with the outside world.[2] The establishment of the Portuguese in the interior made them more attentive to the life of Africans.

Whether by diplomatic or military means, the colonial power established *presidios* and markets in the *sertão*. To organize these new enclaves, civil, military or religious officials were appointed. The colonial authorities in fact had few resources for controlling the *moradores*, who organized the markets and entrepôts. The African rulers supported or rejected their intrusions according to circumstances. Nevertheless, long-distance trade, which consisted of the exchange of slaves for Indian cloth and European manufactured products, conferred a character of permanence and normality on relations between the coast and the interior. It was the governor of Angola, D. Francisco Inocêncio de Sousa Coutinho (1764–72), who realized the importance of long-distance trade as a means of establishing relations with the *sertão* that accorded with the 'enlightenment of reason'. Although the slave trade was not challenged, the type of relations that he established with the African chiefs included respect for the individual, political negotiation based on 'common sense' and the hope of rule by 'religion, industry and civility'.[3]

By the beginning of the nineteenth century, cultures and societies deeply marked by the events of the previous century survived in the zone between Luanda, Benguela and the Zambezi.[4] Both European and African slave traders

524

were showing signs of weakness and decline. In the *sertão* of Benguela the resident traders lived together in buildings defended by strong palisades. They surrounded themselves with a mixed clientele, free men and slaves, cut off from their societies of origin and devoted to long-distance trade.[5]

The interaction between colonial and African societies proceeded geographically by way of movements in the contact zone. Colonial policy oscillated between two strategies: penetrating the African market or waiting on the coast for indigenous traders to arrive. The second option, pursued sporadically, caused a break in trade: traditional products rapidly replaced European products. The flow from the contact zone to the interior reached its peak in about 1770 and then stagnated until the 1830s. The new colonial order gradually replaced the autonomy of the isolated *moradores* and *sertanejos*. But the old stone fortifications of the African chiefdoms[6] vigorously opposed colonial legislation. The lack of control on the part of the colonial authorities did not stop long-distance trade. Indeed, on the contrary, it favoured lasting ties, provided an impetus towards dialogue and accentuated the degree of interdependence between trading partners. African societies played a key role by welcoming into their territories isolated individuals who did not represent colonial sovereignty.

ABOLITION OF SLAVERY AND THE RECONVERSION OF MARKETS

In 1836, the government adopted important legislation on the abolition of slavery and the protection of trade between the African colonies and Lisbon. International relations, determined by the complementarity between industrial economies and suppliers of raw materials, led to a weakening of the triangle of trade, thereby strengthening the direct link with Portugal. Major upheavals ensued in the overseas economy and in relations between the colonial power and African rulers. The colonial authorities demonstrated their inability to implement the new legislation.[7] Moving to replace slavery by raw materials implied the reconversion of a whole chain of middlemen who were not prepared for it. This drove the bourgeoisies of Luanda and Benguela to despair, and they emigrated to Brazil with their capital. A profound crisis ensued in the trading posts of the long-distance trade, and they went into decline. When European cloth ceased to arrive, the people rapidly resumed their traditional clothing,[8] while beads and shells long served as decoration or currency.

The administrative or commercial agents of the *sertão* had founded Luso-African families. Some households, whose origins go back to the eighteenth century, survived the crises by developing their capacity to build relations both with Africans and with the colonizers. When the travelling salesmen received the order to abandon the markets of the *sertão*, they left their mixed-race families behind. The youngest children were quickly absorbed by the mother's family.[9] Between 1836 and 1846, the contact zone shrank abruptly, a shift precipitated by the disruption of the slave trade. African cultures regained some ground. The cultural traits transmitted by the Luso-African families of the eighteenth century were absorbed, along with the mulatto children.

The slave trade having been declared illegal, the colonial authorities taxed legal exports in order to maintain customs revenues. The clandestine export of slaves continued until 1850. However, by about 1845, some firms had changed over to the export of natural produce. But obtaining raw materials in large quantities and at competitive prices depended on the capacity of the wholesalers and all the slave trading networks to adapt. In order to study long-distance trade, we shall look at the line of penetration which, starting from Benguela, spread out in several directions right into Central Africa. Of all the lines of penetration in the Portuguese colonies, this was the one that offered the most extensive and busiest network.[10] Ivory was the commodity that contributed the most to freeing the Portuguese colonial economy from its dependence on America.

A new generation of commercial agents, uncorrupted by slavery, emerged, demonstrating its ability to apply the new trading guidelines. The *sertanejos* had credit with the White wholesalers and authority with the indigenous traders. The functions of middlemen became more complex and their position grew stronger. They exchanged cloth, firearms, beads, ironmongery and shells[11] for ivory, wax and other natural products. In concert with the African chiefs, the *sertanejos* drew up rules to underpin peaceful and enduring relations. The ivory trade involved ponderous trading machinery: purchases were made farther and farther inland and the powerful caravans, duly armed, employed large numbers of men. Thus, the Ovimbundu took part in it in their thousands. The king himself organized his caravans[12] or combined them with others for better protection. By stepping up the services they provided in the entrepôts, they gained more and more control over the long-distance trade. Bié, Kasanje, Punto Andongo, Ambaca and Cambambe for Angola, Zumbo and Tete for Mozambique, were the starting-points for distant areas. Other social groups actively participated in the development of trade: small shippers, *macota* responsible for large caravans, middlemen *pombeiros* playing a major role in administration and trade.

The caravan trade also relied on networks of relations built up by the elites of the various communities of Central Africa. After its success among the *sertanejo*, reconversion of the economy also required the adaptation of the suppliers' structures. The line of penetration which had been advancing since the end of the eighteenth century from Tete towards the kingdom of Cazembe, was still uneven.[13] The Muiza who engaged in the ivory trade began to turn to Zanzibar in about 1830,[14] while the wholesalers in the Zambezi region handed back foreign trade to Africans. In Angola, between 1845 and 1870, the distances covered by the Luso-African trading caravans grew enormously. In a quarter of a century, they established contacts with numerous small chiefdoms in Central Africa. After raids designed to capture slaves, the chiefs engaged in elephant hunting and exploiting natural products. External demand for commodities formerly held in contempt, changed the way labour was organized: the composition of tribute changed, and traditional utensils and foodstuffs became valued supplements to high-value products such as ivory and wax.

Extensive indigenous economic zones began to take shape in central Africa.[15] The three largest ones were linked to international trade through trading posts established in Angola, at the Cape and in Zanzibar. At the beginning of the 1850s, the Arab-Swahili of Zanzibar met Portuguese-Africans coming from Angola in the Congo basin; the English, coming from the Cape, made contact with them on the middle Zambezi a decade later.[16] On the edges of the economic zones were contact zones subject to the pressures of European demand and African supply. They were also determined by the antagonisms of foreign actors. Given the vastness of Central Africa and the distance from the leading centres, the great commercial networks of Luanda, Benguela and the Cape were in competition by 1860 and confronted one another violently two decades later. In situations of fierce competition and/or lack of security, the movements of economic zones hardened. Without coinciding geographically, the outward-oriented economic zones and African political formations were superimposed on one another in a dangerous state of coexistence, motivated by mutual interests. Hence the frontiers were fluctuating: they moved forwards or backwards without directly getting involved in local politics. The longevity of the relations established between a few hundred foreigners and the local peoples implied the acceptance of clear-cut rules of the game: the king saw to it that his monopoly over foreign trade was respected and the *sertanejo* disciplined his employees in exchange for protection by the political authorities.

Only respect for the rules kept paths open and maintained the security and regularity of markets and a degree of mutual loyalty between customers and suppliers. The 1880s saw a weakening of the large political groupings in Central Africa that had come to play the role of stable interlocutors in dealing with international trade. This fact allowed foreigners to meddle in local problems, thereby helping to aggravate them. The international trade in raw materials strongly influenced population movements and political changes in the region. Thus, the suzerains demanded ever higher tribute in order to meet the growing demand for ivory and the demands of the aristocracies. They became indebted to traders in order to reward their courtiers and political supporters with ever more costly European goods. In the last quarter of the nineteenth century, the weakening of the power of the old oligarchies had a knock-on effect on the expansion of extractive activities. In order to exploit rubber, the Chokwe drove the peoples of the Lunda Empire towards the sources of the Zambezi. Sudden movements of this type began to occur everywhere. African chiefs, facing threats of violence, turned for help to caravan organizers, and they, moved by their desire for booty, got involved in the conflicts. Relations became unpredictable: the rules of the former partners were being constantly ignored and relations of trust broken, removing any possibility of understanding between the exogenous economic zones and African political formations.

EXCHANGE OF TECHNIQUES, PRACTICES AND KNOWLEDGE

By about 1850, the Portuguese had acquired both empirical and scientific knowledge of Africa. The life-stories of settlers and other adventurers enable us today to look at the African cultures of that time in a historical perspective. European observers proved excellent in the description of material culture. They admired African techniques of making tools, whose effectiveness and/or beauty they acknowledged. Such was the case with fishing-nets, hunting-traps, hives, canoes, kitchen utensils and farming, weaving and metalworking techniques.[17] Traders closely observed the objects and techniques and tried to adopt them. In the medical context, for example, until the development of quinine,

Europeans used natural African medicaments and resorted to the magical-cum-religious practices of healers.

The introduction of new habits of dress was more rapid among the aristocracies of the powerful chiefdoms than among the peoples of decentralized political organizations. Among the Barotse, a European cloth trader acknowledged that 'cloth was of no use to those people', as their clothes made from hides were so comfortable; the Amboela used Western fabrics as currency; among the Kuba, European fabrics served only to mark the social hierarchy;[18] to clothe themselves, the Muiza preferred dressed tree bark.[19] Fabrics made from palm fibres (*viniferous raffia*) had all the qualities required to compete with European types of cloth, 'those standardized spider-webs'.

Peoples who were in direct contact with the Portuguese adopted firearms at a very early date. Learning how to handle and maintain weapons, mastering how they were made and the possibility of repairing them with local materials, all helped facilitate their acceptance. All these stages were gone through at different times, depending on the region and the circumstances, by African hunters, warriors and metalworkers. Their position, which was already important in some societies, became predominant: demand for their services rose, as did the price of their labour.[20] Elephant hunters were, along with caravan organizers, the first Africans to use firearms. Warriors adopted them subsequently. Through hunting rituals, these foreign objects became integrated into the traditional system of magico-religious values.[21] Right down to the 1880s Africans learned to know the different qualities of weapons and powders exchanged for the products of gathering. Political power depended increasingly on the strength given by firearms. Thus, strong political confederations weakened in the face of powerfully armed peoples. The Chokwe and Cazembe peoples extracted excellent quality iron to make high-quality utensils[22] and firearms. They successfully profited from trade between Europe and Africa: as suppliers of raw materials, elephant hunters, collectors of gum and wax, but also skilled metalworkers and weavers, they imposed themselves as partners, not contenting themselves with selling everyday articles, but supplying high-quality craft products and specialized services. Conversely, their Lunda neighbours, subjects of the powerful empire of the Mwant Yav, had poorly skilled metalworkers producing poor quality guns. By 1880, the superiority of the material culture of the Chokwe over that of the Lunda[23] was patent, heralding the fall of that old hegemony which came about in 1887.[24]

Farming, fishing and cattle-herding reached a high degree of skill among some peoples. Farming in wet and flooded areas had been developed by the Lozi on the banks of the middle Zambezi and the Amboela on the upper Cuxibi, a tributary of the Cuando. The *sertanejos* who travelled through these regions regularly were able to observe farm work all year round. Waterways were used not only for farming and fishing but also as a means of communication and a means of defence against enemies. The Lozi lived on the alluvial soil in the dry season and on the riverbanks and the islands in times of flooding; their canoes, dug out of tree trunks, could carry thirty-five people and heavy cargoes.[25] The Amboela lived permanently on the river to protect themselves from wild animals and enemies, and the houses built on piles, very close together, allowed only small canoes to move about. Enemies could not enter the area without risk.[26]

The interaction between the coast and the interior led to a shift in food habits.[27] Imported edible plants spread rapidly wherever their production proved locally possible. In this vast area, cassava was already by the nineteenth century the basic foodstuff from the coast to Central Africa.[28] Other edible plants were spread by caravans (tomatoes, marrows, maize, bananas, sweet potatoes, several varieties of beans), as were certain infectious human illnesses (smallpox, measles, syphilis) and epizootic diseases. The pineapple, which had come from America, moved rapidly from the Congo to Luanda. Sugar cane arrived on the east coast of Africa from India, and on the west coast through Madeira and Sao Tome and Principe. By the middle of the nineteenth century, these two well-acclimatized plants were growing wild between the Cafue and Aruangua rivers.[29]

While slavery stole away its children, Africa took foreign plants and enriched its food patterns. It learned how to use firearms, absorbed by European hybrids and took over their teachings. Once legitimized by religion, the objects became part of everyday life, ritual dances, the symbols of social status and art, sculpture in particular. Craft objects, both sacred and profane, used both African and European materials.

At Ambaca, the Africans adopted writing in the course of the seventeenth century. The chiefs communicated with the Portuguese authorities or traders through writings in the Portuguese language. To do this they learned Portuguese or used the services of permanent secretaries and travelling writers. The *mestizo* families that had come into being had their children educated. Orphans of a Portuguese father and an African mother would stay under the protection of a colleague settled in the region.[30] 'The land is traversed in every direction by an active exchange of letters and notes',[31] observed Silva Porto in 1862, referring to Ovimbundu territory.[32] By about 1850 the written word, transmitted through non-formal education, was used by Africans in their dealings with the Portuguese.

THE MODERN GEOGRAPHICAL MOVEMENT (1876) AND AFRICA'S ENTRY INTO MODERNITY

Until 1875, African chiefdoms in the interior could choose their interlocutors, The Portuguese authorities, more concerned about the movement of colonial commodities, did not seek to establish full political and military control. African societies still controlled the dirt tracks, which they might open or close to outsiders, and could choose the type of relations that they wanted to have with them. Africa was entering modernity under rules largely established by Africans themselves in the face of external pressure. As a result, we may speak of 'an indigenous, autochthonous production of modernity'.[33]

The role of intermediary between the coast and the interior gradually fell on the local peoples. At the beginning of the 1870s, the Ovimbundu demonstrated their capacity to manage long-distance trade by themselves. At that time, a demand arose on the international market for gum, a product that did not require the sort of major resources that the trade in ivory did. *Pombeiros* and shippers marketed it, the entrepôt companies made their resources available: the gum trade, unlike the ivory trade, was not under the control of the lineage hierarchy.[34] The African market, controlled by the big chiefdoms, warmly welcomed the new middlemen, encouraging commercial activity directed from the interior to the coast. There are still in existence announcements of consignments organized by rulers holding a monopoly over the extraction of products.[35] These transactions enabled the Africans to get a picture of the net profits of *sertanejo* trade. The agreement between the Portuguese and the African chiefs to protect this trade took concrete shape, in the 1890s, with the construction of the Benguela railway to Katanga, with international capital and technicians. Hence after 1885, any move to establish contacts was countered by the systematic colonization of Africa.

European expansion in the nineteenth century had essentially three aspects: scientific, technological and economic. In Africa, the Portuguese[36] combined empirical and scientific curiosity with the traditional slave-trade subject to only loose state control. This state of affairs continued until the time when other European nations embarked on colonization in Africa using the powerful means that the Industrial Revolution made available to them. From that point onwards, scientific exploitation enjoyed the official backing of the University and the Royal Academy of Sciences.

In 1797, the mathematician Lacerda e Almeida was the first Portuguese scientist to attempt to cross Africa but, not having any quinine, he died of fever at Cazembe. By the end of the eighteenth century the Portuguese had assembled the necessary material conditions to undertake the crossing of Africa with the involvement of experienced men, and two black *pombeiros*, assimilated by Luso-African society, with a great deal of experience of travelling on foot and capable of keeping a log book, were the guides. This crossing of Africa was possible thanks to the African chiefs who opened the way to their fellows in the name of Portugal (1802–14). The log of the *pombeiros*, which came to light in 1843, enabled European geographers to fill previously unknown blank spaces on the map of Africa. The government then became concerned to protect geographical exploration, which had been left to private initiative for almost three decades.

But the traditional trade, the irreplaceable handmaiden of geographical discovery, proved unsuited to consolidating the underpinnings of colonial power at a time when, the 1876 Brussels conference and the 1885 Berlin conference having placed colonial expansion on the agenda of the European powers, scientific and military expeditions became an indissociable part of the competition for economic, cultural and political superiority in the world. Between 1850 and 1876, scientific exploratory missions crossed paths in Central Africa and likewise crossed the paths taken by the *sertanejos*. This showed up the absence of the Portuguese from this competition, a situation revealed in 1853 when the great British explorer Livingstone met the intrepid *sertanejo* Silva Porto in the Barotse kingdom. Their meeting did show, however, that the knowledge acquired by the Portuguese was no small asset for Europe in its quest for answers to its questions about the African continent.

But the reports of Silva Porto and those like him in the *sertão* were out of date in terms of the aims of the new international policy. In 1876, the Sociedade de Geografia de Lisboa and the Ministry of the Navy and Overseas Territories quickly mounted a well-equipped expedition that was entrusted to qualified officers of the Navy and the Army.[37] The scientists measured, observed and drew maps, thus providing precise answers to Europe's questions about the use of modern techniques in colonial expansion. But the explorers, who passed quickly by, judged the indigenous people by European criteria, and their writings, by transmitting snapshots of African societies at a particular time, helped to forge a false view of Africa. Conversely, the writings of the *sertanejos*, ordinary habitués of the bush, acute observers broken to the realities of African life, retain some value. Nevertheless, the geographical movement promoted the comparative study of the various societies, and the scientific explorers came more and more to be regarded as the instruments of European expansion in Africa.

Portugal made efforts to update its means of action in Africa. Establishing settlers on the spot continued to be regarded as the most reliable means of influence, and petty traders, Luso-Africans, deportees and poor settlers all continued to relate to Africans through selective adaptation. But Lisbon no longer had any need for these personal experiences as arguments in international diplomatic meetings. The habitués of the *sertão* were no longer sought out or welcomed by cultural institutions and politicians. Those relations which had, for more than a century, acted as a source of information and training had been pushed into the background.

THE SCRAMBLE FOR AFRICA: THE DIRECT IMPACT ON AUTONOMOUS AFRICAN DEVELOPMENT

The new international law, imposed by the Berlin conference (1885), compelled the Portuguese government to undertake more centralizing action in its African colonies. The steamship, and shortly afterwards the telegraph, enabled it to control the colonial governments more easily. In the urban centres, administrative and military jobs reserved for natives, Luso-Africans, Whites or mestizos, in the absence of Portuguese immigrants, came under threat,[38] local interests were pushed into the background and 'Angolense' families were treated with contempt.

In the 1840s, prohibition of the slave trade had led to condemnation of those who had engaged in it. In fact, the accused were not always those really responsible, and many of them were unjustly convicted. Some took refuge in Brazil and those who stayed were banned from employment in the civil service, denied promotion in the army and systematically replaced by incompetent immigrants.[39] These developments, which Orlando Ribeiro called 'the failure of the colonization of Angola',[40] were denounced for the first time in 1848. The first signs of a radicalization of the opposition between the Europeans and the 'Angolenses' appeared, even though the latter were white.[41] Schools, newspapers and publishing houses closed. The Luso-Africans, who had once had access to education, saw their children doomed to ignorance.[42]

But the administrative centralization did not evolve in a straight line. In the 1860s, the 'Angolenses' made contact with fellow citizens who had emigrated to Brazil and other colonies. An intellectual elite organized itself in Cape Verde and Mozambique. Newspapers such as *O Independente* in Praia and *A Civilizacão da Africa Portuguesa* in Luanda denounced the injustices and errors perpetrated by the authorities. The introduction of the telephone in 1890 increased administrative centralization and the colonial authorities carried out orders diligently. At the beginning of the twentieth century, in colonial societies, the Luso-African stratum underwent a process of subordination. Orlando Ribeiro clearly expresses what was happening: 'an elite to which senior officials, prosperous traders and intellectuals belonged . . . which the immigration of Portuguese with their families pushed aside instead of absorbing'.[43]

The external impact on African societies was, until 1885, indirect, limited and dependent on administrative centres established on the coast. After the Berlin conference, the colonial nations put direct pressure on Africa. Portugal aligned itself with the other conquering nations, with the watchword: 'Let us do as the English do': 'pacify' populations, mechanize transport, open communication routes, carry out public works and build schools, hospitals, vaccination centres and religious missions.[44] Implementation of this programme highlighted the technical and financial inability of the Portuguese authorities to develop the vast territories they claimed in the hinterland.

The leading commercial centres of the coastal towns were transferred to former entrepôts in the *sertão*. Traditional Luso-African trade and all forms of exchange were affected by it. The autonomy of Africans in trading networks rapidly declined.[45] Military occupation of the hinterland and the opening of communication routes precipitated the collapse of traditional political structures. After 1890, 'pacification' attracted trading companies, creating what amounted to a 'migratory movement towards the interior'.[46]

The monopoly that Africans had held over the extraction of natural produce, long respected by the *sertanejo* trade, was challenged: it was urgent to take over the last link in the commercial network linking Africa to the international economy. The destructive hunts organized by the Europeans had serious effects on wildlife, and even undermined the magical and religious system. Equally laden with consequences was the removal after 1890 of the former *sertanejo*, the transporter of commodity-currencies, in favour of the *sertanejo* who was a producer of alcohol, which became the main exchange currency in the *sertão*.[47] The trading firms were closely supervised by the colonial authorities and the natives, replaced as middlemen, lost contact with the outside world.[48]

The staking out of colonial zones of influence eliminated political formations and transformed pre-colonial socio-economic areas. The borders of African kingdoms, traditionally defined by relations of vassalage, were now governed by European international law, leading to serious disputes with results that are still with us today. Notwithstanding the presence of the colonial power, the persistence of an 'indigenous political geography'[49] could not be glossed over. Despite the internal upheavals and the lack of security of communication routes, the local aristocracies did not remain passive spectators. They were not always easy partners and were able to put up resistance and use diplomacy. 'It is not always possible to ascertain who is using whom in this kind of situation'.[50]

Having no support from capitalists, who showed little interest, Portugal sought to put into practice the 'humanist idea of civilizing and assimilating the African savage', with the funds available in the state treasury. Religious missions were also an effective instrument of 'civilization' because of the speed with which they worked, their independence and their low costs.[51] The Huila mission, founded in 1881 by the Congregation of the Holy Spirit, was a 'laboratory mission', which from 1889 embarked on a movement to expand towards the eastern border of Angola.[52]

Contacts between Catholic missionaries and African societies were limited to the preservation of good neighbourly relations, without any interpenetration. The missionaries did not properly understand that the world of Africans was pervaded by the sacred and that the whole rhythm of social life was marked by rituals. They would not hear of converted Africans continuing to live in traditional society. The missionaries created a protected Christian area where the powers of lineages and ancestors could not penetrate. The first catechumens were young people uprooted from their lineage by slavery and ransomed by Christian charity. The growth of this Christian social fabric, open to the local cultures, led to the emergence of religious syncretism.[53] The Christian area ultimately reproduced an Africanized, messianic and prophetic Christianity.

Prolonged relations extending over centuries between Africans and Portuguese were reflected in shared experiences of struggle and collaboration. Meanwhile, Africa assimilated second-generation Whites and *mestizos*, adopted writing, selected objects, learned techniques, adapted religion, broadened its political, geographical and ethnic view of the world and evaluated, as best as it could, its own territory and the geo-strategic role that it might play internationally. It selected external elements to construct its own modernity. It was no longer simply a market for raw materials, or a continent that was a mere receptacle for trading. It had knowledge of its own to share which was unknown to Europeans. But colonization settled Europeans on the spot to decide the fate of Africans. Mastery of the new technologies was no longer passed on to them, leading to a regression of productive and creative capacities among them.

But Africa's deep-seated knowledge resisted and survived the collapse of political and social structures, the imposition of objects and habits, the seizure of land and property, the uprooting of populations and the dispersal of lineages. The technological and financial inabilities of Portugal, a poor country, favoured the maintaining of human relationships and the accumulation of experiences that were gradually absorbed by Africans. Africa's entry into modernity had been interrupted by the brutal impact of colonization, which wiped out its capacities for initiative and creativity. Our study of the time when Africa was master of its directions, its preferences and its choices will perhaps produce the beginning of a response to the question of the capacity of this continent to make its mark in the modern world.

NOTES

1 The Senegal, Gambia, São Domingos Rivers and the Rio Grande and Rio Nunez.

2 Even on the coast of Mozambique, it was the Arabs who travelled to Monomotapa.

3 D. Francisco I. de Sousa Coutinho, 'Memórias do reino de Angola 1773 e 1775', *Arquivos de Angola*, Luanda, Vol. IV, No. 49, January 1939.

4 'Many of these early traders and their descendants were subsequently incorporated into the Umbundu stock, and in some instances whole communities of them', Gladwyn M. Childs, *Umbundu Kinship and Character*, London, 1949, pp. 197–8.

5 Jean-Luc Vellut, 'Notes sur le Luanda et la frontière luso-africaine (1700–1900)', *Etudes d'Histoire Africaine*, Université National du Zaïre, III, 1972, p. 97.

6 Carlos Ervedosa, 1980, *Arqueologia Angolana*, Ediçoes 70, pp. 395–426.

7 Mário António de Oliveira, 1981, *Alguns Aspectos de Administraçao de Angola em Época de Reformas (1834–51)*, Lisbon, pp. 33, 104–8. Skirts made from tree bark.

8 This African stage 'of a circuit made up of a trade in and out' has often been overlooked. Jean-Luc Vellut, 1989, 'L'économie internationale des côtes de Guinée inférieure au XIXème siècle', *I Reuniaõ International de História de Africa. Relação Europa-Africa no. 3° Quartel do Séc. XIX*, Instituto de Investigaçao Cientifica Tropical, Lisbon, pp. 142–3.

9 J. Rodrigues Graça, 1890, 'Expediçao ao Muatiânvua-Diário de António Ferreira da Silva Porto', 1986, Vol. I, introdução e notas de Maria Emilia Madeira Santos, Coimbra.

10 See *Viagens e Apontamentos de um Portuense em Africa. Diário de António Ferreira da Silva Porto*, 1986, Vol. I, introdução e notas de Maria Emilia Madeira Santos, Coimbra.

11 Shells/currency: *zimbos*, cowries, *mandés* or *pandes*.

12 Childs, 1949, *Umbundu Kingship*, p. 200.

13 A. C. Pedroso Camito, 1854, *O Muata-Cazembe e os Povos Maraves, Chevas, Muízas, membas, Lundas e outros de Africa Austral. Diário de Expedição Portugesa Comandada pelo Major Monteiro e Dirigida àquele Imperador nos anos de 1831 e 1832*, Lisbon.

14 *Ibid.* pp. 219–20.

15 J.-L. Vellut, 1980, 'Africa Central do Oeste em Véspera da Partilha Colonial: um Esboço Histórico Século XIX', *Africa*, S. Paulo, pp. 110ff.

16 *Viagens e Apontamentos de un Portuense em Africa. Diário de António Ferreira da Silva Porto*, 1986, Vol. I, introdução, pp. 117ff.

17 Biblioteca Pública Municipal do Porto, *Diário de Silva Porto*, 1864, Vol. III, p. 119.

18 Biblioteca Pública Municipal do Porto, *Diário de Silva Porto*, 1868, Vol. V, p. 44.

19 Camito, 1854, *Muata Cazember*, pp. 146–7 and 217.

20 M. E. Madeira Santos, 1989, *Tecnologias em Presença: Manufacturas Europeias e Artefactos Africans (c. 1850–80)*, Reunião International de História de Africa, Lisbon, pp. 207–40.

21 Camito, 1854, *Muata Cazember*, pp. 38–9.

22 Biblioteca Pública Municipal do Porto, *Diário de Silva Porto*, 1880, Vol. XIX.

23 A. Augusto de Carvalho, 1894, *Viagem à Mussumba do Muatiânvua*, Vol. IV, Lisbon, p. 793.

24 Paiva Couceiro, 1892, *Relatório da Viagem entre Baikundo e as Terras do Mucusso*, Lisbon, pp. 73–5.

25 Biblioteca Pública Municipal do Porto, *Diário de Silva Porto*, 1863, Vol. III, pp. 256ff.

26 Jean-Pierre Chrétien, 1988, 'The Historical Dimension of Alimentary Practices in Africa', *Diogènes*, No. 144, pp. 92–3.

27 *Diário de Silva Porto, Viagens e Apontamentos, 1861, Vol. II* (forthcoming).

28 *Ibid.*

29 *Diário de Silva Porto, Viagens e Apontamentos, 1861, Vol. II* (forthcoming).

30 *Ibid.*

31 *Ibid.*

32 Jean Copans, 1990, *La longue marche de la modernité africaine, savoirs intellectuels, démocratie*, Karthala, Paris, p. 229.

33 Jean-Luc Vellut, 1982, 'Notes sur le Lunda', p. 141.

34 Biblioteca Pública Municipal do Porto, *Viagens e apontamentos*, Vol. VII, p. 141.

35 This topic has been studied by M. E. Madeira Santos, 1988, *Viagens de exploração terrestre dos Portugueses em África*, IICT, 2nd edn, Lisbon, pp. 175ff.

36 Hermenigildo Capello, Roberto Ivens and Alexandre Serpa Pinto.

37 Fernando Albuquerque Mourao, 1989, *As duas Vertentes do Processo no Século XIX: Idealismo e Realismo*, RIHA, Lisbon, p. 40.

38 Carlos Pacheco, 1990, *José da Silva Maia Ferreira. O Homen e a sua Época*, Unao de Escritores Angolanos, Luanda, p. 201.

39 J. A. de Carvalho Menesses, 1848, *Demonstração Geografica e Politica do Territorío Portugeêz na Guiné Inferior, que Abrange o Reino de Angola Benguella e suas Dependências*, Rio de Janeiro, pp. 27ff.

40 Orlando Ribeiro, 1981, *A Colonização de Angola e o seu fracasso*, Impresa Nacional, Lisbon.

41 J. A. de Carvalho Meneses, 1848, pp. 123 and 151.

42 *Ibid.*, pp. 35, 165.

43 Orlando Ribeiro, 1981, pp. 132–3.

44 M. E. Madeira Santos, 1988, pp. 294–6, 360–2. Between 1880 and 1902 railways were built between Luanda and Ambaca, Laurenço Marques and Pretoria, from Beira towards Salisbury and from Benguela towards Katanga. River navigation using steamships began on the Cuenza, the Zambezi and the Shire and the telegraph network was extended.

45 Francisco Paulo Cid, 1892, 'Relatório do Governador', p. 14.

46 Augusto Bastos, 1912, *Monografia da Catumbela*, Lisbon, pp. 36, 43.

47 Adelino Torres, 1991, pp. 233–4, 247.

48 *Memória sobre a Colónia Portuguensa no Lobale*, 1903, Questão do Bãrotse, Lisbon.

49 Ilidio do Amaral, 1981, 'Entre o Cunene e o Cubango, ou a propósito de uma fronteira africana', *Garcia de Porta, sér. Geog.*, Vol. 6, Nos. 1–2, Lisbon, p. 19.

50 J.-L. Vellut, 1987, 'Résistances et espaces de liberté dans l'histoire coloniale du Zaïre': avant la march à l'indépendance, ca. 1876–1945'. In C. Coquery-Vidrovitch, A. Forest and H. Weiss (eds) *Rébellion-révolution au Zaïre 1963–65*, Vol. I, Harmattan, Paris, pp. 29ff.

51 *Missoes de Angola. Parecer e proposta da comissao Africana*, Lisbon, Sociedade de Geografia de Lisboa, n.d., pp. 3–4.

52 *Relatório do Padre José Maria Antunes ao Minitro do Ultramar, 1 de Dezembro de 1894, Spiritana Monumenta Africana, Série Africana, Angola (Ediçao de António Brásio)*, Louvain, Editions Enauwelaerts, 1970, Vol. IV (1890–1903), p. 251.

53 Carlos Estermen, 1893, *Etnografia de Angola (sudoeste e centro)*, Vol. I, IICT, Lisbon, pp. 453–83.

15.6
SOUTHERN AFRICA

Ngwabi Bhebe

INTRODUCTION

This section on Southern Africa covers Botswana, Lesotho, Malawi, Namibia, South Africa, Swaziland, Zambia and Zimbabwe, and will be discussed under five themes which also played a decisive role in providing Southern Africa with a cultural, socio-economic, and political infrastructure. These were *proto-difaqane/-mfecane*; the expansion of the missionary and traders frontier; the Boer Trek or migration into the interior from the Cape Colony; the discovery of vast mineral deposits at Kimberley in the Rand in the imposition of colonial rule. *Mfecane or difaqane* refers to the violent disruptions and demographic changes that engulfed Zululand first and then the whole of Southern Africa. Until recently *mfecane* was dated to the beginning of the nineteenth century and attributed to the Zulu king Shaka. Following Julian Cobbing's work historians of the sub-region have revisited and revised their views on the causes of *mfecane* and are even dating its origins to the mid-eighteenth century, if not earlier. The causes of the upheavals are seen now as internally generated among the northern Nguni and externally produced in the north-eastern Cape colonial frontier and in the trading port and hinterland of the Delagoa Bay.[1] The tracing of the *mfecane or difaqane* to earlier than the beginning of the nineteenth century has prompted historians now to speak of *mfecane/difaqane* proper, as referring to the struggle for the control of northern Zululand first between Zwide and Dingiswayo and then between Zwide and Shaka the one hand, and then to speak of the *proto-mfecane/proto-difaqane* from 1750 to 1822 on the other.[2]

PROTO-DIFAQANE/-MFECANE

A number of factors were associated with the *proto-difaqane/-mfecane*. The first was international trade, whose axis was the Mozambique coast where it was instituted by Swahili traders who were doing business as far south as Sofala as early as the eighth century. By the mid-eighteenth century, the Portuguese had long replaced the Swahili, even though their trading ports were also visited by Dutch, French and English traders. Over generations trade routes had opened up between the interior of Southern Africa and the Mozambican coast to serve as channels for European and Asiatic imports, such as beads, cloth, porcelain, fire-arms, etc., and for African exports, including gold, copper, ivory, furs, hides, ostrich feathers, etc. The economies that generated and absorbed these commodities in the interior

were state managed, so that the tendency was for ambitious royal lineage leaders, whose people straddled or lived next to trade routes or within areas endowed with any of the export resources, to struggle to dominate the production and export of the commodities or to tax the traffic that passed through their territories. Moreover, optimal production and control of export resources were ensured by population sizes, so that the larger the state the larger was the productive labour and the army which doubled up as a military force and a hunting instrument. Both occupations withdrew male labour from food production, leaving women and children in the latter employment. Women, who were also vital for the reproduction of the group, were secured either by raiding for them from neighbouring societies or by paying for them with cattle bride wealth. The net effect of the struggle by different lineage leaders and their followers to increase their territories, populations, and cattle and to control local and international trade and trade routes was to produce violent competition among Southern African societies.

The following areas emerged as vortices in the subregion, whose violent upheavals produced large-scale migrations and territorial aggrandizements: the Zimbabwe plateau, northern Transvaal, southern and west-central Transvaal and the adjacent south, eastern Botswana, the Cape Colony and Delagoa Bay hinterland. On the Zimbabwe plateau, Changamires's Rozvi state, having eclipsed the earlier Mutapa and Torwa empires, dominated trade with the Portuguese via Zumbo in the Zambezi valley and the Savi and Limpopo river valley trade routes. Changamire's Rozvi eruptions of civil wars, raids and resultant refugee migrations impacted on the Sotho/Tswana and Venda in the south and south-west and produced similar waves further on, so that Neil Parsons is compelled to speak of 'the period of increasing violence about 1770–1820 from the Zambezi southwards'.[3]

In the northern Transvaal, among the Venda, Lovedu, and Pedi, the northern Rozvi shock waves converged with the waves originating from the south among the Sotho/Tswana. Moreover the Venda, Pedi and Lovedu were in rich hunting grounds and were blessed with rich copper and iron deposits, which they mined for the itinerant Remba, who in turn smelted the ores and manufactured weapons, implements and items of adornment for trading locally and internationally.[4] These people, too, either straddled or lived near coastal-interior trade routes. Large Venda, Lovedu and Pedi kingdoms emerged in the Soutpansberg and Steelpoort valley out of the struggles to control and monopolize wealth generated locally and internationally, coupled also with the impact of Sotho-Tswana and Changamires Rozvi, who brought a culture of state building. Thus the Lovedu trace their political aggregation under Mudjaji rain-queens and the introduction of the 'fire' circumcision to the immigration of the Rozvi from Changamire; while the Venda trace the genesis of their Singo chiefdoms to the coming of the Shona also from the Zimbabwe plateau. Both cultures adopted stone building from the same direction. In the meantime, the impact of the Sotho-Tswana was more on the Pedi, where the Kgatla imposed their rule and built a powerful kingdom whose wealth rested partially on the east-west trade carried by the Pedi themselves and the Tsonga from Delagoa Bay and Inhambane.[5]

Proto-difaqane among the Sotho-Tswana is considered by both historians and archaeologists to have reached its climax from 1770 to 1820.[6] During this violent period the Sotho-Tswana were at each other's throats trying to wrestle from one another grazing lands, hunting grounds, permanent watering places, monopoly over local and external trade, cattle and women. Chiefs developed an unusual appetite for Asiatic and European goods brought by ox wagon traders and by human caravans to be exchanged for ivory, furs, ostrich feathers, copper, etc. By 1820, warfare was endemic among the Sotho-Tswana as chiefs militarized their people in order to raid far and wide for the resources to sustain their consumer appetites and to defend themselves from similarly motivated adversaries.[7]

These upheavals brought about important socio-economic and cultural changes that came to characterize the Sotho-Tswana in the nineteenth and twentieth centuries. Historians and archaeologists agree that population agglomerations which are characteristic of the Sotho-Tswana even today date to the *proto-difaqane* when these people sought protection in urbanized settlements and in defensible locations such as hilltops and caves and even supplemented these with perimeter stone walls.[8] Since this went on at the same time as territorial expansion and the absorption of foreigners, historians believe that this was the time when Sotho-Tswana rulers invented the 'fluid ward system . . . whereby foreigners [were] incorporated into the patrilineal decision-making groups', an efficient incorporation system, which allowed considerable social and political independence to subordinate lineages without threatening the integrity of the whole chiefdom.[9]

Another important feature of the Sotho-Tswana, which worsened their violent competition, was cattle. Cattle were invaluable for the exchange of wives, labour, and cementing loyalty in society.[10]

It is important to understand not only the role of cattle but also that of women and grain. Women were agricultural producers and reproducers of the tribe, and grain provided food and constituted a means to enhance the status of chiefs and other people of power, as status was assessed on the basis of how much grain one could boast. So, chiefs became interested in having plenty of cattle, which provided bride wealth to pay for wives; and in having large number of followers who could provide large armies to raid for cattle and women. Women, agriculture, cattle, and large followings, all became interlinked means of amassing power and enhancing one's status.[11]

Proto-difaqane was a watershed in the Southern African international commercial traffic, which all along had been tilted in favour of the Mozambique coast and now began to flow in increasing volumes to and from the Cape colony. Links with the Mozambican ports were far from being completely severed, since the slave trade, which was now outlawed in the Atlantic in the nineteenth century, increased greatly via these eastern outlets. The Shona and others in the Zambezi basin and the Tsonga further south maintained the East Coast as their source of lucrative international commerce.[12]

The first to appear north of the Orange river and therefore to provide firm links between the Cape Colony and the interior were the Kora, original cattle keepers of the Cape, and the Orlam, Boer migrants, and both groups were hunters and herders and as nomads lived in their ox wagons. In their wake came diverse elements, such as bandits, traders, missionaries, Khoisan, Boers, Griqua, and Coloureds, all of whom pressed upon the Sotho/Tswana and aggravated the violence initiated by *proto-difecane*.

THE CAPE COLONY

Founded by the Dutch East India Company as a halfway station to its East Indian empire in 1652 and taken over by the British at the beginning of the nineteenth century, the Cape was by the end of the eighteenth century a significant European settlement whose economic interests were beginning to be felt in the interior. Its rapid expansion from the immediate hinterland of Cape Town to the Orange River to the north-east and to the east where it abutted against the Sotho/Tswana and the Xhosa, was inherent in its economy. The second and third generations of settlers originally planted by the company to supply its trading ships on their way to the East with fresh foods, abandoned settled life and became migrant cattle herders and competed with the original inhabitants for stock, watering places and grazing areas. Their land tenure system encouraged their nomadism. Each settler who could afford to pay an annual tax of 24 rix dollars to the government (which was never efficient enough to collect it anywhere) was entitled to own land of up to 3,000 *morgen*, which was abandoned for a fresh one on the exhaustion of the old. This practice, together with the practice of every young man who could afford it, on reaching maturity, being also entitled to similar farms, produced a vastly expansive colony and exacerbated competition for resources with the Khoisan. Boer migrants managed with their fire power and horses to overcome, dispossess and to either reduce Khoisan to various forms of abject dependence or to drive them to the periphery of their ever-expanding frontier; hence the Khoisan's forming the vanguard of the Cape colonial expansion among the Sotho-Tswana across the Orange River.[13] Furthermore, up to the beginning of the nineteenth century, the Cape was a slave-owning society, so that the war captives produced by the settlers' conflicts with the Khoisan and refugees escaping Sotho-Tswana conflicts ended up as slaves of white settlers. Before looking at some of the lasting implications of the Cape Colony's expansion into the interior, it is necessary to examine *mfecane* proper as yet another African revolution that laid the cultural infrastructure for Euro-Afro interactions.

MFECANE

There is no agreement on the causes of the *mfecane*, and the point is made by Elizabeth Eldredge, who argues that none of the factors proposed by different writers – such as population pressure, environmental degradation or international trade – on its own adequately explains the outbreak of the *mfecane/difaqane*. Although she does not explicitly anchor her argument in the *proto-difaqane/-mfecane*, her contention is suggestive of a set of causes that accelerated an ongoing revolution rather than initiated it. Indeed, she says, by the end of the eighteenth century African chiefs in Southern Africa had built up considerable power and wealth based on the Indian Ocean coastal trade in ivory, which acknowledges gains achieved during the preceding *proto*-period.[14]

But this accumulation of power and wealth by chiefs, according to Eldredge, was undermined when elephants got weeded out so that these rulers now ran out of taxable alternatives especially, since international trade had not stimulated any corresponding expansion in agricultural output. Chiefs were faced with diminishing revenues unless they resorted to raiding their neighbours' resources. Moreover, trade had already created inequalities among and within African societies by placing wealth in the hands of a few powerful individuals and a few chiefdoms, both of whom used their new wealth to build up strong armies with which again to enrich themselves through raids against their weaker neighbours. Eldredge further suggests that this unequal accumulation of wealth went hand-in-hand with the dislocation of traditional systems of redistribution of resources during times of scarcity. All these factors worsened competition for resources within and among societies during droughts from 1800 to 1803, 1812 and 1816–18.[15] These lean years, according to Eldredge, not only coincided with worsening turmoil but also provoked a political revolution among the northern Nguni.[16] The same droughts hit the Sotho-Tswana west of the Drakensberg and combined with crop and livestock epidemics between 1816 and 1818. Before they could recover from these devastations they were invaded in 1822 by Hlubi refugees fleeing from the *mfecane*, which was now underway among the northern Nguni.[17]

West of the Drakensberg mountains, violence was made worse by the new economic pressures induced by the Cape colonial frontier. As both Julian Cobbing and Eldredge point out, Cape settlers and colonial officials perpetrated violence by promoting slave raiding across the Orange River. Settler violence forced Khoisan and Coloureds to unite and move across the Orange where they were known by various names, such as Bastaards, Kora, and Korana and in the end as Griqua and Bergnaars. White traders supplied them with guns to hunt for ivory, furs, etc., and colonial officials supported them too with guns, expecting them to use the firearms for protecting the frontier. But the Griqua used the firearms to raid Sotho-Tswana for cattle and slaves to sell to the white settlers in the Cape Colony.[18]

The *mfecane-difaqane* revolution was associated with some socio-political and cultural changes throughout most of Southern Africa. The first people to be affected by the changes were Zwide's Ndwandwe, Dingiswayo's Mthethwa, and Shaka's Zulu. All three introduced age-regiments for their armies, a practice perhaps copied from earlier empires such as the Rozvi in the Zimbabwe plateau and the Tembe in the Delagoa Bay hinterland. From an economic point of view, regiments were significant in that they were used as an efficient means of raiding neighbours for livestock and grain, and for group hunting of elephants for their tusks and lions for their skins. From a cultural standpoint, these regiments replaced the circumcision

practice, which had been used to train young men into adulthood among the northern Nguni. Another big change in marital practice was that men were no longer allowed to marry until they had done their military service to the satisfaction of the king, which sometimes delayed their marriage up to the age of thirty. Thus girls were deprived the opportunity to marry men of their own age and forced to marry men much older than themselves and to marry into polygamous families, since men who were allowed to marry after completing their service at any given time were always much fewer in number than girls of marriageable age.[19]

Zwide and his mother introduced innovations that were later copied as national symbols and institutions by others. The monarchy, for instance, was made dual, with the queen mother ruling the kingdom with her son. This was taken over by the Swazi where Thandile, the mother of Swazi king Mswati (1840–68), introduced the system from her Ndwandwe people. All the rulers associated with *mfecane* observed *incwala* (the first fruit ritual) as an annual national ceremony. It was Shaka, however, who put together all these practices and made them into powerful and inspiring symbols of the Zulu nation.[20]

Shaka's methods and the revolutionary achievements of the *mfecane* were dispersed widely in the whole subcontinent, from the Cape Colony to southern Tanzania. When the Ndwandwe were defeated by Shaka in 1818 and forced to abandon their homes, those who escaped death or being absorbed in the Zulu nation, fled north under two of their generals. One of these, Soshangane, decided to carve a home for himself between Delagoa Bay and the lower Zambezi, while his compatriot Zwangendaba raided his way through Mozambique and Zimbabwe until he came to Southern Tanzania, where he died in 1848 and his people then split into the Tuta Ngoni of southern Tanzania, the Mpezeni Ngoni of eastern Zambia, and the Mombera Ngoni of Malawi.[21]

Still in the north, *mfecane* among the northern Nguni also influenced the formation of the Swazi state, under its leader Sobhuza I, who retreated from the Pongola valley to avoid annihilation by the then formidable Ndwandwe and lodged himself in the defensible mountainous centre of Swaziland. Here he initiated the process of conquering and absorbing the Sotho original inhabitants of the country. His son and successor, Mswati, and his mother Thandile welded the nation together by giving it national symbols, traditions and strong government, such as powerful royal medicines that had national significance, *incwala*, and the *libandla* – a national council made up of all adult males of the nation. The conquered Sotho and others learned the language of their conquerors.

Another offshoot of the northern Nguni who became the vehicle of transporting Nguni language and other cultural practices was Mzilikazi, who built the Ndebele nation. He first settled on the Transvaal Highveld but was forced out of there by the Boers and their Griqua allies in 1838 and settled in western Zimbabwe in 1840. Here the Ndebele spread Sindebele – a Nguni language – and other aspects among the Shona speaking people. Almost at the same time as the Ndebele, the Hlubi of Mpangazita also crossed the Drakensburg on to the Highveld and were soon followed by the Ngwane of Mathiwane. It is important to observe at this point that it was the Hlubi, the Ngwane, Ndebele, and the Griqua, who exacerbated violence and warfare among the Highveld Sotho-Tswana and are therefore regarded as having brought about *difaqane* (the enlargement and intensification of warfare).

The *difaqane* turmoil forced some Sotho-Tswana Nguni to break up, and others to amalgamate into large kingdoms. Good examples of broken-up groups were the Hlubi and Ngwane, the initiators of the bloodshed themselves. They clashed over the mastery of the Caledon valley and the Hlubi were crushed in *c.*1824–5, so that the Ngwane victors absorbed some of their survivors while others joined Mzilikazi's Nbebele. In the meantime, Mathiwane led his people to the Pondo country on the eastern Drakensberg, where in 1822 he was defeated at the battle of Mbolompo by a combined force of the British, Xhosa, and Thembu. The Ngwane were reduced to refugees called Mfengu by the Xhosa.

Examples of the amalgamating tendency were the Pedi and the Basotho. Under their king Thulare (1780–1820), the Pedi built, as we have already seen, a powerful kingdom in the Steelpoort valley. Following the death of Thulare, a succession crisis engulfed them, which also coincided with Mzilikazi's Ndebele invasion of their country. Between 1822 and 1823 the Ndebele killed all the sons of Thulare except Sekwati, who retreated with his people into the stronghold of the Lulu mountains, where he revived the kingdom and rebuilt it out of refugees from other victims of *mfecane*.[22]

Similarly, Moshoeshoe of the Basotho, faced with constant attacks in his exposed original Butha Buthe homeland, decided to settle on Thaba Bosiu hill, which could easily be defended. The case of the Sotho-Tswana who undertook long migrations was represented by Sebetwane's Kololo, who, after being elbowed out of southern Transvaal and south-eastern Botswana, decided to go and settle in the south of the Zambezi floodplain in western Zambia. They thus carried Sotho-Tswana culture to southern Central Africa and in fact also took the initiative to open trade with Griqua traders from the Cape Colony and the Ovimbundu, who brought Portuguese goods from Angola.[23]

Thus *mfecane-difaqane*, just like the *proto-difaqane/-mfecane* before it laid a strong cultural-political-economic infrastructure for Southern Africa – an infrastructure that indeed pre-dated the Western impact and its imperialism and colonialism, even though ironically the infrastructure presented a ready basis for the transmission and advance of those European influences. In fact Western traders, missionaries, colonists, mineralogists, labour recruiters, and of course military strategists, locked on to this Nguni and Sotho-Tswana network from the south, all the time taking advantage of the relative commercial-cultural edge of the Cape Colony. A good example of this and a trail-blazer was David Livingstone, who from the beginning followed in the footsteps of the Kololo from Botswana to the southern Zambezi floodplain; and then took advantage of the Kololo trade networks with the Angolan Ovombundu and the Zambezi valley Tonga to explore that region, before following the Ngoni to southern Tanzania. The obvious colonizer was Cecil John Rhodes, who acquired the whole region outside South Africa up to the Copperbelt of Zambia on the basis of treaties he extracted from nearly the same network of post-*mfecane* states or their successors. Rhodes was, however, preceded by missionaries, the Great Trek, and mineral discoveries: developments which in themselves were critical for the cultural and economic transformation of the region.

MISSIONARIES

The London Missionary Society (LMS) pioneered missionary work in the interior of Southern Africa. The first to be touched by this religious frontier of Europe were the Xhosa, among whom the Hollander J. T. van der Kemp preached the gospel and taught agriculture from 1799 until he established a permanent station at Bethelsdorp near Port Elizabeth in 1801. He was followed by more LMS missionaries who decided to settle in the Xhosa country proper. The Methodists who came between 1823 and 1845 decided to go to Pondoland. In the meantime, the missionary frontier had also taken a north-easterly direction, following a British peace expedition sent to the north of the Orange River in 1801. While some of these abandoned their calling for more lucrative occupations, William Anderson remained among the Griqua and eventually acquired an influential political and religious position from 1801 to 1820. When he retired his place was taken over by the more famous Robert Moffat, who moved his centre of operations to the Tlaping town of Kuruman. In 1823 Methodists started work among the Rolong and settled at Thaba Nchu in 1833, and in the same year the Paris Evangelical Missionary Society moved into Lesotho. American Board missionaries, on the recommendation of Robert Moffat, went to preach to the Ndebele and Tswana at Mosega in 1835, while another group of the same mission entered Zululand in 1836. When the Ndebele migrated to Zimbabwe, Robert Moffat again followed them up to establish an LMS station there at the same time as another wing of the same organization was despatched to the Kololo kingdom. The Ngoni challenge in Malawi was taken up by the Free Church of Scotland, when they established Livingstonia Mission in memory of David Livingstone on the shores of Lake Malawi in 1875.[24]

The missionaries' primary aim was to preach the gospel in order to convert Africans to Christianity; in the process, they became vehicles of transmitting Western education and Western industrial habits. Thus mission stations, missionaries and their African helpers found themselves performing several functions, such as literacy teaching, preaching and training people in agriculture, carpentry, building and many other crafts. They also learnt African languages, into which they translated the Bible and other religious texts. Livingstone had emphasized the importance of relieving physical suffering among Africans by means of medical interventions. His message was taken up by nearly all missionary organizations, which tried to include medically trained people among their missionary teams and also built clinics and later hospitals at their stations; some of these hospitals also trained nurses.[25] Missionaries and their families were often the first white people to settle permanently among the interior Africans, and in South Africa they were followed by Boer migrant families during the so-called Great Trek, although the two white groups were not related in their aims and activities.

THE GREAT TREK

The Great Trek was an exodus of Afrikaners from the Cape Colony into the interior of Southern Africa, as they tried to escape what they considered to be restrictive and oppressive British rule, especially its anti-slavery aspects. Their relations with Africans were soured right from the beginning in that they were attracted by the same resources to which African states claimed exclusive rights. Thus, Boers identified Natal-land, claimed by the Zulu and their subjects, as excellent for their arable activities; the Orange Free State and Eastern Transvaal, territories of the Sotho-Tswana, as ideal for their own cattle grazing; and the Venda country in the northern Transvaal as suitable for their hunting. These long-standing sources of conflict were aggravated by Boer raids against African societies for cattle and slaves.

From 1835, Boers moved across the Orange River in large numbers and their first major obstacles seemed to be Mzilikazi's Ndebele and the Zulu, now ruled by Shaka's half-brother Dingane. In November 1837, the Boers and their Tswana and Griqua allies forced Mzilikazi to leave the Transvaal and to go and settle in western Zimbabwe by 1840. In 1838 and in January 1840, Boers combined with Mpande, Dingane's dissident half-brother, to drive Dingane out of the country into Swaziland, where he was murdered. Mpande took over power and ruled as a vassal of the Boers.

The defeat of both the Zulu and the Ndebele, though far from breaking the backbone of African resistance in their interior, opened the way for the Boers to establish their independent republics; the first was Natal, which was dissolved when the British, wanting to block them from having access to the sea, annexed the territory in 1843. On the basis of treaties signed with Sotho-Tswana and Griqua states in 1837, the Boers settled between the Orange and the Vaal rivers. When the British, who had pursued the Boers into the interior, gave up their sovereign claims over them in 1854 and pulled out, the coast was clear for the establishment of the Orange Free State as a Boer republic. In 1859 all Boer factions, which had divided the Transvaal reluctantly, coalesced under one leadership to form the South African Republic.

By the 1850s, therefore, the *mfecane/difaqane*, the Great Trek and British colonial expansion had created a patchwork of African and white independent states and dependent British colonies. Besides the many wars that broke out between Africans and whites, the two racial groups were being drawn together by economic relations arising out of white dependence on African labour, trade relations and the African desire to exploit the new opportunities to earn incomes in European enterprises. These opportunities vastly increased with the discoveries of diamonds at Kimberley in 1868–70 and gold in the Witwatersrand in 1884.

ECONOMIC INTERACTIONS

Shula Marks and Atmore[26] have observed that *mfecane*, the Great Trek and British colonial expansion produced the simultaneous existence of different modes of production and social formations, which included hunting economies, tributary mode of production, quasi-feudal systems and colonial economies, all of which experienced an uneven penetration of capital. In this juxtaposition of variegated societies the one dominant feature was that of powerful African kingdoms and colonial states which were incorporating weaker chiefdoms in order to appropriate their surpluses, a process that was in the end won by the white settlers with the backing of British imperial power.

In terms of modes of production characterizing African societies in the nineteenth-century, Marks and Atmore see these as 'complex social formations', which practised cattle and crop farming by means of simple technologies, on a communal basis but having definite divisions of labour between sexes, between aristocracies and commoners, and chiefs embodying the state. Production was carried out in the homestead which was part of a lineage village whose members cooperated to produce a socially necessary surplus by means of work parties in return for beer and or payment in kind, and they also cooperated in cattle herding and in defence operations. Each lineage ensured its reproduction through acquisition of wives from other lineages, in return for whom cattle were paid as bride wealth. Wives provided agricultural labour and reproduced the lineage. Part of the lineage surplus was diverted to the chief and head of state, who in turn was expected to provide food during national festivals and to provide religious protection and guarantee prosperity for his or her people. Control over cattle gave chiefs and heads of lineage power over their people and the means to expand their followers by paying bride wealth. Thus, the Swazi kings used their cattle to expand their power and Shaka to consolidate his Zulu kingdom. The Mpondo chiefs used a cattle-loaning system to create and maintain clientage relationships.

This state and lineage relationship leads Philip Bonner to characterize these social formations of Southern Africa as made up of the articulation of the lineage or 'patrilineage system' or the 'homestead complex' on the one hand and the tributary authority on the other, which controlled economic resources and their distribution in society. 'Through its appropriation of these resources', Marks and Atmore point out, 'the state – or more precisely, the chief – had vital control over the production and reproduction of the lineages, which made up the social formation'.[27] That was how, in particular, the ruling elite in the Swazi, Ndebele, Ngoni, and Gaza states accumulated wealth, which they, in turn, used to consolidate and expand their power. They built age-regiments by means of which the kings controlled warfare and its loot and captives as well as local production. Warfare, as we have seen, produced women and children who provided labour and the reproduction of the tribe.

Marks and Atmore point out that *mfecane* had the added dimension of conditioning the way African societies in the subregion responded to Western penetration. Those who gained from the *mfecane* by building powerful raiding states – such as the Zulu, Ndebele, Swazi, Pedi and Basotho – resisted subjugation well into the nineteenth century; weaker societies which had always been prey to their more powerful neighbours either remained aloof or actually collaborated with the colonial intruders; yet others, who had become accustomed to paying tribute to their more powerful overlords, now sold or paid their surplus in rent to the newcomers.[28]

To illustrate these various shades of African economic responses to Western expansion we shall look at Natal, Herschel, the Mpondo and the Pedi, and these examples will demonstrate among other things that the integration of African societies into capitalism did not require political subjugation, as the latter action actually ended up stifling dynamic African initiatives. Natal, for instance, shows how Africans there were drawn into the capitalist system of production and did so well as to threaten white producers with their competition. Henry Slater, who has looked at the issue closely, argues that it was that African success, which was also at the root of African reluctance to sell their labour to white farmers, which compelled European farmers to combine with the colonial state in an effort to frustrate

African production by means of legislation at the end of the nineteenth and beginning of the twentieth centuries.[29]

In the Natal Boer republic, Afrikaner settlers allocated themselves farms generously, with some having more than one holding of not less than 3,000 *morgens* each in size. At first, they relied for labour on their own servants, whom they had brought up from the Cape. However, no sooner had the republic established peace with the Zulu raiders than the original African owners of land who had sought refuge elsewhere descended from their mountain to lay claim to the same farms now supposedly owned by the Boers. The republic government was soon terminated by the British annexation of Natal, but the legal pattern had now been established whereby Africans found themselves as squatters with white landlords.

With the coming of British rule the picture changed by introducing more landlords of diverse interests, such as missionaries, absentee speculators, small British farmers, crown lands of the colonial state, and African reserves, so that Africans now had a choice to settle on estates where they could maximize opportunities to pursue their own economic interests. Favourable terms for Africans existed on missionary farms, crown lands, reserves and the holdings of absentee landlords, who made their incomes by charging rent to African occupiers. As long as such options remained open Africans used these limited land privileges to accumulate wealth by the use of their lineage production system; through ivory hunting using the share system whereby whites loaned guns to African hunters in return for a share of the ivory hunted; by exchanging their ivory for cattle; and by selling their produce in the emergent towns of Durban and Pietermaritzburg. Africans became relatively rich, self-sufficient, and reluctant to work for farmers who, in fact, were notorious for the low wages they offered, and on top of that offered stiff competition to white producers in agricultural markets. Commercial farmers began to clamour for ways to remove Africans from independent productive pursuits. Opposed to the farmers were missionaries, the government, which was happy to collect revenue from African producers, and absentee landlords who benefited from the rents paid by their African squatters. At the beginning of the twentieth century, the die was cast when commercial farmers combined with industrial capital based on mining to demand the destruction of the basis of African production, culminating in the Native Land Act of 1913, which severely curtailed African access to productive land.[30]

Another area whose integration into the capitalist mode of production saw Africans respond positively to market forces was the Herschel district, which experienced the rise of an African peasantry in the nineteenth century. Colin Bundy, the authority on the area, shows how the peasants of Herschel adapted their traditional methods to step up agricultural production and then used their surpluses to acquire more efficient instruments of production such as ploughs and wagons. They sold their grain to the burgeoning urban centres in the Cape Colony and the Orange Free State, and when diamond mining started at Kimberley yet other markets arose there and along the railway line. Prosperity of the peasants again showed itself in the inequalities that emerged in Herschel with some people owning vast herds of cattle, as many as twenty fields each, and modern transportation means, especially wagons. More money was made when gold mining started in the Rand, where prices for cattle went up because of the demand for beef and ox teams for wagon transportation.

At the beginning of the twentieth-century Herschel's productive capacity had been deliberately undermined through the colonial government's neglect of investment in public utilities and infrastructure, so that its people were getting impoverished and unable to meet their food requirements.[31]

Unlike Natal and Herschel Africans, the Mpondo and Pedi were outside colonial rule. The Mpondo were not annexed until 1894, by which time they were deeply meshed in the capitalist economy. By the 1860s, they were exporting cattle and hide to Cape colonial traders in return for woollen blankets, liquor, cotton goods, and capital items such as horses and guns which were for hunting ivory and other animal products for export. Soon commerce interpenetrated agriculture so that people began to import more efficient tools of production, such as iron hoes and spades to replace wooden ones. As they colonized heavier, more loamed soils than their traditional sandy ones, the Mpondo started to import ploughs for which they used draught oxen, being taught the technique of yoking them by traders and missionaries. By the 1860s, use of the plough had become general among the Mpondo and they had become integrated into the colonial economy.[32]

Turning to the Pedi, it is not clear when they started to engage in the migrant labour system, but by 1862, resident Berlin missionaries were reporting that hundreds of them were going to work in the Cape Colony in order to acquire guns and cattle. Apparently the practice had so caught on, that on reaching puberty a young man demonstrated his manhood by undertaking the hazardous trip to and from the Cape for work. The whole enterprise was well organized in that workers travelled in groups of 200–500, rested in Moshoeshoe's kingdom where in return for a fee they were looked after, and travelled with their own provisions. Group trips were absolutely necessary to provide protection against attacks by Boers through whose territories they passed, and by greedy chiefs who waylaid the migrants to strip them of their earnings. When diamond mines opened, the Pedi and their Tsonga neighbours supplied the largest number of migrant labourers. Moreover, the Pedi rulers had also taken an interest in the labour system so that they were organizing regiments of workers and entering into labour agreements with recruiters in return for a slice of the workers' earnings.[33] Mining, indeed, had an even bigger impact, not only on the Pedi but on the whole of Southern Africa, so that to complete the picture of the interaction between Africans and the white settlers we should end with the impact of the mining industry.

THE IMPACT OF MINING

Diamonds were discovered near the Vaal-Orange confluence in 1867, and this occasioned the large-scale immigration of diggers to the Griqua country where the alluvial diggings were located. Three years later even bigger deposits were located where Kimberley stands today. These fresh findings required deep mining so that they set the foundation for the South African large-scale mining industry. Within five years well over £1,600,000 worth of diamonds were being exported from the mines. The industry provided employment for Southern Africans of all races, and they were being drawn from as far afield as Zimbabwe, where both Shona and Ndebele young men migrated for short periods to Kimberley to go and earn guns.[34] Mining also attracted immigrants and capital from overseas; encouraged urban population concentration, which served as a big market for local farmers; and prompted construction of railways and other forms of transportation, so that when combined with gold mining in 1885, the impact of the industry on Southern Africa was phenomenal.[35]

Gold mining began in earnest in 1886, and its immediate impact was to intensify the migration of both whites and Africans to Johannesburg. Advanced scientific research and application, sophisticated technical engineering and financial administrative skills were brought to bear on the industry to make it pay, over and above, of course, the fact that in the end it was the availability of cheap African labour that accounted for most of its profits. By 1888, forty-four mines were in production, turning out £1,300,000 worth of gold. Railway construction was intensified so that the Cape line reached the Rand in 1892 and Delagoa Bay was linked with another line in 1895. By 1906, gold mining and related industries, which had been interrupted by the Anglo-Boer war of 1899–1902, had attracted an agglomerated population of 51,000 indentured Chinese labourers, 94,000 Africans from all over Southern Africa, and 18,000 whites.[36]

The mining industry and the railway and road construction all helped to create a huge market for commercial agriculture. Because of the limited productive capacity of farmers, prices for their produce rose, giving them the incentive to develop their holdings. Still they failed to cope with the demand so that in 1899 South Africa was forced to import wheat to meet the food requirements of the urban population. Farmers put the blame on two things – shortage of labour and violent fluctuation of prices for their products. The instability of the agricultural industry, too, was the outcome of droughts and diseases. Once slavery was abolished, white settlers in Southern Africa failed to make the logical move of attracting labour by means of economic incentives, insisting on all sorts of compulsions to force Africans to work for them. They remained opposed to giving decent living wages to their workers, claiming that if they paid good wages Africans would satisfy their target needs too soon and then run away. Francis Wilson rightly points out that this was a false assumption because the supply of labour is not dependent upon the amount of time an individual worker is prepared to work for an employer, but also very much on the number of workers that are ready to offer their labour. Because of the poor wages white farmers were prepared to pay the workers, they suffered chronic labour shortages amidst plenty.[37]

The mining revolution in South Africa had political ramifications for the subcontinent, especially the rejuvenation of British imperialism under the leadership of the financial magnate Cecil John Rhodes, who made his fortune in the Kimberley mines. Between 1888 and 1894 the British government cooperated with Rhodes and his colonizing instrument, the British South Africa Company, to bring the whole area covered by Botswana, Zimbabwe, Zambia and Malawi under British rule. Even before the mopping-up operations of bringing effective rule to these areas were completed, Rhodes and his company set about providing their empire with effective communications and transportation systems. The railway from the Cape reached Vryburg in 1890; Mafeking in 1894; Bulawayo in 1897; Mutare in 1898; Wange in 1903; and the Copperbelt in 1911.[38] The railway system facilitated especially the movement of African labour from Malawi, Zambia, Zimbabwe, Botswana and Mozambique, all destined for the insatiable mines and white farms both in Zimbabwe and South Africa.

CONCLUSION

Thus by the beginning of the twentieth century the unifying cultural and political infrastructure provided in the region by the *proto-difaqane/-mfecane* and the *mfecane* proper were complemented and completed by British imperial rule and the network of the movement of migrant labourers. The huge magnet that pulled the region together and also gave it its economic dynamism was the South African mining industry. To pry Africans out of their economic self-sufficiency and to herd them to the mines and white farms, extra economic and harsh means were adopted now that the whites had political power. Both in South Africa and later in Zimbabwe legislation was adopted to limit land available to Africans, on top of taxes that were instituted everywhere in the subregion and which were imposed not so much to raise revenue but simply to compel Africans to sell their labour for cash. As we have noted, all these efforts served to stifle African economic initiatives in their integration into the global economy so that they were compelled to enter the system as impoverished dependants, a status they still suffer today.

NOTES

1 J. Cobbing, 'The Mfecane as Alibi: Thoughts on Dithakong and Mbolopho', *Journal of African History*, 29 (1988) pp. 487–519; N. Parsons, 'Prelude to *Difaqane* in the Interior of Southern Africa *c*.1600–*c*.1822', in: C. Hamilton (ed.) 1995, *The Mfecane Aftermath: Reconstructive Debates in Southern African History*, Johannesburg: Witwatersrand University Press, pp. 323–49; Andrew Manson, 'Conflict in the Western Highveld/Southern Kalahari *c*.1750–1820', in: Hamilton, *The Mfecane Aftermath*, pp. 351–61; Simon Hall, 'Archaeological Indicators for stress in the Western Transvaal Region between the Seventeenth and the Nineteenth Centuries', in: Hamilton, *The Mfecane Aftermath*, pp. 301–22; E. Eldredge, 'Sources of Conflict in Southern Africa, *c*.1800–30: The *Mfecane* Reconsidered', *Journal of African History*, 33 (1992) pp. 1–35; C. A. Hamilton, 'The Character and Objects of Chaka: A Reconstruction of the Making of Shaka as Mfecane Motor', *Journal of African History*, 33 (1992) pp. 27–63.
2 Parsons, 'Prelude to *Difaqane* in the Interior', pp. 335–48.
3 *Ibid.*, p. 335; See also D. N. Beach, 'The Zimbabwe Plateau and Its Peoples', in: David Birmingham and Phyllis M. Martin (eds) 1983, *History of Central Africa*, Vol. 1, London and New York: Longman, pp. 245–77.
4 N. Parsons, 1993, *A New History of Southern Africa*, 2nd edn, London: Macmillan, p. 40.
5 *Ibid.*, pp. 40–3.
6 *Ibid.*, pp. 50–3; Parsons, 'Prelude to *Difaqane* in the Interior'; Manson, 'Conflict in the Western Highveld/ Southern Kalahari'; Hall, 'Archaeological Indicators'.
7 Parsons, *A New History of Southern Africa*, p. 52
8 Parsons, 'Prelude to *Difaqane* in the Interior'; Manson, 'Conflict in the Western Highveld/Southern Kalahari'; Hall, 'Archaeological Indicators'.

9 Parsons, 'Prelude to *Difaqane* in the Interior', p. 336; Manson, 'Conflict in the Western Highveld/Southern Kalahari', p. 356.

10 Manson, 'Conflict in the Western Highveld/Southern Kalahari', pp. 356–7.

11 Parsons, 'Prelude to *Difaqane* in the Interior', p. 337.

12 Beach, 'The Zimbabwe Plateau', p. 252; Parsons, 'Prelude to the *Difaqane* in the Interior', p. 344.

13 F. Wilson, 'Farming, 1866–99', in: M. Wilson and L. Thompson (eds) 1975, *The Oxford History of South Africa*, Vol. 2, Oxford: Clarendon Press, p.106; M. Legassick, 'The Frontier Tradition in South African Historiography', in: Shula Marks and Antony Atmore (eds) 1980, *Economy and Society in Pre-industrial South Africa*, London: Longman, p. 156.

14 Eldredge, 'Sources of Conflict in Southern Africa', pp. 123–53.

15 *Ibid.*, pp. 153–4.

16 *Ibid.*, p. 155.

17 *Ibid.*, p. 158.

18 *Ibid.*, p.140; Cobbing, 'The *Mfecane* as Alibi', pp. 492–500.

19 Parsons, *A New History of Southern Africa*, pp. 68–70; J. D. Omer-Cooper, 'The Nguni Outburst', in: J. E. Flint (ed.) 1976, *The Cambridge History of Africa, from c.1790 to c.1870*, Vol. 5, Cambridge: Cambridge University Press, pp. 322–6; Eldredge, 'Sources of Conflict in Southern Africa', pp. 152–3.

20 L. Thompson, 'Co-operation and Conflict: The Zulu kingdom and Natal', in: Wilson and Thompson, *The Oxford History of South Africa*, p. 345.

21 J. D. Omer-Cooper, 1996, *The Zulu Aftermath: A Nineteenth-Century Revolution in Bantu Africa*, London: Longman, pp. 86–92.

22 P. Delius, 'Migrant Labour and the Pedi, 1840–80', in: Marks and Atmore, *Economy and Society*, pp. 294–5; Thompson, 'Co-operation and Conflict', pp. 403–4.

23 Omer-Cooper, *The Zulu Aftermath*, pp. 99–127.

24 Jean and John Comaroff, 1991, *Of Revelation and Revolution: Christianity, Colonialism and Consciousness in South Africa*, Vol. 1, Chicago, University of Chicago Press, pp. 46–8; 178–81; Omer-Cooper, *The Zulu Aftermath*, pp. 43, 104, 144; A. J. Willis, 1964, *An Introduction to the History of Central Africa*, London: Oxford University Press, pp. 101–8.

25 T. Tlou and A. Campbell, 1984, *History of Botswana*, Gaborone: Macmillan, pp. 129–41; Lord Hailey, 1957, *An African Survey Revised 1956: A Study of Problems Arising in Africa South of the Sahara*, London: Oxford University Press, pp. 1064–5; Monica Wilson, 'Co-Operation and Conflict: The Eastern Cape', in: Wilson and Thompson, *The Oxford History of South Africa*, Vol. 1, pp. 238–40.

26 Marks and Atmore, 'Introduction', in: Marks and Atmore, *Economy and Society*, pp. 80–101.

27 *Ibid.*, p. 11; see also P. Bonner, 'Classes, the Mode of Production and the State in Pre-colonial Swaziland', in: Marks and Atmore, *Economy and Society*, pp. 80–101.

28 H. Slater, 'The Changing Pattern of Economic Relationships in Rural Natal, 1838–1914', in: Marks and Atmore, *Economy and Society*, pp. 148–59.

29 *Ibid.*

30 *Ibid.*, p. 164.

31 Colin Bundy, 'Peasants in Herscel: A Case Study of a South African Frontier District', in: Marks and Atmore, *Economy and Society*, pp. 211–19.

32 W. Beinart, 'Production and the Material Basis of Chieftainship: Pondoland *c.*1830–80', in: Marks and Atmore, *Economy and Society*, pp. 120–47.

33 P. Delius, 'Migrant Labour and the Pedi, 1840–80', in: Marks and Atmore, *Economy and Society*, pp. 296–308.

34 Beach, 'The Zimbabwe Plateau and Peoples', p. 274.

34 H. Houghton, 'Economic Development, 1865–1965', in: Thompson and Wilson, *The Oxford History of South Africa*, Vol. 2, pp.10–13.

36 *Ibid.*, pp. 14–15.

37 Francis Wilson, 'Farming, 1866–1966', in: Thompson and Wilson, *The Oxford History of South Africa*, Vol. 2, pp. 120–1.

38 John Lunn, 'The Political Economy of Primary Railways Construction in the Rhodesias, 1890–1911', *Journal of African History*, 33 (1992).

SELECTED BIBLIOGRAPHY

ALPERS, E. A. 1975. *Ivory and Slaves in East Central Africa: Changing Patterns of International Trade to the Later Nineteenth Century*. Heinemann, London.

BALLARD, C. 1986. Drought and Economic Distress: South Africa in the 1800s. *Journal of Interdisciplinary History*, Vol. 17, No. 2, pp. 359–78.

BEACH, D. N. 1974. Ndebele Raiders and Shona Power. *Journal of African History*, Vol. 15, pp. 633–51.

——. 1980. *The Shona and Zimbabwe 900–1850: An Outline of Shona History*. Mambo Press, Gweru/Heinemann Educational, London.

——. 1983. The Zimbabwe Plateau and its Peoples. In: Birmingham, D. and Martin, P. M. (eds) *History of Central Africa*. Longman, London.

——. 1984. *Zimbabwe before 1900*. Mambo Press, Gweru.

BEINART, W. 1982. *The Political Economy of Pondoland, 1860–1930*. Cambridge University Press, Cambridge.

BHEBE, N. 1973. Some Aspects of Ndebele Relations with the Shona. *Rhodesian History*, Vol. 4, pp. 31–8.

——. 1978. *Christianity and Traditional Religion in Western Zimbabwe*. Longman, London.

BIRMINGHAM, D.; MARTIN, P. M. (eds) 1983. *History of Central Africa*. Longman, London.

BONNER, P. 1983. *Kinds, Commoners and Concessionaires: The Evolution and Dissolution of the Nineteenth Century Swazi State*. Cambridge University Press, Cambridge/Raven Press, Johannesburg.

COBBING, J. 1974. The Evolution of the Ndebele Amabutho. *Journal of African History*, Vol. 15, No. 4, pp. 607–31.

——. 1977. The Absent Priesthood: Another look at the Rhodesian Risings of 1896–97. *Journal of African History*, Vol. 18, No. 1, pp. 61–84.

——. 1988. The *Mfecane* as alibi: Thoughts on Dithakong and Mbolompo. *Journal of African History*, Vol. 29, No. 3, pp. 487–519.

COMAROFF, J. 1991. *Of Revelation and Revolution: Christianity, Colonialism, and Consciousness in South Africa*. Vol. 1. University of Chicago Press, Chicago and London.

CRAIS, C. C. 1992. *The Making of the Colonial order: White Supremacy and Black Resistance in the Eastern Cape, 1770–1865*. Witwatersrand University Press, Johannesburg.

DAVENPORT, T. R. H. 1977. *South Africa: A Modern History*. University of Toronto Press, Toronto/Macmillan, London.

DELIUS, P. 1983. *The Land Belongs to Us: The Pedi Polity, the Boers, and the British in the Nineteenth Century Transvaal*. Raven Press, Johannesburg.

ELDREDGE, E. A. 1992. Sources of Conflict in Southern Africa, *c.*1800–30. The 'Mfecane' considered. *Journal of African History*, Vol. 33, No. 1, pp. 1–35.

——. 1993. *A South Africa Kingdom: The Pursuit of Security in Nineteenth-century Lesotho*. Cambridge University Press, Cambridge/Witwatersrand University Press, Johannesburg.

ELDREDGE, E. A.; MONTON, F. (eds) 1994. *Slavery in South Africa: Captive Labour on the Dutch Frontier*. Westview Press, Boulder/University of Natal Press, Pietermaritzburg.

ELPHICK, R.; GILIOMEE, H. B. (eds) 1979. *The Shaping of South African Society, 1652–1820*. Maskew Miller Longman, Cape Town.

FLINT, J.; FLINT E. (eds) 1976. *The Cambridge History of Africa, Vol. 5: from c.1790 to 1870*. Cambridge University Press, Cambridge.

——. 1980. Ecological Factors in the Rise of Shaka and the Zulu kingdom. In: Marks, S. and Atmore, A. (eds) *Economy and Society in Pre-industrial South Africa*. Longman, London, pp. 102–19.

GUY, J. J. 1979. *The Destruction of the Zulu Kingdom: The Civil War in Zululand, 1879–84*. Longman, London.

HALL, S. (ed.) 1995. Archaeological Indications for Stress in the Western Transvaal Region between the Seventeenth and Nineteenth Centuries. In: Hamilton, C. *The Mfecane aftermath: Reconstructive Debates in Southern African History*. Witwatersrand University Press, Johannesburg/University of Natal Press, Pietermaritzburg, pp. 307–22.

HAMILTON, C. (ed.) 1995. *The Mfecane Aftermath: Reconstructive Debates in Southern African History*. Witwatersrand University Press, Johannesburg/University of Natal Press, Pietermaritzburg.

LYE, W. F.; MURRAY, C. 1980. *Transformations on the Highveld: The Tswana and Southern Sotho*. David Philip, Cape Town.

MANSON, A. 1995. Conflict in the Western Highveld/Southern Kalahari, *c.*1750–1820. In: Hamilton, C. *The Mfecane aftermath: Reconstructive Debates in Southern African History*. Witwatersrand University Press, Johannesburg/University of Natal Press, Pietermaritzburg, pp. 351–62.

MARKS, S.; ATMORE, A. (eds) 1980. *Economy and Society in Pre-industrial South Africa*. Longman, London.

MCCRACKEN, J. 1977. *Politics and Christianity in Malawi, 1875 to 1940: The Impact of the Livingstonia Mission in the Northern Province*. Cambridge University Press, Cambridge.

MUDENGE, S. I. G. 1988. *A Political History of Munhumutapa c.1400–1902*. Zimbabwe Publishing House, Harare.

OMER-COOPER, J. D. 1996. *The Zulu Aftermath: A Nineteenth Century Revolution in Bantu Africa*. Longman, London/Ibadan.

PACHAI, B. (ed.) 1973. *Malawi: The History of the Nation*. Longman, London.

PARSONS, N. 1993. *A New History of Southern Africa*. 2nd edn. Macmillan, London.

ROBERTS, A. D. 1976. *A History of Zambia*. Heinemann, London.

SANDERS, P. B. 1975. *Moshoeshoe, Chief of the Sotho*. Heinemann, London.

TLOU, T.; CAMPBELL, A. 1984. *History of Botswana*. Macmillan, Gaborone.

VAIL, L. (ed.) 1989. *The Creation of Tribalism in Southern Africa*. James Currey, London/University of California Press, Berkley and Los Angeles.

WILLS, A. J. 1964. *An Introduction to the History of Central Africa*. Oxford University Press, London.

WILSON, M.; THOMPSON, L. M. (EDS) 1969–71. *The Oxford History of South Africa*. 2 Vols. Clarendon Press, Oxford.

15.7

THE INDIAN OCEAN

Rajaonah V. Faranirina and Christophe Wondji

Rather than the French Revolution, it was the signing of the Treaties of Vienna in 1815 that ushered in a new period in the south-western Indian Ocean. Britain took it upon itself, from Mauritius, to intercept the slave trading that was active in the Mozambique Channel but also affected Reunion up to the middle of the century, and to rein in France's designs on Madagascar. Sir Robert Farquhar, governor of Mauritius, obtained the collaboration of the Malagasy sovereign, Radama I (1810–28), in return for assistance in pursuing his policy of expanding and modernizing the kingdom. With the Anglo-Malagasy Treaty of 1817 abolishing the slave trade in the Kingdom of Madagascar,[1] the island increasingly drew the attention of the Western powers and was opened up to their influence, first via the Mascarene Islands (Mauritius and Reunion).

LEARNING MODERNITY: TAKING A LEAD FROM THE WEST

The 'coffee civilization', which reached its apogee in the eighteenth century in Reunion, shrank inexorably in the nineteenth century with the extraordinary demand for sugar, which also affected the island of Mauritius. An aristocracy of sugar producers, benefiting until the 1860s from the high market prices in Europe, became established in the Mascarenes. Conscious of the fragility of a plantation economy heavily dependent on slavery, itself marked out for abolition, and of the need to modernize the manufacture of sugar so as to meet the competition from sugar beet, the colonists took their lead from the West. They accepted the innovations proposed to them by representatives of European firms selling industrial equipment. They encouraged research, on the spot, by 'sugar technicians'. There can also be said to have been an industrial revolution with the spread of the steam engine. It is thus understandable that, to some extent, the Mascarenes were seen as models for the go-ahead Malagasy elites. The fact is that the modernization of industry was not matched by any revolution in agriculture, where the planters became mired in routine and irrational exploitation requiring large numbers of labourers from Madagascar and especially from India after the emancipation of the slaves.

In 1820, Radama I made it a condition of renewal of the 1817 Treaty that the British government should educate some thirty young people in Britain and Mauritius. Foreigners came to Madagascar from the Mascarenes or Europe, among them the missionaries of the London Missionary Society (LMS), who launched a variety of handicraft activities. However, they had to leave the country when, in 1835, Queen Ranavalona I (1828–61) forbade Christianity and ordered them to teach only arts that were profitable to her people. The Queen nevertheless cultivated her relations with 'useful' foreigners. As a token of satisfaction she promoted two foreigners to a high rank in Merina society – Napoleon de Lastelle, a tax farmer from Mauritius settled in Tamatave province, who was her associate in exploiting an agro-industrial sugar and rum complex, and the Frenchman Jean Laborde, who established various industries, including a cannon foundry, with forges operated by a host of conscripted labourers. Some indigenous workers were able to improve their skills, such as those recruited by the missionaries for the many religious building projects.

These occasional technology transfers did not make up for the decline in local craftwork, since Madagascar became in the course of the century an outlet for the manufactures of the West arriving, in part, from the Mascarenes. The latter islands further exported sugar and rum from a vastly increased number of mills. Schooling, on the other hand, as a basis of evangelization, went ahead in the various islands. In Reunion, education on the French model developed with the aid of the Brothers of the Ecoles Chrétiennes and the Sisters of Saint Joseph of Cluny. But the congregations came up against the reservations of the colonists when, for example, they did away with segregation in school of the children of whites and of those of the emancipated. The whites, likewise, did not want to see coloured monitors, and Creole-speakers at that, taking charge of their children. In addition, the sugar producers did nothing to encourage the schooling of their workers' children.

In Madagascar it was decided to conduct education in the language of the country. The LMS missionaries worked together with Radama I for the transcription of Malagasy. In 1820 the King inaugurated the first school in Antananarivo, but education only started markedly progressing in the 1870s when the government backed evangelization. The establishment of an education ministry and the institution of compulsory schooling in 1881 lent fresh impetus to education in the Kingdom of Madagascar. But parents were wary of schools that provided a pool of labour for the recruitment of soldiers and conscript labourers. The populations of the provinces outside the Imerina region regarded education dispensed by representatives of the central authority as administrative pressure. Although textbooks were issued, logistical and material problems limited the impact of primary education entrusted to

Malagasies, despite their preparation in teacher-training schools of a high standard.

BETWEEN REAPPROPRIATION AND REJECTION OF FOREIGN INFLUENCES

The palaces that the Malagasy sovereigns had built by foreigners incorporated architectural innovations. Radama I chose for his palace, which was fitted up by the Lyon carpenter Louis Gros, the colonial style of the large houses of Mauritius. However, as in the Queen's Palace built by Jean Laborde for Ranavalona I, the space was patterned astrologically around a central pillar in deference to tradition. The palaces were likewise built of wood, symbolizing life, as opposed to stone, the material of tombs. After the conversion of the Malagasy leaders to Christianity in 1869, however, the hewn stone used in the capital for churches in the Norman style became the noble material it already was in Reunion, where for a decade already stone had replaced timber in the building of a great many churches, leaving a distinctly European stamp on the landscape. The missionary James Cameron put a stone facing on the palace of Queen Ranavalona I.[2] He also introduced the Malagasies to the use of bricks and tiles and launched a housing style adopted by the rich, with houses that looked traditional but had a veranda and several rooms, like the bourgeois dwellings of Europe.

Malagasy intellectuals enhanced their culture with the learning they acquired in the West. Raombana (1809–55), who studied in Manchester, wrote a history of his country in English and along Western lines. But this first Malagasy historian was convinced of the ethnic unity of his people and opposed the outlook of European colonial historiography. The settling of the Malagasies also made it possible to preserve the treasures of oral culture, instances being the poems whose collection Ranavalona I encouraged, and historical traditions. There was a big increase in the number of manuscripts in the last quarter of the century, with foreigners like Father Callet in the Imerina region taking part in this work of transcription.

However, in taking the interest they did in local languages and customs, the missionaries were mainly intent on evangelization. The first Malagasy edition of the Bible was published in 1835. At about the same time, Father Monnet, like the pastor Lebrun and Father Laval in Mauritius, undertook the conversion to Christianity of the blacks of Reunion and wrote a catechism in Creole. But the whites were not always supportive of action liable to call their superiority into question. Mass and religious instruction took place at meal times (between noon and 2 p.m. or at the end of the day). To put his message across better, Father Laval used the language of the plantation in his lessons, likening the church to a large dwelling and Christ to the master of the estate.

In Catholic strategy Reunion was to be the centre of a missionary Christianity, in particular for Madagascar, and the Jesuits taught young Malagasies in Reunion. But their overseas work was long confined to the 'small islands' under French domination (Nosy-Be, Sainte-Marie and Mayotte), particularly as Queen Ranavalona I had prohibited the 'religion of the whites', regarded as being liable to subvert the socio-political order, which rested upon ancestor and sampy[3] worship and upon differences in social status. The law was harsh on Christians. Traumatized by persecutions, those who did not renounce their faith had to practise it in secret. The Christians recovered their freedom on the Queen's death, however, and, as of 1869, enjoyed the support of the new Queen, Ranavalona II (1868–83), and the prime minister Rainilaiarivony, both baptized by a Malagasy pastor. Christianity made a strong comeback, while traditional religion declined (the sampy were burned). And evangelization did have some effect, but sometimes in difficult circumstances, for in the Mascarene Islands, those in favour of the abolition of slavery were faced with the hostility of the Creole colonists. Having been abolished in Mauritius in 1835, with compensation for the owners, slavery was ended in Reunion in 1848 under the Second Republic, but the Malagasy sovereigns, concerned though they were about the modernization of their country, had no thoughts of doing away with slavery.

In the circles of emancipated slaves and poor white settlers of Reunion, evangelization gave rise to a popular religion full of vitality, shunning the official conformism and marked, in particular, by an increased number of oratories, the importance of the cult of the Virgin or recourse to intercessors that, while not beatified, were recognized by the church. On the other hand, there was little impact on the increasingly large number of Indians enlisted in Reunion and, above all, Mauritius. While the contracts of employment in the coolie trade provided for a return to India, most of those enlisted in fact never went back, and this led to an 'Indianization' of Mauritius, where the Indians outnumbered the rest of the population by two to one at the beginning of the twentieth century. Although Christianity was said to open the door to social esteem, the Indians were seldom converted but, on the contrary, sought to preserve their identity through the dynamism of their religion. In Reunion they built a large temple and staged sumptuous festivities, but under the watchful eye of the landowners, the church and the authorities, ever afraid of excesses on the occasion of the ritual ceremonies. The Indians, whether Muslim or Hindu, remained deeply attached to their original religion.

The same went for the Malagasies, who assassinated Radama II (1861–3) for his over-liberal attitude to foreigners and practised the traditional cults more zealously in order to check epidemics and famines, which signified the wrath of ancestors against foreign intrusion. Their fervour reached its zenith when the French invaded the country in 1894. People started openly venerating the sampy, which had never before been subjected to such burnings. The resistance started in the Imerina region with the killing of a missionary family in November 1895, on the day of the royal bath (fandroana), the highlight of national religious rituals. And, as though in response to the auto-da-fé of the sampy, Christian religious buildings were destroyed. Resistance to colonial conquest was thus synonymous with the revival of the Malagasy national cultural heritage.

CONQUEST AND OCCUPATION: MADAGASCAR AS A FRENCH COLONY

The exclusive growing of sugar cane exposed the Mascarenes to serious danger, as attested by the long crisis that started in 1863. Its causes were spread evenly between natural disasters, the collapse of sugar prices, production cost problems and the refusal of the planters to set about improving their operations. The difficulties were such, however, that thoughts turned to emigration to South Africa and Madagascar, whereupon the inhabitants of Reunion urged the annexation of Madagascar, which for France was a focal point of interest as from the middle of the nineteenth century.

As we have seen, Madagascar was by then a virtually unified kingdom recognized by the major European powers and jealous of its independence. But it was not to escape the imperialist scramble for power at the end of the century and, under the influence of vested interests in Reunion, the Catholics and the French colonial party, France put paid to the Kingdom's independence after two victorious wars fought in 1883–5 and 1894–5. After installing a French Resident General in Antananarivo, in 1885, and after Great Britain had relinquished its hold on Madagascar in order to assert its protectorate in Zanzibar, France took control of the island and set about methodically conquering the country from 1894 to 1904 under the leadership of General Galliéni. The monarchy was abolished in 1897 and the colonial regime took hold, with all the institutional instruments of domination that sprang up throughout French Africa – the Indigenous Code, forced labour and exorbitant powers of the governors and local administrators.[4]

In its strategy of domination, the colonial authority reappropriated the ingredients of Malagasy culture. It thus revived in part the symbolism of the bath festival, replaced by the celebration of 14 July. But, as the storming of the Bastille was synonymous with freedom, republican France abolished slavery, and this was its first 'civilizing' measure. Other technical innovations were introduced. France laid out roads and built the Antananarivo-Tamatave railway, which fascinated the Malagasies. The works engaged a multitude of statute labourers, particularly for porterage. Furthermore, the colonial authorities dissociated Christianity and civilization, and took over from the Christian missions where medical care was concerned. Galliéni requisitioned the hospital of the Medical Missionary Academy, which trained doctors, opened a medical school and established an indigenous medical assistance service, which did not prevent the amateur midwives, sorcerers, soothsayers and healers from continuing to exercise their art as in the past.

The move towards the secularization of education affected the island and official schools were established, entrusted to primary teachers graduating from the Le Myre de Villiers teacher-training college, a breeding ground for local civil servants. The colonial authorities waged a struggle against the missions in which the freemason Governor General Victor Augagneur (1905–9) was particularly prominent. The disarray of denominational education annoyed the indigenous Christian elite, already disturbed by segregated schooling. The fact was that the authorities had very soon given up any idea of a policy of assimilation as being virtually impossible to implement, and the education provided to the indigenous population differed from that given to Europeans. The Malagasy language enjoyed official status along with French in school curricula but in fact occupied a secondary position.

But this indigenous education, which had not entirely broken with Malagasy culture, was disparaged, as it was not the surest guarantee of advancement in society. In contradistinction to this second-class education, the indigenous elite sought both to upgrade Malagasy culture and attain the quintessence of French civilization. This demand mobilized young intellectuals, especially the Medical School students, who in 1913 founded a secret society, the VVS (Vy, Vata, Sakalika), whose activities formed the nucleus of the national Malagasy movement after the First World War.[5]

NOTES

1 The Kingdom of Madagascar, recognized internationally and led by the sovereigns of Antananarivo, covered two thirds of the island at the end of the century.

2 The palace of Radama I and Manjakamiadana, generally referred to as the Queen's Palace, is part of the *rova* (royal enclosure) of Antananarivo developed between the seventeenth and nineteenth centuries and comprising other palaces, tombs and a Protestant church. The *rova* was badly damaged by fire on 6 November 1995. The Malagasy government is considering rebuilding it with support from UNESCO.

3 In view of the diversity of renderings (idols, talismans, palladia), we prefer to keep to the Malagasy term.

4 See UNESCO's *General History of Africa*, Vol. VII, pp. 245–72.

5 *Vy, Vata, Sakalika* (VVS) means 'Iron, Stone, Ramification'. Cf. *General History of Africa*, UNESCO, Vol. VII.

BIBLIOGRAPHY

AYACHE, S. 1976. *Raombana: l'historien (1809–1855)*. Ambozontany, Fianarantsoa, pp. 510ff.

BELROSE-HUYGHUES, V. 1975. 'Un exemple de syncrétisme esthétique au XIXe siècle: le *Rova* de Tananarive d'Andrianjaka à Radama Ier'. *Omaly sy Anio*, Nos. 1–2, Antananarivo, pp. 173–207.

DESCHAMPS, H. (ed.) 1972. *Histoire de Madagascar*, 4th edn, Berger-Levrault, Paris, pp. 358ff.

DOMENICHINI-RAMIARAMANANA, B. 1983. *Du ohabolana au hainteny*. Karthala, Paris, pp. 665ff.

ESOAVELOMANDROSO, F. V. 1976. 'Langue, culture et colonisation à Madagascar'. *Omaly sy Anio*, Nos. 3–4, Antananarivo, pp. 106–65.

——. 1990. 'Les 14 juillet au temps de la colonisation'. In: G. Jacob, *Regards sur Madagascar et la Révolution Française*. CNAPMAD, Antananarivo, pp. 145–58.

ESOAVELOMANDROSO, M. 1987. 'Madagascar de 1880 à 1939: Initiations et réactions africaines à la conquête et à la domination coloniales'. In: *Histoire générale de l'Afrique*. Vol. VII, Ch. 10, UNESCO, Paris, pp. 245–72.

EVE, P. 1990. *Histoire abrégée de l'enseignement à La Réunion*. Comité de la Culture, de l'Education et de l'Environnement, Région Réunion, Saint-André, pp. 40ff.

——. 1985. *La religion populaire à La Réunion*. 2 Vols. Institut de Linguistique et d'Anthropologie, Université de La Réunion, Saint-Denis, pp. 159–190.

FUMA, S. 1982. *Esclaves et citoyens, Le destin de 62,000 Réunionnais, Histoire de l'insertion sociale des affranchis dans la société réunionnaise*. Documents et Recherches No. 6, Fondation pour la Recherche et le Développement dans l'Océan Indien, Saint-Denis, pp. 175ff.

——. 1989. *Une colonie à sucre, L'économie de La Réunion au XIXe siècle*. Océan Éditions, Saint-André, pp. 412ff.

GERBEAU, H. 1989. 'Le cyclone de la liberté'. In: Cl. Wanquet, *Fragments pour une histoire des économies et sociétés de plantation à La Réunion*. Université de La Réunion, Saint-Denis, pp. 159–224.

——. 1979. 'Quelques aspects de la traite illégale des esclaves à l'île Bourbon au XXe siècle'. *Mouvements de populations dans l'océan Indien*. Honoré Champion, Paris, pp. 273–308.

HÜBSCH, B. 1993 (ed.) *Madagascar et le christianisme*. ACCT-Ambozontany, Fianarantsoa/Karthala, Paris, pp. 518ff.

JACOB, G. 1989–90. 'La révolution industrielle de l'Imerina au XIXe siècle ou l'impossible transfert'. *Omaly sy Anio*, Nos. 29–32, Antananarivo, pp. 225–35.

LEHEMBRE, B. 1984. *L'Ile Maurice*. Karthala, Paris, p. 244.

MARIMOUTOU, M. 1989 'Cabanons et danses de feu: la vie privée des engagés indiens dans les camps réunionnais du XIXe siècle'. In: Cl. Wanquet, *Fragments pour une histoire des économies et sociétés de plantation à La Réunion*. Université de La Réunion, Saint-Denis, pp. 225–50.

MICHEL, J. 1979. *Le Père Jacques Laval, le Saint de l'Île Maurice (1803–1864)*. Beauchesne, Paris, pp. 464ff.

PRUDHOMME, C. 1984. *Histoire religieuse de La Réunion*. Karthala, Paris, pp. 369ff.

RAISON-JOURDE, F. 1991. *Bible et pouvoir à Madagascar au XIXe siècle*. Karthala, Paris, pp. 840ff.

RAJAONAH, F. 1994. 'Modèles européens pour une ville malgache, Antananarivo XIXe–XXe siècle'. Paper presented at *Conférence d'Histoire urbaine*. Ms. (forthcoming 1996). Strasbourg, pp. 12ff.

TOUSSAINT, A. 1961. *Histoire de l'océan Indien*. Presses Universitaires de France, Paris, pp. 286ff.

——. 1972. *Histoire des îles Mascareignes*. Berger-Levrault, Paris, pp. 351ff.

——. 1971. 'Histoire de l'Ile Maurice'. *Que sais-je?*, No. 1449, Presses Universitaires de France, Paris, pp. 128ff.

UNESCO, 1987. *General History of Africa*. Vol. VII. UNESCO, Paris.

15.8

CONCLUSION

Christophe Wondji

The various contributions making up this chapter are interesting for a variety of reasons. They throw new light not only on the major upheavals that took place in Africa, but also on the profound transformations in the life of African societies from the beginning of the nineteenth century to the eve of the First World War. While these contributions show what African civilizations stood for throughout the nineteenth century, their principal merit is twofold: they reveal other as yet unexplored aspects of the sombre history of the brutal colonial conquest of Africa by the European powers in the late nineteenth century, and they raise legitimate questions about the real reasons behind the policies and methods applied by the colonizers to attain their objectives, and the consequences for the African peoples.

When the European explorers came into contact with the peoples living in the interior of the African continent, the latter already had structured social organizations in the form of village communities, kingdoms or empires. The more or less powerful kingdoms encountered across the continent, such as the kingdoms of Dahomey and Bamun, were founded on ancestral values; but it was the empires staunchly Islamic, such as the caliphate of Sokoto, the Fulani empire of the Massina and the Wassulu kingdom of Samori Touré, that dominated the political scene. In the technical and economic field they had developed highly elaborate production methods in metalworking, architecture, farming and the domestication of new plants imported from the Americas and Asia in previous centuries. The savannah, forest lands and Saharan areas traded their different products over long and short distances. In the fields of culture and religion they developed art forms linked to the religion of Islam's ancestors. Young children were educated by means of initiatory rites or in the *medersas*. The same contacts were to be observed on the large island of Madagascar.

But it was events during the period from 1880 to 1914 that would prove fatal to African societies: the conquest, followed by the occupation, of territories by the European imperialistic powers. The special feature of this period was that once the machinery of colonial rule had been put in place, with the exception of Ethiopia which managed to preserve its sovereignty, African societies great and small were dispossessed of the ability to project themselves into the future; to run their own politics; to organize their own economy; and to lead a normal cultural life conducive to technical innovation and artistic creation.

While the methods applied probably differed from one colonizing power to another, there is no doubt that each power wreaked havoc by destroying the vital cultural elements of the 'indigenous' societies that it dominated, sometimes replacing them with new references derived from the colonial culture. The installation of colonial rule also led to the negation of the Black people and the expropriation of the riches found in their land and subsoil, while they themselves were turned into an unpaid workforce of mere slaves. A variety of systems, in particular education systems, were also instituted to ensure more efficient exploitation of sought-after raw materials; and indigenous peoples were won over to the colonizers' cause by means of 'collaboration'. In that respect the most significant events are probably those that took place in the final quarter of the century and the period leading up to the First World War. These include the most important changes and transformations, not only politically and socially but also, to some extent, technologically.

Although to begin with the colonizers talked grandly about the 'need to civilize primitive peoples', in practice things were quite different. The so-called wars of pacification, the introduction of forced labour on plantations, or to build the roads and railways needed for exporting raw materials, resulted in large-scale massacres of people that Adam Hochschild has qualified as 'a crime against humanity' comparable to the Jewish Holocaust.[1] Another enormous crime was the pillaging of the works of art of African societies by the colonial administrators and scientific missions organized throughout the continent. The period 1880–1914 took a heavy toll on African societies: while the revolts against forced labour were usually put down by violent means, they nonetheless increased in number after 1914. The African and Malagasy elite, albeit small in size, would rapidly realize the need for the negation of colonialism and try to organize themselves first in defence against the segregation of the labour laws to which they were subject, and second to fight for the cause of their peoples.

NOTE

1 Hochschild, Adam, King Leopold's Ghost: A Story of Greed, Terror and Heroism in Colonial Africa, Mariner Books, New York, 1998.

16

AUSTRALASIA AND THE PACIFIC

Donald Denoon and Pamela Statham

INTRODUCTION

Australasia and Oceania were the last inhabited regions on earth to come into regular contact with Asia, Europe and the Americas. Created by the break-up of Gondwanaland millennia before *homo sapiens* evolved, the Australian continent and the islands of the Pacific were separated from South East Asia by the Wallace line: no placental animals crossed that barrier before humans entered Australia, perhaps 60,000 years ago. The islands were colonized even later, from west to east, between 40,000 and 2000 years ago. The pioneers of Australia and New Guinea (a single land mass during the last glaciation) presumably travelled by raft, whereas Austronesian and Polynesian navigators used sailing vessels and sophisticated navigation for their later odysseys. Navigating either the Pacific Ocean or the arid centre of Australia was only the first of several daunting problems. Hunters found no animals familiar to them in South East Asia, much vegetation was equally foreign, but during centuries of trial and error, ways were found for survival and the sustainable exploitation of limited resources. Agriculture developed in the islands earlier than in Europe, and taro, yam and sago were later supplemented by the American sweet potato.

Australia was sparsely populated – perhaps a million and a half people in 7,750M acres (7.68M square kilometres), relying on hunting, foraging and fishing – but in parts of the islands with good soil and reliable water (Hawaii, the New Guinea highlands, parts of Fiji and of New Caledonia) dense populations evolved by the eighteenth century. While Australian hunters and gatherers needed few formal structures to resolve disputes within communities organized on kinship lines, many Melanesian communities were mobilized for surplus production and exchanges by 'Big-men', and parts of Polynesia sustained elaborate hierarchies of chief and commoner families. Their isolation was not complete. Makassans visited northern Australia each year to harvest sea slugs; Tidore traders bought slaves from western New Guinea; seventeenth-century Dutch explorers charted the western and northern coasts of Australia; and Spanish rule in the Philippines spilled over into the Caroline and Mariana islands of Micronesia. But these interactions touched only the perimeter of the region, so that most populations were entirely unprepared for the devastating nineteenth century. New Guinea highlanders – a million or more – were still unprepared in the twentieth.

Until the late eighteenth century, European navigation was inexact. Many islands were visited (for example the Dutch sailor Abel Tasman charted Tasmania, Tonga and Fiji in the seventeenth century) but few were precisely mapped, and 'discoveries' were not followed through. The first major impact of European technical advances was the burst of exploration from the 1760s, made possible by the refinement of chronometers and navigational aids. Captain James Cook's brief from the Royal Society in London was to observe the transit of Venus in 1769, from Tahiti, in order to facilitate navigation. His further instructions were to search for *Terra Australis* and to determine whether previously charted parts of western Australia, New Guinea, Tasmania and New Zealand were extremities of the same land mass.

Cook was (and remains) the best-known European explorer of his day. His three voyages between 1768 and 1780 opened the whole Southern Pacific from Hawaii to New Zealand and Australia, to the attention of the European intelligentsia. Their observations of societies differing radically from those of the Old World were at least as challenging as the precise geographical, botanical, zoological and astronomic evidence collected. In the spirit of the Enlightenment, Cook and Joseph Banks (and other gentlemen-scientists) had been careful to record their findings, experiences and reflections. Banks alone compiled twenty-five volumes of cards detailing botanical specimens after the first voyage (Steven, 1988: 10). Although Cook claimed the whole east coast of Australia for Britain in 1770 (bestowing on it the puzzling name of New South Wales), seventeen years passed before that claim was substantiated. Similar claims to Tahiti, the Marquesas and other islands proved equally ephemeral. The continent and the islands then boasted neither the resources nor the strategic significance to engage serious European attention.

FIRST FLEET

Britain's decision to plant convicts in Botany Bay – the area which had most attracted Cook and Banks – embodied several considerations (Martin, 1978). Convicted felons could not be sent to the American colonies after the War of Independence; yet their numbers mounted as punishable offences multiplied, and prison hulks in the Thames made influential Londoners fearful of infection. Meanwhile the Admiralty was perplexed by the problem of protecting shipping en route to the British East India Company base in India. The Spanish empire in the northern Pacific was a declining threat, but Dutch and French incursions still threatened. The valuable trade in spices, tea and silk, made it imperative for Britain to fend off competition. Security could only be achieved if naval ships could be assured of replacement masts, rather than relying on timber shipped around the Cape of Good Hope and vulnerable to the Dutch (at the Cape) or the French (at Mauritius and Reunion) (Frost, 1980). A rumoured alliance between the French and the Dutch in 1786 provoked the Admiralty to revisit Cook's and Banks' report. Botany Bay then acquired virtues. It could be a base from which to claim Norfolk Island where tall pines had been noted, its remoteness offered a destination for transportation, and it might develop into a valuable trade and defence post.

Lord Sydney's 'Heads of a Plan' in 1786 contained detailed orders to initiate the colonization of Australia. They were less precise about the subsequent management of the colony, except that its regulation is 'committed to the care of a discreet officer' (Clark, 1950: 36). As was later made clear to the first governor, Captain Arthur Phillip, this authority extended beyond eastern Australia to all islands of the South Pacific. Convict minders were also to explore territory, claim Norfolk Island, supply naval stores (such as flax and masts) and ensure self-sufficiency in food.

In May 1787 the First Fleet of eleven ships sailed from Portsmouth, carrying 1,450 people (half of them convicts), and arrived at Botany Bay in the following January. Phillip immediately noticed its exposed anchorage, shallows and waterless surroundings, and moved the fleet to Port Jackson's immense harbour, to Sydney Cove, where the Tank Stream brought fresh water and ships could anchor close to shore. On 26 January 1788 the settlement commenced.

The First Fleet, far more than earlier explorations, marked a turning point in the whole region. The port would provision missionaries and resource raiders who had previously had no safe haven. It also heralded two complementary movements which dominated the nineteenth-century history of the region: the extraordinarily rapid growth of new settler societies, especially in temperate regions, and the massive depopulation of indigenous people. These trends were intimately related. Islands whose people repelled outsiders averted population loss; but many islands in the Solomons and Vanuatu (formerly the New Hebrides) were decimated by crowd diseases: smallpox, measles, influenza, gonorrhoea, leprosy, and tuberculosis. Vanuatu lost half its people. The main island of New Caledonia sustained at least 100,000 people in 1800; 1900 saw only a third of that population. Most Polynesian populations fell by at least half – Marquesans fell by about 96 per cent. Aboriginal Australians suffered a similar fate. In New South Wales alone two smallpox epidemics in 1789 and 1829 moved inland, ahead of the people who brought it, and combined with the infertility induced by venereal diseases reduced a population of about 65,000 to 4,000 by 1845 (McArthur, 1967; Butlin, 1994: 136–7; Frost, 1995, ch. 10).

The landing of the First Fleet must have traumatized Aboriginal people on the shores of Sydney harbour. The newcomers were more numerous than those on the *Mayflower*, and the size of the invading group plus their portmanteau of plants, animals and microbes meant the rapid decimation of hunting grounds and indigenous food supplies. Occasional skirmishes had minimal effect on such

a hydra-headed phenomenon and negotiation was difficult, given the different values of each community. The new arrivals were baffling: they placed a higher value on property than on life, and discipline was imposed by floggings and hangings when imported food ran short. Food scarcity was chronic for the first four years, for supplies were damaged on the voyage and seed had to be reserved for planting. Early farming was frustrated by poor soil near Sydney cove, elementary farming equipment, convict inexperience of farming, lack of supervision, insects and flood. Better land was later found inland at Parramatta and allocated to the few emancipists (time-expired convicts) and those of Phillip's marines who remained in the colony.

In June 1790 the second fleet arrived with supplies – and another thousand mouths to feed, half of whom were sick. Among them were the first contingent of the New South Wales Corps, whose officers soon engaged in trade, profiting from the introduction of rum, tea, sugar (and livestock) which were eagerly consumed. The shortage of ready money was overcome by an internal barter system and by government bill purchase of cargoes from incoming ships. When Governor Philip returned to England in 1792, (not to be replaced, by Governor Hunter, until 1795) the officers of the Corps ran the colony. They controlled the commissariat and directed the deployment of convict working parties. Each was granted 100 acres and ten convicts. Their influence has been described as brutal and corrupt, but the officers and other ranks applied their knowledge and management skills to food production, and it was the officers' land grants which soon produced surpluses for the commissariat (Evatt, 1938: 73 ff; Fletcher, 1976: ch. 4).

By the time Hunter acknowledged the officers' monopoly of trade, in 1798, their direct influence was waning. Emancipists were challenging the monopoly, and increased shipping made it more difficult to protect. In response, the officers turned to livestock raising and more lucrative meat production. Indigenous fauna were too difficult to manage, and European livestock were so scarce that for several years it was forbidden to kill female breeding stock (*Historical Records of Australia*). This gaol without walls, dominated by soldiers, was the improbable matrix for the development of a thriving commercial centre.

COMMERCIAL AGRICULTURE AND PASTORALISM

Early Sydney was not just a gaol: it was an entrepot on the shores of the world's greatest ocean, where settlers built sailing vessels and embarked on sealing and bay whaling. Offshoot settlements were all sited on the east coast (as well as Norfolk Island, which had become a penal settlement in February 1788). Governor King sent a detachment to the River Derwent in Tasmania in 1803, and to the River Tamar in 1804, which founded Hobart and Launceston; and in 1804 to Newcastle, north of Sydney. Expanding settlements had far-reaching consequences for the Islands. In 1801 HMS *Porpoise* sailed to Tahiti, returning with 31,000lb of salt pork, which was landed more cheaply and in better condition than pork from Britain, encouraging other expeditions (Hainsworth, 1971: 158).

By the early 1800s, Sydney looked a prosperous little settlement with gardens neatly fenced and a cove full of ships (Hackforth, 1977: esp. 32 and 88). Life for convicts was not bad. They did not wear uniforms, nor were they housed in gaols. Outside the hours of work they were free. Acute food scarcity was behind them, and opportunities abounded for emancipists. A distinctive culture began to emerge among people unified by a long sea passage. The 'honour among thieves' ethic of the London underworld was tempered by Irish humour, passion, volatility and music: almost all the settler's music derived from Ireland or Scotland. The Irish rebellion of 1798 generated convicts with pronounced anti-authoritarian (and anti-English) views. This leaven culminated in the 1804 Battle of Vinegar Hill, when an uprising of Irish convicts and ex-convicts was quashed by the New South Wales Corps. This incident is less well known than the 'Rum Rebellion' of 1808 when officers of the Corps and an orderly band of soldiers deposed Governor Bligh. Bligh's reputation as a martinet rested on his survival of the mutiny on the *Bounty*, and on arrival he had made him himself unpopular by insulting prominent settlers. The Rum Rebellion was ostensibly about the rum trade, but had far more to do with property rights and personality clashes (Ritchie, 1988: xvi). The ensuing second period of military administration differed from the first in that it was more even-handed, but the coup could hardly be ignored. The Corps was recalled, its leaders sent to trial and a new governor (Macquarie) sent to take over.

Macquarie's accession in 1810 is commonly seen as a complete break with the early settlement. This is debatable. Although Macquarie brought his own regiment (the 73rd) with him, over half the NSW Corps remained in the colony. Shipwrights had already built ocean-going vessels and merchants had found partners among overseas ship-owners. Sealing and bay whaling had already proved profitable and Sydney was a regular port of call. Moreover, pioneer work by the MacArthur's and Reverend Samuel Marsden had already shown that fine wool could be grown in the colony. Land was plentiful, since Aboriginal ownership was mainly ignored, the climate was temperate and convict labour was cheap. Experience proved that Australian sheep did not have to be folded at night and constant movement onto new pasture improved wool quality, such that in terms of cost and quality it soon rivalled European wool on British markets. The industry required little labour, apart from shearing. Unlike crop growing, sheep farming was principally a man's world. Shearers' wives and families lived in town, and pastoral families also spent considerable time in the towns. With the introduction of sheep dogs, fencing and dams in the 1860s, labour requirements declined further and, after shearing, involved mostly urban services – bullock teams to bring supplies and carry off the baled wool; insurance and shipping; banks; merchants and storage facilities, and ships. So most employment created by this industry was generated in the ports, and the families of those so employed created additional service needs – all offering more suitable employment for both willing and unwilling immigrants, who generally lacked rural skills.

By 1840 Australia was ringed with British settlements. After Governor King's settlements in Tasmania and Newcastle, occupation moved up and down the coast of New South Wales and inland. One driving force was the desire of the Sydney population to rid themselves of the worst convicts – a move culminating in the end of transportation in 1840 (though convicts were sent to Tasmania until 1852). At first recidivists had been sent to Norfolk Island and Newcastle but, as the former was small and the latter became a port for the rich Hunter Valley, new secure places were sought. Port Macquarie followed Newcastle, but soon proved too near settlement, so plans were laid for a new outpost even further north. In 1824 a penal settlement was established at Moreton Bay near present-day Brisbane. In the same year soldiers and convicts were sent to form an outpost on Melville Island, in northern Australia, to safeguard British shipping and complement British Singapore.

When Governor Darling was given his commission in 1825, New South Wales was redefined to encompass Melville Island. This left all present-day Western Australia unclaimed. Concerned about the need for a dumping ground for recidivists and reports of French interest in the south-west coast, Darling sent soldiers and convicts to establish an outpost at King George's Sound. Arriving on Christmas Day 1827, Major Lockyer claimed the territory surrounding present-day Albany. Meanwhile, word had spread that all was not well on Melville Island. Plans were laid in London to relocate the outpost to the mainland and a ship, commanded by Captain James Stirling, was sent to implement them. Stirling had noted an area on the west coast in the same latitude as Sydney and subsequently explored (and extolled) the territory around the Swan River – fervently advising its immediate colonization. The British Government at first refused, but Stirling's persistence, and the interests of certain British capitalists, led to a change of heart. In June 1829, Swan River Colony, the first non-convict settlement in Australia, was founded under Stirling's command, as a 'private enterprise experiment', where settlers would be attracted by land grants in proportion to the capital assets and labour they introduced.

The experiment nearly failed due to poorly planned Conditions of Settlement, and adverse publicity soon after foundation, which curbed the migrant tide (Cameron, 1979). This bad publicity reflected conditions at the port of Fremantle rather than in the capital, Perth, twelve miles up river, but it meant that under 200 settlers with their servants and families and a small military garrison were left to face similar problems to those in early New South Wales. Predictable food scarcity led settlers to clash with Aboriginal peoples whose hunting grounds they had usurped. The worst of these clashes was in the Murray River district, south of Perth, where in 1834 soldiers and settlers confronted a large tribal group in the 'Battle of Pinjarra'. In retribution for the murder of one white settler, some forty Aborigines were driven into the river and shot (Battye, 1924: 133). This incident provoked shame, and agitation for protection of the native inhabitants, but (as in the islands) the efforts of 'Government Native Protectors' and missionaries were really attempts to Europeanize (or 'civilize') them – forcing them to abandon an ancient lifestyle and culture for one that was unsuited to the Australian environment.

By the 1840s a similar pattern was occurring in Tasmania, Victoria and South Australia. The two earlier settlements in Tasmania had hosted an outward push for land that soon occupied all suitable territory. Clashes between settlers and Aborigines led in November 1828 to the declaration of martial law and, in one of the worst incidents in Australian history, a drive to shoot, capture and incarcerate all native inhabitants (Shaw, 1980: 126ff). Continued British immigration to the island led to increasing land shortage by the 1830s, causing settlers to look north to the mainland and east to New Zealand. In 1835 several Tasmanian pastoralists moved across the Bass Strait into the Port Philip Bay region, where one of them, Batman, purchased land in the Yarra River region from the local Dutigalla tribe. This purchase, a forerunner of later events in New Zealand, directly contravened the British government's assumption of *terra nullius* and was later disallowed (Shaw, 1989: 210–11). But other pastoralists had followed Batman, laid claim to land in the same vicinity and begun building. Largely to facilitate administration, the Sydney government acknowledged the emerging town of Melbourne, which in 1851 became the capital of Victoria.

South Australia was declared a separate colony in 1836, also as a non-convict settlement. Fired by criticisms of government policy in Swan River Colony, the colonial reformer, Edward Gibbon Wakefield, had devised a plan for 'systematic colonization', in which land was to be sold rather than granted and revenues so obtained used to fund immigration. With the support of other British reformists, he chose newly discovered territory around the mouth of the Murray River for its implementation and petitioned the British government to proclaim it a colony. Disappointed when the official Conditions of Settlement did not conform to his specifications, Wakefield disavowed South Australia, although its settlement is still referred to as the 'Wake-fieldian Experiment'. This colony benefited from a more mobile and skilled labour force, sale of land in smaller lots, more suitable introduced capital assets, financial backing from the South Australian Company and, most of all, from a far larger initial population. In two years South Australia, and especially its capital, Adelaide, attracted more immigrants than Swan River had in ten. However, an unwieldy initial administrative structure delayed early progress (Pike, 1967) and South Australia joined all the other colonies in experiencing declining immigration and faltering rural expansion in the early 1840s.

Australia's European population in 1840 stood at only 190,000, though it had grown by over 10 per cent in the 1830s (see Table 15) (Jackson, 1988: 6–7). Subsequent slower growth provoked a time of reckoning in colonial capitals where legislative councils (appointed by the governor) struggled to balance budgets. Most received grants-in-aid from the crown but were under pressure to become self-reliant. Given the 1841 increase in the price of crown land (to £1 per hectare), land sales revenues dwindled. Most tried to offset this by dues, fees and licences in order to overcome the largest constraint – poor overland transport. In the mid-1840s it often cost the same for bullock wagons

Table 15 Australian population growth 1800–1910.

	Population, thousands	Annual percentage increase in preceding ten years
1800	5	9.8
1810	12	8.3
1820	34	11.2
1830	70	7.6
1840	190	10.5
1850	405	7.8
1860	1,146	11.0
1870	1,648	3.7
1880	2,232	31.0
1890	3,151	3.5
1900	3,765	1.8
1910	4,425	1.6

Source: R. V. Jackson *Population History of Australia*, McPhee, Gribble, Melbourne, 1988.

Table 16 Population of Australian capital cities (in thousands) followed by percentage annual rate of increase by decades.

	Melbourne		Sydney		Adelaide		Brisbane		Perth		Hobart	
1851	29	–	54	–	18	–	3	–	–	–	–	–
1861	125	15.7	96	5.9	35	6.9	6	7.2	5	–	25	–
1871	191	4.3	138	3.7	51	3.9	15	9.6	–	–	26	0.4
1881	268	3.4	225	5.0	92	6.1	31	7.6	9	2.8	27	0.4

Source: W. A. Sinclair, *The Process of Economic Development in Australia* (Longman, 1979).

Table 17 Australian balance of trade.

Year to 31 Dec.	Exports	Imports	Trade Balance	Current Account Balance
	22	23	3	8
1861	17.41	17.65	−0.24	−2.5
1862	18.07	20.60	−2.53	−5.0
1863	19.34	21.25	−1.90	−5.1
1864	18.98	20.50	−152	−4.5
1865	19.71	20.66	−0.95	−4.3
1866	18.98	21.31	−2.33	−5.9
1867	19.38	15.96	2.42	−1.3
1868	21.65	18.44	3.21	−0.8
1869	20.07	19.91	0.16	−4.1
1870	18.01	17.83	0.18	−3.7
1871	21.73	17.02	4.71	−0.3
1872	22.52	18.83	3.69	−1.1
1873	26.37	24.57	1.80	−3.0
1874	25.65	24.55	1.10	−4.5
1875	24.98	24.94	0.04	−5.4
1876	23.54	23.96	−0.42	−6.3
1877	23.11	25.80	−2.69	−8.4
1878	23.77	26.18	−2.41	−9.0
1879	21.18	24.23	−3.05	−9.6
1880	27.26	22.94	4.32	−3.0
1881	27.53	29.07	−1.54	−8.8
1882	27.31	36.10	−8.79	−16.8
1883	30.06	35.45	−5.39	−14.7
1884	28.71	36.99	−8.28	−17.9
1885	26.67	36.86	−10.19	−20.5
1886	21.70	34.18	−12.48	−23.0
1887	23.42	29.57	−6.15	−18.8
1888	28.90	36.88	−7.98	−21.4
1889	29.55	37.58	−8.03	−22.7
1890	29.32	35.17	−5.85	−20.7
1891	36.04	37.71	−1.67	−17.0
1892	33.37	30.11	3.26	−11.1
1893	33.23	23.77	9.46	−4.3
1894	32.13	21.90	10.23	−3.2
1895	33.64	23.20	10.44	−3.2
1896	32.96	29.66	3.30	−10.9
1897	37.78	31.96	5.82	−8.0
1898	40.17	31.48	8.69	−5.5
1899	48.60	34.33	14.27	0.9
1900	45.96	41.39	4.57	−10.4

Notes

1 Recorded exports FOB, includes gold and coin; re-exports, excludes transhipments.

2 Recorded imports CIF, excludes transhipments.

3 After deducting transportation costs and interest due to non-residents.

Source: *Australian Historical Statistics*, Fairfax Syme etc., 1988, p. 50.

to carry goods fifty miles inland as it did to ship them from England (Cowan, 1977: 21). Extensive exploration had shown that, apart from the Murray and Darling rivers in New South Wales, Australia generally lacked the system of rivers and inland lakes that facilitated inland transportation elsewhere. The solution was therefore railways, which began in Melbourne in 1854 but had major impact in the 1860s and 1870s on the older colonies, and in the 1880s and 1890s on less populated Queensland and Western Australia (Cowell, 1972: ch. 5).

TRADING, RESOURCE RAIDING, AND THE MISSIONARY FRONTIER

Assisted by the development of ports around Australia, deep-sea whaling (mainly from New England in America) enjoyed its golden age in the early nineteenth century and paved the way for other ventures. Early entrepreneurs, operating mainly out of Sydney and Hobart, engaged in resource raiding. Mobilized by chiefs and overseen by traders, swimming divers collected pearl-shell and turtle-shell. *Beche-de-mer* (sea slugs) were collected and processed, mostly by islanders, for transport to China: by 1830 *beche-de-mer* was Fiji's leading export. Trading vessels employed scores of Europeans and Islanders, making great demands on food and fuel. One beneficiary was the Vunivalu (or war leader) of Bau, an islet off the east coast of Viti Levu in Fiji where vessels called en route to the fishing grounds, for supplies were exchanged for highly prized whales' teeth which consolidated the Vunivalu's influence (Denoon *et al.*, 1997).

Sandalwood was a different proposition since stands were inland and more labour was needed to fell and transport logs. Sandalwood in Hawaii inspired Kamehameha I to grant himself a trading monopoly over high initial profits. When his ventures lost money, he fell back on revenue from pilot and port fees. Sandalwood was also the focus of trade in Fiji, New Caledonia and the New Hebrides. Traders – mostly based in Sydney – devised rewards and penalties to secure cooperation. Islanders were introduced to cloth and nails, then tobacco, alcohol and firearms. Shineberg summarized the nexus as 'teaching islanders to smoke so that Chinese could burn incense – so that Australians could drink tea' (Shineberg, 1967: 151). Using such barter payment ships' masters and traders employed islanders directly, built shore stations, and visited every few months to bring supplies in and ship out shell and wood.

The demographic consequences of trading were severe, since islanders had no natural immunity to most European diseases although endemic yaws conferred some cross-immunity against syphilis and some captains tried to isolate infected sailors. Measles in Fiji, for example, in 1875 killed at least a quarter of the people. But natural history does not fully explain these outcomes. Morbidity seemed to correlate with the intensity of early contact and actual colonial experience: those suffering most being the dispossessed who endured crowding and poor nutrition (Kunitz, 1994). Missionaries also encouraged people to settle in villages, and converts suffered predictable consequences. Islanders often looked to missionaries for medication; but their remedies were limited and Islanders received more consolation than therapy.

Missionaries had more success in influencing ideology and governance in the Polynesian islands. The strange behaviour and unfathomable resources of Europeans had to be explained and assimilated into islanders' cosmologies. Missionaries were the most common sources of perceptions, beginning with the arrival of the London Missionary Society (LMS) at Matavai Bay in 1797. The nearby chief of one of the island's polities befriended the Europeans, who accepted his claim to hegemony and helped in his battles. By his death in 1803 they had acknowledged him as Pomare I, and endorsed the claims of Pomare II, the guarantor of the pork trade. The LMS also pinned their faith to the Pomares. Civil wars peaked in the Battle of Feipi in November 1815, resulting in a unified archipelago, ruled by the Pomares with LMS support. A missionary was the main author of the 1824 constitution which established a parliament and presided over the drafting of laws (Gunson, 1978).

In Tonga the LMS failed until 1826, when Tahitian teachers landed and built a congregation. The decisive initiative was taken by Taufa'ahau, who fought to combine the essential dynastic titles. As George I Tupou (a name reflecting his respect for Britain) he united Tonga and made Methodism almost the state religion. Methodist ministers again assisted in formulating laws (Latukefu, 1974).

When the pioneer Methodist missionary John Williams arrived in Samoa in 1830, Samoans already knew of Christianity through other Islanders, and some chiefs entreated him to send teachers. He put the victorious chief Malietoa Vai'inupo in charge of the mission, but Malietoa was slow to convert. Chiefs hoped for more than spiritual insights: tools, personal clients, and literacy. In Hawaii this order of events was modified. After the Battle of Nu'uanu in 1795, Kamehameha I instituted the centralized kingdom and the Kamehameha dynasty. The indigenous religion was overthrown just before missionaries arrived in the 1820s, whereupon Christianity became the new state religion (Daws, 1968).

Education was part of the missionaries' mandate. Islanders were often more eager for literacy than conversion. Missions founded schools for teachers and missionaries, as well as introducing Islanders to commerce. Church contributions were paid in commodities and Islanders were exhorted to produce for the glory of God, competing to give the largest contributions. From the first, social relations had centred on the foreigners' demands for sexual services, but missionaries intervened in cultural and gender relationships, not only to suppress 'vice' but also to impose Western norms. Island women's social standing and autonomy offended Western assumptions, and missionaries tried to instil Western gender roles by example and by education.

Various circumstances provoked Islanders to change political structures. Ambitious Polynesian chiefs welcomed the chance to extend their authority, and they were materially assisted by many foreigners who regarded hierarchies as incipient monarchies which could facilitate trade, missionization and diplomacy. Naval officers often pressured chiefs to sign treaties guaranteeing the safety and property of foreigners. Reflecting a common aim of early constitutions, that of Cakobau's Fiji included in its purposes 'to preserve the perfect harmony' which should exist between the two races [and] facilitate the increasing European commerce' (Scarr, 1984). Missionaries usually drafted early laws against sexual license, gun peddling and alcohol, but increasingly the legal codes addressed commerce.

Flourishing trade attracted merchant houses. Godeffroy und Sohn of Hamburg sailed in during the 1860s, to place trading agents on shore stations through the central

Pacific. To escape dependence on islander-grown copra, they bought land in Samoa and laid out plantations tended by workers from other islands. The house of Ballande, wine shippers in Bordeaux, built another string of retail outlets, recruited labourers (and carried their rations) from Vietnam to New Caledonia. The English company J. T. Arundel diversified out of Peruvian guano into island trading and nitrate mining; while Burns Philp and Co. also stretched their Queensland coastal trade into the islands. Missionaries often bridged the chasm between companies and island partners, and alliances were sometimes sought by missionaries themselves. When Protestants and Catholics contested the same islands, they sought business partners who shared their affiliation. Many companies acquired a distinctly sectarian tinge. Burns Philp favoured Presbyterian missionaries in Vanuatu, and offered them discounted rates while the pious Catholic Andre Ballande invoked St Anthony to bless his ventures (Denoon *et al.*, 1997).

Swindlers and saints alike depended on local power-holders. The Hawaiian monarchy gave missionaries' sons their start in business. The Pomares in Tahiti created an Anglo-Polynesian, Protestant ascendancy which survived French annexation. A colonial state would serve just as well as a monarchy. Andre Ballande for example aligned himself with the Catholic church, reinforced by his influence as deputy for Bordeaux, and weathered the bitter dispute between church and state at the turn of the century, even having his debts cancelled by a friendly government. Distinctions between economics, religion and politics had little meaning.

The leverage of local power-holders shrank as small traders were either displaced or subordinated by European companies with enough capital to plant their own crops on their own land, recruit workers from other islands and ride out unruly markets. Just as Le Nickel dominated New Caledonian mining, and Pacific Phosphates engorged pro-duction, so Lever took control of Solomon Island copra, while the rest of the region's production was shared by a handful of German and Anglo-Australian firms. Crucial to these large enterprises was the discovery of ways to control land and labour.

Most foreigners believed in private property. Privatizing lands, they argued in Hawaii, would encourage 'improve-ment'. Laws passed in 1850 had devastating effects. The Kuleana Act enabled 'native tenants' to be awarded their lands in fee simple, while another 1850 law gave foreigners the right to own land – so commoners could sell just when foreigners could buy (Linnekin, 1990). In Samoa, during the civil wars of the 1860s and 1870s, Europeans speculated in land sold to them by Samoans without authority. An International Land Commission, meeting from 1892 to 1894, found that, while in Hawaii the burden of proof was on the native claimant, in Samoa the onus was on foreigners who claimed more than double the entire area but were awarded only about one fifth (Ward and Kingdon, 1995).

Tonga's laws and constitution aimed to secure recogni-tion from foreign powers and thereby continued indepen-dence. The Vava'u Code of 1839 committed Tonga to Christianity, prohibiting 'Murder, Theft, Adultery, Fornica-tion and the retailing of Ardent spirits', but was mainly concerned with social and political order. In 1850 the sale of land to foreigners was forbidden. In 1875 'King George' proposed a new constitution to parliament, drafted by the missionary Shirley Baker, which with few modifications, still serves the kingdom.

In Fiji, Bau was a magnet for beachcombers, some of whom became mercenary soldiers of the Vunivalu. By 1861 the Christian Cakobau was Vunivalu, and the foreign community was expanding. Foreign debts were pressing and planters and traders were reluctant to recognize Cakobau. Other chiefs awaited a chance to cast off Bau's hegemony, and some were courted by Enele Ma'afu, leader of a Tongan community under the auspices of Methodism. In June 1871, Cakobau declared himself King of a united Fiji, co-opting Ma'afu as his viceroy and other chiefs and traders as cabinet ministers. The monarchy held together just long enough to cede sovereignty to Britain in 1875, when Fiji became the headquarters of British interests.

NEW ZEALAND

The tides of European settlement, trade and evangelization converged on the exceptional natural resources of New Zealand from the 1790s (Lloyd Pritchard, 1970; Hawke, 1985). Whalers called at the Bay of Islands for water, food and sexual services. Sealing and on-shore bay whaling enterprises, which attracted Australian adventurers, were more consequential as they employed Maoris and bought Maori food. The stimulus of the New South Wales market also fostered wheat, flax production and timber extraction. Like South Australia, New Zealand attracted Wakefield and other enthusiasts for orderly settlement, as well as disorderly settlers from Australia. But Maori societies were already being transformed by the forces which had impinged so heavily on other islands. From 1814 missionaries instructed Maori in European farming methods: growing potatoes and wheat, and a few began herding cattle and sheep. Soon many were well placed to compete commercially with British settlers and benefit from expanding trade. In the early 1820s, however, Maori acquired muskets, and warfare got out of control, while new diseases and enslavement caused drastic depopulation. Since Christianity seemed to be associated with the wealth and strength of Europeans, con-version occurred on a large scale. Nonetheless social changes passed beyond Maori control. In 1840 the first British governor, William Hobson, landed with instructions to secure sovereignty – preferably by treaty. Hobson invited chiefs to Waitangi, where he presented them with a treaty. Signed by over 530 chiefs, the Treaty of Waitangi established British sovereignty, at least morally, by agreement.

Maori tribes retained economic control for a generation after the Treaty. In the 1840s many areas had thriving farms and water mills, and Maori producers traded far afield. By the 1850s tribes owned and operated most of the coastal shipping in the North Island. They supplied the local market with almost all its produce and maintained a large export trade to Australia and the Pacific. Many settlers were affronted by Maori competitors, but they could not take control until they gained access to land. As in other islands, many Maori at first had been willing to sell land to settlers. Even after the Treaty sales did not stop, since some land was lying fallow and many communities wanted settlers as conduits of wealth. However, in the mid-1850s Maori resistance to the sale of land became acute, especially in prosperous areas, for many settlers had switched to exten-sive pastoralism after the market slumped in 1856, so compounding the land scarcity problem.

To deal with the increasing threat to land ownership, Maori united in inter-tribal councils to devise a common strategy. Meetings were at first geared to limit land sales, but soon attention turned to the possibility of a Maori monarchy. The kingship was offered to several chiefs, and in 1858 Potatau Te Wherowhero of the Waikato tribe accepted. At first the King was supported by only twenty-three tribes, for many refused to pledge allegiance fearing racial disharmony and exclusion from the European economy, but they supported the movement's land policy. The extreme Kingites opposed the selling of land in any circumstances, whereas moderates were willing to yield certain disputed blocks for the sake of peace. Some chiefs refused to recognize Potatau as King in the belief that Maori social organization did not allow for such difference in status, while many northern chiefs argued that a Maori kingship was incompatible with the Treaty of Waitangi. The Kingites themselves remained divided on a strategy to counter European aggression. Nevertheless the mere existence of a King influenced inter-ethnic relations throughout New Zealand – Maoridom was more centrally organized than it had been before.

The wars of the 1860s were caused not only by conflict over land. They also concerned the control and management of economic infrastructure. After twelve years of skirmishing between land sellers and landholders, war broke out in Taranaki in March 1860. As soon as a substantial victory was achieved, all troops were transferred to Auckland. The critical question was how the government would respond to the Maori King since some of his adherents had interfered in Taranaki. Potatau died in June 1860, his son Maatutaera was enthroned, and won the allegiance of increasing numbers who became convinced that the settlers were planning to seize their lands. The wars lasted until the end of 1864, and consisted largely of pitched battles in which each tribe made a final stand on its domain. The Kingites made their last stand under chief Rewi at Orakau, where 300 Maori refused to surrender for three days. Their slogan *Ka whawhai tonu ake! Ake! Ake!* (We shall fight on forever! Forever! Forever!) has become a rallying cry in modern Maori protest movements.

The government then confiscated three million acres of the most arable areas of the North Island. Punishing rebels was a mere pretext; confiscations were plainly for the purpose of settlement. Military settlements were established, and an ambitious immigration scheme recruited settlers. Outside the confiscated areas the sale of land was facilitated by establishing the Native Land Court in 1865. Its aim was first to determine land titles on a sub-tribal basis, and then to individualize titles by allotting shares to a maximum of ten owners per block. The confiscations violated the Waitangi Treaty, but Maoris discovered that the Treaty offered no protection. In a leading case in 1877, Judge James Prendergast described the Treaty as 'a simple nullity', setting a precedent which persisted until 1987 (Denoon *et al.*, 1997).

Towards the end of the century it was commonly believed that the Maori were on the verge of extinction. Their number reached its nadir in 1896, when only 42,113 people were enumerated in a census. In 1892 the four Maori Members of Parliament (seated since 1867) set up a parallel Maori Parliament, which accepted the Westminster parliament but sought control over a limited range of affairs. It was not a success. European society ignored what it considered a separatist movement, and many Maori were also uninterested. In part, the lack of enthusiasm resulted from a large-scale movement of Maori into the money economy.

Eventually the division of Maoridom proved fatal. During the last half of the century several young political leaders emerged. Unlike the elderly Maori leaders who distrusted the government outright, they no longer resisted some governmental protection. In 1898 the old guard refused to cooperate further with the younger leaders, and walked out. The Maori Parliament was disbanded in 1902.

GOLD RUSHES

The most profound climacteric in the nineteenth-century Australian economy was the discovery of gold in New South Wales and Victoria in 1851, for it dramatically increased the population of those colonies as well as their ethnic mix and skill base. The first officially to find gold, at Ophir NSW, was Edward Hargraves, fresh from the Californian diggings, who recognized similar gold-bearing localities (Blainey, 1963: 46ff; Bate, 1988: 41ff). Initial diggers were locals, but men from other colonies and overseas quickly joined the rush, especially to the rich fields near Ballarat and Bendigo in Victoria. Californian '49ers became Bendigo '52ers, where they swelled complaints about the 30-shilling annual Licence to Dig imposed by the government in 1851. By October 1853 finds in NSW were becoming rarer and, to stem the tide of departing diggers, NSW lowered its annual licence fee to 10 shillings. In contrast Victoria, facing increasing expenditure on roads, police and postal services, raised the fee to £1 per month and introduced fortnightly licence inspections. With alluvial finds dwindling, miners detested the tax – especially as it did not entitle them to vote – and the level of protest rose. It peaked in December 1854 in the Eureka Stockade, on the Ballarat field, where 150 unlicensed diggers stood up to 400 police and troops – 30 diggers were killed and 100 captured. This event has attained the significance to Australians that the Boston Tea Party has for Americans, and the Australian flag still carries the Eureka Stockade symbol, the stars of the Southern Cross on a blue background. The anti-authoritarian stance of Eureka was emulated by gold thieves, known as bushrangers, the most famous being Ned Kelly. For years they stalked travellers and isolated farmhouses but were protected from police by those who admired their Robin-Hood ethics: rob the rich but harm no woman or child. Their daring exploits to evade capture have entered Australian folklore.

In June 1855, the government of Victoria finally replaced the hated Miners Licence with an export duty and introduced a system of elected members for special gold fields courts. Reflecting increasing tensions between European and Chinese diggers, they also imposed a tax of £10 on all male Chinese immigrants and restricted the numbers of Chinese any one ship could land. Anti-Chinese sentiment stemmed partly from their 'strange' customs and language, but was also linked to their industrious habit of picking over discarded tailings in large all-male groups and succeeding where other diggers had failed. The Victorian action was the first time any colony had restricted immigration, but by 1888 all had passed discriminatory Acts against the Chinese or non-whites in general.

By 1856 most of the alluvial gold had been taken, although numbers on the Victorian fields continued to increase. As all necessities were expensive, life on the fields became more difficult. Most diggers drifted back to Melbourne where they were absorbed into various service, building and manufacturing enterprises catering for the enlarged population; some went to work for the companies that were established to exploit the less accessible underground gold seams, and a few continued their search for the elusive nugget.

The gold rushes built up the pressure of migration and investment, which burst out again with the discovery of gold in New Zealand in 1861. Then, in the late 1860s, the resistance of Maoris in New Zealand (and squatters in Australia) to successful small holding and the diminishing returns from alluvial gold led to a new movement to Queensland. Traditions of these mobile diggers included contempt for Aborigines, hostility towards Chinese and reliance on each other in fields remote from police and provisions. From north Queensland, some Australian diggers crossed the Coral Sea to Papua. Australians also discovered gold in New Caledonia in 1870. The most significant discovery here, however, was nickel. Rothschilds put Société Le Nickel on a sound financial footing and during the 1890s production boomed. The local economy exhibited the paradox of a large indigenous population, a French convict labour force – and a chronic shortage of labour. From the 1860s the gap had been filled by indentured New Hebrideans, and later by Vietnamese (Shineberg, in press) – there was little scope for Australians except as technicians or supervisors.

Papua, by contrast, became an extension of the Queensland mining industry. Early Papuan mining was alluvial, but the exploitation of lodes demanded more capital than local store-keepers could lend. Investment was inhibited by the absence of a legal structure until the British New Guinea administration offered protection for life and property. Thereafter, Australian prospectors focused on the islands in Milne Bay, beginning on Tagula (Sudest) in 1888 when 400 miners descended on a population of about 1,000. Rushes followed to other off-shore islands. Misima and Murua (Woodlark) attracted Australian capital, and promoters in Sydney exploited no-liability companies to engage in 'stock market manipulation, insider trading, exaggeration (if not falsification) of assays...and, ultimately, mismanagement'. Until the development of Misima, the effect of colonial rule was to strengthen the traditions of alluvial mining, to curb violence in Papua – and allow killings in Australian stock markets. The discovery of the mother-lode led to large-scale quartz-mining from 1914, when the largest Australian company, Broken Hill, took over (Nelson, 1976; O'Faircheallaigh, 1982).

Mining was not the only attraction in the islands. Commercial farming in Australia and New Zealand generated sustained demand for fertilizers, such as guano, which was quarried in Peru by Chinese workers. In 1862, when this labour supply was interrupted, the adventurer James Byrne resolved to recruit Melanesians. Poor navigation brought him to Tongareva, 'the one island in all Polynesia where the people were only too eager to be recruited', as their coconut trees were diseased and their missionaries encouraged them to work abroad. Byrne's profits provoked Peruvians to charter any ship which might float, to scour Polynesia for labour. When volunteers were few, islanders were kidnapped. Most vulnerable were small islands (such as Rapanui which lost a third of its people). Some recruits shovelled guano and others worked on plantations and in domestic service. Mercifully the venture lasted only two years, in which 3,634 people left the islands: perhaps one in ten returned, since repatriation was just as haphazard as recruitment (Lal *et al.*, 1994).

Micronesian nitrates began to be exploited soon afterwards. Phosphates were identified on Banaba (Ocean Island) in 1900, and two Banabans were induced to sign a 999-year concession (Williams and MacDonald, 1985). In 1908 a French and British company (the Compagnie Française des Phosphates de l'Océanie, and the Pacific Phosphate Company) joined forces in an integrated operation embracing almost all Pacific nitrate production. On Makatea islet, north-east of Tahiti, 160 to 200 Polynesians had the misfortune to live over phosphates. Banabans not only lost their chance of royalties: they were not employed. Deprived of their lands, islanders were almost forgotten and drifted away, making way for wage labourers (Newbury, 1972). The company then introduced Japanese and Chinese indentured workers. Equally brisk dispossession followed in Nauru (Pacific Phosphate Company, 1906) where locals were involved only to cow mutinous Chinese workers. Of all the catastrophes which befell inhabitants of small islands, phosphates were the worst. Rights to deposits were cheaply bought and there was no need to involve islanders in production. Those who lived near gold at least had a sporting chance to benefit.

PLANTATIONS AND THE LABOUR RESERVE

Pastoral properties in Australia required few workers, and grain and dairy farms were mainly family operations. However, from the 1860s sugar became the export staple in the wet coastal plains of north Queensland – a plantation crop requiring plentiful and cheap labour. The islands of the western Pacific became a 'labour reserve' in the perception of planters: from 1863 until 1904, 62,000 islanders worked in Queensland, most from Vanuatu and the Solomons (Lal *et al.*, 1994). During the 1890s, technical advances made it possible for plantations to yield to family farms, while the Colonial Sugar Refining Company (CSR) processed cane in central mills. This company had large interests in Fiji, whose British governor, Sir Arthur Gordon, had recognized the Island's need for capital and labour, and seen that CSR could provide the first, and indentured Indian labour the second. But Gordon was determined to avoid the dispossession which had occurred in Australia, New Zealand and Hawaii. His solution was to formalize the Great Council of Chiefs to advise the governor on Fijian affairs, to enlist chiefs in rural administration and tax collection, and to guarantee to Fijians the possession of most of their land. A Native Lands Commission assessed settlers' claims, and demarcated land which remained under communal control. The structure was not as benign as it appeared, but it did reconcile the needs of the sugar industry with the authority of the chiefs (Ward and Kingdon, 1995).

For island plantations, land was essential – but elusive. By 1880 when Tahiti was formally annexed it was too late to subvert property rights held by islanders, and there was no scope for large companies. Copra became the staple export, but only a fraction was grown on plantations. This outcome was avoided in New Caledonia, for in 1855 the French colonial government had acquired all lands which were not under cultivation and placed them in the hands of planters and ranchers. They and their indigenous allies were able to put down revolts by the dispossessed. French convicts, introduced from 1850, became the foundation for a society of emancipists and free settlers, creating a capitalist economy on the bases of mining and pastoralism, while the Kanak were evicted to off-shore islands and reserves (Connell, 1987).

Even when land was acquired, labour did not flow. In Samoa, the focal point of German enterprise, the Deutsche Handels-und Plantagen-Gesellschaft company (DHPG) had land, but could not mobilize enough cheap labour. Samoans would not work on plantations and Gilbertese (who recruited readily) were too few. Formal annexation of Western Samoa by Germany in 1900 made little difference to DHPG's dominance in framing and interpreting land and labour policies. As in other island colonies, lack of revenue meant that large companies, with access to capital, could promote development when colonial governments could not.

EROSION OF THE BRITISH INFORMAL EMPIRE

Britain's informal empire in the Pacific rested on its navy, supplied from Sydney. Frail kingdoms and theocracies flourished under that umbrella, and mission families provided the consular services which hinged naval power to island authorities. Three kinds of instability challenged this informal empire: the intrusion of other powerful nations, the increasing number of immigrant settlers, and the expansion of commerce.

From the 1840s French interests were drawn into the region, protected by the French navy. American naval power provoked the re-emergence of Japan and extinguished the decaying Spanish empire, initiating America's own 'Pacific Century'. The new German empire, under Bismarck, was the least of Britain's anxieties. Bismarck doubted whether colonial acquisitions would justify the antagonism of Britain or France. Like the British – but unlike the French – he resisted both tariff protection and colonial annexations.

The greatest sources of instability were British settlers in Australia and New Zealand, and French settlers (caldoches) in New Caledonia, who demanded that their governments annex every known island. European governments were reluctant to risk global conflicts, but they could not ignore increasing disorder, nor simply rebuff their importunate subjects. But responses were minimalist. The (British) Western Pacific High Commission was appended to the Governorship of Fiji, and its authority was largely to advise the Royal Navy (Scarr, 1990). When it proved inadequate, Britain declared protectorates over Papua and the Solomon islands – on condition that Australian and New Zealand colonies foot the bill. When Bismarck decided in 1884 to move from informal empire to protectorates, he tried to operate through chartered companies, until these declared themselves bankrupt.

German traders had dominated the commerce of the central Pacific in the 1870s, mainly through Godeffroys in Samoa, where they ran plantations, bought Samoan-grown copra and handled most trade. They also cornered Tongan copra by agreement with the Methodist mission. Astute in the Pacific, Godeffroys were rash in Europe. They were declared bankrupt in 1879 and bought out by the DHPG. Enduring depressed copra prices through the 1880s and 1890s, and competition from other labour recruiters in Melanesia, DHPG implored Berlin to annex territory to protect their land, labour and trade. Companies willing to act as governments promised annexation without cost.

The largest was the New Guinea Company, commissioned to govern New Guinea in 1884. Land was acquired after perfunctory negotiations, but malaria decimated Company officers; tropical micro-organisms ravished field crops, and indentured Melanesian and Chinese labourers suffered high mortality rates. Only in the Gazelle Peninsula, where planters were already established, did plantations flourish. Bad planning was a consequence of commercial calculations in Hamburg, applied to a task which required negotiations in New Guinea. The effects included massive loss of life and capital. In 1899 the Company surrendered its mandate, and New Guinea became an orthodox colony, where the governor struggled to promote the collective interests of planters, restrain their appetites for labour and curb the mortality rates of workers. By 1914 a prosperous plantation colony had been created in the Bismarck archipelago (Firth, 1983).

Inspired by British Australia, French colonization was markedly less successful (Henningham, 1992). The explorer La Perouse had reached Botany Bay a week after the First Fleet; and in an isolated burst of colonizing enthusiasm, French settlers were landed in the South Island of New Zealand at Akoroa in 1840 – again too late to sustain possession. Instead, they turned to eastern Polynesia, where claims rested on Catholic complaints against Protestant bigotry. The French navy annexed the Marquesas group in 1841 and created a protectorate over Tahiti a year later. New Caledonia was annexed ten years later and became a penal colony modelled on convict-built Australia, notably in the abrogation of Kanakas' rights to land which passed to the government. Little of the main island was suited to European agriculture, but pastoral production flourished and minerals became important. A copper mining company was floated in 1859 with the Rothschilds as major shareholders. In 1880, with further support from Rothschilds, the Société Le Nickel was launched, soon becoming the mainstay of the colonial economy. Rothschilds took complete control in 1890 and nursed Le Nickel through the subsequent world depression.

In the 1880s Protestant missionaries dominated the New Hebrides labour reserve and Australians were urging the British government to annex the group. To forestall that outcome, the French Caledonian Company of the New Hebrides was established, and in 1882 set out to buy the islands piecemeal. By 1886 the Company claimed more than half the entire land area, and had begun to plant French settlers and to encourage Marist missionaries. Much land was 'bought' from Melanesians who had no idea that they were 'selling', and were outraged when settlers arrived. The Caledonian Company eventually failed, but French influence in the New Hebrides endured.

Australian colonists' anxieties about the islands were exacerbated by Japanese adventurers, precipitated into the region when the United States Navy breached the seclusion policy. From Thursday Island to Broome during the 1880s Japanese men were introduced as divers for pearls and pearl-shell, and some bought pearling vessels and dominated the trade. Only racially-restrictive licensing laws prevented them from outright ownership of the whole fleet. By the 1890s, over thirty Japanese women were working on Thursday Island, and others were scattered throughout the dusty towns of northern Australia.

TOWARDS AUSTRALIAN FEDERATION

By the 1890s, land-abundant Australia had become one of the most urbanized countries in the world. Its total population of nearly 4 million, excluding Aboriginal people, was concentrated in a few capital cities, with most in Sydney and Melbourne. The advent of railways had allowed suburbia to grow, just as the capital cities were reaching their walking limits; and wool, Australia's staple export, required little direct labour but generated a great deal of employment in the ports. After the gold rushes of the 1850s the settler population had grown more slowly, natural increase overtaking migration. A second surge from 1880 to 1885 brought in an average 44,000 per year before dwindling to negligible levels during the 1890s (Jackson, 1988: 27). Part of the 1880s surge was made up of Melanesian labour for Queensland sugar plantations and Japanese pearl divers for northern Australia, but most were British immigrants assisted by colonial governments.

In Western Australia the outflow of young men to the eastern gold fields in the 1850s had been offset by the introduction of male convicts, guards and their families, and young free women brought out deliberately to equalize the gender balance. Between 1850 and 1868 (when transportation ceased) 9,635 convicts and a similar number of free immigrants had brought Western Australia's non-Aboriginal population to 22,700 – a number New South Wales reached by 1820. Missing out on the land boom which attracted immigrants to the eastern colonies in the 1880s, the west attracted migrants only in the 1890s with the discovery of gold.

In South Australia (which administered the Northern Territory) various private companies attempted unsuccessfully to establish pastoral ventures and settle the 'top end', until 1870 when the city of Palmerston was proclaimed. (This was re-named Darwin in 1911 when the Northern Territory was made separate.) Among the early settlers were those involved with the British-Australia Overseas Telegraph Company, as the first submarine cable entered Australia at Palmerston in November 1871. Over the next two decades the 'top end' witnessed the remarkable cattle drives of the Duracks and other families, who walked their stock from northern Queensland into the Ord river region of north-west Australia (Durack, 1967).

For much of the period of the long boom (1860–90) Australia benefited from high levels of British investment. In Britain interest rates were low and railway building, previously a profitable investment, was complete. By contrast, investment opportunities in Australia and New Zealand looked promising, especially as most were either backed by government or based on the security of land. Colonial governments floated loans on the London stock exchange to finance railways and other public works, while private banks and finance companies offered investment opportunities in the pastoral industry and land markets So sterling poured into Australia. The ease of borrowing, however, encouraged settlers to move onto marginal lands, governments to build uneconomic railway lines, and speculators to trade in rural and urban land and buildings (Cannon, 1966; Roe 1974). Meanwhile infant manufacturing concerns, initiated after the gold rushes, were unattractive to British and even local investors, and so were largely deprived of the capital needed for expansion. Nonetheless some of Australia's largest and most successful enterprises, such as the Broken Hill Proprietary Company and Myer retailers were born in this period.

With a larger population base and rail links to port cities, agriculture diversified. The timber industry had taken off with the advent of railways, partly due to the demand for sleepers but also because rail solved the problem of overland transport. The quality of Australian hardwoods was already widely known, but a lucrative export trade had to await the development of cheap transport. The cattle industry also benefited from rail, and began to rival wool as a pastoral activity, especially in the northern outreaches of settlement where Aboriginals were trained as stockmen. The production of butter and cheese as well as fresh meat increased even before the invention of refrigerated transport in the 1890s. The wheat industry also expanded through cheap railway freight and from the advent of iron- hulled ships (wooden ships had largely precluded export because of the risk involved if wheat became damp and swelled). During the 1870s and 1880s thousands of acres were planted with wheat, especially in South Australia. Grain growers in all colonies took advantage of the stump-jump plough, invented in South Australia in the 1840s, and the stripper harvester, invented in Victoria in 1883, which stripped, threshed and bagged wheat in one operation. A major hazard – the damage done by introduced rabbits – was addressed by legislation and by the construction of extensive lines of rabbit-proof fencing from 1887.

Drought in New South Wales in the late 1880s placed the first serious strain on the speculative boom in the eastern colonies. Farmers on marginal lands failed to meet debt repayments, forcing most banks to review their lending policies. As they began to retrench and to raise interest rates, they were replaced by land and building finance companies which continued to offer low interest rates. It was one of these – the Premier Building Association of Melbourne – which first struck trouble and suspended operations in 1889. Panic was averted by drawing on British funds; but in the following year the crash of the British House of Baring unnerved already worried investors and led to a flight of capital. This left many Australian institutions on the brink of collapse, precisely when wool export prices were falling and excess capacity in the housing market was being exacerbated by a decline in immigration.

The 1890s depression was an enormous psychological shock. Fifty years of prosperity had fostered the belief that Australia was immune from the ills of the rest of the world. A surge of nationalist sentiment had occurred in the 1880s, including the first attempts to describe an Australian culture, such as Andrew 'Banjo' Paterson's and Henry Lawson's poems, printed alongside political cartoons and critical articles in the new *Bulletin* magazine. The Heidelberg school of painting (Roberts, Streeton, McCubbin and Condor, exhibited first in August 1889) also sought to define the Australian 'difference'. Idealists such as Lane, Archibald and Norton spoke out fiercely for workers' rights, identifying a natural socialism in the bush workers' tradition of 'mateship' espoused by the poets and other writers in the *Bulletin*. These sentiments were echoed in several short-lived but influential newspapers which aimed to popularize the theories of Henry George, Sidney Webb and other socialist thinkers.

The Maritime Strike of 1890 – so-called because it started among waterside workers – developed into a general strike for an eight-hour working day. Starting in August, it was soon supported by 50,000 shearers, seamen, miners and other workers, who held out until November when union funds were exhausted and members and their families were in desperate straits. Most strikers returned to work on the same – or worse – conditions, though employers failed to ban unionism. The strike showed workers that a political voice might achieve more than direct action, and led to the creation of the Australian Labor Party. The demoralizing effect of the strike was followed by the financial collapse, which left at least 30 per cent of workers unemployed.

By early 1894 the depression was lifting, as the eastern colonies began to enjoy side-benefits from the discovery, in Western Australia, of the richest gold fields in the continent's history. Minor discoveries in the 1880s were followed by the announcement in September 1892 that Bayly and Ford had struck gold in Coolgardie; while Paddy Hannan reported an even bigger find at Kalgoorlie in 1893. They had stumbled upon the 'Golden Mile' (Mayman, 1964; Blainey, 1992), an extremely rich seam running between these two desert towns which is still worked today. Thousands of would-be diggers arrived (bringing Western Australia's settler population from 46,000 in 1890 to over 100,000 by 1897), totally unprepared for the 100-mile walk beyond the last rail link and the primitive living conditions on the field.

New techniques of extraction had to be developed, since all previous gold fields had used water in pans or cradles. Here there was no natural water supply: Bore water was briny, and all drinking water had to be brought in by donkey or camel trains. Instead of water, diggers used the winds to separate gold from sand in a 'dry-blower'. The Western Australian gold fields were unusual also, in sustaining none of the fierce anti-Chinese sentiment which had animated diggers in the eastern colonies. The Western Australian government – anxious about Japanese pearlers in the north – had already legislated to restrict non-European immigration south of the 26th parallel (Vanden Driesen, 1986: 134–5). The few non-Europeans who did reach the fields were mainly descendants of earlier migrants, and most turned to the less exciting but more profitable ventures of laundering and food provision. There were also 'Afghans' who accompanied the camel trains introduced to carry supplies over the desert country. To relieve the lack of water, C. Y. O'Connor, the government's chief engineer, planned a 290-mile pipeline to pump fresh water from Perth to Coolgardie, a huge project which was completed in 1903 (Taubman, 1978).

By this time Western Australia was part of the new Australian Commonwealth, initiated on 1 January 1901. Federation was not easy, since the colonies valued their autonomy (not least Western Australia, which had been self-governing only since 1890). A growing number of common concerns were expressed at various Premiers' Conferences, and Sir Henry Parkes, Premier of New South Wales and a great orator, persuaded his colleagues that there would be strength in unity. Defence, immigration (especially the restriction of Asian immigration), transport (there was still no East-West land link) and the increasing patriotism of colonists who felt that Australia was 'different', were the issues which drove the premiers to plan a federal constitution and agree to a national referendum. New Zealand, whose delegates attended earlier conferences, pulled out in 1897. The 'Commonwealth bill' was first put to the south-eastern colonies in 1898 and to all colonial legislatures in 1899. At this stage all except Western Australia favoured the change. In the West, the rural establishment still dominated the legislative assembly and resisted federation. However, the gold fields' population was keen to federate in order to lower costs, and they threatened to secede unless the government agreed to put forward the bill. The premier, John Forrest, yielded and called a referendum

in 1900, where pro-federation votes won two-to-one. By this stage the bill had already been enacted by the British parliament and had received royal assent.

Rivalry between New South Wales and Victoria complicated the choice of a federal capital. Agreement was finally reached that the federal parliament would meet in Melbourne until a capital site was determined, within New South Wales but at least 100 miles from Sydney. Although Canberra was selected in 1908 and its layout planned by the American Walter Burley Griffin, parliament did not move there for twenty years, reflecting the tardy and grudging transfer of resources from the states (Pegrum, 1983).

The Commonwealth's agenda included the definition of Australia's physical boundaries and social composition. These were unclear only in the north-east, where Japanese prostitutes and pearl-divers, Chinese gold-seekers, and Melanesian plantation workers offended the 'White Australia' sentiment of the new federal government. The Pacific Island Labourers Act of the first parliament determined that islanders be repatriated. Sugar producers were forewarned, and the Commonwealth paid a bounty on sugar produced by white workers, so the industry survived the repatriation crisis. Islanders were less fortunate. There had been nearly 10,000 in Queensland in 1901. By 1906 there were only about 4,500. Those whose long residence entitled them to stay found most jobs closed by white labour preference. They continued to practise Christianity and to assimilate culturally to settler society: yet they were largely excluded from that society, with lower standards of living and education, pressed always closer to the even more marginal Aboriginal population (Moore, 1985).

During the 1870s colonial 'management' of Aboriginal and Islander peoples had been reinforced by mission stations. In northern Australia missions were given land to administer as Aboriginal reservations. In the Torres Strait itself, islanders' knowledge of luggers and beche-de-mer had expanded when sailors settled among them, and again when they embraced Christianity. Their knowledge and skills enabled them to take an active part in pearling, and so after the turn of the century both missionaries and Queensland officials resolved to transform them into independent entrepreneurs. This trajectory exempted them from the Aborigines Protection Act, and earned them a civil status like that of the Kanakas – neither white nor Aboriginal. The islanders' distinct legal status was never eroded, and their lands (unlike Aboriginal Australians' lands) were not expropriated.

From the perspective of the new Australian Commonwealth, the important achievement was order – however anomalous – on a remote frontier, and the missions preserved order cheaply. The White Australia immigration policy, introduced with similar intentions, restricted Japanese to limited numbers and to prescribed jobs, and completely halted Chinese immigration. Together with the repatriation of Kanakas, these measures amounted to a gradual ethnic cleansing and tidying.

Insular in some respects, the new Commonwealth Parliament was quite reformist in others. Following New Zealand's and South Australia's lead in enfranchising women on the same terms as men, the new Federal government passed similar legislation in 1902. In another decision which paralleled developments in New Zealand, the Parliament in 1908 linked tariff protection to the payment of 'fair and reasonable wages', a decision that led the following year to the famous 'Harvester Judgement'. In assessing the claim of the Sunshine Harvester Company for tariff protection, Justice Higgans formulated the principle of a minimum or 'basic wage' for unskilled workers that would provide a decent standard of living for a man, his wife and two children. Over the next decade the principle was accepted by all states, and indexed for inflation. Women's wages were excluded until a ruling in 1919 set their minimum at 54 per cent of the male rate, on the grounds that most working females would be single and not require the 'family' or male wage.

By this stage Australians and New Zealanders were beginning to make their mark on the outside world. Although men from the various colonies had served in the Boer war in the 1890s, the call to aid the 'Mother Country' in 1914-18 saw Australians fighting under one flag for the first time – often alongside New Zealanders. Bugle calls through bush towns rallied dozens of raw recruits who with their horses were amassed at Albany, Western Australia, before leaving in November 1914, destined for Egypt, which they were to protect from Turkey – a German ally. The larrikinism of the high-spirited Australians and New Zealanders appalled some of the British officers sent to train them for military action, but under continual fire on the cliffs and hills at Gallipoli (on the Turkish coast) they showed legendary courage and care for wounded comrades. The beachhead was secured for the Allies at enormous human cost, and was followed by attacks on Lone Pine and San Blair. But their position was untenable and soldiers were evacuated – leaving a total of 7,594 fallen Australians behind (*Australians-Events*, 1988). Despite defeat, the bravery of the ANZACs inspired those at home. In folklore, Australia 'came of age' in this war – in Turkey as well as in France and Belgium, where thousands more died repelling the Germans. Every year, the day of remembrance for all fallen soldiers in Australia is still held on the First World War commemorative ANZAC Day.

CONCLUSION

The enthusiastic participation of Australians and New Zealanders in the Great War is one measure of those societies' commitment to the affairs of Europe, and the British Empire in particular. The crisis of war dispelled some of their fanciful pretensions and clarified their place and prospects in a global community. The linkages of indigenous peoples were more problematic and conditional. Some Aboriginal Australians managed to enlist in Australian forces, and New Caledonian Kanakas, Fijians and New Zealand Maori enlisted in the allied cause with fervour; but other islanders were allotted more passive roles. German colonies, along with their inhabitants, were seized for their (slight) strategic value and held thereafter as prizes of war; New Guinea by Australia, Western Samoa by New Zealand, and Micronesia by Japan. Colonists on the whole grasped the role of junior partners in imperial hierarchies, explicitly designating most 'natives' to subordination. European scientific and medical ideas of the period offered justification for this unequal incorporation; It would take at least half a century for the more humane and generous elements of that body of thought to re-shape European ideas about race. During that long interval, indigenous people were to use both protest and cooperation to protect their autonomy, re-build their self esteem and widen their opportunities.

NOTES

1 Since the collection of economic and demographic statistics did not begin in the Islands until the mid-twentieth century, we cannot include the Islands in the statistical appendix to this chapter. The first census in Papua New Guinea, for example, was conducted only in the 1960s; no census was conducted in Irian Jaya during the Dutch era; and economists have not yet discovered how to attribute values to trade and exchange in a non-monetary economy.

2 With a capital injection from William Lever's purchase of Company land claims in the Solomon Islands, the company was restructured as the Pacific Phosphate Company. In 1907 it achieved economies of scale (and market leverage) by securing mining rights in German Nauru. (See Williams and McDonald, 1985).

3 The Pacific Phosphate Company gained a 94-year concession there in 1906.

BIBLIOGRAPHY

APPLEYARD, R. T.; MANFORD, T. 1979. *The Beginning*. University of Western Australia Press.

Australians-Events. 1988. Bicentenary Series, Fairfax Syme & Weldon, p. 126.

BATTYE, J. S. 1924. *Western Australia – a History from its Discovery to the Inauguration of the Commonwealth*. Oxford.

BATE, W. 1988. *Victorian Gold Rushes*. McPhee, Gribble, Melbourne.

BLAINEY, G. 1963. *The Rush that Never Ended*. Melbourne University Press.

——. 1992. *The Golden Mile*. Allen & Unwin.

BONNEMAISON, J. 1986. *Les fondements d'une identité. Territoire, histoire et société dans l'archipel de Vanatu (Mélanésie)*. Vol. 1. Paris, L'arbre et la pirogue. Also published by the University of Hawaii Press, Honolulu, in 1994 as *The Tree and the Canoe: History and Ethnogeography of Tanna*.

BUTLIN, N. 1994. *Economics and the Dreamtime*. Cambridge University Press.

CAMERON, J. M. R. 1979. *Ambition's Fire*. University of Western Australia Press.

CANNON, M. 1966. *The Land Boomers*. Melbourne University Press.

CLARK, C. M. H. 1950. *Documents in Australian History*. Angus & Robertson, Melbourne.

COWAN, P. (ed.) 1977. *A Faithful Picture: The Letters of Eliza and Thomas Brown 1841–1852*. Fremantle Arts Centre Press, pp. 21ff.

COWELL, M. 1972. *Australian Transport*. Paul Hamlyn, Sydney.

CONNELL, J. 1987. *New Caledonia or Kanaky? The Political History of a French Colony*. Australian National University Press, Canberra.

DAWS, G. 1968. *Shoal of Time: a History of the Hawaiian Islands*. University of Hawaii Press, Honolulu.

DENOON, D.; FIRTH, S.; LINNEKIN, J.; MELEISEA, M.; NERO, K. (eds) 1997. *Cambridge History of Pacific Islanders*. Cambridge University Press.

DURACK, M. 1967. *Kings in Grass Castles*. Corgi Books.

EVATT, H. V. 1938. *The Rum Rebellion*. Angus & Robertson, Melbourne.

FIRTH, S. 1983. *New Guinea under the Germans*. Melbourne.

FLETCHER, B. 1976. *Landed Enterprise and Penal Society: A History of Farming and Grazing in New South Wales before 1821*. Sydney University Press.

FROST, A. 1980. *Convicts and Empire: A Naval Question*. Oxford University Press.

——. 1995. *Botany Bay Mirages: Illusions of Australia's Convict Beginnings.* Melbourne University Press, ch. 10, 'Curse of Cain?'.

GUNSON, W. N. 1978. *Messengers of Grace: Evangelical Missionaries in the South Seas, 1797–1860.* Melbourne University Press, pp. 32–88.

HACKFORTH, J. 1977. *The Convict Artists.* Macmillan.

HAINSWORTH, D. 1971. *The Sydney Traders.* Cassell, Sydney.

HAWKE, G. R. 1985. *The Making of New Zealand: An Economic History.* Cambridge University Press.

HENNINGHAM, S. 1992. *France and the South Pacific: A Contemporary History.* Sydney.

Historical Records of Australia. Series 1, Vol. 4, pp. 477ff.

JACKSON, R. V. 1988. *Population History of Australia.* McPhee, Gribble, Melbourne.

KUNITZ, S. 1994. *Disease and Social Diversity: the European Impact on the Health of Non-Europeans.* Oxford University Press.

LAL, B.; MUNRO, D.; BEECHERT, E. (eds) 1994. *Plantation Workers: Resistance and Accommodation.* University of Hawaii Press, Honolulu.

LATUKEFU, S. 1974. *Church and State in Tonga.* Australian National University Press, Canberra.

LINNEKIN, J. 1990. *Sacred Queens and Women of Consequence: Rank, Gender, and Colonialism in the Hawaiian Islands.* University of Michigan Press.

LLOYD PRITCHARD, M. F. 1970. *An Economic History of New Zealand.* Collins, London.

MARTIN, G. (ed.) 1978. *The Founding of Australia.* Hale & Iremonger, Sydney.

MCARTHUR, N. 1967. *Island Populations of the Pacific.* Australian National University Press, Canberra.

MAYMAN, T. 1964. *The Mile that Midas Touched.* Adelaide.

MERLE, I. 1995. *Expériences coloniales: la Nouvelle-Calédonie 1853–1920.* Paris.

MOORE, C. 1985. *Kanaka: A History of Melanesian Mackay.* Port Moresby.

NELSON, H. 1976. *Black, White and Gold: Gold Mining in Papua New Guinea, 1878–1930.* Australian National University Press, Canberra.

NEWBURY, C. 1972. 'The Makatea Phosphate Concession'. In : Ward, R. G. (ed.) *Man in the Pacific Islands.* Oxford.

O' FAIRCHEALLAIGH, C. 1982. *Mining in the Papua New Guinea Economy, 1880–1980.* University of Papua New Guinea, Port Moresby.

PEGRUM, R. 1983. *The Bush Capital: How Australia chose Canberra as its Capital City.* Hale & Iremonger, Sydney.

PIKE, D. 1967. *Paradise of Dissent.* Longmans, London.

RITCHIE, J. 1988. *A Charge of Mutiny.* National Library of Australia.

ROE, J. 1974. *Marvellous Melbourne.* Hicks Smith.

SCARR, D. 1984. *Fiji: A Short History.* Sydney.

——. 1990. *The History of the Pacific Islands: Kingdoms of the Reefs.* Melbourne.

SHAW, A. G. L. 1980. *Sir George Arthur, 1784–1854.* Melbourne University Press.

——. 1989. 'The Founding of Melbourne'. In : Statham, P. (ed.) *Origins of Australia's Capital Cities.* Cambridge University Press.

SHINEBERG, D. 1967. *They Came for Sandalwood.* Melbourne University Press.

——. In press. *New Hebrideans in New Caledonia.* University of Hawaii Press, Honolulu.

STEVEN, M. 1988. *First Impressions: The British Discovery of Australia.* British Museum of Natural History, London, pp. 10ff.

TAUBMAN, M. 1978. *The Chief: A Biography of C. Y. O'Connor.* University of Western Australia Press.

VAN DEN DRIESON, I. 1986. *Essays on Immigration policy and Population in Western Australia 1850–1901.* University of Western Australia Press, pp. 134ff.

WARD, A. 1974. *A Show of Justice.* Australian National University Press, Canberra.

WARD, R. G.; KINGDOM, E. 1995. *Land, Custom and Practice in the South Pacific.* Cambridge University Press.

WILLIAMS, M.; MACDONALD, B. 1985. *The Phosphateers: A History of the British Phosphate Commissioners and the Christmas Island Phosphate Commission. Melbourne.*

D

CONCLUSION

CONCLUSION

Germán Carrera Damas

The most widely accepted view of the nineteenth century is basically that adopted by European historians and historiographers. As a general, if tacit, rule, we have very little idea what that century meant in other historical contexts, except in their relation to the European context, and we underestimate its importance. Of course societies for which the division of history into centuries has no meaning are excluded. Did they experience the nineteenth century as a period which could be distinguished from the preceding centuries? It is not easy to establish this, at least at the present time. It is thus difficult to form a picture of the nineteenth century which can make a legitimate claim to universality.

But this conceptual difficulty also stems from the historical events of the nineteenth century, the first in which the idea of universality was adopted throughout the world, and which ended with the heroic attempts to reach the poles, the last great bastions of *terra incognita,* which were the culmination of Europe's global adventure and laid the basis for the Western/European vision of a universal civilization.

But if we represent this creative adventure as a series of waves of 'universality' radiating outwards from Western Europe we can see that, although the waves were not concentric, they came to cover almost all the planet. As a result, there was established among different societies, cultures and civilizations a system of relationships and links whose nature and intensity were variable, and whose epicentre was the socio-historic and economic dynamics of certain European countries, although it also took firm root in North America.

This planet-wide network was far from homogeneous, although few corners of the world were unaffected by the transformations or disturbances – depending on whether the view was from the centre outwards or from the periphery inwards – which it brought with it. In some areas, including Europe itself, the idea of progress, which infused all the links and relationships formed by this system, had the effect of accelerating the socio-historic process. But although taken as a whole it had a unifying effect – one of whose most obvious signs was perhaps the development of transport and communications, which was linked with the accelerated expansion of economic and cultural requirements – the new system had profoundly traumatic consequences for many societies. Even in Europe it confirmed the dissolution of a socio-political process which until the end of the eighteenth century had in many respects been basically homogeneous. The formation of centres of industrialization in England, France, Germany and Belgium, the rapid development of the great North Sea ports, more extensive and intensive rail coverage, and the emergence of the first international finance centres widened the breach between predominantly agricultural areas and areas engaging in trade and manufacturing. The clearest signs of the dissolution of this homogeneity were connected with the revolutions in North America and France, which historically marked the division between the eighteenth and the nineteenth centuries, and it was intensified by the first industrial revolution.

The most noticeable effect of this process, however, was that the idea of progress thus formed, which ranged from material to spiritual and moral considerations, cast a shadow over the autonomous development of many societies, reoriented it and in several cases invalidated it, subsuming it in the concept of backwardness, the predecessor of the twentieth-century concept of underdevelopment.

Paradoxically, perhaps, in the first of the centuries that can really be described as universal, the closing of the gap between different societies brought about by technological, social and even political advances – for it was the nineteenth century that saw the first laborious stirrings of the modern republic and modern democracy – also gave rise, as a result of the introduction of the world capitalist system, to what was perhaps the deepest and bloodiest breach between different peoples, dug by those modern forms of intersocietal relations that are known as colonialism and imperialism, the first designating primarily the traditional type of European expansion during the first half of the nineteenth century and the second its development in modern times.

Some clarification of the concepts involved may be a useful aid to understanding this combination of historical processes, without detracting from their essential unity. The aim of historians and sociologists, whose approach was generally based on the conviction that the nineteenth century had clearly distinguishing features, was precisely to define that unity. Simón Rodriguez, a Venezuelan social philosopher who witnessed the transition from the eighteenth to the nineteenth century in Europe, published in 1828 a work entitled *Sociedades Americanas en* 1828, in which the following diagnosis of the ills of the nineteenth century is to be found: 'This century is afflicted by an insatiable cupidity which is attended by three types of delirium: trade mania, colonial mania and religious mania'. He was referring to what he perceived as the three driving forces behind the new type of European expansion. Trade mania referred to the movement to generalize free trade and the opening up to trade of the territories reserved for themselves by the earlier empires. Colonial mania was not only what came to be seen as the century's colonialist and imperialist calling, but also the presentation as a force for progress of the settling in the new states of the masses pauperized by the first industrial revolution and the agricultural crisis. Religious mania referred to freedom of worship, understood as intellectual and spiritual freedom, but also seen as a condition for the spread of 'trade mania', as it encouraged the introduction of Protestant traders.

TRANSFORMATION OF HUMANITY AND ITS ENVIRONMENT

Resolute and prodigious progress was made during the nineteenth century in forging a new relationship between human beings and their physical environment. Previously an attitude of expectant curiosity had been dominant, as the means available for changing the environment were limited. But the combination of technological development with the transformation of scientific knowledge accelerated and intensified a process of change which enabled an increasing proportion of humanity to move from a largely passive adjustment to the environment to an increasingly active approach.

This change was due to three factors: social organization, technological capacity and scientific knowledge. The first consisted in new combinations of economic interests which intensified the effects of enterprise, as was demonstrated by the development of the railways and steam navigation. The second consisted in developing machinery which could make unprecedented use of applied energy. Scientific knowledge, last, quickly expanded from the provision of scientific explanations for the technological changes introduced and applied by craftsmen to the exploration of new areas of physics, such as thermodynamics, electricity, light and sound. In the process the significance of the concepts of distance and geographical barrier began to change. The uncertainty associated with the movement of people and goods was dramatically reduced, and distances were increasingly measured in days, as Jules Verne had foreseen. It would be the twentieth century that would measure distance in hours.

The opening of the Suez and Panama canals – the latter at the turn of the century – and the force for expansion offered by the railway network were emblematic of humanity's ability to transform its physical environment on an increasingly vast scale. At the same time the spread of steam navigation and railway transport, giving rise to new forms of cultural expression, symbolized the correlation between humanity's transformation of the physical environment and its own transformation as a result of the changes wrought on its surroundings.

FINAL TRANSPOSITION FROM MEDIEVAL TO MODERN, FROM AGRICULTURAL TO INDUSTRIAL AND FROM RURAL TO URBAN

The after-effects of the revolutionary movements of the end of the eighteenth century, to which we have already referred, set in motion the transposition from a medieval to a modern approach. To return to the image of concentric waves symbolizing the Euro-centric process of universalization which characterized the nineteenth century, it must be recognized that, although relatively close to the epicentre, they effected a transposition from modern to contemporary approaches – to use the Euro-centric system of periodization – the further they travelled the less marked

were the changes set in motion, and signs and factors of different – and sometimes contradictory – historical periods began to coexist. Although a distinguishing feature of European expansion was the imposition of European criteria of civilization, which included attempts to deprive the subjugated societies of their own history, in some cases the difficulties of this civilizing mission were so formidable as to make such coexistence essential, as clearly demonstrated by the examples of India and China.

The shift from an agricultural society to an industrial society is much more obvious than the shift from country dweller to town dweller. Although in both cases account must be taken of the changes in the concepts of the rural environment and the urban environment, the change was more significant for the country dweller, thanks to communications and the development of information. The situation could perhaps be summed up as follows: at the beginning of the nineteenth century the urban environment was differentiated from the rural environment by the gradual deterioration that began immediately outside the ancient city walls. By the end of the century the development of suburban transport and information were pushing the point at which living conditions began to deteriorate further and further away.

Although urbanization, associated with industrialization, was established as a dominant trend in the occupation of territory, the nineteenth century ended with a type of urban life which has been called the ruralization of the city, as industrial growth attracted huge numbers of country dwellers who tried to reproduce the practices of rural culture in a precarious urban setting. In this sense it can be said that in Europe the modern transformation of the city was preceded by the dislocation of the medieval city, which lasted almost into the last third of the nineteenth century. Outside Europe, the expansion of European industry and trade stimulated urbanization, introducing new ideas of comfort and functionality with modern artefacts not associated so much with luxury as with the practical side of everyday life, particularly in ports. Its main effect, however, was to create enclaves mainly engaged in extractive activity.

Particularly towards the end of the century the European city became the symbol of modern urban life, represented by new architectural styles, for both public and privately owned buildings; the transformation of the urban scene by broad avenues; the extension of water supplies, sewage systems and gas, and the installation of public parks and gardens; the general provision of street lighting and urban transport systems, both above and below ground; the proliferation of cultural activities and the wider circulation of the press. The development of sport put the final touch to the dominance of the urban way of life, becoming a focus of attention alongside the religious focus and competing with it.

But the city was also, as Emile Zola imagined it, a huge maw. The transportation in bulk of perishable agricultural goods, and in particular the fact that meat and grain could now be brought in from remote areas, encouraged the concentration of the population in cities. This compensated for the relatively slow development of agricultural technology, although by the end of the century basic cereal production had been mechanized, the domestication of the potato and maize had been completed and the production of sugar from beet became widespread, thus bringing these foodstuffs within reach of the urban masses.

MAIN AREAS IN WHICH TRADITIONAL SOCIAL, ECONOMIC AND CULTURAL FORMS SURVIVED

It is less a case of areas in European societies in which traditional social, economic and cultural forms survived during the nineteenth century than of the slowness with which new forms developed. But the further we are from the epicentre of the process of Western European universalization, the more the society, economy and cultures of the region concerned persist, infiltrated by European expansion. Here the term 'traditional' is not helpful, for two reasons. In the first place because different societies have perceptibly different historical rhythms and in the second because the quality 'traditional' is evaluated in terms of a notion of progress that was alien to those societies.

As far as Europe is concerned a distinction must be drawn between manifestations of the phenomenon of survival of traditional forms in more dynamic societies and the ways in which they survived in less dynamic societies, although the contrasts that can be observed even in this respect can be quite disconcerting, as for example the contrast between the republican form of government in the former colonies and the resurgence of absolutism in the former metropolises, once the Napoleonic hurricane had subsided.

A noteworthy example of this survival of traditional forms, in the areas referred to above, was the modernization and adaptation of those forms to new economic and social requirements, to the point that the latter played a fundamental role in their development. In some cases traditional forms were strengthened by the application of modern elements. This was true of the organization of the military, which was divested of Napoleonic social innovations in order the better to serve the restoration of the monarchy and the prevention of any relapse into republicanism.

But traditional forms could be primary factors in the development of the new society. Perhaps the most eloquent example of this possibility is offered by the institution of slavery in what is called its modern form. This was a European institution, devised to optimize the occupation and exploitation of the colonial territories and populations of America. It mainly involved Indians – and this continued after abolition – and Negroes from Africa. The abolition of slavery and the effective suppression of the slave trade, linked with the ideology of abolitionism, was a product of the nineteenth century and involved a campaign to eradicate traditional forms of slavery which had persisted in some parts of Africa and Asia. Slavery nevertheless continued into the last third of the century (in the United States until 1862; in Brazil until 1888). Abolished in France in 1793 and reinstated by Napoleon in 1802, it was definitively abolished in 1848. After its abolition in England it persisted in Australia and New Zealand under the guise of deportation. As abolition proceeded, serfdom, whose origins went back to the middle ages, continued to exist in large areas of Europe, particularly in Central and Eastern Europe, until almost the third part of the nineteenth century. At the same time, under the 'indentured' labour system, hundreds of thousands of workers left India and China for the British colonies, the United States and some of the countries of Latin America to live and work in conditions which in many respects were scarcely better than those of the slaves.

Recent research has highlighted the role played by slavery in the new economic system, not only in that the slave trade was a source of accumulation but also because of the role played by the plantation economy – which, based on slavery, was an integral part of the functional structure of the international trading system – in the formation and expansion of a vigorous industrial and commercial capitalism.

This process was organically linked to later events involving the social status of work. The formulation of a new work ethic, at a time when manual and intellectual work were being increasingly differentiated, combined with the most immediate effect of mechanization, the replacement of the craft approach by the simplified functionalism of machine operators, to make the nineteenth century a time of great changes in this area. During the first industrial revolution the status of the men, women and children, especially apprentices, who worked in the mines or in spinning and weaving was little better than that of slaves as regards their actual ability to exercise freedom. Organized social protests against these conditions, which were countered by all kinds of repressive measures, led to the emergence of trade unionism, a doctrinal and organizational reworking of the traditional guilds. By the end of the century industrial development was building bridges between manual and intellectual work and calling for the provision of basic instruction for workers and improvements in living and working conditions. The change in the social image of work was organically linked with that of the domestic status and social subordination of women.

From a global point of view, it was in the evolution of political systems that the struggle between modern and traditional forms was most intense, both in Europe and in America. In fact, the sequence of events in this area during the whole nineteenth century could be summed up in the political evolution of France between 1792, with the establishment of the republic, and 1814, with that of the constitutional monarchy, with the re-establishment of a new version of the same regime following the institution of the empire in 1804. In effect, political systems and forms of government reflected a struggle on the one hand between traditional monarchy and the republic and, on the other, between absolutism and constitutional liberalism. In Europe, the century closed with the modernization of the monarchy, under pressure from the revolutionary movements inspired by liberalism and republicanism in 1830 and 1848, with the definitive abandonment of absolutism under the influence of constitutional liberalism. Indeed, the first major attempt at liberalization on a global scale may be considered to have occurred in the second half of the nineteenth century.

Another distinctive nineteenth-century process, the consolidation in Europe of the great nation-states, was inherently linked to the confrontation between different systems of government and different ideologies. National integration in Germany and Italy gave rise to serious conflicts in international politics, initiating important alliances and wars of varying magnitude, the most important of which was the Franco-Prussian war of 1870–1, not only because it marked the consolidation of Germany as a nation but also because it triggered off the Paris Commune (1871) which in turn inspired other radical revolutionary movements. The settlement of this conflict is also considered to be one of the basic causes of the First World War.

In the most dynamic regions of Europe, traditional forms were abandoned as aristocratic monarchical societies evolved and republics gestated. Attempts simply to re-establish absolutism came up against the political legacy of the French Revolution, producing mixed regimes in which moderate liberalism developed and both monarchical and republican forms of government became gradually more democratic. Nevertheless, it was only at the end of the century that the republic appeared to take lasting root in France. Efforts to confer some political status on women and the first calls for their political enfranchisement ran in parallel with this process of liberalization and democratization; however, the century ended without their bearing fruit.

This triumph over traditional social, economic and cultural forms resulted in the development of the bourgeoisie as an entrepreneurial class and in the formation of the industrial proletariat. The entrepreneur ceased to be an isolated individual and merged into management cadres and the mass of shareholders in large companies. In other words, the entrepreneurial approach became the hallmark of an entire social class, affecting all its manifestations. At the same time, the labourers of the first industrial revolution developed from their state of semi-freedom to form the industrial proletariat, leading to the birth of socialist movements which elaborated upon the initial mixture of ideology and religion to produce the revolutionary assertions of the Communist Manifesto of 1848, whose profound and far-reaching effects were to make themselves felt until the end of the following century. Efforts to make the workers' movement a factor contributing to a new order in international relations by having it participate in political processes as an independent, organized force, cutting across frontiers, gave rise to the so-called 'Internationals', and it was through these that general political concepts such as Marxism, social democracy and Leninism became more clearly defined, although the latter rapidly veered off towards a concept of statehood.

One result of this global process, bristling with contradictions, was the individualization of human beings both on a conceptual level and in their gradual transition from objects of social aid to subjects of human and social rights, while at the same time the discovery and practice of institutionalized philanthropy began to emerge.

The creative and renovative thrust of the nineteenth century, which in the more developed societies nourished hopes of a future of unlimited peace and prosperity, also led to the radical transformation of warfare by new technologies, as heralded by the deadly American Civil War (1861–5). The outcome of that war was decided by the industrial development of the North, which had at its disposal a railway network superior to that of the South. It was becoming clear that in future wars modern technological progress, represented by railways, the telegraph, new types of artillery and the mass production of weapons, would be a decisive factor. Navies held the key to the new system of international relationships, and the use during the Civil War of one of the first specially designed battleships marked the beginning of a rapid transformation both of naval engineering and of naval operations, which were dependent on the establishment of a network of coaling stations, a strategic preoccupation which was organically linked to colonial and imperialist expansion.

War became more destructive, although the civilian population was in general spared. The establishment of the Red Cross in 1863, with its threefold mandate as a humanitarian, supranational and international organization, was possibly an outlet for the horror inspired by the renewed and intensified violence of modern warfare.

Beyond the more dynamic countries of Europe, a colourful kaleidoscope of societies was spreading in which urban industrialized civilization was creating nuclei surrounded by expanses of territory in which the pace of economic, social and cultural change continued as before. At the end of the century, the new civilization was mainly confined to the continent of Europe, including the European part of Russia, and North America. In East Asia, Japan offered an exceptional example of the symbiosis of traditional and modern.

In spite of industrial civilization's intrusions, the vast colonial and semi-colonial universe of Africa, Asia and Latin America continued to be subordinate to the more developed European societies. At the end of the century, only Argentina seemed likely to be governed by modern, European-style, nuclei.

THE GREAT GLOBAL DIVIDE: A SUBSTANTIAL INCREASE IN WEALTH CREATES SOCIAL INEQUALITIES WITHIN NATIONS AND GROWING INEQUALITIES BETWEEN RICH AND POOR NATIONS

The growing inequality between nations, as regards their wealth and power, which characterized the nineteenth century, was the result of the first major crisis to befall the empires whose formation had been an important feature of the eighteenth century. At the end of that century, the severing of their colonial links by the British colonies in North America signalled the start of the crisis, which by the beginning of the nineteenth century had rapidly turned into a crisis over monarchy as a system of government. The independence of Haiti in 1804 and of the Spanish colonies in America between 1810 and 1824, threatened the integrity and stability of the French and Spanish empires. The Ottoman Empire unravelled in Europe under pressure from the Serbian revolt in 1804, the Greek revolt in 1829–30, the Bulgarian revolt of 1876 and the Russo-Turkish wars of the same period. These developments made it clear that the traditional empires were indeed in crisis. The growth of nationalism as the expression of a people's will for self-rule could be seen both in the rejection of foreign domination – as observed in the popular Spanish uprising against Napoleon Bonaparte, in the Mexican uprising against European imperialism as represented by Maximilian of Austria, and in the Polish resistance to Russian and German domination – and in the independence movements emerging in the heart of the Ottoman and Austro-Hungarian empires.

The break-up of the Spanish Empire brought to an end a cycle of European history that had lasted for more than three centuries, and encouraged European expansion as we know it today. The new states that emerged had to find their place in an international order in which the restoration of the monarchy and indeed the re-establishment of the former empires was the overriding concern. Although the latter concern had to be abandoned, new forms of domination were being elaborated during the nineteenth century, as was the straightforward occupation of territory – particularly in Africa and Asia – whose impetus was strengthened as armaments, transport and communications became more efficient.

The nineteenth century has been regarded as the century of modern colonialism, which culminated in the emergence of more elaborate forms of imperialism. There were constant struggles between the colonial powers to consolidate their possessions, make good their losses and safeguard their spheres of influence, in particular between Great Britain, France, Holland, Belgium, Russia and the Ottoman Empire. The web of rivalry was further complicated towards the end of the century by the colonial aspirations of Germany and Italy, and later on Japan. The Crimean War (1853–6) was one of the most consummate examples of that struggle. At the same time the colonial wars were spreading further, either to pre-empt bids for independence (the Boer Wars of 1880–1 and 1899–1902), to exact new privileges from colonies and countries subjected to colonial exactions (the Opium Wars of 1839–41 and 1857–8), to acquire new territories (the Sino-Japanese War of 1894–5), to consolidate strategic positions (the Anglo-Russian conflict in Afghanistan and the Russo-Turkish conflict of 1877–8), or to force an opening for trade (the conflict between the United States and Japan which led to the latter's opening to trade in 1854). In North Africa, India and the Sudan, the purpose of the colonial wars was to repress independence movements and movements inspired by religion. Outside the traditional imperial framework, the recently created republic in North America pursued its expansionist plans at the expense of the even more recently created Mexican republic.

The presence and participation of Africa on the world stage in the nineteenth century deserves special attention for the magnitude of the operation involved and for its political and economic significance in relations between the different empires. It seems to have been determined by a combination of different factors, operating simultaneously or in conjunction, whose general effect was to hasten the collapse of autonomous evolutionary processes, already weakened during the previous century by slavery and the first stages of colonialism. These factors included: the dislocation of autochthonous socio-political structures and their replacement by the colonial order; the conversion of societies by Christian missionary activity and the expansion of Islam; the exploitation of raw materials for the world market; and the production of negative cultural stereotypes which had the effect of emphasizing the supremacy of the white race. Essentially these stereotypes reflected a rejection of African societies' resistance, whether active or passive, to colonial intervention, although it also modernized various aspects of their social life, determining global changes, which led to the present configuration of nations. Overall, Africa offered one of the most outstanding examples of European expansion of the nineteenth century, in the last two decades of which almost the whole of the continent was brought under European control.

In ideological terms, the result of the colonial wars and of wars of territorial expansion was to establish a belief in the superiority, not only of Western European civilization, but also of the white race.

The formulation of the Monroe Doctrine in 1823 established the principle of non-interference by the United States in European affairs, in return for European abstention from intervention on the American continent. Its effect was felt in Latin America, which had recently freed itself from its colonial links with Spain. The disastrous attempt by France and Austria, taking advantage of the American Civil War, to restore the monarchy in Mexico was the last direct challenge to the Monroe Doctrine.

Throughout the nineteenth century the gap between poor and rich countries continued to widen. But this is a very general assessment. In actual fact, in rich and poor countries alike a whole range of situations evolved, in response to a multitude of different factors. However, the polarization between wealth and poverty certainly accentuated the difference between the ranges of situations to be found in the rich countries and the poor countries.

The global increase in wealth and the polarization that resulted were a function of the new economy, based on industrialization, the increased regionalization and technicalization of agriculture, and the globalization of trade made possible by the revolution in transport and communications, enshrined in the principle of freedom of the seas. New ways of transporting merchandise meant that economic specialization became geographically determined. This accentuated and increased economic interdependence, in the dual forms of free trade and colonial trade. Because economic and commercial interdependence was put forward under the banner of free trade, it was initially received with great enthusiasm as representing the dissolution of the trade monopolies that were a feature of the empires of the preceding century. However, as the effects of liberalization with regard to the equality (or inequality) of trade arrangements on the development of international trade and the world economy became more tangible, enthusiasm quickly evaporated. Very soon there was a backlash that generated measures to protect the interests of traditional local manufacturers. This backlash has been cited as one of the reasons for the technological stagnation of the weakest economies. However, it scarcely appears to have been a factor, and certainly not the most important one, in impeding the transfer of technology, which was not one of the priorities of European expansion and did not come easily, even between the most developed industrial countries, particularly as regards the nascent chemical industry. As a result, the effectiveness of legal patents has continued to increase.

The establishment of the global capitalist system at the end of the century was both the cause and the effect of the emergence of large companies – generally engaged in prospecting and exploiting vast quantities of mineral products and selling them on the world market. The large oil companies are an excellent example of this process. They came to play a decisive role, not only in the life of the countries in which they carried out their operations, but also in developments in international relations. These rivalries reflected, at a very high level, the confrontations in preceding centuries between the principal European monarchies over control of the African slave trade, as well as between the companies which tended to monopolize colonial trade.

Although the first industrial revolution, symbolized by coal and steam, opened the first major rift between the different societies as regards their development, by the end of the century the second industrial revolution, represented by steel, electricity, oil and the chemical industry, had made the rift insuperable.

The vertiginous and unlimited expansion of the concept of 'needs' was due to economic progress and transformation, and was a highly dynamic factor in cultural development. The revolution in the concept of needs also played a decisive role in social differentiation within the rich countries. Luxury, as an indication of social status, became accessible to an ever-larger section of the population, while simultaneously becoming markedly inaccessible to the vast majority, for whom subsistence was already a distant goal. This resulted in migration *en masse* towards new lands of opportunity. The major European countries had never been so rich, yet neither had they exported so much poverty. Irish, Italian, Spanish, Portuguese and German immigrants played a major role in enriching their host countries and were also powerful agents of cultural diffusion.

Inequality between poor and rich countries was disguised by certain aspects of colonialism and imperialism. The setting up of enclaves that attempted to reproduce metropolitan patterns, and the achievements of the colonial administrations, did not radically change the overall situation. The relative spontaneity with which European cultural patterns were adopted was due to the belief that they held the key to the Europeans' power. The framework of political, economic and cultural relations that existed in the colonial countries and those subject to European predominance, gave rise to the contrasting and conflicting mind-sets which are to a large extent characteristic of the nineteenth century.

THE INTERNATIONALIZATION OF THE SCIENCES, TECHNOLOGY AND CULTURE. THE TRANSFER OF INTELLECTUAL AND TECHNICAL MODELS. TRANSNATIONAL CULTURAL MODELS

During the nineteenth century, there developed a belief that the spread of European patterns of consumption and cultural characteristics among the upper strata of non-European societies would set in motion a durable process of modernization that would herald the advent of a universal civilization. This was the basis for the attempts at modernization advocated by the ideological leaders of those classes and either induced or imposed by those in power, notably in Asia and Latin America. In the latter case, the contrast between civilization and barbarism was used to justify the extermination of many native societies.

The expansion of European domination thanks to the new versions of colonialism and imperialism was regarded by the dominant societies as incontrovertible proof of European technological, scientific and cultural superiority. European domination was therefore advocated as offering an opportunity to take advantage of what was in general regarded as progress in all areas, which gave rise to anti-traditionalist attitudes and movements. Political developments in the Ottoman Empire are a very good example of this type of confrontation.

Although the spread of patterns that had developed in the most advanced European centres was more clearly visible in the economy, the military and technology, it also became very important in the field of science – particularly medical science, civil engineering and architecture, and administrative methods and procedures.

The global capitalist system derived much of the dynamism and strength needed for its expansion from the conjunction of technology, science and industry. This was in turn both a cause and an effect of the new approach to the world introduced by the scientific revolution of the nineteenth century. That revolution was symbolized by 'learning', as the personification of the inquiring mind being led intrepidly on to explore as yet undiscovered realms.

However, it was progress in medical science that held out most promise for the future, as advances were made in chemotherapy and surgery. The shift from traditional curative medicine to the public health approach, reflected in the general availability of the smallpox vaccine, marked a radical change in the idea of social welfare. As regards the individual, a new attitude towards mental illness emphasized the humanitarian side of medical practice.

The adoption of European models in civil engineering and architecture involved not only the use of new technologies and materials, but also architectural aesthetics. The construction of railways and ports spearheaded the spread of the new technologies, and the new materials were used very noticeably in the building of roads and metal structures.

The universal adoption of European administrative methods and procedures, particularly in connection with customs and taxation, meant that they became part of the new international business language. The universalization of European business ideas was regarded as being sufficiently important to merit the introduction of a new specialized branch of education, and the new business schools were considered to be vehicles of modernization. The industrial and technical schools, at all levels, which had spread rapidly throughout Europe, particularly in the most advanced countries, did not follow the example of the business schools.

The nineteenth century established landmarks in all fields of knowledge. A methodological structure for historiography was rapidly built up and a range of new philosophical systems offered explanations of society and social development. Although the individual was the object of particular scientific attention, the study of society was the main focus of innovation. A specific science, sociology, set out to elucidate the profound and far-reaching changes affecting societies, particularly in Europe. At the same time closer contacts between societies and cultures which until then had been almost completely isolated from one another, encouraged the comparative study of different societies, not only in space but also in time, assigning particular fields to anthropology, ethnology and archaeology. This great scientific endeavour gave rise to scientism and historicism, which were at the time ranked among the great philosophical discoveries of Western European civilization: human beings and their natural environment cease to be objects of reflection and become instead objects of investigation. This development was reflected in the associated comparative development of science and philosophy. The new understanding of human beings in society and in the diversity of the global context broadened the spatial framework for their study as archaeology broadened the temporal framework. But perhaps the most important contribution made in these fields was the transformation of the scientific view of humankind affected by theories of evolution. The theories of Darwin and Spencer soon had a following in other countries, where their champions waged the same battle as in the more developed European countries for the assertion of independent scientific thinking. These findings were applied in social practice in quite different, almost contradictory ways. While they basically intensified efforts to free scientific research from religious and ethical inhibitions, they also unleashed outbursts of intolerance and fuelled racist views known generically as Social Darwinism, which became part of the ideology of colonialist and imperial domination.

Likewise, although it encountered significant social resistance, the influence of the scientific revolution made itself increasingly felt in the legal and political spheres. The increase in the amount of information available through the general distribution of newspapers, and the new social idea of education developed in Europe as a result of mechanization, played a fundamental role in these processes. Free, compulsory state education was a reliable way of promoting social progress, while the spread of informal education through the press and books stimulated social and political progress and lessened the differences between rural and urban life.

The opportunities to travel offered by new, safer and more efficient means of transport and communication enriched and extended cultural models to the point that they became universal in scope. A creative process of artistic and cultural interpenetration between different societies was thus set in motion at the same time as, in the richest among them, artists began more and more to work on a professional basis, thus transforming the scope, as well as the social and economic significance of art. The advent of organized tourism was a major factor in generating and disseminating cultural change.

The tendency for cultural changes to be global in their scope affected relations between the different religions. Certain social customs and practices with religious links were categorized as retrograde and denounced for obstructing the progress not only of the peoples concerned, but also of humanity in general. The economic, political and military might of the most developed European countries found in missionary activities an area that complemented their expansionist drive.

Agnostic movements of various derivations used the scientific approach not only to challenge religious domination in spiritual matters, but also to combat the influence exercised by the religious hierarchies on people's minds through education. The battle to free education from religious influences was part of the more general struggle for freedom of thought, and it filtered through into the struggle for political freedom and the exercise of democratic rights. In some countries the conflicts thus initiated led to violence and social upheaval, most notably in some of the new states that had emerged from the ruins of the Spanish Empire.

The century, which began with the most vigorous promotion of freedom of thought and the free exercise of critical faculties, defying religious dogmatism and ideological and political intolerance, closed with another round of that prolonged struggle still in progress.

The recognition of society's creative capacity in the field of technology had very different results. What were soon to be outstanding features of a new era in human development – aeroplanes, submarines, motor cars, radio, cinema and x-rays – were only just being anticipated.

THE FIRST WORLD WAR ENDS AN EPOCH. AMERICA ENTERS A STAGE DOMINATED BY EUROPE. TRANSITION TO VOLUME VII

The generally held belief that the level of political, technological, scientific and cultural development attained by the civilization of the North Atlantic and the global hegemony it had established opened up long-term prospects of peace for humanity, was shown to have been illusory by ensuing events which were largely following tradition in that they were linked with confrontations between empires for the control of vast colonial territories and spheres of influence. These confrontations culminated in a war, which could quite properly be called the 'Great War' or 'World War', not just because thirty-two countries became involved in it, but also because of its radical, far-reaching and prolonged repercussions in military, political and social terms.

Among the most noteworthy of those repercussions were the entry of America, represented by the United States and Canada, onto a world stage that had been dominated by Europe; the setting up of the first self-proclaimed socialist state, as a result of the Russian Revolution; and the first attempt at economic planning.

At the end of the twentieth century, the involvement of America in European affairs has shown itself to be the most lasting of the repercussions of the First World War, having been confirmed in fact by the Second World War. This completed a process of immense historical importance that dated back to the end of the eighteenth century when the British colonies in America gained their independence. It continued with the first war of independence against slavery (in Haiti), the crisis in the Spanish colonies in America and the wars of independence from Spain. It ended with the break-up of the Spanish colonial empire in 1898 and the permanent replacement of European colonialism by North American colonialism on the American continent, thus confirming the loss of America by the European colonial powers, which was to be seen, in global terms, as one of the most significant features of the nineteenth century.

The Russian Revolution of 1917 launched an experiment in social, economic and political restructuring which for a long time was regarded as the way of overcoming major social and economic problems encountered in the broadest range of situations.

The crushing blow dealt to hopes for peace by the 1914–18 war played havoc with the social and political order, but its effect on attitudes was no less powerful. The brutality of chemical warfare, the violence perpetrated against civilians by the massive use of artillery and the blockade of Germany, the enormous number of fatalities and casualties, all found in the new forms of literary and artistic expression an outlet for the most agonizing protests, challenging the sacrifice of what was seen as a false rationality.

CHRONOLOGICAL TABLE

CHRONOLOGICAL TABLE

EUROPE	AFRICA	AMERICA	ASIA	OCEANIA
1500				
			1590 **Japan**, Hideyoshi Toyotomi re-integrates Japan.	
1600				
			1600 **Japan**, Ieyasu Tokugawa comes to power and rules Japan.	
			1630s **Japan**, Tokugawa prohibits Japanese from going abroad and expels Catholics.	
1700				
			1774 **Japan**, *Kaitai Shinsho*, a translation of a Dutch book of anatomy, published.	
			1787 **West Africa**, The first freed Black Slaves settled in Sierra Leone.	
1789 **France** • French Revolution. Constituent Assembly adopted Declaration of Human and Citizens' Rights. • A. L. de Lavoisier: Law of Conservation of Matter. • A. L. de Jussieu: *Genera Plantaarum*. **Britain**, Jeremy Bentham: *The Principles of Morals and Legislation*. **Germany**, M. H. Klaproth: discovered uranium.		1789 **United States**, George Washington elected President. **Colombia**, The Inquisition court in Cartagena prohibited the circulation of Declaration of the Human and Citizens' Rights in the Americas.		
1790 **France**, N. Appert perfected technique of food preservation. **Britain**, E. Burke: *Reflections on the Revolution in France*. Mozart: *The Magic Flute*.				
1791		1791–1793 **West Indies**, Santo-Domingo: General revolt of slaves under Toussaint Louverture. **Canada**, Elective legislatures set up in upper Canada and lower Canada (French).		

Europe	Africa / Middle East	Americas	Asia	Oceania
1792 France, Fall of French Monarchy.		**1792** Mexico, Inauguration of Royal College of Mining.	**1793** Japan, The first envoy from Russia arrives.	**1797** Tahiti, Base for London Missionary Society.
1792–1815 European Wars		**1793** Colombia, Antonio Nariño printed translation of the Declaration of the Rights of Man and the Citizen.		
1793 France • Musée central des arts opened in the Louvre. • C. Chappe invented the optic telegraph.		United States, Eli Whitney invented cotton gin.		
1795 France, Ecole Polytechnique established.		**1794** Venezuela, Simon Rodriguez: (Reflections on the Shortcomings of Primary Education of Caracas).		
1796 Britain • Edward Jenner perfected the anti-smallpox vaccine. • C. F. Hahnemann discovered homeopathy. France, Pierre Laplace: *Exposition du système du monde*. Germany, Johann W. von Goethe 'Wilhelm Meister' novels (→1829).		Latin America, the Convention abolished slavery in all French colonies.		
1798 Britain, Thomas R. Malthus: *Essay on the Principle of Population*.	**1798–1801** Egypt, French occupation: Bonaparte's scientific expedition.	**1799** Venezuela, Arrival of naturalists Alexander von Humboldt (Prussian) and Amadeo Bonpland (French).		
1800 France, Bank of France created by Napoleon. Italy • Alessandro Volta invented the electric battery. • William Herschel discovered infra-red solar rays. • John L. McAdam developed his technique for surfacing roads. Poland, the Society of Friends of Sciences founded.				
1801 J. M. Ritter, discovered ultraviolet rays. Britain, United Kingdom established.	**1801** West Africa, Ousmane Dan Fodio founded Sokoto empire (→1817). Egypt, French left Egypt.	**1801** West Indies, Santo-Domingo, Toussaint Louverture proclaimed general freedom.		

EUROPE (cont.)		AFRICA (cont.)		AMERICA (cont.)		ASIA (cont.)		OCEANIA (cont.)	
1802	Peace of Amiens. **France**, L. J. Gay-Lussac discovered the law of expansion of gases.			1802	**Spanish America**, Telegrafo Mercantil, the first newspaper in the Río de la Plata launched. **West Indies**, Slavery re-established in the French colonies.	1802	**Southeast Asia**, Vietnam under control of the Nguyen dynasty from China.		
1803	**France**, C. L. Berthollet discovered laws of double decomposition between salts, acids and bases. **Britain**, R. Trevithick built first high-pressure steam locomotive.			1803	**Spanish America**, Charles IV sent smallpox vaccine to the Americas. **Colombia**, First astronomy observatory of Americas inaugurated in Santafé de Bogotá. **Haiti**, Jean Jacques Dessalines liberated Haiti and proclaimed a Republic.			1803	**Australia**, Tasmania became British possession.
1804	**France** • Napoleon crowned Emperor. • Civil Code promulgated.			1804	**Haiti**, Proclaimed independence.				
1805	**France**, M. J. Jacquard invented loom to facilitate weaving of figured and brocaded fabrics. **Britain**, British naval victory at Trafalgar, death of Nelson.								
1806	**Germany**, F. Hegel published *Phenomenology of Mind*.			1806	**Argentina**, English driven out of Buenos Aires.	1806	**Japan**, Minor conflict with Russia in Northern Yezo. (→1807).		
1807	**Britain**, Abolition of slave trade in British possessions.			1807	**United States**: Steamboat Clermont on river Hudson.				
1808	**Spain** • Joseph Bonaparte, proclaimed Joseph I King of Spain. • E. L. Malus discovered polarization of light.			1808	**Brazil**, John VI of Portugal arrived in Rio de Janeiro, declared the capital of the Empire.	1808	**Japan**, There were 656 libraries in Edo (Tokyo) and some 300 in Osaka.		
1809	L. Rolando described structure of the brain. **France**, J. B. de Lamarck: presented theory on the evolution of species.	1809	**West Africa**, Mohammed Bello became the Sultan of Sokoto Empire.						
1810	**France**, Adopted the Penal Code of Napoléon I. **Prussia** • Berlin University created. • Ludwig Von Beethoven began his musical work (→1824).	1810	**Indian Ocean**, The British occupied the French Islands: Réunion and Mauritius.	1810	**Mexico**, Miguel Hidalgo, parish priest of Dolores, declared Mexican independence.				

Year		Year		Year		Year	
1811	**France**, Began producing beet sugar.	1811	**North Africa**, Italy invaded Libya.	1811	**Uruguay**, Began struggle for independence under Jose Gervasio Artigas. **Paraguay**, Declared independence under José Gaspar Rodriguez de Francia. **Venezuela**, Declared Independence.		
1812	**France**, Georges Cuvier presented his first palaeontological studies.			1812	**Brazil**, Inaugurated the first theatre in Salvador.		
1812–14	War between Britain and United States of America.						
1813	**England** • Signed agreement with France, Sweden, Spain, Portugal and Holland on abolition of the slave trade. • **The Times** printed on steam press. **Spain**, Francisco de Goya painted *Dos de Mayo y Tres de Mayo*. **Germany**, J. von Fraunhofer invented first spectroscope.			1813	**Argentina**, The Constituent Assembly frees slaves. **Spanish America**, Inquisition abolished by Cortes of Cadiz.		
		1814	**West Africa**, Hamdallayi, capital of Macina Empire founded. **South Africa**, came under British Administration.			1814	**New Zealand**, Church Missionary Society (Anglican) founded.
1815	**Western Europe** • Napoleon defeated at Battle of Waterloo. Monarchy restored in France. • The Congress of Vienna: resettlement of Europe. **France**, *La Société pour l'instruction élémentaire* founded in Paris. **Netherlands**, Former high schools reorganized as state universities.			1815	**Jamaica**, Simon Bolivar published *Letter from Jamaica*.		
1816	**France** • N. Niepce innovation in photography. • René T. H. Laennec invented stethoscope. **Poland**, University of Warsaw founded. **Netherlands**, Reformed Church established as successor to Dutch Reformed Church.	1816	**West Africa, Senegal**: 'mutual instruction' school founded in Saint-Louis.	1816	**Argentina**, Congress declared independence.		

EUROPE (cont.)		AFRICA (cont.)		AMERICA (cont.)		ASIA (cont.)		OCEANIA (cont.)	
1817	**Belgium**, Universities opened at Ghent, Louvain and Liege.	1817	**West Africa**, Bowdich Embassy in Koumassi.	1817	**Uruguay**, Universal education, Promulgated establishing compulsory, free education.				
		1818	**East Africa**, Cloves introduced into Zanzibar, slave trade developed. **Arabian Peninsula**, The Viceroy Mehemet Ali victory over Wahhabites of Hedjaz.						
1819	**Denmark**, H. C. Oersted discovered magnetic effect of electric current. **France**, 'Conservatoire national des arts et metiers' inaugurated in Paris. **Britain**, Gold standard established.							1819	**Tahiti**, Baptism of king Ponnaré II.
		1820	**East Africa**, Mehemet Ali, conquered Sudan, Nubia and Kordofan (→1824).	1820	**Ecuador**, Guayaquil proclaimed independence.	1820	**India**, Rammohan Roy founded the Brahmin Movement in Bengal.	1820	**Hawaii**, American Board of Commissioners for foreign Missions.
1821	**Britain**, Michael Faraday discovered electromagnetic induction and demonstrated electromagnetic rotation.			1821	**Mexico**, The Plan of Iguala set seal on independence. **Colombia** • Establishment of the Republic of Colombia. • Primary schools to be established in larger towns. **Central America**, Guatemala, Nicaragua and El Salvador declared independence. **Panama**, Declared independence from Spain as part of Republic of Colombia. **Dominican Republic**, Declared independence, as a protectorate of Republic of Colombia. **Argentina** • University of Buenos Aires established. • Simon Bolivar's victory over the Spaniards at Carabolo.				

EUROPE (cont.)	AFRICA (cont.)	AMERICA (cont.)	ASIA (cont.)	OCEANIA (cont.)
1827 France, A. M. Ampère, presented mathematical theory on electrodynamics. Germany, Georg S. Ohm, established fundamental law of electric current.	**1827** Egypt, Medical School and Veterinary School founded in Cairo (1827–1829). West Africa, Fourah Bay College founded by Church Missionary Society.	**1827** Venezuela, Faculty of Medicine of Caracas founded.		**1827** Australia, the naturalist Macleay founded the Australian Museum in Sydney.
1828 Germany, Fiedrich Wöhler synthesized urea. France, The first railway between Saint-Etienne and Andrézieux opened.	**1828** West Africa, Mali, Rene Caillé reached Timbuktu. South Africa, equality under law established. British penal Justice Code replaced Dutch Code.	**1828** United States, Democratic Party founded. Colombia, Simón Bolívar became Supreme Head of the Republic. Venezuela, Economic Society of Friends of the Country established. Bolivia, Paraguay and the Banda Oriental, declared independence.		**1828** New Zealand, The British Crown entrusted administration and jurisdiction of the territory to New South Wales of Australia.
1829 France, Joseph Pelletier and Joseph-Bienaimé isolated alkaloids, and perfected quinine. Britain, G. Stephenson with Robert, his son, built *Rocket*, the first tubular boiler steam locomotive. Russia, Nikolai Ivanovich Lobatchevski developed non-Euclidean geometry.	**1829** Egypt, Pharmacological School established.			
1830 France, (Les Trois glorieuses) revolution in Paris. Louis Phillipe became king. Belgium, secession war against Netherlands. Freedom of education included in the constitution of New Kingdom. Britain • Opening of Liverpool to Manchester railway. • B. Thimonnier invented sewing machine. • Achromatic microscope invented. Germany, Carl Friedrich Gauss launched study of earth's magnetism.	**1830** North Africa, France occupied Algeria. East Africa, Arab caravans crossed continent by Nyassa and Katanga. West Africa, Brothers Lander reconnoitred Niger river.	**1830** Mexico, First bank, the Banco de Avío, founded. Colombia, Simón Bolívar resigned as head of the Republic. Venezuela, seceded from Republic of Colombia. United States, William Miller organized religious sect the Seventh Day Aventists.	**1830** China • Hong Xiuquan, in Guangdong created the G-Worshipping Theology. • Triad Lodges established.	**1830** Australia, Western Australia became a British possession.

576

1831	**Britain**, M. Faraday demonstrated electromagnetic induction. **Greece**, Society for Friends of Education set up. **Britain** • British Association for the Advancement of Science held its first meeting. • Chloroform discovered.		**Colombia**, New Granada established as an independent state. **United States**, Church of Jesus Christ of Latter Day Saints (Mormons) established.	**Near East**, Mehemet Ali of Egypt invaded Syria and defeated the Ottoman Empire at Konya.	**Australia**, Adopted policy for immigration assistance. (1831–1842)
1832	**Poland**, Adam Michiewicz published: *Book of the Polish Nation*. **Germany**, Baron Schilling produced first needle telegraph. **Western Europe**, outbreaks of cholera.	**East Africa**, Sultans of Oman settled in Zanzibar.	**Chile**, Venezuelan Andrés Bello declared Chilean citizen.		
1833	**British possessions**: abolition of slavery. **Britain** • Effective Factory Act. • M. Faraday presented the theory of electrolysis. **France**, National higher primary education introduced. **Russia**, Alexander S. Pushkin wrote: *Egeniy Onegin*.	**South Africa**, Beginning of Boers (Great Trek). Creation of Natal, Transvaal, and Orange States. **Egypt**, School of languages founded in Cairo.	**United States**, Anti-slavery society founded.	**Japan**, Hiroshige: Fifty Three Stations of Tōkaido Road. (1833–1834)	
1834	**Germany** • The *Zollverein* (customs union) established. • Discovery of carbolic acid.	**East Africa**, The Rozwi (Zimbabwe) defeated at Mount Mambo by Zwangendaba. **North Africa**, Government of French possessions in North Africa created. Battle against Abd-el Kader in Algeria. **Egypt**, Polytechnic School founded.		**China**, Reverend Doctor Peter Parker, established in Canton hospital and dispensary for poor Chinese patients.	
1835	**France** • Alexis de Tocqueville published: **Democracy in America** (→1840). • Louis Braille invented a written language for the blind. **Belgium**, Brussels Malines railway.		**United States**, Colt revolver patented.		**Australia**, Victoria became a British possession. Melbourne founded.
1836	**Spain**, Cortes authorized government to recognize the new states of the Americas.	**Southwest Africa**, Governor Sa da Bandeira abolished slavery in Angola.	**Mexico**, United States settlers declared the independence of Texas. **Canada**, First railroad opened.		**South Australia**, Became a British possession. Adelaide founded.

EUROPE (cont.)	AFRICA (cont.)	AMERICA (cont.)	ASIA (cont.)	OCEANIA (cont.)
1837 **British**, Queen Victoria crowned.	1837 **North Africa, Algeria,** Capture of Constantine. 'Abd-ul-Qâdir established a kingdom (→1847).	1837 **United States**, Samuel Morse, developed electric telegraph system of communication. **Bolivia**, Peruvian-Bolivian Confederation founded.		
1838 **Ottoman Empire**, Anglo-Ottoman trade treaty signed. **Britain** • Anti-Slavery Association founded. • Screw propeller initiated.		1838 **Nicaragua**, Left Central American Confederation. Honduras and Costa Rica followed. Confederation dissolved. **Brazil**, *Instituto Histórico e Geográfico Brasileiro* founded. **Río de la Plata**, The newspaper *El Iniciador* launched. **Cuba**, The first railway built.	1838 **Arabian Peninsula**, The Britain took port of Aden in Yemen.	
1839 **Britain** • Anti-corn-Law League founded. • Naysmyth invents steam hammer. **France**, Louis Blanc: *De l'organisation du travail*. **Ottoman Empire**, Sultan Abdulmejid declared equality among subjects of the Empire regardless of race or creed. **Russia**, Observatory of Pulkovo founded (later the Russian Centre of Astronomy).		1839 **United States**, John Lowell Institute of Boston founded.	1839 **Near East**, War between Egypt and Ottoman Empire. Mehemet Ali defeated the sultan Mahmoud II in Syria. **Middle East**, First war between Afghans and British. **China**, Opium war (→1842).	
1840 **France**, A. Masson and L. Bréguet invented electric transformer. **Hungary**, Roller-milling of grain introduced.	1840 **East Africa**, Rapid increase of Indian population. **North Africa, Algeria** • General Bugaud became Governor. • Bardo military academy of Algeria created by Governor General.	1840 **Canadian Act of Union** **United States**, C. H. McCormick invented harvester.	1840 **India**, Russian politico-scientific mission sent to Bukhara.	1840 **New Zealand**, Treaty of Waitangi established sovereignty of United Kingdom. British citizenship granted to all inhabitants. **Australia**, Abrogation of deportation of convicts to New South Wales.
1841 Straits Convention between Turkey, France and England. **France**, Law restricting child labour in factories. **Britain**, James P. Joule discovered heating when an electric current flows through a resistance: the Joule effect.	1841 **West Africa, Liberia**, Colony governed by Blacks. **Senegal**, First secondary-level boarding school established in Gorée. **South Africa**, Lovedale Missionary Institution established in the Cape. **Egypt**: Mehemet Ali gains hereditary possession of Egypt and Sudan from the Ottoman Sultan.	1841 **Venezuela**, Publication of *Resumen de la Historia de Venezuela* by Rafael María Baralt and Ramón Díaz, and *Atlas histórico, geográfico, político y estadístico de Venezuela* by Agustín Codazzi. **Chile**, Reopening of University. **Venezuela**, la Sociedad de Amigos del País founded to establish a botanical garden and a natural history museum.		

1842	**Tahiti**, Dupetit-Thomas obtained its transfer for France. **Marquesas Islands**, Occupied by France. **New Caledonia**, Became a French possession.
1843	**Tahiti**, A French protectorate. **Australia**, Free colonists obtain constitutional charters.
1844	**New Zealand**, War between Maoris and Britain.

1842	**China**, Opening of several ports for foreign trade by Nankin treaty. Hong-Kong ceded to the United Kingdom.

1843	**Costa Rica**, The old School House of Santo Tomás became a university. **Río de la Plata**, Institute of History and Geography opened.
1844	**West Indies**, Dominican Republic proclaimed.
1845	**Mexico**, United States troops invaded Mexican territory. **Venezuela**. Spain recognized the Republic of Venezuela. **United States** • Founding of the observatory of Cincinnati. • The New York weekly *The Scientific American* founded.
1846	**United States**, The Smithsonian Institution established.
1847	**Chile**, Publication in Santiago, by Venezuelan Andrés Bello, of *Gramática de la lengua castellana*.

1842	**South Africa**, Boers second Trek; Orange Republic founded.
1843	**South Africa**, Britain annexed Natal.
1844	**North Africa, Morocco**, Franco-Moroccan War. 'Abd-ul-Qādir ceded to France. **Algeria**, creation of *Bureaux Arabes*. Outline of a policy of 'Arab-French' education (→1848). **West Africa**, Amadou Cheikou died; decline of the Macina empire.
1845	**South Africa**, The Ngoni people from the south reached Ufipa. **North Africa, Morocco**, Reforming programmes: reorganization of Qarawiyīn University (→1846).
1846	**North Africa, Morocco**, Inauguration of college of engineering in Fez.
1847	**West Africa**, Liberia proclaimed a sovereign Republic.

1846	**Britain** • Abolition of the *Corn Laws* by Peel. • The first Workers' International held in London.
1847	**Scotland**, James Y. Simpson, revealed effectiveness of chloroform as a general anaesthetic. **Austria**, Semmlwis developed antiseptics.

EUROPE (cont.)		AFRICA (cont.)		AMERICA (cont.)		ASIA (cont.)		OCEANIA (cont.)	
1848	Europe, Year of Revolutions. France, Fall of Orleanist Monarchy. Schoelcher decree abolished slavery in colonies. Germany, National Parliament met in Frankfurt. Britain, Karl Marx and Friedrich Engels published *Communist Manifesto*. Italy, Revolt in Palermo against absolutism of Fernando II, King of Naples.	1848	East Africa, Johannes Rebmann discovered Mount Kilimanjaro.	1848	Canada, The British granted the Canadian colonies responsible government. **United States** • Gold discovered in California. • An initial womens rights convention held in New York. • John Collins Warren successfully performed first operation under general anaesthetic. **Mexico** • Treaty of Guadalupe Hidalgo, ended war with United States. Mexico cedes Texas, New Mexico, and California to United States. • Lucas Alemán published *Historia de México*.			1849–1853	Hawaii, Division of the land (*Mahelé*) between king and government, chiefs and tenants.
		1849	Central Africa, Libreville founded.					1850	Australia, Australian Colonies government Act. New South Wales, Tasmania, South Australia Victoria, Queensland granted regional autonomy.
1850	**Germany** • Hermann von Helmholtz invented ophthalmoscope. • Helmholtz and Frans Cornelis Donders developed ophthalmic optics. • Wilhelm Griesinger and Theodor Bilharz discovered cause of severe anaemia, and causative agent of bilharzia. France, The Falloux Law strengthened the hold of the Catholic Church on public schools. Britain, 10,000 km of railway established.	1850	Henry Barth's Saharan explorations (→1854).	1850	**United States** • Clay's compromise adopted between slave states and abolitionist states. • First colleges for girls, (e.g. Vassar and Wellesley) established. Mexico, First section of Vera Cruz-Mexico City railway inaugurated.	1850	China, Book on anatomy and therapeutics published by Wang Ch'ing-jen.		
1851	**Britain** • First International Exhibition in London. • Julius Reuter founded telegraphic news agency. • A submarine cable linked London with Paris. Ottoman Government established the Society of Knowledge. France, L. Foucault demonstrated the rotation of the earth.	1851	Egypt, A railway built between Alexandria and Cairo. South Africa, War between Boers and Basuto. West Africa, The slave trade prohibited by treaties between England and the kingdoms of Dahomey, Porto-Novo, Badagry and Abe Okuta.			1851	China, T'ai-p'ing rebellion. Iran, Founding of Dar al-Funun college in Tehran.	1851	Australia, Gold discovered in Bathurst and in Bendigo.

1852	**New Zealand**, Autonomous provincial government established.			1852	**United States** • Harriet Beecher Stowe published: *Uncle Tom's Cabin*. • Isaac Singer's sewing machine. **Argentina**, Juan Batista Alberdi published: *Bases y puntos de partida para la organización política de la República Argentina*. **Chile**, The Observatory of Santiago opened.			1852	**France** • Napoleon III Emperor. • Auguste Comte: *Catéchisme positif*. **Britain**, Lord Kelvin: research on refrigeration and cryogenics.
1853	**New Caledonia**, Annexed by France.	1853	**Japan**, American envoy Commodore M. C. Perry visits Japan.	1853	**Venezuela**, Manuel Antonio Carreño published *Manual de Urbanidad y buenas maneras*. **Argentina**, Constitution established.			1853	**Ottoman Empire** • Beginning of Crimean war. • Garabed Balyan designed the Dolmabahçe Palace in Istanbul (→1855). • **France**, L. Pasteur transformed tartaric into racemic acid.
		1854	**Japan**, Kanagawa open port treaty.	1854	**United States**, Republican Party founded. **Venezuela**, Slavery abolished.	1854	**East Africa** • Suez Canal Universal Society founded. • Concession for the Suez Canal given to Ferdinand de Lesseps, French vice-Consul.		
				1855	**Chile**, Promulgation of Civil Code.				
1856	**New Zealand**, Autonomous government established.			1856	**United States** • University of California, Berkeley, founded. • Atlantic cable inaugurated.	1856	**South Africa**, South African Republic founded.	1856	**Ottoman Empire**: Russians defeated in the Crimean war. **France** • Gustave Flaubert published: *Madame Bovary*. • African Missions of Lyon founded. **Germany**, J. Fuhlrott discovered skeleton of Neanderthal man. **Britain** • William H. Perkin discovered synthetic mauve aniline dye when attempting to produce synthetic quinine. • Henry Bessemer developed the 'Converter' for making steel at low cost.

	EUROPE (cont.)	AFRICA (cont.)	AMERICA (cont.)	ASIA (cont.)	OCEANIA (cont.)
1857	**France** • L. Foucault invented the silver–mirror telescope, and the gyroscope. • Charles Baudelaire published: *Les Fleurs du mal.* **West Europe**, building of the Mont-Cenis tunnel between France and Italy started. **Ottoman Empire**, the slave trade forbidden in the empire. **Britain**, the South Kensington Museum of science, arts and industry opened.	**Tunisia**, Muhammad Bey, issued a proclamation of reform. **West Africa, Senegal**, Dakar founded. **Madagascar**, Queen Ranavalona II expelled Europeans from Tananarive.	**Argentina**, Colón Theatre opened.	**India** • Sepoy rebellion against British (→1859). • British India transfered to the Crown. • Sir Jamsetjee Jeejeebhoy School of Art opened in Bombay.	
1858	**Romania**, Unification under Hospodar Alexandre Cuza. **Britain**, Charles Darwin published: *On the origin of species.* **Italy**, Unification of Piedmont.	**East Africa**, John Hanning Speke and Richard Francis Burton discovered Lake Tanganyika and Lake Victoria. **South Africa** • Diamond fields discovered at Kimberley. • First Orange Free state–Lesotho war.		**Southeast Asia**, France occupied Annam. **Japan** • The treaty of diplomatic relations and commerce with five Western states. • Major split within the government initiates domestic political conflict. • Shogunate rejected major daimyos. **Iraq**, Land Code gave right of ownership of state land to those who had right of usufruct.	
1859		**North Africa, Egypt**, Suez Canal started. The Khedivial Geographical Society established. **Morocco**, Spanish–Moroccan War. **West Africa**, First Yoruba paper: *Iwe Irohin* issued.	**United States**, Oil discovered in Pennsylvania.	**Viet Nam**, France occupied Saigon.	
1860	**France**, *Jardin d'acclimatation* opened in Paris.	**East Africa**, Negus Theodoros II defeated at Battle of Magdala and commited suicide. **West Africa**, Dakar, Higher School of Amanzimtote opened. **South Africa**, First batch of Indian *Coolies* imported into Natal.	**United States** • Abraham Lincoln won the presidential election in South Carolina, War of Secession began. • Museum of Comparative Zoology opened at Harvard. **Chile**, Law on provision of free primary education by the state passed.	**Japan**, Samurai assassinated Shogun's regent. **China**, Tongzhi Restoration.	**Australia**, John McDowell Stuart explored south Australia.

1861 **France**, Pierre and Ernest Michaux built velocipede.
Russia, Tsar Alexander II abolished serfdom.
Ottoman Empire, Ottoman Scientific Society founded.

1862 **Prussia**, Otto Von Bismarck appointed Prime Minister.

1863 **France**

- Claude Bernard published: *Introduction to the Study of Medical Experience.*
- Edouard Manet painted the *Picnic.*
- L. Pasteur established the pasteurisation process.

1864 **France**

- Right of Association and right to strike granted to all workers.
- Louis Pasteur proved there is no spontaneous generation of microorganisms, from amorphous matter.

Britain, Meeting of First International in London.
Switzerland, Red Cross and Geneva Convention, set up at instigation of Henry Dunant.
Russia, Statutory recognition of elementary schools.

1865 **Britain**, Lewis Carroll published: *Alice's* Adventures in Wonderland.
Scotland, James Clerk Maxwell succeeded in identifying electromagnetic nature of light.
Britain, Joseph Lister used carbolic acid as an antiseptic.

1861 **Tunisia**, First Constitution in Muslim world enacted.

1862 **West Africa**, Lat Dyor's fight against French expansion.
East Africa, By Treaty of Paris, France and Britain granted sovereignty to States of Zanzibar and Oman.

1861 **United States**, War between the North and South began (→1865).
Mexico, Introduction of the metric decimal system.
Mexico, England, France and Spain agreed to occupy Mexican ports. France decided to pursue the imperial plans of Napoleon III and Maximilian Hapsburg Emperor of Mexico.

1862 **United States**, President Lincoln proclaimed abolition of slavery.

1863 **United States**, Abraham Lincoln issued Emancipation Proclamation.
Venezuela, Adolfo Ernst began positivist science education at the Central University of Venezuela.
Argentina, A system of state schools established to train a political elite.

1865 **United States**

- South capitulated at Appotomax: end of the civil war.
- April 14, President Lincoln assassinated.
- Massachusetts Institute of Technology established.
- Atlantic cable successful.

1861 **India**, Archaeological Survey of India founded.
Near East, Telegraphic line linked Baghdad with Istanbul, Persia and India.

1862 **Southeast Asia**, France annexed lower Cochin China.
China, translation office (Tongwen guan) established in Peking.

1863 **Southeast Asia**, France declared Cambodia a protectorate.
Near East, The Beirut National School opened.

EUROPE (cont.)		AFRICA (cont.)		AMERICA (cont.)		ASIA (cont.)		OCEANIA (cont.)
1866	**Russia** • Fyodor Dostoevsky published: *Crime and Punishment*. • Austro–Prussian war. **France**. Siemens-Martin open-hearth steel.	1866	**Egypt**, School of Irrigation and Architecture founded in Cairo. **East Africa** • Dar es Salaam founded. • David Livingstone, in Zanzibar. **West Africa**, Samori Toure, in Bisandougou, extended his empire over Toron and Wassoulou.	1866	**United States**, The Congress voted equal civil right for black people. **Mexico**. American ultimatum to Emperor Napoleon III for withdrawal of French troops.	1866	**Near East**, The American University of Beirut established. **China**. A medical school established at the Canton Missionary Hospital.	
1867	**France**, Universal Exhibition in Paris. **Germany**, Karl Marx published: *Das kapital*. **Britain** • Joseph Lister announced 'antiseptic principle'. • Benjamin Disraeli introduced electoral reform extending voting rights. **Switzerland**, Zürich University, first in Europe to admit female medical students.	1867	**West Africa**, Ma Ba, Tukuloor's resistance against French invasion. **East Africa**. Karl Mauch discovered gold in Tati (Matabeleland). **North Africa, Lybia**, Turkish administration inaugurated the telegraph. **Algeria**, indigenous school of arts and crafts opened by the French at Fort Napoleon in Kabylia.	1867	**United States** • Alaska bought from Russia. • Western territories granted women's suffrage. **Canada**, Confederation of Canada becomes British Dominion. **Mexico**, June 19, Maximilian executed, after French troops withdraw.	1867	**Japan**, Mutsu–Hito became Emperor; the last Shogun abdicated. **Southeast Asia**, The French merged the two parts of Cochin-China.	
1868	**Ottoman Empire**, Museum opened in Istanbul to promote Turkish Art.	1868	**Egypt**, School of Applied Arts founded in Cairo.	1868	**Cuba**, Independence proclaimed by Carlos Manuel de Céspedes and Francisco Aguilera. **Mexico**, *Sociedad Mexicana de Historia Natural* founded. **Argentina**, The University of Buenos Aires inaugurated Department of Exact Sciences.	1868	**Japan**, Meiji government established.	
1869	**Britain**, The English Science weekly *Nature* founded. **France** • L. G. Perreaux invented the moped. **Russia**, Dmitri Mendeleev published his *Periodic Law of Chemical Elements*. • L. N. Tolstoy published: *War and Peace*. **Austria**, made school attendance compulsory for ages 6 to 14 (or 12).	1869	**Egypt** • Suez Canal opened. • Construction of the Opera House in Cairo.	1869	**United States** • First transcontinental railway linked Atlantic and pacific coasts. • Abolition of child labour. • Baseball, first professional team formed. **Chile**, World's leading producer of copper.		

Year	Europe	Year	Africa	Year	Americas	Year	Asia / Near & Middle East	Year	Oceania / Pacific
1870	France, Franco-Prussian war. French armies defeated. Fall of Napoleon III. Italy, Unification.			1870	United States, John Rockefeller founded Standard Oil Company. Puerto Rico, Launch of pro-independence manifesto 'Country, Justice and Freedom'. Venezuela, General Antonio Guzmán Blanco seized power. Argentina, Domingo Faustino Sarmiento, future President of Argentina, founded the Panama Normal School. Mexico, Gabino Barreda, founded Preparatory School.	1870	India • In Maharashtra, Jyotiba Phule developed critique of Brahmin domination. • Telegraph links India and Europe.		
1871	France, Civil war in Paris; beginning of the Commune. Germany • Bismarck, Chancellor (→1890); universal male suffrage granted. • Mont Cenis, tunnel opened.			1871	Colombia, Colombian Academy of Language founded.	1871	Japan • Daimyo states abolished. • Iwakura Mission to USA and Europe.		
1872	Germany • First anti-clerical law; beginning of *Kulturkampf*. • Postal Museum set up in Berlin. Britain, Cavendish Laboratory established at Cambridge University. Russia, Baku oil industry initiated.			1872	Cuba, José Martí, in exile in Spain, published *La República Española ante la Revolución Cubana*. Argentina, The Scientific Society of Argentina founded.	1872	India, Mayo School of Arts founded in Lahore.		
		1873	Egypt, School for girls established. East Africa, Death of David Livingstone.						
1874	France, Impressionist Exhibition.	1874	West Africa, Ashanti Kingdom defeated. Britain proclaimed emancipation of slaves in the Gold Coast. Central Africa, Stanley started his expedition in Africa, from East to West.			1874	Southeast Asia, Emperor Tu Duc gave France control over Vietnam's foreign relations.	1874	Fiji, Annexed by Britain. Australia, the first trade unions organized.
1875	France • Emile Zola published *Germinal*. • International Bureau of Weights and Measurements established.	1875	Central Africa, French explorer Savorgnan de Brazza found Ogooue Basin.	1875	Mark Twain published *Tom Sawyer*.	1875	Near East, Jesuits founded St. Joseph University in Beirut. Japan, Ryukyu, Bonin, and Kazan islands became part of Japan.		
1876	Ottoman Empire • First attempt to write a Turkish dictionary in Turkish. • Proclamation of first Turkish Constitution. Germany, Robert Kock identified germ, which caused anthrax. Otto gas engine.	1876	International Geographical Conference on colonisation of Africa held in Brussels. West Africa, Senegal: Universal suffrage in four Communes.	1876	United States • Johns Hopkins University founded in Baltimore. • Graham Bell invented the telephone. • Thomas Edison invented Phonograph.	1876	Middle East, First scientific monthly published in Arabic: *al-Muqtataf* (The Selection) founded in Beirut.	1876	Hawaii, Development of sugar cane plantations resulted in treaty between kingdom of Hawaii and United States.

	EUROPE (cont.)	AFRICA (cont.)	AMERICA (cont.)	ASIA (cont.)	OCEANIA (cont.)
1877	**Britain.** Queen Victoria proclaimed Empress of India. **Germany.** Berlin set up *Physikalisch-Technische Reichsanstalt.* **Sweden.** Gustav Laval invented cream separator.	Stanley travelled continent from Zanzibar to Boma in Congo.	**Mexico.** Began work for establishing observatory. **United States** • Former African slaves declared citizens of United States. • Two constitutional amendments (14 and 15) granted adult black males voting rights and equal protection under law.	**Japan** • Last and the biggest rebellion of ex-samurai put down. • Primary schools modelled on the Western pattern proliferated; first 'New Style' university opened in Tokyo. **China.** First general conference of Protestant Missionaries.	**New Caledonia.** First export of nickel and chromium.
1878	**Ottoman Empire.** Treaty of San Stefano signed with Russians. **Prussia.** Congress of Berlin granted: independence to Romania, Serbia and Montenegro. **Bulgaria** created; **Bosnia and Herzegovina** administrered by Austro-Hungary. **Britain.** Sidney Gilchrist Thomas perfected new process in steel production. **France.** L. Pasteur began experiments on cholera with chickens.		**Venezuela.** Businessmen founded Tachira Oil Company. **Argentina.** Academia of Córdoba became National Academy of Sciences.		**New Caledonia.** Revolt led by chief Atai.
1879	**France** • Workers Party created by Jules Guesde. • Auguste Rodin sculpted: *Le penseur* **Russia.** Fyodor Dostoevsky published: *Brothers Karamazov.*	**East Africa.** Protestant and Catholic (Pères Blancs) Missionaries clash in Buganda.	**United States,** Thomas Edison's carbon-filament lamp.		
1880		**North Africa, Algeria:** rapid development of viticulture.			
1881	**Ottoman Empire,** Commission for the Preservation of Monuments of Arab Art established. **France.** Jules Ferry's Law established free primary education. **Britain** • International Medical Congress held in London. • Louis Pasteur used the words 'vaccine' and 'vaccination' for the first time. • Alphonse Laveran discovered a protozoon, the *Plasmodium.*	**North Africa, Tunisia,** French occupation of Algeria. • Art College created in Algiers.			

Year	Europe / Science	Africa	Americas	Asia	Australasia / Pacific
1882	**France** • Primary school made compulsory and non-denominational. • Robert Koch's discovery of the 'tubercle bacillus'.	**East Africa, Britain** occupies Egypt and Sudan. **Central Africa,** King Leopold II of Belgium founded *Congo International Association*.	**Panama,** Digging of Panama Canal began.		**New Zealand,** First frozen meat cargo left Dunedin for London. **Tahiti** annexed by France. **Australia,** Refrigeration process developed for meat.
1883	**Ottoman Empire,** Opening of the Imperial Academy of Fine Arts in Istanbul. **Germany,** R. Koch used Pasteur's process to inoculate against anthrax. He also isolated bacteria responsible for *Vibrio cholerae*. **France** • L. Pasteur produced rabies vaccine for animals, and a cure for hydrophobia. • Zygmunt Wroblewski and Karol Olszewski invented method to liquefy air.	**East Africa,** Emperor Menelik founded Addis Ababa. **West Africa,** Bank of Senegal established.	**Venezuela,** Inauguration of railway from La Guaira to Caracas. **United States,** William Baron Jenney built the first 'skyscraper' in Chicago.	**Southeast Asia,** French occupied Hanoi. • Annam and Tonkin made into French protectorates. **Japan,** Osaka Spinning Mill opened.	
1884	International time zones system established. **Britain,** Universal male suffrage granted. **Germany** • Work accidents became a state responsibility. • Ludwig Knorr, markets febrifuge 'Antipyrin'. **Austria,** Carl Koller invented local anaesthesia (Cocaine). **Britain,** Parson's steam turbine.	Berlin Conference on Partition of Africa (→1885). **South Africa,** First German colony of South-West Africa.	**Argentina,** Free, nondenominational, compulsory primary education for children aged 7 to 13. **United States,** Georges Eastman invented the photographic film.	**China,** War against France. Chinese forces sent to aid Vietnam took Tonkin.	**New Guinea** annexed by Britain. **Australia** • Federal Council established; • Australian Union supported Britain in Sudan.
1885	**France,** Louis Pasteur inoculated first anti-rabies vaccine. **Germany** • Sickness covered by state insurance. • Benz's first motorcar.	**Central Africa** • Congo state founded; • Belgian King Leopold II recognized as sovereign. **Madagascar,** Proclaimed French protectorate. **West Africa,** Dakar-Saint Louis railway opened.	**Canada,** Completion of trans-Canadian railway.	**China,** T'ien-tsin Sino-French treaty. Chinese forces evacuated Tonkin. **Vietnam** became a French protectorate. **Indian Empire,** Formation of the Indian National Congress in Bombay. **Japan,** Tokyo Imperial University founded.	
1886	**Germany** • Heinrich Hertz discovered electromagnetic waves. • Museum of Public Health in Berlin.	Gold discovered in Witwatersrand.	**United States,** Statue of liberty (by French sculptor Bartholdi) erected in New York. **Peru,** Founding of the Universal Confederation of Craftsmen.		

EUROPE (cont.)	AFRICA (cont.)	AMERICA (cont.)	ASIA (cont.)	OCEANIA (cont.)
	1887 West Africa, Binger's journey from Bamako to Grand-Bassam by Sikasso, Ouagadougou and Kong (→1890). South Africa • Johannesburg founded. • Cecil Rhodes created Goldfields of South Africa.	**1887** Chile, The public garden of Santiago created.	**1887** Japan, Fine Arts Academy and Academy of Music founded in Tokyo.	
1888 Scotland, John Dunlop developed the pneumatic tyre. France • Jules Marey demonstrates a cine-camera. • Institut Pasteur founded in Paris. • André and Edouard Michelin founded Michelin Tyre Company. Germany • Invalid and old age state insurance introduced. • Association for popular science established Urania in Berlin.	**1888** Cardinal Lavigerie made responsible for the anti-slavery campaign by Pope Leo XIII.	**1888** Brazil, Emperor Pedro II decreed abolition of slavery.		**1888** Chile annexed Easter Island.
1889 Standard metre and kilogram established. • Anti-slavery Conference held in Brussels. France • The World Fair in Paris. Eiffel Tower erected. • Henri Bergson published: Essai sur les données immédiates de la conscience. Britain, National Physical Laboratory established in London. Ottoman Empire, Young Turk Society is founded.		**1889** Brazil, Pedro II overthrown and Republic proclaimed.	**1889** Near East, Beirut-Damascus railway built.	
1890 France, Clément Ader took first flight by aeroplane. Germany, Fall of Bismarck. Britain, First fully underground railway in London.	**1890** Egypt, Al-Azhar Mosque reformed.	**1890** Argentina, Revolution. • Baring financial crisis. United States, First steel-framed building Chicago.	**1890** Japan • Imperial Diet opened on the basis of the Meiji Constitution. • Boom of railroad construction; nation-wide postal service and telegram networks almost completed. • Shibasaburo Kitazato discovered toxin of tetanus and later invented serotherapy.	**1890** New Zealand, Liberal government established Factories Act, Conciliation and Arbitration Act, and Old Age Pension Act. Australia, 15,000 km of railway tracks laid.

Year	(Europe / Culture & Science)	Year	(Africa)	Year	(Americas)	Year	(Asia)	Year	(Oceania)
1891	**Italy**, Pope Leo III published *Rerum novarum* on Church social doctrine. **Russia**, Beginning of Trans–Siberian Railway construction (→1904). **Britain**, Oscar Wilde published *The Picture of Dorian Gray*. **France**, R. Panhard and E. Levassor built a car run on petrol.	1891	**Central Africa**, French Congo founded. **Egypt**, resident European orientalist painters held first exhibition of paintings at Opera House in Cairo.	1891	**United States**, Thomas Edison used 35 mm film in place of photographic paper.				
1892	**France**, Federation of Trades Union Centres created. **Germany**, R. Diesel perfected diesel motor.	1892	**Central Africa**, Invention of Bamum script writing system during reign of King Njoya (1892/96 →1935).					1892	**Australia**, New gold seams discovered at Colgardie and Kalgoorlie.
1893	**Russia**, Alexander Popov, invented radio antenna, and built first electromagnetic waves receiver.	1893,	**South–West Africa**, Revolts of Matabele, Mashona, Zulu, and Hottentot in Rhodesia (1894).	1893	**United States**, Protectorate established over Hawaii Islands.	1893	**Indochina, Laos**, became French Protectorate and joined Indochina Union.	1893	**New Zealand**, voting rights granted to women. **Hawaii** became pro-American Republic, after a revolution.
1894	**France** • Beginning of Dreyfus affair. • Emile Durkheim: *'Les Règles de la méthode sociologique'*. • Claude Debussy composed: *'Prélude à l'après-midi d'une faune'*. • Charles and Emile Pathé introduce Pathé Phonographs. • Henri Toulouse–Lautrec painted the *Moulin Rouge* series.	1894	**East Africa, Uganda**, became British protectorate.	1894		1894	**Japan**, Sino–Japanese War. Japan gains Taiwan to become an empire with colonies. **China**, Sun Yat-Sen organised in Hawaii China's first modern revolutionary society to set up a Republic.		
1895	**Ottoman Empire**, Armenian massacres began. **France**, Louis and August Lumière designed a cine–camera and projector. **Germany** • Wilhelm Conrad Röntgen discovered X-rays. • Werner von Siemens built first electric locomotive. **Sweden**, Alfred Nobel, inventor of dynamite, instituted The Nobel Prizes.	1895	**West Africa**, The general government of French West Africa (A.O.F.) formed. **Madagascar**, French occupied Tananarivo. **East Africa, Kenya** a British protectorate.	1895	**Cuba**, New uprising by supporters of independence. **Central America**. Honduras, Nicaragua and El Salvador established Greater Republic of Central America.			1895	**Australia**, Voting rights granted to women; Labour Party founded.

	EUROPE (cont.)	AFRICA (cont.)	AMERICA (cont.)	ASIA (cont.)	OCEANIA (cont.)
1896	**Greece**, First Modern Olympic games at Athens. **Italy**, Guglielmo Marconi invented wireless telegraphy. **France**, Henri A. Becquerel observed radiation in uranium. **Russia**, Alexander S. Popov, transmitted first radio message.	**East Africa, Ethiopia**, Emperor Menelik defeated Italian troops at Adoua. Ethiopia became independent. **Madagascar**, France annexed the Island and deported Queen Ranavalona III. **Central Africa**, Njoya King of Bamoum (→1932). **South Africa**, Chimurenga: war for independence fails in Southern Rhodesia.	**Argentina**, Argentine Socialist Party founded. **United States**, Henri Ford's first motor-car.		
1897	**Germany**, Diesel engines manufactured.	**West Africa**, Gold Coast, Aborigines' Rights Protection Society.		**China** ceded two ports to Germany. • Wang Xianqian and Ye dehui founded South Study Society to promote local rights of gentry. **Southeast Asia**, French Indo-China Union became Indochinese government. **Japan**, Kiyoshi Shiga discovered dysentery bacillus.	
1898	**France** • Emile Zola: *'J'accuse'*. • Marie and Pierre Curie isolated the element radium. • F. Löffler and P. Frosch discovered the existence of viruses.	**West Africa** • France captured Almamy Samory Toure, Wassoulou Emperor. • Anglo-French confrontation at Fashoda. **East Africa**, Lord Delamere discovered 'Highlands' in Kenya. **North Africa**, Leonardo da Vinci School of Arts founded by Italian Society of Dante Alighieri.	**Cuba**, Beginning of the Spanish-American War, which led to independence. **Latin America**, Spanish-American War. By treaty of Paris, Spain ceded Puerto Rico, Guam and Philippines to United States, with protectorate over Cuba.	**China** • First party cabinet organized. • The founding of the Guandun Science Society. • Emperor Guangxu issued Hundred-Day Reform dealing with adminstration, education, and economy. **Japan**, First Party cabinet was organized. **Indo-Chinese** • France formed Indo-China, Union comprising Cochin-China, Annam, Tonkin, Cambodia and Laos. • American-Spanish War; Spain ceded Philippines to United States.	**Guam** and **Philippines** occupied by United States after victory against Spain. **Marshall Islands** sold by Spain to Britain. **Bougainville** and **Buka** are allotted to England.
1899	**Netherlands**, First Conference on Peace in the Hague. **Britain**, Patrick Manson started London School of Tropical Medicine.	**Egypt**, Anglo-Egyptian Condominium on Sudan. **South Africa**, Boer War against the British.	**Puerto Rico**, Puerto Rican Republican Party founded, which advocated statehood.		

Year		Year		Year		Year		Year	

1900

1900 — **France**
- Millerand's Law established eleven-hour maximum working day.
- Biggest telescope ever made displayed in Paris.
- *Guide Michelin* founded.

Germany
- Max Planck discovered quantum theory.
- Karl Landsteiner discovered blood groups and described Rhesus factor.
- Ferdinand von Zepplin built his airship.
- Sigmud Freud published *Interpretation of Dreams*.

Ottoman Empire, Public university opened with four faculties.

1900 — **West Africa, Ghana**: the first small hospital opened at Aburi.

Central Africa
- Emir of Bornou kingdom, defeated by the French at Koussri.
- The beginning of the colonization of Chad.

South Africa. Britain annexed Orange State and the Transvaal.

1900 — **United States**, Frederick Taylor instituted scheme of scientific management.

1900 — **China**, Boxer Rebellion against foreigners.
India. Autonomous women's initiatives in education, and demands for voting rights and legal reforms.

1900 — **Australia** helped Britain in war against Boers.

1901 — **France**
- Law allowing rights of association.
- Nobel Prizes were awarded in physics, chemistry and medicine.
- Picasso's first main works.

1901 — **West Africa**
- Ashanti became a British colony.
- The Bank of West Africa (B.A.O.) established.

1901 — **Cuba**, The Constitution of an Independent Republic promulgated. The Congress of the United States approved the protectorate over the new Republic.
United States, National Bureau of Standards created in Washington.
United States, Andrew Carnegie set up in Washington an institution devoted to research.

1901 — **China**
- Treaty between Western Allies (Germany, France, United States) and China.
- Reform began with Empress's decree from exile at Xian.
- Shikai transformed traditional academies into new-style schools in Shandong, Yuan.
- Hang Youwei wrote *Great Commonwealth*, which rejected family values on which Confucian morality was erected.
- New style drama appeared in Shanghai.
Japan, Meiji government opened. Yawata ironworks.

1901 — **Australia**, Australian Commonwealth created and became a British dominion. Law which prohibited Asian men from coming into the country passed.

1902 — **South Africa**, Treaty of Vereeniging between the United Kingdom and Boers, which established British sovereignty.

1902 — **Venezuela**, A fleet from Germany, England and Italy blockaded La Guaira to press for payment of debts.
Argentina, Formulation of the Drago Doctrine, condemning the use of force by big states against small states to collect debts.

1903 — **Ottoman Empire**, Germany obtained concession to build railway between Istanbul and Baghdad.

1903 — **West Africa**, Training School for primary teachers opened in Saint-Louis.

1903 — **Panama**, Independence from Colombia proclaimed.
United States
- Henry Ford opened his first car factory.
- Wilbur Wright realized the first powered heavier than air flight.
- Theodore Roosevelt elected President.

1903 — **Near East**, School of Medicine opened in Damascus.
China, The first cinema.

EUROPE (cont.)	AFRICA (cont.)	AMERICA (cont.)	ASIA (cont.)	OCEANIA (cont.)
1904 Giacomo Puccini composed *Madame Butterfly*. **Anglo-French**, Entente cordiale.	**1904** **West Africa**, Kayes-Niger railway.	**1904** **Panama**, United States promotes Panama Canal construction. **Argentina**, Joaquín V. González proposed a labour code to legalize union activity. **Panama**, Constitution promulgated.	**1904** **Japan** • Russo-Japanese War. • Japan gains southern tip of North East China and northern Sakhalin. • Alternation of bureaucratic cabinet and party cabinet begins. • Hantaro Nagaoka, a founding father of Japanese physics presented model of the atom in 'Nature'. **India**, The Viceroy Lord Curzon (r.1898–1905) authorised Ancient Monuments Preservation Act.	
1905 Albert Einstein published: *Theory of relativity*. **Russia**, First Russian Revolution (→1907); *Duma* created.	**1905** Occupation of Morocco by France. **East Africa**, Insurrection of Maji-Maji against Germany (→1906). **West Africa**, Gold Coast, Attoh Ahuma published: *Memoirs of West Africa Celebrities*.	**1905** **Argentina**, Founding of the University of La Plata. **United States**, President Theodore Roosevelt mediated French-German disputes in Morocco.	**1905** **Japan**, Victory over Russia. **China** • Abolition of the traditional state examination system. • Boycott of American goods to protest against new immigration laws that discriminated against Chinese. • Zhang Zhidong buy back from America the right to build the Hankow-Canton railway construct a railway from Hankow to Sichuan.	**1905–1914** **Australia**, Labour Party declared an eight-hour working day.
1906 **Britain** • The Labour party founded. • Joseph J. Thompson received Nobel Prize of Physics for research into conductivity of gases. **Spain**. Santiago Raamon y Cojal, won Nobel Prize. **Norway** and **Finland**, women granted voting rights.	**1906** **South Africa** • Bambata and Zulu uprising in Natal (→1908). • Civil disobedience campaign under instigation of Gandhi (→1908).	**1906** **United States** • Pure Food and Drug Act passed. • U. Sinclair published: *The Jungle*.	**1906** **China**, Opening of Peking Union Medical College.	**1906** **New Hebrides** became a Franco-British Condominium.
1907				**1907** **New Zealand**, declared British Dominion.
1908 **Ottoman Empire**, Young Turk revolution at Salonica. **Bulgaria**, Ferdinand I became King and proclaimed independence. **Germany**, Ellehamer made first flight. **Britain**, Olympic Games in London.	**1908** **Egypt**, Private University established. **Central Africa**, Congo became a Belgian colony. **West Africa** created the People's Union in Nigeria.		**1908** **Near East, Iraq**: School of Law established in Baghdad. **Korea**, First modern theatre opened in Seoul.	

1909	**Near East**, Anglo-Persian Oil Company established.	1909	**United States**, National Association for the Advancement of Coloured People (NAACP) formed.	1909	**North Africa**: Algiers University founded.	1909	**France**, Louis Bleriot flew across English Channel. **Italy**, Marconi, father of radio, received Nobel Prize. **Britain**, Old age pension established.
1910	**Asia**, Japan annexes Korea.	1910	**Uruguay**, Socialist Party formed. **Mexico**, Francisco I. Madero: *San Luis de Potosí Plan.* **United States**, Washington State gave women the right to vote.	1910	**South Africa**, Britain created South African Union. **Central Africa**, General government of French Equatorial Africa (A.E.F.) formed. **West Africa** • Introduction of cocoa into Ivory Coast. • Creation of Club of Young Senegalese.	1910	**Germany**, Ehrlich developed, with Sahachiro Hata (Japan), first chemotherapeutic agent, the antisyphilitic 'Salvarsan'. **Russia.** Sergi V. Lebedev obtained first sample of synthetic rubber.
1911	**China** • Sun Yat-Sen (1866–1925) became first President of Chinese Republic. • The Provincial Assembly of Sichuan founded Railway Protection League. Meiji Emperor dies. **Near East**, Persia, Art School opened in Tehran. **Japan**, Meiji Emperor dies.	1911	**Uruguay**, Clotilde Luisi first woman to join the diplomatic service as a career civil servant. **Peru**, Iram Bingham discovered Machu-Picchu. **Canada**, 14 April, Wreck of the Titanic.	1911	**North Africa**, Italy invaded Lybia. Ottoman Empire cedes Tripolitania to Italy. **East Africa.** E. Casely Hayford published: *Ethiopia Unbound.* **West Africa**, Conakry-Kourouma railway built.	1911	**Britain**, Sickness insurance Act, passed.
1912	**China**, The year I of the Republic of China inaugurated in Nanjing. • Sun Yat-Sen founded the kuomintang. **Near East**, Law School established in Beirut. **India**, Tagore Rabindranath published *Gitanjali* and won the Nobel Prize for Literature (→1913).	1912	**United States** • Woodrow Wilson elected President. • Illinois: women granted right to vote. **Chile**, The workers' leader Emilio Recabarren founded Workers' Socialist Party. **Cuba**, Third intervention by the United States.	1912	**North Africa**, France, declared Morocco a protectorate. **West Africa**, Unification of Nigeria. **Nigeria** • Anti-slavery and Aborigine Protection Society founded. • Nigerian Civil Servants Union founded.	1912	**Italy** • Universal suffrage established. • G. Marconi produced a continuously oscillating wave, and developed short-wave transmission over long distances.
1913	**Japan**, Ravelojaona published: *Japan and Japanese.*			1913	**Southwest Africa**, The Angolan League (Luanda) founded. **East Africa**, Djibouti/Addis–Ababa railway opened. **Madagascar**, Brickaville-Tanatave railway opened. **West Africa** • Porto-novo-Sákété railway opened. • Microbiology laboratory set up in Saint Louis (Senegal) becomes Institut Pasteur (Dakar). **Egypt.** Muhammad Husayn Haykal *Zaynab.*	1913	**France**, Marcel Proust began: *'A la recherche du temps perdu'.* **Russia** • Igor Stravinski composed *Rite of Spring.* • Petersburg factory produced first airplane by Russian designers.

EUROPE (cont.)		AFRICA (cont.)		AMERICA (cont.)		ASIA (cont.)		OCEANIA (cont.)	
1914	**Austro-Hungary** • 28 June, François-Ferdinand, heir apparent to the throne, assassinated in Sarajevo. • First World War started. **Switzerland,** Socialist Parties Conference at Zimmerwald against the war.	1914	**Egypt** • German–Ottoman offensive over Suez Canal. • Britain officially declared Egypt a protectorate. **West Africa** • Senegal, Blaise Diagne first deputy from Senegal. • French, British, Belgians and South-Africans seized German colonies.	1914	**Mexico,** United States fleet shelled and took Vera Cruz. **Panama,** canal opened under United States control.	1914	**Japan,** World War 1 breaks out. Japan declares war on Germany. Japan occupied German colonies: Qingadao in China and islands in the Pacific. **Austro-Hungary** declared war against Japan.	1914	**Australia,** Australian and New Zealand forces sent to fight in Europe and in Middle East.
						1922	**Japan,** The first Japanese Communist Party established.		
						1924	**Japan,** Alternation of party cabinets begins.		
						1925	**Japan,** Universal Manhood Suffrage Law passed.		
						1931	**Japan,** Manchurian Incident.		

MAPS

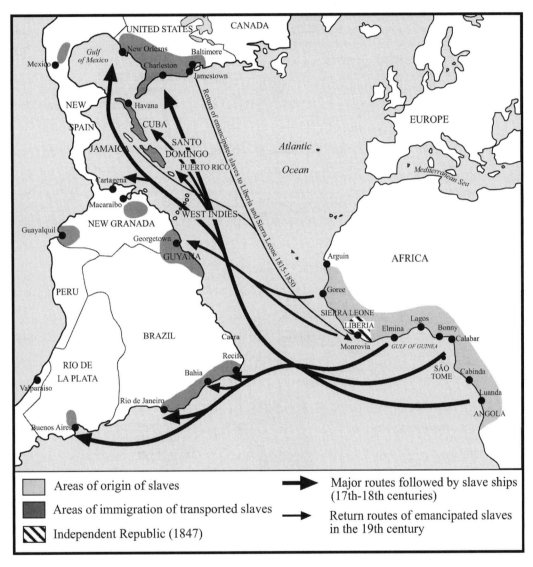

Map 1 'The Slave Trade' (source: Chaliand, G. and Rageau, J. P., 1991. *Atlas des Diasporas*. Editions Odile Jacob, Paris, p.131).

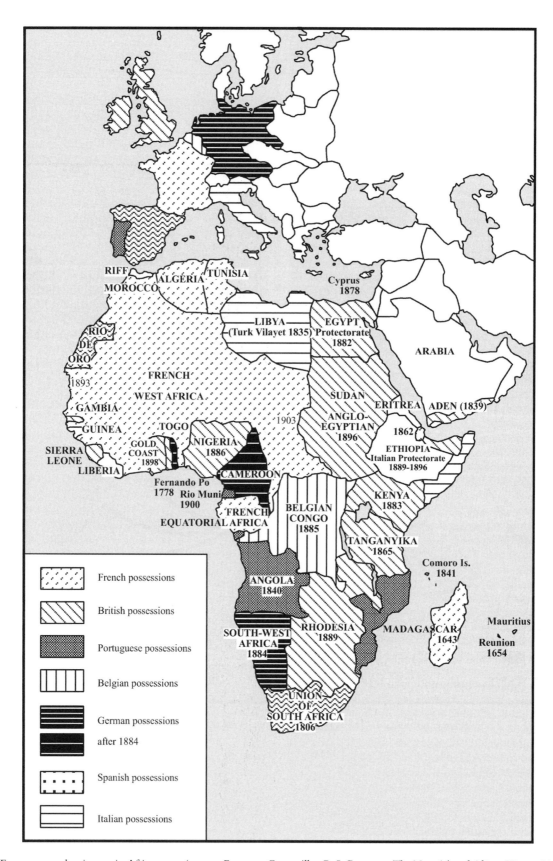

Map 2 European predominance in Africa, 1914 (source: Freeman-Greenville, G. S. P., 1991. *The New Atlas of African History*. Macmillan Press, London, p. 115).

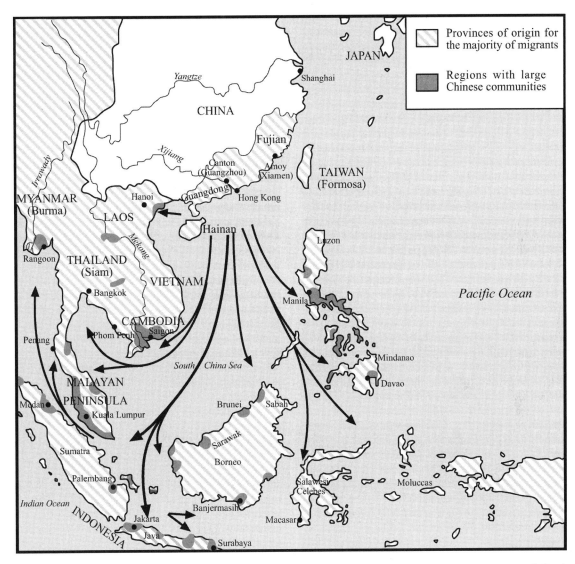

Map 3 South East Asia (regions of traditional immigration of the Chinese, fourteenth to nineteenth centuries) (source: Chaliand, G. and Rageau, J. P., 1991. *Atlas des Diasporas*. Editions Odile Jacob, Paris, p. 131).

Map 4 The Japanese colonial empire, 1895–1945 (source: Duus, P. (ed.) 1988. *The Cambridge History of Japan, Vol. 4: The Twentieth Century*. Cambridge University Press, Cambridge, p. 219).

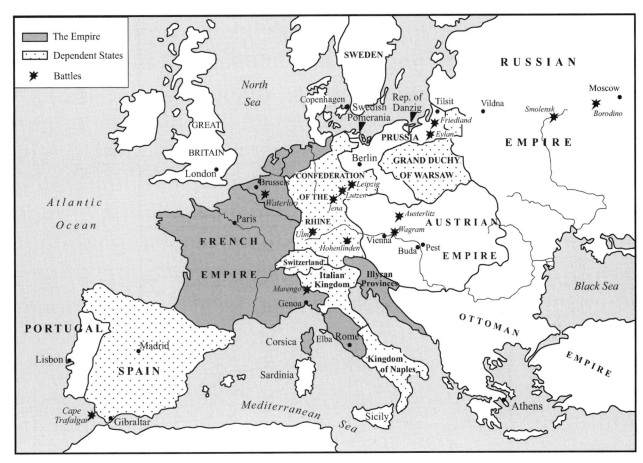

The Empire

Dependent States

Battles

GREAT BRITAIN

London

North Sea

SWEDEN

Copenhagen

Swedish Pomerania

Rep. of Danzig

Tilsit

Vildna

RUSSIAN

Smolensk

Moscow

Borodino

EMPIRE

Atlantic Ocean

Brussels

Waterloo

CONFEDERATION

OF THE

RHINE

Berlin

PRUSSIA

Friedland

Eylau

GRAND DUCHY

OF WARSAW

Paris

FRENCH

EMPIRE

Leipzig

Lutzen

Jena

Ulm

Switzerland

Italian

Kingdom

Hohenlinden

Austerlitz

Wagram

Vienna

Buda

Pest

AUSTRIAN

EMPIRE

Illyran

Provinces

PORTUGAL

Lisbon

Madrid

SPAIN

Marengo

Genoa

Corsica

Elba

Rome

Sardinia

Kingdom

of Naples

Cape Trafalgar

Gibraltar

Mediterranean Sea

Sicily

Athens

OTTOMAN

EMPIRE

Black Sea

Map 5 The Napoleonic empire at its zenith (source: Stuart Woolf, 1990. *Napoléon and the conquest of Europe*, Flammarion, Paris, map '1807–1811', pp. 9–10).

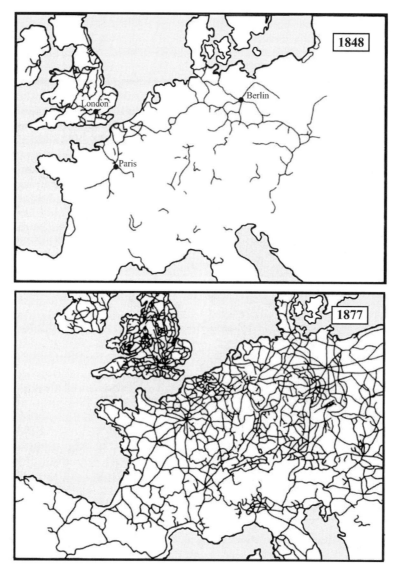

Map 6 Railway map, Western Europe, 1877 (source: Robert Jchnerb, 1955. *Le XIXe siècle. L'apogée de l'expansion européenne (1815–1914)*, 5th edn, 1968, Presses Universitaires de France, Paris, Plate 9, p. 128).

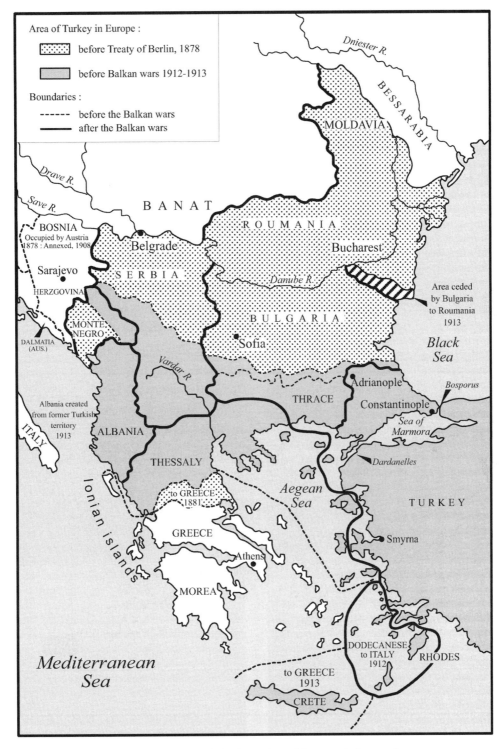

Area of Turkey in Europe :

before Treaty of Berlin, 1878

before Balkan wars 1912-1913

Boundaries :

- - - - before the Balkan wars
———— after the Balkan wars

Dniester R.

BESSARABIA

MOLDAVIA

Drave R.

BANAT

Save R.

ROUMANIA

BOSNIA
Occupied by Austria
1878 : Annexed, 1908

Belgrade

Bucharest

Sarajevo

SERBIA

HERZGOVINA

Danube R.

Area ceded
by Bulgaria
to Roumania
1913

DALMATIA
(AUS.)

MONTE-
NEGRO

BULGARIA

*Black
Sea*

Vardar R

Sofia

Adrianople

THRACE

Bosporus

Albania created
from former Turkish
territory
1913

Constantinople

*Sea of
Marmora*

ITALY

ALBANIA

◄*Dardanelles*

THESSALY

TURKEY

*Aegean
Sea*

to GREECE
1881

Smyrna

GREECE

Ionian islands

Athens

MOREA

DODECANESE
to ITALY
1912

RHODES

*Mediterranean
Sea*

to GREECE
1913

CRETE

Map 7 The Balkan states at the end of the nineteenth and the beginning of the twentieth centuries.

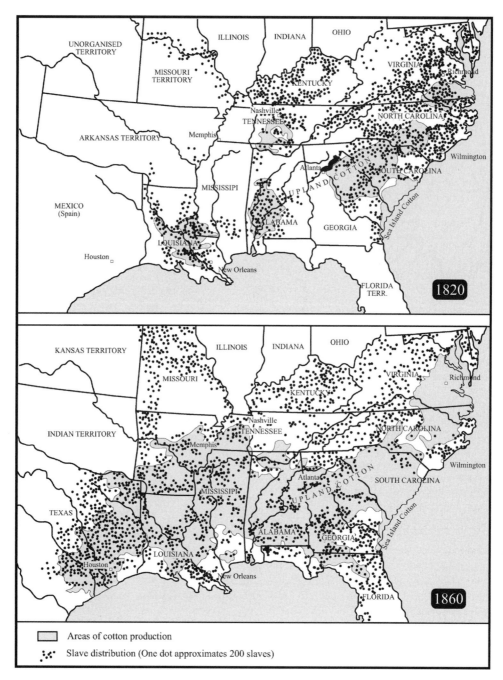

Map 8 The spread of cotton production and slavery in the Southern states of the United States of America (source: Library of Congress).

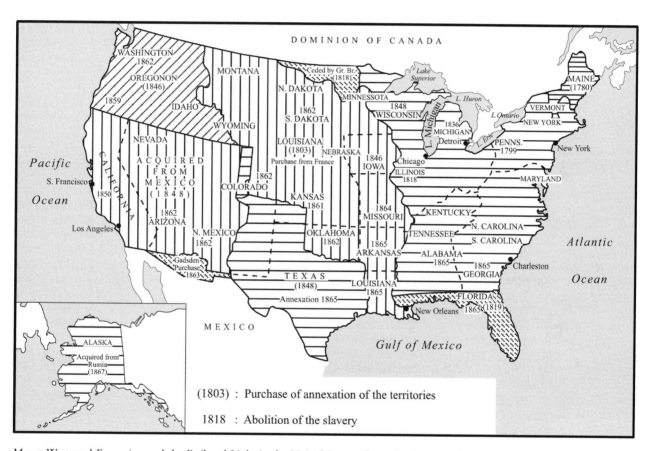

Map 9 Westward Expansion and the Railroad Links in the United States of America (source: Library of Congress).

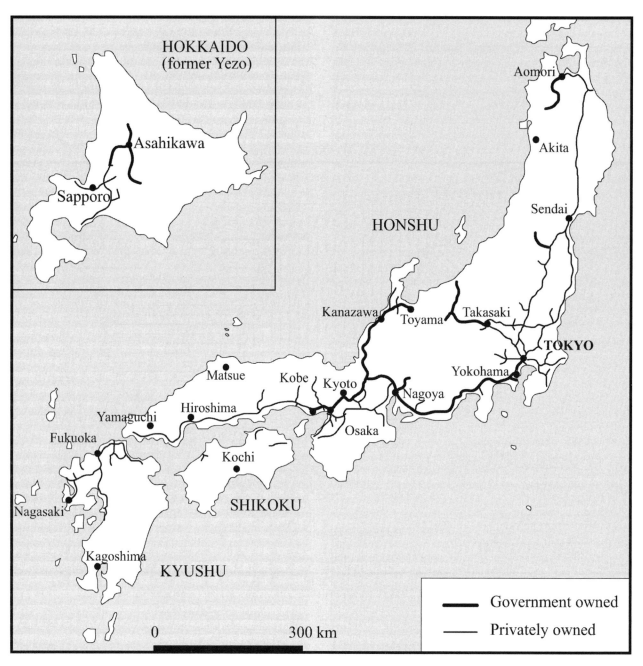

Map 10 The Japanese railway network in 1890 (source: Noda, M., Harada, K., Aoki, E. and Oikawa, Y. (eds) 1986. Nihon no Tetsudo [Japanese Railways], Nihon Keizai Hyoronsha, Tokyo).

Notes:

a Imperial Japan's 'inner territory' consisted of four main islands, Honshu, Kyushu, Shikoku and Hokkaido, along with numerous small islands.

b The first Japanese railway was opened for traffic between Tokyo and Yokohama in 1872. It was extended to Kobe in 1889, when the length of private railways exceeded the length of governmental ones. In 1906, the government bought the main private railways.

Map 11 Formation of major states of modern South East Asia (source: D. J. Steinberg *et al.* 1975. *In Search of Southeast Asia: A Modern History*. Oxford University Press, Kuala Lumpur, between pp. 194 and 195).

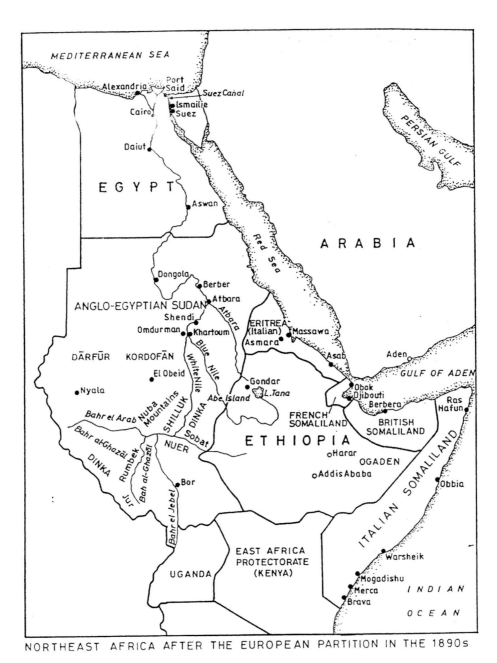

NORTHEAST AFRICA AFTER THE EUROPEAN PARTITION IN THE 1890s

Map 12 Africa south of Sahara towards 1880: Empires, Kingdoms and European settlements (source: E. Coulibaly, Paris, 2001).

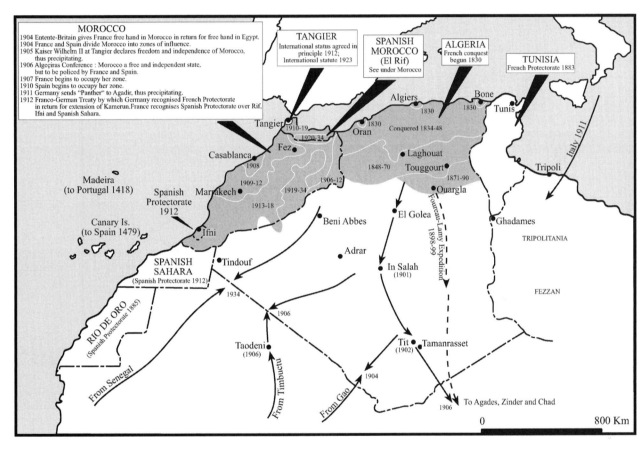

MOROCCO
1904 Entente-Britain gives France free hand in Morocco in return for free hand in Egypt.
1904 France and Spain divide Morocco into zones of influence.
1905 Kaiser Wilhelm II at Tangier declares freedom and independence of Morocco,
  thus precipitating.
1906 Algeciras Conference : Morocco a free and independent state,
  but to be policed by France and Spain.
1907 France begins to occupy her zone.
1910 Spain begins to occupy her zone.
1911 Germany sends "Panther" to Agadir, thus precipitating.
1912 Franco-German Treaty by which Germany recognised French Protectorate
  in return for extension of Kamerun.France recognises Spanish Protectorate over Rif,
  Ifni and Spanish Sahara.

TANGIER
International status agreed in
principle 1912;
International statute 1923

SPANISH
MOROCCO
(El Rif)
See under Morocco

ALGERIA
French conquest
begun 1830

TUNISIA
French Protectorate 1883

Tangier 1910-19
1920-34

Algiers 1830 Bone
1830
Oran 1830 Tunis

Fez Conquered 1834-48

Casablanca 1908 Tripoli

Madeira 1909-12 Laghouat
(to Portugal 1418) 1848-70 Touggourt Italy 1911

Spanish 1906-12 1871-90
Protectorate Marrakech 1919-34 Ouargla
1912 1913-18

Canary Is. Ghadames
(to Spain 1479) Ifni El Golea TRIPOLITANIA

SPANISH Beni Abbes
SAHARA Tindouf
(Spanish Protectorate 1912) In Salah FEZZAN
Adrar (1901)

RIO DE ORO 1934
(Spanish Protectorate 1885) 1906

Taodeni Tit Tamanrasset
(1906) (1902)

From Senegal From Timbuctu From Gao 1904 To Agades, Zinder and Chad
1906

Foureau-Lamy Expedition
1898-99

0 800 Km

Map 13 Africa between 1880 and 1914: People, kingdoms and empires fight against European occupation (source: E. Coulibaly, Paris, 2001).

609

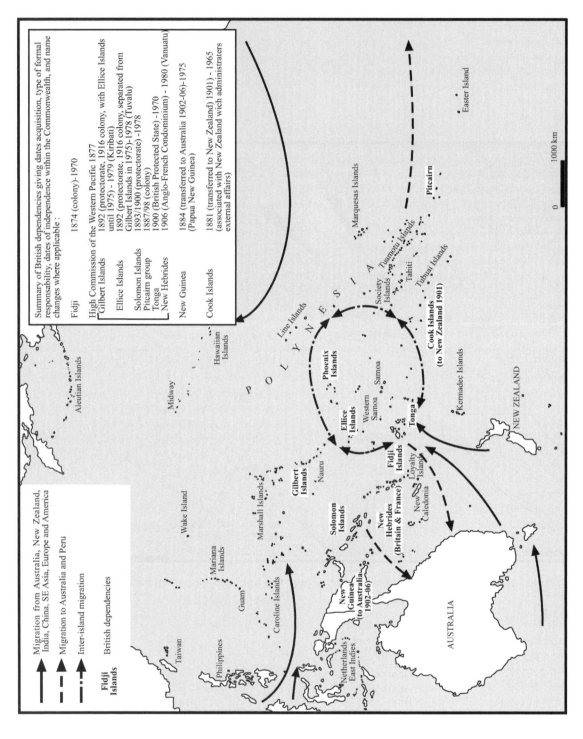

Summary of British dependencies giving dates acquisition, type of formal responsability, dates of independence within the Commonwealth, and name changes where applicable :

Fidji   1874 (colony)-1970

High Commission of the Western Pacific 1877

Gilbert Islands   1892 (protectorate, 1916 colony, with Ellice Islands until 1975) – 1979 (Kiribati)

Ellice Islands   1892 (protectorate, 1916 colony, separated from Gilbert Islands in 1975)-1978 (Tuvalu)

Solomon Islands   1893/1900 (protectorate) -1978

Pitcairn group   1887/98 (colony)

Tonga   1900 (British Protected State) -1970

New Hebrides   1906 (Anglo-French Condominium) - 1980 (Vanuatu)

New Guinea   1884 (transferred to Australia 1902-06)-1975 (Papua New Guinea)

Cook Islands   1881 (transferred to New Zealand 1901) - 1965 (associated with New Zealand wich administraters external affairs)

Migration from Australia, New Zealand, India, China, SE Asia, Europe and America

Migration to Australia and Peru

Inter-island migration

Fidji Islands   British dependencies

Map 14 The Australian colonies and their expansion to the 1850s (source: A. N. Porter (ed.) 1994. *Atlas of British Overseas Expansion*, Routledge, London).

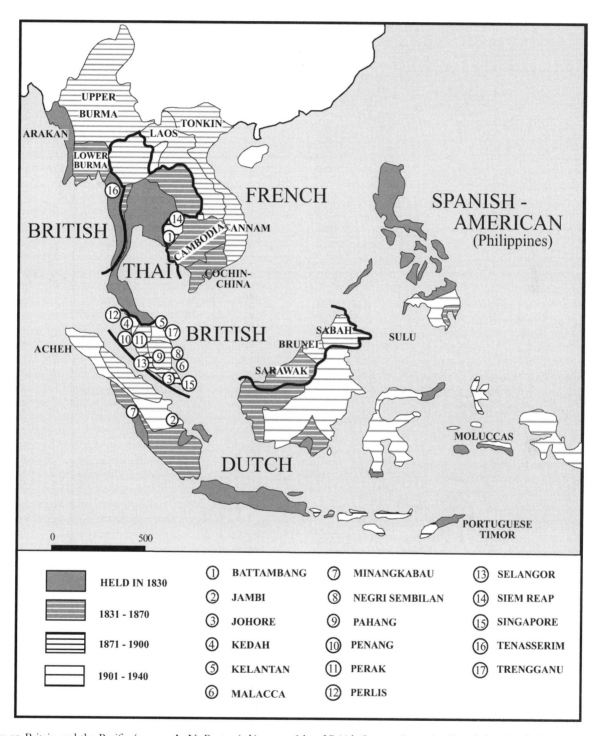

Map 15 Britain and the Pacific (source: A. N. Porter (ed.) 1994. *Atlas of British Overseas Expansion*, Routledge, London).

The map legend reads:

HELD IN 1830
1831 - 1870
1871 - 1900
1901 - 1940

① BATTAMBANG
② JAMBI
③ JOHORE
④ KEDAH
⑤ KELANTAN
⑥ MALACCA
⑦ MINANGKABAU
⑧ NEGRI SEMBILAN
⑨ PAHANG
⑩ PENANG
⑪ PERAK
⑫ PERLIS
⑬ SELANGOR
⑭ SIEM REAP
⑮ SINGAPORE
⑯ TENASSERIM
⑰ TRENGGANU

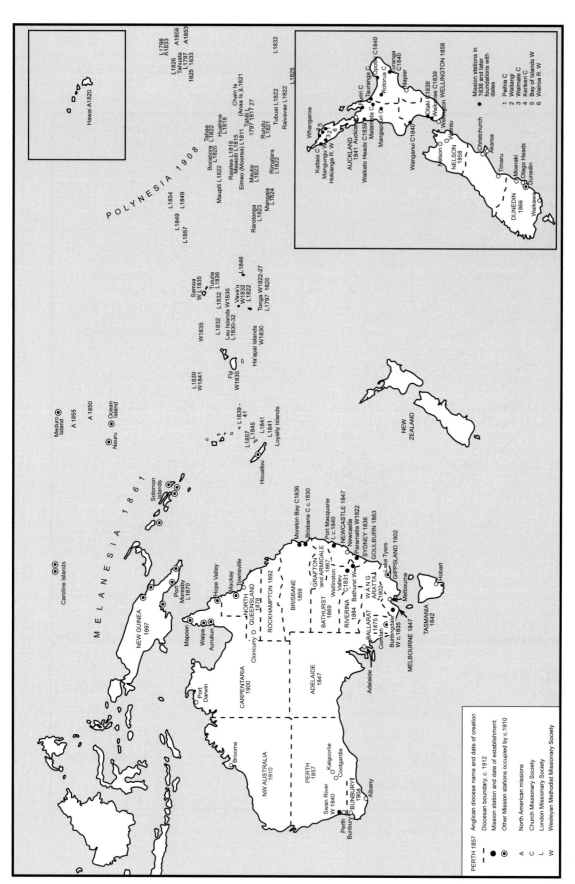

Map 16 Protestant missionary expansion in Australasia and the Pacific to 1914 (source: A. N. Porter (ed.) 1994. *Atlas of British Overseas Expansion*, Routledge, London).

Notes:

a Since the collection of economic and demographic statistics did not begin in the Islands until the mid-twentieth century, we cannot include the islands in the statistical appendix to this chapter.

b The first census in Papua New Guinea, for example, was conducted only in the 1960s; no census was conducted in Irian Jaya during the Dutch era; and economists have not yet discovered how to attribute values to trade and exchange in a non-monetary economy.

INDEX

INDEX

PLATES

Plate 1 Invention of the telephone and its incorporation into domestic life.

Plate 2 A shipload of emigrants setting off for America, 1898.

Plate 3 Engraving, a cane sugar mill (Antilles).

Plate 4 Arnaldo Ferraguti, *The Immigrants.*

Plate 5 Engraving, Russian Peasants (A. Wahlen), nineteenth century (Russia).

Plate 6 Advertisement for a typewriter, nineteenth century.

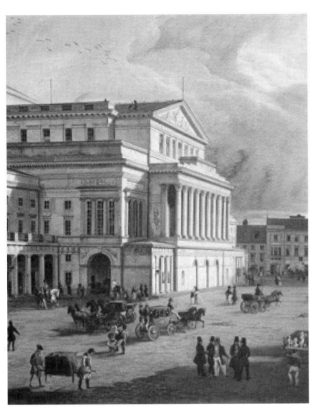

Plate 7 Plaza del Teatro, Warsaw (Poland).

Plate 9 Portrait of Adam Smith, British economist (England).

Plate 8 Modernisation and economic development, 1868, Japan.

Plate 10 Foundry installed near a coal mine.

Plate 12 Zona, *Allegory of the Telegraph*, 1898.

Plate 11 Karl Benz and his assistant in the model patented in 1886.

Plate 13 Equipment to transmit messages by short or long electric signals using an alphabet of dots and dashes created by Samuel Morse.

Plate 15 Advertising poster for Peugeot cars 1892 (France).

Plate 14 The Battleship Hildebrand, Imperial Navy of Germany (source: COVER).

Plate 16 The Bank of England and the London Stock Exchange (England).

Plate 17 A five dollar bill – 1877 (USA) (source: COVER).

Plate 18 The Bank of England.

Plate 19 Lionel Rothschild, the first Jewish Member of Parliament in 1858 (England).

Plate 20 London Stock Market (England) (source: COVER).

Plate 21 Manchester, 1880 (England).

Plate 22 Central Telegraph Office, Manhattan (USA).

Plate 23 Great Eastern repairing the first cable laid in 1858.

Plate 25 Fuller Flatiron Building built in 1902, New York (USA).

Plate 24 The Bessemer converter invented by Henry Bessemer, English industrialist, England (source: CORBIS).

Plate 26 John D. Rockefeller (source: CORBIS).

Plate 28 A Japanese woman choosing fabric to make kimonos (Japan) (source: COVER).

Plate 27 Facade of the Bourse de Commerce in Paris (France).

Plate 29 A cartoon alluding to the American 'antitrust' legislation against the creation of monopolies.

Plate 30 Slum in Newcastle, England, ca. 1880 (England) (source: COVER).

Plate 32 Federico Rossano, *The Harvest* (detail).

Plate 31 Justus von Liebig German chemist, Gliessen, woodcut, 1845 (source: COVER).

Plate 33 Erecting Vines at a French Vineyard (France) (source: COVER).

Plate 34 Poster by Van Caspel for '*Whoogenstraaten & Co.*' (source: COVER).

Plate 35 Newspapers being distributed in a Danish city, nineteenth century (Denmark).

Plate 36 *The Black Village* by Belgian artist Constantin Meunier (1831–1905) (Belgium).

Plate 37 The Working Army, by Luigi Rossi, 1895.

Plate 38 Peasants loading a hay cart, take a break for lunch.

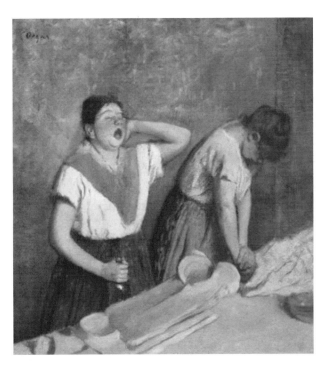

Plate 39 The Pressers, by Edgar Degas, c. 1890, Musée d'Orsay Paris
(France) (source: COVER).

Plate 40 Tuscan girls weaving raffia into hats by Fabbi.

Plate 41 Family of a shoemaker in his workshop.

Plate 42 Machinists working on the looms in an English textile factory, 1874 (England).

Plate 43 Torching of the Royal Arsenal, Paris 24th February 1848, by E. Hagnauer (France).

Plate 44 The Vienna riots in 1848, picture by Goebel (Austria).

Plate 45 Poster for the International Socialists Trade Union Congress of 1896, by Walter Crane 47 The Battle hymn of the Republic dedicated "to the workers" by the French Republic, 1848 (France) (source: COVER).

Plate 46 Poster by Jules Cheret for a Charity Benefit for the *Societe de Secours aux Familles des Marins naufrages*, 1890 (source: COVER).

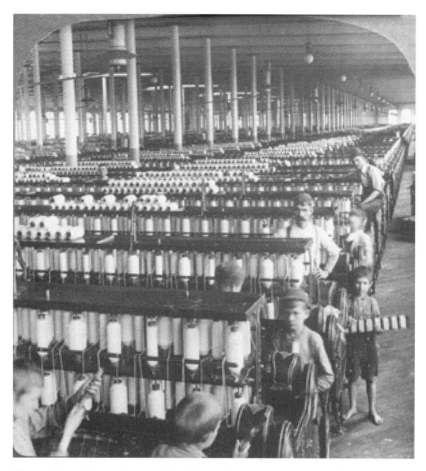

Plate 47 Great Britain, pioneer of the industrial economy introduced safety measures for female and child labourers (England).

Plate 48 Women in a factory, canning oysters, 1893 (source: COVER).

Plate 49 Poster for the central union of French agricultural workers, beginning of the 20th century (France).

Plate 50 Robert Owen, founder of a residential estate for the workers at his textile factory in Scotland (UK).

Plate 51 Karl Marx, photographed in 1875 (Germany).

Plate 52 Bombay in the early twentieth century (India).

Plate 53 Dance of the Chohos, engraving nineteenth century.

Plate 54 Portrait of Robert Fulton.

Plate 55 Railroad workers gather in Promontory, Utah, to celebrate the completion of the first Transcontinental Railway, May 10, 1869.

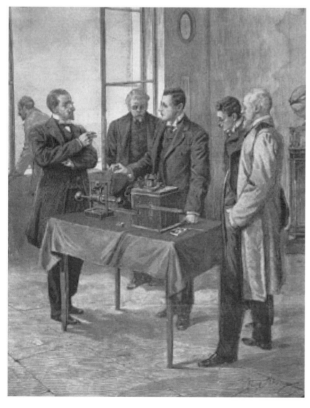

Plate 56 Guglielmo Marconi, inventor of the wireless telegraph, an illustration by Beltrame, 1899.

Plate 57 The telephone, one of its earliest models.

Plate 58 Black workers panning gold from sand in an African river, watched over by a guard with a whip (South-America) (source: COVER).

Plate 59 Mining crew drifting for gold below discovery point in Deadwood, Dakota Territory, photograph, S. J. Morrow, c.a, 1876 (USA).

Plate 60 Portrait of William Godwin, British sociologist and novelist (England).

Plate 61 William Gladstone, 1880 (England).

Plate 62 Napolean III receiving Chinese ambassadors in Fontainbleu (France).

Plate 63 Portrait of Jean Baptiste Leon Say (1826–1896), French economist and statesman (France).

Plate 64 Georg Friedrich List (1789–1846), American economist (USA) (source: COVER).

Plate 65 President Abraham Lincoln visiting soldiers encamped at the Civil War battlefield of Antietam in Maryland, 1st October 1862 (USA).

Plate 66 Women in fashionable dress with umbrella, Leipzig 1870
(Germany).

Plate 67 The Franco-Prussian war.

Plate 68 A barricade at the Porte Maillot, during the Paris Commune, May 1871 (France).

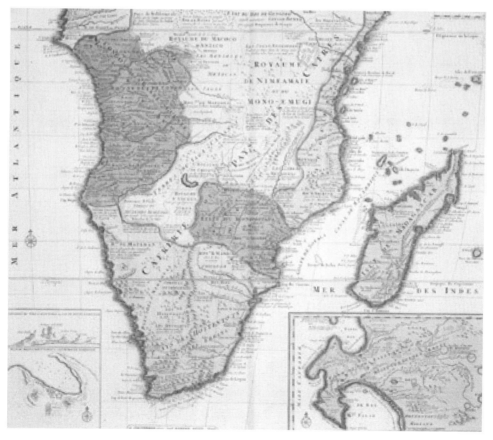

Plate 69 Map of Southern Africa 1790–1800.

Plate 70 This huge pit is all that remains from the first diamond mine in South Africa 1800s.

Plate 71 Benjamin Disraeil, portrait by J. E. Millais (England).

Plate 72 Charles 10th of France entering the church of Notre Dame.

Plate 73 Pademba Road in Freetown, 1856, Sierra Leone.

Plate 74 The ivory trade grew into a thriving business in Zanzibar, second only to the slave trade (Zanzibar).

Plate 75 Abd el-Kader (1808–1838), Algeria.

Plate 76 Portrait of Ferdinand-Marie of Lesseps, by Gabriel Lepaule.

Plate 77 Suez Canal, 1869.

Plate 78 Battle of Isandhlwana in 1879 during the Anglo-Boer War, by an unknown picture.

Plate 80 Sir Henry Bartle Edward Frere, British minister in India, Caricature by Spy (Vanity Fair-Men of the Day no. 68-pub. 1873).

Plate 79 English mounted fusiliers in South Africa, a print, nineteenth century.

Plate 81 Fighting in the Boer War, British soldiers of the Royal Munster Fusiliers shoot from behind sandbags at Honey Kloof, ac. 1900, South Africa (source: COVER).

Plate 83 René Caillé, French explorers (France).

Plate 82 The Scotsman, Mungo Park was the first European to discover Nigeria.

Plate 84 The frontispiece of *The Life and Explorations of Dr. Livingstone*.

Plate 85 Heinrich Barth, German explorer.

Plate 87 A French Colonial Army camp, nineteenth century.

Plate 86 The wedding of Leopold I of Belgium, with Louise Marie of Orléans, 1832.

Plate 88 An exchange of goods between a European with a colonial chest, and a Congolese, around 1900 (Africa).

Plate 89 Portrait of French politician Jules Ferry 1832–1893, collection, Felix Potin, Photograph, ca. 1880s (source: COVER).

Plate 90 British cavalry in the Battle of Omdurman, 1898.

Plate 91 In early California, Chinese immigrants were recruited to work on the railroads (USA) (source: COVER).

Plate 92 The Evil of Opium Smoking–Chinese, opium traders examine blocks of the substance for quality (China).

Plate 93 Cultivation of tea, watercolour on rice paper (China).

Plate 94 Indigenous Indians watering their crop (India).

Plate 95 Communal rice planting, from the series "Famous Views of the Fifty three stations" (Japan).

Plate 96 View of Foreigners in the Trading Compound of Yokohama by Utagawa Sadahide (Japan).

Plate 97 A Japanese fashion illustration, nineteenth century (Japan).

Plate 98 A Japanese print (Japan).

Plate 99 Japanese troops entering Seoul, Korea, 1894.

Plate 100 Japanese porcelain bottle with floral decoration for sake, nineteenth century (Japan).

Plate 101 The phonograph, invented by Thomas Edison, 1877.

Plate 102 Robert Malthus (1766–1834) English economist, engraving by John Linnell (England) (source: COVER).

Plate 103 Cheapside in London, 1986 (England) (source: COVER).

Plate 104 Engraving of James Watt in his Laboratory (England) (source: COVER).

Plate 105 Engraving of a plan of Watt's steam engine (England) (source: COVER).

Plate 106 Crampton Locomotive on the Strasbourg Line, 1849 (source: COVER).

Plate 107 A steam engine with its wagon of fuel (source: UNESCO Library).

Plate 108 Work in a forge, Zanardelli drawing (source: IGDA).

Plate 109 Shutter and lens of a daguerro type Camera, ca. 1840 (source: COVER).

Plate 110 In 1856 Henry Bessemer transformed techniques of steel production with his eponymous converter which blew air directly over the cast iron.

Plate 111 836 Colt Texas Paterson Revolver (source: COVER).

Plate 112 Eiffel Tower, 31 October 1888 – from Le monde illustre,
10 novembreb – (France) (source: UNESCO).

Plate 113 Humphrey Davy, British chemist, in his laboratory (source: UNESCO).

Plate 114 An early Edison Swan lamp and a contemporary value, 1954.

Plate 115 Sir William Henry Perkin (1838–1907), English chemist, ca. 1901 (France).

Plate 116 Tsar Nicolas opened the telegraph line between Saint Petersburgh and Warsaw (Russia) (source: UNESCO Library).

Plate 117 Michael Faraday (1791–1867) English Chemist and Physicist (England) (source: COVER).

Plate 118 An American tractor powered by a Ford internal combustion engine (USA).

Plate 119 Engraving Thomas Alva Edison, with his most popular invention, the phonograph (source: UNESCO Library).

Plate 120 Ernst von Siemens (1816–1892), Engineer.

Plate 122 Inauguration of the first telephone line between New York and Chicago by Alexander Graham Bell (USA)

Plate 121 Frederick W. Taylor (1856–1915), American engineer and economist (USA)

Plate 123 Great Britain introduce convertible agriculture and lightweight iron ploughs, steam-powered threshing machines, and mechanical harvesters, beginning of the nineteenth century (England).

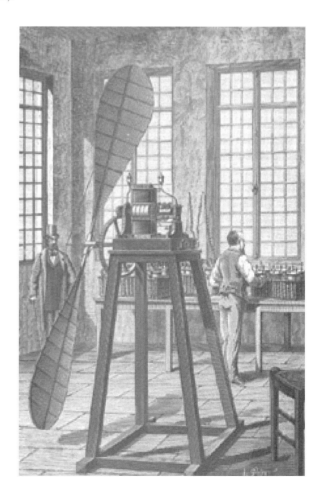

Plate 124 Engraving of an early experiment with a Siemens electric motor and a propeller, 1885 (source: COVER).

Plate 125 Five men make butter in a class at the Hampton Institute in Virginia (USA) (source: COVER).

Plate 126 The Potato Planters, by Jean François Millet.

Plate 127 Richard Cobden, ca. 1860, English Economist and Politician (England) (source: COVER).

Plate 129 Michael Faraday (1791–1867), (England) (source: IGDA).

Plate 128 Using models of celestial spheres astronomers studied movement of stars irrespective of their distance.

Plate 130 Advertising poster for a gas company.

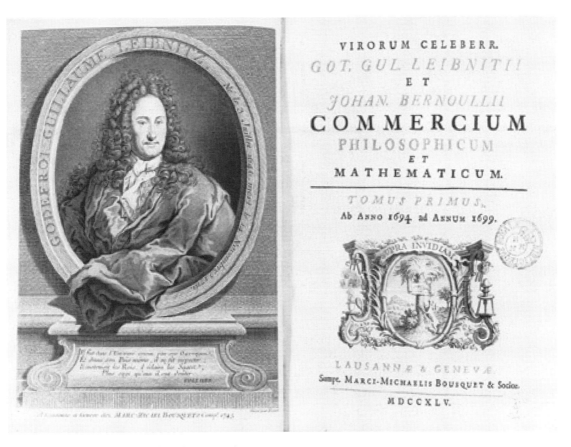

Plate 131 Gottfried Wilhelm Leibniz (1646–1716).

Plate 132 Rene Descartes considered the father of modern philosophy (France).

Plate 133 The Papaya plant and fruit: A hand coloured print of papaya (ca. 1800–1899) (source: COVER).

Plate 134 Portrait of Cartesio.

Plate 135 Interior of Theatre des Italiens in Paris, France, ca. 1851 (source: COVER).

Plate 136 Thomas Hobbes (1588–1679).

Plate 137 Brother Luca Pacioli (1445–1510).

Plate 138 A chess set with pieces made by German company of Weischaubt & Suhne, 1850 (source: COVER).

Plate 139 Sigmund Freud (1856–1939) (source: COVER).

Plate 140 Student accommodation at Harvard University in Massachussetts, 1879, (USA) (source: COVER).

Plate 141 Sigmund Freud, ca. 1935, in his studio in Vienna (Austria) (source: COVER).

Plate 142 A wall paper designed by William Morris, 1870 (source: COVER).

Plate 143 Joseph Ernest Renan (1823–1892), French philosopher, philologist and historian (France) (source: COVER).

Plate 145 Immanuel Kant, German philosopher in his study (Germany) (source: COVER).

Plate 144 Portrait of Karl Frederick Gauss (1777–1855), famed mathematician (source: COVER).

Plate 146 Lazare Carnot, French politician and scientist exiled for his revolutionary activities during the Napoleanic restoration (France) (source: IGDA).

Plate 147 Julius Robert Oppenheimer (1904–1967), American physicist (USA) (source: COVER).

Plate 149 Victorian letterbox, England, ca. 1960–1994 (source: COVER).

Plate 148 A four wheeled Otto cycle, invented by the German scientist Nikolaus August Otto (1832–1891), (Germany) (source: COVER).

Plate 150 Henri Poincaré (1854–1912), French mathematician and astronomer (France) (source: COVER).

Plate 151 Pierre Simon, Marquis of Laplace (1749–1827), French astronomer and mathematician (France) (source: COVER).

Plate 152 Yellow Chrysanthemum, an illustration end of nineteenth century (source: COVER).

Plate 153 Niels Bohr, Nobel Prize winner (source: IGDA).

Plate 155 A 19th century print by F. Gerhard, The Interior of a light filled room, nineteenth century (source: COVER).

Plate 154 Clifton Suspension Bridge in Bristol (England) (source: COVER).

Plate 156 Ernest Rutherford and Hans Wilhelm Geiger at Schuster, Laboratory (source: COVER).

Plate 157 Jons Jacob Berzelius (1779–1848), Swedish chemist (source: COVER).

Plate 158 Red Chilli Peppers, ca. 1800–1899 (source: COVER).

Plate 159 James Prescott Joule (1818–1889), British physicist (source: COVER).

Plate 160 Hendrick Antoon Lorentz (1853–1928), Dutch physicist
(source: COVER).

Plate 161 Max Planck (1858–1947), German physicist (source: COVER).

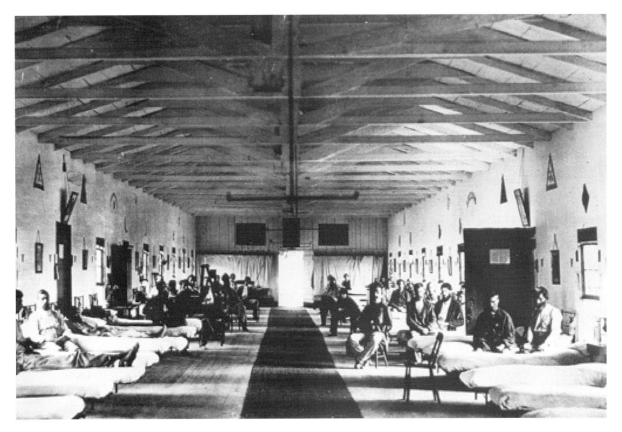

Plate 162 A hospital in Washington, around 1865 (USA) (source: IGDA).

Plate 163 Portrait of Johann Wolfgang von Goethe (1749–1832),
by William Pitt (source: IGDA).

Plate 164 Canadian Doctor William Osler giving a Pathological Seminar in the Old Blockley Laboratory in Baltimore, in 1887. Far left, Charles Walter; with derby, Dr. Mills; shorter man with derby, Dr. Osler; directly in back of Osler, Dr. Ashton; to the right of Osler, Dr. Eshner; to the right of Eshner, Amelia Gilman; to the far right, Kahn (?). From Miss Roberta West's photograph now in possession of Dr. John Croskey (source: COVER).

Plate 165 Ignaz Philipp Semmelweis, a Hungarian doctor who worked in an obstetrics clinic in Vienna (source: COVER).

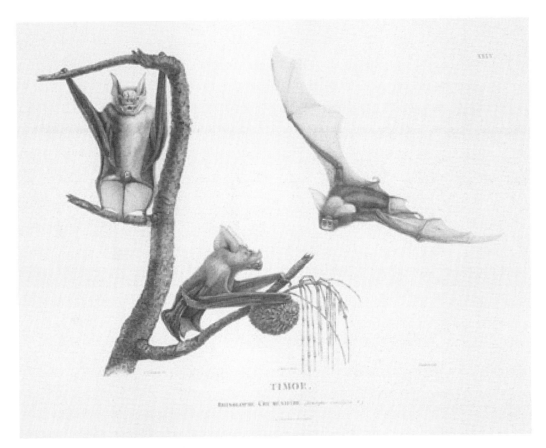

Plate 166 Giant bats from Timor, early nineteenth century (source: COVER).

Plate 167 Louis Pasteur (1822–1895), French chemist and biologist by Albert Edelfelt (source: IGDA).

Plate 168 Louis Pasteur in his laboratory (source: IGDA).

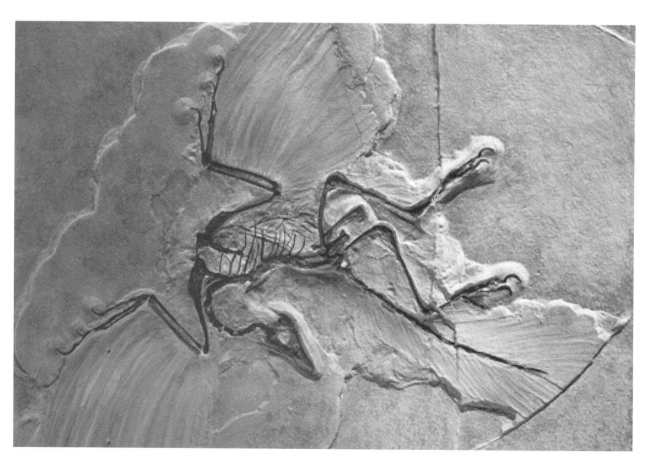

Plate 169 Specimen of Archaeopteryx Casting of Archaeopteryx, the oldest known bird, Berlin (Original fossil located at Humboldt University, Berlin) (source: COVER).

Plate 170 From top to bottom, a long eared owl, a common eagle, and a pelican (illustrations by Robert Hawell, c. 1830) (source: COVER).

Plate 172 The crew of Charles Darwin's ship, the Beagle fishing for sharks (source: COVER).

Plate 171 Charles Robert Darwin, naturalist, in his middle age. (Photo circa 1854) (source: COVER).

Plate 173 Thomas Henry Huxley (1825–1895), the biologist in old age (source: COVER).

Plate 174 Jean Baptiste Pierre Antoine de Monet Lamarck
(1744–1829) French naturalist (France) (source: COVER).

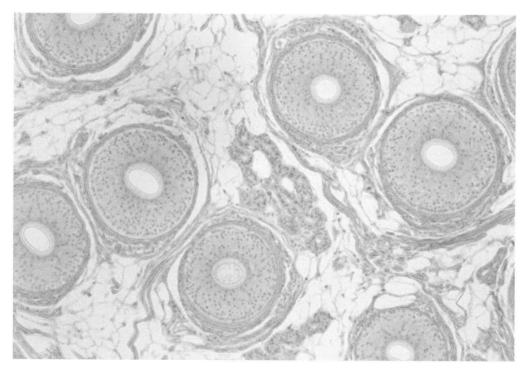

Plate 175 Human Scalp and hair Shafts (source: COVER).

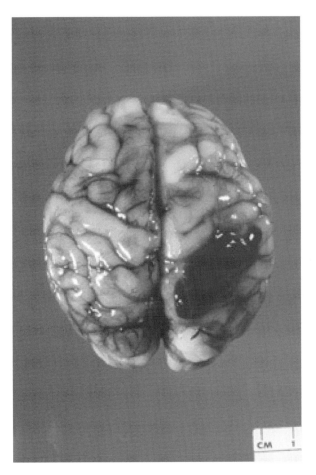

Plate 176 Human brain (source: COVER).

Plate 177 Gregor Johann Mendel (1822–1884), an Austrian monk (source: IGDA).

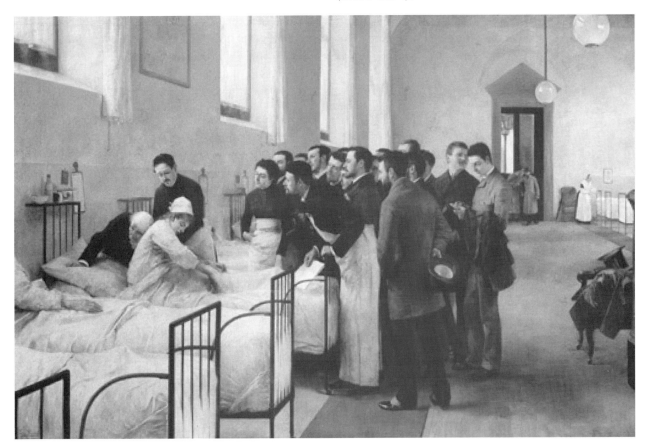

Plate 178 Hospital Visit by Manuel Jiménez Prieto.

Plate 179 Interior of an English hospital in the nineteenth century (England) (source: IGDA).

Plate 180 Robert Koch at the microscope (Germany) (source: IGDA).

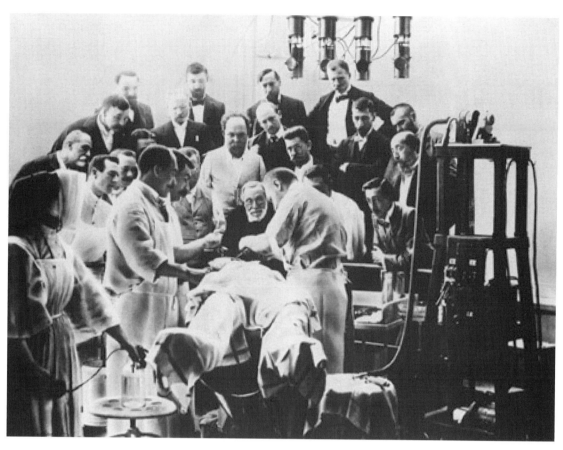

Plate 181 Rudolf Virchow, German pathologist and physiologist in the centre with beard and glasses observing brain surgery at the Sorbonne, Paris in 1900, (France) (source: COVER).

Plate 182 Claude Bernard (1813–1878), French physiologist (source: COVER)

Plate 183 Ivan Petrovitch Pavlov, Russian physiologist (source: IGDA).

Plate 184 Paul Ehrlich, German Doctor (source: IGDA).

Plate 185 Joseph Lister, surgeon and professor (source: UNESCO).

Plate 186 A radiotherapist treats a patient using Rontgen rays, ca. 1916 (source: COVER).

Plate 187 Women gathering medicinal Herbs, Japanese wood-block, by Eisen (source: COVER).

Plate 188 Sun Yat Sen (1867–1925), Chinese revolutionary (China) (source: COVER).

Plate 189 Commodore Matthew Perry (1794–1858) meeting the royal commissioner at Yokahama, 1853 (undated painting) (Japan) (source: COVER).

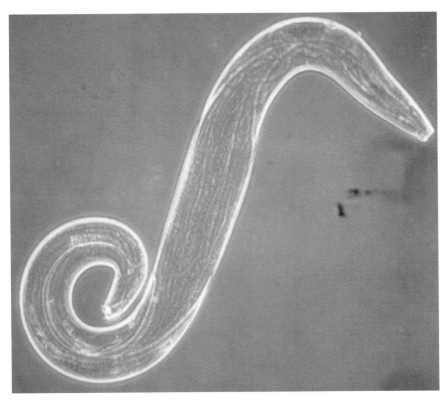

Plate 190 Plasmodium falciparum, the parasite which causes malaria (source: COVER).

Plate 191 William Crawford Gorgas (1854–1920) American army surgeon (source: COVER).

Plate 192 Plague Scene, painted by Théodore Géricault (source: IGDA).

Plate 193 Florence Nightingale, with her sister Frances Parthenope
(source: IGDA).

Plate 194 Emil von Behring (1854–1917) German physiologist (source: COVER).

Plate 195 Charles Darwin (1809–1882) in his later years, 1869 (England) (source: COVER).

Plate 197 Jean-Jacques Rousseau, French encyclopaedist (France) (source: IGDA).

Plate 196 Voltaire, in the Bastille Prison, by François Marie Arouet (source: IGDA).

Plate 198 Portrait of Immanuel Kant (1724–1804) German philosopher, by Hans von Schnorr (source: COVER).

Plate 199 Corot's Studio by J. B. Camile Corot (source: COVER).

Plate 200 Friedrich Schelling, German philosopher (source: IGDA).

Plate 201 Arthur Schopenhauer, German philosopher (source: IGDA).

Plate 202 *Medusa's Pool* by Géricault (source: IGDA).

Plate 203 Henri Bergson, French philosopher and academic (source: IGDA).

Plate 204 Friedrich Nietzsche, painted by Edward Munch (source: IGDA).

Plate 205 Sören Kierkegaard (1813–1855), Danish philosopher (source: COVER).

Plate 206 Isidore Auguste Marie Francois Xavier Comte (1798–1857), French philosopher, ca. 1845.

Plate 207 A Cereus in Bloom, German Print, nineteenth century (Germany) (source: COVER).

Plate 208 A Woman reads to Queen Victoria, Queen of England, as she knits (England) (source: COVER).

Plate 209 Herbert Spencer, positivist (source: COVER).

Plate 210 Engraving Jeremy Bentham, English philosopher (source: COVER).

Plate 211 Mikhail Bakunin, Russian revolutionary (source: IGDA).

Plate 212 Portrait of Karl Marx by Zhang Wun (source: IGDA).

Plate 213 Prince Peter Kropotkin (1842–1921), Russian geographer, sociologist and revolutionary (source: COVER).

Plate 214 Lajos Kosshut, Hungarian patriot (source: IGDA).

Plate 215 Giuseppe Mazzini, Italian politician and writer (source: IGDA).

Plate 216 Thomas Carlyle, English historian and philosopher (source: IGDA).

Abgeordneter Dr. v. Sybel. Nach Photographie.

Plate 217 Heinrich von Sybel, (1817–1895) German historian and politician.

Plate 219 Ahmad Riza, member of the "Young Turks" (source: COVER).

Plate 218 Simon Bolivar, Venezuelan leader (source: IGDA).

Plate 220 A tea store, from Chinese manuscript, nineteenth century (China) (source: IGDA).

Plate 221 Life in the Harem, (Cairo) by John Frederick Lewis (source: COVER).

Plate 222 The Koran of Cairo, written in Moroccan Arabic script (source: COVER).

Plate 223 Nineteenth century Burmese statue of Buddha carved in wood and finished with gold leaf (Myanmar) (source: IGDA).

Plate 224 Aftermath, from Hand to Hand Battle at Sepoy (India) (source: COVER).

Plate 225 Modern Landscape, a print by Utagawa Hiroshige III, from the series "Famous Places on the Tokaido: a record of the process of reform" (Japan) (source: COVER).

Plate 226 Rabindranath Tagore, Indian writer and philosopher (India) (source: IGDA).

Plate 227 Title page of Charles Darwin's The Origin of Species (England) (source: COVER).

Plate 228 Portrait of Emile Durkheim, French professor and philosopher (source: COVER).

Plate 229 The Vatican Council of 1869–70, the opening ceremony (Italy) (source: IGDA).

Plate 230 Ernst Mach (1838–1916), Austrian philosopher and scientist (source: COVER).

Plate 231 The Scream, by Edvard Munch, 1893 (Norway) (source: COVER).

Plate 232 William James (1842–1910), American professor and psychologist (source: COVER).

Plate 233 Friedrich W. Nietzsche (1844–1900), German philosopher (source: COVER).

Plate 234 Artur Schopenhauer (1788–1860), philosopher.

Plate 235 A scene of domestic life, France, ca. 1870 (source: COVER).

Plate 236 Henry Louis Bergson (1859–1941), French philosopher (source: COVER).

Plate 237 Niels Bohr as young man (source: COVER).

Plate 238 Albert Einstein, German physicist (source: IGDA).

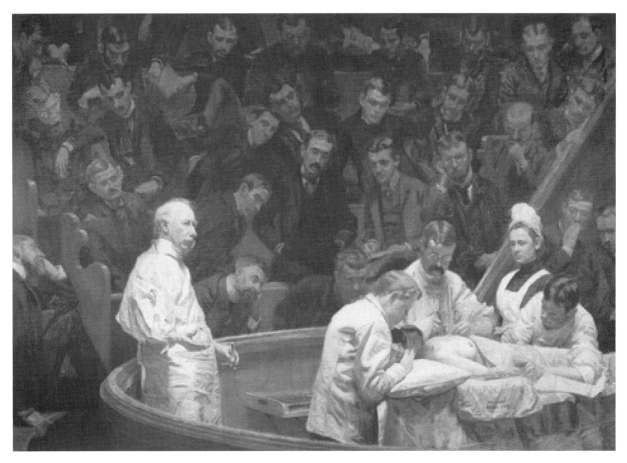

Plate 239 Agnew Clinique, by Thomas Eakins (1889) (source: COVER).

Plate 240 Court of Selim III (source: IGDA).

Plate 241 Students at Edinburgh's Ragged School in a lesson with Reverend Thomas Guthrie, ca 1850 (source: COVER).

Plate 242 Sir Richard Francis Burton, English explorer, orientalist, and writer (source: COVER).

Plate 243 A class room in a school, Washington D. C. ca. 1899 (USA) (source: COVER).

Plate 244 The Country School by Winslow Homer, 1871 (USA) (source: COVER).

Plate 245 John Dewey, the American psychologist (source: COVER).

Plate 246 The Mott street Industrial School, New York, 1885 (USA) (source: COVER).

Plate 247 The Faculty of Engineering at Berkeley founded in 1856 (USA) (source: IGDA).

Plate 248 A French boys school in the nineteenth century (France) (source: IGDA).

Plate 249 Thomas Arnold (1795–1842), English educationalist (England) (source: COVER).

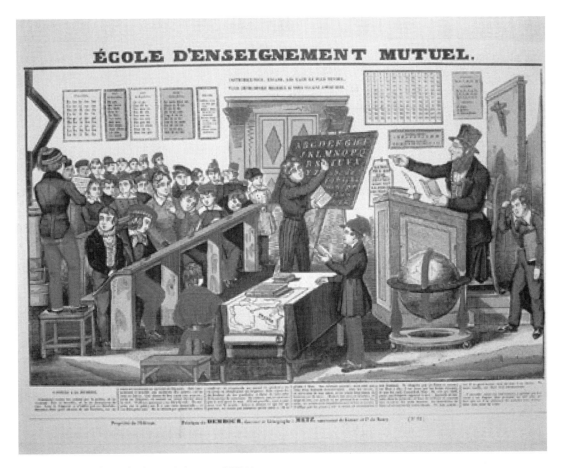

Plate 250 A French Lycée (France) (source: IGDA).

Plate 251 Engraving of a student at Harvard (USA) (source: IGDA).

Plate 252 Students at a Military School in the Ottoman Empire, 1893 (source: COVER).

Plate 253 L'Ecole Polytechnique (France) (source: UNESCO).

Plate 254 Claude-Louis Berthollet, French scientist (source: IGDA).

Plate 255 Portrait of Georges Léopold Cuvier, French naturalist (source: IGDA).

Plate 256 Alexander von Humboldt, German naturalist and geographer, 1803 (source: IGDA).

Plate 257 A Freshman's Ball at the University of Vienna, nineteenth century (Austria) (source: IGDA).

Plate 258 Hans Christian Oersted, Danish Physicist, 1819 (Denmark).

Plate 259 A Meeting of the College of Physicians in London, a Cartoon by T. Rowlandson, 1808 (England) (source: COVER).

Plate 260 William Siemens (1823–1883) German engineer and industrialist (source: COVER).

Plate 261 Engraving of Virgo from Celestial Atlas by Alexander Jamieson, 1822 (source: COVER).

Plate 262 Alfred Nobel (source: IGDA).

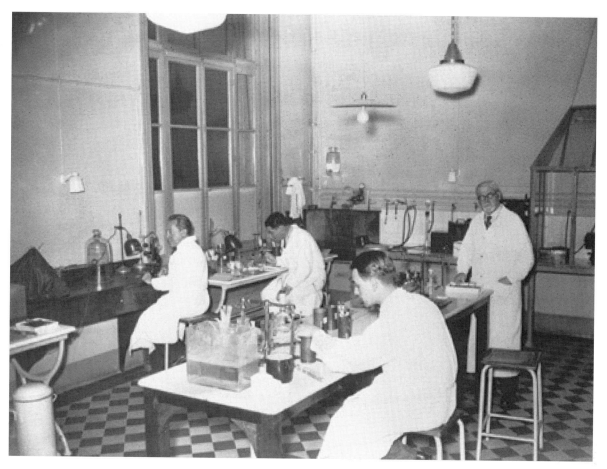

Plate 263 Scientists work in the laboratory at the Pasteur Institute in Paris (France) (source: COVER).

Plate 264 Benjamin Franklin, American politician, physicist and writer, eighteenth century (source: IGDA).

Plate 265 Andrew Carnegie (source: COVER).

Plate 266 Entrance Hall at Van Eetvelde House, 1897, Brussels (Belgium) (source: IGDA).

Plate 268 Camille Flammarion, French Physicist (1842–1925) (source: COVER).

Plate 267 Remington typewriter, 1878 (source: IGDA).

Plate 269 Widow of the French Astronomer, Camille Flammarion (source: COVER).

Plate 270 Samuel Taylor Coleridge, British poet (England) (source: COVER).

Plate 271 Sir Charles Lyell (1797–1875), Scottish Geologist (source: COVER).

Plate 272 "The great industrial exhibition of 1851, The British Nave" by Joseph Nash (England) (source: COVER).

Plate 273 Palm Houses in Kew Gardens, London, (England) (source: COVER).

Plate 274 Exposition Universelle Palais de l'optique, Poster by Georges Paul Leroux (source: COVER).

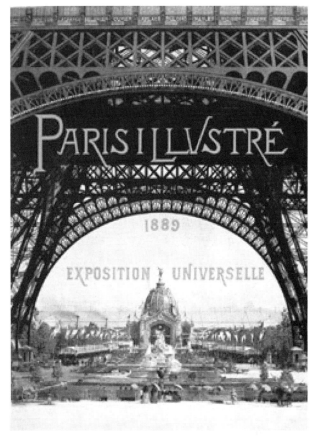

Plate 275 Poster for the 1889 World Exposition in Paris (France) (source: COVER).

Plate 277 Louis Agassiz (1807–1873) Swiss naturalist, ca. 1800s (source: COVER).

Plate 276 Asa Gray (1810–1888), American Botanist (source: COVER).

Plate 278 Sir Joseph Norman Lockyer (1836–1920), British astronomer (source: COVER).

Plate 279 Arearea, 1892, by Paul Gauigin.

Plate 280 An upper class bed room in a European house, nineteenth century (source: COVER).

Plate 281 Pair of Candelabra, ca.1850–1860 (source: COVER).

Plate 282 Hipolyte-Adolphe Taine (1828–93), French philosopher, historian and critic.

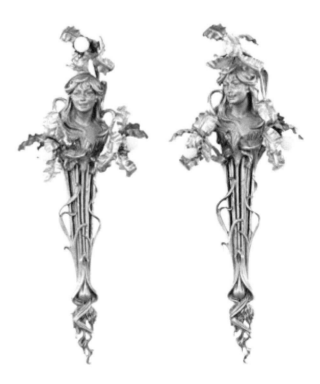

Plate 283 Decorative bronze lamps in the Art Nouveau style, early twentieth century.

Plate 284 Liberty Leading the People, 1830, by Eugene Delacroix (France) (source: COVER).

Plate 285 The Kiss, (1907–08), Gustav Klimt, Austrian painter.

Plate 286 John Ruskin (1819–1900) (England).

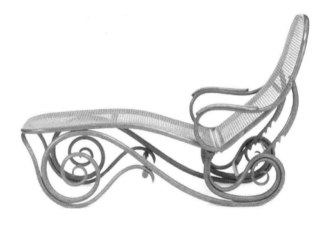

Plate 288 Chaise Longue, Michael Thonet (1796–1871), German furniture designer (source: COVER).

Plate 287 Statue of Liberty, (1874–1886), by Fréderic Auguste Bartholdi (USA) (source: COVER).

Plate 289 A chair by Charles Rennie Mackintosh (1868–1928), Scottish exponent of Art nouveau.

Plate 290 Glyptothek Art Museum in Konigsplatz, Munich, 1846–70, by the German architect, Leo von Klenze.

Plate 291 The Tower of Big Ben in the city of London (England) (source: COVER).

Plate 292 Bust of Eugenie Fiocre, by Jean-Bapstiste Carpeaux (1827–1875), French sculptor and painter.

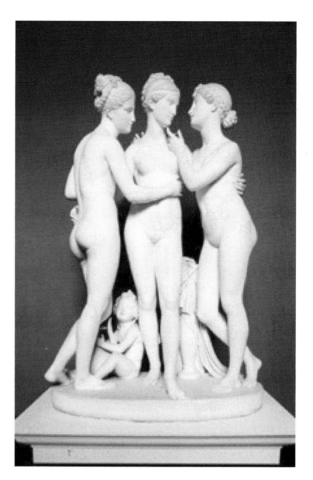

Plate 294 The Three Graces, by Bertel Thorvaldsen.

Plate 293 Cupid and Psyche by Antonio Canova (1757–1822).

Plate 295 The Eiffel Tower, Paris, 1887–1889, by Gustave Eiffel (France).

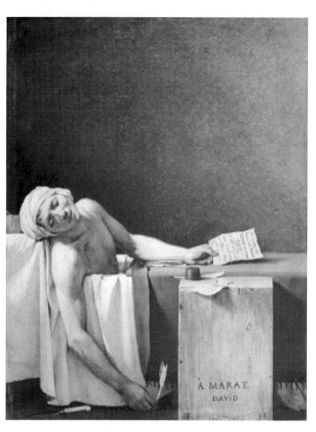

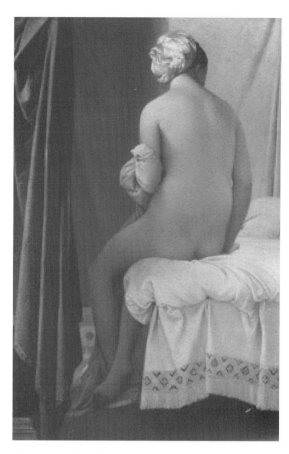

Plate 296 The Murder of Marat, 1793, by Jacques Louis David (France).

Plate 297 The Valpinçon Bather, 1808, by Jean Marie Joseph Ingres (France).

Plate 298 The Third of May, 1808: The Execution of the Defenders of Madrid, By Francisco de Goya (Spain).

Plate 299 Italy and Germany, 1811–1829 by Overbeck.

Plate 300 "L'Amata", by Dante Gabriel Rosetti (1828–1882).

Plate 301 Ludwig van Beethoven (1770–1827), German composer.

Plate 302 Poster for the opera *Tosca*, by the Italian composer Giacomo Puccini (1858–1924).

Plate 304 Portrait of Karl Maria von Weber (1786–1826), German composer.

Plate 303 Poster for the opera *The Damnation of Faust*, by Hector Berlioz (1803–1869), French composer.

Plate 305 Poster by the French designer, Jules Cheret.

Plate 306 Composers Johannes Brahms (1833–1897), German composer (left) with Johann Strauss (1825–1899), Austrian composer (right).

Plate 307 Portrait of the Italian composer Giuseppe Verdi (1813–1901), by Giovanni Boldini (1842–1931).

Plate 308 Staircase in the Hotel Tassel, rue Paul-Emile Janson, Brussels, 1893, by the architect Victor Horta (Belgium).

Plate 310 Little Dancer, Aged Fourteen, 1881, by Edgar Degas (France).

Plate 309 A detail of one of the towers of the Sagrada Familia (below) and a detail of the entrance to Park Gell (centre), in Barcelona, both by architect Antonio Gaudi (1852–1926) (Spain) (source: COVER).

Plate 311 The Kiss, 1886, Auguste Rodin (France).

Plate 312   Moulin de la Galette, 1876, by Pierre Auguste Renoir (France).

Plate 313   The Star, 1878, by Edgar Degas (France).

Plate 314 *The Cardplayers*, by Paul Cezanne (1890–1895) (France).

Plate 315 *The Cot, 1872*, by Berthe Morisot (France).

Plate 316 *Selfportrait, 1888*, Vincent van Gogh.

Plate 317   A Sunday Afternoon on the Island of La Grande Jatte, 1884, by Georges Seurat (France).

Plate 318   The Prioress' Tale, by Sir Edward Coley Burne-Jones.

Plate 319 George Sand (1804–1876), the French writer.

Plate 320 Art Nouveau table lamp, by Louis Majorelle (1859–1926), glass designed by Antonio Daum (1864–1930) (France).

Plate 322 Cover illustration of the programme of the Russian Ballet to the music of "l'apres-midi d'un faune", composed by Claude A. Debussy.

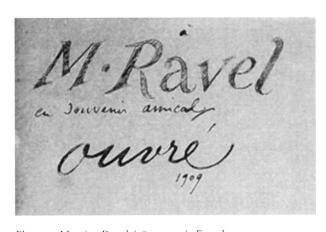

Plate 321 Maurice Ravel (1875–1937), French composer.

Plate 323 Jacob Grimm (1785–1863), German writer.

Plate 324 Lord Byron (1788–1824), British romantic poet.

Plate 326 Pamphlet by the French romantic writer Francois-René, Viscount of Chateaubriand (1768–1848) (France).

Plate 325 Madame de Staël (1766–1817), French writer.

Plate 327 Victor Hugo (1802–1885), French writer.

Plate 328 Stendhal (1783–1842), French writer.

Plate 330 A Magazine illustration of a scene from *The Three Musketeers* (France).

Plate 329 Portrait of Alessandro Manzoni (1785–1873), Italian writer by Francesco Hayez.

Plate 331 Franz Grillparzer (1791–1872), Austrian playwright.

Plate 332 Gustave Flaubert (1821–1880), French novelist.

Plate 334 Mark Twain (1835–1910), American writer.

Plate 333 The Bronte Sisters, (left to right) Anne, Emily and Charlotte, by Patrick Branwell (England).

Plate 335 Heinrich Heine (1797–1856), German poet.

Plate 336 The Traveller Above the Sea of Clouds by Friederich, 1818, German painter.

Plate 338 Giovanni Verga (1840–1922), Italian novelist and playwright.

GUY DE MAUPASSANT

Bel-Ami

Illustrations de
FERDINAND BAC

PARIS
PAUL OLLENDORFF, ÉDITEUR

Plate 337 Cover of a contemporary edition of the novel Bel Ami by Guy de Maupassant (1850–1893) (France).

Plate 339 Benito Pérez Galdos (1843–1920), Spanish writer.

Plate 340 Portrait of Henrik Ibsen (1828–1906), Norwegian playwright by Erik Werenskiold.

Plate 341 Poster for the play La figlia di Lorio (Daughter of Lorio) by Gabrielle D'Annunzio (1863–1938).

Plate 342 A reading with Anton Pavlovic Chekhov (1860–1904), Russian writer.

Plate 343 The Reading by Theo van Rysselbergh, 1903.

Plate 344 Divan Japonais by Henry de Toulouse-Lautrec (1864–1901) (France).

Plate 345 Oscar Wilde (1854–1900) Irish playwright.

Plate 346 Detail from A corner of the table by Henry Fantin-Latour (1836–1904).

Plate 347 Paul Verlaine and Jean Moréas (1856–1910) in a Poster
for the 7eme Exposition du salon des 100, December 1894.

Plate 348 Portrait of Paul Claudel (1868–1955), French poet.

Plate 349 Portrait of William Butler Yeats (1865–1939), Irish poet and play write by John Butler Yeats (1839–1922).

Plate 351 Thomas Stearns Eliot (1888–1965), Anglo-American poet.

Plate 350 Paul Adam (1862–1920), French writer, photographed by Domac.

Plate 352 Paul Valery, French poet by Blanche, 1913 (France).

Plate 353 Cover of a collection of sonnets by Maurice Maeterlink (1862–1949), Belgian writer.

Plate 354 Portrait of Marcel Proust (1871–1922) by J. E. Blanche.

Plate 355 Le Dejeuner sur l'Herbe by Edouard Manet (France).

Plate 356 Portrait of Pierre Joseph Proudhon and his son, French writer by Gustave Courbet, 1865.

Plate 357 Domingo Faustino Sarmiento, President of the Republic Argentine (1868–1874) (Argentina) (source: COVER).

Don Gabriel Garcia Moreno.

Plate 358 Engraving, Gabriel Garcia Moreno (1821–1875) (source: COVER).

Plate 359 Passengers on La Capital Traction and Electric Company line, as they pass through a town (source: COVER).

Plate 360 Estacion Constitucion, Buenos Aires (Argentina) (source: COVER).

Plate 361 Moneda Palace in Santiago de Chille (Chille).

Plate 362 Indigenous Mexicans, nineteenth century (Mexico).

Plate 363 Engraving, South American Indians, by Gallo Gallina, ca. 1823–1834 (source: COVER).

Plate 364 Ancient Peruvian Priest (Peru) (source: COVER).

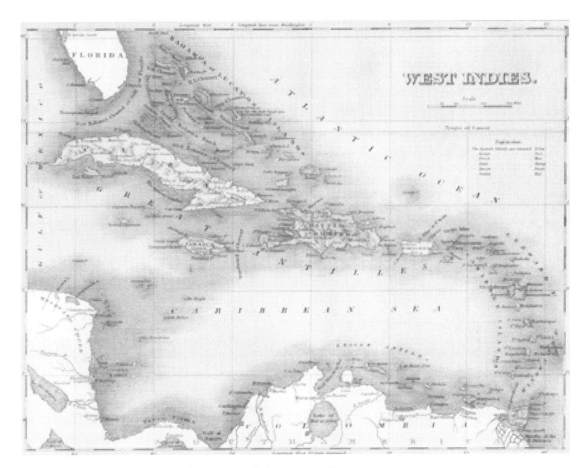

Plate 365 1826 Map of the West Indies (West Indies) (source: COVER).

Plate 366 Agostino Godazzi (1793–1859), Italian geographer.

Plate 367 Figures by a River, Lima Beyond by Johann Moritz Rugendas, 1843 (source: COVER).

Plate 368 José Maria Velasco (1840–1912) Mexican painter.

Plate 369 Peasant Man and Woman by Jose Agustin Arrieta, nineteenth century (Mexico) (source: COVER).

Plate 370 Ornate staircases in Palacio Postal, Mexico city's main post office (source: COVER).

A SIDI-BEL-ABBÉS — LE DRAPEAU DE LA LÉGION ÉTRANGÈRE DÉCORÉ DE LA LÉGION D'HONNEUR

Plate 371 Foreign Legion at Sidi-Bel-Abbes, 1906 (source: COVER).

Plate 372 Poster by Hugo d'Alesi, ca. 1900 (Tunisia) (source: COVER).

Plate 373 French soldiers in Algeria, 1880 (Algeria) (source: COVER).

Plate 374 Dusk on the Galata Bridge with the Yeni Valide Mosque in the Background, Istanbul by David Solomon (source: COVER).

Plate 375 Procession in Cairo's Main Square by Thomas Milton, ca. 1820 (Egypt) (source: COVER).

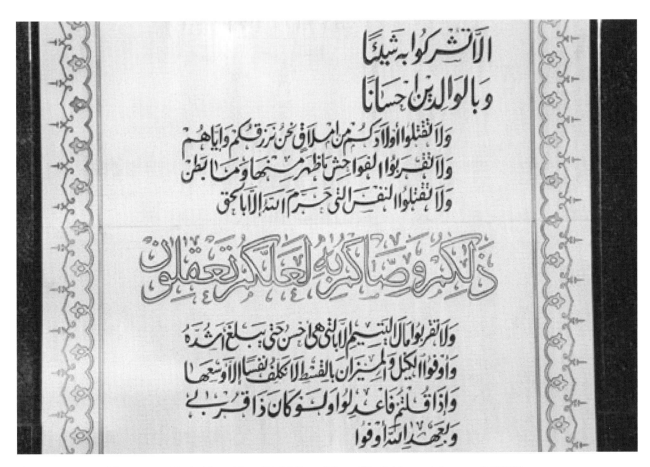

Plate 376 A page of the Koran with Arabic writing, (Abdel Raouf Hasan Khalil Museum) (source: COVER).

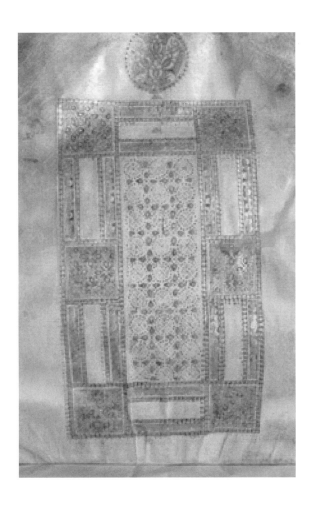

Plate 377 Page from the Koran (Iran) (source: COVER).

Plate 378 Portrait of Fath Ali Shah (1797–1834) (Iran) (source: COVER).

Plate 379 A Young Qajar Prince and his Entourage by Abu' l Hasan, 1860 (source: COVER).

Plate 380 The conquest of Sétif by General Galbois.

Plate 381 A Caféteria in Istanbul, 1850 (Turkey) (source: COVER).

Plate 382 Qajar period ceiling painting and Mosaicwork (Iran) (source: COVER).

Plate 383 Chinese Canton Mandarin porcelain Seats, nineteenth century (China) (source: COVER).

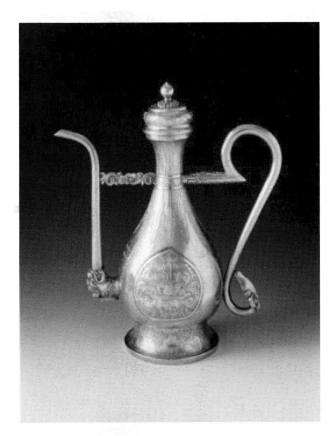

Plate 384 Gold ewer from the Imperial Summer Palace at Beijing, 1852 (China).

Plate 385 Detail from a tapestry, depicting a couple taking tea, eighteenth century (China).

Plate 386 Chinese porcelain vase, nineteenth century (China).

Plate 387 Detail from A Love Scene, Indian Kishangarh, ca. 1880 (India) (source: COVER).

Plate 388 Chattar Manzil Palace (1803–1827), Lucknow (India) (source: COVER).

Plate 389 Rabindranath Tagore, Indian poet (India) (source: COVER).

Plate 390 Ramakrishna (1836–1886), Hindu Saint like figure (India) (source: COVER).

Plate 391 Decorated hexagonal porcelain stool, from Canton (China) (source: COVER).

Plate 392 Statuette of a Court Lady, Qing Dynasty (China) (source: COVER).

Plate 393 A Chinese Couple Outside the Palace of the Moon by Totoya Hokkei, 1830–1839 (China) (source: COVER).

Plate 394 Walking Buddha, nineteenth century (Thailand) (source: COVER).

Plate 395 Wat Phra Kaeo with Colossi of Wirunhok 1782–1784, Grand Palace Bangkok (Thailand) (source: COVER).

Plate 396 Caparisoned Elephant (National Museum, Bangkok, Thailand) (source: COVER).

Plate 397 Detail of a Japanese porcelain vase, nineteenth century (Japan) (source: IGDA).

Plate 398 Engraving by Ando Hiroshige, 1857, from the series "One hundred Views of edo", Ohashi Bridge in the rain in Atake (Japan).

Plate 399 Japanese lacquered Boxes, nineteenth century (Japan) (source: IGDA).

Plate 400 Korean dresser, nineteenth century (Korea) (source: IGDA).

Plate 401 Japanese print, 1888 (Japan) (source: IGDA).

Plate 402 Japanese Fan, nineteenth century (Japan) (source: IGDA).

Plate 403 Japanese ceramic vase from Yokohama, Edo/Meiji period (Japan) (source: IGDA).

Plate 405 Western style stone houses in Tokyo from the series-Famous Places on the Tokaido, print by Utagawa Hiroshige (Japan) (source: COVER).

Plate 404 Women Soliciting Travellers in Goyu, by Utagawa Hiroshige from his famous series *The 53 stages of Tokaido* (Japan) (source: COVER).

Plate 406 A White Glazed Reticulated Brush Pot, Yi Dynasty, nineteenth century (source: COVER).

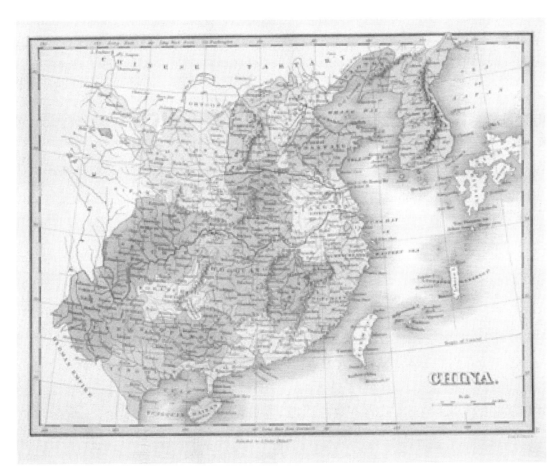

Plate 407 Map of China, 1826 (source: COVER).

Plate 408 Colonel Sato, Disguised as a Korean, Reconnoiters the Yalu Shore, by Migata Toshihide, 1895 (source: COVER).

Plate 409 Qing Dynasty ivory Head of a Bodhisattva (China) (source: COVER).

Plate 410 Icon of Our Saviour the Pantocrator from the Workshop of Pavel Ovchinnikow, 1881 (Russia) (source: COVER).

Plate 411 The Boston rebellion (USA) (source: IGDA).

Plate 412 Battle of Lexington, between colonial and British troops (USA) (source: IGDA).

Plate 413 Battle of Waterloo (source: IGDA).

Plate 414 Gregory XVI, pope from 1831–1846 (source: IGDA).

Plate 415 Mount Athos monastery (Greece) (source: IGDA).

Plate 416 An orthodox priest collecting offerings at the entrance of a church, 1858, by Amadeo Preziosi (source: COVER).

Plate 417 Group of orthodox Armenian priests, around 1870 (source: COVER).

Plate 418 Fyodor Mikhaylovich Dostoyevsky, Russian writer
(source: COVER).

Plate 419 "Priest and Women in Lima" by Collignon, Devilliers, 1848 (source: COVER).

Plate 420 Engraving, John Eliot (1604–1690), Apostle to the Indians, preaches to a group of Native Americans (Ballou's Pict. 1856) (source: COVER).

Plate 422 "Pretre de la Cote-d'or interrogeant le Destin" 1811 (Ghana) (source: COVER).

Plate 421 Agustin de Iturbide entering Mexico City (Mexico) (source: IGDA).

Plate 423 David Livingstone, Scottish explorer and missionary (source: IGDA).

Plate 424 Sir Henry Morton Stanley, English explorer (source: IGDA).

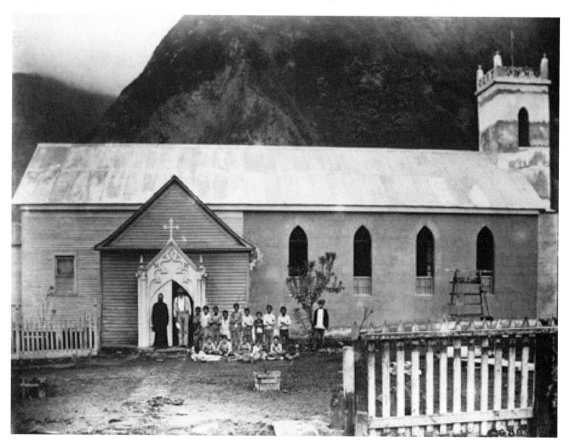

Plate 425 Father Damien (1840–1889) stands with patients outside his church on Molokai Island (source: COVER).

Plate 426 Portrait of Girls in a Missionary School, 1890, Lima (Peru) (source: COVER).

Plate 427 "Missionary on Sandwich Island" (source: COVER).

Plate 428 Postcard of a Christian Mission in Japan: preaching by means of banners, 1909 (Japan) (source: COVER).

Plate 429 A group of people attend a religious service in Nirchinska, 1885 (Russia) (source: COVER).

Plate 430 Abdel Kader, Algerian leader, proclaimed Emir of the Oranesado tribes, 1832 (Algeria) (source: IGDA).

Plate 431 Turkish tapestry, late eighteenth century (Turkey) (source: IGDA).

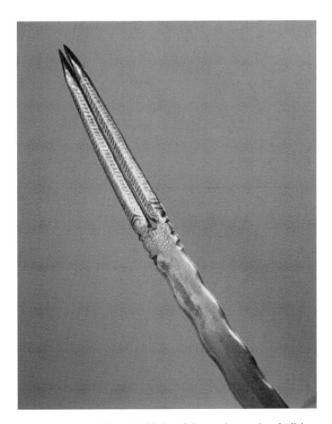

Plate 432 Detail of the split blade of the mythic spade of Allah.

Plate 433 A decorative relief from the Regent's Mosque in Shiraz (Iran).

Plate 434 The God Krishna and his favourite pastor, Radha (India) (source: COVER).

Plate 435 Railway and the increase in migration, Beltrame engraving for a newspaper.

Plate 436 Iron and Coal by Bell Scott.

Plate 437 Les Halles, the central power plant in Paris (France).

Plate 438 The Sirius, first steam-powered transatlantic crossing, 1838.

Plate 439 Saint-Germain station in Paris (France).

Plate 440 Harvesting and Preparation of Mulberry Leaves for Silkworm Culture by Women, print by Utamaro, 1794–1806 (Japan).

Plate 441 Japanese Imari Vase and Pair of Kutani Vases with Samurai nineteenth century (Japan).

Plate 442 An advertisement for Kodak photographic machine (source: CORBIS).

Plate 443 Thomas Edison in his laboratory, A Beltrame illustration for the Sunday edition of Corriere, in 1902.